CYBER CLASSROOM STUDENT ACCESS CARD

Congratulations! Thank you for purchasing a new copy of *Small C++ How to Program Fifth Edition*, by Deitel and Deitel. The access code below provides you with full access to the Cyber Classroom that accompanies this text. You now have full access to all student support areas including:

- Hours of detailed, expert audio descriptions of thousands of lines of code that help to reinforce important concepts
- An abundance of self-assessment material, including practice exams, hundreds of programming exercises, and self-review questions and answers
- A lab manual featuring lab exercises as well as pre- and post-lab activities
- Student solutions to approximately half of the exercises in the textbook

To access the *Small* C++ *How to Program Cyber Classroom* for the first time:

You need to register online using a computer with an Internet connection and a Web browser. The registration process takes just a few minutes and only needs to be completed once.

1. Go to `http://www.prenhall.com/deitel/cyberclassroom`.
2. Find *Small C++ How to Program Fifth Edition Cyber Classroom* and click "**Access the Cyber Classroom**".
3. Click "**register**" under the student area.
4. Use a coin to scratch off the gray coating below and reveal your student access code. ** *Do not use a knife or other sharp object, which can damage the code.*

5. On the registration page, enter your student access code. Do not type the dashes. You may use lower or uppercase letters.
6. Follow the on-screen instructions. If you need help during the online registration process, simply click the **Need Help?** icon.
7. Once your personal Login Name and Password are confirmed, you can begin using the *Small C++ How to Program Fifth Edition Cyber Classroom*!

To login to the *Small* C++ *How to Program Cyber Classroom* for the first time after you register:

Please visit `http://www.prenhall.com/deitel/cyberclassroom` and click "**Access the Cyber Classroom**" under *Small C++ How to Program Fifth Edition Cyber Classroom*. Click "login" under the student section. When prompted, provide your login name and password created during the registration process.

IMPORTANT The access code on this page can only be used once to establish a subscription to the *Small C++ How to Program Fifth Edition Cyber Classroom*. If this access code has already been scratched off, it may no longer be valid. If this is the case, you can purchase a subscription by going to `http://www.prenhall.com/deitel/cyberclassroom`, and clicking on "Purchase" under the appropriate book title.

Upper Saddle River, NJ 07458
www.prenhall.com

SMALL C++

HOW TO PROGRAM

FIFTH EDITION

How To Program Series

Advanced Java™ 2 Platform How to Program
C How to Program, 4/E
C++ How to Program, 5/E
C# How to Program
e-Business and e-Commerce How to Program
Internet and World Wide Web How to Program, 3/E
Java How to Program, 6/E
Small C++ How to Program, 5/E
Small Java™ How to Program, 6/E
Perl How to Program
Python How to Program
Visual C++® .NET How to Program
Visual Basic® 6 How to Program
Visual Basic® .NET How to Program, 2/E
Wireless Internet & Mobile Business How to Program
XML How to Program

Simply Series

Simply C++: An Application-Driven
   Tutorial Approach
Simply C#: An Application-Driven
   Tutorial Approach
Simply Java™ Programming: An
   Application-Driven Tutorial Approach
Simply Visual Basic® .NET: An
   Application Driven Tutorial Approach
   (Visual Studio .NET 2002 Edition)
Simply Visual Basic® .NET: An
   Application Driven Tutorial Approach
   (Visual Studio .NET 2003 Edition)

For Managers Series

e-Business and e-Commerce for
   Managers

.NET How to Program Series

C# How to Program
Visual Basic® .NET How to Program, 2/E
Visual C++® .NET How to Program

Visual Studio® Series

C# How to Program
Visual Basic® .NET How to Program, 2/E
Getting Started with Microsoft® Visual
   C++® 6 with an Introduction to MFC
Visual Basic® 6 How to Program

Also Available

e-books
CourseCompass, WebCT and
   Blackboard support
Pearson Choices: SafariX

Multimedia Cyber Classroom and Web-Based Training Series

C++ Multimedia Cyber Classroom, 5/E

C# Multimedia Cyber Classroom

e-Business and e-Commerce Multimedia Cyber Classroom

Internet and World Wide Web Multimedia Cyber Classroom, 2/E

Java™ Multimedia Cyber Classroom, 6/E

Perl Multimedia Cyber Classroom

Python Multimedia Cyber Classroom

Visual Basic® 6 Multimedia Cyber Classroom

Visual Basic® .NET Multimedia Cyber Classroom, 2/E

Wireless Internet & Mobile Business Programming Multimedia Cyber Classroom

XML Multimedia Cyber Classroom

The Complete Training Course Series

The Complete C++ Training Course, 4/E

The Complete C# Training Course

The Complete e-Business and e-Commerce Programming Training Course

The Complete Internet and World Wide Web Programming Training Course, 2/E

The Complete Java™ 2 Training Course, 5/E

The Complete Perl Training Course

The Complete Python Training Course

The Complete Visual Basic® 6 Training Course

The Complete Visual Basic® .NET Training Course, 2/E

The Complete Wireless Internet & Mobile Business Programming Training Course

The Complete XML Programming Training Course

To follow the Deitel publishing program, please register at:

> www.deitel.com/newsletter/subscribe.html

for the free *DEITEL® BUZZ ONLINE* e-mail newsletter.

To communicate with the authors, send e-mail to:

> deitel@deitel.com

For information on corporate on-site seminars offered by Deitel & Associates, Inc. worldwide, visit:

> www.deitel.com or write to deitel@deitel.com

For continuing updates on Prentice Hall/Deitel publications visit:

> www.deitel.com,
> www.prenhall.com/deitel or
> www.InformIT.com/deitel

Library of Congress Cataloging-in-Publication Data
On file

Vice President and Editorial Director, ECS: *Marcia J. Horton*
Senior Acquisitions Editor: *Kate Hargett*
Associate Editor: *Jennifer Cappello*
Assistant Editor: *Sarah Parker*
Editorial Assistant: *Michael Giacobbe*
Executive Managing Editor: *Vince O'Brien*
Managing Editor: *Tom Manshreck*
Production Editor: *John F. Lovell*
Production Editor, Media: *Bob Engelhardt*
Production Assistant: *Asha Rohra*
Director of Creative Services: *Paul Belfanti*
A/V Production Editor: *Xiaohong Zhu*
Art Studio: *Artworks, York, PA*
Art Director: *Geoffrey Cassar*
Cover Design: *Abbey S. Deitel, Harvey M. Deitel, Mark Goss (Electric Soup Studios), Geoffrey Cassar*
Interior Design: *Harvey M. Deitel, Geoffrey Cassar*
Assistant Manufacturing Manager: *Michael Bell*
Manufacturing Buyer: *Lisa McDowell*
Marketing Manager: *Pamela Hersperger*
Marketing Assistant: *Barrie Reinhold*

© 2005 by Pearson Education, Inc.
Upper Saddle River, New Jersey 07458

The authors and publisher of this book have used their best efforts in preparing this book. These efforts include the development, research, and testing of the theories and programs to determine their effectiveness. The authors and publisher make no warranty of any kind, expressed or implied, with regard to these programs or to the documentation contained in this book. The authors and publisher shall not be liable in any event for incidental or consequential damages in connection with, or arising out of, the furnishing, performance, or use of these programs.

Many of the designations used by manufacturers and sellers to distinguish their products are claimed as trademarks and registered trademarks. Where those designations appear in this book, and Prentice Hall and the authors were aware of a trademark claim, the designations have been printed in initial caps or all caps. All product names mentioned remain trademarks or registered trademarks of their respective owners.

All rights reserved. No part of this book may be reproduced, in any form or by any means,
without permission in writing from the publisher.

Printed in the United States of America

10 9 8 7 6 5 4 3 2

ISBN 0-13-185758-4

Pearson Education Ltd., *London*
Pearson Education Australia Pty. Ltd., *Sydney*
Pearson Education Singapore, Pte. Ltd.
Pearson Education North Asia Ltd., *Hong Kong*
Pearson Education Canada, Inc., *Toronto*
Pearson Educacion de Mexico, S.A. de C.V.
Pearson Education–Japan, *Tokyo*
Pearson Education Malaysia, Pte. Ltd.
Pearson Education, Inc., *Upper Saddle River, New Jersey*

SMALL C++

HOW TO PROGRAM

FIFTH EDITION

H. M. Deitel

Deitel & Associates, Inc.

P. J. Deitel

Deitel & Associates, Inc.

Upper Saddle River, New Jersey 07458

Trademarks

Borland and C++ Builder are trademarks or registered trademarks of Borland.

Cygwin is a trademark and copyrighted work of Red Hat, Inc. in the United States and other countries.

Dive Into is a registered trademark of Deitel & Associates, Inc.

GNU is a trademark of the Free Software Foundation.

Java and all Java-based marks are trademarks or registered trademarks of Sun Microsystems, Inc. in the United States and other countries. Pearson Education is independent of Sun Microsystems, Inc.

Linux is a registered trademark of Linus Torvalds.

Microsoft, Microsoft® Internet Explorer and the Windows logo are either registered trademarks or trademarks of Microsoft Corporation in the United States and/or other countries.

Object Management Group, OMG, Unified Modeling Language and UML are trademarks of Object Management Group, Inc.

To:

Stephen Clamage

Chairman of the J16 committee, "Programming Language C++" that is responsible for the C++ standard; Senior Staff Engineer, Sun Microsystems, Inc., Software Division.

Don Kostuch

Independent Consultant

and Mike Miller

Former Vice Chairman and Core Language Working Group Chairman of the J16 committee, "Programming Language C++;" Software Design Engineer, Edison Design Group, Inc.

For your mentorship, friendship, and tireless devotion to insisting that we "get it right" and helping us do so.

It is a privilege to work with such consummate C++ professionals.

Harvey M. Deitel and Paul J. Deitel

Contents

Preface   xvii

Before You Begin   xliii

1 Introduction to Computers, the Internet and World Wide Web   1

1.1   Introduction   2
1.2   What Is a Computer?   3
1.3   Computer Organization   4
1.4   Early Operating Systems   5
1.5   Personal, Distributed and Client/Server Computing   5
1.6   The Internet and the World Wide Web   6
1.7   Machine Languages, Assembly Languages and High-Level Languages   6
1.8   History of C and C++   8
1.9   C++ Standard Library   8
1.10 History of Java   9
1.11 FORTRAN, COBOL, Pascal and Ada   10
1.12 Basic, Visual Basic, Visual C++, C# and .NET   11
1.13 Key Software Trend: Object Technology   11
1.14 Typical C++ Development Environment   12
1.15 Notes About C++ and *Small C++ How to Program, 5/e*   15
1.16 Test-Driving a C++ Application   16
1.17 Introduction to Object Technology and the UML   22
1.18 Wrap-Up   27
1.19 Web Resources   28

2 Introduction to C++ Programming   36

2.1   Introduction   37
2.2   First Program in C++: Printing a Line of Text   37
2.3   Modifying Our First C++ Program   41
2.4   Another C++ Program: Adding Integers   42
2.5   Memory Concepts   46
2.6   Arithmetic   48
2.7   Decision Making: Equality and Relational Operators   51
2.8   Wrap-Up   56

3   Introduction to Classes and Objects   65

3.1	Introduction	66
3.2	Classes, Objects, Member Functions and Data Members	66
3.3	Overview of the Chapter Examples	68
3.4	Defining a Class with a Member Function	68
3.5	Defining a Member Function with a Parameter	72
3.6	Data Members, *set* Functions and *get* Functions	75
3.7	Initializing Objects with Constructors	82
3.8	Placing a Class in a Separate File for Reusability	86
3.9	Separating Interface from Implementation	90
3.10	Validating Data with *set* Functions	96
3.11	Wrap-Up	101

4   Control Statements: Part 1   108

4.1	Introduction	109
4.2	Algorithms	109
4.3	Pseudocode	110
4.4	Control Structures	111
4.5	if Selection Statement	115
4.6	if...else Double-Selection Statement	116
4.7	while Repetition Statement	121
4.8	Formulating Algorithms: Counter-Controlled Repetition	123
4.9	Formulating Algorithms: Sentinel-Controlled Repetition	129
4.10	Formulating Algorithms: Nested Control Statements	140
4.11	Assignment Operators	145
4.12	Increment and Decrement Operators	145
4.13	Wrap-Up	149

5   Control Statements: Part 2   164

5.1	Introduction	165
5.2	Essentials of Counter-Controlled Repetition	165
5.3	for Repetition Statement	167
5.4	Examples Using the for Statement	172
5.5	do...while Repetition Statement	176
5.6	switch Multiple-Selection Statement	178
5.7	break and continue Statements	188
5.8	Logical Operators	190
5.9	Confusing Equality (==) and Assignment (=) Operators	195
5.10	Structured Programming Summary	196
5.11	Wrap-Up	201

6   Functions and an Introduction to Recursion   211

6.1	Introduction	212
6.2	Program Components in C++	213
6.3	Math Library Functions	214

6.4	Function Definitions with Multiple Parameters	216
6.5	Function Prototypes and Argument Coercion	221
6.6	C++ Standard Library Header Files	223
6.7	Case Study: Random Number Generation	225
6.8	Case Study: Game of Chance and Introducing enum	231
6.9	Storage Classes	235
6.10	Scope Rules	238
6.11	Function Call Stack and Activation Records	241
6.12	Functions with Empty Parameter Lists	245
6.13	Inline Functions	246
6.14	References and Reference Parameters	248
6.15	Default Arguments	253
6.16	Unary Scope Resolution Operator	255
6.17	Function Overloading	256
6.18	Function Templates	259
6.19	Recursion	261
6.20	Example Using Recursion: Fibonacci Series	265
6.21	Recursion vs. Iteration	268
6.22	Wrap-Up	271

7   Arrays and Vectors — **292**

7.1	Introduction	293
7.2	Arrays	294
7.3	Declaring Arrays	295
7.4	Examples Using Arrays	296
7.5	Passing Arrays to Functions	312
7.6	Case Study: Class GradeBook Using an Array to Store Grades	317
7.7	Searching Arrays with Linear Search	324
7.8	Sorting Arrays with Insertion Sort	325
7.9	Multidimensional Arrays	328
7.10	Case Study: Class GradeBook Using a Two-Dimensional Array	331
7.11	Introduction to C++ Standard Library Class Template vector	338
7.12	Wrap-Up	343

8   Pointers and Pointer-Based Strings — **360**

8.1	Introduction	361
8.2	Pointer Variable Declarations and Initialization	362
8.3	Pointer Operators	363
8.4	Passing Arguments to Functions by Reference with Pointers	366
8.5	Using const with Pointers	370
8.6	Selection Sort Using Pass-by-Reference	377
8.7	sizeof Operators	380
8.8	Pointer Expressions and Pointer Arithmetic	383
8.9	Relationship Between Pointers and Arrays	386

8.10   Arrays of Pointers   390
8.11   Case Study: Card Shuffling and Dealing Simulation   391
8.12   Function Pointers   397
8.13   Introduction to Pointer-Based String Processing   402
     8.13.1   Fundamentals of Characters and Pointer-Based Strings   403
     8.13.2   String Manipulation Functions of the String-Handling Library   405
8.14   Wrap-Up   413

9   Classes: A Deeper Look, Part 1   439

9.1   Introduction   440
9.2   Time Class Case Study   441
9.3   Class Scope and Accessing Class Members   446
9.4   Separating Interface from Implementation   448
9.5   Access Functions and Utility Functions   450
9.6   Time Class Case Study: Constructors with Default Arguments   452
9.7   Destructors   458
9.8   When Constructors and Destructors Are Called   459
9.9   Time Class Case Study: Subtle Trap—Returning a Reference to
     a private Data Member   462
9.10   Default Memberwise Assignment   465
9.11   Software Reusability   467
9.12   Wrap-Up   468

10   Classes: A Deeper Look, Part 2   474

10.1   Introduction   475
10.2   const (Constant) Objects and const Member Functions   475
10.3   Composition: Objects as Members of Classes   485
10.4   friend Functions and friend Classes   492
10.5   Using the this Pointer   496
10.6   Dynamic Memory Management with Operators new and delete   501
10.7   static Class Members   503
10.8   Data Abstraction and Information Hiding   509
     10.8.1   Example: Array Abstract Data Type   510
     10.8.2   Example: String Abstract Data Type   511
     10.8.3   Example: Queue Abstract Data Type   511
10.9   Container Classes and Iterators   512
10.10   Proxy Classes   513
10.11   Wrap-Up   516

11   Operator Overloading; String and Array Objects   522

11.1   Introduction   523
11.2   Fundamentals of Operator Overloading   524
11.3   Restrictions on Operator Overloading   525

11.4   Operator Functions as Class Members vs. Global Functions   527
11.5   Overloading Stream Insertion and Stream Extraction Operators   528
11.6   Overloading Unary Operators   532
11.7   Overloading Binary Operators   532
11.8   Case Study: Array Class   533
11.9   Converting between Types   545
11.10 Case Study: String Class   546
11.11 Overloading ++ and --   558
11.12 Case Study: A Date Class   560
11.13 Standard Library Class string   564
11.14 explicit Constructors   568
11.15 Wrap-Up   572

12 Object-Oriented Programming: Inheritance   584

12.1   Introduction   585
12.2   Base Classes and Derived Classes   586
12.3   protected Members   589
12.4   Relationship between Base Classes and Derived Classes   589
       12.4.1   Creating and Using a CommissionEmployee Class   590
       12.4.2   Creating a BasePlusCommissionEmployee Class Without Using
                Inheritance   595
       12.4.3   Creating a CommissionEmployee–BasePlusCommissionEmployee
                Inheritance Hierarchy   601
       12.4.4   CommissionEmployee–BasePlusCommissionEmployee Inheritance
                Hierarchy Using protected Data   606
       12.4.5   CommissionEmployee–BasePlusCommissionEmployee Inheritance
                Hierarchy Using private Data   613
12.5   Constructors and Destructors in Derived Classes   621
12.6   public, protected and private Inheritance   629
12.7   Software Engineering with Inheritance   629
12.8   Wrap-Up   631

13 Object-Oriented Programming: Polymorphism   637

13.1   Introduction   638
13.2   Polymorphism Examples   640
13.3   Relationships Among Objects in an Inheritance Hierarchy   641
       13.3.1   Invoking Base-Class Functions from Derived-Class Objects   641
       13.3.2   Aiming Derived-Class Pointers at Base-Class Objects   649
       13.3.3   Derived-Class Member-Function Calls via Base-Class Pointers   650
       13.3.4   Virtual Functions   652
       13.3.5   Summary of the Allowed Assignments Between Base-Class
                and Derived-Class Objects and Pointers   658
13.4   Type Fields and switch Statements   658
13.5   Abstract Classes and Pure virtual Functions   659

13.6	Case Study: Payroll System Using Polymorphism	661
	13.6.1 Creating Abstract Base Class `Employee`	663
	13.6.2 Creating Concrete Derived Class `SalariedEmployee`	666
	13.6.3 Creating Concrete Derived Class `HourlyEmployee`	668
	13.6.4 Creating Concrete Derived Class `CommissionEmployee`	671
	13.6.5 Creating Indirect Concrete Derived Class `BasePlusCommissionEmployee`	673
	13.6.6 Demonstrating Polymorphic Processing	675
13.7	(Optional) Polymorphism, Virtual Function and Dynamic Binding "Under the Hood"	679
13.8	Case Study: Payroll System Using Polymorphism and Run-Time Type Information with Downcasting, `dynamic_cast`, `typeid` and `type_info`	683
13.9	Virtual Destructors	686
13.10	Wrap-Up	687

A Operator Precedence and Associativity Chart 692
A.1	Operator Precedence	692

B ASCII Character Set 695

C Fundamental Types 696

D Number Systems 698
D.1	Introduction	699
D.2	Abbreviating Binary Numbers as Octal and Hexadecimal Numbers	702
D.3	Converting Octal and Hexadecimal Numbers to Binary Numbers	703
D.4	Converting from Binary, Octal or Hexadecimal to Decimal	703
D.5	Converting from Decimal to Binary, Octal or Hexadecimal	704
D.6	Negative Binary Numbers: Two's Complement Notation	706

E C++ Internet and Web Resources 711
E.1	Resources	711
E.2	Tutorials	713
E.3	FAQs	713
E.4	Visual C++	713
E.5	Newsgroups	714
E.6	Compilers and Development Tools	714

F Using the Visual Studio® .NET Debugger 715
F.1	Introduction	716
F.2	Breakpoints and the **Continue** Command	716
F.3	The **Locals** and **Watch** Windows	722

F.4   Controlling Execution Using the **Step Into**, **Step Over**, **Step Out**
       and **Continue** Commands   725
F.5   The **Autos** Window   728
F.6   Wrap-Up   729

G   Using the GNU™ C++ Debugger   732

G.1   Introduction   733
G.2   Breakpoints and the run, stop, continue and print Commands   733
G.3   The print and set Commands   740
G.4   Controlling Execution Using the step, finish and next Commands   742
G.5   The watch Command   744
G.6   Wrap-Up   747

Bibliography   750

Index   756

Preface

"Be faithful in small things because it is in them that your strength lies."
—Mother Teresa

Welcome to C++ programming and *Small C++ How to Program, Fifth Edition*! C++ is a world-class programming language for developing industrial-strength, high-performance computer applications. At Deitel & Associates, we write college-level computer science textbooks and professional reference books. *Small C++ How to Program, Fifth Edition* was a joy to create. Our goal was to design a smaller, lower-priced book for one-semester introductory (CS1) courses based on the major revision of our book *C++ How to Program, Fifth Edition*. *Small C++ How to Program, Fifth Edition* focuses on the core concepts and features of C++ covered in Chapters 1–13 of *C++ How to Program, 5/e*.

We believe that this book and its support materials have everything instructors and students need for an informative, interesting, challenging and entertaining C++ educational experience. In this Preface, we overview the many features of *Small C++ How to Program, 5/e*. The *Tour of the Book* section of the Preface gives instructors, students and professionals a sense of *Small C++ How to Program, 5/e*'s coverage of C++ and object-oriented programming. We also overview various conventions used in the book, such as syntax coloring the code examples, "code washing" and code highlighting. We provide information about free compilers available on the Web. We also discuss the comprehensive suite of educational materials that help instructors maximize their students' learning experience, including the *Instructor's Resource CD*, PowerPoint® Slide lecture notes, course management systems, SafariX (Pearson Education's WebBook publications) and more.

Features of Small C++ How to Program, 5/e

To create *Small C++ How to Program, 5/e*, we put the previous edition of *C++ How to Program* under the microscope. The new edition has many compelling features:

- **Major Content Revisions.** All the chapters have been significantly updated and upgraded. We tuned the writing for clarity and precision. We also adjusted our use of C++ terminology in accordance with the ANSI/ISO C++ standard document that defines the language.

- **Smaller Chapters.** Larger chapters have been divided into smaller, more manageable chapters (e.g., Chapter 1 of the Fourth Edition has been split into Chapters 1–2; Chapter 2 of the Fourth Edition is now Chapters 4–5).

- **Early Classes and Objects Approach.** We changed to an early classes and objects pedagogy. Students are introduced to the basic concepts and terminology of object technology in Chapter 1. In the previous edition, students began developing customized, reusable classes and objects in Chapter 6, but in this edition, they do so in our completely new Chapter 3. Chapters 4–7 have been carefully rewritten from an "early classes and objects" perspective. This new edition is object oriented, where appropriate, from the start and throughout the text. Moving the discussion of objects and classes to earlier chapters gets students "thinking about objects" immediately and mastering these concepts more completely. Object-oriented programming is not trivial by any means, but it's fun to write object-oriented programs, and students can see immediate results.

- **Integrated Case Studies.** We added several case studies spanning multiple sections and chapters that often build on a class introduced earlier in the book to demonstrate new programming concepts taught later in the book. These case studies include the development of the GradeBook class in Chapters 3–7, the Time class in several sections of Chapters 9–10 and the Employee class in Chapters 12–13.

- **Integrated GradeBook Case Study.** We have added a new GradeBook case study to reinforce our early classes and objects presentation. The case study uses classes and objects in Chapters 3–7 to incrementally build a GradeBook class that represents an instructor's grade book and performs various calculations based on a set of student grades, such as calculating the average grade, finding the maximum and minimum, and printing a bar chart.

- **Essential Topics for CS1.** *Small C++ How to Program, 5/e* focuses on core C++ concepts presented in CS1 courses. It is designed for first courses in computing and is appropriate for Computer Science and Information Systems courses. The book is information-rich enough for the first two courses at many schools.

- **Unified Modeling Language™ 2.0 (UML 2.0)—Introducing the UML 2.0.** The Unified Modeling Language (UML) has become the preferred graphical modeling language for designing object-oriented systems. All the UML diagrams in the book comply with the new UML 2.0 specification. We use UML class diagrams to visually represent classes and their inheritance relationships, and we use UML activity diagrams to demonstrate the flow of control in each of C++'s control statements.

- **Compilation and Linking Process for Multiple-Source-File Programs.** Chapter 3 includes a diagram and discussion of the compilation and linking process that produces an executable application.

- **Function Call Stack Explanation.** In Chapter 6, we provide a detailed discussion (with illustrations) of the function call stack and activation records to explain how C++ is able to keep track of which function is currently executing, how automatic variables of functions are maintained in memory and how a function knows where to return after it completes execution.

- **Early Introduction of C++ Standard Library string and vector Objects.** The string and vector classes are used to make earlier examples more object-oriented.

- **Class string.** We use class string instead of C-like pointer-based char * strings for most string manipulations throughout the book. We continue to include discussions of char * strings in Chapters 8, 10, 11 and 22 to give students practice with pointer manipulations, to illustrate dynamic memory allocation with new and delete, to build our own String class and to prepare students for assignments in industry where they will work with char * strings in C and C++ legacy code.

- **Class Template vector.** We use class template `vector` instead of C-like pointer-based array manipulations throughout the book. We continue to discuss C-like pointer-based arrays in Chapter 7 to prepare students for working with C and C++ legacy code in industry and to use as a basis for building our own customized `Array` class in Chapter 11, Operator Overloading; String and Array Objects.

- **Tuned Treatment of Inheritance and Polymorphism.** Chapters 12–13 have been carefully tuned, making the treatment of inheritance and polymorphism clearer and more accessible for students who are new to OOP. An `Employee` hierarchy replaces the `Point/Circle/Cylinder` hierarchy used in prior editions to introduce inheritance and polymorphism. This new hierarchy is more natural.

- **Discussion and Illustration of How Polymorphism Works "Under the Hood."** Chapter 13 contains a detailed diagram and explanation of how C++ can implement polymorphism, `virtual` functions and dynamic binding internally. This gives students a solid understanding of how these capabilities really work. More importantly, it helps students appreciate the overhead of polymorphism—in terms of additional memory consumption and processor time. This helps students determine when to use polymorphism and when to avoid it.

- **ANSI/ISO C++ Standard Compliance.** We have audited our presentation against the most recent ANSI/ISO C++ standard document for completeness and accuracy. [*Note:* If you need additional technical details on C++, you may want to read the C++ standard document. An electronic PDF copy of the C++ standard document, number INCITS/ISO/IEC 14882-2003, is available for $18 at `webstore.ansi.org/ansidocstore/default.asp`.]

- **New Debugger Appendices.** We include two new "Using the Debugger" appendices: Appendix F, Using the Visual C++ .NET Debugger, and Appendix G, Using the GNU C++ Debugger.

- To keep this book small and focused on first courses, we removed the optional ten-section OOD/UML case study that appears in *C++ How to Program, 5/e.*

- **New Interior Design.** Working with the creative services team at Prentice Hall, we redesigned the interior styles for our *How to Program* Series. The new fonts are easier on the eyes and the new art package is more appropriate for the more detailed illustrations. We now place the defining occurrence of each key term both in the text and in the index in blue, bold style text for easier reference. We emphasize on-screen components in the bold Helvetica font (e.g., the **File** menu) and emphasize C++ program text in the Lucida font (e.g., `int x = 5`).

- **Syntax Coloring.** We syntax color all the C++ code, which is consistent with most C++ integrated development environments and code editors. This greatly improves code readability—an especially important goal, given that this book contains 8,720 lines of code. Our syntax-coloring conventions are as follows:

```
comments appear in green
keywords appear in dark blue
constants and literal values appear in light blue
errors appear in red
all other code appears in black
```

- **Code Highlighting.** Extensive code highlighting makes it easy for readers to locate each program's new features and helps students review the material rapidly when preparing for exams or labs.

- **"Code washing."** This is our term for using extensive and meaningful comments, using meaningful identifiers, applying uniform indentation conventions, aligning curly braces vertically, using a `// end...` comment on every line with a right curly brace and using vertical spacing to highlight significant program units such as control statements and functions. This process results in programs that are easy to read and self-documenting. We have extensively "code washed" all the source-code programs in both the text and the book's ancillaries. We have worked hard to make our code exemplary.

- **Code Testing on Multiple Platforms.** We tested the code examples on various popular C++ platforms. For the most part, all of the examples in this book port easily to all popular ANSI/ISO standard-compliant compilers. We will post any problems at www.deitel.com/books/scpphtp5/index.html.

- **Errors and Warnings Shown for Multiple Platforms.** For programs that intentionally contain errors to illustrate a key concept, we show the error messages that result on several popular platforms.

- **Large Review Team.** The book has been carefully scrutinized by a team of 21 distinguished academic and industry reviewers.

- **Free Web-Based *Cyber Classroom*.** We've converted our popular interactive multimedia version of the text (which we call a *Cyber Classroom*) from a for-sale, CD-based product to a free online supplement, available with the purchase of a new book. For used books, students can purchase an online access kit by searching for the book at prenhall.com.

- **Free Student Solutions Manual.** We've converted our Student Solutions Manual, which contains solutions to approximately half of the exercises, from a for-sale softcover book to an online supplement included with the *Cyber Classroom*.

- **Free Lab Manual.** We've converted our Lab Manual, *C++ in the Lab*, from a for-sale softcover book to an online supplement included with the *Cyber Classroom*.

As you read this book, if you have questions, send an e-mail to deitel@deitel.com; we will respond promptly. Please visit our Web site, www.deitel.com and be sure to sign up for the free *DEITEL® Buzz Online* e-mail newsletter at www.deitel.com/newsletter/subscribe.html for updates to this book and the latest information on C++. We also use the Web site and the newsletter to keep our readers and industry clients informed of the latest news on Deitel publications and services. Please check the following Web site regularly for errata, updates regarding the C++ software, free downloads and other resources:

www.deitel.com/books/scpphtp5/index.html

Teaching Approach

Small C++ How to Program, 5/e contains an abundant collection of examples, exercises and projects drawn from many fields to provide the student with a chance to solve interesting real-world problems. The book concentrates on the principles of good software engineering and stresses program clarity. We avoid arcane terminology and syntax specifications in favor of teaching by example. We are educators who teach programming languages courses in industry classrooms worldwide. Dr. Harvey M. Deitel has 20 years of college teaching experience, including serving as chairman of the Computer Science Department at Boston College, and 15 years of industry teaching experience. Paul Deitel has 12 years of industry teaching experience. The Deitels have taught C++ courses at all levels to the government, industry, military and academic clients of Deitel & Associates.

Learning C++ using the LIVE-CODE Approach

Small C++ How to Program, 5/e, is loaded with C++ programs—each new concept is presented in the context of a complete working C++ program that is immediately followed by one or more sample executions showing the program's inputs and outputs. This style exemplifies the way we teach and write about programming. We call this method of teaching and writing the LIVE-CODE Approach. *We use programming languages to teach programming languages.* Reading the examples in the text is much like typing and running them on a computer. We provide all the source code for the book's examples at `www.deitel.com` and on the accompanying CD—making it easy for students to run each example as they study it.

World Wide Web Access

All the source-code examples for *Small C++ How to Program, 5/e,* (and our other publications) are available on the Internet as downloads from

> `www.deitel.com`

Registration is quick and easy, and the downloads are free. We suggest downloading all the examples (or copying them from the CD included in the back of this book), then running each program as you read the corresponding text. Making changes to the examples and immediately seeing the effects of those changes is a great way to enhance your C++ learning experience.

Objectives

Each chapter begins with a statement of objectives. This lets students know what to expect and gives them an opportunity, after reading the chapter, to determine if they have met these objectives. This is a confidence builder and a source of positive reinforcement.

Quotations

The learning objectives are followed by quotations. Some are humorous, some philosophical and some offer interesting insights. We hope that you will enjoy relating the quotations to the chapter material. Many of the quotations are worth a second look after reading the chapter.

Outline

The chapter outline helps students approach the material in a top-down fashion, so they can anticipate what is to come, and set a comfortable and effective learning pace.

8,720 Lines of Syntax-Colored Code in 124 Example Programs with Live Sample Program Inputs and Outputs

Our LIVE-CODE programs range in size from just a few lines of code to substantial larger examples. Each program is followed by a window containing the input/output dialogue produced when the program is run, so students can confirm that the programs run as expected. Relating outputs to the program statements that produce them is an excellent way to learn and to reinforce concepts. Our programs demonstrate the diverse features of C++. The code is line-numbered and syntax colored—with C++ keywords, comments and other program text appearing in different colors. This facilitates reading the code—students will especially appreciate the syntax coloring when they read the larger programs.

402 Illustrations/Figures

An abundance of charts, tables, line drawings, programs and program outputs is included. We model the flow of control in control statements with UML activity diagrams. UML class diagrams model the data members, constructors and member functions of classes.

403 Programming Tips

We include programming tips to help students focus on important aspects of program development. We highlight these tips in the form of *Good Programming Practices*, *Common Programming Errors*, *Performance Tips*, *Portability Tips*, *Software Engineering Observations* and *Error-Prevention Tips*. These tips and practices represent the best we have gleaned from a combined six decades of programming and teaching experience. One of our students, a mathematics major, told us that she feels this approach is like the highlighting of axioms, theorems, lemmas and corollaries in mathematics books—it provides a basis on which to build good software.

Good Programming Practices

Good Programming Practices *are tips for writing clear programs. These techniques help students produce programs that are more readable, self-documenting and easier to maintain.*

Common Programming Errors

Students who are new to programming (or a programming language) tend to make certain errors frequently. Focusing on these Common Programming Errors *reduces the likelihood that students will make the same mistakes and shortens long lines outside instructors' offices during office hours!*

Performance Tips

In our experience, teaching students to write clear and understandable programs is by far the most important goal for a first programming course. But students want to write the programs that run the fastest, use the least memory, require the smallest number of keystrokes or dazzle in other nifty ways. Students really care about performance. They want to know what they can do to "turbo charge" their programs. So we highlight opportunities for improving program performance—making programs run faster or minimizing the amount of memory that they occupy.

Portability Tips

Software development is a complex and expensive activity. Organizations that develop software must often produce versions customized to a variety of computers and operating systems. So there is a strong emphasis today on portability, i.e., on producing software that will run on a variety of computer systems with few, if any, changes. Some programmers assume that if they implement an application in standard C++, the application will be portable. This simply is not the case. Achieving portability requires careful and cautious design. There are many pitfalls. We include Portability Tips to help students write portable code and to provide insights on how C++ achieves its high degree of portability.

Software Engineering Observations

The object-oriented programming paradigm necessitates a complete rethinking of the way we build software systems. C++ is an effective language for achieving good software engineering. The Software Engineering Observations *highlight architectural and design issues that affect the construction of software systems, especially large-scale systems. Much of what the student learns here will be useful in upper-level courses and in industry as the student begins to work with large, complex real-world systems.*

Error-Prevention Tips

When we first designed this "tip type," we thought we would use it strictly to tell people how to test and debug C++ programs. In fact, many of the tips describe aspects of C++ that reduce the likelihood of "bugs" and thus simplify the testing and debugging processes.

Wrap-Up Sections

Each chapter ends with additional pedagogical devices. New in this edition, each chapter ends with a brief "wrap-up" section that recaps the topics that were presented. The wrap-ups also help the student transition to the next chapter.

Summary (567 Summary bullets)

We present a thorough, bullet-list-style summary at the end of every chapter. On average, there are 43 summary bullets per chapter. This focuses the student's review and reinforces key concepts.

Terminology (969 Terms)

We include an alphabetized list of the important terms defined in each chapter—again, for further reinforcement. There is an average of 64 terms per chapter. Each term also appears in the index, and the defining occurrence of each term is highlighted in the index with a blue, bold page number so the student can locate the definitions of terms quickly.

333 Self-Review Exercises and Answers (Count Includes Separate Parts)

Extensive self-review exercises and answers are included for self-study. This gives the student a chance to build confidence with the material and prepare for the regular exercises. We encourage students to do all the self-review exercises and check their answers.

543 Exercises (Solutions in Instructor's Manual; Count Includes Separate Parts)

Each chapter concludes with a substantial set of exercises including simple recall of important terminology and concepts; writing individual C++ statements; writing small portions of C++ functions and classes; writing complete C++ functions, classes and programs; and writing major term projects. The large number of exercises enables instructors to tailor their courses to the unique needs of their audiences and to vary course assignments each semester. Instructors can use these exercises to form homework assignments, short quizzes and major examinations. The solutions for the vast majority of the exercises are included on the *Instructor's Resource CD (IRCD),* which is *available only to instructors* through their Prentice Hall representatives. [**NOTE: Please do not write to us requesting the Instructor's CD. Distribution of this ancillary is limited strictly to college instructors teaching from the book. Instructors may obtain the solutions manual only from their Prentice Hall representatives.**] Students will have access to approximately half the exercises in the book in the free, Web-based *Cyber Classroom* which will be available in late spring 2005. For more information about the *Cyber Classroom*, please visit www.deitel.com or sign up for the free *Deitel® Buzz Online* e-mail newsletter at www.deitel.com/newsletter/subscribe.html.

Approximately 2900 Index Entries

We have included an extensive index. This helps students find terms or concepts by keyword. The index is useful to people reading the book for the first time and is especially useful to practicing programmers who use the book as a reference.

"Double Indexing" of All C++ LIVE-CODE Examples

Small C++ How to Program, 5/e has 124 live-code examples and 543 exercises (including separate parts). We have double-indexed each of the live-code examples and most of the more substantial exercises. For every source-code program in the book, we indexed the figure caption both alphabetically and as a subindex item under "Examples." This makes it easier to find examples that include particular features. The more substantial exercises are also indexed both alphabetically and as subindex items under "Exercises."

Tour of the Book

In this section, we take a tour of the many capabilities of C++ you will study in *Small C++ How to Program, 5/e*. Note that each of the chapters in this book depends on the preceding chapters except Chapter 11, Operator Overloading; String and Array Objects, which can be skipped and covered after either Chapter 12 or 13.

Chapter 1—Introduction to Computers, the Internet and World Wide Web— discusses what computers are, how they work and how they are programmed. The chapter gives a brief history of the development of programming languages from machine languages to assembly languages and high-level languages. The origin of the C++ programming language is discussed. The chapter includes an introduction to a typical C++ programming environment. We walk readers through a "test drive" of a typical C++ application on Windows and Linux systems. Our free *Dive-Into™ Series* publications, which discuss compiling and running C++ applications on various platforms, are available for download at www.deitel.com/books/cpphtp5/index.html. Chapter 1 concludes with an introduction to basic object technology concepts and terminology and the Unified Modeling Language.

Chapter 2—Introduction to C++ Programming—provides a lightweight introduction to programming applications in the C++ programming language. The chapter introduces nonprogrammers to basic programming concepts and constructs. The programs in this chapter illustrate how to display data on the screen and how to obtain data from the user at the keyboard. Chapter 2 ends with detailed treatments of decision making and arithmetic operations.

Chapter 3—Introduction to Classes and Objects—is the "featured" chapter for the new edition. It provides a friendly early introduction to classes and objects. Carefully developed and completely new in this edition, Chapter 3 gets students working with object orientation comfortably from the start. It was developed with the guidance of a distinguished team of industry and academic reviewers. We introduce classes, objects, member functions, constructors and data members using a series of simple real-world examples. We develop a well-engineered framework for organizing object-oriented programs in C++. First, we motivate the notion of classes with a simple example. Then we present a carefully paced sequence of seven complete working programs to demonstrate creating and using your own classes. These examples begin our **integrated case study on developing a grade-book class** that instructors can use to maintain student test scores. This case study is enhanced over the next several chapters, culminating with the version presented in Chapter 7, Arrays and Vectors. The **GradeBook class case study** describes how to define a class and how to use it to create an object. The case study discusses how to declare and define member functions to implement the class's behaviors, how to declare data members to implement the class's attributes and how to call an object's member functions to make them perform their tasks. We introduce C++ Standard Library class string and create string objects to store the name of the course that a GradeBook object represents. Chapter 3 explains the differences between data members of a class and local variables of a function and how to use a constructor to ensure that an object's data is initialized when the object is created. We show how to promote software reusability by separating a class definition from the client code (e.g., function main) that uses the class. We also introduce another fundamental principle of good software engineering—separating interface from implementation. The chapter includes a detailed diagram and discussion explaining the compilation and linking process that produces an executable application.

Chapter 4—Control Statements: Part 1—focuses on the program-development process involved in creating useful classes. The chapter discusses how to take a problem statement and develop a working C++ program from it, including performing intermediate steps in pseudocode. The chapter introduces some simple control statements for decision making (if and if...else) and repetition (while). We examine counter-controlled and sentinel-controlled repetition using the **GradeBook class** from Chapter 3, and introduce C++'s increment, decrement and assignment operators. The chapter includes **two enhanced versions of the GradeBook class**, each based on Chapter 3's final version. These versions each include a member function that uses control statements to calculate the average of a set of student grades. In the first version, the member function uses counter-controlled repetition to input 10 student grades from the user, then determines the average grade. In the second version, the member function uses sentinel-controlled repetition to input an arbitrary number of grades from the user, then calculates the average of the grades that were entered. The chapter uses simple UML activity diagrams to show the flow of control through each of the control statements.

Chapter 5—Control Statements: Part 2—continues the discussion of C++ control statements with examples of the for repetition statement, the do...while repetition statement, the switch selection statement, the break statement and the continue statement. We create an **enhanced version of class GradeBook** that uses a switch statement to count the number of A, B, C, D and F grades entered by the user. This version uses sentinel-controlled repetition to input the grades. While reading the grades from the user, a member function modifies data members that keep track of the count of grades in each letter grade category. Another member function of the class then uses these data members to display a summary report based on the grades entered. The chapter includes a discussion of logical operators.

Chapter 6—Functions and an Introduction to Recursion—takes a deeper look inside objects and their member functions. We discuss C++ standard-library functions and examine more closely how students can build their own functions. The techniques presented in Chapter 6 are essential to the production of properly organized programs, especially the kinds of larger programs and software that system programmers and application programmers are likely to develop in real-world applications. The "divide and conquer" strategy is presented as an effective means for solving complex problems by dividing them into simpler interacting components. The chapter's first example continues the **GradeBook class case study** with an example of a function with multiple parameters. Students enjoy the chapter's treatment of random numbers and simulation, and the discussion of the dice game of craps, which makes elegant use of control statements. The chapter discusses the so-called "C++ enhancements to C," including `inline` functions, reference parameters, default arguments, the unary scope resolution operator, function overloading and function templates. We also present C++'s call-by-value and call-by-reference capabilities. The header files table introduces many of the header files that the reader will use throughout the book. In this new edition, we provide a detailed discussion (with illustrations) of the function call stack and activation records to explain how C++ is able to keep track of which function is currently executing, how automatic variables of functions are maintained in memory and how a function knows where to return after it completes execution. The chapter offers a solid introduction to recursion and includes a table summarizing the recursion examples and exercises distributed throughout the remainder of the book. Some texts leave recursion for a chapter late in the book; we feel this topic is best covered gradually throughout the text. The extensive collection of exercises at the end of the chapter includes several classic recursion problems including the Towers of Hanoi.

Chapter 7—Arrays and Vectors—explains how to process lists and tables of values. We discuss the structuring of data in arrays of data items of the same type and demonstrate how arrays facilitate the tasks performed by objects. The early sections of this chapter use C-style, pointer-based arrays, which, as you will see in Chapter 8, are really pointers to the array contents in memory. We then present arrays as full-fledged objects in the last section of the chapter, where we introduce the C++ Standard Library `vector` class template—a robust array data structure. The chapter presents numerous examples of both one-dimensional arrays and two-dimensional arrays. Examples in the chapter investigate various common array manipulations, printing bar charts, sorting data and passing arrays to functions. The chapter includes the **final two GradeBook case study sections**, in which we use arrays to store student grades for the duration of a program's execution. Previous versions of the class process a set of grades entered by the user, but do not maintain the individual grade values in data members of the class. In this chapter, we use arrays to enable an object of the `GradeBook` class to maintain a set of grades in memory, thus eliminating the need to repeatedly input the same set of grades. The first version of the class stores the grades in a one-dimensional array and can produce a report containing the average of the grades, the minimum and maximum grades and a bar chart representing the grade distribution. The second version (i.e., the final version in the case study) uses a two-dimensional array to store the grades of a number of students on multiple exams in a semester. This version can calculate each student's semester average, as well as the minimum and maximum grades across all grades received for the semester. The class also produces a bar chart displaying the overall grade distribution for the semester. Another key feature of this chapter is the discussion of elementary sorting and searching techniques. The end-of-chapter exercises include a variety of interesting and challenging problems, such as improved sorting techniques, the design of a simple airline reservations system, an introduction to the concept of turtle graphics (made famous in the LOGO language) and the Knight's Tour and Eight Queens problems that introduce the notion of heuristic programming widely employed in the field of artificial intelligence. The exercises conclude with many recursion problems including selection sort, palindromes, linear search, the Eight Queens, printing an array, printing a string backwards and finding the minimum value in an array.

Chapter 8—Pointers and Pointer-Based Strings—presents one of the most powerful features of the C++ language—pointers. The chapter provides detailed explanations of pointer operators, call by reference, pointer expressions, pointer arithmetic, the relationship between pointers and arrays, arrays of pointers and pointers to functions. Chapter 8 demonstrates how to use `const` with pointers to enforce the principle of least privilege to build more robust software. We also introduce and using the `sizeof` operator to determine the size of a data type or data items in bytes during program compilation. There is an intimate relationship between pointers, arrays and C-style strings in C++, so we introduce basic C-style string-manipulation concepts and discuss some of the most popular C-style string-handling functions, such as `getline` (input a line of text), `strcpy` and `strncpy` (copy a string), `strcat` and `strncat` (concatenate two strings), `strcmp` and `strncmp` (compare two strings), `strtok` ("tokenize" a string into its pieces) and `strlen` (return the length of a string). In this new edition, we use `string` objects (introduced in Chapter 3) in place of C-style, `char *` pointer-based strings wherever possible. However, we include `char *` strings in Chapter 8 to help the reader master pointers and prepare for the professional world in which the reader will see a great deal of C legacy code that has been implemented over the last three decades. Thus, the reader will become familiar with the two most prevalent methods of creating and manipulating strings in C++. Many people find that the topic of pointers is, by far, the most difficult part of an introductory programming course. In C and "raw C++," arrays and strings are pointers to array and string contents in memory (even function names are pointers). Studying this chapter carefully should reward you with a deep understanding of pointers. The chapter is loaded with challenging exercises. The chapter exercises include a simulation of the classic race between the tortoise and the hare, card-shuffling and dealing algorithms, recursive quicksort and recursive maze traversals. A special section entitled "Building Your Own Computer" also is included. This section explains machine-language programming and proceeds with a project involving the design and implementation of a computer simulator that leads the student to write and run machine-language programs. This unique feature of the text will be especially useful to the reader who wants to understand how computers really work. Our students enjoy this project and often implement substantial enhancements, many of which are suggested in the exercises. A second special section includes challenging string-manipulation exercises related to text analysis, word processing, printing dates in various formats, check protection, writing the word equivalent of a check amount, Morse Code and metric-to-English conversions.

Chapter 9—Classes: A Deeper Look, Part 1—continues our discussion of object-oriented programming. This chapter uses a rich `Time` class case study to illustrate accessing class members, separating interface from implementation, using access functions and utility functions, initializing objects with constructors, destroying objects with destructors, assignment by default memberwise copy and software reusability. Students learn the order in which constructors and destructors are called during the lifetime of an object. A modification of the `Time` case study demonstrates the problems that can occur when a member function returns a reference to a `private` data member, which breaks the encapsulation of the class. The chapter exercises challenge the student to develop classes for times, dates, rectangles, and playing tic-tac-toe. Students generally enjoy game-playing programs. Mathematically inclined readers will enjoy the exercises on creating class Complex (for complex numbers), class Rational (for rational numbers) and class HugeInteger (for arbitrarily large integers).

Chapter 10—Classes: A Deeper Look, Part 2—continues the study of classes and presents additional object-oriented programming concepts. The chapter discusses declaring and using constant objects, constant member functions, composition—the process of building classes that have objects of other classes as members, friend functions and friend classes that have special access rights to the private and protected members of classes, the this pointer, which enables an object to know its own address, dynamic memory allocation, static class members for containing and manipulating class-wide data, examples of popular abstract data types (arrays, strings and queues), container classes and iterators. In our discussion of const objects, we mention keyword mutable which is used in a subtle manner to enable modification of "non-visible" implementation in const objects. We discuss dynamic memory allocation using new and delete. When new fails, the program terminates by default because new "throws an exception" in standard C++. We motivate the discussion of static class members with a video-game-based example. We emphasize how important it is to hide implementation details from clients of a class; then, we discuss proxy classes, which provide a means of hiding implementation (including the private data in class headers) from clients of a class. The chapter exercises include developing a saving-account class and a class for holding sets of integers.

Chapter 11—Operator Overloading; String and Array Objects—presents one of the most popular topics in our C++ courses. Students really enjoy this material. They find it a perfect match with the detailed discussion of crafting valuable classes in Chapters 9 and 10. Operator overloading enables the programmer to tell the compiler how to use existing operators with objects of new types. C++ already knows how to use these operators with objects of built-in types, such as integers, floats and characters. But suppose that we create a new String class—what would the plus sign mean when used between String objects? Many programmers use + with strings to mean concatenation. In Chapter 11, the programmer will learn how to "overload" the plus sign, so when it is written between two String objects in an expression, the compiler will generate a function call to an "operator function" that will concatenate the two Strings. The chapter discusses the fundamentals of operator overloading, restrictions in operator overloading, overloading with class member functions vs. with nonmember functions, overloading unary and binary operators and converting between types. Chapter 11 features a collection of substantial case studies including an array class, a String class, a date class, a huge integer class and a complex numbers class (the last two appear with full source code in the exercises). Mathematically inclined students will enjoy creating the polynomial class in the exercises. This material is different from most programming languages and courses. Operator overloading is a complex topic, but an enriching one. Using operator overloading wisely helps you add extra "polish" to your classes. The discussions of class Array and class String are particularly valuable to students who have already used the C++ Standard Library string class and vector class template that provide similar capabilities. The exercises encourage the student to add operator overloading to classes Complex, Rational and HugeInteger to enable convenient manipulation of objects of these classes with operator symbols—as in mathematics—rather than with function calls as the student did in the Chapter 10 exercises.

Chapter 12—Object-Oriented Programming: Inheritance—introduces one of the most fundamental capabilities of object-oriented programming languages—inheritance: a form of software reusability in which new classes are developed quickly and easily by absorbing the capabilities of existing classes and adding appropriate new capabilities. In the context of an **Employee hierarchy** case study, this substantially revised chapter presents a five-example sequence demonstrating `private` data, `protected` data and good software engineering with inheritance. We begin by demonstrating a class with `private` data members and `public` member functions to manipulate that data. Next, we implement a second class with additional capabilities, intentionally and tediously duplicating much of the first example's code. The third example begins our discussion of inheritance and software reuse—we use the class from the first example as a base class and quickly and simply inherit its data and functionality into a new derived class. This example introduces the inheritance mechanism and demonstrates that a derived class cannot access its base class's `private` members directly. This motivates our fourth example, in which we introduce `protected` data in the base class and demonstrate that the derived class can indeed access the `protected` data inherited from the base class. The last example in the sequence demonstrates proper software engineering by defining the base class's data as `private` and using the base class's `public` member functions (that were inherited by the derived class) to manipulate the base class's `private` data in the derived class. The chapter discusses the notions of base classes and derived classes, `protected` members, `public` inheritance, `protected` inheritance, `private` inheritance, direct base classes, indirect base classes, constructors and destructors in base classes and derived classes, and software engineering with inheritance. The chapter also compares inheritance (the *is-a* relationship) with composition (the *has-a* relationship) and introduces the *uses-a* and *knows-a* relationships.

Chapter 13—Object-Oriented Programming: Polymorphism—deals with another fundamental capability of object-oriented programming: polymorphic behavior. The completely revised Chapter 13 builds on the inheritance concepts presented in Chapter 12 and focuses on the relationships among classes in a class hierarchy and the powerful processing capabilities that these relationships enable. When many classes are related to a common base class through inheritance, each derived-class object may be treated as a base-class object. This enables programs to be written in a simple and general manner independent of the specific types of the derived-class objects. New kinds of objects can be handled by the same program, thus making systems more extensible. Polymorphism enables programs to eliminate complex `switch` logic in favor of simpler "straight-line" logic. A screen manager of a video game, for example, can send a `draw` message to every object in a linked list of objects to be drawn. Each object knows how to draw itself. An object of a new class can be added to the program without modifying that program (as long as that new object also knows how to draw itself). The chapter discusses the mechanics of achieving polymorphic behavior via `virtual` functions. It distinguishes between abstract classes (from which objects cannot be instantiated) and concrete classes (from which objects can be instantiated). Abstract classes are useful for providing an inheritable interface to classes throughout the hierarchy. We demonstrate abstract classes and polymorphic behavior by revisiting the **Employee hierarchy** of Chapter 12. We introduce an abstract `Employee` base class, from which classes `CommissionEmployee`, `Hourly-Employee` and `SalariedEmployee` inherit directly and class `BasePlusCommission-Employee` inherits indirectly. In the past, our professional audiences have insisted that we provide a deeper explanation that shows precisely how polymorphism is implemented in C++, and hence, precisely what execution time and memory "costs" are incurred when programming with this powerful capability. We responded by developing an illustration and a precise explanation of the *vtables* (virtual function tables) that the C++ compiler builds automatically to support polymorphism. To conclude, we introduce run-time type information (RTTI) and dynamic casting, which enable a program to determine an object's type at execution time, then act on that object accordingly. Using RTTI and dynamic casting, we give a 10% pay increase to employees of a specific type, then calculate the earnings for such employees. For all other employee types, we calculate their earnings polymorphically.

Appendix A—Operator Precedence and Associativity Chart—presents the complete set of C++ operator symbols, in which each operator appears on a line by itself with its operator symbol, its name and its associativity.

Appendix B—ASCII Character Set—All the programs in this book use the ASCII character set, which is presented in this appendix.

Appendix C—Fundamental Types—lists all fundamental types defined in the *C++ Standard*.

Appendix D—Number Systems—discusses the binary, octal, decimal and hexadecimal number systems. It considers how to convert numbers between bases and explains the one's complement and two's complement binary representations.

Appendix E—C++ Internet and Web Resources—contains a listing of valuable C++ resources, such as demos, information about popular compilers (including "freebies"), books, articles, conferences, job banks, journals, magazines, help, tutorials, FAQs (frequently asked questions), newsgroups, Web-based courses, product news and C++ development tools.

Appendix F—Using the Visual C++ .NET Debugger—demonstrates key features of the Visual Studio .NET Debugger, which allows a programmer to monitor the execution of applications to locate and remove logic errors. The appendix presents step-by-step instructions, so students learn how to use the debugger in a hands-on manner.

Appendix G—Using the GNU C++ Debugger—demonstrates key features of the GNU C++ Debugger, which allows a programmer to monitor the execution of applications to locate and remove logic errors. The appendix presents step-by-step instructions, so students learn how to use the debugger in a hands-on manner.

Bibliography—lists over 100 books and articles to encourage the student to do further reading on C++ and OOP.

Index—The comprehensive index enables the reader to locate by keyword any term or concept throughout the text.

Software Bundled with Small C++ How to Program, 5/e

For the academic educational market only, this textbook is available in a value pack with Microsoft® Visual C++ .NET 2003 Standard Edition integrated development environment as a free supplement. There is no time limit for using the software. [*Note:* If you are a professional using this publication, you will have to either purchase the necessary software to build and run the applications in this textbook or download one of the many free compilers available online.][*Note:* If you are a student in a course for which this book is the required textbook, you must purchase your book from your college bookstore to ensure that you get the value pack with the software. College bookstores will need to order the books directly from Prentice Hall to get the value pack with the software. A caution—used books may not include the software.]

Free C++ Compilers and Trial-Edition C++ Compilers on the Web

Many C++ compilers are available for download from the Web. We discuss several that are available for free or as free-trial versions. Please keep in mind that in many cases, the trial-edition software cannot be used after the (often brief) trial period has expired.

One popular organization that develops free software is the GNU Project (www.gnu.org), originally created to develop a free operating system similar to UNIX. GNU offers developer resources, including editors, debuggers and compilers. Many developers use the GCC (GNU Compiler Collection) compilers, available for download from gcc.gnu.org. The GCC contains compilers for C, C++, Java and other languages. The GCC compiler is a command-line compiler (i.e., it does not provide a graphical user interface). Many Linux and UNIX systems come with the GCC compiler installed. Red Hat has developed Cygwin (www.cygwin.com), an emulator that allows developers to use UNIX commands on Windows. Cygwin includes the GCC compiler.

Borland provides a Windows-based C++ developer product called C++Builder (www.borland.com/cbuilder/cppcomp/index.html). The basic C++Builder compiler (a command-line compiler) is free for download. Borland also provides several versions of C++Builder that contain graphical user interfaces (GUIs). These GUIs are formally called integrated development environments (IDEs) and enable the developer to edit, debug and test programs quickly and conveniently. Using an IDE, many of the tasks that involved tedious commands can now be executed via menus and buttons. Some of these products are available on a free-trial basis. For more information on C++Builder, visit

> www.borland.com/products/downloads/download_cbuilder.html

For Linux developers, Borland provides the Borland Kylix development environment. The Borland Kylix Open Edition, which includes an IDE, can be downloaded from

> www.borland.com/products/downloads/download_kylix.html

Borland also provides C++BuilderX—a cross-platform integrated C++ development environment. The free Personal Edition is available from

> www.borland.com/products/downloads/download_cbuilderx.html

The command-line compiler (version 5.6.4) that comes with C++BuilderX was one of several compilers we used to test the programs in this book. Many of the downloads available from Borland require users to register.

The Digital Mars C++ Compiler (www.digitalmars.com), is available for Windows and DOS, and includes tutorials and documentation. Readers can download a command-line or IDE version of the compiler. The DJGPP C/C++ development system is available for computers running DOS. DJGPP stands for DJ's GNU Programming Platform, where DJ is for DJ Delorie, the creator of DJGPP. Information on DJGPP can be found at www.delorie.com/djgpp. Locations where the compiler can be downloaded at are provided at www.delorie.com/djgpp/getting.html.

For a list of other compilers that are available free for download, visit the following sites:

```
www.thefreecountry.com/compilers/cpp.shtml
www.compilers.net
```

Warnings and Error Messages on Older C++ Compilers

The programs in this book are designed to be used with compilers that support standard C++. However, there are variations among compilers that may cause occasional warnings or errors. In addition, though the standard specifies various situations that require errors to be generated, it does not specify the messages that compilers should issue. Warnings and error messages vary among compilers—this is normal.

Some older C++ compilers, such as Microsoft Visual C++ 6, Borland C++ 5.5 and various earlier versions of GNU C++, generate error or warning messages in places where newer compilers do not. Although most of the examples in this book will work with these older compilers, there are a few examples that need minor modifications to work with older compilers. The Web site for this book (www.deitel.com/books/scpphtp5/index.html) lists the warnings and error messages that are produced by several older compilers and what, if anything, you can do to fix the warnings and errors.

Notes Regarding **using** *Declarations and C Standard Library Functions*

The C++ Standard Library includes the functions from the C Standard Library. According to the C++ standard document, the contents of the header files that come from the C Standard Library are part of the "std" namespace. Some compilers (old and new) generate error messages when using declarations are encountered for C functions. We will post a list of these issues at www.deitel.com/books/scpphtp5/index.html.

DIVE-INTO™ Series Tutorials for Popular C++ Environments

Our free *Dive-Into™* Series publications, which are available with the resources for *Small C++ How to Program, 5/e* at www.deitel.com/books/downloads.html, help students and instructors familiarize themselves with various C++ development tools. These publications include:

- *Dive-Into Microsoft® Visual C++® 6*
- *Dive-Into Microsoft® Visual C++® .NET*
- *Dive-Into Borland™ C++Builder™ Compiler* (command-line version)
- *Dive-Into Borland™ C++Builder™ Personal* (IDE version)
- *Dive-Into GNU C++ on Linux* and *Dive-Into GNU C++ via Cygwin on Windows* (Cygwin is a UNIX emulator for Windows. It includes the GNU C++ compiler)

Each of these tutorials shows how to compile, execute and debug C++ applications in that particular compiler product. Many of these documents also provide step-by-step instructions with screenshots to help readers install the software. Each document overviews the compiler and its online documentation.

Teaching Resources for *Small C++ How to Program, 5/e*

Small C++ How to Program, 5/e, has extensive resources for instructors. The *Instructor's Resource CD (IRCD)* contains the *Solutions Manual* with solutions to the vast majority of the end-of-chapter exercises, a *Test Item File* of multiple-choice questions (approximately two per book section) and PowerPoint slides containing all the code and figures in the text, plus bulleted items that summarize the key points in the text. Instructors can customize the slides. [*Note:* The IRCD is *available only to instructors* through their Prentice Hall representatives. To find your local sales representative, visit

    `vig.prenhall.com/replocator`

If you need additional help or if you have any questions about the IRCD, please email us at `deitel@deitel.com`. We will respond promptly.]

C++ Multimedia Cyber Classroom, 5/e, Online

C++ How to Program, 5/e and *Small C++ How to Program, 5/e* each include a free, Web-based interactive multimedia ancillary to the book—*The C++ Multimedia Cyber Classroom, 5/e*—available with the purchase of a new book. Our Web-based *Cyber Classroom* will include audio walkthroughs of code examples in the text, solutions to about half of the exercises in the book, a free lab manual and more. For more information about the new Web-based *Cyber Classroom*, please visit our Web site at `www.deitel.com` or sign up for the free *Deitel® Buzz Online* e-mail newsletter at

    `www.deitel.com/newsletter/subscribe.html`.

Students who use our *Cyber Classrooms* tell us that they like the interactivity and that the *Cyber Classroom* is a powerful reference tool. Professors tell us that their students enjoy using the *Cyber Classroom* and consequently spend more time on the courses, mastering more of the material than in textbook-only courses. For a complete list of our current CD-ROM-based *Cyber Classrooms*, see the *Deitel® Series* page at the beginning of this book, the product listing and ordering information at the end of this book, or visit `www.deitel.com`, `www.prenhall.com/deitel` or `www.InformIT.com/deitel`.

C++ in the Lab

C++ in the Lab: Lab Manual to Accompany C++ How to Program, 5/e, our online lab manual that is now part of the *Cyber Classroom*, complements *C++ How to Program, 5/e,* and *Small C++ How to Program, 5/e,* with hands-on lab assignments designed to reinforce students' comprehension of lecture material. *C++ in the Lab* will be available with new books purchased from Prentice Hall for fall 2005 classes. This lab manual is designed for closed laboratories—regularly scheduled classes supervised by an instructor. Closed laboratories provide an excellent learning environment, because students can use concepts presented in class to solve carefully designed lab problems. Instructors are better able to measure the students' understanding of the material by monitoring the students' progress in lab. This lab manual also can be used for open laboratories, homework and for self-study.

Chapters 1–13 in the lab manual are divided into *Prelab Activities, Lab Exercises* and *Postlab Activities*. Each chapter contains objectives that introduce the lab's key topics and an assignment checklist for students to mark which exercises the instructor has assigned.

Solutions to the lab manual's *Prelab Activities, Lab Exercises* and *Postlab Activities* are available in electronic form. Instructors can obtain these materials from their regular Prentice Hall representatives; the solutions are not available to students.

Prelab Activities

Prelab Activities are intended to be completed by students after studying each chapter of *Small C++ How to Program, 5/e*. *Prelab Activities* test students' understanding of the textbook material and prepare students for the programming exercises in the lab session. The exercises focus on important terminology and programming concepts and are effective for self-review. *Prelab Activities* include *Matching Exercises, Fill-in-the-Blank Exercises, Short-Answer Questions, Programming-Output Exercises* (determine what short code segments do without actually running the program) and *Correct-the-Code Exercises* (identify and correct all errors in short code segments).

Lab Exercises

The most important section in each chapter is the *Lab Exercises*. These teach students how to apply the material learned in *Small C++ How to Program, 5/e*, and prepare them for writing C++ programs. Each lab contains one or more lab exercises and a debugging problem. The *Lab Exercises* contain the following:

- *Lab Objectives* highlight specific concepts on which the lab exercise focuses.

- *Problem Descriptions* provide the details of the exercise and hints to help students implement the program.

- *Sample Outputs* illustrate the desired program behavior, which further clarifies the problem descriptions and aids the students with writing programs.

- *Program Templates* take complete C++ programs and replace key lines of code with comments describing the missing code.

- *Problem-Solving Tips* highlight key issues that students need to consider when solving the lab exercises.

- *Follow-Up Questions and Activities* ask students to modify solutions to lab exercises, write new programs that are similar to their lab-exercise solutions or explain the implementation choices that were made when solving lab exercises.

- *Debugging Problems* consist of blocks of code that contain syntax errors and/or logic errors. These alert students to the types of errors they are likely to encounter while programming.

Postlab Activities

Professors typically assign *Postlab Activities* to reinforce key concepts or to provide students with more programming experience outside the lab. *Postlab Activities* test the students' understanding of the *Prelab* and *Lab Exercise* material, and ask students to apply their knowledge to creating programs from scratch. The section provides two types of programming activities: coding exercises and programming challenges. Coding exercises are short and serve as review after the *Prelab Activities* and *Lab Exercises* have been completed. The coding exercises ask students to write programs or program segments using key concepts from the textbook. *Programming Challenges* allow students to apply their knowledge to substantial programming exercises. Hints, sample outputs and pseudocode are provided to aid students with these problems. Students who successfully complete the *Programming Challenges* for a chapter have mastered the chapter material. Answers to the programming challenges are available at www.deitel.com/books/downloads.html.

CourseCompass^{SM}, WebCT™ and Blackboard™

Selected content from the Deitels' introductory programming language *How to Program* series textbooks, including *Small C++ How to Program, 5/e*, is available to integrate into various popular course management systems, including CourseCompass, Blackboard and WebCT. Course management systems help faculty create, manage and use sophisticated Web-based educational tools and programs. Instructors can save hours of inputting data by using the Deitel course-management-systems content.

Blackboard, CourseCompass and WebCT offer:

- **Features to create and customize an online course**, such as areas to post course information (e.g., policies, syllabi, announcements, assignments, grades, performance evaluations and progress tracking), class and student management tools, a gradebook, reporting tools, page tracking, a calendar and assignments.

- **Communication tools** to help create and maintain interpersonal relationships between students and instructors, including chat rooms, whiteboards, document sharing, bulletin boards and private e-mail.

- **Flexible testing tools** that allow an instructor to create online quizzes and tests from questions directly linked to the text, and that grade and track results effectively. All tests can be inputted into the gradebook for efficient course management. WebCT also allows instructors to administer timed online quizzes.

- **Support materials** for instructors are available in print and online formats.

In addition to the types of tools found in Blackboard and WebCT, CourseCompass from Prentice Hall includes:

- **CourseCompass course home page**, which makes the course as easy to navigate as a book. An expandable table of contents allows instructors to view course content at a glance and to link to any section.

- **Hosting on Prentice Hall's centralized servers**, which allows course administrators to avoid separate licensing fees or server-space issues. Access to Prentice Hall technical support is available.

- **"How Do I" online-support sections** are available for users who need help personalizing course sites, including step-by-step instructions for adding PowerPoint slides, video and more.

- **Instructor Quick Start Guide** helps instructors create online courses using a simple, step-by-step process.

To view free online demonstrations and learn more about these Course Management Systems, which support Deitel content, visit the following Web sites:

- Blackboard: www.blackboard.com and www.prenhall.com/blackboard

- WebCT: www.webct.com and www.prenhall.com/webct

- CourseCompass: www.coursecompass.com and www.prenhall.com/coursecompass

PearsonChoices

Today's students have increasing demands on their time and money, and they need to be resourceful about how, when and where they study. Pearson/Prentice Hall, a division of Pearson Education, has responded to that need by creating PearsonChoices to allow faculty and students to choose from a variety of textbook formats and prices.

Small C++ How to Program, 5/e is our alternative print edition to *C++ How to Program, 5/e*. *Small C++ How to Program, 5/e* is a smaller text that is focused on Computer Science 1 (CS1) programming courses and is priced lower than our 24-chapter *C++ How to Program, 5/e* and other competing texts in the CS1 market.

Chapters in Both **Small C++ How to Program, 5/e** *and* **C++ How to Program, 5/e**
Chapter 1—Introduction to Computers, the Internet and World Wide Web
Chapter 2—Introduction to C++ Programming
Chapter 3—Introduction to Classes and Objects
Chapter 4—Control Statements: Part 1
Chapter 5—Control Statements: Part 2
Chapter 6—Functions and an Introduction to Recursion
Chapter 7—Arrays and Vectors
Chapter 8—Pointers and Pointer-Based Strings
Chapter 9—Classes: A Deeper Look, Part 1
Chapter 10—Classes: A Deeper Look, Part 2
Chapter 11—Operator Overloading: String and Array Objects
Chapter 12—Object-Oriented Programming: Inheritance
Chapter 13—Object-Oriented Programming: Polymorphism

Appendices in Both **Small C++ How to Program, 5/e** *and* **C++ How to Program, 5/e**
Operator Precedence and Associativity Chart
ASCII Character Set
Fundamental Types
Number Systems
C++ Internet and Web Resources
Using the Visual C++ .NET Debugger
Using the GNU C++ Debugger

Chapters in Only **C++ How to Program, 5/e**
Chapter 14—Templates
Chapter 15—Stream Input/Output
Chapter 16—Exception Handling
Chapter 17—File Processing
Chapter 18—Class `string` and String Stream Processing
Chapter 19—Web Programming
Chapter 20—Searching and Sorting
Chapter 21—Data Structures
Chapter 22—Bits, Characters, Streams and Structures
Chapter 23—Standard Template Library
Chapter 24—Other Topics

Appendices in Only **C++ How to Program, 5/e**
C Legacy-Code Topics
Preprocessor
ATM Case Study Code
UML 2 Diagrams
Introduction to XHTML
XHTML Special Characters

SafariX WebBooks

SafariX Textbooks Online is a new service for college students looking to save money on required or recommended textbooks for academic courses. This secure WebBooks platform creates a new option in the higher education market; an additional choice for students alongside conventional textbooks and online learning services. Pearson provides students with a WebBook at 50% of the cost of its conventional print equivalent.

SafariX WebBooks are viewed through a Web browser connected to the Internet. No special plug-ins are required and no applications need to be downloaded. Students simply log in, purchase access and begin studying. With SafariX Textbooks Online students can search the text, make notes online, print out reading assignments that incorporate their professors' lecture notes and bookmark important passages they want to review later. They can navigate easily to a page number, reading assignment, or chapter. The Table of Contents of each WebBook appears in the left hand column alongside the text.

We are pleased to offer students the *Small C++ How to Program, 5/e* SafariX WebBook available for fall 2005 classes. Visit www.pearsonchoices.com for more information. Other Deitel titles available as SafariX WebBooks include *Java How to Program, 6/e, Small Java How to Program, 6/e, C++ How to Program, 5/e* and *Simply C++: An Application-Driven Tutorial Approach.* Visit www.safarix.com/tour.html for more information.

THE DEITEL® *Buzz Online* Free E-mail Newsletter

Our free e-mail newsletter, the DEITEL® *Buzz Online* is sent to approximately 38,000 opt-in, registered subscribers and includes commentary on industry trends and developments, links to free articles and resources from our published books and upcoming publications, product-release schedules, errata, challenges, anecdotes, information on our corporate instructor-led training courses and more. It's also our way to notify our readers rapidly about issues related to *Small C++ How to Program, 5/e.* To subscribe, visit

    www.deitel.com/newsletter/subscribe.html

Acknowledgments

One of the great pleasures of writing a textbook is acknowledging the efforts of many people whose names may not appear on the cover, but whose hard work, cooperation, friendship and understanding were crucial to the production of the book. Many people at Deitel & Associates, Inc. devoted long hours to working with us on this project.

- Andrew B. Goldberg is a graduate of Amherst College, where he earned a bachelor's degree in Computer Science. Andrew updated Chapters 1–13 based on the book's new early-classes presentation and other content revisions.

- Jeff Listfield is a Computer Science graduate of Harvard College. Jeff contributed to Appendices A–C, F and G.

- Cheryl Yaeger graduated from Boston University in three years with a bachelor's degree in Computer Science. Cheryl contributed to Chapters 4, 6, 8, 9 and 13.

- Barbara Deitel, Chief Financial Officer at Deitel & Associates, Inc. researched the quotes at the beginning of each chapter and applied copyedits to the book.

- Abbey Deitel, President of Deitel & Associates, Inc., is an Industrial Management graduate of Carnegie Mellon University. She contributed to the Preface and Chapter 1. She applied copyedits to several chapters in the book, managed the review process and suggested the theme and bug names for the cover of the book.

- Christi Kelsey is a graduate of Purdue University with a bachelor's degree in Management and a minor in Information Systems. Christi contributed to the Preface and Chapter 1. She edited the Index, paged the manuscript and coordinated many aspects of our publishing relationship with Prentice Hall.

We are fortunate to have worked on this project with the talented and dedicated team of publishing professionals at Prentice Hall. We especially appreciate the extraordinary efforts of our Computer Science Editor, Kate Hargett and her boss and our mentor in publishing—Marcia Horton, Editorial Director of Prentice Hall's Engineering and Computer Science Division. Jennifer Cappello did an extraordinary job recruiting the review team and managing the review process from the Prentice Hall side. Vince O'Brien, Tom Manshreck and John Lovell did a marvelous job managing the production of the book. The talents of Paul Belfanti, Carole Anson, Xiaohong Zhu and Geoffrey Cassar are evident in the redesign of the book's interior and the new cover art, and Sarah Parker managed the publication of the book's extensive ancillary package.

We sincerely appreciate the efforts of our fifth-edition reviewers and our fourth-edition post-publication reviewers:

Academic Reviewers
Karen Arlien, Bismarck State College
David Branigan, DeVry University, Illinois
Jimmy Chen, Salt Lake Community College
Martin Dulberg, North Carolina State University
Ric Heishman, Northern Virginia Community College
Richard Holladay, San Diego Mesa College
William Honig, Loyola University
Earl LaBatt, OPNET Technologies, Inc.; University of New Hampshire
Brian Larson, Modesto Junior College
Gavin Osborne, Saskatchewan Institute of Applied Science and Technology
Donna Reese, Mississippi State University

Industry Reviewers
Curtis Green, Boeing Integrated Defense Systems
James Huddleston, Independent Consultant
Ed James-Beckham, Borland Software Corporation
Don Kostuch, Independent Consultant

Kriang Lerdsuwanakij, Siemens Limited
William Mike Miller, Edison Design Group, Inc.
Mark Schimmel, Borland International
Vicki Scott, Metrowerks
James Snell, Boeing Integrated Defense Systems
Raymond Stephenson, Microsoft

C++ 4/e Post-Publication Reviewers
Butch Anton, Wi-Tech Consulting
Karen Arlien, Bismarck State College
Jimmy Chen, Salt Lake Community College
Martin Dulberg, North Carolina State University
William Honig, Loyola University
Don Kostuch, Independent Consultant
Earl LaBatt, OPNET Technologies, Inc./ University of New Hampshire
Brian Larson, Modesto Junior College
Kriang Lerdsuwanakij, Siemens Limited
Robert Myers, Florida State University
Gavin Osborne, Saskatchewan Institute of Applied Science and Technology
Wolfgang Pelz, The University of Akron
David Papurt, Independent Consultant
Donna Reese, Mississippi State University
Catherine Wyman, DeVry University, Phoenix
Salih Yurttas, Texas A&M University

Under a tight time schedule, they scrutinized every aspect of the text and made countless suggestions for improving the accuracy and completeness of the presentation.

Well, there you have it! Welcome to the exciting world of C++ and object-oriented programming. We hope you enjoy this look at contemporary computer programming. Good luck! As you read the book, we would sincerely appreciate your comments, criticisms, corrections and suggestions for improving the text. Please address all correspondence to:

deitel@deitel.com

We will respond promptly, and we will post corrections and clarifications on :

www.deitel.com/books/scpphtp5/index.html

We hope you enjoy learning with *Small C++ How to Program, Fifth Edition* as much as we enjoyed writing it!

Dr. Harvey M. Deitel
Paul J. Deitel

About the Authors

Dr. Harvey M. Deitel, Chairman and Chief Strategy Officer of Deitel & Associates, Inc., has 43 years experience in the computing field, including extensive industry and academic experience. Dr. Deitel earned B.S. and M.S. degrees from the Massachusetts Institute of Technology and a Ph.D. from Boston University. He worked on the pioneering virtual-memory operating-systems projects at IBM and MIT that developed techniques now widely implemented in systems such as UNIX, Linux and Windows XP. He has 20 years of college teaching experience, including earning tenure and serving as the Chairman of the Computer Science Department at Boston College before founding Deitel & Associates, Inc., with his son, Paul J. Deitel. Dr. Deitel has delivered hundreds of professional seminars to major corporations, academic institutions, government organizations and the military. He and Paul are the co-authors of several dozen books and multimedia packages and they are writing many more. With translations published in Japanese, German, Russian, Spanish, Traditional Chinese, Simplified Chinese, Korean, French, Polish, Italian, Portuguese, Greek, Urdu and Turkish, the Deitels' texts have earned international recognition.

Paul J. Deitel, CEO and Chief Technical Officer of Deitel & Associates, Inc., is a graduate of MIT's Sloan School of Management, where he studied Information Technology. Through Deitel & Associates, Inc., he has delivered C++, Java, C, Internet and World Wide Web courses to industry clients including IBM, Sun Microsystems, Dell, Lucent Technologies, Fidelity, NASA at the Kennedy Space Center, the National Severe Storm Laboratory, PalmSource, White Sands Missile Range, Rogue Wave Software, Boeing, Stratus, Cambridge Technology Partners, TJX, One Wave, Hyperion Software, Adra Systems, Entergy, CableData Systems and many other organizations. Paul is one of the world's most experienced Java and C++ corporate trainers having taught over 100 professional Java and C++ training courses. He has also lectured on C++ and Java for the Boston Chapter of the Association for Computing Machinery. He and his father, Dr. Harvey M. Deitel, are the world's best-selling Computer Science textbook authors.

About Deitel & Associates, Inc.

Deitel & Associates, Inc., is an internationally recognized corporate training and content-creation organization specializing in computer programming languages, Internet/World Wide Web software technology and object technology education. The company provides instructor-led courses on major programming languages and platforms such as Java, Advanced Java, C, C++, .NET programming languages, XML, Perl, Python; object technology; and Internet and World Wide Web programming. The founders of Deitel & Associates, Inc., are Dr. Harvey M. Deitel and Paul J. Deitel. The company's clients include many of the world's largest computer companies, government agencies, branches of the military and business organizations. Through its 29-year publishing partnership with Prentice Hall, Deitel & Associates, Inc. publishes leading-edge programming textbooks, professional books, interactive multimedia *Cyber Classrooms*, *Complete Training Courses*, Web-based training courses and course management systems e-content for popular CMSs such as WebCT, Blackboard and Pearson's CourseCompass. Deitel & Associates, Inc., and the authors can be reached via e-mail at:

    deitel@deitel.com

To learn more about Deitel & Associates, Inc., its publications and its worldwide *DIVE INTO*™ Series Corporate Training curriculum, see the last few pages of this book or visit:

    www.deitel.com

and subscribe to the free _DEITEL® Buzz Online_ e-mail newsletter at:

```
www.deitel.com/newsletter/subscribe.html
```

Individuals wishing to purchase Deitel books, Cyber Classrooms, Complete Training Courses and Web-based training courses can do so through:

```
www.deitel.com/books/index.html
```

Bulk orders by corporations and academic institutions should be placed directly with Prentice Hall. See the last few pages of this book for worldwide ordering details.

Before You Begin

Please follow the instructions in this section to ensure that the book's examples are copied properly to your computer before you begin using this book.

Font and Naming Conventions

We use fonts to distinguish between on-screen components (such as menu names and menu items) and C++ code or commands. Our convention is to emphasize on-screen components in a sans-serif bold **Helvetica** font (for example, **File** menu) and to emphasize C++ code and commands in a sans-serif `Lucida` font (for example, `cout << "Hello";`).

Resources on the CD That Accompanies Small C++ How to Program, Fifth Edition

The CD that accompanies this book includes:

- Hundreds of C++ LIVE-CODE examples

- Links to free C++ compilers and integrated development environments (IDEs)

- Hundreds of Web resources, including general references, tutorials, FAQs and newsgroups.

If you have any questions, please feel free to email us at `deitel@deitel.com`. We will respond promptly.

Copying and Organizing Files

All of the examples for *Small C++ How to Program, Fifth Edition* are included on the CD that accompanies this book. Follow the steps in the next section, *Copying the Book Examples from the CD*, to copy the `examples` directory from the CD onto your hard drive. We suggest that you work from your hard drive rather than your CD drive for two reasons: The CD is read-only, so you cannot save your applications to the book's CD, and files can be accessed faster from a hard drive than from a CD. The examples from the book are also available for download from:

```
www.deitel.com/books/scpphtp5/index.html
www.prenhall.com/deitel
```

We assume for the purpose of this Before You Begin section that you are using a computer running Microsoft Windows. Screen shots in the following section might differ slightly from what you see on your computer, depending on whether you are using Windows 2000 or Windows XP. If you are running a different operating system and have questions about copying the example files to your computer, please see your instructor.

Copying the Book Examples from the CD

1. *Inserting the CD.* Insert the CD that accompanies *Small C++ How To Program, Fifth Edition* into your computer's CD drive. The window displayed in Fig. 1 should appear. If the page appears, proceed to *Step 3* of this section. If the page does not appear, proceed to *Step 2*.

2. *Opening the CD directory using My Computer.* If the page shown in Fig. 1 does not appear, double click the **My Computer** icon on your desktop. In the **My Computer** window, double click your CD-ROM drive (Fig. 2) to load the CD (Fig. 1).

3. *Opening the CD-ROM directory.* If the page in Fig. 1 does appear, click the **Browse CD Contents** link (Fig. 1) to access the CD's contents.

4. *Copying the examples directory.* Right click the newly copied examples directory (Fig. 3), then select **Copy**. Next, go to **My Computer** and double click the **C:** drive. Select the **Edit** menu's **Paste** option to copy the directory and its contents from the CD to your **C:** drive. [*Note*: We save the examples to the **C:** drive and refer to this drive throughout the text. You may choose to save your files to a different drive based on your computer's setup, the setup in your school's lab or your personal preferences. If you are working in a computer lab, please see your instructor for more information to confirm where the examples should be saved.]

The book example files you copied onto your computer from the CD are read-only. Next, you will remove the read-only property so you can modify and run the examples.

Changing the Read-Only Property of Files

1. *Opening the Properties dialog.* Right click the examples directory and select **Properties** from the menu. The **examples Properties** dialog appears (Fig. 4).

2. *Changing the read-only property.* In the **Attributes** section of this dialog, click the box next to **Read-only** to remove the check mark (Fig. 5). Click **Apply** to apply the changes.

3. *Changing the property for all files.* Clicking **Apply** will display the **Confirm Attribute Changes** window (Fig. 6). In this window, click the radio button next to **Apply changes to this folder, subfolders and files** and click **OK** to remove the read-only property for all of the files and directories in the examples directory.

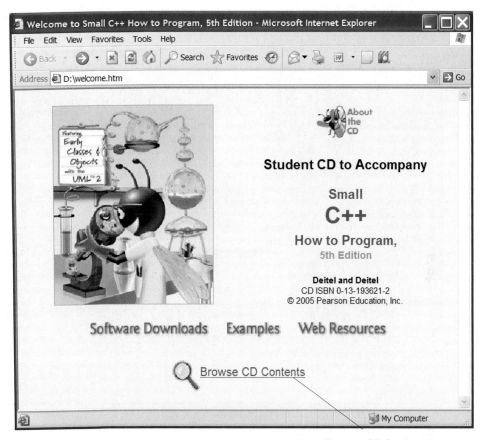

Click the **Browse CD Contents**

Fig. 1 | Welcome page for Small C++ How to Program CD.

Selected CD-ROM drive

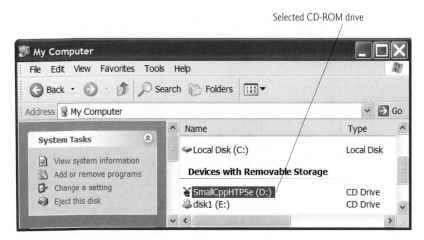

Fig. 2 | Locating the CD-ROM drive.

Right click the
examples directory

Select **Copy**

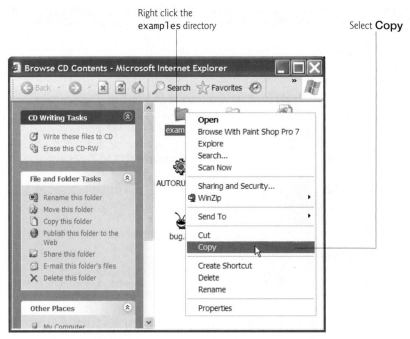

Fig. 3 | Copying the **examples** directory.

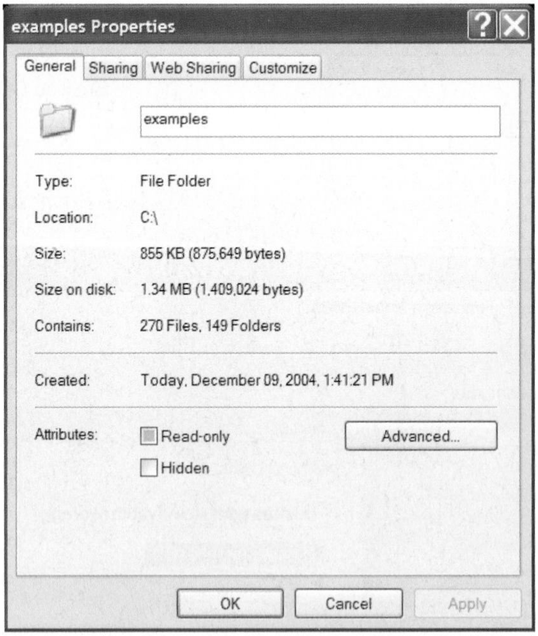

Fig. 4 | **examples Properties** dialog.

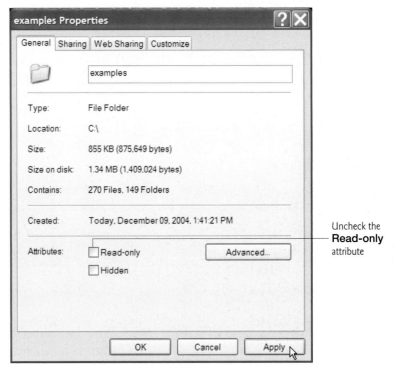

Fig. 5 | Unchecking the **Read-only** check box.

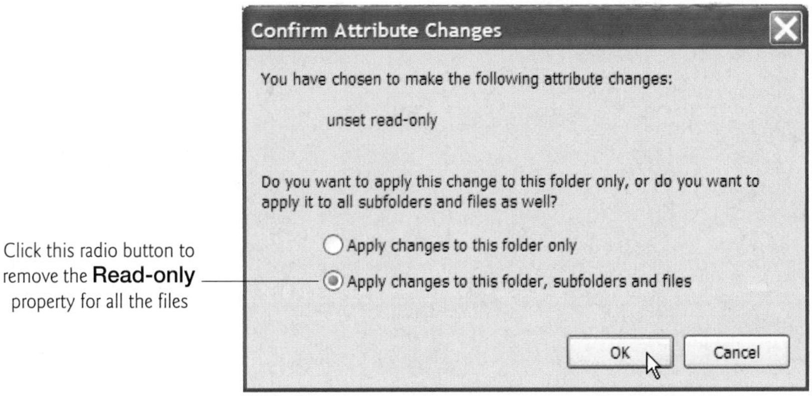

Fig. 6 | Removing read-only for all the files in the `examples` directory.

You are now ready to begin your C++ studies with *Small C++ How to Program*. We hope you enjoy the book! You can reach us easily at `deitel@deitel.com`. We will respond promptly.

Introduction to Computers, the Internet and World Wide Web

The chief merit of language is clearness.
—Galen

Our life is frittered away by detail. ... Simplify, simplify.
—Henry David Thoreau

He had a wonderful talent for packing thought close, and rendering it portable.
—Thomas B. Macaulay

Man is still the most extraordinary computer of all.
—John F. Kennedy

OBJECTIVES

In this chapter you will learn:

- Basic hardware and software concepts.
- Basic object-technology concepts, such as classes, objects, attributes, behaviors, encapsulation and inheritance.
- The different types of programming languages.
- Which programming languages are most widely used.
- A typical C++ program development environment.
- The history of the industry-standard object-oriented system modeling language, the UML.
- The history of the Internet and the World Wide Web.
- To test-drive C++ applications in two popular C++ environments—GNU C++ running on Linux and Microsoft's Visual C++® .NET running on Windows® XP.

Outline

1.1   Introduction

1.2   What Is a Computer?

1.3   Computer Organization

1.4   Early Operating Systems

1.5   Personal, Distributed and Client/Server Computing

1.6   The Internet and the World Wide Web

1.7   Machine Languages, Assembly Languages and High-Level Languages

1.8   History of C and C++

1.9   C++ Standard Library

1.10 History of Java

1.11 FORTRAN, COBOL, Pascal and Ada

1.12 Basic, Visual Basic, Visual C++, C# and .NET

1.13 Key Software Trend: Object Technology

1.14 Typical C++ Development Environment

1.15 Notes About C++ and Small C++ How to Program, 5/e

1.16 Test-Driving a C++ Application

1.17 Introduction to Object Technology and the UML

1.18 Wrap-Up

1.19 Web Resources

Summary | Terminology | Self-Review Exercises | Answers to Self-Review Exercises | Exercises

1.1 Introduction

Welcome to C++! We have worked hard to create what we hope you will find to be an informative, entertaining and challenging learning experience. C++ is a powerful computer programming language that is appropriate for technically oriented people with little or no programming experience and for experienced programmers to use in building substantial information systems. *Small C++ How to Program, Fifth Edition*, is an effective learning tool for each of these audiences.

The core of the book emphasizes achieving program *clarity* through the proven techniques of object-oriented programming—this is an "early classes and objects" book—nonprogrammers will learn programming the right way from the beginning. The presentation is clear, straightforward and abundantly illustrated. We teach C++ features in the context of complete working C++ programs and show the outputs produced when those programs are run on a computer—we call this the live-code approach. The example programs are included on the CD that accompanies this book, or you may download them from www.deitel.com or www.prenhall.com/deitel.

The early chapters introduce the fundamentals of computers, computer programming and the C++ computer programming language, providing a solid foundation for the deeper treatment of C++ in the later chapters. Experienced programmers tend to read the early chapters quickly, then find the treatment of C++ in the remainder of the book both rigorous and challenging.

Most people are at least somewhat familiar with the exciting things computers do. Using this textbook, you will learn how to command computers to do those things. Computers (often referred to as hardware) are controlled by software (i.e., the instructions you write to command the computer to perform actions and make decisions). C++ is one of today's most popular software development languages. This text provides an introduction to programming in the version of C++ standardized in the United States through the American National Standards Institute (ANSI) and worldwide through the efforts of the International Organization for Standardization (ISO).

Computer use is increasing in almost every field of endeavor. Computing costs have been decreasing dramatically due to rapid developments in both hardware and software technologies. Computers that might have filled large rooms and cost millions of dollars a few decades ago can now be inscribed on silicon chips smaller than a fingernail, costing a few dollars each. (Those large computers were called mainframes and are widely used today in business, government and industry.) Fortunately, silicon is one of the most abundant materials on earth—it's an ingredient in common sand. Silicon chip technology has made computing so economical that about a billion general-purpose computers are in use worldwide, helping people in business, industry and government, and in their personal lives.

Over the years, many programmers learned the programming methodology called structured programming. You will learn structured programming and an exciting newer methodology, object-oriented programming. Why do we teach both? Object orientation is the key programming methodology used by programmers today. You will create and work with many software objects in this text. You will discover however, that their internal structure is often built using structured-programming techniques. Also, the logic of manipulating objects is occasionally expressed with structured programming.

You are embarking on a challenging and rewarding path. As you proceed, if you have any questions, please send e-mail to

    deitel@deitel.com

We will respond promptly. To keep up to date with C++ developments at Deitel & Associates, please register for our free e-mail newsletter, the *Deitel® Buzz Online,* at

    www.deitel.com/newsletter/subscribe.html

We hope that you will enjoy learning with *C++ How to Program, Fifth Edition.*

1.2 What Is a Computer?

A computer is a device capable of performing computations and making logical decisions at speeds millions (even billions) of times faster than human beings can. For example, many of today's personal computers can perform a billion additions per second. A person operating a desk calculator could spend an entire lifetime performing calculations and still not complete as many calculations as a powerful personal computer can perform in one second! (Points to ponder: How would you know whether the person added the numbers correctly? How would you know whether the computer added the numbers correctly?) Today's fastest supercomputers can perform trillions of additions per second!

Computers process data under the control of sets of instructions called computer programs. These programs guide the computer through orderly sets of actions specified by people called computer programmers.

A computer consists of various devices referred to as hardware (e.g., the keyboard, screen, mouse, hard disk, memory, DVDs and processing units). The programs that run on a computer are referred to as software. Hardware costs have been declining dramatically in recent years, to the point that personal computers have become a commodity. In this book, you will learn a proven methodology that is reducing software development costs—object-oriented programming.

1.3 Computer Organization

Regardless of differences in physical appearance, virtually every computer may be envisioned as divided into six logical units or sections:

1. **Input unit.** This is the "receiving" section of the computer. It obtains information (data and computer programs) from input devices and places this information at the disposal of the other units for processing. Most information is entered into computers through keyboards and mouse devices. Information also can be entered in many other ways, including by speaking to your computer, scanning images and having your computer receive information from a network, such as the Internet.

2. **Output unit.** This is the "shipping" section of the computer. It takes information that the computer has processed and places it on various output devices to make the information available for use outside the computer. Most information output from computers today is displayed on screens, printed on paper or used to control other devices. Computers also can output their information to networks, such as the Internet.

3. **Memory unit.** This is the rapid-access, relatively low-capacity "warehouse" section of the computer. It stores computer programs while they are being executed. It retains information that has been entered through the input unit, so that it will be immediately available for processing when needed. The memory unit also retains processed information until it can be placed on output devices by the output unit. Information in the memory unit is typically lost when the computer's power is turned off. The memory unit is often called either memory or primary memory. [Historically, this unit has been called "core memory," but that term is fading from use today.]

4. **Arithmetic and logic unit (ALU).** This is the "manufacturing" section of the computer. It is responsible for performing calculations, such as addition, subtraction, multiplication and division. It contains the decision mechanisms that allow the computer, for example, to compare two items from the memory unit to determine whether they are equal.

5. **Central processing unit (CPU).** This is the "administrative" section of the computer. It coordinates and supervises the operation of the other sections. The CPU tells the input unit when information should be read into the memory unit, tells the ALU when information from the memory unit should be used in calculations and tells the output unit when to send information from the memory unit to certain output devices. Many of today's computers have multiple CPUs and, hence, can perform many operations simultaneously—such computers are called multiprocessors.

6. Secondary storage unit. This is the long-term, high-capacity "warehousing" section of the computer. Programs or data not actively being used by the other units normally are placed on secondary storage devices, such as your hard drive, until they are again needed, possibly hours, days, months or even years later. Information in secondary storage takes much longer to access than information in primary memory, but the cost per unit of secondary storage is much less than that of primary memory. Other secondary storage devices include CDs and DVDs, which can hold hundreds of millions of characters and billions of characters, respectively.

1.4 Early Operating Systems

Early computers could perform only one job or task at a time. This is often called single-user batch processing. The computer runs a single program at a time while processing data in groups or batches. In these early systems, users generally submitted their jobs to a computer center on decks of punched cards and often had to wait hours or even days before printouts were returned to their desks.

Software systems called operating systems were developed to make using computers more convenient. Early operating systems smoothed and speeded up the transition between jobs, and hence increased the amount of work, or throughput, computers could process.

As computers became more powerful, it became evident that single-user batch processing was inefficient, because so much time was spent waiting for slow input/output devices to complete their tasks. It was thought that many jobs or tasks could *share* the resources of the computer to achieve better utilization. This is achieved by multiprogramming. Multiprogramming involves the simultaneous operation of many jobs that are competing to share the computer's resources. With early multiprogramming operating systems, users still submitted jobs on decks of punched cards and waited hours or days for results.

In the 1960s, several groups in industry and the universities pioneered timesharing operating systems. Timesharing is a special case of multiprogramming in which users access the computer through terminals, typically devices with keyboards and screens. Dozens or even hundreds of users share the computer at once. The computer actually does not run them all simultaneously. Rather, it runs a small portion of one user's job, then moves on to service the next user, perhaps providing service to each user several times per second. Thus, the users' programs *appear* to be running simultaneously. An advantage of timesharing is that user requests receive almost immediate responses.

1.5 Personal, Distributed and Client/Server Computing

In 1977, Apple Computer popularized personal computing. Computers became so economical that people could buy them for their own personal or business use. In 1981, IBM, the world's largest computer vendor, introduced the IBM Personal Computer. This quickly legitimized personal computing in business, industry and government organizations, as IBM mainframes were heavily used.

These computers were "stand-alone" units—people transported disks back and forth between them to share information (often called "sneakernet"). Although early personal computers were not powerful enough to timeshare several users, these machines could be linked together in computer networks, sometimes over telephone lines and sometimes in local area networks (LANs) within an organization. This led to the phenomenon of distributed computing, in which an organization's computing, instead of being performed only at some central computer installation, is distributed over networks to the sites where the organization's work is performed. Personal computers were powerful enough to handle the computing requirements of individual users as well as the basic communications tasks of passing information between computers electronically.

Today's personal computers are as powerful as the million-dollar machines of just a few decades ago. The most powerful desktop machines—called workstations—provide individual users with enormous capabilities. Information is shared easily across computer networks, where computers called file servers offer a common data store that may be used by client computers distributed throughout the network, hence the term client/server computing. C++ has become widely used for writing software for operating systems, for computer networking and for distributed client/server applications. Today's popular operating systems such as UNIX, Linux, Mac OS X and Microsoft's Windows-based systems provide the kinds of capabilities discussed in this section.

1.6 The Internet and the World Wide Web

The Internet—a global network of computers—was initiated almost four decades ago with funding supplied by the U.S. Department of Defense. Originally designed to connect the main computer systems of about a dozen universities and research organizations, the Internet today is accessible by computers worldwide.

With the introduction of the World Wide Web—which allows computer users to locate and view multimedia-based documents on almost any subject over the Internet—the Internet has exploded into one of the world's premier communication mechanisms.

The Internet and the World Wide Web are surely among humankind's most important and profound creations. In the past, most computer applications ran on computers that were not connected to one another. Today's applications can be written to communicate among the world's computers. The Internet mixes computing and communications technologies. It makes our work easier. It makes information instantly and conveniently accessible worldwide. It enables individuals and local small businesses to get worldwide exposure. It is changing the way business is done. People can search for the best prices on virtually any product or service. Special-interest communities can stay in touch with one another. Researchers can be made instantly aware of the latest breakthroughs.

1.7 Machine Languages, Assembly Languages and High-Level Languages

Programmers write instructions in various programming languages, some directly understandable by computers and others requiring intermediate translation steps. Hundreds of computer languages are in use today. These may be divided into three general types:

1. Machine languages

2. Assembly languages

3. High-level languages

Any computer can directly understand only its own machine language. Machine language is the "natural language" of a computer and as such is defined by its hardware design. [*Note:* Machine language is often referred to as object code. This term predates "object-oriented programming." These two uses of "object" are unrelated.] Machine languages generally consist of strings of numbers (ultimately reduced to 1s and 0s) that instruct computers to perform their most elementary operations one at a time. Machine languages are machine dependent (i.e., a particular machine language can be used on only one type of computer). Such languages are cumbersome for humans, as illustrated by the following section of an early machine-language program that adds overtime pay to base pay and stores the result in gross pay:

```
+1300042774
+1400593419
+1200274027
```

Machine-language programming was simply too slow, tedious and error-prone for most programmers. Instead of using the strings of numbers that computers could directly understand, programmers began using English-like abbreviations to represent elementary operations. These abbreviations formed the basis of assembly languages. Translator programs called assemblers were developed to convert early assembly-language programs to machine language at computer speeds. The following section of an assembly-language program also adds overtime pay to base pay and stores the result in gross pay:

```
load    basepay
add     overpay
store   grosspay
```

Although such code is clearer to humans, it is incomprehensible to computers until translated to machine language.

Computer usage increased rapidly with the advent of assembly languages, but programmers still had to use many instructions to accomplish even the simplest tasks. To speed the programming process, high-level languages were developed in which single statements could be written to accomplish substantial tasks. Translator programs called compilers convert high-level language programs into machine language. High-level languages allow programmers to write instructions that look almost like everyday English and contain commonly used mathematical notations. A payroll program written in a high-level language might contain a statement such as

```
grossPay = basePay + overTimePay;
```

From the programmer's standpoint, obviously, high-level languages are preferable to machine and assembly language. C, C++, Microsoft's .NET languages (e.g., Visual Basic .NET, Visual C++ .NET and C#) and Java are among the most widely used high-level programming languages.

The process of compiling a high-level language program into machine language can take a considerable amount of computer time. Interpreter programs were developed to execute high-level language programs directly, although much more slowly. Interpreters are popular in program development environments in which new features are being added and errors corrected. Once a program is fully developed, a compiled version can be produced to run most efficiently.

1.8 History of C and C++

C++ evolved from C, which evolved from two previous programming languages, BCPL and B. BCPL was developed in 1967 by Martin Richards as a language for writing operating-systems software and compilers for operating systems. Ken Thompson modeled many features in his language B after their counterparts in BCPL and used B to create early versions of the UNIX operating system at Bell Laboratories in 1970.

The C language was evolved from B by Dennis Ritchie at Bell Laboratories. C uses many important concepts of BCPL and B. C initially became widely known as the development language of the UNIX operating system. Today, most operating systems are written in C and/or C++. C is now available for most computers and is hardware independent. With careful design, it is possible to write C programs that are portable to most computers.

The widespread use of C with various kinds of computers (sometimes called hardware platforms) unfortunately led to many variations. This was a serious problem for program developers, who needed to write portable programs that would run on several platforms. A standard version of C was needed. The American National Standards Institute (ANSI) cooperated with the International Organization for Standardization (ISO) to standardize C worldwide; the joint standard document was published in 1990 and is referred to as *ANSI/ISO 9899: 1990*.

Portability Tip 1.1

Because C is a standardized, hardware-independent, widely available language, applications written in C often can be run with little or no modification on a wide range of computer systems.

C++, an extension of C, was developed by Bjarne Stroustrup in the early 1980s at Bell Laboratories. C++ provides a number of features that "spruce up" the C language, but more importantly, it provides capabilities for object-oriented programming.

A revolution is brewing in the software community. Building software quickly, correctly and economically remains an elusive goal, and this at a time when the demand for new and more powerful software is soaring. Objects are essentially reusable software components that model items in the real world. Software developers are discovering that using a modular, object-oriented design and implementation approach can make them much more productive than they can be with previous popular programming techniques. Object-oriented programs are easier to understand, correct and modify.

1.9 C++ Standard Library

C++ programs consist of pieces called classes and functions. You can program each piece that you may need to form a C++ program. However, most C++ programmers take advantage of the rich collections of existing classes and functions in the C++ Standard Library. Thus, there are really two parts to learning the C++ "world." The first is learning the C++ language itself; the second is learning how to use the classes and functions in the C++ Standard Library. Throughout the book, we discuss many of these classes and functions. P J. Plauger's book, *The Standard C Library* (Upper Saddle River, NJ: Prentice Hall PTR, 1992), is a must read for programmers who need a deep understanding of the ANSI C library functions that are included in C++, how to implement them and how to use them to write portable code. The standard class libraries generally are provided by compiler vendors. Many special-purpose class libraries are supplied by independent software vendors.

Software Engineering Observation 1.1

Use a "building-block" approach to create programs. Avoid reinventing the wheel. Use existing pieces wherever possible. Called software reuse, this practice is central to object-oriented programming.

Software Engineering Observation 1.2

When programming in C++, you typically will use the following building blocks: Classes and functions from the C++ Standard Library, classes and functions you and your colleagues create and classes and functions from various popular third-party libraries.

We include many Software Engineering Observations throughout the book to explain concepts that affect and improve the overall architecture and quality of software systems. We also highlight other kinds of tips, including Good Programming Practices (to help you write programs that are clearer, more understandable, more maintainable and easier to test and debug—or remove programming errors), Common Programming Errors (problems to watch out for and avoid), Performance Tips (techniques for writing programs that run faster and use less memory), Portability Tips (techniques to help you write programs that can run, with little or no modification, on a variety of computers— these tips also include general observations about how C++ achieves its high degree of portability) and Error-Prevention Tips (techniques for removing bugs from your programs and, more important, techniques for writing bug-free programs in the first place). Many of these are only guidelines. You will, no doubt, develop your own preferred programming style.

The advantage of creating your own functions and classes is that you will know exactly how they work. You will be able to examine the C++ code. The disadvantage is the time-consuming and complex effort that goes into designing, developing and maintaining new functions and classes that are correct and that operate efficiently.

Performance Tip 1.1

Using C++ Standard Library functions and classes instead of writing your own versions can improve program performance, because they are written carefully to perform efficiently. This technique also shortens program development time.

Portability Tip 1.2

Using C++ Standard Library functions and classes instead of writing your own improves program portability, because they are included in every C++ implementation.

1.10 History of Java

Microprocessors are having a profound impact in intelligent consumer electronic devices. Recognizing this, Sun Microsystems in 1991 funded an internal corporate research project code-named Green. The project resulted in the development of a C++-based language that its creator, James Gosling, called Oak after an oak tree outside his window at Sun. It was later discovered that there already was a computer language called Oak. When a group of Sun people visited a local coffee shop, the name Java was suggested and it stuck.

The Green project ran into some difficulties. The marketplace for intelligent consumer electronic devices did not develop in the early 1990s as quickly as Sun had anticipated. The project was in danger of being canceled. By sheer good fortune, the World Wide Web exploded in popularity in 1993, and Sun saw the immediate potential of using Java to add dynamic content (e.g., interactivity, animations and the like) to Web pages. This breathed new life into the project.

Sun formally announced Java in 1995. Java generated immediate interest in the business community because of the phenomenal success of the World Wide Web. Java is now used to develop large-scale enterprise applications, to enhance the functionality of Web servers (the computers that provide the content we see in our Web browsers), to provide applications for consumer devices (such as cell phones, pagers and personal digital assistants) and for many other purposes. Current versions of C++, such as Microsoft®'s Visual C++® .NET and Borland®'s C++Builder™, have similar capabilities.

1.11 FORTRAN, COBOL, Pascal and Ada

Hundreds of high-level languages have been developed, but only a few have achieved broad acceptance. FORTRAN (FORmula TRANslator) was developed by IBM Corporation in the mid-1950s to be used for scientific and engineering applications that require complex mathematical computations. FORTRAN is still widely used, especially in engineering applications.

COBOL (COmmon Business Oriented Language) was developed in the late 1950s by computer manufacturers, the U.S. government and industrial computer users. COBOL is used for commercial applications that require precise and efficient manipulation of large amounts of data. Much business software is still programmed in COBOL.

During the 1960s, many large software development efforts encountered severe difficulties. Software deliveries were typically late, costs greatly exceeded budgets and the finished products were unreliable. People began to realize that software development was a far more complex activity than they had imagined. Research in the 1960s resulted in the evolution of structured programming—a disciplined approach to writing programs that are clearer, easier to test and debug and easier to modify than large programs produced with previous techniques.

One of the more tangible results of this research was the development of the Pascal programming language by Professor Niklaus Wirth in 1971. Named after the seventeenth-century mathematician and philosopher Blaise Pascal, it was designed for teaching structured programming and rapidly became the preferred programming language in most colleges. Pascal lacks many features needed in commercial, industrial and government applications, so it has not been widely accepted in these environments.

The Ada programming language was developed under the sponsorship of the U.S. Department of Defense (DOD) during the 1970s and early 1980s. Hundreds of separate languages were being used to produce the DOD's massive command-and-control software systems. The DOD wanted a single language that would fill most of its needs. The Ada language was named after Lady Ada Lovelace, daughter of the poet Lord Byron. Lady Lovelace is credited with writing the world's first computer program in the early 1800s (for the Analytical Engine mechanical computing device designed by Charles Babbage). One important capability of Ada, called multitasking, allows programmers to specify that many activities are to occur in parallel. Java, through a technique called multithreading, also enables programmers to write programs with parallel activities. Although multithreading is not part of standard C++, it is available through various add-on class libraries.

1.12 Basic, Visual Basic, Visual C++, C# and .NET

The BASIC (Beginner's All-purpose Symbolic Instruction Code) programming language was developed in the mid-1960s at Dartmouth College as a means of writing simple programs. BASIC's primary purpose was to familiarize novices with programming techniques. Microsoft's Visual Basic language, introduced in the early 1990s to simplify the development of Microsoft Windows applications, has become one of the most popular programming languages in the world.

Microsoft's latest development tools are part of its corporate-wide strategy for integrating the Internet and the Web into computer applications. This strategy is implemented in Microsoft's .NET platform, which provides developers with the capabilities they need to create and run computer applications that can execute on computers distributed across the Internet. Microsoft's three primary programming languages are Visual Basic .NET (based on the original BASIC), Visual C++ .NET (based on C++) and C# (a new language based on C++ and Java that was developed expressly for the .NET platform). Developers using .NET can write software components in the language they are most familiar with and then form applications by combining those components with components written in any .NET language.

1.13 Key Software Trend: Object Technology

One of the authors, Harvey Deitel, remembers the great frustration that was felt in the 1960s by software development organizations, especially those working on large-scale projects. During his undergraduate years, he had the privilege of working summers at a leading computer vendor on the teams developing timesharing, virtual memory operating systems. This was a great experience for a college student. But, in the summer of 1967, reality set in when the company "decommitted" from producing as a commercial product the particular system on which hundreds of people had been working for many years. It was difficult to get this software right. Software is "complex stuff."

Improvements to software technology did emerge with the benefits of structured programming (and the related disciplines of structured systems analysis and design) being realized in the 1970s. Not until the technology of object-oriented programming became widely used in the 1990s, though, did software developers finally feel they had the necessary tools for making major strides in the software development process.

Actually, object technology dates back to the mid 1960s. The C++ programming language, developed at AT&T by Bjarne Stroustrup in the early 1980s, is based on two languages—C, which initially was developed at AT&T to implement the UNIX operating system in the early 1970s, and Simula 67, a simulation programming language developed in Europe and released in 1967. C++ absorbed the features of C and added Simula's capabilities for creating and manipulating objects. Neither C nor C++ was originally intended for wide use beyond the AT&T research laboratories. But grass roots support rapidly developed for each.

What are objects and why are they special? Actually, object technology is a packaging scheme that helps us create meaningful software units. These can be large and are highly focussed on particular applications areas. There are date objects, time objects, paycheck objects, invoice objects, audio objects, video objects, file objects, record objects and so on. In fact, almost any noun can be reasonably represented as an object.

We live in a world of objects. Just look around you. There are cars, planes, people, animals, buildings, traffic lights, elevators and the like. Before object-oriented languages appeared, programming languages (such as FORTRAN, COBOL, Pascal, Basic and C) were focussed on actions (verbs) rather than on things or objects (nouns). Programmers living in a world of objects programmed primarily using verbs. This made it awkward to write programs. Now, with the availability of popular object-oriented languages such as C++ and Java, programmers continue to live in an object-oriented world and can program in an object-oriented manner. This is a more natural process than procedural programming and has resulted in significant productivity enhancements.

A key problem with procedural programming is that the program units do not easily mirror real-world entities effectively, so these units are not particularly reusable. It is not unusual for programmers to "start fresh" on each new project and have to write similar software "from scratch." This wastes time and money, as people repeatedly "reinvent the wheel." With object technology, the software entities created (called classes), if properly designed, tend to be much more reusable on future projects. Using libraries of reusable componentry, such as MFC (Microsoft Foundation Classes), Microsoft's .NET Framework Class Library and those produced by Rogue Wave and many other software development organizations, can greatly reduce the amount of effort required to implement certain kinds of systems (compared to the effort that would be required to reinvent these capabilities on new projects).

Software Engineering Observation 1.3

Extensive class libraries of reusable software components are available over the Internet and the World Wide Web. Many of these libraries are available at no charge.

Some organizations report that the key benefit object-oriented programming gives them is not software reuse. Rather, they indicate that it tends to produce software that is more understandable, better organized and easier to maintain, modify and debug. This can be significant, because it has been estimated that as much as 80 percent of software costs are associated not with the original efforts to develop the software, but with the continued evolution and maintenance of that software throughout its lifetime.

Whatever the perceived benefits of object orientation are, it is clear that object-oriented programming will be the key programming methodology for the next several decades.

1.14 Typical C++ Development Environment

Let's consider the steps in creating and executing a C++ application using a C++ development environment (illustrated in Fig. 1.1). C++ systems generally consist of three parts: a program development environment, the language and the C++ Standard Library. C++ programs typically go through six phases: edit, preprocess, compile, link, load and execute. The following discussion explains a typical C++ program development environment. [*Note:* On our Web site at www.deitel.com/books/downloads.html, we provide *DEITEL®* *DIVE INTO™ Series* publications to help you begin using several popular C++ development tools, including Borland® C++Builder™, Microsoft® Visual C++® 6, Microsoft® Visual C++® .NET, GNU C++ on Linux and GNU C++ on the Cygwin™ UNIX® environment for Windows®. We will make other *DIVE INTO™ Series* publications available as instructors request them.]

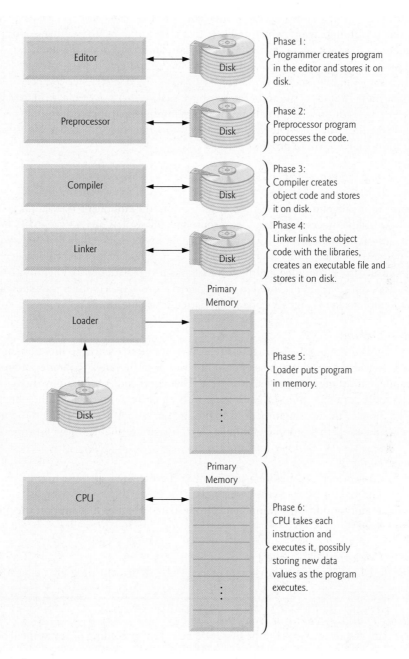

Fig. 1.1 | Typical C++ environment.

Phase 1: Creating a Program

Phase 1 consists of editing a file with an **editor program** (normally known simply as an **editor**). You type a C++ program (typically referred to as **source code**) using the editor, make any necessary corrections and save the program on a secondary storage device, such as your hard drive. C++ source code file names often end with the .cpp, .cxx, .cc or .C extensions (note that C is in uppercase) which indicate that a file contains C++ source code. See the documentation for your C++ environment for more information on file-name extensions.

Two editors widely used on UNIX systems are vi and emacs. C++ software packages for Microsoft Windows such as Borland C++ (www.borland.com), Metrowerks CodeWarrior (www.metrowerks.com) and Microsoft Visual C++ (www.msdn.microsoft.com/visualc/) have editors integrated into the programming environment. You can also use a simple text editor, such as Notepad in Windows, to write your C++ code. We assume the reader knows how to edit a program.

Phases 2 and 3: Preprocessing and Compiling a C++ Program
In phase 2, the programmer gives the command to compile the program. In a C++ system, a preprocessor program executes automatically before the compiler's translation phase begins (so we call preprocessing phase 2 and compiling phase 3). The C++ preprocessor obeys commands called preprocessor directives, which indicate that certain manipulations are to be performed on the program before compilation. These manipulations usually include other text files to be compiled and perform various text replacements. The most common preprocessor directives are discussed in this book. In phase 3, the compiler translates the C++ program into machine-language code (also referred to as object code).

Phase 4: Linking
Phase 4 is called linking. C++ programs typically contain references to functions and data defined elsewhere, such as in the standard libraries or in the private libraries of groups of programmers working on a particular project. The object code produced by the C++ compiler typically contains "holes" due to these missing parts. A linker links the object code with the code for the missing functions to produce an executable image (with no missing pieces). If the program compiles and links correctly, an executable image is produced.

Phase 5: Loading
Phase 5 is called loading. Before a program can be executed, it must first be placed in memory. This is done by the loader, which takes the executable image from disk and transfers it to memory. Additional components from shared libraries that support the program are also loaded.

Phase 6: Execution
Finally, the computer, under the control of its CPU, executes the program one instruction at a time.

Problems That May Occur at Execution Time
Programs do not always work on the first try. Each of the preceding phases can fail because of various errors that we discuss throughout the book. For example, an executing program might attempt to divide by zero (an illegal operation for whole-number arithmetic in C++). This would cause the C++ program to display an error message. If this occurs, you would have to return to the edit phase, make the necessary corrections and proceed through the remaining phases again to determine that the corrections fix the problem(s).

Most programs in C++ input and/or output data. Certain C++ functions take their input from cin (the standard input stream; pronounced "see-in"), which is normally the keyboard, but cin can be redirected to another device. Data is often output to cout (the standard output stream; pronounced "see-out"), which is normally the computer screen, but cout can be redirected to another device. When we say that a program prints a result, we normally mean that the result is displayed on a screen. Data may be output to other devices, such as disks and hardcopy printers. There is also a standard error stream referred to as cerr. The cerr stream (normally connected to the screen) is used for displaying error messages. It is common for users to assign cout to a device other than the screen while keeping cerr assigned to the screen, so that normal outputs are separated from errors.

Common Programming Error 1.1

Errors like division by zero occur as a program runs, so they are called runtime errors or execution-time errors. Fatal runtime errors cause programs to terminate immediately without having successfully performed their jobs. Nonfatal runtime errors allow programs to run to completion, often producing incorrect results. [Note: On some systems, divide-by-zero is not a fatal error. Please see your system documentation.]

1.15 Notes About C++ and Small C++ How to Program, 5/e

Experienced C++ programmers sometimes take pride in being able to create some weird, contorted, convoluted usage of the language. This is a poor programming practice. It makes programs more difficult to read, more likely to behave strangely, more difficult to test and debug, and more difficult to adapt to changing requirements. This book is geared for novice programmers, so we stress program *clarity*. The following is our first "good programming practice."

Good Programming Practice 1.1

Write your C++ programs in a simple and straightforward manner. This is sometimes referred to as KIS ("keep it simple"). Do not "stretch" the language by trying bizarre usages.

You have heard that C and C++ are portable languages, and that programs written in C and C++ can run on many different computers. *Portability is an elusive goal.* The ANSI C standard document contains a lengthy list of portability issues, and complete books have been written that discuss portability.

Portability Tip 1.3

Although it is possible to write portable programs, there are many problems among different C and C++ compilers and different computers that can make portability difficult to achieve. Writing programs in C and C++ does not guarantee portability. The programmer often will need to deal directly with compiler and computer variations. As a group, these are sometimes called platform variations.

We have audited our presentation against the ANSI/ISO C++ standard document for completeness and accuracy. However, C++ is a rich language, and there are some features we have not covered. If you need additional technical details on C++, you may want to read the C++ standard document, which can be ordered from the ANSI Web site at

webstore.ansi.org/ansidocstore/default.asp

The title of the document is "Information Technology – Programming Languages – C++" and its document number is INCITS/ISO/IEC 14882-2003.

We have included an extensive bibliography of books and papers on C++ and object-oriented programming. We also have included a C++ Resources appendix containing many Internet and Web sites relating to C++ and object-oriented programming. We have listed several Web sites in Section 1.19 including links to free C++ compilers, resource sites and some fun C++ games and game programming tutorials.

Good Programming Practice 1.2

Read the manuals for the version of C++ you are using. Refer to these manuals frequently to be sure you are aware of the rich collection of C++ features and that you are using them correctly.

Good Programming Practice 1.3

Your computer and compiler are good teachers. If after reading your C++ language manual, you still are not sure how a feature of C++ works, experiment using a small "test program" and see what happens. Set your compiler options for "maximum warnings." Study each message that the compiler generates and correct the programs to eliminate the messages.

1.16 Test-Driving a C++ Application

In this section, you will run and interact with your first C++ application. You will begin by running an entertaining guess-the-number game, which picks a number from 1 to 1000 and prompts you to guess the number. If your guess is correct, the game ends. If your guess is not correct, the application indicates whether your guess is higher or lower than the correct number. There is no limit on the number of guesses you can make. [*Note:* For this test drive only, we have modified this application from the exercise you will be asked to create in Chapter 6, Functions and an Introduction to Recursion. Typically this application selects different numbers for you to guess each time you run it, because it chooses the numbers to guess at random. Our modified application chooses the same "correct" guesses every time you execute the program. This allows you to use the same guesses and see the same results that we show as we walk you through interacting with your first C++ application.]

We will demonstrate running a C++ application in two ways—using the Windows XP **Command Prompt** and using a shell on Linux (similar to a Windows **Command Prompt**). The application runs similarly on both platforms. Many development environments are available in which readers can compile, build and run C++ applications, such as Borland's C++Builder, Metrowerks, GNU C++, Microsoft Visual C++ .NET, etc. While we don't test-drive each of these environments, we do provide information in Section 1.19 regarding free C++ compilers available for download on the Internet. Please see your instructor for information on your specific development environment. Also, we provide several *Dive-Into*™ *Series* publications to help you get started with various C++ compliers. These are available free for download at www.deitel.com/books/scpphtp5/index.html.

In the following steps, you will run the application and enter various numbers to guess the correct number. The elements and functionality that you see in this application are typical of those you will learn to program in this book. Throughout the book, we use fonts to distinguish between features you see on the screen (e.g., the **Command Prompt**) and elements that are not directly related to the screen. Our convention is to emphasize screen features like titles and menus (e.g., the **File** menu) in a semibold **sans-serif Helvetica** font and to emphasize file names, text displayed by an application and values you should enter into an application (e.g., GuessNumber or 500), in a sans-serif Lucida font. As you have noticed, the defining occurrence of each term is set in blue, heavy bold. For the figures in this section, we highlight the user input required by each step and point out significant parts of the application. To make these features more visible, we have modified the background color of the **Command Prompt** window (for the Windows test-drive only). To modify the colors of the **Command Prompt** on your system, open a **Command Prompt**, then right click the title bar and select **Properties**. In the **"Command Prompt" Properties** dialog box that appears, click the **Colors** tab, and select your preferred text and background colors.]

Running a C++ application from the Windows XP Command Prompt

1. *Checking your setup.* Read the *Before You Begin* section at the beginning of this textbook to make sure that you have copied the book's examples to your hard drive correctly.

2. *Locating the completed application.* Open a **Command Prompt** window. For readers using Windows 95, 98 or 2000, select **Start > Programs > Accessories > Command Prompt**. For Windows XP users, select **Start > All Programs > Accessories > Command Prompt**. To change to your completed **GuessNumber** application directory, type **cd C:\examples\ch01\GuessNumber\Windows**, then press *Enter* (Fig. 1.2). The command cd is used to change directories.

3. *Running the GuessNumber application.* Now that you are in the directory that contains the **GuessNumber** application, type the command **GuessNumber** (Fig. 1.3) and press *Enter*. [*Note:* GuessNumber.exe is the actual name of the application; however, Windows assumes the .exe extension by default.]

4. *Entering your first guess.* The application displays "Please type your first guess.", then displays a question mark (?) as a prompt on the next line (Fig. 1.3). At the prompt, enter **500** (Fig. 1.4).

5. *Entering another guess.* The application displays "Too high. Try again.", meaning that the value you entered is greater than the number the application chose as the correct guess. So, you should enter a lower number for your next guess. At the prompt, enter **250** (Fig. 1.5). The application again displays "Too high. Try again.", because the value you entered is still greater than the number that the correct guess.

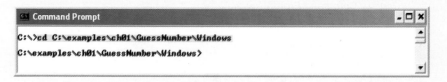

Fig. 1.2 | Opening a **Command Prompt** window and changing the directory.

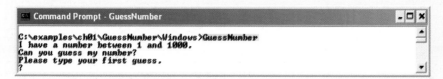

Fig. 1.3 | Running the **GuessNumber** application.

```
Command Prompt - GuessNumber                                    _ □ ×

C:\examples\ch01\GuessNumber\Windows>GuessNumber
I have a number between 1 and 1000.
Can you guess my number?
Please type your first guess.
? 500
Too high. Try again.
?
```

Fig. 1.4 | Entering your first guess.

```
Command Prompt - GuessNumber                                    _ □ ×

C:\examples\ch01\GuessNumber\Windows>GuessNumber
I have a number between 1 and 1000.
Can you guess my number?
Please type your first guess.
? 500
Too high. Try again.
? 250
Too high. Try again.
? _
```

Fig. 1.5 | Entering a second guess and receiving feedback.

6. **Entering additional guesses.** Continue to play the game by entering values until you guess the correct number. Once you guess the answer, the application will display "Excellent! You guessed the number!" (Fig. 1.6).

7. **Playing the game again or exiting the application.** After guessing the correct number, the application asks if you would like to play another game (Fig. 1.6). At the "Would you like to play again (y or n)?" prompt, entering the one character **y** causes the application to choose a new number and displays the message "Please enter your first guess." followed by a question mark prompt (Fig. 1.7) so you can make your first guess in the new game. Entering the character **n** ends the application and returns you to the application's directory at the **Command Prompt** (Fig. 1.8). Each time you execute this application from the beginning (i.e., *Step 3*), it will choose the same numbers for you to guess.

8. **Close the Command Prompt window.**

```
Command Prompt - GuessNumber                                    _ □ ×
Too high. Try again.
? 125
Too high. Try again.
? 62
Too high. Try again.
? 31
Too low. Try again.
? 46
Too high. Try again.
? 39
Too low. Try again.
? 42

Excellent! You guessed the number!
Would you like to play again (y or n)? _
```

Fig. 1.6 | Entering additional guesses and guessing the correct number.

```
Command Prompt · GuessNumber                                    _ □ ×

Excellent! You guessed the number!
Would you like to play again (y or n)? y

I have a number between 1 and 1000.
Can you guess my number?
Please type your first guess.
?
```

Fig. 1.7 | Playing the game again.

```
Command Prompt                                                  _ □ ×

Excellent! You guessed the number!
Would you like to play again (y or n)? n

C:\examples\ch01\GuessNumber\Windows>_
```

Fig. 1.8 | Exiting the game.

Running a C++ Application Using GNU C++ with Linux

For this test drive, we assume that you know how to copy the examples into your home directory. Please see your instructor if you have any questions regarding copying the files to your Linux system. Also, for the figures in this section, we use a bold highlight to point out the user input required by each step. The prompt in the shell on our system uses the tilde (~) character to represent the home directory and each prompt ends with the dollar sign ($) character. The prompt will vary among Linux systems.

1. Locating the completed application. From a Linux shell, change to the completed **GuessNumber** application directory (Fig. 1.9) by typing

   cd Examples\ch01\GuessNumber\GNU_Linux

   then pressing *Enter*. The command cd is used to change directories.

2. *Compiling the GuessNumber application.* To run an application on the GNU C++ compiler, it must first be compiled by typing

   g++ GuessNumber.cpp -o GuessNumber

   as in Fig. 1.10. The preceding command compiles the application and produces an executable file called GuessNumber.

3. *Running the GuessNumber application.* To run the executable file GuessNumber, type ./GuessNumber at the next prompt, then press *Enter* (Fig. 1.11).

```
~$ cd examples/ch01/GuessNumber/GNU_Linux
~/examples/ch01/GuessNumber/GNU_Linux$
```

Fig. 1.9 | Changing to the **GuessNumber** application's directory after logging in to your Linux account.

```
~/examples/ch01/GuessNumber/GNU_Linux$ g++ GuessNumber.cpp -o GuessNumber
~/examples/ch01/GuessNumber/GNU_Linux$
```

Fig. 1.10 | Compiling the **GuessNumber** application using the g++ command.

```
~/examples/ch01/GuessNumber/GNU_Linux$ ./GuessNumber
I have a number between 1 and 1000.
Can you guess my number?
Please type your first guess.
?
```

Fig. 1.11 | Running the **GuessNumber** application.

4. *Entering your first guess.* The application displays "Please type your first guess.", then displays a question mark (?) as a prompt on the next line (Fig. 1.11). At the prompt, enter **500** (Fig. 1.12). [*Note:* This is the same application that we modified and test-drove for Windows, but the outputs could vary, based on the compiler being used.]

5. *Entering another guess.* The application displays "Too high. Try again.", meaning that the value you entered is greater than the number the application chose as the correct guess (Fig. 1.12). At the next prompt, enter **250** (Fig. 1.13). This time the application displays "Too low. Try again.", because the value you entered is less than the correct guess.

6. *Entering additional guesses.* Continue to play the game (Fig. 1.14) by entering values until you guess the correct number. When you guess the answer, the application displays "Excellent! You guessed the number!" (Fig. 1.14).

```
~/examples/ch01/GuessNumber/GNU_Linux$ ./GuessNumber
I have a number between 1 and 1000.
Can you guess my number?
Please type your first guess.
? 500
Too high. Try again.
?
```

Fig. 1.12 | Entering an initial guess.

```
~/examples/ch01/GuessNumber/GNU_Linux$ ./GuessNumber
I have a number between 1 and 1000.
Can you guess my number?
Please type your first guess.
? 500
Too high. Try again.
? 250
Too low. Try again.
?
```

Fig. 1.13 | Entering a second guess and receiving feedback.

```
Too low. Try again.
? 375
Too low. Try again.
? 437
Too high. Try again.
? 406
Too high. Try again.
? 391
Too high. Try again.
? 383
Too low. Try again.
? 387
Too high. Try again.
? 385
Too high. Try again.
? 384

Excellent! You guessed the number.
Would you like to play again (y or n)?
```

Fig. 1.14 | Entering additional guesses and guessing the correct number.

7. ***Playing the game again or exiting the application.*** After guessing the correct number, the application asks if you would like to play another game. At the "Would you like to play again (y or n)?" prompt, entering the one character **y** causes the application to choose a new number and displays the message "Please enter your first guess." followed by a question mark prompt (Fig. 1.15) so you can make your first guess in the new game. Entering the character **n** ends the application and returns you to the application's directory in the shell (Fig. 1.16). Each time you execute this application from the beginning (i.e., *Step 3*), it will choose the same numbers for you to guess.

```
Excellent! You guessed the number.
Would you like to play again (y or n)? y

I have a number between 1 and 1000.
Can you guess my number?
Please type your first guess.
?
```

Fig. 1.15 | Playing the game again.

```
Excellent! You guessed the number.
Would you like to play again (y or n)? n

~/examples/ch01/GuessNumber/GNU_Linux$
```

Fig. 1.16 | Exiting the game.

1.17 Introduction to Object Technology and the UML

Now we begin our early introduction to object orientation, a natural way of thinking about the world and writing computer programs. Our goal here is to help you develop an object-oriented way of thinking and to introduce you to the Unified Modeling Language™ (UML™)—a graphical language that allows people who design object-oriented software systems to use an industry-standard notation to represent them.

Basic Object Technology Concepts

We begin our introduction to object orientation with some key terminology. Everywhere you look in the real world you see objects—people, animals, plants, cars, planes, buildings, computers and so on. Humans think in terms of objects. Telephones, houses, traffic lights, microwave ovens and water coolers are just a few more objects we see around us every day.

We sometimes divide objects into two categories: animate and inanimate. Animate objects are "alive" in some sense—they move around and do things. Inanimate objects, on the other hand, do not move on their own. Objects of both types, however, have some things in common. They all have attributes (e.g., size, shape, color and weight), and they all exhibit behaviors (e.g., a ball rolls, bounces, inflates and deflates; a baby cries, sleeps, crawls, walks and blinks; a car accelerates, brakes and turns; a towel absorbs water). We will study the kinds of attributes and behaviors that software objects have.

Humans learn about existing objects by studying their attributes and observing their behaviors. Different objects can have similar attributes and can exhibit similar behaviors. Comparisons can be made, for example, between babies and adults and between humans and chimpanzees.

Object-oriented design (OOD) models software in terms similar to those that people use to describe real-world objects. It takes advantage of class relationships, where objects of a certain class, such as a class of vehicles, have the same characteristics—cars, trucks, little red wagons and roller skates have much in common. OOD takes advantage of inheritance relationships, where new classes of objects are derived by absorbing characteristics of existing classes and adding unique characteristics of their own. An object of class "convertible" certainly has the characteristics of the more general class "automobile," but more specifically, the roof goes up and down.

Object-oriented design provides a natural and intuitive way to view the software design process—namely, modeling objects by their attributes, behaviors and interrelationships just as we describe real-world objects. OOD also models communication between objects. Just as people send messages to one another (e.g., a sergeant commands a soldier to stand at attention), objects also communicate via messages. A bank account object may receive a message to decrease its balance by a certain amount because the customer has withdrawn that amount of money.

OOD encapsulates (i.e., wraps) attributes and operations (behaviors) into objects—an object's attributes and operations are intimately tied together. Objects have the property of information hiding. This means that objects may know how to communicate with one another across well-defined interfaces, but normally they are not allowed to know how other objects are implemented—implementation details are hidden within the objects themselves. We can drive a car effectively, for instance, without knowing the details of how engines, transmissions, brakes and exhaust systems work internally—as long as we know how to use the accelerator pedal, the brake pedal, the steering wheel and so on. Information hiding, as we will see, is crucial to good software engineering.

Languages like C++ are object oriented. Programming in such a language is called object-oriented programming (OOP), and it allows computer programmers to implement an object-oriented design as a working software system. Languages like C, on the other hand, are procedural, so programming tends to be action oriented. In C, the unit of programming is the function. In C++, the unit of programming is the class from which objects are eventually instantiated (an OOP term for "created"). C++ classes contain functions that implement operations and data that implements attributes.

C programmers concentrate on writing functions. Programmers group actions that perform some common task into functions, and group functions to form programs. Data is certainly important in C, but the view is that data exists primarily in support of the actions that functions perform. The verbs in a system specification help the C programmer determine the set of functions that will work together to implement the system.

Classes, Data Members and Member Functions

C++ programmers concentrate on creating their own user-defined types called classes. Each class contains data as well as the set of functions that manipulate that data and provide services to clients (i.e., other classes or functions that use the class). The data components of a class are called data members. For example, a bank account class might include an account number and a balance. The function components of a class are called member functions (typically called methods in other object-oriented programming languages such as Java). For example, a bank account class might include member functions to make a deposit (increasing the balance), make a withdrawal (decreasing the balance) and inquire what the current balance is. The programmer uses built-in types (and other user-defined types) as the "building blocks" for constructing new user-defined types (classes). The nouns in a system specification help the C++ programmer determine the set of classes from which objects are created that work together to implement the system.

Classes are to objects as blueprints are to houses—a class is a "plan" for building an object of the class. Just as we can build many houses from one blueprint, we can instantiate (create) many objects from one class. You cannot cook meals in the kitchen of a blueprint; you can cook meals in the kitchen of a house. You cannot sleep in the bedroom of a blueprint; you can sleep in the bedroom of a house.

Classes can have relationships with other classes. For example, in an object-oriented design of a bank, the "bank teller" class needs to relate to other classes, such as the "customer" class, the "cash drawer" class, the "safe" class, and so on. These relationships are called associations.

Packaging software as classes makes it possible for future software systems to reuse the classes. Groups of related classes are often packaged as reusable components. Just as realtors often say that the three most important factors affecting the price of real estate are "location, location and location," people in the software development community often say that the three most important factors affecting the future of software development are "reuse, reuse and reuse."

Software Engineering Observation 1.4

Reuse of existing classes when building new classes and programs saves time, money and effort. Reuse also helps programmers build more reliable and effective systems, because existing classes and components often have gone through extensive testing, debugging and performance tuning.

Indeed, with object technology, you can build much of the new software you will need by combining existing classes, just as automobile manufacturers combine interchangeable parts. Each new class you create will have the potential to become a valuable software asset that you and other programmers can reuse to speed and enhance the quality of future software development efforts.

Introduction to Object-Oriented Analysis and Design (OOAD)

Soon you will be writing programs in C++. How will you create the code for your programs? Perhaps, like many beginning programmers, you will simply turn on your computer and start typing. This approach may work for small programs (like the ones we present in the early chapters of the book), but what if you were asked to create a software system to control thousands of automated teller machines for a major bank? Or what if you were asked to work on a team of 1,000 software developers building the next generation of the U.S. air traffic control system? For projects so large and complex, you could not simply sit down and start writing programs.

To create the best solutions, you should follow a detailed process for analyzing your project's requirements (i.e., determining *what* the system is supposed to do) and developing a design that satisfies them (i.e., deciding *how* the system should do it). Ideally, you would go through this process and carefully review the design (or have your design reviewed by other software professionals) before writing any code. If this process involves analyzing and designing your system from an object-oriented point of view, it is called object-oriented analysis and design (OOAD). Experienced programmers know that analysis and design can save many hours by helping avoid an ill-planned system development approach that has to be abandoned partway through its implementation, possibly wasting considerable time, money and effort.

OOAD is the generic term for the process of analyzing a problem and developing an approach for solving it. Small problems like the ones discussed in these first few chapters do not require an exhaustive OOAD process. It may be sufficient, before we begin writing C++ code, to write pseudocode—an informal text-based means of expressing program logic. It is not actually a programming language, but we can use it as a kind of outline to guide us as we write our code. We introduce pseudocode in Chapter 4.

As problems and the groups of people solving them increase in size, the methods of OOAD quickly become more appropriate than pseudocode. Ideally, a group should agree on a strictly defined process for solving its problem and a uniform way of communicating the results of that process to one another. Although many different OOAD processes exist, a single graphical language for communicating the results of *any* OOAD process has come into wide use. This language, known as the Unified Modeling Language (UML), was developed in the mid-1990s under the initial direction of three software methodologists: Grady Booch, James Rumbaugh and Ivar Jacobson.

History of the UML

In the 1980s, increasing numbers of organizations began using OOP to build their applications, and a need developed for a standard OOAD process. Many methodologists—including Booch, Rumbaugh and Jacobson—individually produced and promoted separate processes to satisfy this need. Each process had its own notation, or "language" (in the form of graphical diagrams), to convey the results of analysis and design.

By the early 1990s, different organizations, and even divisions within the same organization, were using their own unique processes and notations. At the same time, these organizations also wanted to use software tools that would support their particular processes. Software vendors found it difficult to provide tools for so many processes. Clearly, a standard notation and standard processes were needed.

In 1994, James Rumbaugh joined Grady Booch at Rational Software Corporation (now a division of IBM), and the two began working to unify their popular processes. They soon were joined by Ivar Jacobson. In 1996, the group released early versions of the UML to the software engineering community and requested feedback. Around the same time, an organization known as the Object Management Group™ (OMG™) invited submissions for a common modeling language. The OMG (www.omg.org) is a nonprofit organization that promotes the standardization of object-oriented technologies by issuing guidelines and specifications, such as the UML. Several corporations—among them HP, IBM, Microsoft, Oracle and Rational Software—had already recognized the need for a common modeling language. In response to the OMG's request for proposals, these companies formed UML Partners—the consortium that developed the UML version 1.1 and submitted it to the OMG. The OMG accepted the proposal and, in 1997, assumed responsibility for the continuing maintenance and revision of the UML. In March 2003, the OMG released UML version 1.5. The UML version 2—which had been adopted and was in the process of being finalized at the time of this publication—marks the first major revision since the 1997 version 1.1 standard. Many books, modeling tools and industry experts are already using the UML version 2, so we present UML version 2 terminology and notation throughout this book.

What Is the UML?

The Unified Modeling Language is now the most widely used graphical representation scheme for modeling object-oriented systems. It has indeed unified the various popular notational schemes. Those who design systems use the language (in the form of diagrams) to model their systems, as we do throughout this book.

An attractive feature of the UML is its flexibility. The UML is extensible (i.e., capable of being enhanced with new features) and is independent of any particular OOAD process. UML modelers are free to use various processes in designing systems, but all developers can now express their designs with one standard set of graphical notations.

Internet and Web UML Resources

For more information about the UML, refer to the following Web sites.

www.uml.org

This UML resource page from the Object Management Group (OMG) provides specification documents for the UML and other object-oriented technologies.

www.ibm.com/software/rational/uml

This is the UML resource page for IBM Rational—the successor to the Rational Software Corporation (the company that created the UML).

www-306.ibm.com/software/rational/uml/

Lists frequently asked questions about the UML, provided by IBM Rational.

www.softdocwiz.com/Dictionary.htm

Hosts the Unified Modeling Language Dictionary, which lists and defines all terms used in the UML.

`www-306.ibm.com/software/rational/offerings/design.html`
Provides information about IBM Rational software available for designing systems. Provides downloads of 30-day trial versions of several products, such as IBM Rational Rose® XDE Developer.

`www.embarcadero.com/products/describe/index.html`
Provides a 15-day trial license for the Embarcadero Technologies® UML modeling tool Describe.™

`www.borland.com/together/index.html`
Provides a free 30-day license to download a trial version of Borland® Together® Control-Center™—a software development tool that supports the UML.

`www.ilogix.com/rhapsody/rhapsody.cfm`
Provides a free 30-day license to download a trial version of I-Logix Rhapsody®—a UML 2-based model-driven development environment.

`argouml.tigris.org`
Contains information and downloads for ArgoUML, a free open-source UML tool.

`www.objectsbydesign.com/books/booklist.html`
Lists books on the UML and object-oriented design.

`www.objectsbydesign.com/tools/umltools_byCompany.html`
Lists software tools that use the UML, such as IBM Rational Rose, Embarcadero Describe, Sparx Systems Enterprise Architect, I-Logix Rhapsody and Gentleware Poseidon for UML.

`www.ootips.org/ood-principles.html`
Provides answers to the question, "What Makes a Good Object-Oriented Design?"

`www.cetus-links.org/oo_uml.html`
Introduces the UML and provides links to numerous UML resources.

`www.agilemodeling.com/essays/umlDiagrams.htm`
Provides in-depth descriptions and tutorials on each of the 13 UML 2 diagram types.

Recommended Readings

Many books on the UML have been published. The following recommended books provide information about object-oriented design with the UML.

Arlow, J., and I. Neustadt. *UML and the Unified Process: Practical Object-Oriented Analysis and Design.* London: Pearson Education Ltd., 2002.

Booch, G. *Object-Oriented Analysis and Design with Applications,* Third Edition. Boston: Addison-Wesley, 2004.

Eriksson, H., et al. *UML 2 Toolkit.* New York: John Wiley, 2003.

Fowler, M. *UML Distilled, Third Edition: A Brief Guide to the Standard Object Modeling Language.* Boston: Addison-Wesley, 2004.

Kruchten, P. *The Rational Unified Process: An Introduction.* Boston: Addison-Wesley, 2004.

Larman, C. *Applying UML and Patterns: An Introduction to Object-Oriented Analysis and Design,* Second Edition. Upper Saddle River, NJ: Prentice Hall, 2002.

Roques, P. *UML in Practice: The Art of Modeling Software Systems Demonstrated Through Worked Examples and Solutions.* New York: John Wiley, 2004.

Rosenberg, D., and K. Scott. *Applying Use Case Driven Object Modeling with UML: An Annotated e-Commerce Example.* Reading, MA: Addison-Wesley, 2001.

Rumbaugh, J., I. Jacobson and G. Booch. *The Complete UML Training Course.* Upper Saddle River, NJ: Prentice Hall, 2000.

Rumbaugh, J., I. Jacobson and G. Booch. *The Unified Modeling Language Reference Manual*. Reading, MA: Addison-Wesley, 1999.

Rumbaugh, J., I. Jacobson and G. Booch. *The Unified Software Development Process*. Reading, MA: Addison-Wesley, 1999.

Rumbaugh, J., I. Jacobson and G. Booch. *The Unified Modeling Language User Guide*. Reading, MA: Addison-Wesley, 1999.

For additional books on the UML, visit www.amazon.com or www.bn.com. IBM Rational, formerly Rational Software Corporation, also provides a recommended-reading list for UML books at www.ibm.com/software/rational/info/technical/books.jsp.

Section 1.17 Self-Review Exercises

1.1   List three examples of real-world objects that we did not mention. For each object, list several attributes and behaviors.

1.2   Pseudocode is _____.
   a) another term for OOAD
   b) a programming language used to display UML diagrams
   c) an informal means of expressing program logic
   d) a graphical representation scheme for modeling object-oriented systems

1.3   The UML is used primarily to _____.
   a) test object-oriented systems
   b) design object-oriented systems
   c) implement object-oriented systems
   d) Both a and b

Answers to Section 1.17 Self-Review Exercises

1.1   [*Note:* Answers may vary.] a) A television's attributes include the size of the screen, the number of colors it can display, its current channel and its current volume. A television turns on and off, changes channels, displays video and plays sounds. b) A coffee maker's attributes include the maximum volume of water it can hold, the time required to brew a pot of coffee and the temperature of the heating plate under the coffee pot. A coffee maker turns on and off, brews coffee and heats coffee. c) A turtle's attributes include its age, the size of its shell and its weight. A turtle walks, retreats into its shell, emerges from its shell and eats vegetation.

1.2   c.

1.3   b.

1.18 Wrap-Up

This chapter introduced basic hardware and software concepts, and explored C++'s role in developing distributed client/server applications. You studied the history of the Internet and the World Wide Web. We discussed the different types of programming languages, their history and which programming languages are most widely used. We also discussed the C++ Standard Library which contains reusable classes and functions that help C++ programmers create portable C++ programs.

   We presented basic object technology concepts, including classes, objects, attributes, behaviors, encapsulation and inheritance. You also learned about the history and purpose of the UML—the industry-standard graphical language for modeling software systems.

You learned the typical steps for creating and executing a C++ application. Finally, you "test-drove" a sample C++ application similar to the types of applications you will learn to program in this book.

In the next chapter, you will create your first C++ applications. You will see several examples that demonstrate how programs display messages on the screen and obtain information from the user at the keyboard for processing. We analyze and explain each example to help you ease your way into C++ programming.

1.19 Web Resources

This section provides many Web resources that will be useful to you as you learn C++. The sites include C++ resources, C++ development tools for students and professionals and some links to fun games built with C++. This section also lists our own Web sites where you can find downloads and resources associated with this book. You will find additional Web Resources in Appendix E.

Deitel & Associates Web Sites

www.deitel.com/books/scpphtp5/index.html
The Deitel & Associates *C++ How to Program, Fifth Edition* site. Here you will find links to the book's examples (also included on the CD that accompanies the book) and other resources, such as our free *Dive Into*™ guides that help you get started with several C++ integrated development environments (IDEs).

www.deitel.com
Please check the Deitel & Associates site for updates, corrections and additional resources for all Deitel publications.

www.deitel.com/newsletter/subscribe.html
Please visit this site to subscribe for the *Deitel*® *Buzz Online* e-mail newsletter to follow the Deitel & Associates publishing program.

www.prenhall.com/deitel
Prentice Hall's site for Deitel publications. Here you will find detailed product information, sample chapters and *Companion Web Sites* containing book- and chapter-specific resources for students and instructors.

Compilers and Development Tools

www.thefreecountry.com/compilers/cpp.shtml
This site lists free C and C++ compilers for a variety of operating systems.

msdn.microsoft.com/visualc
The *Microsoft Visual C++* site provides product information, overviews, supplemental materials and ordering information for the Visual C++ compiler.

www.borland.com/cbuilder/
This is a link to the *Borland C++Builder*. A free command-line version is available for download.

www.compilers.net
Compilers.net is designed to help users locate compilers.

developer.intel.com/software/products/compilers/cwin/index.htm
An evaluation download of the *Intel C++ compiler* is available at this site.

`www.symbian.com/developer/development/cppdev.html`
Symbian provides a C++ Developer's Pack and links to various resources, including code and development tools for C++ programmers implementing mobile applications for the Symbian operating system, which is popular on devices such as mobile phones.

Resources
`www.hal9k.com/cug`
The *C/C++ Users Group (CUG)* site contains C++ resources, journals, shareware and freeware.
`www.devx.com`
DevX is a comprehensive resource for programmers that provides the latest news, tools and techniques for various programming languages. The *C++ Zone* offers tips, discussion forums, technical help and online newsletters.
`www.acm.org/crossroads/xrds3-2/ovp32.html`
The Association for Computing Machinery (ACM) site offers a comprehensive listing of C++ resources, including recommended texts, journals and magazines, published standards, newsletters, FAQs and newsgroups.
`www.accu.informika.ru/resources/public/terse/cpp.htm`
The Association of C & C++ Users (ACCU) site contains links to C++ tutorials, articles, developer information, discussions and book reviews.
`www.cuj.com`
The *C/C++ User's Journal* is an online magazine that contains articles, tutorials and downloads. The site features news about C++, forums and links to information about development tools.
`www.research.att.com/~bs/homepage.html`
This is the site for Bjarne Stroustrup, designer of the C++ programming language. This site provides a list of C++ resources, FAQs and other useful C++ information.

Games
`www.codearchive.com/list.php?go=0708`
This site has several C++ games available for download.
`www.mathtools.net/C_C__/Games/`
This site includes links to numerous games built with C++. The source code for most of the games is available for download.
`www.forum.nokia.com/main/0,6566,050_20,00.html`
Visit this Nokia site to learn how to use C++ to program games for some Nokia wireless devices.

Summary

- The various devices that comprise a computer system are referred to as hardware.
- The computer programs that run on a computer are referred to as software.
- A computer is capable of performing computations and making logical decisions at speeds millions (even billions) of times faster than human beings can.
- Computers process data under the control of sets of instructions called computer programs, which guide the computer through orderly sets of actions specified by computer programmers.

- The input unit is the "receiving" section of the computer. It obtains information from input devices and places it at the disposal of the other units for processing.

- The output unit is the "shipping" section of the computer. It takes information processed by the computer and places it on output devices to make it available for use outside the computer.

- The memory unit is the rapid-access, relatively low-capacity "warehouse" section of the computer. It retains information that has been entered through the input unit, making it immediately available for processing when needed, and retains information that has already been processed until it can be placed on output devices by the output unit.

- The arithmetic and logic unit (ALU) is the "manufacturing" section of the computer. It is responsible for performing calculations and making decisions.

- The central processing unit (CPU) is the "administrative" section of the computer. It coordinates and supervises the operation of the other sections.

- The secondary storage unit is the long-term, high-capacity "warehousing" section of the computer. Programs or data not being used by the other units are normally placed on secondary storage devices (e.g., disks) until they are needed, possibly hours, days, months or even years later.

- Operating systems were developed to help make it more convenient to use computers.

- Multiprogramming involves the sharing of a computer's resources among the jobs competing for its attention, so that the jobs appear to run simultaneously.

- With distributed computing, an organization's computing is distributed over networks to the sites where the work of the organization is performed.

- Any computer can directly understand only its own machine language, which generally consist of strings of numbers that instruct computers to perform their most elementary operations.

- English-like abbreviations form the basis of assembly languages. Translator programs called assemblers convert assembly-language programs to machine language.

- Compilers translate high-level language programs into machine-language programs. High-level languages (like C++) contain English words and conventional mathematical notations.

- Interpreter programs directly execute high-level language programs, eliminating the need to compile them into machine language.

- C++ evolved from C, which evolved from two previous programming languages, BCPL and B.

- C++ is an extension of C developed by Bjarne Stroustrup in the early 1980s at Bell Laboratories. C++ enhances the C language and provides capabilities for object-oriented programming.

- Objects are reusable software components that model items in the real world. Using a modular, object-oriented design and implementation approach can make software development groups more productive than with previous programming techniques.

- C++ programs consist of pieces called classes and functions. You can program each piece you may need to form a C++ program. However, most C++ programmers take advantage of the rich collections of existing classes and functions in the C++ Standard Library.

- Java is used to create dynamic and interactive content for Web pages, develop enterprise applications, enhance Web server functionality, provide applications for consumer devices and more.

- FORTRAN (FORmula TRANslator) was developed by IBM Corporation in the mid-1950s for scientific and engineering applications that require complex mathematical computations.

- COBOL (COmmon Business Oriented Language) was developed in the late 1950s by a group of computer manufacturers and government and industrial computer users. COBOL is used primarily for commercial applications that require precise and efficient data manipulation.

- Ada was developed under the sponsorship of the United States Department of Defense (DOD) during the 1970s and early 1980s. Ada provides multitasking, which allows programmers to specify that many activities are to occur in parallel.

- The BASIC (Beginner's All-Purpose Symbolic Instruction Code) programming language was developed in the mid-1960s at Dartmouth College as a language for writing simple programs. BASIC's primary purpose was to familiarize novices with programming techniques.

- Microsoft's Visual Basic was introduced in the early 1990s to simplify the process of developing Microsoft Windows applications.

- Microsoft has a corporate-wide strategy for integrating the Internet and the Web into computer applications. This strategy is implemented in Microsoft's .NET platform.

- The .NET platform's three primary programming languages are Visual Basic .NET (based on the original BASIC), Visual C++ .NET (based on C++) and C# (a new language based on C++ and Java that was developed expressly for the .NET platform).

- .NET developers can write software components in their preferred language, then form applications by combining those components with components written in any .NET language.

- C++ systems generally consist of three parts: a program development environment, the language and the C++ Standard Library.

- C++ programs typically go through six phases: *edit, preprocess, compile, link, load* and *execute.*

- C++ source code file names often end with the .cpp, .cxx, .cc or .C extensions.

- A preprocessor program executes automatically before the compiler's translation phase begins. The C++ preprocessor obeys commands called preprocessor directives, which indicate that certain manipulations are to be performed on the program before compilation.

- The object code produced by the C++ compiler typically contains "holes" due to references to functions and data defined elsewhere. A linker links the object code with the code for the missing functions to produce an executable image (with no missing pieces).

- The loader takes the executable image from disk and transfers it to memory for execution.

- Most programs in C++ input and/or output data. Data is often input from cin (the standard input stream) which is normally the keyboard, but cin can be redirected from another device. Data is often output to cout (the standard output stream), which is normally the computer screen, but cout can be redirected to another device. The cerr stream is used to display error messages.

- The Unified Modeling Language (UML) is a graphical language that allows people who build systems to represent their object-oriented designs in a common notation.

- Object-oriented design (OOD) models software components in terms of real-world objects. It takes advantage of class relationships, where objects of a certain class have the same characteristics. It also takes advantage of inheritance relationships, where newly created classes of objects are derived by absorbing characteristics of existing classes and adding unique characteristics of their own. OOD encapsulates data (attributes) and functions (behavior) into objects—the data and functions of an object are intimately tied together.

- Objects have the property of information hiding—objects normally are not allowed to know how other objects are implemented.

- Object-oriented programming (OOP) allows programmers to implement object-oriented designs as working systems.

- C++ programmers create their own user-defined types called classes. Each class contains data (known as data members) and the set of functions (known as member functions) that manipulate that data and provide services to clients.

- Classes can have relationships with other classes. These relationships are called associations.
- Packaging software as classes makes it possible for future software systems to reuse the classes. Groups of related classes are often packaged as reusable components.
- An instance of a class is called an object.
- With object technology, programmers can build much of the software they will need by combining standardized, interchangeable parts called classes.
- The process of analyzing and designing a system from an object-oriented point of view is called object-oriented analysis and design (OOAD).

Terminology

action
Ada
American National Standards Institute (ANSI)
analysis
ANSI/ISO standard C
ANSI/ISO standard C++
arithmetic and logic unit (ALU)
assembler
assembly language
association
attribute of an object
BASIC (Beginner's All-Purpose
     Instruction Code)
batch processing
behavior of an object
Booch, Grady
C
C++
C++ Standard Library
C#
central processing unit (CPU)
class
client
client/server computing
COBOL (COmmon Business
     Oriented Language)
compile phase
compiler
component
computer
computer program
computer programmer
core memory
data
data member
debug
decision
design

distributed computing
dynamic content
edit phase
editor
encapsulate
executable image
execute phase
extensible
file server
FORTRAN (FORmula TRANslator)
function
hardware
hardware platform
high-level language
information hiding
inheritance
input device
input unit
input/output (I/O)
instantiate
interface
International Organization for
     Standardization (ISO)
Internet
interpreter
Jacobson, Ivar
Java
link phase
linker
live-code approach
load phase
loader
local area networks (LANs)
logical unit
machine dependent
machine independent
machine language
member function

memory	primary memory
memory unit	procedural programming
method	pseudocode
MFC (Microsoft Foundation Classes)	Rational Software Corporation
Microsoft's .NET Framework Class Library	requirements document
multiprocessor	Rumbaugh, James
multiprogramming	runtime errors or execution-time errors
multitasking	secondary storage unit
multithreading	software
.NET platform	software reuse
object	source code
object code	structured programming
Object Management Group (OMG)	structured systems analysis and design
object-oriented analysis and design (OOAD)	supercomputer
object-oriented design (OOD)	task
object-oriented programming (OOP)	throughput
operating system	timesharing
operation	translation
output device	translator program
output unit	Unified Modeling Language (UML)
personal computing	user-defined type
platform	Visual Basic .NET
portable	Visual C++ .NET
preprocess phase	workstation
preprocessor directives	World Wide Web

Self-Review Exercises

1.1   Fill in the blanks in each of the following:

a) The company that popularized personal computing was _____.

b) The computer that made personal computing legitimate in business and industry was the _____.

c) Computers process data under the control of sets of instructions called computer _____.

d) The six key logical units of the computer are the _____, _____, _____, _____, _____ and the _____.

e) The three classes of languages discussed in the chapter are _____, _____, and _____.

f) The programs that translate high-level language programs into machine language are called _____.

g) C is widely known as the development language of the _____ operating system.

h) The _____ language was developed by Wirth for teaching structured programming.

i) The Department of Defense developed the Ada language with a capability called _____, which allows programmers to specify that many activities can proceed in parallel.

1.2   Fill in the blanks in each of the following sentences about the C++ environment.

a) C++ programs are normally typed into a computer using a(n) _____ program.

b) In a C++ system, a(n) _____ program executes before the compiler's translation phase begins.

    c) The _____ program combines the output of the compiler with various library functions to produce an executable image.

    d) The _____ program transfers the executable image of a C++ program from disk to memory.

1.3   Fill in the blanks in each of the following statements (based on Section 1.17):

    a) Objects have the property of _____—although objects may know how to communicate with one another across well-defined interfaces, they normally are not allowed to know how other objects are implemented.

    b) C++ programmers concentrate on creating _____, which contain data members and the member functions that manipulate those data members and provide services to clients.

    c) Classes can have relationships with other classes. These relationships are called _____.

    d) The process of analyzing and designing a system from an object-oriented point of view is called _____.

    e) OOD also takes advantage of _____ relationships, where new classes of objects are derived by absorbing characteristics of existing classes, then adding unique characteristics of their own.

    f) _____ is a graphical language that allows people who design software systems to use an industry-standard notation to represent them.

    g) The size, shape, color and weight of an object are considered _____ of the object.

Answers to Self-Review Exercises

1.1   a) Apple. b) IBM Personal Computer. c) programs. d) input unit, output unit, memory unit, arithmetic and logic unit, central processing unit, secondary storage unit. e) machine languages, assembly languages and high-level languages. f) compilers. g) UNIX. h) Pascal. i) multitasking.

1.2   a) editor. b) preprocessor. c) linker. d) loader.

1.3   a) information hiding. b) classes. c) associations. d) object-oriented analysis and design (OOAD). e) inheritance. f) The Unified Modeling Language (UML). g) attributes.

Exercises

1.4   Categorize each of the following items as either hardware or software:

    a) CPU

    b) C++ compiler

    c) ALU

    d) C++ preprocessor

    e) input unit

    f) an editor program

1.5   Why might you want to write a program in a machine-independent language instead of a machine-dependent language? Why might a machine-dependent language be more appropriate for writing certain types of programs?

1.6   Fill in the blanks in each of the following statements:

    a) Which logical unit of the computer receives information from outside the computer for use by the computer? _____.

    b) The process of instructing the computer to solve specific problems is called _____.

   c) What type of computer language uses English-like abbreviations for machine-language instructions? _____.

   d) Which logical unit of the computer sends information that has already been processed by the computer to various devices so that the information may be used outside the computer? _____.

   e) Which logical unit of the computer retains information? _____.

   f) Which logical unit of the computer performs calculations? _____.

   g) Which logical unit of the computer makes logical decisions? _____.

   h) The level of computer language most convenient to the programmer for writing programs quickly and easily is _____.

   i) The only language that a computer directly understands is called that computer's _____.

   j) Which logical unit of the computer coordinates the activities of all the other logical units? _____.

1.7   Why is so much attention today focused on object-oriented programming in general and C++ in particular?

1.8   Distinguish between the terms fatal error and nonfatal error. Why might you prefer to experience a fatal error rather than a nonfatal error?

1.9   Give a brief answer to each of the following questions:

   a) Why does this text discuss structured programming in addition to object-oriented programming?

   b) What are the typical steps (mentioned in the text) of an object-oriented design process?

   c) What kinds of messages do people send to one another?

   d) Objects send messages to one another across well-defined interfaces. What interfaces does a car radio (object) present to its user (a person object)?

1.10   You are probably wearing on your wrist one of the world's most common types of objects—a watch. Discuss how each of the following terms and concepts applies to the notion of a watch: object, attributes, behaviors, class, inheritance (consider, for example, an alarm clock), abstraction, modeling, messages, encapsulation, interface, information hiding, data members and member functions.

2

Introduction to C++ Programming

Featuring Early Classes & Objects with the UML™ 2

What's in a name?
that which we call a rose
By any other name
would smell as sweet.
—William Shakespeare

When faced with a decision,
I always ask, "What would
be the most fun?"
—Peggy Walker

"Take some more tea," the
March Hare said to Alice,
very earnestly. "I've had
nothing yet, "Alice replied in
an offended tone: "so I can't
take more." "You mean you
can't take less," said the
Hatter: "it's very easy to take
more than nothing."
—Lewis Carroll

High thoughts must have
high language.
—Aristophanes

OBJECTIVES

In this chapter you will learn:

- To write simple computer programs in C++.
- To write simple input and output statements.
- To use fundamental types.
- Basic computer memory concepts.
- To use arithmetic operators.
- The precedence of arithmetic operators.
- To write simple decision-making statements.

Outline

2.1 Introduction

2.2 First Program in C++: Printing a Line of Text

2.3 Modifying Our First C++ Program

2.4 Another C++ Program: Adding Integers

2.5 Memory Concepts

2.6 Arithmetic

2.7 Decision Making: Equality and Relational Operators

2.8 Wrap-Up

Summary | Terminology | Self-Review Exercises | Answers to Self-Review Exercises | Exercises

2.1 Introduction

We now introduce C++ programming, which facilitates a disciplined approach to program design. Most of the C++ programs you will study in this book process information and display results. In this chapter, we present five examples that demonstrate how your programs can display messages and obtain information from the user for processing. The first three examples simply display messages on the screen. The next is a program that obtains two numbers from a user, calculates their sum and displays the result. The accompanying discussion shows you how to perform various arithmetic calculations and save their results for later use. The fifth example demonstrates decision-making fundamentals by showing you how to compare two numbers, then display messages based on the comparison results. We analyze each program one line at a time to help you ease your way into C++ programming. To help you apply the skills you learn here, we provide many programming problems in the chapter's exercises.

2.2 First Program in C++: Printing a Line of Text

C++ uses notations that may appear strange to nonprogrammers. We now consider a simple program that prints a line of text (Fig. 2.1). This program illustrates several important features of the C++ language. We consider each line in detail.

Lines 1 and 2

```
// Fig. 2.1: fig02_01.cpp
// Text-printing program.
```

each begin with //, indicating that the remainder of each line is a comment. Programmers insert comments to document programs and also help people read and understand them. Comments do not cause the computer to perform any action when the program is run—they are ignored by the C++ compiler and do not cause any machine-language object code to be generated. The comment `Text-printing program` describes the purpose of the program. A comment beginning with // is called a single-line comment because it terminates at the end of the current line. [*Note:* C++ programmers also may use C's style in which a comment—possibly containing many lines—begins with the pair of characters /* and ends with */.]

```
 1   // Fig. 2.1: fig02_01.cpp
 2   // Text-printing program.
 3   #include <iostream> // allows program to output data to the screen
 4
 5   // function main begins program execution
 6   int main()
 7   {
 8      std::cout << "Welcome to C++!\n"; // display message
 9
10      return 0; // indicate that program ended successfully
11
12   } // end function main
```

```
Welcome to C++!
```

Fig. 2.1 | Text-printing program.

Good Programming Practice 2.1

Every program should begin with a comment that describes the purpose of the program, author, date and time. (We are not showing the author, date and time in this book's programs because this information would be redundant.)

Line 3

```
#include <iostream> // allows program to output data to the screen
```

is a preprocessor directive, which is a message to the C++ preprocessor (introduced in Section 1.14). Lines that begin with # are processed by the preprocessor before the program is compiled. This line notifies the preprocessor to include in the program the contents of the input/output stream header file <iostream>. This file must be included for any program that outputs data to the screen or inputs data from the keyboard using C++-style stream input/output. The program in Fig. 2.1 outputs data to the screen, as we will soon see. We discuss header files in more detail in Chapter 6.

Common Programming Error 2.1

Forgetting to include the <iostream> header file in a program that inputs data from the keyboard or outputs data to the screen causes the compiler to issue an error message, because the compiler cannot recognize references to the stream components (e.g., cout).

Line 4 is simply a blank line. Programmers use blank lines, space characters and tab characters (i.e., "tabs") to make programs easier to read. Together, these characters are known as white space. White-space characters are normally ignored by the compiler. In this chapter and several that follow, we discuss conventions for using white-space characters to enhance program readability.

Good Programming Practice 2.2

Use blank lines and space characters to enhance program readability.

Line 5

```
// function main begins program execution
```

is another single-line comment indicating that program execution begins at the next line.
Line 6

```
int main()
```

is a part of every C++ program. The parentheses after `main` indicate that `main` is a program
building block called a **function**. C++ programs typically consist of one or more functions
and classes (as you will learn in Chapter 3). Exactly one function in every program must
be `main`. Figure 2.1 contains only one function. C++ programs begin executing at function
`main`, even if `main` is not the first function in the program. The keyword `int` to the left of
`main` indicates that `main` "returns" an integer (whole number) value. A **keyword** is a word
in code that is reserved by C++ for a specific use. The complete list of C++ keywords can
be found in Fig. 4.3. We will explain what it means for a function to "return a value" when
we demonstrate how to create your own functions in Section 3.5 and when we study functions in greater depth in Chapter 6. For now, simply include the keyword `int` to the left
of `main` in each of your programs.

The **left brace**, **{**, (line 7) must begin the **body** of every function. A corresponding
right brace, **}**, (line 12) must end each function's body. Line 8

```
std::cout << "Welcome to C++!\n"; // display message
```

instructs the computer to **perform an action**—namely, to print the **string** of characters
contained between the double quotation marks. A string is sometimes called a **character
string**, a **message** or a **string literal**. We refer to characters between double quotation
marks simply as **strings**. White-space characters in strings are not ignored by the compiler.

The entire line 8, including `std::cout`, the `<<` **operator**, the string `"Welcome to
C++!\n"` and the **semicolon** (`;`), is called a **statement**. Every C++ statement must end with
a semicolon (also known as the **statement terminator**). Preprocessor directives (like
`#include`) do not end with a semicolon. Output and input in C++ are accomplished with
streams of characters. Thus, when the preceding statement is executed, it sends the stream
of characters `Welcome to C++!\n` to the **standard output stream object**—`std::cout`—
which is normally "connected" to the screen.

Notice that we placed `std::` before `cout`. This is required when we use names that we've
brought into the program by the preprocessor directive `#include <iostream>`. The notation
`std::cout` specifies that we are using a name, in this case `cout`, that belongs to "namespace"
`std`. The names `cin` (the standard input stream) and `cerr` (the standard error stream)—
introduced in Chapter 1—also belong to namespace `std`. Namespaces are an advanced C++
feature that we discuss in depth in Chapter 24 of our sister book, *C++ How to Program, 5/e*.
For now, you should simply remember to include `std::` before each mention of `cout`, `cin`
and `cerr` in a program. This can be cumbersome—in Fig. 2.13, we introduce the `using` declaration, which will enable us to omit `std::` before each use of a name in the `std` namespace.

The `<<` operator is referred to as the **stream insertion operator**. When this program
executes, the value to the right of the operator, the right **operand**, is inserted in the output
stream. Notice that the operator points in the direction of where the data goes. The characters of the right operand normally print exactly as they appear between the double

quotes. Notice, however, that the characters \n are not printed on the screen. The backslash (\) is called an escape character. It indicates that a "special" character is to be output. When a backslash is encountered in a string of characters, the next character is combined with the backslash to form an escape sequence. The escape sequence \n means newline. It causes the cursor (i.e., the current screen-position indicator) to move to the beginning of the next line on the screen. Some other common escape sequences are listed in Fig. 2.2.

 Common Programming Error 2.2

Omitting the semicolon at the end of a C++ statement is a syntax error. (Again, preprocessor directives do not end in a semicolon.) The syntax of a programming language specifies the rules for creating a proper program in that language. A syntax error occurs when the compiler encounters code that violates C++'s language rules (i.e., its syntax). The compiler normally issues an error message to help the programmer locate and fix the incorrect code. Syntax errors are also called compiler errors, compile-time errors or compilation errors, because the compiler detects them during the compilation phase. You will be unable to execute your program until you correct all the syntax errors in it. As you will see, some compilation errors are not syntax errors.

Line 10

```
return 0; // indicate that program ended successfully
```

is one of several means we will use to exit a function. When the return statement is used at the end of main, as shown here, the value 0 indicates that the program has terminated successfully. In Chapter 6 we discuss functions in detail, and the reasons for including this statement will become clear. For now, simply include this statement in each program, or the compiler may produce a warning on some systems. The right brace, }, (line 12) indicates the end of function main.

Good Programming Practice 2.3

Many programmers make the last character printed by a function a newline (\n). This ensures that the function will leave the screen cursor positioned at the beginning of a new line. Conventions of this nature encourage software reusability—a key goal in software development.

Escape sequence	Description
\n	Newline. Position the screen cursor to the beginning of the next line.
\t	Horizontal tab. Move the screen cursor to the next tab stop.
\r	Carriage return. Position the screen cursor to the beginning of the current line; do not advance to the next line.
\a	Alert. Sound the system bell.
\\	Backslash. Used to print a backslash character.
\'	Single quote. Use to print a single quote character.
\"	Double quote. Used to print a double quote character.

Fig. 2.2 | Escape sequences.

Good Programming Practice 2.4

Indent the entire body of each function one level within the braces that delimit the body of the function. This makes a program's functional structure stand out and helps make the program easier to read.

Good Programming Practice 2.5

Set a convention for the size of indent you prefer, then apply it uniformly. The tab key may be used to create indents, but tab stops may vary. We recommend using either 1/4-inch tab stops or (preferably) three spaces to form a level of indent.

2.3 Modifying Our First C++ Program

This section continues our introduction to C++ programming with two examples, showing how to modify the program in Fig. 2.1 to print text on one line by using multiple statements and to print text on several lines by using a single statement.

Printing a Single Line of Text with Multiple Statements

Welcome to C++! can be printed several ways. For example, Fig. 2.3 performs stream insertion in multiple statements (lines 8–9), yet produces the same output as the program of Fig. 2.1. [*Note:* From this point forward, we use a darker shade of gray than the code table background to highlight the key features each program introduces.] Each stream insertion resumes printing where the previous one stopped. The first stream insertion (line 8) prints Welcome followed by a space, and the second stream insertion (line 9) begins printing on the same line immediately following the space. In general, C++ allows the programmer to express statements in a variety of ways.

Printing Multiple Lines of Text with a Single Statement

A single statement can print multiple lines by using newline characters, as in line 8 of Fig. 2.4. Each time the \n (newline) escape sequence is encountered in the output stream, the screen cursor is positioned to the beginning of the next line. To get a blank line in your output, place two newline characters back to back, as in line 8.

```cpp
1   // Fig. 2.3: fig02_03.cpp
2   // Printing a line of text with multiple statements.
3   #include <iostream> // allows program to output data to the screen
4
5   // function main begins program execution
6   int main()
7   {
8      std::cout << "Welcome ";
9      std::cout << "to C++!\n";
10
11     return 0; // indicate that program ended successfully
12
13  } // end function main
```

```
Welcome to C++!
```

Fig. 2.3 | Printing a line of text with multiple statements.

```
 1   // Fig. 2.4: fig02_04.cpp
 2   // Printing multiple lines of text with a single statement.
 3   #include <iostream> // allows program to output data to the screen
 4
 5   // function main begins program execution
 6   int main()
 7   {
 8      std::cout << "Welcome\nto\n\n C++!\n";
 9
10      return 0; // indicate that program ended successfully
11
12   } // end function main
```

```
Welcome
to

C++!
```

Fig. 2.4 | Printing multiple lines of text with a single statement.

2.4 Another C++ Program: Adding Integers

Our next program uses the input stream object `std::cin` and the stream extraction operator, `>>`, to obtain two integers typed by a user at the keyboard, computes the sum of these values and outputs the result using `std::cout`. Figure 2.5 shows the program and sample inputs and outputs. Note that we highlight the user's input in bold.

The comments in lines 1 and 2

```
// Fig. 2.5: fig02_05.cpp
// Addition program that displays the sum of two numbers.
```

state the name of the file and the purpose of the program. The C++ preprocessor directive

```
#include <iostream> // allows program to perform input and output
```

in line 3 includes the contents of the `iostream` header file in the program.

The program begins execution with function `main` (line 6). The left brace (line 7) marks the beginning of `main`'s body and the corresponding right brace (line 25) marks the end of `main`.

Lines 9–11

```
int number1; // first integer to add
int number2; // second integer to add
int sum; // sum of number1 and number2
```

are declarations. The identifiers `number1`, `number2` and `sum` are the names of variables. A variable is a location in the computer's memory where a value can be stored for use by a program. These declarations specify that the variables `number1`, `number2` and `sum` are data of type `int`, meaning that these variables will hold integer values, i.e., whole numbers such as 7, –11, 0 and 31914. All variables must be declared with a name and a data type before they can be used in a program. Several variables of the same type may be declared in one

```
1   // Fig. 2.5: fig02_05.cpp
2   // Addition program that displays the sum of two numbers.
3   #include <iostream> // allows program to perform input and output
4
5   // function main begins program execution
6   int main()
7   {
8      // variable declarations
9      int number1; // first integer to add
10     int number2; // second integer to add
11     int sum; // sum of number1 and number2
12
13     std::cout << "Enter first integer: "; // prompt user for data
14     std::cin >> number1; // read first integer from user into number1
15
16     std::cout << "Enter second integer: "; // prompt user for data
17     std::cin >> number2; // read second integer from user into number2
18
19     sum = number1 + number2; // add the numbers; store result in sum
20
21     std::cout << "Sum is " << sum << std::endl; // display sum; end line
22
23     return 0; // indicate that program ended successfully
24
25  } // end function main
```

```
Enter first integer: 45
Enter second integer: 72
Sum is 117
```

Fig. 2.5 | Addition program that displays the sum of two integers entered at the keyboard.

declaration or in multiple declarations. We could have declared all three variables in one declaration as follows:

```
int number1, number2, sum;
```

This makes the program less readable and prevents us from providing comments that describe each variable's purpose. If more than one name is declared in a declaration (as shown here), the names are separated by commas (,). This is referred to as a comma-separated list.

Good Programming Practice 2.6

Place a space after each comma (,) to make programs more readable.

Good Programming Practice 2.7

Some programmers prefer to declare each variable on a separate line. This format allows for easy insertion of a descriptive comment next to each declaration.

We will soon discuss the data type `double` for specifying real numbers, and the data type `char` for specifying character data. Real numbers are numbers with decimal points, such as 3.4, 0.0 and –11.19. A `char` variable may hold only a single lowercase letter, a single uppercase letter, a single digit or a single special character (e.g., $ or *). Types such as `int`, `double` and `char` are often called fundamental types, primitive types or built-in types. Fundamental-type names are keywords and therefore must appear in all lowercase letters. Appendix C contains the complete list of fundamental types.

A variable name (such as `number1`) is any valid identifier that is not a keyword. An identifier is a series of characters consisting of letters, digits and underscores (_) that does not begin with a digit. C++ is case sensitive—uppercase and lowercase letters are different, so `a1` and `A1` are different identifiers.

Portability Tip 2.1

C++ allows identifiers of any length, but your C++ implementation may impose some restrictions on the length of identifiers. Use identifiers of 31 characters or fewer to ensure portability.

Good Programming Practice 2.8

Choosing meaningful identifiers helps make a program self-documenting—a person can understand the program simply by reading it rather than having to refer to manuals or comments.

Good Programming Practice 2.9

Avoid using abbreviations in identifiers. This promotes program readability.

Good Programming Practice 2.10

Avoid identifiers that begin with underscores and double underscores, because C++ compilers may use names like that for their own purposes internally. This will prevent names you choose from being confused with names the compilers choose.

Error-Prevention Tip 2.1

Languages like C++ are "moving targets." As they evolve, more keywords could be added to the language. Avoid using "loaded" words like "object" as identifiers. Even though "object" is not currently a keyword in C++, it could become one; therefore, future compiling with new compilers could break existing code.

Declarations of variables can be placed almost anywhere in a program, but they must appear before their corresponding variables are used in the program. For example, in the program of Fig. 2.5, the declaration in line 9

```
int number1; // first integer to add
```

could have been placed immediately before line 14

```
std::cin >> number1; // read first integer from user into number1
```

the declaration in line 10

```
int number2; // second integer to add
```

could have been placed immediately before line 17

```
std::cin >> number2; // read second integer from user into number2
```

and the declaration in line 11

```
int sum; // sum of number1 and number2
```

could have been placed immediately before line 19

```
sum = number1 + number2; // add the numbers; store result in sum
```

Good Programming Practice 2.11

Always place a blank line between a declaration and adjacent executable statements. This makes the declarations stand out in the program and contributes to program clarity.

Good Programming Practice 2.12

If you prefer to place declarations at the beginning of a function, separate them from the executable statements in that function with one blank line to highlight where the declarations end and the executable statements begin.

Line 13

```
std::cout << "Enter first integer: "; // prompt user for data
```

prints the string Enter first integer: (also known as a string literal or a literal) on the screen. This message is called a prompt because it directs the user to take a specific action. We like to pronounce the preceding statement as "std::cout *gets* the character string "Enter first integer: "." Line 14

```
std::cin >> number1; // read first integer from user into number1
```

uses the input stream object cin (of namespace std) and the stream extraction operator, >>, to obtain a value from the keyboard. Using the stream extraction operator with std::cin takes character input from the standard input stream, which is usually the keyboard. We like to pronounce the preceding statement as, "std::cin *gives* a value to number1" or simply "std::cin *gives* number1."

Error-Prevention Tip 2.2

Programs should validate the correctness of all input values to prevent erroneous information from affecting a program's calculations.

When the computer executes the preceding statement, it waits for the user to enter a value for variable number1. The user responds by typing an integer (as characters), then pressing the *Enter* key (sometimes called the *Return* key) to send the characters to the computer. The computer converts the character representation of the number to an integer and assigns (copies) this number (or value) to the variable number1. Any subsequent references to number1 in this program will use this same value.

The std::cout and std::cin stream objects facilitate interaction between the user and the computer. Because this interaction resembles a dialog, it is often called conversational computing or interactive computing.

Line 16

```
std::cout << "Enter second integer: "; // prompt user for data
```

prints Enter second integer: on the screen, prompting the user to take action. Line 17

```
std::cin >> number2; // read second integer from user into number2
```

obtains a value for variable number2 from the user.

The assignment statement in line 19

```
sum = number1 + number2; // add the numbers; store result in sum
```

calculates the sum of the variables number1 and number2 and assigns the result to variable sum using the assignment operator =. The statement is read as, "sum *gets* the value of number1 + number2." Most calculations are performed in assignment statements. The = operator and the + operator are called binary operators because each has two operands. In the case of the + operator, the two operands are number1 and number2. In the case of the preceding = operator, the two operands are sum and the value of the expression number1 + number2.

Good Programming Practice 2.13

Place spaces on either side of a binary operator. This makes the operator stand out and makes the program more readable.

Line 21

```
std::cout << "Sum is " << sum << std::endl; // display sum; end line
```

displays the character string Sum is followed by the numerical value of variable sum followed by std::endl—a so-called stream manipulator. The name endl is an abbreviation for "end line" and belongs to namespace std. The std::endl stream manipulator outputs a newline, then "flushes the output buffer." This simply means that, on some systems where outputs accumulate in the machine until there are enough to "make it worthwhile" to display on the screen, std::endl forces any accumulated outputs to be displayed at that moment. This can be important when the outputs are prompting the user for an action, such as entering data.

Note that the preceding statement outputs multiple values of different types. The stream insertion operator "knows" how to output each type of data. Using multiple stream insertion operators (<<) in a single statement is referred to as concatenating, chaining or cascading stream insertion operations. It is unnecessary to have multiple statements to output multiple pieces of data.

Calculations can also be performed in output statements. We could have combined the statements in lines 19 and 21 into the statement

```
std::cout << "Sum is " << number1 + number2 << std::endl;
```

thus eliminating the need for the variable sum.

A powerful feature of C++ is that users can create their own data types called classes (we introduce this capability in Chapter 3 and explore it in depth in Chapters 9 and10). Users can then "teach" C++ how to input and output values of these new data types using the >> and << operators (this is called operator overloading—a topic we explore in Chapter 11).

2.5 Memory Concepts

Variable names such as number1, number2 and sum actually correspond to locations in the computer's memory. Every variable has a name, a type, a size and a value.

In the addition program of Fig. 2.5, when the statement

```
std::cin >> number1; // read first integer from user into number1
```

in line 14 is executed, the characters typed by the user are converted to an integer that is placed into a memory location to which the name number1 has been assigned by the C++

compiler. Suppose the user enters the number 45 as the value for number1. The computer will place 45 into location number1, as shown in Fig. 2.6.

Whenever a value is placed in a memory location, the value overwrites the previous value in that location; thus, placing a new value into a memory location is said to be destructive.

Returning to our addition program, when the statement

```
std::cin >> number2; // read second integer from user into number2
```

in line 17 is executed, suppose the user enters the value 72. This value is placed into location number2, and memory appears as in Fig. 2.7. Note that these locations are not necessarily adjacent in memory.

Once the program has obtained values for number1 and number2, it adds these values and places the sum into variable sum. The statement

```
sum = number1 + number2; // add the numbers; store result in sum
```

that performs the addition also replaces whatever value was stored in sum. This occurs when the calculated sum of number1 and number2 is placed into location sum (without regard to what value may already be in sum; that value is lost). After sum is calculated, memory appears as in Fig. 2.8. Note that the values of number1 and number2 appear exactly as they did before they were used in the calculation of sum. These values were used, but not destroyed, as the computer performed the calculation. Thus, when a value is read out of a memory location, the process is nondestructive.

number1	45

Fig. 2.6 | Memory location showing the name and value of variable number1.

number1	45
number2	72

Fig. 2.7 | Memory locations after storing values for number1 and number2.

number1	45
number2	72
sum	117

Fig. 2.8 | Memory locations after calculating and storing the sum of number1 and number2.

2.6 **Arithmetic**

Most programs perform arithmetic calculations. Figure 2.9 summarizes the C++ arithmetic operators. Note the use of various special symbols not used in algebra. The asterisk (*) indicates multiplication and the percent sign (%) is the modulus operator that will be discussed shortly. The arithmetic operators in Fig. 2.9 are all binary operators, i.e., operators that take two operands. For example, the expression number1 + number2 contains the binary operator + and the two operands number1 and number2.

Integer division (i.e., where both the numerator and the denominator are integers) yields an integer quotient; for example, the expression 7 / 4 evaluates to 1 and the expression 17 / 5 evaluates to 3. Note that any fractional part in integer division is discarded (i.e., truncated)—no rounding occurs.

C++ provides the modulus operator, %, that yields the remainder after integer division. The modulus operator can be used only with integer operands. The expression x % y yields the remainder after x is divided by y. Thus, 7 % 4 yields 3 and 17 % 5 yields 2. In later chapters, we discuss many interesting applications of the modulus operator, such as determining whether one number is a multiple of another (a special case of this is determining whether a number is odd or even).

Common Programming Error 2.3

Attempting to use the modulus operator (%) with noninteger operands is a compilation error.

Arithmetic Expressions in Straight-Line Form

Arithmetic expressions in C++ must be entered into the computer in straight-line form. Thus, expressions such as "a divided by b" must be written as a / b, so that all constants, variables and operators appear in a straight line. The algebraic notation

$$\frac{a}{b}$$

is generally not acceptable to compilers, although some special-purpose software packages do exist that support more natural notation for complex mathematical expressions.

Parentheses for Grouping Subexpressions

Parentheses are used in C++ expressions in the same manner as in algebraic expressions. For example, to multiply a times the quantity b + c we write a * (b + c).

C++ operation	C++ arithmetic operator	Algebraic expression	C++ expression
Addition	+	$f + 7$	f + 7
Subtraction	–	$p - c$	p - c
Multiplication	*	bm or $b \cdot m$	b * m
Division	/	x / y or $\frac{x}{y}$ or $x \div y$	x / y
Modulus	%	$r \bmod s$	r % s

Fig. 2.9 | Arithmetic operators.

Rules of Operator Precedence

C++ applies the operators in arithmetic expressions in a precise sequence determined by the following rules of operator precedence, which are generally the same as those followed in algebra:

1. Operators in expressions contained within pairs of parentheses are evaluated first. Thus, *parentheses may be used to force the order of evaluation to occur in any sequence desired by the programmer.* Parentheses are said to be at the "highest level of precedence." In cases of nested, or embedded, parentheses, such as

   ```
   ( ( a + b ) + c )
   ```

   the operators in the innermost pair of parentheses are applied first.

2. Multiplication, division and modulus operations are applied next. If an expression contains several multiplication, division and modulus operations, operators are applied from left to right. Multiplication, division and modulus are said to be on the same level of precedence.

3. Addition and subtraction operations are applied last. If an expression contains several addition and subtraction operations, operators are applied from left to right. Addition and subtraction also have the same level of precedence.

The set of rules of operator precedence defines the order in which C++ applies operators. When we say that certain operators are applied from left to right, we are referring to the associativity of the operators. For example, in the expression

```
a + b + c
```

the addition operators (+) associate from left to right, so a + b is calculated first, then c is added to that sum to determine the value of the whole expression. We will see that some operators associate from right to left. Figure 2.10 summarizes these rules of operator precedence. This table will be expanded as additional C++ operators are introduced. A complete precedence chart is included in Appendix A.

Operator(s)	Operation(s)	Order of evaluation (precedence)
( )	Parentheses	Evaluated first. If the parentheses are nested, the expression in the innermost pair is evaluated first. If there are several pairs of parentheses "on the same level" (i.e., not nested), they are evaluated left to right.
* / %	Multiplication Division Modulus	Evaluated second. If there are several, they are evaluated left to right.
+ -	Addition Subtraction	Evaluated last. If there are several, they are evaluated left to right.

Fig. 2.10 | Precedence of arithmetic operators.

Sample Algebraic and C++ Expressions

Now consider several expressions in light of the rules of operator precedence. Each example lists an algebraic expression and its C++ equivalent. The following is an example of an arithmetic mean (average) of five terms:

Algebra: $\quad m = \dfrac{a + b + c + d + e}{5}$

C++: $\quad$ m = (a + b + c + d + e) / 5;

The parentheses are required because division has higher precedence than addition. The entire quantity (a + b + c + d + e) is to be divided by 5. If the parentheses are erroneously omitted, we obtain a + b + c + d + e / 5, which evaluates incorrectly as

$$\iota + b + c + d + \dfrac{e}{5}$$

The following is an example of the equation of a straight line:

Algebra: $\quad y = mx + b$

C++: $\quad$ y = m * x + b;

No parentheses are required. The multiplication is applied first because multiplication has a higher precedence than addition.

The following example contains modulus (%), multiplication, division, addition, subtraction and assignment operations:

Algebra: $\quad z = pr \% q + w/x - y$

C++: $\quad$ z = p * r % q + w / x - y;
$\qquad\qquad$ ⑥   ①   ②   ④   ③   ⑤

The circled numbers under the statement indicate the order in which C++ applies the operators. The multiplication, modulus and division are evaluated first in left-to-right order (i.e., they associate from left to right) because they have higher precedence than addition and subtraction. The addition and subtraction are applied next. These are also applied left to right. Then the assignment operator is applied.

Evaluation of a Second-Degree Polynomial

To develop a better understanding of the rules of operator precedence, consider the evaluation of a second-degree polynomial ($y = ax^2 + bx + c$):

$\qquad$ y = a * x * x + b * x + c;
$\qquad\quad$ ⑥   ①   ②   ④   ③   ⑤

The circled numbers under the statement indicate the order in which C++ applies the operators. There is no arithmetic operator for exponentiation in C++, so we have represented x^2 as x * x. We will soon discuss the standard library function pow ("power") that performs exponentiation. Because of some subtle issues related to the data types required by pow, we defer a detailed explanation of pow until Chapter 6.

Common Programming Error 2.4

*Some programming languages use operators ** or ∧ to represent exponentiation. C++ does not support these exponentiation operators; using them for exponentiation results in errors.*

Suppose variables a, b, c and x in the preceding second-degree polynomial are initialized as follows: a = 2, b = 3, c = 7 and x = 5. Figure 2.11 illustrates the order in which the operators are applied.

As in algebra, it is acceptable to place unnecessary parentheses in an expression to make the expression clearer. These are called redundant parentheses. For example, the preceding assignment statement could be parenthesized as follows:

```
y = ( a * x * x ) + ( b * x ) + c;
```

Good Programming Practice 2.14

Using redundant parentheses in complex arithmetic expressions can make the expressions clearer.

2.7 Decision Making: Equality and Relational Operators

This section introduces a simple version of C++'s if statement that allows a program to make a decision based on the truth or falsity of some condition. If the condition is met, i.e., the condition is true, the statement in the body of the if statement is executed. If the condition is not met, i.e., the condition is false, the body statement is not executed. We will see an example shortly.

Step 1.	y = 2 * 5 * 5 + 3 * 5 + 7;	*(Leftmost multiplication)*
	2 * 5 is 10	
Step 2.	y = 10 * 5 + 3 * 5 + 7;	*(Leftmost multiplication)*
	10 * 5 is 50	
Step 3.	y = 50 + 3 * 5 + 7;	*(Multiplication before addition)*
	3 * 5 is 15	
Step 4.	y = 50 + 15 + 7;	*(Leftmost addition)*
	50 + 15 is 65	
Step 5.	y = 65 + 7;	*(Last addition)*
	65 + 7 is 72	
Step 6.	y = 72	*(Last operation—place 72 in y)*

Fig. 2.11 | Order in which a second-degree polynomial is evaluated.

Conditions in if statements can be formed by using the equality operators and relational operators summarized in Fig. 2.12. The relational operators all have the same level of precedence and associate left to right. The equality operators both have the same level of precedence, which is lower than that of the relational operators, and associate left to right.

Common Programming Error 2.5

A syntax error will occur if any of the operators ==, !=, >= and <= appears with spaces between its pair of symbols.

Common Programming Error 2.6

Reversing the order of the pair of symbols in any of the operators !=, >= and <= (by writing them as =!, => and =<, respectively) is normally a syntax error. In some cases, writing != as =! will not be a syntax error, but almost certainly will be a logic error that has an effect at execution time. You will understand why when you learn about logical operators in Chapter 5. A fatal logic error causes a program to fail and terminate prematurely. A nonfatal logic error allows a program to continue executing, but usually produces incorrect results.

Common Programming Error 2.7

Confusing the equality operator == with the assignment operator = results in logic errors. The equality operator should be read "is equal to," and the assignment operator should be read "gets" or "gets the value of" or "is assigned the value of." Some people prefer to read the equality operator as "double equals." As we discuss in Section 5.9, confusing these operators may not necessarily cause an easy-to-recognize syntax error, but may cause extremely subtle logic errors.

The following example uses six if statements to compare two numbers input by the user. If the condition in any of these if statements is satisfied, the output statement associated with that if statement is executed. Figure 2.13 shows the program and the input/output dialogs of three sample executions.

Standard algebraic equality or relational operator	C++ equality or relational operator	Sample C++ condition	Meaning of C++ condition
Relational operators			
>	>	x > y	x is greater than y
<	<	x < y	x is less than y
≥	>=	x >= y	x is greater than or equal to y
≤	<=	x <= y	x is less than or equal to y
Equality operators			
=	==	x == y	x is equal to y
≠	!=	x != y	x is not equal to y

Fig. 2.12 | Equality and relational operators.

Lines 6–8

```
using std::cout; // program uses cout
using std::cin;  // program uses cin
using std::endl; // program uses endl
```

are **using** declarations that eliminate the need to repeat the std:: prefix as we did in earlier programs. Once we insert these using declarations, we can write cout instead of
std::cout, cin instead of std::cin and endl instead of std::endl, respectively, in the
remainder of the program. [*Note:* From this point forward in the book, each example contains one or more using declarations.]

```
 1   // Fig. 2.13: fig02_13.cpp
 2   // Comparing integers using if statements, relational operators
 3   // and equality operators.
 4   #include <iostream> // allows program to perform input and output
 5
 6   using std::cout; // program uses cout
 7   using std::cin;  // program uses cin
 8   using std::endl; // program uses endl
 9
10   // function main begins program execution
11   int main()
12   {
13      int number1; // first integer to compare
14      int number2; // second integer to compare
15
16      cout << "Enter two integers to compare: "; // prompt user for data
17      cin >> number1 >> number2; // read two integers from user
18
19      if ( number1 == number2 )
20         cout << number1 << " == " << number2 << endl;
21
22      if ( number1 != number2 )
23         cout << number1 << " != " << number2 << endl;
24
25      if ( number1 < number2 )
26         cout << number1 << " < " << number2 << endl;
27
28      if ( number1 > number2 )
29         cout << number1 << " > " << number2 << endl;
30
31      if ( number1 <= number2 )
32         cout << number1 << " <= " << number2 << endl;
33
34      if ( number1 >= number2 )
35         cout << number1 << " >= " << number2 << endl;
36
37      return 0; // indicate that program ended successfully
38
39   } // end function main
```

Fig. 2.13 | Equality and relational operators. (Part 1 of 2.)

```
Enter two integers to compare: 3 7
3 != 7
3 < 7
3 <= 7
```

```
Enter two integers to compare: 22 12
22 != 12
22 > 12
22 >= 12
```

```
Enter two integers to compare: 7 7
7 == 7
7 <= 7
7 >= 7
```

Fig. 2.13 | Equality and relational operators. (Part 2 of 2.)

Good Programming Practice 2.15

Place using *declarations immediately after the* #include *to which they refer.*

Lines 13–14

```
int number1; // first integer to compare
int number2; // second integer to compare
```

declare the variables used in the program. Remember that variables may be declared in one declaration or in multiple declarations.

The program uses cascaded stream extraction operations (line 17) to input two integers. Remember that we are allowed to write cin (instead of std::cin) because of line 7. First a value is read into variable number1, then a value is read into variable number2.

The if statement at lines 19–20

```
if ( number1 == number2 )
    cout << number1 << " == " << number2 << endl;
```

compares the values of variables number1 and number2 to test for equality. If the values are equal, the statement at line 20 displays a line of text indicating that the numbers are equal. If the conditions are true in one or more of the if statements starting at lines 22, 25, 28, 31 and 34, the corresponding body statement displays an appropriate line of text.

Notice that each if statement in Fig. 2.13 has a single statement in its body and that each body statement is indented. In Chapter 4 we show how to specify if statements with multiple-statement bodies (by enclosing the body statements in a pair of braces, { }, creating what is called a compound statement or a block).

Good Programming Practice 2.16

Indent the statement(s) in the body of an if *statement to enhance readability.*

Good Programming Practice 2.17

For readability, there should be no more than one statement per line in a program.

Common Programming Error 2.8

Placing a semicolon immediately after the right parenthesis after the condition in an if state-ment is often a logic error (although not a syntax error). The semicolon causes the body of the if statement to be empty, so the if statement performs no action, regardless of whether or not its condition is true. Worse yet, the original body statement of the if statement now would become a statement in sequence with the if statement and would always execute, often causing the pro-gram to produce incorrect results.

Note the use of white space in Fig. 2.13. Recall that white-space characters, such as tabs, newlines and spaces, are normally ignored by the compiler. So, statements may be split over several lines and may be spaced according to the programmer's preferences. It is a syntax error to split identifiers, strings (such as "hello") and constants (such as the number 1000) over several lines.

Common Programming Error 2.9

It is a syntax error to split an identifier by inserting white-space characters (e.g., writing main as ma in).

Good Programming Practice 2.18

A lengthy statement may be spread over several lines. If a single statement must be split across lines, choose meaningful breaking points, such as after a comma in a comma-separated list, or after an operator in a lengthy expression. If a statement is split across two or more lines, indent all subsequent lines and left-align the group.

Figure 2.14 shows the precedence and associativity of the operators introduced in this chapter. The operators are shown top to bottom in decreasing order of precedence. Notice that all these operators, with the exception of the assignment operator =, associate from left to right. Addition is left-associative, so an expression like x + y + z is evaluated as if it had been written (x + y) + z. The assignment operator = associates from right to left, so an expression such as x = y = 0 is evaluated as if it had been written x = (y = 0), which, as we will soon see, first assigns 0 to y then assigns the result of that assignment—0—to x.

Operators				Associativity	Type
()				left to right	parentheses
*	/	%		left to right	multiplicative
+	-			left to right	additive
<<	>>			left to right	stream insertion/extraction
<	<=	>	>=	left to right	relational
==	!=			left to right	equality
=				right to left	assignment

Fig. 2.14 | Precedence and associativity of the operators discussed so far.

Good Programming Practice 2.19

Refer to the operator precedence and associativity chart when writing expressions containing many operators. Confirm that the operators in the expression are performed in the order you expect. If you are uncertain about the order of evaluation in a complex expression, break the expression into smaller statements or use parentheses to force the order of evaluation, exactly as you would do in an algebraic expression. Be sure to observe that some operators such as assignment (=) associate right to left rather than left to right.

2.8 Wrap-Up

You learned many important features of C++ in this chapter, including displaying data on the screen, inputting data from the keyboard and declaring variables of fundamental types. In particular, you learned to use the output stream object cout and the input stream object cin to build simple interactive programs. We explained how variables are stored in and retrieved from memory. You also learned how to use arithmetic operators to perform calculations. We discussed the order in which C++ applies operators (i.e., the rules of operator precedence), as well as the associativity of the operators. You also learned how C++'s if statement allows a program to make decisions. Finally, we introduced the equality and relational operators, which you use to form conditions in if statements.

The non-object-oriented applications presented here introduced you to basic programming concepts. As you will see in Chapter 3, C++ applications typically contain just a few lines of code in function main—these statements normally create the objects that perform the work of the application, then the objects "take over from there." In Chapter 3, you will learn how to implement your own classes and use objects of those classes in applications.

Summary

- Single-line comments begin with //. Programmers insert comments to document programs and improve their readability.

- Comments do not cause the computer to perform any action when the program is run—they are ignored by the C++ compiler and do not cause any machine-language object code to be generated.

- A preprocessor directive begins with # and is a message to the C++ preprocessor. Preprocessor directives are processed by the preprocessor before the program is compiled and don't end with a semicolon as C++ statements do.

- The line #include <iostream> tells the C++ preprocessor to include the contents of the input/output stream header file in the program. This file contains information necessary to compile programs that use std::cin and std::cout and operators << and >>.

- Programmers use white space (i.e., blank lines, space characters and tab characters) to make programs easier to read. White-space characters are ignored by the compiler.

- C++ programs begin executing at the function main, even if main does not appear first in the program.

- The keyword int to the left of main indicates that main "returns" an integer value.

- A left brace, {, must begin the body of every function. A corresponding right brace, }, must end each function's body.

- A string in double quotes is sometimes referred to as a character string, message or string literal. White-space characters in strings are not ignored by the compiler.

- Every statement must end with a semicolon (also known as the statement terminator).
- Output and input in C++ are accomplished with streams of characters.
- The output stream object `std::cout`—normally connected to the screen—is used to output data. Multiple data items can be output by concatenating stream insertion (`<<`) operators.
- The input stream object `std::cin`—normally connected to the keyboard—is used to input data. Multiple data items can be input by concatenating stream extraction (`>>`) operators.
- The `std::cout` and `std::cin` stream objects facilitate interaction between the user and the computer. Because this interaction resembles a dialog, it is often called conversational computing or interactive computing.
- The notation `std::cout` specifies that we are using a name, in this case `cout`, that belongs to "namespace" `std`.
- When a backslash (i.e., an escape character) is encountered in a string of characters, the next character is combined with the backslash to form an escape sequence.
- The escape sequence \n means newline. It causes the cursor (i.e., the current screen-position indicator) to move to the beginning of the next line on the screen.
- A message that directs the user to take a specific action is known as a prompt.
- C++ keyword `return` is one of several means to exit a function.
- All variables in a C++ program must be declared before they can be used.
- A variable name in C++ is any valid identifier that is not a keyword. An identifier is a series of characters consisting of letters, digits and underscores (_). Identifiers cannot start with a digit. C++ identifiers can be any length; however, some systems and/or C++ implementations may impose some restrictions on the length of identifiers.
- C++ is case sensitive.
- Most calculations are performed in assignment statements.
- A variable is a location in the computer's memory where a value can be stored for use by a program.
- Variables of type `int` hold integer values, i.e., whole numbers such as 7, –11, 0, 31914.
- Every variable stored in the computer's memory has a name, a value, a type and a size.
- Whenever a new value is placed in a memory location, the process is destructive; i.e., the new value replaces the previous value in that location. The previous value is lost.
- When a value is read from memory, the process is nondestructive; i.e., a copy of the value is read, leaving the original value undisturbed in the memory location.
- The `std::endl` stream manipulator outputs a newline, then "flushes the output buffer."
- C++ evaluates arithmetic expressions in a precise sequence determined by the rules of operator precedence and associativity.
- Parentheses may be used to force the order of evaluation to occur in any sequence desired by the programmer.
- Integer division (i.e., both the numerator and the denominator are integers) yields an integer quotient. Any fractional part in integer division is truncated—no rounding occurs.
- The modulus operator, `%`, yields the remainder after integer division. The modulus operator can be used only with integer operands.
- The `if` statement allows a program to make a decision when a certain condition is met. The format for an `if` statement is

```
if ( condition )
   statement;
```

If the condition is true, the statement in the body of the if is executed. If the condition is not met, i.e., the condition is false, the body statement is skipped.

- Conditions in if statements are commonly formed by using equality operators and relational operators. The result of using these operators is always the value true or false.
- The declaration

```
using std::cout;
```

is a using declaration that eliminates the need to repeat the std:: prefix. Once we include this using declaration, we can write cout instead of std::cout in the remainder of a program.

Terminology

/* ... */ comment (C-style comment)
// comment
arithmetic operator
assignment operator (=)
associativity of operators
binary operator
block
body of a function
cascading stream insertion operations
case sensitive
chaining stream insertion operations
character string
cin object
comma-separated list
comment (//)
compilation error
compiler error
compile-time error
compound statement
concatenating stream insertion operations
condition
cout object
cursor
data type
decision
declaration
destructive write
equality operators
 == "is equal to"
 != "is not equal to"
escape character (\)
escape sequence
exit a function
fatal error
function
identifier
if statement
input/output stream header file <iostream>
int data type

integer (int)
integer division
left-to-right associativity
literal
logic error
main function
memory
memory location
message
modulus operator (%)
multiplication operator (*)
nested parentheses
newline character (\n)
nondestructive read
nonfatal logic error
operand
operator
operator associativity
parentheses ()
perform an action
precedence
preprocessor directive
prompt
redundant parentheses
relational operators
 < "is less than"
 <= "is less than or equal to"
 > "is greater than"
 >= "is greater than or equal to"
return statement
rules of operator precedence
self-documenting program
semicolon (;) statement terminator
standard input stream object (cin)
standard output stream object (cout)
statement
statement terminator (;)
stream
stream insertion operator (<<)

stream extraction operator (>>)   syntax error
stream manipulator   using declaration
string   variable
string literal   white space

Self-Review Exercises

2.1 Fill in the blanks in each of the following.
   a) Every C++ program begins execution at the function _____.
   b) The _____ begins the body of every function and the _____ ends the body of every function.
   c) Every C++ statement ends with a(n) _____.
   d) The escape sequence \n represents the _____ character, which causes the cursor to position to the beginning of the next line on the screen.
   e) The _____ statement is used to make decisions.

2.2 State whether each of the following is *true* or *false*. If *false*, explain why. Assume the statement using std::cout; is used.
   a) Comments cause the computer to print the text after the // on the screen when the program is executed.
   b) The escape sequence \n, when output with cout and the stream insertion operator, causes the cursor to position to the beginning of the next line on the screen.
   c) All variables must be declared before they are used.
   d) All variables must be given a type when they are declared.
   e) C++ considers the variables number and NuMbEr to be identical.
   f) Declarations can appear almost anywhere in the body of a C++ function.
   g) The modulus operator (%) can be used only with integer operands.
   h) The arithmetic operators *, /, %, + and – all have the same level of precedence.
   i) A C++ program that prints three lines of output must contain three statements using cout and the stream insertion operator.

2.3 Write a single C++ statement to accomplish each of the following (assume that using declarations have not been used):
   a) Declare the variables c, thisIsAVariable, q76354 and number to be of type int.
   b) Prompt the user to enter an integer. End your prompting message with a colon (:) followed by a space and leave the cursor positioned after the space.
   c) Read an integer from the user at the keyboard and store the value entered in integer variable age.
   d) If the variable number is not equal to 7, print "The variable number is not equal to 7".
   e) Print the message "This is a C++ program" on one line.
   f) Print the message "This is a C++ program" on two lines. End the first line with C++.
   g) Print the message "This is a C++ program" with each word on a separate line.
   h) Print the message "This is a C++ program" with each word separated from the next by a tab.

2.4 Write a statement (or comment) to accomplish each of the following (assume that using declarations have been used):
   a) State that a program calculates the product of three integers.
   b) Declare the variables x, y, z and result to be of type int (in separate statements).
   c) Prompt the user to enter three integers.
   d) Read three integers from the keyboard and store them in the variables x, y and z.

e) Compute the product of the three integers contained in variables x, y and z, and assign the result to the variable result.

f) Print "The product is " followed by the value of the variable result.

g) Return a value from main indicating that the program terminated successfully.

2.5   Using the statements you wrote in Exercise 2.4, write a complete program that calculates and displays the product of three integers. Add comments to the code where appropriate. [*Note:* You will need to write the necessary using declarations.]

2.6   Identify and correct the errors in each of the following statements (assume that the statement using std::cout; is used):

a) ```
   if (c < 7);
       cout << "c is less than 7\n";
   ```

b) ```
   if ( c => 7 )
       cout << "c is equal to or greater than 7\n";
   ```

Answers to Self-Review Exercises

2.1   a) main.   b) left brace ({), right brace (}).   c) semicolon.   d) newline.   e) if.

2.2   a) False. Comments do not cause any action to be performed when the program is executed. They are used to document programs and improve their readability.

b) True.

c) True.

d) True.

e) False. C++ is case sensitive, so these variables are unique.

f) True.

g) True.

h) False. The operators *, / and % have the same precedence, and the operators + and - have a lower precedence.

i) False. A single cout statement with multiple \n escape sequences can print several lines.

2.3   a) `int c, thisIsAVariable, q76354, number;`

b) `std::cout << "Enter an integer: ";`

c) `std::cin >> age;`

d) ```
   if (number != 7)
       std::cout << "The variable number is not equal to 7\n";
   ```

e) `std::cout << "This is a C++ program\n";`

f) `std::cout << "This is a C++\nprogram\n";`

g) `std::cout << "This\nis\na\nC++\nprogram\n";`

h) `std::cout << "This\tis\ta\tC++\tprogram\n";`

**2.4**    a) `// Calculate the product of three integers`

b) ```
   int x;
   int y;
   int z;
   int result;
   ```

c) `cout << "Enter three integers: ";`

d) `cin >> x >> y >> z;`

e) `result = x * y * z;`

f) `cout << "The product is " << result << endl;`

g) `return 0;`

2.5   (See program below)

```
 1  // Calculate the product of three integers
 2  #include <iostream> // allows program to perform input and output
 3
 4  using std::cout; // program uses cout
 5  using std::cin; // program uses cin
 6  using std::endl; // program uses endl
 7
 8  // function main begins program execution
 9  int main()
10  {
11     int x; // first integer to multiply
12     int y; // second integer to multiply
13     int z; // third integer to multiply
14     int result; // the product of the three integers
15
16     cout << "Enter three integers: "; // prompt user for data
17     cin >> x >> y >> z; // read three integers from user
18     result = x * y * z; // multiply the three integers; store result
19     cout << "The product is " << result << endl; // print result; end line
20
21     return 0; // indicate program executed successfully
22  } // end function main
```

2.6   a) Error: Semicolon after the right parenthesis of the condition in the if statement.
Correction: Remove the semicolon after the right parenthesis. [*Note:* The result of this error is that the output statement will be executed whether or not the condition in the if statement is true.] The semicolon after the right parenthesis is a null (or empty) statement—a statement that does nothing. We will learn more about the null statement in the next chapter.

   b) Error: The relational operator =>.
Correction: Change => to >=, and you may want to change "equal to or greater than" to "greater than or equal to" as well.

Exercises

2.7   Discuss the meaning of each of the following objects:
   a) std::cin
   b) std::cout

2.8   Fill in the blanks in each of the following:
   a) _____ are used to document a program and improve its readability.
   b) The object used to print information on the screen is _____.
   c) A C++ statement that makes a decision is _____.
   d) Most calculations are normally performed by _____ statements.
   e) The _____ object inputs values from the keyboard.

2.9   Write a single C++ statement or line that accomplishes each of the following:
   a) Print the message "Enter two numbers".
   b) Assign the product of variables b and c to variable a.
   c) State that a program performs a payroll calculation (i.e., use text that helps to document a program).
   d) Input three integer values from the keyboard into integer variables a, b and c.

2.10 State which of the following are *true* and which are *false*. If *false*, explain your answers.
a) C++ operators are evaluated from left to right.
b) The following are all valid variable names: _under_bar_, m928134, t5, j7, her_sales, his_account_total, a, b, c, z, z2.
c) The statement cout << "a = 5;"; is a typical example of an assignment statement.
d) A valid C++ arithmetic expression with no parentheses is evaluated from left to right.
e) The following are all invalid variable names: 3g, 87, 67h2, h22, 2h.

2.11 Fill in the blanks in each of the following:
a) What arithmetic operations are on the same level of precedence as multiplication? _____.
b) When parentheses are nested, which set of parentheses is evaluated first in an arithmetic expression? _____.
c) A location in the computer's memory that may contain different values at various times throughout the execution of a program is called a _____.

2.12 What, if anything, prints when each of the following C++ statements is performed? If nothing prints, then answer "nothing." Assume x = 2 and y = 3.
a) cout << x;
b) cout << x + x;
c) cout << "x=";
d) cout << "x = " << x;
e) cout << x + y << " = " << y + x;
f) z = x + y;
g) cin >> x >> y;
h) // cout << "x + y = " << x + y;
i) cout << "\n";

2.13 Which of the following C++ statements contain variables whose values are replaced?
a) cin >> b >> c >> d >> e >> f;
b) p = i + j + k + 7;
c) cout << "variables whose values are replaced";
d) cout << "a = 5";

2.14 Given the algebraic equation $y = ax^3 + 7$, which of the following, if any, are correct C++ statements for this equation?
a) y = a * x * x * x + 7;
b) y = a * x * x * (x + 7);
c) y = (a * x) * x * (x + 7);
d) y = (a * x) * x * x + 7;
e) y = a * (x * x * x) + 7;
f) y = a * x * (x * x + 7);

2.15 State the order of evaluation of the operators in each of the following C++ statements and show the value of x after each statement is performed.
a) x = 7 + 3 * 6 / 2 - 1;
b) x = 2 % 2 + 2 * 2 - 2 / 2;
c) x = (3 * 9 * (3 + (9 * 3 / (3))));

2.16 Write a program that asks the user to enter two numbers, obtains the two numbers from the user and prints the sum, product, difference, and quotient of the two numbers.

2.17 Write a program that prints the numbers 1 to 4 on the same line with each pair of adjacent numbers separated by one space. Do this several ways:

     a) Using one statement with one stream insertion operator.

     b) Using one statement with four stream insertion operators.

     c) Using four statements.

2.18 Write a program that asks the user to enter two integers, obtains the numbers from the user, then prints the larger number followed by the words "is larger." If the numbers are equal, print the message "These numbers are equal."

2.19 Write a program that inputs three integers from the keyboard and prints the sum, average, product, smallest and largest of these numbers. The screen dialog should appear as follows:

```
Input three different integers: 13 27 14
Sum is 54
Average is 18
Product is 4914
Smallest is 13
Largest is 27
```

2.20 Write a program that reads in the radius of a circle as an integer and prints the circle's diameter, circumference and area. Use the constant value 3.14159 for π. Do all calculations in output statements. [*Note:* In this chapter, we have discussed only integer constants and variables. In Chapter 4 we discuss floating-point numbers, i.e., values that can have decimal points.]

2.21 Write a program that prints a box, an oval, an arrow and a diamond as follows:

```
*********        ***             *                *
*       *       *   *           ***             *   *
*       *      *     *         *****           *     *
*       *      *     *           *            *       *
*       *      *     *           *            *       *
*       *      *     *           *            *       *
*       *      *     *           *             *     *
*       *       *   *            *              *   *
*********        ***             *                *
```

2.22 What does the following code print?

```
cout << "*\n**\n***\n****\n*****" << endl;
```

2.23 Write a program that reads in five integers and determines and prints the largest and the smallest integers in the group. Use only the programming techniques you learned in this chapter.

2.24 Write a program that reads an integer and determines and prints whether it is odd or even. [*Hint:* Use the modulus operator. An even number is a multiple of two. Any multiple of two leaves a remainder of zero when divided by 2.]

2.25 Write a program that reads in two integers and determines and prints if the first is a multiple of the second. [*Hint:* Use the modulus operator.]

2.26 Display the following checkerboard pattern with eight output statements, then display the same pattern using as few statements as possible.

```
*  *  *  *  *  *  *
 *  *  *  *  *  *  *
*  *  *  *  *  *  *
 *  *  *  *  *  *  *
*  *  *  *  *  *  *
 *  *  *  *  *  *  *
*  *  *  *  *  *  *
 *  *  *  *  *  *  *
```

2.27   Here is a peek ahead. In this chapter you learned about integers and the type int. C++ can also represent uppercase letters, lowercase letters and a considerable variety of special symbols. C++ uses small integers internally to represent each different character. The set of characters a computer uses and the corresponding integer representations for those characters is called that computer's character set. You can print a character by enclosing that character in single quotes, as with

```
cout << 'A'; // print an uppercase A
```

You can print the integer equivalent of a character using static_cast as follows:

```
cout << static_cast< int >( 'A' ); // print 'A' as an integer
```

This is called a cast operation (we formally introduce casts in Chapter 4). When the preceding statement executes, it prints the value 65 (on systems that use the ASCII character set). Write a program that prints the integer equivalent of a character typed at the keyboard. Test your program several times using uppercase letters, lowercase letters, digits and special characters (like $).

2.28   Write a program that inputs a five-digit integer, separates the integer into its individual digits and prints the digits separated from one another by three spaces each. [*Hint:* Use the integer division and modulus operators.] For example, if the user types in 42339, the program should print:

```
4   2   3   3   9
```

2.29   Using only the techniques you learned in this chapter, write a program that calculates the squares and cubes of the integers from 0 to 10 and uses tabs to print the following neatly formatted table of values:

```
integer square  cube
0       0       0
1       1       1
2       4       8
3       9       27
4       16      64
5       25      125
6       36      216
7       49      343
8       64      512
9       81      729
10      100     1000
```

3

Introduction to Classes and Objects

You will see something new.
Two things. And I call them
Thing One and Thing Two.
—Dr. Theodor Scuss Geisel

Nothing can have value
without being an object of
utility.
—Karl Marx

Your public servants serve
you right.
—Adlai E. Stevenson

Knowing how to answer one
who speaks,
To reply to one who sends a
message.
—Amenemope

OBJECTIVES

In this chapter you will learn:

- What classes, objects, member functions and data members are.

- How to define a class and use it to create an object.

- How to define member functions in a class to implement the class's behaviors.

- How to declare data members in a class to implement the class's attributes.

- How to call a member function of an object to make that member function perform its task.

- The differences between data members of a class and local variables of a function.

- How to use a constructor to ensure that an object's data is initialized when the object is created.

- How to engineer a class to separate its interface from its implementation and encourage reuse.

Outline

3.1   Introduction

3.2   Classes, Objects, Member Functions and Data Members

3.3   Overview of the Chapter Examples

3.4   Defining a Class with a Member Function

3.5   Defining a Member Function with a Parameter

3.6   Data Members, set Functions and get Functions

3.7   Initializing Objects with Constructors

3.8   Placing a Class in a Separate File for Reusability

3.9   Separating Interface from Implementation

3.10   Validating Data with set Functions

3.11   Wrap-Up

Summary | Terminology | Self-Review Exercises | Answers to Self-Review Exercises | Exercises

3.1 Introduction

In Chapter 2, you created simple programs that displayed messages to the user, obtained information from the user, performed calculations and made decisions. In this chapter, you will begin writing programs that employ the basic concepts of object-oriented programming that we introduced in Section 1.17. One common feature of every program in Chapter 2 was that all the statements that performed tasks were located in function main. Typically, the programs you develop in this book will consist of function main and one or more classes, each containing data members and member functions. If you become part of a development team in industry, you might work on software systems that contain hundreds, or even thousands, of classes. In this chapter, we develop a simple, well-engineered framework for organizing object-oriented programs in C++.

First, we motivate the notion of classes with a real-world example. Then we present a carefully paced sequence of seven complete working programs to demonstrate creating and using your own classes. These examples begin our integrated case study on developing a grade-book class that instructors can use to maintain student test scores. This case study is enhanced over the next several chapters, culminating with the version presented in Chapter 7, Arrays and Vectors.

3.2 Classes, Objects, Member Functions and Data Members

Let's begin with a simple analogy to help you reinforce your understanding from Section 1.17 of classes and their contents. Suppose you want to drive a car and make it go faster by pressing down on its accelerator pedal. What must happen before you can do this? Well, before you can drive a car, someone has to design it and build it. A car typically begins as engineering drawings, similar to the blueprints used to design a house. These drawings include the design for an accelerator pedal that the driver will use to make the car go faster. In a sense, the pedal "hides" the complex mechanisms that actually make the car go faster, just as the brake pedal "hides" the mechanisms that slow the car, the steering wheel "hides" the mechanisms that turn the car and so on. This enables people with little or no knowledge of how cars are engineered to drive a car easily, simply by using the accelerator pedal, the brake pedal, the steering wheel, the transmission shifting mechanism and other such simple and user-friendly "interfaces" to the car's complex internal mechanisms.

Unfortunately, you cannot drive the engineering drawings of a car—before you can drive a car, it must be built from the engineering drawings that describe it. A completed car will have an actual accelerator pedal to make the car go faster. But even that's not enough—the car will not accelerate on its own, so the driver must press the accelerator pedal to tell the car to go faster.

Now let's use our car example to introduce the key object-oriented programming concepts of this section. Performing a task in a program requires a function (such as main, as described in Chapter 2). The function describes the mechanisms that actually perform its tasks. The function hides from its user the complex tasks that it performs, just as the accelerator pedal of a car hides from the driver the complex mechanisms of making the car go faster. In C++, we begin by creating a program unit called a class to house a function, just as a car's engineering drawings house the design of an accelerator pedal. Recall from Section 1.17 that a function belonging to a class is called a member function. In a class, you provide one or more member functions that are designed to perform the class's tasks. For example, a class that represents a bank account might contain one member function to deposit money into the account, another to withdraw money from the account and a third to inquire what the current account balance is.

Just as you cannot drive an engineering drawing of a car, you cannot "drive" a class. Just as someone has to build a car from its engineering drawings before you can actually drive the car, you must create an object of a class before you can get a program to perform the tasks the class describes. That is one reason C++ is known as an object-oriented programming language. Note also that just as *many* cars can be built from the same engineering drawing, *many* objects can be built from the same class.

When you drive a car, pressing its gas pedal sends a message to the car to perform a task—that is, make the car go faster. Similarly, you send messages to an object—each message is known as a member-function call and tells a member function of the object to perform its task. This is often called requesting a service from an object.

Thus far, we have used the car analogy to introduce classes, objects and member functions. In addition to the capabilities a car provides, it also has many attributes, such as its color, the number of doors, the amount of gas in its tank, its current speed and its total miles driven (i.e., its odometer reading). Like the car's capabilities, these attributes are represented as part of a car's design in its engineering diagrams. As you drive a car, these attributes are always associated with the car. Every car maintains its own attributes. For example, each car knows how much gas is in its own gas tank, but not how much is in the tanks of other cars. Similarly, an object has attributes that are carried with the object as it is used in a program. These attributes are specified as part of the object's class. For example, a bank account object has a balance attribute that represents the amount of money in the account. Each bank account object knows the balance in the account it represents, but not the balances of the other accounts in the bank. Attributes are specified by the class's data members.

3.3 Overview of the Chapter Examples

The remainder of this chapter presents seven simple examples that demonstrate the concepts we introduced in the context of the car analogy. These examples, summarized below, incrementally build a GradeBook class to demonstrate these concepts:

1. The first example presents a GradeBook class with one member function that simply displays a welcome message when it is called. We then show how to create an object of that class and call the member function so that it displays the welcome message.

2. The second example modifies the first by allowing the member function to receive a course name as a so-called argument. Then, the member function displays the course name as part of the welcome message.

3. The third example shows how to store the course name in a GradeBook object. For this version of the class, we also show how to use member functions to set the course name in the object and get the course name from the object.

4. The fourth example demonstrates how the data in a GradeBook object can be initialized when the object is created—the initialization is performed by a special member function called the class's constructor. This example also demonstrates that each GradeBook object maintains its own course name data member.

5. The fifth example modifies the fourth by demonstrating how to place class GradeBook into a separate file to enable software reusability.

6. The sixth example modifies the fifth by demonstrating the good software-engineering principle of separating the interface of the class from its implementation. This makes the class easier to modify without affecting any clients of the class's objects—that is, any classes or functions that call the member functions of the class's objects from outside the objects.

7. The last example enhances class GradeBook by introducing data validation, which ensures that data in an object adheres to a particular format or is in a proper value range. For example, a Date object would require a month value in the range 1–12. In this GradeBook example, the member function that sets the course name for a GradeBook object ensures that the course name is 25 characters or fewer. If not, the member function uses only the first 25 characters of the course name and displays a warning message.

Note that the GradeBook examples in this chapter do not actually process or store grades. We begin processing grades with class GradeBook in Chapter 4 and we store grades in a GradeBook object in Chapter 7, Arrays and Vectors.

3.4 Defining a Class with a Member Function

We begin with an example (Fig. 3.1) that consists of class GradeBook, which represents a grade book that an instructor can use to maintain student test scores, and a main function (lines 20–25) that creates a GradeBook object. This is the first in a series of graduated examples leading up to a fully functional GradeBook class in Chapter 7, Arrays and Vectors. Function main uses this object and its member function to display a message on the screen welcoming the instructor to the grade-book program.

```
 1   // Fig. 3.1: fig03_01.cpp
 2   // Define class GradeBook with a member function displayMessage;
 3   // Create a GradeBook object and call its displayMessage function.
 4   #include <iostream>
 5   using std::cout;
 6   using std::endl;
 7
 8   // GradeBook class definition
 9   class GradeBook
10   {
11   public:
12      // function that displays a welcome message to the GradeBook user
13      void displayMessage()
14      {
15         cout << "Welcome to the Grade Book!" << endl;
16      } // end function displayMessage
17   }; // end class GradeBook
18
19   // function main begins program execution
20   int main()
21   {
22      GradeBook myGradeBook; // create a GradeBook object named myGradeBook
23      myGradeBook.displayMessage(); // call object's displayMessage function
24      return 0; // indicate successful termination
25   } // end main
```

```
Welcome to the Grade Book!
```

Fig. 3.1 | Defining class GradeBook with a member function, creating a GradeBook object and calling its member function.

First we describe how to define a class and a member function. Then we explain how an object is created and how to call a member function of an object. The first few examples contain function main and the GradeBook class it uses in the same file. Later in the chapter, we introduce more sophisticated ways to structure your programs to achieve better software engineering.

Class *GradeBook*

Before function main (lines 20–25) can create an object of class GradeBook, we must tell the compiler what member functions and data members belong to the class. This is known as defining a class. The GradeBook class definition (lines 9–17) contains a member function called displayMessage (lines 13–16) that displays a message on the screen (line 15). Recall that a class is like a blueprint—so we need to make an object of class GradeBook (line 22) and call its displayMessage member function (line 23) to get line 15 to execute and display the welcome message. We'll soon explain lines 22–23 in detail.

The class definition begins at line 9 with the keyword class followed by the class name GradeBook. By convention, the name of a user-defined class begins with a capital letter, and for readability, each subsequent word in the class name begins with a capital letter. This capitalization style is often referred to as camel case, because the pattern of uppercase and lowercase letters resembles the silhouette of a camel.

Every class's body is enclosed in a pair of left and right braces ({ and }), as in lines 10 and 17. The class definition terminates with a semicolon (line 17).

Common Programming Error 3.1

Forgetting the semicolon at the end of a class definition is a syntax error.

Recall that the function main is always called automatically when you execute a program. Most functions do not get called automatically. As you will soon see, you must call member function displayMessage explicitly to tell it to perform its task.

Line 11 contains the access-specifier label public:. The keyword public is called an access specifier. Lines 13–16 define member function displayMessage. This member function appears after access specifier public: to indicate that the function is "available to the public"—that is, it can be called by other functions in the program and by member functions of other classes. Access specifiers are always followed by a colon (:). For the remainder of the text, when we refer to the access specifier public, we will omit the colon as we did in this sentence. Section 3.6 introduces a second access specifier, private (again, we omit the colon in our discussions, but include it in our programs).

Each function in a program performs a task and may return a value when it completes its task—for example, a function might perform a calculation, then return the result of that calculation. When you define a function, you must specify a return type to indicate the type of the value returned by the function when it completes its task. In line 13, keyword void to the left of the function name displayMessage is the function's return type. Return type void indicates that displayMessage will perform a task but will not return (i.e., give back) any data to its calling function (in this example, main, as we'll see in a moment) when it completes its task. (In Fig. 3.5, you will see an example of a function that returns a value.)

The name of the member function, displayMessage, follows the return type. By convention, function names begin with a lowercase first letter and all subsequent words in the name begin with a capital letter. The parentheses after the member function name indicate that this is a function. An empty set of parentheses, as shown in line 13, indicates that this member function does not require additional data to perform its task. You will see an example of a member function that does require additional data in Section 3.5. Line 13 is commonly referred to as the function header. Every function's body is delimited by left and right braces ({ and }), as in lines 14 and 16.

The body of a function contains statements that perform the function's task. In this case, member function displayMessage contains one statement (line 15) that displays the message "Welcome to the Grade Book!". After this statement executes, the function has completed its task.

Common Programming Error 3.2

Returning a value from a function whose return type has been declared void is a compilation error.

Common Programming Error 3.3

Defining a function inside another function is a syntax error.

*Testing Class **GradeBook***

Next, we'd like to use class GradeBook in a program. As you learned in Chapter 2, function main begins the execution of every program. Lines 20–25 of Fig. 3.1 contain the main function that will control our program's execution.

In this program, we'd like to call class GradeBook's displayMessage member function to display the welcome message. Typically, you cannot call a member function of a class until you create an object of that class. (As you will learn in Section 10.7, static member functions are an exception.) Line 22 creates an object of class GradeBook called myGrade-Book. Note that the variable's type is GradeBook—the class we defined in lines 9–17. When we declare variables of type int, as we did in Chapter 2, the compiler knows what int is—it's a fundamental type. When we write line 22, however, the compiler does not automatically know what type GradeBook is—it's a user-defined type. Thus, we must tell the compiler what GradeBook is by including the class definition, as we did in lines 9–17. If we omitted these lines, the compiler would issue an error message (such as "'GradeBook': undeclared identifier" in Microsoft Visual C++ .NET or "'GradeBook': undeclared" in GNU C++). Each new class you create becomes a new type that can be used to create objects. Programmers can define new class types as needed; this is one reason why C++ is known as an extensible language.

Line 23 calls the member function displayMessage (defined in lines 13–16) using variable myGradeBook followed by the dot operator (.), the function name displayMessage and an empty set of parentheses. This call causes the displayMessage function to perform its task. At the beginning of line 23, "myGradeBook." indicates that main should use the GradeBook object that was created in line 22. The empty parentheses in line 13 indicate that member function displayMessage does not require additional data to perform its task. (In Section 3.5, you'll see how to pass data to a function.) When displayMessage completes its task, function main continues executing at line 24, which indicates that main performed its tasks successfully. This is the end of main, so the program terminates.

*UML Class Diagram for Class **GradeBook***

Recall from Section 1.17 that the UML is a graphical language used by programmers to represent their object-oriented systems in a standardized manner. In the UML, each class is modeled in a class diagram as a rectangle with three compartments. Figure 3.2 presents a UML class diagram for class GradeBook of Fig. 3.1. The top compartment contains the name of the class, centered horizontally and in boldface type. The middle compartment contains the class's attributes, which correspond to data members in C++. In Fig. 3.2 the middle compartment is empty, because the version of class GradeBook in Fig. 3.1 does not have any attributes. (Section 3.6 presents a version of the GradeBook class that does have an attribute.) The bottom compartment contains the class's operations, which correspond

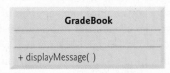

Fig. 3.2 | UML class diagram indicating that class GradeBook has a public displayMessage operation.

to member functions in C++. The UML models operations by listing the operation name followed by a set of parentheses. The class GradeBook has only one member function, displayMessage, so the bottom compartment of Fig. 3.2 lists one operation with this name. Member function displayMessage does not require additional information to perform its tasks, so the parentheses following displayMessage in the class diagram are empty, just as they are in the member function's header in line 13 of Fig. 3.1. The plus sign (+) in front of the operation name indicates that displayMessage is a public operation in the UML (i.e., a public member function in C++). We frequently use UML class diagrams to summarize class attributes and operations.

3.5 Defining a Member Function with a Parameter

In our car analogy from Section 3.2, we mentioned that pressing a car's gas pedal sends a message to the car to perform a task—make the car go faster. But how fast should the car accelerate? As you know, the farther down you press the pedal, the faster the car accelerates. So the message to the car includes both the task to perform and additional information that helps the car perform the task. This additional information is known as a parameter—the value of the parameter helps the car determine how fast to accelerate. Similarly, a member function can require one or more parameters that represent additional data it needs to perform its task. A function call supplies values—called arguments—for each of the function's parameters. For example, to make a deposit into a bank account, suppose a deposit member function of an Account class specifies a parameter that represents the deposit amount. When the deposit member function is called, an argument value representing the deposit amount is copied to the member function's parameter. The member function then adds that amount to the account balance.

Defining and Testing Class **GradeBook**

Our next example (Fig. 3.3) redefines class GradeBook (lines 14–23) with a displayMessage member function (lines 18–22) that displays the course name as part of the welcome message. The new displayMessage member function requires a parameter (courseName in line 18) that represents the course name to output.

Before discussing the new features of class GradeBook, let's see how the new class is used in main (lines 26–40). Line 28 creates a variable of type string called nameOfCourse that will be used to store the course name entered by the user. A variable of type string represents a string of characters such as "CS101 Introduction to C++ Programming". A string is actually an object of the C++ Standard Library class string. This class is defined in header file <string>, and the name string, like cout, belongs to namespace std. To enable line 28 to compile, line 9 includes the <string> header file. Note that the using declaration in line 10 allows us to simply write string in line 28 rather than std::string. For now, you can think of string variables like variables of other types such as int. You will learn about additional string capabilities in Section 3.10.

Line 29 creates an object of class GradeBook named myGradeBook. Line 32 prompts the user to enter a course name. Line 33 reads the name from the user and assigns it to the nameOfCourse variable, using the library function getline to perform the input. Before we explain this line of code, let's explain why we cannot simply write

```
cin >> nameOfCourse;
```

```
1   // Fig. 3.3: fig03_03.cpp
2   // Define class GradeBook with a member function that takes a parameter;
3   // Create a GradeBook object and call its displayMessage function.
4   #include <iostream>
5   using std::cout;
6   using std::cin;
7   using std::endl;
8
9   #include <string> // program uses C++ standard string class
10  using std::string;
11  using std::getline;
12
13  // GradeBook class definition
14  class GradeBook
15  {
16  public:
17     // function that displays a welcome message to the GradeBook user
18     void displayMessage( string courseName )
19     {
20        cout << "Welcome to the grade book for\n" << courseName << "!"
21           << endl;
22     } // end function displayMessage
23  }; // end class GradeBook
24
25  // function main begins program execution
26  int main()
27  {
28     string nameOfCourse; // string of characters to store the course name
29     GradeBook myGradeBook; // create a GradeBook object named myGradeBook
30
31     // prompt for and input course name
32     cout << "Please enter the course name:" << endl;
33     getline( cin, nameOfCourse ); // read a course name with blanks
34     cout << endl; // output a blank line
35
36     // call myGradeBook's displayMessage function
37     // and pass nameOfCourse as an argument
38     myGradeBook.displayMessage( nameOfCourse );
39     return 0; // indicate successful termination
40  } // end main
```

```
Please enter the course name:
CS101 Introduction to C++ Programming

Welcome to the grade book for
CS101 Introduction to C++ Programming!
```

Fig. 3.3 | Defining class GradeBook with a member function that takes a parameter.

to obtain the course name. In our sample program execution, we use the course name "CS101 Introduction to C++ Programming," which contains multiple words. (Recall that we highlight user-supplied input in bold.) When cin is used with the stream extraction operator, it reads characters until the first white-space character is reached. Thus, only

"CS101" would be read by the preceding statement. The rest of the course name would have to be read by subsequent input operations.

In this example, we'd like the user to type the complete course name and press *Enter* to submit it to the program, and we'd like to store the entire course name in the string variable nameOfCourse. The function call getline(cin, nameOfCourse) in line 33 reads characters (including the space characters that separate the words in the input) from the standard input stream object cin (i.e., the keyboard) until the newline character is encountered, places the characters in the string variable nameOfCourse and discards the newline character. Note that when you press *Enter* while typing program input, a newline is inserted in the input stream. Also note that the <string> header file must be included in the program to use function getline and that the name getline belongs to namespace std.

Line 38 calls myGradeBook's displayMessage member function. The nameOfCourse variable in parentheses is the argument that is passed to member function displayMessage so that it can perform its task. The value of variable nameOfCourse in main becomes the value of member function displayMessage's parameter courseName in line 18. When you execute this program, notice that member function displayMessage outputs as part of the welcome message the course name you type (in our sample execution, CS101 Introduction to C++ Programming).

More on Arguments and Parameters

To specify that a function requires data to perform its task, you place additional information in the function's parameter list, which is located in the parentheses following the function name. The parameter list may contain any number of parameters, including none at all (represented by empty parentheses as in Fig. 3.1, line 13) to indicate that a function does not require any parameters. Member function displayMessage's parameter list (Fig. 3.3, line 18) declares that the function requires one parameter. Each parameter should specify a type and an identifier. In this case, the type string and the identifier courseName indicate that member function displayMessage requires a string to perform its task. The member function body uses the parameter courseName to access the value that is passed to the function in the function call (line 38 in main). Lines 20–21 display parameter courseName's value as part of the welcome message. Note that the parameter variable's name (line 18) can be the same as or different from the argument variable's name (line 38)—you'll learn why in Chapter 6, Functions and an Introduction to Recursion.

A function can specify multiple parameters by separating each parameter from the next with a comma (we'll see an example in Figs. 6.4–6.5). The number and order of arguments in a function call must match the number and order of parameters in the parameter list of the called member function's header. Also, the argument types in the function call must match the types of the corresponding parameters in the function header. (As you will learn in subsequent chapters, an argument's type and its corresponding parameter's type need not always be identical, but they must be "consistent.") In our example, the one string argument in the function call (i.e., nameOfCourse) exactly matches the one string parameter in the member-function definition (i.e., courseName).

 Common Programming Error 3.4

Placing a semicolon after the right parenthesis enclosing the parameter list of a function definition is a syntax error.

Common Programming Error 3.5

Defining a function parameter again as a local variable in the function is a compilation error.

Good Programming Practice 3.1

To avoid ambiguity, do not use the same names for the arguments passed to a function and the corresponding parameters in the function definition.

Good Programming Practice 3.2

Choosing meaningful function names and meaningful parameter names makes programs more readable and helps avoid excessive use of comments.

Updated UML Class Diagram for Class GradeBook

The UML class diagram of Fig. 3.4 models class GradeBook of Fig. 3.3. Like the class GradeBook defined in Fig. 3.1, this GradeBook class contains public member function displayMessage. However, this version of displayMessage has a parameter. The UML models a parameter by listing the parameter name, followed by a colon and the parameter type in the parentheses following the operation name. The UML has its own data types similar to those of C++. The UML is language-independent—it is used with many different programming languages—so its terminology does not exactly match that of C++. For example, the UML type String corresponds to the C++ type string. Member function displayMessage of class GradeBook (Fig. 3.3; lines 18–22) has a string parameter named courseName, so Fig. 3.4 lists courseName : String between the parentheses following the operation name displayMessage. Note that this version of the GradeBook class still does not have any data members.

3.6 Data Members, set Functions and get Functions

In Chapter 2, we declared all of a program's variables in its main function. Variables declared in a function definition's body are known as local variables and can be used only from the line of their declaration in the function to the immediately following closing right brace (}) of the function definition. A local variable must be declared before it can be used in a function. A local variable cannot be accessed outside the function in which it is declared. When a function terminates, the values of its local variables are lost. (You will see an exception to this in Chapter 6 when we discuss static local variables.) Recall from Section 3.2 that an object has attributes that are carried with it as it is used in a program. Such attributes exist throughout the life of the object.

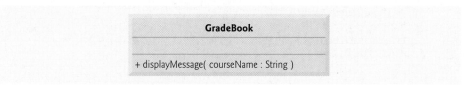

Fig. 3.4 | UML class diagram indicating that class GradeBook has a displayMessage operation with a courseName parameter of UML type String.

A class normally consists of one or more member functions that manipulate the attributes that belong to a particular object of the class. Attributes are represented as variables in a class definition. Such variables are called data members and are declared inside a class definition but outside the bodies of the class's member-function definitions. Each object of a class maintains its own copy of its attributes in memory. The example in this section demonstrates a GradeBook class that contains a courseName data member to represent a particular GradeBook object's course name.

GradeBook Class with a Data Member, a set Function and a get Function

In our next example, class GradeBook (Fig. 3.5) maintains the course name as a data member so that it can be used or modified at any time during a program's execution. The class contains member functions setCourseName, getCourseName and displayMessage. Member function setCourseName stores a course name in a GradeBook data member—member function getCourseName obtains a GradeBook's course name from that data member. Member function displayMessage—which now specifies no parameters—still displays a welcome message that includes the course name. However, as you will see, the function now obtains the course name by calling another function in the same class—getCourseName.

```
 I   // Fig. 3.5: fig03_05.cpp
 2   // Define class GradeBook that contains a courseName data member
 3   // and member functions to set and get its value;
 4   // Create and manipulate a GradeBook object with these functions.
 5   #include <iostream>
 6   using std::cout;
 7   using std::cin;
 8   using std::endl;
 9
10   #include <string> // program uses C++ standard string class
11   using std::string;
12   using std::getline;
13
14   // GradeBook class definition
15   class GradeBook
16   {
17   public:
18      // function that sets the course name
19      void setCourseName( string name )
20      {
21         courseName = name; // store the course name in the object
22      } // end function setCourseName
23
24      // function that gets the course name
25      string getCourseName()
26      {
27         return courseName; // return the object's courseName
28      } // end function getCourseName
29
```

Fig. 3.5 | Defining and testing class GradeBook with a data member and set and get functions. (Part 1 of 2.)

```
30       // function that displays a welcome message
31       void displayMessage()
32       {
33          // this statement calls getCourseName to get the
34          // name of the course this GradeBook represents
35          cout << "Welcome to the grade book for\n" << getCourseName() << "!"
36             << endl;
37       } // end function displayMessage
38    private:
39       string courseName; // course name for this GradeBook
40    }; // end class GradeBook
41
42    // function main begins program execution
43    int main()
44    {
45       string nameOfCourse; // string of characters to store the course name
46       GradeBook myGradeBook; // create a GradeBook object named myGradeBook
47
48       // display initial value of courseName
49       cout << "Initial course name is: " << myGradeBook.getCourseName()
50          << endl;
51
52       // prompt for, input and set course name
53       cout << "\nPlease enter the course name:" << endl;
54       getline( cin, nameOfCourse ); // read a course name with blanks
55       myGradeBook.setCourseName( nameOfCourse ); // set the course name
56
57       cout << endl; // outputs a blank line
58       myGradeBook.displayMessage(); // display message with new course name
59       return 0; // indicate successful termination
60    } // end main
```

```
Initial course name is:

Please enter the course name:
CS101 Introduction to C++ Programming

Welcome to the grade book for
CS101 Introduction to C++ Programming!
```

Fig. 3.5 | Defining and testing class `GradeBook` with a data member and set and get functions. (Part 2 of 2.)

 Good Programming Practice 3.3

Place a blank line between member-function definitions to enhance program readability.

A typical instructor teaches more than one course, each with its own course name. Line 39 declares that `courseName` is a variable of type `string`. Because the variable is declared in the class definition (lines 15–40) but outside the bodies of the class's member-function definitions (lines 19–22, 25–28 and 31–37), line 39 is a declaration for a data member. Every instance (i.e., object) of class `GradeBook` contains one copy of each of the class's data members. For example, if there are two `GradeBook` objects, each object has its own copy of courseName (one per object), as we'll see in the example of Fig. 3.7. A benefit of making courseName a data member is that all the member functions of the class (in this case, GradeBook) can manipulate any data members that appear in the class definition (in this case, courseName).

Access Specifiers **public** and **private**

Most data member declarations appear after the access-specifier label private: (line 38). Like public, keyword private is an access specifier. Variables or functions declared after access specifier private (and before the next access specifier) are accessible only to member functions of the class for which they are declared. Thus, data member courseName can be used only in member functions setCourseName, getCourseName and displayMessage of (every object of) class GradeBook. Data member courseName, because it is private, cannot be accessed by functions outside the class (such as main) or by member functions of other classes in the program. Attempting to access data member courseName in one of these program locations with an expression such as myGradeBook.courseName would result in a compilation error containing a message similar to

```
cannot access private member declared in class 'GradeBook'
```

Software Engineering Observation 3.1

As a rule of thumb, data members should be declared private and member functions should be declared public. (We will see that it is appropriate to declare certain member functions private, if they are to be accessed only by other member functions of the class.)

Common Programming Error 3.6

An attempt by a function, which is not a member of a particular class (or a friend of that class, as we will see in Chapter 10), to access a private member of that class is a compilation error.

The default access for class members is private so all members after the class header and before the first access specifier are private. The access specifiers public and private may be repeated, but this is unnecessary and can be confusing.

Good Programming Practice 3.4

Despite the fact that the public and private access specifiers may be repeated and intermixed, list all the public members of a class first in one group and then list all the private members in another group. This focuses the client's attention on the class's public interface, rather than on the class's implementation.

Good Programming Practice 3.5

If you choose to list the private members first in a class definition, explicitly use the private access specifier despite the fact that private is assumed by default. This improves program clarity.

Declaring data members with access specifier private is known as data hiding. When a program creates (instantiates) an object of class GradeBook, data member courseName is encapsulated (hidden) in the object and can be accessed only by member functions of the object's class. In class GradeBook, member functions setCourseName and getCourseName manipulate the data member courseName directly (and displayMessage could do so if necessary).

Software Engineering Observation 3.2

We will learn in Chapter 10, Classes: A Deeper Look, Part 2, that functions and classes declared by a class to be friends *can* access the private *members of the class.*

Error-Prevention Tip 3.1

Making the data members of a class private *and the member functions of the class* public *facilitates debugging because problems with data manipulations are localized to either the class's member functions or the* friends *of the class.*

Member Functions *setCourseName and getCourseName*

Member function setCourseName (defined in lines 19–22) does not return any data when it completes its task, so its return type is void. The member function receives one parameter—name—which represents the course name that will be passed to it as an argument (as we will see in line 55 of main). Line 21 assigns name to data member courseName. In this example, setCourseName does not attempt to validate the course name—i.e., the function does not check that the course name adheres to any particular format or follows any other rules regarding what a "valid" course name looks like. Suppose, for instance, that a university can print student transcripts containing course names of only 25 characters or fewer. In this case, we might want class GradeBook to ensure that its data member courseName never contains more than 25 characters. We discuss basic validation techniques in Section 3.10.

Member function getCourseName (defined in lines 25–28) returns a particular Grade-Book object's courseName. The member function has an empty parameter list, so it does not require additional data to perform its task. The function specifies that it returns a string. When a function that specifies a return type other than void is called and completes its task, the function returns a result to its calling function. For example, when you go to an automated teller machine (ATM) and request your account balance, you expect the ATM to give you back a value that represents your balance. Similarly, when a statement calls member function getCourseName on a GradeBook object, the statement expects to receive the GradeBook's course name (in this case, a string, as specified by the function's return type). If you have a function square that returns the square of its argument, the statement

```
int result = square( 2 );
```

returns 4 from function square and initializes the variable result with the value 4. If you have a function maximum that returns the largest of three integer arguments, the statement

```
int biggest = maximum( 27, 114, 51 );
```

returns 114 from function maximum and initializes variable biggest with the value 114.

Common Programming Error 3.7

Forgetting to return a value from a function that is supposed to return a value is a compilation error.

Note that the statements at lines 21 and 27 each use variable courseName (line 39) even though it was not declared in any of the member functions. We can use courseName in the member functions of class GradeBook because courseName is a data member of the class. Also note that the order in which member functions are defined does not determine when they are called at execution time. So member function getCourseName could be defined before member function setCourseName.

Member Function `displayMessage`

Member function `displayMessage` (lines 31–37) does not return any data when it completes its task, so its return type is `void`. The function does not receive parameters, so its parameter list is empty. Lines 35–36 output a welcome message that includes the value of data member `courseName`. Line 35 calls member function `getCourseName` to obtain the value of `courseName`. Note that member function `displayMessage` could also access data member `courseName` directly, just as member functions `setCourseName` and `getCourseName` do. We explain shortly why we choose to call member function `getCourseName` to obtain the value of `courseName`.

Testing Class **GradeBook**

The `main` function (lines 43–60) creates one object of class `GradeBook` and uses each of its member functions. Line 46 creates a `GradeBook` object named `myGradeBook`. Lines 49–50 display the initial course name by calling the object's `getCourseName` member function. Note that the first line of the output does not show a course name, because the object's `courseName` data member (i.e., a `string`) is initially empty—by default, the initial value of a `string` is the so-called *empty string*, i.e., a string that does not contain any characters. Nothing appears on the screen when an empty string is displayed.

Line 53 prompts the user to enter a course name. Local `string` variable `nameOfCourse` (declared in line 45) is set to the course name entered by the user, which is obtained by the call to the `getline` function (line 54). Line 55 calls object `myGradeBook`'s `setCourseName` member function and supplies `nameOfCourse` as the function's argument. When the function is called, the argument's value is copied to parameter `name` (line 19) of member function `setCourseName` (lines 19–22). Then the parameter's value is assigned to data member `courseName` (line 21). Line 57 skips a line in the output; then line 58 calls object `myGradeBook`'s `displayMessage` member function to display the welcome message containing the course name.

Software Engineering with Set and Get Functions

A class's `private` data members can be manipulated only by member functions of that class (and by "friends" of the class, as we will see in Chapter 10, Classes: A Deeper Look, Part 2). So a client of an object—that is, any class or function that calls the object's member functions from outside the object—calls the class's `public` member functions to request the class's services for particular objects of the class. This is why the statements in function `main` (Fig. 3.5, lines 43–60) call member functions `setCourseName`, `getCourseName` and `displayMessage` on a `GradeBook` object. Classes often provide `public` member functions to allow clients of the class to *set* (i.e., assign values to) or *get* (i.e., obtain the values of) `private` data members. The names of these member functions need not begin with *set* or *get*, but this naming convention is common. In this example, the member function that *sets* the `courseName` data member is called `setCourseName`, and the member function that *gets* the value of the `courseName` data member is called `getCourseName`. Note that *set* functions are also sometimes called **mutators** (because they mutate, or change, values), and *get* functions are also sometimes called **accessors** (because they access values).

Recall that declaring data members with access specifier `private` enforces data hiding. Providing `public` *set* and *get* functions allows clients of a class to access the hidden data, but only *indirectly*. The client knows that it is attempting to modify or obtain an object's data, but the client does not know how the object performs these operations. In some cases, a class may internally represent a piece of data one way, but expose that data to clients in a different way. For example, suppose a Clock class represents the time of day as a private int data member time that stores the number of seconds since midnight. However, when a client calls a Clock object's getTime member function, the object could return the time with hours, minutes and seconds in a string in the format "HH:MM:SS". Similarly, suppose the Clock class provides a *set* function named setTime that takes a string parameter in the "HH:MM:SS" format. Using advanced string capabilities, the setTime function could convert this string to a number of seconds, which the function stores in its private data member. The *set* function could also check that the value it receives represents a valid time (e.g., "12:30:45" is valid but "42:85:70" is not). The *set* and *get* functions allow a client to interact with an object, but the object's private data remains safely encapsulated (i.e., hidden) in the object itself.

The *set* and *get* functions of a class also should be used by other member functions within the class to manipulate the class's private data, although these member functions *can* access the private data directly. In Fig. 3.5, member functions setCourseName and getCourseName are public member functions, so they are accessible to clients of the class, as well as to the class itself. Member function displayMessage calls member function getCourseName to obtain the value of data member courseName for display purposes, even though displayMessage can access courseName directly—accessing a data member via its *get* function creates a better, more robust class (i.e., a class that is easier to maintain and less likely to stop working). If we decide to change the data member courseName in some way, the displayMessage definition will not require modification—only the bodies of the *get* and *set* functions that directly manipulate the data member will need to change. For example, suppose we decide that we want to represent the course name as two separate data members—courseNumber (e.g., "CS101") and courseTitle (e.g., "Introduction to C++ Programming"). Member function displayMessage can still issue a single call to member function getCourseName to obtain the full course to display as part of the welcome message. In this case, getCourseName would need to build and return a string containing the courseNumber followed by the courseTitle. Member function displayMessage would continue to display the complete course title "CS101 Introduction to C++ Programming," because it is unaffected by the change to the class's data members. The benefits of calling a *set* function from another member function of a class will become clear when we discuss validation in Section 3.10.

Good Programming Practice 3.6

Always try to localize the effects of changes to a class's data members by accessing and manipulating the data members through their get and set functions. Changes to the name of a data member or the data type used to store a data member then affect only the corresponding get and set functions, but not the callers of those functions.

Software Engineering Observation 3.3

It is important to write programs that are understandable and easy to maintain. Change is the rule rather than the exception. Programmers should anticipate that their code will be modified.

Software Engineering Observation 3.4

The class designer need not provide set or get functions for each private data item; these capabilities should be provided only when appropriate. If a service is useful to the client code, that service should typically be provided in the class's public interface.

GradeBook's UML Class Diagram with a Data Member and* set *and* get *Functions
Figure 3.6 contains an updated UML class diagram for the version of class GradeBook in
Fig. 3.5. This diagram models class GradeBook's data member courseName as an attribute
in the middle compartment of the class. The UML represents data members as attributes
by listing the attribute name, followed by a colon and the attribute type. The UML type
of attribute courseName is String, which corresponds to string in C++. Data member
courseName is private in C++, so the class diagram lists a minus sign (–) in front of the
corresponding attribute's name. The minus sign in the UML is equivalent to the private
access specifier in C++. Class GradeBook contains three public member functions, so the
class diagram lists three operations in the third compartment. Recall that the plus (+) sign
before each operation name indicates that the operation is public in C++. Operation set-
CourseName has a String parameter called name. The UML indicates the return type of an
operation by placing a colon and the return type after the parentheses following the operation name. Member function getCourseName of class GradeBook (Fig. 3.5) has a string
return type in C++, so the class diagram shows a String return type in the UML. Note
that operations setCourseName and displayMessage do not return values (i.e., they return
void), so the UML class diagram does not specify a return type after the parentheses of
these operations. The UML does not use void as C++ does when a function does not return a value.

3.7 Initializing Objects with Constructors

As mentioned in Section 3.6, when an object of class GradeBook (Fig. 3.5) is created, its
data member courseName is initialized to the empty string by default. What if you want
to provide a course name when you create a GradeBook object? Each class you declare can
provide a constructor that can be used to initialize an object of the class when the object
is created. A constructor is a special member function that must be defined with the same
name as the class, so that the compiler can distinguish it from the class's other member
functions. An important difference between constructors and other functions is that constructors cannot return values, so they cannot specify a return type (not even void). Normally, constructors are declared public. The term "constructor" is often abbreviated as
"ctor" in the literature—we prefer not to use this abbreviation.

C++ requires a constructor call for each object that is created, which helps ensure that
the object is initialized properly before it is used in a program—the constructor call occurs
implicitly when the object is created. In any class that does not explicitly include a constructor, the compiler provides a default constructor—that is, a constructor with no

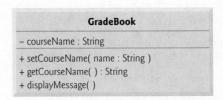

Fig. 3.6 | UML class diagram for class GradeBook with a private courseName attribute and
public operations setCourseName, getCourseName and displayMessage.

parameters. For example, when line 46 of Fig. 3.5 creates a GradeBook object, the default constructor is called, because the declaration of myGradeBook does not specify any constructor arguments. The default constructor provided by the compiler creates a GradeBook object without giving any initial values to the object's data members. [*Note:* For data members that are objects of other classes, the default constructor implicitly calls each data member's default constructor to ensure that the data member is initialized properly. In fact, this is why the string data member courseName (in Fig. 3.5) was initialized to the empty string—the default constructor for class string sets the string's value to the empty string. In Section 10.3, you will learn more about initializing data members that are objects of other classes.]

In the example of Fig. 3.7, we specify a course name for a GradeBook object when the object is created (line 49). In this case, the argument "CS101 Introduction to C++ Programming" is passed to the GradeBook object's constructor (lines 17–20) and used to initialize the courseName. Figure 3.7 defines a modified GradeBook class containing a constructor with a string parameter that receives the initial course name.

```cpp
1   // Fig. 3.7: fig03_07.cpp
2   // Instantiating multiple objects of the GradeBook class and using
3   // the GradeBook constructor to specify the course name
4   // when each GradeBook object is created.
5   #include <iostream>
6   using std::cout;
7   using std::endl;
8
9   #include <string> // program uses C++ standard string class
10  using std::string;
11
12  // GradeBook class definition
13  class GradeBook
14  {
15  public:
16     // constructor initializes courseName with string supplied as argument
17     GradeBook( string name )
18     {
19        setCourseName( name ); // call set function to initialize courseName
20     } // end GradeBook constructor
21
22     // function to set the course name
23     void setCourseName( string name )
24     {
25        courseName = name; // store the course name in the object
26     } // end function setCourseName
27
28     // function to get the course name
29     string getCourseName()
30     {
31        return courseName; // return object's courseName
32     } // end function getCourseName
```

Fig. 3.7 | Instantiating multiple objects of the GradeBook class and using the GradeBook constructor to specify the course name when each GradeBook object is created. (Part I of 2.)

```
33
34      // display a welcome message to the GradeBook user
35      void displayMessage()
36      {
37         // call getCourseName to get the courseName
38         cout << "Welcome to the grade book for\n" << getCourseName()
39            << "!" << endl;
40      } // end function displayMessage
41   private:
42      string courseName; // course name for this GradeBook
43   }; // end class GradeBook
44
45   // function main begins program execution
46   int main()
47   {
48      // create two GradeBook objects
49      GradeBook gradeBook1( "CS101 Introduction to C++ Programming" );
50      GradeBook gradeBook2( "CS102 Data Structures in C++" );
51
52      // display initial value of courseName for each GradeBook
53      cout << "gradeBook1 created for course: " << gradeBook1.getCourseName()
54         << "\ngradeBook2 created for course: " << gradeBook2.getCourseName()
55         << endl;
56      return 0; // indicate successful termination
57   } // end main
```

```
gradeBook1 created for course: CS101 Introduction to C++ Programming
gradeBook2 created for course: CS102 Data Structures in C++
```

Fig. 3.7 | Instantiating multiple objects of the `GradeBook` class and using the `GradeBook` constructor to specify the course name when each `GradeBook` object is created. (Part 2 of 2.)

Defining a Constructor

Lines 17–20 of Fig. 3.7 define a constructor for class `GradeBook`. Notice that the constructor has the same name as its class, `GradeBook`. A constructor specifies in its parameter list the data it requires to perform its task. When you create a new object, you place this data in the parentheses that follow the object name (as we did in lines 49–50). Line 17 indicates that class `GradeBook`'s constructor has a `string` parameter called `name`. Note that line 17 does not specify a return type, because constructors cannot return values (or even `void`).

Line 19 in the constructor's body passes the constructor's parameter `name` to member function `setCourseName`, which assigns a value to data member `courseName`. The `setCourseName` member function (lines 23–26) simply assigns its parameter `name` to the data member `courseName`, so you might be wondering why we bother making the call to `setCourseName` in line 19—the constructor certainly could perform the assignment `courseName = name`. In Section 3.10, we modify `setCourseName` to perform validation (ensuring that, in this case, the `courseName` is 25 or fewer characters in length). At that point the benefits of calling `setCourseName` from the constructor will become clear. Note that both the constructor (line 17) and the `setCourseName` function (line 23) use a parameter called `name`. You can use the same parameter names in different functions because the parameters are local to each function; they do not interfere with one another.

*Testing Class **GradeBook***

Lines 46–57 of Fig. 3.7 define the main function that tests class GradeBook and demonstrates initializing GradeBook objects using a constructor. Line 49 in function main creates and initializes a GradeBook object called gradeBook1. When this line executes, the Grade-Book constructor (lines 17–20) is called (implicitly by C++) with the argument "CS101 Introduction to C++ Programming" to initialize gradeBook1's course name. Line 50 repeats this process for the GradeBook object called gradeBook2, this time passing the argument "CS102 Data Structures in C++" to initialize gradeBook2's course name. Lines 53–54 use each object's getCourseName member function to obtain the course names and show that they were indeed initialized when the objects were created. The output confirms that each GradeBook object maintains its own copy of data member courseName.

Two Ways to Provide a Default Constructor for a Class

Any constructor that takes no arguments is called a default constructor. A class gets a default constructor in one of two ways:

1. The compiler implicitly creates a default constructor in a class that does not define a constructor. Such a default constructor does not initialize the class's data members, but does call the default constructor for each data member that is an object of another class. [*Note:* An uninitialized variable typically contains a "garbage" value (e.g., an uninitialized int variable might contain -858993460, which is likely to be an incorrect value for that variable in most programs).]

2. The programmer explicitly defines a constructor that takes no arguments. Such a default constructor will perform the initialization specified by the programmer and will call the default constructor for each data member that is an object of another class.

If the programmer defines a constructor with arguments, C++ will not implicitly create a default constructor for that class. Note that for each version of class GradeBook in Fig. 3.1, Fig. 3.3 and Fig. 3.5 the compiler implicitly defined a default constructor.

Error–Prevention Tip 3.2

Unless no initialization of your class's data members is necessary (almost never), provide a constructor to ensure that your class's data members are initialized with meaningful values when each new object of your class is created.

Software Engineering Observation 3.5

Data members can be initialized in a constructor of the class or their values may be set later after the object is created. However, it is a good software engineering practice to ensure that an object is fully initialized before the client code invokes the object's member functions. In general, you should not rely on the client code to ensure that an object gets initialized properly.

*Adding the Constructor to Class **GradeBook**'s UML Class Diagram*

The UML class diagram of Fig. 3.8 models class GradeBook of Fig. 3.7, which has a constructor with a name parameter of type string (represented by type String in the UML). Like operations, the UML models constructors in the third compartment of a class in a class diagram. To distinguish a constructor from a class's operations, the UML places the word "constructor" between guillemets (« and ») before the constructor's name. It is customary to list the class's constructor before other operations in the third compartment.

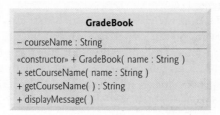

Fig. 3.8 | UML class diagram indicating that class GradeBook has a constructor with a name parameter of UML type String.

3.8 Placing a Class in a Separate File for Reusability

We have developed class GradeBook as far as we need to for now from a programming perspective, so let's consider some software engineering issues. One of the benefits of creating class definitions is that, when packaged properly, our classes can be reused by programmers—potentially worldwide. For example, we can reuse C++ Standard Library type string in any C++ program by including the header file <string> in the program (and, as we will see, by being able to link to the library's object code).

Unfortunately, programmers who wish to use our GradeBook class cannot simply include the file from Fig. 3.7 in another program. As you learned in Chapter 2, function main begins the execution of every program, and every program must have exactly one main function. If other programmers include the code from Fig. 3.7, they get extra baggage—our main function—and their programs will then have two main functions. When they attempt to compile their programs, the compiler will indicate an error because, again, each program can have only one main function. For example, attempting to compile a program with two main functions in Microsoft Visual C++ .NET produces the error

```
error C2084: function 'int main(void)' already has a body
```

when the compiler tries to compile the second main function it encounters. Similarly, the GNU C++ compiler produces the error

```
redefinition of 'int main()'
```

These errors indicate that a program already has a main function. So, placing main in the same file with a class definition prevents that class from being reused by other programs. In this section, we demonstrate how to make class GradeBook reusable by separating it into another file from the main function.

Header Files

Each of the previous examples in the chapter consists of a single .cpp file, also known as a source-code file, that contains a GradeBook class definition and a main function. When building an object-oriented C++ program, it is customary to define reusable source code (such as a class) in a file that by convention has a .h filename extension—known as a header file. Programs use #include preprocessor directives to include header files and take advantage of reusable software components, such as type string provided in the C++ Standard Library and user-defined types like class GradeBook.

In our next example, we separate the code from Fig. 3.7 into two files—GradeBook.h (Fig. 3.9) and fig03_10.cpp (Fig. 3.10). As you look at the header file in Fig. 3.9, notice that it contains only the GradeBook class definition (lines 11–41) and lines 3–8, which allow class GradeBook to use cout, endl and type string. The main function that uses class GradeBook is defined in the source-code file fig03_10.cpp (Fig. 3.10) at lines 10–21. To help you prepare for the larger programs you will encounter later in this book and in industry, we often use a separate source-code file containing function main to test our classes (this is called a **driver program**). You will soon learn how a source-code file with main can use the class definition found in a header file to create objects of a class.

Including a Header File That Contains a User-Defined Class

A header file such as GradeBook.h (Fig. 3.9) cannot be used to begin program execution, because it does not contain a main function. If you try to compile and link GradeBook.h by itself to create an executable application, Microsoft Visual C++ .NET will produce the linker error message:

```
error LNK2019: unresolved external symbol _main referenced in
function _mainCRTStartup
```

```
1   // Fig. 3.9: GradeBook.h
2   // GradeBook class definition in a separate file from main.
3   #include <iostream>
4   using std::cout;
5   using std::endl;
6
7   #include <string> // class GradeBook uses C++ standard string class
8   using std::string;
9
10  // GradeBook class definition
11  class GradeBook
12  {
13  public:
14     // constructor initializes courseName with string supplied as argument
15     GradeBook( string name )
16     {
17        setCourseName( name ); // call set function to initialize courseName
18     } // end GradeBook constructor
19
20     // function to set the course name
21     void setCourseName( string name )
22     {
23        courseName = name; // store the course name in the object
24     } // end function setCourseName
25
26     // function to get the course name
27     string getCourseName()
28     {
29        return courseName; // return object's courseName
30     } // end function getCourseName
31
```

Fig. 3.9 | GradeBook class definition. (Part 1 of 2.)

```
32        // display a welcome message to the GradeBook user
33        void displayMessage()
34        {
35           // call getCourseName to get the courseName
36           cout << "Welcome to the grade book for\n" << getCourseName()
37              << "!" << endl;
38        } // end function displayMessage
39     private:
40        string courseName; // course name for this GradeBook
41     }; // end class GradeBook
```

Fig. 3.9 | GradeBook class definition. (Part 2 of 2.)

Running GNU C++ on Linux produces a linker error message containing:

```
undefined reference to 'main'
```

This error indicates that the linker could not locate the program's main function. To test class GradeBook (defined in Fig. 3.9), you must write a separate source-code file containing a main function (such as Fig. 3.10) that instantiates and uses objects of the class.

Recall from Section 3.4 that, while the compiler knows what fundamental data types like int are, the compiler does not know what a GradeBook is because it is a user-defined type. In fact, the compiler does not even know the classes in the C++ Standard Library. To help it understand how to use a class, we must explicitly provide the compiler with the class's definition—that's why, for example, to use type string, a program must include

```
 1    // Fig. 3.10: fig03_10.cpp
 2    // Including class GradeBook from file GradeBook.h for use in main.
 3    #include <iostream>
 4    using std::cout;
 5    using std::endl;
 6
 7    #include "GradeBook.h" // include definition of class GradeBook
 8
 9    // function main begins program execution
10    int main()
11    {
12       // create two GradeBook objects
13       GradeBook gradeBook1( "CS101 Introduction to C++ Programming" );
14       GradeBook gradeBook2( "CS102 Data Structures in C++" );
15
16       // display initial value of courseName for each GradeBook
17       cout << "gradeBook1 created for course: " << gradeBook1.getCourseName()
18          << "\ngradeBook2 created for course: " << gradeBook2.getCourseName()
19          << endl;
20       return 0; // indicate successful termination
21    } // end main
```

```
gradeBook1 created for course: CS101 Introduction to C++ Programming
gradeBook2 created for course: CS102 Data Structures in C++
```

Fig. 3.10 | Including class GradeBook from file GradeBook.h for use in main.

the `<string>` header file. This enables the compiler to determine the amount of memory that it must reserve for each object of the class and ensure that a program calls the class's member functions correctly.

To create `GradeBook` objects `gradeBook1` and `gradeBook2` in lines 13–14 of Fig. 3.10, the compiler must know the size of a `GradeBook` object. While objects conceptually contain data members and member functions, C++ objects typically contain only data. The compiler creates only one copy of the class's member functions and shares that copy among all the class's objects. Each object, of course, needs its own copy of the class's data members, because their contents can vary among objects (such as two different `BankAccount` objects having two different `balance` data members). The member function code, however, is not modifiable, so it can be shared among all objects of the class. Therefore, the size of an object depends on the amount of memory required to store the class's data members. By including `GradeBook.h` in line 7, we give the compiler access to the information it needs (Fig. 3.9, line 40) to determine the size of a `GradeBook` object and to determine whether objects of the class are used correctly (in lines 13–14 and 17–18 of Fig. 3.10).

Line 7 instructs the C++ preprocessor to replace the directive with a copy of the contents of `GradeBook.h` (i.e., the `GradeBook` class definition) *before* the program is compiled. When the source-code file `fig03_10.cpp` is compiled, it now contains the `GradeBook` class definition (because of the `#include`), and the compiler is able to determine how to create `GradeBook` objects and see that their member functions are called correctly. Now that the class definition is in a header file (without a `main` function), we can include that header in *any* program that needs to reuse our `GradeBook` class.

How Header Files Are Located

Notice that the name of the `GradeBook.h` header file in line 7 of Fig. 3.10 is enclosed in quotes (" ") rather than angle brackets (< >). Normally, a program's source-code files and user-defined header files are placed in the same directory. When the preprocessor encounters a header file name in quotes (e.g., `"GradeBook.h"`), the preprocessor attempts to locate the header file in the same directory as the file in which the `#include` directive appears. If the preprocessor cannot find the header file in that directory, it searches for it in the same location(s) as the C++ Standard Library header files. When the preprocessor encounters a header file name in angle brackets (e.g., `<iostream>`), it assumes that the header is part of the C++ Standard Library and does not look in the directory of the program that is being preprocessed.

Error-Prevention Tip 3.3

To ensure that the preprocessor can locate header files correctly, `#include` preprocessor directives should place the names of user-defined header files in quotes (e.g., `"GradeBook.h"`) and place the names of C++ Standard Library header files in angle brackets (e.g., `<iostream>`).

Additional Software Engineering Issues

Now that class `GradeBook` is defined in a header file, the class is reusable. Unfortunately, placing a class definition in a header file as in Fig. 3.9 still reveals the entire implementation of the class to the class's clients—`GradeBook.h` is simply a text file that anyone can open and read. Conventional software engineering wisdom says that to use an object of a class, the client code needs to know only what member functions to call, what arguments to provide to each member function and what return type to expect from each member function. The client code does not need to know how those functions are implemented.

If client code does know how a class is implemented, the client code programmer might write client code based on the class's implementation details. Ideally, if that implementation changes, the class's clients should not have to change. Hiding the class's implementation details makes it easier to change the class's implementation while minimizing, and hopefully eliminating, changes to client code.

In Section 3.9, we show how to break up the GradeBook class into two files so that

1. the class is reusable

2. the clients of the class know what member functions the class provides, how to call them and what return types to expect

3. the clients do not know how the class's member functions are implemented.

3.9 Separating Interface from Implementation

In the preceding section, we showed how to promote software reusability by separating a class definition from the client code (e.g., function main) that uses the class. We now introduce another fundamental principle of good software engineering—separating interface from implementation.

Interface of a Class

Interfaces define and standardize the ways in which things such as people and systems interact with one another. For example, a radio's controls serve as an interface between the radio's users and its internal components. The controls allow users to perform a limited set of operations (such as changing the station, adjusting the volume, and choosing between AM and FM stations). Various radios may implement these operations differently—some provide push buttons, some provide dials and some support voice commands. The interface specifies *what* operations a radio permits users to perform but does not specify *how* the operations are implemented inside the radio.

Similarly, the interface of a class describes *what* services a class's clients can use and how to *request* those services, but not *how* the class carries out the services. A class's interface consists of the class's public member functions (also known as the class's **public services**). For example, class GradeBook's interface (Fig. 3.9) contains a constructor and member functions setCourseName, getCourseName and displayMessage. GradeBook's clients (e.g., main in Fig. 3.10) use these functions to request the class's services. As you will soon see, you can specify a class's interface by writing a class definition that lists only the member function names, return types and parameter types.

Separating the Interface from the Implementation

In our prior examples, each class definition contained the complete definitions of the class's public member functions and the declarations of its private data members. However, it is better software engineering to define member functions outside the class definition, so that their implementation details can be hidden from the client code. This practice ensures that programmers do not write client code that depends on the class's implementation details. If they were to do so, the client code would be more likely to "break" if the class's implementation changed.

The program of Figs. 3.11–3.13 separates class GradeBook's interface from its implementation by splitting the class definition of Fig. 3.9 into two files—the header file

GradeBook.h (Fig. 3.11) in which class GradeBook is defined, and the source-code file GradeBook.cpp (Fig. 3.12) in which GradeBook's member functions are defined. By convention, member-function definitions are placed in a source-code file of the same base name (e.g., GradeBook) as the class's header file but with a .cpp filename extension. The source-code file fig03_13.cpp (Fig. 3.13) defines function main (the client code). The code and output of Fig. 3.13 are identical to that of Fig. 3.10. Figure 3.14 shows how this three-file program is compiled from the perspectives of the GradeBook class programmer and the client-code programmer—we will explain this figure in detail.

GradeBook.h: *Defining a Class's Interface with Function Prototypes*

Header file GradeBook.h (Fig. 3.11) contains another version of GradeBook's class definition (lines 9–18). This version is similar to the one in Fig. 3.9, but the function definitions in Fig. 3.9 are replaced here with function prototypes (lines 12–15) that describe the class's public interface without revealing the class's member function implementations. A function prototype is a declaration of a function that tells the compiler the function's name, its return type and the types of its parameters. Note that the header file still specifies the class's private data member (line 17) as well. Again, the compiler must know the data members of the class to determine how much memory to reserve for each object of the class. Including the header file GradeBook.h in the client code (line 8 of Fig. 3.13) provides the compiler with the information it needs to ensure that the client code calls the member functions of class GradeBook correctly.

The function prototype in line 12 (Fig. 3.12) indicates that the constructor requires one string parameter. Recall that constructors do not have return types, so no return type appears in the function prototype. Member function setCourseName's function prototype (line 13) indicates that setCourseName requires a string parameter and does not return a value (i.e., its return type is void). Member function getCourseName's function prototype (line 14) indicates that the function does not require parameters and returns a string.

```
 1   // Fig. 3.11: GradeBook.h
 2   // GradeBook class definition. This file presents GradeBook's public
 3   // interface without revealing the implementations of GradeBook's member
 4   // functions, which are defined in GradeBook.cpp.
 5   #include <string> // class GradeBook uses C++ standard string class
 6   using std::string;
 7
 8   // GradeBook class definition
 9   class GradeBook
10   {
11   public:
12      GradeBook( string ); // constructor that initializes courseName
13      void setCourseName( string ); // function that sets the course name
14      string getCourseName(); // function that gets the course name
15      void displayMessage(); // function that displays a welcome message
16   private:
17      string courseName; // course name for this GradeBook
18   }; // end class GradeBook
```

Fig. 3.11 | GradeBook class definition containing function prototypes that specify the interface of the class.

Finally, member function `displayMessage`'s function prototype (line 15) specifies that `displayMessage` does not require parameters and does not return a value. These function prototypes are the same as the corresponding function headers in Fig. 3.9, except that the parameter names (which are optional in prototypes) are not included and each function prototype must end with a semicolon.

Common Programming Error 3.8

Forgetting the semicolon at the end of a function prototype is a syntax error.

Good Programming Practice 3.7

Although parameter names in function prototypes are optional (they are ignored by the compiler), many programmers use these names for documentation purposes.

Error-Prevention Tip 3.4

Parameter names in a function prototype (which, again, are ignored by the compiler) can be misleading if wrong or confusing names are used. For this reason, many programmers create function prototypes by copying the first line of the corresponding function definitions (when the source code for the functions is available), then appending a semicolon to the end of each prototype.

GradeBook.cpp: *Defining Member Functions in a Separate Source-Code File*

Source-code file `GradeBook.cpp` (Fig. 3.12) defines class `GradeBook`'s member functions, which were declared in lines 12–15 of Fig. 3.11. The member-function definitions appear in lines 11–34 and are nearly identical to the member-function definitions in lines 15–38 of Fig. 3.9.

Notice that each member function name in the function headers (lines 11, 17, 23 and 29) is preceded by the class name and `::`, which is known as the binary scope resolution operator. This "ties" each member function to the (now separate) `GradeBook` class definition, which declares the class's member functions and data members. Without "Grade-Book::" preceding each function name, these functions would not be recognized by the compiler as member functions of class `GradeBook`—the compiler would consider them "free" or "loose" functions, like `main`. Such functions cannot access `GradeBook`'s `private` data or call the class's member functions, without specifying an object. So, the compiler would not be able to compile these functions. For example, lines 19 and 25 that access variable `courseName` would cause compilation errors because `courseName` is not declared as a local variable in each function—the compiler would not know that `courseName` is already declared as a data member of class `GradeBook`.

Common Programming Error 3.9

When defining a class's member functions outside that class, omitting the class name and binary scope resolution operator (::) preceding the function names causes compilation errors.

To indicate that the member functions in `GradeBook.cpp` are part of class `GradeBook`, we must first include the `GradeBook.h` header file (line 8 of Fig. 3.12). This allows us to access the class name `GradeBook` in the `GradeBook.cpp` file. When compiling Grade-Book.cpp, the compiler uses the information in `GradeBook.h` to ensure that

```
 1   // Fig. 3.12: GradeBook.cpp
 2   // GradeBook member-function definitions. This file contains
 3   // implementations of the member functions prototyped in GradeBook.h.
 4   #include <iostream>
 5   using std::cout;
 6   using std::endl;
 7
 8   #include "GradeBook.h" // include definition of class GradeBook
 9
10   // constructor initializes courseName with string supplied as argument
11   GradeBook::GradeBook( string name )
12   {
13      setCourseName( name ); // call set function to initialize courseName
14   } // end GradeBook constructor
15
16   // function to set the course name
17   void GradeBook::setCourseName( string name )
18   {
19      courseName = name; // store the course name in the object
20   } // end function setCourseName
21
22   // function to get the course name
23   string GradeBook::getCourseName()
24   {
25      return courseName; // return object's courseName
26   } // end function getCourseName
27
28   // display a welcome message to the GradeBook user
29   void GradeBook::displayMessage()
30   {
31      // call getCourseName to get the courseName
32      cout << "Welcome to the grade book for\n" << getCourseName()
33         << "!" << endl;
34   } // end function displayMessage
```

Fig. 3.12 | GradeBook member-function definitions represent the implementation of class GradeBook.

1. the first line of each member function (lines 11, 17, 23 and 29) matches its prototype in the GradeBook.h file—for example, the compiler ensures that getCourseName accepts no parameters and returns a string.

2. each member function knows about the class's data members and other member functions—for example, lines 19 and 25 can access variable courseName because it is declared in GradeBook.h as a data member of class GradeBook, and lines 13 and 32 can call functions setCourseName and getCourseName, respectively, because each is declared as a member function of the class in GradeBook.h (and because these calls conform with the corresponding prototypes).

*Testing Class **GradeBook***
Figure 3.13 performs the same GradeBook object manipulations as Fig. 3.10. Separating GradeBook's interface from the implementation of its member functions does not affect

```
 1   // Fig. 3.13: fig03_13.cpp
 2   // GradeBook class demonstration after separating
 3   // its interface from its implementation.
 4   #include <iostream>
 5   using std::cout;
 6   using std::endl;
 7
 8   #include "GradeBook.h" // include definition of class GradeBook
 9
10   // function main begins program execution
11   int main()
12   {
13      // create two GradeBook objects
14      GradeBook gradeBook1( "CS101 Introduction to C++ Programming" );
15      GradeBook gradeBook2( "CS102 Data Structures in C++" );
16
17      // display initial value of courseName for each GradeBook
18      cout << "gradeBook1 created for course: " << gradeBook1.getCourseName()
19         << "\ngradeBook2 created for course: " << gradeBook2.getCourseName()
20         << endl;
21      return 0; // indicate successful termination
22   } // end main
```

```
gradeBook1 created for course: CS101 Introduction to C++ Programming
gradeBook2 created for course: CS102 Data Structures in C++
```

Fig. 3.13 | GradeBook class demonstration after separating its interface from its implementation.

the way that this client code uses the class. It affects only how the program is compiled and linked, which we discuss in detail shortly.

As in Fig. 3.10, line 8 of Fig. 3.13 includes the GradeBook.h header file so that the compiler can ensure that GradeBook objects are created and manipulated correctly in the client code. Before executing this program, the source-code files in Fig. 3.12 and Fig. 3.13 must both be compiled, then linked together—that is, the member-function calls in the client code need to be tied to the implementations of the class's member functions—a job performed by the linker.

The Compilation and Linking Process

The diagram in Fig. 3.14 shows the compilation and linking process that results in an executable GradeBook application that can be used by instructors. Often a class's interface and implementation will be created and compiled by one programmer and used by a separate programmer who implements the class's client code. So, the diagram shows what is required by both the class-implementation programmer and the client-code programmer. The dashed lines in the diagram show the pieces required by the class-implementation programmer, the client-code programmer and the GradeBook application user, respectively. [*Note:* Figure 3.14 is not a UML diagram.]

A class-implementation programmer responsible for creating a reusable GradeBook class creates the header file GradeBook.h and source-code file GradeBook.cpp that #includes the

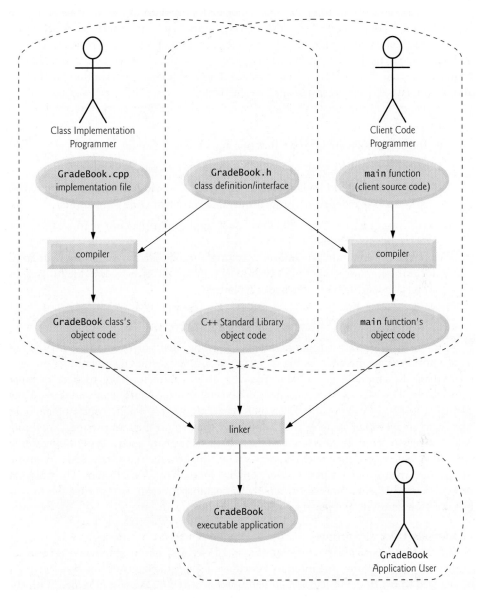

Fig. 3.14 | Compilation and linking process that produces an executable application.

header file, then compiles the source-code file to create GradeBook's object code. To hide the implementation details of GradeBook's member functions, the class-implementation programmer would provide the client-code programmer with the header file GradeBook.h (which specifies the class's interface and data members) and the object code for class Grade-Book which contains the machine-language instructions that represent GradeBook's member functions. The client-code programmer is not given GradeBook's source-code file, so the client remains unaware of how GradeBook's member functions are implemented.

The client code needs to know only GradeBook's interface to use the class and must be able to link its object code. Since the interface of the class is part of the class definition in the GradeBook.h header file, the client-code programmer must have access to this file and #include it in the client's source-code file. When the client code is compiled, the compiler uses the class definition in GradeBook.h to ensure that the main function creates and manipulates objects of class GradeBook correctly.

To create the executable GradeBook application to be used by instructors, the last step is to link

1. the object code for the main function (i.e., the client code)

2. the object code for class GradeBook's member function implementations

3. the C++ Standard Library object code for the C++ classes (e.g., string) used by the class implementation programmer and the client-code programmer.

The linker's output is the executable GradeBook application that instructors can use to manage their students' grades.

For further information on compiling multiple-source-file programs, see your compiler's documentation or study the Dive-Into™ publications that we provide for various C++ compilers at www.deitel.com/books/cpphtp5.

3.10 Validating Data with set Functions

In Section 3.6, we introduced *set* functions for allowing clients of a class to modify the value of a private data member. In Fig. 3.5, class GradeBook defines member function set-CourseName to simply assign a value received in its parameter name to data member courseName. This member function does not ensure that the course name adheres to any particular format or follows any other rules regarding what a "valid" course name looks like. As we stated earlier, suppose that a university can print student transcripts containing course names of only 25 characters or less. If the university uses a system containing GradeBook objects to generate the transcripts, we might want class GradeBook to ensure that its data member courseName never contains more than 25 characters. The program of Figs. 3.15–3.17 enhances class GradeBook's member function setCourseName to perform this validation (also known as validity checking).

GradeBook Class Definition
Notice that GradeBook's class definition (Fig. 3.15)—and hence, its interface—is identical to that of Fig. 3.11. Since the interface remains unchanged, clients of this class need not be changed when the definition of member function setCourseName is modified. This enables clients to take advantage of the improved GradeBook class simply by linking the client code to the updated GradeBook's object code.

Validating the Course Name with GradeBook Member Function *setCourseName*
The enhancement to class GradeBook is in the definition of setCourseName (Fig. 3.16, lines 18–31). The if statement in lines 20–21 determines whether parameter name contains a valid course name (i.e., a string of 25 or fewer characters). If the course name is valid, line 21 stores the course name in data member courseName. Note the expression name.length() in line 20. This is a member-function call just like myGradeBook.display-Message(). The C++ Standard Library's string class defines a member function length

```
 1    // Fig. 3.15: GradeBook.h
 2    // GradeBook class definition presents the public interface of
 3    // the class. Member-function definitions appear in GradeBook.cpp.
 4    #include <string> // program uses C++ standard string class
 5    using std::string;
 6
 7    // GradeBook class definition
 8    class GradeBook
 9    {
10    public:
11       GradeBook( string ); // constructor that initializes a GradeBook object
12       void setCourseName( string ); // function that sets the course name
13       string getCourseName(); // function that gets the course name
14       void displayMessage(); // function that displays a welcome message
15    private:
16       string courseName; // course name for this GradeBook
17    }; // end class GradeBook
```

Fig. 3.15 | GradeBook class definition.

```
 1    // Fig. 3.16: GradeBook.cpp
 2    // Implementations of the GradeBook member-function definitions.
 3    // The setCourseName function performs validation.
 4    #include <iostream>
 5    using std::cout;
 6    using std::endl;
 7
 8    #include "GradeBook.h" // include definition of class GradeBook
 9
10    // constructor initializes courseName with string supplied as argument
11    GradeBook::GradeBook( string name )
12    {
13       setCourseName( name ); // validate and store courseName
14    } // end GradeBook constructor
15
16    // function that sets the course name;
17    // ensures that the course name has at most 25 characters
18    void GradeBook::setCourseName( string name )
19    {
20       if ( name.length() <= 25 ) // if name has 25 or fewer characters
21          courseName = name; // store the course name in the object
22
23       if ( name.length() > 25 ) // if name has more than 25 characters
24       {
25          // set courseName to first 25 characters of parameter name
26          courseName = name.substr( 0, 25 ); // start at 0, length of 25
27
28          cout << "Name \"" << name << "\" exceeds maximum length (25).\n"
29             << "Limiting courseName to first 25 characters.\n" << endl;
30       } // end if
31    } // end function setCourseName
```

Fig. 3.16 | Member-function definitions for class GradeBook with a set function that validates the length of data member courseName. (Part 1 of 2.)

```
32
33   // function to get the course name
34   string GradeBook::getCourseName()
35   {
36      return courseName; // return object's courseName
37   } // end function getCourseName
38
39   // display a welcome message to the GradeBook user
40   void GradeBook::displayMessage()
41   {
42      // call getCourseName to get the courseName
43      cout << "Welcome to the grade book for\n" << getCourseName()
44         << "!" << endl;
45   } // end function displayMessage
```

Fig. 3.16 | Member-function definitions for class GradeBook with a set function that validates the length of data member courseName. (Part 2 of 2.)

that returns the number of characters in a string object. Parameter name is a string object, so the call name.length() returns the number of characters in name. If this value is less than or equal to 25, name is valid and line 21 executes.

The if statement in lines 23–30 handles the case in which setCourseName receives an invalid course name (i.e., a name that is more than 25 characters long). Even if parameter name is too long, we still want to leave the GradeBook object in a consistent state—that is, a state in which the object's data member courseName contains a valid value (i.e., a string of 25 characters or less). Thus, we truncate (i.e., shorten) the specified course name and assign the first 25 characters of name to the courseName data member (unfortunately, this could truncate the course name awkwardly). Standard class string provides member function substr (short for "substring") that returns a new string object created by copying part of an existing string object. The call in line 26 (i.e., name.substr(0, 25)) passes two integers (0 and 25) to name's member function substr. These arguments indicate the portion of the string name that substr should return. The first argument specifies the starting position in the original string from which characters are copied—the first character in every string is considered to be at position 0. The second argument specifies the number of characters to copy. Therefore, the call in line 26 returns a 25-character substring of name starting at position 0 (i.e., the first 25 characters in name). For example, if name holds the value "CS101 Introduction to Programming in C++", substr returns "CS101 Introduction to Pro". After the call to substr, line 26 assigns the substring returned by substr to data member courseName. In this way, member function setCourseName ensures that courseName is always assigned a string containing 25 or fewer characters. If the member function has to truncate the course name to make it valid, lines 28–29 display a warning message.

Note that the if statement in lines 23–30 contains two body statements—one to set the courseName to the first 25 characters of parameter name and one to print an accompanying message to the user. We want both of these statements to execute when name is too long, so we place them in a pair of braces, { }. Recall from Chapter 2 that this creates a block. You will learn more about placing multiple statements in the body of a control statement in Chapter 4.

Note that the cout statement in lines 28–29 could also appear without a stream insertion operator at the start of the second line of the statement, as in:

```
cout << "Name \"" << name << "\" exceeds maximum length (25).\n"
    "Limiting courseName to first 25 characters.\n" << endl;
```

The C++ compiler combines adjacent string literals, even if they appear on separate lines of a program. Thus, in the statement above, the C++ compiler would combine the string literals "\" exceeds maximum length (25).\n" and "Limiting courseName to first 25 characters.\n" into a single string literal that produces output identical to that of lines 28–29 in Fig. 3.16. This behavior allows you to print lengthy strings by breaking them across lines in your program without including additional stream insertion operations.

Testing Class GradeBook

Figure 3.17 demonstrates the modified version of class GradeBook (Figs. 3.15–3.16) featuring validation. Line 14 creates a GradeBook object named gradeBook1. Recall that the

```
 1   // Fig. 3.17: fig03_17.cpp
 2   // Create and manipulate a GradeBook object; illustrate validation.
 3   #include <iostream>
 4   using std::cout;
 5   using std::endl;
 6
 7   #include "GradeBook.h" // include definition of class GradeBook
 8
 9   // function main begins program execution
10   int main()
11   {
12      // create two GradeBook objects;
13      // initial course name of gradeBook1 is too long
14      GradeBook gradeBook1( "CS101 Introduction to Programming in C++" );
15      GradeBook gradeBook2( "CS102 C++ Data Structures" );
16
17      // display each GradeBook's courseName
18      cout << "gradeBook1's initial course name is: "
19         << gradeBook1.getCourseName()
20         << "\ngradeBook2's initial course name is: "
21         << gradeBook2.getCourseName() << endl;
22
23      // modify myGradeBook's courseName (with a valid-length string)
24      gradeBook1.setCourseName( "CS101 C++ Programming" );
25
26      // display each GradeBook's courseName
27      cout << "\ngradeBook1's course name is: "
28         << gradeBook1.getCourseName()
29         << "\ngradeBook2's course name is: "
30         << gradeBook2.getCourseName() << endl;
31      return 0; // indicate successful termination
32   } // end main
```

Fig. 3.17 | Creating and manipulating a GradeBook object in which the course name is limited to 25 characters in length. (Part 1 of 2.)

```
Name "CS101 Introduction to Programming in C++" exceeds maximum length (25).
Limiting courseName to first 25 characters.

gradeBook1's initial course name is: CS101 Introduction to Pro
gradeBook2's initial course name is: CS102 C++ Data Structures

gradeBook1's course name is: CS101 C++ Programming
gradeBook2's course name is: CS102 C++ Data Structures
```

Fig. 3.17 | Creating and manipulating a GradeBook object in which the course name is limited to 25 characters in length. (Part 2 of 2.)

GradeBook constructor calls member function setCourseName to initialize data member courseName. In previous versions of the class, the benefit of calling setCourseName in the constructor was not evident. Now, however, the constructor takes advantage of the validation provided by setCourseName. The constructor simply calls setCourseName, rather than duplicating its validation code. When line 14 of Fig. 3.17 passes an initial course name of "CS101 Introduction to Programming in C++" to the GradeBook constructor, the constructor passes this value to setCourseName, where the actual initialization occurs. Because this course name contains more than 25 characters, the body of the second if statement executes, causing courseName to be initialized to the truncated 25-character course name "CS101 Introduction to Pro" (the truncated part is highlighted in red in line 14). Notice that the output in Fig. 3.17 contains the warning message output by lines 28–29 of Fig. 3.16 in member function setCourseName. Line 15 creates another GradeBook object called gradeBook2—the valid course name passed to the constructor is exactly 25 characters.

Lines 18–21 of Fig. 3.17 display the truncated course name for gradeBook1 (we highlight this in red in the program output) and the course name for gradeBook2. Line 24 calls gradeBook1's setCourseName member function directly, to change the course name in the GradeBook object to a shorter name that does not need to be truncated. Then, lines 27–30 output the course names for the GradeBook objects again.

Additional Notes on Set *Functions*
A public *set* function such as setCourseName should carefully scrutinize any attempt to modify the value of a data member (e.g., courseName) to ensure that the new value is appropriate for that data item. For example, an attempt to *set* the day of the month to 37 should be rejected, an attempt to *set* a person's weight to zero or a negative value should be rejected, an attempt to *set* a grade on an exam to 185 (when the proper range is zero to 100) should be rejected, etc.

Software Engineering Observation 3.6

Making data members private and controlling access, especially write access, to those data members through public member functions helps ensure data integrity.

Error-Prevention Tip 3.5

The benefits of data integrity are not automatic simply because data members are made private—the programmer must provide appropriate validity checking and report the errors.

Software Engineering Observation 3.7

Member functions that set the values of private *data should verify that the intended new values are proper; if they are not, the* set *functions should place the* private *data members into an appropriate state.*

A class's *set* functions can return values to the class's clients indicating that attempts were made to assign invalid data to objects of the class. A client of the class can test the return value of a *set* function to determine whether the client's attempt to modify the object was successful and to take appropriate action. To keep the program of Figs. 3.15–3.17 simple at this early point in the book, setCourseName in Fig. 3.16 just prints an appropriate message on the screen.

3.11 Wrap-Up

In this chapter, you learned how to create user-defined classes, and how to create and use objects of those classes. In particular, we declared data members of a class to maintain data for each object of the class. We also defined member functions that operate on that data. You learned how to call an object's member functions to request the services it provides and how to pass data to those member functions as arguments. We discussed the difference between a local variable of a member function and a data member of a class. We also showed how to use a constructor to specify the initial values for an object's data members. You learned how to separate the interface of a class from its implementation to promote good software engineering. We also presented a diagram that shows the files that class-implementation programmers and client-code programmers need to compile the code they write. We demonstrated how *set* functions can be used to validate an object's data and ensure that objects are maintained in a consistent state. In addition, UML class diagrams were used to model classes and their constructors, member functions and data members. In the next chapter, we begin our introduction to control statements, which specify the order in which a function's actions are performed.

Summary

- Performing a task in a program requires a function. The function hides from its user the complex tasks that it performs.
- A function in a class is known as a member function and performs one of the class's tasks.
- You must create an object of a class before a program can perform the tasks the class describes. That is one reason C++ is known as an object-oriented programming language.
- Each message sent to an object is a member-function call that tells the object to perform a task.
- An object has attributes that are carried with the object as it is used in a program. These attributes are specified as data members in the object's class.
- A class definition contains the data members and member functions that define the class's attributes and behaviors, respectively.
- A class definition begins with the keyword class followed immediately by the class name.
- By convention, the name of a user-defined class begins with a capital letter and, for readability, each subsequent word in the class name begins with a capital letter.
- Every class's body is enclosed in a pair of braces ({ and }) and ends with a semicolon.

- Member functions that appear after access specifier `public` can be called by other functions in a program and by member functions of other classes.

- Access specifiers are always followed by a colon (:).

- Keyword `void` is a special return type which indicates that a function will perform a task but will not return any data to its calling function when it completes its task.

- By convention, function names begin with a lowercase first letter and all subsequent words in the name begin with a capital letter.

- An empty set of parentheses after a function name indicates that the function does not require additional data to perform its task.

- Every function's body is delimited by left and right braces ({ and }).

- Typically, you cannot call a member function until you create an object of its class.

- Each new class you create becomes a new type in C++ that can be used to declare variables and create objects. This is one reason why C++ is known as an extensible language.

- A member function can require one or more parameters that represent additional data it needs to perform its task. A function call supplies arguments for each of the function's parameters.

- A member function is called by following the object name with a dot operator (.), the function name and a set of parentheses containing the function's arguments.

- A variable of C++ Standard Library class `string` represents a string of characters. This class is defined in header file `<string>`, and the name `string` belongs to namespace `std`.

- Function `getline` (from header `<string>`) reads characters from its first argument until a newline character is encountered, then places the characters (not including the newline) in the `string` variable specified as its second argument. The newline character is discarded.

- A parameter list may contain any number of parameters, including none at all (represented by empty parentheses) to indicate that a function does not require any parameters.

- The number of arguments in a function call must match the number of parameters in the parameter list of the called member function's header. Also, the argument types in the function call must be consistent with the types of the corresponding parameters in the function header.

- Variables declared in a function's body are local variables and can be used only from the point of their declaration in the function to the immediately following closing right brace (}). When a function terminates, the values of its local variables are lost.

- A local variable must be declared before it can be used in a function. A local variable cannot be accessed outside the function in which it is declared.

- Data members normally are `private`. Variables or functions declared `private` are accessible only to member functions of the class in which they are declared.

- When a program creates (instantiates) an object of a class, its `private` data members are encapsulated (hidden) in the object and can be accessed only by member functions of the object's class.

- When a function that specifies a return type other than `void` is called and completes its task, the function returns a result to its calling function.

- By default, the initial value of a `string` is the empty string—i.e., a string that does not contain any characters. Nothing appears on the screen when an empty string is displayed.

- Classes often provide `public` member functions to allow clients of the class to *set* or *get* `private` data members. The names of these member functions normally begin with *set* or *get*.

- Providing `public` *set* and *get* functions allows clients of a class to indirectly access the hidden data. The client knows that it is attempting to modify or obtain an object's data, but the client does not know how the object performs these operations.

- The *set* and *get* functions of a class also should be used by other member functions within the class to manipulate the class's private data, although these member functions *can* access the private data directly. If the class's data representation is changed, member functions that access the data only via the *set* and *get* functions will not require modification—only the bodies of the *set* and *get* functions that directly manipulate the data member will need to change.

- A public *set* function should carefully scrutinize any attempt to modify the value of a data member to ensure that the new value is appropriate for that data item.

- Each class you declare should provide a constructor to initialize an object of the class when the object is created. A constructor is a special member function that must be defined with the same name as the class, so that the compiler can distinguish it from the class's other member functions.

- A difference between constructors and functions is that constructors cannot return values, so they cannot specify a return type (not even void). Normally, constructors are declared public.

- C++ requires a constructor call at the time each object is created, which helps ensure that every object is initialized before it is used in a program.

- A constructor that takes no arguments is a default constructor. In any class that does not include a constructor, the compiler provides a default constructor. The class programmer can also define a default constructor explicitly. If the programmer defines a constructor for a class, C++ will not create a default constructor.

- Class definitions, when packaged properly, can be reused by programmers worldwide.

- It is customary to define a class in a header file that has a .h filename extension.

- If the class's implementation changes, the class's clients should not be required to change.

- Interfaces define and standardize the ways in which things such as people and systems interact.

- The interface of a class describes the public member functions (also known as public services) that are made available to the class's clients. The interface describes *what* services clients can use and how to *request* those services, but does not specify *how* the class carries out the services.

- A fundamental principle of good software engineering is to separate interface from implementation. This makes programs easier to modify. Changes in the class's implementation do not affect the client as long as the class's interface originally provided to the client remains unchanged.

- A function prototype contains a function's name, its return type and the number, types and order of the parameters the function expects to receive.

- Once a class is defined and its member functions are declared (via function prototypes), the member functions should be defined in a separate source-code file

- For each member function defined outside of its corresponding class definition, the function name must be preceded by the class name and the binary scope resolution operator (::).

- Class string's length member function returns the number of characters in a string object.

- Class string's member function substr (short for "substring") returns a new string object created by copying part of an existing string object. The function's first argument specifies the starting position in the original string from which characters are copied. Its second argument specifies the number of characters to copy.

- In the UML, each class is modeled in a class diagram as a rectangle with three compartments. The top compartment contains the class name, centered horizontally in boldface. The middle compartment contains the class's attributes (data members in C++). The bottom compartment contains the class's operations (member functions and constructors in C++).

- The UML models operations by listing the operation name followed by a set of parentheses. A plus sign (+) preceding the operation name indicates a public operation in the UML (i.e., a public member function in C++).

- The UML models a parameter of an operation by listing the parameter name, followed by a colon and the parameter type between the parentheses following the operation name.

- The UML has its own data types. Not all the UML data types have the same names as the corresponding C++ types. The UML type String corresponds to the C++ type string.

- The UML represents data members as attributes by listing the attribute name, followed by a colon and the attribute type. Private attributes are preceded by a minus sign (–) in the UML.

- The UML indicates the return type of an operation by placing a colon and the return type after the parentheses following the operation name.

- UML class diagrams do not specify return types for operations that do not return values.

- The UML models constructors as operations in a class diagram's third compartment. To distinguish a constructor from a class's operations, the UML places the word "constructor" between guillemets (« and ») before the constructor's name.

Terminology

access specifier
accessor
argument
attribute (UML)
binary scope resolution operator (::)
body of a class definition
calling function (caller)
camel case
class definition
class diagram (UML)
class-implementation programmer
client-code programmer
client of an object or class
compartment in a class diagram (UML)
consistent state
constructor
data hiding
data member
default constructor
default precision
defining a class
dot operator (.)
empty string
extensible language
function call
function header
function prototype
get function
getline function of <string> library
guillemets, « and » (UML)
header file
implementation of a class

instance of a class
interface of a class
invoke a member function
length member function of class string
local variable
member function
member-function call
message (send to an object)
minus (–) sign (UML)
mutator
object code
operation (UML)
operation parameter (UML)
parameter
parameter list
plus (+) sign (UML)
precision
private access specifier
public access specifier
public services of a class
return type
separate interface from implementation
set function
software engineering
source-code file
string class
<string> header file
substr member function of class string
UML class diagram
validation
validity checking
void return type

Self-Review Exercises

3.1 Fill in the blanks in each of the following:

a) A house is to a blueprint as a(n) _____ is to a class.

b) Every class definition contains keyword _____ followed immediately by the class's name.

c) A class definition is typically stored in a file with the _____ filename extension.

d) Each parameter in a function header should specify both a(n) _____ and a(n) _____.

e) When each object of a class maintains its own copy of an attribute, the variable that represents the attribute is also known as a(n) _____.

f) Keyword `public` is a(n) _____.

g) Return type _____ indicates that a function will perform a task but will not return any information when it completes its task.

h) Function _____ from the `<string>` library reads characters until a newline character is encountered, then copies those characters into the specified `string`.

i) When a member function is defined outside the class definition, the function header must include the class name and the _____, followed by the function name to "tie" the member function to the class definition.

j) The source-code file and any other files that use a class can include the class's header file via an _____ preprocessor directive.

3.2 State whether each of the following is *true* or *false*. If *false*, explain why.

a) By convention, function names begin with a capital letter and all subsequent words in the name begin with a capital letter.

b) Empty parentheses following a function name in a function prototype indicate that the function does not require any parameters to perform its task.

c) Data members or member functions declared with access specifier `private` are accessible to member functions of the class in which they are declared.

d) Variables declared in the body of a particular member function are known as data members and can be used in all member functions of the class.

e) Every function's body is delimited by left and right braces ({ and }).

f) Any source-code file that contains `int main()` can be used to execute a program.

g) The types of arguments in a function call must match the types of the corresponding parameters in the function prototype's parameter list.

3.3 What is the difference between a local variable and a data member?

3.4 Explain the purpose of a function parameter. What is the difference between a parameter and an argument?

Answers to Self-Review Exercises

3.1 a) object. b) `class`. c) `.h` d) type, name. e) data member. f) access specifier. g) `void`. h) `getline`. i) binary scope resolution operator (`::`). j) `#include`.

3.2 a) False. By convention, function names begin with a lowercase letter and all subsequent words in the name begin with a capital letter. b) True. c) True. d) False. Such variables are called local variables and can be used only in the member function in which they are declared. e) True. f) True. g) True.

3.3 A local variable is declared in the body of a function and can be used only from the point at which it is declared to the immediately following closing brace. A data member is declared in a class definition, but not in the body of any of the class's member functions. Every object (instance) of a class has a separate copy of the class's data members. Also, data members are accessible to all member functions of the class.

3.4   A parameter represents additional information that a function requires to perform its task. Each parameter required by a function is specified in the function header. An argument is the value supplied in the function call. When the function is called, the argument value is passed into the function parameter so that the function can perform its task.

Exercises

3.5   Explain the difference between a function prototype and a function definition.

3.6   What is a default constructor? How are an object's data members initialized if a class has only an implicitly defined default constructor?

3.7   Explain the purpose of a data member.

3.8   What is a header file? What is a source-code file? Discuss the purpose of each.

3.9   Explain how a program could use class `string` without inserting a `using` declaration.

3.10   Explain why a class might provide a *set* function and a *get* function for a data member.

3.11   *(Modifying Class GradeBook)* Modify class `GradeBook` (Figs. 3.11–3.12) as follows:
   a) Include a second `string` data member that represents the course instructor's name.
   b) Provide a *set* function to change the instructor's name and a *get* function to retrieve it.
   c) Modify the constructor to specify two parameters—one for the course name and one for the instructor's name.
   d) Modify member function `displayMessage` such that it first outputs the welcome message and course name, then outputs `"This course is presented by: "` followed by the instructor's name.

Use your modified class in a test program that demonstrates the class's new capabilities.

3.12   *(Account Class)* Create a class called `Account` that a bank might use to represent customers' bank accounts. Your class should include one data member of type `int` to represent the account balance. [*Note:* In subsequent chapters, we'll use numbers that contain decimal points (e.g., 2.75)—called floating-point values—to represent dollar amounts.] Your class should provide a constructor that receives an initial balance and uses it to initialize the data member. The constructor should validate the initial balance to ensure that it is greater than or equal to 0. If not, the balance should be set to 0 and the constructor should display an error message, indicating that the initial balance was invalid. The class should provide three member functions. Member function `credit` should add an amount to the current balance. Member function `debit` should withdraw money from the `Account` and should ensure that the debit amount does not exceed the `Account`'s balance. If it does, the balance should be left unchanged and the function should print a message indicating `"Debit amount exceeded account balance."` Member function `getBalance` should return the current balance. Create a program that creates two `Account` objects and tests the member functions of class `Account`.

3.13   *(Invoice Class)* Create a class called `Invoice` that a hardware store might use to represent an invoice for an item sold at the store. An `Invoice` should include four pieces of information as data members—a part number (type `string`), a part description (type `string`), a quantity of the item being purchased (type `int`) and a price per item (type `int`). [*Note:* In subsequent chapters, we'll use numbers that contain decimal points (e.g., 2.75)—called floating-point values—to represent dollar amounts.] Your class should have a constructor that initializes the four data members. Provide a *set* and a *get* function for each data member. In addition, provide a member function named `getInvoiceAmount` that calculates the invoice amount (i.e., multiplies the quantity by the price per item), then returns the amount as an `int` value. If the quantity is not positive, it should be set to 0. If the price per item is not positive, it should be set to 0. Write a test program that demonstrates class `Invoice`'s capabilities.

3.14   *(Employee Class)* Create a class called `Employee` that includes three pieces of information as data members—a first name (type `string`), a last name (type `string`) and a monthly salary (type `int`). [*Note:* In subsequent chapters, we'll use numbers that contain decimal points (e.g., 2.75)—called floating-point values—to represent dollar amounts.] Your class should have a constructor that initializes the three data members. Provide a *set* and a *get* function for each data member. If the monthly salary is not positive, set it to 0. Write a test program that demonstrates class `Employee`'s capabilities. Create two `Employee` objects and display each object's *yearly* salary. Then give each `Employee` a 10 percent raise and display each `Employee`'s yearly salary again.

3.15   *(Date Class)* Create a class called `Date` that includes three pieces of information as data members—a month (type `int`), a day (type `int`) and a year (type `int`). Your class should have a constructor with three parameters that uses the parameters to initialize the three data members. For the purpose of this exercise, assume that the values provided for the year and day are correct, but ensure that the month value is in the range 1–12; if it is not, set the month to 1. Provide a *set* and a *get* function for each data member. Provide a member function `displayDate` that displays the month, day and year separated by forward slashes (/). Write a test program that demonstrates class `Date`'s capabilities.

4

Control Statements: Part 1

Featuring
Early
Classes &
Objects
with the
UML™ 2

Let's all move one place on.
—Lewis Carroll

The wheel is come full circle.
—William Shakespeare

Who can control his fate?
—William Shakespeare

How many apples fell on Newton's head before he took the hint!
—Robert Frost

All the evolution we know of proceeds from the vague to the definite.
—Charles Sanders Peirce

OBJECTIVES

In this chapter you will learn:

- Basic problem-solving techniques.

- To develop algorithms through the process of top-down, stepwise refinement.

- To use the `if` and `if...else` selection statements to choose among alternative actions.

- To use the `while` repetition statement to execute statements in a program repeatedly.

- Counter-controlled repetition and sentinel-controlled repetition.

- To use the increment, decrement and assignment operators.

Outline

4.1 Introduction

4.2 Algorithms

4.3 Pseudocode

4.4 Control Structures

4.5 `if` Selection Statement

4.6 `if...else` Double-Selection Statement

4.7 `while` Repetition Statement

4.8 Formulating Algorithms: Counter-Controlled Repetition

4.9 Formulating Algorithms: Sentinel-Controlled Repetition

4.10 Formulating Algorithms: Nested Control Statements

4.11 Assignment Operators

4.12 Increment and Decrement Operators

4.13 Wrap-Up

Summary | Terminology | Self-Review Exercises | Answers to Self-Review Exercises | Exercises

4.1 Introduction

Before writing a program to solve a problem, we must have a thorough understanding of the problem and a carefully planned approach to solving it. When writing a program, we must also understand the types of building blocks that are available and employ proven program construction techniques. In this chapter and in Chapter 5, Control Statements: Part 2, we discuss these issues in presenting of the theory and principles of structured programming. The concepts presented here are crucial to building effective classes and manipulating objects.

In this chapter, we introduce C++'s `if`, `if...else` and `while` statements, three of the building blocks that allow programmers to specify the logic required for member functions to perform their tasks. We devote a portion of this chapter (and Chapters 5 and 7) to further developing the `GradeBook` class introduced in Chapter 3. In particular, we add a member function to the `GradeBook` class that uses control statements to calculate the average of a set of student grades. Another example demonstrates additional ways to combine control statements to solve a similar problem. We introduce C++'s assignment operators and explore C++'s increment and decrement operators. These additional operators abbreviate and simplify many program statements.

4.2 Algorithms

Any solvable computing problem can be solved by the execution of a series of actions in a specific order. A procedure for solving a problem in terms of

1. the actions to execute and

2. the order in which these actions execute

is called an algorithm. The following example demonstrates that correctly specifying the order in which the actions execute is important.

Consider the "rise-and-shine algorithm" followed by one junior executive for getting out of bed and going to work: (1) Get out of bed, (2) take off pajamas, (3) take a shower,

(4) get dressed, (5) eat breakfast, (6) carpool to work. This routine gets the executive to work well prepared to make critical decisions. Suppose that the same steps are performed in a slightly different order: (1) Get out of bed, (2) take off pajamas, (3) get dressed, (4) take a shower, (5) eat breakfast, (6) carpool to work. In this case, our junior executive shows up for work soaking wet. Specifying the order in which statements (actions) execute in a computer program is called program control. This chapter investigates program control using C++'s control statements.

4.3 Pseudocode

Pseudocode (or "fake" code) is an artificial and informal language that helps programmers develop algorithms without having to worry about the strict details of C++ language syntax. The pseudocode we present here is particularly useful for developing algorithms that will be converted to structured portions of C++ programs. Pseudocode is similar to everyday English; it is convenient and user friendly, although it is not an actual computer programming language.

Pseudocode does not execute on computers. Rather, it helps the programmer "think out" a program before attempting to write it in a programming language, such as C++. This chapter provides several examples of how to use pseudocode to develop C++ programs.

The style of pseudocode we present consists purely of characters, so programmers can type pseudocode conveniently, using any editor program. The computer can produce a freshly printed copy of a pseudocode program on demand. A carefully prepared pseudocode program can easily be converted to a corresponding C++ program. In many cases, this simply requires replacing pseudocode statements with C++ equivalents.

Pseudocode normally describes only executable statements, which cause specific actions to occur after a programmer converts a program from pseudocode to C++ and the program is run on a computer. Declarations (that do not have initializers or do not involve constructor calls) are not executable statements. For example, the declaration

```
int i;
```

tells the compiler variable i's type and instructs the compiler to reserve space in memory for the variable. This declaration does not cause any action—such as input, output or a calculation—to occur when the program executes. We typically do not include variable declarations in our pseudocode. However, some programmers choose to list variables and mention their purposes at the beginning of pseudocode programs.

We now look at an example of pseudocode that may be written to help a programmer create the addition program of Fig. 2.5. This pseudocode (Fig. 4.1) corresponds to the algorithm that inputs two integers from the user, adds these integers and displays their sum. Although we show the complete pseudocode listing here, we will show how to create pseudocode from a problem statement later in the chapter.

Lines 1–2 correspond to the statements in lines 13–14 of Fig. 2.5. Notice that the pseudocode statements are simply English statements that convey what task is to be performed in C++. Likewise, lines 4–5 correspond to the statements in lines 16–17 of Fig. 2.5 and lines 7–8 correspond to the statements in lines 19 and 21 of Fig. 2.5.

1	*Prompt the user to enter the first integer*
2	*Input the first integer*
3	
4	*Prompt the user to enter the second integer*
5	*Input the second integer*
6	
7	*Add first integer and second integer, store result*
8	*Display result*

Fig. 4.1 | Pseudocode for the addition program of Fig. 2.5.

There are a few important aspects of the pseudocode in Fig. 4.1. Notice that the pseudocode corresponds to code only in function `main`. This occurs because pseudocode is normally used for algorithms, not complete programs. In this case, the pseudocode is used to represent the algorithm. The function in which this code is placed is not important to the algorithm itself. For the same reason, line 23 of Fig. 2.5 (the `return` statement) is not included in the pseudocode—this `return` statement is placed at the end of every `main` function and is not important to the algorithm. Finally, lines 9–11 of Fig. 2.5 are not included in the pseudocode because these variable declarations are not executable statements.

4.4 **Control Structures**

Normally, statements in a program execute one after the other in the order in which they are written. This is called sequential execution. Various C++ statements we will soon discuss enable the programmer to specify that the next statement to execute may be other than the next one in sequence. This is called transfer of control.

During the 1960s, it became clear that the indiscriminate use of transfers of control was the root of much difficulty experienced by software development groups. The finger of blame was pointed at the goto statement, which allows the programmer to specify a transfer of control to one of a wide range of possible destinations in a program (creating what is often called "spaghetti code"). The notion of so-called structured programming became almost synonymous with "goto elimination."

The research of Böhm and Jacopini[1] demonstrated that programs could be written without any goto statements. It became the challenge of the era for programmers to shift their styles to "goto-less programming." It was not until the 1970s that programmers started taking structured programming seriously. The results have been impressive, as software development groups have reported reduced development times, more frequent on-time delivery of systems and more frequent within-budget completion of software projects. The key to these successes is that structured programs are clearer, are easier to debug, test and modify and are more likely to be bug-free in the first place.

Böhm and Jacopini's work demonstrated that all programs could be written in terms of only three control structures, namely, the sequence structure, the selection structure and the repetition structure. The term "control structures" comes from the field of com-

---

1. Böhm, C., and G. Jacopini, "Flow Diagrams, Turing Machines, and Languages with Only Two Formation Rules," *Communications of the ACM*, Vol. 9, No. 5, May 1966, pp. 366–371.

puter science. When we introduce C++'s implementations of control structures, we will refer to them in the terminology of the C++ standard document[2] as "control statements."

Sequence Structure in C++

The sequence structure is built into C++. Unless directed otherwise, the computer executes C++ statements one after the other in the order in which they are written—that is, in sequence. The Unified Modeling Language (UML) activity diagram of Fig. 4.2 illustrates a typical sequence structure in which two calculations are performed in order. C++ allows us to have as many actions as we want in a sequence structure. As we will soon see, anywhere a single action may be placed, we may place several actions in sequence.

In this figure, the two statements involve adding a grade to a total variable and adding the value 1 to a counter variable. Such statements might appear in a program that takes the average of several student grades. To calculate an average, the total of the grades being averaged is divided by the number of grades. A counter variable would be used to keep track of the number of values being averaged. You will see similar statements in the program of Section 4.8.

Activity diagrams are part of the UML. An activity diagram models the workflow (also called the activity) of a portion of a software system. Such workflows may include a portion of an algorithm, such as the sequence structure in Fig. 4.2. Activity diagrams are composed of special-purpose symbols, such as action state symbols (a rectangle with its left and right sides replaced with arcs curving outward), diamonds and small circles; these symbols are connected by transition arrows, which represent the flow of the activity.

Like pseudocode, activity diagrams help programmers develop and represent algorithms, although many programmers prefer pseudocode. Activity diagrams clearly show how control structures operate.

Consider the sequence-structure activity diagram of Fig. 4.2. It contains two action states that represent actions to perform. Each action state contains an action expression—e.g., "add grade to total" or "add 1 to counter"—that specifies a particular action to perform. Other actions might include calculations or input/output operations. The arrows

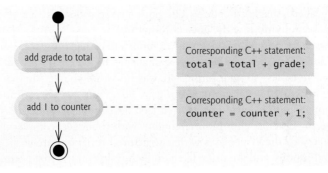

Fig. 4.2 | Sequence-structure activity diagram.

---

2. This document is more specifically known as *NCITS/ISO/IEC 14882-2003 Programming languages—C++* and is available for download (for a fee) at: webstore.ansi.org/ansidocstore/product.asp?sku=INCITS%2FISO%2FIEC+14882%2D2003.

in the activity diagram are called transition arrows. These arrows represent transitions, which indicate the order in which the actions represented by the action states occur—the program that implements the activities illustrated by the activity diagram in Fig. 4.2 first adds grade to total, then adds 1 to counter.

The solid circle located at the top of the activity diagram represents the activity's initial state—the beginning of the workflow before the program performs the modeled activities. The solid circle surrounded by a hollow circle that appears at the bottom of the activity diagram represents the final state—the end of the workflow after the program performs its activities.

Figure 4.2 also includes rectangles with the upper-right corners folded over. These are called notes in the UML. Notes are explanatory remarks that describe the purpose of symbols in the diagram. Notes can be used in any UML diagram—not just activity diagrams. Figure 4.2 uses UML notes to show the C++ code associated with each action state in the activity diagram. A dotted line connects each note with the element that the note describes. Activity diagrams normally do not show the C++ code that implements the activity. We use notes for this purpose here to illustrate how the diagram relates to C++ code. For more information on the UML, visit www.uml.org.

Selection Statements in C++

C++ provides three types of selection statements (discussed in this chapter and Chapter 5). The if selection statement either performs (selects) an action if a condition (predicate) is true or skips the action if the condition is false. The if...else selection statement performs an action if a condition is true or performs a different action if the condition is false. The switch selection statement (Chapter 5) performs one of many different actions, depending on the value of an integer expression.

The if selection statement is a single-selection statement because it selects or ignores a single action (or, as we will soon see, a single group of actions). The if...else statement is called a double-selection statement because it selects between two different actions (or groups of actions). The switch selection statement is called a multiple-selection statement because it selects among many different actions (or groups of actions).

Repetition Statements in C++

C++ provides three types of repetition statements (also called looping statements or loops) that enable programs to perform statements repeatedly as long as a condition (called the loop-continuation condition) remains true. The repetition statements are the while, do...while and for statements. (Chapter 5 presents the do...while and for statements.) The while and for statements perform the action (or group of actions) in their bodies zero or more times—if the loop-continuation condition is initially false, the action (or group of actions) will not execute. The do...while statement performs the action (or group of actions) in its body at least once.

Each of the words if, else, switch, while, do and for is a C++ keyword. These words are reserved by the C++ programming language to implement various features, such as C++'s control statements. Keywords must not be used as identifiers, such as variable names. Figure 4.3 contains a complete list of C++ keywords.

C++ Keywords

Keywords common to the C and C++ programming languages

auto	break	case	char	const
continue	default	do	double	else
enum	extern	float	for	goto
if	int	long	register	return
short	signed	sizeof	static	struct
switch	typedef	union	unsigned	void
volatile	while			

C++-only keywords

and	and_eq	asm	bitand	bitor
bool	catch	class	compl	const_cast
delete	dynamic_cast	explicit	export	false
friend	inline	mutable	namespace	new
not	not_eq	operator	or	or_eq
private	protected	public	reinterpret_cast	static_cast
template	this	throw	true	try
typeid	typename	using	virtual	wchar_t
xor	xor_eq			

Fig. 4.3 | C++ keywords.

Common Programming Error 4.1

Using a keyword as an identifier is a syntax error.

Common Programming Error 4.2

Spelling a keyword with any uppercase letters is a syntax error. All of C++'s keywords contain only lowercase letters.

Summary of Control Statements in C++

C++ has only three kinds of control structures, which from this point forward we refer to as control statements: the sequence statement, selection statements (three types—if, if...else and switch) and repetition statements (three types—while, for and do...while). Each C++ program combines as many of these control statements as is appropriate for the algorithm the program implements. As with the sequence statement of Fig. 4.2, we can model each control statement as an activity diagram. Each diagram contains an initial state and a final state, which represent a control statement's entry point and exit point, respectively. These single-entry/single-exit control statements make it easy to build programs—the control statements are attached to one another by connecting the exit point of one to the entry point of the next. This is similar to the way a child stacks building blocks, so we call this control-statement stacking. We will learn shortly that there is only one other way to connect control statements—called control-statement nesting, in which one control statement is contained inside another. Thus, algorithms in C++ programs are constructed from only three kinds of control statements, combined in only two ways. This is the essence of simplicity.

Software Engineering Observation 4.1

Any C++ program we will ever build can be constructed from only seven different types of control statements (sequence, if, if...else, switch, while, do...while and for) combined in only two ways (control-statement stacking and control-statement nesting).

4.5 if Selection Statement

Programs use selection statements to choose among alternative courses of action. For example, suppose the passing grade on an exam is 60. The pseudocode statement

> *If student's grade is greater than or equal to 60*
> > *Print "Passed"*

determines whether the condition "student's grade is greater than or equal to 60" is true or false. If the condition is true, then "Passed" is printed and the next pseudocode statement in order is "performed" (remember that pseudocode is not a real programming language). If the condition is false, the print statement is ignored and the next pseudocode statement in order is performed. Note that the second line of this selection statement is indented. Such indentation is optional, but it is recommended because it emphasizes the inherent structure of structured programs. When you convert your pseudocode into C++ code, the C++ compiler ignores white-space characters (like blanks, tabs and newlines) used for indentation and vertical spacing.

Good Programming Practice 4.1

Consistently applying reasonable indentation conventions throughout your programs greatly improves program readability. We suggest three blanks per indent. Some people prefer using tabs but these can vary across editors, causing a program written on one editor to align differently when used with another.

The preceding pseudocode *If* statement can be written in C++ as

```
if ( grade >= 60 )
   cout << "Passed";
```

Notice that the C++ code corresponds closely to the pseudocode. This is one of the properties of pseudocode that makes it such a useful program development tool.

Figure 4.4 illustrates the single-selection if statement. It contains what is perhaps the most important symbol in an activity diagram—the diamond or decision symbol, which indicates that a decision is to be made. A decision symbol indicates that the workflow will continue along a path determined by the symbol's associated guard conditions, which can be true or false. Each transition arrow emerging from a decision symbol has a guard condition (specified in square brackets above or next to the transition arrow). If a particular guard condition is true, the workflow enters the action state to which that transition arrow points. In Fig. 4.4, if the grade is greater than or equal to 60, the program prints "Passed" to the screen, then transitions to the final state of this activity. If the grade is less than 60, the program immediately transitions to the final state without displaying a message.

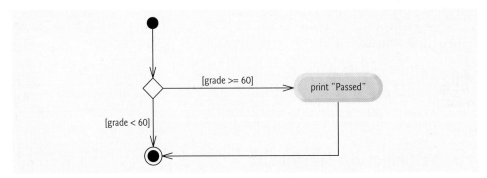

Fig. 4.4 | `if` single-selection statement activity diagram.

We learned in Chapter 1 that decisions can be based on conditions containing relational or equality operators. Actually, in C++, a decision can be based on any expression—if the expression evaluates to zero, it is treated as false; if the expression evaluates to nonzero, it is treated as true. C++ provides the data type `bool` for variables that can hold only the values `true` and `false`—each of these is a C++ keyword.

Portability Tip 4.1

For compatibility with earlier versions of C, which used integers for Boolean values, the `bool` value `true` also can be represented by any nonzero value (compilers typically use 1) and the `bool` value `false` also can be represented as the value zero.

Note that the `if` statement is a single-entry/single-exit statement. We will see that the activity diagrams for the remaining control statements also contain initial states, transition arrows, action states that indicate actions to perform, decision symbols (with associated guard conditions) that indicate decisions to be made and final states. This is consistent with the action/decision model of programming we have been emphasizing.

We can envision seven bins, each containing only empty UML activity diagrams of one of the seven types of control statements. The programmer's task, then, is assembling a program from the activity diagrams of as many of each type of control statement as the algorithm demands, combining the activity diagrams in only two possible ways (stacking or nesting), then filling in the action states and decisions with action expressions and guard conditions in a manner appropriate to form a structured implementation for the algorithm. We will discuss the variety of ways in which actions and decisions may be written.

4.6 `if...else` Double-Selection Statement

The `if` single-selection statement performs an indicated action only when the condition is `true`; otherwise the action is skipped. The `if...else` double-selection statement allows the programmer to specify an action to perform when the condition is true and a different action to perform when the condition is `false`. For example, the pseudocode statement

> *If student's grade is greater than or equal to 60*
> > *Print "Passed"*
>
> *Else*
> > *Print "Failed"*

prints "Passed" if the student's grade is greater than or equal to 60, but prints "Failed" if the student's grade is less than 60. In either case, after printing occurs, the next pseudocode statement in sequence is "performed."

The preceding pseudocode *If...Else* statement can be written in C++ as

```
if ( grade >= 60 )
    cout << "Passed";
else
    cout << "Failed";
```

Note that the body of the else is also indented. Whatever indentation convention you choose should be applied consistently throughout your programs. It is difficult to read programs that do not obey uniform spacing conventions.

Good Programming Practice 4.2

Indent both body statements of an if...else statement.

Good Programming Practice 4.3

If there are several levels of indentation, each level should be indented the same additional amount of space.

Figure 4.5 illustrates the flow of control in the if...else statement. Once again, note that (besides the initial state, transition arrows and final state) the only other symbols in the activity diagram represent action states and decisions. We continue to emphasize this action/decision model of computing. Imagine again a deep bin of empty UML activity diagrams of double-selection statements—as many as the programmer might need to stack and nest with the activity diagrams of other control statements to form a structured implementation of an algorithm. The programmer fills in the action states and decision symbols with action expressions and guard conditions appropriate to the algorithm.

Conditional Operator (?:)

C++ provides the conditional operator (?:), which is closely related to the if...else statement. The conditional operator is C++'s only ternary operator—it takes three operands. The operands, together with the conditional operator, form a conditional expression. The

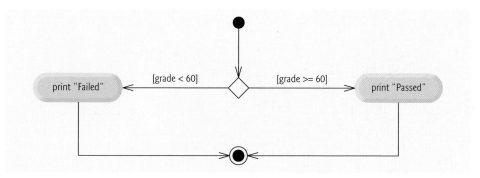

Fig. 4.5 | if...else double-selection statement activity diagram.

first operand is a condition, the second operand is the value for the entire conditional expression if the condition is `true` and the third operand is the value for the entire conditional expression if the condition is `false`. For example, the output statement

```
cout << ( grade >= 60 ? "Passed" : "Failed" );
```

contains a conditional expression, `grade >= 60 ? "Passed" : "Failed"`, that evaluates to the string `"Passed"` if the condition `grade >= 60` is `true`, but evaluates to the string `"Failed"` if the condition is `false`. Thus, the statement with the conditional operator performs essentially the same as the preceding `if...else` statement. As we will see, the precedence of the conditional operator is low, so the parentheses in the preceding expression are required.

Error-Prevention Tip 4.1

To avoid precedence problems (and for clarity), place conditional expressions (that appear in larger expressions) in parentheses.

The values in a conditional expression also can be actions to execute. For example, the following conditional expression also prints `"Passed"` or `"Failed"`:

```
grade >= 60 ? cout << "Passed" : cout << "Failed";
```

The preceding conditional expression is read, "If `grade` is greater than or equal to 60, then `cout << "Passed"`; otherwise, `cout << "Failed"`." This, too, is comparable to the preceding `if...else` statement. Conditional expressions can appear in some program locations where `if...else` statements cannot.

Nested `if...else` Statements

Nested `if...else` statements test for multiple cases by placing `if...else` selection statements inside other `if...else` selection statements. For example, the following pseudocode `if...else` statement prints A for exam grades greater than or equal to 90, B for grades in the range 80 to 89, C for grades in the range 70 to 79, D for grades in the range 60 to 69 and F for all other grades:

> *If student's grade is greater than or equal to 90*
>> *Print "A"*
> *Else*
>> *If student's grade is greater than or equal to 80*
>>> *Print "B"*
>> *Else*
>>> *If student's grade is greater than or equal to 70*
>>>> *Print "C"*
>>> *Else*
>>>> *If student's grade is greater than or equal to 60*
>>>>> *Print "D"*
>>>> *Else*
>>>>> *Print "F"*

This pseudocode can be written in C++ as

```
if ( studentGrade >= 90 ) // 90 and above gets "A"
   cout << "A";
else
   if ( studentGrade >= 80 ) // 80-89 gets "B"
      cout << "B";
   else
      if ( studentGrade >= 70 ) // 70-79 gets "C"
         cout << "C";
      else
         if ( studentGrade >= 60 ) // 60-69 gets "D"
            cout << "D";
         else // less than 60 gets "F"
            cout << "F";
```

If studentGrade is greater than or equal to 90, the first four conditions will be true, but only the cout statement after the first test will execute. After that cout executes, the program skips the else-part of the "outermost" if...else statement. Most C++ programmers prefer to write the preceding if...else statement as

```
if ( studentGrade >= 90 ) // 90 and above gets "A"
   cout << "A";
else if ( studentGrade >= 80 ) // 80-89 gets "B"
   cout << "B";
else if ( studentGrade >= 70 ) // 70-79 gets "C"
   cout << "C";
else if ( studentGrade >= 60 ) // 60-69 gets "D"
   cout << "D";
else // less than 60 gets "F"
   cout << "F";
```

The two forms are identical except for the spacing and indentation, which the compiler ignores. The latter form is popular because it avoids deep indentation of the code to the right. Such indentation often leaves little room on a line, forcing lines to be split and decreasing program readability.

Performance Tip 4.1

A nested if...else statement can perform much faster than a series of single-selection if statements because of the possibility of early exit after one of the conditions is satisfied.

Performance Tip 4.2

In a nested if...else statement, test the conditions that are more likely to be true at the beginning of the nested if...else statement. This will enable the nested if...else statement to run faster and exit earlier than testing infrequently occurring cases first.

Dangling-else Problem

The C++ compiler always associates an else with the immediately preceding if unless told to do otherwise by the placement of braces ({ and }). This behavior can lead to what is referred to as the dangling-else problem. For example,

```
if ( x > 5 )
   if ( y > 5 )
      cout << "x and y are > 5";
else
   cout << "x is <= 5";
```

appears to indicate that if x is greater than 5, the nested if statement determines whether y is also greater than 5. If so, "x and y are > 5" is output. Otherwise, it appears that if x is not greater than 5, the else part of the if...else outputs "x is <= 5".

Beware! This nested if...else statement does not execute as it appears. The compiler actually interprets the statement as

```
if ( x > 5 )
   if ( y > 5 )
      cout << "x and y are > 5";
   else
      cout << "x is <= 5";
```

in which the body of the first if is a nested if...else. The outer if statement tests whether x is greater than 5. If so, execution continues by testing whether y is also greater than 5. If the second condition is true, the proper string—"x and y are > 5"—is displayed. However, if the second condition is false, the string "x is <= 5" is displayed, even though we know that x is greater than 5.

To force the nested if...else statement to execute as it was originally intended, we must write it as follows:

```
if ( x > 5 )
{
   if ( y > 5 )
      cout << "x and y are > 5";
}
else
   cout << "x is <= 5";
```

The braces ({}) indicate to the compiler that the second if statement is in the body of the first if and that the else is associated with the first if. Exercise 4.23 and Exercise 4.24 further investigate the dangling-else problem.

Blocks

The if selection statement normally expects only one statement in its body. Similarly, the if and else parts of an if...else statement each expect only one body statement. To include several statements in the body of an if or in either part of an if...else, enclose the statements in braces ({ and }). A set of statements contained within a pair of braces is called a compound statement or a block. We use the term "block" from this point forward.

Software Engineering Observation 4.2

A block can be placed anywhere in a program that a single statement can be placed.

The following example includes a block in the else part of an if...else statement.

```
if ( studentGrade >= 60 )
   cout << "Passed.\n";
else
{
   cout << "Failed.\n";
   cout << "You must take this course again.\n";
}
```

In this case, if `studentGrade` is less than 60, the program executes both statements in the body of the `else` and prints

```
Failed.
You must take this course again.
```

Notice the braces surrounding the two statements in the `else` clause. These braces are important. Without the braces, the statement

```
cout << "You must take this course again.\n";
```

would be outside the body of the `else` part of the `if` and would execute regardless of whether the grade is less than 60. This is an example of a logic error.

Common Programming Error 4.3

Forgetting one or both of the braces that delimit a block can lead to syntax errors or logic errors in a program.

Good Programming Practice 4.4

Always putting the braces in an `if...else` statement (or any control statement) helps prevent their accidental omission, especially when adding statements to an `if` or `else` clause at a later time. To avoid omitting one or both of the braces, some programmers prefer to type the beginning and ending braces of blocks even before typing the individual statements within the braces.

Just as a block can be placed anywhere a single statement can be placed, it is also possible to have no statement at all—called a null statement (or an empty statement). The null statement is represented by placing a semicolon (;) where a statement would normally be.

Common Programming Error 4.4

Placing a semicolon after the condition in an `if` statement leads to a logic error in single-selection `if` statements and a syntax error in double-selection `if...else` statements (when the `if` part contains an actual body statement).

4.7 `while` Repetition Statement

A repetition statement (also called a looping statement or a loop) allows the programmer to specify that a program should repeat an action while some condition remains true. The pseudocode statement

> *While there are more items on my shopping list*
> *Purchase next item and cross it off my list*

describes the repetition that occurs during a shopping trip. The condition, "there are more items on my shopping list" is either true or false. If it is true, then the action, "Purchase next item and cross it off my list" is performed. This action will be performed repeatedly while the condition remains true. The statement contained in the *While* repetition statement constitutes the body of the *While*, which can be a single statement or a block. Eventually, the condition will become false (when the last item on the shopping list has been purchased and crossed off the list). At this point, the repetition terminates, and the first pseudocode statement after the repetition statement executes.

As an example of C++'s while repetition statement, consider a program segment designed to find the first power of 3 larger than 100. Suppose the integer variable product has been initialized to 3. When the following while repetition statement finishes executing, product contains the result:

```
int product = 3;

while ( product <= 100 )
   product = 3 * product;
```

When the while statement begins execution, the value of product is 3. Each repetition of the while statement multiplies product by 3, so product takes on the values 9, 27, 81 and 243 successively. When product becomes 243, the while statement condition—product <= 100—becomes false. This terminates the repetition, so the final value of product is 243. At this point, program execution continues with the next statement after the while statement.

Common Programming Error 4.5

Not providing, in the body of a while statement, an action that eventually causes the condition in the while to become false normally results in a logic error called an infinite loop, *in which the repetition statement never terminates. This can make a program appear to "hang" or "freeze" if the loop body does not contain statements that interact with the user.*

The UML activity diagram of Fig. 4.6 illustrates the flow of control that corresponds to the preceding while statement. Once again, the symbols in the diagram (besides the initial state, transition arrows, a final state and three notes) represent an action state and a decision. This diagram also introduces the UML's merge symbol, which joins two flows of activity into one flow of activity. The UML represents both the merge symbol and the decision symbol as diamonds. In this diagram, the merge symbol joins the transitions from the initial state and from the action state, so they both flow into the decision that determines whether the loop should begin (or continue) executing. The decision and merge symbols can be distinguished by the number of "incoming" and "outgoing" transition arrows. A decision symbol has one transition arrow pointing to the diamond and two or more transition arrows pointing out from the diamond to indicate possible transitions from that point. In addition, each transition arrow pointing out of a decision symbol has a guard condition next to it. A merge symbol has two or more transition arrows pointing to the diamond and only one transition arrow pointing from the diamond, to indicate multiple activity flows merging to continue the activity. Note that, unlike the decision symbol, the merge symbol does not have a counterpart in C++ code. None of the transition arrows associated with a merge symbol have guard conditions.

The diagram of Fig. 4.6 clearly shows the repetition of the while statement discussed earlier in this section. The transition arrow emerging from the action state points to the merge, which transitions back to the decision that is tested each time through the loop until the guard condition product > 100 becomes true. Then the while statement exits (reaches its final state) and control passes to the next statement in sequence in the program.

Imagine a deep bin of empty UML while repetition statement activity diagrams—as many as the programmer might need to stack and nest with the activity diagrams of other control statements to form a structured implementation of an algorithm. The programmer fills in the action states and decision symbols with action expressions and guard conditions appropriate to the algorithm.

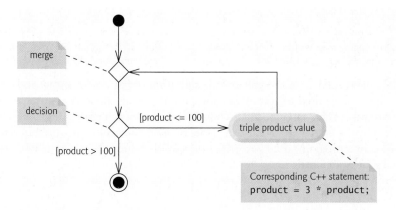

Fig. 4.6 | while repetition statement UML activity diagram.

Performance Tip 4.3

Many of the performance tips we mention in this text result in only small improvements, so the reader might be tempted to ignore them. However, a small performance improvement for code that executes many times in a loop can result in substantial overall performance improvement.

4.8 Formulating Algorithms: Counter-Controlled Repetition

To illustrate how programmers develop algorithms, this section and Section 4.9 solve two variations of a class average problem. Consider the following problem statement:

> *A class of ten students took a quiz. The grades (integers in the range 0 to 100) for this quiz are available to you. Calculate and display the total of all student grades and the class average on the quiz.*

The class average is equal to the sum of the grades divided by the number of students. The algorithm for solving this problem on a computer must input each of the grades, calculate the average and print the result.

Pseudocode Algorithm with Counter-Controlled Repetition

Let's use pseudocode to list the actions to execute and specify the order in which these actions should occur. We use counter-controlled repetition to input the grades one at a time. This technique uses a variable called a counter to control the number of times a group of statements will execute (also known as the number of iterations of the loop).

Counter-controlled repetition is often called definite repetition because the number of repetitions is known before the loop begins executing. In this example, repetition terminates when the counter exceeds 10. This section presents a fully developed pseudocode algorithm (Fig. 4.7) and a version of class GradeBook (Fig. 4.8–Fig. 4.9) that implements the algorithm in a C++ member function. The section then presents an application (Fig. 4.10) that demonstrates the algorithm in action. In Section 4.9 we demonstrate how to use pseudocode to develop such an algorithm from scratch.

> **Software Engineering Observation 4.3**
>
> *Experience has shown that the most difficult part of solving a problem on a computer is developing the algorithm for the solution. Once a correct algorithm has been specified, the process of producing a working C++ program from the algorithm is normally straightforward.*

Note the references in the pseudocode algorithm of Fig. 4.7 to a total and a counter. A total is a variable used to accumulate the sum of several values. A counter is a variable used to count—in this case, the grade counter indicates which of the 10 grades is about to be entered by the user. Variables used to store totals are normally initialized to zero before being used in a program; otherwise, the sum would include the previous value stored in the total's memory location.

```
 1   Set total to zero
 2   Set grade counter to one
 3
 4   While grade counter is less than or equal to ten
 5       Prompt the user to enter the next grade
 6       Input the next grade
 7       Add the grade into the total
 8       Add one to the grade counter
 9
10   Set the class average to the total divided by ten
11   Print the total of the grades for all students in the class
12   Print the class average
```

Fig. 4.7 | Pseudocode algorithm that uses counter-controlled repetition to solve the class average problem.

```cpp
 1   // Fig. 4.8: GradeBook.h
 2   // Definition of class GradeBook that determines a class average.
 3   // Member functions are defined in GradeBook.cpp
 4   #include <string> // program uses C++ standard string class
 5   using std::string;
 6
 7   // GradeBook class definition
 8   class GradeBook
 9   {
10   public:
11      GradeBook( string ); // constructor initializes course name
12      void setCourseName( string ); // function to set the course name
13      string getCourseName(); // function to retrieve the course name
14      void displayMessage(); // display a welcome message
15      void determineClassAverage(); // averages grades entered by the user
16   private:
17      string courseName; // course name for this GradeBook
18   }; // end class GradeBook
```

Fig. 4.8 | Class average problem using counter-controlled repetition: GradeBook header file.

```cpp
 1   // Fig. 4.9: GradeBook.cpp
 2   // Member-function definitions for class GradeBook that solves the
 3   // class average program with counter-controlled repetition.
 4   #include <iostream>
 5   using std::cout;
 6   using std::cin;
 7   using std::endl;
 8
 9   #include "GradeBook.h" // include definition of class GradeBook
10
11   // constructor initializes courseName with string supplied as argument
12   GradeBook::GradeBook( string name )
13   {
14      setCourseName( name ); // validate and store courseName
15   } // end GradeBook constructor
16
17   // function to set the course name;
18   // ensures that the course name has at most 25 characters
19   void GradeBook::setCourseName( string name )
20   {
21      if ( name.length() <= 25 ) // if name has 25 or fewer characters
22         courseName = name; // store the course name in the object
23      else // if name is longer than 25 characters
24      { // set courseName to first 25 characters of parameter name
25         courseName = name.substr( 0, 25 ); // select first 25 characters
26         cout << "Name \"" << name << "\" exceeds maximum length (25).\n"
27            << "Limiting courseName to first 25 characters.\n" << endl;
28      } // end if...else
29   } // end function setCourseName
30
31   // function to retrieve the course name
32   string GradeBook::getCourseName()
33   {
34      return courseName;
35   } // end function getCourseName
36
37   // display a welcome message to the GradeBook user
38   void GradeBook::displayMessage()
39   {
40      cout << "Welcome to the grade book for\n" << getCourseName() << "!\n"
41         << endl;
42   } // end function displayMessage
43
44   // determine class average based on 10 grades entered by user
45   void GradeBook::determineClassAverage()
46   {
47      int total; // sum of grades entered by user
48      int gradeCounter; // number of the grade to be entered next
49      int grade; // grade value entered by user
50      int average; // average of grades
51
```

Fig. 4.9 | Class average problem using counter-controlled repetition: GradeBook source code file. (Part 1 of 2.)

```
52        // initialization phase
53        total = 0; // initialize total
54        gradeCounter = 1; // initialize loop counter
55
56        // processing phase
57        while ( gradeCounter <= 10 ) // loop 10 times
58        {
59           cout << "Enter grade: "; // prompt for input
60           cin >> grade; // input next grade
61           total = total + grade; // add grade to total
62           gradeCounter = gradeCounter + 1; // increment counter by 1
63        } // end while
64
65        // termination phase
66        average = total / 10; // integer division yields integer result
67
68        // display total and average of grades
69        cout << "\nTotal of all 10 grades is " << total << endl;
70        cout << "Class average is " << average << endl;
71     } // end function determineClassAverage
```

Fig. 4.9 | Class average problem using counter-controlled repetition: GradeBook source code file. (Part 2 of 2.)

Enhancing GradeBook Validation

Before we discuss the implementation of the class average algorithm, let's consider an enhancement we made to our GradeBook class. In Fig. 3.16, our setCourseName member function would validate the course name by first testing if the course name's length was less than or equal to 25 characters, using an if statement. If this was true, the course name would be set. This code was then followed by another if statement that tested if the course name's length was larger than 25 characters (in which case the course name would be shortened). Notice that the second if statement's condition is the exact opposite of the first if statement's condition. If one condition evaluates to true, the other must evaluate to false. Such a situation is ideal for an if...else statement, so we have modified our code, replacing the two if statements with one if...else statement (lines 21–28 of Fig. 4.9).

Implementing Counter-Controlled Repetition in Class GradeBook

Class GradeBook (Fig. 4.8–Fig. 4.9) contains a constructor (declared in line 11 of Fig. 4.8 and defined in lines 12–15 of Fig. 4.9) that assigns a value to the class's instance variable courseName (declared in line 17 of Fig. 4.8). Lines 19–29, 32–35 and 38–42 of Fig. 4.9 define member functions setCourseName, getCourseName and displayMessage, respectively. Lines 45–71 define member function determineClassAverage, which implements the class average algorithm described by the pseudocode in Fig. 4.7.

Lines 47–50 declare local variables total, gradeCounter, grade and average to be of type int. Variable grade stores the user input. Notice that the preceding declarations appear in the body of member function determineClassAverage.

In this chapter's versions of class GradeBook, we simply read and process a set of grades. The averaging calculation is performed in member function determineClassAverage using local variables—we do not preserve any information about student grades in the

```
 1   // Fig. 4.10: fig04_10.cpp
 2   // Create GradeBook object and invoke its determineClassAverage function.
 3   #include "GradeBook.h" // include definition of class GradeBook
 4
 5   int main()
 6   {
 7      // create GradeBook object myGradeBook and
 8      // pass course name to constructor
 9      GradeBook myGradeBook( "CS101 C++ Programming" );
10
11      myGradeBook.displayMessage(); // display welcome message
12      myGradeBook.determineClassAverage(); // find average of 10 grades
13      return 0; // indicate successful termination
14   } // end main
```

```
Welcome to the grade book for
CS101 C++ Programming

Enter grade: 67
Enter grade: 78
Enter grade: 89
Enter grade: 67
Enter grade: 87
Enter grade: 98
Enter grade: 93
Enter grade: 85
Enter grade: 82
Enter grade: 100

Total of all 10 grades is 846
Class average is 84
```

Fig. 4.10 | Class average problem using counter-controlled repetition: Creating an object of class GradeBook (Fig. 4.8–Fig. 4.9) and invoking its determineClassAverage member function.

class's instance variables. In Chapter 7, Arrays and Vectors, we modify class GradeBook to maintain the grades in memory using an instance variable that refers to a data structure known as an array. This allows a GradeBook object to perform various calculations on the same set of grades without requiring the user to enter the grades multiple times.

 Good Programming Practice 4.5

Separate declarations from other statements in functions with a blank line for readability.

Lines 53–54 initialize total to 0 and gradeCounter to 1. Note that variables total and gradeCounter are initialized before they are used in a calculation. Counter variables normally are initialized to zero or one, depending on their use (we will present examples showing each possibility). An uninitialized variable contains a "garbage" value (also called an undefined value)—the value last stored in the memory location reserved for that variable. Variables grade and average (for the user input and calculated average, respectively) need not be initialized here—their values will be assigned as they are input or calculated later in the function.

Common Programming Error 4.6

Not initializing counters and totals can lead to logic errors.

Error-Prevention Tip 4.2

Initialize each counter and total, either in its declaration or in an assignment statement. Totals are normally initialized to 0. Counters are normally initialized to 0 or 1, depending on how they are used (we will show examples of when to use 0 and when to use 1).

Good Programming Practice 4.6

Declare each variable on a separate line with its own comment to make programs more readable.

Line 57 indicates that the while statement should continue looping (also called iterating) as long as gradeCounter's value is less than or equal to 10. While this condition remains true, the while statement repeatedly executes the statements between the braces that delimit its body (lines 58–63).

Line 59 displays the prompt "Enter grade: ". This line corresponds to the pseudocode statement *"Prompt the user to enter the next grade."* Line 60 reads the grade entered by the user and assigns it to variable grade. This line corresponds to the pseudocode statement *"Input the next grade."* Recall that variable grade was not initialized earlier in the program, because the program obtains the value for grade from the user during each iteration of the loop. Line 61 adds the new grade entered by the user to the total and assigns the result to total, which replaces its previous value.

Line 62 adds 1 to gradeCounter to indicate that the program has processed a grade and is ready to input the next grade from the user. Incrementing gradeCounter eventually causes gradeCounter to exceed 10. At that point the while loop terminates because its condition (line 57) becomes false.

When the loop terminates, line 66 performs the averaging calculation and assigns its result to the variable average. Line 69 displays the text "Total of all 10 grades is " followed by variable total's value. Line 70 then displays the text "Class average is " followed by variable average's value. Member function determineClassAverage, then returns control to the calling function (i.e., main in Fig. 4.10).

Demonstrating Class GradeBook

Figure 4.10 contains this application's main function, which creates an object of class GradeBook and demonstrates its capabilities. Line 9 of Fig. 4.10 creates a new GradeBook object called myGradeBook. The string in line 9 is passed to the GradeBook constructor (lines 12–15 of Fig. 4.9). Line 11 of Fig. 4.10 calls myGradeBook's displayMessage member function to display a welcome message to the user. Line 12 then calls myGradeBook's determineClassAverage member function to allow the user to enter 10 grades, for which the member function then calculates and prints the average—the member function performs the algorithm shown in the pseudocode of Fig. 4.7.

Notes on Integer Division and Truncation

The averaging calculation performed by member function determineClassAverage in response to the function call at line 12 in Fig. 4.10 produces an integer result. The program's output indicates that the sum of the grade values in the sample execution is 846, which, when divided by 10, should yield 84.6—a number with a decimal point. However, the result of the calculation `total / 10` (line 66 of Fig. 4.9) is the integer 84, because `total` and 10 are both integers. Dividing two integers results in integer division—any fractional part of the calculation is lost (i.e., truncated). We will see how to obtain a result that includes a decimal point from the averaging calculation in the next section.

Common Programming Error 4.7

Assuming that integer division rounds (rather than truncates) can lead to incorrect results. For example, 7 ÷ 4, which yields 1.75 in conventional arithmetic, truncates to 1 in integer arithmetic, rather than rounding to 2.

In Fig. 4.9, if line 66 used `gradeCounter` rather than 10 for the calculation, the output for this program would display an incorrect value, 76. This occurs because in the final iteration of the `while` statement, `gradeCounter` was incremented to the value 11 in line 62.

Common Programming Error 4.8

Using a loop's counter-control variable in a calculation after the loop often causes a common logic error called an off-by-one-error. In a counter-controlled loop that counts up by one each time through the loop, the loop terminates when the counter's value is one higher than its last legitimate value (i.e., 11 in the case of counting from 1 to 10).

4.9 Formulating Algorithms: Sentinel-Controlled Repetition

Let us generalize the class average problem. Consider the following problem:

Develop a class average program that processes grades for an arbitrary number of students each time it is run.

In the previous class average example, the problem statement specified the number of students, so the number of grades (10) was known in advance. In this example, no indication is given of how many grades the user will enter during the program's execution. The program must process an arbitrary number of grades. How can the program determine when to stop the input of grades? How will it know when to calculate and print the class average?

One way to solve this problem is to use a special value called a sentinel value (also called a signal value, a dummy value or a flag value) to indicate "end of data entry." The user types grades in until all legitimate grades have been entered. The user then types the sentinel value to indicate that the last grade has been entered. Sentinel-controlled repetition is often called indefinite repetition because the number of repetitions is not known before the loop begins executing.

Clearly, the sentinel value must be chosen so that it cannot be confused with an acceptable input value. Grades on a quiz are normally nonnegative integers, so –1 is an acceptable sentinel value for this problem. Thus, a run of the class average program might process a stream of inputs such as 95, 96, 75, 74, 89 and –1. The program would then compute and print the class average for the grades 95, 96, 75, 74 and 89. Since –1 is the sentinel value, it should not enter into the averaging calculation.

Common Programming Error 4.9

Choosing a sentinel value that is also a legitimate data value is a logic error.

Developing the Pseudocode Algorithm with Top-Down, Stepwise Refinement: The Top and First Refinement

We approach the class average program with a technique called top-down, stepwise refinement, a technique that is essential to the development of well-structured programs. We begin with a pseudocode representation of the *top*—a single statement that conveys the overall function of the program:

> *Determine the class average for the quiz*

The top is, in effect, a *complete* representation of a program. Unfortunately, the top (as in this case) rarely conveys sufficient detail from which to write a program. So we now begin the refinement process. We divide the top into a series of smaller tasks and list these in the order in which they need to be performed. This results in the following first refinement.

> *Initialize variables*
> *Input, sum and count the quiz grades*
> *Calculate and print the total of all student grades and the class average*

This refinement uses only the sequence structure—the steps listed should execute in order, one after the other.

 Software Engineering Observation 4.4

Each refinement, as well as the top itself, is a complete specification of the algorithm; only the level of detail varies.

 Software Engineering Observation 4.5

Many programs can be divided logically into three phases: an initialization phase that initializes the program variables; a processing phase that inputs data values and adjusts program variables (such as counters and totals) accordingly; and a termination phase that calculates and outputs the final results.

Proceeding to the Second Refinement

The preceding *Software Engineering Observation* is often all you need for the first refinement in the top-down process. To proceed to the next level of refinement, i.e., the second refinement, we commit to specific variables. In this example, we need a running total of the numbers, a count of how many numbers have been processed, a variable to receive the value of each grade as it is input by the user and a variable to hold the calculated average. The pseudocode statement

> *Initialize variables*

can be refined as follows:

> *Initialize total to zero*
> *Initialize counter to zero*

Only the variables *total* and *counter* need to be initialized before they are used. The variables *average* and *grade* (for the calculated average and the user input, respectively) need not be initialized, because their values will be replaced as they are calculated or input.

The pseudocode statement

Input, sum and count the quiz grades

requires a repetition statement (i.e., a loop) that successively inputs each grade. We do not know in advance how many grades are to be processed, so we will use sentinel-controlled repetition. The user enters legitimate grades one at a time. After entering the last legitimate grade, the user enters the sentinel value. The program tests for the sentinel value after each grade is input and terminates the loop when the user enters the sentinel value. The second refinement of the preceding pseudocode statement is then

Prompt the user to enter the first grade
Input the first grade (possibly the sentinel)

While the user has not yet entered the sentinel
    Add this grade into the running total
    Add one to the grade counter
    Prompt the user to enter the next grade
    Input the next grade (possibly the sentinel)

In pseudocode, we do not use braces around the statements that form the body of the *While* structure. We simply indent the statements under the *While* to show that they belong to the *While*. Again, pseudocode is only an informal program development aid.

The pseudocode statement

Calculate and print the total of all student grades and the class average

can be refined as follows:

If the counter is not equal to zero
    Set the average to the total divided by the counter
    Print the total of the grades for all students in the class
    Print the class average
else
    Print "No grades were entered"

We are careful here to test for the possibility of division by zero—normally a fatal logic error that, if undetected, would cause the program to fail (often called "bombing" or "crashing"). The complete second refinement of the pseudocode for the class average problem is shown in Fig. 4.11.

Common Programming Error 4.10

An attempt to divide by zero normally causes a fatal runtime error.

Error-Prevention Tip 4.3

When performing division by an expression whose value could be zero, explicitly test for this possibility and handle it appropriately in your program (such as by printing an error message) rather than allowing the fatal error to occur.

In Fig. 4.7 and Fig. 4.11, we include some blank lines and indentation in the pseudocode to make it more readable. The blank lines separate the pseudocode algorithms into their various phases, and the indentation emphasizes the control statement bodies.

1	*Initialize total to zero*
2	*Initialize counter to zero*
3	
4	*Prompt the user to enter the first grade*
5	*Input the first grade (possibly the sentinel)*
6	
7	*While the user has not yet entered the sentinel*
8	*Add this grade into the running total*
9	*Add one to the grade counter*
10	*Prompt the user to enter the next grade*
11	*Input the next grade (possibly the sentinel)*
12	
13	*If the counter is not equal to zero*
14	*Set the average to the total divided by the counter*
15	*Print the total of the grades for all students in the class*
16	*Print the class average*
17	*else*
18	*Print "No grades were entered"*

Fig. 4.11 | Class average problem pseudocode algorithm with sentinel-controlled repetition.

The pseudocode algorithm in Fig. 4.11 solves the more general class average problem. This algorithm was developed after only two levels of refinement. Sometimes more levels are necessary.

Software Engineering Observation 4.6

Terminate the top-down, stepwise refinement process when the pseudocode algorithm is specified in sufficient detail for you to be able to convert the pseudocode to C++. Normally, implementing the C++ program is then straightforward.

Software Engineering Observation 4.7

Many experienced programmers write programs without ever using program development tools like pseudocode. These programmers feel that their ultimate goal is to solve the problem on a computer and that writing pseudocode merely delays the production of final outputs. Although this method might work for simple and familiar problems, it can lead to serious difficulties in large, complex projects.

Implementing Sentinel-Controlled Repetition in Class *GradeBook*

Figures 4.12 and 4.13 show the C++ class GradeBook containing member function determineClassAverage that implements the pseudocode algorithm of Fig. 4.11 (this class is demonstrated in Fig. 4.14). Although each grade entered is an integer, the averaging calculation is likely to produce a number with a decimal point—in other words, a real number or floating-point number (e.g., 7.33, 0.0975 or 1000.12345). The type int cannot represent such a number, so this class must use another type to do so. C++ provides several data types for storing floating-point numbers in memory, including float and double. The primary difference between these types is that, compared to float variables, double variables can store numbers with larger magnitude and finer detail (i.e., more digits to the right of the decimal point—also known as the number's **precision**). This program introduces a special operator called a **cast operator** to force the averaging calculation to produce a floating-point numeric result. These features are explained in detail as we discuss the program.

In this example, we see that control statements can be stacked on top of one another (in sequence) just as a child stacks building blocks. The while statement (lines 67–75 of Fig. 4.13) is immediately followed by an if...else statement (lines 78–90) in sequence. Much of the code in this program is identical to the code in Fig. 4.9, so we concentrate on the new features and issues.

```
1   // Fig. 4.12: GradeBook.h
2   // Definition of class GradeBook that determines a class average.
3   // Member functions are defined in GradeBook.cpp
4   #include <string> // program uses C++ standard string class
5   using std::string;
6
7   // GradeBook class definition
8   class GradeBook
9   {
10  public:
11     GradeBook( string ); // constructor initializes course name
12     void setCourseName( string ); // function to set the course name
13     string getCourseName(); // function to retrieve the course name
14     void displayMessage(); // display a welcome message
15     void determineClassAverage(); // averages grades entered by the user
16  private:
17     string courseName; // course name for this GradeBook
18  }; // end class GradeBook
```

Fig. 4.12 | Class average problem using sentinel-controlled repetition: GradeBook header file.

```
1   // Fig. 4.13: GradeBook.cpp
2   // Member-function definitions for class GradeBook that solves the
3   // class average program with sentinel-controlled repetition.
4   #include <iostream>
5   using std::cout;
6   using std::cin;
7   using std::endl;
8   using std::fixed; // ensures that decimal point is displayed
9
10  #include <iomanip> // parameterized stream manipulators
11  using std::setprecision; // sets numeric output precision
12
13  // include definition of class GradeBook from GradeBook.h
14  #include "GradeBook.h"
15
```

Fig. 4.13 | Class average problem using sentinel-controlled repetition: GradeBook source code file. (Part 1 of 3.)

```
16   // constructor initializes courseName with string supplied as argument
17   GradeBook::GradeBook( string name )
18   {
19      setCourseName( name ); // validate and store courseName
20   } // end GradeBook constructor
21
22   // function to set the course name;
23   // ensures that the course name has at most 25 characters
24   void GradeBook::setCourseName( string name )
25   {
26      if ( name.length() <= 25 ) // if name has 25 or fewer characters
27         courseName = name; // store the course name in the object
28      else // if name is longer than 25 characters
29      { // set courseName to first 25 characters of parameter name
30         courseName = name.substr( 0, 25 ); // select first 25 characters
31         cout << "Name \"" << name << "\" exceeds maximum length (25).\n"
32            << "Limiting courseName to first 25 characters.\n" << endl;
33      } // end if...else
34   } // end function setCourseName
35
36   // function to retrieve the course name
37   string GradeBook::getCourseName()
38   {
39      return courseName;
40   } // end function getCourseName
41
42   // display a welcome message to the GradeBook user
43   void GradeBook::displayMessage()
44   {
45      cout << "Welcome to the grade book for\n" << getCourseName() << "!\n"
46         << endl;
47   } // end function displayMessage
48
49   // determine class average based on 10 grades entered by user
50   void GradeBook::determineClassAverage()
51   {
52      int total; // sum of grades entered by user
53      int gradeCounter; // number of grades entered
54      int grade; // grade value
55      double average; // number with decimal point for average
56
57      // initialization phase
58      total = 0; // initialize total
59      gradeCounter = 0; // initialize loop counter
60
61      // processing phase
62      // prompt for input and read grade from user
63      cout << "Enter grade or -1 to quit: ";
64      cin >> grade; // input grade or sentinel value
65
```

Fig. 4.13 | Class average problem using sentinel-controlled repetition: GradeBook source code file. (Part 2 of 3.)

```
66    // loop until sentinel value read from user
67    while ( grade != -1 ) // while grade is not -1
68    {
69       total = total + grade; // add grade to total
70       gradeCounter = gradeCounter + 1; // increment counter
71
72       // prompt for input and read next grade from user
73       cout << "Enter grade or -1 to quit: ";
74       cin >> grade; // input grade or sentinel value
75    } // end while
76
77    // termination phase
78    if ( gradeCounter != 0 ) // if user entered at least one grade...
79    {
80       // calculate average of all grades entered
81       average = static_cast< double >( total ) / gradeCounter;
82
83       // display total and average (with two digits of precision)
84       cout << "\nTotal of all " << gradeCounter << " grades entered is "
85          << total << endl;
86       cout << "Class average is " << setprecision( 2 ) << fixed << average
87          << endl;
88    } // end if
89    else // no grades were entered, so output appropriate message
90       cout << "No grades were entered" << endl;
91 } // end function determineClassAverage
```

Fig. 4.13 | Class average problem using sentinel-controlled repetition: GradeBook source code file. (Part 3 of 3.)

```
1    // Fig. 4.14: fig04_14.cpp
2    // Create GradeBook object and invoke its determineClassAverage function.
3
4    // include definition of class GradeBook from GradeBook.h
5    #include "GradeBook.h"
6
7    int main()
8    {
9       // create GradeBook object myGradeBook and
10      // pass course name to constructor
11      GradeBook myGradeBook( "CS101 C++ Programming" );
12
13      myGradeBook.displayMessage(); // display welcome message
14      myGradeBook.determineClassAverage(); // find average of 10 grades
15      return 0; // indicate successful termination
16   } // end main
```

Fig. 4.14 | Class average problem using sentinel-controlled repetition: Creating an object of class GradeBook (Fig. 4.12–Fig. 4.13) and invoking its determineClassAverage member function. (Part 1 of 2.)

```
Welcome to the grade book for
CS101 C++ Programming

Enter grade or -1 to quit: 97
Enter grade or -1 to quit: 88
Enter grade or -1 to quit: 72
Enter grade or -1 to quit: -1

Total of all 3 grades entered is 257
Class average is 85.67
```

Fig. 4.14 | Class average problem using sentinel-controlled repetition: Creating an object of class GradeBook (Fig. 4.12–Fig. 4.13) and invoking its determineClassAverage member function. (Part 2 of 2.)

Line 55 declares the double variable average. Recall that we used an int variable in the preceding example to store the class average. Using type double in the current example allows us to store the class average calculation's result as a floating-point number. Line 59 initializes the variable gradeCounter to 0, because no grades have been entered yet. Remember that this program uses sentinel-controlled repetition. To keep an accurate record of the number of grades entered, the program increments variable gradeCounter only when the user enters a valid grade value (i.e., not the sentinel value) and the program completes the processing of the grade. Finally, notice that both input statements (lines 64 and 74) are preceded by an output statement that prompts the user for input.

Good Programming Practice 4.7

Prompt the user for each keyboard input. The prompt should indicate the form of the input and any special input values. For example, in a sentinel-controlled loop, the prompts requesting data entry should explicitly remind the user what the sentinel value is.

Program Logic for Sentinel-Controlled Repetition vs. Counter-Controlled Repetition
Compare the program logic for sentinel-controlled repetition in this application with that for counter-controlled repetition in Fig. 4.9. In counter-controlled repetition, each iteration of the while statement (lines 57–63 of Fig. 4.9) reads a value from the user, for the specified number of iterations. In sentinel-controlled repetition, the program reads the first value (lines 63–64 of Fig. 4.13) before reaching the while. This value determines whether the program's flow of control should enter the body of the while. If the condition of the while is false, the user entered the sentinel value, so the body of the while does not execute (i.e., no grades were entered). If, on the other hand, the condition is true, the body begins execution, and the loop adds the grade value to the total (line 69). Then lines 73–74 in the loop's body input the next value from the user. Next, program control reaches the closing right brace (}) of the body at line 75, so execution continues with the test of the while's condition (line 67). The condition uses the most recent grade input by the user to determine whether the loop's body should execute again. Note that the value of variable grade is always input from the user immediately before the program tests the while condition. This allows the program to determine whether the value just input is the sentinel value *before* the program processes that value (i.e., adds it to the total and incre-

ments `gradeCounter`). If the sentinel value is input, the loop terminates, and the program does not add –1 to the `total`.

After the loop terminates, the `if...else` statement at lines 78–90 executes. The condition at line 78 determines whether any grades were entered. If none were, the `else` part (lines 89–90) of the `if...else` statement executes and displays the message "No grades were entered" and the member function returns control to the calling function.

Notice the block in the `while` loop in Fig. 4.13. Without the braces, the last three statements in the body of the loop would fall outside the loop, causing the computer to interpret this code incorrectly, as follows:

```
// loop until sentinel value read from user
while ( grade != -1 )
   total = total + grade; // add grade to total
gradeCounter = gradeCounter + 1; // increment counter

// prompt for input and read next grade from user
cout << "Enter grade or -1 to quit: ";
cin >> grade;
```

This would cause an infinite loop in the program if the user did not input –1 for the first grade (at line 64).

Common Programming Error 4.11

Omitting the braces that delimit a block can lead to logic errors, such as infinite loops. To prevent this problem, some programmers enclose the body of every control statement in braces, even if the body contains only a single statement.

Floating-Point Number Precision and Memory Requirements

Variables of type `float` represent single-precision floating-point numbers and have seven significant digits on most 32-bit systems today. Variables of type `double` represent double-precision floating-point numbers. These require twice as much memory as `float` variables and provide 15 significant digits on most 32-bit systems today—approximately double the precision of `float` variables. For the range of values required by most programs, variables of type `float` should suffice, but you can use `double` to "play it safe." In some programs, even variables of type `double` will be inadequate—such programs are beyond the scope of this book. Most programmers represent floating-point numbers with type `double`. In fact, C++ treats all floating-point numbers you type in a program's source code (such as 7.33 and 0.0975) as `double` values by default. Such values in the source code are known as floating-point constants. See Appendix C, Fundamental Types, for the ranges of values for `float`s and `double`s.

Floating-point numbers often arise as a result of division. In conventional arithmetic, when we divide 10 by 3, the result is 3.3333333..., with the sequence of 3s repeating infinitely. The computer allocates only a fixed amount of space to hold such a value, so clearly the stored floating-point value can be only an approximation.

Common Programming Error 4.12

Using floating-point numbers in a manner that assumes they are represented exactly (e.g., using them in comparisons for equality) can lead to incorrect results. Floating-point numbers are represented only approximately by most computers.

Although floating-point numbers are not always 100% precise, they have numerous applications. For example, when we speak of a "normal" body temperature of 98.6, we do not need to be precise to a large number of digits. When we read the temperature on a thermometer as 98.6, it may actually be 98.5999473210643. Calling this number simply 98.6 is fine for most applications involving body temperatures. Due to the imprecise nature of floating-point numbers, type `double` is preferred over type `float`, because `double` variables can represent floating-point numbers more accurately. For this reason, we use type `double` throughout the book.

Converting Between Fundamental Types Explicitly and Implicitly

The variable `average` is declared to be of type `double` (line 55 of Fig. 4.13) to capture the fractional result of our calculation. However, `total` and `gradeCounter` are both integer variables. Recall that dividing two integers results in integer division, in which any fractional part of the calculation is lost (i.e., truncated). In the following statement:

```
average = total / gradeCounter;
```

the division calculation is performed first, so the fractional part of the result is lost before it is assigned to `average`. To perform a floating-point calculation with integer values, we must create temporary values that are floating-point numbers for the calculation. C++ provides the unary cast operator to accomplish this task. Line 81 uses the cast operator `static_cast< double >( total )` to create a *temporary* floating-point copy of its operand in parentheses—`total`. Using a cast operator in this manner is called explicit conversion. The value stored in `total` is still an integer.

The calculation now consists of a floating-point value (the temporary `double` version of `total`) divided by the integer `gradeCounter`. The C++ compiler knows how to evaluate only expressions in which the data types of the operands are identical. To ensure that the operands are of the same type, the compiler performs an operation called promotion (also called implicit conversion) on selected operands. For example, in an expression containing values of data types `int` and `double`, C++ promotes `int` operands to `double` values. In our example, we are treating `total` as a `double` (by using the unary cast operator), so the compiler promotes `gradeCounter` to `double`, allowing the calculation to be performed—the result of the floating-point division is assigned to `average`. In Chapter 6, Functions and an Introduction to Recursion, we discuss all the fundamental data types and their order of promotion.

 Common Programming Error 4.13

The cast operator can be used to convert between fundamental numeric types, such as `int` and `double`, and between related class types (as we discuss in Chapter 13, Object-Oriented Programming: Polymorphism). Casting to the wrong type may cause compilation errors or runtime errors.

Cast operators are available for use with every data type and with class types as well. The `static_cast` operator is formed by following keyword `static_cast` with angle brackets (< and >) around a data type name. The cast operator is a unary operator—an operator that takes only one operand. In Chapter 2, we studied the binary arithmetic operators. C++ also supports unary versions of the plus (+) and minus (-) operators, so that the programmer can write such expressions as -7 or +5. Cast operators have higher precedence than other unary operators, such as unary + and unary -. This precedence is higher than that of the multiplicative operators *, / and %, and lower than that of parentheses. We indicate the cast operator with the notation `static_cast< ` *type* ` >()` in our precedence charts (see, for example, Fig. 4.22).

Formatting for Floating-Point Numbers

The formatting capabilities in Fig. 4.13 are discussed here briefly and explained in depth in Chapter 15 of *C++ How to Program, 5/e*. The call to `setprecision` in line 86 (with an argument of 2) indicates that `double` variable `average` should be printed with two digits of precision to the right of the decimal point (e.g., 92.37). This call is referred to as a parameterized stream manipulator (because of the 2 in parentheses). Programs that use these calls must contain the preprocessor directive (line 10)

```
#include <iomanip>
```

Line 11 specifies the names from the `<iomanip>` header file that are used in this program. Note that `endl` is a nonparameterized stream manipulator (because it is not followed by a value or expression in parentheses) and does not require the `<iomanip>` header file. If the precision is not specified, floating-point values are normally output with six digits of precision (i.e., the default precision on most 32-bit systems today), although we will see an exception to this in a moment.

The stream manipulator `fixed` (line 86) indicates that floating-point values should be output in so-called fixed-point format, as opposed to scientific notation. Scientific notation is a way of displaying a number as a floating-point number between the values of 1 and 10, multiplied by a power of 10. For instance, the value 3,100 would be displayed in scientific notation as 3.1×10^3. Scientific notation is useful when displaying values that are very large or very small. Fixed-point formatting, on the other hand, is used to force a floating-point number to display a specific number of digits. Specifying fixed-point formatting also forces the decimal point and trailing zeros to print, even if the value is a whole number amount, such as 88.00. Without the fixed-point formatting option, such a value prints in C++ as 88 without the trailing zeros and without the decimal point. When the stream manipulators `fixed` and `setprecision` are used in a program, the printed value is rounded to the number of decimal positions indicated by the value passed to `setprecision` (e.g., the value 2 in line 86), although the value in memory remains unaltered. For example, the values 87.946 and 67.543 are output as 87.95 and 67.54, respectively. Note that it also is possible to force a decimal point to appear by using stream manipulator `showpoint`. If `showpoint` is specified without `fixed`, then trailing zeros will not print. Like `endl`, stream manipulators `fixed` and `showpoint` are nonparameterized and do not require the `<iomanip>` header file. Both can be found in header `<iostream>`.

Lines 86 and 87 of Fig. 4.13 output the class average. In this example, we display the class average rounded to the nearest hundredth and output it with exactly two digits to the right of the decimal point. The parameterized stream manipulator (line 86) indicates that variable `average`'s value should be displayed with two digits of precision to the right of the decimal point—indicated by `setprecision( 2 )`. The three grades entered during the sample execution of the program in Fig. 4.14 total 257, which yields the average 85.666666.... The parameterized stream manipulator `setprecision` causes the value to be rounded to the specified number of digits. In this program, the average is rounded to the hundredths position and displayed as `85.67`.

4.10 Formulating Algorithms: Nested Control Statements

For the next example, we once again formulate an algorithm by using pseudocode and top-down, stepwise refinement, and write a corresponding C++ program. We have seen that control statements can be stacked on top of one another (in sequence) just as a child stacks building blocks. In this case study, we examine the only other structured way control statements can be connected, namely, by nesting one control statement within another.

Consider the following problem statement:

A college offers a course that prepares students for the state licensing exam for real estate brokers. Last year, ten of the students who completed this course took the exam. The college wants to know how well its students did on the exam. You have been asked to write a program to summarize the results. You have been given a list of these 10 students. Next to each name is written a 1 if the student passed the exam or a 2 if the student failed.

Your program should analyze the results of the exam as follows:

1. Input each test result (i.e., a 1 or a 2). Display the prompting message "Enter result" each time the program requests another test result.

2. Count the number of test results of each type.

3. Display a summary of the test results indicating the number of students who passed and the number who failed.

4. If more than eight students passed the exam, print the message "Raise tuition."

After reading the problem statement carefully, we make the following observations:

1. The program must process test results for 10 students. A counter-controlled loop can be used because the number of test results is known in advance.

2. Each test result is a number—either a 1 or a 2. Each time the program reads a test result, the program must determine whether the number is a 1 or a 2. We test for a 1 in our algorithm. If the number is not a 1, we assume that it is a 2. (Exercise 4.20 considers the consequences of this assumption.)

3. Two counters are used to keep track of the exam results—one to count the number of students who passed the exam and one to count the number of students who failed the exam.

4. After the program has processed all the results, it must decide whether more than eight students passed the exam.

Let us proceed with top-down, stepwise refinement. We begin with a pseudocode representation of the top:

Analyze exam results and decide whether tuition should be raised

Once again, it is important to emphasize that the top is a *complete* representation of the program, but several refinements are likely to be needed before the pseudocode evolves naturally into a C++ program.

Our first refinement is

Initialize variables
Input the 10 exam results, and count passes and failures
Print a summary of the exam results and decide if tuition should be raised

Here, too, even though we have a complete representation of the entire program, further refinement is necessary. We now commit to specific variables. Counters are needed to record the passes and failures, a counter will be used to control the looping process and a variable is needed to store the user input. The last variable is not initialized, because its value is read from the user during each iteration of the loop.

The pseudocode statement

> *Initialize variables*

can be refined as follows:

> *Initialize passes to zero*
> *Initialize failures to zero*
> *Initialize student counter to one*

Notice that only the counters are initialized at the start of the algorithm.

The pseudocode statement

> *Input the 10 exam results, and count passes and failures*

requires a loop that successively inputs the result of each exam. Here it is known in advance that there are precisely 10 exam results, so counter-controlled looping is appropriate. Inside the loop (i.e., nested within the loop), an if...else statement will determine whether each exam result is a pass or a failure and will increment the appropriate counter. The refinement of the preceding pseudocode statement is then

> *While student counter is less than or equal to 10*
> > *Prompt the user to enter the next exam result*
> > *Input the next exam result*
>
> > *If the student passed*
> > > *Add one to passes*
> > *Else*
> > > *Add one to failures*
>
> > *Add one to student counter*

We use blank lines to isolate the *If...Else* control structure, which improves readability.

The pseudocode statement

> *Print a summary of the exam results and decide whether tuition should be raised*

can be refined as follows:

> *Print the number of passes*
> *Print the number of failures*
>
> *If more than eight students passed*
> > *Print "Raise tuition"*

The complete second refinement appears in Fig. 4.15. Notice that blank lines are also used to set off the *While* structure for program readability. This pseudocode is now sufficiently refined for conversion to C++.

Conversion to Class Analysis

The C++ class that implements the pseudocode algorithm is shown in Fig. 4.16–Fig. 4.17, and two sample executions appear in Fig. 4.18.

```
 1    Initialize passes to zero
 2    Initialize failures to zero
 3    Initialize student counter to one
 4
 5    While student counter is less than or equal to 10
 6        Prompt the user to enter the next exam result
 7        Input the next exam result
 8
 9        If the student passed
10            Add one to passes
11        Else
12            Add one to failures
13
14        Add one to student counter
15
16    Print the number of passes
17    Print the number of failures
18
19    If more than eight students passed
20        Print "Raise tuition"
```

Fig. 4.15 | Pseudocode for examination-results problem.

```
 1    // Fig. 4.16: Analysis.h
 2    // Definition of class Analysis that analyzes examination results.
 3    // Member function is defined in Analysis.cpp
 4
 5    // Analysis class definition
 6    class Analysis
 7    {
 8    public:
 9        void processExamResults(); // process 10 students' examination results
10    }; // end class Analysis
```

Fig. 4.16 | Examination-results problem: `Analysis` header file.

```
 1    // Fig. 4.17: Analysis.cpp
 2    // Member-function definitions for class Analysis that
 3    // analyzes examination results.
 4    #include <iostream>
 5    using std::cout;
 6    using std::cin;
 7    using std::endl;
```

Fig. 4.17 | Examination-results problem: Nested control statements in `Analysis` source code file. (Part I of 2.)

```cpp
8
9   // include definition of class Analysis from Analysis.h
10  #include "Analysis.h"
11
12  // process the examination results of 10 students
13  void Analysis::processExamResults()
14  {
15     // initializing variables in declarations
16     int passes = 0; // number of passes
17     int failures = 0; // number of failures
18     int studentCounter = 1; // student counter
19     int result; // one exam result (1 = pass, 2 = fail)
20
21     // process 10 students using counter-controlled loop
22     while ( studentCounter <= 10 )
23     {
24        // prompt user for input and obtain value from user
25        cout << "Enter result (1 = pass, 2 = fail): ";
26        cin >> result; // input result
27
28        // if...else nested in while
29        if ( result == 1 )         // if result is 1,
30           passes = passes + 1;    // increment passes;
31        else                       // else result is not 1, so
32           failures = failures + 1; // increment failures
33
34        // increment studentCounter so loop eventually terminates
35        studentCounter = studentCounter + 1;
36     } // end while
37
38     // termination phase; display number of passes and failures
39     cout << "Passed " << passes << "\nFailed " << failures << endl;
40
41     // determine whether more than eight students passed
42     if ( passes > 8 )
43        cout << "Raise tuition " << endl;
44  } // end function processExamResults
```

Fig. 4.17 | Examination-results problem: Nested control statements in Analysis source code file. (Part 2 of 2.)

```cpp
1   // Fig. 4.18: fig04_18.cpp
2   // Test program for class Analysis.
3   #include "Analysis.h" // include definition of class Analysis
4
5   int main()
6   {
7      Analysis application; // create Analysis object
8      application.processExamResults(); // call function to process results
9      return 0; // indicate successful termination
10  } // end main
```

Fig. 4.18 | Test program for class Analysis. (Part 1 of 2.)

```
Enter result (1 = pass, 2 = fail): 1
Enter result (1 = pass, 2 = fail): 1
Enter result (1 = pass, 2 = fail): 1
Enter result (1 = pass, 2 = fail): 1
Enter result (1 = pass, 2 = fail): 2
Enter result (1 = pass, 2 = fail): 1
Enter result (1 = pass, 2 = fail): 1
Enter result (1 = pass, 2 = fail): 1
Enter result (1 = pass, 2 = fail): 1
Enter result (1 = pass, 2 = fail): 1
Passed 9
Failed 1
Raise tuition
```

```
Enter result (1 = pass, 2 = fail): 1
Enter result (1 = pass, 2 = fail): 2
Enter result (1 = pass, 2 = fail): 2
Enter result (1 = pass, 2 = fail): 1
Enter result (1 = pass, 2 = fail): 1
Enter result (1 = pass, 2 = fail): 1
Enter result (1 = pass, 2 = fail): 2
Enter result (1 = pass, 2 = fail): 1
Enter result (1 = pass, 2 = fail): 1
Enter result (1 = pass, 2 = fail): 2
Passed 6
Failed 4
```

Fig. 4.18 | Test program for class `Analysis`. (Part 2 of 2.)

Lines 16–18 of Fig. 4.17 declare the variables that member function `processExamResults` of class `Analysis` uses to process the examination results. Note that we have taken advantage of a feature of C++ that allows variable initialization to be incorporated into declarations (`passes` is initialized to 0, `failures` is initialized to 0 and `studentCounter` is initialized to 1). Looping programs may require initialization at the beginning of each repetition; such reinitialization normally would be performed by assignment statements rather than in declarations or by moving the declarations inside the loop bodies.

The `while` statement (lines 22–36) loops 10 times. During each iteration, the loop inputs and processes one exam result. Notice that the `if...else` statement (lines 29–32) for processing each result is nested in the `while` statement. If the `result` is 1, the `if...else` statement increments `passes`; otherwise, it assumes the `result` is 2 and increments `failures`. Line 35 increments `studentCounter` before the loop condition is tested again at line 22. After 10 values have been input, the loop terminates and line 39 displays the number of `passes` and the number of `failures`. The `if` statement at lines 42–43 determines whether more than eight students passed the exam and, if so, outputs the message `"Raise Tuition"`.

Demonstrating Class *Analysis*

Figure 4.18 creates an `Analysis` object (line 7) and invokes the object's `processExamResults` member function (line 8) to process a set of exam results entered by the user. Figure 4.18 shows the input and output from two sample executions of the program. At the end of the first sample execution, the condition at line 42 of member function pro-cessExamResults in Fig. 4.17 is true—more than eight students passed the exam, so the program outputs a message indicating that the tuition should be raised.

4.11 Assignment Operators

C++ provides several assignment operators for abbreviating assignment expressions. For example, the statement

    c = c + 3;

can be abbreviated with the addition assignment operator += as

    c += 3;

The += operator adds the value of the expression on the right of the operator to the value of the variable on the left of the operator and stores the result in the variable on the left of the operator. Any statement of the form

    variable = variable operator expression;

in which the same *variable* appears on both sides of the assignment operator and *operator* is one of the binary operators +, -, *, /, or % (or others we'll discuss later in the text), can be written in the form

    variable operator= expression;

Thus the assignment c += 3 adds 3 to c. Figure 4.19 shows the arithmetic assignment operators, sample expressions using these operators and explanations.

4.12 Increment and Decrement Operators

In addition to the arithmetic assignment operators, C++ also provides two unary operators for adding 1 to or subtracting 1 from the value of a numeric variable. These are the unary increment operator, ++, and the unary decrement operator, --, which are summarized in Fig. 4.20. A program can increment by 1 the value of a variable called c using the increment operator, ++, rather than the expression c = c + 1 or c += 1. An increment or decrement operator that is prefixed to (placed before) a variable is referred to as the prefix

Assignment operator	Sample expression	Explanation	Assigns
Assume: int c = 3, d = 5, e = 4, f = 6, g = 12;			
+=	c += 7	c = c + 7	10 to c
-=	d -= 4	d = d - 4	1 to d
*=	e *= 5	e = e * 5	20 to e
/=	f /= 3	f = f / 3	2 to f
%=	g %= 9	g = g % 9	3 to g

Fig. 4.19 | Arithmetic assignment operators.

Operator	Called	Sample expression	Explanation
++	preincrement	++a	Increment a by 1, then use the new value of a in the expression in which a resides.
++	postincrement	a++	Use the current value of a in the expression in which a resides, then increment a by 1.
--	predecrement	--b	Decrement b by 1, then use the new value of b in the expression in which b resides.
--	postdecrement	b--	Use the current value of b in the expression in which b resides, then decrement b by 1.

Fig. 4.20 | Increment and decrement operators.

increment or prefix decrement operator, respectively. An increment or decrement operator that is postfixed to (placed after) a variable is referred to as the postfix increment or postfix decrement operator, respectively.

Using the prefix increment (or decrement) operator to add (or subtract) 1 from a variable is known as preincrementing (or predecrementing) the variable. Preincrementing (or predecrementing) causes the variable to be incremented (decremented) by 1, and then the new value of the variable is used in the expression in which it appears. Using the postfix increment (or decrement) operator to add (or subtract) 1 from a variable is known as postincrementing (or postdecrementing) the variable. Postincrementing (or postdecrementing) causes the current value of the variable to be used in the expression in which it appears, and then the variable's value is incremented (decremented) by 1.

 Good Programming Practice 4.8

Unlike binary operators, the unary increment and decrement operators should be placed next to their operands, with no intervening spaces.

Figure 4.21 demonstrates the difference between the prefix increment and postfix increment versions of the ++ increment operator. The decrement operator (--) works similarly. Note that this example does not contain a class, but just a source code file with function main performing all the application's work. In this chapter and in Chapter 3, you have seen examples consisting of one class (including the header and source code files for this class), as well as another source code file testing the class. This source code file contained function main, which created an object of the class and called its member functions. In this example, we simply want to show the mechanics of the ++ operator, so we use only one source code file with function main. Occasionally, when it does not make sense to try to create a reusable class to demonstrate a simple concept, we will use a mechanical example contained entirely within the main function of a single source code file.

Line 12 initializes the variable c to 5, and line 13 outputs c's initial value. Line 14 outputs the value of the expression c++. This expression postincrements the variable c, so c's original value (5) is output, then c's value is incremented. Thus, line 14 outputs c's initial value (5) again. Line 15 outputs c's new value (6) to prove that the variable's value was indeed incremented in line 14.

```cpp
1   // Fig. 4.21: fig04_21.cpp
2   // Preincrementing and postincrementing.
3   #include <iostream>
4   using std::cout;
5   using std::endl;
6
7   int main()
8   {
9      int c;
10
11     // demonstrate postincrement
12     c = 5; // assign 5 to c
13     cout << c << endl; // print 5
14     cout << c++ << endl; // print 5 then postincrement
15     cout << c << endl; // print 6
16
17     cout << endl; // skip a line
18
19     // demonstrate preincrement
20     c = 5; // assign 5 to c
21     cout << c << endl; // print 5
22     cout << ++c << endl; // preincrement then print 6
23     cout << c << endl; // print 6
24     return 0; // indicate successful termination
25  } // end main
```

```
5
5
6

5
6
6
```

Fig. 4.21 | Preincrementing and postincrementing.

Line 20 resets c's value to 5, and line 21 outputs c's value. Line 22 outputs the value of the expression ++c. This expression preincrements c, so its value is incremented, then the new value (6) is output. Line 23 outputs c's value again to show that the value of c is still 6 after line 22 executes.

The arithmetic assignment operators and the increment and decrement operators can be used to simplify program statements. The three assignment statements in Fig. 4.17

```cpp
passes = passes + 1;
failures = failures + 1;
studentCounter = studentCounter + 1;
```

can be written more concisely with assignment operators as

```cpp
passes += 1;
failures += 1;
studentCounter += 1;
```

with prefix increment operators as

```
++passes;
++failures;
++studentCounter;
```

or with postfix increment operators as

```
passes++;
failures++;
studentCounter++;
```

Note that, when incrementing (++) or decrementing (--) of a variable occurs in a statement by itself, the preincrement and postincrement forms have the same effect, and the predecrement and postdecrement forms have the same effect. It is only when a variable appears in the context of a larger expression that preincrementing the variable and postincrementing the variable have different effects (and similarly for predecrementing and postdecrementing).

Common Programming Error 4.14

Attempting to use the increment or decrement operator on an expression other than a modifiable variable name or reference, e.g., writing ++(x + 1), is a syntax error.

Figure 4.22 shows the precedence and associativity of the operators introduced to this point. The operators are shown top-to-bottom in decreasing order of precedence. The second column indicates the associativity of the operators at each level of precedence. Notice that the conditional operator (?:), the unary operators preincrement (++), predecrement (--), plus (+) and minus (-), and the assignment operators =, +=, -=, *=, /= and %= associate from right to left. All other operators in the operator precedence chart of Fig. 4.22 associate from left to right. The third column names the various groups of operators.

Operators						Associativity	Type
( )						left to right	parentheses
++	--	static_cast< *type* >( )				left to right	unary (postfix)
++	--	+	-			right to left	unary (prefix)
*	/	%				left to right	multiplicative
+	-					left to right	additive
<<	>>					left to right	insertion/extraction
<	<=	>	>=			left to right	relational
==	!=					left to right	equality
?:						right to left	conditional
=	+=	-=	*=	/=	%=	right to left	assignment

Fig. 4.22 | Operator precedence for the operators encountered so far in the text.

4.13 Wrap-Up

This chapter presented basic problem-solving techniques that programmers use in building classes and developing member functions for these classes. We demonstrated how to construct an algorithm (i.e., an approach to solving a problem) in pseudocode, then how to refine the algorithm through several phases of pseudocode development, resulting in C++ code that can be executed as part of a function. You learned how to use top-down, stepwise refinement to plan out the specific actions that a function must perform and the order in which the function must perform them.

You learned that only three types of control structures—sequence, selection and repetition—are needed to develop any algorithm. We demonstrated two of C++'s selection statements—the `if` single-selection statement and the `if...else` double-selection statement. The `if` statement is used to execute a set of statements based on a condition—if the condition is true, the statements execute; if it is not, the statements are skipped. The `if...else` double-selection statement is used to execute one set of statements if a condition is true, and another set of statements if the condition is false. We then discussed the `while` repetition statement, where a set of statements are executed repeatedly as long as a condition is true. We used control-statement stacking to total and compute the average of a set of student grades with counter- and sentinel-controlled repetition, and we used control-statement nesting to analyze and make decisions based on a set of exam results. We introduced assignment operators, which can be used for abbreviating statements. We presented the increment and decrement operators, which can be used to add or subtract the value 1 from a variable. In Chapter 5, Control Statements: Part 2, we continue our discussion of control statements, introducing the `for`, `do...while` and `switch` statements.

Summary

- An algorithm is a procedure for solving a problem in terms of the actions to execute and the order in which to execute them.

- Specifying the order in which statements (actions) execute in a program is called program control.

- Pseudocode helps a programmer think out a program before attempting to write it in a programming language.

- Activity diagrams are part of the Unified Modeling Language (UML)—an industry standard for modeling software systems.

- An activity diagram models the workflow (also called the activity) of a software system.

- Activity diagrams are composed of special-purpose symbols, such as action state symbols, diamonds and small circles. These symbols are connected by transition arrows that represent the flow of the activity.

- Like pseudocode, activity diagrams help programmers develop and represent algorithms.

- An action state is represented as a rectangle with its left and right sides replaced with arcs curving outward. The action expression appears inside the action state.

- The arrows in an activity diagram represent transitions, which indicate the order in which the actions represented by action states occur.

- The solid circle located at the top of an activity diagram represents the initial state—the beginning of the workflow before the program performs the modeled actions.

- The solid circle surrounded by a hollow circle that appears at the bottom of the activity diagram represents the final state—the end of the workflow after the program performs its actions.

- Rectangles with the upper-right corners folded over are called notes in the UML. Notes are explanatory remarks that describe the purpose of symbols in the diagram. A dotted line connects each note with the element that the note describes.

- A diamond or decision symbol in an activity diagram indicates that a decision is to be made. The workflow will continue along a path determined by the symbol's associated guard conditions, which can be true or false. Each transition arrow emerging from a decision symbol has a guard condition (specified in square brackets next to the transition arrow). If a guard condition is true, the workflow enters the action state to which the transition arrow points.

- A diamond in an activity diagram also represents the merge symbol, which joins two flows of activity into one. A merge symbol has two or more transition arrows pointing to the diamond and only one transition arrow pointing from the diamond, to indicate multiple activity flows merging to continue the activity.

- Top-down, stepwise refinement is a process for refining pseudocode by maintaining a complete representation of the program during each refinement.

- There are three types of control structures—sequence, selection and repetition.

- The sequence structure is built into C++—by default, statements execute in the order they appear.

- A selection structure chooses among alternative courses of action.

- The if single-selection statement either performs (selects) an action if a condition is true, or skips the action if the condition is false.

- The if...else double-selection statement performs (selects) an action if a condition is true and performs a different action if the condition is false.

- To include several statements in an if's body (or the body of an else for an if...else statement), enclose the statements in braces ({ and }). A set of statements contained within a pair of braces is called a block. A block can be placed anywhere in a program that a single statement can be placed.

- A null statement, indicating that no action is to be taken, is indicated by a semicolon (;).

- A repetition statement specifies that an action is to be repeated while some condition remains true.

- A value that contains a fractional part is referred to as a floating-point number and is represented approximately by data types such as float and double.

- Counter-controlled repetition is used when the number of repetitions is known before a loop begins executing, i.e., when there is definite repetition.

- The unary cast operator static_cast can be used to create a temporary floating-point copy of its operand.

- Unary operators take only one operand; binary operators take two.

- The parameterized stream manipulator setprecision indicates the number of digits of precision that should be displayed to the right of the decimal point.

- The stream manipulator fixed indicates that floating-point values should be output in so-called fixed-point format, as opposed to scientific notation.

- Sentinel-controlled repetition is used when the number of repetitions is not known before a loop begins executing, i.e., when there is indefinite repetition.

- A nested control statement appears in the body of another control statement.

- C++ provides the arithmetic assignment operators +=, -=, *=, /= and %= for abbreviating assignment expressions.

- The increment operator, ++, and the decrement operator, --, increment or decrement a variable by 1, respectively. If the operator is prefixed to the variable, the variable is incremented or decremented by 1 first, and then its new value is used in the expression in which it appears. If the operator is postfixed to the variable, the variable is first used in the expression in which it appears, and then the variable's value is incremented or decremented by 1.

Terminology

action
action expression
action state
action state symbol
action/decision model of programming
activity diagram
addition assignment operator (+=)
algorithm
approximation of floating-point numbers
arithmetic assignment operators
arrow symbol
assignment operators
associate from left to right
associate from right to left
averaging calculation
binary arithmetic operator
block
"bombing"
bool
cast operator
compound statement
conditional expression
conditional operator (?:)
control statement
control-statement nesting
control-statement stacking
counter
counter-controlled repetition
"crashing"
dangling-else problem
decision symbol
decrement operator (--)
default precision
definite repetition
diamond symbol
dotted line
double data type
double-precision floating-point number
double-selection statement
dummy value
empty statement
executable statement
explicit conversion
fatal logic error
final state
first refinement
fixed-point format
fixed stream manipulator
flag value

float data type
floating-point constant
floating-point number
"garbage" value
goto elimination
goto statement
if...else double-selection statement
implicit conversion
increment operator (++)
indefinite repetition
initial state
integer division
integer promotion
iterating
iterations of a loop
keywords
loop
loop-continuation condition
loop iterations
loop nested within a loop
looping statement
merge symbol
multiple-selection statement
nested control statement
nonparameterized stream manipulator
note
null statement
object-oriented design (OOD)
off-by-one error
operand
operator precedence
order in which actions should execute
parameterized stream manipulator
postdecrement
postfix decrement operator
postfix increment operator
postincrement
precision
predecrement
prefix decrement operator
prefix increment operator
preincrement
procedure
program control
promotion
pseudocode
repetition statement
rounding
scientific notation

second refinement
selection statement
sentinel-controlled repetition
sentinel value
sequence statement
sequence-statement activity diagram
sequential execution
setprecision stream manipulator
showpoint stream manipulator
signal value
single-entry/single-exit control statement
single-selection if statement
single-precision floating-point number
small circle symbol
solid circle symbol
stream manipulator

structured programming
ternary operator
top
top-down, stepwise refinement
total
transfer of control
transition
transition arrow symbol
truncate
unary cast operator
unary minus (–) operator
unary operator
unary plus (+) operator
undefined value
while repetition statement
workflow of a portion of a software system

Self-Review Exercises

4.1   Answer each of the following questions.
   a) All programs can be written in terms of three types of control structures: _____,
       _____ and _____.
   b) The _____ selection statement is used to execute one action when a condition is
       true or a different action when that condition is false.
   c) Repeating a set of instructions a specific number of times is called _____ repetition.
   d) When it is not known in advance how many times a set of statements will be repeated,
       a(n) _____ value can be used to terminate the repetition.

4.2   Write four different C++ statements that each add 1 to integer variable x.

4.3   Write C++ statements to accomplish each of the following:
   a) In one statement, assign the sum of the current value of x and y to z and postincrement
       the value of x.
   b) Determine whether the value of the variable count is greater than 10. If it is, print
       "Count is greater than 10."
   c) Predecrement the variable x by 1, then subtract it from the variable total.
   d) Calculate the remainder after q is divided by divisor and assign the result to q. Write
       this statement two different ways.

4.4   Write C++ statements to accomplish each of the following tasks.
   a) Declare variables sum and x to be of type int.
   b) Set variable x to 1.
   c) Set variable sum to 0.
   d) Add variable x to variable sum and assign the result to variable sum.
   e) Print "The sum is: " followed by the value of variable sum.

4.5   Combine the statements that you wrote in Exercise 4.4 into a program that calculates and
prints the sum of the integers from 1 to 10. Use the while statement to loop through the calculation
and increment statements. The loop should terminate when the value of x becomes 11.

4.6   State the values of each variable after the calculation is performed. Assume that, when each
statement begins executing, all variables have the integer value 5.
   a) product *= x++;
   b) quotient /= ++x;

4.7   Write single C++ statements that do the following:
   a) Input integer variable x with cin and >>.
   b) Input integer variable y with cin and >>.
   c) Set integer variable i to 1.
   d) Set integer variable power to 1.
   e) Multiply variable power by x and assign the result to power.
   f) Postincrement variable i by 1.
   g) Determine whether i is less than or equal to y.
   h) Output integer variable power with cout and <<.

4.8   Write a C++ program that uses the statements in Exercise 4.7 to calculate x raised to the y power. The program should have a while repetition statement.

4.9   Identify and correct the errors in each of the following:
   a) while (c <= 5)
       {
           product *= c;
           c++;
   b) cin << value;
   c) if (gender == 1)
           cout << "Woman" << endl;
       else;
           cout << "Man" << endl;

4.10   What is wrong with the following while repetition statement?

```
while ( z >= 0 )
    sum += z;
```

Answers to Self-Review Exercises

4.1   a) Sequence, selection and repetition. b) if...else. c) Counter-controlled or definite. d) Sentinel, signal, flag or dummy.

4.2   x = x + 1;
       x += 1;
       ++x;
       x++;

4.3   a) z = x++ + y;
       b) if (count > 10)
               cout << "Count is greater than 10" << endl;
       c) total -= --x;
       d) q %= divisor;
           q = q % divisor;

4.4   a) int sum;
           int x;
       b) x = 1;
       c) sum = 0;
       d) sum += x;
           or
           sum = sum + x;
       e) cout << "The sum is: " << sum << endl;

4.5   See the following code:

```
 1   // Exercise 4.5 Solution: ex04_05.cpp
 2   // Calculate the sum of the integers from 1 to 10.
 3   #include <iostream>
 4   using std::cout;
 5   using std::endl;
 6
 7   int main()
 8   {
 9      int sum; // stores sum of integers 1 to 10
10      int x; // counter
11
12      x = 1; // count from 1
13      sum = 0; // initialize sum
14
15      while ( x <= 10 ) // loop 10 times
16      {
17         sum += x; // add x to sum
18         x++; // increment x
19      } // end while
20
21      cout << "The sum is: " << sum << endl;
22      return 0; // indicate successful termination
23   } // end main
```

```
The sum is: 55
```

4.6   a) product = 25, x = 6;
       b) quotient = 0, x = 6;

```
 1   // Exercise 4.6 Solution: ex04_06.cpp
 2   // Calculate the value of product and quotient.
 3   #include <iostream>
 4   using std::cout;
 5   using std::endl;
 6
 7   int main()
 8   {
 9      int x = 5;
10      int product = 5;
11      int quotient = 5;
12
13      // part a
14      product *= x++; // part a statement
15      cout << "Value of product after calculation: " << product << endl;
16      cout << "Value of x after calculation: " << x << endl << endl;
17
18      // part b
19      x = 5; // reset value of x
20      quotient /= ++x; // part b statement
21      cout << "Value of quotient after calculation: " << quotient << endl;
22      cout << "Value of x after calculation: " << x << endl << endl;
23      return 0; // indicate successful termination
24   } // end main
```

```
Value of product after calculation: 25
Value of x after calculation: 6

Value of quotient after calculation: 0
Value of x after calculation: 6
```

4.7　a) cin >> x;
　　b) cin >> y;
　　c) i = 1;
　　d) power = 1;
　　e) power *= x;
　　　 or
　　　 power = power * x;
　　f) i++;
　　g) if (i <= y)
　　h) cout << power << endl;

4.8　See the following code:

```cpp
1   // Exercise 4.8 Solution: ex04_08.cpp
2   // Raise x to the y power.
3   #include <iostream>
4   using std::cout;
5   using std::cin;
6   using std::endl;
7
8   int main()
9   {
10     int x; // base
11     int y; // exponent
12     int i; // counts from 1 to y
13     int power; // used to calculate x raised to power y
14
15     i = 1; // initialize i to begin counting from 1
16     power = 1; // initialize power
17
18     cout << "Enter base as an integer: ";  // prompt for base
19     cin >> x; // input base
20
21     cout << "Enter exponent as an integer: "; // prompt for exponent
22     cin >> y; // input exponent
23
24     // count from 1 to y and multiply power by x each time
25     while ( i <= y )
26     {
27        power *= x;
28        i++;
29     } // end while
30
31     cout << power << endl; // display result
32     return 0; // indicate successful termination
33  } // end main
```

```
Enter base as an integer: 2
Enter exponent as an integer: 3
8
```

4.9 a) Error: Missing the closing right brace of the while body.
Correction: Add closing right brace after the statement c++;.
b) Error: Used stream insertion instead of stream extraction.
Correction: Change << to >>.
c) Error: Semicolon after else results in a logic error. The second output statement will always be executed.
Correction: Remove the semicolon after else.

4.10 The value of the variable z is never changed in the while statement. Therefore, if the loop-continuation condition (z >= 0) is initially true, an infinite loop is created. To prevent the infinite loop, z must be decremented so that it eventually becomes less than 0.

Exercises

4.11 Identify and correct the error(s) in each of the following:

a) ```
if (age >= 65);
    cout << "Age is greater than or equal to 65" << endl;
else
    cout << "Age is less than 65 << endl";
```

b) ```
if ( age >= 65 )
    cout << "Age is greater than or equal to 65" << endl;
else;
    cout << "Age is less than 65 << endl";
```

c) ```
int x = 1, total;

while (x <= 10)
{
   total += x;
   x++;
}
```

d) ```
While ( x <= 100 )
    total += x;
    x++;
```

e) ```
while (y > 0)
{
   cout << y << endl;
   y++;
}
```

**4.12** What does the following program print?

```
1   // Exercise 4.12: ex04_12.cpp
2   // What does this program print?
3   #include <iostream>
4   using std::cout;
5   using std::endl;
```
```

```
6
7   int main()
8   {
9      int y; // declare y
10     int x = 1; // initialize x
11     int total = 0; // initialize total
12
13     while ( x <= 10 ) // loop 10 times
14     {
15        y = x * x; // perform calculation
16        cout << y << endl; // output result
17        total += y; // add y to total
18        x++; // increment counter x
19     } // end while
20
21     cout << "Total is " << total << endl; // display result
22     return 0; // indicate successful termination
23  } // end main
```

For Exercise 4.13 to Exercise 4.16, perform each of these steps:
   a) Read the problem statement.
   b) Formulate the algorithm using pseudocode and top-down, stepwise refinement.
   c) Write a C++ program.
   d) Test, debug and execute the C++ program.

4.13   Drivers are concerned with the mileage obtained by their automobiles. One driver has kept track of several tankfuls of gasoline by recording miles driven and gallons used for each tankful. Develop a C++ program that uses a while statement to input the miles driven and gallons used for each tankful. The program should calculate and display the miles per gallon obtained for each tankful and print the combined miles per gallon obtained for all tankfuls up to this point.

```
Enter the miles used (-1 to quit): 287
Enter gallons: 13
MPG this tankful: 22.076923
Total MPG: 22.076923

Enter the miles used (-1 to quit): 200
Enter gallons: 10
MPG this tankful: 20.000000
Total MPG: 21.173913

Enter the miles used (-1 to quit): 120
Enter gallons: 5
MPG this tankful: 24.000000
Total MPG: 21.678571

Enter miles (-1 to quit): -1
```

4.14   Develop a C++ program that will determine whether a department-store customer has exceeded the credit limit on a charge account. For each customer, the following facts are available:
   a) Account number (an integer)

    b) Balance at the beginning of the month
    c) Total of all items charged by this customer this month
    d) Total of all credits applied to this customer's account this month
    e) Allowed credit limit

The program should use a while statement to input each of these facts, calculate the new balance (= beginning balance + charges – credits) and determine whether the new balance exceeds the customer's credit limit. For those customers whose credit limit is exceeded, the program should display the customer's account number, credit limit, new balance and the message "Credit Limit Exceeded."

```
Enter account number (-1 to end): 100
Enter beginning balance: 5394.78
Enter total charges: 1000.00
Enter total credits: 500.00
Enter credit limit: 5500.00
New balance is 5894.78
Account:      100
Credit limit: 5500.00
Balance:      5894.78
Credit Limit Exceeded.

Enter Account Number (or -1 to quit): 200
Enter beginning balance: 1000.00
Enter total charges: 123.45
Enter total credits: 321.00
Enter credit limit: 1500.00
New balance is 802.45

Enter Account Number (or -1 to quit): 300
Enter beginning balance: 500.00
Enter total charges: 274.73
Enter total credits: 100.00
Enter credit limit: 800.00
New balance is 674.73

Enter Account Number (or -1 to quit): -1
```

4.15 One large chemical company pays its salespeople on a commission basis. The salespeople each receive $200 per week plus 9 percent of their gross sales for that week. For example, a salesperson who sells $5000 worth of chemicals in a week receives $200 plus 9 percent of $5000, or a total of $650. Develop a C++ program that uses a while statement to input each salesperson's gross sales for last week and calculates and displays that salesperson's earnings. Process one salesperson's figures at a time.

```
Enter sales in dollars (-1 to end): 5000.00
Salary is: $650.00

Enter sales in dollars (-1 to end): 6000.00
Salary is: $740.00

Enter sales in dollars (-1 to end): 7000.00
Salary is: $830.00

Enter sales in dollars (-1 to end): -1
```

4.16 Develop a C++ program that uses a `while` statement to determine the gross pay for each of several employees. The company pays "straight time" for the first 40 hours worked by each employee and pays "time-and-a-half" for all hours worked in excess of 40 hours. You are given a list of the employees of the company, the number of hours each employee worked last week and the hourly rate of each employee. Your program should input this information for each employee and should determine and display the employee's gross pay.

```
Enter hours worked (-1 to end): 39
Enter hourly rate of the worker ($00.00): 10.00
Salary is $390.00

Enter hours worked (-1 to end): 40
Enter hourly rate of the worker ($00.00): 10.00
Salary is $400.00

Enter hours worked (-1 to end): 41
Enter hourly rate of the worker ($00.00): 10.00
Salary is $415.00

Enter hours worked (-1 to end): -1
```

4.17 The process of finding the largest number (i.e., the maximum of a group of numbers) is used frequently in computer applications. For example, a program that determines the winner of a sales contest inputs the number of units sold by each salesperson. The salesperson who sells the most units wins the contest. Write a pseudocode program, then a C++ program that uses a `while` statement to determine and print the largest number of 10 numbers input by the user. Your program should use three variables, as follows:

counter:	A counter to count to 10 (i.e., to keep track of how many numbers have been input and to determine when all 10 numbers have been processed).
number:	The current number input to the program.
largest:	The largest number found so far.

4.18 Write a C++ program that uses a `while` statement and the tab escape sequence `\t` to print the following table of values:

```
N       10*N    100*N   1000*N

1       10      100     1000
2       20      200     2000
3       30      300     3000
4       40      400     4000
5       50      500     5000
```

4.19 Using an approach similar to that in Exercise 4.17, find the *two* largest values among the 10 numbers. [*Note:* You must input each number only once.]

4.20 The examination-results program of Fig. 4.16–Fig. 4.18 assumes that any value input by the user that is not a 1 must be a 2. Modify the application to validate its inputs. On any input, if the value entered is other than 1 or 2, keep looping until the user enters a correct value.

4.21   What does the following program print?

```
1   // Exercise 4.21: ex04_21.cpp
2   // What does this program print?
3   #include <iostream>
4   using std::cout;
5   using std::endl;
6
7   int main()
8   {
9      int count = 1; // initialize count
10
11     while ( count <= 10 ) // loop 10 times
12     {
13        // output line of text
14        cout << ( count % 2 ? "****" : "++++++++" ) << endl;
15        count++; // increment count
16     } // end while
17
18     return 0; // indicate successful termination
19  } // end main
```

4.22   What does the following program print?

```
1   // Exercise 4.22: ex04_22.cpp
2   // What does this program print?
3   #include <iostream>
4   using std::cout;
5   using std::endl;
6
7   int main()
8   {
9      int row = 10; // initialize row
10     int column; // declare column
11
12     while ( row >= 1 ) // loop until row < 1
13     {
14        column = 1; // set column to 1 as iteration begins
15
16        while ( column <= 10 ) // loop 10 times
17        {
18           cout << ( row % 2 ? "<" : ">" ); // output
19           column++; // increment column
20        } // end inner while
21
22        row--; // decrement row
23        cout << endl; // begin new output line
24     } // end outer while
25
26     return 0; // indicate successful termination
27  } // end main
```

4.23   *(Dangling-Else Problem)* State the output for each of the following when x is 9 and y is 11 and when x is 11 and y is 9. Note that the compiler ignores the indentation in a C++ program. The C++ compiler always associates an `else` with the previous `if` unless told to do otherwise by the placement of braces {}. On first glance, the programmer may not be sure which `if` and `else` match, so this is referred to as the "dangling-else" problem. We eliminated the indentation from the following code to make the problem more challenging. [*Hint:* Apply indentation conventions you have learned.]

a)
```
if ( x < 10 )
if ( y > 10 )
cout << "*****" << endl;
else
cout << "#####" << endl;
cout << "$$$$$" << endl;
```

b)
```
if ( x < 10 )
{
if ( y > 10 )
cout << "*****" << endl;
}
else
{
cout << "#####" << endl;
cout << "$$$$$" << endl;
}
```

4.24   *(Another Dangling-Else Problem)* Modify the following code to produce the output shown. Use proper indentation techniques. You must not make any changes other than inserting braces. The compiler ignores indentation in a C++ program. We eliminated the indentation from the following code to make the problem more challenging. [*Note:* It is possible that no modification is necessary.]

```
if ( y == 8 )
if ( x == 5 )
cout << "@@@@@" << endl;
else
cout << "#####" << endl;
cout << "$$$$$" << endl;
cout << "&&&&&" << endl;
```

a) Assuming x = 5 and y = 8, the following output is produced.

```
@@@@@
$$$$$
&&&&&
```

b) Assuming x = 5 and y = 8, the following output is produced.

```
@@@@@
```

c) Assuming x = 5 and y = 8, the following output is produced.

```
@@@@@
&&&&&
```

d) Assuming x = 5 and y = 7, the following output is produced. [*Note:* The last three output statements after the `else` are all part of a block.]

```
#####
$$$$$
&&&&&
```

4.25   Write a program that reads in the size of the side of a square and then prints a hollow square of that size out of asterisks and blanks. Your program should work for squares of all side sizes between 1 and 20. For example, if your program reads a size of 5, it should print

```
*****
*   *
*   *
*   *
*****
```

4.26   A palindrome is a number or a text phrase that reads the same backwards as forwards. For example, each of the following five-digit integers is a palindrome: 12321, 55555, 45554 and 11611. Write a program that reads in a five-digit integer and determines whether it is a palindrome. [*Hint:* Use the division and modulus operators to separate the number into its individual digits.]

4.27   Input an integer containing only 0s and 1s (i.e., a "binary" integer) and print its decimal equivalent. Use the modulus and division operators to pick off the "binary" number's digits one at a time from right to left. Much as in the decimal number system, where the rightmost digit has a positional value of 1, the next digit left has a positional value of 10, then 100, then 1000, and so on, in the binary number system the rightmost digit has a positional value of 1, the next digit left has a positional value of 2, then 4, then 8, and so on. Thus the decimal number 234 can be interpreted as 2 * 100 + 3 * 10 + 4 * 1. The decimal equivalent of binary 1101 is 1 * 1 + 0 * 2 + 1 * 4 + 1 * 8 or 1 + 0 + 4 + 8, or 13. [*Note:* The reader not familiar with binary numbers might wish to refer to Appendix D.]

4.28   Write a program that displays the checkerboard pattern shown below. Your program must use only three output statements, one of each of the following forms:

```
cout << "* ";
cout << ' ';
cout << endl;
```

```
* * * * * * * *
 * * * * * * * *
* * * * * * * *
 * * * * * * * *
* * * * * * * *
 * * * * * * * *
* * * * * * * *
 * * * * * * * *
```

4.29   Write a program that prints the powers of the integer 2, namely 2, 4, 8, 16, 32, 64, etc. Your `while` loop should not terminate (i.e., you should create an infinite loop). To do this, simply use the keyword true as the expression for the while statement. What happens when you run this program?

4.30 Write a program that reads the radius of a circle (as a double value) and computes and prints the diameter, the circumference and the area. Use the value 3.14159 for π.

4.31 What is wrong with the following statement? Provide the correct statement to accomplish what the programmer was probably trying to do.

```
cout << ++( x + y );
```

4.32 Write a program that reads three nonzero double values and determines and prints whether they could represent the sides of a triangle.

4.33 Write a program that reads three nonzero integers and determines and prints whether they could be the sides of a right triangle.

4.34 *(Cryptography)* A company wants to transmit data over the telephone, but is concerned that its phones could be tapped. All of the data are transmitted as four-digit integers. The company has asked you to write a program that encrypts the data so that it can be transmitted more securely. Your program should read a four-digit integer and encrypt it as follows: Replace each digit by *(the sum of that digit plus 7) modulus 10*. Then, swap the first digit with the third, swap the second digit with the fourth and print the encrypted integer. Write a separate program that inputs an encrypted four-digit integer and decrypts it to form the original number.

4.35 The factorial of a nonnegative integer n is written $n!$ (pronounced "n factorial") and is defined as follows:

$$n! = n \cdot (n-1) \cdot (n-2) \cdot \ldots \cdot 1 \quad \text{(for values of } n \text{ greater than to 1)}$$

and

$$n! = 1 \quad \text{(for } n = 0 \text{ or } n = 1\text{)}.$$

For example, $5! = 5 \cdot 4 \cdot 3 \cdot 2 \cdot 1$, which is 120. Use while statements in each of the following:

    a) Write a program that reads a nonnegative integer and computes and prints its factorial.

    b) Write a program that estimates the value of the mathematical constant e by using the formula:

$$e = 1 + \frac{1}{1!} + \frac{1}{2!} + \frac{1}{3!} + \ldots$$

        Prompt the user for the desired accuracy of e (i.e., the number of terms in the summation).

    c) Write a program that computes the value of e^x by using the formula

$$e^x = 1 + \frac{x}{1!} + \frac{x^2}{2!} + \frac{x^3}{3!} + \ldots$$

        Prompt the user for the desired accuracy of e (i.e., the number of terms in the summation).

5

Control Statements: Part 2

Not everything that can be counted counts, and not every thing that counts can be counted.
—Albert Einstein

Who can control his fate?
—William Shakespeare

The used key is always bright.
—Benjamin Franklin

Intelligence ... is the faculty of making artificial objects, especially tools to make tools.
—Henri Bergson

Every advantage in the past is judged in the light of the final issue.
—Demosthenes

OBJECTIVES

In this chapter you will learn:

■ The essentials of counter-controlled repetition.

■ To use the **for** and **do...while** repetition statements to execute statements in a program repeatedly.

■ To understand multiple selection using the **switch** selection statement.

■ To use the **break** and **continue** program control statements to alter the flow of control.

■ To use the logical operators to form complex conditional expressions in control statements.

■ To avoid the consequences of confusing the equality and assignment operators.

Outline

5.1 Introduction

5.2 Essentials of Counter-Controlled Repetition

5.3 `for` Repetition Statement

5.4 Examples Using the `for` Statement

5.5 `do...while` Repetition Statement

5.6 `switch` Multiple-Selection Statement

5.7 `break` and `continue` Statements

5.8 Logical Operators

5.9 Confusing Equality (`==`) and Assignment (`=`) Operators

5.10 Structured Programming Summary

5.11 Wrap-Up

Summary | Terminology | Self-Review Exercises | Answers to Self-Review Exercises | Exercises

5.1 Introduction

Chapter 4 began our introduction to the types of building blocks that are available for problem solving. We used those building blocks to employ proven program construction techniques. In this chapter, we continue our presentation of the theory and principles of structured programming by introducing C++'s remaining control statements. The control statements we study here and in Chapter 4 will help us in building and manipulating objects. We continue our early emphasis on object-oriented programming that began with a discussion of basic concepts in Chapter 1 and extensive object-oriented code examples and exercises in Chapters 3–4.

In this chapter, we demonstrate the `for`, `do...while` and `switch` statements. Through a series of short examples using `while` and `for`, we explore the essentials of counter-controlled repetition. We devote a portion of the chapter to expanding the `GradeBook` class presented in Chapters 3–4. In particular, we create a version of class `GradeBook` that uses a `switch` statement to count the number of A, B, C, D and F grades in a set of letter grades entered by the user. We introduce the `break` and `continue` program control statements. We discuss the logical operators, which enable programmers to use more powerful conditional expressions in control statements. We also examine the common error of confusing the equality (`==`) and assignment (`=`) operators, and how to avoid it. Finally, we summarize C++'s control statements and the proven problem-solving techniques presented in this chapter and Chapter 4.

5.2 Essentials of Counter-Controlled Repetition

This section uses the `while` repetition statement introduced in Chapter 4 to formalize the elements required to perform counter-controlled repetition. Counter-controlled repetition requires

1. the *name* of a control variable (or loop counter)

2. the *initial value* of the control variable

3. the loop-continuation condition that tests for the final value of the control variable (i.e., whether looping should continue)

4. the increment (or decrement) by which the control variable is modified each time through the loop.

Consider the simple program in Fig. 5.1, which prints the numbers from 1 to 10. The declaration at line 9 *names* the control variable (counter), declares it to be an integer, reserves space for it in memory and sets it to an *initial value* of 1. Declarations that require initialization are, in effect, executable statements. In C++, it is more precise to call a declaration that also reserves memory—as the preceding declaration does—a definition. Because definitions are declarations, too, we will use the term "declaration" except when the distinction is important.

The declaration and initialization of counter (line 9) also could have been accomplished with the statements

```
int counter; // declare control variable
counter = 1; // initialize control variable to 1
```

We use both methods of initializing variables.

Line 14 *increments* the loop counter by 1 each time the loop's body is performed. The loop-continuation condition (line 11) in the while statement determines whether the value of the control variable is less than or equal to 10 (the final value for which the condition is true). Note that the body of this while executes even when the control variable is 10. The loop terminates when the control variable is greater than 10 (i.e., when counter becomes 11).

```cpp
1   // Fig. 5.1: fig05_01.cpp
2   // Counter-controlled repetition.
3   #include <iostream>
4   using std::cout;
5   using std::endl;
6
7   int main()
8   {
9      int counter = 1; // declare and initialize control variable
10
11     while ( counter <= 10 ) // loop-continuation condition
12     {
13        cout << counter << " ";
14        counter++; // increment control variable by 1
15     } // end while
16
17     cout << endl; // output a newline
18     return 0; // successful termination
19  } // end main
```

```
1 2 3 4 5 6 7 8 9 10
```

Fig. 5.1 | Counter-controlled repetition.

Figure 5.1 can be made more concise by initializing counter to 0 and by replacing the while statement with

```
while ( ++counter <= 10 ) // loop-continuation condition
    cout << counter << " ";
```

This code saves a statement, because the incrementing is done directly in the while condition before the condition is tested. Also, the code eliminates the braces around the body of the while, because the while now contains only one statement. Coding in such a condensed fashion takes some practice and can lead to programs that are more difficult to read, debug, modify and maintain.

Common Programming Error 5.1

Floating-point values are approximate, so controlling counting loops with floating-point variables can result in imprecise counter values and inaccurate tests for termination.

Error-Prevention Tip 5.1

Control counting loops with integer values.

Good Programming Practice 5.1

Put a blank line before and after each control statement to make it stand out in the program.

Good Programming Practice 5.2

Too many levels of nesting can make a program difficult to understand. As a rule, try to avoid using more than three levels of indentation.

Good Programming Practice 5.3

Vertical spacing above and below control statements and indentation of the bodies of control statements within the control statement headers give programs a two-dimensional appearance that greatly improves readability.

5.3 for Repetition Statement

Section 5.2 presented the essentials of counter-controlled repetition. The while statement can be used to implement any counter-controlled loop. C++ also provides the **for repetition statement**, which specifies the counter-controlled repetition details in a single line of code. To illustrate the power of for, let us rewrite the program of Fig. 5.1. The result is shown in Fig. 5.2.

When the for statement (lines 11–12) begins executing, the control variable counter is declared and initialized to 1. Then, the loop-continuation condition counter <= 10 is checked. The initial value of counter is 1, so the condition is satisfied and the body statement (line 12) prints the value of counter, namely 1. Then, the expression counter++ increments control variable counter and the loop begins again with the loop-continuation test. The control variable is now equal to 2, so the final value is not exceeded and the program performs the body statement again. This process continues until the loop body has executed 10 times and the control variable counter is incremented to 11—this causes the loop-continuation test (line 11 between the semicolons) to fail and repetition to terminate. The program continues by performing the first statement after the for statement (in this case, the output statement at line 14).

```
 1    // Fig. 5.2: fig05_02.cpp
 2    // Counter-controlled repetition with the for statement.
 3    #include <iostream>
 4    using std::cout;
 5    using std::endl;
 6
 7    int main()
 8    {
 9        // for statement header includes initialization,
10        // loop-continuation condition and increment.
11        for ( int counter = 1; counter <= 10; counter++ )
12            cout << counter << " ";
13
14        cout << endl; // output a newline
15        return 0; // indicate successful termination
16    } // end main
```

```
1 2 3 4 5 6 7 8 9 10
```

Fig. 5.2 | Counter-controlled repetition with the `for` statement.

for *Statement Header Components*

Figure 5.3 takes a closer look at the `for` statement header (line 11) of Fig. 5.2. Notice that the `for` statement header "does it all"—it specifies each of the items needed for counter-controlled repetition with a control variable. If there is more than one statement in the body of the `for`, braces are required to enclose the body of the loop.

Notice that Fig. 5.2 uses the loop-continuation condition `counter <= 10`. If the programmer incorrectly wrote `counter < 10`, then the loop would execute only 9 times. This is a common off-by-one error.

 Common Programming Error 5.2

Using an incorrect relational operator or using an incorrect final value of a loop counter in the condition of a `while` or `for` statement can cause off-by-one errors.

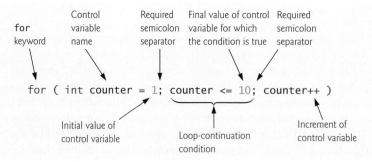

Fig. 5.3 | `for` statement header components.

Good Programming Practice 5.4

Using the final value in the condition of a while *or* for *statement and using the* <= *relational operator will help avoid off-by-one errors. For a loop used to print the values 1 to 10, for example, the loop-continuation condition should be* counter <= 10 *rather than* counter < 10 *(which is an off-by-one error) or* counter < 11 *(which is nevertheless correct). Many programmers prefer so-called* zero-based counting, *in which, to count 10 times through the loop,* counter *would be initialized to zero and the loop-continuation test would be* counter < 10.

The general form of the for statement is

> for (*initialization*; *loopContinuationCondition*; *increment*)
>   *statement*

where the *initialization* expression initializes the loop's control variable, *loopContinuation-Condition* determines whether the loop should continue executing (this condition typically contains the final value of the control variable for which the condition is true) and *increment* increments the control variable. In most cases, the for statement can be represented by an equivalent while statement, as follows:

> *initialization*;
>
> while (*loopContinuationCondition*)
> {
>   *statement*
>   *increment*;
> }

There is an exception to this rule, which we will discuss in Section 5.7.

If the *initialization* expression in the for statement header declares the control variable (i.e., the control variable's type is specified before the variable name), the control variable can be used only in the body of the for statement—the control variable will be unknown outside the for statement. This restricted use of the control variable name is known as the variable's scope. The scope of a variable specifies where it can be used in a program. Scope is discussed in detail in Chapter 6, Functions and an Introduction to Recursion.

Common Programming Error 5.3

When the control variable of a for *statement is declared in the initialization section of the* for *statement header, using the control variable after the body of the statement is a compilation error.*

Portability Tip 5.1

In the C++ standard, the scope of the control variable declared in the initialization section of a for *statement differs from the scope in older C++ compilers. In pre-standard compilers, the scope of the control variable does not terminate at the end of the block defining the body of the* for *statement; rather, the scope terminates at the end of the block that encloses the* for *statement. C++ code created with prestandard C++ compilers can break when compiled on standard-compliant compilers. If you are working with prestandard compilers and you want to be sure your code will work with standard-compliant compilers, there are two defensive programming strategies you can use: either declare control variables with different names in every* for *statement, or, if you prefer to use the same name for the control variable in several* for *statements, declare the control variable before the first* for *statement.*

As we will see, the *initialization* and *increment* expressions can be comma-separated lists of expressions. The commas, as used in these expressions, are comma operators, which guarantee that lists of expressions evaluate from left to right. The comma operator has the lowest precedence of all C++ operators. The value and type of a comma-separated list of expressions is the value and type of the rightmost expression in the list. The comma operator most often is used in `for` statements. Its primary application is to enable the programmer to use multiple initialization expressions and/or multiple increment expressions. For example, there may be several control variables in a single `for` statement that must be initialized and incremented.

Good Programming Practice 5.5

Place only expressions involving the control variables in the initialization and increment sections of a `for` statement. Manipulations of other variables should appear either before the loop (if they should execute only once, like initialization statements) or in the loop body (if they should execute once per repetition, like incrementing or decrementing statements).

The three expressions in the `for` statement header are optional (but the two semicolon separators are required). If the *loopContinuationCondition* is omitted, C++ assumes that the condition is true, thus creating an infinite loop. One might omit the *initialization* expression if the control variable is initialized earlier in the program. One might omit the *increment* expression if the increment is calculated by statements in the body of the `for` or if no increment is needed. The increment expression in the `for` statement acts as a stand-alone statement at the end of the body of the `for`. Therefore, the expressions

```
counter = counter + 1
counter += 1
++counter
counter++
```

are all equivalent in the incrementing portion of the `for` statement (when no other code appears there). Many programmers prefer the form `counter++`, because `for` loops evaluate the increment expression after the loop body executes. The postincrementing form therefore seems more natural. The variable being incremented here does not appear in a larger expression, so both preincrementing and postincrementing actually have the same effect.

Common Programming Error 5.4

Using commas instead of the two required semicolons in a `for` header is a syntax error.

Common Programming Error 5.5

Placing a semicolon immediately to the right of the right parenthesis of a `for` header makes the body of that `for` statement an empty statement. This is usually a logic error.

Software Engineering Observation 5.1

Placing a semicolon immediately after a `for` header is sometimes used to create a so-called delay loop. Such a `for` loop with an empty body still loops the indicated number of times, doing nothing other than the counting. For example, you might use a delay loop to slow down a program that is producing outputs on the screen too quickly for you to read them. Be careful though, because such a time delay will vary among systems with different processor speeds.

The initialization, loop-continuation condition and increment expressions of a for statement can contain arithmetic expressions. For example, if x = 2 and y = 10, and x and y are not modified in the loop body, the for header

```
for ( int j = x; j <= 4 * x * y; j += y / x )
```

is equivalent to

```
for ( int j = 2; j <= 80; j += 5 )
```

The "increment" of a for statement can be negative, in which case it is really a decrement and the loop actually counts downward (as shown in Section 5.4).

If the loop-continuation condition is initially false, the body of the for statement is not performed. Instead, execution proceeds with the statement following the for.

Frequently, the control variable is printed or used in calculations in the body of a for statement, but this is not required. It is common to use the control variable for controlling repetition while never mentioning it in the body of the for statement.

Error-Prevention Tip 5.2

Although the value of the control variable can be changed in the body of a for statement, avoid doing so, because this practice can lead to subtle logic errors.

for *Statement UML Activity Diagram*

The for statement's UML activity diagram is similar to that of the while statement (Fig. 4.6). Figure 5.4 shows the activity diagram of the for statement in Fig. 5.2. The diagram makes it clear that initialization occurs once before the loop-continuation test is

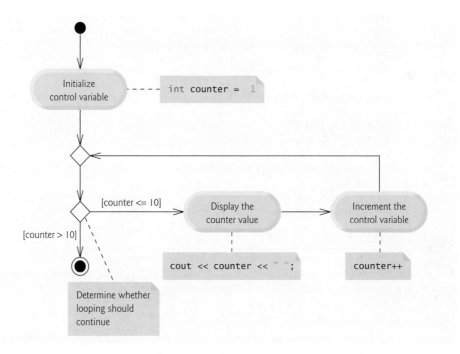

Fig. 5.4 | UML activity diagram for the for statement in Fig. 5.2.

evaluated the first time, and that incrementing occurs each time through the loop *after* the body statement executes. Note that (besides an initial state, transition arrows, a merge, a final state and several notes) the diagram contains only action states and a decision. Imagine, again, that the programmer has a bin of empty for statement UML activity diagrams—as many as the programmer might need to stack and nest with the activity diagrams of other control statements to form a structured implementation of an algorithm. The programmer fills in the action states and decision symbols with action expressions and guard conditions appropriate to the algorithm.

5.4 Examples Using the for Statement

The following examples show methods of varying the control variable in a for statement. In each case, we write the appropriate for statement header. Note the change in the relational operator for loops that decrement the control variable.

a) Vary the control variable from 1 to 100 in increments of 1.

```
for ( int i = 1; i <= 100; i++ )
```

b) Vary the control variable from 100 down to 1 in increments of -1 (that is, decrements of 1).

```
for ( int i = 100; i >= 1; i-- )
```

c) Vary the control variable from 7 to 77 in steps of 7.

```
for ( int i = 7; i <= 77; i += 7 )
```

d) Vary the control variable from 20 down to 2 in steps of -2.

```
for ( int i = 20; i >= 2; i -= 2 )
```

e) Vary the control variable over the following sequence of values: 2, 5, 8, 11, 14, 17, 20.

```
for ( int i = 2; i <= 20; i += 3 )
```

f) Vary the control variable over the following sequence of values: 99, 88, 77, 66, 55, 44, 33, 22, 11, 0.

```
for ( int i = 99; i >= 0; i -= 11 )
```

 Common Programming Error 5.6

Not using the proper relational operator in the loop-continuation condition of a loop that counts downward (such as incorrectly using i <= 1 instead of i >= 1 in a loop counting down to 1) is usually a logic error that yields incorrect results when the program runs.

Application: Summing the Even Integers from 2 to 20

The next two examples provide simple applications of the for statement. The program of Fig. 5.5 uses a for statement to sum the even integers from 2 to 20. Each iteration of the loop (lines 12–13) adds the current value of the control variable number to variable total.

```
1   // Fig. 5.5: fig05_05.cpp
2   // Summing integers with the for statement.
3   #include <iostream>
4   using std::cout;
5   using std::endl;
6
7   int main()
8   {
9      int total = 0; // initialize total
10
11     // total even integers from 2 through 20
12     for ( int number = 2; number <= 20; number += 2 )
13        total += number;
14
15     cout << "Sum is " << total << endl; // display results
16     return 0; // successful termination
17   } // end main
```

```
Sum is 110
```

Fig. 5.5 | Summing integers with the **for** statement.

Note that the body of the for statement in Fig. 5.5 actually could be merged into the increment portion of the for header by using the comma operator as follows:

```
for ( int number = 2; // initialization
      number <= 20; // loop continuation condition
      total += number, number += 2 ) // total and increment
   ; // empty body
```

Good Programming Practice 5.6

Although statements preceding a for and statements in the body of a for often can be merged into the for header, doing so can make the program more difficult to read, maintain, modify and debug.

Good Programming Practice 5.7

Limit the size of control statement headers to a single line, if possible.

Application: Compound Interest Calculations

The next example computes compound interest using a for statement. Consider the following problem statement:

> *A person invests $1000.00 in a savings account yielding 5 percent interest. Assuming that all interest is left on deposit in the account, calculate and print the amount of money in the account at the end of each year for 10 years. Use the following formula for determining these amounts:*
> $$a = p (1 + r)^n$$
> *where*
> > p *is the original amount invested (i.e., the principal),*
> > r *is the annual interest rate,*
> > n *is the number of years and*
> > a *is the amount on deposit at the end of the nth year.*

This problem involves a loop that performs the indicated calculation for each of the 10 years the money remains on deposit. The solution is shown in Fig. 5.6.

The for statement (lines 28–35) executes its body 10 times, varying a control variable from 1 to 10 in increments of 1. C++ does not include an exponentiation operator, so we use the standard library function pow (line 31) for this purpose. The function pow(x, y) calculates the value of x raised to the yth power. In this example, the algebraic expression $(1 + r)^{n}$ is written as pow(1.0 + rate, year), where variable rate represents r and variable year represents n. Function pow takes two arguments of type double and returns a double value.

This program will not compile without including header file <cmath> (line 12). Function pow requires two double arguments. Note that year is an integer. Header <cmath>

```cpp
1   // Fig. 5.6: fig05_06.cpp
2   // Compound interest calculations with for.
3   #include <iostream>
4   using std::cout;
5   using std::endl;
6   using std::fixed;
7
8   #include <iomanip>
9   using std::setw; // enables program to set a field width
10  using std::setprecision;
11
12  #include <cmath> // standard C++ math library
13  using std::pow; // enables program to use function pow
14
15  int main()
16  {
17     double amount; // amount on deposit at end of each year
18     double principal = 1000.0; // initial amount before interest
19     double rate = .05; // interest rate
20
21     // display headers
22     cout << "Year" << setw( 21 ) << "Amount on deposit" << endl;
23
24     // set floating-point number format
25     cout << fixed << setprecision( 2 );
26
27     // calculate amount on deposit for each of ten years
28     for ( int year = 1; year <= 10; year++ )
29     {
30        // calculate new amount for specified year
31        amount = principal * pow( 1.0 + rate, year );
32
33        // display the year and the amount
34        cout << setw( 4 ) << year << setw( 21 ) << amount << endl;
35     } // end for
36
37     return 0; // indicate successful termination
38  } // end main
```

Fig. 5.6 | Compound interest calculations with for. (Part 1 of 2.)

```
Year     Amount on deposit
  1             1050.00
  2             1102.50
  3             1157.63
  4             1215.51
  5             1276.28
  6             1340.10
  7             1407.10
  8             1477.46
  9             1551.33
 10             1628.89
```

Fig. 5.6 | Compound interest calculations with for. (Part 2 of 2.)

includes information that tells the compiler to convert the value of year to a temporary double representation before calling the function. This information is contained in pow's function prototype. Chapter 6 provides a summary of other math library functions.

 Common Programming Error 5.7

In general, forgetting to include the appropriate header file when using standard library functions (e.g., <cmath> in a program that uses math library functions) is a compilation error.

A Caution about Using Type **double** for Monetary Amounts

Notice that lines 17–19 declare the variables amount, principal and rate to be of type double. We have done this for simplicity because we are dealing with fractional parts of dollars, and we need a type that allows decimal points in its values. Unfortunately, this can cause trouble. Here is a simple explanation of what can go wrong when using float or double to represent dollar amounts (assuming setprecision(2) is used to specify two digits of precision when printing): Two dollar amounts stored in the machine could be 14.234 (which prints as 14.23) and 18.673 (which prints as 18.67). When these amounts are added, they produce the internal sum 32.907, which prints as 32.91. Thus your printout could appear as

```
  14.23
+ 18.67
-------
  32.91
```

but a person adding the individual numbers as printed would expect the sum 32.90! You have been warned!

 Good Programming Practice 5.8

Do not use variables of type float or double to perform monetary calculations. The imprecision of floating-point numbers can cause errors that result in incorrect monetary values. In the Exercises, we explore the use of integers to perform monetary calculations. [Note: Some third-party vendors sell C++ class libraries that perform precise monetary calculations. We include several URLs in Appendix E.]

Using Stream Manipulators to Format Numeric Output

The output statement at line 25 before the for loop and the output statement at line 34 in the for loop combine to print the values of the variables year and amount with the formatting specified by the parameterized stream manipulators `setprecision` and `setw` and the nonparameterized stream manipulator `fixed`. The stream manipulator `setw( 4 )` specifies that the next value output should appear in a field width of 4—i.e., `cout` prints the value with at least 4 character positions. If the value to be output is less than 4 character positions wide, the value is right justified in the field by default. If the value to be output is more than 4 character positions wide, the field width is extended to accommodate the entire value. To indicate that values should be output left justified, simply output nonparameterized stream manipulator `left` (found in header `<iostream>`). Right justification can be restored by outputting nonparameterized stream manipulator `right`.

The other formatting in the output statements indicates that variable `amount` is printed as a fixed-point value with a decimal point (specified in line 25 with the stream manipulator `fixed`) right justified in a field of 21 character positions (specified in line 34 with `setw( 21 )`) and two digits of precision to the right of the decimal point (specified in line 25 with manipulator `setprecision( 2 )`). We applied the stream manipulators `fixed` and `setprecision` to the output stream (i.e., `cout`) before the `for` loop because these format settings remain in effect until they are changed—such settings are called sticky settings. Thus, they do not need to be applied during each iteration of the loop. However, the field width specified with `setw` applies only to the next value output. We discuss C++'s powerful input/output formatting capabilities in detail in Chapter 15 of *C++ How to Program*.

Note that the calculation `1.0 + rate`, which appears as an argument to the `pow` function, is contained in the body of the `for` statement. In fact, this calculation produces the same result during each iteration of the loop, so repeating it is wasteful—it should be performed once before the loop.

Performance Tip 5.1

Avoid placing expressions whose values do not change inside loops—but, even if you do, many of today's sophisticated optimizing compilers will automatically place such expressions outside the loops in the generated machine-language code.

Performance Tip 5.2

Many compilers contain optimization features that improve the performance of the code you write, but it is still better to write good code from the start.

For fun, be sure to try our Peter Minuit problem in Exercise 5.29. This problem demonstrates the wonders of compound interest.

5.5 do...while Repetition Statement

The do...while repetition statement is similar to the `while` statement. In the `while` statement, the loop-continuation condition test occurs at the beginning of the loop before the body of the loop executes. The do...while statement tests the loop-continuation condition *after* the loop body executes; therefore, the loop body always executes at least once. When a do...while terminates, execution continues with the statement after the `while` clause. Note that it is not necessary to use braces in the do...while statement if there is only one statement in the body; however, most programmers include the braces to avoid confusion between the `while` and do...while statements. For example,

```
while ( condition )
```

normally is regarded as the header of a while statement. A do...while with no braces around the single statement body appears as

```
do
    statement
while ( condition );
```

which can be confusing. The last line—while(*condition*);—might be misinterpreted by the reader as a while statement containing as its body an empty statement. Thus, the do...while with one statement is often written as follows to avoid confusion:

```
do
{
    statement
} while ( condition );
```

Good Programming Practice 5.9

Always including braces in a do...while statement helps eliminate ambiguity between the while statement and the do...while statement containing one statement.

Figure 5.7 uses a do...while statement to print the numbers 1–10. Upon entering the do...while statement, line 13 outputs counter's value and line 14 increments counter. Then the program evaluates the loop-continuation test at the bottom of the loop (line 15). If the condition is true, the loop continues from the first body statement in the do...while (line 13). If the condition is false, the loop terminates and the program continues with the next statement after the loop (line 17).

do...while Statement UML Activity Diagram

Figure 5.8 contains the UML activity diagram for the do...while statement. This diagram makes it clear that the loop-continuation condition is not evaluated until after the loop performs the loop-body action states at least once. Compare this activity diagram with that

```cpp
1   // Fig. 5.7: fig05_07.cpp
2   // do...while repetition statement.
3   #include <iostream>
4   using std::cout;
5   using std::endl;
6
7   int main()
8   {
9       int counter = 1; // initialize counter
10
11      do
12      {
13          cout << counter << " "; // display counter
14          counter++; // increment counter
15      } while ( counter <= 10 ); // end do...while
16
17      cout << endl; // output a newline
18      return 0; // indicate successful termination
19  } // end main
```

Fig. 5.7 | do...while repetition statement. (Part 1 of 2.)

```
1 2 3 4 5 6 7 8 9 10
```

Fig. 5.7 | do...while repetition statement. (Part 2 of 2.)

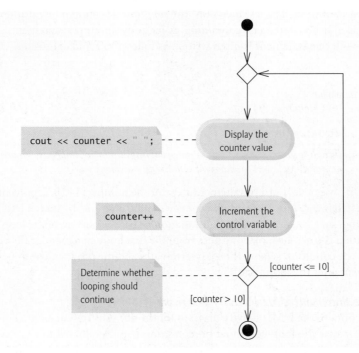

Fig. 5.8 | UML activity diagram for the do...while repetition statement of Fig. 5.7.

of the while statement (Fig. 4.6). Again, note that (besides an initial state, transition arrows, a merge, a final state and several notes) the diagram contains only action states and a decision. Imagine, again, that the programmer has access to a bin of empty do...while statement UML activity diagrams—as many as the programmer might need to stack and nest with the activity diagrams of other control statements to form a structured implementation of an algorithm. The programmer fills in the action states and decision symbols with action expressions and guard conditions appropriate to the algorithm.

5.6 switch Multiple-Selection Statement

We discussed the if single-selection statement and the if...else double-selection statement in Chapter 4. C++ provides the switch multiple-selection statement to perform many different actions based on the possible values of a variable or expression. Each action is associated with the value of a constant integral expression (i.e., any combination of character constants and integer constants that evaluates to a constant integer value) that the variable or expression on which the switch is based may assume.

GradeBook Class with switch Statement to Count A, B, C, D and F Grades

In the next example, we present an enhanced version of the GradeBook class introduced in Chapter 3 and further developed in Chapter 4. The new version of the class asks the user to enter a set of letter grades, then displays a summary of the number of students who received each grade. The class uses a switch to determine whether each grade entered is an A, B, C, D or F and to increment the appropriate grade counter. Class GradeBook is defined in Fig. 5.9, and its member-function definitions appear in Fig. 5.10. Figure 5.11 shows sample inputs and outputs of the main program that uses class GradeBook to process a set of grades.

Like earlier versions of the class definition, the GradeBook class definition (Fig. 5.9) contains function prototypes for member functions setCourseName (line 13), getCourseName (line 14) and displayMessage (line 15), as well as the class's constructor (line 12). The class definition also declares private data member courseName (line 19).

Class GradeBook (Fig. 5.9) now contains five additional private data members (lines 20–24)—counter variables for each grade category (i.e., A, B, C, D and F). The class also contains two additional public member functions—inputGrades and displayGradeReport. Member function inputGrades (declared in line 16) reads an arbitrary number of letter grades from the user using sentinel-controlled repetition and updates the appropriate grade counter for each grade entered. Member function displayGradeReport (declared in line 17) outputs a report containing the number of students who received each letter grade.

Source-code file GradeBook.cpp (Fig. 5.10) contains the member-function definitions for class GradeBook. Notice that lines 16–20 in the constructor initialize the five

```
 1   // Fig. 5.9: GradeBook.h
 2   // Definition of class GradeBook that counts A, B, C, D and F grades.
 3   // Member functions are defined in GradeBook.cpp
 4
 5   #include <string> // program uses C++ standard string class
 6   using std::string;
 7
 8   // GradeBook class definition
 9   class GradeBook
10   {
11   public:
12      GradeBook( string ); // constructor initializes course name
13      void setCourseName( string ); // function to set the course name
14      string getCourseName(); // function to retrieve the course name
15      void displayMessage(); // display a welcome message
16      void inputGrades(); // input arbitrary number of grades from user
17      void displayGradeReport(); // display a report based on the grades
18   private:
19      string courseName; // course name for this GradeBook
20      int aCount; // count of A grades
21      int bCount; // count of B grades
22      int cCount; // count of C grades
23      int dCount; // count of D grades
24      int fCount; // count of F grades
25   }; // end class GradeBook
```

Fig. 5.9 | GradeBook class definition.

```
 1   // Fig. 5.10: GradeBook.cpp
 2   // Member-function definitions for class GradeBook that
 3   // uses a switch statement to count A, B, C, D and F grades.
 4   #include <iostream>
 5   using std::cout;
 6   using std::cin;
 7   using std::endl;
 8
 9   #include "GradeBook.h" // include definition of class GradeBook
10
11   // constructor initializes courseName with string supplied as argument;
12   // initializes counter data members to 0
13   GradeBook::GradeBook( string name )
14   {
15      setCourseName( name ); // validate and store courseName
16      aCount = 0; // initialize count of A grades to 0
17      bCount = 0; // initialize count of B grades to 0
18      cCount = 0; // initialize count of C grades to 0
19      dCount = 0; // initialize count of D grades to 0
20      fCount = 0; // initialize count of F grades to 0
21   } // end GradeBook constructor
22
23   // function to set the course name; limits name to 25 or fewer characters
24   void GradeBook::setCourseName( string name )
25   {
26      if ( name.length() <= 25 ) // if name has 25 or fewer characters
27         courseName = name; // store the course name in the object
28      else // if name is longer than 25 characters
29      { // set courseName to first 25 characters of parameter name
30         courseName = name.substr( 0, 25 ); // select first 25 characters
31         cout << "Name \"" << name << "\" exceeds maximum length (25).\n"
32            << "Limiting courseName to first 25 characters.\n" << endl;
33      } // end if...else
34   } // end function setCourseName
35
36   // function to retrieve the course name
37   string GradeBook::getCourseName()
38   {
39      return courseName;
40   } // end function getCourseName
41
42   // display a welcome message to the GradeBook user
43   void GradeBook::displayMessage()
44   {
45      // this statement calls getCourseName to get the
46      // name of the course this GradeBook represents
47      cout << "Welcome to the grade book for\n" << getCourseName() << "!\n"
48         << endl;
49   } // end function displayMessage
50
```

Fig. 5.10 | GradeBook class uses switch statement to count letter grades A, B, C, D and F. (Part 1 of 3.)

```
51   // input arbitrary number of grades from user; update grade counter
52   void GradeBook::inputGrades()
53   {
54      int grade; // grade entered by user
55
56      cout << "Enter the letter grades." << endl
57         << "Enter the EOF character to end input." << endl;
58
59      // loop until user types end-of-file key sequence
60      while ( ( grade = cin.get() ) != EOF )
61      {
62         // determine which grade was entered
63         switch ( grade ) // switch statement nested in while
64         {
65            case 'A': // grade was uppercase A
66            case 'a': // or lowercase a
67               aCount++; // increment aCount
68               break; // necessary to exit switch
69
70            case 'B': // grade was uppercase B
71            case 'b': // or lowercase b
72               bCount++; // increment bCount
73               break; // exit switch
74
75            case 'C': // grade was uppercase C
76            case 'c': // or lowercase c
77               cCount++; // increment cCount
78               break; // exit switch
79
80            case 'D': // grade was uppercase D
81            case 'd': // or lowercase d
82               dCount++; // increment dCount
83               break; // exit switch
84
85            case 'F': // grade was uppercase F
86            case 'f': // or lowercase f
87               fCount++; // increment fCount
88               break; // exit switch
89
90            case '\n': // ignore newlines,
91            case '\t': // tabs,
92            case ' ': // and spaces in input
93               break; // exit switch
94
95            default: // catch all other characters
96               cout << "Incorrect letter grade entered."
97                  << " Enter a new grade." << endl;
98               break; // optional; will exit switch anyway
99         } // end switch
100     } // end while
101  } // end function inputGrades
```

Fig. 5.10 | GradeBook class uses switch statement to count letter grades A, B, C, D and F. (Part 2 of 3.)

```
102
103   // display a report based on the grades entered by user
104   void GradeBook::displayGradeReport()
105   {
106      // output summary of results
107      cout << "\n\nNumber of students who received each letter grade:"
108         << "\nA: " << aCount // display number of A grades
109         << "\nB: " << bCount // display number of B grades
110         << "\nC: " << cCount // display number of C grades
111         << "\nD: " << dCount // display number of D grades
112         << "\nF: " << fCount // display number of F grades
113         << endl;
114   } // end function displayGradeReport
```

Fig. 5.10 | GradeBook class uses switch statement to count letter grades A, B, C, D and F. (Part 3 of 3.)

grade counters to 0—when a GradeBook object is first created, no grades have been entered yet. As you will soon see, these counters are incremented in member function input-Grades as the user enters grades. The definitions of member functions setCourseName, getCourseName and displayMessage are identical to those found in the earlier versions of class GradeBook. Let's consider the new GradeBook member functions in detail.

Reading Character Input

The user enters letter grades for a course in member function inputGrades (lines 52–101). Inside the while header, at line 60, the parenthesized assignment (grade = cin.get()) executes first. The cin.get() function reads one character from the keyboard and stores that character in integer variable grade (declared in line 54). Characters normally are stored in variables of type **char**; however, characters can be stored in any integer data type, because they are represented as 1-byte integers in the computer. Thus, we can treat a character either as an integer or as a character, depending on its use. For example, the statement

```
cout << "The character (" << 'a' << ") has the value "
   << static_cast< int > ( 'a' ) << endl;
```

prints the character a and its integer value as follows:

```
The character (a) has the value 97
```

The integer 97 is the character's numerical representation in the computer. Most computers today use the ASCII (American Standard Code for Information Interchange) character set, in which 97 represents the lowercase letter 'a'. A table of the ASCII characters and their decimal equivalents is presented in Appendix B.

Assignment statements as a whole have the value that is assigned to the variable on the left side of the =. Thus, the value of the assignment expression grade = cin.get() is the same as the value returned by cin.get() and assigned to the variable grade.

The fact that assignment statements have values can be useful for assigning the same value to several variables. For example,

```
a = b = c = 0;
```

first evaluates the assignment c = 0 (because the = operator associates from right to left). The variable b is then assigned the value of the assignment c = 0 (which is 0). Then, the variable a is assigned the value of the assignment b = (c = 0) (which is also 0). In the program, the value of the assignment grade = cin.get() is compared with the value of EOF (a symbol whose acronym stands for "end-of-file"). We use EOF (which normally has the value –1) as the sentinel value. *However, you do not type the value –1, nor do you type the letters EOF as the sentinel value.* Rather, you type a system-dependent keystroke combination that means "end-of-file" to indicate that you have no more data to enter. EOF is a symbolic integer constant defined in the <iostream> header file. If the value assigned to grade is equal to EOF, the while loop (lines 60–100) terminates. We have chosen to represent the characters entered into this program as ints, because EOF has an integer value.

On UNIX/Linux systems and many others, end-of-file is entered by typing

    <ctrl> d

on a line by itself. This notation means to press and hold down the *Ctrl* key, then press the *d* key. On other systems such as Microsoft Windows, end-of-file can be entered by typing

    <ctrl> z

[*Note:* In some cases, you must press *Enter* after the preceding key sequence. Also, the characters ^Z sometimes appear on the screen to represent end-of-file, as is shown in Fig. 5.11.]

Portability Tip 5.2

The keystroke combinations for entering end-of-file are system dependent.

Portability Tip 5.3

Testing for the symbolic constant EOF rather than –1 makes programs more portable. The ANSI/ISO C standard, from which C++ adopts the definition of EOF, states that EOF is a negative integral value (but not necessarily –1), so EOF could have different values on different systems.

In this program, the user enters grades at the keyboard. When the user presses the *Enter* (or *Return*) key, the characters are read by the cin.get() function, one character at a time. If the character entered is not end-of-file, the flow of control enters the switch statement (lines 63–99), which increments the appropriate letter-grade counter based on the grade entered.

switch Statement Details

The switch statement consists of a series of case labels and an optional default case. These are used in this example to determine which counter to increment, based on a grade. When the flow of control reaches the switch, the program evaluates the expression in the parentheses (i.e., grade) following keyword switch (line 63). This is called the controlling expression. The switch statement compares the value of the controlling expression with each case label. Assume the user enters the letter C as a grade. The program compares C to each case in the switch. If a match occurs (case 'C': at line 75), the program executes the statements for that case. For the letter C, line 77 increments cCount by 1. The break statement (line 78) causes program control to proceed with the first statement after the switch—in this program, control transfers to line 100. This line marks the end of the body of the while loop that inputs grades (lines 60–100), so control flows to the while's condition (line 60) to determine whether the loop should continue executing.

The cases in our switch explicitly test for the lowercase and uppercase versions of the letters A, B, C, D and F. Note the cases at lines 65–66 that test for the values 'A' and 'a' (both of which represent the grade A). Listing cases consecutively in this manner with no statements between them enables the cases to perform the same set of statements—when the controlling expression evaluates to either 'A' or 'a', the statements at lines 67–68 will execute. Note that each case can have multiple statements. The switch selection statement differs from other control statements in that it does not require braces around multiple statements in each case.

Without break statements, each time a match occurs in the switch, the statements for that case and subsequent cases execute until a break statement or the end of the switch is encountered. This is often referred to as "falling through" to the statements in subsequent cases. (This feature is perfect for writing a concise program that displays the iterative song "The Twelve Days of Christmas" in Exercise 5.28.)

Common Programming Error 5.8

Forgetting a break statement when one is needed in a switch statement is a logic error.

Common Programming Error 5.9

Omitting the space between the word case and the integral value being tested in a switch statement can cause a logic error. For example, writing case3: instead of writing case 3: simply creates an unused label. We will say more about this in. In this situation, the switch statement will not perform the appropriate actions when the switch's controlling expression has a value of 3.

Providing a **default** Case

If no match occurs between the controlling expression's value and a case label, the default case (lines 95–98) executes. We use the default case in this example to process all controlling-expression values that are neither valid grades nor newline, tab or space characters (we discuss how the program handles these white-space characters shortly). If no match occurs, the default case executes, and lines 96–97 print an error message indicating that an incorrect letter grade was entered. If no match occurs in a switch statement that does not contain a default case, program control simply continues with the first statement after the switch.

Good Programming Practice 5.10

Provide a default case in switch statements. Cases not explicitly tested in a switch statement without a default case are ignored. Including a default case focuses the programmer on the need to process exceptional conditions. There are situations in which no default processing is needed. Although the case clauses and the default case clause in a switch statement can occur in any order, it is common practice to place the default clause last.

Good Programming Practice 5.11

In a switch statement that lists the default clause last, the default clause does not require a break statement. Some programmers include this break for clarity and for symmetry with other cases.

Ignoring Newline, Tab and Blank Characters in Input

Note that lines 90–93 in the switch statement of Fig. 5.10 cause the program to skip newline, tab and blank characters. Reading characters one at a time can cause some problems. To have the program read the characters, we must send them to the computer by pressing the *Enter* key on the keyboard. This places a newline character in the input after the character we wish to process. Often, this newline character must be specially processed to make the program work correctly. By including the preceding cases in our switch statement, we prevent the error message in the default case from being printed each time a newline, tab or space is encountered in the input.

Common Programming Error 5.10

Not processing newline and other white-space characters in the input when reading characters one at a time can cause logic errors.

Testing Class GradeBook

Figure 5.11 creates a GradeBook object (line 9). Line 11 invokes the object's display-Message member function to output a welcome message to the user. Line 12 invokes the object's inputGrades member function to read a set of grades from the user and keep track of the number of students who received each grade. Note that the input/output window in Fig. 5.11 shows an error message displayed in response to entering an invalid grade (i.e., E). Line 13 invokes GradeBook member function displayGradeReport (defined in lines 104–114 of Fig. 5.10), which outputs a report based on the grades entered (as in the output in Fig. 5.11).

switch Statement UML Activity Diagram

Figure 5.12 shows the UML activity diagram for the general switch multiple-selection statement. Most switch statements use a break in each case to terminate the switch statement after processing the case. Figure 5.12 emphasizes this by including break statements in the activity diagram. Without the break statement, control would not transfer to the first statement after the switch statement after a case is processed. Instead, control would transfer to the next case's actions.

```cpp
1   // Fig. 5.11: fig05_11.cpp
2   // Create GradeBook object, input grades and display grade report.
3
4   #include "GradeBook.h" // include definition of class GradeBook
5
6   int main()
7   {
8      // create GradeBook object
9      GradeBook myGradeBook( "CS101 C++ Programming" );
10
11     myGradeBook.displayMessage(); // display welcome message
12     myGradeBook.inputGrades(); // read grades from user
13     myGradeBook.displayGradeReport(); // display report based on grades
14     return 0; // indicate successful termination
15  } // end main
```

Fig. 5.11 | Creating a GradeBook object and calling its member functions. (Part 1 of 2.)

```
Welcome to the grade book for
CS101 C++ Programming!

Enter the letter grades.
Enter the EOF character to end input.
a
B
c
C
A
d
f
C
E
Incorrect letter grade entered. Enter a new grade.
D
A
b
^Z


Number of students who received each letter grade:
A: 3
B: 2
C: 3
D: 2
F: 1
```

Fig. 5.11 | Creating a GradeBook object and calling its member functions. (Part 2 of 2.)

The diagram makes it clear that the break statement at the end of a case causes control to exit the switch statement immediately. Again, note that (besides an initial state, transition arrows, a final state and several notes) the diagram contains action states and decisions. Also, note that the diagram uses merge symbols to merge the transitions from the break statements to the final state.

Imagine, again, that the programmer has a bin of empty switch statement UML activity diagrams—as many as the programmer might need to stack and nest with the activity diagrams of other control statements to form a structured implementation of an algorithm. The programmer fills in the action states and decision symbols with action expressions and guard conditions appropriate to the algorithm. Note that, although nested control statements are common, it is rare to find nested switch statements in a program.

When using the switch statement, remember that it can be used only for testing a *constant* integral expression—any combination of character constants and integer constants that evaluates to a constant integer value. A character constant is represented as the specific character in single quotes, such as 'A'. An integer constant is simply an integer value. Also, each case label can specify only one constant integral expression.

 Common Programming Error 5.11

Specifying an expression including variables (e.g., a + b) in a switch statement's case label is a syntax error.

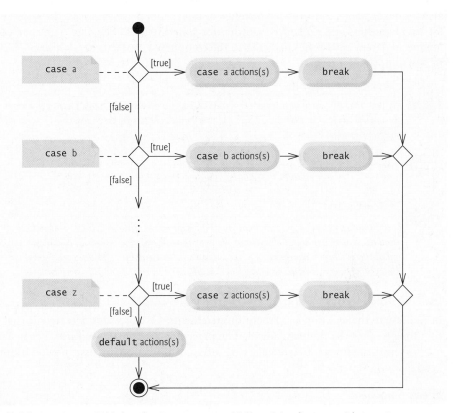

Fig. 5.12 | switch multiple-selection statement UML activity diagram with break statements.

 Common Programming Error 5.12

Providing identical case labels in a switch statement is a compilation error. Providing case labels containing different expressions that evaluate to the same value also is a compilation error. For example, placing case 4 + 1: and case 3 + 2: in the same switch statement is a compilation error, because these are both equivalent to case 5:.

In Chapter 13, we present a more elegant way to implement switch logic. We will use a technique called polymorphism to create programs that are often clearer, more concise, easier to maintain and easier to extend than programs that use switch logic.

Notes on Data Types

C++ has flexible data type sizes (see Appendix C, Fundamental Types). Different applications, for example, might need integers of different sizes. C++ provides several data types to represent integers. The range of integer values for each type depends on the particular computer's hardware. In addition to the types int and char, C++ provides the types short (an abbreviation of short int) and long (an abbreviation of long int). The minimum range of values for short integers is –32,768 to 32,767. For the vast majority of integer calculations, long integers are sufficient. The minimum range of values for long integers is -2,147,483,648 to –2,147,483,647. On most computers, ints are equivalent either to short or to long. The range of values for an int is at least the same as that for short integers and no larger than that for long integers. The data type char can be used to represent any of the characters in the computer's character set. It also can be used to represent small integers.

Portability Tip 5.4

Because ints can vary in size between systems, use long integers if you expect to process integers outside the range –32,768 to 32,767 and you would like to run the program on several different computer systems.

Performance Tip 5.3

If memory is at a premium, it might be desirable to use smaller integer sizes.

Performance Tip 5.4

Using smaller integer sizes can result in a slower program if the machine's instructions for manipulating them are not as efficient as those for the natural-size integers, i.e., integers whose size equals the machine's word size (e.g., 32 bits on a 32-bit machine, 64 bits on a 64-bit machine). Always test proposed efficiency "upgrades" to be sure they really improve performance.

5.7 break and continue Statements

In addition to the selection and repetition statements, C++ provides statements break and continue to alter the flow of control. The preceding section showed how break can be used to terminate a switch statement's execution. This section discusses how to use break in a repetition statement.

break *Statement*

The break statement, when executed in a while, for, do...while or switch statement, causes immediate exit from that statement. Program execution continues with the next statement. Common uses of the break statement are to escape early from a loop or to skip the remainder of a switch statement (as in Fig. 5.10). Figure 5.13 demonstrates the break statement (line 14) exiting a for repetition statement.

```cpp
 1   // Fig. 5.13: fig05_13.cpp
 2   // break statement exiting a for statement.
 3   #include <iostream>
 4   using std::cout;
 5   using std::endl;
 6
 7   int main()
 8   {
 9      int count; // control variable also used after loop terminates
10
11      for ( count = 1; count <= 10; count++ ) // loop 10 times
12      {
13         if ( count == 5 )
14            break; // break loop only if x is 5
15
16         cout << count << " ";
17      } // end for
```

Fig. 5.13 | break statement exiting a for statement. (Part 1 of 2.)

```
18
19       cout << "\nBroke out of loop at count = " << count << endl;
20       return 0; // indicate successful termination
21  } // end main
```

```
1 2 3 4
Broke out of loop at count = 5
```

Fig. 5.13 | break statement exiting a for statement. (Part 2 of 2.)

When the if statement detects that count is 5, the break statement executes. This terminates the for statement, and the program proceeds to line 19 (immediately after the for statement), which displays a message indicating the value of the control variable that terminated the loop. The for statement fully executes its body only four times instead of 10. Note that the control variable count is defined outside the for statement header, so that we can use the control variable both in the body of the loop and after the loop completes its execution.

continue *Statement*

The continue statement, when executed in a while, for or do...while statement, skips the remaining statements in the body of that statement and proceeds with the next iteration of the loop. In while and do...while statements, the loop-continuation test evaluates immediately after the continue statement executes. In the for statement, the increment expression executes, then the loop-continuation test evaluates.

Figure 5.14 uses the continue statement (line 12) in a for statement to skip the output statement (line 14) when the nested if (lines 11–12) determines that the value of count is 5. When the continue statement executes, program control continues with the increment of the control variable in the for header (line 9) and loops five more times.

```
1   // Fig. 5.14: fig05_14.cpp
2   // continue statement terminating an iteration of a for statement.
3   #include <iostream>
4   using std::cout;
5   using std::endl;
6
7   int main()
8   {
9      for ( int count = 1; count <= 10; count++ ) // loop 10 times
10     {
11        if ( count == 5 ) // if count is 5,
12           continue;      // skip remaining code in loop
13
14        cout << count << " ";
15     } // end for
16
17     cout << "\nUsed continue to skip printing 5" << endl;
18     return 0; // indicate successful termination
19  } // end main
```

Fig. 5.14 | continue statement terminating a single iteration of a for statement. (Part 1 of 2.)

```
1 2 3 4 6 7 8 9 10
Used continue to skip printing 5
```

Fig. 5.14 | continue statement terminating a single iteration of a for statement. (Part 2 of 2.)

In Section 5.3, we stated that the while statement could be used in most cases to represent the for statement. The one exception occurs when the increment expression in the while statement follows the continue statement. In this case, the increment does not execute before the program tests the loop-continuation condition, and the while does not execute in the same manner as the for.

Good Programming Practice 5.12

Some programmers feel that break and continue violate structured programming. The effects of these statements can be achieved by structured programming techniques we soon will learn, so these programmers do not use break and continue. Most programmers consider the use of break in switch statements acceptable.

Performance Tip 5.5

The break and continue statements, when used properly, perform faster than do the corresponding structured techniques.

Software Engineering Observation 5.2

There is a tension between achieving quality software engineering and achieving the best-performing software. Often, one of these goals is achieved at the expense of the other. For all but the most performance-intensive situations, apply the following rule of thumb: First, make your code simple and correct; then make it fast and small, but only if necessary.

5.8 Logical Operators

So far we have studied only simple conditions, such as counter <= 10, total > 1000 and number != sentinelValue. We expressed these conditions in terms of the relational operators >, <, >= and <=, and the equality operators == and !=. Each decision tested precisely one condition. To test multiple conditions while making a decision, we performed these tests in separate statements or in nested if or if...else statements.

C++ provides logical operators that are used to form more complex conditions by combining simple conditions. The logical operators are && (logical AND), || (logical OR) and ! (logical NOT, also called logical negation).

Logical AND (&&) Operator

Suppose that we wish to ensure that two conditions are *both* true before we choose a certain path of execution. In this case, we can use the && (logical AND) operator, as follows:

```
if ( gender == 1 && age >= 65 )
    seniorFemales++;
```

This if statement contains two simple conditions. The condition gender == 1 is used here to determine whether a person is a female. The condition age >= 65 determines whether a person is a senior citizen. The simple condition to the left of the && operator evaluates first, because the precedence of == is higher than the precedence of &&. If necessary, the simple condition to the right of the && operator evaluates next, because the precedence of >= is higher than the precedence of &&. As we will discuss shortly, the right side of a logical AND expression is evaluated only if the left side is true. The if statement then considers the combined condition

```
gender == 1 && age >= 65
```

This condition is true if and only if both of the simple conditions are true. Finally, if this combined condition is indeed true, the statement in the if statement's body increments the count of seniorFemales. If either of the simple conditions is false (or both are), then the program skips the incrementing and proceeds to the statement following the if. The preceding combined condition can be made more readable by adding redundant parentheses:

```
( gender == 1 ) && ( age >= 65 )
```

 Common Programming Error 5.13

Although 3 < x < 7 is a mathematically correct condition, it does not evaluate as you might expect in C++. Use (3 < x && x < 7) to get the proper evaluation in C++.

Figure 5.15 summarizes the && operator. The table shows all four possible combinations of false and true values for *expression1* and *expression2*. Such tables are often called truth tables. C++ evaluates to false or true all expressions that include relational operators, equality operators and/or logical operators.

Logical OR (||) Operator

Now let us consider the || (logical OR) operator. Suppose we wish to ensure at some point in a program that either *or* both of two conditions are true before we choose a certain path of execution. In this case, we use the || operator, as in the following program segment:

```
if ( ( semesterAverage >= 90 ) || ( finalExam >= 90 ) )
   cout << "Student grade is A" << endl;
```

This preceding condition also contains two simple conditions. The simple condition semesterAverage >= 90 evaluates to determine whether the student deserves an "A" in the course because of a solid performance throughout the semester. The simple condition finalExam >= 90 evaluates to determine whether the student deserves an "A" in the course because of an outstanding performance on the final exam. The if statement then considers the combined condition

```
( semesterAverage >= 90 ) || ( finalExam >= 90 )
```

expression1	expression2	expression1 && expression2
false	false	false
false	true	false
true	false	false
true	true	true

Fig. 5.15 | && (logical AND) operator truth table.

and awards the student an "A" if either or both of the simple conditions are `true`. Note that the message "`Student grade is A`" prints unless both of the simple conditions are `false`. Figure 5.16 is a truth table for the logical OR operator (`||`).

The `&&` operator has a higher precedence than the `||` operator. Both operators associate from left to right. An expression containing `&&` or `||` operators evaluates only until the truth or falsehood of the expression is known. Thus, evaluation of the expression

```
( gender == 1 ) && ( age >= 65 )
```

stops immediately if `gender` is not equal to 1 (i.e., the entire expression is `false`) and continues if `gender` is equal to 1 (i.e., the entire expression could still be `true` if the condition `age >= 65` is `true`). This performance feature for the evaluation of logical AND and logical OR expressions is called short-circuit evaluation.

> ### Performance Tip 5.6
>
> *In expressions using operator &&, if the separate conditions are independent of one another, make the condition most likely to be `false` the leftmost condition. In expressions using operator ||, make the condition most likely to be `true` the leftmost condition. This use of short-circuit evaluation can reduce a program's execution time.*

Logical Negation (!) Operator

C++ provides the `!` (logical NOT, also called logical negation) operator to enable a programmer to "reverse" the meaning of a condition. Unlike the `&&` and `||` binary operators, which combine two conditions, the unary logical negation operator has only a single condition as an operand. The unary logical negation operator is placed before a condition when we are interested in choosing a path of execution if the original condition (without the logical negation operator) is `false`, such as in the following program segment:

```
if ( !( grade == sentinelValue ) )
   cout << "The next grade is " << grade << endl;
```

The parentheses around the condition `grade == sentinelValue` are needed because the logical negation operator has a higher precedence than the equality operator.

In most cases, the programmer can avoid using logical negation by expressing the condition with an appropriate relational or equality operator. For example, the preceding `if` statement also can be written as follows:

```
if ( grade != sentinelValue )
   cout << "The next grade is " << grade << endl;
```

expression1	expression2	expression1 || expression2
false	false	false
false	true	true
true	false	true
true	true	true

Fig. 5.16 | `||` (logical OR) operator truth table.

This flexibility often can help a programmer express a condition in a more "natural" or convenient manner. Figure 5.17 is a truth table for the logical negation operator (!).

Logical Operators Example

Figure 5.18 demonstrates the logical operators by producing their truth tables. The output shows each expression that is evaluated and its bool result. By default, bool values true and false are displayed by cout and the stream insertion operator as 1 and 0, respectively. However, we use stream manipulator boolalpha in line 11 to specify that the value of

expression	!expression
false	true
true	false

Fig. 5.17 | ! (logical negation) operator truth table.

```
 1   // Fig. 5.18: fig05_18.cpp
 2   // Logical operators.
 3   #include <iostream>
 4   using std::cout;
 5   using std::endl;
 6   using std::boolalpha; // causes bool values to print as "true" or "false"
 7
 8   int main()
 9   {
10      // create truth table for && (logical AND) operator
11      cout << boolalpha << "Logical AND (&&)"
12         << "\nfalse && false: " << ( false && false )
13         << "\nfalse && true: " << ( false && true )
14         << "\ntrue && false: " << ( true && false )
15         << "\ntrue && true: " << ( true && true ) << "\n\n";
16
17      // create truth table for || (logical OR) operator
18      cout << "Logical OR (||)"
19         << "\nfalse || false: " << ( false || false )
20         << "\nfalse || true: " << ( false || true )
21         << "\ntrue || false: " << ( true || false )
22         << "\ntrue || true: " << ( true || true ) << "\n\n";
23
24      // create truth table for ! (logical negation) operator
25      cout << "Logical NOT (!)"
26         << "\n!false: " << ( !false )
27         << "\n!true: " << ( !true ) << endl;
28      return 0; // indicate successful termination
29   } // end main
```

Fig. 5.18 | Logical operators. (Part I of 2.)

```
Logical AND (&&)
false && false: false
false && true: false
true && false: false
true && true: true

Logical OR (||)
false || false: false
false || true: true
true || false: true
true || true: true

Logical NOT (!)
!false: true
!true: false
```

Fig. 5.18 | Logical operators. (Part 2 of 2.)

each bool expression should be displayed either as the word "true" or the word "false." For example, the result of the expression false && false in line 12 is false, so the second line of output includes the word "false." Lines 11–15 produce the truth table for &&. Lines 18–22 produce the truth table for ||. Lines 25–27 produce the truth table for !.

Summary of Operator Precedence and Associativity
Figure 5.19 adds the logical operators to the operator precedence and associativity chart. The operators are shown from top to bottom, in decreasing order of precedence.

Operators						Associativity	Type
()						left to right	parentheses
++	--	static_cast< *type* >()				left to right	unary (postfix)
++	--	+	-	!		right to left	unary (prefix)
*	/	%				left to right	multiplicative
+	-					left to right	additive
<<	>>					left to right	insertion/extraction
<	<=	>	>=			left to right	relational
==	!=					left to right	equality
&&						left to right	logical AND
||						left to right	logical OR
?:						right to left	conditional
=	+=	-=	*=	/=	%=	right to left	assignment
,						left to right	comma

Fig. 5.19 | Operator precedence and associativity.

5.9 Confusing Equality (==) and Assignment (=) Operators

There is one type of error that C++ programmers, no matter how experienced, tend to make so frequently that we feel it requires a separate section. That error is accidentally swapping the operators == (equality) and = (assignment). What makes these swaps so damaging is the fact that they ordinarily do not cause syntax errors. Rather, statements with these errors tend to compile correctly and the programs run to completion, often generating incorrect results through runtime logic errors. [*Note:* Some compilers issue a warning when = is used in a context where == normally is expected.]

There are two aspects of C++ that contribute to these problems. One is that any expression that produces a value can be used in the decision portion of any control statement. If the value of the expression is zero, it is treated as `false`, and if the value is nonzero, it is treated as `true`. The second is that assignments produce a value—namely, the value assigned to the variable on the left side of the assignment operator. For example, suppose we intend to write

```
if ( payCode == 4 )
    cout << "You get a bonus!" << endl;
```

but we accidentally write

```
if ( payCode = 4 )
    cout << "You get a bonus!" << endl;
```

The first `if` statement properly awards a bonus to the person whose payCode is equal to 4. The second `if` statement—the one with the error—evaluates the assignment expression in the `if` condition to the constant 4. Any nonzero value is interpreted as `true`, so the condition in this `if` statement is always `true` and the person always receives a bonus regardless of what the actual paycode is! Even worse, the paycode has been modified when it was only supposed to be examined!

Common Programming Error 5.14

Using operator == for assignment and using operator = for equality are logic errors.

Error-Prevention Tip 5.3

Programmers normally write conditions such as x == 7 with the variable name on the left and the constant on the right. By reversing these so that the constant is on the left and the variable name is on the right, as in 7 == x, the programmer who accidentally replaces the == operator with = will be protected by the compiler. The compiler treats this as a compilation error, because you can't change the value of a constant. This will prevent the potential devastation of a runtime logic error.

Variable names are said to be *lvalues* (for "left values") because they can be used on the left side of an assignment operator. Constants are said to be *rvalues* (for "right values") because they can be used on only the right side of an assignment operator. Note that *lvalues* can also be used as *rvalues*, but not vice versa.

There is another equally unpleasant situation. Suppose the programmer wants to assign a value to a variable with a simple statement like

```
x = 1;
```

but instead writes

```
x == 1;
```

Here, too, this is not a syntax error. Rather, the compiler simply evaluates the conditional expression. If x is equal to 1, the condition is true and the expression evaluates to the value true. If x is not equal to 1, the condition is false and the expression evaluates to the value false. Regardless of the expression's value, there is no assignment operator, so the value simply is lost. The value of x remains unaltered, probably causing an execution-time logic error. Unfortunately, we do not have a handy trick available to help you with this problem!

Error-Prevention Tip 5.4

Use your text editor to search for all occurrences of = in your program and check that you have the correct assignment operator or logical operator in each place.

5.10 Structured Programming Summary

Just as architects design buildings by employing the collective wisdom of their profession, so should programmers design programs. Our field is younger than architecture is, and our collective wisdom is considerably sparser. We have learned that structured programming produces programs that are easier than unstructured programs to understand, test, debug, modify, and even prove correct in a mathematical sense.

Figure 5.20 uses activity diagrams to summarize C++'s control statements. The initial and final states indicate the single entry point and the single exit point of each control statement. Arbitrarily connecting individual symbols in an activity diagram can lead to unstructured programs. Therefore, the programming profession uses only a limited set of control statements that can be combined in only two simple ways to build structured programs.

For simplicity, only single-entry/single-exit control statements are used—there is only one way to enter and only one way to exit each control statement. Connecting control statements in sequence to form structured programs is simple—the final state of one control statement is connected to the initial state of the next control statement—that is, the control statements are placed one after another in a program. We have called this "control-statement stacking." The rules for forming structured programs also allow for control statements to be nested.

Figure 5.21 shows the rules for forming structured programs. The rules assume that action states may be used to indicate any action. The rules also assume that we begin with the so-called simplest activity diagram (Fig. 5.22), consisting of only an initial state, an action state, a final state and transition arrows.

Applying the rules of Fig. 5.21 always results in an activity diagram with a neat, building-block appearance. For example, repeatedly applying Rule 2 to the simplest activity diagram results in an activity diagram containing many action states in sequence (Fig. 5.23). Rule 2 generates a stack of control statements, so let us call Rule 2 the stacking rule. [*Note:* The vertical dashed lines in Fig. 5.23 are not part of the UML. We use them to separate the four activity diagrams that demonstrate Rule 2 of Fig. 5.21 being applied.]

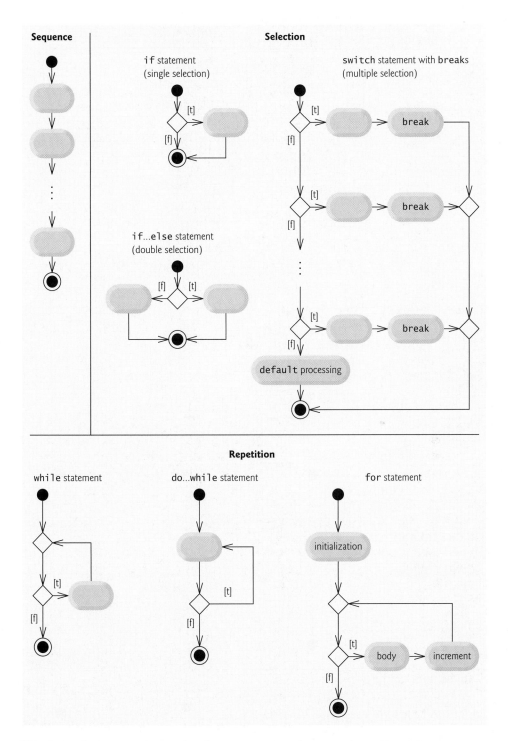

Fig. 5.20 | C++'s single-entry/single-exit sequence, selection and repetition statements.

Rules for Forming Structured Programs

1) Begin with the "simplest activity diagram" (Fig. 5.22).

2) Any action state can be replaced by two action states in sequence.

3) Any action state can be replaced by any control statement (sequence, if, if...else, switch, while, do...while or for).

4) Rules 2 and 3 can be applied as often as you like and in any order.

Fig. 5.21 | Rules for forming structured programs.

Fig. 5.22 | Simplest activity diagram.

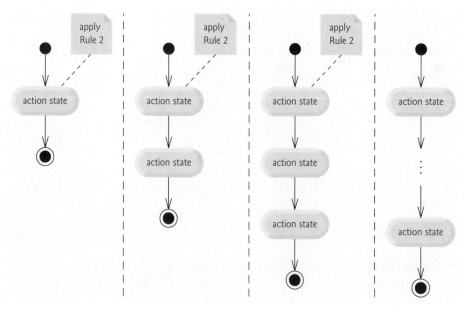

Fig. 5.23 | Repeatedly applying Rule 2 of Fig. 5.21 to the simplest activity diagram.

Rule 3 is called the nesting rule. Repeatedly applying Rule 3 to the simplest activity diagram results in an activity diagram with neatly nested control statements. For example, in Fig. 5.24, the action state in the simplest activity diagram is replaced with a double-selection (if...else) statement. Then Rule 3 is applied again to the action states in the double-selection statement, replacing each of these action states with a double-selection statement. The dashed action-state symbols around each of the double-selection statements represent an action state that was replaced in the preceding activity diagram. [*Note:* The dashed arrows and dashed action state symbols shown in Fig. 5.24 are not part of the UML.

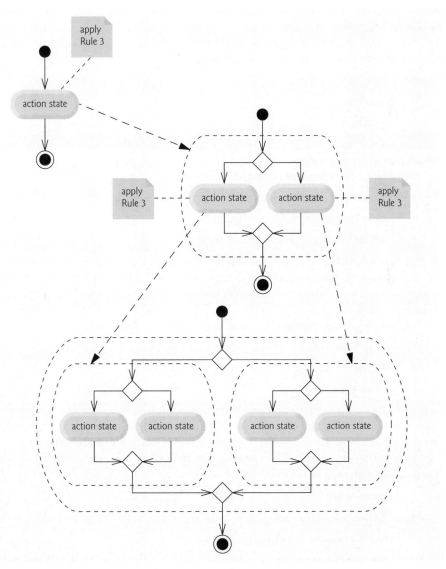

Fig. 5.24 | Applying Rule 3 of Fig. 5.21 to the simplest activity diagram several times.

They are used here as pedagogic devices to illustrate that any action state may be replaced with a control statement.]

Rule 4 generates larger, more involved and more deeply nested statements. The diagrams that emerge from applying the rules in Fig. 5.21 constitute the set of all possible activity diagrams and hence the set of all possible structured programs. The beauty of the structured approach is that we use only seven simple single-entry/single-exit control statements and assemble them in only two simple ways.

If the rules in Fig. 5.21 are followed, an activity diagram with illegal syntax (such as that in Fig. 5.25) cannot be created. If you are uncertain about whether a particular diagram is legal, apply the rules of Fig. 5.21 in reverse to reduce the diagram to the simplest activity diagram. If it is reducible to the simplest activity diagram, the original diagram is structured; otherwise, it is not.

Structured programming promotes simplicity. Böhm and Jacopini have given us the result that only three forms of control are needed:

- Sequence
- Selection
- Repetition

The sequence structure is trivial. Simply list the statements to execute in the order in which they should execute.

Selection is implemented in one of three ways:

- `if` statement (single selection)
- `if...else` statement (double selection)
- `switch` statement (multiple selection)

It is straightforward to prove that the simple `if` statement is sufficient to provide any form of selection—everything that can be done with the `if...else` statement and the `switch` statement can be implemented (although perhaps not as clearly and efficiently) by combining `if` statements.

Repetition is implemented in one of three ways:

- `while` statement
- `do...while` statement
- `for` statement

It is straightforward to prove that the `while` statement is sufficient to provide any form of repetition. Everything that can be done with the `do...while` statement and the `for` statement can be done (although perhaps not as smoothly) with the `while` statement.

Combining these results illustrates that any form of control ever needed in a C++ program can be expressed in terms of the following:

- sequence
- `if` statement (selection)
- `while` statement (repetition)

and that these control statements can be combined in only two ways—stacking and nesting. Indeed, structured programming promotes simplicity.

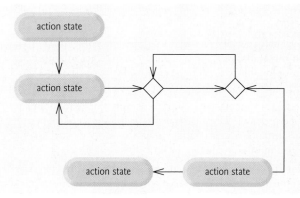

Fig. 5.25 | Activity diagram with illegal syntax.

5.11 Wrap-Up

In this chapter, we completed our introduction to C++'s control statements, which enable programmers to control the flow of execution in functions. Chapter 4 discussed the `if`, `if...else` and `while` statements. The current chapter demonstrated C++'s remaining control statements—`for`, `do...while` and `switch`. We have shown that any algorithm can be developed using combinations of the sequence structure (i.e., statements listed in the order in which they should execute), the three types of selection statements—`if`, `if...else` and `switch`—and the three types of repetition statements—`while`, `do...while` and `for`. In this chapter and Chapter 4, we have discussed how programmers can combine these building blocks to utilize proven program construction and problem-solving techniques. This chapter also introduced C++'s logical operators, which enable programmers to use more complex conditional expressions in control statements. Finally, we examined the common errors of confusing the equality and assignment operators and provided suggestions for avoiding these errors.

In Chapter 3, we introduced C++ programming with the basic concepts of objects, classes and member functions. Chapter 4 and this chapter provided a thorough introduction to the types of control statements that programmers typically use to specify program logic in functions. In Chapter 6, we examine functions in greater depth.

Summary

- In C++, it is more precise to call a declaration that also reserves memory a definition.
- The `for` repetition statement handles all the details of counter-controlled repetition. The general format of the `for` statement is

    ```
    for ( initialization; loopContinuationCondition; increment )
        statement
    ```

    where *initialization* initializes the loop's control variable, *loopContinuationCondition* is the condition that determines whether the loop should continue executing and *increment* increments the control variable.

- Typically, for statements are used for counter-controlled repetition and while statements are used for sentinel-controlled repetition.

- The scope of a variable specifies where it can be used in a program. For example, a control variable declared in the header of a for statement can be used only in the body of the for statement—the control variable will be unknown outside the for statement.

- The initialization and increment expressions in a for statement header can be comma-separated lists of expressions. The commas, as used in these expressions, are comma operators, which guarantee that lists of expressions evaluate from left to right. The comma operator has the lowest precedence of all C++ operators. The value and type of a comma-separated list of expressions is the value and type of the rightmost expression in the list.

- The initialization, loop-continuation condition and increment expressions of a for statement can contain arithmetic expressions. Also, the increment of a for statement can be negative, in which case it is really a decrement and the loop counts downward.

- If the loop-continuation condition in a for header is initially false, the body of the for statement is not performed. Instead, execution proceeds with the statement following the for.

- Standard library function pow(x, y) calculates the value of x raised to the yth power. Function pow takes two arguments of type double and returns a double value.

- Parameterized stream manipulator setw specifies the field width in which the next value output should appear. The value is right justified in the field by default. If the value to be output is larger than the field width, the field width is extended to accommodate the entire value. Nonparameterized stream manipulator left (found in header <iostream>) can be used to cause a value to be left justified in a field and right can be used to restore right justification.

- Sticky settings are those output-formatting settings that remain in effect until they are changed.

- The do...while repetition statement tests the loop-continuation condition at the end of the loop, so the body of the loop will be executed at least once. The format for the do...while statement is

```
do
{
    statement
} while ( condition );
```

- The switch multiple-selection statement performs different actions based on the possible values of a variable or expression. Each action is associated with the value of a constant integral expression (i.e., any combination of character constants and integer constants that evaluates to a constant integer value) that the variable or expression on which the switch is based may assume.

- The switch statement consists of a series of case labels and an optional default case.

- The cin.get() function reads one character from the keyboard. Characters normally are stored in variables of type char; however, characters can be stored in any integer data type, because they are represented as 1-byte integers in the computer. Thus, a character can be treated either as an integer or as a character, depending on its use.

- The end-of-file indicator is a system-dependent keystroke combination that specifies that there is no more data to input. EOF is a symbolic integer constant defined in the <iostream> header file that indicates "end-of-file."

- The expression in the parentheses following keyword switch is called the controlling expression of the switch. The switch statement compares the value of the controlling expression with each case label.

- Listing cases consecutively with no statements between them enables the cases to perform the same set of statements.

- Each case can have multiple statements. The switch selection statement differs from other control statements in that it does not require braces around multiple statements in each case.

- The switch statement can be used only for testing a constant integral expression. A character constant is represented as the specific character in single quotes, such as 'A'. An integer constant is simply an integer value. Also, each case label can specify only one constant integral expression.

- C++ provides several data types to represent integers—int, char, short and long. The range of integer values for each type depends on the particular computer's hardware.

- The break statement, when executed in one of the repetition statements (for, while and do...while), causes immediate exit from the statement.

- The continue statement, when executed in one of the repetition statements (for, while and do...while), skips any remaining statements in the body of the repetition statement and proceeds with the next iteration of the loop. In a while or do...while statement, execution continues with the next evaluation of the condition. In a for statement, execution continues with the increment expression in the for statement header.

- Logical operators enable programmers to form complex conditions by combining simple conditions. The logical operators are && (logical AND), || (logical OR) and ! (logical NOT, also called logical negation).

- The && (logical AND) operator ensures that two conditions are *both* true before choosing a certain path of execution.

- The || (logical OR) operator ensures that either *or* both of two conditions are true before choosing a certain path of execution.

- An expression containing && or || operators evaluates only until the truth or falsehood of the expression is known. This performance feature for the evaluation of logical AND and logical OR expressions is called short-circuit evaluation.

- The ! (logical NOT, also called logical negation) operator enables a programmer to "reverse" the meaning of a condition. The unary logical negation operator is placed before a condition to choose a path of execution if the original condition (without the logical negation operator) is false. In most cases, the programmer can avoid using logical negation by expressing the condition with an appropriate relational or equality operator.

- When used as a condition, any nonzero value implicitly converts to true; 0 (zero) implicitly converts to false.

- By default, bool values true and false are displayed by cout as 1 and 0, respectively. Stream manipulator boolalpha specifies that the value of each bool expression should be displayed as either the word "true" or the word "false."

- Any form of control ever needed in a C++ program can be expressed in terms of sequence, selection and repetition statements, and these can be combined in only two ways—stacking and nesting.

Terminology

!, logical NOT operator	constant integral expression
&&, logical AND operator	continue statement
||, logical OR operator	controlling expression of a switch
ASCII character set	decrement a control variable
boolalpha stream manipulator	default case in switch
break statement	definition
case label	delay loop
char fundamental type	field width
comma operator	final value of a control variable

for repetition statement

for header

increment a control variable

initial value of a control variable

left justification

left stream manipulator

logical AND (&&)

logical negation (!)

logical NOT (!)

logical operator

logical OR (||)

loop-continuation condition

lvalue ("left value")

name of a control variable

nesting rule

off-by-one error

right justification

right stream manipulator

rvalue ("right value")

scope of a variable

setw stream manipulator

short-circuit evaluation

simple condition

stacking rule

standard library function pow

sticky setting

switch multiple-selection statement

truth table

zero-based counting

Self-Review Exercises

5.1   State whether the following are *true* or *false*. If the answer is *false*, explain why.

a) The default case is required in the switch selection statement.

b) The break statement is required in the default case of a switch selection statement to exit the switch properly.

c) The expression (x > y && a < b) is true if either the expression x > y is true or the expression a < b is true.

d) An expression containing the || operator is true if either or both of its operands are true.

5.2   Write a C++ statement or a set of C++ statements to accomplish each of the following:

a) Sum the odd integers between 1 and 99 using a for statement. Assume the integer variables sum and count have been declared.

b) Print the value 333.546372 in a field width of 15 characters with precisions of 1, 2 and 3. Print each number on the same line. Left-justify each number in its field. What three values print?

c) Calculate the value of 2.5 raised to the power 3 using function pow. Print the result with a precision of 2 in a field width of 10 positions. What prints?

d) Print the integers from 1 to 20 using a while loop and the counter variable x. Assume that the variable x has been declared, but not initialized. Print only 5 integers per line. [*Hint:* Use the calculation x % 5. When the value of this is 0, print a newline character; otherwise, print a tab character.]

e) Repeat Exercise 5.2 (d) using a for statement.

5.3   Find the error(s) in each of the following code segments and explain how to correct it (them).

```
a) x = 1;
   while ( x <= 10 );
      x++;
   }
b) for ( y = .1; y != 1.0; y += .1 )
      cout << y << endl;
c) switch ( n )
   {
      case 1:
         cout << "The number is 1" << endl;
```

```
    case 2:
        cout << "The number is 2" << endl;
        break;
    default:
        cout << "The number is not 1 or 2" << endl;
        break;
}
```

d) The following code should print the values 1 to 10.

```
n = 1;
while ( n < 10 )
    cout << n++ << endl;
```

Answers to Self-Review Exercises

5.1   a) False. The `default` case is optional. If no default action is needed, then there is no need for a `default` case. Nevertheless, it is considered good software engineering to always provide a `default` case.

b) False. The `break` statement is used to exit the `switch` statement. The `break` statement is not required when the `default` case is the last case. Nor will the `break` statement be required if having control proceed with the next case makes sense.

c) False. When using the `&&` operator, both of the relational expressions must be `true` for the entire expression to be `true`.

d) True.

5.2   a)
```
sum = 0;
for ( count = 1; count <= 99; count += 2 )
    sum += count;
```
b)
```
cout << fixed << left
    << setprecision( 1 ) << setw( 15 ) << 333.546372
    << setprecision( 2 ) << setw( 15 ) << 333.546372
    << setprecision( 3 ) << setw( 15 ) << 333.546372
    << endl;
```
Output is:
```
333.5          333.55         333.546
```
c)
```
cout << fixed << setprecision( 2 )
    << setw( 10 ) << pow( 2.5, 3 )
    << endl;
```
Output is:
```
    15.63
```
d)
```
x = 1;

while ( x <= 20 )
{
    cout << x;

    if ( x % 5 == 0 )
        cout << endl;
    else
        cout << '\t';

    x++;
}
```

e)
```
for ( x = 1; x <= 20; x++ )
{
    cout << x;

    if ( x % 5 == 0 )
        cout << endl;
    else
        cout << '\t';
}
```

or

```
for ( x = 1; x <= 20; x++ )
{
    if ( x % 5 == 0 )
        cout << x << endl;
    else
        cout << x << '\t';
}
```

5.3   a) Error: The semicolon after the while header causes an infinite loop.
Correction: Replace the semicolon by a {, or remove both the ; and the }.
     b) Error: Using a floating-point number to control a for repetition statement.
Correction: Use an integer and perform the proper calculation in order to get the values you desire.

```
for ( y = 1; y != 10; y++ )
    cout << ( static_cast< double >( y ) / 10 ) << endl;
```

     c) Error: Missing break statement in the first case.
Correction: Add a break statement at the end of the statements for the first case. Note that this is not an error if the programmer wants the statement of case 2: to execute every time the case 1: statement executes.
     d) Error: Improper relational operator used in the while repetition-continuation condition.
Correction: Use <= rather than <, or change 10 to 11.

Exercises

5.4   Find the error(s) in each of the following:
     a)
```
For ( x = 100, x >= 1, x++ )
    cout << x << endl;
```
     b) The following code should print whether integer value is odd or even:
```
switch ( value % 2 )
{
    case 0:
        cout << "Even integer" << endl;
    case 1:
        cout << "Odd integer" << endl;
}
```

c) The following code should output the odd integers from 19 to 1:

```
for ( x = 19; x >= 1; x += 2 )
    cout << x << endl;
```

d) The following code should output the even integers from 2 to 100:

```
counter = 2;

do
{
    cout << counter << endl;
    counter += 2;
} While ( counter < 100 );
```

5.5   Write a program that uses a for statement to sum a sequence of integers. Assume that the first integer read specifies the number of values remaining to be entered. Your program should read only one value per input statement. A typical input sequence might be

>   5 100 200 300 400 500

where the 5 indicates that the subsequent 5 values are to be summed.

5.6   Write a program that uses a for statement to calculate and print the average of several integers. Assume the last value read is the sentinel 9999. A typical input sequence might be

>   10 8 11 7 9 9999

indicating that the program should calculate the average of all the values preceding 9999.

5.7   What does the following program do?

```
1   // Exercise 5.7: ex05_07.cpp
2   // What does this program print?
3   #include <iostream>
4   using std::cout;
5   using std::cin;
6   using std::endl;
7
8   int main()
9   {
10      int x; // declare x
11      int y; // declare y
12
13      // prompt user for input
14      cout << "Enter two integers in the range 1-20: ";
15      cin >> x >> y;  // read values for x and y
16
17      for ( int i = 1; i <= y; i++ ) // count from 1 to y
18      {
19          for ( int j = 1; j <= x; j++ ) // count from 1 to x
20              cout << '@'; // output @
21
22          cout << endl; // begin new line
23      } // end outer for
24
25      return 0; // indicate successful termination
26   } // end main
```

5.8   Write a program that uses a for statement to find the smallest of several integers. Assume that the first value read specifies the number of values remaining and that the first number is not one of the integers to compare.

5.9   Write a program that uses a for statement to calculate and print the product of the odd integers from 1 to 15.

5.10   The factorial function is used frequently in probability problems. Using the definition of factorial in Exercise 4.35, write a program that uses a for statement to evaluate the factorials of the integers from 1 to 5. Print the results in tabular format. What difficulty might prevent you from calculating the factorial of 20?

5.11   Modify the compound interest program of Section 5.4 to repeat its steps for the interest rates 5 percent, 6 percent, 7 percent, 8 percent, 9 percent and 10 percent. Use a for statement to vary the interest rate.

5.12   Write a program that uses for statements to print the following patterns separately, one below the other. Use for loops to generate the patterns. All asterisks (*) should be printed by a single statement of the form cout << '*'; (this causes the asterisks to print side by side). [*Hint:* The last two patterns require that each line begin with an appropriate number of blanks. *Extra credit:* Combine your code from the four separate problems into a single program that prints all four patterns side by side by making clever use of nested for loops.]

```
(a)              (b)              (c)              (d)
*                **********       **********                *
**               *********        *********                **
***              ********         ********                ***
****             *******          *******                ****
*****            ******           ******                *****
******           *****            *****                ******
*******          ****             ****                *******
********          ***             ***                ********
*********          **             **                *********
**********          *             *                **********
```

5.13   One interesting application of computers is the drawing of graphs and bar charts. Write a program that reads five numbers (each between 1 and 30). Assume that the user enters only valid values. For each number that is read, your program should print a line containing that number of adjacent asterisks. For example, if your program reads the number 7, it should print *******.

5.14   A mail order house sells five different products whose retail prices are: product 1 — $2.98, product 2—$4.50, product 3—$9.98, product 4—$4.49 and product 5—$6.87. Write a program that reads a series of pairs of numbers as follows:
   a) product number
   b) quantity sold
Your program should use a switch statement to determine the retail price for each product. Your program should calculate and display the total retail value of all products sold. Use a sentinel-controlled loop to determine when the program should stop looping and display the final results.

5.15   Modify the GradeBook program of Fig. 5.9–Fig. 5.11 so that it calculates the grade-point average for the set of grades. A grade of A is worth 4 points, B is worth 3 points, etc.

5.16   Modify the program in Fig. 5.6 so it uses only integers to calculate the compound interest. [*Hint:* Treat all monetary amounts as integral numbers of pennies. Then "break" the result into its dollar portion and cents portion by using the division and modulus operations. Insert a period.]

5.17 Assume i = 1, j = 2, k = 3 and m = 2. What does each of the following statements print? Are the parentheses necessary in each case?

a) `cout << ( i == 1 ) << endl;`
b) `cout << ( j == 3 ) << endl;`
c) `cout << ( i >= 1 && j < 4 ) << endl;`
d) `cout << ( m <= 99 && k < m ) << endl;`
e) `cout << ( j >= i || k == m ) << endl;`
f) `cout << ( k + m < j || 3 - j >= k ) << endl;`
g) `cout << ( !m ) << endl;`
h) `cout << ( !( j - m ) ) << endl;`
i) `cout << ( !( k > m ) ) << endl;`

5.18 Write a program that prints a table of the binary, octal and hexadecimal equivalents of the decimal numbers in the range 1 through 256. If you are not familiar with these number systems, read Appendix D, Number Systems, first.

5.19 Calculate the value of π from the infinite series

$$\pi = 4 - \frac{4}{3} + \frac{4}{5} - \frac{4}{7} + \frac{4}{9} - \frac{4}{11} + \cdots$$

Print a table that shows the approximate value of π after each of the first 1,000 terms of this series.

5.20 *(Pythagorean Triples)* A right triangle can have sides that are all integers. A set of three integer values for the sides of a right triangle is called a Pythagorean triple. These three sides must satisfy the relationship that the sum of the squares of two of the sides is equal to the square of the hypotenuse. Find all Pythagorean triples for side1, side2 and hypotenuse all no larger than 500. Use a triple-nested for loop that tries all possibilities. This is an example of brute force computing. You will learn in more advanced computer-science courses that there are many interesting problems for which there is no known algorithmic approach other than sheer brute force.

5.21 A company pays its employees as managers (who receive a fixed weekly salary), hourly workers (who receive a fixed hourly wage for up to the first 40 hours they work and "time-and-a-half"— 1.5 times their hourly wage—for overtime hours worked), commission workers (who receive $250 plus 5.7 percent of their gross weekly sales), or pieceworkers (who receive a fixed amount of money per item for each of the items they produce—each pieceworker in this company works on only one type of item). Write a program to compute the weekly pay for each employee. You do not know the number of employees in advance. Each type of employee has its own pay code: Managers have code 1, hourly workers have code 2, commission workers have code 3 and pieceworkers have code 4. Use a switch to compute each employee's pay according to that employee's paycode. Within the switch, prompt the user (i.e., the payroll clerk) to enter the appropriate facts your program needs to calculate each employee's pay according to that employee's paycode.

5.22 *(De Morgan's Laws)* In this chapter, we discussed the logical operators &&, || and !. De Morgan's laws can sometimes make it more convenient for us to express a logical expression. These laws state that the expression !(*condition1* && *condition2*) is logically equivalent to the expression (!*condition1* || !*condition2*). Also, the expression !(*condition1* || *condition2*) is logically equivalent to the expression (!*condition1* && !*condition2*). Use De Morgan's laws to write equivalent expressions for each of the following, then write a program to show that the original expression and the new expression in each case are equivalent:

a) `!( x < 5 ) && !( y >= 7 )`
b) `!( a == b ) || !( g != 5 )`
c) `!( ( x <= 8 ) && ( y > 4 ) )`
d) `!( ( i > 4 ) || ( j <= 6 ) )`

5.23   Write a program that prints the following diamond shape. You may use output statements that print either a single asterisk (*) or a single blank. Maximize your use of repetition (with nested for statements) and minimize the number of output statements.

```
       *
      ***
     *****
    *******
   *********
    *******
     *****
      ***
       *
```

5.24   Modify the program you wrote in Exercise 5.23 to read an odd number in the range 1 to 19 to specify the number of rows in the diamond, then display a diamond of the appropriate size.

5.25   A criticism of the break and continue statements is that each is unstructured. Actually they statements can always be replaced by structured statements, although doing so can be awkward. Describe in general how you would remove any break statement from a loop in a program and replace it with some structured equivalent. [*Hint:* The break statement leaves a loop from within the body of the loop. Another way to leave is by failing the loop-continuation test. Consider using in the loop-continuation test a second test that indicates "early exit because of a 'break' condition."] Use the technique you developed here to remove the break statement from the program of Fig. 5.13.

5.26   What does the following program segment do?

```
1   for ( int i = 1; i <= 5; i++ )
2   {
3      for ( int j = 1; j <= 3; j++ )
4      {
5         for ( int k = 1; k <= 4; k++ )
6            cout << '*';
7
8         cout << endl;
9      } // end inner for
10
11      cout << endl;
12   } // end outer for
```

5.27   Describe in general how you would remove any continue statement from a loop in a program and replace it with some structured equivalent. Use the technique you developed here to remove the continue statement from the program of Fig. 5.14.

5.28   *("The Twelve Days of Christmas" Song)* Write a program that uses repetition and switch statements to print the song "The Twelve Days of Christmas." One switch statement should be used to print the day (i.e., "First," "Second," etc.). A separate switch statement should be used to print the remainder of each verse. Visit the Web site www.12days.com/library/carols/12daysofxmas.htm for the complete lyrics to the song.

5.29   *(Peter Minuit Problem)* Legend has it that, in 1626, Peter Minuit purchased Manhattan Island for $24.00 in barter. Did he make a good investment? To answer this question, modify the compound interest program of Fig. 5.6 to begin with a principal of $24.00 and to calculate the amount of interest on deposit if that money had been kept on deposit until this year (e.g., 379 years through 2005). Place the for loop that performs the compound interest calculation in an outer for loop that varies the interest rate from 5 percent to 10 percent to observe the wonders of compound interest.

Functions and an Introduction to Recursion

Featuring
Early
Classes &
Objects
with the
UML™ 2

Form ever follows function.
—Louis Henri Sullivan

E pluribus unum.
(One composed of many.)
—Virgil

O! call back yesterday, bid time return.
—William Shakespeare

Call me Ishmael.
—Herman Melville

When you call me that, smile!
—Owen Wister

Answer me in one word.
—William Shakespeare

There is a point at which methods devour themselves.
—Frantz Fanon

Life can only be understood backwards; but it must be lived forwards.
—Soren Kierkegaard

OBJECTIVES

In this chapter you will learn:

- To construct programs modularly from functions.
- To use common math functions available in the C++ Standard Library.
- To create functions with multiple parameters.
- The mechanisms for passing information between functions and returning results.
- How the function call/return mechanism is supported by the function call stack and activation records.
- To use random number generation to implement game-playing applications.
- How the visibility of identifiers is limited to specific regions of programs.
- To write and use recursive functions, i.e., functions that call themselves.

Outline

6.1 Introduction

6.2 Program Components in C++

6.3 Math Library Functions

6.4 Function Definitions with Multiple Parameters

6.5 Function Prototypes and Argument Coercion

6.6 C++ Standard Library Header Files

6.7 Case Study: Random Number Generation

6.8 Case Study: Game of Chance and Introducing **enum**

6.9 Storage Classes

6.10 Scope Rules

6.11 Function Call Stack and Activation Records

6.12 Functions with Empty Parameter Lists

6.13 Inline Functions

6.14 References and Reference Parameters

6.15 Default Arguments

6.16 Unary Scope Resolution Operator

6.17 Function Overloading

6.18 Function Templates

6.19 Recursion

6.20 Example Using Recursion: Fibonacci Series

6.21 Recursion vs. Iteration

6.22 Wrap-Up

Summary | Terminology | Self-Review Exercises | Answers to Self-Review Exercises | Exercises

6.1 Introduction

Most computer programs that solve real-world problems are much larger than the programs presented in the first few chapters of this book. Experience has shown that the best way to develop and maintain a large program is to construct it from small, simple pieces, or components. This technique is called divide and conquer. We introduced functions (as program pieces) in Chapter 3. In this chapter, we study functions in more depth. We emphasize how to declare and use functions to facilitate the design, implementation, operation and maintenance of large programs.

We will overview a portion of the C++ Standard Library's math functions, showing several that require more than one parameter. Next, you will learn how to declare a function with than one parameter. We will also present additional information about function prototypes and how the compiler uses them to convert the type of an argument in a function call to the type specified in a function's parameter list, if necessary.

Next, we'll take a brief diversion into simulation techniques with random number generation and develop a version of the casino dice game called craps that uses most of the programming techniques you have learned to this point in the book.

We then present C++'s storage classes and scope rules. These determine the period during which an object exists in memory and where its identifier can be referenced in a program. You will also learn how C++ is able to keep track of which function is currently executing, how parameters and other local variables of functions are maintained in memory and how a function knows where to return after it completes execution. We discuss two topics that help improve program performance—inline functions that can eliminate the overhead of a function call and reference parameters that can be used to pass large data items to functions efficiently.

Many of the applications you develop will have more than one function of the same name. This technique, called function overloading, is used by programmers to implement functions that perform similar tasks for arguments of different types or possibly for different numbers of arguments. We consider function templates—a mechanism for defining a family of overloaded functions. The chapter concludes with a discussion of functions that call themselves, either directly, or indirectly (through another function)—a topic called recursion that is discussed at length in upper-level computer science courses.

6.2 Program Components in C++

C++ programs are typically written by combining new functions and classes the programmer writes with "prepackaged" functions and classes available in the C++ Standard Library. In this chapter, we concentrate on functions.

The C++ Standard Library provides a rich collection of functions for performing common mathematical calculations, string manipulations, character manipulations, input/output, error checking and many other useful operations. This makes the programmer's job easier, because these functions provide many of the capabilities programmers need. The C++ Standard Library functions are provided as part of the C++ programming environment.

Software Engineering Observation 6.1

Read the documentation for your compiler to familiarize yourself with the functions and classes in the C++ Standard Library.

Functions (called methods or procedures in other programming languages) allow the programmer to modularize a program by separating its tasks into self-contained units. You have used functions in every program you have written. These functions are sometimes referred to as user-defined functions or programmer-defined functions. The statements in the function bodies are written only once, are reused from perhaps several locations in a program and are hidden from other functions.

There are several motivations for modularizing a program with functions. One is the divide-and-conquer approach, which makes program development more manageable by constructing programs from small, simple pieces. Another is software reusability—using existing functions as building blocks to create new programs. For example, in earlier programs, we did not have to define how to read a line of text from the keyboard—C++ provides this capability via the getline function of the <string> header file. A third motivation is to avoid repeating code. Also, dividing a program into meaningful functions makes the program easier to debug and maintain.

Software Engineering Observation 6.2

To promote software reusability, every function should be limited to performing a single, well-defined task, and the name of the function should express that task effectively. Such functions make programs easier to write, test, debug and maintain.

Error-Prevention Tip 6.1

A small function that performs one task is easier to test and debug than a larger function that performs many tasks.

Software Engineering Observation 6.3

If you cannot choose a concise name that expresses a function's task, your function might be attempting to perform too many diverse tasks. It is usually best to break such a function into several smaller functions.

As you know, a function is invoked by a function call, and when the called function completes its task, it either returns a result or simply returns control to the caller. An analogy to this program structure is the hierarchical form of management (Figure 6.1). A boss (similar to the calling function) asks a worker (similar to the called function) to perform a task and report back (i.e., return) the results after completing the task. The boss function does not know how the worker function performs its designated tasks. The worker may also call other worker functions, unbeknownst to the boss. This hiding of implementation details promotes good software engineering. Figure 6.1 shows the `boss` function communicating with several worker functions in a hierarchical manner. The `boss` function divides the responsibilities among the various `worker` functions. Note that `worker1` acts as a "boss function" to `worker4` and `worker5`.

6.3 Math Library Functions

As you know, a class can provide member functions that perform the services of the class. For example, in Chapters 3–5, you have called the member functions of various versions of a `GradeBook` object to display the `GradeBook`'s welcome message, to set its course name, to obtain a set of grades and to calculate the average of those grades.

Sometimes functions are not members of a class. Such functions are called global functions. Like a class's member functions, the function prototypes for global functions

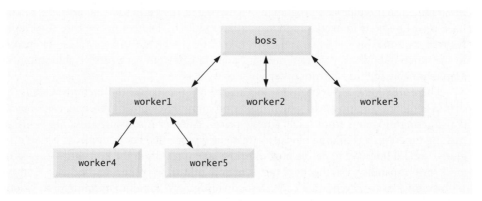

Fig. 6.1 | Hierarchical boss function/worker function relationship.

are placed in header files, so that the global functions can be reused in any program that includes the header file and that can link to the function's object code. For example, recall that we used function pow of the <cmath> header file to raise a value to a power in Figure 5.6. We introduce various functions from the <cmath> header file here to present the concept of global functions that do not belong to a particular class. In this chapter and in subsequent chapters, we use a combination of global functions (such as main) and classes with member functions to implement our example programs.

The <cmath> header file provides a collection of functions that enable you to perform common mathematical calculations. For example, you can calculate the square root of 900.0 with the function call

```
sqrt( 900.0 )
```

The preceding expression evaluates to 30.0. Function sqrt takes an argument of type double and returns a double result. Note that there is no need to create any objects before calling function sqrt. Also note that *all* functions in the <cmath> header file are global functions—therefore, each is called simply by specifying the name of the function followed by parentheses containing the function's arguments.

Function arguments may be constants, variables or more complex expressions. If c = 13.0, d = 3.0 and f = 4.0, then the statement

```
cout << sqrt( c + d * f ) << endl;
```

calculates and prints the square root of 13.0 + 3.0 * 4.0 = 25.0—namely, 5.0. Some math library functions are summarized in Fig. 6.2. In the figure, the variables x and y are of type double.

Function	Description	Example
ceil(x)	rounds x to the smallest integer not less than x	ceil(9.2) is 10.0 ceil(-9.8) is -9.0
cos(x)	trigonometric cosine of x (x in radians)	cos(0.0) is 1.0
exp(x)	exponential function e^x	exp(1.0) is 2.71828 exp(2.0) is 7.38906
fabs(x)	absolute value of x	fabs(5.1) is 5.1 fabs(0.0) is 0.0 fabs(-8.76) is 8.76
floor(x)	rounds x to the largest integer not greater than x	floor(9.2) is 9.0 floor(-9.8) is -10.0
fmod(x, y)	remainder of x/y as a floating-point number	fmod(2.6, 1.2) is 0.2
log(x)	natural logarithm of x (base e)	log(2.718282) is 1.0 log(7.389056) is 2.0

Fig. 6.2 | Math library functions. (Part I of 2.)

Function	Description	Example
log10(x)	logarithm of *x* (base 10)	log10(10.0) is 1.0 log10(100.0) is 2.0
pow(x, y)	*x* raised to power *y* (x^y)	pow(2, 7) is 128 pow(9, .5) is 3
sin(x)	trigonometric sine of *x* (*x* in radians)	sin(0.0) is 0
sqrt(x)	square root of *x* (where *x* is a nonnegative value)	sqrt(9.0) is 3.0
tan(x)	trigonometric tangent of *x* (*x* in radians)	tan(0.0) is 0

Fig. 6.2 | Math library functions. (Part 2 of 2.)

6.4 Function Definitions with Multiple Parameters

Chapters 3–5 presented classes containing simple functions that had at most one parameter. Functions often require more than one piece of information to perform their tasks. We now consider functions with multiple parameters.

The program in Figs. 6.3–6.5 modifies our GradeBook class by including a user-defined function called maximum that determines and returns the largest of three int values. When the application begins execution, the main function (lines 5–14 of Fig. 6.5) creates one object of class GradeBook (line 8) and calls the object's inputGrades member function (line 11) to read three integer grades from the user. In class GradeBook's implementation file (Fig. 6.4), lines 54–55 of member function inputGrades prompt the user to enter three integer values and read them from the user. Line 58 calls member function maximum (defined in lines 62–75). Function maximum determines the largest value, then the return statement (line 74) returns that value to the point at which function inputGrades invoked maximum (line 58). Member function inputGrades then stores maximum's return value in data member maximumGrade. This value is then output by calling function displayGradeReport (line 12 of Fig. 6.5). [*Note:* We named this function displayGradeReport because subsequent versions of class GradeBook will use this function to display a complete grade report, including the maximum and minimum grades.] In Chapter 7, Arrays and Vectors, we'll enhance the GradeBook to process an arbitrary number of grades.

```
1   // Fig. 6.3: GradeBook.h
2   // Definition of class GradeBook that finds the maximum of three grades.
3   // Member functions are defined in GradeBook.cpp
4   #include <string> // program uses C++ standard string class
5   using std::string;
6
```

Fig. 6.3 | GradeBook header file. (Part 1 of 2.)

```
7    // GradeBook class definition
8    class GradeBook
9    {
10   public:
11      GradeBook( string ); // constructor initializes course name
12      void setCourseName( string ); // function to set the course name
13      string getCourseName(); // function to retrieve the course name
14      void displayMessage(); // display a welcome message
15      void inputGrades(); // input three grades from user
16      void displayGradeReport(); // display a report based on the grades
17      int maximum( int, int, int ); // determine max of 3 values
18   private:
19      string courseName; // course name for this GradeBook
20      int maximumGrade; // maximum of three grades
21   }; // end class GradeBook
```

Fig. 6.3 | GradeBook header file. (Part 2 of 2.)

```
1    // Fig. 6.4: GradeBook.cpp
2    // Member-function definitions for class GradeBook that
3    // determines the maximum of three grades.
4    #include <iostream>
5    using std::cout;
6    using std::cin;
7    using std::endl;
8
9    #include "GradeBook.h" // include definition of class GradeBook
10
11   // constructor initializes courseName with string supplied as argument;
12   // initializes studentMaximum to 0
13   GradeBook::GradeBook( string name )
14   {
15      setCourseName( name ); // validate and store courseName
16      maximumGrade = 0; // this value will be replaced by the maximum grade
17   } // end GradeBook constructor
18
19   // function to set the course name; limits name to 25 or fewer characters
20   void GradeBook::setCourseName( string name )
21   {
22      if ( name.length() <= 25 ) // if name has 25 or fewer characters
23         courseName = name; // store the course name in the object
24      else // if name is longer than 25 characters
25      { // set courseName to first 25 characters of parameter name
26         courseName = name.substr( 0, 25 ); // select first 25 characters
27         cout << "Name \"" << name << "\" exceeds maximum length (25).\n"
28            << "Limiting courseName to first 25 characters.\n" << endl;
29      } // end if...else
30   } // end function setCourseName
31
```

Fig. 6.4 | GradeBook class defines function maximum. (Part 1 of 2.)

```
32   // function to retrieve the course name
33   string GradeBook::getCourseName()
34   {
35      return courseName;
36   } // end function getCourseName
37
38   // display a welcome message to the GradeBook user
39   void GradeBook::displayMessage()
40   {
41      // this statement calls getCourseName to get the
42      // name of the course this GradeBook represents
43      cout << "Welcome to the grade book for\n" << getCourseName() << "!\n"
44         << endl;
45   } // end function displayMessage
46
47   // input three grades from user; determine maximum
48   void GradeBook::inputGrades()
49   {
50      int grade1; // first grade entered by user
51      int grade2; // second grade entered by user
52      int grade3; // third grade entered by user
53
54      cout << "Enter three integer grades: ";
55      cin >> grade1 >> grade2 >> grade3;
56
57      // store maximum in member studentMaximum
58      maximumGrade = maximum( grade1, grade2, grade3 );
59   } // end function inputGrades
60
61   // returns the maximum of its three integer parameters
62   int GradeBook::maximum( int x, int y, int z )
63   {
64      int maximumValue = x; // assume x is the largest to start
65
66      // determine whether y is greater than maximumValue
67      if ( y > maximumValue )
68         maximumValue = y; // make y the new maximumValue
69
70      // determine whether z is greater than maximumValue
71      if ( z > maximumValue )
72         maximumValue = z; // make z the new maximumValue
73
74      return maximumValue;
75   } // end function maximum
76
77   // display a report based on the grades entered by user
78   void GradeBook::displayGradeReport()
79   {
80      // output maximum of grades entered
81      cout << "Maximum of grades entered: " << maximumGrade << endl;
82   } // end function displayGradeReport
```

Fig. 6.4 | GradeBook class defines function maximum. (Part 2 of 2.)

```
1   // Fig. 6.5: fig06_05.cpp
2   // Create GradeBook object, input grades and display grade report.
3   #include "GradeBook.h" // include definition of class GradeBook
4
5   int main()
6   {
7      // create GradeBook object
8      GradeBook myGradeBook( "CS101 C++ Programming" );
9
10     myGradeBook.displayMessage(); // display welcome message
11     myGradeBook.inputGrades(); // read grades from user
12     myGradeBook.displayGradeReport(); // display report based on grades
13     return 0; // indicate successful termination
14  } // end main
```

```
Welcome to the grade book for
CS101 C++ Programming!

Enter three integer grades: 86 67 75
Maximum of grades entered: 86
```

```
Welcome to the grade book for
CS101 C++ Programming!

Enter three integer grades: 67 86 75
Maximum of grades entered: 86
```

```
Welcome to the grade book for
CS101 C++ Programming!

Enter three integer grades: 67 75 86
Maximum of grades entered: 86
```

Fig. 6.5 | Demonstrating function maximum.

Software Engineering Observation 6.4

The commas used in line 58 of Fig. 6.4 to separate the arguments to function maximum are not comma operators as discussed in Section 5.3. The comma operator guarantees that its operands are evaluated left to right. The order of evaluation of a function's arguments, however, is not specified by the C++ standard. Thus, different compilers can evaluate function arguments in different orders. The C++ standard does guarantee that all arguments in a function call are evaluated before the called function executes.

Portability Tip 6.1

Sometimes when a function's arguments are more involved expressions, such as those with calls to other functions, the order in which the compiler evaluates the arguments could affect the values of one or more of the arguments. If the evaluation order changes between compilers, the argument values passed to the function could vary, causing subtle logic errors.

Error-Prevention Tip 6.2

If you have doubts about the order of evaluation of a function's arguments and whether the order would affect the values passed to the function, evaluate the arguments in separate assignment statements before the function call, assign the result of each expression to a local variable, then pass those variables as arguments to the function.

The prototype of member function maximum (Fig. 6.3, line 17) indicates that the function returns an integer value, that the function's name is maximum and that the function requires three integer parameters to accomplish its task. Function maximum's header (Fig. 6.4, line 62) matches the function prototype and indicates that the parameter names are x, y and z. When maximum is called (Fig. 6.4, line 58), the parameter x is initialized with the value of the argument grade1, the parameter y is initialized with the value of the argument grade2 and the parameter z is initialized with the value of the argument grade3. There must be one argument in the function call for each parameter (also called a formal parameter) in the function definition.

Notice that multiple parameters are specified in both the function prototype and the function header as a comma-separated list. The compiler refers to the function prototype to check that calls to maximum contain the correct number and types of arguments and that the types of the arguments are in the correct order. In addition, the compiler uses the prototype to ensure that the value returned by the function can be used correctly in the expression that called the function (e.g., a function call that returns void cannot be used as the right side of an assignment statement). Each argument must be consistent with the type of the corresponding parameter. For example, a parameter of type double can receive values like 7.35, 22 or –0.03456, but not a string like "hello". If the arguments passed to a function do not match the types specified in the function's prototype, the compiler attempts to convert the arguments to those types. Section 6.5 discusses this conversion.

Common Programming Error 6.1

Declaring method parameters of the same type as double x, y instead of double x, double y is a syntax error—an explicit type is required for each parameter in the parameter list.

Common Programming Error 6.2

Compilation errors occur if the function prototype, function header and function calls do not all agree in the number, type and order of arguments and parameters, and in the return type.

Software Engineering Observation 6.5

A function that has many parameters may be performing too many tasks. Consider dividing the function into smaller functions that perform the separate tasks. Limit the function header to one line if possible.

To determine the maximum value (lines 62–75 of Fig. 6.4), we begin with the assumption that parameter x contains the largest value, so line 64 of function maximum declares local variable maximumValue and initializes it with the value of parameter x. Of course, it is possible that parameter y or z contains the actual largest value, so we must compare each of these values with maximumValue. The if statement at lines 67–68 determines whether y is greater than maximumValue and, if so, assigns y to maximumValue. The if statement at lines 71–72 determines whether z is greater than maximumValue and, if so, assigns z to `maximumValue`. At this point the largest of the three values is in `maximumValue`, so line 74 returns that value to the call in line 58. When program control returns to the point in the program where `maximum` was called, `maximum`'s parameters x, y and z are no longer accessible to the program. We'll see why in the next section.

There are three ways to return control to the point at which a function was invoked. If the function does not return a result (i.e., the function has a `void` return type), control returns when the program reaches the function-ending right brace, or by execution of the statement

```
return;
```

If the function does return a result, the statement

```
return expression;
```

evaluates *expression* and returns the value of *expression* to the caller.

6.5 Function Prototypes and Argument Coercion

A function prototype (also called a function declaration) tells the compiler the name of a function, the type of data returned by the function, the number of parameters the function expects to receive, the types of those parameters and the order in which the parameters of those types are expected.

Software Engineering Observation 6.6

Function prototypes are required in C++. Use #include preprocessor directives to obtain function prototypes for the C++ Standard Library functions from the header files for the appropriate libraries (e.g., the prototype for math function sqrt is in header file <cmath>; a partial list of C++ Standard Library header files appears in Section 6.6). Also use #include to obtain header files containing function prototypes written by you or your group members.

Common Programming Error 6.3

If a function is defined before it is invoked, then the function's definition also serves as the function's prototype, so a separate prototype is unnecessary. If a function is invoked before it is defined, and that function does not have a function prototype, a compilation error occurs.

Software Engineering Observation 6.7

Always provide function prototypes, even though it is possible to omit them when functions are defined before they are used (in which case the function header acts as the function prototype as well). Providing the prototypes avoids tying the code to the order in which functions are defined (which can easily change as a program evolves).

Function Signatures

The portion of a function prototype that includes the name of the function and the types of its arguments is called the function signature or simply the signature. The function signature does not specify the function's return type. Function in the same scope must have unique signatures. The scope of a function is the region of a program in which the function is known and accessible. We'll say more about scope in Section 6.10.

Common Programming Error 6.4

It is a compilation error if two functions in the same scope have the same signature but different return types.

In Fig. 6.3, if the function prototype in line 17 had been written

```
void maximum( int, int, int );
```

the compiler would report an error, because the void return type in the function prototype would differ from the int return type in the function header. Similarly, such a prototype would cause the statement

```
cout << maximum( 6, 9, 0 );
```

to generate a compilation error, because that statement depends on maximum to return a value to be displayed.

Argument Coercion

An important feature of function prototypes is argument coercion—i.e., forcing arguments to the appropriate types specified by the parameter declarations. For example, a program can call a function with an integer argument, even though the function prototype specifies a double argument—the function will still work correctly.

Argument Promotion Rules

Sometimes, argument values that do not correspond precisely to the parameter types in the function prototype can be converted by the compiler to the proper type before the function is called. These conversions occur as specified by C++'s promotion rules. The promotion rules indicate how to convert between types without losing data. An int can be converted to a double without changing its value. However, a double converted to an int truncates the fractional part of the double value. Keep in mind that double variables can hold numbers of much greater magnitude than int variables, so the loss of data may be considerable. Values may also be modified when converting large integer types to small integer types (e.g., long to short), signed to unsigned or unsigned to signed.

The promotion rules apply to expressions containing values of two or more data types; such expressions are also referred to as mixed-type expressions. The type of each value in a mixed-type expression is promoted to the "highest" type in the expression (actually a temporary version of each value is created and used for the expression—the original values remain unchanged). Promotion also occurs when the type of a function argument does not match the parameter type specified in the function definition or prototype. Figure 6.6 lists the fundamental data types in order from "highest type" to "lowest type."

Converting values to lower fundamental types can result in incorrect values. Therefore, a value can be converted to a lower fundamental type only by explicitly assigning the value to a variable of lower type (some compilers will issue a warning in this case) or by using a cast operator (see Section 4.9). Function argument values are converted to the parameter types in a function prototype as if they were being assigned directly to variables of those types. If a square function that uses an integer parameter is called with a floating-

Data types
long double
double
float
unsigned long int   (synonymous with unsigned long)
long int   (synonymous with long)
unsigned int   (synonymous with unsigned)
int
unsigned short int   (synonymous with unsigned short)
short int   (synonymous with short)
unsigned char
char
bool

Fig. 6.6 | Promotion hierarchy for fundamental data types.

point argument, the argument is converted to int (a lower type), and square could return an incorrect value. For example, square(4.5) returns 16, not 20.25.

Common Programming Error 6.5

Converting from a higher data type in the promotion hierarchy to a lower type, or between signed and unsigned, can corrupt the data value, causing a loss of information.

Common Programming Error 6.6

It is a compilation error if the arguments in a function call do not match the number and types of the parameters declared in the corresponding function prototype. It is also an error if the number of arguments in the call matches, but the arguments cannot be implicitly converted to the expected types.

6.6 C++ Standard Library Header Files

The C++ Standard Library is divided into many portions, each with its own header file. The header files contain the function prototypes for the related functions that form each portion of the library. The header files also contain definitions of various class types and functions, as well as constants needed by those functions. A header file "instructs" the compiler on how to interface with library and user-written components.

Figure 6.7 lists some common C++ Standard Library header files. The table indicates which of these header files we use in this book. Many other header files are used in Chapters 15-23 of our sister book, *C++ How to Program, 5/e*. Header file names ending in .h are "old-style" header files that have been superseded by the C++ Standard Library header files. We use only the C++ Standard Library versions of each header file in this book to ensure that our examples will work on most standard C++ compilers.

C++ Standard Library header file	Explanation
<iostream>	Contains function prototypes for the C++ standard input and standard output functions, introduced in Chapter 2. This header file replaces header file <iostream.h>.
<iomanip>	Contains function prototypes for stream manipulators that format streams of data. This header file is first used in Section 4.9. This header file replaces header file <iomanip.h>.
<cmath>	Contains function prototypes for math library functions (discussed in Section 6.3). This header file replaces header file <math.h>.
<cstdlib>	Contains function prototypes for conversions of numbers to text, text to numbers, memory allocation, random numbers and various other utility functions. Portions of the header file are covered in Section 6.7. This header file replaces header file <stdlib.h>.
<ctime>	Contains function prototypes and types for manipulating the time and date. This header file replaces header file <time.h>. This header file is used in Section 6.7.
<vector>, <list>, <deque>, <queue>, <stack>, <map>, <set>, <bitset>	These header files contain classes that implement the C++ Standard Library containers. Containers store data during a program's execution. The <vector> header is introduced in Chapter 7, Arrays and Vectors.
<cctype>	Contains function prototypes for functions that test characters for certain properties (such as whether the character is a digit or a punctuation), and function prototypes for functions that can be used to convert lowercase letters to uppercase letters and vice versa. This header file replaces header file <ctype.h>. These topics are introduced in Chapter 8, Pointers and Pointer-Based Strings.
<cstring>	Contains function prototypes for C-style string-processing functions. This header file replaces header file <string.h>. This header file is used in Chapter 11, Operator Overloading; String and Array Objects.
<typeinfo>	Contains classes for runtime type identification (determining data types at execution time). This header file is discussed in Section 13.8.
<exception>, <stdexcept>	These header files contain classes that are used for exception handling, a technique that allows a program to resolve (or handle) problems that occur during its execution.

Fig. 6.7 | C++ Standard Library header files. (Part 1 of 2.)

C++ Standard Library header file	Explanation
`<memory>`	Contains classes and functions used by the C++ Standard Library to allocate memory to the C++ Standard Library containers.
`<fstream>`	Contains function prototypes for functions that perform input from files on disk and output to files on disk. This header file replaces header file `<fstream.h>`.
`<string>`	Contains the definition of class `string` from the C++ Standard Library (introduced in Chapter 3).
`<sstream>`	Contains function prototypes for functions that perform input from strings in memory and output to strings in memory.
`<functional>`	Contains classes and functions used by C++ Standard Library algorithms.
`<iterator>`	Contains classes for accessing data in the C++ Standard Library containers.
`<algorithm>`	Contains functions for manipulating data in C++ Standard Library containers.
`<cassert>`	Contains macros for adding diagnostics that aid program debugging. This replaces header file `<assert.h>` from pre-standard C++.
`<cfloat>`	Contains the floating-point size limits of the system. This header file replaces header file `<float.h>`.
`<climits>`	Contains the integral size limits of the system. This header file replaces header file `<limits.h>`.
`<cstdio>`	Contains function prototypes for the C-style standard input/output library functions and information used by them. This header file replaces header file `<stdio.h>`.
`<locale>`	Contains classes and functions normally used by stream processing to process data in the natural form for different languages (e.g., monetary formats, sorting strings, character presentation, etc.).
`<limits>`	Contains classes for defining the numerical data type limits on each computer platform.
`<utility>`	Contains classes and functions that are used by many C++ Standard Library header files.

Fig. 6.7 | C++ Standard Library header files. (Part 2 of 2.)

6.7 Case Study: Random Number Generation

We now take a brief and hopefully entertaining diversion into a popular programming application, namely simulation and game playing. In this and the next section, we develop a game-playing program that includes multiple functions. The program uses many of the control statements and concepts discussed to this point.

The element of chance can be introduced into computer applications by using the C++ Standard Library function rand.

Consider the following statement:

```
i = rand();
```

The function rand generates an unsigned integer between 0 and RAND_MAX (a symbolic constant defined in the <cstdlib> header file). The value of RAND_MAX must be at least 32767—the maximum positive value for a two-byte (16-bit) integer. For GNU C++, the value of RAND_MAX is 214748647; for Visual Studio, the value of RAND_MAX is 32767. If rand truly produces integers at random, every number between 0 and RAND_MAX has an equal *chance* (or probability) of being chosen each time rand is called.

The range of values produced directly by the function rand often is different than what a specific application requires. For example, a program that simulates coin tossing might require only 0 for "heads" and 1 for "tails." A program that simulates rolling a six-sided die would require random integers in the range 1 to 6. A program that randomly predicts the next type of spaceship (out of four possibilities) that will fly across the horizon in a video game might require random integers in the range 1 through 4.

Rolling a Six-Sided Die

To demonstrate rand, let us develop a program (Fig. 6.8) to simulate 20 rolls of a six-sided die and print the value of each roll. The function prototype for the rand function is in <cstdlib>. To produce integers in the range 0 to 5, we use the modulus operator (%) with rand as follows:

```
rand() % 6
```

This is called scaling. The number 6 is called the scaling factor. We then shift the range of numbers produced by adding 1 to our previous result. Figure 6.8 confirms that the results are in the range 1 to 6.

```
1   // Fig. 6.8: fig06_08.cpp
2   // Shifted and scaled random integers.
3   #include <iostream>
4   using std::cout;
5   using std::endl;
6
7   #include <iomanip>
8   using std::setw;
9
10  #include <cstdlib> // contains function prototype for rand
11  using std::rand;
12
13  int main()
14  {
```

Fig. 6.8 | Shifted, scaled integers produced by 1 + rand() % 6. (Part 1 of 2.)

```
15     // loop 20 times
16     for ( int counter = 1; counter <= 20; counter++ )
17     {
18        // pick random number from 1 to 6 and output it
19        cout << setw( 10 ) << ( 1 + rand() % 6 );
20
21        // if counter is divisible by 5, start a new line of output
22        if ( counter % 5 == 0 )
23           cout << endl;
24     } // end for
25
26     return 0; // indicates successful termination
27  } // end main
```

6	6	5	5	6
5	1	1	5	3
6	6	2	4	2
6	2	3	4	1

Fig. 6.8 | Shifted, scaled integers produced by `1 + rand() % 6`. (Part 2 of 2.)

Rolling a Six-Sided Die 6,000,000 Times

To show that the numbers produced by function `rand` occur with approximately equal likelihood, Fig. 6.9 simulates 6,000,000 rolls of a die. Each integer in the range 1 to 6 should appear approximately 1,000,000 times. This is confirmed by the output window at the end of Fig. 6.9.

```
1   // Fig. 6.9: fig06_09.cpp
2   // Roll a six-sided die 6,000,000 times.
3   #include <iostream>
4   using std::cout;
5   using std::endl;
6
7   #include <iomanip>
8   using std::setw;
9
10  #include <cstdlib> // contains function prototype for rand
11  using std::rand;
12
13  int main()
14  {
15     int frequency1 = 0; // count of 1s rolled
16     int frequency2 = 0; // count of 2s rolled
17     int frequency3 = 0; // count of 3s rolled
18     int frequency4 = 0; // count of 4s rolled
19     int frequency5 = 0; // count of 5s rolled
20     int frequency6 = 0; // count of 6s rolled
21
22     int face; // stores most recently rolled value
23
```

Fig. 6.9 | Rolling a six-sided die 6,000,000 times. (Part 1 of 2.)

```
24    // summarize results of 6,000,000 rolls of a die
25    for ( int roll = 1; roll <= 6000000; roll++ )
26    {
27       face = 1 + rand() % 6; // random number from 1 to 6
28
29       // determine roll value 1-6 and increment appropriate counter
30       switch ( face )
31       {
32          case 1:
33             ++frequency1; // increment the 1s counter
34             break;
35          case 2:
36             ++frequency2; // increment the 2s counter
37             break;
38          case 3:
39             ++frequency3; // increment the 3s counter
40             break;
41          case 4:
42             ++frequency4; // increment the 4s counter
43             break;
44          case 5:
45             ++frequency5; // increment the 5s counter
46             break;
47          case 6:
48             ++frequency6; // increment the 6s counter
49             break;
50          default: // invalid value
51             cout << "Program should never get here!";
52       } // end switch
53    } // end for
54
55    cout << "Face" << setw( 13 ) << "Frequency" << endl; // output headers
56    cout << "    1" << setw( 13 ) << frequency1
57       << "\n    2" << setw( 13 ) << frequency2
58       << "\n    3" << setw( 13 ) << frequency3
59       << "\n    4" << setw( 13 ) << frequency4
60       << "\n    5" << setw( 13 ) << frequency5
61       << "\n    6" << setw( 13 ) << frequency6 << endl;
62    return 0; // indicates successful termination
63 } // end main
```

```
Face      Frequency
  1        999702
  2       1000823
  3        999378
  4        998898
  5       1000777
  6       1000422
```

Fig. 6.9 | Rolling a six-sided die 6,000,000 times. (Part 2 of 2.)

As the program output shows, we can simulate the rolling of a six-sided die by scaling and shifting the values produced by rand. Note that the program should never get to the default case (lines 50–51) provided in the switch structure, because the switch's controlling expression (face) always has values in the range 1–6; however, we provide the default case as a matter of good practice. After we study arrays in Chapter 7, we show how to replace the entire switch structure in Fig. 6.9 elegantly with a single-line statement.

Error-Prevention Tip 6.3

Provide a default case in a switch to catch errors even if you are absolutely, positively certain that you have no bugs!

Randomizing the Random Number Generator
Executing the program of Fig. 6.8 again produces

6	6	5	5	6
5	1	1	5	3
6	6	2	4	2
6	2	3	4	1

Notice that the program prints exactly the same sequence of values shown in Fig. 6.8. How can these be random numbers? Ironically, this repeatability is an important characteristic of function rand. When debugging a simulation program, this repeatability is essential for proving that corrections to the program work properly.

Function rand actually generates pseudorandom numbers. Repeatedly calling rand produces a sequence of numbers that appears to be random. However, the sequence repeats itself each time the program executes. Once a program has been thoroughly debugged, it can be conditioned to produce a different sequence of random numbers for each execution. This is called randomizing and is accomplished with the C++ Standard Library function srand. Function srand takes an unsigned integer argument and seeds the rand function to produce a different sequence of random numbers for each execution of the program.

Figure 6.10 demonstrates function srand. The program uses the data type unsigned, which is short for unsigned int. An int is stored in at least two bytes of memory (typically four bytes of memory on today's popular 32-bit systems) and can have positive and negative values. A variable of type unsigned int is also stored in at least two bytes of memory. A two-byte unsigned int can have only nonnegative values in the range 0–65535. A four-byte unsigned int can have only nonnegative values in the range 0–4294967295. Function srand takes an unsigned int value as an argument. The function prototype for the srand function is in header file <cstdlib>.

```
1   // Fig. 6.10: fig06_10.cpp
2   // Randomizing die-rolling program.
3   #include <iostream>
4   using std::cout;
5   using std::cin;
6   using std::endl;
7
```

Fig. 6.10 | Randomizing the die-rolling program. (Part 1 of 2.)

```
8   #include <iomanip>
9   using std::setw;
10
11  #include <cstdlib> // contains prototypes for functions srand and rand
12  using std::rand;
13  using std::srand;
14
15  int main()
16  {
17     unsigned seed; // stores the seed entered by the user
18
19     cout << "Enter seed: ";
20     cin >> seed;
21     srand( seed ); // seed random number generator
22
23     // loop 10 times
24     for ( int counter = 1; counter <= 10; counter++ )
25     {
26        // pick random number from 1 to 6 and output it
27        cout << setw( 10 ) << ( 1 + rand() % 6 );
28
29        // if counter is divisible by 5, start a new line of output
30        if ( counter % 5 == 0 )
31           cout << endl;
32     } // end for
33
34     return 0; // indicates successful termination
35  } // end main
```

```
Enter seed: 67
        6         1         4         6         2
        1         6         1         6         4
```

```
Enter seed: 432
        4         6         3         1         6
        3         1         5         4         2
```

```
Enter seed: 67
        6         1         4         6         2
        1         6         1         6         4
```

Fig. 6.10 | Randomizing the die-rolling program. (Part 2 of 2.)

Let us run the program several times and observe the results. Notice that the program produces a *different* sequence of random numbers each time it executes, provided that the user enters a different seed. We used the same seed in the first and third sample outputs, so the same series of 10 numbers is displayed in each of those outputs.

To randomize without having to enter a seed each time, we may use a statement like

```
srand( time( 0 ) );
```

This causes the computer to read its clock to obtain the value for the seed. Function `time` (with the argument 0 as written in the preceding statement) returns the current time as the number of seconds since January 1, 1970 at midnight Greenwich Mean Time (GMT). This value is converted to an `unsigned` integer and used as the seed to the random number generator. The function prototype for `time` is in `<ctime>`.

Common Programming Error 6.7

Calling function `srand` more than once in a program restarts the pseudorandom number sequence and can affect the randomness of the numbers produced by `rand`.

Generalized Scaling and Shifting of Random Numbers

Previously, we demonstrated how to write a single statement to simulate the rolling of a six-sided die with the statement

```
face = 1 + rand() % 6;
```

which always assigns an integer (at random) to variable `face` in the range $1 \leq \text{face} \leq 6$. Note that the width of this range (i.e., the number of consecutive integers in the range) is 6 and the starting number in the range is 1. Referring to the preceding statement, we see that the width of the range is determined by the number used to scale `rand` with the modulus operator (i.e., 6), and the starting number of the range is equal to the number (i.e., 1) that is added to the expression `rand % 6`. We can generalize this result as

```
number = shiftingValue + rand() % scalingFactor;
```

where *shiftingValue* is equal to the first number in the desired range of consecutive integers and *scalingFactor* is equal to the width of the desired range of consecutive integers. The exercises show that it is possible to choose integers at random from sets of values other than ranges of consecutive integers.

Common Programming Error 6.8

Using `srand` in place of `rand` to attempt to generate random numbers is a compilation error— function `srand` does not return a value.

6.8 Case Study: Game of Chance and Introducing enum

One of the most popular games of chance is a dice game known as "craps," which is played in casinos and back alleys worldwide. The rules of the game are straightforward:

A player rolls two dice. Each die has six faces. These faces contain 1, 2, 3, 4, 5 and 6 spots. After the dice have come to rest, the sum of the spots on the two upward faces is calculated. If the sum is 7 or 11 on the first roll, the player wins. If the sum is 2, 3 or 12 on the first roll (called "craps"), the player loses (i.e., the "house" wins). If the sum is 4, 5, 6, 8, 9 or 10 on the first roll, then that sum becomes the player's "point." To win, you must continue rolling the dice until you "make your point." The player loses by rolling a 7 before making the point.

The program in Fig. 6.11 simulates the game of craps.

In the rules of the game, notice that the player must roll two dice on the first roll and on all subsequent rolls. We define function `rollDice` (lines 71–83) to roll the dice and compute and print their sum. Function `rollDice` is defined once, but it is called from two places (lines 27 and 51) in the program. Interestingly, `rollDice` takes no arguments, so we have indicated an empty parameter list in the prototype (line 14) and in the function header (line 71). Function rollDice does return the sum of the two dice, so return type int is indicated in the function prototype and function header.

```cpp
1   // Fig. 6.11: fig06_11.cpp
2   // Craps simulation.
3   #include <iostream>
4   using std::cout;
5   using std::endl;
6
7   #include <cstdlib> // contains prototypes for functions srand and rand
8   using std::rand;
9   using std::srand;
10
11  #include <ctime> // contains prototype for function time
12  using std::time;
13
14  int rollDice(); // rolls dice, calculates amd displays sum
15
16  int main()
17  {
18     // enumeration with constants that represent the game status
19     enum Status { CONTINUE, WON, LOST }; // all caps in constants
20
21     int myPoint; // point if no win or loss on first roll
22     Status gameStatus; // can contain CONTINUE, WON or LOST
23
24     // randomize random number generator using current time
25     srand( time( 0 ) );
26
27     int sumOfDice = rollDice(); // first roll of the dice
28
29     // determine game status and point (if needed) based on first roll
30     switch ( sumOfDice )
31     {
32        case 7: // win with 7 on first roll
33        case 11: // win with 11 on first roll
34           gameStatus = WON;
35           break;
36        case 2: // lose with 2 on first roll
37        case 3: // lose with 3 on first roll
38        case 12: // lose with 12 on first roll
39           gameStatus = LOST;
40           break;
41        default: // did not win or lose, so remember point
42           gameStatus = CONTINUE; // game is not over
43           myPoint = sumOfDice; // remember the point
44           cout << "Point is " << myPoint << endl;
45           break; // optional at end of switch
46     } // end switch
47
```

Fig. 6.11 | Craps simulation. (Part 1 of 3.)

```
48      // while game is not complete
49      while ( gameStatus == CONTINUE ) // not WON or LOST
50      {
51         sumOfDice = rollDice(); // roll dice again
52
53         // determine game status
54         if ( sumOfDice == myPoint ) // win by making point
55            gameStatus = WON;
56         else
57            if ( sumOfDice == 7 ) // lose by rolling 7 before point
58               gameStatus = LOST;
59      } // end while
60
61      // display won or lost message
62      if ( gameStatus == WON )
63         cout << "Player wins" << endl;
64      else
65         cout << "Player loses" << endl;
66
67      return 0; // indicates successful termination
68   } // end main
69
70   // roll dice, calculate sum and display results
71   int rollDice()
72   {
73      // pick random die values
74      int die1 = 1 + rand() % 6; // first die roll
75      int die2 = 1 + rand() % 6; // second die roll
76
77      int sum = die1 + die2; // compute sum of die values
78
79      // display results of this roll
80      cout << "Player rolled " << die1 << " + " << die2
81         << " = " << sum << endl;
82      return sum; // end function rollDice
83   } // end function rollDice
```

```
Player rolled 2 + 5 = 7
Player wins
```

```
Player rolled 6 + 6 = 12
Player loses
```

```
Player rolled 3 + 3 = 6
Point is 6
Player rolled 5 + 3 = 8
Player rolled 4 + 5 = 9
Player rolled 2 + 1 = 3
Player rolled 1 + 5 = 6
Player wins
```

Fig. 6.11 | Craps simulation. (Part 2 of 3.)

```
Player rolled 1 + 3 = 4
Point is 4
Player rolled 4 + 6 = 10
Player rolled 2 + 4 = 6
Player rolled 6 + 4 = 10
Player rolled 2 + 3 = 5
Player rolled 2 + 4 = 6
Player rolled 1 + 1 = 2
Player rolled 4 + 4 = 8
Player rolled 4 + 3 = 7
Player loses
```

Fig. 6.11 | Craps simulation. (Part 3 of 3.)

The game is reasonably involved. The player may win or lose on the first roll or on any subsequent roll. The program uses variable gameStatus to keep track of this. Variable gameStatus is declared to be of new type Status. Line 19 declares a user-defined type called an enumeration. An enumeration, introduced by the keyword enum and followed by a type name (in this case, Status), is a set of integer constants represented by identifiers. The values of these enumeration constants start at 0, unless specified otherwise, and increment by 1. In the preceding enumeration, the constant CONTINUE has the value 0, WON has the value 1 and LOST has the value 2. The identifiers in an enum must be unique, but separate enumeration constants can have the same integer value (we show how to accomplish this momentarily).

Good Programming Practice 6.1

Capitalize the first letter of an identifier used as a user-defined type name.

Good Programming Practice 6.2

Use only uppercase letters in the names of enumeration constants. This makes these constants stand out in a program and reminds the programmer that enumeration constants are not variables.

Variables of user-defined type Status can be assigned only one of the three values declared in the enumeration. When the game is won, the program sets variable gameStatus to WON (lines 34 and 55). When the game is lost, the program sets variable gameStatus to LOST (lines 39 and 58). Otherwise, the program sets variable gameStatus to CONTINUE (line 42) to indicate that the dice must be rolled again.

Another popular enumeration is

```
enum Months { JAN = 1, FEB, MAR, APR, MAY, JUN, JUL, AUG,
    SEP, OCT, NOV, DEC };
```

which creates user-defined type Months with enumeration constants representing the months of the year. The first value in the preceding enumeration is explicitly set to 1, so the remaining values increment from 1, resulting in the values 1 through 12. Any enumeration constant can be assigned an integer value in the enumeration definition, and subsequent enumeration constants each have a value 1 higher than the preceding constant in the list until the next explicit setting.

After the first roll, if the game is won or lost, the program skips the body of the `while` statement (lines 49–59) because `gameStatus` is not equal to `CONTINUE`. The program proceeds to the `if...else` statement at lines 62–65, which prints `"Player wins"` if `gameStatus` is equal to `WON` and `"Player loses"` if `gameStatus` is equal to `LOST`.

After the first roll, if the game is not over, the program saves the sum in `myPoint` (line 43). Execution proceeds with the `while` statement, because `gameStatus` is equal to `CONTINUE`. During each iteration of the `while`, the program calls `rollDice` to produce a new sum. If sum matches `myPoint`, the program sets `gameStatus` to `WON` (line 55), the `while`-test fails, the `if...else` statement prints `"Player wins"` and execution terminates. If `sum` is equal to 7, the program sets `gameStatus` to `LOST` (line 58), the `while`-test fails, the `if...else` statement prints `"Player loses"` and execution terminates.

Note the interesting use of the various program control mechanisms we have discussed. The craps program uses two functions—main and `rollDice`—and the `switch`, `while`, `if...else`, nested `if...else` and nested `if` statements. In the exercises, we investigate various interesting characteristics of the game of craps.

Good Programming Practice 6.3

Using enumerations rather than integer constants can make programs clearer and more maintainable. You can set the value of an enumeration constant once in the enumeration declaration.

Common Programming Error 6.9

Assigning the integer equivalent of an enumeration constant to a variable of the enumeration type is a compilation error.

Common Programming Error 6.10

After an enumeration constant has been defined, attempting to assign another value to the enumeration constant is a compilation error.

6.9 Storage Classes

The programs you have seen so far use identifiers for variable names. The attributes of variables include name, type, size and value. This chapter also uses identifiers as names for user-defined functions. Actually, each identifier in a program has other attributes, including storage class, scope and linkage.

C++ provides five storage-class specifiers: `auto`, `register`, `extern`, `mutable` and `static`. This section discusses storage-class specifiers `auto`, `register`, `extern` and `static`. Storage-class specifier `mutable` (discussed in detail in Chapter 24 of our sister book, *C++ How to Program, 5/e*) is used exclusively with classes.

Storage Class, Scope and Linkage

An identifier's storage class determines the period during which that identifier exists in memory. Some identifiers exist briefly, some are repeatedly created and destroyed and others exist for the entire execution of a program. This section discusses two storage classes: static and automatic.

An identifier's scope is where the identifier can be referenced in a program. Some identifiers can be referenced throughout a program; others can be referenced from only limited portions of a program. Section 6.10 discusses the scope of identifiers.

An identifier's linkage determines whether an identifier is known only in the source file where it is declared or across multiple files that are compiled, then linked together. An identifier's storage-class specifier helps determine its storage class and linkage.

Storage Class Categories

The storage-class specifiers can be split into two storage classes: automatic storage class and static storage class. Keywords `auto` and `register` are used to declare variables of the automatic storage class. Such variables are created when program execution enters the block in which they are defined, they exist while the block is active and they are destroyed when the program exits the block.

Local Variables

Only local variables of a function can be of automatic storage class. A function's local variables and parameters normally are of automatic storage class. The storage class specifier `auto` explicitly declares variables of automatic storage class. For example, the following declaration indicates that `double` variables x and y are local variables of automatic storage class—they exist only in the nearest enclosing pair of curly braces within the body of the function in which the definition appears:

```
auto double x, y;
```

Local variables are of automatic storage class by default, so keyword `auto` rarely is used. For the remainder of the text, we refer to variables of automatic storage class simply as automatic variables.

Performance Tip 6.1

Automatic storage is a means of conserving memory, because automatic storage class variables exist in memory only when the block in which they are defined is executing.

Software Engineering Observation 6.8

Automatic storage is an example of the principle of least privilege, which is fundamental to good software engineering. In the context of an application, the principle states that code should be granted only the amount of privilege and access that it needs to accomplish its designated task, but no more. Why should we have variables stored in memory and accessible when they are not needed?

Register Variables

Data in the machine-language version of a program is normally loaded into registers for calculations and other processing.

Performance Tip 6.2

The storage-class specifier `register` can be placed before an automatic variable declaration to suggest that the compiler maintain the variable in one of the computer's high-speed hardware registers rather than in memory. If intensely used variables such as counters or totals are maintained in hardware registers, the overhead of repeatedly loading the variables from memory into the registers and storing the results back into memory is eliminated.

Common Programming Error 6.11

Using multiple storage-class specifiers for an identifier is a syntax error. Only one storage class specifier can be applied to an identifier. For example, if you include register, *do not also include* auto.

The compiler might ignore register declarations. For example, there might not be a sufficient number of registers available for the compiler to use. The following definition *suggests* that the integer variable counter be placed in one of the computer's registers; regardless of whether the compiler does this, counter is initialized to 1:

```
register int counter = 1;
```

The register keyword can be used only with local variables and function parameters.

Performance Tip 6.3

Often, register *is unnecessary. Today's optimizing compilers are capable of recognizing frequently used variables and can decide to place them in registers without needing a* register *declaration from the programmer.*

Static Storage Class

Keywords extern and static declare identifiers for variables of the static storage class and for functions. Static-storage-class variables exist from the point at which the program begins execution and last for the duration of the program. A static-storage-class variable's storage is allocated when the program begins execution. Such a variable is initialized once when its declaration is encountered. For functions, the name of the function exists when the program begins execution, just as for all other functions. However, even though the variables and the function names exist from the start of program execution, this does not mean that these identifiers can be used throughout the program. Storage class and scope (where a name can be used) are separate issues, as we will see in Section 6.10.

Identifiers with Static Storage Class

There are two types of identifiers with static storage class—external identifiers (such as global variables and global function names) and local variables declared with the storage class specifier static. Global variables are created by placing variable declarations outside any class or function definition. Global variables retain their values throughout the execution of the program. Global variables and global functions can be referenced by any function that follows their declarations or definitions in the source file.

Software Engineering Observation 6.9

Declaring a variable as global rather than local allows unintended side effects to occur when a function that does not need access to the variable accidentally or maliciously modifies it. This is another example of the principle of least privilege. In general, except for truly global resources such as cin *and* cout, *the use of global variables should be avoided except in certain situations with unique performance requirements.*

Software Engineering Observation 6.10

Variables used only in a particular function should be declared as local variables in that function rather than as global variables.

Local variables declared with the keyword `static` are still known only in the function in which they are declared, but, unlike automatic variables, `static` local variables retain their values when the function returns to its caller. The next time the function is called, the `static` local variables contain the values they had when the function last completed execution. The following statement declares local variable `count` to be `static` and to be initialized to 1:

```
static int count = 1;
```

All numeric variables of the static storage class are initialized to zero if they are not explicitly initialized by the programmer, but it is nevertheless a good practice to explicitly initialize all variables.

Storage-class specifiers `extern` and `static` have special meaning when they are applied explicitly to external identifiers such as global variables and global function names. These uses of `extern` and `static` are discussed in Appendix E, C Legacy Code Topics, of our sister book, *C++ How to Program, 5/e*.

6.10 Scope Rules

The portion of the program where an identifier can be used is known as its scope. For example, when we declare a local variable in a block, it can be referenced only in that block and in blocks nested within that block. This section discusses four scopes for an identifier—function scope, file scope, block scope and function-prototype scope. Later we will see one other scope—class scope (Chapter 9). C++ defines one other scope—namespace scope—that we discuss in Chapter 24 of our sister book, *C++ How to Program, 5/e*).

An identifier declared outside any function or class has file scope. Such an identifier is "known" in all functions from the point at which it is declared until the end of the file. Global variables, function definitions and function prototypes placed outside a function all have file scope.

Labels (identifiers followed by a colon such as `start:`) are the only identifiers with function scope. Labels can be used anywhere in the function in which they appear, but cannot be referenced outside the function body. Labels are used in `goto` statements (Appendix E). Labels are implementation details that functions hide from one another.

Identifiers declared inside a block have block scope. Block scope begins at the identifier's declaration and ends at the terminating right brace (}) of the block in which the identifier is declared. Local variables have block scope, as do function parameters, which are also local variables of the function. Any block can contain variable declarations. When blocks are nested and an identifier in an outer block has the same name as an identifier in an inner block, the identifier in the outer block is "hidden" until the inner block terminates. While executing in the inner block, the inner block sees the value of its own local identifier and not the value of the identically named identifier in the enclosing block. Local variables declared `static` still have block scope, even though they exist from the time the program begins execution. Storage duration does not affect the scope of an identifier.

The only identifiers with function prototype scope are those used in the parameter list of a function prototype. As mentioned previously, function prototypes do not require names in the parameter list—only types are required. Names appearing in the parameter list of a function prototype are ignored by the compiler. Identifiers used in a function prototype can be reused elsewhere in the program without ambiguity. In a single prototype, a particular identifier can be used only once.

Common Programming Error 6.12

Accidentally using the same name for an identifier in an inner block that is used for an identifier in an outer block, when in fact the programmer wants the identifier in the outer block to be active for the duration of the inner block, is normally a logic error.

Good Programming Practice 6.4

Avoid variable names that hide names in outer scopes. This can be accomplished by avoiding the use of duplicate identifiers in a program.

The program of Fig. 6.12 demonstrates scoping issues with global variables, automatic local variables and static local variables.

```
1   // Fig. 6.12: fig06_12.cpp
2   // A scoping example.
3   #include <iostream>
4   using std::cout;
5   using std::endl;
6
7   void useLocal( void ); // function prototype
8   void useStaticLocal( void ); // function prototype
9   void useGlobal( void ); // function prototype
10
11  int x = 1; // global variable
12
13  int main()
14  {
15     int x = 5; // local variable to main
16
17     cout << "local x in main's outer scope is " << x << endl;
18
19     { // start new scope
20        int x = 7; // hides x in outer scope
21
22        cout << "local x in main's inner scope is " << x << endl;
23     } // end new scope
24
25     cout << "local x in main's outer scope is " << x << endl;
26
27     useLocal(); // useLocal has local x
28     useStaticLocal(); // useStaticLocal has static local x
29     useGlobal(); // useGlobal uses global x
30     useLocal(); // useLocal reinitializes its local x
31     useStaticLocal(); // static local x retains its prior value
32     useGlobal(); // global x also retains its value
33
34     cout << "\nlocal x in main is " << x << endl;
35     return 0; // indicates successful termination
36  } // end main
37
```

Fig. 6.12 | Scoping example. (Part 1 of 2.)

```
38   // useLocal reinitializes local variable x during each call
39   void useLocal( void )
40   {
41      int x = 25; // initialized each time useLocal is called
42
43      cout << "\nlocal x is " << x << " on entering useLocal" << endl;
44      x++;
45      cout << "local x is " << x << " on exiting useLocal" << endl;
46   } // end function useLocal
47
48   // useStaticLocal initializes static local variable x only the
49   // first time the function is called; value of x is saved
50   // between calls to this function
51   void useStaticLocal( void )
52   {
53      static int x = 50; // initialized first time useStaticLocal is called
54
55      cout << "\nlocal static x is " << x << " on entering useStaticLocal"
56         << endl;
57      x++;
58      cout << "local static x is " << x << " on exiting useStaticLocal"
59         << endl;
60   } // end function useStaticLocal
61
62   // useGlobal modifies global variable x during each call
63   void useGlobal( void )
64   {
65      cout << "\nglobal x is " << x << " on entering useGlobal" << endl;
66      x *= 10;
67      cout << "global x is " << x << " on exiting useGlobal" << endl;
68   } // end function useGlobal
```

```
local x in main's outer scope is 5
local x in main's inner scope is 7
local x in main's outer scope is 5

local x is 25 on entering useLocal
local x is 26 on exiting useLocal

local static x is 50 on entering useStaticLocal
local static x is 51 on exiting useStaticLocal

global x is 1 on entering useGlobal
global x is 10 on exiting useGlobal

local x is 25 on entering useLocal
local x is 26 on exiting useLocal

local static x is 51 on entering useStaticLocal
local static x is 52 on exiting useStaticLocal

global x is 10 on entering useGlobal
global x is 100 on exiting useGlobal

local x in main is 5
```

Fig. 6.12 | Scoping example. (Part 2 of 2.)

Line 11 declares and initializes global variable x to 1. This global variable is hidden in any block (or function) that declares a variable named x. In main, line 15 declares a local variable x and initializes it to 5. Line 17 outputs this variable to show that the global x is hidden in main. Next, lines 19–23 define a new block in main in which another local variable x is initialized to 7 (line 20). Line 22 outputs this variable to show that it hides x in the outer block of main. When the block exits, the variable x with value 7 is destroyed automatically. Next, line 25 outputs the local variable x in the outer block of main to show that it is no longer hidden.

To demonstrate other scopes, the program defines three functions, each of which takes no arguments and returns nothing. Function useLocal (lines 39–46) declares automatic variable x (line 41) and initializes it to 25. When the program calls useLocal, the function prints the variable, increments it and prints it again before the function returns program control to its caller. Each time the program calls this function, the function recreates automatic variable x and reinitializes it to 25.

Function useStaticLocal (lines 51–60) declares static variable x and initializes it to 50. Local variables declared as static retain their values even when they are out of scope (i.e., the function in which they are declared is not executing). When the program calls useStaticLocal, the function prints x, increments it and prints it again before the function returns program control to its caller. In the next call to this function, static local variable x contains the value 51. The initialization in line 53 occurs only once—the first time useStaticLocal is called.

Function useGlobal (lines 63–68) does not declare any variables. Therefore, when it refers to variable x, the global x (preceding main) is used. When the program calls use-Global, the function prints the global variable x, multiplies it by 10 and prints again before the function returns program control to its caller. The next time the program calls useGlobal, the global variable has its modified value, 10. After executing functions use-Local, useStaticLocal and useGlobal twice each, the program prints the local variable x in main again to show that none of the function calls modified the value of x in main, because the functions all referred to variables in other scopes.

6.11 Function Call Stack and Activation Records

To understand how C++ performs function calls, we first need to consider a data structure (i.e., collection of related data items) known as a stack. Think of a stack as analogous to a pile of dishes. When a dish is placed on the pile, it is normally placed at the top (referred to as pushing the dish onto the stack). Similarly, when a dish is removed from the pile, it is normally removed from the top (referred to as popping the dish off the stack). Stacks are known as last-in, first-out (LIFO) data structures—the last item pushed (inserted) on the stack is the first item popped (removed) from the stack.

One of the most important mechanisms for computer science students to understand is the function call stack (sometimes referred to as the program execution stack). This data structure—working "behind the scenes"—supports the function call/return mechanism. It also supports the creation, maintenance and destruction of each called function's automatic variables. We explained the last-in, first-out (LIFO) behavior of stacks with our dish-stacking example. As we'll see in Figs. 6.14–6.16, this LIFO behavior is exactly what a function does when returning to the function that called it.

As each function is called, it may, in turn, call other functions, which may, in turn, call other functions—all before any of the functions returns. Each function eventually must return control to the function that called it. So, somehow, we must keep track of the return addresses that each function needs to return control to the function that called it. The function call stack is the perfect data structure for handling this information. Each time a function calls another function, an entry is pushed onto the stack. This entry, called a stack frame or an activation record, contains the return address that the called function needs to return to the calling function. It also contains some additional information we will soon discuss. If the called function returns, instead of calling another function before returning, the stack frame for the function call is popped, and control transfers to the return address in the popped stack frame.

The beauty of the call stack is that each called function always finds the information it needs to return to its caller at the top of the call stack. And, if a function makes a call to another function, a stack frame for the new function call is simply pushed onto the call stack. Thus, the return address required by the newly called function to return to its caller is now located at the top of the stack.

The stack frames have another important responsibility. Most functions have automatic variables—parameters and any local variables the function declares. Automatic variables need to exist while a function is executing. They need to remain active if the function makes calls to other functions. But when a called function returns to its caller, the called function's automatic variables need to "go away." The called function's stack frame is a perfect place to reserve the memory for the called function's automatic variables. That stack frame exists as long as the called function is active. When the called function returns—and no longer needs its local automatic variables—its stack frame is popped from the stack, and those local automatic variables are no longer known to the program.

Of course, the amount of memory in a computer is finite, so only a certain amount of memory can be used to store activation records on the function call stack. If more function calls occur than can have their activation records stored on the function call stack, an error known as stack overflow occurs.

Function Call Stack in Action

So, as we have seen, the call stack and activation records support the function call/return mechanism and the creation and destruction of automatic variables. Now let's consider how the call stack supports the operation of a square function called by main (lines 11–17 of Fig. 6.13). First the operating system calls main—this pushes an activation record onto the stack (shown in Fig. 6.14). The activation record tells main how to return to the

```
1   // Fig. 6.13: fig06_13.cpp
2   // square function used to demonstrate the function
3   // call stack and activation records.
4   #include <iostream>
5   using std::cin;
6   using std::cout;
7   using std::endl;
8
```

Fig. 6.13 | square function used to demonstrate the function call stack and activation records. (Part 1 of 2.)

```
 9   int square( int ); // prototype for function square
10
11   int main()
12   {
13      int a = 10; // value to square (local automatic variable in main)
14
15      cout << a << " squared: " << square( a ) << endl; // display a squared
16      return 0; // indicate successful termination
17   } // end main
18
19   // returns the square of an integer
20   int square( int x ) // x is a local variable
21   {
22      return x * x; // calculate square and return result
23   } // end function square
```

```
10 squared: 100
```

Fig. 6.13 | `square` function used to demonstrate the function call stack and activation records. (Part 2 of 2.)

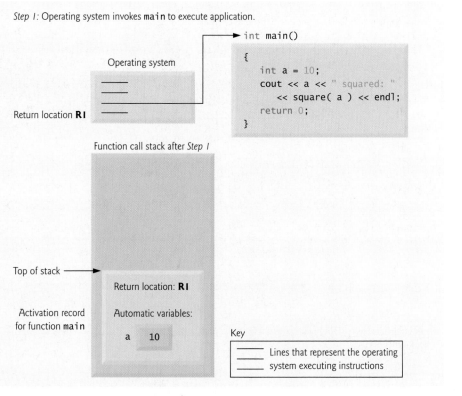

Fig. 6.14 | Function call stack after the operating system invokes `main` to execute the application.

operating system (i.e., transfer to return address R1) and contains the space for main's automatic variable (i.e., a, which is initialized to 10).

Function main—before returning to the operating system—now calls function square in line 15 of Fig. 6.13. This causes a stack frame for square (lines 20–23) to be pushed onto the function call stack (Fig. 6.15). This stack frame contains the return address that square needs to return to main (i.e., R2) and the memory for square's automatic variable (i.e., x).

After square calculates the square of its argument, it needs to return to main—and no longer needs the memory for its automatic variable x. So the stack is popped—giving square the return location in main (i.e., R2) and losing square's automatic variable. Figure 6.16 shows the function call stack after square's activation record has been popped.

Function main now displays the result of calling square (line 15), then executes the return statement (line 16). This causes the activation record for main to be popped from the stack. This gives main the address it needs to return to the operating system (i.e., R1 in Fig. 6.14) and causes the memory for main's automatic variable (i.e., a) to become unavailable.

You have now seen how valuable the notion of the stack data structure is in implementing a key mechanism that supports program execution. Data structures have many

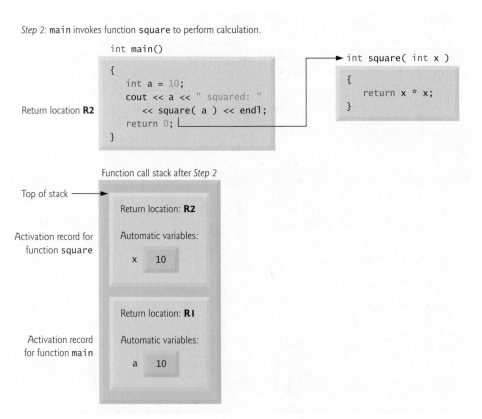

Fig. 6.15 | Function call stack after main invokes function square to perform the calculation.

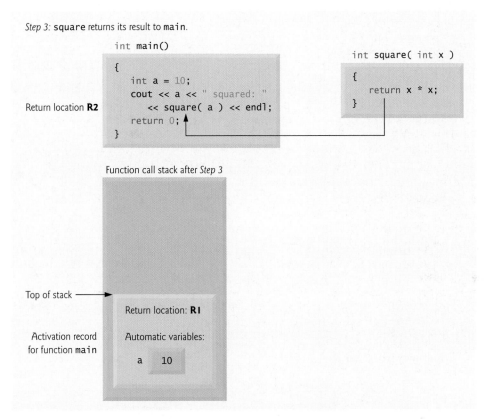

Step 3: `square` returns its result to `main`.

Function call stack after *Step 3*

Top of stack

Activation record
for function `main`

Fig. 6.16 | Function call stack after function `square` returns to `main`.

important applications in computer science. We discuss stacks, queues, lists, trees and other data structures in Chapter 21, Data Structures, and Chapter 23, Standard Template Library (STL) of our sister book, *C++ How to Program, 5/e.*

6.12 Functions with Empty Parameter Lists

In C++, an empty parameter list is specified by writing either `void` or nothing at all in parentheses. The prototype

```
void print();
```

specifies that function `print` does not take arguments and does not return a value. Figure 6.17 demonstrates both ways to declare and use functions with empty parameter lists.

Portability Tip 6.2

The meaning of an empty function parameter list in C++ is dramatically different than in C. In C, it means all argument checking is disabled (i.e., the function call can pass any arguments it wants). In C++, it means that the function explicitly takes no arguments. Thus, C programs using this feature might cause compilation errors when compiled in C++.

```
1   // Fig. 6.17: fig06_17.cpp
2   // Functions that take no arguments.
3   #include <iostream>
4   using std::cout;
5   using std::endl;
6
7   void function1(); // function that takes no arguments
8   void function2( void ); // function that takes no arguments
9
10  int main()
11  {
12     function1(); // call function1 with no arguments
13     function2(); // call function2 with no arguments
14     return 0; // indicates successful termination
15  } // end main
16
17  // function1 uses an empty parameter list to specify that
18  // the function receives no arguments
19  void function1()
20  {
21     cout << "function1 takes no arguments" << endl;
22  } // end function1
23
24  // function2 uses a void parameter list to specify that
25  // the function receives no arguments
26  void function2( void )
27  {
28     cout << "function2 also takes no arguments" << endl;
29  } // end function2
```

```
function1 takes no arguments
function2 also takes no arguments
```

Fig. 6.17 | Functions that take no arguments.

 Common Programming Error 6.13

C++ programs do not compile unless function prototypes are provided for every function or each function is defined before it is called.

6.13 Inline Functions

Implementing a program as a set of functions is good from a software engineering stand-point, but function calls involve execution-time overhead. C++ provides inline functions to help reduce function call overhead—especially for small functions. Placing the qualifier inline before a function's return type in the function definition "advises" the compiler to generate a copy of the function's code in place (when appropriate) to avoid a function call. The trade-off is that multiple copies of the function code are inserted in the program (often making the program larger) rather than there being a single copy of the function to which control is passed each time the function is called. The compiler can ignore the inline qualifier and typically does so for all but the smallest functions.

Software Engineering Observation 6.11

Any change to an inline function could require all clients of the function to be recompiled. This can be significant in some program development and maintenance situations.

Good Programming Practice 6.5

The inline qualifier should be used only with small, frequently used functions.

Performance Tip 6.4

Using inline functions can reduce execution time but may increase program size.

Figure 6.18 uses inline function cube (lines 11–14) to calculate the volume of a cube of side side. Keyword const in the parameter list of function cube (line 11) tells the compiler that the function does not modify variable side. This ensures that the value of side is not changed by the function when the calculation is performed. (Keyword const is discussed in detail in Chapter 7, Chapter 8 and Chapter 10.) Notice that the complete definition of function cube appears before it is used in the program. This is required so that the compiler knows how to expand a cube function call into its inlined code. For this reason, reusable inline functions are typically placed in header files, so that their definitions can be included in each source file that uses them.

Software Engineering Observation 6.12

The const qualifier should be used to enforce the principle of least privilege. Using the principle of least privilege to properly design software can greatly reduce debugging time and improper side effects and can make a program easier to modify and maintain.

```cpp
1   // Fig. 6.18: fig06_18.cpp
2   // Using an inline function to calculate the volume of a cube.
3   #include <iostream>
4   using std::cout;
5   using std::cin;
6   using std::endl;
7
8   // Definition of inline function cube. Definition of function appears
9   // before function is called, so a function prototype is not required.
10  // First line of function definition acts as the prototype.
11  inline double cube( const double side )
12  {
13     return side * side * side; // calculate cube
14  } // end function cube
15
16  int main()
17  {
18     double sideValue; // stores value entered by user
19     cout << "Enter the side length of your cube: ";
20     cin >> sideValue; // read value from user
21
```

Fig. 6.18 | inline function that calculates the volume of a cube. (Part 1 of 2.)

```
22        // calculate cube of sideValue and display result
23        cout << "Volume of cube with side "
24           << sideValue << " is " << cube( sideValue ) << endl;
25        return 0; // indicates successful termination
26     } // end main
```

```
Enter the side length of your cube: 3.5
Volume of cube with side 3.5 is 42.875
```

Fig. 6.18 | `inline` function that calculates the volume of a cube. (Part 2 of 2.)

6.14 References and Reference Parameters

Two ways to pass arguments to functions in many programming languages are pass-by-value and pass-by-reference. When an argument is passed by value, a *copy* of the argument's value is made and passed (on the function call stack) to the called function. Changes to the copy do not affect the original variable's value in the caller. This prevents the accidental side effects that so greatly hinder the development of correct and reliable software systems. Each argument that has been passed in the programs in this chapter so far has been passed by value.

Performance Tip 6.5

One disadvantage of pass-by-value is that, if a large data item is being passed, copying that data can take a considerable amount of execution time and memory space.

Reference Parameters

This section introduces reference parameters—the first of two means C++ provides for performing pass-by-reference. With pass-by-reference, the caller gives the called function the ability to access the caller's data directly, and to modify that data if the called function chooses to do so.

Performance Tip 6.6

Pass-by-reference is good for performance reasons, because it can eliminate the pass-by-value overhead of copying large amounts of data.

Software Engineering Observation 6.13

Pass-by-reference can weaken security, because the called function can corrupt the caller's data.

Later, we will show how to achieve the performance advantage of pass-by-reference while simultaneously achieving the software engineering advantage of protecting the caller's data from corruption.

A reference parameter is an alias for its corresponding argument in a function call. To indicate that a function parameter is passed by reference, simply follow the parameter's type in the function prototype by an ampersand (&); use the same convention when listing the parameter's type in the function header. For example, the following declaration in a function header

```
int &count
```

when read from right to left is pronounced "count is a reference to an int." In the function call, simply mention the variable by name to pass it by reference. Then, mentioning the variable by its parameter name in the body of the called function actually refers to the original variable in the calling function, and the original variable can be modified directly by the called function. As always, the function prototype and header must agree.

Passing Arguments by Value and by Reference

Figure 6.19 compares pass-by-value and pass-by-reference with reference parameters. The "styles" of the arguments in the calls to function squareByValue and function squareByReference are identical—both variables are simply mentioned by name in the function calls. Without checking the function prototypes or function definitions, it is not possible to tell from the calls alone whether either function can modify its arguments. Because function prototypes are mandatory, however, the compiler has no trouble resolving the ambiguity.

```cpp
1   // Fig. 6.19: fig06_19.cpp
2   // Comparing pass-by-value and pass-by-reference with references.
3   #include <iostream>
4   using std::cout;
5   using std::endl;
6
7   int squareByValue( int ); // function prototype (value pass)
8   void squareByReference( int & ); // function prototype (reference pass)
9
10  int main()
11  {
12     int x = 2; // value to square using squareByValue
13     int z = 4; // value to square using squareByReference
14
15     // demonstrate squareByValue
16     cout << "x = " << x << " before squareByValue\n";
17     cout << "Value returned by squareByValue: "
18        << squareByValue( x ) << endl;
19     cout << "x = " << x << " after squareByValue\n" << endl;
20
21     // demonstrate squareByReference
22     cout << "z = " << z << " before squareByReference" << endl;
23     squareByReference( z );
24     cout << "z = " << z << " after squareByReference" << endl;
25     return 0; // indicates successful termination
26  } // end main
27
28  // squareByValue multiplies number by itself, stores the
29  // result in number and returns the new value of number
30  int squareByValue( int number )
31  {
32     return number *= number; // caller's argument not modified
33  } // end function squareByValue
34
```

Fig. 6.19 | Passing arguments by value and by reference. (Part 1 of 2.)

```
35   // squareByReference multiplies numberRef by itself and stores the result
36   // in the variable to which numberRef refers in function main
37   void squareByReference( int &numberRef )
38   {
39      numberRef *= numberRef; // caller's argument modified
40   } // end function squareByReference
```

```
x = 2 before squareByValue
Value returned by squareByValue: 4
x = 2 after squareByValue

z = 4 before squareByReference
z = 16 after squareByReference
```

Fig. 6.19 | Passing arguments by value and by reference. (Part 2 of 2.)

Common Programming Error 6.14

Because reference parameters are mentioned only by name in the body of the called function, the programmer might inadvertently treat reference parameters as pass-by-value parameters. This can cause unexpected side effects if the original copies of the variables are changed by the function.

Chapter 8 discusses pointers; pointers enable an alternate form of pass-by-reference in which the style of the call clearly indicates pass-by-reference (and the potential for modifying the caller's arguments).

Performance Tip 6.7

For passing large objects, use a constant reference parameter to simulate the appearance and security of pass-by-value and avoid the overhead of passing a copy of the large object.

Software Engineering Observation 6.14

Many programmers do not bother to declare parameters passed by value as const, even though the called function should not be modifying the passed argument. Keyword const in this context would protect only a copy of the original argument, not the original argument itself, which when passed by value is safe from modification by the called function.

To specify a reference to a constant, place the const qualifier before the type specifier in the parameter declaration.

Note in line 37 of Fig. 6.19 the placement of & in the parameter list of function squareByReference. Some C++ programmers prefer to write int& numberRef.

Software Engineering Observation 6.15

For the combined reasons of clarity and performance, many C++ programmers prefer that modifiable arguments be passed to functions by using pointers (which we study in Chapter 8), small nonmodifiable arguments be passed by value and large nonmodifiable arguments be passed to functions by using references to constants.

References as Aliases within a Function
References can also be used as aliases for other variables within a function (although they typically are used with functions as shown in Fig. 6.19). For example, the code

```
int count = 1; // declare integer variable count
int &cRef = count; // create cRef as an alias for count
cRef++; // increment count (using its alias cRef)
```

increments variable count by using its alias cRef. Reference variables must be initialized in their declarations (see Fig. 6.20 and Fig. 6.21) and cannot be reassigned as aliases to other variables. Once a reference is declared as an alias for another variable, all operations supposedly performed on the alias (i.e., the reference) are actually performed on the original variable. The alias is simply another name for the original variable. Taking the address of a reference and comparing references do not cause syntax errors; rather, each operation actually occurs on the variable for which the reference is an alias. Unless it is a reference to a constant, a reference argument must be an *lvalue* (e.g., a variable name), not a constant or expression that returns an *rvalue* (e.g., the result of a calculation). See Section 5.9 for definitions of the terms *lvalue* and *rvalue*.

```
1   // Fig. 6.20: fig06_20.cpp
2   // References must be initialized.
3   #include <iostream>
4   using std::cout;
5   using std::endl;
6
7   int main()
8   {
9      int x = 3;
10     int &y = x; // y refers to (is an alias for) x
11
12     cout << "x = " << x << endl << "y = " << y << endl;
13     y = 7; // actually modifies x
14     cout << "x = " << x << endl << "y = " << y << endl;
15     return 0; // indicates successful termination
16  } // end main
```

```
x = 3
y = 3
x = 7
y = 7
```

Fig. 6.20 | Initializing and using a reference.

```
1   // Fig. 6.21: fig06_21.cpp
2   // References must be initialized.
3   #include <iostream>
4   using std::cout;
5   using std::endl;
6
7   int main()
8   {
9      int x = 3;
10     int &y; // Error: y must be initialized
```

Fig. 6.21 | Uninitialized reference causes a syntax error. (Part 1 of 2.)

```
11
12    cout << "x = " << x << endl << "y = " << y << endl;
13    y = 7;
14    cout << "x = " << x << endl << "y = " << y << endl;
15    return 0; // indicates successful termination
16 } // end main
```

Borland C++ command-line compiler error message:

```
Error E2304 C:\scpphtp5_examples\ch06\Fig06_21\fig06_21.cpp 10:
    Reference variable 'y' must be initialized in function main()
```

Microsoft Visual C++ compiler error message:

```
C:\scpphtp5_examples\ch06\Fig06_21\fig06_21.cpp(10) : error C2530: 'y' :
    references must be initialized
```

GNU C++ compiler error message:

```
fig06_21.cpp:10: error: 'y' declared as a reference but not initialized
```

Fig. 6.21 | Uninitialized reference causes a syntax error. (Part 2 of 2.)

Returning a Reference from a Function

Functions can return references, but this can be dangerous. When returning a reference to a variable declared in the called function, the variable should be declared `static` within that function. Otherwise, the reference refers to an automatic variable that is discarded when the function terminates; such a variable is said to be "undefined," and the program's behavior is unpredictable. References to undefined variables are called dangling references.

 Common Programming Error 6.15

Not initializing a reference variable when it is declared is a compilation error, unless the declaration is part of a function's parameter list. Reference parameters are initialized when the function in which they are declared is called.

 Common Programming Error 6.16

Attempting to reassign a previously declared reference to be an alias to another variable is a logic error. The value of the other variable is simply assigned to the variable for which the reference is already an alias.

 Common Programming Error 6.17

Returning a reference to an automatic variable in a called function is a logic error. Some compilers issue a warning when this occurs.

Error Messages for Uninitialized References

Note that the C++ standard does not specify the error messages that compilers use to indicate particular errors. For this reason, Fig. 6.21 shows the error messages produced by the Borland C++ 5.5 command-line compiler, Microsoft Visual C++.NET compiler and GNU C++ compiler when a reference is not initialized.

6.15 Default Arguments

It is not uncommon for a program to invoke a function repeatedly with the same argument value for a particular parameter. In such cases, the programmer can specify that such a parameter has a **default argument**, i.e., a default value to be passed to that parameter. When a program omits an argument for a parameter with a default argument in a function call, the compiler rewrites the function call and inserts the default value of that argument to be passed as an argument to the function call.

Default arguments must be the rightmost (trailing) arguments in a function's parameter list. When calling a function with two or more default arguments, if an omitted argument is not the rightmost argument in the argument list, then all arguments to the right of that argument also must be omitted. Default arguments should be specified with the first occurrence of the function name—typically, in the function prototype. If the function prototype is omitted because the function definition also serves as the prototype, then the default arguments should be specified in the function header. Default values can be any expression, including constants, global variables or function calls. Default arguments also can be used with `inline` functions.

Figure 6.22 demonstrates using default arguments in calculating the volume of a box. The function prototype for `boxVolume` (line 8) specifies that all three parameters have been given default values of 1. Note that we provided variable names in the function prototype for readability. As always, variable names are not required in function prototypes.

 Common Programming Error 6.18

It is a compilation error to specify default arguments in both a function's prototype and header.

```
1   // Fig. 6.22: fig06_22.cpp
2   // Using default arguments.
3   #include <iostream>
4   using std::cout;
5   using std::endl;
6
7   // function prototype that specifies default arguments
8   int boxVolume( int length = 1, int width = 1, int height = 1 );
9
10  int main()
11  {
12     // no arguments--use default values for all dimensions
13     cout << "The default box volume is: " << boxVolume();
14
15     // specify length; default width and height
16     cout << "\n\nThe volume of a box with length 10,\n"
17        << "width 1 and height 1 is: " << boxVolume( 10 );
18
19     // specify length and width; default height
20     cout << "\n\nThe volume of a box with length 10,\n"
21        << "width 5 and height 1 is: " << boxVolume( 10, 5 );
22
```

Fig. 6.22 | Default arguments to a function. (Part 1 of 2.)

```
23      // specify all arguments
24      cout << "\n\nThe volume of a box with length 10,\n"
25          << "width 5 and height 2 is: " << boxVolume( 10, 5, 2 )
26          << endl;
27      return 0; // indicates successful termination
28   } // end main
29
30   // function boxVolume calculates the volume of a box
31   int boxVolume( int length, int width, int height )
32   {
33      return length * width * height;
34   } // end function boxVolume
```

```
The default box volume is: 1

The volume of a box with length 10,
width 1 and height 1 is: 10

The volume of a box with length 10,
width 5 and height 1 is: 50

The volume of a box with length 10,
width 5 and height 2 is: 100
```

Fig. 6.22 | Default arguments to a function. (Part 2 of 2.)

The first call to boxVolume (line 13) specifies no arguments, thus using all three default values of 1. The second call (line 17) passes a length argument, thus using default values of 1 for the width and height arguments. The third call (line 21) passes arguments for length and width, thus using a default value of 1 for the height argument. The last call (line 25) passes arguments for length, width and height, thus using no default values. Note that any arguments passed to the function explicitly are assigned to the function's parameters from left to right. Therefore, when boxVolume receives one argument, the function assigns the value of that argument to its length parameter (i.e., the leftmost parameter in the parameter list). When boxVolume receives two arguments, the function assigns the values of those arguments to its length and width parameters in that order. Finally, when boxVolume receives all three arguments, the function assigns the values of those arguments to its length, width and height parameters, respectively.

Good Programming Practice 6.6

Using default arguments can simplify writing function calls. However, some programmers feel that explicitly specifying all arguments is clearer.

Software Engineering Observation 6.16

If the default values for a function change, all client code using the function must be recompiled.

Common Programming Error 6.19

Specifying and attempting to use a default argument that is not a rightmost (trailing) argument (while not simultaneously defaulting all the rightmost arguments) is a syntax error.

6.16 Unary Scope Resolution Operator

It is possible to declare local and global variables of the same name. C++ provides the unary scope resolution operator (::) to access a global variable when a local variable of the same name is in scope. The unary scope resolution operator cannot be used to access a local variable of the same name in an outer block. A global variable can be accessed directly without the unary scope resolution operator if the name of the global variable is not the same as that of a local variable in scope.

Figure 6.23 demonstrates the unary scope resolution operator with local and global variables of the same name (lines 7 and 11). To emphasize that the local and global versions of variable number are distinct, the program declares one variable of type int and the other double.

Using the unary scope resolution operator (::) with a given variable name is optional when the only variable with that name is a global variable.

Common Programming Error 6.20

It is an error to attempt to use the unary scope resolution operator (::) to access a nonglobal variable in an outer block. If no global variable with that name exists, a compilation error occurs. If a global variable with that name exists, this is a logic error, because the program will refer to the global variable when you intended to access the nonglobal variable in the outer block.

Good Programming Practice 6.7

Always using the unary scope resolution operator (::) to refer to global variables makes programs easier to read and understand, because it makes it clear that you are intending to access a global variable rather than a nonglobal variable.

```cpp
1   // Fig. 6.23: fig06_23.cpp
2   // Using the unary scope resolution operator.
3   #include <iostream>
4   using std::cout;
5   using std::endl;
6
7   int number = 7; // global variable named number
8
9   int main()
10  {
11      double number = 10.5; // local variable named number
12
13      // display values of local and global variables
14      cout << "Local double value of number = " << number
15          << "\nGlobal int value of number = " << ::number << endl;
16      return 0; // indicates successful termination
17  } // end main
```

```
Local double value of number = 10.5
Global int value of number = 7
```

Fig. 6.23 | Unary scope resolution operator.

Software Engineering Observation 6.17

Always using the unary scope resolution operator (::) to refer to global variables makes programs easier to modify by reducing the risk of name collisions with nonglobal variables.

Error-Prevention Tip 6.4

Always using the unary scope resolution operator (::) to refer to a global variable eliminates possible logic errors that might occur if a nonglobal variable hides the global variable.

Error-Prevention Tip 6.5

Avoid using variables of the same name for different purposes in a program. Although this is allowed in various circumstances, it can lead to errors.

6.17 Function Overloading

C++ enables several functions of the same name to be defined, as long as these functions have different sets of parameters (at least as far as the parameter types or the number of parameters or the order of the parameter types are concerned). This capability is called function overloading. When an overloaded function is called, the C++ compiler selects the proper function by examining the number, types and order of the arguments in the call. Function overloading is commonly used to create several functions of the same name that perform similar tasks, but on different data types. For example, many functions in the math library are overloaded for different numeric data types.[1]

Good Programming Practice 6.8

Overloading functions that perform closely related tasks can make programs more readable and understandable.

*Overloaded **square** Functions*
Figure 6.24 uses overloaded square functions to calculate the square of an int (lines 8–12) and the square of a double (lines 15–19). Line 23 invokes the int version of function square by passing the literal value 7. C++ treats whole number literal values as type int by default. Similarly, line 25 invokes the double version of function square by passing the literal value 7.5, which C++ treats as a double value by default. In each case the compiler chooses the proper function to call, based on the type of the argument. The last two lines of the output window confirm that the proper function was called in each case.

```
 I   // Fig. 6.24: fig06_24.cpp
 2   // Overloaded functions.
 3   #include <iostream>
 4   using std::cout;
 5   using std::endl;
 6
```

Fig. 6.24 | Overloaded square functions. (Part 1 of 2.)

---

1. The C++ standard requires float, double and long double overloaded versions of the math library functions discussed in Section 6.3.

```
7    // function square for int values
8    int square( int x )
9    {
10       cout << "square of integer " << x << " is ";
11       return x * x;
12   } // end function square with int argument
13
14   // function square for double values
15   double square( double y )
16   {
17       cout << "square of double " << y << " is ";
18       return y * y;
19   } // end function square with double argument
20
21   int main()
22   {
23       cout << square( 7 ); // calls int version
24       cout << endl;
25       cout << square( 7.5 ); // calls double version
26       cout << endl;
27       return 0; // indicates successful termination
28   } // end main
```

```
square of integer 7 is 49
square of double 7.5 is 56.25
```

Fig. 6.24 | Overloaded `square` functions. (Part 2 of 2.)

How the Compiler Differentiates Overloaded Functions

Overloaded functions are distinguished by their signatures. A signature is a combination of a function's name and its parameter types (in order). The compiler encodes each function identifier with the number and types of its parameters (sometimes referred to as name mangling or name decoration) to enable type-safe linkage. Type-safe linkage ensures that the proper overloaded function is called and that the types of the arguments conform to the types of the parameters.

Figure 6.25 was compiled with the Borland C++ 5.6.4 command-line compiler. Rather than showing the execution output of the program (as we normally would), we show the mangled function names produced in assembly language by Borland C++. Each mangled name begins with @ followed by the function name. The function name is then separated from the mangled parameter list by $q. In the parameter list for function nothing2 (line 25; see the fourth output line), c represents a char, i represents an int, rf represents a float & (i.e., a reference to a float) and rd represents a double & (i.e., a reference to a double). In the parameter list for function nothing1, i represents an int, f represents a float, c represents a char and ri represents an int &. The two square functions are distinguished by their parameter lists; one specifies d for double and the other specifies i for int. The return types of the functions are not specified in the mangled names. Overloaded functions can have different return types, but if they do, they must also have different parameter lists. Again, you cannot have two functions with the same signa-

```
1   // Fig. 6.25: fig06_25.cpp
2   // Name mangling.
3
4   // function square for int values
5   int square( int x )
6   {
7      return x * x;
8   } // end function square
9
10  // function square for double values
11  double square( double y )
12  {
13     return y * y;
14  } // end function square
15
16  // function that receives arguments of types
17  // int, float, char and int &
18  void nothing1( int a, float b, char c, int &d )
19  {
20     // empty function body
21  } // end function nothing1
22
23  // function that receives arguments of types
24  // char, int, float & and double &
25  int nothing2( char a, int b, float &c, double &d )
26  {
27     return 0;
28  } // end function nothing2
29
30  int main()
31  {
32     return 0; // indicates successful termination
33  } // end main
```

```
@square$qi
@square$qd
@nothing1$qifcri
@nothing2$qcirfrd
_main
```

Fig. 6.25 | Name mangling to enable type-safe linkage.

ture and different return types. Note that function name mangling is compiler specific. Also note that function main is not mangled, because it cannot be overloaded.

 Common Programming Error 6.21

Creating overloaded functions with identical parameter lists and different return types is a compilation error.

The compiler uses only the parameter lists to distinguish between functions of the same name. Overloaded functions need not have the same number of parameters. Programmers should use caution when overloading functions with default parameters, because this may cause ambiguity.

Common Programming Error 6.22

A function with default arguments omitted might be called identically to another overloaded function; this is a compilation error. For example, having in a program both a function that explicitly takes no arguments and a function of the same name that contains all default arguments results in a compilation error when an attempt is made to use that function name in a call passing no arguments. The compiler does not know which version of the function to choose.

Overloaded Operators
In Chapter 11, we discuss how to overload operators to define how they should operate on objects of user-defined data types. (In fact, we have been using many overloaded operators to this point, including the stream insertion operator << and the stream extraction operator >>, each of which is overloaded to be able to display data of all the fundamental types. We say more about overloading << and >> to be able to handle objects of user-defined types in Chapter 11.) Section 6.18 introduces function templates for automatically generating overloaded functions that perform identical tasks on different data types.

6.18 Function Templates

Overloaded functions are normally used to perform similar operations that involve different program logic on different data types. If the program logic and operations are identical for each data type, overloading may be performed more compactly and conveniently by using function templates. The programmer writes a single function template definition. Given the argument types provided in calls to this function, C++ automatically generates separate function template specializations to handle each type of call appropriately. Thus, defining a single function template essentially defines a whole family of overloaded functions.

Figure 6.26 contains the definition of a function template (lines 4–18) for a maximum function that determines the largest of three values. All function template definitions begin with the template keyword (line 4) followed by a template parameter list to the function template enclosed in angle brackets (< and >). Every parameter in the template

```
1   // Fig. 6.26: maximum.h
2   // Definition of function template maximum.
3
4   template < class T >  // or template< typename T >
5   T maximum( T value1, T value2, T value3 )
6   {
7      T maximumValue = value1; // assume value1 is maximum
8
9      // determine whether value2 is greater than maximumValue
10     if ( value2 > maximumValue )
11        maximumValue = value2;
12
13     // determine whether value3 is greater than maximumValue
14     if ( value3 > maximumValue )
15        maximumValue = value3;
16
17     return maximumValue;
18  } // end function template maximum
```

Fig. 6.26 | Function template maximum header file.

parameter list (often referred to as a formal type parameter) is preceded by keyword type-name or keyword class (which are synonyms). The formal type parameters are place-holders for fundamental types or user-defined types. These placeholders are used to specify the types of the function's parameters (line 5), to specify the function's return type (line 5) and to declare variables within the body of the function definition (line 7). A function template is defined like any other function, but uses the formal type parameters as place-holders for actual data types.

The function template in Fig. 6.26 declares a single formal type parameter T (line 4) as a placeholder for the type of the data to be tested by function maximum. The name of a type parameter must be unique in the template parameter list for a particular template def-inition. When the compiler detects a maximum invocation in the program source code, the type of the data passed to maximum is substituted for T throughout the template definition, and C++ creates a complete function for determining the maximum of three values of the specified data type. Then the newly created function is compiled. Thus, templates are a means of code generation.

Common Programming Error 6.23

Not placing keyword class or keyword typename before every formal type parameter of a func-tion template (e.g., writing < class S, T > instead of < class S, class T >) is a syntax error.

Figure 6.27 uses the maximum function template (lines 20, 30 and 40) to determine the largest of three int values, three double values and three char values.

```cpp
1   // Fig. 6.27: fig06_27.cpp
2   // Function template maximum test program.
3   #include <iostream>
4   using std::cout;
5   using std::cin;
6   using std::endl;
7
8   #include "maximum.h" // include definition of function template maximum
9
10  int main()
11  {
12     // demonstrate maximum with int values
13     int int1, int2, int3;
14
15     cout << "Input three integer values: ";
16     cin >> int1 >> int2 >> int3;
17
18     // invoke int version of maximum
19     cout << "The maximum integer value is: "
20        << maximum( int1, int2, int3 );
21
22     // demonstrate maximum with double values
23     double double1, double2, double3;
24
25     cout << "\n\nInput three double values: ";
26     cin >> double1 >> double2 >> double3;
```

Fig. 6.27 | Demonstrating function template maximum. (Part 1 of 2.)

```
27
28      // invoke double version of maximum
29      cout << "The maximum double value is: "
30         << maximum( double1, double2, double3 );
31
32      // demonstrate maximum with char values
33      char char1, char2, char3;
34
35      cout << "\n\nInput three characters: ";
36      cin >> char1 >> char2 >> char3;
37
38      // invoke char version of maximum
39      cout << "The maximum character value is: "
40         << maximum( char1, char2, char3 ) << endl;
41      return 0; // indicates successful termination
42   } // end main
```

```
Input three integer values: 1 2 3
The maximum integer value is: 3

Input three double values: 3.3 2.2 1.1
The maximum double value is: 3.3

Input three characters: A C B
The maximum character value is: C
```

Fig. 6.27 | Demonstrating function template `maximum`. (Part 2 of 2.)

In Fig. 6.27, three functions are created as a result of the calls in lines 20, 30 and 40—expecting three `int` values, three `double` values and three `char` values, respectively. The function template specialization created for type `int` replaces each occurrence of T with `int` as follows:

```
int maximum( int value1, int value2, int value3 )
{
   int maximumValue = value1;

   // determine whether value2 is greater than maximumValue
   if ( value2 > maximumValue )
      maximumValue = value2;

   // determine whether value3 is greater than maximumValue
   if ( value3 > maximumValue )
      maximumValue = value3;

   return maximumValue;
} // end function template maximum
```

6.19 Recursion

The programs we have discussed are generally structured as functions that call one another in a disciplined, hierarchical manner. For some problems, it is useful to have functions call themselves. A recursive function is a function that calls itself, either directly, or indirectly (through another function).[2] Recursion is an important topic discussed at length in upper-level computer science courses. This section and the next present simple examples of recursion. This book contains an extensive treatment of recursion. Figure 6.33 (at the end of Section 6.21) summarizes the recursion examples and exercises in the book.

We first consider recursion conceptually, then examine two programs containing recursive functions. Recursive problem-solving approaches have a number of elements in common. A recursive function is called to solve a problem. The function actually knows how to solve only the simplest case(s), or so-called base case(s). If the function is called with a base case, the function simply returns a result. If the function is called with a more complex problem, it typically divides the problem into two conceptual pieces—a piece that the function knows how to do and a piece that it does not know how to do. To make recursion feasible, the latter piece must resemble the original problem, but be a slightly simpler or slightly smaller version. This new problem looks like the original problem, so the function launches (calls) a fresh copy of itself to work on the smaller problem—this is referred to as a recursive call and is also called the recursion step. The recursion step often includes the keyword `return`, because its result will be combined with the portion of the problem the function knew how to solve to form a result that will be passed back to the original caller, possibly `main`.

The recursion step executes while the original call to the function is still open, i.e., it has not yet finished executing. The recursion step can result in many more such recursive calls, as the function keeps dividing each new subproblem with which the function is called into two conceptual pieces. In order for the recursion to eventually terminate, each time the function calls itself with a slightly simpler version of the original problem, this sequence of smaller and smaller problems must eventually converge on the base case. At that point, the function recognizes the base case and returns a result to the previous copy of the function, and a sequence of returns ensues all the way up the line until the original function call eventually returns the final result to `main`. All of this sounds quite exotic compared to the kind of "conventional" problem solving we have been using to this point. As an example of these concepts at work, let us write a recursive program to perform a popular mathematical calculation.

The factorial of a nonnegative integer n, written $n!$ (and pronounced "n factorial"), is the product

$$n \cdot (n-1) \cdot (n-2) \cdot \ldots \cdot 1$$

with $1!$ equal to 1, and $0!$ defined to be 1. For example, $5!$ is the product $5 \cdot 4 \cdot 3 \cdot 2 \cdot 1$, which is equal to 120.

The factorial of an integer, `number`, greater than or equal to 0, can be calculated iteratively (nonrecursively) by using a `for` statement as follows:

```
factorial = 1;

for ( int counter = number; counter >= 1; counter-- )
   factorial *= counter;
```

---

2. Although many compilers allow function `main` to call itself, Section 3.6.1, paragraph 3, of the C++ standard document indicates that `main` should not be called within a program. Its sole purpose is to be the starting point for program execution.

A recursive definition of the factorial function is arrived at by observing the following relationship:

$n! = n \cdot (n - 1)!$

For example, 5! is clearly equal to 5 * 4! as is shown by the following:

$5! = 5 \cdot 4 \cdot 3 \cdot 2 \cdot 1$
$5! = 5 \cdot (4 \cdot 3 \cdot 2 \cdot 1)$
$5! = 5 \cdot (4!)$

The evaluation of 5! would proceed as shown in Fig. 6.28. Figure 6.28(a) shows how the succession of recursive calls proceeds until 1! is evaluated to be 1, which terminates the recursion. Figure 6.28(b) shows the values returned from each recursive call to its caller until the final value is calculated and returned.

The program of Fig. 6.29 uses recursion to calculate and print the factorials of the integers 0–10. (The choice of the data type unsigned long is explained momentarily.) The recursive function factorial (lines 23–29) first determines whether the terminating condition number <= 1 (line 25) is true. If number is indeed less than or equal to 1, function factorial returns 1 (line 26), no further recursion is necessary and the function terminates. If number is greater than 1, line 28 expresses the problem as the product of number and a recursive call to factorial evaluating the factorial of number - 1. Note that factorial(number - 1) is a slightly simpler problem than the original calculation factorial(number).

Function factorial has been declared to receive a parameter of type unsigned long and return a result of type unsigned long. This is shorthand notation for unsigned long

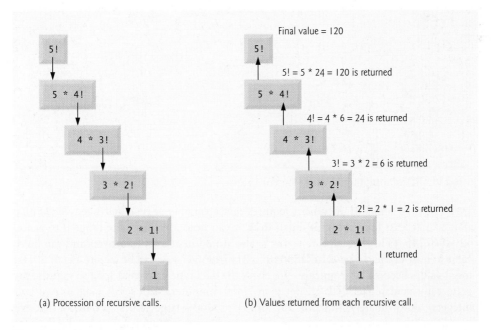

(a) Procession of recursive calls.   (b) Values returned from each recursive call.

Fig. 6.28 | Recursive evaluation of 5!.

```
1   // Fig. 6.29: fig06_29.cpp
2   // Testing the recursive factorial function.
3   #include <iostream>
4   using std::cout;
5   using std::endl;
6
7   #include <iomanip>
8   using std::setw;
9
10  unsigned long factorial( unsigned long ); // function prototype
11
12  int main()
13  {
14     // calculate the factorials of 0 through 10
15     for ( int counter = 0; counter <= 10; counter++ )
16        cout << setw( 2 ) << counter << "! = " << factorial( counter )
17           << endl;
18
19     return 0; // indicates successful termination
20  } // end main
21
22  // recursive definition of function factorial
23  unsigned long factorial( unsigned long number )
24  {
25     if ( number <= 1 ) // test for base case
26        return 1; // base cases: 0! = 1 and 1! = 1
27     else // recursion step
28        return number * factorial( number - 1 );
29  } // end function factorial
```

```
 0! = 1
 1! = 1
 2! = 2
 3! = 6
 4! = 24
 5! = 120
 6! = 720
 7! = 5040
 8! = 40320
 9! = 362880
10! = 3628800
```

Fig. 6.29 | Demonstrating function `factorial`.

int. The C++ standard document requires that a variable of type unsigned long int be stored in at least four bytes (32 bits); thus, it can hold a value in the range 0 to at least 4294967295. (The data type long int is also stored in at least four bytes and can hold a value at least in the range –2147483648 to 2147483647.) As can be seen in Fig. 6.29, factorial values become large quickly. We chose the data type unsigned long so that the program can calculate factorials greater than 7! on computers with small (such as two-byte) integers. Unfortunately, function factorial produces large values so quickly that even unsigned long does not help us compute many factorial values before even the size of an unsigned long variable is exceeded.

The exercises explore using variables of data type `double` to calculate factorials of larger numbers. This points to a weakness in most programming languages, namely, that the languages are not easily extended to handle the unique requirements of various applications. As we will see when we discuss object-oriented programming in more depth, C++ is an extensible language that allows us to create classes that can represent arbitrarily large integers if we wish. Such classes already are available in popular class libraries,[3] and we work on similar classes of our own in Exercise 9.14 and Exercise 11.5.

Common Programming Error 6.24

Either omitting the base case, or writing the recursion step incorrectly so that it does not converge on the base case, causes "infinite" recursion, eventually exhausting memory. This is analogous to the problem of an infinite loop in an iterative (nonrecursive) solution.

6.20 Example Using Recursion: Fibonacci Series

The Fibonacci series

0, 1, 1, 2, 3, 5, 8, 13, 21, ...

begins with 0 and 1 and has the property that each subsequent Fibonacci number is the sum of the previous two Fibonacci numbers.

The series occurs in nature and, in particular, describes a form of spiral. The ratio of successive Fibonacci numbers converges on a constant value of 1.618.... This number, too, frequently occurs in nature and has been called the golden ratio or the golden mean. Humans tend to find the golden mean aesthetically pleasing. Architects often design windows, rooms and buildings whose length and width are in the ratio of the golden mean. Postcards are often designed with a golden mean length/width ratio.

The Fibonacci series can be defined recursively as follows:

fibonacci(0) = 0
fibonacci(1) = 1
fibonacci(n) = fibonacci($n - 1$) + fibonacci($n - 2$)

The program of Fig. 6.30 calculates the nth Fibonacci number recursively by using function `fibonacci`. Notice that Fibonacci numbers also tend to become large quickly, although slower than factorials do. Therefore, we chose the data type `unsigned long` for the parameter type and the return type in function `fibonacci`. Figure 6.30 shows the execution of the program, which displays the Fibonacci values for several numbers.

The application begins with a `for` statement that calculates and displays the Fibonacci values for the integers 0–10 and is followed by three calls to calculate the Fibonacci values of the integers 20, 30 and 35 (lines 18–20). The calls to `fibonacci` (lines 15, 18, 19 and 20) from `main` are not recursive calls, but the calls from line 30 of `fibonacci` are recursive. Each time the program invokes `fibonacci` (lines 25–31), the function immediately tests the base case to determine whether `number` is equal to 0 or 1 (line 27). If this is true, line 28 returns `number`. Interestingly, if `number` is greater than 1, the recursion step (line 30) generates *two* recursive calls, each for a slightly smaller problem than the original call to `fibonacci`. Figure 6.31 shows how function `fibonacci` would evaluate `fibonacci( 3 )`.

---

3. Such classes can be found at shoup.net/ntl, cliodhna.cop.uop.edu/~hetrick/c-sources.html and www.trumphurst.com/cpplibs/datapage.phtml?category='intro'.

```cpp
1    // Fig. 6.30: fig06_30.cpp
2    // Testing the recursive fibonacci function.
3    #include <iostream>
4    using std::cout;
5    using std::cin;
6    using std::endl;
7
8    unsigned long fibonacci( unsigned long ); // function prototype
9
10   int main()
11   {
12      // calculate the fibonacci values of 0 through 10
13      for ( int counter = 0; counter <= 10; counter++ )
14         cout << "fibonacci( " << counter << " ) = "
15            << fibonacci( counter ) << endl;
16
17      // display higher fibonacci values
18      cout << "fibonacci( 20 ) = " << fibonacci( 20 ) << endl;
19      cout << "fibonacci( 30 ) = " << fibonacci( 30 ) << endl;
20      cout << "fibonacci( 35 ) = " << fibonacci( 35 ) << endl;
21      return 0; // indicates successful termination
22   } // end main
23
24   // recursive method fibonacci
25   unsigned long fibonacci( unsigned long number )
26   {
27      if ( ( number == 0 ) || ( number == 1 ) ) // base cases
28         return number;
29      else // recursion step
30         return fibonacci( number - 1 ) + fibonacci( number - 2 );
31   } // end function fibonacci
```

```
fibonacci( 0 ) = 0
fibonacci( 1 ) = 1
fibonacci( 2 ) = 1
fibonacci( 3 ) = 2
fibonacci( 4 ) = 3
fibonacci( 5 ) = 5
fibonacci( 6 ) = 8
fibonacci( 7 ) = 13
fibonacci( 8 ) = 21
fibonacci( 9 ) = 34
fibonacci( 10 ) = 55
fibonacci( 20 ) = 6765
fibonacci( 30 ) = 832040
fibonacci( 35 ) = 9227465
```

Fig. 6.30 | Demonstrating function `fibonacci`.

This figure raises some interesting issues about the order in which C++ compilers will evaluate the operands of operators. This is a separate issue from the order in which operators are applied to their operands, namely, the order dictated by the rules of operator precedence and associativity. Figure 6.31 shows that evaluating `fibonacci( 3 )` causes two

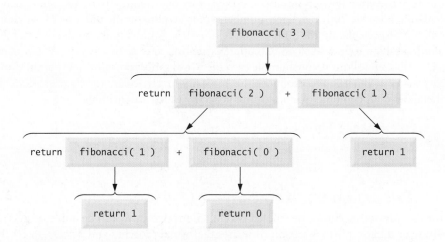

Fig. 6.31 | Set of recursive calls to function `fibonacci`.

recursive calls, namely, `fibonacci( 2 )` and `fibonacci( 1 )`. But in what order are these calls made?

Most programmers simply assume that the operands are evaluated left to right. The C++ language does not specify the order in which the operands of most operators (including +) are to be evaluated. Therefore, the programmer must make no assumption about the order in which these calls execute. The calls could in fact execute `fibonacci( 2 )` first, then `fibonacci( 1 )`, or they could execute in the reverse order: `fibonacci( 1 )`, then `fibonacci( 2 )`. In this program and in most others, it turns out that the final result would be the same. However, in some programs the evaluation of an operand can have side effects (changes to data values) that could affect the final result of the expression.

The C++ language specifies the order of evaluation of the operands of only four operators—namely, &&, ||, the comma (,) operator and ?:. The first three are binary operators whose two operands are guaranteed to be evaluated left to right. The last operator is C++'s only ternary operator. Its leftmost operand is always evaluated first; if it evaluates to non-zero (true), the middle operand evaluates next and the last operand is ignored; if the leftmost operand evaluates to zero (false), the third operand evaluates next and the middle operand is ignored.

Common Programming Error 6.25

Writing programs that depend on the order of evaluation of the operands of operators other than &&, ||, ?: and the comma (,) operator can lead to logic errors.

Portability Tip 6.3

Programs that depend on the order of evaluation of the operands of operators other than &&, ||, ?: and the comma (,) operator can function differently on systems with different compilers.

A word of caution is in order about recursive programs like the one we use here to generate Fibonacci numbers. Each level of recursion in function `fibonacci` has a doubling effect on the number of function calls; i.e., the number of recursive calls that are required to calculate the nth Fibonacci number is on the order of 2^n. This rapidly gets out of hand. Calculating only the 20th Fibonacci number would require on the order of 2^{20} or about a million calls, calculating the 30th Fibonacci number would require on the order of 2^{30} or about a billion calls, and so on. Computer scientists refer to this as exponential complexity. Problems of this nature humble even the world's most powerful computers! Complexity issues in general, and exponential complexity in particular, are discussed in detail in the upper-level computer science course generally called "Algorithms."

Performance Tip 6.8

Avoid Fibonacci-style recursive programs that result in an exponential "explosion" of calls.

6.21 Recursion vs. Iteration

In the two previous sections, we studied two functions that easily can be implemented recursively or iteratively. This section compares the two approaches and discusses why the programmer might choose one approach over the other in a particular situation.

Both iteration and recursion are based on a control statement: Iteration uses a repetition structure; recursion uses a selection structure. Both iteration and recursion involve repetition: Iteration explicitly uses a repetition structure; recursion achieves repetition through repeated function calls. Iteration and recursion both involve a termination test: Iteration terminates when the loop-continuation condition fails; recursion terminates when a base case is recognized. Iteration with counter-controlled repetition and recursion both gradually approach termination: Iteration modifies a counter until the counter assumes a value that makes the loop-continuation condition fail; recursion produces simpler versions of the original problem until the base case is reached. Both iteration and recursion can occur infinitely: An infinite loop occurs with iteration if the loop-continuation test never becomes false; infinite recursion occurs if the recursion step does not reduce the problem during each recursive call in a manner that converges on the base case.

To illustrate the differences between iteration and recursion, let us examine an iterative solution to the factorial problem (Fig. 6.32). Note that a repetition statement is used (lines 28–29 of Fig. 6.32) rather than the selection statement of the recursive solution (lines 24–27 of Fig. 6.29). Note that both solutions use a termination test. In the recursive solution, line 24 tests for the base case. In the iterative solution, line 28 tests the loop-continuation condition—if the test fails, the loop terminates. Finally, note that instead of producing simpler versions of the original problem, the iterative solution uses a counter that is modified until the loop-continuation condition becomes false.

```cpp
1   // Fig. 6.32: fig06_32.cpp
2   // Testing the iterative factorial function.
3   #include <iostream>
4   using std::cout;
5   using std::endl;
6
7   #include <iomanip>
8   using std::setw;
```

Fig. 6.32 | Iterative factorial solution. (Part 1 of 2.)

```
 9
10   unsigned long factorial( unsigned long ); // function prototype
11
12   int main()
13   {
14      // calculate the factorials of 0 through 10
15      for ( int counter = 0; counter <= 10; counter++ )
16         cout << setw( 2 ) << counter << "! = " << factorial( counter )
17            << endl;
18
19      return 0;
20   } // end main
21
22   // iterative function factorial
23   unsigned long factorial( unsigned long number )
24   {
25      unsigned long result = 1;
26
27      // iterative declaration of function factorial
28      for ( unsigned long i = number; i >= 1; i-- )
29         result *= i;
30
31      return result;
32   } // end function factorial
```

```
 0! = 1
 1! = 1
 2! = 2
 3! = 6
 4! = 24
 5! = 120
 6! = 720
 7! = 5040
 8! = 40320
 9! = 362880
10! = 3628800
```

Fig. 6.32 | Iterative factorial solution. (Part 2 of 2.)

Recursion has many negatives. It repeatedly invokes the mechanism, and conse-quently the overhead, of function calls. This can be expensive in both processor time and memory space. Each recursive call causes another copy of the function (actually only the function's variables) to be created; this can consume considerable memory. Iteration nor-mally occurs within a function, so the overhead of repeated function calls and extra memory assignment is omitted. So why choose recursion?

Software Engineering Observation 6.18

Any problem that can be solved recursively can also be solved iteratively (nonrecursively). A recursive approach is normally chosen in preference to an iterative approach when the recursive approach more naturally mirrors the problem and results in a program that is easier to understand and debug. Another reason to choose a recursive solution is that an iterative solution is not apparent.

Performance Tip 6.9

Avoid using recursion in performance situations. Recursive calls take time and consume additional memory.

Common Programming Error 6.26

Accidentally having a nonrecursive function call itself, either directly or indirectly (through another function), is a logic error.

Most programming textbooks introduce recursion much later than we have done here. We feel that recursion is a sufficiently rich and complex topic that it is better to introduce it earlier and spread the examples over the remainder of the text. Figure 6.33 summarizes the recursion examples and exercises in the text.

Location in Text	Recursion Examples and Exercises
Chapter 6	
Section 6.19, Fig. 6.29	Factorial function
Section 6.19, Fig. 6.30	Fibonacci function
Exercise 6.7	Sum of two integers
Exercise 6.40	Raising an integer to an integer power
Exercise 6.42	Towers of Hanoi
Exercise 6.44	Visualizing recursion
Exercise 6.45	Greatest common divisor
Exercise 6.50, Exercise 6.51	Mystery "What does this program do?" exercise
Chapter 7	
Exercise 7.18	Mystery "What does this program do?" exercise
Exercise 7.21	Mystery "What does this program do?" exercise
Exercise 7.31	Selection sort
Exercise 7.32	Determine whether a string is a palindrome
Exercise 7.33	Linear search
Exercise 7.34	Binary search
Exercise 7.35	Eight Queens
Exercise 7.36	Print an array
Exercise 7.37	Print a string backward
Exercise 7.38	Minimum value in an array
Chapter 8	
Exercise 8.24	Quicksort
Exercise 8.25	Maze traversal
Exercise 8.26	Generating Mazes Randomly
Exercise 8.27	Mazes of Any Size

Fig. 6.33 | Summary of recursion examples and exercises in the text.

6.22 Wrap-Up

In this chapter, you learned more about the details of function declarations. Functions have different pieces, such as the function prototype, function signature, function header and function body. You learned about argument coercion, or the forcing of arguments to the appropriate types specified by the parameter declarations of a function. We demonstrated how to use functions rand and srand to generate sets of random numbers that can be used for simulations. You also learned about the scope of variables, or the portion of a program where an identifier can be used. Two different ways to pass arguments to functions were covered—pass-by-value and pass-by-reference. For pass-by-reference, references are used as an alias to a variable. You learned that multiple functions in one class can be overloaded by providing functions with the same name and different signatures. Such functions can be used to perform the same or similar tasks, using different types or different numbers of parameters. We then demonstrated a simpler way of overloading functions using function templates, where a function is defined once but can be used for several different types. You were then introduced to the concept of recursion, where a function calls itself to solve a problem.

In Chapter 7, you will learn how to maintain lists and tables of data in arrays. You will see a more elegant array-based implementation of the dice-rolling application and two enhanced versions of our GradeBook case study that you studied in Chapters 3–5 that will use arrays to store the actual grades entered.

Summary

- Experience has shown that the best way to develop and maintain a large program is to construct it from small, simple pieces, or components. This technique is called divide and conquer.

- C++ programs are typically written by combining new functions and classes the programmer writes with "prepackaged" functions and classes available in the C++ Standard Library.

- Functions allow the programmer to modularize a program by separating its tasks into self-contained units.

- The statements in the function bodies are written only once, are reused from perhaps several locations in a program and are hidden from other functions.

- The compiler refers to the function prototype to check that calls to a method contain the correct number and types of arguments, that the types of the arguments are in the correct order and that the value returned by the function can be used correctly in the expression that called the function.

- There are three ways to return control to the point at which a function was invoked. If the function does not return a result, control returns when the program reaches the function-ending right brace, or by execution of the statement

    ```
    return;
    ```

    If the function does return a result, the statement

    ```
    return expression;
    ```

    evaluates *expression* and returns the value of *expression* to the caller.

- A function prototype tells the compiler the name of a function, the type of data returned by that function, the number of parameters the function expects to receive, the types of those parameters and the order in which the parameters of those types are expected.

- The portion of a function prototype that includes the name of the function and the types of its arguments is called the function signature or simply the signature.

- An important feature of function prototypes is argument coercion—i.e., forcing arguments to the appropriate types specified by the parameter declarations.

- Argument values that do not correspond precisely to the parameter types in the function prototype can be converted by the compiler to the proper type as specified by C++'s promotion rules. The promotion rules indicate how to convert between types without losing data.

- The element of chance can be introduced into computer applications by using the C++ Standard Library function rand.

- Function rand actually generates pseudorandom numbers. Calling rand repeatedly produces a sequence of numbers that appears to be random. However, the sequence repeats itself each time the program executes.

- Once a program has been thoroughly debugged, it can be conditioned to produce a different sequence of random numbers for each execution. This is called randomizing and is accomplished with the C++ Standard Library function srand.

- Function srand takes an unsigned integer argument and seeds the rand function to produce a different sequence of random numbers for each execution of the program.

- Random numbers in a range can be generated with

    number = *shiftingValue* + rand() % *scalingFactor*;

  where *shiftingValue* is equal to the first number in the desired range of consecutive integers and *scalingFactor* is equal to the width of the desired range of consecutive integers.

- An enumeration, introduced by the keyword enum and followed by a type name, is a set of integer constants represented by identifiers. The values of these enumeration constants start at 0, unless specified otherwise, and increment by 1.

- An identifier's storage class determines the period during which that identifier exists in memory.

- An identifier's scope is where the identifier can be referenced in a program.

- An identifier's linkage determines whether an identifier is known only in the source file where it is declared or across multiple files that are compiled, then linked together.

- Keywords auto and register are used to declare variables of the automatic storage class. Such variables are created when program execution enters the block in which they are defined, they exist while the block is active and they are destroyed when the program exits the block.

- Only local variables of a function can be of automatic storage class.

- The storage class specifier auto explicitly declares variables of automatic storage class. Local variables are of automatic storage class by default, so keyword auto rarely is used.

- Keywords extern and static declare identifiers for variables of the static storage class and for functions. Static-storage-class variables exist from the point at which the program begins execution and last for the duration of the program.

- A static-storage-class variable's storage is allocated when the program begins execution. Such a variable is initialized once when its declaration is encountered. For functions, the name of the function exists when the program begins execution, just as for all other functions.

- There are two types of identifiers with static storage class—external identifiers (such as global variables and global function names) and local variables declared with the storage class specifier static.

- Global variables are created by placing variable declarations outside any class or function definition. Global variables retain their values throughout the execution of the program. Global variables and global functions can be referenced by any function that follows their declarations or definitions in the source file.

- Local variables declared with the keyword static are still known only in the function in which they are declared, but, unlike automatic variables, static local variables retain their values when the function returns to its caller. The next time the function is called, the static local variables contain the values they had when the function last completed execution.

- An identifier declared outside any function or class has file scope.

- Labels are the only identifiers with function scope. Labels can be used anywhere in the function in which they appear, but cannot be referenced outside the function body.

- Identifiers declared inside a block have block scope. Block scope begins at the identifier's declaration and ends at the terminating right brace (}) of the block in which the identifier is declared.

- The only identifiers with function-prototype scope are those used in the parameter list of a function prototype.

- Stacks are known as last-in, first-out (LIFO) data structures—the last item pushed (inserted) on the stack is the first item popped (removed) from the stack.

- One of the most important mechanisms for computer science students to understand is the function call stack (sometimes referred to as the program execution stack). This data structure supports the function call/return mechanism.

- The function call stack also supports the creation, maintenance and destruction of each called function's automatic variables.

- Each time a function calls another function, an entry is pushed onto the stack. This entry, called a stack frame or an activation record, contains the return address that the called function needs to return to the calling function, as well as the automatic variables for the function call.

- The stack frame exists as long as the called function is active. When the called function returns— and no longer needs its local automatic variables—its stack frame is popped from the stack, and those local automatic variables are no longer known to the program.

- In C++, an empty parameter list is specified by writing either void or nothing in parentheses.

- C++ provides inline functions to help reduce function call overhead—especially for small functions. Placing the qualifier inline before a function's return type in the function definition "advises" the compiler to generate a copy of the function's code in place to avoid a function call.

- Two ways to pass arguments to functions in many programming languages are pass-by-value and pass-by-reference.

- When an argument is passed by value, a *copy* of the argument's value is made and passed (on the function call stack) to the called function. Changes to the copy do not affect the original variable's value in the caller.

- With pass-by-reference, the caller gives the called function the ability to access the caller's data directly and to modify it if the called function chooses to do so.

- A reference parameter is an alias for its corresponding argument in a function call.

- To indicate that a function parameter is passed by reference, simply follow the parameter's type in the function prototype by an ampersand (&); use the same convention when listing the parameter's type in the function header.

- Once a reference is declared as an alias for another variable, all operations supposedly performed on the alias (i.e., the reference) are actually performed on the original variable. The alias is simply another name for the original variable.

- It is not uncommon for a program to invoke a function repeatedly with the same argument value for a particular parameter. In such cases, the programmer can specify that such a parameter has a default argument, i.e., a default value to be passed to that parameter.

- When a program omits an argument for a parameter with a default argument, the compiler rewrites the function call and inserts the default value of that argument to be passed as an argument to the function call.
- Default arguments must be the rightmost (trailing) arguments in a function's parameter list.
- Default arguments should be specified with the first occurrence of the function name—typically, in the function prototype.
- C++ provides the unary scope resolution operator (::) to access a global variable when a local variable of the same name is in scope.
- C++ enables several functions of the same name to be defined, as long as these functions have different sets of parameters. This capability is called function overloading.
- When an overloaded function is called, the C++ compiler selects the proper function by examining the number, types and order of the arguments in the call.
- Overloaded functions are distinguished by their signatures.
- The compiler encodes each function identifier with the number and types of its parameters to enable type-safe linkage. Type-safe linkage ensures that the proper overloaded function is called and that the types of the arguments conform to the types of the parameters.
- Overloaded functions are normally used to perform similar operations that involve different program logic on different data types. If the program logic and operations are identical for each data type, overloading may be performed more compactly and conveniently using function templates.
- The programmer writes a single function template definition. Given the argument types provided in calls to this function, C++ automatically generates separate function template specializations to handle each type of call appropriately. Thus, defining a single function template essentially defines a family of overloaded functions.
- All function template definitions begin with the `template` keyword followed by a template parameter list to the function template enclosed in angle brackets (< and >).
- The formal type parameters are placeholders for fundamental types or user-defined types. These placeholders are used to specify the types of the function's parameters, to specify the function's return type and to declare variables within the body of the function definition.
- A recursive function is a function that calls itself, either directly or indirectly.
- A recursive function knows how to solve only the simplest case(s), or so-called base case(s). If the function is called with a base case, the function simply returns a result.
- If the function is called with a more complex problem, the function typically divides the problem into two conceptual pieces—a piece that the function knows how to do and a piece that it does not know how to do. To make recursion feasible, the latter piece must resemble the original problem, but be a slightly simpler or slightly smaller version of it.
- In order for the recursion to eventually terminate, each time the function calls itself with a slightly simpler version of the original problem, this sequence of smaller and smaller problems must eventually converge on the base case.
- The ratio of successive Fibonacci numbers converges on a constant value of 1.618.... This number frequently occurs in nature and has been called the golden ratio or the golden mean.
- Iteration and recursion have many similarities: both are based on a control statement, involve repetition, involve a termination test, gradually approach termination and can occur infinitely.
- Recursion has many negatives. It repeatedly invokes the mechanism, and consequently the overhead, of function calls. This can be expensive in both processor time and memory space. Each recursive call causes another copy of the function (actually only the function's variables) to be created; this can consume considerable memory.

Terminology

& to declare reference
activation record
alias
argument coercion
auto storage-class specifier
automatic local variable
automatic storage class
base case(s)
block scope
class scope
converge on a base case
dangling reference
default argument
divide-and-conquer approach
enum keyword
enumeration
enumeration constant
exponential complexity
extern storage-class specifier
factorial
Fibonacci series
file scope
formal parameter
formal type parameter
function call stack
function declaration
function definition
function name
function overloading
function prototype
function-prototype scope
function scope
function signature
function template
function template specialization
function call overhead
global function
global variable
golden mean
golden ratio
"highest" type
infinite loop
infinite recursion
initializing a reference
inline function
inline keyword
inner block
integral size limits
invoke a method

iteration
iterative solution
label
LIFO (last-in, first-out)
linkage
"lowest type"
mandatory function prototypes
mangled function name
methods
mixed-type expression
modularizing a program with functions
mutable storage-class specifier
name decoration
name mangling
name of a variable
namespace scope
nested blocks
numerical data type limits
optimizing compiler
out of scope
outer block
overloading
parameter
pass-by-reference
pass-by-value
pop off a stack
"prepackaged" functions
principle of least privilege
procedure
program execution stack
programmer-defined function
promotion rules
pseudorandom numbers
push onto a stack
rand function
RAND_MAX symbolic constant
random number
randomizing
recursion
recursion overhead
recursion step
recursive call
recursive evaluation
recursive function
recursive solution
reference parameter
reference to a constant
reference to an automatic variable
register storage-class specifier

repeatability of function rand
returning a reference from a function
rightmost (trailing) arguments
scaling
scaling factor
scope of an identifier
seed
seed function rand
sequence of random numbers
shift a range of numbers
shifted, scaled integers
shifting value
side effect of an expression
signature
software reuse
srand function
stack
stack frame
stack overflow
static keyword
static local variable
static storage class

static storage-class specifier
storage class
storage-class specifiers
template definition
template function
template keyword
template parameter list
terminating condition
terminating right brace (}) of a block
termination test
truncate fractional part of a double
type name (enumerations)
type of a variable
type parameter
type-safe linkage
unary scope resolution operator (::)
user-defined function
user-defined type
validate a function call
void return type
width of random number range

Self-Review Exercises

6.1   Answer each of the following:
   a) Program components in C++ are called _____ and_____.
   b) A function is invoked with a(n) _____.
   c) A variable that is known only within the function in which it is defined is called a(n) _____.
   d) The _____ statement in a called function passes the value of an expression back to the calling function.
   e) The keyword _____ is used in a function header to indicate that a function does not return a value or to indicate that a function contains no parameters.
   f) The _____ of an identifier is the portion of the program in which the identifier can be used.
   g) The three ways to return control from a called function to a caller are _____, _____ and _____.
   h) A(n) _____ allows the compiler to check the number, types and order of the arguments passed to a function.
   i) Function _____ is used to produce random numbers.
   j) Function _____ is used to set the random number seed to randomize a program.
   k) The storage-class specifiers are mutable, _____, _____, _____ and _____.
   l) Variables declared in a block or in the parameter list of a function are assumed to be of storage class _____ unless specified otherwise.
   m) Storage-class specifier _____ is a recommendation to the compiler to store a variable in one of the computer's registers.
   n) A variable declared outside any block or function is a(n) _____ variable.
   o) For a local variable in a function to retain its value between calls to the function, it must be declared with the _____ storage-class specifier.

p) The six possible scopes of an identifier are _____, _____, _____, _____, _____ and _____.

q) A function that calls itself either directly or indirectly (i.e., through another function) is a(n) _____ function.

r) A recursive function typically has two components: One that provides a means for the recursion to terminate by testing for a(n) _____ case and one that expresses the problem as a recursive call for a slightly simpler problem than the original call.

s) In C++, it is possible to have various functions with the same name that operate on different types or numbers of arguments. This is called function _____.

t) The _____ enables access to a global variable with the same name as a variable in the current scope.

u) The _____ qualifier is used to declare read-only variables.

v) A function _____ enables a single function to be defined to perform a task on many different data types.

6.2   For the program in Fig. 6.34, state the scope (either function scope, file scope, block scope or function-prototype scope) of each of the following elements:

a) The variable x in main.

b) The variable y in cube.

c) The function cube.

d) The function main.

e) The function prototype for cube.

f) The identifier y in the function prototype for cube.

6.3   Write a program that tests whether the examples of the math library function calls shown in Fig. 6.2 actually produce the indicated results.

```
1   // Exercise 6.2: Ex06_02.cpp
2   #include <iostream>
3   using std::cout;
4   using std::endl;
5
6   int cube( int y ); // function prototype
7
8   int main()
9   {
10     int x;
11
12     for ( x = 1; x <= 10; x++ ) // loop 10 times
13        cout << cube( x ) << endl; // calculate cube of x and output results
14
15     return 0; // indicates successful termination
16  } // end main
17
18  // definition of function cube
19  int cube( int y )
20  {
21     return y * y * y;
22  } // end function cube
```

Fig. 6.34 | Program for Exercise 6.2

6.4   Give the function header for each of the following functions:
   a) Function hypotenuse that takes two double-precision, floating-point arguments, side1 and side2, and returns a double-precision, floating-point result.
   b) Function smallest that takes three integers, x, y and z, and returns an integer.
   c) Function instructions that does not receive any arguments and does not return a value. [*Note:* Such functions are commonly used to display instructions to a user.]
   d) Function intToDouble that takes an integer argument, number, and returns a double-precision, floating-point result.

6.5   Give the function prototype for each of the following:
   a) The function described in Exercise 6.4(a).
   b) The function described in Exercise 6.4(b).
   c) The function described in Exercise 6.4(c).
   d) The function described in Exercise 6.4(d).

6.6   Write a declaration for each of the following:
   a) Integer count that should be maintained in a register. Initialize count to 0.
   b) Double-precision, floating-point variable lastVal that is to retain its value between calls to the function in which it is defined.

6.7   Find the error in each of the following program segments, and explain how the error can be corrected (see also Exercise 6.53):
   a) ```
      int g(void)
      {
          cout << "Inside function g" << endl;
          int h(void)
          {
              cout << "Inside function h" << endl;
          }
      }
      ```
   b) ```
      int sum( int x, int y )
      {
          int result;

          result = x + y;
      }
      ```
   c) ```
      int sum(int n)
      {
          if (n == 0)
              return 0;
          else
              n + sum(n - 1);
      }
      ```
   d) ```
      void f( double a );
      {
          float a;
          cout << a << endl;
      }
      ```
   e) ```
      void product(void)
      {
          int a;
      ```
      ```

```
              int b;
              int c;
              int result;
              cout << "Enter three integers: ";
              cin >> a >> b >> c;
              result = a * b * c;
              cout << "Result is " << result;
              return result;
           }
```

6.8   Why would a function prototype contain a parameter type declaration such as `double &`?

6.9   (True/False) All arguments to function calls in C++ are passed by value.

6.10   Write a complete program that prompts the user for the radius of a sphere, and calculates and prints the volume of that sphere. Use an `inline` function `sphereVolume` that returns the result of the following expression: `( 4.0 / 3.0 ) * 3.14159 * pow( radius, 3 )`.

Answers to Self-Review Exercises

6.1   a) functions, classes. b) function call. c) local variable. d) return. e) void. f) scope. g) return;, return *expression*; or encounter the closing right brace of a function. h) function prototype. i) rand. j) srand. k) auto, register, extern, static. l) auto. m) register. n) global. o) static. p) function scope, file scope, block scope, function-prototype scope, class scope, namespace scope.   q) recursive. r) base. s) overloading. t) unary scope resolution operator (::). u) const. v) template.

6.2   a) block scope. b) block scope. c) file scope. d) file scope. e) file scope. f) function-prototype scope.

6.3   See the following program:

```cpp
1  // Exercise 6.3: Ex06_03.cpp
2  // Testing the math library functions.
3  #include <iostream>
4  using std::cout;
5  using std::endl;
6  using std::fixed;
7
8  #include <iomanip>
9  using std::setprecision;
10
11 #include <cmath>
12 using namespace std;
13
14 int main()
15 {
16    cout << fixed << setprecision( 1 );
17
18    cout << "sqrt(" << 900.0 << ") = " << sqrt( 900.0 )
19       << "\nsqrt(" << 9.0 << ") = " << sqrt( 9.0 );
20    cout << "\nexp(" << 1.0 << ") = " << setprecision( 6 )
21       << exp( 1.0 ) << "\nexp(" << setprecision( 1 ) << 2.0
22       << ") = " << setprecision( 6 ) << exp( 2.0 );
23    cout << "\nlog(" << 2.718282 << ") = " << setprecision( 1 )
```

```
24              << log( 2.718282 )
25              << "\nlog(" << setprecision( 6 ) << 7.389056 << ") = "
26              << setprecision( 1 ) << log( 7.389056 );
27      cout << "\nlog10(" << 1.0 << ") = " << log10( 1.0 )
28              << "\nlog10(" << 10.0 << ") = " << log10( 10.0 )
29              << "\nlog10(" << 100.0 << ") = " << log10( 100.0 ) ;
30      cout << "\nfabs(" << 13.5 << ") = " << fabs( 13.5 )
31              << "\nfabs(" << 0.0 << ") = " << fabs( 0.0 )
32              << "\nfabs(" << -13.5 << ") = " << fabs( -13.5 );
33      cout << "\nceil(" << 9.2 << ") = " << ceil( 9.2 )
34              << "\nceil(" << -9.8 << ") = " << ceil( -9.8 );
35      cout << "\nfloor(" << 9.2 << ") = " << floor( 9.2 )
36              << "\nfloor(" << -9.8 << ") = " << floor( -9.8 );
37      cout << "\npow(" << 2.0 << ", " << 7.0 << ") = "
38              << pow( 2.0, 7.0 ) << "\npow(" << 9.0 << ", "
39              << 0.5 << ") = " << pow( 9.0, 0.5 );
40      cout << setprecision(3) << "\nfmod("
41              << 13.675 << ", " << 2.333 << ") = "
42              << fmod( 13.675, 2.333 ) << setprecision( 1 );
43      cout << "\nsin(" << 0.0 << ") = " << sin( 0.0 );
44      cout << "\ncos(" << 0.0 << ") = " << cos( 0.0 );
45      cout << "\ntan(" << 0.0 << ") = " << tan( 0.0 ) << endl;
46      return 0; // indicates successful termination
47  } // end main
```

```
sqrt(900.0) = 30.0
sqrt(9.0) = 3.0
exp(1.0) = 2.718282
exp(2.0) = 7.389056
log(2.718282) = 1.0
log(7.389056) = 2.0
log10(1.0) = 0.0
log10(10.0) = 1.0
log10(100.0) = 2.0
fabs(13.5) = 13.5
fabs(0.0) = 0.0
fabs(-13.5) = 13.5
ceil(9.2) = 10.0
ceil(-9.8) = -9.0
floor(9.2) = 9.0
floor(-9.8) = -10.0
pow(2.0, 7.0) = 128.0
pow(9.0, 0.5) = 3.0
fmod(13.675, 2.333) = 2.010
sin(0.0) = 0.0
cos(0.0) = 1.0
tan(0.0) = 0.0
```

6.4   a) `double hypotenuse( double side1, double side2 )`
      b) `int smallest( int x, int y, int z )`
      c) `void instructions( void ) // in C++ (void) can be written ()`
      d) `double intToDouble( int number )`

6.5   a) `double hypotenuse( double, double );`
      b) `int smallest( int, int, int );`

    c) `void instructions( void ); // in C++ (void) can be written ()`
    d) `double intToDouble( int );`

6.6   a) `register int count = 0;`
    b) `static double lastVal;`

6.7   a) Error: Function h is defined in function g.
        Correction: Move the definition of h out of the definition of g.
    b) Error: The function is supposed to return an integer, but does not.
        Correction: Delete variable `result` and place the following statement in the function:

           `return x + y;`

    c) Error: The result of n + sum(n - 1) is not returned; sum returns an improper result.
        Correction: Rewrite the statement in the `else` clause as

           `return n + sum( n - 1 );`

    d) Errors: Semicolon after the right parenthesis that encloses the parameter list, and re-defining the parameter a in the function definition.
        Corrections: Delete the semicolon after the right parenthesis of the parameter list, and delete the declaration `float a;`.
    e) Error: The function returns a value when it is not supposed to.
        Correction: Eliminate the `return` statement.

6.8   This creates a reference parameter of type "reference to `double`" that enables the function to modify the original variable in the calling function.

6.9   False. C++ enables pass-by-reference using reference parameters (and pointers, as we discuss in Chapter 8).

6.10   See the following program:

```cpp
1   // Exercise 6.10 Solution: Ex06_10.cpp
2   // Inline function that calculates the volume of a sphere.
3   #include <iostream>
4   using std::cin;
5   using std::cout;
6   using std::endl;
7
8   #include <cmath>
9   using std::pow;
10
11  const double PI = 3.14159; // define global constant PI
12
13  // calculates volume of a sphere
14  inline double sphereVolume( const double radius )
15  {
16      return 4.0 / 3.0 * PI * pow( radius, 3 );
17  } // end inline function sphereVolume
18
19  int main()
20  {
21      double radiusValue;
22
23      // prompt user for radius
24      cout << "Enter the length of the radius of your sphere: ";
25      cin >> radiusValue; // input radius
```

```
26
27        // use radiusValue to calculate volume of sphere and display result
28        cout << "Volume of sphere with radius " << radiusValue
29            << " is " << sphereVolume( radiusValue ) << endl;
30        return 0; // indicates successful termination
31    } // end main
```

Exercises

6.11 Show the value of x after each of the following statements is performed:

 a) x = fabs(7.5)
 b) x = floor(7.5)
 c) x = fabs(0.0)
 d) x = ceil(0.0)
 e) x = fabs(-6.4)
 f) x = ceil(-6.4)
 g) x = ceil(-fabs(-8 + floor(-5.5)))

6.12 A parking garage charges a $2.00 minimum fee to park for up to three hours. The garage charges an additional $0.50 per hour for each hour *or part thereof* in excess of three hours. The maximum charge for any given 24-hour period is $10.00. Assume that no car parks for longer than 24 hours at a time. Write a program that calculates and prints the parking charges for each of three customers who parked their cars in this garage yesterday. You should enter the hours parked for each customer. Your program should print the results in a neat tabular format and should calculate and print the total of yesterday's receipts. The program should use the function calculateCharges to determine the charge for each customer. Your outputs should appear in the following format:

Car	Hours	Charge
1	1.5	2.00
2	4.0	2.50
3	24.0	10.00
TOTAL	29.5	14.50

6.13 An application of function floor is rounding a value to the nearest integer. The statement

    y = floor(x + .5);

rounds the number x to the nearest integer and assigns the result to y. Write a program that reads several numbers and uses the preceding statement to round each of these numbers to the nearest integer. For each number processed, print both the original number and the rounded number.

6.14 Function floor can be used to round a number to a specific decimal place. The statement

    y = floor(x * 10 + .5) / 10;

rounds x to the tenths position (the first position to the right of the decimal point). The statement

    y = floor(x * 100 + .5) / 100;

rounds x to the hundredths position (the second position to the right of the decimal point). Write a program that defines four functions to round a number x in various ways:

 a) roundToInteger(number)
 b) roundToTenths(number)
 c) roundToHundredths(number)
 d) roundToThousandths(number)

For each value read, your program should print the original value, the number rounded to the nearest integer, the number rounded to the nearest tenth, the number rounded to the nearest hundredth and the number rounded to the nearest thousandth.

6.15   Answer each of the following questions:
   a)   What does it mean to choose numbers "at random?"
   b)   Why is the rand function useful for simulating games of chance?
   c)   Why would you randomize a program by using srand? Under what circumstances is it desirable not to randomize?
   d)   Why is it often necessary to scale or shift the values produced by rand?
   e)   Why is computerized simulation of real-world situations a useful technique?

6.16   Write statements that assign random integers to the variable n in the following ranges:
   a) $1 \leq n \leq 2$
   b) $1 \leq n \leq 100$
   c) $0 \leq n \leq 9$
   d) $1000 \leq n \leq 1112$
   e) $-1 \leq n \leq 1$
   f) $-3 \leq n \leq 11$

6.17   For each of the following sets of integers, write a single statement that prints a number at random from the set:
   a)   2, 4, 6, 8, 10.
   b)   3, 5, 7, 9, 11.
   c)   6, 10, 14, 18, 22.

6.18   Write a function integerPower(base, exponent) that returns the value of

$$base^{\ exponent}$$

For example, integerPower(3, 4) = 3 * 3 * 3 * 3. Assume that *exponent* is a positive, non-zero integer and that *base* is an integer. The function integerPower should use for or while to control the calculation. Do not use any math library functions.

6.19   *(Hypotenuse)* Define a function hypotenuse that calculates the length of the hypotenuse of a right triangle when the other two sides are given. Use this function in a program to determine the length of the hypotenuse for each of the triangles shown below. The function should take two double arguments and return the hypotenuse as a double.

Triangle	Side 1	Side 2
1	3.0	4.0
2	5.0	12.0
3	8.0	15.0

6.20   Write a function multiple that determines for a pair of integers whether the second is a multiple of the first. The function should take two integer arguments and return true if the second is a multiple of the first, false otherwise. Use this function in a program that inputs a series of pairs of integers.

6.21   Write a program that inputs a series of integers and passes them one at a time to function even, which uses the modulus operator to determine whether an integer is even. The function should take an integer argument and return true if the integer is even and false otherwise.

6.22   Write a function that displays at the left margin of the screen a solid square of asterisks whose side is specified in integer parameter side. For example, if side is 4, the function displays the following:

```
****
****
****
****
```

6.23   Modify the function created in Exercise 6.22 to form the square out of whatever character is contained in character parameter fillCharacter. Thus, if side is 5 and fillCharacter is #, then this function should print the following:

```
#####
#####
#####
#####
#####
```

6.24   Use techniques similar to those developed in Exercise 6.22 and Exercise 6.23 to produce a program that graphs a wide range of shapes.

6.25   Write program segments that accomplish each of the following:
a) Calculate the integer part of the quotient when integer a is divided by integer b.
b) Calculate the integer remainder when integer a is divided by integer b.
c) Use the program pieces developed in (a) and (b) to write a function that inputs an integer between 1 and 32767 and prints it as a series of digits, each pair of which is separated by two spaces. For example, the integer 4562 should print as follows:

```
4  5  6  2
```

6.26   Write a function that takes the time as three integer arguments (hours, minutes and seconds) and returns the number of seconds since the last time the clock "struck 12." Use this function to calculate the amount of time in seconds between two times, both of which are within one 12-hour cycle of the clock.

6.27   *(Celsius and Fahrenheit Temperatures)* Implement the following integer functions:
a) Function celsius returns the Celsius equivalent of a Fahrenheit temperature.
b) Function fahrenheit returns the Fahrenheit equivalent of a Celsius temperature.
c) Use these functions to write a program that prints charts showing the Fahrenheit equivalents of all Celsius temperatures from 0 to 100 degrees, and the Celsius equivalents of all Fahrenheit temperatures from 32 to 212 degrees. Print the outputs in a neat tabular format that minimizes the number of lines of output while remaining readable.

6.28   Write a program that inputs three double-precision, floating-point numbers and passes them to a function that returns the smallest number.

6.29   *(Perfect Numbers)* An integer is said to be a *perfect number* if the sum of its factors, including 1 (but not the number itself), is equal to the number. For example, 6 is a perfect number, because 6 = 1 + 2 + 3. Write a function perfect that determines whether parameter number is a perfect number. Use this function in a program that determines and prints all the perfect numbers between 1 and 1000. Print the factors of each perfect number to confirm that the number is indeed perfect. Challenge the power of your computer by testing numbers much larger than 1000.

6.30   *(PrimeNumbers)* An integer is said to be *prime* if it is divisible by only 1 and itself. For example, 2, 3, 5 and 7 are prime, but 4, 6, 8 and 9 are not.
   a)   Write a function that determines whether a number is prime.
   b)   Use this function in a program that determines and prints all the prime numbers between 2 and 10,000. How many of these numbers do you really have to test before being sure that you have found all the primes?
   c)   Initially, you might think that $n/2$ is the upper limit for which you must test to see whether a number is prime, but you need only go as high as the square root of n. Why? Rewrite the program, and run it both ways. Estimate the performance improvement.

6.31   *(Reverse Digits)* Write a function that takes an integer value and returns the number with its digits reversed. For example, given the number 7631, the function should return 1367.

6.32   The *greatest common divisor (GCD)* of two integers is the largest integer that evenly divides each of the numbers. Write a function gcd that returns the greatest common divisor of two integers.

6.33   Write a function qualityPoints that inputs a student's average and returns 4 if a student's average is 90–100, 3 if the average is 80–89, 2 if the average is 70–79, 1 if the average is 60–69 and 0 if the average is lower than 60.

6.34   Write a program that simulates coin tossing. For each toss of the coin, the program should print Heads or Tails. Let the program toss the coin 100 times and count the number of times each side of the coin appears. Print the results. The program should call a separate function flip that takes no arguments and returns 0 for tails and 1 for heads. [*Note:* If the program realistically simulates the coin tossing, then each side of the coin should appear approximately half the time.]

6.35   *(Computers in Education)* Computers are playing an increasing role in education. Write a program that helps an elementary school student learn multiplication. Use rand to produce two positive one-digit integers. It should then type a question such as

        How much is 6 times 7?

The student then types the answer. Your program checks the student's answer. If it is correct, print "Very good!", then ask another multiplication question. If the answer is wrong, print "No. Please try again.", then let the student try the same question repeatedly until the student finally gets it right.

6.36   *(Computer Assisted Instruction)* The use of computers in education is referred to as *computer-assisted instruction* (CAI). One problem that develops in CAI environments is student fatigue. This can be eliminated by varying the computer's dialogue to hold the student's attention. Modify the program of Exercise 6.35 so the various comments are printed for each correct answer and each incorrect answer as follows:
   Responses to a correct answer

        Very good!
        Excellent!
        Nice work!
        Keep up the good work!

   Responses to an incorrect answer

        No. Please try again.
        Wrong. Try once more.

```
Don't give up!
No. Keep trying.
```

Use the random number generator to choose a number from 1 to 4 to select an appropriate response to each answer. Use a `switch` statement to issue the responses.

6.37 More sophisticated computer-aided instruction systems monitor the student's performance over a period of time. The decision to begin a new topic often is based on the student's success with previous topics. Modify the program of Exercise 6.36 to count the number of correct and incorrect responses typed by the student. After the student types 10 answers, your program should calculate the percentage of correct responses. If the percentage is lower than 75 percent, your program should print "Please ask your instructor for extra help" and terminate.

6.38 *(Guess the Number Game)* Write a program that plays the game of "guess the number" as follows: Your program chooses the number to be guessed by selecting an integer at random in the range 1 to 1000. The program then displays the following:

```
I have a number between 1 and 1000.
Can you guess my number?
Please type your first guess.
```

The player then types a first guess. The program responds with one of the following:

```
1. Excellent! You guessed the number!
   Would you like to play again (y or n)?
2. Too low. Try again.
3. Too high. Try again.
```

If the player's guess is incorrect, your program should loop until the player finally gets the number right. Your program should keep telling the player Too high or Too low to help the player "zero in" on the correct answer.

6.39 Modify the program of Exercise 6.38 to count the number of guesses the player makes. If the number is 10 or fewer, print "Either you know the secret or you got lucky!" If the player guesses the number in 10 tries, then print "Ahah! You know the secret!" If the player makes more than 10 guesses, then print "You should be able to do better!" Why should it take no more than 10 guesses? Well, with each "good guess" the player should be able to eliminate half of the numbers. Now show why any number from 1 to 1000 can be guessed in 10 or fewer tries.

6.40 Write a recursive function power(base, exponent) that, when invoked, returns

$$base^{exponent}$$

For example, power(3, 4) = 3 * 3 * 3 * 3. Assume that exponent is an integer greater than or equal to 1. *Hint:* The recursion step would use the relationship

$$base^{exponent} = base \cdot base^{exponent - 1}$$

and the terminating condition occurs when exponent is equal to 1, because

$$base^1 = base$$

6.41 *(Fibonacci Series)* The Fibonacci series

$$0, 1, 1, 2, 3, 5, 8, 13, 21, \ldots$$

begins with the terms 0 and 1 and has the property that each succeeding term is the sum of the two preceding terms. (a) Write a *nonrecursive* function fibonacci(n) that calculates the nth Fibonacci number. (b) Determine the largest int Fibonacci number that can be printed on your system. Modify the program of part (a) to use double instead of int to calculate and return Fibonacci numbers, and use this modified program to repeat part (b).

6.42   *(Towers of Hanoi)* In this chapter, you studied functions that can be easily implemented both recursively and iteratively. In this exercise, we present a problem whose recursive solution demonstrates the elegance of recursion, and whose iterative solution may not be as apparent.

The Towers of Hanoi is one of the most famous classic problems every budding computer scientist must grapple with. Legend has it that in a temple in the Far East, priests are attempting to move a stack of golden disks from one diamond peg to another (Fig. 6.35). The initial stack has 64 disks threaded onto one peg and arranged from bottom to top by decreasing size. The priests are attempting to move the stack from one peg to another under the constraints that exactly one disk is moved at a time and at no time may a larger disk be placed above a smaller disk. Three pegs are provided, one being used for temporarily holding disks. Supposedly, the world will end when the priests complete their task, so there is little incentive for us to facilitate their efforts.

Let us assume that the priests are attempting to move the disks from peg 1 to peg 3. We wish to develop an algorithm that prints the precise sequence of peg-to-peg disk transfers.

If we were to approach this problem with conventional methods, we would rapidly find ourselves hopelessly knotted up in managing the disks. Instead, attacking this problem with recursion in mind allows the steps to be simple. Moving n disks can be viewed in terms of moving only $n - 1$ disks (hence, the recursion), as follows:

a) Move $n - 1$ disks from peg 1 to peg 2, using peg 3 as a temporary holding area.

b) Move the last disk (the largest) from peg 1 to peg 3.

c) Move the $n - 1$ disks from peg 2 to peg 3, using peg 1 as a temporary holding area.

The process ends when the last task involves moving $n = 1$ disk (i.e., the base case). This task is accomplished by simply moving the disk, without the need for a temporary holding area.

Write a program to solve the Towers of Hanoi problem. Use a recursive function with four parameters:

a) The number of disks to be moved

b) The peg on which these disks are initially threaded

c) The peg to which this stack of disks is to be moved

d) The peg to be used as a temporary holding area

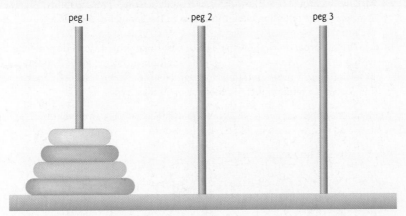

Fig. 6.35 | Towers of Hanoi for the case with four disks.

Your program should print the precise instructions it will take to move the disks from the starting peg to the destination peg. For example, to move a stack of three disks from peg 1 to peg 3, your program should print the following series of moves:

$1 \rightarrow 3$ (This means move one disk from peg 1 to peg 3.)
$1 \rightarrow 2$
$3 \rightarrow 2$
$1 \rightarrow 3$
$2 \rightarrow 1$
$2 \rightarrow 3$
$1 \rightarrow 3$

6.43 Any program that can be implemented recursively can be implemented iteratively, although sometimes with more difficulty and less clarity. Try writing an iterative version of the Towers of Hanoi. If you succeed, compare your iterative version with the recursive version developed in Exercise 6.42. Investigate issues of performance, clarity and your ability to demonstrate the correctness of the programs.

6.44 *(Visualizing Recursion)* It is interesting to watch recursion "in action." Modify the factorial function of Fig. 6.29 to print its local variable and recursive call parameter. For each recursive call, display the outputs on a separate line and add a level of indentation. Do your utmost to make the outputs clear, interesting and meaningful. Your goal here is to design and implement an output format that helps a person understand recursion better. You may want to add such display capabilities to the many other recursion examples and exercises throughout the text.

6.45 *(Recursive Greatest Common Divisor)* The greatest common divisor of integers x and y is the largest integer that evenly divides both x and y. Write a recursive function gcd that returns the greatest common divisor of x and y, defined recursively as follows: If y is equal to 0, then gcd(x, y) is x; otherwise, gcd(x, y) is gcd(y, x % y), where % is the modulus operator. [*Note:* For this algorithm, x must be larger than y.]

6.46 Can main be called recursively on your system? Write a program containing a function main. Include static local variable count and initialize it to 1. Postincrement and print the value of count each time main is called. Compile your program. What happens?

6.47 Exercises 6.35–6.37 developed a computer-assisted instruction program to teach an elementary school student multiplication. This exercise suggests enhancements to that program.
   a) Modify the program to allow the user to enter a grade-level capability. A grade level of 1 means to use only single-digit numbers in the problems, a grade level of 2 means to use numbers as large as two digits, etc.
   b) Modify the program to allow the user to pick the type of arithmetic problems he or she wishes to study. An option of 1 means addition problems only, 2 means subtraction problems only, 3 means multiplication problems only, 4 means division problems only and 5 means a random mix of problems of all these types.

6.48 Write function distance that calculates the distance between two points *(x1, y1)* and *(x2, y2)*. All numbers and return values should be of type double.

6.49 What is wrong with the following program?

```
1   // Exercise 6.49: ex06_49.cpp
2   // What is wrong with this program?
3   #include <iostream>
4   using std::cin;
5   using std::cout;
```

```
6
7   int main()
8   {
9      int c;
10
11     if ( ( c = cin.get() ) != EOF )
12     {
13        main();
14        cout << c;
15     } // end if
16
17     return 0; // indicates successful termination
18  } // end main
```

6.50   What does the following program do?

```
1   // Exercise 6.50: ex06_50.cpp
2   // What does this program do?
3   #include <iostream>
4   using std::cout;
5   using std::cin;
6   using std::endl;
7
8   int mystery( int, int ); // function prototype
9
10  int main()
11  {
12     int x, y;
13
14     cout << "Enter two integers: ";
15     cin >> x >> y;
16     cout << "The result is " << mystery( x, y ) << endl;
17
18     return 0; // indicates successful termination
19  } // end main
20
21  // Parameter b must be a positive integer to prevent infinite recursion
22  int mystery( int a, int b )
23  {
24     if ( b == 1 ) // base case
25        return a;
26     else // recursion step
27        return a + mystery( a, b - 1 );
28  } // end function mystery
```

6.51   After you determine what the program of Exercise 6.50 does, modify the program to function properly after removing the restriction that the second argument be nonnegative.

6.52   Write a program that tests as many of the math library functions in Fig. 6.2 as you can. Exercise each of these functions by having your program print out tables of return values for a diversity of argument values.

6.53   Find the error in each of the following program segments and explain how to correct it:
a) `float cube( float ); // function prototype`

```
double cube( float number ) // function definition
{
   return number * number * number;
}
```

b) `register auto int x = 7;`
c) `int randomNumber = srand();`
d) `float y = 123.45678;`
   `int x;`

   `x = y;`
   `cout << static_cast< float >( x ) << endl;`
e) `double square( double number )`
   ```
   {
      double number;
      return number * number;
   }
   ```
f) `int sum( int n )`
   ```
   {
      if ( n == 0 )
         return 0;
      else
         return n + sum( n );
   }
   ```

6.54   Modify the craps program of Fig. 6.11 to allow wagering. Package as a function the portion of the program that runs one game of craps. Initialize variable bankBalance to 1000 dollars. Prompt the player to enter a wager. Use a while loop to check that wager is less than or equal to bankBalance and, if not, prompt the user to reenter wager until a valid wager is entered. After a correct wager is entered, run one game of craps. If the player wins, increase bankBalance by wager and print the new bankBalance. If the player loses, decrease bankBalance by wager, print the new bankBalance, check on whether bankBalance has become zero and, if so, print the message "Sorry. You busted!" As the game progresses, print various messages to create some "chatter" such as "Oh, you're going for broke, huh?", "Aw cmon, take a chance!" or "You're up big. Now's the time to cash in your chips!".

6.55   Write a C++ program that prompts the user for the radius of a circle then calls inline function circleArea to calculate the area of that circle.

6.56   Write a complete C++ program with the two alternate functions specified below, of which each simply triples the variable count defined in main. Then compare and contrast the two approaches. These two functions are
   a) function tripleByValue that passes a copy of count by value, triples the copy and returns the new value and
   a) function tripleByReference that passes count by reference via a reference parameter and triples the original value of count through its alias (i.e., the reference parameter).

6.57   What is the purpose of the unary scope resolution operator?

6.58   Write a program that uses a function template called min to determine the smaller of two arguments. Test the program using integer, character and floating-point number arguments.

6.59 Write a program that uses a function template called max to determine the largest of three arguments. Test the program using integer, character and floating-point number arguments.

6.60 Determine whether the following program segments contain errors. For each error, explain how it can be corrected. [*Note:* For a particular program segment, it is possible that no errors are present in the segment.]

a)
```
template < class A >
int sum( int num1, int num2, int num3 )
{
    return num1 + num2 + num3;
}
```

b)
```
void printResults( int x, int y )
{
    cout << "The sum is " << x + y << '\n';
    return x + y;
}
```

c)
```
template < A >
A product( A num1, A num2, A num3 )
{
    return num1 * num2 * num3;
}
```

d)
```
double cube( int );
int cube( int );
```

7

Arrays and
Vectors

Now go, write it
before them in a table,
and note it in a book.
—Isaiah 30:8

To go beyond is as
wrong as to fall short.
—Confucius

Begin at the beginning, ...
and go on till you come to
the end: then stop.
—Lewis Carroll

OBJECTIVES

In this chapter you will learn:

- To use the array data structure to represent a set of related data items.
- To use arrays to store, sort and search lists and tables of values.
- To declare arrays, initialize arrays and refer to the individual elements of arrays.
- To pass arrays to functions.
- Basic searching and sorting techniques.
- To declare and manipulate multidimensional arrays.
- To use C++ Standard Library class template **vector**.

Outline

7.1 Introduction

7.2 Arrays

7.3 Declaring Arrays

7.4 Examples Using Arrays

7.5 Passing Arrays to Functions

7.6 Case Study: Class GradeBook Using an Array to Store Grades

7.7 Searching Arrays with Linear Search

7.8 Sorting Arrays with Insertion Sort

7.9 Multidimensional Arrays

7.10 Case Study: Class GradeBook Using a Two-Dimensional Array

7.11 Introduction to C++ Standard Library Class Template vector

7.12 Wrap-Up

Summary | Terminology | Self-Review Exercises | Answers to Self-Review Exercises | Exercises | Recursion Exercises | vector Exercises

7.1 Introduction

This chapter introduces the important topic of data structures—collections of related data items. Arrays are data structures consisting of related data items of the same type. You learned about classes in Chapter 3. In Chapter 9, we discuss the notion of structures. Structures and classes are each capable of holding related data items of possibly different types. Arrays, structures and classes are "static" entities in that they remain the same size throughout program execution. (They may, of course, be of automatic storage class and hence be created and destroyed each time the blocks in which they are defined are entered and exited.)

After discussing how arrays are declared, created and initialized, this chapter presents a series of practical examples that demonstrate several common array manipulations. We then explain how character strings (represented until now by string objects) can also be represented by character arrays. We present an example of searching arrays to find particular elements. The chapter also introduces one of the most important computing applications—sorting data (i.e., putting the data in some particular order). Two sections of the chapter enhance the case study of class GradeBook in Chapters 3–6. In particular, we use arrays to enable the class to maintain a set of grades in memory and analyze student grades from multiple exams in a semester—two capabilities that were absent from previous versions of the GradeBook class. These and other chapter examples demonstrate the ways in which arrays allow programmers to organize and manipulate data.

The style of arrays we use throughout most of this chapter are C-style pointer-based arrays. (We will study pointers in Chapter 8.) In the final section of this chapter, we will cover arrays as full-fledged objects called vectors. We will discover that these object-based arrays are safer and more versatile than the C-like, pointer-based arrays we discuss in the early part of this chapter.

7.2 Arrays

An array is a consecutive group of memory locations that all have the same type. To refer to a particular location or element in the array, we specify the name of the array and the position number of the particular element in the array.

Figure 7.1 shows an integer array called c. This array contains 12 elements. A program refers to any one of these elements by giving the name of the array followed by the position number of the particular element in square brackets ([]). The position number is more formally called a subscript or index (this number specifies the number of elements from the beginning of the array). The first element in every array has subscript 0 (zero) and is sometimes called the zeroth element. Thus, the elements of array c are c[0] (pronounced "c sub zero"), c[1], c[2] and so on. The highest subscript in array c is 11, which is 1 less than 12—the number of elements in the array. Array names follow the same conventions as other variable names, i.e., they must be identifiers.

A subscript must be an integer or integer expression (using any integral type). If a program uses an expression as a subscript, then the program evaluates the expression to determine the subscript. For example, if we assume that variable a is equal to 5 and that variable b is equal to 6, then the statement

        c[a + b] += 2;

adds 2 to array element c[11]. Note that a subscripted array name is an *lvalue*—it can be used on the left side of an assignment, just as non-array variable names can.

Let us examine array c in Fig. 7.1 more closely. The name of the entire array is c. The 12 elements of array c are referred to as c[0], c[1], c[2], ..., c[11]. The value of c[0] is -45, the value of c[1] is 6, the value of c[2] is 0, the value of c[7] is 62, and

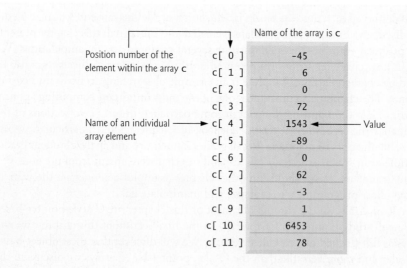

Fig. 7.1 | Array of 12 elements

the value of c[11] is 78. To print the sum of the values contained in the first three elements of array c, we would write

```
cout << c[ 0 ] + c[ 1 ] + c[ 2 ] << endl;
```

To divide the value of c[6] by 2 and assign the result to the variable x, we would write

```
x = c[ 6 ] / 2;
```

Common Programming Error 7.1

It is important to note the difference between the "seventh element of the array" and "array element 7." Array subscripts begin at 0, so the "seventh element of the array" has a subscript of 6, while "array element 7" has a subscript of 7 and is actually the eighth element of the array. Unfortunately, this distinction frequently is a source of off-by-one errors. To avoid such errors, we refer to specific array elements explicitly by their array name and subscript number (e.g., c[6] or c[7]).

The brackets used to enclose the subscript of an array are actually an operator in C++. Brackets have the same level of precedence as parentheses. Figure 7.2 shows the precedence and associativity of the operators introduced so far. Note that brackets ([]) have been added to the first row of Fig. 7.2. The operators are shown top to bottom in decreasing order of precedence with their associativity and type.

7.3 Declaring Arrays

Arrays occupy space in memory. The programmer specifies the type of the elements and the number of elements required by an array as follows:

type arrayName[*arraySize*];

Operators	Associativity	Type
() []	left to right	highest
++ -- static_cast< *type* >(*operand*)	left to right	unary (postfix)
++ -- + - !	right to left	unary (prefix)
* / %	left to right	multiplicative
+ -	left to right	additive
<< >>	left to right	insertion/extraction
< <= > >=	left to right	relational
== !=	left to right	equality
&&	left to right	logical AND
||	left to right	logical OR
?:	right to left	conditional
= += -= *= /= %=	right to left	assignment
,	left to right	comma

Fig. 7.2 | Operator precedence and associativity.

and the compiler reserves the appropriate amount of memory. The *arraySize* must be an integer constant greater than zero. For example, to tell the compiler to reserve 12 elements for integer array c, use the declaration

```
int c[ 12 ]; // c is an array of 12 integers
```

Memory can be reserved for several arrays with a single declaration. The following declaration reserves 100 elements for the integer array b and 27 elements for the integer array x.

```
int b[ 100 ], // b is an array of 100 integers
    x[ 27 ]; // x is an array of 27 integers
```

 Good Programming Practice 7.1

We prefer to declare one array per declaration for readability, modifiability and ease of commenting.

Arrays can be declared to contain values of any non-reference data type. For example, an array of type char can be used to store a character string. Until now, we have used string objects to store character strings. Section 7.4 introduces using character arrays to store strings. Character strings and their similarity to arrays (a relationship C++ inherited from C), and the relationship between pointers and arrays, are discussed in Chapter 8.

7.4 Examples Using Arrays

This section presents many examples that demonstrate how to declare arrays, how to initialize arrays and how to perform many common array manipulations.

Declaring an Array and Using a Loop to Initialize the Array's Elements
The program in Fig. 7.3 declares 10-element integer array n (line 12). Lines 15–16 use a for statement to initialize the array elements to zeros. The first output statement (line 18) displays the column headings for the columns printed in the subsequent for statement (lines 21–22), which prints the array in tabular format. Remember that setw specifies the field width in which only the *next* value is to be output.

Initializing an Array in a Declaration with an Initializer List
The elements of an array also can be initialized in the array declaration by following the array name with an equals sign and a comma-separated list (enclosed in braces) of initializers. The program in Fig. 7.4 uses an initializer list to initialize an integer array with 10 values (line 13) and prints the array in tabular format (lines 15–19).

If there are fewer initializers than elements in the array, the remaining array elements are initialized to zero. For example, the elements of array n in Fig. 7.3 could have been initialized to zero with the declaration

```
int n[ 10 ] = { 0 }; // initialize elements of array n to 0
```

The declaration explicitly initializes the first element to zero and implicitly initializes the remaining nine elements to zero, because there are fewer initializers than elements in the array. Automatic arrays are not implicitly initialized to zero although static arrays are. The programmer must at least initialize the first element to zero with an initializer list for the remaining elements to be implicitly set to zero. The initialization method shown in Fig. 7.3 can be performed repeatedly as a program executes.

```
 1   // Fig. 7.3: fig07_03.cpp
 2   // Initializing an array.
 3   #include <iostream>
 4   using std::cout;
 5   using std::endl;
 6
 7   #include <iomanip>
 8   using std::setw;
 9
10   int main()
11   {
12      int n[ 10 ]; // n is an array of 10 integers
13
14      // initialize elements of array n to 0
15      for ( int i = 0; i < 10; i++ )
16         n[ i ] = 0; // set element at location i to 0
17
18      cout << "Element" << setw( 13 ) << "Value" << endl;
19
20      // output each array element's value
21      for ( int j = 0; j < 10; j++ )
22         cout << setw( 7 ) << j << setw( 13 ) << n[ j ] << endl;
23
24      return 0; // indicates successful termination
25   } // end main
```

```
Element        Value
      0            0
      1            0
      2            0
      3            0
      4            0
      5            0
      6            0
      7            0
      8            0
      9            0
```

Fig. 7.3 | Initializing an array's elements to zeros and printing the array.

```
 1   // Fig. 7.4: fig07_04.cpp
 2   // Initializing an array in a declaration.
 3   #include <iostream>
 4   using std::cout;
 5   using std::endl;
 6
 7   #include <iomanip>
 8   using std::setw;
 9
10   int main()
11   {
```

Fig. 7.4 | Initializing the elements of an array in its declaration. (Part 1 of 2.)

```
12      // use initializer list to initialize array n
13      int n[ 10 ] = { 32, 27, 64, 18, 95, 14, 90, 70, 60, 37 };
14
15      cout << "Element" << setw( 13 ) << "Value" << endl;
16
17      // output each array element's value
18      for ( int i = 0; i < 10; i++ )
19         cout << setw( 7 ) << i << setw( 13 ) << n[ i ] << endl;
20
21      return 0; // indicates successful termination
22   } // end main
```

```
Element        Value
      0           32
      1           27
      2           64
      3           18
      4           95
      5           14
      6           90
      7           70
      8           60
      9           37
```

Fig. 7.4 | Initializing the elements of an array in its declaration. (Part 2 of 2.)

If the array size is omitted from a declaration with an initializer list, the compiler determines the number of elements in the array by counting the number of elements in the initializer list. For example,

```
int n[] = { 1, 2, 3, 4, 5 };
```

creates a five-element array.

If the array size and an initializer list are specified in an array declaration, the number of initializers must be less than or equal to the array size. The array declaration

```
int n[ 5 ] = { 32, 27, 64, 18, 95, 14 };
```

causes a compilation error, because there are six initializers and only five array elements.

Common Programming Error 7.2

Providing more initializers in an array initializer list than there are elements in the array is a compilation error.

Common Programming Error 7.3

Forgetting to initialize the elements of an array whose elements should be initialized is a logic error.

Specifying an Array's Size with a Constant Variable and Setting Array Elements with Calculations

Figure 7.5 sets the elements of a 10-element array s to the even integers 2, 4, 6, ..., 20 (lines 17–18) and prints the array in tabular format (lines 20–24). These numbers are generated (line 18) by multiplying each successive value of the loop counter by 2 and adding 2.

```
1   // Fig. 7.5: fig07_05.cpp
2   // Set array s to the even integers from 2 to 20.
3   #include <iostream>
4   using std::cout;
5   using std::endl;
6
7   #include <iomanip>
8   using std::setw;
9
10  int main()
11  {
12     // constant variable can be used to specify array size
13     const int arraySize = 10;
14
15     int s[ arraySize ]; // array s has 10 elements
16
17     for ( int i = 0; i < arraySize; i++ ) // set the values
18        s[ i ] = 2 + 2 * i;
19
20     cout << "Element" << setw( 13 ) << "Value" << endl;
21
22     // output contents of array s in tabular format
23     for ( int j = 0; j < arraySize; j++ )
24        cout << setw( 7 ) << j << setw( 13 ) << s[ j ] << endl;
25
26     return 0; // indicates successful termination
27  } // end main
```

```
Element        Value
      0            2
      1            4
      2            6
      3            8
      4           10
      5           12
      6           14
      7           16
      8           18
      9           20
```

Fig. 7.5 | Generating values to be placed into elements of an array.

Line 13 uses the **const** qualifier to declare a so-called constant variable arraySize with the value 10. Constant variables must be initialized with a constant expression when they are declared and cannot be modified thereafter (as shown in Fig. 7.6 and Fig. 7.7). Constant variables are also called named constants or read-only variables.

Common Programming Error 7.4

Not assigning a value to a constant variable when it is declared is a compilation error.

Common Programming Error 7.5

Assigning a value to a constant variable in an executable statement is a compilation error.

```
 1  // Fig. 7.6: fig07_06.cpp
 2  // Using a properly initialized constant variable.
 3  #include <iostream>
 4  using std::cout;
 5  using std::endl;
 6
 7  int main()
 8  {
 9     const int x = 7; // initialized constant variable
10
11     cout << "The value of constant variable x is: " << x << endl;
12
13     return 0; // indicates successful termination
14  } // end main
```

```
The value of constant variable x is: 7
```

Fig. 7.6 | Initializing and using a constant variable.

```
 1  // Fig. 7.7: fig07_07.cpp
 2  // A const variable must be initialized.
 3
 4  int main()
 5  {
 6     const int x; // Error: x must be initialized
 7
 8     x = 7; // Error: cannot modify a const variable
 9
10     return 0; // indicates successful termination
11  } // end main
```

Borland C++ command-line compiler error message:

```
Error E2304 fig07_07.cpp 6: Constant variable 'x' must be initialized
    in function main()
Error E2024 fig07_07.cpp 8: Cannot modify a const object in function main()
```

Microsoft Visual C++.NET compiler error message:

```
C:\scpphtp5_examples\ch07\fig07_07.cpp(6) : error C2734: 'x' : const object
    must be initialized if not extern
C:\scpphtp5_examples\ch07\fig07_07.cpp(8) : error C2166: l-value specifies
    const object
```

GNU C++ compiler error message:

```
fig07_07.cpp:6: error: uninitialized const `x'
fig07_07.cpp:8: error: assignment of read-only variable `x'
```

Fig. 7.7 | const variables must be initialized.

Constant variables can be placed anywhere a constant expression is expected. In Fig. 7.5, constant variable `arraySize` specifies the size of array `s` in line 15.

Common Programming Error 7.6

Only constants can be used to declare the size of automatic and static arrays. Not using a constant for this purpose is a compilation error.

Using constant variables to specify array sizes makes programs more scalable. In Fig. 7.5, the first `for` statement could fill a 1000-element array by simply changing the value of `arraySize` in its declaration from 10 to 1000. If the constant variable `arraySize` had not been used, we would have to change lines 15, 17 and 23 of the program to scale the program to handle 1000 array elements. As programs get larger, this technique becomes more useful for writing clearer, easier-to-modify programs.

Software Engineering Observation 7.1

Defining the size of each array as a constant variable instead of a literal constant can make programs more scalable.

Good Programming Practice 7.2

Defining the size of an array as a constant variable instead of a literal constant makes programs clearer. This technique eliminates so-called magic numbers. For example, repeatedly mentioning the size 10 in array-processing code for a 10-element array gives the number 10 an artificial significance and can unfortunately confuse the reader when the program includes other 10s that have nothing to do with the array size.

Summing the Elements of an Array

Often, the elements of an array represent a series of values to be used in a calculation. For example, if the elements of an array represent exam grades, a professor may wish to total the elements of the array and use that sum to calculate the class average for the exam. The examples using class `GradeBook` later in the chapter, namely Figs. 7.16–7.17 and Figs. 7.23–7.24, use this technique.

The program in Fig. 7.8 sums the values contained in the 10-element integer array a. The program declares, creates and initializes the array at line 10. The `for` statement (lines 14–15) performs the calculations. The values being supplied as initializers for array a also could be read into the program from the user at the keyboard, or from a file on disk. For example, the `for` statement

```
for ( int j = 0; j < arraySize; j++ )
   cin >> a[ j ];
```

reads one value at a time from the keyboard and stores the value in element a[j].

```
1   // Fig. 7.8: fig07_08.cpp
2   // Compute the sum of the elements of the array.
3   #include <iostream>
4   using std::cout;
5   using std::endl;
6
```

Fig. 7.8 | Computing the sum of the elements of an array. (Part 1 of 2.)

```
7    int main()
8    {
9       const int arraySize = 10; // constant variable indicating size of array
10      int a[ arraySize ] = { 87, 68, 94, 100, 83, 78, 85, 91, 76, 87 };
11      int total = 0;
12
13      // sum contents of array a
14      for ( int i = 0; i < arraySize; i++ )
15         total += a[ i ];
16
17      cout << "Total of array elements: " << total << endl;
18
19      return 0; // indicates successful termination
20   } // end main
```

```
Total of array elements: 849
```

Fig. 7.8 | Computing the sum of the elements of an array. (Part 2 of 2.)

Using Bar Charts to Display Array Data Graphically

Many programs present data to users in a graphical manner. For example, numeric values are often displayed as bars in a bar chart. In such a chart, longer bars represent proportionally larger numeric values. One simple way to display numeric data graphically is with a bar chart that shows each numeric value as a bar of asterisks (*).

Professors often like to examine the distribution of grades on an exam. A professor might graph the number of grades in each of several categories to visualize the grade distribution. Suppose the grades were 87, 68, 94, 100, 83, 78, 85, 91, 76 and 87. Note that there was one grade of 100, two grades in the 90s, four grades in the 80s, two grades in the 70s, one grade in the 60s and no grades below 60. Our next program (Fig. 7.9) stores this grade distribution data in an array of 11 elements, each corresponding to a category of grades. For example, n[0] indicates the number of grades in the range 0–9, n[7] indicates the number of grades in the range 70–79 and n[10] indicates the number of grades of 100. The two versions of class GradeBook later in the chapter (Figs. 7.16–7.17 and Figs. 7.23–7.24) contain code that calculates these grade frequencies based on a set of grades. For now, we manually create the array by looking at the set of grades.

```
1    // Fig. 7.9: fig07_09.cpp
2    // Bar chart printing program.
3    #include <iostream>
4    using std::cout;
5    using std::endl;
6
7    #include <iomanip>
8    using std::setw;
9
10   int main()
11   {
12      const int arraySize = 11;
```

Fig. 7.9 | Bar chart printing program. (Part 1 of 2.)

```
13        int n[ arraySize ] = { 0, 0, 0, 0, 0, 0, 1, 2, 4, 2, 1 };
14
15        cout << "Grade distribution:" << endl;
16
17        // for each element of array n, output a bar of the chart
18        for ( int i = 0; i < arraySize; i++ )
19        {
20           // output bar labels ("0-9:", ..., "90-99:", "100:" )
21           if ( i == 0 )
22              cout << "  0-9: ";
23           else if ( i == 10 )
24              cout << "  100: ";
25           else
26              cout << i * 10 << "-" << ( i * 10 ) + 9 << ": ";
27
28           // print bar of asterisks
29           for ( int stars = 0; stars < n[ i ]; stars++ )
30              cout << '*';
31
32           cout << endl; // start a new line of output
33        } // end outer for
34
35        return 0; // indicates successful termination
36     } // end main
```

```
Grade distribution:
   0-9:
  10-19:
  20-29:
  30-39:
  40-49:
  50-59:
  60-69: *
  70-79: **
  80-89: ****
  90-99: **
   100: *
```

Fig. 7.9 | Bar chart printing program. (Part 2 of 2.)

The program reads the numbers from the array and graphs the information as a bar chart. The program displays each grade range followed by a bar of asterisks indicating the number of grades in that range. To label each bar, lines 21–26 output a grade range (e.g., "70-79: ") based on the current value of counter variable i. The nested for statement (lines 29–30) outputs the bars. Note the loop-continuation condition at line 29 (stars < n[i]). Each time the program reaches the inner for, the loop counts from 0 up to n[i], thus using a value in array n to determine the number of asterisks to display. In this example, n[0]–n[5] contain zeros because no students received a grade below 60. Thus, the program displays no asterisks next to the first six grade ranges.

Common Programming Error 7.7

Although it is possible to use the same control variable in a for statement and a second for statement nested inside, this is confusing and can lead to logic errors.

Using the Elements of an Array as Counters

Sometimes, programs use counter variables to summarize data, such as the results of a survey. In Fig. 6.9, we used separate counters in our die-rolling program to track the number of occurrences of each side of a die as the program rolled the die 6,000,000 times. An array version of this program is shown in Fig. 7.10.

```cpp
1   // Fig. 7.10: fig07_10.cpp
2   // Roll a six-sided die 6,000,000 times.
3   #include <iostream>
4   using std::cout;
5   using std::endl;
6
7   #include <iomanip>
8   using std::setw;
9
10  #include <cstdlib>
11  using std::rand;
12  using std::srand;
13
14  #include <ctime>
15  using std::time;
16
17  int main()
18  {
19     const int arraySize = 7; // ignore element zero
20     int frequency[ arraySize ] = { 0 };
21
22     srand( time( 0 ) ); // seed random number generator
23
24     // roll die 6,000,000 times; use die value as frequency index
25     for ( int roll = 1; roll <= 6000000; roll++ )
26        frequency[ 1 + rand() % 6 ]++;
27
28     cout << "Face" << setw( 13 ) << "Frequency" << endl;
29
30     // output each array element's value
31     for ( int face = 1; face < arraySize; face++ )
32        cout << setw( 4 ) << face << setw( 13 ) << frequency[ face ]
33           << endl;
34
35     return 0; // indicates successful termination
36  } // end main
```

```
Face     Frequency
   1       1000167
   2       1000149
   3       1000152
   4        998748
   5        999626
   6       1001158
```

Fig. 7.10 | Die-rolling program using an array instead of `switch`.

Figure 7.10 uses the array frequency (line 20) to count the occurrences of each side of the die. *The single statement in line 26 of this program replaces the switch statement in lines 30–52 of Fig. 6.9.* Line 26 uses a random value to determine which frequency element to increment during each iteration of the loop. The calculation in line 26 produces a random subscript from 1 to 6, so array frequency must be large enough to store six counters. However, we use a seven-element array in which we ignore frequency[0]—it is more logical to have the die face value 1 increment frequency[1] than frequency[0]. Thus, each face value is used as a subscript for array frequency. We also replace lines 56–61 of Fig. 6.9 by looping through array frequency to output the results (lines 31–33).

Using Arrays to Summarize Survey Results

Our next example (Fig. 7.11) uses arrays to summarize the results of data collected in a survey. Consider the following problem statement:

> *Forty students were asked to rate the quality of the food in the student cafeteria on a scale of 1 to 10 (1 meaning awful and 10 meaning excellent). Place the 40 responses in an integer array and summarize the results of the poll.*

This is a typical array-processing application. We wish to summarize the number of responses of each type (i.e., 1 through 10). The array responses (lines 17–19) is a 40-element integer array of the students' responses to the survey. Note that array responses is declared const, as its values do not (and should not) change. We use an 11-element array frequency (line 22) to count the number of occurrences of each response. Each element of the array is used as a counter for one of the survey responses and is initialized to zero. As in Fig. 7.10, we ignore frequency[0].

```cpp
 1   // Fig. 7.11: fig07_11.cpp
 2   // Student poll program.
 3   #include <iostream>
 4   using std::cout;
 5   using std::endl;
 6
 7   #include <iomanip>
 8   using std::setw;
 9
10   int main()
11   {
12      // define array sizes
13      const int responseSize = 40; // size of array responses
14      const int frequencySize = 11; // size of array frequency
15
16      // place survey responses in array responses
17      const int responses[ responseSize ] = { 1, 2, 6, 4, 8, 5, 9, 7, 8,
18         10, 1, 6, 3, 8, 6, 10, 3, 8, 2, 7, 6, 5, 7, 6, 8, 6, 7,
19         5, 6, 6, 5, 6, 7, 5, 6, 4, 8, 6, 8, 10 };
20
21      // initialize frequency counters to 0
22      int frequency[ frequencySize ] = { 0 };
23
```

Fig. 7.11 | Poll analysis program. (Part 1 of 2.)

```
24        // for each answer, select responses element and use that value
25        // as frequency subscript to determine element to increment
26        for ( int answer = 0; answer < responseSize; answer++ )
27           frequency[ responses[ answer ] ]++;
28
29        cout << "Rating" << setw( 17 ) << "Frequency" << endl;
30
31        // output each array element's value
32        for ( int rating = 1; rating < frequencySize; rating++ )
33           cout << setw( 6 ) << rating << setw( 17 ) << frequency[ rating ]
34              << endl;
35
36        return 0; // indicates successful termination
37     } // end main
```

Rating	Frequency
1	2
2	2
3	2
4	2
5	5
6	11
7	5
8	7
9	1
10	3

Fig. 7.11 | Poll analysis program. (Part 2 of 2.)

Software Engineering Observation 7.2

The const *qualifier should be used to enforce the principle of least privilege. Using the principle of least privilege to properly design software can greatly reduce debugging time and improper side effects and can make a program easier to modify and maintain.*

Good Programming Practice 7.3

Strive for program clarity. It is sometimes worthwhile to trade off the most efficient use of memory or processor time in favor of writing clearer programs.

Performance Tip 7.1

Sometimes performance considerations far outweigh clarity considerations.

The first for statement (lines 26–27) takes the responses one at a time from the array responses and increments one of the 10 counters in the frequency array (frequency[1] to frequency[10]). The key statement in the loop is line 27, which increments the appropriate frequency counter, depending on the value of responses[answer].

Let's consider several iterations of the for loop. When control variable answer is 0, the value of responses[answer] is the value of responses[0] (i.e., 1 in line 17), so the program interprets frequency[responses[answer]]++ as

```
frequency[ 1 ]++
```

which increments the value in array element 1. To evaluate the expression, start with the value in the innermost set of square brackets (answer). Once you know answer's value (which is the value of the loop control variable in line 26), plug it into the expression and evaluate the next outer set of square brackets (i.e., responses[answer], which is a value selected from the responses array in lines 17–19). Then use the resulting value as the subscript for the frequency array to specify which counter to increment.

When answer is 1, responses[answer] is the value of responses[1], which is 2, so the program interprets frequency[responses[answer]]++ as

```
frequency[ 2 ]++
```

which increments array element 2.

When answer is 2, responses[answer] is the value of responses[2], which is 6, so the program interprets frequency[responses[answer]]++ as

```
frequency[ 6 ]++
```

which increments array element 6, and so on. Regardless of the number of responses processed in the survey, the program requires only an 11-element array (ignoring element zero) to summarize the results, because all the response values are between 1 and 10 and the subscript values for an 11-element array are 0 through 10.

If the data in the responses array had contained an invalid value, such as 13, the program would have attempted to add 1 to frequency[13], which is outside the bounds of the array. *C++ has no array bounds checking to prevent the computer from referring to an element that does not exist.* Thus, an executing program can "walk off" either end of an array without warning. The programmer should ensure that all array references remain within the bounds of the array.

Common Programming Error 7.8

Referring to an element outside the array bounds is an execution-time logic error. It is not a syntax error.

Error-Prevention Tip 7.1

When looping through an array, the array subscript should never go below 0 and should always be less than the total number of elements in the array (one less than the size of the array). Make sure that the loop-termination condition prevents accessing elements outside this range.

Portability Tip 7.1

The (normally serious) effects of referencing elements outside the array bounds are system dependent. Often this results in changes to the value of an unrelated variable or a fatal error that terminates program execution.

C++ is an extensible language. Section 7.11 presents C++ Standard Library class template vector, which enables programmers to perform many operations that are not available for C++'s built-in arrays. For example, we will be able to compare vectors directly and assign one vector to another. In Chapter 11, we extend C++ further by implementing an array as a user-defined class of our own. This new array definition will enable us to input and output entire arrays with cin and cout, initialize arrays when they are created, prevent access to out-of-range array elements and change the range of subscripts (and even their subscript type) so that the first element of an array is not required to be element 0. We will even be able to use noninteger subscripts.

Error-Prevention Tip 7.2

In Chapter 11, we will see how to develop a class representing a "smart array," which checks that all subscript references are in bounds at runtime. Using such smart data types helps eliminate bugs.

Using Character Arrays to Store and Manipulate Strings

To this point, we have discussed only integer arrays. However, arrays may be of any type. We now introduce storing character strings in character arrays. Recall that, starting in Chapter 3, we have been using `string` objects to store character strings, such as the course name in our `GradeBook` class. A string such as "hello" is actually an array of characters. While `string` objects are convenient to use and reduce the potential for errors, character arrays that represent strings have several unique features, which we discuss in this section. As you continue your study of C++, you may encounter C++ capabilities that require you to use character arrays in preference to `string` objects. You may also be asked to update existing code using character arrays.

A character array can be initialized using a string literal. For example, the declaration

```
char string1[] = "first";
```

initializes the elements of array `string1` to the individual characters in the string literal `"first"`. The size of array `string1` in the preceding declaration is determined by the compiler based on the length of the string. It is important to note that the string `"first"` contains five characters *plus* a special string-termination character called the null character. Thus, array `string1` actually contains six elements. The character constant representation of the null character is `'\0'` (backslash followed by zero). All strings represented by character arrays end with this character. A character array representing a string should always be declared large enough to hold the number of characters in the string and the terminating null character.

Character arrays also can be initialized with individual character constants in an initializer list. The preceding declaration is equivalent to the more tedious form

```
char string1[] = { 'f', 'i', 'r', 's', 't', '\0' };
```

Note the use of single quotes to delineate each character constant. Also, note that we explicitly provided the terminating null character as the last initializer value. Without it, this array would simply represent an array of characters, not a string. As we discuss in Chapter 8, not providing a terminating null character for a string can cause logic errors.

Because a string is an array of characters, we can access individual characters in a string directly with array subscript notation. For example, `string1[ 0 ]` is the character `'f'`, `string1[ 3 ]` is the character `'s'` and `string1[ 5 ]` is the null character.

We also can input a string directly into a character array from the keyboard using `cin` and `>>`. For example, the declaration

```
char string2[ 20 ];
```

creates a character array capable of storing a string of 19 characters and a terminating null character. The statement

```
cin >> string2;
```

reads a string from the keyboard into `string2` and appends the null character to the end of the string input by the user. Note that the preceding statement provides only the name of the array and no information about the size of the array. It is the programmer's responsibility to ensure that the array into which the string is read is capable of holding any string the user types at the keyboard. By default, `cin` reads characters from the keyboard until the first white-space character is encountered—regardless of the array size. Thus, inputting data with `cin` and `>>` can insert data beyond the end of the array (see Section 8.13 for information on preventing insertion beyond the end of a `char` array).

 Common Programming Error 7.9

Not providing `cin >>` with a character array large enough to store a string typed at the keyboard can result in loss of data in a program and other serious runtime errors.

A character array representing a null-terminated string can be output with `cout` and `<<`. The statement

```
cout << string2;
```

prints the array `string2`. Note that `cout <<`, like `cin >>`, does not care how large the character array is. The characters of the string are output until a terminating null character is encountered. [*Note:* `cin` and `cout` assume that character arrays should be processed as strings terminated by null characters; `cin` and `cout` do not provide similar input and output processing capabilities for other array types.]

Figure 7.12 demonstrates initializing a character array with a string literal, reading a string into a character array, printing a character array as a string and accessing individual characters of a string.

```
 1   // Fig. 7.12: fig07_12.cpp
 2   // Treating character arrays as strings.
 3   #include <iostream>
 4   using std::cout;
 5   using std::cin;
 6   using std::endl;
 7
 8   int main()
 9   {
10      char string1[ 20 ]; // reserves 20 characters
11      char string2[] = "string literal"; // reserves 15 characters
12
13      // read string from user into array string1
14      cout << "Enter the string \"hello there\": ";
15      cin >> string1; // reads "hello" [space terminates input]
16
17      // output strings
18      cout << "string1 is: " << string1 << "\nstring2 is: " << string2;
19
20      cout << "\nstring1 with spaces between characters is:\n";
```

Fig. 7.12 | Character arrays processed as strings. (Part 1 of 2.)

```
21
22      // output characters until null character is reached
23      for ( int i = 0; string1[ i ] != '\0'; i++ )
24          cout << string1[ i ] << ' ';
25
26      cin >> string1; // reads "there"
27      cout << "\nstring1 is: " << string1 << endl;
28
29      return 0; // indicates successful termination
30  } // end main
```

```
Enter the string "hello there": hello there
string1 is: hello
string2 is: string literal
string1 with spaces between characters is:
h e l l o
string1 is: there
```

Fig. 7.12 | Character arrays processed as strings. (Part 2 of 2.)

Lines 23–24 of Fig. 7.12 use a for statement to loop through the string1 array and print the individual characters separated by spaces. The condition in the for statement, string1[i] != '\0', is true until the loop encounters the terminating null character of the string.

Static Local Arrays and Automatic Local Arrays

Chapter 6 discussed the storage class specifier static. A static local variable in a function definition exists for the duration of the program, but is visible only in the function body.

Performance Tip 7.2

We can apply static to a local array declaration so that the array is not created and initialized each time the program calls the function and is not destroyed each time the function terminates in the program. This can improve performance, especially when using large arrays.

A program initializes static local arrays when their declarations are first encountered. If a static array is not initialized explicitly by the programmer, each element of that array is initialized to zero by the compiler when the array is created. Recall that C++ does not perform such default initialization for automatic variables.

Figure 7.13 demonstrates function staticArrayInit (lines 25–41) with a static local array (line 28) and function automaticArrayInit (lines 44–60) with an automatic local array (line 47).

```
1   // Fig. 7.13: fig07_13.cpp
2   // Static arrays are initialized to zero.
3   #include <iostream>
4   using std::cout;
5   using std::endl;
6
7   void staticArrayInit( void ); // function prototype
```

Fig. 7.13 | static array initialization and automatic array initialization. (Part 1 of 3.)

```
 8   void automaticArrayInit( void ); // function prototype
 9
10   int main()
11   {
12      cout << "First call to each function:\n";
13      staticArrayInit();
14      automaticArrayInit();
15
16      cout << "\n\nSecond call to each function:\n";
17      staticArrayInit();
18      automaticArrayInit();
19      cout << endl;
20
21      return 0; // indicates successful termination
22   } // end main
23
24   // function to demonstrate a static local array
25   void staticArrayInit( void )
26   {
27      // initializes elements to 0 first time function is called
28      static int array1[ 3 ]; // static local array
29
30      cout << "\nValues on entering staticArrayInit:\n";
31
32      // output contents of array1
33      for ( int i = 0; i < 3; i++ )
34         cout << "array1[" << i << "] = " << array1[ i ] << "   ";
35
36      cout << "\nValues on exiting staticArrayInit:\n";
37
38      // modify and output contents of array1
39      for ( int j = 0; j < 3; j++ )
40         cout << "array1[" << j << "] = " << ( array1[ j ] += 5 ) << "   ";
41   } // end function staticArrayInit
42
43   // function to demonstrate an automatic local array
44   void automaticArrayInit( void )
45   {
46      // initializes elements each time function is called
47      int array2[ 3 ] = { 1, 2, 3 }; // automatic local array
48
49      cout << "\n\nValues on entering automaticArrayInit:\n";
50
51      // output contents of array2
52      for ( int i = 0; i < 3; i++ )
53         cout << "array2[" << i << "] = " << array2[ i ] << "   ";
54
55      cout << "\nValues on exiting automaticArrayInit:\n";
56
57      // modify and output contents of array2
58      for ( int j = 0; j < 3; j++ )
59         cout << "array2[" << j << "] = " << ( array2[ j ] += 5 ) << "   ";
60   } // end function automaticArrayInit
```

Fig. 7.13 | static array initialization and automatic array initialization. (Part 2 of 3.)

```
First call to each function:

Values on entering staticArrayInit:
array1[0] = 0   array1[1] = 0   array1[2] = 0
Values on exiting staticArrayInit:
array1[0] = 5   array1[1] = 5   array1[2] = 5

Values on entering automaticArrayInit:
array2[0] = 1   array2[1] = 2   array2[2] = 3
Values on exiting automaticArrayInit:
array2[0] = 6   array2[1] = 7   array2[2] = 8

Second call to each function:

Values on entering staticArrayInit:
array1[0] = 5   array1[1] = 5   array1[2] = 5
Values on exiting staticArrayInit:
array1[0] = 10   array1[1] = 10   array1[2] = 10

Values on entering automaticArrayInit:
array2[0] = 1   array2[1] = 2   array2[2] = 3
Values on exiting automaticArrayInit:
array2[0] = 6   array2[1] = 7   array2[2] = 8
```

Fig. 7.13 | `static` array initialization and automatic array initialization. (Part 3 of 3.)

Function `staticArrayInit` is called twice (lines 13 and 17). The `static` local array is initialized to zero by the compiler the first time the function is called. The function prints the array, adds 5 to each element and prints the array again. The second time the function is called, the `static` array contains the modified values stored during the first function call. Function `automaticArrayInit` also is called twice (lines 14 and 18). The elements of the automatic local array are initialized (line 47) with the values 1, 2 and 3. The function prints the array, adds 5 to each element and prints the array again. The second time the function is called, the array elements are reinitialized to 1, 2 and 3. The array has automatic storage class, so the array is recreated during each call to `automaticArrayInit`.

 Common Programming Error 7.10

Assuming that elements of a function's local static array are initialized every time the function is called can lead to logic errors in a program.

7.5 Passing Arrays to Functions

To pass an array argument to a function, specify the name of the array without any brackets. For example, if array `hourlyTemperatures` has been declared as

```
int hourlyTemperatures[ 24 ];
```

the function call

```
modifyArray( hourlyTemperatures, 24 );
```

passes array `hourlyTemperatures` and its size to function `modifyArray`. When passing an array to a function, the array size is normally passed as well, so the function can process the specific number of elements in the array. (Otherwise, we would need to build this knowledge into the called function itself or, worse yet, place the array size in a global variable.) In Section 7.11, when we present C++ Standard Library class template `vector` to represent a more robust type of array, you will see that the size of a `vector` is built in—every `vector` object "knows" its own size, which can be obtained by invoking the `vector` object's `size` member function. Thus, when we pass a `vector` *object* into a function, we will not have to pass the size of the `vector` as an argument.

C++ passes arrays to functions by reference—the called functions can modify the element values in the callers' original arrays. The value of the name of the array is the address in the computer's memory of the first element of the array. Because the starting address of the array is passed, the called function knows precisely where the array is stored in memory. Therefore, when the called function modifies array elements in its function body, it is modifying the actual elements of the array in their original memory locations.

> **Performance Tip 7.3**
>
> *Passing arrays by reference makes sense for performance reasons. If arrays were passed by value, a copy of each element would be passed. For large, frequently passed arrays, this would be time consuming and would require considerable storage for the copies of the array elements.*

Although entire arrays are passed by reference, individual array elements are passed by value exactly as simple variables are. Such simple single pieces of data are called scalars or scalar quantities. To pass an element of an array to a function, use the subscripted name of the array element as an argument in the function call. In Chapter 6, we showed how to pass scalars (i.e., individual variables and array elements) by reference with references. In Chapter 8, we show how to pass scalars by reference with pointers.

For a function to receive an array through a function call, the function's parameter list must specify that the function expects to receive an array. For example, the function header for function `modifyArray` might be written as

```
void modifyArray( int b[], int arraySize )
```

indicating that `modifyArray` expects to receive the address of an array of integers in parameter b and the number of array elements in parameter `arraySize`. The size of the array is not required between the array brackets. If it is included, the compiler ignores it. Because C++ passes arrays to functions by reference, when the called function uses the array name b, it will in fact be referring to the actual array in the caller (i.e., array `hourlyTemperatures` discussed at the beginning of this section).

Note the strange appearance of the function prototype for `modifyArray`

```
void modifyArray( int [], int );
```

This prototype could have been written

```
void modifyArray( int anyArrayName[], int anyVariableName );
```

but, as we learned in Chapter 3, C++ compilers ignore variable names in prototypes. Remember, the prototype tells the compiler the number of arguments and the type of each argument (in the order in which the arguments are expected to appear).

The program in Fig. 7.14 demonstrates the difference between passing an entire array and passing an array element. Lines 22–23 print the five original elements of integer array a. Line 28 passes a and its size to function modifyArray (lines 45–50), which multiplies each of a's elements by 2 (through parameter b). Then, lines 32–33 print array a again in main. As the output shows, the elements of a are indeed modified by modifyArray. Next, line 36 prints the value of scalar a[3], then line 38 passes element a[3] to function modifyElement (lines 54–58), which multiplies its parameter by 2 and prints the new value. Note that when line 39 again prints a[3] in main, the value has not been modified, because individual array elements are passed by value.

```cpp
1   // Fig. 7.14: fig07_14.cpp
2   // Passing arrays and individual array elements to functions.
3   #include <iostream>
4   using std::cout;
5   using std::endl;
6
7   #include <iomanip>
8   using std::setw;
9
10  void modifyArray( int [], int ); // appears strange
11  void modifyElement( int );
12
13  int main()
14  {
15     const int arraySize = 5; // size of array a
16     int a[ arraySize ] = { 0, 1, 2, 3, 4 }; // initialize array a
17
18     cout << "Effects of passing entire array by reference:"
19        << "\n\nThe values of the original array are:\n";
20
21     // output original array elements
22     for ( int i = 0; i < arraySize; i++ )
23        cout << setw( 3 ) << a[ i ];
24
25     cout << endl;
26
27     // pass array a to modifyArray by reference
28     modifyArray( a, arraySize );
29     cout << "The values of the modified array are:\n";
30
31     // output modified array elements
32     for ( int j = 0; j < arraySize; j++ )
33        cout << setw( 3 ) << a[ j ];
34
35     cout << "\n\n\nEffects of passing array element by value:"
36        << "\n\na[3] before modifyElement: " << a[ 3 ] << endl;
37
38     modifyElement( a[ 3 ] ); // pass array element a[ 3 ] by value
39     cout << "a[3] after modifyElement: " << a[ 3 ] << endl;
```

Fig. 7.14 | Passing arrays and individual array elements to functions. (Part 1 of 2.)

```
40
41       return 0; // indicates successful termination
42    } // end main
43
44    // in function modifyArray, "b" points to the original array "a" in memory
45    void modifyArray( int b[], int sizeOfArray )
46    {
47       // multiply each array element by 2
48       for ( int k = 0; k < sizeOfArray; k++ )
49          b[ k ] *= 2;
50    } // end function modifyArray
51
52    // in function modifyElement, "e" is a local copy of
53    // array element a[ 3 ] passed from main
54    void modifyElement( int e )
55    {
56       // multiply parameter by 2
57       cout << "Value of element in modifyElement: " << ( e *= 2 ) << endl;
58    } // end function modifyElement
```

```
Effects of passing entire array by reference:

The values of the original array are:
   0   1   2   3   4
The values of the modified array are:
   0   2   4   6   8


Effects of passing array element by value:

a[3] before modifyElement: 6
Value of element in modifyElement: 12
a[3] after modifyElement: 6
```

Fig. 7.14 | Passing arrays and individual array elements to functions. (Part 2 of 2.)

There may be situations in your programs in which a function should not be allowed to modify array elements. C++ provides the type qualifier const that can be used to prevent modification of array values in the caller by code in a called function. When a function specifies an array parameter that is preceded by the const qualifier, the elements of the array become constant in the function body, and any attempt to modify an element of the array in the function body results in a compilation error. This enables the programmer to prevent accidental modification of array elements in the function's body.

Figure 7.15 demonstrates the const qualifier. Function tryToModifyArray (lines 21–26) is defined with parameter const int b[], which specifies that array b is constant and cannot be modified. Each of the three attempts by the function to modify array b's elements (lines 23–25) results in a compilation error. The Microsoft Visual C++.NET compiler, for example, produces the error "l-value specifies const object." [*Note:* The C++ standard defines an "object" as any "region of storage," thus including variables or array elements of fundamental data types as well as instances of classes (what we've been

```
 1   // Fig. 7.15: fig07_15.cpp
 2   // Demonstrating the const type qualifier.
 3   #include <iostream>
 4   using std::cout;
 5   using std::endl;
 6
 7   void tryToModifyArray( const int [] ); // function prototype
 8
 9   int main()
10   {
11      int a[] = { 10, 20, 30 };
12
13      tryToModifyArray( a );
14      cout << a[ 0 ] << ' ' << a[ 1 ] << ' ' << a[ 2 ] << '\n';
15
16      return 0; // indicates successful termination
17   } // end main
18
19   // In function tryToModifyArray, "b" cannot be used
20   // to modify the original array "a" in main.
21   void tryToModifyArray( const int b[] )
22   {
23      b[ 0 ] /= 2; // error
24      b[ 1 ] /= 2; // error
25      b[ 2 ] /= 2; // error
26   } // end function tryToModifyArray
```

Borland C++ command-line compiler error message:

```
Error E2024 fig07_15.cpp 23: Cannot modify a const object
   in function tryToModifyArray(const int * const)
Error E2024 fig07_15.cpp 24: Cannot modify a const object
   in function tryToModifyArray(const int * const)
Error E2024 fig07_15.cpp 25: Cannot modify a const object
   in function tryToModifyArray(const int * const)
```

Microsoft Visual C++.NET compiler error message:

```
C:\scpphtp5_examples\ch07\fig07_15.cpp(23) : error C2166: l-value specifies
   const object
C:\scpphtp5_examples\ch07\fig07_15.cpp(24) : error C2166: l-value specifies
   const object
C:\scpphtp5_examples\ch07\fig07_15.cpp(25) : error C2166: l-value specifies
   const object
```

GNU C++ compiler error message:

```
fig07_15.cpp:23: error: assignment of read-only location
fig07_15.cpp:24: error: assignment of read-only location
fig07_15.cpp:25: error: assignment of read-only location
```

Fig. 7.15 | const type qualifier applied to an array parameter.

calling objects).] This message indicates that using a const object (e.g., b[0]) as an *lvalue* is an error—you cannot assign a new value to a const object by placing it on the left of an assignment operator. Note that compiler error messages vary between compilers (as shown in Fig. 7.15). The const qualifier will be discussed again in Chapter 10.

Common Programming Error 7.11

Forgetting that arrays in the caller are passed by reference, and hence can be modified in called functions, may result in logic errors.

Software Engineering Observation 7.3

Applying the const type qualifier to an array parameter in a function definition to prevent the original array from being modified in the function body is another example of the principle of least privilege. Functions should not be given the capability to modify an array unless it is absolutely necessary.

7.6 Case Study: Class GradeBook Using an Array to Store Grades

This section further evolves class GradeBook, introduced in Chapter 3 and expanded in Chapters 4–6. Recall that this class represents a grade book used by a professor to store and analyze a set of student grades. Previous versions of the class process a set of grades entered by the user, but do not maintain the individual grade values in data members of the class. Thus, repeat calculations require the user to reenter the same grades. One way to solve this problem would be to store each grade entered in an individual data member of the class. For example, we could create data members grade1, grade2, ..., grade10 in class GradeBook to store 10 student grades. However, the code to total the grades and determine the class average would be cumbersome. In this section, we solve this problem by storing grades in an array.

Storing Student Grades in an Array in Class *GradeBook*
The version of class GradeBook (Figs. 7.16–7.17) presented here uses an array of integers to store the grades of several students on a single exam. This eliminates the need to repeatedly input the same set of grades. Array grades is declared as a data member in line 29 of Fig. 7.16—therefore, each GradeBook object maintains its own set of grades.

```
1   // Fig. 7.16: GradeBook.h
2   // Definition of class GradeBook that uses an array to store test grades.
3   // Member functions are defined in GradeBook.cpp
4
5   #include <string> // program uses C++ Standard Library string class
6   using std::string;
7
8   // GradeBook class definition
9   class GradeBook
10  {
11  public:
12      // constant -- number of students who took the test
13      const static int students = 10; // note public data
```

Fig. 7.16 | Definition of class GradeBook using an array to store test grades. (Part 1 of 2.)

```
14
15      // constructor initializes course name and array of grades
16      GradeBook( string, const int [] );
17
18      void setCourseName( string ); // function to set the course name
19      string getCourseName(); // function to retrieve the course name
20      void displayMessage(); // display a welcome message
21      void processGrades(); // perform various operations on the grade data
22      int getMinimum(); // find the minimum grade for the test
23      int getMaximum(); // find the maximum grade for the test
24      double getAverage(); // determine the average grade for the test
25      void outputBarChart(); // output bar chart of grade distribution
26      void outputGrades(); // output the contents of the grades array
27   private:
28      string courseName; // course name for this grade book
29      int grades[ students ]; // array of student grades
30   }; // end class GradeBook
```

Fig. 7.16 | Definition of class **GradeBook** using an array to store test grades. (Part 2 of 2.)

```
1    // Fig. 7.17: GradeBook.cpp
2    // Member-function definitions for class GradeBook that
3    // uses an array to store test grades.
4    #include <iostream>
5    using std::cout;
6    using std::cin;
7    using std::endl;
8    using std::fixed;
9
10   #include <iomanip>
11   using std::setprecision;
12   using std::setw;
13
14   #include "GradeBook.h" // GradeBook class definition
15
16   // constructor initializes courseName and grades array
17   GradeBook::GradeBook( string name, const int gradesArray[] )
18   {
19      setCourseName( name ); // initialize courseName
20
21      // copy grades from gradeArray to grades data member
22      for ( int grade = 0; grade < students; grade++ )
23         grades[ grade ] = gradesArray[ grade ];
24   } // end GradeBook constructor
25
26   // function to set the course name
27   void GradeBook::setCourseName( string name )
28   {
29      courseName = name; // store the course name
30   } // end function setCourseName
31
```

Fig. 7.17 | **GradeBook** class member functions manipulating an array of grades. (Part 1 of 4.)

```
32    // function to retrieve the course name
33    string GradeBook::getCourseName()
34    {
35       return courseName;
36    } // end function getCourseName
37
38    // display a welcome message to the GradeBook user
39    void GradeBook::displayMessage()
40    {
41       // this statement calls getCourseName to get the
42       // name of the course this GradeBook represents
43       cout << "Welcome to the grade book for\n" << getCourseName() << "!"
44          << endl;
45    } // end function displayMessage
46
47    // perform various operations on the data
48    void GradeBook::processGrades()
49    {
50       // output grades array
51       outputGrades();
52
53       // call function getAverage to calculate the average grade
54       cout << "\nClass average is " << setprecision( 2 ) << fixed <<
55          getAverage() << endl;
56
57       // call functions getMinimum and getMaximum
58       cout << "Lowest grade is " << getMinimum() << "\nHighest grade is "
59          << getMaximum() << endl;
60
61       // call function outputBarChart to print grade distribution chart
62       outputBarChart();
63    } // end function processGrades
64
65    // find minimum grade
66    int GradeBook::getMinimum()
67    {
68       int lowGrade = 100; // assume lowest grade is 100
69
70       // loop through grades array
71       for ( int grade = 0; grade < students; grade++ )
72       {
73          // if current grade lower than lowGrade, assign it to lowGrade
74          if ( grades[ grade ] < lowGrade )
75             lowGrade = grades[ grade ]; // new lowest grade
76       } // end for
77
78       return lowGrade; // return lowest grade
79    } // end function getMinimum
80
81    // find maximum grade
82    int GradeBook::getMaximum()
83    {
84       int highGrade = 0; // assume highest grade is 0
```

Fig. 7.17 | GradeBook class member functions manipulating an array of grades. (Part 2 of 4.)

```
85
86      // loop through grades array
87      for ( int grade = 0; grade < students; grade++ )
88      {
89         // if current grade higher than highGrade, assign it to highGrade
90         if ( grades[ grade ] > highGrade )
91            highGrade = grades[ grade ]; // new highest grade
92      } // end for
93
94      return highGrade; // return highest grade
95   } // end function getMaximum
96
97   // determine average grade for test
98   double GradeBook::getAverage()
99   {
100     int total = 0; // initialize total
101
102     // sum grades in array
103     for ( int grade = 0; grade < students; grade++ )
104        total += grades[ grade ];
105
106     // return average of grades
107     return static_cast< double >( total ) / students;
108  } // end function getAverage
109
110  // output bar chart displaying grade distribution
111  void GradeBook::outputBarChart()
112  {
113     cout << "\nGrade distribution:" << endl;
114
115     // stores frequency of grades in each range of 10 grades
116     const int frequencySize = 11;
117     int frequency[ frequencySize ] = { 0 };
118
119     // for each grade, increment the appropriate frequency
120     for ( int grade = 0; grade < students; grade++ )
121        frequency[ grades[ grade ] / 10 ]++;
122
123     // for each grade frequency, print bar in chart
124     for ( int count = 0; count < frequencySize; count++ )
125     {
126        // output bar labels ("0-9:", ..., "90-99:", "100:" )
127        if ( count == 0 )
128           cout << "  0-9: ";
129        else if ( count == 10 )
130           cout << "  100: ";
131        else
132           cout << count * 10 << "-" << ( count * 10 ) + 9 << ": ";
133
134        // print bar of asterisks
135        for ( int stars = 0; stars < frequency[ count ]; stars++ )
136           cout << '*';
```

Fig. 7.17 | GradeBook class member functions manipulating an array of grades. (Part 3 of 4.)

```
137
138          cout << endl; // start a new line of output
139      } // end outer for
140  } // end function outputBarChart
141
142  // output the contents of the grades array
143  void GradeBook::outputGrades()
144  {
145      cout << "\nThe grades are:\n\n";
146
147      // output each student's grade
148      for ( int student = 0; student < students; student++ )
149          cout << "Student " << setw( 2 ) << student + 1 << ": " << setw( 3 )
150              << grades[ student ] << endl;
151  } // end function outputGrades
```

Fig. 7.17 | GradeBook class member functions manipulating an array of grades. (Part 4 of 4.)

Note that the size of the array in line 29 of Fig. 7.16 is specified by public const static data member students (declared in line 13). This data member is public so that it is accessible to the clients of the class. We will soon see an example of a client program using this constant. Declaring students with the const qualifier indicates that this data member is constant—its value cannot be changed after being initialized. Keyword static in this variable declaration indicates that the data member is shared by all objects of the class—all GradeBook objects store grades for the same number of students. Recall from Section 3.6 that when each object of a class maintains its own copy of an attribute, the variable that represents the attribute is also known as a data member—each object (instance) of the class has a separate copy of the variable in memory. There are variables for which each object of a class does not have a separate copy. That is the case with static data members, which are also known as class variables. When objects of a class containing static data members are created, all the objects of that class share one copy of the class's static data members. A static data member can be accessed within the class definition and the member-function definitions just like any other data member. As you will soon see, a public static data member can also be accessed outside of the class, even when no objects of the class exist, using the class name followed by the binary scope resolution operator (::) and the name of the data member. You will learn more about static data members in Chapter 10.

The class's constructor (declared in line 16 of Fig. 7.16 and defined in lines 17–24 of Fig. 7.17) has two parameters—the name of the course and an array of grades. When a program creates a GradeBook object (e.g., line 13 of fig07_18.cpp), the program passes an existing int array to the constructor, which copies the values in the passed array to the data member grades (lines 22–23 of Fig. 7.17). The grade values in the passed array could have been input from a user or read from a file on disk. In our test program, we simply initialize an array with a set of grade values (Fig. 7.18, lines 10–11). Once the grades are stored in data member grades of class GradeBook, all the class's member functions can access the grades array as needed to perform various calculations.

```
1   // Fig. 7.18: fig07_18.cpp
2   // Creates GradeBook object using an array of grades.
3
4   #include "GradeBook.h" // GradeBook class definition
5
6   // function main begins program execution
7   int main()
8   {
9      // array of student grades
10     int gradesArray[ GradeBook::students ] =
11        { 87, 68, 94, 100, 83, 78, 85, 91, 76, 87 };
12
13     GradeBook myGradeBook(
14        "CS101 Introduction to C++ Programming", gradesArray );
15     myGradeBook.displayMessage();
16     myGradeBook.processGrades();
17     return 0;
18  } // end main
```

```
Welcome to the grade book for
CS101 Introduction to C++ Programming!

The grades are:

Student  1:  87
Student  2:  68
Student  3:  94
Student  4: 100
Student  5:  83
Student  6:  78
Student  7:  85
Student  8:  91
Student  9:  76
Student 10:  87

Class average is 84.90
Lowest grade is 68
Highest grade is 100

Grade distribution:
  0-9:
 10-19:
 20-29:
 30-39:
 40-49:
 50-59:
 60-69: *
 70-79: **
 80-89: ****
 90-99: **
   100: *
```

Fig. 7.18 | Creates a GradeBook object using an array of grades, then invokes member function processGrades to analyze them.

Member function processGrades (declared in line 21 of Fig. 7.16 and defined in lines 48–63 of Fig. 7.17) contains a series of member function calls that output a report summarizing the grades. Line 51 calls member function outputGrades to print the contents of the array grades. Lines 148–150 in member function outputGrades use a for statement to output each student's grade. Although array indices start at 0, a professor would typically number students starting at 1. Thus, lines 149–150 output student + 1 as the student number to produce grade labels "Student 1: ", "Student 2: ", and so on.

Member function processGrades next calls member function getAverage (lines 54–55) to obtain the average of the grades in the array. Member function getAverage (declared in line 24 of Fig. 7.16 and defined in lines 98–108) uses a for statement to total the values in array grades before calculating the average. Note that the averaging calculation in line 107 uses const static data member students to determine the number of grades being averaged.

Lines 58–59 in member function processGrades call member functions getMinimum and getMaximum to determine the lowest and highest grades of any student on the exam, respectively. Let us examine how member function getMinimum finds the lowest grade. Because the highest grade allowed is 100, we begin by assuming that 100 is the lowest grade (line 68). Then, we compare each of the elements in the array to the lowest grade, looking for smaller values. Lines 71–76 in member function getMinimum loop through the array, and lines 74–75 compare each grade to lowGrade. If a grade is less than lowGrade, lowGrade is set to that grade. When line 78 executes, lowGrade contains the lowest grade in the array. Member function getMaximum (lines 82–95) works similarly to member function getMinimum.

Finally, line 62 in member function processGrades calls member function output-BarChart to print a distribution chart of the grade data using a technique similar to that in Fig. 7.9. In that example, we manually calculated the number of grades in each category (i.e., 0–9, 10–19, …, 90–99 and 100) by simply looking at a set of grades. In this example, lines 120–121 use a technique similar to that in Fig. 7.10 and Fig. 7.11 to calculate the frequency of grades in each category. Line 117 declares and creates array frequency of 11 ints to store the frequency of grades in each grade category. For each grade in array grades, lines 120–121 increment the appropriate element of the frequency array. To determine which element to increment, line 121 divides the current grade by 10 using integer division. For example, if grade is 85, line 121 increments frequency[8] to update the count of grades in the range 80–89. Lines 124–139 next print the bar chart (see Fig. 7.18) based on the values in array frequency. Like lines 29–30 of Fig. 7.9, lines 135–136 of Fig. 7.17 use a value in array frequency to determine the number of asterisks to display in each bar.

Testing Class *GradeBook*

The program of Fig. 7.18 creates an object of class GradeBook (Figs. 7.16–7.17) using the int array gradesArray (declared and initialized in lines 10–11). Note that we use the binary scope resolution operator (::) in the expression "GradeBook::students" (line 10) to access class GradeBook's static constant students. We use this constant here to create an array that is the same size as array grades stored as a data member in class GradeBook. Lines 13–14 pass a course name and gradesArray to the GradeBook constructor. Line 15 displays a welcome message, and line 16 invokes the GradeBook object's processGrades member function. The output reveals the summary of the 10 grades in myGradeBook.

7.7 **Searching Arrays with Linear Search**

Often a programmer will be working with large amounts of data stored in arrays. It may be necessary to determine whether an array contains a value that matches a certain key value. The process of finding a particular element of an array is called searching. In this section we discuss the simple linear search. Exercise 7.33 at the end of this chapter asks you to implement a recursive version of the linear search. To learn about the more complex, yet more efficient, binary search, please visit en.wikipedia.org/wiki/Binary_search.

Linear Search

The linear search (Fig. 7.19, lines 37–44) compares each element of an array with a search key (line 40). Because the array is not in any particular order, it is just as likely that the value will be found in the first element as the last. On average, therefore, the program must compare the search key with half the elements of the array. To determine that a value is not in the array, the program must compare the search key to every element in the array.

The linear searching method works well for small arrays or for unsorted arrays (i.e., arrays whose elements are in no particular order). However, for large arrays, linear searching is inefficient. If the array is sorted (e.g., its elements are in ascending order), you can use the high-speed binary search technique (en.wikipedia.org/wiki/Binary_search).

```
1   // Fig. 7.19: fig07_19.cpp
2   // Linear search of an array.
3   #include <iostream>
4   using std::cout;
5   using std::cin;
6   using std::endl;
7
8   int linearSearch( const int [], int, int ); // prototype
9
10  int main()
11  {
12     const int arraySize = 100; // size of array a
13     int a[ arraySize ]; // create array a
14     int searchKey; // value to locate in array a
15
16     for ( int i = 0; i < arraySize; i++ )
17        a[ i ] = 2 * i; // create some data
18
19     cout << "Enter integer search key: ";
20     cin >> searchKey;
21
22     // attempt to locate searchKey in array a
23     int element = linearSearch( a, searchKey, arraySize );
24
25     // display results
26     if ( element != -1 )
27        cout << "Found value in element " << element << endl;
28     else
29        cout << "Value not found" << endl;
```

Fig. 7.19 | Linear search of an array. (Part 1 of 2.)

```
30
31      return 0; // indicates successful termination
32   } // end main
33
34   // compare key to every element of array until location is
35   // found or until end of array is reached; return subscript of
36   // element if key or -1 if key not found
37   int linearSearch( const int array[], int key, int sizeOfArray )
38   {
39      for ( int j = 0; j < sizeOfArray; j++ )
40         if ( array[ j ] == key ) // if found,
41            return j; // return location of key
42
43      return -1; // key not found
44   } // end function linearSearch
```

```
Enter integer search key: 36
Found value in element 18
```

```
Enter integer search key: 37
Value not found
```

Fig. 7.19 | Linear search of an array. (Part 2 of 2.)

7.8 Sorting Arrays with Insertion Sort

Sorting data (i.e., placing the data into some particular order such as ascending or descending) is one of the most important computing applications. A bank sorts all checks by account number so that it can prepare individual bank statements at the end of each month. Telephone companies sort their phone directories by last name and, within that, by first name to make it easy to find phone numbers. Virtually every organization must sort some data and, in many cases, massive amounts of data. Sorting data is an intriguing problem that has attracted some of the most intense research efforts in the field of computer science. In this chapter, we discuss a simple sorting scheme. In the exercises, we investigate more complex schemes that yield superior performance.

 **Performance Tip 7.4**

Sometimes, simple algorithms perform poorly. Their virtue is that they are easy to write, test and debug. More complex algorithms are sometimes needed to realize optimal performance.

Insertion Sort

The program in Fig. 7.20 sorts the values of the 10-element array data into ascending order. The technique we use is called **insertion sort**—a simple, but inefficient, sorting algorithm. The first iteration of this algorithm takes the second element and, if it is less than the first element, swaps it with the first element (i.e., the program *inserts* the second element in front of the first element). The second iteration looks at the third element and inserts it into the correct position with respect to the first two elements, so all three elements are in order. At the ith iteration of this algorithm, the first i elements in the original array will be sorted.

Line 13 of Fig. 7.20 declares and initializes array data with the following values:

    34   56   4   10   77   51   93   30   5   52

The program first looks at data[0] and data[1], whose values are 34 and 56, respectively. These two elements are already in order, so the program continues—if they were out of order, the program would swap them.

```cpp
1   // Fig. 7.20: fig07_20.cpp
2   // This program sorts an array's values into ascending order.
3   #include <iostream>
4   using std::cout;
5   using std::endl;
6
7   #include <iomanip>
8   using std::setw;
9
10  int main()
11  {
12     const int arraySize = 10; // size of array a
13     int data[ arraySize ] = { 34, 56, 4, 10, 77, 51, 93, 30, 5, 52 };
14     int insert; // temporary variable to hold element to insert
15
16     cout << "Unsorted array:\n";
17
18     // output original array
19     for ( int i = 0; i < arraySize; i++ )
20        cout << setw( 4 ) << data[ i ];
21
22     // insertion sort
23     // loop over the elements of the array
24     for ( int next = 1; next < arraySize; next++ )
25     {
26        insert = data[ next ]; // store the value in the current element
27
28        int moveItem = next; // initialize location to place element
29
30        // search for the location in which to put the current element
31        while ( ( moveItem > 0 ) && ( data[ moveItem - 1 ] > insert ) )
32        {
33           // shift element one slot to the right
34           data[ moveItem ] = data[ moveItem - 1 ];
35           moveItem--;
36        } // end while
37
38        data[ moveItem ] = insert; // place inserted element into the array
39     } // end for
40
41     cout << "\nSorted array:\n";
```

Fig. 7.20 | Sorting an array with insertion sort. (Part 1 of 2.)

```
42
43      // output sorted array
44      for ( int i = 0; i < arraySize; i++ )
45         cout << setw( 4 ) << data[ i ];
46
47      cout << endl;
48      return 0; // indicates successful termination
49  } // end main
```

```
Unsorted array:
  34  56   4  10  77  51  93  30   5  52
Sorted array:
   4   5  10  30  34  51  52  56  77  93
```

Fig. 7.20 | Sorting an array with insertion sort. (Part 2 of 2.)

In the second iteration, the program looks at the value of data[2], 4. This value is less than 56, so the program stores 4 in a temporary variable and moves 56 one element to the right. The program then checks and determines that 4 is less than 34, so it moves 34 one element to the right. The program has now reached the beginning of the array, so it places 4 in data[0]. The array now is

    4   34   56   10   77   51   93   30   5   52

In the third iteration, the program stores the value of data[3], 10, in a temporary variable. Then the program compares 10 to 56 and moves 56 one element to the right because it is larger than 10. The program then compares 10 to 34, moving 34 right one element. When the program compares 10 to 4, it observes that 10 is larger than 4 and places 10 in data[1]. The array now is

    4   10   34   56   77   51   93   30   5   52

Using this algorithm, at the ith iteration, the first i elements of the original array are sorted. They may not be in their final locations, however, because smaller values may be located later in the array.

The sorting is performed by the for statement in lines 24–39 that loops over the elements of the array. In each iteration, line 26 temporarily stores in variable insert (declared in line 14) the value of the element that will be inserted into the sorted portion of the array. Line 28 declares and initializes the variable moveItem, which keeps track of where to insert the element. Lines 31–36 loop to locate the correct position where the element should be inserted. The loop terminates either when the program reaches the front of the array or when it reaches an element that is less than the value to be inserted. Line 34 moves an element to the right, and line 35 decrements the position at which to insert the next element. After the while loop ends, line 38 inserts the element into place. When the for statement in lines 24–39 terminates, the elements of the array are sorted.

The chief virtue of the insertion sort is that it is easy to program; however, it runs slowly. This becomes apparent when sorting large arrays. In the exercises, we will investigate some alternate algorithms for sorting an array.

7.9 Multidimensional Arrays

Multidimensional arrays with two dimensions are often used to represent tables of values consisting of information arranged in rows and columns. To identify a particular table element, we must specify two subscripts. By convention, the first identifies the element's row and the second identifies the element's column. Arrays that require two subscripts to identify a particular element are called two-dimensional arrays or 2-D arrays. Note that multidimensional arrays can have more than two dimensions (i.e., subscripts). Figure 7.21 illustrates a two-dimensional array, a. The array contains three rows and four columns, so it is said to be a 3-by-4 array. In general, an array with m rows and n columns is called an *m-by-n* array.

Every element in array a is identified in Fig. 7.21 by an element name of the form a[i][j], where a is the name of the array, and i and j are the subscripts that uniquely identify each element in a. Notice that the names of the elements in row 0 all have a first subscript of 0; the names of the elements in column 3 all have a second subscript of 3.

Common Programming Error 7.12

Referencing a two-dimensional array element a[x][y] incorrectly as a[x, y] is an error. Actually, a[x, y] is treated as a[y], because C++ evaluates the expression x, y (containing a comma operator) simply as y (the last of the comma-separated expressions).

A multidimensional array can be initialized in its declaration much like a one-dimensional array. For example, a two-dimensional array b with values 1 and 2 in its row 0 elements and values 3 and 4 in its row 1 elements could be declared and initialized with

```
int b[ 2 ][ 2 ] = { { 1, 2 }, { 3, 4 } };
```

The values are grouped by row in braces. So, 1 and 2 initialize b[0][0] and b[0][1], respectfully, and 3 and 4 initialize b[1][0] and b[1][1], respectfully. If there are not enough initializers for a given row, the remaining elements of that row are initialized to 0. Thus, the declaration

```
int b[ 2 ][ 2 ] = { { 1 }, { 3, 4 } };
```

initializes b[0][0] to 1, b[0][1] to 0, b[1][0] to 3 and b[1][1] to 4.

Figure 7.22 demonstrates initializing two-dimensional arrays in declarations. Lines 11–13 declare three arrays, each with two rows and three columns.

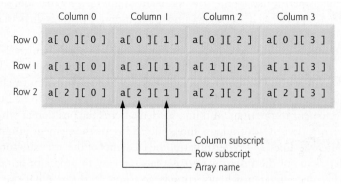

Fig. 7.21 | Two-dimensional array with three rows and four columns.

```
1   // Fig. 7.22: fig07_22.cpp
2   // Initializing multidimensional arrays.
3   #include <iostream>
4   using std::cout;
5   using std::endl;
6
7   void printArray( const int [][ 3 ] ); // prototype
8
9   int main()
10  {
11     int array1[ 2 ][ 3 ] = { { 1, 2, 3 }, { 4, 5, 6 } };
12     int array2[ 2 ][ 3 ] = { 1, 2, 3, 4, 5 };
13     int array3[ 2 ][ 3 ] = { { 1, 2 }, { 4 } };
14
15     cout << "Values in array1 by row are:" << endl;
16     printArray( array1 );
17
18     cout << "\nValues in array2 by row are:" << endl;
19     printArray( array2 );
20
21     cout << "\nValues in array3 by row are:" << endl;
22     printArray( array3 );
23     return 0; // indicates successful termination
24  } // end main
25
26  // output array with two rows and three columns
27  void printArray( const int a[][ 3 ] )
28  {
29     // loop through array's rows
30     for ( int i = 0; i < 2; i++ )
31     {
32        // loop through columns of current row
33        for ( int j = 0; j < 3; j++ )
34           cout << a[ i ][ j ] << ' ';
35
36        cout << endl; // start new line of output
37     } // end outer for
38  } // end function printArray
```

```
Values in array1 by row are:
1 2 3
4 5 6

Values in array2 by row are:
1 2 3
4 5 0

Values in array3 by row are:
1 2 0
4 0 0
```

Fig. 7.22 | Initializing multidimensional arrays.

The declaration of array1 (line 11) provides six initializers in two sublists. The first sublist initializes row 0 of the array to the values 1, 2 and 3; and the second sublist initializes row 1 of the array to the values 4, 5 and 6. If the braces around each sublist are removed from the array1 initializer list, the compiler initializes the elements of row 0 followed by the elements of row 1, yielding the same result.

The declaration of array2 (line 12) provides only five initializers. The initializers are assigned to row 0, then row 1. Any elements that do not have an explicit initializer are initialized to zero, so array2[1][2] is initialized to zero.

The declaration of array3 (line 13) provides three initializers in two sublists. The sublist for row 0 explicitly initializes the first two elements of row 0 to 1 and 2; the third element is implicitly initialized to zero. The sublist for row 1 explicitly initializes the first element to 4 and implicitly initializes the last two elements to zero.

The program calls function printArray to output each array's elements. Notice that the function definition (lines 27–38) specifies the parameter const int a[][3]. When a function receives a one-dimensional array as an argument, the array brackets are empty in the function's parameter list. The size of the first dimension (i.e., the number of rows) of a two-dimensional array is not required either, but all subsequent dimension sizes are required. The compiler uses these sizes to determine the locations in memory of elements in multidimensional arrays. All array elements are stored consecutively in memory, regardless of the number of dimensions. In a two-dimensional array, row 0 is stored in memory followed by row 1. In a two-dimensional array, each row is a one-dimensional array. To locate an element in a particular row, the function must know exactly how many elements are in each row so it can skip the proper number of memory locations when accessing the array. Thus, when accessing a[1][2], the function knows to skip row 0's three elements in memory to get to row 1. Then, the function accesses element 2 of that row.

Many common array manipulations use for repetition statements. For example, the following for statement sets all the elements in row 2 of array a in Fig. 7.21 to zero:

```
for ( column = 0; column < 4; column++ )
    a[ 2 ][ column ] = 0;
```

The for statement varies only the second subscript (i.e., the column subscript). The preceding for statement is equivalent to the following assignment statements:

```
a[ 2 ][ 0 ] = 0;
a[ 2 ][ 1 ] = 0;
a[ 2 ][ 2 ] = 0;
a[ 2 ][ 3 ] = 0;
```

The following nested for statement determines the total of all the elements in array a:

```
total = 0;

for ( row = 0; row < 3; row++ )

    for ( column = 0; column < 4; column++ )
        total += a[ row ][ column ];
```

The for statement totals the elements of the array one row at a time. The outer for statement begins by setting row (i.e., the row subscript) to 0, so the elements of row 0 may be totaled by the inner for statement. The outer for statement then increments row to 1, so the elements of row 1 can be totaled. Then, the outer for statement increments row to 2, so the elements of row 2 can be totaled. When the nested for statement terminates, total contains the sum of all the array elements.

7.10 Case Study: Class GradeBook Using a Two-Dimensional Array

In Section 7.6, we presented class GradeBook (Figs. 7.16–7.17), which used a one-dimensional array to store student grades on a single exam. In most semesters, students take several exams. Professors are likely to want to analyze grades across the entire semester, both for a single student and for the class as a whole.

Storing Student Grades in a Two-Dimensional Array in Class *GradeBook*

Figures 7.23–7.24 contain a version of class GradeBook that uses a two-dimensional array grades to store the grades of a number of students on multiple exams. Each row of the array represents a single student's grades for the entire course, and each column represents all the grades the students earned for one particular exam. A client program, such as fig07_25.cpp, passes the array as an argument to the GradeBook constructor. In this example, we use a ten-by-three array containing ten students' grades on three exams.

Five member functions (declared in lines 23–27 of Fig. 7.23) perform array manipulations to process the grades. Each of these member functions is similar to its counterpart in the earlier one-dimensional array version of class GradeBook (Figs. 7.16–7.17). Member function getMinimum (defined in lines 65–82 of Fig. 7.24) determines the lowest grade of any student for the semester. Member function getMaximum (defined in lines 85–102 of Fig. 7.24) determines the highest grade of any student for the semester. Member function getAverage (lines 105–115 of Fig. 7.24) determines a particular student's semester average. Member function outputBarChart (lines 118–149 of Fig. 7.24) outputs a bar chart of the distribution of all student grades for the semester. Member function output-Grades (lines 152–177 of Fig. 7.24) outputs the two-dimensional array in a tabular format, along with each student's semester average.

```
1    // Fig. 7.23: GradeBook.h
2    // Definition of class GradeBook that uses a
3    // two-dimensional array to store test grades.
4    // Member functions are defined in GradeBook.cpp
5    #include <string> // program uses C++ Standard Library string class
6    using std::string;
7
8    // GradeBook class definition
9    class GradeBook
10   {
11   public:
12      // constants
13      const static int students = 10; // number of students
14      const static int tests = 3; // number of tests
15
16      // constructor initializes course name and array of grades
17      GradeBook( string, const int [][ tests ] );
18
19      void setCourseName( string ); // function to set the course name
20      string getCourseName(); // function to retrieve the course name
```

Fig. 7.23 | Definition of class GradeBook with a two-dimensional array to store grades. (Part 1 of 2.)

```
21      void displayMessage(); // display a welcome message
22      void processGrades(); // perform various operations on the grade data
23      int getMinimum(); // find the minimum grade in the grade book
24      int getMaximum(); // find the maximum grade in the grade book
25      double getAverage( const int [], const int ); // find average of grades
26      void outputBarChart(); // output bar chart of grade distribution
27      void outputGrades(); // output the contents of the grades array
28   private:
29      string courseName; // course name for this grade book
30      int grades[ students ][ tests ]; // two-dimensional array of grades
31   }; // end class GradeBook
```

Fig. 7.23 | Definition of class GradeBook with a two-dimensional array to store grades. (Part 2 of 2.)

```
1    // Fig. 7.24: GradeBook.cpp
2    // Member-function definitions for class GradeBook that
3    // uses a two-dimensional array to store grades.
4    #include <iostream>
5    using std::cout;
6    using std::cin;
7    using std::endl;
8    using std::fixed;
9
10   #include <iomanip> // parameterized stream manipulators
11   using std::setprecision; // sets numeric output precision
12   using std::setw; // sets field width
13
14   // include definition of class GradeBook from GradeBook.h
15   #include "GradeBook.h"
16
17   // two-argument constructor initializes courseName and grades array
18   GradeBook::GradeBook( string name, const int gradesArray[][ tests ] )
19   {
20      setCourseName( name ); // initialize courseName
21
22      // copy grades from gradeArray to grades
23      for ( int student = 0; student < students; student++ )
24
25         for ( int test = 0; test < tests; test++ )
26            grades[ student ][ test ] = gradesArray[ student ][ test ];
27   } // end two-argument GradeBook constructor
28
29   // function to set the course name
30   void GradeBook::setCourseName( string name )
31   {
32      courseName = name; // store the course name
33   } // end function setCourseName
```

Fig. 7.24 | GradeBook class member-function definitions manipulating a two-dimensional array of grades. (Part I of 4.)

```
34
35   // function to retrieve the course name
36   string GradeBook::getCourseName()
37   {
38      return courseName;
39   } // end function getCourseName
40
41   // display a welcome message to the GradeBook user
42   void GradeBook::displayMessage()
43   {
44      // this statement calls getCourseName to get the
45      // name of the course this GradeBook represents
46      cout << "Welcome to the grade book for\n" << getCourseName() << "!"
47         << endl;
48   } // end function displayMessage
49
50   // perform various operations on the data
51   void GradeBook::processGrades()
52   {
53      // output grades array
54      outputGrades();
55
56      // call functions getMinimum and getMaximum
57      cout << "\nLowest grade in the grade book is " << getMinimum()
58         << "\nHighest grade in the grade book is " << getMaximum() << endl;
59
60      // output grade distribution chart of all grades on all tests
61      outputBarChart();
62   } // end function processGrades
63
64   // find minimum grade
65   int GradeBook::getMinimum()
66   {
67      int lowGrade = 100; // assume lowest grade is 100
68
69      // loop through rows of grades array
70      for ( int student = 0; student < students; student++ )
71      {
72         // loop through columns of current row
73         for ( int test = 0; test < tests; test++ )
74         {
75            // if current grade less than lowGrade, assign it to lowGrade
76            if ( grades[ student ][ test ] < lowGrade )
77               lowGrade = grades[ student ][ test ]; // new lowest grade
78         } // end inner for
79      } // end outer for
80
81      return lowGrade; // return lowest grade
82   } // end function getMinimum
83
```

Fig. 7.24 | GradeBook class member-function definitions manipulating a two-dimensional array of grades. (Part 2 of 4.)

```
84   // find maximum grade
85   int GradeBook::getMaximum()
86   {
87      int highGrade = 0; // assume highest grade is 0
88
89      // loop through rows of grades array
90      for ( int student = 0; student < students; student++ )
91      {
92         // loop through columns of current row
93         for ( int test = 0; test < tests; test++ )
94         {
95            // if current grade greater than lowGrade, assign it to highGrade
96            if ( grades[ student ][ test ] > highGrade )
97               highGrade = grades[ student ][ test ]; // new highest grade
98         } // end inner for
99      } // end outer for
100
101     return highGrade; // return highest grade
102  } // end function getMaximum
103
104  // determine average grade for particular set of grades
105  double GradeBook::getAverage( const int setOfGrades[], const int grades )
106  {
107     int total = 0; // initialize total
108
109     // sum grades in array
110     for ( int grade = 0; grade < grades; grade++ )
111        total += setOfGrades[ grade ];
112
113     // return average of grades
114     return static_cast< double >( total ) / grades;
115  } // end function getAverage
116
117  // output bar chart displaying grade distribution
118  void GradeBook::outputBarChart()
119  {
120     cout << "\nOverall grade distribution:" << endl;
121
122     // stores frequency of grades in each range of 10 grades
123     const int frequencySize = 11;
124     int frequency[ frequencySize ] = { 0 };
125
126     // for each grade, increment the appropriate frequency
127     for ( int student = 0; student < students; student++ )
128
129        for ( int test = 0; test < tests; test++ )
130           ++frequency[ grades[ student ][ test ] / 10 ];
131
132     // for each grade frequency, print bar in chart
133     for ( int count = 0; count < frequencySize; count++ )
134     {
```

Fig. 7.24 | GradeBook class member-function definitions manipulating a two-dimensional array of grades. (Part 3 of 4.)

```
135            // output bar label ("0-9:", ..., "90-99:", "100:" )
136            if ( count == 0 )
137               cout << "   0-9: ";
138            else if ( count == 10 )
139               cout << "  100: ";
140            else
141               cout << count * 10 << "-" << ( count * 10 ) + 9 << ": ";
142
143            // print bar of asterisks
144            for ( int stars = 0; stars < frequency[ count ]; stars++ )
145               cout << '*';
146
147            cout << endl; // start a new line of output
148         } // end outer for
149      } // end function outputBarChart
150
151      // output the contents of the grades array
152      void GradeBook::outputGrades()
153      {
154         cout << "\nThe grades are:\n\n";
155         cout << "              "; // align column heads
156
157         // create a column heading for each of the tests
158         for ( int test = 0; test < tests; test++ )
159            cout << "Test " << test + 1 << "  ";
160
161         cout << "Average" << endl; // student average column heading
162
163         // create rows/columns of text representing array grades
164         for ( int student = 0; student < students; student++ )
165         {
166            cout << "Student " << setw( 2 ) << student + 1;
167
168            // output student's grades
169            for ( int test = 0; test < tests; test++ )
170               cout << setw( 8 ) << grades[ student ][ test ];
171
172            // call member function getAverage to calculate student's average;
173            // pass row of grades and the value of tests as the arguments
174            double average = getAverage( grades[ student ], tests );
175            cout << setw( 9 ) << setprecision( 2 ) << fixed << average << endl;
176         } // end outer for
177      } // end function outputGrades
```

Fig. 7.24 | GradeBook class member-function definitions manipulating a two-dimensional array of grades. (Part 4 of 4.)

Member functions getMinimum, getMaximum, outputBarChart and outputGrades each loop through array grades by using nested for statements For example, consider the nested for statement in member function getMinimum (lines 70–79). The outer for statement begins by setting student (i.e., the row subscript) to 0, so the elements of row 0 can be compared with variable lowGrade in the body of the inner for statement. The inner for statement loops through the grades of a particular row and compares each grade with lowGrade. If a grade is less than lowGrade, lowGrade is set to that grade. The outer for statement then increments the row subscript to 1. The elements of row 1 are compared with variable lowGrade. The outer for statement then increments the row subscript to 2, and the elements of row 2 are compared with variable lowGrade. This repeats until all rows of grades have been traversed. When execution of the nested statement is complete, low-Grade contains the smallest grade in the two-dimensional array. Member function get-Maximum works similarly to member function getMinimum.

Member function outputBarChart in Fig. 7.24 is nearly identical to the one in Fig. 7.17. However, to output the overall grade distribution for a whole semester, the member function uses a nested for statement (lines 127–130) to create the one-dimensional array frequency based on all the grades in the two-dimensional array. The rest of the code in each of the two outputBarChart member functions that displays the chart is identical.

Member function outputGrades (lines 152–177) also uses nested for statements to output values of the array grades, in addition to each student's semester average. The output in Fig. 7.25 shows the result, which resembles the tabular format of a professor's physical grade book. Lines 158–159 print the column headings for each test. We use a counter-controlled for statement so that we can identify each test with a number. Similarly, the for statement in lines 164–176 first outputs a row label using a counter variable to identify each student (line 166). Although array indices start at 0, note that lines 159 and 166 output

```
1   // Fig. 7.25: fig07_25.cpp
2   // Creates GradeBook object using a two-dimensional array of grades.
3
4   #include "GradeBook.h" // GradeBook class definition
5
6   // function main begins program execution
7   int main()
8   {
9      // two-dimensional array of student grades
10     int gradesArray[ GradeBook::students ][ GradeBook::tests ] =
11        { { 87, 96, 70 },
12          { 68, 87, 90 },
13          { 94, 100, 90 },
14          { 100, 81, 82 },
15          { 83, 65, 85 },
16          { 78, 87, 65 },
17          { 85, 75, 83 },
18          { 91, 94, 100 },
19          { 76, 72, 84 },
20          { 87, 93, 73 } };
21
22     GradeBook myGradeBook(
23        "CS101 Introduction to C++ Programming", gradesArray );
24     myGradeBook.displayMessage();
25     myGradeBook.processGrades();
26     return 0; // indicates successful termination
27  } // end main
```

Fig. 7.25 | Creates a GradeBook object using a two-dimensional array of grades, then invokes member function processGrades to analyze them. (Part 1 of 2.)

```
Welcome to the grade book for
CS101 Introduction to C++ Programming!

The grades are:

            Test 1  Test 2  Test 3  Average
Student  1     87      96      70    84.33
Student  2     68      87      90    81.67
Student  3     94     100      90    94.67
Student  4    100      81      82    87.67
Student  5     83      65      85    77.67
Student  6     78      87      65    76.67
Student  7     85      75      83    81.00
Student  8     91      94     100    95.00
Student  9     76      72      84    77.33
Student 10     87      93      73    84.33

Lowest grade in the grade book is 65
Highest grade in the grade book is 100

Overall grade distribution:
   0-9:
  10-19:
  20-29:
  30-39:
  40-49:
  50-59:
  60-69: ***
  70-79: ******
  80-89: ***********
  90-99: *******
   100: ***
```

Fig. 7.25 | Creates a GradeBook object using a two-dimensional array of grades, then invokes member function processGrades to analyze them. (Part 2 of 2.)

test + 1 and student + 1, respectively, to produce test and student numbers starting at 1 (see Fig. 7.25). The inner for statement in lines 169–170 uses the outer for statement's counter variable student to loop through a specific row of array grades and output each student's test grade. Finally, line 174 obtains each student's semester average by passing the current row of grades (i.e., grades[student]) to member function getAverage.

Member function getAverage (lines 105–115) takes two arguments—a one-dimensional array of test results for a particular student and the number of test results in the array. When line 174 calls getAverage, the first argument is grades[student], which specifies that a particular row of the two-dimensional array grades should be passed to getAverage. For example, based on the array created in Fig. 7.25, the argument grades[1] represents the three values (a one-dimensional array of grades) stored in row 1 of the two-dimensional array grades. A two-dimensional array can be considered an array whose elements are one-dimensional arrays. Member function getAverage calculates the sum of the array elements, divides the total by the number of test results and returns the floating-point result as a double value (line 114).

Testing Class GradeBook

The program in Fig. 7.25 creates an object of class GradeBook (Figs. 7.23–7.24) using the two-dimensional array of ints named gradesArray (declared and initialized in lines 10–20). Note that line 10 accesses class GradeBook's static constants students and tests to indicate the size of each dimension of array gradesArray. Lines 22–23 pass a course name and gradesArray to the GradeBook constructor. Lines 24–25 then invoke myGradeBook's displayMessage and processGrades member functions to display a welcome message and obtain a report summarizing the students' grades for the semester, respectively.

7.11 Introduction to C++ Standard Library Class Template vector

We now introduce C++ Standard Library class template vector, which represents a more robust type of array featuring many additional capabilities. As you will see in later chapters and in more advanced C++ courses, C-style pointer-based arrays (i.e., the type of arrays presented thus far) have great potential for errors. For example, as mentioned earlier, a program can easily "walk off" either end of an array, because C++ does not check whether subscripts fall outside the range of an array. Two arrays cannot be meaningfully compared with equality operators or relational operators. As you will learn in Chapter 8, pointer variables (known more commonly as pointers) contain memory addresses as their values. Array names are simply pointers to where the arrays begin in memory, and, of course, two arrays will always be at different memory locations. When an array is passed to a general-purpose function designed to handle arrays of any size, the size of the array must be passed as an additional argument. Furthermore, one array cannot be assigned to another with the assignment operator(s)—array names are const pointers, and, as you will learn in Chapter 8, a constant pointer cannot be used on the left side of an assignment operator. These and other capabilities certainly seem like "naturals" for dealing with arrays, but C++ does not provide such capabilities. However, the C++ Standard Library provides class template vector to allow programmers to create a more powerful and less error-prone alternative to arrays. In Chapter 11, Operator Overloading; String and Array Objects, we present the means to implement such array capabilities as those provided by vector. You will learn how to customize operators for use with your own classes (a technique known as operator overloading).

The vector class template is available to anyone building applications with C++. The notations that the vector example uses might be unfamiliar to you, because vectors use template notation. Recall that Section 6.18 discussed function templates. Class templates are an advanced features of C++ beyond the scope of this book. However, you should feel comfortable using class template vector by mimicking the syntax in the example we show in this section.

The program of Fig. 7.26 demonstrates capabilities provided by C++ Standard Library class template vector that are not available for C-style pointer-based arrays. Standard class template vector provides many of the same features as the Array class that we construct in Chapter 11, Operator Overloading; String and Array Objects. Standard class template vector is defined in header <vector> (line 11) and belongs to namespace std (line 12).

Lines 19–20 create two vector objects that store values of type int—integers1 contains seven elements, and integers2 contains 10 elements. By default, all the elements of each vector object are set to 0. Note that vectors can be defined to store any data type, by replacing int in vector< int > with the appropriate data type. This notation, which specifies the type stored in the vector, is similar to the template notation that Section 6.18 introduced with function templates.

```cpp
 1   // Fig. 7.26: fig07_26.cpp
 2   // Demonstrating C++ Standard Library class template vector.
 3   #include <iostream>
 4   using std::cout;
 5   using std::cin;
 6   using std::endl;
 7
 8   #include <iomanip>
 9   using std::setw;
10
11   #include <vector>
12   using std::vector;
13
14   void outputVector( const vector< int > & ); // display the vector
15   void inputVector( vector< int > & ); // input values into the vector
16
17   int main()
18   {
19      vector< int > integers1( 7 );  // 7-element vector< int >
20      vector< int > integers2( 10 ); // 10-element vector< int >
21
22      // print integers1 size and contents
23      cout << "Size of vector integers1 is " << integers1.size()
24         << "\nvector after initialization:" << endl;
25      outputVector( integers1 );
26
27      // print integers2 size and contents
28      cout << "\nSize of vector integers2 is " << integers2.size()
29         << "\nvector after initialization:" << endl;
30      outputVector( integers2 );
31
32      // input and print integers1 and integers2
33      cout << "\nEnter 17 integers:" << endl;
34      inputVector( integers1 );
35      inputVector( integers2 );
36
37      cout << "\nAfter input, the vectors contain:\n"
38         << "integers1:" << endl;
39      outputVector( integers1 );
40      cout << "integers2:" << endl;
41      outputVector( integers2 );
42
43      // use inequality (!=) operator with vector objects
44      cout << "\nEvaluating: integers1 != integers2" << endl;
45
46      if ( integers1 != integers2 )
47         cout << "integers1 and integers2 are not equal" << endl;
48
```

Fig. 7.26 | C++ Standard Library class template vector. (Part 1 of 4.)

```
49      // create vector integers3 using integers1 as an
50      // initializer; print size and contents
51      vector< int > integers3( integers1 ); // copy constructor
52
53      cout << "\nSize of vector integers3 is " << integers3.size()
54         << "\nvector after initialization:" << endl;
55      outputVector( integers3 );
56
57      // use overloaded assignment (=) operator
58      cout << "\nAssigning integers2 to integers1:" << endl;
59      integers1 = integers2; // integers1 is larger than integers2
60
61      cout << "integers1:" << endl;
62      outputVector( integers1 );
63      cout << "integers2:" << endl;
64      outputVector( integers2 );
65
66      // use equality (==) operator with vector objects
67      cout << "\nEvaluating: integers1 == integers2" << endl;
68
69      if ( integers1 == integers2 )
70         cout << "integers1 and integers2 are equal" << endl;
71
72      // use square brackets to create rvalue
73      cout << "\nintegers1[5] is " << integers1[ 5 ];
74
75      // use square brackets to create lvalue
76      cout << "\n\nAssigning 1000 to integers1[5]" << endl;
77      integers1[ 5 ] = 1000;
78      cout << "integers1:" << endl;
79      outputVector( integers1 );
80
81      // attempt to use out-of-range subscript
82      cout << "\nAttempt to assign 1000 to integers1.at( 15 )" << endl;
83      integers1.at( 15 ) = 1000; // ERROR: out of range
84      return 0;
85   } // end main
86
87   // output vector contents
88   void outputVector( const vector< int > &array )
89   {
90      size_t i; // declare control variable
91
92      for ( i = 0; i < array.size(); i++ )
93      {
94         cout << setw( 12 ) << array[ i ];
95
96         if ( ( i + 1 ) % 4 == 0 ) // 4 numbers per row of output
97            cout << endl;
98      } // end for
99
```

Fig. 7.26 | C++ Standard Library class template vector. (Part 2 of 4.)

```
100     if ( i % 4 != 0 )
101         cout << endl;
102  } // end function outputVector
103
104  // input vector contents
105  void inputVector( vector< int > &array )
106  {
107     for ( size_t i = 0; i < array.size(); i++ )
108         cin >> array[ i ];
109  } // end function inputVector
```

```
Size of vector integers1 is 7
vector after initialization:
            0              0            0            0
            0              0            0

Size of vector integers2 is 10
vector after initialization:
            0              0            0            0
            0              0            0            0
            0              0

Enter 17 integers:
1 2 3 4 5 6 7 8 9 10 11 12 13 14 15 16 17

After input, the vectors contain:
integers1:
            1              2            3            4
            5              6            7
integers2:
            8              9           10           11
           12             13           14           15
           16             17

Evaluating: integers1 != integers2
integers1 and integers2 are not equal

Size of vector integers3 is 7
vector after initialization:
            1              2            3            4
            5              6            7

Assigning integers2 to integers1:
integers1:
            8              9           10           11
           12             13           14           15
           16             17
integers2:
            8              9           10           11
           12             13           14           15
           16             17

Evaluating: integers1 == integers2
integers1 and integers2 are equal
```

(continued at top of next page...)

Fig. 7.26 | C++ Standard Library class template vector. (Part 3 of 4.)

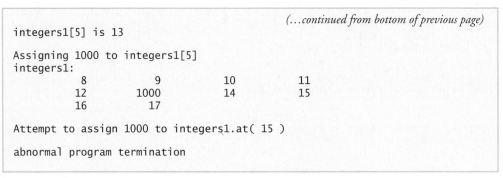

(...continued from bottom of previous page)

```
integers1[5] is 13

Assigning 1000 to integers1[5]
integers1:
            8          9         10         11
           12       1000         14         15
           16         17

Attempt to assign 1000 to integers1.at( 15 )

abnormal program termination
```

Fig. 7.26 | C++ Standard Library class template vector. (Part 4 of 4.)

Line 23 uses vector member function `size` to obtain the size (i.e., the number of elements) of `integers1`. Line 25 passes `integers1` to function `outputVector` (lines 88–102), which uses square brackets (`[]`) to obtain the value in each element of the vector as a value that can be used for output. Note the resemblance of this notation to the notation used to access the value of an array element. Lines 28 and 30 perform the same tasks for `integers2`.

Member function `size` of class template vector returns the number of elements in a vector as a value of type `size_t` (which represents the type `unsigned int` on many systems). As a result, line 90 declares the control variable `i` to be of type `size_t`, too. On some compilers, declaring `i` as an `int` causes the compiler to issue a warning message, since the loop-continuation condition (line 92) would compare a `signed` value (i.e., `int i`) and an `unsigned` value (i.e., a value of type `size_t` returned by function `size`).

Lines 34–35 pass `integers1` and `integers2` to function `inputVector` (lines 105–109) to read values for each vector's elements from the user. Function `inputVector` uses square brackets (`[]`) to obtain *lvalues* that can be used to store the input values in each element of the vector.

Line 46 demonstrates that vector objects can be compared directly with the `!=` operator. If the contents of two vectors are not equal, the operator returns `true`; otherwise, the operator returns `false`.

C++ Standard Library class template vector allows programmers to create a new vector object that is initialized with the contents of an existing vector. Line 51 creates a vector object (`integers3`) and initializes it with a copy of `integers1`. This invokes vector's so-called copy constructor to perform the copy operation. You will learn about copy constructors in detail in Chapter 11. Lines 53 and 55 output the size and contents of `integers3` to demonstrate that it was initialized correctly.

Line 59 assigns `integers2` to `integers1`, demonstrating that the assignment (`=`) operator can be used with vector objects. Lines 62 and 64 output the contents of both objects to show that they now contain identical values. Line 69 then compares `integers1` to `integers2` with the equality (`==`) operator to determine whether the contents of the two objects are equal after the assignment in line 59 (which they are).

Lines 73 and 77 demonstrate that a program can use square brackets (`[]`) to obtain a vector element as an *unmodifiable lvalue* and as a *modifiable lvalue*, respectively. An unmodifiable *lvalue* is an expression that identifies an object in memory (such as an element in a vector), but cannot be used to modify that object. A modifiable *lvalue* also identifies an object in memory, but can be used to modify the object. As is the case with C-style pointer-based arrays, C++ does not perform any bounds checking when `vector` elements are accessed with square brackets. Therefore, the programmer must ensure that operations using `[]` do not accidentally attempt to manipulate elements outside the bounds of the `vector`. Standard class template `vector` does, however, provide bounds checking in its member function `at`, which "throws an exception." if its argument is an invalid subscript. By default, this causes a C++ program to terminate. If the subscript is valid, function `at` returns the element at the specified location as a modifiable *lvalue* or an unmodifiable *lvalue*, depending on the context (non-`const` or `const`) in which the call appears. Line 83 demonstrates a call to function `at` with an invalid subscript.

In this section, we demonstrated the C++ Standard Library class template `vector`, a robust, reusable class that can replace C-style pointer-based arrays. In Chapter 11, you will see that `vector` achieves many of its capabilities by "overloading" C++'s built-in operators, and you will learn how to customize operators for use with your own classes in similar ways. For example, we create an `Array` class that, like class template `vector`, improves upon basic array capabilities. Our `Array` class also provides additional features, such as the ability to input and output entire arrays with operators `>>` and `<<`, respectively.

7.12 Wrap-Up

This chapter began our introduction to data structures, exploring the use of arrays and vectors to store data in and retrieve data from lists and tables of values. The chapter examples demonstrated how to declare an array, initialize an array and refer to individual elements of an array. We also illustrated how to pass arrays to functions and how to use the `const` qualifier to enforce the principle of least privilege. Chapter examples also presented basic searching and sorting techniques. You learned how to declare and manipulate multidimensional arrays. Finally, we demonstrated the capabilities of C++ Standard Library class template `vector`, which provides a more robust alternative to arrays.

We have now introduced the basic concepts of classes, objects, control statements, functions and arrays. In Chapter 8, we present one of C++'s most powerful features—the pointer. Pointers keep track of where data and functions are stored in memory, which allows us to manipulate those items in interesting ways. After introducing basic pointer concepts, we examine in detail the close relationship among arrays, pointers and strings.

Summary

- Data structures are collections of related data items. Arrays are data structures consisting of related data items of the same type. Arrays are "static" entities in that they remain the same size throughout program execution. (They may, of course, be of automatic storage class and hence be created and destroyed each time the blocks in which they are defined are entered and exited.)
- An array is a consecutive group of memory locations that share the same type.
- To refer to a particular location or element in an array, we specify the name of the array and the position number of the particular element in the array.
- A program refers to any one of an array's elements by giving the name of the array followed by the position number of the particular element in square brackets (`[]`). The position number is more formally called a subscript or index (this number specifies the number of elements from the beginning of the array).
- The first element in every array has subscript zero and is sometimes called the zeroth element.

- A subscript must be an integer or integer expression (using any integral type).
- It is important to note the difference between the "seventh element of the array" and "array element 7." Array subscripts begin at 0, so the "seventh element of the array" has a subscript of 6, while "array element 7" has a subscript of 7 and is actually the eighth element of the array. This distinction frequently is a source of off-by-one errors.
- The brackets used to enclose the subscript of an array are an operator in C++. Brackets have the same level of precedence as parentheses.
- Arrays occupy space in memory. The programmer specifies the type of each element and the number of elements required by an array as follows:

      type arrayName[*arraySize*];

  and the compiler reserves the appropriate amount of memory.
- Arrays can be declared to contain any data type. For example, an array of type char can be used to store a character string.
- The elements of an array can be initialized in the array declaration by following the array name with an equals sign and an initializer list—a comma-separated list (enclosed in braces) of constant initializers. When initializing an array with an initializer list, if there are fewer initializers than elements in the array, the remaining elements are initialized to zero.
- If the array size is omitted from a declaration with an initializer list, the compiler determines the number of elements in the array by counting the number of elements in the initializer list.
- If the array size and an initializer list are specified in an array declaration, the number of initializers must be less than or equal to the array size. Providing more initializers in an array initializer list than there are elements in the array is a compilation error.
- Constants must be initialized with a constant expression when they are declared and cannot be modified thereafter. Constants can be placed anywhere a constant expression is expected.
- C++ has no array bounds checking to prevent the computer from referring to an element that does not exist. Thus, an executing program can "walk off" either end of an array without warning. Programmers should ensure that all array references remain within the bounds of the array.
- A character array can be initialized using a string literal. The size of a character array is determined by the compiler based on the length of the string *plus* a special string-termination character called the null character (represented by the character constant '\0').
- All strings represented by character arrays end with the null character. A character array representing a string should always be declared large enough to hold the number of characters in the string and the terminating null character.
- Character arrays also can be initialized with individual character constants in an initializer list.
- Individual characters in a string can be accessed directly with array subscript notation.
- A string can be input directly into a character array from the keyboard using cin and >>.
- A character array representing a null-terminated string can be output with cout and <<.
- A static local variable in a function definition exists for the duration of the program but is visible only in the function body.
- A program initializes static local arrays when their declarations are first encountered. If a static array is not initialized explicitly by the programmer, each element of that array is initialized to zero by the compiler when the array is created.

- To pass an array argument to a function, specify the name of the array without any brackets. To pass an element of an array to a function, use the subscripted name of the array element as an argument in the function call.

- Arrays are passed to functions by reference—the called functions can modify the element values in the callers' original arrays. The value of the name of the array is the address in the computer's memory of the first element of the array. Because the starting address of the array is passed, the called function knows precisely where the array is stored in memory.

- Individual array elements are passed by value exactly as simple variables are. Such simple single pieces of data are called scalars or scalar quantities.

- To receive an array argument, a function's parameter list must specify that the function expects to receive an array. The size of the array is not required between the array brackets.

- C++ provides the type qualifier const that can be used to prevent modification of array values in the caller by code in a called function. When an array parameter is preceded by the const qualifier, the elements of the array become constant in the function body, and any attempt to modify an element of the array in the function body results in a compilation error.

- The linear search compares each element of an array with a search key. Because the array is not in any particular order, it is just as likely that the value will be found in the first element as the last. On average, therefore, a program must compare the search key with half the elements of the array. To determine that a value is not in the array, the program must compare the search key to every element in the array. The linear searching method works well for small arrays and is acceptable for unsorted arrays.

- An array can be sorted using insertion sort. The first iteration of this algorithm takes the second element and, if it is less than the first element, swaps it with the first element (i.e., the program *inserts* the second element in front of the first element). The second iteration looks at the third element and inserts it into the correct position with respect to the first two elements, so all three elements are in order. At the ith iteration of this algorithm, the first i elements in the original array will be sorted. For small arrays, the insertion sort is acceptable, but for larger arrays it is inefficient compared to other more sophisticated sorting algorithms.

- Multidimensional arrays with two dimensions are often used to represent tables of values consisting of information arranged in rows and columns.

- Arrays that require two subscripts to identify a particular element are called two-dimensional arrays. An array with m rows and n columns is called an *m-by-n* array.

- C++ Standard Library class template vector represents a more robust alternative to arrays featuring many capabilities that are not provided for C-style pointer-based arrays.

- By default, all the elements of an integer vector object are set to 0.

- A vector can be defined to store any data type using a declaration of the form

    vector< *type* > *name*(*size*);

- Member function size of class template vector returns the number of elements in the vector on which it is invoked.

- The value of an element of a vector can be accessed or modified using square brackets ([]).

- Objects of standard class template vector can be compared directly with the equality (==) and inequality (!=) operators. The assignment (=) operator can also be used with vector objects.

- An unmodifiable *lvalue* is an expression that identifies an object in memory (such as an element in a vector), but cannot be used to modify that object. A modifiable *lvalue* also identifies an object in memory, but can be used to modify the object.
- Standard class template vector provides bounds checking in its member function at, which "throws an exception" if its argument is an invalid subscript. By default, this causes a C++ program to terminate.

Terminology

2-D array	null character (`'\0'`)
a[i]	off-by-one error
a[i][j]	one-dimensional array
array	pass-by-reference
array initializer list	passing arrays to functions
at member function of vector	position number
bounds checking	read-only variables
column of a two-dimensional array	row of a two-dimensional array
column subscript	row subscript
const type qualifier	scalability
constant variable	scalar
data structure	scalar quantity
declare an array	search an array
element of an array	search key
index	size member function of vector
index zero	sort an array
initialize an array	square brackets []
initializer	static data member
initializer list	string represented by a character array
insertion sort	subscript
key value	table of values
linear search of an array	tabular format
magic number	two-dimensional array
m-by-*n* array	unmodifiable *lvalue*
modifiable *lvalue*	value of an element
multidimensional array	vector (C++ Standard Library class template)
name of an array	"walk off" an array
named constant	zeroth element

Self-Review Exercises

7.1 Answer each of the following:
  a) Lists and tables of values can be stored in _____ or _____.
  b) The elements of an array are related by the fact that they have the same _____ and _____.
  c) The number used to refer to a particular element of an array is called its _____.
  d) A(n) _____ should be used to declare the size of an array, because it makes the program more scalable.
  e) The process of placing the elements of an array in order is called _____ the array.
  f) The process of determining if an array contains a particular key value is called _____ the array.

g) An array that uses two subscripts is referred to as a(n) _____ array.

7.2 State whether the following are *true* or *false*. If the answer is *false*, explain why.
a) An array can store many different types of values.
b) An array subscript should normally be of data type `float`.
c) If there are fewer initializers in an initializer list than the number of elements in the array, the remaining elements are initialized to the last value in the initializer list.
d) It is an error if an initializer list contains more initializers than there are elements in the array.
e) An individual array element that is passed to a function and modified in that function will contain the modified value when the called function completes execution.

7.3 Write one or more statements that perform the following tasks for and array called `fractions`:
a) Define a constant variable `arraySize` initialized to 10.
b) Declare an array with `arraySize` elements of type `double`, and initialize the elements to 0.
c) Name the fourth element of the array.
d) Refer to array element 4.
e) Assign the value `1.667` to array element 9.
f) Assign the value `3.333` to the seventh element of the array.
g) Print array elements 6 and 9 with two digits of precision to the right of the decimal point, and show the output that is actually displayed on the screen.
h) Print all the array elements using a `for` statement. Define the integer variable `i` as a control variable for the loop. Show the output.

7.4 Answer the following questions regarding an array called `table`:
a) Declare the array to be an integer array and to have 3 rows and 3 columns. Assume that the constant variable `arraySize` has been defined to be 3.
b) How many elements does the array contain?
c) Use a `for` repetition statement to initialize each element of the array to the sum of its subscripts. Assume that the integer variables `i` and `j` are declared as control variables.
d) Write a program segment to print the values of each element of array `table` in tabular format with 3 rows and 3 columns. Assume that the array was initialized with the declaration

```
int table[ arraySize ][ arraySize ] = { { 1, 8 }, { 2, 4, 6 }, { 5 } };
```

and the integer variables `i` and `j` are declared as control variables. Show the output.

7.5 Find the error in each of the following program segments and correct the error:
a) `#include <iostream>;`
b) `arraySize = 10; // arraySize was declared const`
c) Assume that `int b[ 10 ] = { 0 };`
```
for ( int i = 0; i <= 10; i++ )
    b[ i ] = 1;
```
d) Assume that `int a[ 2 ][ 2 ] = { { 1, 2 }, { 3, 4 } };`
```
a[ 1, 1 ] = 5;
```

Answers to Self-Review Exercises

7.1 a) arrays, vectors. b) name, type. c) subscript (or index). d) constant variable. e) sorting. f) searching. g) two-dimensional.

7.2 a) False. An array can store only values of the same type.
b) False. An array subscript should be an integer or an integer expression.

c) False. The remaining elements are initialized to zero.

d) True.

e) False. Individual elements of an array are passed by value. If the entire array is passed to a function, then any modifications will be reflected in the original.

7.3 a) `const int arraySize = 10;`

b) `double fractions[ arraySize ] = { 0.0 };`

c) `fractions[ 3 ]`

d) `fractions[ 4 ]`

e) `fractions[ 9 ] = 1.667;`

f) `fractions[ 6 ] = 3.333;`

g) `cout << fixed << setprecision( 2 );`
   `cout << fractions[ 6 ] << ' ' << fractions[ 9 ] << endl;`
   Output: 3.33 1.67.

h) `for ( int i = 0; i < arraySize; i++ )`
   `    cout << "fractions[" << i << "] = " << fractions[ i ] << endl;`
   Output:
   `fractions[ 0 ] = 0.0`
   `fractions[ 1 ] = 0.0`
   `fractions[ 2 ] = 0.0`
   `fractions[ 3 ] = 0.0`
   `fractions[ 4 ] = 0.0`
   `fractions[ 5 ] = 0.0`
   `fractions[ 6 ] = 3.333`
   `fractions[ 7 ] = 0.0`
   `fractions[ 8 ] = 0.0`
   `fractions[ 9 ] = 1.667`

7.4 a) `int table[ arraySize ][ arraySize ];`

b) Nine.

c) `for ( i = 0; i < arraySize; i++ )`

   `    for ( j = 0; j < arraySize; j++ )`
   `        table[ i ][ j ] = i + j;`

d) `cout << "    [0]  [1]  [2]" << endl;`

   `for ( int i = 0; i < arraySize; i++ ) {`
   `    cout << '[' << i << "] ";`

   `    for ( int j = 0; j < arraySize; j++ )`
   `        cout << setw( 3 ) << table[ i ][ j ] << "  ";`

   `    cout << endl;`

   Output:

	[0]	[1]	[2]
[0]	1	8	0
[1]	2	4	6
[2]	5	0	0

7.5 a) Error: Semicolon at end of #include preprocessor directive.
     Correction: Eliminate semicolon.

b) Error: Assigning a value to a constant variable using an assignment statement.
   Correction: Initialize the constant variable in a `const int arraySize` declaration.
c) Error: Referencing an array element outside the bounds of the array (`b[10]`).
   Correction: Change the final value of the control variable to 9.
d) Error: Array subscripting done incorrectly.
   Correction: Change the statement to `a[ 1 ][ 1 ] = 5;`

Exercises

7.6 Fill in the blanks in each of the following:
a) The names of the four elements of array p (`int p[ 4 ];`) are _____, _____, _____ and _____.
b) Naming an array, stating its type and specifying the number of elements in the array is called _____ the array.
c) By convention, the first subscript in a two-dimensional array identifies an element's _____ and the second subscript identifies an element's _____.
d) An *m*-by-*n* array contains _____ rows, _____ columns and _____ elements.
e) The name of the element in row 3 and column 5 of array d is _____.

7.7 Determine whether each of the following is *true* or *false*. If *false*, explain why.
a) To refer to a particular location or element within an array, we specify the name of the array and the value of the particular element.
b) An array declaration reserves space for the array.
c) To indicate that 100 locations should be reserved for integer array p, the programmer writes the declaration

    p[100];

d) A for statement must be used to initialize the elements of a 15-element array to zero.
e) Nested for statements must be used to total the elements of a two-dimensional array.

7.8 Write C++ statements to accomplish each of the following:
a) Display the value of element 6 of character array f.
b) Input a value into element 4 of one-dimensional floating-point array b.
c) Initialize each of the 5 elements of one-dimensional integer array g to 8.
d) Total and print the elements of floating-point array c of 100 elements.
e) Copy array a into the first portion of array b. Assume `double a[ 11 ], b[ 34 ];`
f) Determine and print the smallest and largest values contained in 99-element floating-point array w.

7.9 Consider a 2-by-3 integer array t.
a) Write a declaration for t.
b) How many rows does t have?
c) How many columns does t have?
d) How many elements does t have?
e) Write the names of all the elements in row 1 of t.
f) Write the names of all the elements in column 2 of t.
g) Write a single statement that sets the element of t in row 1 and column 2 to zero.
h) Write a series of statements that initialize each element of t to zero. Do not use a loop.
i) Write a nested for statement that initializes each element of t to zero.
j) Write a statement that inputs the values for the elements of t from the terminal.
k) Write a series of statements that determine and print the smallest value in array t.

l) Write a statement that displays the elements in row 0 of t.

m) Write a statement that totals the elements in column 3 of t.

n) Write a series of statements that prints the array t in neat, tabular format. List the column subscripts as headings across the top and list the row subscripts at the left of each row.

7.10   Use a one-dimensional array to solve the following problem. A company pays its salespeople on a commission basis. The salespeople each receive $200 per week plus 9 percent of their gross sales for that week. For example, a salesperson who grosses $5000 in sales in a week receives $200 plus 9 percent of $5000, or a total of $650. Write a program (using an array of counters) that determines how many of the salespeople earned salaries in each of the following ranges (assume that each salesperson's salary is truncated to an integer amount):

a) $200–$299

b) $300–$399

c) $400–$499

d) $500–$599

e) $600–$699

f) $700–$799

g) $800–$899

h) $900–$999

i) $1000 and over

7.11   *(Bubble Sort)* In the bubble sort algorithm, smaller values gradually "bubble" their way upward to the top of the array like air bubbles rising in water, while the larger values sink to the bottom. The bubble sort makes several passes through the array. On each pass, successive pairs of elements are compared. If a pair is in increasing order (or the values are identical), we leave the values as they are. If a pair is in decreasing order, their values are swapped in the array. Write a program that sorts an array of 10 integers using bubble sort.

7.12   The bubble sort described in Exercise 7.11 is inefficient for large arrays. Make the following simple modifications to improve the performance of the bubble sort:

a) After the first pass, the largest number is guaranteed to be in the highest-numbered element of the array; after the second pass, the two highest numbers are "in place," and so on. Instead of making nine comparisons on every pass, modify the bubble sort to make eight comparisons on the second pass, seven on the third pass, and so on.

b) The data in the array may already be in the proper order or near-proper order, so why make nine passes if fewer will suffice? Modify the sort to check at the end of each pass if any swaps have been made. If none have been made, then the data must already be in the proper order, so the program should terminate. If swaps have been made, then at least one more pass is needed.

7.13   Write single statements that perform the following one-dimensional array operations:

a) Initialize the 10 elements of integer array counts to zero.

b) Add 1 to each of the 15 elements of integer array bonus.

c) Read 12 values for double array monthlyTemperatures from the keyboard.

d) Print the 5 values of integer array bestScores in column format.

7.14   Find the error(s) in each of the following statements:

a) Assume that: char str[5];

```
cin >> str; // user types "hello"
```

b) Assume that: int a[3];

```
cout << a[ 1 ] << " " << a[ 2 ] << " " << a[ 3 ] << endl;
```

c) double f[3] = { 1.1, 10.01, 100.001, 1000.0001 };

d) Assume that: `double d[ 2 ][ 10 ];`

   `d[ 1, 9 ] = 2.345;`

7.15 Use a one-dimensional array to solve the following problem. Read in 20 numbers, each of which is between 10 and 100, inclusive. As each number is read, validate it and store it in the array only if it is not a duplicate of a number already read. After reading all the values, display only the unique values that the user entered. Provide for the "worst case" in which all 20 numbers are different. Use the smallest possible array to solve this problem.

7.16 Label the elements of a 3-by-5 one-dimensional array `sales` to indicate the order in which they are set to zero by the following program segment:

```
for ( row = 0; row < 3; row++ )

    for ( column = 0; column < 5; column++ )
        sales[ row ][ column ] = 0;
```

7.17 Write a program that simulates the rolling of two dice. The program should use `rand` to roll the first die and should use `rand` again to roll the second die. The sum of the two values should then be calculated. [*Note:* Each die can show an integer value from 1 to 6, so the sum of the two values will vary from 2 to 12, with 7 being the most frequent sum and 2 and 12 being the least frequent sums.] Figure 7.27 shows the 36 possible combinations of the two dice. Your program should roll the two dice 36,000 times. Use a one-dimensional array to tally the numbers of times each possible sum appears. Print the results in a tabular format. Also, determine if the totals are reasonable (i.e., there are six ways to roll a 7, so approximately one-sixth of all the rolls should be 7).

	1	2	3	4	5	6
1	2	3	4	5	6	7
2	3	4	5	6	7	8
3	4	5	6	7	8	9
4	5	6	7	8	9	10
5	6	7	8	9	10	11
6	7	8	9	10	11	12

Fig. 7.27 | The 36 possible outcomes of rolling two dice.

7.18 What does the following program do?

```
1   // Ex. 7.18: Ex07_18.cpp
2   // What does this program do?
3   #include <iostream>
4   using std::cout;
5   using std::endl;
6
7   int whatIsThis( int [], int ); // function prototype
8
9   int main()
10  {
11      const int arraySize = 10;
12      int a[ arraySize ] = { 1, 2, 3, 4, 5, 6, 7, 8, 9, 10 };
```

```
13
14      int result = whatIsThis( a, arraySize );
15
16      cout << "Result is " << result << endl;
17      return 0; // indicates successful termination
18   } // end main
19
20   // What does this function do?
21   int whatIsThis( int b[], int size )
22   {
23      if ( size == 1 ) // base case
24         return b[ 0 ];
25      else // recursive step
26         return b[ size - 1 ] + whatIsThis( b, size - 1 );
27   } // end function whatIsThis
```

7.19   Modify the program of Fig. 6.11 to play 1000 games of craps. The program should keep track of the statistics and answer the following questions:

a)   How many games are won on the 1st roll, 2nd roll, ..., 20th roll, and after the 20th roll?

b)   How many games are lost on the 1st roll, 2nd roll, ..., 20th roll, and after the 20th roll?

c)   What are the chances of winning at craps? [*Note:* You should discover that craps is one of the fairest casino games. What do you suppose this means?]

d)   What is the average length of a game of craps?

e)   Do the chances of winning improve with the length of the game?

7.20   (*Airline Reservations System*) A small airline has just purchased a computer for its new automated reservations system. You have been asked to program the new system. You are to write a program to assign seats on each flight of the airline's only plane (capacity: 10 seats).

Your program should display the following menu of alternatives—Please type 1 for "First Class" and Please type 2 for "Economy". If the person types 1, your program should assign a seat in the first class section (seats 1-5). If the person types 2, your program should assign a seat in the economy section (seats 6-10). Your program should print a boarding pass indicating the person's seat number and whether it is in the first class or economy section of the plane.

Use a one-dimensional array to represent the seating chart of the plane. Initialize all the elements of the array to 0 to indicate that all seats are empty. As each seat is assigned, set the corresponding elements of the array to 1 to indicate that the seat is no longer available.

Your program should, of course, never assign a seat that has already been assigned. When the first class section is full, your program should ask the person if it is acceptable to be placed in the economy section (and vice versa). If yes, then make the appropriate seat assignment. If no, then print the message "Next flight leaves in 3 hours."

7.21   What does the following program do?

```
1    // Ex. 7.21: Ex07_21.cpp
2    // What does this program do?
3    #include <iostream>
4    using std::cout;
5    using std::endl;
6
7    void someFunction( int [], int, int ); // function prototype
```

```
8
9   int main()
10  {
11      const int arraySize = 10;
12      int a[ arraySize ] = { 1, 2, 3, 4, 5, 6, 7, 8, 9, 10 };
13
14      cout << "The values in the array are:" << endl;
15      someFunction( a, 0, arraySize );
16      cout << endl;
17      return 0; // indicates successful termination
18  } // end main
19
20  // What does this function do?
21  void someFunction( int b[], int current, int size )
22  {
23      if ( current < size )
24      {
25          someFunction( b, current + 1, size );
26          cout << b[ current ] << "   ";
27      } // end if
28  } // end function someFunction
```

7.22   Use a two-dimensional array to solve the following problem. A company has four salespeople (1 to 4) who sell five different products (1 to 5). Once a day, each salesperson passes in a slip for each different type of product sold. Each slip contains the following:

    a)   The salesperson number

    b)   The product number

    c)   The total dollar value of that product sold that day

Thus, each salesperson passes in between 0 and 5 sales slips per day. Assume that the information from all of the slips for last month is available. Write a program that will read all this information for last month's sales and summarize the total sales by salesperson by product. All totals should be stored in the two-dimensional array sales. After processing all the information for last month, print the results in tabular format with each of the columns representing a particular salesperson and each of the rows representing a particular product. Cross total each row to get the total sales of each product for last month; cross total each column to get the total sales by salesperson for last month. Your tabular printout should include these cross totals to the right of the totaled rows and to the bottom of the totaled columns.

7.23   (*Turtle Graphics*) The Logo language, which is popular among elementary school children, made the concept of *turtle graphics* famous. Imagine a mechanical turtle that walks around the room under the control of a C++ program. The turtle holds a pen in one of two positions, up or down. While the pen is down, the turtle traces out shapes as it moves; while the pen is up, the turtle moves about freely without writing anything. In this problem, you will simulate the operation of the turtle and create a computerized sketchpad as well.

    Use a 20-by-20 array floor that is initialized to zeros. Read commands from an array that contains them. Keep track of the current position of the turtle at all times and whether the pen is currently up or down. Assume that the turtle always starts at position (0, 0) of the floor with its pen up. The set of turtle commands your program must process are shown in Fig. 7.28.

    Suppose that the turtle is somewhere near the center of the floor. The following "program" would draw and print a 12-by-12 square and end with the pen in the up position:

Command	Meaning
1	Pen up
2	Pen down
3	Turn right
4	Turn left
5,10	Move forward 10 spaces (or a number other than 10)
6	Print the 20-by-20 array
9	End of data (sentinel)

Fig. 7.28 | Turtle graphics commands.

```
2
5,12
3
5,12
3
5,12
3
5,12
1
6
9
```

As the turtle moves with the pen down, set the appropriate elements of array floor to 1's. When the 6 command (print) is given, wherever there is a 1 in the array, display an asterisk or some other character you choose. Wherever there is a zero, display a blank. Write a program to implement the turtle graphics capabilities discussed here. Write several turtle graphics programs to draw interesting shapes. Add other commands to increase the power of your turtle graphics language.

7.24 (*Knight's Tour*) One of the more interesting puzzlers for chess buffs is the Knight's Tour problem. The question is this: Can the chess piece called the knight move around an empty chessboard and touch each of the 64 squares once and only once? We study this intriguing problem in depth in this exercise.

The knight makes L-shaped moves (over two in one direction and then over one in a perpendicular direction). Thus, from a square in the middle of an empty chessboard, the knight can make eight different moves (numbered 0 through 7) as shown in Fig. 7.29.

    a) Draw an 8-by-8 chessboard on a sheet of paper and attempt a Knight's Tour by hand. Put a 1 in the first square you move to, a 2 in the second square, a 3 in the third, etc. Before starting the tour, estimate how far you think you will get, remembering that a full tour consists of 64 moves. How far did you get? Was this close to your estimate?

    b) Now let us develop a program that will move the knight around a chessboard. The board is represented by an 8-by-8 two-dimensional array board. Each of the squares is initialized to zero. We describe each of the eight possible moves in terms of both their horizontal and vertical components. For example, a move of type 0, as shown in Fig. 7.29, consists of moving two squares horizontally to the right and one square vertically upward. Move 2 consists of moving one square horizontally to the left and two squares vertically upward. Horizontal moves to the left and vertical moves upward are indicated with negative numbers. The eight moves may be described by two one-dimensional arrays, horizontal and vertical, as follows:

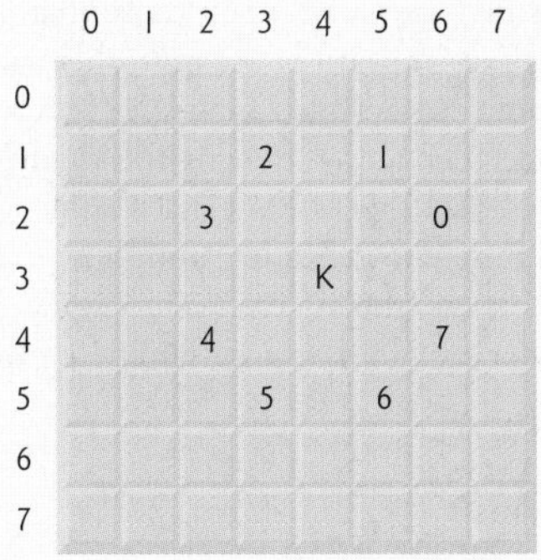

Fig. 7.29 | The eight possible moves of the knight.

```
horizontal[ 0 ] = 2
horizontal[ 1 ] = 1
horizontal[ 2 ] = -1
horizontal[ 3 ] = -2
horizontal[ 4 ] = -2
horizontal[ 5 ] = -1
horizontal[ 6 ] = 1
horizontal[ 7 ] = 2

vertical[ 0 ] = -1
vertical[ 1 ] = -2
vertical[ 2 ] = -2
vertical[ 3 ] = -1
vertical[ 4 ] = 1
vertical[ 5 ] = 2
vertical[ 6 ] = 2
vertical[ 7 ] = 1
```

Let the variables currentRow and currentColumn indicate the row and column of the knight's current position. To make a move of type moveNumber, where moveNumber is between 0 and 7, your program uses the statements

```
currentRow += vertical[ moveNumber ];
currentColumn += horizontal[ moveNumber ];
```

Keep a counter that varies from 1 to 64. Record the latest count in each square the knight moves to. Remember to test each potential move to see if the knight has already visited that square, and, of course, test every potential move to make sure that the knight does not land off the chessboard. Now write a program to move the knight around the chessboard. Run the program. How many moves did the knight make?

c) After attempting to write and run a Knight's Tour program, you have probably developed some valuable insights. We will use these to develop a heuristic (or strategy) for moving the knight. Heuristics do not guarantee success, but a carefully developed heuristic greatly improves the chance of success. You may have observed that the outer squares are more troublesome than the squares nearer the center of the board. In fact, the most troublesome, or inaccessible, squares are the four corners.

Intuition may suggest that you should attempt to move the knight to the most troublesome squares first and leave open those that are easiest to get to, so when the board gets congested near the end of the tour, there will be a greater chance of success.

We may develop an "accessibility heuristic" by classifying each square according to how accessible it is and then always moving the knight to the square (within the knight's L-shaped moves, of course) that is most inaccessible. We label a two-dimensional array `accessibility` with numbers indicating from how many squares each particular square is accessible. On a blank chessboard, each center square is rated as 8, each corner square is rated as 2 and the other squares have accessibility numbers of 3, 4 or 6 as follows:

```
2  3  4  4  4  4  3  2
3  4  6  6  6  6  4  3
4  6  8  8  8  8  6  4
4  6  8  8  8  8  6  4
4  6  8  8  8  8  6  4
4  6  8  8  8  8  6  4
3  4  6  6  6  6  4  3
2  3  4  4  4  4  3  2
```

Now write a version of the Knight's Tour program using the accessibility heuristic. At any time, the knight should move to the square with the lowest accessibility number. In case of a tie, the knight may move to any of the tied squares. Therefore, the tour may begin in any of the four corners. [*Note:* As the knight moves around the chessboard, your program should reduce the accessibility numbers as more and more squares become occupied. In this way, at any given time during the tour, each available square's accessibility number will remain equal to precisely the number of squares from which that square may be reached.] Run this version of your program. Did you get a full tour? Now modify the program to run 64 tours, one starting from each square of the chessboard. How many full tours did you get?

d) Write a version of the Knight's Tour program which, when encountering a tie between two or more squares, decides what square to choose by looking ahead to those squares reachable from the "tied" squares. Your program should move to the square for which the next move would arrive at a square with the lowest accessibility number.

7.25 (*Knight's Tour: Brute Force Approaches*) In Exercise 7.24, we developed a solution to the Knight's Tour problem. The approach used, called the "accessibility heuristic," generates many solutions and executes efficiently.

As computers continue increasing in power, we will be able to solve more problems with sheer computer power and relatively unsophisticated algorithms. This is the "brute force" approach to problem solving.

a) Use random number generation to enable the knight to walk around the chessboard (in its legitimate L-shaped moves, of course) at random. Your program should run one tour and print the final chessboard. How far did the knight get?

b) Most likely, the preceding program produced a relatively short tour. Now modify your program to attempt 1000 tours. Use a one-dimensional array to keep track of the number of tours of each length. When your program finishes attempting the 1000 tours, it should print this information in neat tabular format. What was the best result?

c) Most likely, the preceding program gave you some "respectable" tours, but no full tours. Now "pull all the stops out" and simply let your program run until it produces a full tour. [*Caution:* This version of the program could run for hours on a powerful computer.] Once again, keep a table of the number of tours of each length, and print this table when the first full tour is found. How many tours did your program attempt before producing a full tour? How much time did it take?

d) Compare the brute force version of the Knight's Tour with the accessibility heuristic version. Which required a more careful study of the problem? Which algorithm was more difficult to develop? Which required more computer power? Could we be certain (in advance) of obtaining a full tour with the accessibility heuristic approach? Could we be certain (in advance) of obtaining a full tour with the brute force approach? Argue the pros and cons of brute force problem solving in general.

7.26 (*Eight Queens*) Another puzzler for chess buffs is the Eight Queens problem. Simply stated: Is it possible to place eight queens on an empty chessboard so that no queen is "attacking" any other, i.e., no two queens are in the same row, the same column, or along the same diagonal? Use the thinking developed in Exercise 7.24 to formulate a heuristic for solving the Eight Queens problem. Run your program. [*Hint:* It is possible to assign a value to each square of the chessboard indicating how many squares of an empty chessboard are "eliminated" if a queen is placed in that square. Each of the corners would be assigned the value 22, as in Fig. 7.30.] Once these "elimination numbers" are placed in all 64 squares, an appropriate heuristic might be: Place the next queen in the square with the smallest elimination number. Why is this strategy intuitively appealing?

7.27 (*Eight Queens: Brute Force Approaches*) In this exercise, you will develop several brute-force approaches to solving the Eight Queens problem introduced in Exercise 7.26.
a) Solve the Eight Queens exercise, using the random brute force technique developed in Exercise 7.25.
b) Use an exhaustive technique, i.e., try all possible combinations of eight queens on the chessboard.
c) Why do you suppose the exhaustive brute force approach may not be appropriate for solving the Knight's Tour problem?
d) Compare and contrast the random brute force and exhaustive brute force approaches in general.

7.28 (*Knight's Tour: Closed-Tour Test*) In the Knight's Tour, a full tour occurs when the knight makes 64 moves touching each square of the chess board once and only once. A closed tour occurs when the 64th move is one move away from the location in which the knight started the tour. Modify the Knight's Tour program you wrote in Exercise 7.24 to test for a closed tour if a full tour has occurred.

7.29 (*The Sieve of Eratosthenes*) A prime integer is any integer that is evenly divisible only by itself and 1. The Sieve of Eratosthenes is a method of finding prime numbers. It operates as follows:

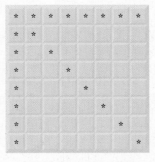

Fig. 7.30 | The 22 squares eliminated by placing a queen in the upper-left corner.

a) Create an array with all elements initialized to 1 (true). Array elements with prime subscripts will remain 1. All other array elements will eventually be set to zero. You will ignore elements 0 and 1 in this exercise.

b) Starting with array subscript 2, every time an array element is found whose value is 1, loop through the remainder of the array and set to zero every element whose subscript is a multiple of the subscript for the element with value 1. For array subscript 2, all elements beyond 2 in the array that are multiples of 2 will be set to zero (subscripts 4, 6, 8, 10, etc.); for array subscript 3, all elements beyond 3 in the array that are multiples of 3 will be set to zero (subscripts 6, 9, 12, 15, etc.); and so on.

When this process is complete, the array elements that are still set to one indicate that the subscript is a prime number. These subscripts can then be printed. Write a program that uses an array of 1000 elements to determine and print the prime numbers between 2 and 999. Ignore element 0 of the array.

7.30   (*Bucket Sort*) A bucket sort begins with a one-dimensional array of positive integers to be sorted and a two-dimensional array of integers with rows subscripted from 0 to 9 and columns subscripted from 0 to $n - 1$, where n is the number of values in the array to be sorted. Each row of the two-dimensional array is referred to as a bucket. Write a function bucketSort that takes an integer array and the array size as arguments and performs as follows:

a) Place each value of the one-dimensional array into a row of the bucket array based on the value's ones digit. For example, 97 is placed in row 7, 3 is placed in row 3 and 100 is placed in row 0. This is called a "distribution pass."

b) Loop through the bucket array row by row, and copy the values back to the original array. This is called a "gathering pass." The new order of the preceding values in the one-dimensional array is 100, 3 and 97.

c) Repeat this process for each subsequent digit position (tens, hundreds, thousands, etc.).

On the second pass, 100 is placed in row 0, 3 is placed in row 0 (because 3 has no tens digit) and 97 is placed in row 9. After the gathering pass, the order of the values in the one-dimensional array is 100, 3 and 97. On the third pass, 100 is placed in row 1, 3 is placed in row zero and 97 is placed in row zero (after the 3). After the last gathering pass, the original array is now in sorted order.

Note that the two-dimensional array of buckets is 10 times the size of the integer array being sorted. This sorting technique provides better performance than a insertion sort, but requires much more memory. The insertion sort requires space for only one additional element of data. This is an example of the space–time trade-off: The bucket sort uses more memory than the insertion sort, but performs better. This version of the bucket sort requires copying all the data back to the original array on each pass. Another possibility is to create a second two-dimensional bucket array and repeatedly swap the data between the two bucket arrays.

Recursion Exercises

7.31   (*Selection Sort*) A selection sort searches an array looking for the smallest element. Then, the smallest element is swapped with the first element of the array. The process is repeated for the subarray beginning with the second element of the array. Each pass of the array results in one element being placed in its proper location. This sort performs comparably to the insertion sort—for an array of n elements, $n - 1$ passes must be made, and for each subarray, $n - 1$ comparisons must be made to find the smallest value. When the subarray being processed contains one element, the array is sorted. Write recursive function selectionSort to perform this algorithm.

7.32   (*Palindromes*) A palindrome is a string that is spelled the same way forward and backward. Some examples of palindromes are "radar," "able was i ere i saw elba" and (if blanks are ignored) "a man a plan a canal panama." Write a recursive function testPalindrome that returns true if the string stored in the array is a palindrome, and false otherwise. The function should ignore spaces and punctuation in the string.

7.33   (*Linear Search*) Modify the program in Fig. 7.19 to use recursive function linearSearch to perform a linear search of the array. The function should receive an integer array and the size of the array as arguments. If the search key is found, return the array subscript; otherwise, return −1.

7.34   (*Eight Queens*) Modify the Eight Queens program you created in Exercise 7.26 to solve the problem recursively.

7.35   (*Print an array*) Write a recursive function printArray that takes an array, a starting subscript and an ending subscript as arguments and returns nothing. The function should stop processing and return when the starting subscript equals the ending subscript.

7.36   (*Print a string backward*) Write a recursive function stringReverse that takes a character array containing a string and a starting subscript as arguments, prints the string backward and returns nothing. The function should stop processing and return when the terminating null character is encountered.

7.37   (*Find the minimum value in an array*) Write a recursive function recursiveMinimum that takes an integer array, a starting subscript and an ending subscript as arguments, and returns the smallest element of the array. The function should stop processing and return when the starting subscript equals the ending subscript.

vector Exercises

7.38   Use a vector of integers to solve the problem described in Exercise 7.10.

7.39   Modify the dice-rolling program you created in Exercise 7.17 to use a vector to store the numbers of times each possible sum of the two dice appears.

7.40   (*Find the minimum value in a vector*) Modify your solution to Exercise 7.37 to find the minimum value in a vector instead of an array.

8

Pointers and Pointer-Based Strings

Addresses are given to us to conceal our whereabouts.
—Saki (H. H. Munro)

By indirection find direction out.
—William Shakespeare

*Many things, having full reference
To one consent, may work contrariously.*
—William Shakespeare

You will find it a very good practice always to verify your references, sir!
—Dr. Routh

OBJECTIVES

In this chapter you will learn:

- What pointers are.
- The similarities and differences between pointers and references and when to use each.
- To use pointers to pass arguments to functions by reference.
- To use pointer-based C-style strings.
- The close relationships among pointers, arrays and C-style strings.
- To use pointers to functions.
- To declare and use arrays of C-style strings.

Outline

8.1   Introduction

8.2   Pointer Variable Declarations and Initialization

8.3   Pointer Operators

8.4   Passing Arguments to Functions by Reference with Pointers

8.5   Using `const` with Pointers

8.6   Selection Sort Using Pass-by-Reference

8.7   `sizeof` Operators

8.8   Pointer Expressions and Pointer Arithmetic

8.9   Relationship Between Pointers and Arrays

8.10 Arrays of Pointers

8.11 Case Study: Card Shuffling and Dealing Simulation

8.12 Function Pointers

8.13 Introduction to Pointer-Based String Processing

    8.13.1 Fundamentals of Characters and Pointer-Based Strings

    8.13.2 String Manipulation Functions of the String-Handling Library

8.14 Wrap-Up

Summary | Terminology | Self-Review Exercises | Answers to Self-Review Exercises | Exercises | Special Section: Building Your Own Computer | More Pointer Exercises | String-Manipulation Exercises | Special Section: Advanced String-Manipulation Exercises | A Challenging String-Manipulation Project

8.1 Introduction

This chapter discusses one of the most powerful features of the C++ programming language, the pointer. In Chapter 6, we saw that references can be used to perform pass-by-reference. Pointers also enable pass-by-reference and can be used to create and manipulate dynamic data structures (i.e., data structures that can grow and shrink), such as linked lists, queues, stacks and trees. This chapter explains basic pointer concepts and reinforces the intimate relationship among arrays and pointers. The view of arrays as pointers derives from the C programming language. As we saw in Chapter 7, C++ Standard Library class `vector` provides an implementation of arrays as full-fledged objects.

Similarly, C++ actually offers two types of strings—`string` class objects (which we have been using since Chapter 3) and C-style, `char *` pointer-based strings. This chapter on pointers discusses `char *` strings to deepen your knowledge of pointers. In fact, the null-terminated strings that we introduced in Section 7.4 and used in Fig. 7.12 are `char *` pointer-based strings. This chapter also includes a substantial collection of string-processing exercises that use `char *`strings. C-style, `char *` pointer-based strings are widely used in legacy C and C++ systems. So, if you work with legacy C or C++ systems, you may be required to manipulate these `char *` pointer-based strings.

We will examine the use of pointers with classes in Chapter 13, Object-Oriented Programming: Polymorphism, where we will see that the so-called "polymorphic processing" of object-oriented programming is performed with pointers and references.

8.2 Pointer Variable Declarations and Initialization

Pointer variables contain memory addresses as their values. Normally, a variable directly contains a specific value. However, a pointer contains the memory address of a variable that, in turn, contains a specific value. In this sense, a variable name directly references a value, and a pointer indirectly references a value (Fig. 8.1). Referencing a value through a pointer is often called indirection. Note that diagrams typically represent a pointer as an arrow from the variable that contains an address to the variable located at that address in memory.

Pointers, like any other variables, must be declared before they can be used. For example, for the pointer in Fig. 8.1, the declaration

```
int *countPtr, count;
```

declares the variable countPtr to be of type int * (i.e., a pointer to an int value) and is read, "countPtr is a pointer to int" or "countPtr points to an object of type int." Also, variable count in the preceding declaration is declared to be an int, not a pointer to an int. The * in the declaration applies only to countPtr. Each variable being declared as a pointer must be preceded by an asterisk (*). For example, the declaration

```
double *xPtr, *yPtr;
```

indicates that both xPtr and yPtr are pointers to double values. When * appears in a declaration, it is not an operator; rather, it indicates that the variable being declared is a pointer. Pointers can be declared to point to objects of any data type.

Common Programming Error 8.1

*Assuming that the * used to declare a pointer distributes to all variable names in a declaration's comma-separated list of variables can lead to errors. Each pointer must be declared with the * prefixed to the name (either with or without a space in between—the compiler ignores the space). Declaring only one variable per declaration helps avoid these types of errors and improves program readability.*

Good Programming Practice 8.1

Although it is not a requirement, including the letters Ptr in pointer variable names makes it clear that these variables are pointers and that they must be handled appropriately.

Pointers should be initialized either when they are declared or in an assignment. A pointer may be initialized to 0, NULL or an address. A pointer with the value 0 or NULL

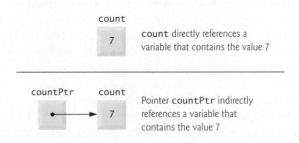

Fig. 8.1 | Directly and indirectly referencing a variable.

points to nothing and is known as a null pointer. Symbolic constant NULL is defined in header file <iostream> (and in several other standard library header files) to represent the value 0. Initializing a pointer to NULL is equivalent to initializing a pointer to 0, but in C++, 0 is used by convention. When 0 is assigned, it is converted to a pointer of the appropriate type. The value 0 is the only integer value that can be assigned directly to a pointer variable without casting the integer to a pointer type first. Assigning a variable's numeric address to a pointer is discussed in Section 8.3.

Error-Prevention Tip 8.1

Initialize pointers to prevent pointing to unknown or uninitialized areas of memory.

8.3 Pointer Operators

The address operator (&) is a unary operator that returns the memory address of its operand. For example, assuming the declarations

```
int y = 5; // declare variable y
int *yPtr; // declare pointer variable yPtr
```

the statement

```
yPtr = &y; // assign address of y to yPtr
```

assigns the address of the variable y to pointer variable yPtr. Then variable yPtr is said to "point to" y. Now, yPtr indirectly references variable y's value. Note that the use of the & in the preceding assignment statement is not the same as the use of the & in a reference variable declaration, which is always preceded by a data-type name.

Figure 8.2 shows a schematic representation of memory after the preceding assignment. The "pointing relationship" is indicated by drawing an arrow from the box that represents the pointer yPtr in memory to the box that represents the variable y in memory.

Figure 8.3 shows another representation of the pointer in memory, assuming that integer variable y is stored at memory location 600000 and that pointer variable yPtr is stored at memory location 500000. The operand of the address operator must be an *lvalue* (i.e., something to which a value can be assigned, such as a variable name or a reference); the address operator cannot be applied to constants or to expressions that do not result in references.

The * operator, commonly referred to as the indirection operator or dereferencing operator, returns a synonym (i.e., an alias or a nickname) for the object to which its pointer operand points. For example (referring again to Fig. 8.2), the statement

```
cout << *yPtr << endl;
```

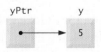

Fig. 8.2 | Graphical representation of a pointer pointing to a variable in memory.

Fig. 8.3 | Representation of y and yPtr in memory.

prints the value of variable y, namely, 5, just as the statement

```
cout << y << endl;
```

would. Using * in this manner is called dereferencing a pointer. Note that a dereferenced pointer may also be used on the left side of an assignment statement, as in

```
*yPtr = 9;
```

which would assign 9 to y in Fig. 8.3. The dereferenced pointer may also be used to receive an input value as in

```
cin >> *yPtr;
```

which places the input value in y. The dereferenced pointer is an *lvalue*.

Common Programming Error 8.2

Dereferencing a pointer that has not been properly initialized or that has not been assigned to point to a specific location in memory could cause a fatal execution-time error, or it could accidentally modify important data and allow the program to run to completion, possibly with incorrect results.

Common Programming Error 8.3

An attempt to dereference a variable that is not a pointer is a compilation error.

Common Programming Error 8.4

Dereferencing a null pointer is normally a fatal execution-time error.

The program in Fig. 8.4 demonstrates the & and * pointer operators. Memory locations are output by << in this example as hexadecimal (i.e., base-16) integers. (See Appendix D, Number Systems, for more information on hexadecimal integers.) Note that the hexadecimal memory addresses output by this program are compiler and operating-system dependent, so you may get different results when you run the program.

Portability Tip 8.1

The format in which a pointer is output is compiler dependent. Some systems output pointer values as hexadecimal integers, while others use decimal integers.

Notice that the address of a (line 15) and the value of aPtr (line 16) are identical in the output, confirming that the address of a is indeed assigned to the pointer variable aPtr. The & and * operators are inverses of one another—when they are both applied consecutively to aPtr in either order, they "cancel one another out" and the same result (the value in aPtr) is printed.

```
 1   // Fig. 8.4: fig08_04.cpp
 2   // Using the & and * operators.
 3   #include <iostream>
 4   using std::cout;
 5   using std::endl;
 6
 7   int main()
 8   {
 9      int a; // a is an integer
10      int *aPtr; // aPtr is an int * -- pointer to an integer
11
12      a = 7; // assigned 7 to a
13      aPtr = &a; // assign the address of a to aPtr
14
15      cout << "The address of a is " << &a
16         << "\nThe value of aPtr is " << aPtr;
17      cout << "\n\nThe value of a is " << a
18         << "\nThe value of *aPtr is " << *aPtr;
19      cout << "\n\nShowing that * and & are inverses of "
20         << "each other.\n&*aPtr = " << &*aPtr
21         << "\n*&aPtr = " << *&aPtr << endl;
22      return 0; // indicates successful termination
23   } // end main
```

```
The address of a is 0012F580
The value of aPtr is 0012F580

The value of a is 7
The value of *aPtr is 7

Showing that * and & are inverses of each other.
&*aPtr = 0012F580
*&aPtr = 0012F580
```

Fig. 8.4 | Pointer operators & and *.

Figure 8.5 lists the precedence and associativity of the operators introduced to this point. Note that the address operator (&) and the dereferencing operator (*) are unary operators on the third level of precedence in the chart.

Operators	Associativity	Type
() []	left to right	highest
++ -- static_cast< *type* >(*operand*)	left to right	unary (postfix)
++ -- + - ! & *	right to left	unary (prefix)
* / %	left to right	multiplicative
+ -	left to right	additive

Fig. 8.5 | Operator precedence and associativity. (Part 1 of 2.)

Operators						Associativity	Type
<<	>>					left to right	insertion/extraction
<	<=	>	>=			left to right	relational
==	!=					left to right	equality
&&						left to right	logical AND
||						left to right	logical OR
?:						right to left	conditional
=	+=	-=	*=	/=	%=	right to left	assignment
,						left to right	comma

Fig. 8.5 | Operator precedence and associativity. (Part 2 of 2.)

8.4 Passing Arguments to Functions by Reference with Pointers

There are three ways in C++ to pass arguments to a function—pass-by-value, pass-by-reference with reference arguments and pass-by-reference with pointer arguments. Chapter 6 compared and contrasted pass-by-value and pass-by-reference with reference arguments. In this section, we explain pass-by-reference with pointer arguments.

As we saw in Chapter 6, return can be used to return one value from a called function to a caller (or to return control from a called function without passing back a value). We also saw that arguments can be passed to a function using reference arguments. Such arguments enable the called function to modify the original values of the arguments in the caller. Reference arguments also enable programs to pass large data objects to a function and avoid the overhead of passing the objects by value (which, of course, requires making a copy of the object). Pointers, like references, also can be used to modify one or more variables in the caller or to pass pointers to large data objects to avoid the overhead of passing the objects by value.

In C++, programmers can use pointers and the indirection operator (*) to accomplish pass-by-reference (exactly as pass-by-reference is done in C programs, because C does not have references). When calling a function with an argument that should be modified, the address of the argument is passed. This is normally accomplished by applying the address operator (&) to the name of the variable whose value will be modified.

As we saw in Chapter 7, arrays are not passed using operator &, because the name of the array is the starting location in memory of the array (i.e., an array name is already a pointer). The name of an array, arrayName, is equivalent to &arrayName[0]. When the address of a variable is passed to a function, the indirection operator (*) can be used in the function to form a synonym for the name of the variable—this in turn can be used to modify the value of the variable at that location in the caller's memory.

Figure 8.6 and Fig. 8.7 present two versions of a function that cubes an integer—cubeByValue and cubeByReference. Figure 8.6 passes variable number by value to function cubeByValue (line 15). Function cubeByValue (lines 21–24) cubes its argument and passes the new value back to main using a return statement (line 23). The new value is

```
 1   // Fig. 8.6: fig08_06.cpp
 2   // Cube a variable using pass-by-value.
 3   #include <iostream>
 4   using std::cout;
 5   using std::endl;
 6
 7   int cubeByValue( int ); // prototype
 8
 9   int main()
10   {
11      int number = 5;
12
13      cout << "The original value of number is " << number;
14
15      number = cubeByValue( number ); // pass number by value to cubeByValue
16      cout << "\nThe new value of number is " << number << endl;
17      return 0; // indicates successful termination
18   } // end main
19
20   // calculate and return cube of integer argument
21   int cubeByValue( int n )
22   {
23      return n * n * n; // cube local variable n and return result
24   } // end function cubeByValue
```

```
The original value of number is 5
The new value of number is 125
```

Fig. 8.6 | Pass-by-value used to cube a variable's value.

assigned to number (line 15) in main. Note that the calling function has the opportunity to examine the result of the function call before modifying variable number's value. For example, in this program, we could have stored the result of cubeByValue in another variable, examined its value and assigned the result to number only after determining that the returned value was reasonable.

Figure 8.7 passes the variable number to function cubeByReference using pass-by-reference with a pointer argument (line 15)—the address of number is passed to the function. Function cubeByReference (lines 22–25) specifies parameter nPtr (a pointer to int) to receive its argument. The function dereferences the pointer and cubes the value to which nPtr points (line 24). This directly changes the value of number in main.

 Common Programming Error 8.5

Not dereferencing a pointer when it is necessary to do so to obtain the value to which the pointer points is an error.

A function receiving an address as an argument must define a pointer parameter to receive the address. For example, the header for function cubeByReference (line 22) specifies that cubeByReference receives the address of an int variable (i.e., a pointer to an int) as an argument, stores the address locally in nPtr and does not return a value.

The function prototype for cubeByReference (line 7) contains int * in parentheses. As with other variable types, it is not necessary to include names of pointer parameters in

```
1   // Fig. 8.7: fig08_07.cpp
2   // Cube a variable using pass-by-reference with a pointer argument.
3   #include <iostream>
4   using std::cout;
5   using std::endl;
6
7   void cubeByReference( int * ); // prototype
8
9   int main()
10  {
11     int number = 5;
12
13     cout << "The original value of number is " << number;
14
15     cubeByReference( &number ); // pass number address to cubeByReference
16
17     cout << "\nThe new value of number is " << number << endl;
18     return 0; // indicates successful termination
19  } // end main
20
21  // calculate cube of *nPtr; modifies variable number in main
22  void cubeByReference( int *nPtr )
23  {
24     *nPtr = *nPtr * *nPtr * *nPtr; // cube *nPtr
25  } // end function cubeByReference
```

```
The original value of number is 5
The new value of number is 125
```

Fig. 8.7 | Pass-by-reference with a pointer argument used to cube a variable's value.

function prototypes. Parameter names included for documentation purposes are ignored by the compiler.

Figures 8.8–8.9 analyze graphically the execution of the programs in Fig. 8.6 and Fig. 8.7, respectively.

Software Engineering Observation 8.1

Use pass-by-value to pass arguments to a function unless the caller explicitly requires that the called function directly modify the value of the argument variable in the caller. This is another example of the principle of least privilege.

In the function header and in the prototype for a function that expects a one-dimensional array as an argument, the pointer notation in the parameter list of cubeByReference may be used. The compiler does not differentiate between a function that receives a pointer and a function that receives a one-dimensional array. This, of course, means that the function must "know" when it is receiving an array or simply a single variable for which it is to perform pass-by-reference. When the compiler encounters a function parameter for a one-dimensional array of the form int b[], the compiler converts the parameter to the pointer notation int *b (pronounced "b is a pointer to an integer"). Both forms of declaring a function parameter as a one-dimensional array are interchangeable.

Step 1: Before `main` calls `cubeByValue`:

```
int main()                              number       int cubeByValue( int n )
{                                                     {
   int number = 5;                        5              return n * n * n;
                                                      }
   number = cubeByValue( number );                                        n
}
                                                                    undefined
```

Step 2: After `cubeByValue` receives the call:

```
int main()                              number       int cubeByValue( int n )
{                                                     {
   int number = 5;                        5              return n * n * n;
                                                      }
   number = cubeByValue( number );                                        n
}
                                                                          5
```

Step 3: After `cubeByValue` cubes parameter `n` and before `cubeByValue` returns to `main`:

```
int main()                              number       int cubeByValue( int n )
{                                                     {                  125
   int number = 5;                        5              return n * n * n;
                                                      }
   number = cubeByValue( number );                                        n
}                                                                         5
```

Step 4: After `cubeByValue` returns to `main` and before assigning the result to `number`:

```
int main()                              number       int cubeByValue( int n )
{                                                     {
   int number = 5;                        5              return n * n * n;
                    125                               }
   number = cubeByValue( number );                                        n
}
                                                                    undefined
```

Step 5: After `main` completes the assignment to `number`:

```
int main()                              number       int cubeByValue( int n )
{                                                     {
   int number = 5;                       125             return n * n * n;
      125              125                            }
   number = cubeByValue( number );                                        n
}
                                                                    undefined
```

Fig. 8.8 | Pass-by-value analysis of the program of Fig. 8.6.

Step 1: Before `main` calls `cubeByReference`:

```
int main()                          number
{
    int number = 5;                  5

    cubeByReference( &number );
}
```

```
void cubeByReference( int *nPtr )
{
    *nPtr = *nPtr * *nPtr * *nPtr;
}
                                    nPtr

                                 undefined
```

Step 2: After `cubeByReference` receives the call and before `*nPtr` is cubed:

```
int main()                          number
{
    int number = 5;                  5

    cubeByReference( &number );
}
```

```
void cubeByReference( int *nPtr )
{
    *nPtr = *nPtr * *nPtr * *nPtr;
}
                                    nPtr

call establishes this pointer
```

Step 3: After `*nPtr` is cubed and before program control returns to `main`:

```
int main()                          number
{
    int number = 5;                 125

    cubeByReference( &number );
}
```

```
void cubeByReference( int *nPtr )
{                        125

    *nPtr = *nPtr * *nPtr * *nPtr;
}
                                    nPtr
called function modifies caller's
variable
```

Fig. 8.9 | Pass-by-reference analysis (with a pointer argument) of the program of Fig. 8.7.

8.5 Using const with Pointers

Recall that the const qualifier enables the programmer to inform the compiler that the value of a particular variable should not be modified.

Portability Tip 8.2

Although const is well defined in ANSI C and C++, some compilers do not enforce it properly. So a good rule is, "Know your compiler."

Over the years, a large base of legacy code was written in early versions of C that did not use const, because it was not available. For this reason, there are great opportunities for improvement in the software engineering of old (also called "legacy") C code. Also, many programmers currently using ANSI C and C++ do not use const in their programs, because they began programming in early versions of C. These programmers are missing many opportunities for good software engineering.

Many possibilities exist for using (or not using) const with function parameters. How do you choose the most appropriate of these possibilities? Let the principle of least privilege be your guide. Always award a function enough access to the data in its parameters to accomplish its specified task, but no more. This section discusses how to combine const with pointer declarations to enforce the principle of least privilege.

Chapter 6 explained that when a function is called using pass-by-value, a copy of the argument (or arguments) in the function call is made and passed to the function. If the copy is modified in the function, the original value is maintained in the caller without change. In many cases, a value passed to a function is modified so the function can accomplish its task. However, in some instances, the value should not be altered in the called function, even though the called function manipulates only a copy of the original value.

For example, consider a function that takes a one-dimensional array and its size as arguments and subsequently prints the array. Such a function should loop through the array and output each array element individually. The size of the array is used in the function body to determine the highest subscript of the array so the loop can terminate when the printing completes. The size of the array does not change in the function body, so it should be declared const. Of course, because the array is only being printed, it, too, should be declared const. This is especially important because an entire array is *always* passed by reference and could easily be changed in the called function.

Software Engineering Observation 8.2

If a value does not (or should not) change in the body of a function to which it is passed, the parameter should be declared const to ensure that it is not accidentally modified.

If an attempt is made to modify a const value, a warning or an error is issued, depending on the particular compiler.

Error-Prevention Tip 8.2

Before using a function, check its function prototype to determine the parameters that it can modify.

There are four ways to pass a pointer to a function: a nonconstant pointer to nonconstant data (Fig. 8.10), a nonconstant pointer to constant data (Fig. 8.11 and Fig. 8.12), a constant pointer to nonconstant data (Fig. 8.13) and a constant pointer to constant data (Fig. 8.14). Each combination provides a different level of access privileges.

Nonconstant Pointer to Nonconstant Data
The highest access is granted by a nonconstant pointer to nonconstant data—the data can be modified through the dereferenced pointer, and the pointer can be modified to point to other data. The declaration for a nonconstant pointer to nonconstant data does not include const. Such a pointer can be used to receive a null-terminated string in a function that changes the pointer value to process (and possibly modify) each character in the string. Recall from Section 7.4 that a null-terminated string can be placed in a character array that contains the characters of the string and a null character indicating where the string ends.

In Fig. 8.10, function convertToUppercase (lines 25–34) declares parameter sPtr (line 25) to be a nonconstant pointer to nonconstant data (again, const is not used). The function processes one character at a time from the null-terminated string stored in character array phrase (lines 27–33). Keep in mind that a character array's name is really equivalent to a pointer to the first character of the array, so passing phrase as an argument to convertToUppercase is possible. Function islower (line 29) takes a character argument

```cpp
1   // Fig. 8.10: fig08_10.cpp
2   // Converting lowercase letters to uppercase letters
3   // using a non-constant pointer to non-constant data.
4   #include <iostream>
5   using std::cout;
6   using std::endl;
7
8   #include <cctype> // prototypes for islower and toupper
9   using std::islower;
10  using std::toupper;
11
12  void convertToUppercase( char * );
13
14  int main()
15  {
16     char phrase[] = "characters and $32.98";
17
18     cout << "The phrase before conversion is: " << phrase;
19     convertToUppercase( phrase );
20     cout << "\nThe phrase after conversion is:  " << phrase << endl;
21     return 0; // indicates successful termination
22  } // end main
23
24  // convert string to uppercase letters
25  void convertToUppercase( char *sPtr )
26  {
27     while ( *sPtr != '\0' ) // loop while current character is not '\0'
28     {
29        if ( islower( *sPtr ) ) // if character is lowercase,
30           *sPtr = toupper( *sPtr ); // convert to uppercase
31
32        sPtr++; // move sPtr to next character in string
33     } // end while
34  } // end function convertToUppercase
```

```
The phrase before conversion is: characters and $32.98
The phrase after conversion is:  CHARACTERS AND $32.98
```

Fig. 8.10 | Converting a string to uppercase.

and returns true if the character is a lowercase letter and false otherwise. Characters in the range 'a' through 'z' are converted to their corresponding uppercase letters by function toupper (line 30); others remain unchanged—function toupper takes one character as an argument. If the character is a lowercase letter, the corresponding uppercase letter is returned; otherwise, the original character is returned. Function toupper and function islower are part of the character-handling library <cctype>. After processing one character, line 32 increments sPtr by 1 (this would not be possible if sPtr were declared const). When operator ++ is applied to a pointer that points to an array, the memory address stored in the pointer is modified to point to the next element of the array (in this case, the next character in the string). Adding one to a pointer is one valid operation in pointer arithmetic, which is covered in detail in Section 8.8 and Section 8.9.

Nonconstant Pointer to Constant Data

A nonconstant pointer to constant data is a pointer that can be modified to point to any data item of the appropriate type, but the data to which it points cannot be modified through that pointer. Such a pointer might be used to receive an array argument to a function that will process each element of the array, but should not be allowed to modify the data. For example, function printCharacters (lines 22–26 of Fig. 8.11) declares parameter sPtr (line 22) to be of type const char *, so that it can receive a null-terminated pointer-based string. The declaration is read from right to left as "sPtr is a pointer to a character constant." The body of the function uses a for statement (lines 24–25) to output each character in the string until the null character is encountered. After each character is printed, pointer sPtr is incremented to point to the next character in the string (this works because the pointer is not const). Function main creates char array phrase to be passed to printCharacters. Again, we can pass the array phrase to printCharacters because the name of the array is really a pointer to the first character in the array.

Figure 8.12 demonstrates the compilation error messages produced when attempting to compile a function that receives a nonconstant pointer to constant data, then tries to use that pointer to modify the data. [*Note:* Remember that compiler error messages vary among compilers.]

```cpp
1   // Fig. 8.11: fig08_11.cpp
2   // Printing a string one character at a time using
3   // a non-constant pointer to constant data.
4   #include <iostream>
5   using std::cout;
6   using std::endl;
7
8   void printCharacters( const char * ); // print using pointer to const data
9
10  int main()
11  {
12     const char phrase[] = "print characters of a string";
13
14     cout << "The string is:\n";
15     printCharacters( phrase ); // print characters in phrase
16     cout << endl;
17     return 0; // indicates successful termination
18  } // end main
19
20  // sPtr can be modified, but it cannot modify the character to which
21  // it points, i.e., sPtr is a "read-only" pointer
22  void printCharacters( const char *sPtr )
23  {
24     for ( ; *sPtr != '\0'; sPtr++ ) // no initialization
25        cout << *sPtr; // display character without modification
26  } // end function printCharacters
```

```
The string is:
print characters of a string
```

Fig. 8.11 | Printing a string one character at a time using a nonconstant pointer to constant data.

```
1   // Fig. 8.12: fig08_12.cpp
2   // Attempting to modify data through a
3   // non-constant pointer to constant data.
4
5   void f( const int * ); // prototype
6
7   int main()
8   {
9      int y;
10
11     f( &y ); // f attempts illegal modification
12     return 0; // indicates successful termination
13  } // end main
14
15  // xPtr cannot modify the value of constant variable to which it points
16  void f( const int *xPtr )
17  {
18     *xPtr = 100; // error: cannot modify a const object
19  } // end function f
```

Borland C++ command-line compiler error message:

```
Error E2024 fig08_12.cpp 18:
   Cannot modify a const object in function f(const int *)
```

Microsoft Visual C++ compiler error message:

```
c:\scpphtp5_examples\ch08\Fig08_12\fig08_12.cpp(18) :
   error C2166: l-value specifies const object
```

GNU C++ compiler error message:

```
fig08_12.cpp: In function `void f(const int*)':
fig08_12.cpp:18: error: assignment of read-only location
```

Fig. 8.12 | Attempting to modify data through a nonconstant pointer to constant data.

As we know, arrays are aggregate data types that store related data items of the same type under one name. When a function is called with an array as an argument, the array is passed to the function by reference. However, objects are always passed by value—a copy of the entire object is passed. This requires the execution-time overhead of making a copy of each data item in the object and storing it on the function call stack. When an object must be passed to a function, we can use a pointer to constant data (or a reference to constant data) to get the performance of pass-by-reference and the protection of pass-by-value. When a pointer to an object is passed, only a copy of the address of the object must be made; the object itself is not copied. On a machine with four-byte addresses, a copy of four bytes of memory is made rather than a copy of a possibly large object.

Performance Tip 8.1

If they do not need to be modified by the called function, pass large objects using pointers to constant data or references to constant data, to obtain the performance benefits of pass-by-reference.

> ### Software Engineering Observation 8.3
> *Pass large objects using pointers to constant data, or references to constant data, to obtain the security of pass-by-value.*

Constant Pointer to Nonconstant Data

A constant pointer to nonconstant data is a pointer that always points to the same memory location; the data at that location can be modified through the pointer. This is the default for an array name. An array name is a constant pointer to the beginning of the array. All data in the array can be accessed and changed by using the array name and array subscripting. A constant pointer to nonconstant data can be used to receive an array as an argument to a function that accesses array elements using array subscript notation. Pointers that are declared const must be initialized when they are declared. (If the pointer is a function parameter, it is initialized with a pointer that is passed to the function.) The program of Fig. 8.13 attempts to modify a constant pointer. Line 11 declares pointer ptr to be of type int * const. The declaration in the figure is read from right to left as "ptr is a constant pointer to a nonconstant integer." The pointer is initialized with the address of integer variable x. Line 14 attempts to assign the address of y to ptr, but the compiler generates an error message. Note that no error occurs when line 13 assigns the value 7 to

```
1   // Fig. 8.13: fig08_13.cpp
2   // Attempting to modify a constant pointer to non-constant data.
3
4   int main()
5   {
6      int x, y;
7
8      // ptr is a constant pointer to an integer that can
9      // be modified through ptr, but ptr always points to the
10     // same memory location.
11     int * const ptr = &x; // const pointer must be initialized
12
13     *ptr = 7; // allowed: *ptr is not const
14     ptr = &y; // error: ptr is const; cannot assign to it a new address
15     return 0; // indicates successful termination
16  } // end main
```

Borland C++ command-line compiler error message:

```
Error E2024 fig08_13.cpp 14: Cannot modify a const object in function main()s
```

Microsoft Visual C++ compiler error message:

```
c:\scpphtp5_examples\ch08\Fig08_13\fig08_13.cpp(14) : error C2166:
   l-value specifies const object
```

GNU C++ compiler error message:

```
fig08_13.cpp: In function `int main()':
fig08_13.cpp:14: error: assignment of read-only variable `ptr'
```

Fig. 8.13 | Attempting to modify a constant pointer to nonconstant data.

*ptr—the nonconstant value to which ptr points can be modified using the dereferenced ptr, even though ptr itself has been declared const.

Common Programming Error 8.6

Not initializing a pointer that is declared const is a compilation error.

Constant Pointer to Constant Data

The least amount of access privilege is granted by a constant pointer to constant data. Such a pointer always points to the same memory location, and the data at that memory location cannot be modified using the pointer. This is how an array should be passed to a function that only reads the array, using array subscript notation, and does not modify the array. The program of Fig. 8.14 declares pointer variable ptr to be of type const int * const (line 14). This declaration is read from right to left as "ptr is a constant pointer to an integer constant." The figure shows the error messages generated when an attempt is

```
 1   // Fig. 8.14: fig08_14.cpp
 2   // Attempting to modify a constant pointer to constant data.
 3   #include <iostream>
 4   using std::cout;
 5   using std::endl;
 6
 7   int main()
 8   {
 9      int x = 5, y;
10
11      // ptr is a constant pointer to a constant integer.
12      // ptr always points to the same location; the integer
13      // at that location cannot be modified.
14      const int *const ptr = &x;
15
16      cout << *ptr << endl;
17
18      *ptr = 7; // error: *ptr is const; cannot assign new value
19      ptr = &y; // error: ptr is const; cannot assign new address
20      return 0; // indicates successful termination
21   } // end main
```

Borland C++ command-line compiler error message:

```
Error E2024 fig08_14.cpp 18: Cannot modify a const object in function main()
Error E2024 fig08_14.cpp 19: Cannot modify a const object in function main()
```

Microsoft Visual C++ compiler error message:

```
c:\scpphtp5_examples\ch08\Fig08_14\fig08_14.cpp(18) : error C2166:
   l-value specifies const object
c:\scpphtp5_examples\ch08\Fig08_14\fig08_14.cpp(19) : error C2166:
   l-value specifies const object
```

Fig. 8.14 | Attempting to modify a constant pointer to constant data. (Part 1 of 2.)

GNU C++ compiler error message:

```
fig08_14.cpp: In function `int main()':
fig08_14.cpp:18: error: assignment of read-only location
fig08_14.cpp:19: error: assignment of read-only variable `ptr'
```

Fig. 8.14 | Attempting to modify a constant pointer to constant data. (Part 2 of 2.)

made to modify the data to which ptr points (line 18) and when an attempt is made to modify the address stored in the pointer variable (line 19). Note that no errors occur when the program attempts to dereference ptr, or when the program attempts to output the value to which ptr points (line 16), because neither the pointer nor the data it points to is being modified in this statement.

8.6 Selection Sort Using Pass-by-Reference

In this section, we define a sorting program to demonstrate passing arrays and individual array elements by reference. We use the selection sort algorithm, which is an easy-to-program, but unfortunately inefficient, sorting algorithm. The first iteration of the algorithm selects the smallest element in the array and swaps it with the first element. The second iteration selects the second-smallest element (which is the smallest element of the remaining elements) and swaps it with the second element. The algorithm continues until the last iteration selects the second-largest element and swaps it with the second-to-last index, leaving the largest element in the last index. After the ith iteration, the smallest i items of the array will be sorted into increasing order in the first i elements of the array.

As an example, consider the array

34	56	4	10	77	51	93	30	5	52

A program that implements selection sort first determines the smallest element (4) of this array, which is contained in element 2. The program swaps the 4 with the element 0 (34), resulting in

4	56	**34**	10	77	51	93	30	5	52

[*Note:* We use bold to highlight the values that were swapped.] The program then determines the smallest value of the remaining elements (all elements except 4), which is 5, contained in element 8. The program swaps the 5 with the element 1 (56), resulting in

4	**5**	34	10	77	51	93	30	**56**	52

On the third iteration, the program determines the next smallest value (10) and swaps it with the element 2 (34).

4	5	**10**	**34**	77	51	93	30	56	52

The process continues until the array is fully sorted.

4	5	10	30	34	51	52	56	77	93

Note that after the first iteration, the smallest element is in the first position. After the second iteration, the two smallest elements are in order in the first two positions. After the third iteration, the three smallest elements are in order in the first three positions.

Figure 8.15 implements selection sort using two functions—selectionSort and swap. Function selectionSort (lines 36–53) sorts the array. Line 38 declares the variable smallest, which will store the index of the smallest element in the remaining array. Lines 41–52 loop size - 1 times. Line 43 sets the index of the smallest element to the current index. Lines 46–49 loop over the remaining elements in the array. For each of these elements, line 48 compares its value to the value of the smallest element. If the current element is smaller than the smallest element, line 49 assigns the current element's index to smallest. When this loop finishes, smallest will contain the index of the smallest element in the remaining array. Line 51 calls function swap (lines 57–62) to place the smallest remaining element in the next spot in the array (i.e., exchange the array elements array[i] and array[smallest]).

Let us now look more closely at function swap. Remember that C++ enforces information hiding between functions, so swap does not have access to individual array elements in selectionSort. Because selectionSort *wants* swap to have access to the array elements to be swapped, selectionSort passes each of these elements to swap by refer-

```
1   // Fig. 8.15: fig08_15.cpp
2   // This program puts values into an array, sorts the values into
3   // ascending order and prints the resulting array.
4   #include <iostream>
5   using std::cout;
6   using std::endl;
7
8   #include <iomanip>
9   using std::setw;
10
11  void selectionSort( int * const, const int ); // prototype
12  void swap( int * const, int * const ); // prototype
13
14  int main()
15  {
16     const int arraySize = 10;
17     int a[ arraySize ] = { 2, 6, 4, 8, 10, 12, 89, 68, 45, 37 };
18
19     cout << "Data items in original order\n";
20
21     for ( int i = 0; i < arraySize; i++ )
22        cout << setw( 4 ) << a[ i ];
23
24     selectionSort( a, arraySize ); // sort the array
25
26     cout << "\nData items in ascending order\n";
27
28     for ( int j = 0; j < arraySize; j++ )
29        cout << setw( 4 ) << a[ j ];
30
31     cout << endl;
32     return 0; // indicates successful termination
33  } // end main
```

Fig. 8.15 | Selection sort with pass-by-reference. (Part 1 of 2.)

```
34
35   // function to sort an array
36   void selectionSort( int * const array, const int size )
37   {
38      int smallest; // index of smallest element
39
40      // loop over size - 1 elements
41      for ( int i = 0; i < size - 1; i++ )
42      {
43         smallest = i; // first index of remaining array
44
45         // loop to find index of smallest element
46         for ( int index = i + 1; index < size; index++ )
47
48            if ( array[ index ] < array[ smallest ] )
49               smallest = index;
50
51         swap( &array[ i ], &array[ smallest ] );
52      } // end if
53   } // end function selectionSort
54
55   // swap values at memory locations to which
56   // element1Ptr and element2Ptr point
57   void swap( int * const element1Ptr, int * const element2Ptr )
58   {
59      int hold = *element1Ptr;
60      *element1Ptr = *element2Ptr;
61      *element2Ptr = hold;
62   } // end function swap
```

```
Data items in original order
   2   6   4   8  10  12  89  68  45  37
Data items in ascending order
   2   4   6   8  10  12  37  45  68  89
```

Fig. 8.15 | Selection sort with pass-by-reference. (Part 2 of 2.)

ence—the address of each array element is passed explicitly. Although entire arrays are passed by reference, individual array elements are scalars and are ordinarily passed by value. Therefore, selectionSort uses the address operator (&) on each array element in the swap call (line 51) to effect pass-by-reference. Function swap (lines 57–62) receives &array[i] in pointer variable element1Ptr. Information hiding prevents swap from "knowing" the name array[i], but swap can use *element1Ptr as a synonym for array[i]. Thus, when swap references *element1Ptr, it is actually referencing array[i] in selectionSort. Similarly, when swap references *element2Ptr, it is actually referencing array[smallest] in selectionSort.

Even though swap is not allowed to use the statements

```
hold = array[ i ];
array[ i ] = array[ smallest ];
array[ smallest ] = hold;
```

precisely the same effect is achieved by

```
int hold = *element1Ptr;
*element1Ptr = *element2Ptr;
*element2Ptr = hold;
```

in the swap function of Fig. 8.15.

Several features of function selectionSort should be noted. The function header (line 36) declares array as int * const array, rather than int array[], to indicate that function selectionSort receives a one-dimensional array as an argument. Both parameter array's pointer and parameter size are declared const to enforce the principle of least privilege. Although parameter size receives a copy of a value in main and modifying the copy cannot change the value in main, selectionSort does not need to alter size to accomplish its task—the array size remains fixed during the execution of selectionSort. Therefore, size is declared const to ensure that it is not modified. If the size of the array were to be modified during the sorting process, the sorting algorithm would not run correctly.

Note that function selectionSort receives the size of the array as a parameter, because the function must have that information to sort the array. When a pointer-based array is passed to a function, only the memory address of the first element of the array is received by the function; the array size must be passed separately to the function.

By defining function selectionSort to receive the array size as a parameter, we enable the function to be used by any program that sorts one-dimensional int arrays of arbitrary size. The size of the array could have been programmed directly into the function, but this would restrict the function to processing an array of a specific size and reduce the function's reusability—only programs processing one-dimensional int arrays of the specific size "hard coded" into the function could use the function.

Software Engineering Observation 8.4

When passing an array to a function, also pass the size of the array (rather than building into the function knowledge of the array size). This makes the function more reusable.

8.7 sizeof Operators

C++ provides the unary operator sizeof to determine the size of an array (or of any other data type, variable or constant) in bytes during program compilation. When applied to the name of an array, as in Fig. 8.16 (line 14), the sizeof operator returns the total number of bytes in the array as a value of type size_t (an alias for unsigned int on most compilers). Note that this is different from the size of a vector< int >, for example, which is the number of integer elements in the vector. The computer we used to compile this program stores variables of type double in 8 bytes of memory, and array is declared to have 20 elements (line 12), so array uses 160 bytes in memory. When applied to a pointer parameter (line 24) in a function that receives an array as an argument, the sizeof operator returns the size of the pointer in bytes (4), not the size of the array.

Common Programming Error 8.7

Using the sizeof operator in a function to find the size in bytes of an array parameter results in the size in bytes of a pointer, not the size in bytes of the array.

```
 1   // Fig. 8.16: fig08_16.cpp
 2   // Sizeof operator when used on an array name
 3   // returns the number of bytes in the array.
 4   #include <iostream>
 5   using std::cout;
 6   using std::endl;
 7
 8   size_t getSize( double * ); // prototype
 9
10   int main()
11   {
12      double array[ 20 ]; // 20 doubles; occupies 160 bytes on our system
13
14      cout << "The number of bytes in the array is " << sizeof( array );
15
16      cout << "\nThe number of bytes returned by getSize is "
17         << getSize( array ) << endl;
18      return 0; // indicates successful termination
19   } // end main
20
21   // return size of ptr
22   size_t getSize( double *ptr )
23   {
24      return sizeof( ptr );
25   } // end function getSize
```

```
The number of bytes in the array is 160
The number of bytes returned by getSize is 4
```

Fig. 8.16 | `sizeof` operator when applied to an array name returns the number of bytes in the array.

[*Note:* When the Borland C++ compiler is used to compile Fig. 8.16, the compiler generates the warning message "Parameter 'ptr' is never used in function get-Size(double *)." This warning occurs because `sizeof` is actually a compile-time operator; thus, variable `ptr` is not used in the function's body at execution time. Many compilers issue warnings like this to let you know that a variable is not being used so that you can either remove it from your code or modify your code to use the variable properly. Similar messages occur in Fig. 8.17 with various compilers.]

The number of elements in an array also can be determined using the results of two `sizeof` operations. For example, consider the following array declaration:

```
double realArray[ 22 ];
```

If variables of data type `double` are stored in eight bytes of memory, array `realArray` contains a total of 176 bytes. To determine the number of elements in the array, the following expression can be used:

```
sizeof realArray / sizeof( double ) // calculate number of elements
```

The expression determines the number of bytes in array `realArray` (176) and divides that value by the number of bytes used in memory to store a `double` value (8); the result is the number of elements in `realArray` (22).

Determining the Sizes of the Fundamental Types, an Array and a Pointer
The program of Fig. 8.17 uses the sizeof operator to calculate the number of bytes used to store most of the standard data types. Notice that, in the output, the types double and long double have the same size. Types may have different sizes based on the system the

```cpp
1   // Fig. 8.17: fig08_17.cpp
2   // Demonstrating the sizeof operator.
3   #include <iostream>
4   using std::cout;
5   using std::endl;
6
7   int main()
8   {
9      char c; // variable of type char
10     short s; // variable of type short
11     int i; // variable of type int
12     long l; // variable of type long
13     float f; // variable of type float
14     double d; // variable of type double
15     long double ld; // variable of type long double
16     int array[ 20 ]; // array of int
17     int *ptr = array; // variable of type int *
18
19     cout << "sizeof c = " << sizeof c
20        << "\tsizeof(char) = " << sizeof( char )
21        << "\nsizeof s = " << sizeof s
22        << "\tsizeof(short) = " << sizeof( short )
23        << "\nsizeof i = " << sizeof i
24        << "\tsizeof(int) = " << sizeof( int )
25        << "\nsizeof l = " << sizeof l
26        << "\tsizeof(long) = " << sizeof( long )
27        << "\nsizeof f = " << sizeof f
28        << "\tsizeof(float) = " << sizeof( float )
29        << "\nsizeof d = " << sizeof d
30        << "\tsizeof(double) = " << sizeof( double )
31        << "\nsizeof ld = " << sizeof ld
32        << "\tsizeof(long double) = " << sizeof( long double )
33        << "\nsizeof array = " << sizeof array
34        << "\nsizeof ptr = " << sizeof ptr << endl;
35     return 0; // indicates successful termination
36  } // end main
```

```
sizeof c = 1      sizeof(char) = 1
sizeof s = 2      sizeof(short) = 2
sizeof i = 4      sizeof(int) = 4
sizeof l = 4      sizeof(long) = 4
sizeof f = 4      sizeof(float) = 4
sizeof d = 8      sizeof(double) = 8
sizeof ld = 8     sizeof(long double) = 8
sizeof array = 80
sizeof ptr = 4
```

Fig. 8.17 | sizeof operator used to determine standard data type sizes.

program is run on. On another system, for example, double and long double may be defined to be of different sizes.

Portability Tip 8.3

The number of bytes used to store a particular data type may vary between systems. When writing programs that depend on data type sizes, and that will run on several computer systems, use sizeof to determine the number of bytes used to store the data types.

Operator sizeof can be applied to any variable name, type name or constant value. When sizeof is applied to a variable name (which is not an array name) or a constant value, the number of bytes used to store the specific type of variable or constant is returned. Note that the parentheses used with sizeof are required only if a type name (e.g., int) is supplied as its operand. The parentheses used with sizeof are not required when sizeof's operand is a variable name or constant. Remember that sizeof is an operator, not a function, and that it has its effect at compile time, not execution time.

Common Programming Error 8.8

Omitting the parentheses in a sizeof operation when the operand is a type name is a compilation error.

Performance Tip 8.2

Because sizeof is a compile-time unary operator, not an execution-time operator, using sizeof does not negatively impact execution performance.

Error-Prevention Tip 8.3

To avoid errors associated with omitting the parentheses around the operand of operator sizeof, many programmers include parentheses around every sizeof operand.

8.8 Pointer Expressions and Pointer Arithmetic

Pointers are valid operands in arithmetic expressions, assignment expressions and comparison expressions. However, not all the operators normally used in these expressions are valid with pointer variables. This section describes the operators that can have pointers as operands and how these operators are used with pointers.

Several arithmetic operations may be performed on pointers. A pointer may be incremented (++) or decremented (--), an integer may be added to a pointer (+ or +=), an integer may be subtracted from a pointer (- or -=) or one pointer may be subtracted from another.

Assume that array int v[5] has been declared and that its first element is at memory location 3000. Assume that pointer vPtr has been initialized to point to v[0] (i.e., the value of vPtr is 3000). Figure 8.18 diagrams this situation for a machine with four-byte integers. Note that vPtr can be initialized to point to array v with either of the following statements (because the name of an array is equivalent to the address of its first element):

```
int *vPtr = v;
int *vPtr = &v[ 0 ];
```

Portability Tip 8.4

Most computers today have two-byte or four-byte integers. Some of the newer machines use eight-byte integers. Because the results of pointer arithmetic depend on the size of the objects a pointer points to, pointer arithmetic is machine dependent.

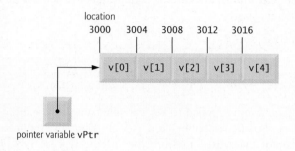

Fig. 8.18 | Array v and a pointer variable vPtr that points to v.

In conventional arithmetic, the addition 3000 + 2 yields the value 3002. This is normally not the case with pointer arithmetic. When an integer is added to, or subtracted from, a pointer, the pointer is not simply incremented or decremented by that integer, but by that integer times the size of the object to which the pointer refers. The number of bytes depends on the object's data type. For example, the statement

```
vPtr += 2;
```

would produce 3008 (3000 + 2 * 4), assuming that an int is stored in four bytes of memory. In the array v, vPtr would now point to v[2] (Fig. 8.19). If an integer is stored in two bytes of memory, then the preceding calculation would result in memory location 3004 (3000 + 2 * 2). If the array were of a different data type, the preceding statement would increment the pointer by twice the number of bytes it takes to store an object of that data type. When performing pointer arithmetic on a character array, the results will be consistent with regular arithmetic, because each character is one byte long.

If vPtr had been incremented to 3016, which points to v[4], the statement

```
vPtr -= 4;
```

would set vPtr back to 3000—the beginning of the array. If a pointer is being incremented or decremented by one, the increment (++) and decrement (--) operators can be used. Each of the statements

```
++vPtr;
vPtr++;
```

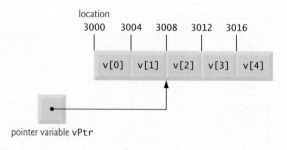

Fig. 8.19 | Pointer vPtr after pointer arithmetic.

increments the pointer to point to the next element of the array. Each of the statements

```
--vPtr;
vPtr--;
```

decrements the pointer to point to the previous element of the array.

Pointer variables pointing to the same array may be subtracted from one another. For example, if vPtr contains the location 3000 and v2Ptr contains the address 3008, the statement

```
x = v2Ptr - vPtr;
```

would assign to x the number of array elements from vPtr to v2Ptr—in this case, 2. Pointer arithmetic is meaningless unless performed on a pointer that points to an array. We cannot assume that two variables of the same type are stored contiguously in memory unless they are adjacent elements of an array.

Common Programming Error 8.9

Using pointer arithmetic on a pointer that does not refer to an array of values is a logic error.

Common Programming Error 8.10

Subtracting or comparing two pointers that do not refer to elements of the same array is a logic error.

Common Programming Error 8.11

Using pointer arithmetic to increment or decrement a pointer such that the pointer refers to an element past the end of the array or before the beginning of the array is normally a logic error.

A pointer can be assigned to another pointer if both pointers are of the same type. Otherwise, a cast operator must be used to convert the value of the pointer on the right of the assignment to the pointer type on the left of the assignment. The exception to this rule is the pointer to void (i.e., void *), which is a generic pointer capable of representing any pointer type. All pointer types can be assigned to a pointer of type void * without casting. However, a pointer of type void * cannot be assigned directly to a pointer of another type—the pointer of type void * must first be cast to the proper pointer type.

Software Engineering Observation 8.5

Nonconstant pointer arguments can be passed to constant pointer parameters. This is helpful when the body of a program uses a nonconstant pointer to access data, but does not want that data to be modified by a function called in the body of the program.

A void * pointer cannot be dereferenced. For example, the compiler "knows" that a pointer to int refers to four bytes of memory on a machine with four-byte integers, but a pointer to void simply contains a memory address for an unknown data type—the precise number of bytes to which the pointer refers and the type of the data are not known by the compiler. The compiler must know the data type to determine the number of bytes to be dereferenced for a particular pointer—for a pointer to void, this number of bytes cannot be determined from the type.

Common Programming Error 8.12

*Assigning a pointer of one type to a pointer of another (other than void *) without casting the first pointer to the type of the second pointer is a compilation error.*

Common Programming Error 8.13

*All operations on a void * pointer are compilation errors, except comparing void * pointers with other pointers, casting void * pointers to valid pointer types and assigning addresses to void * pointers.*

Pointers can be compared using equality and relational operators. Comparisons using relational operators are meaningless unless the pointers point to members of the same array. Pointer comparisons compare the addresses stored in the pointers. A comparison of two pointers pointing to the same array could show, for example, that one pointer points to a higher numbered element of the array than the other pointer does. A common use of pointer comparison is determining whether a pointer is 0 (i.e., the pointer is a null pointer—it does not point to anything).

8.9 Relationship Between Pointers and Arrays

Arrays and pointers are intimately related in C++ and may be used *almost* interchangeably. An array name can be thought of as a constant pointer. Pointers can be used to do any operation involving array subscripting.

Assume the following declarations:

```
int b[ 5 ]; // create 5-element int array b
int *bPtr; // create int pointer bPtr
```

Because the array name (without a subscript) is a (constant) pointer to the first element of the array, we can set bPtr to the address of the first element in array b with the statement

```
bPtr = b; // assign address of array b to bPtr
```

This is equivalent to taking the address of the first element of the array as follows:

```
bPtr = &b[ 0 ]; // also assigns address of array b to bPtr
```

Array element b[3] can alternatively be referenced with the pointer expression

```
*( bPtr + 3 )
```

The 3 in the preceding expression is the offset to the pointer. When the pointer points to the beginning of an array, the offset indicates which element of the array should be referenced, and the offset value is identical to the array subscript. The preceding notation is referred to as pointer/offset notation. The parentheses are necessary, because the precedence of * is higher than the precedence of +. Without the parentheses, the above expression would add 3 to the value of *bPtr (i.e., 3 would be added to b[0], assuming that bPtr points to the beginning of the array). Just as the array element can be referenced with a pointer expression, the address

```
&b[ 3 ]
```

can be written with the pointer expression

```
bPtr + 3
```

The array name can be treated as a pointer and used in pointer arithmetic. For example, the expression

```
*( b + 3 )
```

also refers to the array element b[3]. In general, all subscripted array expressions can be written with a pointer and an offset. In this case, pointer/offset notation was used with the name of the array as a pointer. Note that the preceding expression does not modify the array name in any way; b still points to the first element in the array.

Pointers can be subscripted exactly as arrays can. For example, the expression

```
bPtr[ 1 ]
```

refers to the array element b[1]; this expression uses pointer/subscript notation.

Remember that an array name is a constant pointer; it always points to the beginning of the array. Thus, the expression

```
b += 3
```

causes a compilation error, because it attempts to modify the value of the array name (a constant) with pointer arithmetic.

Common Programming Error 8.14

Although array names are pointers to the beginning of the array and pointers can be modified in arithmetic expressions, array names cannot be modified in arithmetic expressions, because array names are constant pointers.

Good Programming Practice 8.2

For clarity, use array notation instead of pointer notation when manipulating arrays.

Figure 8.20 uses the four notations discussed in this section for referring to array elements—array subscript notation, pointer/offset notation with the array name as a pointer, pointer subscript notation and pointer/offset notation with a pointer—to accomplish the same task, namely printing the four elements of the integer array b.

```cpp
1   // Fig. 8.20: fig08_20.cpp
2   // Using subscripting and pointer notations with arrays.
3   #include <iostream>
4   using std::cout;
5   using std::endl;
6
7   int main()
8   {
9       int b[] = { 10, 20, 30, 40 }; // create 4-element array b
10      int *bPtr = b; // set bPtr to point to array b
11
12      // output array b using array subscript notation
13      cout << "Array b printed with:\n\nArray subscript notation\n";
```

Fig. 8.20 | Referencing array elements with the array name and with pointers. (Part 1 of 2.)

```
14
15      for ( int i = 0; i < 4; i++ )
16         cout << "b[" << i << "] = " << b[ i ] << '\n';
17
18      // output array b using the array name and pointer/offset notation
19      cout << "\nPointer/offset notation where "
20         << "the pointer is the array name\n";
21
22      for ( int offset1 = 0; offset1 < 4; offset1++ )
23         cout << "*(b + " << offset1 << ") = " << *( b + offset1 ) << '\n';
24
25      // output array b using bPtr and array subscript notation
26      cout << "\nPointer subscript notation\n";
27
28      for ( int j = 0; j < 4; j++ )
29         cout << "bPtr[" << j << "] = " << bPtr[ j ] << '\n';
30
31      cout << "\nPointer/offset notation\n";
32
33      // output array b using bPtr and pointer/offset notation
34      for ( int offset2 = 0; offset2 < 4; offset2++ )
35         cout << "*(bPtr + " << offset2 << ") = "
36            << *( bPtr + offset2 ) << '\n';
37
38      return 0; // indicates successful termination
39   } // end main
```

```
Array b printed with:

Array subscript notation
b[0] = 10
b[1] = 20
b[2] = 30
b[3] = 40

Pointer/offset notation where the pointer is the array name
*(b + 0) = 10
*(b + 1) = 20
*(b + 2) = 30
*(b + 3) = 40

Pointer subscript notation
bPtr[0] = 10
bPtr[1] = 20
bPtr[2] = 30
bPtr[3] = 40

Pointer/offset notation
*(bPtr + 0) = 10
*(bPtr + 1) = 20
*(bPtr + 2) = 30
*(bPtr + 3) = 40
```

Fig. 8.20 | Referencing array elements with the array name and with pointers. (Part 2 of 2.)

To further illustrate the interchangeability of arrays and pointers, let us look at the two string-copying functions—copy1 and copy2—in the program of Fig. 8.21. Both functions copy a string into a character array. After a comparison of the function prototypes for copy1 and copy2, the functions appear identical (because of the interchangeability of arrays and pointers). These functions accomplish the same task, but they are implemented differently.

```cpp
 1   // Fig. 8.21: fig08_21.cpp
 2   // Copying a string using array notation and pointer notation.
 3   #include <iostream>
 4   using std::cout;
 5   using std::endl;
 6
 7   void copy1( char *, const char * ); // prototype
 8   void copy2( char *, const char * ); // prototype
 9
10   int main()
11   {
12      char string1[ 10 ];
13      char *string2 = "Hello";
14      char string3[ 10 ];
15      char string4[] = "Good Bye";
16
17      copy1( string1, string2 ); // copy string2 into string1
18      cout << "string1 = " << string1 << endl;
19
20      copy2( string3, string4 ); // copy string4 into string3
21      cout << "string3 = " << string3 << endl;
22      return 0; // indicates successful termination
23   } // end main
24
25   // copy s2 to s1 using array notation
26   void copy1( char * s1, const char * s2 )
27   {
28      // copying occurs in the for header
29      for ( int i = 0; ( s1[ i ] = s2[ i ] ) != '\0'; i++ )
30         ; // do nothing in body
31   } // end function copy1
32
33   // copy s2 to s1 using pointer notation
34   void copy2( char *s1, const char *s2 )
35   {
36      // copying occurs in the for header
37      for ( ; ( *s1 = *s2 ) != '\0'; s1++, s2++ )
38         ; // do nothing in body
39   } // end function copy2
```

```
string1 = Hello
string3 = Good Bye
```

Fig. 8.21 | String copying using array notation and pointer notation.

Function copy1 (lines 26–31) uses array subscript notation to copy the string in s2 to the character array s1. The function declares an integer counter variable i to use as the array subscript. The for statement header (line 29) performs the entire copy operation— its body is the empty statement. The header specifies that i is initialized to zero and incremented by one on each iteration of the loop. The condition in the for, (s1[i] = s2[i]) != '\0', performs the copy operation character by character from s2 to s1. When the null character is encountered in s2, it is assigned to s1, and the loop terminates, because the null character is equal to '\0'. Remember that the value of an assignment statement is the value assigned to its left operand.

Function copy2 (lines 34–39) uses pointers and pointer arithmetic to copy the string in s2 to the character array s1. Again, the for statement header (line 37) performs the entire copy operation. The header does not include any variable initialization. As in function copy1, the condition (*s1 = *s2) != '\0' performs the copy operation. Pointer s2 is dereferenced, and the resulting character is assigned to the dereferenced pointer s1. After the assignment in the condition, the loop increments both pointers, so they point to the next element of array s1 and the next character of string s2, respectively. When the loop encounters the null character in s2, the null character is assigned to the dereferenced pointer s1 and the loop terminates. Note that the "increment portion" of this for statement has two increment expressions separated by a comma operator.

The first argument to both copy1 and copy2 must be an array large enough to hold the string in the second argument. Otherwise, an error may occur when an attempt is made to write into a memory location beyond the bounds of the array (recall that when using pointer-based arrays, there is no "built-in" bounds checking). Also, note that the second parameter of each function is declared as const char * (a pointer to a character constant—i.e., a constant string). In both functions, the second argument is copied into the first argument—characters are copied from the second argument one at a time, but the characters are never modified. Therefore, the second parameter is declared to point to a constant value to enforce the principle of least privilege—neither function needs to modify the second argument, so neither function is allowed to modify the second argument.

8.10 Arrays of Pointers

Arrays may contain pointers. A common use of such a data structure is to form an array of pointer-based strings, referred to simply as a string array. Each entry in the array is a string, but in C++ a string is essentially a pointer to its first character, so each entry in an array of strings is simply a pointer to the first character of a string. Consider the declaration of string array suit that might be useful in representing a deck of cards:

```
const char *suit[ 4 ] =
    { "Hearts", "Diamonds", "Clubs", "Spades" };
```

The suit[4] portion of the declaration indicates an array of four elements. The const char * portion of the declaration indicates that each element of array suit is of type "pointer to char constant data." The four values to be placed in the array are "Hearts", "Diamonds", "Clubs" and "Spades". Each is stored in memory as a null-terminated character string that is one character longer than the number of characters between quotes. The four strings are seven, nine, six and seven characters long (including their terminating null characters), respectively. Although it appears as though these strings are being placed in the suit array, only pointers are actually stored in the array, as shown in Fig. 8.22. Each pointer points to the first character of its corresponding string. Thus, even though the suit array is fixed in size, it provides access to character strings of any length. This flexibility is one example of C++'s powerful data-structuring capabilities.

The suit strings could be placed into a two-dimensional array, in which each row represents one suit and each column represents one of the letters of a suit name. Such a data structure must have a fixed number of columns per row, and that number must be as large as the largest string. Therefore, considerable memory is wasted when we store a large number of strings, of which most are shorter than the longest string. We use arrays of strings to help represent a deck of cards in the next section.

String arrays are commonly used with command-line arguments that are passed to function main when a program begins execution. Such arguments follow the program name when a program is executed from the command line. A typical use of command-line arguments is to pass options to a program. For example, from the command line on a Windows computer, the user can type

```
dir /P
```

to list the contents of the current directory and pause after each screen of information. When the dir command executes, the option /P is passed to dir as a command-line argument. Such arguments are placed in a string array that main receives as an argument.

8.11 Case Study: Card Shuffling and Dealing Simulation

This section uses random-number generation to develop a card shuffling and dealing simulation program. This program can then be used as a basis for implementing programs that play specific card games. To reveal some subtle performance problems, we have intentionally used suboptimal shuffling and dealing algorithms. In the exercises, we develop more efficient algorithms.

Using the top-down, stepwise-refinement approach, we develop a program that will shuffle a deck of 52 playing cards and then deal each of the 52 cards. The top-down approach is particularly useful in attacking larger, more complex problems than we have seen in the early chapters.

We use a 4-by-13 two-dimensional array deck to represent the deck of playing cards (Fig. 8.23). The rows correspond to the suits—row 0 corresponds to hearts, row 1 to diamonds, row 2 to clubs and row 3 to spades. The columns correspond to the face values of

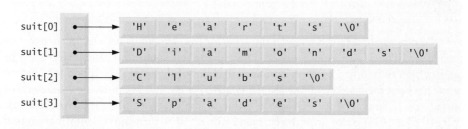

Fig. 8.22 | Graphical representation of the suit array.

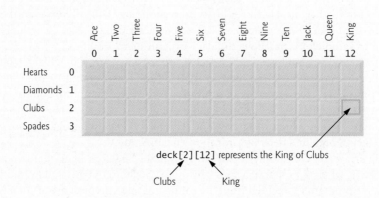

Fig. 8.23 | Two-dimensional array representation of a deck of cards.

the cards—columns 0 through 9 correspond to faces ace through 10, respectively, and columns 10 through 12 correspond to jack, queen and king, respectively. We shall load the string array `suit` with character strings representing the four suits (as in Fig. 8.22) and the string array `face` with character strings representing the 13 face values.

This simulated deck of cards may be shuffled as follows. First the array `deck` is initialized to zeros. Then, a `row` (0–3) and a `column` (0–12) are each chosen at random. The number 1 is inserted in array element `deck[ row ][ column ]` to indicate that this card is going to be the first one dealt from the shuffled deck. This process continues with the numbers 2, 3, …, 52 being randomly inserted in the `deck` array to indicate which cards are to be placed second, third, …, and 52nd in the shuffled deck. As the `deck` array begins to fill with card numbers, it is possible that a card will be selected twice (i.e., `deck[ row ][ column ]` will be nonzero when it is selected). This selection is simply ignored, and other `row`s and `column`s are repeatedly chosen at random until an unselected card is found. Eventually, the numbers 1 through 52 will occupy the 52 slots of the `deck` array. At this point, the deck of cards is fully shuffled.

This shuffling algorithm could execute for an indefinitely long period if cards that have already been shuffled are repeatedly selected at random. This phenomenon is known as indefinite postponement (also called starvation). In the exercises, we discuss a better shuffling algorithm that eliminates the possibility of indefinite postponement.

Performance Tip 8.3

Sometimes algorithms that emerge in a "natural" way can contain subtle performance problems such as indefinite postponement. Seek algorithms that avoid indefinite postponement.

To deal the first card, we search the array for the element `deck[ row ][ column ]` that matches 1. This is accomplished with a nested `for` statement that varies `row` from 0 to 3 and `column` from 0 to 12. What card does that slot of the array correspond to? The `suit` array has been preloaded with the four suits, so to get the suit, we print the character string `suit[ row ]`. Similarly, to get the face value of the card, we print the character string `face[ column ]`. We also print the character string `" of "`. Printing this information in the proper order enables us to print each card in the form `"King of Clubs"`, `"Ace of Diamonds"` and so on.

Let us proceed with the top-down, stepwise-refinement process. The top is simply

Shuffle and deal 52 cards

Our first refinement yields

Initialize the suit array
Initialize the face array
Initialize the deck array
Shuffle the deck
Deal 52 cards

"Shuffle the deck" may be expanded as follows:

For each of the 52 cards
    Place card number in randomly selected unoccupied slot of deck

"Deal 52 cards" may be expanded as follows:

For each of the 52 cards
    Find card number in deck array and print face and suit of card

Incorporating these expansions yields our complete second refinement:

Initialize the suit array
Initialize the face array
Initialize the deck array

For each of the 52 cards
    Place card number in randomly selected unoccupied slot of deck

For each of the 52 cards
    Find card number in deck array and print face and suit of card

"Place card number in randomly selected unoccupied slot of deck" may be expanded as follows:

Choose slot of deck randomly

While chosen slot of deck has been previously chosen
    Choose slot of deck randomly

Place card number in chosen slot of deck

"Find card number in deck array and print face and suit of card" may be expanded as follows:

For each slot of the deck array
    If slot contains card number
        Print the face and suit of the card

Incorporating these expansions yields our third refinement (Fig. 8.24):

This completes the refinement process. Figures 8.25–8.27 contain the card shuffling and dealing program and a sample execution. Lines 61–67 of function deal (Fig. 8.26) implement lines 1–2 of Fig. 8.24. The constructor (lines 22–35 of Fig. 8.26) implements lines 1–3 of Fig. 8.24. Function shuffle (lines 38–55 of Fig. 8.26) implements lines 5–11 of Fig. 8.24. Function deal (lines 58–88 of Fig. 8.26) implements lines 13–16 of Fig. 8.24. Note the output formatting used in function deal (lines 81–83 of Fig. 8.26).

```
 1   Initialize the suit array
 2   Initialize the face array
 3   Initialize the deck array
 4
 5   For each of the 52 cards
 6       Choose slot of deck randomly
 7
 8       While slot of deck has been previously chosen
 9           Choose slot of deck randomly
10
11       Place card number in chosen slot of deck
12
13   For each of the 52 cards
14       For each slot of deck array
15           If slot contains desired card number
16               Print the face and suit of the card
```

Fig. 8.24 | Pseudocode algorithm for card shuffling and dealing program.

```
 1   // Fig. 8.25: DeckOfCards.h
 2   // Definition of class DeckOfCards that
 3   // represents a deck of playing cards.
 4
 5   // DeckOfCards class definition
 6   class DeckOfCards
 7   {
 8   public:
 9      DeckOfCards(); // constructor initializes deck
10      void shuffle(); // shuffles cards in deck
11      void deal(); // deals cards in deck
12   private:
13      int deck[ 4 ][ 13 ]; // represents deck of cards
14   }; // end class DeckOfCards
```

Fig. 8.25 | DeckOfCards header file.

```
 1   // Fig. 8.26: DeckOfCards.cpp
 2   // Member-function definitions for class DeckOfCards that simulates
 3   // the shuffling and dealing of a deck of playing cards.
 4   #include <iostream>
 5   using std::cout;
 6   using std::left;
 7   using std::right;
 8
 9   #include <iomanip>
10   using std::setw;
11
```

Fig. 8.26 | Definitions of member functions for shuffling and dealing. (Part 1 of 3.)

```cpp
12  #include <cstdlib> // prototypes for rand and srand
13  using std::rand;
14  using std::srand;
15
16  #include <ctime> // prototype for time
17  using std::time;
18
19  #include "DeckOfCards.h" // DeckOfCards class definition
20
21  // DeckOfCards default constructor initializes deck
22  DeckOfCards::DeckOfCards()
23  {
24     // loop through rows of deck
25     for ( int row = 0; row <= 3; row++ )
26     {
27        // loop through columns of deck for current row
28        for ( int column = 0; column <= 12; column++ )
29        {
30           deck[ row ][ column ] = 0; // initialize slot of deck to 0
31        } // end inner for
32     } // end outer for
33
34     srand( time( 0 ) ); // seed random number generator
35  } // end DeckOfCards default constructor
36
37  // shuffle cards in deck
38  void DeckOfCards::shuffle()
39  {
40     int row; // represents suit value of card
41     int column; // represents face value of card
42
43     // for each of the 52 cards, choose a slot of the deck randomly
44     for ( int card = 1; card <= 52; card++ )
45     {
46        do // choose a new random location until unoccupied slot is found
47        {
48           row = rand() % 4; // randomly select the row
49           column = rand() % 13; // randomly select the column
50        } while( deck[ row ][ column ] != 0 ); // end do...while
51
52        // place card number in chosen slot of deck
53        deck[ row ][ column ] = card;
54     } // end for
55  } // end function shuffle
56
57  // deal cards in deck
58  void DeckOfCards::deal()
59  {
60     // initialize suit array
61     static const char *suit[ 4 ] =
62        { "Hearts", "Diamonds", "Clubs", "Spades" };
63
```

Fig. 8.26 | Definitions of member functions for shuffling and dealing. (Part 2 of 3.)

```
64    // initialize face array
65    static const char *face[ 13 ] =
66       { "Ace", "Deuce", "Three", "Four", "Five", "Six", "Seven",
67       "Eight", "Nine", "Ten", "Jack", "Queen", "King" };
68
69    // for each of the 52 cards
70    for ( int card = 1; card <= 52; card++ )
71    {
72       // loop through rows of deck
73       for ( int row = 0; row <= 3; row++ )
74       {
75          // loop through columns of deck for current row
76          for ( int column = 0; column <= 12; column++ )
77          {
78             // if slot contains current card, display card
79             if ( deck[ row ][ column ] == card )
80             {
81                cout << setw( 5 ) << right << face[ column ]
82                   << " of " << setw( 8 ) << left << suit[ row ]
83                   << ( card % 2 == 0 ? '\n' : '\t' );
84             } // end if
85          } // end innermost for
86       } // end inner for
87    } // end outer for
88    } // end function deal
```

Fig. 8.26 | Definitions of member functions for shuffling and dealing. (Part 3 of 3.)

The output statement outputs the face right justified in a field of five characters and outputs the suit left justified in a field of eight characters (Fig. 8.27). The output is printed in two-column format—if the card being output is in the first column, a tab is output after the card to move to the second column (line 83); otherwise, a newline is output.

There is also a weakness in the dealing algorithm. Once a match is found, even if it is found on the first try, the two inner for statements continue searching the remaining elements of deck for a match. In the exercises, we correct this deficiency.

```
1    // Fig. 8.27: fig08_27.cpp
2    // Card shuffling and dealing program.
3    #include "DeckOfCards.h" // DeckOfCards class definition
4
5    int main()
6    {
7       DeckOfCards deckOfCards; // create DeckOfCards object
8
9       deckOfCards.shuffle(); // shuffle the cards in the deck
10      deckOfCards.deal(); // deal the cards in the deck
11      return 0; // indicates successful termination
12   } // end main
```

Fig. 8.27 | Card shuffling and dealing program. (Part 1 of 2.)

```
 Nine of Spades      Seven of Clubs
 Five of Spades      Eight of Clubs
Queen of Diamonds    Three of Hearts
 Jack of Spades       Five of Diamonds
 Jack of Diamonds    Three of Diamonds
Three of Clubs         Six of Clubs
  Ten of Clubs        Nine of Diamonds
  Ace of Hearts      Queen of Hearts
Seven of Spades      Deuce of Spades
  Six of Hearts      Deuce of Clubs
  Ace of Clubs       Deuce of Diamonds
 Nine of Hearts      Seven of Diamonds
  Six of Spades      Eight of Diamonds
  Ten of Spades       King of Hearts
 Four of Clubs         Ace of Spades
  Ten of Hearts      Four of Spades
Eight of Hearts      Eight of Spades
 Jack of Hearts        Ten of Diamonds
 Four of Diamonds     King of Diamonds
Seven of Hearts       King of Spades
Queen of Spades      Four of Hearts
 Nine of Clubs         Six of Diamonds
Deuce of Hearts       Jack of Clubs
 King of Clubs       Three of Spades
Queen of Clubs        Five of Clubs
 Five of Hearts        Ace of Diamonds
```

Fig. 8.27 | Card shuffling and dealing program. (Part 2 of 2.)

8.12 Function Pointers

A pointer to a function contains the address of the function in memory. In Chapter 7, we saw that the name of an array is actually the address in memory of the first element of the array. Similarly, the name of a function is actually the starting address in memory of the code that performs the function's task. Pointers to functions can be passed to functions, returned from functions, stored in arrays and assigned to other function pointers.

Multipurpose Selection Sort Using Function Pointers
To illustrate the use of pointers to functions, Fig. 8.28 modifies the selection sort program of Fig. 8.15. Figure 8.28 consists of main (lines 17–55) and the functions selectionSort (lines 59–76), swap (lines 80–85), ascending (lines 89–92) and descending (lines 96–99). Function selectionSort receives a pointer to a function—either function ascending or function descending—as an argument in addition to the integer array to sort and the size of the array. Functions ascending and descending determine the sorting order. The program prompts the user to choose whether the array should be sorted in ascending order or in descending order (lines 24–26). If the user enters 1, a pointer to function ascending is passed to function selectionSort (line 37), causing the array to be sorted into increasing order. If the user enters 2, a pointer to function descending is passed to function selectionSort (line 45), causing the array to be sorted into decreasing order.

The following parameter appears in line 60 of selectionSort's function header:

```
bool ( *compare )( int, int )
```

This parameter specifies a pointer to a function. The keyword `bool` indicates that the function being pointed to returns a `bool` value. The text (`*compare`) indicates the name of the pointer to the function (the `*` indicates that parameter `compare` is a pointer). The text (`int`, `int`) indicates that the function pointed to by compare takes two integer arguments. Parentheses are needed around `*compare` to indicate that `compare` is a pointer to a function. If we had not included the parentheses, the declaration would have been

```
bool *compare( int, int )
```

which declares a function that receives two integers as parameters and returns a pointer to a `bool` value.

```
1   // Fig. 8.28: fig08_28.cpp
2   // Multipurpose sorting program using function pointers.
3   #include <iostream>
4   using std::cout;
5   using std::cin;
6   using std::endl;
7
8   #include <iomanip>
9   using std::setw;
10
11  // prototypes
12  void selectionSort( int [], const int, bool (*)( int, int ) );
13  void swap( int * const, int * const );
14  bool ascending( int, int ); // implements ascending order
15  bool descending( int, int ); // implements descending order
16
17  int main()
18  {
19     const int arraySize = 10;
20     int order; // 1 = ascending, 2 = descending
21     int counter; // array index
22     int a[ arraySize ] = { 2, 6, 4, 8, 10, 12, 89, 68, 45, 37 };
23
24     cout << "Enter 1 to sort in ascending order,\n"
25        << "Enter 2 to sort in descending order: ";
26     cin >> order;
27     cout << "\nData items in original order\n";
28
29     // output original array
30     for ( counter = 0; counter < arraySize; counter++ )
31        cout << setw( 4 ) << a[ counter ];
32
33     // sort array in ascending order; pass function ascending
34     // as an argument to specify ascending sorting order
35     if ( order == 1 )
36     {
37        selectionSort( a, arraySize, ascending );
38        cout << "\nData items in ascending order\n";
39     } // end if
40
```

Fig. 8.28 | Multipurpose sorting program using function pointers. (Part 1 of 3.)

```
41      // sort array in descending order; pass function descending
42      // as an argument to specify descending sorting order
43      else
44      {
45         selectionSort( a, arraySize, descending );
46         cout << "\nData items in descending order\n";
47      } // end else part of if...else
48
49      // output sorted array
50      for ( counter = 0; counter < arraySize; counter++ )
51         cout << setw( 4 ) << a[ counter ];
52
53      cout << endl;
54      return 0; // indicates successful termination
55   } // end main
56
57   // multipurpose selection sort; the parameter compare is a pointer to
58   // the comparison function that determines the sorting order
59   void selectionSort( int work[], const int size,
60                       bool (*compare)( int, int ) )
61   {
62      int smallestOrLargest; // index of smallest (or largest) element
63
64      // loop over size - 1 elements
65      for ( int i = 0; i < size - 1; i++ )
66      {
67         smallestOrLargest = i; // first index of remaining vector
68
69         // loop to find index of smallest (or largest) element
70         for ( int index = i + 1; index < size; index++ )
71            if ( !(*compare)( work[ smallestOrLargest ], work[ index ] ) )
72               smallestOrLargest = index;
73
74         swap( &work[ smallestOrLargest ], &work[ i ] );
75      } // end if
76   } // end function selectionSort
77
78   // swap values at memory locations to which
79   // element1Ptr and element2Ptr point
80   void swap( int * const element1Ptr, int * const element2Ptr )
81   {
82      int hold = *element1Ptr;
83      *element1Ptr = *element2Ptr;
84      *element2Ptr = hold;
85   } // end function swap
86
87   // determine whether element a is less than
88   // element b for an ascending order sort
89   bool ascending( int a, int b )
90   {
91      return a < b; // returns true if a is less than b
92   } // end function ascending
93
```

Fig. 8.28 | Multipurpose sorting program using function pointers. (Part 2 of 3.)

```
94    // determine whether element a is greater than
95    // element b for a descending order sort
96    bool descending( int a, int b )
97    {
98       return a > b; // returns true if a is greater than b
99    } // end function descending
```

```
Enter 1 to sort in ascending order,
Enter 2 to sort in descending order: 1

Data items in original order
    2    6    4    8   10   12   89   68   45   37
Data items in ascending order
    2    4    6    8   10   12   37   45   68   89
```

```
Enter 1 to sort in ascending order,
Enter 2 to sort in descending order: 2

Data items in original order
    2    6    4    8   10   12   89   68   45   37
Data items in descending order
   89   68   45   37   12   10    8    6    4    2
```

Fig. 8.28 | Multipurpose sorting program using function pointers. (Part 3 of 3.)

The corresponding parameter in the function prototype of selectionSort is

```
bool (*)( int, int )
```

Note that only types have been included. As always, for documentation purposes, the programmer can include names that the compiler will ignore.

The function passed to selectionSort is called in line 71 as follows:

```
( *compare )( work[ smallestOrLargest ], work[ index ] )
```

Just as a pointer to a variable is dereferenced to access the value of the variable, a pointer to a function is dereferenced to execute the function. The parentheses around *compare are again necessary—if they were left out, the * operator would attempt to dereference the value returned from the function call. The call to the function could have been made without dereferencing the pointer, as in

```
compare( work[ smallestOrLargest ], work[ index ] )
```

which uses the pointer directly as the function name. We prefer the first method of calling a function through a pointer, because it explicitly illustrates that compare is a pointer to a function that is dereferenced to call the function. The second method of calling a function through a pointer makes it appear as though compare is the name of an actual function in the program. This may be confusing to a user of the program who would like to see the definition of function compare and finds that it is not defined in the file.

Arrays of Pointers to Functions

One use of function pointers is in menu-driven systems. For example, a program might prompt a user to select an option from a menu by entering an integer values. The user's choice can be used as a subscript into an array of function pointers, and the pointer in the array can be used to call the function.

Figure 8.29 provides a mechanical example that demonstrates declaring and using an array of pointers to functions. The program defines three functions—function0, function1 and function2—that each take an integer argument and do not return a value. Line 17 stores pointers to these three functions in array f. In this case, all the functions to which the array points must have the same return type and same parameter types. The declaration in line 17 is read beginning in the leftmost set of parentheses as, "f is an array of three pointers to functions that each take an int as an argument and return void." The

```cpp
1   // Fig. 8.29: fig08_29.cpp
2   // Demonstrating an array of pointers to functions.
3   #include <iostream>
4   using std::cout;
5   using std::cin;
6   using std::endl;
7
8   // function prototypes -- each function performs similar actions
9   void function0( int );
10  void function1( int );
11  void function2( int );
12
13  int main()
14  {
15     // initialize array of 3 pointers to functions that each
16     // take an int argument and return void
17     void (*f[ 3 ])( int ) = { function0, function1, function2 };
18
19     int choice;
20
21     cout << "Enter a number between 0 and 2, 3 to end: ";
22     cin >> choice;
23
24     // process user's choice
25     while ( ( choice >= 0 ) && ( choice < 3 ) )
26     {
27        // invoke the function at location choice in
28        // the array f and pass choice as an argument
29        (*f[ choice ])( choice );
30
31        cout << "Enter a number between 0 and 2, 3 to end: ";
32        cin >> choice;
33     } // end while
34
35     cout << "Program execution completed." << endl;
36     return 0; // indicates successful termination
37  } // end main
```

Fig. 8.29 | Array of pointers to functions. (Part 1 of 2.)

```
38
39   void function0( int a )
40   {
41      cout << "You entered " << a << " so function0 was called\n\n";
42   } // end function function0
43
44   void function1( int b )
45   {
46      cout << "You entered " << b << " so function1 was called\n\n";
47   } // end function function1
48
49   void function2( int c )
50   {
51      cout << "You entered " << c << " so function2 was called\n\n";
52   } // end function function2
```

```
Enter a number between 0 and 2, 3 to end: 0
You entered 0 so function0 was called

Enter a number between 0 and 2, 3 to end: 1
You entered 1 so function1 was called

Enter a number between 0 and 2, 3 to end: 2
You entered 2 so function2 was called

Enter a number between 0 and 2, 3 to end: 3
Program execution completed.
```

Fig. 8.29 | Array of pointers to functions. (Part 2 of 2.)

array is initialized with the names of the three functions (which, again, are pointers). The program prompts the user to enter a number between 0 and 2, or 3 to terminate. When the user enters a value between 0 and 2, the value is used as the subscript into the array of pointers to functions. Line 29 invokes one of the functions in array f. In the call, f[choice] selects the pointer at location choice in the array. The pointer is dereferenced to call the function, and choice is passed as the argument to the function. Each function prints its argument's value and its function name to indicate that the function is called correctly. In the exercises, you will develop a menu-driven system. We will see in Chapter 13, Object-Oriented Programming: Polymorphism, that arrays of pointers to functions are used by compiler developers to implement the mechanisms that support virtual functions—the key technology behind polymorphism.

8.13 Introduction to Pointer-Based String Processing

In this section, we introduce some common C++ Standard Library functions that facilitate string processing. The techniques discussed here are appropriate for developing text editors, word processors, page layout software, computerized typesetting systems and other kinds of text-processing software. We have already used the C++ Standard Library string class in several examples to represent strings as full-fledged objects. For example, the GradeBook class case study in Chapters 3–7 represents a course name using a string object. Although using string objects is usually straightforward, we use null-terminated, pointer-based strings in this section. Many C++ Standard Library functions operate only on null-terminated, pointer-based strings, which are more complicated to use than `string` objects. Also, if you work with legacy C++ programs, you may be required to manipulate these pointer-based strings.

8.13.1 Fundamentals of Characters and Pointer-Based Strings

Characters are the fundamental building blocks of C++ source programs. Every program is composed of a sequence of characters that—when grouped together meaningfully—is interpreted by the compiler as a series of instructions used to accomplish a task. A program may contain character constants. A character constant is an integer value represented as a character in single quotes. The value of a character constant is the integer value of the character in the machine's character set. For example, `'z'` represents the integer value of z (122 in the ASCII character set; see Appendix B), and `'\n'` represents the integer value of newline (10 in the ASCII character set).

A string is a series of characters treated as a single unit. A string may include letters, digits and various special characters such as +, -, *, /and $. String literals, or string constants, in C++ are written in double quotation marks as follows:

```
"John Q. Doe"             (a name)
"9999 Main Street"        (a street address)
"Maynard, Massachusetts"  (a city and state)
"(201) 555-1212"          (a telephone number)
```

A pointer-based string in C++ is an array of characters ending in the null character (`'\0'`), which marks where the string terminates in memory. A string is accessed via a pointer to its first character. The value of a string is the address of its first character. Thus, in C++, it is appropriate to say that *a string is a constant pointer*—in fact, a pointer to the string's first character. In this sense, strings are like arrays, because an array name is also a pointer to its first element.

A string literal may be used as an initializer in the declaration of either a character array or a variable of type `char *`. The declarations

```
char color[] = "blue";
const char *colorPtr = "blue";
```

each initialize a variable to the string `"blue"`. The first declaration creates a five-element array `color` containing the characters `'b'`, `'l'`, `'u'`, `'e'` and `'\0'`. The second declaration creates pointer variable `colorPtr` that points to the letter b in the string `"blue"` (which ends in `'\0'`) somewhere in memory. String literals have `static` storage class (they exist for the duration of the program) and may or may not be shared if the same string literal is referenced from multiple locations in a program. Also, string literals in C++ are constant—their characters cannot be modified.

The declaration `char color[] = "blue";` could also be written

```
char color[] = { 'b', 'l', 'u', 'e', '\0' };
```

When declaring a character array to contain a string, the array must be large enough to store the string and its terminating null character. The preceding declaration determines the size of the array, based on the number of initializers provided in the initializer list.

Common Programming Error 8.15

Not allocating sufficient space in a character array to store the null character that terminates a string is an error.

Common Programming Error 8.16

Creating or using a C-style string that does not contain a terminating null character can lead to logic errors.

Error-Prevention Tip 8.4

When storing a string of characters in a character array, be sure that the array is large enough to hold the largest string that will be stored. C++ allows strings of any length to be stored. If a string is longer than the character array in which it is to be stored, characters beyond the end of the array will overwrite data in memory following the array, leading to logic errors.

A string can be read into a character array using stream extraction with `cin`. For example, the following statement can be used to read a string into character array `word[ 20 ]`:

```
cin >> word;
```

The string entered by the user is stored in `word`. The preceding statement reads characters until a white-space character or end-of-file indicator is encountered. Note that the string should be no longer than 19 characters to leave room for the terminating null character. The `setw` stream manipulator can be used to ensure that the string read into `word` does not exceed the size of the array. For example, the statement

```
cin >> setw( 20 ) >> word;
```

specifies that `cin` should read a maximum of 19 characters into array `word` and save the 20th location in the array to store the terminating null character for the string. The `setw` stream manipulator applies only to the next value being input. If more than 19 characters are entered, the remaining characters are not saved in `word`, but will be read in and can be stored in another variable.

In some cases, it is desirable to input an entire line of text into an array. For this purpose, C++ provides the function `cin.getline` in header file `<iostream>`. In Chapter 3 you were introduced to the similar function `getline` from header file `<string>`, which read input until a newline character was entered, and stored the input (without the newline character) into a `string` specified as an argument. The `cin.getline` function takes three arguments—a character array in which the line of text will be stored, a length and a delimiter character. For example, the program segment

```
char sentence[ 80 ];
cin.getline( sentence, 80, '\n' );
```

declares array `sentence` of 80 characters and reads a line of text from the keyboard into the array. The function stops reading characters when the delimiter character `'\n'` is encountered, when the end-of-file indicator is entered or when the number of characters read so far is one less than the length specified in the second argument. (The last character in the array is reserved for the terminating null character.) If the delimiter character is encountered, it is read and discarded. The third argument to `cin.getline` has `'\n'` as a default value, so the preceding function call could have been written as follows:

```
cin.getline( sentence, 80 );
```

Chapter 15, Stream Input/Output, of our sister book, *C++ How to Program, 5/e*, provides a detailed discussion of `cin.getline` and other input/output functions.

Common Programming Error 8.17

Processing a single character as a `char *` string can lead to a fatal runtime error. A `char *` string is a pointer—probably a respectably large integer. However, a character is a small integer (ASCII values range 0–255). On many systems, dereferencing a `char` value causes an error, because low memory addresses are reserved for special purposes such as operating system interrupt handlers—so "memory access violations" occur.

Common Programming Error 8.18

Passing a string as an argument to a function when a character is expected is a compilation error.

8.13.2 String Manipulation Functions of the String-Handling Library

The string-handling library provides many useful functions for manipulating string data, comparing strings, searching strings for characters and other strings, tokenizing strings (separating strings into logical pieces such as the separate words in a sentence) and determining the length of strings. This section presents some common string-manipulation functions of the string-handling library (from the C++ standard library). The functions are summarized in Fig. 8.30; then each is used in a live-code example. The prototypes for these functions are located in header file `<cstring>`.

Function prototype	Function description
`char *strcpy( char *s1, const char *s2 );`	
	Copies the string s2 into the character array s1. The value of s1 is returned.
`char *strncpy( char *s1, const char *s2, size_t n );`	
	Copies at most n characters of the string s2 into the character array s1. The value of s1 is returned.
`char *strcat( char *s1, const char *s2 );`	
	Appends the string s2 to s1. The first character of s2 overwrites the terminating null character of s1. The value of s1 is returned.
`char *strncat( char *s1, const char *s2, size_t n );`	
	Appends at most n characters of string s2 to string s1. The first character of s2 overwrites the terminating null character of s1. The value of s1 is returned.
`int strcmp( const char *s1, const char *s2 );`	
	Compares the string s1 with the string s2. The function returns a value of zero, less than zero (usually –1) or greater than zero (usually 1) if s1 is equal to, less than or greater than s2, respectively.

Fig. 8.30 | String-manipulation functions of the string-handling library. (Part 1 of 2.)

Function prototype	Function description
`int strncmp( const char *s1, const char *s2, size_t n );`	
	Compares up to n characters of the string s1 with the string s2. The function returns zero, less than zero or greater than zero if the n-character portion of s1 is equal to, less than or greater than the corresponding n-character portion of s2, respectively.
`char *strtok( char *s1, const char *s2 );`	
	A sequence of calls to strtok breaks string s1 into "tokens"—logical pieces such as words in a line of text. The string is broken up based on the characters contained in string s2. For instance, if we were to break the string "this:is:a:string" into tokens based on the character ':', the resulting tokens would be "this", "is", "a" and "string". Function strtok returns only one token at a time, however. The first call contains s1 as the first argument, and subsequent calls to continue tokenizing the same string contain NULL as the first argument. A pointer to the current token is returned by each call. If there are no more tokens when the function is called, NULL is returned.
`size_t strlen( const char *s );`	
	Determines the length of string s. The number of characters preceding the terminating null character is returned.

Fig. 8.30 | String-manipulation functions of the string-handling library. (Part 2 of 2.)

Note that several functions in Fig. 8.30 contain parameters with data type `size_t`. This type is defined in the header file `<cstring>` to be an unsigned integral type such as unsigned `int` or unsigned `long`.

Common Programming Error 8.19

Forgetting to include the <cstring> header file when using functions from the string-handling library causes compilation errors.

Copying Strings with *strcpy* and *strncpy*

Function `strcpy` copies its second argument—a string—into its first argument—a character array that must be large enough to store the string and its terminating null character, (which is also copied). Function `strncpy` is equivalent to strcpy, except that strncpy specifies the number of characters to be copied from the string into the array. Note that function strncpy does not necessarily copy the terminating null character of its second argument—a terminating null character is written only if the number of characters to be copied is at least one more than the length of the string. For example, if "test" is the second argument, a terminating null character is written only if the third argument to strncpy is at least 5 (four characters in "test" plus one terminating null character). If the third argument is larger than 5, null characters are appended to the array until the total number of characters specified by the third argument is written.

Common Programming Error 8.20

When using strncpy, the terminating null character of the second argument (a char * string) will not be copied if the number of characters specified by strncpy's third argument is not greater than the second argument's length. In that case, a fatal error may occur if the programmer does not manually terminate the resulting char * string with a null character.

Figure 8.31 uses strcpy (line 17) to copy the entire string in array x into array y and uses strncpy (line 23) to copy the first 14 characters of array x into array z. Line 24 appends a null character ('\0') to array z, because the call to strncpy in the program does not write a terminating null character. (The third argument is less than the string length of the second argument plus one.)

Concatenating Strings with *strcat* and *strncat*

Function strcat appends its second argument (a string) to its first argument (a character array containing a string). The first character of the second argument replaces the null character ('\0') that terminates the string in the first argument. The programmer must ensure that the array used to store the first string is large enough to store the combination of the

```cpp
1   // Fig. 8.31: fig08_31.cpp
2   // Using strcpy and strncpy.
3   #include <iostream>
4   using std::cout;
5   using std::endl;
6
7   #include <cstring> // prototypes for strcpy and strncpy
8   using std::strcpy;
9   using std::strncpy;
10
11  int main()
12  {
13     char x[] = "Happy Birthday to You"; // string length 21
14     char y[ 25 ];
15     char z[ 15 ];
16
17     strcpy( y, x ); // copy contents of x into y
18
19     cout << "The string in array x is: " << x
20        << "\nThe string in array y is: " << y << '\n';
21
22     // copy first 14 characters of x into z
23     strncpy( z, x, 14 ); // does not copy null character
24     z[ 14 ] = '\0'; // append '\0' to z's contents
25
26     cout << "The string in array z is: " << z << endl;
27     return 0; // indicates successful termination
28  } // end main
```

```
The string in array x is: Happy Birthday to You
The string in array y is: Happy Birthday to You
The string in array z is: Happy Birthday
```

Fig. 8.31 | strcpy and strncpy.

first string, the second string and the terminating null character (copied from the second string). Function **strncat** appends a specified number of characters from the second string to the first string and appends a terminating null character to the result. The program of Fig. 8.32 demonstrates function strcat (lines 19 and 29) and function strncat (line 24).

```
1   // Fig. 8.32: fig08_32.cpp
2   // Using strcat and strncat.
3   #include <iostream>
4   using std::cout;
5   using std::endl;
6
7   #include <cstring> // prototypes for strcat and strncat
8   using std::strcat;
9   using std::strncat;
10
11  int main()
12  {
13     char s1[ 20 ] = "Happy "; // length 6
14     char s2[] = "New Year "; // length 9
15     char s3[ 40 ] = "";
16
17     cout << "s1 = " << s1 << "\ns2 = " << s2;
18
19     strcat( s1, s2 ); // concatenate s2 to s1 (length 15)
20
21     cout << "\n\nAfter strcat(s1, s2):\ns1 = " << s1 << "\ns2 = " << s2;
22
23     // concatenate first 6 characters of s1 to s3
24     strncat( s3, s1, 6 ); // places '\0' after last character
25
26     cout << "\n\nAfter strncat(s3, s1, 6):\ns1 = " << s1
27        << "\ns3 = " << s3;
28
29     strcat( s3, s1 ); // concatenate s1 to s3
30     cout << "\n\nAfter strcat(s3, s1):\ns1 = " << s1
31        << "\ns3 = " << s3 << endl;
32     return 0; // indicates successful termination
33  } // end main
```

```
s1 = Happy
s2 = New Year

After strcat(s1, s2):
s1 = Happy New Year
s2 = New Year

After strncat(s3, s1, 6):
s1 = Happy New Year
s3 = Happy

After strcat(s3, s1):
s1 = Happy New Year
s3 = Happy Happy New Year
```

Fig. 8.32 | strcat and strncat.

Comparing Strings with **strcmp** *and* **strncmp**

Figure 8.33 compares three strings using strcmp (lines 21, 22 and 23) and strncmp (lines 26, 27 and 28). Function strcmp compares its first string argument with its second string argument character by character. The function returns zero if the strings are equal, a negative value if the first string is less than the second string and a positive value if the first string is greater than the second string. Function strncmp is equivalent to strcmp, except that strncmp compares up to a specified number of characters. Function strncmp stops comparing characters if it reaches the null character in one of its string arguments. The program prints the integer value returned by each function call.

 Common Programming Error 8.21

Assuming that strcmp and strncmp return one (a true value) when their arguments are equal is a logic error. Both functions return zero (C++'s false value) for equality. Therefore, when testing two strings for equality, the result of the strcmp or strncmp function should be compared with zero to determine whether the strings are equal.

To understand just what it means for one string to be "greater than" or "less than" another string, consider the process of alphabetizing a series of last names. The reader would, no doubt, place "Jones" before "Smith," because the first letter of "Jones" comes

```
1   // Fig. 8.33: fig08_33.cpp
2   // Using strcmp and strncmp.
3   #include <iostream>
4   using std::cout;
5   using std::endl;
6
7   #include <iomanip>
8   using std::setw;
9
10  #include <cstring> // prototypes for strcmp and strncmp
11  using std::strcmp;
12  using std::strncmp;
13
14  int main()
15  {
16     char *s1 = "Happy New Year";
17     char *s2 = "Happy New Year";
18     char *s3 = "Happy Holidays";
19
20     cout << "s1 = " << s1 << "\ns2 = " << s2 << "\ns3 = " << s3
21        << "\n\nstrcmp(s1, s2) = " << setw( 2 ) << strcmp( s1, s2 )
22        << "\nstrcmp(s1, s3) = " << setw( 2 ) << strcmp( s1, s3 )
23        << "\nstrcmp(s3, s1) = " << setw( 2 ) << strcmp( s3, s1 );
24
25     cout << "\n\nstrncmp(s1, s3, 6) = " << setw( 2 )
26        << strncmp( s1, s3, 6 ) << "\nstrncmp(s1, s3, 7) = " << setw( 2 )
27        << strncmp( s1, s3, 7 ) << "\nstrncmp(s3, s1, 7) = " << setw( 2 )
28        << strncmp( s3, s1, 7 ) << endl;
29     return 0; // indicates successful termination
30  } // end main
```

Fig. 8.33 | strcmp and strncmp. (Part 1 of 2.)

```
s1 = Happy New Year
s2 = Happy New Year
s3 = Happy Holidays

strcmp(s1, s2) =  0
strcmp(s1, s3) =  1
strcmp(s3, s1) = -1

strncmp(s1, s3, 6) =  0
strncmp(s1, s3, 7) =  1
strncmp(s3, s1, 7) = -1
```

Fig. 8.33 | strcmp and strncmp. (Part 2 of 2.)

before the first letter of "Smith" in the alphabet. But the alphabet is more than just a list of 26 letters—it is an ordered list of characters. Each letter occurs in a specific position within the list. "Z" is more than just a letter of the alphabet; "Z" is specifically the 26th letter of the alphabet.

How does the computer know that one letter comes before another? All characters are represented inside the computer as numeric codes; when the computer compares two strings, it actually compares the numeric codes of the characters in the strings.

In an effort to standardize character representations, most computer manufacturers have designed their machines to utilize one of two popular coding schemes—ASCII or EBCDIC. Recall that ASCII stands for "American Standard Code for Information Interchange." EBCDIC stands for "Extended Binary Coded Decimal Interchange Code." There are other coding schemes, but these two are the most popular.

ASCII and EBCDIC are called character codes, or character sets. Most readers of this book will be using desktop or notebook computers that use the ASCII character set. IBM mainframe computers use the EBCDIC character set. As Internet and World Wide Web usage becomes pervasive, the newer Unicode character set is growing rapidly in popularity. For more information on Unicode, visit www.unicode.org. String and character manipulations actually involve the manipulation of the appropriate numeric codes and not the characters themselves. This explains the interchangeability of characters and small integers in C++. Since it is meaningful to say that one numeric code is greater than, less than or equal to another numeric code, it becomes possible to relate various characters or strings to one another by referring to the character codes. Appendix B contains the ASCII character codes.

Portability Tip 8.5

The internal numeric codes used to represent characters may be different on different computers, because these computers may use different character sets.

Portability Tip 8.6

Do not explicitly test for ASCII codes, as in if (rating == 65); rather, use the corresponding character constant, as in if (rating == 'A').

[*Note:* With some compilers, functions strcmp and strncmp always return -1, 0 or 1, as in the sample output of Fig. 8.33. With other compilers, these functions return 0 or the difference between the numeric codes of the first characters that differ in the strings being compared. For example, when s1 and s3 are compared, the first characters that differ between them are the first character of the second word in each string—N (numeric code 78) in s1 and H (numeric code 72) in s3, respectively. In this case, the return value will be 6 (or -6 if s3 is compared to s1).]

Tokenizing a String with strtok

Function strtok breaks a string into a series of tokens. A token is a sequence of characters separated by delimiting characters (usually spaces or punctuation marks). For example, in a line of text, each word can be considered a token, and the spaces separating the words can be considered delimiters.

Multiple calls to strtok are required to break a string into tokens (assuming that the string contains more than one token). The first call to strtok contains two arguments, a string to be tokenized and a string containing characters that separate the tokens (i.e., delimiters). Line 19 in Fig. 8.34 assigns to tokenPtr a pointer to the first token in sentence. The second argument, " ", indicates that tokens in sentence are separated by spaces. Function strtok searches for the first character in sentence that is not a delimiting character (space). This begins the first token. The function then finds the next delimiting character in the string and replaces it with a null ('\0') character. This terminates the cur-

```cpp
1   // Fig. 8.34: fig08_34.cpp
2   // Using strtok.
3   #include <iostream>
4   using std::cout;
5   using std::endl;
6
7   #include <cstring> // prototype for strtok
8   using std::strtok;
9
10  int main()
11  {
12     char sentence[] = "This is a sentence with 7 tokens";
13     char *tokenPtr;
14
15     cout << "The string to be tokenized is:\n" << sentence
16        << "\n\nThe tokens are:\n\n";
17
18     // begin tokenization of sentence
19     tokenPtr = strtok( sentence, " " );
20
21     // continue tokenizing sentence until tokenPtr becomes NULL
22     while ( tokenPtr != NULL )
23     {
24        cout << tokenPtr << '\n';
25        tokenPtr = strtok( NULL, " " ); // get next token
26     } // end while
27
28     cout << "\nAfter strtok, sentence = " << sentence << endl;
29     return 0; // indicates successful termination
30  } // end main
```

Fig. 8.34 | strtok. (Part 1 of 2.)

```
The string to be tokenized is:
This is a sentence with 7 tokens

The tokens are:

This
is
a
sentence
with
7
tokens

After strtok, sentence = This
```

Fig. 8.34 | strtok. (Part 2 of 2.)

rent token. Function strtok saves (in a static variable) a pointer to the next character following the token in sentence and returns a pointer to the current token.

Subsequent calls to strtok to continue tokenizing sentence contain NULL as the first argument (line 25). The NULL argument indicates that the call to strtok should continue tokenizing from the location in sentence saved by the last call to strtok. Note that strtok maintains this saved information in a manner that is not visible to the programmer. If no tokens remain when strtok is called, strtok returns NULL. The program of Fig. 8.34 uses strtok to tokenize the string "This is a sentence with 7 tokens". The program prints each token on a separate line. Line 28 outputs sentence after tokenization. Note that *strtok modifies the input string*; therefore, a copy of the string should be made if the program requires the original after the calls to strtok. When sentence is output after tokenization, note that only the word "This" prints, because strtok replaced each blank in sentence with a null character ('\0') during the tokenization process.

Common Programming Error 8.22

Not realizing that strtok modifies the string being tokenized and then attempting to use that string as if it were the original unmodified string is a logic error.

Determining String Lengths

Function strlen takes a string as an argument and returns the number of characters in the string—the terminating null character is not included in the length. The length is also the index of the null character. The program of Fig. 8.35 demonstrates function strlen.

```
1   // Fig. 8.35: fig08_35.cpp
2   // Using strlen.
3   #include <iostream>
4   using std::cout;
5   using std::endl;
6
```

Fig. 8.35 | strlen returns the length of a char * string. (Part 1 of 2.)

```
 7   #include <cstring> // prototype for strlen
 8   using std::strlen;
 9
10   int main()
11   {
12      char *string1 = "abcdefghijklmnopqrstuvwxyz";
13      char *string2 = "four";
14      char *string3 = "Boston";
15
16      cout << "The length of \"" << string1 << "\" is " << strlen( string1 )
17         << "\nThe length of \"" << string2 << "\" is " << strlen( string2 )
18         << "\nThe length of \"" << string3 << "\" is " << strlen( string3 )
19         << endl;
20      return 0; // indicates successful termination
21   } // end main
```

```
The length of "abcdefghijklmnopqrstuvwxyz" is 26
The length of "four" is 4
The length of "Boston" is 6
```

Fig. 8.35 | `strlen` returns the length of a `char` * string. (Part 2 of 2.)

8.14 Wrap-Up

In this chapter we provided a detailed introduction into pointers, or variables that contain memory addresses as their values. We began by demonstrating how to declare and initialize pointers. You saw how to use the address operator (&) to assign the address of a variable to a pointer and the indirection operator (*) to access the data stored in the variable indirectly referenced by a pointer. We discussed passing arguments by reference using both pointer arguments and reference arguments.

You learned how to use const with pointers to enforce the principle of least privilege. We demonstrated using nonconstant pointers to nonconstant data, nonconstant pointers to constant data, constant pointers to nonconstant data and constant pointers to constant data. We then used selection sort to demonstrate passing arrays and individual array elements by reference. We discussed to the sizeof operator, which can be used to determine the size of a data type in bytes during program compilation.

We continued by demonstrating how to use pointers in arithmetic and comparison expressions. You saw that pointer arithmetic can be used to jump from one element of an array to another. You learned how to use arrays of pointers, and more specifically string arrays (an array of strings). We then continued by discussing function pointers, which enable programmers to pass functions as parameters. We concluded the chapter with a discussion of several C++ functions that manipulate pointer-based strings. You learned string processing capabilities such as copying strings, tokenizing strings and determining the length of strings.

In the next chapter, we begin our in-depth treatment of classes. You will learn about the scope of a class's members, and how to keep objects in a consistent state. You will also learn about using special member functions called constructors and destructors, which execute when an object is created and destroyed, respectively.

Summary

- Pointers are variables that contain as their values memory addresses of other variables.
- The declaration

    ```
    int *ptr;
    ```

    declares `ptr` to be a pointer to a variable of type `int` and is read, "`ptr` is a pointer to `int`." The `*` as used here in a declaration indicates that the variable is a pointer.
- There are three values that can be used to initialize a pointer: `0`, `NULL` or an address of an object of the same type. Initializing a pointer to `0` and initializing that same pointer to `NULL` are identical—`0` is the convention in C++.
- The only integer that can be assigned to a pointer without casting is zero.
- The `&` (address) operator returns the memory address of its operand.
- The operand of the address operator must be a variable name (or another *lvalue*); the address operator cannot be applied to constants or to expressions that do not return a reference.
- The `*` operator, referred to as the indirection (or dereferencing) operator, returns a synonym, alias or nickname for the name of the object that its operand points to in memory. This is called dereferencing the pointer.
- When calling a function with an argument that the caller wants the called function to modify, the address of the argument may be passed. The called function then uses the indirection operator (`*`) to dereference the pointer and modify the value of the argument in the calling function.
- A function receiving an address as an argument must have a pointer as its corresponding parameter.
- The `const` qualifier enables the programmer to inform the compiler that the value of a particular variable cannot be modified through the specified identifier. If an attempt is made to modify a `const` value, the compiler issues either a warning or an error, depending on the particular compiler.
- There are four ways to pass a pointer to a function—a nonconstant pointer to nonconstant data, a nonconstant pointer to constant data, a constant pointer to nonconstant data and a constant pointer to constant data.
- The value of the array name is the address of (a pointer to) the array's first element.
- To pass a single element of an array by reference using pointers, pass the address of the specific array element.
- C++ provides unary operator `sizeof` to determine the size of an array (or of any other data type, variable or constant) in bytes at compile time.
- When applied to the name of an array, the `sizeof` operator returns the total number of bytes in the array as an integer.
- The arithmetic operations that may be performed on pointers are incrementing (`++`) a pointer, decrementing (`--`) a pointer, adding (`+` or `+=`) an integer to a pointer, subtracting (`-` or `-=`) an integer from a pointer and subtracting one pointer from another.
- When an integer is added or subtracted from a pointer, the pointer is incremented or decremented by that integer times the size of the object to which the pointer refers.
- Pointers can be assigned to one another if both pointers are of the same type. Otherwise, a cast must be used. The exception to this is a `void *` pointer, which is a generic pointer type that can hold pointer values of any type. Pointers to `void` can be assigned pointers of other types. A `void *` pointer can be assigned to a pointer of another type only with an explicit type cast.
- The only valid operations on a `void *` pointer are comparing `void *` pointers with other pointers, assigning addresses to `void *` pointers and casting `void *` pointers to valid pointer types.

- Pointers can be compared using the equality and relational operators. Comparisons using relational operators are meaningful only if the pointers point to members of the same array.

- Pointers that point to arrays can be subscripted exactly as array names can.

- In pointer/offset notation, if the pointer points to the first element of the array, the offset is the same as an array subscript.

- All subscripted array expressions can be written with a pointer and an offset, using either the name of the array as a pointer or using a separate pointer that points to the array.

- Arrays may contain pointers.

- A pointer to a function is the address where the code for the function resides.

- Pointers to functions can be passed to functions, returned from functions, stored in arrays and assigned to other pointers.

- A common use of function pointers is in so-called menu-driven systems. The function pointers are used to select which function to call for a particular menu item.

- Function strcpy copies its second argument—a string—into its first argument—a character array. The programmer must ensure that the target array is large enough to store the string and its terminating null character.

- Function strncpy is equivalent to strcpy, except that a call to strncpy specifies the number of characters to be copied from the string into the array. The terminating null character will be copied only if the number of characters to be copied is at least one more than the length of the string.

- Function strcat appends its second string argument—including the terminating null character—to its first string argument. The first character of the second string replaces the null ('\0') character of the first string. The programmer must ensure that the target array used to store the first string is large enough to store both the first string and the second string.

- Function strncat is equivalent to strcat, except that a call to strncat appends a specified number of characters from the second string to the first string. A terminating null character is appended to the result.

- Function strcmp compares its first string argument with its second string argument character by character. The function returns zero if the strings are equal, a negative value if the first string is less than the second string and a positive value if the first string is greater than the second string.

- Function strncmp is equivalent to strcmp, except that strncmp compares a specified number of characters. If the number of characters in one of the strings is less than the number of characters specified, strncmp compares characters until the null character in the shorter string is encountered.

- A sequence of calls to strtok breaks a string into tokens that are separated by characters contained in a second string argument. The first call specifies the string to be tokenized as the first argument, and subsequent calls to continue tokenizing the same string specify NULL as the first argument. The function returns a pointer to the current token from each call. If there are no more tokens when strtok is called, NULL is returned.

- Function strlen takes a string as an argument and returns the number of characters in the string—the terminating null character is not included in the length of the string.

Terminology

& (address operator)

* (pointer dereference or indirection operator)

'\0' (null character)

address operator (&)

array of pointers to functions

ASCII (American Standard Code for Information Interchange)

calling functions by reference

character code

character constant

command-line arguments

comparing strings

concatenating strings

const with function parameters

constant pointer

constant pointer to constant data

constant pointer to nonconstant data

copying strings

decrement a pointer

delimiter character

dereference a 0 pointer

dereference a pointer

dereferencing operator (*)

directly reference a value

EBCDIC (Extended Binary Coded Decimal Interchange Code)

function pointer

getline function of cin

increment a pointer

indefinite postponement

indirection

indirection (*) operator

indirectly reference a value

interchangeability of arrays and pointers

islower function (<cctype>)

modify a constant pointer

modify address stored in pointer variable

nonconstant pointer to constant data

nonconstant pointer to nonconstant data

null character ('\0')

null pointer

null-terminated string

offset to a pointer

pass-by-reference with pointer arguments

pass-by-reference with reference arguments

pointer arithmetic

pointer-based strings

pointer dereference (*) operator

pointer subtraction

pointer to a function

reference to constant data

referencing array elements

selection sort algorithm

size_t type

sizeof operator

special characters

starvation

strcat function of header file <cstring>

strcmp function of header file <cstring>

strcpy function of header file <cstring>

string array

string being tokenized

string constant

string copying

strlen function of header file <cstring>

strncat function of header file <cstring>

strncmp function of header file <cstring>

strncpy function of header file <cstring>

strtok function of header file <cstring>

terminating null character

token

tokenizing strings

toupper function (<cctype>)

Self-Review Exercises

8.1 Answer each of the following:
  a) A pointer is a variable that contains as its value the _____ of another variable.
  b) The three values that can be used to initialize a pointer are _____, _____ and _____.
  c) The only integer that can be assigned directly to a pointer is _____.

8.2 State whether the following are *true* or *false*. If the answer is *false*, explain why.
  a) The address operator & can be applied only to constants and to expressions.
  b) A pointer that is declared to be of type void * can be dereferenced.
  c) Pointers of different types can never be assigned to one another without a cast operation.

8.3 For each of the following, write C++ statements that perform the specified task. Assume that double-precision, floating-point numbers are stored in eight bytes and that the starting address of the array is at location 1002500 in memory. Each part of the exercise should use the results of previous parts where appropriate.

a) Declare an array of type double called numbers with 10 elements, and initialize the elements to the values 0.0, 1.1, 2.2, ..., 9.9. Assume that the symbolic constant SIZE has been defined as 10.

b) Declare a pointer nPtr that points to a variable of type double.

c) Use a for statement to print the elements of array numbers using array subscript notation. Print each number with one position of precision to the right of the decimal point.

d) Write two separate statements that each assign the starting address of array numbers to the pointer variable nPtr.

e) Use a for statement to print the elements of array numbers using pointer/offset notation with pointer nPtr.

f) Use a for statement to print the elements of array numbers using pointer/offset notation with the array name as the pointer.

g) Use a for statement to print the elements of array numbers using pointer/subscript notation with pointer nPtr.

h) Refer to the fourth element of array numbers using array subscript notation, pointer/offset notation with the array name as the pointer, pointer subscript notation with nPtr and pointer/offset notation with nPtr.

i) Assuming that nPtr points to the beginning of array numbers, what address is referenced by nPtr + 8? What value is stored at that location?

j) Assuming that nPtr points to numbers[5], what address is referenced by nPtr after nPtr -= 4 is executed? What is the value stored at that location?

8.4   For each of the following, write a single statement that performs the specified task. Assume that floating-point variables number1 and number2 have been declared and that number1 has been initialized to 7.3. Assume that variable ptr is of type char *. Assume that arrays s1 and s2 are each 100-element char arrays that are initialized with string literals.

a) Declare the variable fPtr to be a pointer to an object of type double.

b) Assign the address of variable number1 to pointer variable fPtr.

c) Print the value of the object pointed to by fPtr.

d) Assign the value of the object pointed to by fPtr to variable number2.

e) Print the value of number2.

f) Print the address of number1.

g) Print the address stored in fPtr. Is the value printed the same as the address of number1?

h) Copy the string stored in array s2 into array s1.

i) Compare the string in s1 with the string in s2, and print the result.

j) Append the first 10 characters from the string in s2 to the string in s1.

k) Determine the length of the string in s1, and print the result.

l) Assign to ptr the location of the first token in s2. The tokens delimiters are commas (,).

8.5   Perform the task specified by each of the following statements:

a) Write the function header for a function called exchange that takes two pointers to double-precision, floating-point numbers x and y as parameters and does not return a value.

b) Write the function prototype for the function in part (a).

c) Write the function header for a function called evaluate that returns an integer and that takes as parameters integer x and a pointer to function poly. Function poly takes an integer parameter and returns an integer.

d) Write the function prototype for the function in part (c).

e) Write two statements that each initialize character array vowel with the string of vowels, "AEIOU".

8.6   Find the error in each of the following program segments. Assume the following declarations and statements:

```
int *zPtr;       // zPtr will reference array z
int *aPtr = 0;
void *sPtr = 0;
int number;
int z[ 5 ] = { 1, 2, 3, 4, 5 };
```

a) ++zPtr;
b) // use pointer to get first value of array
   number = zPtr;
c) // assign array element 2 (the value 3) to number
   number = *zPtr[2];
d) // print entire array z
   for (int i = 0; i <= 5; i++)
       cout << zPtr[i] << endl;
e) // assign the value pointed to by sPtr to number
   number = *sPtr;
f) ++z;
g) char s[10];
   cout << strncpy(s, "hello", 5) << endl;
h) char s[12];
   strcpy(s, "Welcome Home");
i) if (strcmp(string1, string2))
       cout << "The strings are equal" << endl;

8.7   What (if anything) prints when each of the following statements is performed? If the statement contains an error, describe the error and indicate how to correct it. Assume the following variable declarations:

```
char s1[ 50 ] = "jack";
char s2[ 50 ] = "jill";
char s3[ 50 ];
```

a) cout << strcpy(s3, s2) << endl;
b) cout << strcat(strcat(strcpy(s3, s1), " and "), s2)
       << endl;
c) cout << strlen(s1) + strlen(s2) << endl;
d) cout << strlen(s3) << endl;

Answers to Self-Review Exercises

8.1   a) address. b) 0, NULL, an address. c) 0.

8.2   a) False. The operand of the address operator must be an *lvalue*; the address operator cannot be applied to constants or to expressions that do not result in references.

b) False. A pointer to void cannot be dereferenced. Such a pointer does not have a type that enables the compiler to determine the number of bytes of memory to dereference and the type of the data to which the pointer points.

c) False. Pointers of any type can be assigned to void pointers. Pointers of type void can be assigned to pointers of other types only with an explicit type cast.

8.3   a) double numbers[SIZE] = { 0.0, 1.1, 2.2, 3.3, 4.4, 5.5, 6.6, 7.7, 8.8, 9.9 };
b) double *nPtr;
c) cout << fixed << showpoint << setprecision(1);
   for (int i = 0; i < SIZE; i++)
       cout << numbers[i] << ' ';

d) `nPtr = numbers;`
   `nPtr = &numbers[ 0 ];`

e) `cout << fixed << showpoint << setprecision( 1 );`
   `for ( int j = 0; j < SIZE; j++ )`
   `    cout << *( nPtr + j ) << ' ';`

f) `cout << fixed << showpoint << setprecision( 1 );`
   `for ( int k = 0; k < SIZE; k++ )`
   `    cout << *( numbers + k ) << ' ';`

g) `cout << fixed << showpoint << setprecision( 1 );`
   `for ( int m = 0; m < SIZE; m++ )`
   `    cout << nPtr[ m ] << ' ';`

h) `numbers[ 3 ]`
   `*( numbers + 3 )`
   `nPtr[ 3 ]`
   `*( nPtr + 3 )`

i) The address is 1002500 + 8 * 8 = 1002564. The value is 8.8.

j) The address of `numbers[ 5 ]` is 1002500 + 5 * 8 = 1002540.
   The address of `nPtr -= 4` is 1002540 - 4 * 8 = 1002508.
   The value at that location is 1.1.

8.4 a) `double *fPtr;`

     b) `fPtr = &number1;`

     c) `cout << "The value of *fPtr is " << *fPtr << endl;`

     d) `number2 = *fPtr;`

     e) `cout << "The value of number2 is " << number2 << endl;`

     f) `cout << "The address of number1 is " << &number1 << endl;`

     g) `cout << "The address stored in fPtr is " << fPtr << endl;`
        Yes, the value is the same.

     h) `strcpy( s1, s2 );`

     i) `cout << "strcmp(s1, s2) = " << strcmp( s1, s2 ) << endl;`

     j) `strncat( s1, s2, 10 );`

     k) `cout << "strlen(s1) = " << strlen( s1 ) << endl;`

     l) `ptr = strtok( s2, "," );`

8.5 a) `void exchange( double *x, double *y )`

     b) `void exchange( double *, double * );`

     c) `int evaluate( int x, int (*poly)( int ) )`

     d) `int evaluate( int, int (*)( int ) );`

     e) `char vowel[] = "AEIOU";`
        `char vowel[] = { 'A', 'E', 'I', 'O', 'U', '\0' };`

8.6 a) Error: zPtr has not been initialized.
        Correction: Initialize zPtr with `zPtr = z;`

     b) Error: The pointer is not dereferenced.
        Correction: Change the statement to `number = *zPtr;`

     c) Error: `zPtr[ 2 ]` is not a pointer and should not be dereferenced.
        Correction: Change `*zPtr[ 2 ]` to `zPtr[ 2 ]`.

     d) Error: Referring to an array element outside the array bounds with pointer subscripting.
        Correction: To prevent this, change the relational operator in the for statement to <.

     e) Error: Dereferencing a void pointer.
        Correction: To dereference the void pointer, it must first be cast to an integer pointer.
        Change the statement to `number = *static_cast< int * >( sPtr );`

    f) Error: Trying to modify an array name with pointer arithmetic.

       Correction: Use a pointer variable instead of the array name to accomplish pointer arithmetic, or subscript the array name to refer to a specific element.

    g) Error: Function strncpy does not write a terminating null character to array s, because its third argument is equal to the length of the string "hello".

       Correction: Make 6 the third argument of strncpy or assign '\0' to s[5] to ensure that the terminating null character is added to the string.

    h) Error: Character array s is not large enough to store the terminating null character.

       Correction: Declare the array with more elements.

    i) Error: Function strcmp will return 0 if the strings are equal; therefore, the condition in the if statement will be false, and the output statement will not be executed.

       Correction: Explicitly compare the result of strcmp with 0 in the condition of the if statement.

8.7   a) jill

       b) jack and jill

       c) 8

       d) 13

Exercises

8.8   State whether the following are *true* or *false*. If *false*, explain why.

    a) Two pointers that point to different arrays cannot be compared meaningfully.

    b) Because the name of an array is a pointer to the first element of the array, array names can be manipulated in precisely the same manner as pointers.

8.9   For each of the following, write C++ statements that perform the specified task. Assume that unsigned integers are stored in two bytes and that the starting address of the array is at location 1002500 in memory.

    a) Declare an array of type unsigned int called values with five elements, and initialize the elements to the even integers from 2 to 10. Assume that the symbolic constant SIZE has been defined as 5.

    b) Declare a pointer vPtr that points to an object of type unsigned int.

    c) Use a for statement to print the elements of array values using array subscript notation.

    d) Write two separate statements that assign the starting address of array values to pointer variable vPtr.

    e) Use a for statement to print the elements of array values using pointer/offset notation.

    f) Use a for statement to print the elements of array values using pointer/offset notation with the array name as the pointer.

    g) Use a for statement to print the elements of array values by subscripting the pointer to the array.

    h) Refer to the fifth element of values using array subscript notation, pointer/offset notation with the array name as the pointer, pointer subscript notation and pointer/offset notation.

    i) What address is referenced by vPtr + 3? What value is stored at that location?

    j) Assuming that vPtr points to values[4], what address is referenced by vPtr -= 4? What value is stored at that location?

8.10   For each of the following, write a single statement that performs the specified task. Assume that long integer variables value1 and value2 have been declared and value1 has been initialized to 200000.

    a) Declare the variable longPtr to be a pointer to an object of type long.

    b) Assign the address of variable value1 to pointer variable longPtr.

    c) Print the value of the object pointed to by longPtr.

    d) Assign the value of the object pointed to by longPtr to variable value2.

    e) Print the value of value2.

    f) Print the address of value1.

    g) Print the address stored in longPtr. Is the value printed the same as value1's address?

8.11   Perform the task specified by each of the following statements:

    a) Write the function header for function zero that takes a long integer array parameter bigIntegers and does not return a value.

    b) Write the function prototype for the function in part (a).

    c) Write the function header for function add1AndSum that takes an integer array parameter oneTooSmall and returns an integer.

    d) Write the function prototype for the function described in part (c).

Note: Exercise 8.12 through Exercise 8.15 are reasonably challenging. Once you have solved these problems, you ought to be able to implement many popular card games.

8.12   Modify the program in Fig. 8.27 so that the card dealing function deals a five-card poker hand. Then write functions to accomplish each of the following:

    a) Determine whether the hand contains a pair.

    b) Determine whether the hand contains two pairs.

    c) Determine whether the hand contains three of a kind (e.g., three jacks).

    d) Determine whether the hand contains four of a kind (e.g., four aces).

    e) Determine whether the hand contains a flush (i.e., all five cards of the same suit).

    f) Determine whether the contains a straight (i.e., five cards of consecutive face values).

8.13   Use the functions developed in Exercise 8.12 to write a program that deals two five-card poker hands, evaluates each hand and determines which is the better hand.

8.14   Modify the program developed in Exercise 8.13 so that it can simulate the dealer. The dealer's five-card hand is dealt "face down" so the player cannot see it. The program should then evaluate the dealer's hand, and, based on the quality of the hand, the dealer should draw one, two or three more cards to replace the corresponding number of unneeded cards in the original hand. The program should then reevaluate the dealer's hand. [*Caution:* This is a difficult problem!]

8.15   Modify the program developed in Exercise 8.14 so that it handles the dealer's hand, but the player is allowed to decide which cards of the player's hand to replace. The program should then evaluate both hands and determine who wins. Now use this new program to play 20 games against the computer. Who wins more games, you or the computer? Have one of your friends play 20 games against the computer. Who wins more games? Based on the results of these games, make appropriate modifications to refine your poker-playing program. [*Note:* This, too, is a difficult problem.] Play 20 more games. Does your modified program play a better game?

8.16   In the card shuffling and dealing program of Figs. 8.25–8.27, we intentionally used an inefficient shuffling algorithm that introduced the possibility of indefinite postponement. In this problem, you will create a high-performance shuffling algorithm that avoids indefinite postponement.

    Modify Figs. 8.25–8.27 as follows. Initialize the deck array as shown in Fig. 8.36. Modify the shuffle function to loop row by row and column by column through the array, touching every element once. Each element should be swapped with a randomly selected element of the array. Print the resulting array to determine whether the deck is satisfactorily shuffled (as in Fig. 8.37, for example). You may want your program to call the shuffle function several times to ensure a satisfactory shuffle.

    Note that, although the approach in this problem improves the shuffling algorithm, the dealing algorithm still requires searching the deck array for card 1, then card 2, then card 3 and so on. Worse yet, even after the dealing algorithm locates and deals the card, the algorithm continues searching through the remainder of the deck. Modify the program of Figs. 8.25–8.27 so that once a card is dealt, no further attempts are made to match that card number, and the program immediately proceeds with dealing the next card.

	0	1	2	3	4	5	6	7	8	9	10	11	12
Unshuffled deck array													
0	1	2	3	4	5	6	7	8	9	10	11	12	13
1	14	15	16	17	18	19	20	21	22	23	24	25	26
2	27	28	29	30	31	32	33	34	35	36	37	38	39
3	40	41	42	43	44	45	46	47	48	49	50	51	52

Fig. 8.36 | Unshuffled deck array.

	0	1	2	3	4	5	6	7	8	9	10	11	12
Sample shuffled deck array													
0	19	40	27	25	36	46	10	34	35	41	18	2	44
1	13	28	14	16	21	30	8	11	31	17	24	7	1
2	12	33	15	42	43	23	45	3	29	32	4	47	26
3	50	38	52	39	48	51	9	5	37	49	22	6	20

Fig. 8.37 | Sample shuffled deck array.

8.17 (*Simulation: The Tortoise and the Hare*) In this exercise, you will re-create the classic race of the tortoise and the hare. You will use random number generation to develop a simulation of this memorable event.

Our contenders begin the race at "square 1" of 70 squares. Each square represents a possible position along the race course. The finish line is at square 70. The first contender to reach or pass square 70 is rewarded with a pail of fresh carrots and lettuce. The course weaves its way up the side of a slippery mountain, so occasionally the contenders lose ground.

There is a clock that ticks once per second. With each tick of the clock, your program should adjust the position of the animals according to the rules in Fig. 8.38.

Use variables to keep track of the positions of the animals (i.e., position numbers are 1–70). Start each animal at position 1 (i.e., the "starting gate"). If an animal slips left before square 1, move the animal back to square 1.

Generate the percentages in the preceding table by producing a random integer i in the range $1 \le i \le 10$. For the tortoise, perform a "fast plod" when $1 \le i \le 5$, a "slip" when $6 \le i \le 7$ or a "slow plod" when $8 \le i \le 10$. Use a similar technique to move the hare.

Begin the race by printing

```
BANG !!!!!
AND THEY'RE OFF !!!!!
```

For each tick of the clock (i.e., each repetition of a loop), print a 70-position line showing the letter T in the tortoise's position and the letter H in the hare's position. Occasionally, the contenders land on the same square. In this case, the tortoise bites the hare and your program should print OUCH!!! beginning at that position. All print positions other than the T, the H or the OUCH!!! (in case of a tie) should be blank.

After printing each line, test if either animal has reached or passed square 70. If so, print the winner and terminate the simulation. If the tortoise wins, print TORTOISE WINS!!! YAY!!! If the

Animal	Move type	Percentage of the time	Actual move
Tortoise	Fast plod	50%	3 squares to the right
	Slip	20%	6 squares to the left
	Slow plod	30%	1 square to the right
Hare	Sleep	20%	No move at all
	Big hop	20%	9 squares to the right
	Big slip	10%	12 squares to the left
	Small hop	30%	1 square to the right
	Small slip	20%	2 squares to the left

Fig. 8.38 | Rules for moving the tortoise and the hare.

hare wins, print `Hare wins`. Yuch. If both animals win on the same clock tick, you may want to favor the tortoise (the "underdog"), or you may want to print `It's a tie`. If neither animal wins, perform the loop again to simulate the next tick of the clock. When you are ready to run your program, assemble a group of fans to watch the race. You'll be amazed how involved the audience gets!

Special Section: Building Your Own Computer

In the next several problems, we take a temporary diversion away from the world of high-level-language programming. We "peel open" a computer and look at its internal structure. We introduce machine-language programming and write several machine-language programs. To make this an especially valuable experience, we then build a computer (using software-based *simulation*) on which you can execute your machine-language programs!

8.18   (*Machine-Language Programming*) Let us create a computer we will call the Simpletron. As its name implies, it is a simple machine, but, as we will soon see, it is a powerful one as well. The Simpletron runs programs written in the only language it directly understands, that is, Simpletron Machine Language, or SML for short.

The Simpletron contains an *accumulator*—a "special register" in which information is put before the Simpletron uses that information in calculations or examines it in various ways. All information in the Simpletron is handled in terms of *words*. A word is a signed four-digit decimal number, such as +3364, -1293, +0007, -0001, etc. The Simpletron is equipped with a 100-word memory, and these words are referenced by their location numbers 00, 01, ..., 99.

Before running an SML program, we must *load*, or place, the program into memory. The first instruction (or statement) of every SML program is always placed in location 00. The simulator will start executing at this location.

Each instruction written in SML occupies one word of the Simpletron's memory; thus, instructions are signed four-digit decimal numbers. Assume that the sign of an SML instruction is always plus, but the sign of a data word may be either plus or minus. Each location in the Simpletron's memory may contain an instruction, a data value used by a program or an unused (and hence undefined) area of memory. The first two digits of each SML instruction are the *operation code* that specifies the operation to be performed. SML operation codes are shown in Fig. 8.39.

The last two digits of an SML instruction are the *operand*—the address of the memory location containing the word to which the operation applies.

Operation code	Meaning
Input/output operations	
`const int READ = 10;`	Read a word from the keyboard into a specific location in memory.
`const int WRITE = 11;`	Write a word from a specific location in memory to the screen.
Load and store operations	
`const int LOAD = 20;`	Load a word from a specific location in memory into the accumulator.
`const int STORE = 21;`	Store a word from the accumulator into a specific location in memory.
Arithmetic operations	
`const int ADD = 30;`	Add a word from a specific location in memory to the word in the accumulator (leave result in accumulator).
`const int SUBTRACT = 31;`	Subtract a word from a specific location in memory from the word in the accumulator (leave result in accumulator).
`const int DIVIDE = 32;`	Divide a word from a specific location in memory into the word in the accumulator (leave result in accumulator).
`const int MULTIPLY = 33;`	Multiply a word from a specific location in memory by the word in the accumulator (leave result in accumulator).
Transfer-of-control operations	
`const int BRANCH = 40;`	Branch to a specific location in memory.
`const int BRANCHNEG = 41;`	Branch to a specific location in memory if the accumulator is negative.
`const int BRANCHZERO = 42;`	Branch to a specific location in memory if the accumulator is zero.
`const int HALT = 43;`	Halt—the program has completed its task.

Fig. 8.39 | Simpletron Machine Language (SML) operation codes.

Now let us consider two simple SML programs. The first SML program (Fig. 8.40) reads two numbers from the keyboard and computes and prints their sum. The instruction +1007 reads the first number from the keyboard and places it into location 07 (which has been initialized to zero). Instruction +1008 reads the next number into location 08. The *load* instruction, +2007, places (copies) the first number into the accumulator, and the *add* instruction, +3008, adds the second number to the number in the accumulator. *All SML arithmetic instructions leave their results in the accumulator.* The *store* instruction, +2109, places (copies) the result back into memory location 09. Then the *write* instruction, +1109, takes the number and prints it (as a signed four-digit decimal number). The *halt* instruction, +4300, terminates execution.

Location	Number	Instruction
00	+1007	(Read A)
01	+1008	(Read B)
02	+2007	(Load A)
03	+3008	(Add B)
04	+2109	(Store C)
05	+1109	(Write C)
06	+4300	(Halt)
07	+0000	(Variable A)
08	+0000	(Variable B)
09	+0000	(Result C)

Fig. 8.40 | SML Example 1.

The SML program in Fig. 8.41 reads two numbers from the keyboard, then determines and prints the larger value. Note the use of the instruction +4107 as a conditional transfer of control, much the same as C++'s if statement.

Now write SML programs to accomplish each of the following tasks:

a) Use a sentinel-controlled loop to read positive numbers and compute and print their sum. Terminate input when a negative number is entered.

b) Use a counter-controlled loop to read seven numbers, some positive and some negative, and compute and print their average.

c) Read a series of numbers, and determine and print the largest number. The first number read indicates how many numbers should be processed.

Location	Number	Instruction
00	+1009	(Read A)
01	+1010	(Read B)
02	+2009	(Load A)
03	+3110	(Subtract B)
04	+4107	(Branch negative to 07)
05	+1109	(Write A)
06	+4300	(Halt)
07	+1110	(Write B)
08	+4300	(Halt)
09	+0000	(Variable A)
10	+0000	(Variable B)

Fig. 8.41 | SML Example 2.

8.19 (*Computer Simulator*) It may at first seem outrageous, but in this problem you are going to build your own computer. No, you will not be soldering components together. Rather, you will use the powerful technique of *software-based simulation* to create a *software model* of the Simpletron. You will not be disappointed. Your Simpletron simulator will turn the computer you are using into a Simpletron, and you actually will be able to run, test and debug the SML programs you wrote in Exercise 8.18.

When you run your Simpletron simulator, it should begin by printing

```
*** Welcome to Simpletron! ***

*** Please enter your program one instruction ***
*** (or data word) at a time. I will type the ***
*** location number and a question mark (?).   ***
*** You then type the word for that location.  ***
*** Type the sentinel -99999 to stop entering  ***
*** your program. ***
```

Your program should simulate the Simpletron's memory with a single-subscripted, 100-element array memory. Now assume that the simulator is running, and let us examine the dialog as we enter the program of Example 2 of Exercise 8.18:

```
00 ? +1009
01 ? +1010
02 ? +2009
03 ? +3110
04 ? +4107
05 ? +1109
06 ? +4300
07 ? +1110
08 ? +4300
09 ? +0000
10 ? +0000
11 ? -99999

*** Program loading completed ***
*** Program execution begins  ***
```

Note that the numbers to the right of each ? in the preceding dialog represent the SML program instructions input by the user.

The SML program has now been placed (or loaded) into array memory. Now the Simpletron executes your SML program. Execution begins with the instruction in location 00 and, like C++, continues sequentially, unless directed to some other part of the program by a transfer of control.

Use variable accumulator to represent the accumulator register. Use variable counter to keep track of the location in memory that contains the instruction being performed. Use variable operationCode to indicate the operation currently being performed (i.e., the left two digits of the instruction word). Use variable operand to indicate the memory location on which the current instruction operates. Thus, operand is the rightmost two digits of the instruction currently being performed. Do not execute instructions directly from memory. Rather, transfer the next instruction to be performed from memory to a variable called instructionRegister. Then "pick off" the left two digits and place them in operationCode, and "pick off" the right two digits and place them in operand. When Simpletron begins execution, the special registers are all initialized to zero.

Now let us "walk through" the execution of the first SML instruction, +1009 in memory location 00. This is called an *instruction execution cycle.*

The counter tells us the location of the next instruction to be performed. We *fetch* the contents of that location from memory by using the C++ statement

```
instructionRegister = memory[ counter ];
```

The operation code and operand are extracted from the instruction register by the statements

```
operationCode = instructionRegister / 100;
operand = instructionRegister % 100;
```

Now, the Simpletron must determine that the operation code is actually a *read* (versus a *write*, a *load*, etc.). A switch differentiates among the 12 operations of SML.

In the switch statement, the behavior of various SML instructions is simulated as shown in Fig. 8.42 (we leave the others to the reader).

The *halt* instruction also causes the Simpletron to print the name and contents of each register, as well as the complete contents of memory. Such a printout is often called a *computer dump* (and, no, a computer dump is not a place where old computers go). To help you program your dump function, a sample dump format is shown in Fig. 8.43. Note that a dump after executing a Simpletron program would show the actual values of instructions and data values at the moment execution terminated. To format numbers with their sign as shown in the dump, use stream manipulator showpos. To disable the display of the sign, use stream manipulator noshowpos. For numbers that have fewer than four digits, you can format numbers with leading zeros between the sign and the value by using the following statement before outputting the value:

```
cout << setfill( '0' ) << internal;
```

Parameterized stream manipulator setfill (from header <iomanip>) specifies the fill character that will appear between the sign and the value when a number is displayed with a field width of five characters but does not have four digits. (One position in the field width is reserved for the sign.) Stream manipulator internal indicates that the fill characters should appear between the sign and the numeric value .

read:	`cin >> memory[ operand ];`
load:	`accumulator = memory[ operand ];`
add:	`accumulator += memory[ operand ];`
branch:	We will discuss the branch instructions shortly.
halt:	This instruction prints the message `*** Simpletron execution terminated ***`

Fig. 8.42 | Behavior of SML instructions.

```
REGISTERS:
accumulator          +0000
counter                 00
instructionRegister  +0000
operationCode           00
operand                 00

MEMORY:
        0      1      2      3      4      5      6      7      8      9
 0  +0000  +0000  +0000  +0000  +0000  +0000  +0000  +0000  +0000  +0000
10  +0000  +0000  +0000  +0000  +0000  +0000  +0000  +0000  +0000  +0000
20  +0000  +0000  +0000  +0000  +0000  +0000  +0000  +0000  +0000  +0000
30  +0000  +0000  +0000  +0000  +0000  +0000  +0000  +0000  +0000  +0000
40  +0000  +0000  +0000  +0000  +0000  +0000  +0000  +0000  +0000  +0000
50  +0000  +0000  +0000  +0000  +0000  +0000  +0000  +0000  +0000  +0000
60  +0000  +0000  +0000  +0000  +0000  +0000  +0000  +0000  +0000  +0000
70  +0000  +0000  +0000  +0000  +0000  +0000  +0000  +0000  +0000  +0000
80  +0000  +0000  +0000  +0000  +0000  +0000  +0000  +0000  +0000  +0000
90  +0000  +0000  +0000  +0000  +0000  +0000  +0000  +0000  +0000  +0000
```

Fig. 8.43 | A sample dump.

Let us proceed with the execution of our program's first instruction—+1009 in location 00. As we have indicated, the switch statement simulates this by performing the C++ statement

```
cin >> memory[ operand ];
```

A question mark (?) should be displayed on the screen before the cin statement executes to prompt the user for input. The Simpletron waits for the user to type a value and press the *Enter* key. The value is then read into location 09.

At this point, simulation of the first instruction is complete. All that remains is to prepare the Simpletron to execute the next instruction. The instruction just performed was not a transfer of control, so we need merely increment the instruction counter register as follows:

```
++counter;
```

This completes the simulated execution of the first instruction. The entire process (i.e., the instruction execution cycle) begins anew with the fetch of the next instruction to execute.

Now let us consider how to simulate the branching instructions (i.e., the transfers of control). All we need to do is adjust the value in the instruction counter appropriately. Therefore, the unconditional branch instruction (40) is simulated in the switch as

```
counter = operand;
```

The conditional "branch if accumulator is zero" instruction is simulated as

```
if ( accumulator == 0 )
    counter = operand;
```

At this point, you should implement your Simpletron simulator and run each of the SML programs you wrote in Exercise 8.18. You may embellish SML with additional features and provide for these in your simulator.

Your simulator should check for various types of errors. During the program loading phase, for example, each number the user types into the Simpletron's memory must be in the range -9999 to +9999. Your simulator should use a while loop to test that each number entered is in this range and, if not, keep prompting the user to reenter the number until the user enters a correct number.

During the execution phase, your simulator should check for various serious errors, such as attempts to divide by zero, attempts to execute invalid operation codes, accumulator overflows (i.e., arithmetic operations resulting in values larger than +9999 or smaller than -9999) and the like. Such serious errors are called fatal errors. When a fatal error is detected, your simulator should print an error message such as

```
*** Attempt to divide by zero ***
*** Simpletron execution abnormally terminated ***
```

and should print a full computer dump in the format we have discussed previously. This will help the user locate the error in the program.

More Pointer Exercises

8.20   Modify the card shuffling and dealing program of Figs. 8.25–8.27 so the shuffling and dealing operations are performed by the same function (shuffleAndDeal). The function should contain one nested looping statement that is similar to function shuffle in Fig. 8.26.

8.21   What does this program do?

```
 1   // Ex. 8.21: ex08_21.cpp
 2   // What does this program do?
 3   #include <iostream>
 4   using std::cout;
 5   using std::cin;
 6   using std::endl;
 7
 8   void mystery1( char *, const char * ); // prototype
 9
10   int main()
11   {
12      char string1[ 80 ];
13      char string2[ 80 ];
14
15      cout << "Enter two strings: ";
16      cin >> string1 >> string2;
17      mystery1( string1, string2 );
18      cout << string1 << endl;
19      return 0; // indicates successful termination
20   } // end main
21
22   // What does this function do?
23   void mystery1( char *s1, const char *s2 )
24   {
25      while ( *s1 != '\0' )
26         ++s1;
27
28      for ( ; *s1 = *s2; s1++, s2++ )
29         ; // empty statement
30   } // end function mystery1
```

8.22   What does this program do?

```
 1   // Ex. 8.22: ex08_22.cpp
 2   // What does this program do?
 3   #include <iostream>
 4   using std::cout;
 5   using std::cin;
 6   using std::endl;
 7
 8   int mystery2( const char * ); // prototype
 9
10   int main()
11   {
12      char string1[ 80 ];
13
14      cout << "Enter a string: ";
15      cin >> string1;
16      cout << mystery2( string1 ) << endl;
17      return 0; // indicates successful termination
18   } // end main
19
```

```
20    // What does this function do?
21    int mystery2( const char *s )
22    {
23       int x;
24
25       for ( x = 0; *s != '\0'; s++ )
26          ++x;
27
28       return x;
29    } // end function mystery2
```

8.23   Find the error in each of the following segments. If the error can be corrected, explain how.

a) `int *number;`
    `cout << number << endl;`

b) `double *realPtr;`
    `long *integerPtr;`
    `integerPtr = realPtr;`

c) `int * x, y;`
    `x = y;`

d) `char s[] = "this is a character array";`
    `for ( ; *s != '\0'; s++)`
    `   cout << *s << ' ';`

e) `short *numPtr, result;`
    `void *genericPtr = numPtr;`
    `result = *genericPtr + 7;`

f) `double x = 19.34;`
    `double xPtr = &x;`
    `cout << xPtr << endl;`

g) `char *s;`
    `cout << s << endl;`

8.24   (*Quicksort*) You have previously seen the sorting techniques of the bucket sort and selection sort. We now present the recursive sorting technique called Quicksort. The basic algorithm for a single-subscripted array of values is as follows:

a) *Partitioning Step:* Take the first element of the unsorted array and determine its final location in the sorted array (i.e., all values to the left of the element in the array are less than the element, and all values to the right of the element in the array are greater than the element). We now have one element in its proper location and two unsorted subarrays.

b) *Recursive Step:* Perform *Step 1* on each unsorted subarray.

Each time *Step 1* is performed on a subarray, another element is placed in its final location of the sorted array, and two unsorted subarrays are created. When a subarray consists of one element, that subarray must be sorted; therefore, that element is in its final location.

The basic algorithm seems simple enough, but how do we determine the final position of the first element of each subarray? As an example, consider the following set of values (the element in bold is the partitioning element—it will be placed in its final location in the sorted array):

37 2 6 4 89 8 10 12 68 45

a) Starting from the rightmost element of the array, compare each element with **37** until an element less than **37** is found. Then swap **37** and that element. The first element less than **37** is 12, so **37** and 12 are swapped. The values now reside in the array as follows:

12 2 6 4 89 8 10 **37** 68 45

Element 12 is in italics to indicate that it was just swapped with **37**.

b) Starting from the left of the array, but beginning with the element after 12, compare each element with **37** until an element greater than **37** is found. Then swap **37** and that element. The first element greater than **37** is 89, so **37** and 89 are swapped. The values now reside in the array as follows:

12   2   6   4   **37**   8   10   *89*   68   45

c) Starting from the right, but beginning with the element before 89, compare each element with **37** until an element less than **37** is found. Then swap **37** and that element. The first element less than **37** is 10, so **37** and 10 are swapped. The values now reside in the array as follows:

12   2   6   4   *10*   8   **37**   89   68   45

d) Starting from the left, but beginning with the element after 10, compare each element with **37** until an element greater than **37** is found. Then swap **37** and that element. There are no more elements greater than **37**, so when we compare **37** with itself, we know that **37** has been placed in its final location of the sorted array.

Once the partition has been applied to the array, there are two unsorted subarrays. The subarray with values less than 37 contains 12, 2, 6, 4, 10 and 8. The subarray with values greater than 37 contains 89, 68 and 45. The sort continues with both subarrays being partitioned in the same manner as the original array.

Based on the preceding discussion, write recursive function quickSort to sort a single-subscripted integer array. The function should receive as arguments an integer array, a starting subscript and an ending subscript. Function partition should be called by quickSort to perform the partitioning step.

8.25   (*Maze Traversal*) The grid of hashes (#) and dots (.) in Fig. 8.44 is a two-dimensional array representation of a maze. In the two-dimensional array, the hashes represent the walls of the maze and the dots represent squares in the possible paths through the maze. Moves can be made only to a location in the array that contains a dot.

There is a simple algorithm for walking through a maze that guarantees finding the exit (assuming that there is an exit). If there is not an exit, you will arrive at the starting location again. Place your right hand on the wall to your right and begin walking forward. Never remove your hand from the wall. If the maze turns to the right, you follow the wall to the right. As long as you do not remove your hand from the wall, eventually you will arrive at the exit of the maze. There may be a shorter path than the one you have taken, but you are guaranteed to get out of the maze if you follow the algorithm.

Fig. 8.44 | Two-dimensional array representation of a maze.

Write recursive function `mazeTraverse` to walk through the maze. The function should receive arguments that include a 12-by-12 character array representing the maze and the starting location of the maze. As `mazeTraverse` attempts to locate the exit from the maze, it should place the character X in each square in the path. The function should display the maze after each move, so the user can watch as the maze is solved.

8.26 (*Generating Mazes Randomly*) Write a function `mazeGenerator` that takes as an argument a two-dimensional 12-by-12 character array and randomly produces a maze. The function should also provide the starting and ending locations of the maze. Try your function `mazeTraverse` from Exercise 8.25, using several randomly generated mazes.

8.27 (*Mazes of Any Size*) Generalize functions `mazeTraverse` and `mazeGenerator` of Exercise 8.25 and Exercise 8.26 to process mazes of any width and height.

8.28 (*Modifications to the Simpletron Simulator*) In Exercise 8.19, you wrote a software simulation of a computer that executes programs written in Simpletron Machine Language (SML). In this exercise, we propose several modifications and enhancements to the Simpletron Simulator. Some of the following modifications and enhancements may be required to execute the programs produced by the compiler. [*Note:* Some modifications may conflict with others and therefore must be done separately.]

a) Extend the Simpletron Simulator's memory to contain 1000 memory locations to enable the Simpletron to handle larger programs.

b) Allow the simulator to perform modulus calculations. This requires an additional Simpletron Machine Language instruction.

c) Allow the simulator to perform exponentiation calculations. This requires an additional Simpletron Machine Language instruction.

d) Modify the simulator to use hexadecimal values rather than integer values to represent Simpletron Machine Language instructions.

e) Modify the simulator to allow output of a newline. This requires an additional Simpletron Machine Language instruction.

f) Modify the simulator to process floating-point values in addition to integer values.

g) Modify the simulator to handle string input. [*Hint:* Each Simpletron word can be divided into two groups, each holding a two-digit integer. Each two-digit integer represents the ASCII decimal equivalent of a character. Add a machine-language instruction that will input a string and store the string beginning at a specific Simpletron memory location. The first half of the word at that location will be a count of the number of characters in the string (i.e., the length of the string). Each succeeding half-word contains one ASCII character expressed as two decimal digits. The machine-language instruction converts each character into its ASCII equivalent and assigns it to a half-word.]

h) Modify the simulator to handle output of strings stored in the format of part (g). [*Hint:* Add a machine-language instruction that will print a string beginning at a certain Simpletron memory location. The first half of the word at that location is a count of the number of characters in the string (i.e., the length of the string). Each succeeding half-word contains one ASCII character expressed as two decimal digits. The machine-language instruction checks the length and prints the string by translating each two-digit number into its equivalent character.]

i) Modify the simulator to include instruction `SML_DEBUG` that prints a memory dump after each instruction executes. Give `SML_DEBUG` an operation code of 44. The word +4401 turns on debug mode, and +4400 turns off debug mode.

8.29   What does this program do?

```
1   // Ex. 8.29: ex08_29.cpp
2   // What does this program do?
3   #include <iostream>
4   using std::cout;
5   using std::cin;
6   using std::endl;
7
8   bool mystery3( const char *, const char * ); // prototype
9
10  int main()
11  {
12     char string1[ 80 ], string2[ 80 ];
13
14     cout << "Enter two strings: ";
15     cin >> string1 >> string2;
16     cout << "The result is " << mystery3( string1, string2 ) << endl;
17     return 0; // indicates successful termination
18  } // end main
19
20  // What does this function do?
21  bool mystery3( const char *s1, const char *s2 )
22  {
23     for ( ; *s1 != '\0' && *s2 != '\0'; s1++, s2++ )
24
25        if ( *s1 != *s2 )
26           return false;
27
28     return true;
29  } // end function mystery3
```

String-Manipulation Exercises

[*Note:* The following exercises should be implemented using C-style, pointer-based strings.]

8.30   Write a program that uses function strcmp to compare two strings input by the user. The program should state whether the first string is less than, equal to or greater than the second string.

8.31   Write a program that uses function strncmp to compare two strings input by the user. The program should input the number of characters to compare. The program should state whether the first string is less than, equal to or greater than the second string.

8.32   Write a program that uses random number generation to create sentences. The program should use four arrays of pointers to char called article, noun, verb and preposition. The program should create a sentence by selecting a word at random from each array in the following order: article, noun, verb, preposition, article and noun. As each word is picked, it should be concatenated to the previous words in an array that is large enough to hold the entire sentence. The words should be separated by spaces. When the final sentence is output, it should start with a capital letter and end with a period. The program should generate 20 such sentences.

The arrays should be filled as follows: The article array should contain the articles "the", "a", "one", "some" and "any"; the noun array should contain the nouns "boy", "girl", "dog", "town" and "car"; the verb array should contain the verbs "drove", "jumped", "ran", "walked" and "skipped"; the preposition array should contain the prepositions "to", "from", "over", "under" and "on".

After completing the program, modify it to produce a short story consisting of several of these sentences. (How about the possibility of a random term-paper writer!)

8.33 *(Limericks)* A limerick is a humorous five-line verse in which the first and second lines rhyme with the fifth, and the third line rhymes with the fourth. Using techniques similar to those developed in Exercise 8.32, write a C++ program that produces random limericks. Polishing this program to produce good limericks is a challenging problem, but the result will be worth the effort!

8.34 Write a program that encodes English language phrases into pig Latin. Pig Latin is a form of coded language often used for amusement. Many variations exist in the methods used to form pig Latin phrases. For simplicity, use the following algorithm: To form a pig-Latin phrase from an English-language phrase, tokenize the phrase into words with function strtok. To translate each English word into a pig-Latin word, place the first letter of the English word at the end of the English word and add the letters "ay." Thus, the word "jump" becomes "umpjay," the word "the" becomes "hetay" and the word "computer" becomes "omputercay." Blanks between words remain as blanks. Assume that the English phrase consists of words separated by blanks, there are no punctuation marks and all words have two or more letters. Function printLatinWord should display each word. [*Hint:* Each time a token is found in a call to strtok, pass the token pointer to function printLatinWord and print the pig-Latin word.]

8.35 Write a program that inputs a telephone number as a string in the form (555) 555-5555. The program should use function strtok to extract the area code as a token, the first three digits of the phone number as a token, and the last four digits of the phone number as a token. The seven digits of the phone number should be concatenated into one string. Both the area code and the phone number should be printed.

8.36 Write a program that inputs a line of text, tokenizes the line with function strtok and outputs the tokens in reverse order.

8.37 Use the string-comparison functions discussed in Section 8.13.2 and the techniques for sorting arrays developed in Chapter 7 to write a program that alphabetizes a list of strings. Use the names of 10 or 15 towns in your area as data for your program.

8.38 Write two versions of each string copy and string-concatenation function in Fig. 8.30. The first version should use array subscripting, and the second should use pointers and pointer arithmetic.

8.39 Write two versions of each string-comparison function in Fig. 8.30. The first version should use array subscripting, and the second should use pointers and pointer arithmetic.

8.40 Write two versions of function strlen in Fig. 8.30. The first version should use array subscripting, and the second should use pointers and pointer arithmetic.

Special Section: Advanced String-Manipulation Exercises

The preceding exercises are keyed to the text and designed to test the reader's understanding of fundamental string-manipulation concepts. This section includes a collection of intermediate and advanced string-manipulation exercises. The reader should find these problems challenging, yet enjoyable. The problems vary considerably in difficulty. Some require an hour or two of program writing and implementation. Others are useful for lab assignments that might require two or three weeks of study and implementation. Some are challenging term projects.

8.41 *(Text Analysis)* The availability of computers with string-manipulation capabilities has resulted in some rather interesting approaches to analyzing the writings of great authors. Much attention has been focused on whether William Shakespeare ever lived. Some scholars believe there is substantial evidence indicating that Christopher Marlowe or other authors actually penned the masterpieces attributed to Shakespeare. Researchers have used computers to find similarities in the writings of these two authors. This exercise examines three methods for analyzing texts with a computer. Note that thousands of texts, including Shakespeare, are available online at www.gutenberg.org.

a) Write a program that reads several lines of text from the keyboard and prints a table indicating the number of occurrences of each letter of the alphabet in the text. For example, the phrase

```
To be, or not to be: that is the question:
```

contains one "a," two "b's," no "c's," etc.

b) Write a program that reads several lines of text and prints a table indicating the number of one-letter words, two-letter words, three-letter words, etc., appearing in the text. For example, the phrase

```
Whether 'tis nobler in the mind to suffer
```

contains the following word lengths and occurrences:

Word length	Occurrences
1	0
2	2
3	1
4	2 (including 'tis)
5	0
6	2
7	1

c) Write a program that reads several lines of text and prints a table indicating the number of occurrences of each different word in the text. The first version of your program should include the words in the table in the same order in which they appear in the text. For example, the lines

```
To be, or not to be: that is the question:
Whether 'tis nobler in the mind to suffer
```

contain the words "to" three times, the word "be" two times, the word "or" once, etc. A more interesting (and useful) printout should then be attempted in which the words are sorted alphabetically.

8.42 *(Word Processing)* One important function in word-processing systems is *type justification*—the alignment of words to both the left and right margins of a page. This generates a professional-looking document that gives the appearance of being set in type rather than prepared on a typewriter. Type justification can be accomplished on computer systems by inserting blank characters between each of the words in a line so that the rightmost word aligns with the right margin.

Write a program that reads several lines of text and prints this text in type-justified format. Assume that the text is to be printed on paper 8 1/2 inches wide and that one-inch margins are to be allowed on both the left and right sides. Assume that the computer prints 10 characters to the horizontal inch. Therefore, your program should print 6-1/2 inches of text, or 65 characters per line.

8.43 *(Printing Dates in Various Formats)* Dates are commonly printed in several different formats in business correspondence. Two of the more common formats are

```
07/21/1955
July 21, 1955
```

Write a program that reads a date in the first format and prints that date in the second format.

8.44 *(Check Protection)* Computers are frequently employed in check-writing systems such as payroll and accounts-payable applications. Many strange stories circulate regarding weekly paychecks being printed (by mistake) for amounts in excess of $1 million. Weird amounts are printed by computerized check-writing systems, because of human error or machine failure. Systems designers build controls into their systems to prevent such erroneous checks from being issued.

Another serious problem is the intentional alteration of a check amount by someone who intends to cash a check fraudulently. To prevent a dollar amount from being altered, most computerized check-writing systems employ a technique called *check protection.*

Checks designed for imprinting by computer contain a fixed number of spaces in which the computer may print an amount. Suppose that a paycheck contains eight blank spaces in which the computer is supposed to print the amount of a weekly paycheck. If the amount is large, then all eight of those spaces will be filled, for example,

```
1,230.60    (check amount)
--------
12345678    (position numbers)
```

On the other hand, if the amount is less than $1000, then several of the spaces would ordinarily be left blank. For example,

```
  99.87
--------
12345678
```

contains three blank spaces. If a check is printed with blank spaces, it is easier for someone to alter the amount of the check. To prevent a check from being altered, many check-writing systems insert *leading asterisks* to protect the amount as follows:

```
***99.87
--------
12345678
```

Write a program that inputs a dollar amount to be printed on a check and then prints the amount in check-protected format with leading asterisks if necessary. Assume that nine spaces are available for printing an amount.

8.45 *(Writing the Word Equivalent of a Check Amount)* Continuing the discussion of the previous example, we reiterate the importance of designing check-writing systems to prevent alteration of check amounts. One common security method requires that the check amount be both written in numbers and "spelled out" in words. Even if someone is able to alter the numerical amount of the check, it is extremely difficult to change the amount in words.

Write a program that inputs a numeric check amount and writes the word equivalent of the amount. Your program should be able to handle check amounts as large as $99.99. For example, the amount 112.43 should be written as

```
ONE HUNDRED TWELVE and 43/100
```

8.46   *(Morse Code)* Perhaps the most famous of all coding schemes is the Morse code, developed by Samuel Morse in 1832 for use with the telegraph system. The Morse code assigns a series of dots and dashes to each letter of the alphabet, each digit and a few special characters (such as period, comma, colon and semicolon). In sound-oriented systems, the dot represents a short sound, and the dash represents a long sound. Other representations of dots and dashes are used with light-oriented systems and signal-flag systems.

Separation between words is indicated by a space, or, quite simply, the absence of a dot or dash. In a sound-oriented system, a space is indicated by a short period of time during which no sound is transmitted. The international version of the Morse code appears in Fig. 8.45.

Write a program that reads an English-language phrase and encodes it into Morse code. Also write a program that reads a phrase in Morse code and converts it into the English-language equivalent. Use one blank between each Morse-coded letter and three blanks between each Morse-coded word.

Character	Code	Character	Code
A	.-	N	-.
B	-...	O	---
C	-.-.	P	.--.
D	-..	Q	--.-
E	.	R	.-.
F	..-.	S	...
G	--.	T	-
H	....	U	..-
I	..	V	...-
J	.---	W	.--
K	-.-	X	-..-
L	.-..	Y	-.--
M	--	Z	--..
Digits			
1	.----	6	-....
2	..---	7	--...
3	...--	8	---..
4	....-	9	----.
5	.....	0	-----

Fig. 8.45 | Morse code alphabet.

8.47   *(A Metric Conversion Program)* Write a program that will assist the user with metric conversions. Your program should allow the user to specify the names of the units as strings (i.e., centimeters, liters, grams, etc., for the metric system and inches, quarts, pounds, etc., for the English system) and should respond to simple questions such as

```
"How many inches are in 2 meters?"
"How many liters are in 10 quarts?"
```

Your program should recognize invalid conversions. For example, the question

```
"How many feet are in 5 kilograms?"
```

is not meaningful, because "feet" are units of length, while "kilograms" are units of weight.

A Challenging String-Manipulation Project

8.48   *(A Crossword Puzzle Generator)* Most people have worked a crossword puzzle, but few have ever attempted to generate one. Generating a crossword puzzle is a difficult problem. It is suggested here as a string-manipulation project requiring substantial sophistication and effort. There are many issues that the programmer must resolve to get even the simplest crossword puzzle generator program working. For example, how does one represent the grid of a crossword puzzle inside the computer? Should one use a series of strings, or should two-dimensional arrays be used? The programmer needs a source of words (i.e., a computerized dictionary) that can be directly referenced by the program. In what form should these words be stored to facilitate the complex manipulations required by the program? The really ambitious reader will want to generate the "clues" portion of the puzzle, in which the brief hints for each "across" word and each "down" word are printed for the puzzle worker. Merely printing a version of the blank puzzle itself is not a simple problem.

Classes: A Deeper Look, Part I

My object all sublime
I shall achieve in time.
—W. S. Gilbert

Is it a world to hide virtues
in?
—William Shakespeare

Don't be "consistent," but be
simply true.
—Oliver Wendell Holmes, Jr.

This above all: to thine own
self be true.
—William Shakespeare

OBJECTIVES

In this chapter you will learn:

- How to use a preprocessor wrapper to prevent multiple definition errors caused by including more than one copy of a header file in a source-code file.

- To understand class scope and accessing class members via the name of an object, a reference to an object or a pointer to an object.

- To define constructors with default arguments.

- How destructors are used to perform "termination housekeeping" on an object before it is destroyed.

- When constructors and destructors are called and the order in which they are called.

- The logic errors that may occur when a `public` member function of a class returns a reference to `private` data.

- To assign the data members of one object to those of another object by default memberwise assignment.

Outline

9.1 Introduction

9.2 **Time** Class Case Study

9.3 Class Scope and Accessing Class Members

9.4 Separating Interface from Implementation

9.5 Access Functions and Utility Functions

9.6 **Time** Class Case Study: Constructors with Default Arguments

9.7 Destructors

9.8 When Constructors and Destructors Are Called

9.9 **Time** Class Case Study: A Subtle Trap—Returning a Reference to a **private** Data Member

9.10 Default Memberwise Assignment

9.11 Software Reusability

9.12 Wrap-Up

Summary | Terminology | Self-Review Exercises | Answers to Self-Review Exercises | Exercises

9.1 Introduction

In the preceding chapters, we introduced many basic terms and concepts of C++ object-oriented programming. We also discussed our program development methodology: We selected appropriate attributes and behaviors for each class and specified the manner in which objects of our classes collaborated with objects of C++ Standard Library classes to accomplish each program's overall goals.

In this chapter, we take a deeper look at classes. We use an integrated Time class case study in this chapter (three examples) and Chapter 10 (two examples) to demonstrate several class construction features. We begin with a Time class that reviews several of the features presented in the preceding chapters. The example also demonstrates an important C++ software engineering concept—using a "preprocessor wrapper" in header files to prevent the code in the header from being included into the same source code file more than once. Since a class can be defined only once, using such preprocessor directives prevents multiple definition errors.

Next, we discuss class scope and the relationships among members of a class. We also demonstrate how client code can access a class's public members via three types of "handles"—the name of an object, a reference to an object or a pointer to an object. As you will see, object names and references can be used with the dot (.) member selection operator to access a public member, and pointers can be used with the arrow (->) member selection operator.

We discuss access functions that can read or display data in an object. A common use of access functions is to test the truth or falsity of conditions—such functions are known as predicate functions. We also demonstrate the notion of a utility function (also called a helper function)—a private member function that supports the operation of the class's public member functions, but is not intended for use by clients of the class.

In the second example of the Time class case study, we demonstrate how to pass arguments to constructors and show how default arguments can be used in a constructor to enable client code to initialize objects of a class using a variety of arguments. Next, we discuss a special member function called a destructor that is part of every class and is used to perform "termination housekeeping" on an object before the object is destroyed. We then demonstrate the order in which constructors and destructors are called, because your programs' correctness depends on using properly initialized objects that have not yet been destroyed.

Our last example of the Time class case study in this chapter shows a dangerous programming practice in which a member function returns a reference to private data. We discuss how this breaks the encapsulation of a class and allows client code to directly access an object's data. This last example shows that objects of the same class can be assigned to one another using default memberwise assignment, which copies the data members in the object on the right side of the assignment into the corresponding data members of the object on the left side of the assignment. The chapter concludes with a discussion of software reusability.

9.2 Time Class Case Study

Our first example (Figs. 9.1–9.3) creates class Time and a driver program that tests the class. You have already created several classes in this book. In this section, we review many of the concepts covered in Chapter 3 and demonstrate an important C++ software engineering concept—using a "preprocessor wrapper" in header files to prevent the code in the header from being included into the same source code file more than once. Since a class can be defined only once, using such preprocessor directives prevents multiple-definition errors.

```
 1  // Fig. 9.1: Time.h
 2  // Declaration of class Time.
 3  // Member functions are defined in Time.cpp
 4
 5  // prevent multiple inclusions of header file
 6  #ifndef TIME_H
 7  #define TIME_H
 8
 9  // Time class definition
10  class Time
11  {
12  public:
13     Time(); // constructor
14     void setTime( int, int, int ); // set hour, minute and second
15     void printUniversal(); // print time in universal-time format
16     void printStandard(); // print time in standard-time format
17  private:
18     int hour; // 0 - 23 (24-hour clock format)
19     int minute; // 0 - 59
20     int second; // 0 - 59
21  }; // end class Time
22
23  #endif
```

Fig. 9.1 | Time class definition.

***Time* Class Definition**

The class definition (Fig. 9.1) contains prototypes (lines 13–16) for member functions `Time`, `setTime`, `printUniversal` and `printStandard`. The class includes `private` integer members `hour`, `minute` and `second` (lines 18–20). Class `Time`'s `private` data members can be accessed only by its four member functions. Chapter 12 introduces a third access specifier, `protected`, as we study inheritance and the part it plays in object-oriented programming.

Good Programming Practice 9.1

For clarity and readability, use each access specifier only once in a class definition. Place `public` members first, where they are easy to locate.

Software Engineering Observation 9.1

Each element of a class should have `private` visibility unless it can be proven that the element needs `public` visibility. This is another example of the principle of least privilege.

In Fig. 9.1, note that the class definition is enclosed in the following preprocessor wrapper (lines 5–7 and 23):

```
// prevent multiple inclusions of header file
#ifndef TIME_H
#define TIME_H
   ...
#endif
```

When we build larger programs, other definitions and declarations will also be placed in header files. The preceding preprocessor wrapper prevents the code between `#ifndef` (which means "if not defined") and `#endif` from being included if the name `TIME_H` has been defined. If the header has not been included previously in a file, the name `TIME_H` is defined by the `#define` directive and the header file statements are included. If the header has been included previously, `TIME_H` is defined already and the header file is not included again. Attempts to include a header file multiple times (inadvertently) typically occur in large programs with many header files that may themselves include other header files. [*Note:* The commonly used convention for the symbolic constant name in the preprocessor directives is simply the header file name in upper case with the underscore character replacing the period.]

Error-Prevention Tip 9.1

Use `#ifndef`, `#define` and `#endif` preprocessor directives to form a preprocessor wrapper that prevents header files from being included more than once in a program.

Good Programming Practice 9.2

Use the name of the header file in upper case with the period replaced by an underscore in the `#ifndef` and `#define` preprocessor directives of a header file.

***Time* Class Member Functions**

In Fig. 9.2, the `Time` constructor (lines 14–17) initializes the data members to 0 (i.e., the universal-time equivalent of 12 AM). This ensures that the object begins in a consistent state. Invalid values cannot be stored in the data members of a `Time` object, because the constructor is called when the `Time` object is created, and all subsequent attempts by a client to modify

```
 1   // Fig. 9.2: Time.cpp
 2   // Member-function definitions for class Time.
 3   #include <iostream>
 4   using std::cout;
 5
 6   #include <iomanip>
 7   using std::setfill;
 8   using std::setw;
 9
10   #include "Time.h" // include definition of class Time from Time.h
11
12   // Time constructor initializes each data member to zero.
13   // Ensures all Time objects start in a consistent state.
14   Time::Time()
15   {
16      hour = minute = second = 0;
17   } // end Time constructor
18
19   // set new Time value using universal time; ensure that
20   // the data remains consistent by setting invalid values to zero
21   void Time::setTime( int h, int m, int s )
22   {
23      hour = ( h >= 0 && h < 24 ) ? h : 0; // validate hour
24      minute = ( m >= 0 && m < 60 ) ? m : 0; // validate minute
25      second = ( s >= 0 && s < 60 ) ? s : 0; // validate second
26   } // end function setTime
27
28   // print Time in universal-time format (HH:MM:SS)
29   void Time::printUniversal()
30   {
31      cout << setfill( '0' ) << setw( 2 ) << hour << ":"
32         << setw( 2 ) << minute << ":" << setw( 2 ) << second;
33   } // end function printUniversal
34
35   // print Time in standard-time format (HH:MM:SS AM or PM)
36   void Time::printStandard()
37   {
38      cout << ( ( hour == 0 || hour == 12 ) ? 12 : hour % 12 ) << ":"
39         << setfill( '0' ) << setw( 2 ) << minute << ":" << setw( 2 )
40         << second << ( hour < 12 ? " AM" : " PM" );
41   } // end function printStandard
```

Fig. 9.2 | Time class member-function definitions.

the data members are scrutinized by function setTime (discussed shortly). Finally, it is important to note that the programmer can define several overloaded constructors for a class.

The data members of a class cannot be initialized where they are declared in the class body. It is strongly recommended that these data members be initialized by the class's constructor (as there is no default initialization for fundamental-type data members). Data members can also be assigned values by Time's *set* functions. [*Note:* Chapter 10 demonstrates that only a class's static const data members of integral or enum types can be initialized in the class's body.]

Common Programming Error 9.1

Attempting to initialize a non-static data member of a class explicitly in the class definition is a syntax error.

Function setTime (lines 21–26) is a public function that declares three int parameters and uses them to set the time. A conditional expression tests each argument to determine whether the value is in a specified range. For example, the hour value (line 23) must be greater than or equal to 0 and less than 24, because the universal-time format represents hours as integers from 0 to 23 (e.g., 1 PM is hour 13 and 11 PM is hour 23; midnight is hour 0 and noon is hour 12). Similarly, both minute and second values (lines 24 and 25) must be greater than or equal to 0 and less than 60. Any values outside these ranges are set to zero to ensure that a Time object always contains consistent data—that is, the object's data values are always kept in range, even if the values provided as arguments to function setTime were incorrect. In this example, zero is a consistent value for hour, minute and second.

A value passed to setTime is a correct value if it is in the allowed range for the member it is initializing. So, any number in the range 0–23 would be a correct value for the hour. A correct value is always a consistent value. However, a consistent value is not necessarily a correct value. If setTime sets hour to 0 because the argument received was out of range, then hour is correct only if the current time is coincidentally midnight.

Function printUniversal (lines 29–33 of Fig. 9.2) takes no arguments and outputs the date in universal-time format, consisting of three colon-separated pairs of digits—for the hour, minute and second, respectively. For example, if the time were 1:30:07 PM, function printUniversal would return 13:30:07. Note that line 31 uses parameterized stream manipulator setfill to specify the fill character that is displayed when an integer is output in a field wider than the number of digits in the value. By default, the fill characters appear to the left of the digits in the number. In this example, if the minute value is 2, it will be displayed as 02, because the fill character is set to zero ('0'). If the number being output fills the specified field, the fill character will not be displayed. Note that, once the fill character is specified with setfill, it applies for all subsequent values that are displayed in fields wider than the value being displayed (i.e., setfill is a "sticky" setting). This is in contrast to setw, which applies only to the next value displayed (setw is a "nonsticky" setting).

Error-Prevention Tip 9.2

Each sticky setting (such as a fill character or floating-point precision) should be restored to its previous setting when it is no longer needed. Failure to do so may result in incorrectly formatted output later in a program.

Function printStandard (lines 36–41) takes no arguments and outputs the date in standard-time format, consisting of the hour, minute and second values separated by colons and followed by an AM or PM indicator (e.g., 1:27:06 PM). Like function printUniversal, function printStandard uses setfill('0') to format the minute and second as two digit values with leading zeros if necessary. Line 38 uses a conditional operator (?:) to determine the value of hour to be displayed—if the hour is 0 or 12 (AM or PM), it appears as 12; otherwise, the hour appears as a value from 1 to 11. The conditional operator in line 40 determines whether AM or PM will be displayed.

Defining Member Functions Outside the Class Definition; Class Scope

Even though a member function declared in a class definition may be defined outside that class definition (and "tied" to the class via the binary scope resolution operator), that member function is still within that class's scope; i.e., its name is known only to other members of the class unless referred to via an object of the class, a reference to an object of the class, a pointer to an object of the class or the binary scope resolution operator. We will say more about class scope shortly.

If a member function is defined in the body of a class definition, the C++ compiler attempts to inline calls to the member function. Member functions defined outside a class definition can be inlined by explicitly using keyword `inline`. Remember that the compiler reserves the right not to inline any function.

Performance Tip 9.1

Defining a member function inside the class definition inlines the member function (if the compiler chooses to do so). This can improve performance.

Software Engineering Observation 9.2

Defining a small member function inside the class definition does not promote the best software engineering, because clients of the class will be able to see the implementation of the function, and the client code must be recompiled if the function definition changes.

Software Engineering Observation 9.3

Only the simplest and most stable member functions (i.e., whose implementations are unlikely to change) should be defined in the class header.

Member Functions vs. Global Functions

It is interesting that the `printUniversal` and `printStandard` member functions take no arguments. This is because these member functions implicitly know that they are to print the data members of the particular `Time` object for which they are invoked. This can make member function calls more concise than conventional function calls in procedural programming.

Software Engineering Observation 9.4

Using an object-oriented programming approach can often simplify function calls by reducing the number of parameters to be passed. This benefit of object-oriented programming derives from the fact that encapsulating data members and member functions within an object gives the member functions the right to access the data members.

Software Engineering Observation 9.5

Member functions are usually shorter than functions in non-object-oriented programs, because the data stored in data members have ideally been validated by a constructor or by member functions that store new data. Because the data is already in the object, the member-function calls often have no arguments or at least have fewer arguments than typical function calls in non-object-oriented languages. Thus, the calls are shorter, the function definitions are shorter and the function prototypes are shorter. This facilitates many aspects of program development.

Error-Prevention Tip 9.3

The fact that member function calls generally take either no arguments or substantially fewer arguments than conventional function calls in non-object-oriented languages reduces the likelihood of passing the wrong arguments, the wrong types of arguments or the wrong number of arguments.

*Using Class **Time***

Once class Time has been defined, it can be used as a type in object, array, pointer and reference declarations as follows:

```
Time sunset; // object of type Time
Time arrayOfTimes[ 5 ], // array of 5 Time objects
Time &dinnerTime = sunset; // reference to a Time object
Time *timePtr = &dinnerTime, // pointer to a Time object
```

Figure 9.3 uses class Time. Line 12 instantiates a single object of class Time called t. When the object is instantiated, the Time constructor is called to initialize each private data member to 0. Then, lines 16 and 18 print the time in universal and standard formats to confirm that the members were initialized properly. Line 20 sets a new time by calling member function setTime, and lines 24 and 26 print the time again in both formats. Line 28 attempts to use setTime to set the data members to invalid values—function setTime recognizes this and sets the invalid values to 0 to maintain the object in a consistent state. Finally, lines 33 and 35 print the time again in both formats.

Looking Ahead to Composition and Inheritance

Often, classes do not have to be created "from scratch." Rather, they can include objects of other classes as members or they may be derived from other classes that provide attributes and behaviors the new classes can use. Such software reuse can greatly enhance programmer productivity and simplify code maintenance. Including class objects as members of other classes is called composition (or aggregation) and is discussed in Chapter 10. Deriving new classes from existing classes is called inheritance and is discussed in Chapter 12.

Object Size

People new to object-oriented programming often suppose that objects must be quite large because they contain data members and member functions. Logically, this is true—the programmer may think of objects as containing data and functions (and our discussion has certainly encouraged this view); physically, however, this is not true.

Performance Tip 9.2

Objects contain only data, so objects are much smaller than if they also contained member functions. Applying operator sizeof to a class name or to an object of that class will report only the size of the class's data members. The compiler creates one copy (only) of the member functions separate from all objects of the class. All objects of the class share this one copy. Each object, of course, needs its own copy of the class's data, because the data can vary among the objects. The function code is nonmodifiable (also called reentrant code or pure procedure) and, hence, can be shared among all objects of one class.

9.3 Class Scope and Accessing Class Members

A class's data members (variables declared in the class definition) and member functions (functions declared in the class definition) belong to that class's scope. Nonmember functions are defined at file scope.

Within a class's scope, class members are immediately accessible by all of that class's member functions and can be referenced by name. Outside a class's scope, public class members are referenced through one of the handles on an object—an object name, a reference to an object or a pointer to an object. The type of the object, reference or pointer

```
 1   // Fig. 9.3: fig09_03.cpp
 2   // Program to test class Time.
 3   // NOTE: This file must be compiled with Time.cpp.
 4   #include <iostream>
 5   using std::cout;
 6   using std::endl;
 7
 8   #include "Time.h" // include definition of class Time from Time.h
 9
10   int main()
11   {
12      Time t; // instantiate object t of class Time
13
14      // output Time object t's initial values
15      cout << "The initial universal time is ";
16      t.printUniversal(); // 00:00:00
17      cout << "\nThe initial standard time is ";
18      t.printStandard(); // 12:00:00 AM
19
20      t.setTime( 13, 27, 6 ); // change time
21
22      // output Time object t's new values
23      cout << "\n\nUniversal time after setTime is ";
24      t.printUniversal(); // 13:27:06
25      cout << "\nStandard time after setTime is ";
26      t.printStandard(); // 1:27:06 PM
27
28      t.setTime( 99, 99, 99 ); // attempt invalid settings
29
30      // output t's values after specifying invalid values
31      cout << "\n\nAfter attempting invalid settings:"
32         << "\nUniversal time: ";
33      t.printUniversal(); // 00:00:00
34      cout << "\nStandard time: ";
35      t.printStandard(); // 12:00:00 AM
36      cout << endl;
37      return 0;
38   } // end main
```

```
The initial universal time is 00:00:00
The initial standard time is 12:00:00 AM

Universal time after setTime is 13:27:06
Standard time after setTime is 1:27:06 PM

After attempting invalid settings:
Universal time: 00:00:00
Standard time: 12:00:00 AM
```

Fig. 9.3 | Program to test class Time.

specifies the interface (i.e., the member functions) accessible to the client. [*Note:* We will see in Chapter 10 that an implicit handle is inserted by the compiler on every reference to a data member or member function from within an object.]

Member functions of a class can be overloaded, but only by other member functions of that class. To overload a member function, simply provide in the class definition a prototype for each version of the overloaded function, and provide a separate function definition for each version of the function.

Variables declared in a member function have block scope and are known only to that function. If a member function defines a variable with the same name as a variable with class scope, the class-scope variable is hidden by the block-scope variable in the block scope. Such a hidden variable can be accessed by preceding the variable name with the class name followed by the scope resolution operator (::). Hidden global variables can be accessed with the unary scope resolution operator (see Chapter 6).

The dot member selection operator (.) is preceded by an object's name or with a reference to an object to access the object's members. The arrow member selection operator (->) is preceded by a pointer to an object to access the object's members.

Figure 9.4 uses a simple class called Count (lines 8–25) with private data member x of type int (line 24), public member function setX (lines 12–15) and public member function print (lines 18–21) to illustrate accessing the members of a class with the member selection operators. For simplicity, we have included this small class in the same file as the main function that uses it. Lines 29–31 create three variables related to type Count—counter (a Count object), counterPtr (a pointer to a Count object) and counterRef (a reference to a Count object). Variable counterRef refers to counter, and variable counterPtr points to counter. In lines 34–35 and 38–39, note that the program can invoke member functions setX and print by using the dot (.) member selection operator preceded by either the name of the object (counter) or a reference to the object (counterRef, which is an alias for counter). Similarly, lines 42–43 demonstrate that the program can invoke member functions setX and print by using a pointer (countPtr) and the arrow (->) member selection operator.

9.4 Separating Interface from Implementation

In Chapter 3, we began by including a class's definition and member-function definitions in one file. We then demonstrated separating this code into two files—a header file for the class definition (i.e., the class's interface) and a source code file for the class's member-function definitions (i.e., the class's implementation). Recall that this makes it easier to modify programs—as far as clients of a class are concerned, changes in the class's implementation do not affect the client as long as the class's interface originally provided to the client remains unchanged.

Software Engineering Observation 9.6

Clients of a class do not need access to the class's source code in order to use the class. The clients do, however, need to be able to link to the class's object code (i.e., the compiled version of the class). This encourages independent software vendors (ISVs) to provide class libraries for sale or license. The ISVs provide in their products only the header files and the object modules. No proprietary information is revealed—as would be the case if source code were provided. The C++ user community benefits by having more ISV-produced class libraries available.

Actually, things are not quite this rosy. Header files do contain some portions of the implementation and hints about others. Inline member functions, for example, need to be in a header file, so that when the compiler compiles a client, the client can include the

```
1   // Fig. 9.4: fig09_04.cpp
2   // Demonstrating the class member access operators . and ->
3   #include <iostream>
4   using std::cout;
5   using std::endl;
6
7   // class Count definition
8   class Count
9   {
10  public: // public data is dangerous
11     // sets the value of private data member x
12     void setX( int value )
13     {
14        x = value;
15     } // end function setX
16
17     // prints the value of private data member x
18     void print()
19     {
20        cout << x << endl;
21     } // end function print
22
23  private:
24     int x;
25  }; // end class Count
26
27  int main()
28  {
29     Count counter; // create counter object
30     Count *counterPtr = &counter; // create pointer to counter
31     Count &counterRef = counter; // create reference to counter
32
33     cout << "Set x to 1 and print using the object's name: ";
34     counter.setX( 1 ); // set data member x to 1
35     counter.print(); // call member function print
36
37     cout << "Set x to 2 and print using a reference to an object: ";
38     counterRef.setX( 2 ); // set data member x to 2
39     counterRef.print(); // call member function print
40
41     cout << "Set x to 3 and print using a pointer to an object: ";
42     counterPtr->setX( 3 ); // set data member x to 3
43     counterPtr->print(); // call member function print
44     return 0;
45  } // end main
```

```
Set x to 1 and print using the object's name: 1
Set x to 2 and print using a reference to an object: 2
Set x to 3 and print using a pointer to an object: 3
```

Fig. 9.4 | Accessing an object's member functions through each type of object handle—the object's name, a reference to the object and a pointer to the object.

inline function definition in place. A class's private members are listed in the class definition in the header file, so these members are visible to clients even though the clients may not access the private members. In Chapter 10, we show how to use a "proxy class" to hide even the private data of a class from clients of the class.

Software Engineering Observation 9.7

Information important to the interface to a class should be included in the header file. Information that will be used only internally in the class and will not be needed by clients of the class should be included in the unpublished source file. This is yet another example of the principle of least privilege.

9.5 Access Functions and Utility Functions

Access functions can read or display data. Another common use for access functions is to test the truth or falsity of conditions—such functions are often called predicate functions. An example of a predicate function would be an isEmpty function for any container class—a class capable of holding many objects—such as a linked list, a stack or a queue. A program might test isEmpty before attempting to read another item from the container object. An isFull predicate function might test a container-class object to determine whether it has no additional room. Useful predicate functions for our Time class might be isAM and isPM.

The program of Figs. 9.5–9.7 demonstrates the notion of a utility function (also called a helper function). A utility function is not part of a class's public interface; rather, it is a private member function that supports the operation of the class's public member functions. Utility functions are not intended to be used by clients of a class (but can be used by friends of a class, as we will see in Chapter 10).

Class SalesPerson (Fig. 9.5) declares an array of 12 monthly sales figures (line 16) and the prototypes for the class's constructor and member functions that manipulate the array.

In Fig. 9.6, the SalesPerson constructor (lines 15–19) initializes array sales to zero. The public member function setSales (lines 36–43) sets the sales figure for one month

```
1   // Fig. 9.5: SalesPerson.h
2   // SalesPerson class definition.
3   // Member functions defined in SalesPerson.cpp.
4   #ifndef SALESP_H
5   #define SALESP_H
6
7   class SalesPerson
8   {
9   public:
10      SalesPerson(); // constructor
11      void getSalesFromUser(); // input sales from keyboard
12      void setSales( int, double ); // set sales for a specific month
13      void printAnnualSales(); // summarize and print sales
14   private:
15      double totalAnnualSales(); // prototype for utility function
16      double sales[ 12 ]; // 12 monthly sales figures
17   }; // end class SalesPerson
18
19   #endif
```

Fig. 9.5 | SalesPerson class definition.

```
 1   // Fig. 9.6: SalesPerson.cpp
 2   // Member functions for class SalesPerson.
 3   #include <iostream>
 4   using std::cout;
 5   using std::cin;
 6   using std::endl;
 7   using std::fixed;
 8
 9   #include <iomanip>
10   using std::setprecision;
11
12   #include "SalesPerson.h" // include SalesPerson class definition
13
14   // initialize elements of array sales to 0.0
15   SalesPerson::SalesPerson()
16   {
17      for ( int i = 0; i < 12; i++ )
18         sales[ i ] = 0.0;
19   } // end SalesPerson constructor
20
21   // get 12 sales figures from the user at the keyboard
22   void SalesPerson::getSalesFromUser()
23   {
24      double salesFigure;
25
26      for ( int i = 1; i <= 12; i++ )
27      {
28         cout << "Enter sales amount for month " << i << ": ";
29         cin >> salesFigure;
30         setSales( i, salesFigure );
31      } // end for
32   } // end function getSalesFromUser
33
34   // set one of the 12 monthly sales figures; function subtracts
35   // one from month value for proper subscript in sales array
36   void SalesPerson::setSales( int month, double amount )
37   {
38      // test for valid month and amount values
39      if ( month >= 1 && month <= 12 && amount > 0 )
40         sales[ month - 1 ] = amount; // adjust for subscripts 0-11
41      else // invalid month or amount value
42         cout << "Invalid month or sales figure" << endl;
43   } // end function setSales
44
45   // print total annual sales (with the help of utility function)
46   void SalesPerson::printAnnualSales()
47   {
48      cout << setprecision( 2 ) << fixed
49         << "\nThe total annual sales are: $"
50         << totalAnnualSales() << endl; // call utility function
51   } // end function printAnnualSales
52
```

Fig. 9.6 | SalesPerson class member-function definitions. (Part 1 of 2.)

```
53   // private utility function to total annual sales
54   double SalesPerson::totalAnnualSales()
55   {
56      double total = 0.0; // initialize total
57
58      for ( int i = 0; i < 12; i++ ) // summarize sales results
59         total += sales[ i ]; // add month i sales to total
60
61      return total;
62   } // end function totalAnnualSales
```

Fig. 9.6 | SalesPerson class member-function definitions. (Part 2 of 2.)

in array sales. The public member function printAnnualSales (lines 46–51) prints the total sales for the last 12 months. The private utility function totalAnnualSales (lines 54–62) totals the 12 monthly sales figures for the benefit of printAnnualSales. Member function printAnnualSales edits the sales figures into monetary format.

In Fig. 9.7, notice that the application's main function includes only a simple sequence of member-function calls—there are no control statements. The logic of manipulating the sales array is completely encapsulated in class SalesPerson's member functions.

Software Engineering Observation 9.8

A phenomenon of object-oriented programming is that once a class is defined, creating and manipulating objects of that class often involve issuing only a simple sequence of member-function calls—few, if any, control statements are needed. By contrast, it is common to have control statements in the implementation of a class's member functions.

9.6 Time Class Case Study: Constructors with Default Arguments

The program of Figs. 9.8–9.10 enhances class Time to demonstrate how arguments are implicitly passed to a constructor. The constructor defined in Fig. 9.2 initialized hour,

```
1    // Fig. 9.7: fig09_07.cpp
2    // Demonstrating a utility function.
3    // Compile this program with SalesPerson.cpp
4
5    // include SalesPerson class definition from SalesPerson.h
6    #include "SalesPerson.h"
7
8    int main()
9    {
10      SalesPerson s; // create SalesPerson object s
11
12      s.getSalesFromUser(); // note simple sequential code;
13      s.printAnnualSales(); // no control statements in main
14      return 0;
15   } // end main
```

Fig. 9.7 | Utility function demonstration. (Part 1 of 2.)

```
Enter sales amount for month 1: 5314.76
Enter sales amount for month 2: 4292.38
Enter sales amount for month 3: 4589.83
Enter sales amount for month 4: 5534.03
Enter sales amount for month 5: 4376.34
Enter sales amount for month 6: 5698.45
Enter sales amount for month 7: 4439.22
Enter sales amount for month 8: 5893.57
Enter sales amount for month 9: 4909.67
Enter sales amount for month 10: 5123.45
Enter sales amount for month 11: 4024.97
Enter sales amount for month 12: 5923.92

The total annual sales are: $60120.59
```

Fig. 9.7 | Utility function demonstration. (Part 2 of 2.)

```cpp
1   // Fig. 9.8: Time.h
2   // Declaration of class Time.
3   // Member functions defined in Time.cpp.
4
5   // prevent multiple inclusions of header file
6   #ifndef TIME_H
7   #define TIME_H
8
9   // Time abstract data type definition
10  class Time
11  {
12  public:
13     Time( int = 0, int = 0, int = 0 ); // default constructor
14
15     // set functions
16     void setTime( int, int, int ); // set hour, minute, second
17     void setHour( int ); // set hour (after validation)
18     void setMinute( int ); // set minute (after validation)
19     void setSecond( int ); // set second (after validation)
20
21     // get functions
22     int getHour(); // return hour
23     int getMinute(); // return minute
24     int getSecond(); // return second
25
26     void printUniversal(); // output time in universal-time format
27     void printStandard(); // output time in standard-time format
28  private:
29     int hour; // 0 - 23 (24-hour clock format)
30     int minute; // 0 - 59
31     int second; // 0 - 59
32  }; // end class Time
33
34  #endif
```

Fig. 9.8 | Time class containing a constructor with default arguments.

minute and second to 0 (i.e., midnight in universal time). Like other functions, construc-tors can specify default arguments. Line 13 of Fig. 9.8 declares the Time constructor to in-clude default arguments, specifying a default value of zero for each argument passed to the constructor. In Fig. 9.9, lines 14–17 define the new version of the Time constructor that

```cpp
1   // Fig. 9.9: Time.cpp
2   // Member-function definitions for class Time.
3   #include <iostream>
4   using std::cout;
5
6   #include <iomanip>
7   using std::setfill;
8   using std::setw;
9
10  #include "Time.h" // include definition of class Time from Time.h
11
12  // Time constructor initializes each data member to zero;
13  // ensures that Time objects start in a consistent state
14  Time::Time( int hr, int min, int sec )
15  {
16     setTime( hr, min, sec ); // validate and set time
17  } // end Time constructor
18
19  // set new Time value using universal time; ensure that
20  // the data remains consistent by setting invalid values to zero
21  void Time::setTime( int h, int m, int s )
22  {
23     setHour( h ); // set private field hour
24     setMinute( m ); // set private field minute
25     setSecond( s ); // set private field second
26  } // end function setTime
27
28  // set hour value
29  void Time::setHour( int h )
30  {
31     hour = ( h >= 0 && h < 24 ) ? h : 0; // validate hour
32  } // end function setHour
33
34  // set minute value
35  void Time::setMinute( int m )
36  {
37     minute = ( m >= 0 && m < 60 ) ? m : 0; // validate minute
38  } // end function setMinute
39
40  // set second value
41  void Time::setSecond( int s )
42  {
43     second = ( s >= 0 && s < 60 ) ? s : 0; // validate second
44  } // end function setSecond
45
```

Fig. 9.9 | Time class member-function definitions including a constructor that takes arguments. (Part I of 2.)

```
46    // return hour value
47    int Time::getHour()
48    {
49       return hour;
50    } // end function getHour
51
52    // return minute value
53    int Time::getMinute()
54    {
55       return minute;
56    } // end function getMinute
57
58    // return second value
59    int Time::getSecond()
60    {
61       return second;
62    } // end function getSecond
63
64    // print Time in universal-time format (HH:MM:SS)
65    void Time::printUniversal()
66    {
67       cout << setfill( '0' ) << setw( 2 ) << getHour() << ":"
68          << setw( 2 ) << getMinute() << ":" << setw( 2 ) << getSecond();
69    } // end function printUniversal
70
71    // print Time in standard-time format (HH:MM:SS AM or PM)
72    void Time::printStandard()
73    {
74       cout << ( ( getHour() == 0 || getHour() == 12 ) ? 12 : getHour() % 12 )
75          << ":" << setfill( '0' ) << setw( 2 ) << getMinute()
76          << ":" << setw( 2 ) << getSecond() << ( hour < 12 ? " AM" : " PM" );
77    } // end function printStandard
```

Fig. 9.9 | Time class member-function definitions including a constructor that takes arguments. (Part 2 of 2.)

receives values for parameters hr, min and sec that will be used to initialize private data members hour, minute and second, respectively. Note that class Time provides *set* and *get* functions for each data member. The Time constructor now calls setTime, which calls the setHour, setMinute and setSecond functions to validate and assign values to the data members. The default arguments to the constructor ensure that, even if no values are provided in a constructor call, the constructor still initializes the data members to maintain the Time object in a consistent state. A constructor that defaults all its arguments is also a default constructor—i.e., a constructor that can be invoked with no arguments. There can be a maximum of one default constructor per class.

In Fig. 9.9, line 16 of the constructor calls member function setTime with the values passed to the constructor (or the default values). Function setTime calls setHour to ensure that the value supplied for hour is in the range 0–23, then calls setMinute and setSecond to ensure that the values for minute and second are each in the range 0–59. If a value is out of range, that value is set to zero (to ensure that each data member remains in a consistent state). Note that, using C++'s exception handling capabilities, it is possible to "throw and exception." We do this in Chapter 16 of our sister book, *C++ How to Program, 5/e*

Note that the Time constructor could be written to include the same statements as member function setTime, or even the individual statements in the setHour, setMinute and setSecond functions. Calling setHour, setMinute and setSecond from the constructor may be slightly more efficient because the extra call to setTime would be eliminated. Similarly, copying the code from lines 31, 37 and 43 into constructor would eliminate the overhead of calling setTime, setHour, setMinute and setSecond. Coding the Time constructor or member function setTime as a copy of the code in lines 31, 37 and 43 would make maintenance of this class more difficult. If the implementations of setHour, setMinute and setSecond were to change, the implementation of any member function that duplicates lines 31, 37 and 43 would have to change accordingly. Having the Time constructor call setTime and having setTime call setHour, setMinute and set-Second enables us to limit the changes to code that validates the hour, minute or second to the corresponding *set* function. This reduces the likelihood of errors when altering the class's implementation. Also, the performance of the Time constructor and setTime can be enhanced by explicitly declaring them inline or by defining them in the class definition (which implicitly inlines the function definition).

Software Engineering Observation 9.9

If a member function of a class already provides all or part of the functionality required by a constructor (or other member function) of the class, call that member function from the constructor (or other member function). This simplifies the maintenance of the code and reduces the likelihood of an error if the implementation of the code is modified. As a general rule: Avoid repeating code.

Software Engineering Observation 9.10

Any change to the default argument values of a function requires the client code to be recompiled (to ensure that the program still functions correctly).

Function main in Fig. 9.10 initializes five Time objects—one with all three arguments defaulted in the implicit constructor call (line 11), one with one argument specified (line

```
 1   // Fig. 9.10: fig09_10.cpp
 2   // Demonstrating a default constructor for class Time.
 3   #include <iostream>
 4   using std::cout;
 5   using std::endl;
 6
 7   #include "Time.h" // include definition of class Time from Time.h
 8
 9   int main()
10   {
11       Time t1; // all arguments defaulted
12       Time t2( 2 ); // hour specified; minute and second defaulted
13       Time t3( 21, 34 ); // hour and minute specified; second defaulted
14       Time t4( 12, 25, 42 ); // hour, minute and second specified
15       Time t5( 27, 74, 99 ); // all bad values specified
16
```

Fig. 9.10 | Constructor with default arguments. (Part 1 of 2.)

```
17      cout << "Constructed with:\n\nt1: all arguments defaulted\n  ";
18      t1.printUniversal(); // 00:00:00
19      cout << "\n  ";
20      t1.printStandard(); // 12:00:00 AM
21
22      cout << "\n\nt2: hour specified; minute and second defaulted\n  ";
23      t2.printUniversal(); // 02:00:00
24      cout << "\n  ";
25      t2.printStandard(); // 2:00:00 AM
26
27      cout << "\n\nt3: hour and minute specified; second defaulted\n  ";
28      t3.printUniversal(); // 21:34:00
29      cout << "\n  ";
30      t3.printStandard(); // 9:34:00 PM
31
32      cout << "\n\nt4: hour, minute and second specified\n  ";
33      t4.printUniversal(); // 12:25:42
34      cout << "\n  ";
35      t4.printStandard(); // 12:25:42 PM
36
37      cout << "\n\nt5: all invalid values specified\n  ";
38      t5.printUniversal(); // 00:00:00
39      cout << "\n  ";
40      t5.printStandard(); // 12:00:00 AM
41      cout << endl;
42      return 0;
43   } // end main
```

```
Constructed with:

t1: all arguments defaulted
  00:00:00
  12:00:00 AM

t2: hour specified; minute and second defaulted
  02:00:00
  2:00:00 AM

t3: hour and minute specified; second defaulted
  21:34:00
  9:34:00 PM

t4: hour, minute and second specified
  12:25:42
  12:25:42 PM

t5: all invalid values specified
  00:00:00
  12:00:00 AM
```

Fig. 9.10 | Constructor with default arguments. (Part 2 of 2.)

12), one with two arguments specified (line 13), one with three arguments specified (line 14) and one with three invalid arguments specified (line 15). Then the program displays each object in universal-time and standard-time formats.

Notes Regarding Class *Time's* Set *and* Get *Functions and Constructor*

Time's *set* and *get* functions are called throughout the body of the class. In particular, function setTime (lines 21–26 of Fig. 9.9) calls functions setHour, setMinute and setSecond, and functions printUniversal and printStandard call functions getHour, getMinute and get-Second in line 67–68 and lines 74–76, respectively. In each case, these functions could have accessed the class's private data directly without calling the *set* and *get* functions. However, consider changing the representation of the time from three int values (requiring 12 bytes of memory) to a single int value representing the total number of seconds that have elapsed since midnight (requiring only four bytes of memory). If we made such a change, only the bodies of the functions that access the private data directly would need to change—in particular, the individual *set* and *get* functions for the hour, minute and second. There would be no need to modify the bodies of functions setTime, printUniversal or printStandard, because they do not access the data directly. Designing the class in this manner reduces the likelihood of programming errors when altering the class's implementation.

Similarly, the Time constructor could be written to include a copy of the appropriate statements from function setTime. Doing so may be slightly more efficient, because the extra constructor call and call to setTime are eliminated. However, duplicating statements in multiple functions or constructors makes changing the class's internal data representation more difficult. Having the Time constructor call function setTime directly requires any changes to the implementation of setTime to be made only once.

Common Programming Error 9.2

A constructor can call other member functions of the class, such as set *or* get *functions, but because the constructor is initializing the object, the data members may not yet be in a consistent state. Using data members before they have been properly initialized can cause logic errors.*

9.7 Destructors

A destructor is another type of special member function. The name of the destructor for a class is the tilde character (~) followed by the class name. This naming convention has intuitive appeal, because as we will see in a later chapter, the tilde operator is the bitwise complement operator, and, in a sense, the destructor is the complement of the constructor. Note that a destructor is often referred to with the abbreviation "dtor" in the literature. We prefer not to use this abbreviation.

A class's destructor is called implicitly when an object is destroyed. This occurs, for example, as an automatic object is destroyed when program execution leaves the scope in which that object was instantiated. *The destructor itself does not actually release the object's memory*—it performs termination housekeeping before the system reclaims the object's memory, so the memory may be reused to hold new objects.

A destructor receives no parameters and returns no value. A destructor may not specify a return type—not even void. A class may have only one destructor—destructor overloading is not allowed.

Common Programming Error 9.3

It is a syntax error to attempt to pass arguments to a destructor, to specify a return type for a destructor (even void *cannot be specified), to return values from a destructor or to overload a destructor.*

Even though destructors have not been provided for the classes presented so far, every class has a destructor. If the programmer does not explicitly provide a destructor, the compiler creates an "empty" destructor. [*Note:* We will see that such an implicitly created destructor does, in fact, perform important operations on objects that are created through composition (Chapter 10) and inheritance (Chapter 12).] In Chapter 11, we will build destructors appropriate for classes whose objects contain dynamically allocated memory (e.g., for arrays and strings) or use other system resources (e.g., files on disk). We discuss how to dynamically allocate and deallocate memory in Chapter 10.

Software Engineering Observation 9.11

As we will see in the remainder of the book, constructors and destructors have much greater prominence in C++ and object-oriented programming than is possible to convey after only our brief introduction here.

9.8 When Constructors and Destructors Are Called

Constructors and destructors are called implicitly by the compiler. The order in which these function calls occur depends on the order in which execution enters and leaves the scopes where the objects are instantiated. Generally, destructor calls are made in the reverse order of the corresponding constructor calls, but as we will see in Figs. 9.11–9.13, the storage classes of objects can alter the order in which destructors are called.

Constructors are called for objects defined in global scope before any other function (including `main`) in that file begins execution (although the order of execution of global object constructors between files is not guaranteed). The corresponding destructors are called when `main` terminates. Function `exit` forces a program to terminate immediately and does not execute the destructors of automatic objects. The function often is used to terminate a program when an error is detected in the input or if a file to be processed by the program cannot be opened. Function `abort` performs similarly to function `exit` but forces the program to terminate immediately, without allowing the destructors of any objects to be called. Function `abort` is usually used to indicate an abnormal termination of the program.

The constructor for an automatic local object is called when execution reaches the point where that object is defined—the corresponding destructor is called when execution leaves the object's scope (i.e., the block in which that object is defined has finished executing). Constructors and destructors for automatic objects are called each time execution enters and leaves the scope of the object. Destructors are not called for automatic objects if the program terminates with a call to function `exit` or function `abort`.

The constructor for a `static` local object is called only once, when execution first reaches the point where the object is defined—the corresponding destructor is called when `main` terminates or the program calls function `exit`. Global and `static` objects are destroyed in the reverse order of their creation. Destructors are not called for `static` objects if the program terminates with a call to function `abort`.

The program of Figs. 9.11–9.13 demonstrates the order in which constructors and destructors are called for objects of class `CreateAndDestroy` (Fig. 9.11 and Fig. 9.12) of various storage classes in several scopes. Each object of class `CreateAndDestroy` contains (lines 16–17) an integer (`objectID`) and a `string` (`message`) that are used in the program's output to identify the object. This mechanical example is purely for pedagogic purposes. For this reason, line 23 of the destructor in Fig. 9.12 determines whether the object being destroyed has an `objectID` value 1 or 6 and, if so, outputs a newline character. This line helps make the program's output easier to follow.

```
1   // Fig. 9.11: CreateAndDestroy.h
2   // Definition of class CreateAndDestroy.
3   // Member functions defined in CreateAndDestroy.cpp.
4   #include <string>
5   using std::string;
6
7   #ifndef CREATE_H
8   #define CREATE_H
9
10  class CreateAndDestroy
11  {
12  public:
13     CreateAndDestroy( int, string ); // constructor
14     ~CreateAndDestroy(); // destructor
15  private:
16     int objectID; // ID number for object
17     string message; // message describing object
18  }; // end class CreateAndDestroy
19
20  #endif
```

Fig. 9.11 | CreateAndDestroy class definition.

```
1   // Fig. 9.12: CreateAndDestroy.cpp
2   // Member-function definitions for class CreateAndDestroy.
3   #include <iostream>
4   using std::cout;
5   using std::endl;
6
7   #include "CreateAndDestroy.h"// include CreateAndDestroy class definition
8
9   // constructor
10  CreateAndDestroy::CreateAndDestroy( int ID, string messageString )
11  {
12     objectID = ID; // set object's ID number
13     message = messageString; // set object's descriptive message
14
15     cout << "Object " << objectID << "  constructor runs  "
16        << message << endl;
17  } // end CreateAndDestroy constructor
18
19  // destructor
20  CreateAndDestroy::~CreateAndDestroy()
21  {
22     // output newline for certain objects; helps readability
23     cout << ( objectID == 1 || objectID == 6 ? "\n" : "" );
24
25     cout << "Object " << objectID << "  destructor runs  "
26        << message << endl;
27  } // end ~CreateAndDestroy destructor
```

Fig. 9.12 | CreateAndDestroy class member-function definitions.

Figure 9.13 defines object first (line 12) in global scope. Its constructor is actually called before any statements in main execute and its destructor is called at program termination after the destructors for all other objects have run.

Function main (lines 14–26) declares three objects. Objects second (line 17) and fourth (line 23) are local automatic objects, and object third (line 18) is a static local object. The constructor for each of these objects is called when execution reaches the point where that object is declared. The destructors for objects fourth and then second are called (i.e., the reverse of the order in which their constructors were called) when execution reaches the end of main. Because object third is static, it exists until program termination. The destructor for object third is called before the destructor for global object first, but after all other objects are destroyed.

Function create (lines 29–36) declares three objects—fifth (line 32) and seventh (line 34) as local automatic objects, and sixth (line 33) as a static local object. The

```
 1   // Fig. 9.13: fig09_13.cpp
 2   // Demonstrating the order in which constructors and
 3   // destructors are called.
 4   #include <iostream>
 5   using std::cout;
 6   using std::endl;
 7
 8   #include "CreateAndDestroy.h" // include CreateAndDestroy class definition
 9
10   void create( void ); // prototype
11
12   CreateAndDestroy first( 1, "(global before main)" ); // global object
13
14   int main()
15   {
16      cout << "\nMAIN FUNCTION: EXECUTION BEGINS" << endl;
17      CreateAndDestroy second( 2, "(local automatic in main)" );
18      static CreateAndDestroy third( 3, "(local static in main)" );
19
20      create(); // call function to create objects
21
22      cout << "\nMAIN FUNCTION: EXECUTION RESUMES" << endl;
23      CreateAndDestroy fourth( 4, "(local automatic in main)" );
24      cout << "\nMAIN FUNCTION: EXECUTION ENDS" << endl;
25      return 0;
26   } // end main
27
28   // function to create objects
29   void create( void )
30   {
31      cout << "\nCREATE FUNCTION: EXECUTION BEGINS" << endl;
32      CreateAndDestroy fifth( 5, "(local automatic in create)" );
33      static CreateAndDestroy sixth( 6, "(local static in create)" );
34      CreateAndDestroy seventh( 7, "(local automatic in create)" );
35      cout << "\nCREATE FUNCTION: EXECUTION ENDS" << endl;
36   } // end function create
```

Fig. 9.13 | Order in which constructors and destructors are called. (Part 1 of 2.)

```
Object 1    constructor runs    (global before main)

MAIN FUNCTION: EXECUTION BEGINS
Object 2    constructor runs    (local automatic in main)
Object 3    constructor runs    (local static in main)

CREATE FUNCTION: EXECUTION BEGINS
Object 5    constructor runs    (local automatic in create)
Object 6    constructor runs    (local static in create)
Object 7    constructor runs    (local automatic in create)

CREATE FUNCTION: EXECUTION ENDS
Object 7    destructor runs     (local automatic in create)
Object 5    destructor runs     (local automatic in create)

MAIN FUNCTION: EXECUTION RESUMES
Object 4    constructor runs    (local automatic in main)

MAIN FUNCTION: EXECUTION ENDS
Object 4    destructor runs     (local automatic in main)
Object 2    destructor runs     (local automatic in main)

Object 6    destructor runs     (local static in create)
Object 3    destructor runs     (local static in main)

Object 1    destructor runs     (global before main)
```

Fig. 9.13 | Order in which constructors and destructors are called. (Part 2 of 2.)

destructors for objects `seventh` and then `fifth` are called (i.e., the reverse of the order in which their constructors were called) when `create` terminates. Because `sixth` is `static`, it exists until program termination. The destructor for `sixth` is called before the destructors for `third` and `first`, but after all other objects are destroyed.

9.9 Time Class Case Study: A Subtle Trap—Returning a Reference to a `private` Data Member

A reference to an object is an alias for the name of the object and, hence, may be used on the left side of an assignment statement. In this context, the reference makes a perfectly acceptable *lvalue* that can receive a value. One way to use this capability (unfortunately!) is to have a `public` member function of a class return a reference to a `private` data member of that class. Note that if a function returns a `const` reference, that reference cannot be used as a modifiable *lvalue*.

The program of Figs. 9.14–9.16 uses a simplified `Time` class (Fig. 9.14 and Fig. 9.15) to demonstrate returning a reference to a `private` data member with member function `badSetHour` (declared in Fig. 9.14 at line 15 and defined in Fig. 9.15 at lines 29–33). Such a reference return actually makes a call to member function `badSetHour` an alias for `private` data member `hour`! The function call can be used in any way that the `private` data member can be used, including as an *lvalue* in an assignment statement, thus enabling clients of the class to clobber the class's `private` data at will! Note that the same problem would occur if a pointer to the `private` data were to be returned by the function.

```
 1   // Fig. 9.14: Time.h
 2   // Declaration of class Time.
 3   // Member functions defined in Time.cpp
 4
 5   // prevent multiple inclusions of header file
 6   #ifndef TIME_H
 7   #define TIME_H
 8
 9   class Time
10   {
11   public:
12      Time( int = 0, int = 0, int = 0 );
13      void setTime( int, int, int );
14      int getHour();
15      int &badSetHour( int ); // DANGEROUS reference return
16   private:
17      int hour;
18      int minute;
19      int second;
20   }; // end class Time
21
22   #endif
```

Fig. 9.14 | Returning a reference to a private data member.

```
 1   // Fig. 9.15: Time.cpp
 2   // Member-function definitions for Time class.
 3   #include "Time.h" // include definition of class Time
 4
 5   // constructor function to initialize private data;
 6   // calls member function setTime to set variables;
 7   // default values are 0 (see class definition)
 8   Time::Time( int hr, int min, int sec )
 9   {
10      setTime( hr, min, sec );
11   } // end Time constructor
12
13   // set values of hour, minute and second
14   void Time::setTime( int h, int m, int s )
15   {
16      hour = ( h >= 0 && h < 24 ) ? h : 0; // validate hour
17      minute = ( m >= 0 && m < 60 ) ? m : 0; // validate minute
18      second = ( s >= 0 && s < 60 ) ? s : 0; // validate second
19   } // end function setTime
20
21   // return hour value
22   int Time::getHour()
23   {
24      return hour;
25   } // end function getHour
26
```

Fig. 9.15 | Returning a reference to a private data member. (Part 1 of 2.)

```
27   // POOR PROGRAMMING PRACTICE:
28   // Returning a reference to a private data member.
29   int &Time::badSetHour( int hh )
30   {
31      hour = ( hh >= 0 && hh < 24 ) ? hh : 0;
32      return hour; // DANGEROUS reference return
33   } // end function badSetHour
```

Fig. 9.15 | Returning a reference to a `private` data member. (Part 2 of 2.)

Figure 9.16 declares `Time` object `t` (line 12) and reference `hourRef` (line 15), which is initialized with the reference returned by the call `t.badSetHour(20)`. Line 17 displays the value of the alias `hourRef`. This shows how `hourRef` breaks the encapsulation of the class—statements in `main` should not have access to the `private` data of the class. Next, line 18 uses the alias to set the value of `hour` to 30 (an invalid value) and line 19 displays the value returned by function `getHour` to show that assigning a value to `hourRef` actually modifies the `private` data in the `Time` object `t`. Finally, line 23 uses the `badSetHour` function call itself as an *lvalue* and assigns 74 (another invalid value) to the reference returned by the function.

```
1    // Fig. 9.16: fig09_16.cpp
2    // Demonstrating a public member function that
3    // returns a reference to a private data member.
4    #include <iostream>
5    using std::cout;
6    using std::endl;
7
8    #include "Time.h" // include definition of class Time
9
10   int main()
11   {
12      Time t; // create Time object
13
14      // initialize hourRef with the reference returned by badSetHour
15      int &hourRef = t.badSetHour( 20 ); // 20 is a valid hour
16
17      cout << "Valid hour before modification: " << hourRef;
18      hourRef = 30; // use hourRef to set invalid value in Time object t
19      cout << "\nInvalid hour after modification: " << t.getHour();
20
21      // Dangerous: Function call that returns
22      // a reference can be used as an lvalue!
23      t.badSetHour( 12 ) = 74; // assign another invalid value to hour
24
25      cout << "\n\n************************************************************\n"
26         << "POOR PROGRAMMING PRACTICE!!!!!!!!!\n"
27         << "t.badSetHour( 12 ) as an lvalue, invalid hour: "
28         << t.getHour()
29         << "\n************************************************************" << endl;
30      return 0;
31   } // end main
```

Fig. 9.16 | Returning a reference to a `private` data member. (Part 1 of 2.)

```
Valid hour before modification: 20
Invalid hour after modification: 30

****************************************************
POOR PROGRAMMING PRACTICE!!!!!!!!
t.badSetHour( 12 ) as an lvalue, invalid hour: 74
****************************************************
```

Fig. 9.16 | Returning a reference to a `private` data member. (Part 2 of 2.)

Line 28 again displays the value returned by function `getHour` to show that assigning a value to the result of the function call in line 23 modifies the `private` data in the `Time` object `t`.

 Error-Prevention Tip 9.4

Returning a reference or a pointer to a `private` data member breaks the encapsulation of the class and makes the client code dependent on the representation of the class's data. So, returning pointers or references to `private` data is a dangerous practice that should be avoided.

9.10 Default Memberwise Assignment

The assignment operator (=) can be used to assign an object to another object of the same type. By default, such assignment is performed by memberwise assignment—each data member of the object on the right of the assignment operator is assigned individually to the same data member in the object on the left of the assignment operator. Figures 9.17–9.18 define class `Date` for use in this example. Line 20 of Fig. 9.19 uses default memberwise assignment to assign the data members of `Date` object `date1` to the

```
1   // Fig. 9.17: Date.h
2   // Declaration of class Date.
3   // Member functions are defined in Date.cpp
4
5   // prevent multiple inclusions of header file
6   #ifndef DATE_H
7   #define DATE_H
8
9   // class Date definition
10  class Date
11  {
12  public:
13     Date( int = 1, int = 1, int = 2000 ); // default constructor
14     void print();
15  private:
16     int month;
17     int day;
18     int year;
19  }; // end class Date
20
21  #endif
```

Fig. 9.17 | `Date` class header file.

```cpp
1  // Fig. 9.18: Date.cpp
2  // Member-function definitions for class Date.
3  #include <iostream>
4  using std::cout;
5  using std::endl;
6
7  #include "Date.h" // include definition of class Date from Date.h
8
9  // Date constructor (should do range checking)
10 Date::Date( int m, int d, int y )
11 {
12    month = m;
13    day = d;
14    year = y;
15 } // end constructor Date
16
17 // print Date in the format mm/dd/yyyy
18 void Date::print()
19 {
20    cout << month << '/' << day << '/' << year;
21 } // end function print
```

Fig. 9.18 | Date class member-function definitions.

```cpp
1  // Fig. 9.19: fig09_19.cpp
2  // Demonstrating that class objects can be assigned
3  // to each other using default memberwise assignment.
4  #include <iostream>
5  using std::cout;
6  using std::endl;
7
8  #include "Date.h" // include definition of class Date from Date.h
9
10 int main()
11 {
12    Date date1( 7, 4, 2004 );
13    Date date2; // date2 defaults to 1/1/2000
14
15    cout << "date1 = ";
16    date1.print();
17    cout << "\ndate2 = ";
18    date2.print();
19
20    date2 = date1; // default memberwise assignment
21
22    cout << "\n\nAfter default memberwise assignment, date2 = ";
23    date2.print();
24    cout << endl;
25    return 0;
26 } // end main
```

Fig. 9.19 | Default memberwise assignment. (Part I of 2.)

```
date1 = 7/4/2004
date2 = 1/1/2000

After default memberwise assignment, date2 = 7/4/2004
```

Fig. 9.19 | Default memberwise assignment. (Part 2 of 2.)

corresponding data members of Date object date2. In this case, the month member of date1 is assigned to the month member of date2, the day member of date1 is assigned to the day member of date2 and the year member of date1 is assigned to the year member of date2. [*Caution:* Memberwise assignment can cause serious problems when used with a class whose data members contain pointers to dynamically allocated memory; we discuss these problems in Chapter 11 and show how to deal with them.] Notice that the Date constructor does not contain any error checking; we leave this to the exercises.

Objects may be passed as function arguments and may be returned from functions. Such passing and returning is performed using pass-by-value by default—a copy of the object is passed or returned. In such cases, C++ creates a new object and uses a copy constructor to copy the original object's values into the new object. For each class, the compiler provides a default copy constructor that copies each member of the original object into the corresponding member of the new object. Like memberwise assignment, copy constructors can cause serious problems when used with a class whose data members contain pointers to dynamically allocated memory. Chapter 11 discusses how programmers can define a customized copy constructor that properly copies objects containing pointers to dynamically allocated memory.

Performance Tip 9.3

Passing an object by value is good from a security standpoint, because the called function has no access to the original object in the caller, but pass-by-value can degrade performance when making a copy of a large object. An object can be passed by reference by passing either a pointer or a reference to the object. Pass-by-reference offers good performance but is weaker from a security standpoint, because the called function is given access to the original object. Pass-by-const-reference is a safe, good-performing alternative (this can be implemented with a const reference parameter or with a pointer-to-const-data parameter).

9.11 Software Reusability

People who write object-oriented programs concentrate on implementing useful classes. There is a tremendous motivation to capture and catalog classes so that they can be accessed by large segments of the programming community. Many substantial class libraries exist and others are being developed worldwide. Software is increasingly being constructed from existing, well-defined, carefully tested, well-documented, portable, high-performance, widely available components. This kind of software reusability speeds the development of powerful, high-quality software. Rapid applications development (RAD) through the mechanisms of reusable componentry has become an important field.

Significant problems must be solved, however, before the full potential of software reusability can be realized. We need cataloging schemes, licensing schemes, protection mechanisms to ensure that master copies of classes are not corrupted, description schemes so that designers of new systems can easily determine whether existing objects meet their needs, browsing mechanisms to determine what classes are available and how closely they meet software developer requirements and the like. Many interesting research and development problems need to be solved. There is great motivation to solve these problems, because the potential value of their solutions is enormous.

9.12 Wrap-Up

This chapter deepened our coverage of classes, using a rich Time class case study to introduce several new features of classes. You saw that member functions are usually shorter than global functions because member functions can directly access an object's data members, so the member functions can receive fewer arguments than functions in procedural programming languages. You learned how to use the arrow operator to access an object's members via a pointer of the object's class type.

You learned that member functions have class scope—i.e., the member function's name is known only to other members of the class unless referred to via an object of the class, a reference to an object of the class, a pointer to an object of the class or the binary scope resolution operator. We also discussed access functions (commonly used to retrieve the values of data members or to test the truth or falsity of conditions) and utility functions (private member functions that support the operation of the class's public member functions).

You learned that a constructor can specify default arguments that enable it to be called in a variety of ways. You also learned that any constructor that can be called with no arguments is a default constructor and that there can be a maximum of one default constructor per class. We discussed destructors and their purpose of performing termination housekeeping on an object of a class before that object is destroyed. We also demonstrated the order in which an object's constructors and destructors are called.

We demonstrated the problems that can occur when a member function returns a reference to a private data member, which breaks the encapsulation of the class. We also showed that objects of the same type can be assigned to one another using default memberwise assignment. Finally, we discussed the benefits of using class libraries to enhance the speed with which code can be created and to increase the quality of software.

Chapter 10 presents additional class features. We will demonstrate how const can be used to indicate that a member function does not modify an object of a class. You will learn how to build classes with composition—that is, classes that contain objects of other classes as members. We'll show how a class can allow so-called "friend" functions to access the class's non-public members. We'll also show how a class's non-static member functions can use a special pointer named this to access an object's members. Next, you'll learn how to use C++'s new and delete operators, which enable programmers to obtain and release memory as necessary during a program's execution.

Summary

- The preprocessor directives #ifndef (which means "if not defined") and #endif are used to prevent multiple inclusions of a header file. If the code between these directives has not previously been included in an application, #define defines a name that can be used to prevent future inclusions, and the code is included in the source code file.

- Data members of a class cannot be initialized where they are declared in the class body (except for a class's static const data members of integral or enum types as you'll see in Chapter 10). It is strongly recommended that these data members be initialized by the class's constructor (as there is no default initialization for data members of fundamental types).

- Stream manipulator `setfill` specifies the fill character that is displayed when an integer is output in a field that is wider than the number of digits in the value.

- By default, the fill characters appear before the digits in the number.

- Stream manipulator `setfill` is a "sticky" setting, meaning that once the fill character is set, it applies for all subsequent fields being printed.

- Even though a member function declared in a class definition may be defined outside that class definition (and "tied" to the class via the binary scope resolution operator), that member function is still within that class's scope; i.e., its name is known only to other members of the class unless referred to via an object of the class, a reference to an object of the class or a pointer to an object of the class.

- If a member function is defined in the body of a class definition, the C++ compiler attempts to inline calls to the member function.

- Classes do not have to be created "from scratch." Rather, they can include objects of other classes as members or they may be derived from other classes that provide attributes and behaviors the new classes can use. Including class objects as members of other classes is called composition.

- A class's data members and member functions belong to that class's scope.

- Nonmember functions are defined at file scope.

- Within a class's scope, class members are immediately accessible by all of that class's member functions and can be referenced by name.

- Outside a class's scope, class members are referenced through one of the handles on an object— an object name, a reference to an object or a pointer to an object.

- Member functions of a class can be overloaded, but only by other member functions of that class.

- To overload a member function, provide in the class definition a prototype for each version of the overloaded function, and provide a separate definition for each version of the function.

- Variables declared in a member function have block scope and are known only to that function.

- If a member function defines a variable with the same name as a variable with class scope, the class-scope variable is hidden by the block-scope variable in the block scope.

- The dot member selection operator (`.`) is preceded by an object's name or by a reference to an object to access the object's `public` members.

- The arrow member selection operator (`->`) is preceded by a pointer to an object to access that object's `public` members.

- Header files do contain some portions of the implementation and hints about others. Inline member functions, for example, need to be in a header file, so that when the compiler compiles a client, the client can include the `inline` function definition in place.

- A class's `private` members that are listed in the class definition in the header file are visible to clients, even though the clients may not access the `private` members.

- A utility function (also called a helper function) is a `private` member function that supports the operation of the class's `public` member functions. Utility functions are not intended to be used by clients of a class (but can be used by `friend`s of a class).

- Like other functions, constructors can specify default arguments.

- A class's destructor is called implicitly when an object of the class is destroyed.

- The name of the destructor for a class is the tilde (`~`) character followed by the class name.

- A destructor does not actually release an object's storage—it performs termination housekeeping before the system reclaims an object's memory, so the memory may be reused to hold new objects.

- A destructor receives no parameters and returns no value. A class may have only one destructor.

- If the programmer does not explicitly provide a destructor, the compiler creates an "empty" destructor, so every class has exactly one destructor.

- The order in which constructors and destructors are called depends on the order in which execution enters and leaves the scopes where the objects are instantiated.

- Generally, destructor calls are made in the reverse order of the corresponding constructor calls, but the storage classes of objects can alter the order in which destructors are called.

- A reference to an object is an alias for the name of the object and, hence, may be used on the left side of an assignment statement. In this context, the reference makes a perfectly acceptable *lvalue* that can receive a value. One way to use this capability (unfortunately!) is to have a `public` member function of a class return a reference to a `private` data member of that class. If the function returns a `const` reference, then the reference cannot be used as a modifiable *lvalue*.

- The assignment operator (=) can be used to assign an object to another object of the same type. By default, such assignment is performed by memberwise assignment—each member of the object on the right of the assignment operator is assigned individually to the same member in the object on the left of the assignment operator.

- Objects may be passed as function arguments and may be returned from functions. Such passing and returning is performed using pass-by-value by default—a copy of the object is passed or returned. In such cases, C++ creates a new object and uses a copy constructor to copy the original object's values into the new object. We explain these in detail in Chapter 11, Operator Overloading; String and Array Objects.

- For each class, the compiler provides a default copy constructor that copies each member of the original object into the corresponding member of the new object.

- Many substantial class libraries exist, and others are being developed worldwide.

- Software reusability speeds the development of powerful, high-quality software. Rapid applications development (RAD) through the mechanisms of reusable componentry has become an important field.

Terminology

abort function
access function
aggregation
arrow member selection operator (->)
assigning class objects
class libraries
class scope
composition
copy constructor
default arguments with constructors
default memberwise assignment
#define preprocessor directive
derive one class from another
destructor
#endif preprocessor directive
exit function
file scope
fill character

handle on an object
helper function
#ifndef preprocessor directive
implicit handle on an object
inheritance
initializer
memberwise assignment
name handle on an object
object handle
object leaves scope
order in which constructors and destructors are called
overloaded constructor
overloaded member function
pass an object by value
pointer handle on an object
predicate function
preprocessor wrapper

pure procedure
rapid application development (RAD)
reentrant code
reference handle on an object
reusable componentry

`setfill` parameterized stream manipulator
software asset
termination housekeeping
tilde character (~) in a destructor name

Self-Review Exercises

9.1 Fill in the blanks in each of the following:

a) Class members are accessed via the _____ operator in conjunction with the name of an object (or reference to an object) of the class or via the _____ operator in conjunction with a pointer to an object of the class.

b) Class members specified as _____ are accessible only to member functions of the class and `friends` of the class.

c) Class members specified as _____ are accessible anywhere an object of the class is in scope.

d) _____ can be used to assign an object of a class to another object of the same class.

9.2 Find the error(s) in each of the following and explain how to correct it (them):

a) Assume the following prototype is declared in class `Time`:

```
void ~Time( int );
```

b) The following is a partial definition of class `Time`:

```
class Time
{
public:
   // function prototypes

private:
   int hour = 0;
   int minute = 0;
   int second = 0;
}; // end class Time
```

c) Assume the following prototype is declared in class `Employee`:

```
int Employee( const char *, const char * );
```

Answers to Self-Review Exercises

9.1 a) dot (.), arrow (->). b) `private`. c) `public`. d) Default memberwise assignment (performed by the assignment operator).

9.2 a) Error: Destructors are not allowed to return values (or even specify a return type) or take arguments.
Correction: Remove the return type `void` and the parameter `int` from the declaration.

b) Error: Members cannot be explicitly initialized in the class definition.
Correction: Remove the explicit initialization from the class definition and initialize the data members in a constructor.

c) Error: Constructors are not allowed to return values.
Correction: Remove the return type `int` from the declaration.

Exercises

9.3 What is the purpose of the scope resolution operator?

9.4 *(Enhancing Class `Time`)* Provide a constructor that is capable of using the current time from the `time()` function—declared in the C++ Standard Library header `<ctime>`—to initialize an object of the `Time` class.

9.5 *(Complex Class)* Create a class called `Complex` for performing arithmetic with complex numbers. Write a program to test your class.

Complex numbers have the form

> realPart + imaginaryPart * *i*

where *i* is

$$\sqrt{-1}$$

Use `double` variables to represent the `private` data of the class. Provide a constructor that enables an object of this class to be initialized when it is declared. The constructor should contain default values in case no initializers are provided. Provide `public` member functions that perform the following tasks:

   a) Adding two `Complex` numbers: The real parts are added together and the imaginary parts are added together.
   b) Subtracting two `Complex` numbers: The real part of the right operand is subtracted from the real part of the left operand, and the imaginary part of the right operand is subtracted from the imaginary part of the left operand.
   c) Printing `Complex` numbers in the form (a, b), where a is the real part and b is the imaginary part.

9.6 *(Rational Class)* Create a class called `Rational` for performing arithmetic with fractions. Write a program to test your class.

Use integer variables to represent the `private` data of the class—the `numerator` and the `denominator`. Provide a constructor that enables an object of this class to be initialized when it is declared. The constructor should contain default values in case no initializers are provided and should store the fraction in reduced form. For example, the fraction

$$\frac{2}{4}$$

would be stored in the object as 1 in the `numerator` and 2 in the `denominator`. Provide `public` member functions that perform each of the following tasks:

   a) Adding two `Rational` numbers. The result should be stored in reduced form.
   b) Subtracting two `Rational` numbers. The result should be stored in reduced form.
   c) Multiplying two `Rational` numbers. The result should be stored in reduced form.
   d) Dividing two `Rational` numbers. The result should be stored in reduced form.
   e) Printing `Rational` numbers in the form a/b, where a is the numerator and b is the denominator.
   f) Printing `Rational` numbers in floating-point format.

9.7 *(Enhancing Class Time)* Modify the `Time` class of Figs. 9.8–9.9 to include a `tick` member function that increments the time stored in a `Time` object by one second. The `Time` object should always remain in a consistent state. Write a program that tests the `tick` member function in a loop that prints the time in standard format during each iteration of the loop to illustrate that the `tick` member function works correctly. Be sure to test the following cases:

   a) Incrementing into the next minute.
   b) Incrementing into the next hour.
   c) Incrementing into the next day (i.e., 11:59:59 PM to 12:00:00 AM).

9.8 *(Enhancing Class Date)* Modify the `Date` class of Figs. 9.17–9.18 to perform error checking on the initializer values for data members `month`, `day` and `year`. Also, provide a member function `nextDay` to increment the day by one. The `Date` object should always remain in a consistent state. Write a program that tests function `nextDay` in a loop that prints the date during each iteration to illustrate that `nextDay` works correctly. Be sure to test the following cases:

a) Incrementing into the next month.
b) Incrementing into the next year.

9.9   *(Combining Class Time and Class Date)* Combine the modified Time class of Exercise 9.7 and the modified Date class of Exercise 9.8 into one class called DateAndTime. (In Chapter 12, we will discuss inheritance, which will enable us to accomplish this task quickly without modifying the existing class definitions.) Modify the tick function to call the nextDay function if the time increments into the next day. Modify functions printStandard and printUniversal to output the date and time. Write a program to test the new class DateAndTime. Specifically, test incrementing the time into the next day.

9.10   *(Returning Error Indicators from Class Time's set Functions)* Modify the *set* functions in the Time class of Figs. 9.8–9.9 to return appropriate error values if an attempt is made to *set* a data member of an object of class Time to an invalid value. Write a program that tests your new version of class Time. Display error messages when *set* functions return error values.

9.11   *(Rectangle Class)* Create a class Rectangle with attributes length and width, each of which defaults to 1. Provide member functions that calculate the perimeter and the area of the rectangle. Also, provide *set* and *get* functions for the length and width attributes. The *set* functions should verify that length and width are each floating-point numbers larger than 0.0 and less than 20.0.

9.12   *(Enhancing Class Rectangle)* Create a more sophisticated Rectangle class than the one you created in Exercise 9.11. This class stores only the Cartesian coordinates of the four corners of the rectangle. The constructor calls a *set* function that accepts four sets of coordinates and verifies that each of these is in the first quadrant with no single *x*- or *y*-coordinate larger than 20.0. The *set* function also verifies that the supplied coordinates do, in fact, specify a rectangle. Provide member functions that calculate the length, width, perimeter and area. The length is the larger of the two dimensions. Include a predicate function square that determines whether the rectangle is a square.

9.13   *(Enhancing Class Rectangle)* Modify class Rectangle from Exercise 9.12 to include a draw function that displays the rectangle inside a 25-by-25 box enclosing the portion of the first quadrant in which the rectangle resides. Include a setFillCharacter function to specify the character out of which the body of the rectangle will be drawn. Include a setPerimeterCharacter function to specify the character that will be used to draw the border of the rectangle. If you feel ambitious, you might include functions to scale the size of the rectangle, rotate it, and move it around within the designated portion of the first quadrant.

9.14   *(HugeInteger Class)* Create a class HugeInteger that uses a 40-element array of digits to store integers as large as 40 digits each. Provide member functions input, output, add and substract. For comparing HugeInteger objects, provide functions isEqualTo, isNotEqualTo, isGreaterThan, isLessThan, isGreaterThanOrEqualTo and isLessThanOrEqualTo—each of these is a "predicate" function that simply returns true if the relationship holds between the two HugeIntegers and returns false if the relationship does not hold. Also, provide a predicate function isZero. If you feel ambitious, provide member functions multiply, divide and modulus.

9.15   *(TicTacToe Class)* Create a class TicTacToe that will enable you to write a complete program to play the game of tic-tac-toe. The class contains as private data a 3-by-3 two-dimensional array of integers. The constructor should initialize the empty board to all zeros. Allow two human players. Wherever the first player moves, place a 1 in the specified square. Place a 2 wherever the second player moves. Each move must be to an empty square. After each move, determine whether the game has been won or is a draw. If you feel ambitious, modify your program so that the computer makes the moves for one of the players. Also, allow the player to specify whether he or she wants to go first or second. If you feel exceptionally ambitious, develop a program that will play three-dimensional tic-tac-toe on a 4-by-4-by-4 board. [*Caution:* This is an extremely challenging project that could take many weeks of effort!]

10

Classes: A Deeper Look, Part 2

*But what, to serve our
private ends,
Forbids the cheating of our
friends?*
—Charles Churchill

*Instead of this absurd
division into sexes they ought
to class people as static and
dynamic.*
—Evelyn Waugh

*Have no friends not equal to
yourself.*
—Confucius

OBJECTIVES

In this chapter you will learn:

- To specify **const** (constant) objects and **const** member functions.

- To create objects composed of other objects.

- To use **friend** functions and **friend** classes.

- To use the **this** pointer.

- To create and destroy objects dynamically with operators **new** and **delete**, respectively.

- To use **static** data members and member functions.

- The concept of a container class.

- The notion of iterator classes that walk through the elements of container classes.

- To use proxy classes to hide implementation details from a class's clients.

Outline

10.1   Introduction

10.2   const (Constant) Objects and const Member Functions

10.3   Composition: Objects as Members of Classes

10.4   friend Functions and friend Classes

10.5   Using the this Pointer

10.6   Dynamic Memory Management with Operators new and delete

10.7   static Class Members

10.8   Data Abstraction and Information Hiding

    10.8.1   Example: Array Abstract Data Type

    10.8.2   Example: String Abstract Data Type

    10.8.3   Example: Queue Abstract Data Type

10.9   Container Classes and Iterators

10.10   Proxy Classes

10.11   Wrap-Up

Summary | Terminology | Self-Review Exercises | Answers to Self-Review Exercises | Exercises

10.1   Introduction

In this chapter, we continue our study of classes and data abstraction with several more advanced topics. We use const objects and const member functions to prevent modifications of objects and enforce the principle of least privilege. We discuss composition—a form of reuse in which a class can have objects of other classes as members. Next, we introduce friendship, which enables a class designer to specify non-member functions that can access class's non-public members—a technique that is often used in operator overloading (Chapter 11) for performance reasons. We discuss a special pointer (called this), which is an implicit argument to each of a class's non-static member functions that allows those member functions to access the correct object's data members and other non-static member functions. We then discuss dynamic memory management and show how to create and destroy objects dynamically with the new and delete operators. Next, we motivate the need for static class members and show how to use static data members and member functions in your own classes. Finally, we show how to create a proxy class to hide the implementation details of a class (including its private data members) from clients of the class.

Recall that Chapter 3 introduced C++ Standard Library class string to represent strings as full-fledged class objects. In this chapter, however, we use the pointer-based strings we introduced in Chapter 8 to help the reader master pointers and prepare for the professional world in which the reader will see a great deal of C legacy code implemented over the last two decades. Thus, the reader will become familiar with the two most prevalent methods of creating and manipulating strings in C++.

10.2   const (Constant) Objects and const Member Functions

We have emphasized the principle of least privilege as one of the most fundamental principles of good software engineering. Let us see how this principle applies to objects.

Some objects need to be modifiable and some do not. The programmer may use keyword `const` to specify that an object is not modifiable and that any attempt to modify the object should result in a compilation error. The statement

```
const Time noon( 12, 0, 0 );
```

declares a `const` object `noon` of class `Time` and initializes it to 12 noon.

Software Engineering Observation 10.1

Declaring an object as `const` helps enforce the principle of least privilege. Attempts to modify the object are caught at compile time rather than causing execution-time errors. Using `const` properly is crucial to proper class design, program design and coding.

Performance Tip 10.1

Declaring variables and objects `const` can improve performance—today's sophisticated optimizing compilers can perform certain optimizations on constants that cannot be performed on variables.

C++ compilers disallow member function calls for `const` objects unless the member functions themselves are also declared `const`. This is true even for *get* member functions that do not modify the object. In addition, the compiler does not allow member functions declared `const` to modify the object.

A function is specified as `const` *both* in its prototype (Fig. 10.1; lines 19–24) and in its definition (Fig. 10.2; lines 47, 53, 59 and 65) by inserting the keyword `const` after the function's parameter list and, in the case of the function definition, before the left brace that begins the function body.

Common Programming Error 10.1

Defining as `const` a member function that modifies a data member of an object is a compilation error.

Common Programming Error 10.2

Defining as `const` a member function that calls a non-const member function of the class on the same instance of the class is a compilation error.

Common Programming Error 10.3

Invoking a non-const member function on a `const` object is a compilation error.

Software Engineering Observation 10.2

A `const` member function can be overloaded with a non-const version. The compiler chooses which overloaded member function to use based on the object on which the function is invoked. If the object is `const`, the compiler uses the `const` version. If the object is not `const`, the compiler uses the non-const version.

An interesting problem arises for constructors and destructors, each of which typically modifies objects. The `const` declaration is not allowed for constructors and destructors. A constructor must be allowed to modify an object so that the object can be initialized properly. A destructor must be able to perform its termination housekeeping chores before an object's memory is reclaimed by the system.

Common Programming Error 10.4

Attempting to declare a constructor or destructor const is a compilation error.

Defining and Using const Member Functions

The program of Figs. 10.1–10.3 modifies class Time of Figs. 9.9–9.10 by making its *get* functions and printUniversal function const. In the header file Time.h (Fig. 10.1), lines 19–21 and 24 now include keyword const after each function's parameter list. The corresponding definition of each function in Fig. 10.2 (lines 47, 53, 59 and 65, respectively) also specifies keyword const after each function's parameter list.

Figure 10.3 instantiates two Time objects—non-const object wakeUp (line 7) and const object noon (line 8). The program attempts to invoke non-const member functions setHour (line 13) and printStandard (line 20) on the const object noon. In each case, the compiler generates an error message. The program also illustrates the three other member-function-call combinations on objects—a non-const member function on a non-const object (line 11), a const member function on a non-const object (line 15) and a const member function on a const object (lines 17–18). The error messages generated

```
I    // Fig. 10.1: Time.h
2    // Definition of class Time.
3    // Member functions defined in Time.cpp.
4    #ifndef TIME_H
5    #define TIME_H
6
7    class Time
8    {
9    public:
10      Time( int = 0, int = 0, int = 0 ); // default constructor
11
12      // set functions
13      void setTime( int, int, int ); // set time
14      void setHour( int ); // set hour
15      void setMinute( int ); // set minute
16      void setSecond( int ); // set second
17
18      // get functions (normally declared const)
19      int getHour() const; // return hour
20      int getMinute() const; // return minute
21      int getSecond() const; // return second
22
23      // print functions (normally declared const)
24      void printUniversal() const; // print universal time
25      void printStandard(); // print standard time (should be const)
26    private:
27      int hour; // 0 - 23 (24-hour clock format)
28      int minute; // 0 - 59
29      int second; // 0 - 59
30    }; // end class Time
31
32    #endif
```

Fig. 10.1 | Time class definition with const member functions.

for non-const member functions called on a const object are shown in the output window. Notice that, although some current compilers issue only warning messages for lines 13 and 20 (thus allowing this program to be executed), we consider these warnings to be errors—the ANSI/ISO C++ standard disallows the invocation of a non-const member function on a const object.

```cpp
1   // Fig. 10.2: Time.cpp
2   // Member-function definitions for class Time.
3   #include <iostream>
4   using std::cout;
5
6   #include <iomanip>
7   using std::setfill;
8   using std::setw;
9
10  #include "Time.h" // include definition of class Time
11
12  // constructor function to initialize private data;
13  // calls member function setTime to set variables;
14  // default values are 0 (see class definition)
15  Time::Time( int hour, int minute, int second )
16  {
17     setTime( hour, minute, second );
18  } // end Time constructor
19
20  // set hour, minute and second values
21  void Time::setTime( int hour, int minute, int second )
22  {
23     setHour( hour );
24     setMinute( minute );
25     setSecond( second );
26  } // end function setTime
27
28  // set hour value
29  void Time::setHour( int h )
30  {
31     hour = ( h >= 0 && h < 24 ) ? h : 0; // validate hour
32  } // end function setHour
33
34  // set minute value
35  void Time::setMinute( int m )
36  {
37     minute = ( m >= 0 && m < 60 ) ? m : 0; // validate minute
38  } // end function setMinute
39
40  // set second value
41  void Time::setSecond( int s )
42  {
43     second = ( s >= 0 && s < 60 ) ? s : 0; // validate second
44  } // end function setSecond
45
```

Fig. 10.2 | Time class member-function definitions, including const member functions. (Part 1 of 2.)

```
46    // return hour value
47    int Time::getHour() const // get functions should be const
48    {
49       return hour;
50    } // end function getHour
51
52    // return minute value
53    int Time::getMinute() const
54    {
55       return minute;
56    } // end function getMinute
57
58    // return second value
59    int Time::getSecond() const
60    {
61       return second;
62    } // end function getSecond
63
64    // print Time in universal-time format (HH:MM:SS)
65    void Time::printUniversal() const
66    {
67       cout << setfill( '0' ) << setw( 2 ) << hour << ":"
68          << setw( 2 ) << minute << ":" << setw( 2 ) << second;
69    } // end function printUniversal
70
71    // print Time in standard-time format (HH:MM:SS AM or PM)
72    void Time::printStandard() // note lack of const declaration
73    {
74       cout << ( ( hour == 0 || hour == 12 ) ? 12 : hour % 12 )
75          << ":" << setfill( '0' ) << setw( 2 ) << minute
76          << ":" << setw( 2 ) << second << ( hour < 12 ? " AM" : " PM" );
77    } // end function printStandard
```

Fig. 10.2 | `Time` class member-function definitions, including `const` member functions. (Part 2 of 2.)

```
1     // Fig. 10.3: fig10_03.cpp
2     // Attempting to access a const object with non-const member functions.
3     #include "Time.h" // include Time class definition
4
5     int main()
6     {
7        Time wakeUp( 6, 45, 0 ); // non-constant object
8        const Time noon( 12, 0, 0 ); // constant object
9
10                             // OBJECT        MEMBER FUNCTION
11       wakeUp.setHour( 18 );  // non-const    non-const
12
13       noon.setHour( 12 );    // const        non-const
14
15       wakeUp.getHour();      // non-const    const
```

Fig. 10.3 | `const` objects and `const` member functions. (Part 1 of 2.)

```
16
17      noon.getMinute();        // const        const
18      noon.printUniversal();   // const        const
19
20      noon.printStandard();    // const        non-const
21      return 0;
22   } // end main
```

Borland C++ command-line compiler error messages:

```
Warning W8037 fig10_03.cpp 13: Non-const function Time::setHour(int)
   called for const object in function main()
Warning W8037 fig10_03.cpp 20: Non-const function Time::printStandard()
   called for const object in function main()
```

Microsoft Visual C++.NET compiler error messages:

```
C:\scpphtp5_examples\ch10\Fig10_01_03\fig10_03.cpp(13) : error C2662:
   'Time::setHour' : cannot convert 'this' pointer from 'const Time' to
   'Time &'
      Conversion loses qualifiers
C:\scpphtp5_examples\ch10\Fig10_01_03\fig10_03.cpp(20) : error C2662:
   'Time::printStandard' : cannot convert 'this' pointer from 'const Time' to
   'Time &'
      Conversion loses qualifiers
```

GNU C++ compiler error messages:

```
fig10_03.cpp:13: error: passing `const Time' as `this' argument of
   `void Time::setHour(int)' discards qualifiers
fig10_03.cpp:20: error: passing `const Time' as `this' argument of
   `void Time::printStandard()' discards qualifiers
```

Fig. 10.3 | const objects and const member functions. (Part 2 of 2.)

Notice that even though a constructor must be a non-const member function (Fig. 10.2, lines 15–18), it can still be used to initialize a const object (Fig. 10.3, line 8). The definition of the Time constructor (Fig. 10.2, lines 15–18) shows that the Time constructor calls another non-const member function—setTime (lines 21–26)—to perform the initialization of a Time object. Invoking a non-const member function from the constructor call as part of the initialization of a const object is allowed. The "constness" of a const object is enforced from the time the constructor completes initialization of the object until that object's destructor is called.

Also notice that line 20 in Fig. 10.3 generates a compilation error even though member function printStandard of class Time does not modify the object on which it is invoked. The fact that a member function does not modify an object is not sufficient to indicate that the function is constant function—the function must explicitly be declared const.

*Initializing a **const** Data Member with a Member Initializer*

The program of Figs. 10.4–10.6 introduces using member initializer syntax. All data members *can* be initialized using member initializer syntax, but const data members and

```
 1  // Fig. 10.4: Increment.h
 2  // Definition of class Increment.
 3  #ifndef INCREMENT_H
 4  #define INCREMENT_H
 5
 6  class Increment
 7  {
 8  public:
 9     Increment( int c = 0, int i = 1 ); // default constructor
10
11     // function addIncrement definition
12     void addIncrement()
13     {
14        count += increment;
15     } // end function addIncrement
16
17     void print() const; // prints count and increment
18  private:
19     int count;
20     const int increment; // const data member
21  }; // end class Increment
22
23  #endif
```

Fig. 10.4 | Increment class definition containing non-const data member count and const data member increment.

```
 1  // Fig. 10.5: Increment.cpp
 2  // Member-function definitions for class Increment demonstrate using a
 3  // member initializer to initialize a constant of a built-in data type.
 4  #include <iostream>
 5  using std::cout;
 6  using std::endl;
 7
 8  #include "Increment.h" // include definition of class Increment
 9
10  // constructor
11  Increment::Increment( int c, int i )
12     : count( c ), // initializer for non-const member
13       increment( i ) // required initializer for const member
14  {
15     // empty body
16  } // end constructor Increment
17
18  // print count and increment values
19  void Increment::print() const
20  {
21     cout << "count = " << count << ", increment = " << increment << endl;
22  } // end function print
```

Fig. 10.5 | Member initializer used to initialize a constant of a built-in data type.

```
1   // Fig. 10.6: fig10_06.cpp
2   // Program to test class Increment.
3   #include <iostream>
4   using std::cout;
5
6   #include "Increment.h" // include definition of class Increment
7
8   int main()
9   {
10     Increment value( 10, 5 );
11
12     cout << "Before incrementing: ";
13     value.print();
14
15     for ( int j = 1; j <= 3; j++ )
16     {
17        value.addIncrement();
18        cout << "After increment " << j << ": ";
19        value.print();
20     } // end for
21
22     return 0;
23  } // end main
```

```
Before incrementing: count = 10, increment = 5
After increment 1: count = 15, increment = 5
After increment 2: count = 20, increment = 5
After increment 3: count = 25, increment = 5
```

Fig. 10.6 | Invoking an Increment object's print and addIncrement member functions.

data members that are references *must* be initialized using member initializers. Later in this chapter, we will see that member objects must be initialized this way as well. In Chapter 12 when we study inheritance, we will see that base-class portions of derived classes also must be initialized this way.

The constructor definition (Fig. 10.5, lines 11–16) uses a member initializer list to initialize class Increment's data members—non-const integer count and const integer increment (declared in lines 19–20 of Fig. 10.4). Member initializers appear between a constructor's parameter list and the left brace that begins the constructor's body. The member initializer list (Fig. 10.5, lines 12–13) is separated from the parameter list with a colon (:). Each member initializer consists of the data member name followed by parentheses containing the member's initial value. In this example, count is initialized with the value of constructor parameter c and increment is initialized with the value of constructor parameter i. Note that multiple member initializers are separated by commas. Also, note that the member initializer list executes before the body of the constructor executes.

Software Engineering Observation 10.3

A const object cannot be modified by assignment, so it must be initialized. When a data member of a class is declared const, a member initializer must be used to provide the constructor with the initial value of the data member for an object of the class. The same is true for references.

Erroneously Attempting to Initialize a const Data Member with an Assignment
The program of Figs. 10.7–10.9 illustrates the compilation errors caused by attempting to initialize const data member increment with an assignment statement (Fig. 10.8, line 14) in the Increment constructor's body rather than with a member initializer. Note that line 13 of Fig. 10.8 does not generate a compilation error, because count is not declared const. Also note that the compilation errors produced by Microsoft Visual C++.NET refer to int data member increment as a "const object." The ANSI/ISO C++ standard defines an "object" as any "region of storage." Like instances of classes, fundamental-type variables also occupy space in memory, so they are often referred to as "objects."

Common Programming Error 10.5

Not providing a member initializer for a const data member is a compilation error.

Software Engineering Observation 10.4

Constant data members (const objects and const variables) and data members declared as references must be initialized with member initializer syntax; assignments for these types of data in the constructor body are not allowed.

Note that function print (Fig. 10.8, lines 18–21) is declared const. It might seem strange to label this function const, because a program probably will never have a const Increment object. However, it is possible that a program will have a const reference to an Increment object or a pointer to const that points to an Increment object. Typically, this occurs when objects of class Increment are passed to functions or returned from functions. In these cases, only the const member functions of class Increment can be called through the reference or pointer. Thus, it is reasonable to declare function print as const—doing so prevents errors in these situations where an Increment object is treated as a const object.

Error-Prevention Tip 10.1

Declare as const all of a class's member functions that do not modify the object in which they operate. Occasionally this may seem inappropriate, because you will have no intention of creating const objects of that class or accessing objects of that class through const references or pointers to const. Declaring such member functions const does offer a benefit, though. If the member function is inadvertently written to modify the object, the compiler will issue an error message.

```
1   // Fig. 10.7: Increment.h
2   // Definition of class Increment.
3   #ifndef INCREMENT_H
4   #define INCREMENT_H
5
6   class Increment
7   {
8   public:
9      Increment( int c = 0, int i = 1 ); // default constructor
10
```

Fig. 10.7 | Increment class definition containing non-const data member count and const data member increment. (Part 1 of 2.)

```
11      // function addIncrement definition
12      void addIncrement()
13      {
14          count += increment;
15      } // end function addIncrement
16
17      void print() const; // prints count and increment
18   private:
19      int count;
20      const int increment; // const data member
21   }; // end class Increment
22
23   #endif
```

Fig. 10.7 | Increment class definition containing non-const data member count and const data member increment. (Part 2 of 2.)

```
1    // Fig. 10.8: Increment.cpp
2    // Attempting to initialize a constant of
3    // a built-in data type with an assignment.
4    #include <iostream>
5    using std::cout;
6    using std::endl;
7
8    #include "Increment.h" // include definition of class Increment
9
10   // constructor; constant member 'increment' is not initialized
11   Increment::Increment( int c, int i )
12   {
13      count = c; // allowed because count is not constant
14      increment = i; // ERROR: Cannot modify a const object
15   } // end constructor Increment
16
17   // print count and increment values
18   void Increment::print() const
19   {
20      cout << "count = " << count << ", increment = " << increment << endl;
21   } // end function print
```

Fig. 10.8 | Erroneous attempt to initialize a constant of a built-in data type by assignment.

```
1    // Fig. 10.9: fig10_09.cpp
2    // Program to test class Increment.
3    #include <iostream>
4    using std::cout;
5
6    #include "Increment.h" // include definition of class Increment
7
8    int main()
9    {
```

Fig. 10.9 | Program to test class Increment generates compilation errors. (Part 1 of 2.)

```
10      Increment value( 10, 5 );
11
12      cout << "Before incrementing: ";
13      value.print();
14
15      for ( int j = 1; j <= 3; j++ )
16      {
17         value.addIncrement();
18         cout << "After increment " << j << ": ";
19         value.print();
20      } // end for
21
22      return 0;
23   } // end main
```

Borland C++ command-line compiler error message:

```
Error E2024 Increment.cpp 14: Cannot modify a const object in function
   Increment::Increment(int,int)
```

Microsoft Visual C++.NET compiler error messages:

```
C:\cpphtp5_examples\ch10\Fig10_07_09\Increment.cpp(12) : error C2758:
   'Increment::increment' : must be initialized in constructor
base/member initializer list
       C:\cpphtp5_examples\ch10\Fig10_07_09\Increment.h(20) :
          see declaration of 'Increment::increment'
C:\cpphtp5_examples\ch10\Fig10_07_09\Increment.cpp(14) : error C2166:
   l-value specifies const object
```

GNU C++ compiler error messages:

```
Increment.cpp:12: error: uninitialized member 'Increment::increment' with
   'const' type 'const int'
Increment.cpp:14: error: assignment of read-only data-member
   `Increment::increment'
```

Fig. 10.9 | Program to test class `Increment` generates compilation errors. (Part 2 of 2.)

10.3 Composition: Objects as Members of Classes

An `AlarmClock` object needs to know when it is supposed to sound its alarm, so why not include a `Time` object as a member of the `AlarmClock` class? Such a capability is called composition and is sometimes referred to as a *has-a* relationship. A class can have objects of other classes as members.

Software Engineering Observation 10.5

A common form of software reusability is composition, in which a class has objects of other classes as members.

When an object is created, its constructor is called automatically. Previously, we saw how to pass arguments to the constructor of an object we created in `main`. This section shows how an object's constructor can pass arguments to member-object constructors, which is accomplished via member initializers. Member objects are constructed in the order in which they are declared in the class definition (not in the order they are listed in the constructor's member initializer list) and before their enclosing class objects (sometimes called host objects) are constructed.

The program of Figs. 10.10–10.14 uses class Date (Figs. 10.10–10.11) and class Employee (Figs. 10.12–10.13) to demonstrate objects as members of other objects. The definition of class Employee (Fig. 10.12) contains private data members firstName, lastName, birthDate and hireDate. Members birthDate and hireDate are const objects of class Date, which contains private data members month, day and year. The Employee constructor's header (Fig. 10.13, lines 18–21) specifies that the constructor receives four parameters (first, last, dateOfBirth and dateOfHire). The first two parameters are used in the constructor's body to initialize the character arrays firstName and lastName. The last two parameters are passed via member initializers to the constructor for class Date. The colon (:) in the header separates the member initializers from the parameter list. The member initializers specify the Employee constructor parameters being passed to the constructors of the member Date objects. Parameter dateOfBirth is passed to object birthDate's constructor (Fig. 10.13, line 20), and parameter dateOfHire is passed to object hireDate's constructor (Fig. 10.13, line 21). Again, member initializers are separated by commas. As you study class Date (Fig. 10.10), notice that the class does not provide a constructor that receives a parameter of type Date. So, how is the member initializer list in class Employee's constructor able to initialize the birthDate and hireDate objects by passing Date object's to their Date constructors? As we mentioned in Chapter 9, the compiler provides each class with a default copy constructor that copies each member of the constructor's argument object into the corresponding member of the object being initialized. Chapter 11 discusses how programmers can define customized copy constructors.

```
1   // Fig. 10.10: Date.h
2   // Date class definition; Member functions defined in Date.cpp
3   #ifndef DATE_H
4   #define DATE_H
5
6   class Date
7   {
8   public:
9      Date( int = 1, int = 1, int = 1900 ); // default constructor
10     void print() const; // print date in month/day/year format
11     ~Date(); // provided to confirm destruction order
12   private:
13     int month; // 1-12 (January-December)
14     int day; // 1-31 based on month
15     int year; // any year
16
17     // utility function to check if day is proper for month and year
18     int checkDay( int ) const;
19   }; // end class Date
20
21   #endif
```

Fig. 10.10 | Date class definition.

Figure 10.14 creates two `Date` objects (lines 11–12) and passes them as arguments to the constructor of the `Employee` object created in line 13. Line 16 outputs the `Employee` object's data. When each `Date` object is created in lines 11–12, the `Date` constructor defined at lines 11–28 of Fig. 10.11 displays a line of output to show that the constructor was called (see the first two lines of the sample output). [*Note:* Line 13 of Fig. 10.14 causes two additional `Date` constructor calls that do not appear in the program's output. When each of the `Employee`'s `Date` member object's is initialized in the `Employee` constructor's member initializer list, the default copy constructor for class `Date` is called. This constructor is defined implicitly by the compiler and does not contain any output statements to demonstrate when it is called. We discuss copy constructors and default copy constructors in detail in Chapter 11.]

```cpp
1   // Fig. 10.11: Date.cpp
2   // Member-function definitions for class Date.
3   #include <iostream>
4   using std::cout;
5   using std::endl;
6
7   #include "Date.h" // include Date class definition
8
9   // constructor confirms proper value for month; calls
10  // utility function checkDay to confirm proper value for day
11  Date::Date( int mn, int dy, int yr )
12  {
13     if ( mn > 0 && mn <= 12 ) // validate the month
14        month = mn;
15     else
16     {
17        month = 1; // invalid month set to 1
18        cout << "Invalid month (" << mn << ") set to 1.\n";
19     } // end else
20
21     year = yr; // could validate yr
22     day = checkDay( dy ); // validate the day
23
24     // output Date object to show when its constructor is called
25     cout << "Date object constructor for date ";
26     print();
27     cout << endl;
28  } // end Date constructor
29
30  // print Date object in form month/day/year
31  void Date::print() const
32  {
33     cout << month << '/' << day << '/' << year;
34  } // end function print
35
36  // output Date object to show when its destructor is called
37  Date::~Date()
38  {
```

Fig. 10.11 | Date class member-function definitions. (Part 1 of 2.)

```
39          cout << "Date object destructor for date ";
40          print();
41          cout << endl;
42       } // end ~Date destructor
43
44       // utility function to confirm proper day value based on
45       // month and year; handles leap years, too
46       int Date::checkDay( int testDay ) const
47       {
48          static const int daysPerMonth[ 13 ] =
49             { 0, 31, 28, 31, 30, 31, 30, 31, 31, 30, 31, 30, 31 };
50
51          // determine whether testDay is valid for specified month
52          if ( testDay > 0 && testDay <= daysPerMonth[ month ] )
53             return testDay;
54
55          // February 29 check for leap year
56          if ( month == 2 && testDay == 29 && ( year % 400 == 0 ||
57             ( year % 4 == 0 && year % 100 != 0 ) ) )
58             return testDay;
59
60          cout << "Invalid day (" << testDay << ") set to 1.\n";
61          return 1; // leave object in consistent state if bad value
62       } // end function checkDay
```

Fig. 10.11 | Date class member-function definitions. (Part 2 of 2.)

```
1    // Fig. 10.12: Employee.h
2    // Employee class definition.
3    // Member functions defined in Employee.cpp.
4    #ifndef EMPLOYEE_H
5    #define EMPLOYEE_H
6
7    #include "Date.h" // include Date class definition
8
9    class Employee
10   {
11   public:
12      Employee( const char * const, const char * const,
13         const Date &, const Date & );
14      void print() const;
15      ~Employee(); // provided to confirm destruction order
16   private:
17      char firstName[ 25 ];
18      char lastName[ 25 ];
19      const Date birthDate; // composition: member object
20      const Date hireDate; // composition: member object
21   }; // end class Employee
22
23   #endif
```

Fig. 10.12 | Employee class definition showing composition.

```
1   // Fig. 10.13: Employee.cpp
2   // Member-function definitions for class Employee.
3   #include <iostream>
4   using std::cout;
5   using std::endl;
6
7   #include <cstring> // strlen and strncpy prototypes
8   using std::strlen;
9   using std::strncpy;
10
11  #include "Employee.h" // Employee class definition
12  #include "Date.h" // Date class definition
13
14  // constructor uses member initializer list to pass initializer
15  // values to constructors of member objects birthDate and hireDate
16  // [Note: This invokes the so-called "default copy constructor" which the
17  // C++ compiler provides implicitly.]
18  Employee::Employee( const char * const first, const char * const last,
19     const Date &dateOfBirth, const Date &dateOfHire )
20     : birthDate( dateOfBirth ), // initialize birthDate
21       hireDate( dateOfHire ) // initialize hireDate
22  {
23     // copy first into firstName and be sure that it fits
24     int length = strlen( first );
25     length = ( length < 25 ? length : 24 );
26     strncpy( firstName, first, length );
27     firstName[ length ] = '\0';
28
29     // copy last into lastName and be sure that it fits
30     length = strlen( last );
31     length = ( length < 25 ? length : 24 );
32     strncpy( lastName, last, length );
33     lastName[ length ] = '\0';
34
35     // output Employee object to show when constructor is called
36     cout << "Employee object constructor: "
37        << firstName << ' ' << lastName << endl;
38  } // end Employee constructor
39
40  // print Employee object
41  void Employee::print() const
42  {
43     cout << lastName << ", " << firstName << "  Hired: ";
44     hireDate.print();
45     cout << "  Birthday: ";
46     birthDate.print();
47     cout << endl;
48  } // end function print
49
50  // output Employee object to show when its destructor is called
51  Employee::~Employee()
52  {
```

Fig. 10.13 | Employee class member-function definitions, including constructor with a member initializer list. (Part 1 of 2.)

```
53       cout << "Employee object destructor: "
54          << lastName << ", " << firstName << endl;
55    } // end ~Employee destructor
```

Fig. 10.13 | `Employee` class member-function definitions, including constructor with a member initializer list. (Part 2 of 2.)

```
 1    // Fig. 10.14: fig10_14.cpp
 2    // Demonstrating composition--an object with member objects.
 3    #include <iostream>
 4    using std::cout;
 5    using std::endl;
 6
 7    #include "Employee.h" // Employee class definition
 8
 9    int main()
10    {
11       Date birth( 7, 24, 1949 );
12       Date hire( 3, 12, 1988 );
13       Employee manager( "Bob", "Blue", birth, hire );
14
15       cout << endl;
16       manager.print();
17
18       cout << "\nTest Date constructor with invalid values:\n";
19       Date lastDayOff( 14, 35, 1994 ); // invalid month and day
20       cout << endl;
21       return 0;
22    } // end main
```

```
Date object constructor for date 7/24/1949
Date object constructor for date 3/12/1988
Employee object constructor: Bob Blue

Blue, Bob  Hired: 3/12/1988  Birthday: 7/24/1949

Test Date constructor with invalid values:
Invalid month (14) set to 1.
Invalid day (35) set to 1.
Date object constructor for date 1/1/1994

Date object destructor for date 1/1/1994
Employee object destructor: Blue, Bob
Date object destructor for date 3/12/1988
Date object destructor for date 7/24/1949
Date object destructor for date 3/12/1988
Date object destructor for date 7/24/1949
```

Fig. 10.14 | Member-object initializers.

Class `Date` and class `Employee` each include a destructor (lines 37–42 of Fig. 10.11 and lines 51–55 of Fig. 10.13, respectively) that prints a message when an object of its class is destroyed. This enables us to confirm in the program output that objects are constructed from the inside out and destroyed in the reverse order from the outside in (i.e., the Date member objects are destroyed after the Employee object that contains them). Notice the last four lines in the output of Fig. 10.14. The last two lines are the outputs of the Date destructor running on Date objects hire (line 12) and birth (line 11), respectively. These outputs confirm that the three objects created in main are destructed in the reverse of the order in which they were constructed. (The Employee destructor output is five lines from the bottom.) The fourth and third lines from the bottom of the output window show the destructors running for the Employee's member objects hireDate (Fig. 10.12, line 20) and birthDate (Fig. 10.12, line 19). These outputs confirm that the Employee object is destructed from the outside in—i.e., the Employee destructor runs first (output shown five lines from the bottom of the output window), then the member objects are destructed in the reverse order from which they were constructed. Again, the outputs in Fig. 10.14 did not show the constructors running for these objects, because these were the default copy constructors provided by the C++ compiler.

A member object does not need to be initialized explicitly through a member initializer. If a member initializer is not provided, the member object's default constructor will be called implicitly. Values, if any, established by the default constructor can be overridden by *set* functions. However, for complex initialization, this approach may require significant additional work and time.

Common Programming Error 10.6

A compilation error occurs if a member object is not initialized with a member initializer and the member object's class does not provide a default constructor (i.e., the member object's class defines one or more constructors, but none is a default constructor).

Performance Tip 10.2

Initialize member objects explicitly through member initializers. This eliminates the overhead of "doubly initializing" member objects—once when the member object's default constructor is called and again when set *functions are called in the constructor body (or later) to initialize the member object.*

Software Engineering Observation 10.6

If a class member is an object of another class, making that member object public *does not violate the encapsulation and hiding of that member object's* private *members. However, it does violate the encapsulation and hiding of the containing class's implementation, so member objects of class types should still be* private, *like all other data members.*

In line 26 of Fig. 10.11, notice the call to Date member function print. Many member functions of classes in C++ require no arguments. This is because each member function contains an implicit handle (in the form of a pointer) to the object on which it operates. We discuss the implicit pointer, which is represented by keyword this, in Section 10.5.

Class Employee uses two 25-character arrays (Fig. 10.12, lines 17–18) to represent the first name and last name of the Employee. These arrays may waste space for names shorter than 24 characters. (Remember, one character in each array is for the terminating null character, '\0', of the string.) Also, names longer than 24 characters must be truncated to fit in these fixed-size character arrays. Section 10.7 presents another version of class Employee that dynamically creates the exact amount of space required to hold the first and the last name.

Note that the simplest way to represent an `Employee`'s first and last name using the exact amount of space required is to use two `string` objects (C++ Standard Library class `string` was introduced in Chapter 3). If we did this, the `Employee` constructor would appear as follows

```
Employee::Employee( const string &first, const string &last,
   const Date &dateOfBirth, const Date &dateOfHire )
   : firstName( first), // initialize firstName
     lastName( last ), // initialize lastName
     birthDate( dateOfBirth ), // initialize birthDate
     hireDate( dateOfHire ) // initialize hireDate
{
   // output Employee object to show when constructor is called
   cout << "Employee object constructor: "
      << firstName << ' ' << lastName << endl;
} // end Employee constructor
```

Notice that data members `firstName` and `lastName` (now `string` objects) are initialized through member initializers. The `Employee` classes presented in Chapters 12–13 use `string` objects in this fashion. In this chapter, we use pointer-based strings to provide the reader with additional exposure to pointer manipulation.

10.4 `friend` Functions and `friend` Classes

A `friend function` of a class is defined outside that class's scope, yet has the right to access the non-`public` (and `public`) members of the class. Standalone functions or entire classes may be declared to be friends of another class.

Using `friend` functions can enhance performance. This section presents a mechanical example of how a `friend` function works. Later in the book, `friend` functions are used to overload operators for use with class objects (Chapter 11). It is also common to use `friend` functions to create iterator classes. Objects of an iterator class can successively select items or perform an operation on items in a container class object (see Section 10.9). Objects of container classes can store items. Using friends is often appropriate when a member function cannot be used for certain operations, as we will see in Chapter 11.

To declare a function as a friend of a class, precede the function prototype in the class definition with keyword `friend`. To declare all member functions of class `ClassTwo` as friends of class `ClassOne`, place a declaration of the form

```
friend class ClassTwo;
```

in the definition of class `ClassOne`.

Software Engineering Observation 10.7

Even though the prototypes for `friend` functions appear in the class definition, friends are not member functions.

Software Engineering Observation 10.8

Member access notions of private, protected and public are not relevant to friend declarations, so `friend` declarations can be placed anywhere in a class definition.

Good Programming Practice 10.1

Place all friendship declarations first inside the class definition's body and do not precede them with any access specifier.

Friendship is granted, not taken—i.e., for class B to be a friend of class A, class A must explicitly declare that class B is its friend. Also, the friendship relation is neither symmetric nor transitive; i.e., if class A is a friend of class B, and class B is a friend of class C, you cannot infer that class B is a friend of class A (again, friendship is not symmetric), that class C is a friend of class B (also because friendship is not symmetric), or that class A is a friend of class C (friendship is not transitive).

Software Engineering Observation 10.9

Some people in the OOP community feel that "friendship" corrupts information hiding and weakens the value of the object-oriented design approach. In this text, we identify several examples of the responsible use of friendship.

Modifying a Class's **private** Data With a Friend Function

Figure 10.15 is a mechanical example in which we define friend function setX to set the private data member x of class Count. Note that the friend declaration (line 10) appears first (by convention) in the class definition, even before public member functions are declared. Again, this friend declaration can appear anywhere in the class.

```cpp
1  // Fig. 10.15: fig10_15.cpp
2  // Friends can access private members of a class.
3  #include <iostream>
4  using std::cout;
5  using std::endl;
6
7  // Count class definition
8  class Count
9  {
10    friend void setX( Count &, int ); // friend declaration
11 public:
12    // constructor
13    Count()
14       : x( 0 ) // initialize x to 0
15    {
16       // empty body
17    } // end constructor Count
18
19    // output x
20    void print() const
21    {
22       cout << x << endl;
23    } // end function print
24 private:
25    int x; // data member
26 }; // end class Count
27
```

Fig. 10.15 | Friends can access private members of a class. (Part 1 of 2.)

```
28  // function setX can modify private data of Count
29  // because setX is declared as a friend of Count (line 10)
30  void setX( Count &c, int val )
31  {
32     c.x = val; // allowed because setX is a friend of Count
33  } // end function setX
34
35  int main()
36  {
37     Count counter; // create Count object
38
39     cout << "counter.x after instantiation: ";
40     counter.print();
41
42     setX( counter, 8 ); // set x using a friend function
43     cout << "counter.x after call to setX friend function: ";
44     counter.print();
45     return 0;
46  } // end main
```

```
counter.x after instantiation: 0
counter.x after call to setX friend function: 8
```

Fig. 10.15 | Friends can access `private` members of a class. (Part 2 of 2.)

Function setX (lines 30–33) is a C-style, stand-alone function—it is not a member function of class Count. For this reason, when setX is invoked for object counter, line 42 passes counter as an argument to setX rather than using a handle (such as the name of the object) to call the function, as in

```
counter.setX( 8 );
```

As we mentioned, Fig. 10.15 is a mechanical example of using the friend construct. It would normally be appropriate to define function setX as a member function of class Count. It would also normally be appropriate to separate the program of Fig. 10.15 into three files:

1. A header file (e.g., Count.h) containing the Count class definition, which in turn contains the prototype of friend function setX

2. An implementation file (e.g., Count.cpp) containing the definitions of class Count's member functions and the definition of friend function setX

3. A test program (e.g., fig10_15.cpp) with main

*Erroneously Attempting to Modify a **private** Member with a Non-**friend** Function*
The program of Fig. 10.16 demonstrates the error messages produced by the compiler when non-friend function cannotSetX (lines 29–32) is called to modify private data member x.

It is possible to specify overloaded functions as friends of a class. Each overloaded function intended to be a friend must be explicitly declared in the class definition as a friend of the class.

```
1   // Fig. 10.16: fig10_16.cpp
2   // Non-friend/non-member functions cannot access private data of a class.
3   #include <iostream>
4   using std::cout;
5   using std::endl;
6
7   // Count class definition (note that there is no friendship declaration)
8   class Count
9   {
10  public:
11     // constructor
12     Count()
13        : x( 0 ) // initialize x to 0
14     {
15        // empty body
16     } // end constructor Count
17
18     // output x
19     void print() const
20     {
21        cout << x << endl;
22     } // end function print
23  private:
24     int x; // data member
25  }; // end class Count
26
27  // function cannotSetX tries to modify private data of Count,
28  // but cannot because the function is not a friend of Count
29  void cannotSetX( Count &c, int val )
30  {
31     c.x = val; // ERROR: cannot access private member in Count
32  } // end function cannotSetX
33
34  int main()
35  {
36     Count counter; // create Count object
37
38     cannotSetX( counter, 3 ); // cannotSetX is not a friend
39     return 0;
40  } // end main
```

Borland C++ command-line compiler error message:

```
Error E2247 Fig10_16/fig10_16.cpp 31: 'Count::x' is not accessible in
   function cannotSetX(Count &,int)
```

Microsoft Visual C++.NET compiler error messages:

```
C:\cpphtp5_examples\ch10\Fig10_16\fig10_16.cpp(31) : error C2248: 'Count::x'
   : cannot access private member declared in class 'Count'
      C:\scpphtp5_examples\ch10\Fig10_16\fig10_16.cpp(24) : see declaration
         of 'Count::x'
      C:\scpphtp5_examples\ch10\Fig10_16\fig10_16.cpp(9) : see declaration
         of 'Count'
```

Fig. 10.16 | Non-friend/nonmember functions cannot access private members. (Part 1 of 2.)

GNU C++ compiler error messages:

```
fig10_16.cpp:24: error: `int Count::x' is private
fig10_16.cpp:31: error: within this context
```

Fig. 10.16 | Non-friend/nonmember functions cannot access `private` members. (Part 2 of 2.)

10.5 Using the `this` Pointer

We have seen that an object's member functions can manipulate the object's data. How do member functions know which object's data members to manipulate? Every object has access to its own address through a pointer called `this` (a C++ keyword). An object's `this` pointer is not part of the object itself—i.e., the size of the memory occupied by the `this` pointer is not reflected in the result of a `sizeof` operation on the object. Rather, the `this` pointer is passed (by the compiler) as an implicit argument to each of the object's non-static member functions. Section 10.7 introduces `static` class members and explains why the `this` pointer is *not* implicitly passed to `static` member functions.

Objects use the `this` pointer implicitly (as we have done to this point) or explicitly to reference their data members and member functions. The type of the `this` pointer depends on the type of the object and whether the member function in which `this` is used is declared `const`. For example, in a nonconstant member function of class `Employee`, the `this` pointer has type `Employee * const` (a constant pointer to a nonconstant `Employee` object). In a constant member function of the class `Employee`, the `this` pointer has the data type `const Employee * const` (a constant pointer to a constant `Employee` object).

Our first example in this section shows implicit and explicit use of the `this` pointer; later in this chapter and in Chapter 11, we show some substantial and subtle examples of using `this`.

Implicitly and Explicitly Using the `this` Pointer to Access an Object's Data Members
Figure 10.17 demonstrates the implicit and explicit use of the `this` pointer to enable a member function of class `Test` to print the `private` data x of a `Test` object.

For illustration purposes, member function `print` (lines 25–37) first prints x by using the `this` pointer implicitly (line 28)—only the name of the data member is specified. Then `print` uses two different notations to access x through the `this` pointer—the arrow

```
 1   // Fig. 10.17: fig10_17.cpp
 2   // Using the this pointer to refer to object members.
 3   #include <iostream>
 4   using std::cout;
 5   using std::endl;
 6
 7   class Test
 8   {
 9   public:
10      Test( int = 0 ); // default constructor
11      void print() const;
```

Fig. 10.17 | `this` pointer implicitly and explicitly accessing an object's members. (Part 1 of 2.)

```
12   private:
13      int x;
14   }; // end class Test
15
16   // constructor
17   Test::Test( int value )
18      : x( value ) // initialize x to value
19   {
20      // empty body
21   } // end constructor Test
22
23   // print x using implicit and explicit this pointers;
24   // the parentheses around *this are required
25   void Test::print() const
26   {
27      // implicitly use the this pointer to access the member x
28      cout << "        x = " << x;
29
30      // explicitly use the this pointer and the arrow operator
31      // to access the member x
32      cout << "\n  this->x = " << this->x;
33
34      // explicitly use the dereferenced this pointer and
35      // the dot operator to access the member x
36      cout << "\n(*this).x = " << ( *this ).x << endl;
37   } // end function print
38
39   int main()
40   {
41      Test testObject( 12 ); // instantiate and initialize testObject
42
43      testObject.print();
44      return 0;
45   } // end main
```

```
        x = 12
  this->x = 12
(*this).x = 12
```

Fig. 10.17 | this pointer implicitly and explicitly accessing an object's members. (Part 2 of 2.)

operator (->) off the this pointer (line 32) and the dot operator (.) off the dereferenced this pointer (line 36).

Note the parentheses around *this (line 36) when used with the dot member selection operator (.). The parentheses are required because the dot operator has higher precedence than the * operator. Without the parentheses, the expression *this.x would be evaluated as if it were parenthesized as *(this.x), which is a compilation error, because the dot operator cannot be used with a pointer.

One interesting use of the this pointer is to prevent an object from being assigned to itself. As we will see in Chapter 11, self-assignment can cause serious errors when the object contains pointers to dynamically allocated storage.

Common Programming Error 10.7

Attempting to use the member selection operator (.) with a pointer to an object is a compilation error—the dot member selection operator may be used only with an lvalue *such as an object's name, a reference to an object or a dereferenced pointer to an object.*

Using the **this** Pointer to Enable Cascaded Function Calls

Another use of the this pointer is to enable cascaded member-function calls in which multiple functions are invoked in the same statement (as in line 14 of Fig. 10.20). The program of Figs. 10.18–10.20 modifies class Time's *set* functions setTime, setHour, setMinute and setSecond such that each returns a reference to a Time object to enable cascaded member-function calls. Notice in Fig. 10.19 that the last statement in the body of each of these member functions returns *this (lines 26, 33, 40 and 47) into a return type of Time &.

The program of Fig. 10.20 creates Time object t (line 11), then uses it in cascaded member-function calls (lines 14 and 26). Why does the technique of returning *this as a reference work? The dot operator (.) associates from left to right, so line 14 first evaluates t.setHour(18) then returns a reference to object t as the value of this function call. The remaining expression is then interpreted as

```
t.setMinute( 30 ).setSecond( 22 );
```

The t.setMinute(30) call executes and returns a reference to the object t. The remaining expression is interpreted as

```
t.setSecond( 22 );
```

Line 26 also uses cascading. The calls must appear in the order shown in line 26, because printStandard as defined in the class does not return a reference to t. Placing the call to printStandard before the call to setTime in line 26 results in a compilation error. Chapter 11 presents several practical examples of using cascaded function calls. One such example uses multiple << operators with cout to output multiple values in a single statement.

```
1   // Fig. 10.18: Time.h
2   // Cascading member function calls.
3
4   // Time class definition.
5   // Member functions defined in Time.cpp.
6   #ifndef TIME_H
7   #define TIME_H
8
9   class Time
10  {
11  public:
12     Time( int = 0, int = 0, int = 0 ); // default constructor
13
14     // set functions (the Time & return types enable cascading)
15     Time &setTime( int, int, int ); // set hour, minute, second
16     Time &setHour( int ); // set hour
17     Time &setMinute( int ); // set minute
18     Time &setSecond( int ); // set second
19
```

Fig. 10.18 | Time class definition modified to enable cascaded member-function calls. (Part 1 of 2.)

```
20      // get functions (normally declared const)
21      int getHour() const; // return hour
22      int getMinute() const; // return minute
23      int getSecond() const; // return second
24
25      // print functions (normally declared const)
26      void printUniversal() const; // print universal time
27      void printStandard() const; // print standard time
28  private:
29      int hour; // 0 - 23 (24-hour clock format)
30      int minute; // 0 - 59
31      int second; // 0 - 59
32  }; // end class Time
33
34  #endif
```

Fig. 10.18 | Time class definition modified to enable cascaded member-function calls. (Part 2 of 2.)

```
1   // Fig. 10.19: Time.cpp
2   // Member-function definitions for Time class.
3   #include <iostream>
4   using std::cout;
5
6   #include <iomanip>
7   using std::setfill;
8   using std::setw;
9
10  #include "Time.h" // Time class definition
11
12  // constructor function to initialize private data;
13  // calls member function setTime to set variables;
14  // default values are 0 (see class definition)
15  Time::Time( int hr, int min, int sec )
16  {
17      setTime( hr, min, sec );
18  } // end Time constructor
19
20  // set values of hour, minute, and second
21  Time &Time::setTime( int h, int m, int s ) // note Time & return
22  {
23      setHour( h );
24      setMinute( m );
25      setSecond( s );
26      return *this; // enables cascading
27  } // end function setTime
28
29  // set hour value
30  Time &Time::setHour( int h ) // note Time & return
31  {
```

Fig. 10.19 | Time class member-function definitions modified to enable cascaded member-function calls. (Part 1 of 2.)

```
32        hour = ( h >= 0 && h < 24 ) ? h : 0; // validate hour
33        return *this; // enables cascading
34    } // end function setHour
35
36    // set minute value
37    Time &Time::setMinute( int m ) // note Time & return
38    {
39        minute = ( m >= 0 && m < 60 ) ? m : 0; // validate minute
40        return *this; // enables cascading
41    } // end function setMinute
42
43    // set second value
44    Time &Time::setSecond( int s ) // note Time & return
45    {
46        second = ( s >= 0 && s < 60 ) ? s : 0; // validate second
47        return *this; // enables cascading
48    } // end function setSecond
49
50    // get hour value
51    int Time::getHour() const
52    {
53        return hour;
54    } // end function getHour
55
56    // get minute value
57    int Time::getMinute() const
58    {
59        return minute;
60    } // end function getMinute
61
62    // get second value
63    int Time::getSecond() const
64    {
65        return second;
66    } // end function getSecond
67
68    // print Time in universal-time format (HH:MM:SS)
69    void Time::printUniversal() const
70    {
71        cout << setfill( '0' ) << setw( 2 ) << hour << ":"
72            << setw( 2 ) << minute << ":" << setw( 2 ) << second;
73    } // end function printUniversal
74
75    // print Time in standard-time format (HH:MM:SS AM or PM)
76    void Time::printStandard() const
77    {
78        cout << ( ( hour == 0 || hour == 12 ) ? 12 : hour % 12 )
79            << ":" << setfill( '0' ) << setw( 2 ) << minute
80            << ":" << setw( 2 ) << second << ( hour < 12 ? " AM" : " PM" );
81    } // end function printStandard
```

Fig. 10.19 | Time class member-function definitions modified to enable cascaded member-function calls. (Part 2 of 2.)

```
1   // Fig. 10.20: fig10_20.cpp
2   // Cascading member function calls with the this pointer.
3   #include <iostream>
4   using std::cout;
5   using std::endl;
6
7   #include "Time.h" // Time class definition
8
9   int main()
10  {
11     Time t; // create Time object
12
13     // cascaded function calls
14     t.setHour( 18 ).setMinute( 30 ).setSecond( 22 );
15
16     // output time in universal and standard formats
17     cout << "Universal time: ";
18     t.printUniversal();
19
20     cout << "\nStandard time: ";
21     t.printStandard();
22
23     cout << "\n\nNew standard time: ";
24
25     // cascaded function calls
26     t.setTime( 20, 20, 20 ).printStandard();
27     cout << endl;
28     return 0;
29  } // end main
```

```
Universal time: 18:30:22
Standard time: 6:30:22 PM

New standard time: 8:20:20 PM
```

Fig. 10.20 | Cascading member-function calls.

10.6 Dynamic Memory Management with Operators new and delete

C++ enables programmers to control the allocation and deallocation of memory in a program for any built-in or user-defined type. This is known as dynamic memory management and is performed with operators new and delete. Recall that class Employee (Figs. 10.12–10.13) uses two 25-character arrays to represent the first and last name of an Employee. The Employee class definition (Fig. 10.12) must specify the number of elements in each of these arrays when it declares them as data members, because the size of the data members dictates the amount of memory required to store an Employee object. As we discussed earlier, these arrays may waste space for names shorter than 24 characters. Also, names longer than 24 characters must be truncated to fit in these fixed-size arrays.

Wouldn't it be nice if we could use arrays containing exactly the number of elements needed to store an Employee's first and last name? Dynamic memory management allows us to do exactly that. As you will see in the example of Section 10.7, if we replace array data members firstName and lastName with pointers to char, we can use the new operator to dynamically allocate (i.e., reserve) the exact amount of memory required to hold each name at execution time. Dynamically allocating memory in this fashion causes an array (or any other built-in or user-defined type) to be created in the free store (sometimes called the heap)—a region of memory assigned to each program for storing objects created at execution time. Once the memory for an array is allocated in the free store, we can gain access to it by aiming a pointer at the first element of the array. When we no longer need the array, we can return the memory to the free store by using the delete operator to deallocate (i.e., release) the memory, which can then be reused by future new operations.

Again, we present the modified Employee class as described here in the example of Section 10.7. First, we present the details of using the new and delete operators to dynamically allocate memory to store objects, fundamental types and arrays.

Consider the following declaration and statement:

```
Time *timePtr;
timePtr = new Time;
```

The new operator allocates storage of the proper size for an object of type Time, calls the default constructor to initialize the object and returns a pointer of the type specified to the right of the new operator (i.e., a Time *). Note that new can be used to dynamically allocate any fundamental type (such as int or double) or class type. If new is unable to find sufficient space in memory for the object, it indicates that an error occurred by "throwing an exception." Exception handling is covered in detail in Chapter 16 of our sister book, *C++ How to Program, 5/e*. When a program does not "catch" an exception, the program terminates immediately. [*Note:* The new operator returns a 0 pointer in versions of C++ prior to the ANSI/ISO standard. We use the standard version of operator new throughout this book.]

To destroy a dynamically allocated object and free the space for the object, use the delete operator as follows:

```
delete timePtr;
```

This statement first calls the destructor for the object to which timePtr points, then deallocates the memory associated with the object. After the preceding statement, the memory can be reused by the system to allocate other objects.

Common Programming Error 10.8

Not releasing dynamically allocated memory when it is no longer needed can cause the system to run out of memory prematurely. This is sometimes called a "memory leak."

C++ allows you to provide an initializer for a newly created fundamental-type variable, as in

```
double *ptr = new double( 3.14159 );
```

which initializes a newly created double to 3.14159 and assigns the resulting pointer to ptr. The same syntax can be used to specify a comma-separated list of arguments to the constructor of an object. For example,

```
Time *timePtr = new Time( 12, 45, 0 );
```

initializes a newly created Time object to 12:45 PM and assigns the resulting pointer to timePtr.

As discussed earlier, the new operator can be used to allocate arrays dynamically. For example, a 10-element integer array can be allocated and assigned to gradesArray as follows:

```
int *gradesArray = new int[ 10 ];
```

which declares pointer gradesArray and assigns it a pointer to the first element of a dynamically allocated 10-element array of integers. Recall that the size of an array created at compile time must be specified using a constant integral expression. However, the size of a dynamically allocated array can be specified using *any* integral expression that can be evaluated at execution time. Also note that, when allocating an array of objects dynamically, the programmer cannot pass arguments to each object's constructor. Instead, each object in the array is initialized by its default constructor. To delete the dynamically allocated array to which gradesArray points, use the statement

```
delete [] gradesArray;
```

The preceding statement deallocates the array to which gradesArray points. If the pointer in the preceding statement points to an array of objects, the statement first calls the destructor for every object in the array, then deallocates the memory. If the preceding statement did not include the square brackets ([]) and gradesArray pointed to an array of objects, only the first object in the array would receive a destructor call.

Common Programming Error 10.9

Using delete instead of delete [] for arrays of objects can lead to runtime logic errors. To ensure that every object in the array receives a destructor call, always delete memory allocated as an array with operator delete []. Similarly, always delete memory allocated as an individual element with operator delete.

10.7 static Class Members

There is an important exception to the rule that each object of a class has its own copy of all the data members of the class. In certain cases, only one copy of a variable should be shared by all objects of a class. A **static data member** is used for these and other reasons. Such a variable represents "class-wide" information (i.e., a property of the class shared by all instances, not a property of a specific object of the class). The declaration of a static member begins with keyword static. Recall that the versions of class GradeBook in Chapter 7 use static data members to store constants representing the number of grades that all GradeBook objects can hold.

Let us further motivate the need for static class-wide data with an example. Suppose that we have a video game with Martians and other space creatures. Each Martian tends to be brave and willing to attack other space creatures when the Martian is aware that there are at least five Martians present. If fewer than five are present, each Martian becomes cowardly. So each Martian needs to know the martianCount. We could endow each instance of class `Martian` with `martianCount` as a data member. If we do, every `Martian` will have a separate copy of the data member. Every time we create a new `Martian`, we will have to update the data member `martianCount` in all `Martian` objects. Doing this would require every `Martian` object to have, or have access to, handles to all other `Martian` objects in memory. This wastes space with the redundant copies and wastes time in updating the separate copies. Instead, we declare `martianCount` to be `static`. This makes `martian-Count` class-wide data. Every `Martian` can access `martianCount` as if it were a data member of the `Martian`, but only one copy of the `static` variable `martianCount` is maintained by C++. This saves space. We save time by having the `Martian` constructor increment `static` variable `martianCount` and having the `Martian` destructor decrement `martianCount`. Because there is only one copy, we do not have to increment or decrement separate copies of `martianCount` for each `Martian` object.

Performance Tip 10.3

Use `static` data members to save storage when a single copy of the data for all objects of a class will suffice.

Although they may seem like global variables, a class's `static` data members have class scope. Also, `static` members can be declared `public`, `private` or `protected`. A fundamental-type `static` data member is initialized by default to 0. If you want a different initial value, a `static` data member can be initialized *once* (and only once). A `const static` data member of `int` or `enum` type can be initialized in its declaration in the class definition. However, all other `static` data members must be defined at file scope (i.e., outside the body of the class definition) and can be initialized only in those definitions. Note that `static` data members of class types (i.e., `static` member objects) that have default constructors need not be initialized because their default constructors will be called.

A class's `private` and `protected` `static` members are normally accessed through `public` member functions of the class or through `friend`s of the class. (In Chapter 12, we will see that a class's `private` and `protected` `static` members can also be accessed through `protected` member functions of the class.) A class's `static` members exist even when no objects of that class exist. To access a `public` `static` class member when no objects of the class exist, simply prefix the class name and the binary scope resolution operator (`::`) to the name of the data member. For example, if our preceding variable `martian-Count` is `public`, it can be accessed with the expression `Martian::martianCount` when there are no `Martian` objects. (Of course, using `public` data is discouraged.)

A class's `public` `static` class members can also be accessed through any object of that class using the object's name, the dot operator and the name of the member (e.g., `myMartian.martianCount`). To access a `private` or `protected` `static` class member when no objects of the class exist, provide a `public` `static` member function and call the function by prefixing its name with the class name and binary scope resolution operator. (As we will see in Chapter 12, a `protected` `static` member function can serve this purpose, too.) A `static` member function is a service of the *class*, not of a specific object of the class.

Software Engineering Observation 10.10

A class's `static` data members and `static` member functions exist and can be used even if no objects of that class have been instantiated.

The program of Figs. 10.21–10.23 demonstrates a private static data member called count (Fig. 10.21, line 21) and a public static member function called getCount (Fig. 10.21, line 15). In Fig. 10.22, line 14 defines and initializes the data member count to zero at file scope and lines 18–21 define static member function getCount. Notice that neither line 14 nor line 18 includes keyword static, yet both lines refer to static class members. When static is applied to an item at file scope, that item becomes known only in that file. The static members of the class need to be available from any client code that accesses the file, so we cannot declare them static in the .cpp file—we declare them static only in the .h file. Data member count maintains a count of the number of objects of class Employee that have been instantiated. When objects of class Employee exist, member count can be referenced through any member function of an Employee object—in Fig. 10.22, count is referenced by both line 33 in the constructor and line 48 in the destructor. Also, note that since count is an int, it could have been initialized in the header file at line 21 of Fig. 10.21.

Common Programming Error 10.10

It is a compilation error to include keyword static in the definition of a static data members at file scope.

In Fig. 10.22, note the use of the new operator (lines 27 and 30) in the Employee constructor to dynamically allocate the correct amount of memory for members firstName and lastName. If the new operator is unable to fulfill the request for memory for one or both of these character arrays, the program will terminate immediately.

```
1   // Fig. 10.21: Employee.h
2   // Employee class definition.
3   #ifndef EMPLOYEE_H
4   #define EMPLOYEE_H
5
6   class Employee
7   {
8   public:
9      Employee( const char * const, const char * const ); // constructor
10     ~Employee(); // destructor
11     const char *getFirstName() const; // return first name
12     const char *getLastName() const; // return last name
13
14     // static member function
15     static int getCount(); // return number of objects instantiated
16   private:
17     char *firstName;
18     char *lastName;
19
20     // static data
21     static int count; // number of objects instantiated
22   }; // end class Employee
23
24   #endif
```

Fig. 10.21 | Employee class definition with a static data member to track the number of Employee objects in memory.

Also note in Fig. 10.22 that the implementations of functions getFirstName (lines 52–58) and getLastName (lines 61–67) return pointers to const character data. In this

```cpp
1   // Fig. 10.22: Employee.cpp
2   // Member-function definitions for class Employee.
3   #include <iostream>
4   using std::cout;
5   using std::endl;
6
7   #include <cstring> // strlen and strcpy prototypes
8   using std::strlen;
9   using std::strcpy;
10
11  #include "Employee.h" // Employee class definition
12
13  // define and initialize static data member at file scope
14  int Employee::count = 0;
15
16  // define static member function that returns number of
17  // Employee objects instantiated (declared static in Employee.h)
18  int Employee::getCount()
19  {
20     return count;
21  } // end static function getCount
22
23  // constructor dynamically allocates space for first and last name and
24  // uses strcpy to copy first and last names into the object
25  Employee::Employee( const char * const first, const char * const last )
26  {
27     firstName = new char[ strlen( first ) + 1 ];
28     strcpy( firstName, first );
29
30     lastName = new char[ strlen( last ) + 1 ];
31     strcpy( lastName, last );
32
33     count++; // increment static count of employees
34
35     cout << "Employee constructor for " << firstName
36        << ' ' << lastName << " called." << endl;
37  } // end Employee constructor
38
39  // destructor deallocates dynamically allocated memory
40  Employee::~Employee()
41  {
42     cout << "~Employee() called for " << firstName
43        << ' ' << lastName << endl;
44
45     delete [] firstName; // release memory
46     delete [] lastName; // release memory
47
48     count--; // decrement static count of employees
49  } // end ~Employee destructor
```

Fig. 10.22 | Employee class member-function definitions. (Part 1 of 2.)

```
50
51   // return first name of employee
52   const char *Employee::getFirstName() const
53   {
54      // const before return type prevents client from modifying
55      // private data; client should copy returned string before
56      // destructor deletes storage to prevent undefined pointer
57      return firstName;
58   } // end function getFirstName
59
60   // return last name of employee
61   const char *Employee::getLastName() const
62   {
63      // const before return type prevents client from modifying
64      // private data; client should copy returned string before
65      // destructor deletes storage to prevent undefined pointer
66      return lastName;
67   } // end function getLastName
```

Fig. 10.22 | Employee class member-function definitions. (Part 2 of 2.)

implementation, if the client wishes to retain a copy of the first name or last name, the client is responsible for copying the dynamically allocated memory in the Employee object after obtaining the pointer to const character data from the object. It is also possible to implement getFirstName and getLastName, so the client is required to pass a character array and the size of the array to each function. Then the functions could copy the first or last name into the character array provided by the client. Once again, note that we could have used class string here to return a copy of a string object to the caller rather than returning a pointer to the private data.

Figure 10.23 uses static member function getCount to determine the number of Employee objects currently instantiated. Note that when no objects are instantiated in the program, the Employee::getCount() function call is issued (lines 14 and 38). However, when objects are instantiated, function getCount can be called through either of the objects, as shown in the statement at lines 22–23, which uses pointer e1Ptr to invoke function getCount. Note that using e2Ptr->getCount() or Employee::getCount() in line 23 would produce the same result, because getCount always accesses the same static member count.

```
1    // Fig. 10.23: fig10_23.cpp
2    // Driver to test class Employee.
3    #include <iostream>
4    using std::cout;
5    using std::endl;
6
7    #include "Employee.h" // Employee class definition
8
9    int main()
10   {
```

Fig. 10.23 | static data member tracking the number of objects of a class. (Part 1 of 2.)

```
11      // use class name and binary scope resolution operator to
12      // access static number function getCount
13      cout << "Number of employees before instantiation of any objects is "
14         << Employee::getCount() << endl; // use class name
15
16      // use new to dynamically create two new Employees
17      // operator new also calls the object's constructor
18      Employee *e1Ptr = new Employee( "Susan", "Baker" );
19      Employee *e2Ptr = new Employee( "Robert", "Jones" );
20
21      // call getCount on first Employee object
22      cout << "Number of employees after objects are instantiated is "
23         << e1Ptr->getCount();
24
25      cout << "\n\nEmployee 1: "
26         << e1Ptr->getFirstName() << " " << e1Ptr->getLastName()
27         << "\nEmployee 2: "
28         << e2Ptr->getFirstName() << " " << e2Ptr->getLastName() << "\n\n";
29
30      delete e1Ptr; // deallocate memory
31      e1Ptr = 0; // disconnect pointer from free-store space
32      delete e2Ptr; // deallocate memory
33      e2Ptr = 0; // disconnect pointer from free-store space
34
35      // no objects exist, so call static member function getCount again
36      // using the class name and the binary scope resolution operator
37      cout << "Number of employees after objects are deleted is "
38         << Employee::getCount() << endl;
39      return 0;
40   } // end main
```

```
Number of employees before instantiation of any objects is 0
Employee constructor for Susan Baker called.
Employee constructor for Robert Jones called.
Number of employees after objects are instantiated is 2

Employee 1: Susan Baker
Employee 2: Robert Jones

~Employee() called for Susan Baker
~Employee() called for Robert Jones
Number of employees after objects are deleted is 0
```

Fig. 10.23 | static data member tracking the number of objects of a class. (Part 2 of 2.)

 Software Engineering Observation 10.11

Some organizations specify in their software engineering standards that all calls to static member functions be made using the class name and not an object handle.

A member function should be declared static if it does not access non-static data members or non-static member functions of the class. Unlike non-static member functions, a static member function does not have a this pointer, because static data members and static member functions exist independently of any objects of a class. The `this` pointer must refer to a specific object of the class, and when a `static` member function is called, there might not be any objects of its class in memory.

Common Programming Error 10.11

Using the `this` pointer in a `static` member function is a compilation error.

Common Programming Error 10.12

Declaring a `static` member function `const` is a compilation error. The `const` qualifier indicates that a function cannot modify the contents of the object in which it operates, but `static` member functions exist and operate independently of any objects of the class.

Lines 18–19 of Fig. 10.23 use operator `new` to dynamically allocate two `Employee` objects. Remember that the program will terminate immediately if it is unable to allocate one or both of these objects. When each `Employee` object is allocated, its constructor is called. When `delete` is used at lines 30 and 32 to deallocate the two `Employee` objects, each object's destructor is called.

Error-Prevention Tip 10.2

After deleting dynamically allocated memory, set the pointer that referred to that memory to 0. This disconnects the pointer from the previously allocated space on the free store. This space in memory could still contain information, despite having been deleted. By setting the pointer to 0, the program loses any access to that free-store space, which, in fact, could have already been re-allocated for a different purpose. If you didn't set the pointer to 0, your code could inadvertently access this new information, causing extremely subtle, nonrepeatable logic errors.

10.8 Data Abstraction and Information Hiding

A class normally hides its implementation details from its clients. This is called information hiding. As an example of information hiding, let us consider the stack data structure introduced in Section 6.11.

Stacks can be implemented with arrays and with other data structures, such as linked lists. A client of a stack class need not be concerned with the stack's implementation. The client knows only that when data items are placed in the stack, they will be recalled in last-in, first-out order. The client cares about *what* functionality a stack offers, not about *how* that functionality is implemented. This concept is referred to as data abstraction. Although programmers might know the details of a class's implementation, they should not write code that depends on these details. This enables a particular class (such as one that implements a stack and its operations, *push* and *pop*) to be replaced with another version without affecting the rest of the system. As long as the `public` services of the class do not change (i.e., every original `public` member function still has the same prototype in the new class definition), the rest of the system is not affected.

Many programming languages emphasize actions. In these languages, data exists to support the actions that programs must take. Data is "less interesting" than actions. Data is "crude." Only a few built-in data types exist, and it is difficult for programmers to create their own types. C++ and the object-oriented style of programming elevate the importance of data. The primary activities of object-oriented programming in C++ are the creation of types (i.e., classes) and the expression of the interactions among objects of those types. To create languages that emphasize data, the programming-languages community needed to formalize some notions about data. The formalization we consider here is the notion of abstract data types (ADTs), which improve the program development process.

What is an abstract data type? Consider the built-in type int, which most people would associate with an integer in mathematics. Rather, an int is an abstract representation of an integer. Unlike mathematical integers, computer ints are fixed in size. For example, type int on today's popular 32-bit machines is typically limited to the range –2,147,483,648 to +2,147,483,647. If the result of a calculation falls outside this range, an "overflow" error occurs and the computer responds in some machine-dependent manner. It might, for example, "quietly" produce an incorrect result, such as a value too large to fit in an int variable (commonly called arithmetic overflow). Mathematical integers do not have this problem. Therefore, the notion of a computer int is only an approximation of the notion of a real-world integer. The same is true with double.

Even char is an approximation; char values are normally eight-bit patterns of ones and zeros; these patterns look nothing like the characters they represent, such as a capital Z, a lowercase z, a dollar sign ($), a digit (5), and so on. Values of type char on most computers are quite limited compared with the range of real-world characters. The seven-bit ASCII character set (Appendix B) provides for 128 different character values. This is inadequate for representing languages such as Japanese and Chinese that require thousands of characters. As Internet and World Wide Web usage becomes pervasive, the newer Unicode character set is growing rapidly in popularity, owing to its ability to represent the characters of most languages. For more information on Unicode, visit www.unicode.org.

The point is that even the built-in data types provided with programming languages like C++ are really only approximations or imperfect models of real-world concepts and behaviors. We have taken int for granted until this point, but now you have a new perspective to consider. Types like int, double, char and others are all examples of abstract data types. They are essentially ways of representing real-world notions to some satisfactory level of precision within a computer system.

An abstract data type actually captures two notions: A data representation and the operations that can be performed on those data. For example, in C++, an int contains an integer value (data) and provides addition, subtraction, multiplication, division and modulus operations (among others)—division by zero is undefined. These allowed operations perform in a manner sensitive to machine parameters, such as the fixed word size of the underlying computer system. Another example is the notion of negative integers, whose operations and data representation are clear, but the operation of taking the square root of a negative integer is undefined. In C++, the programmer uses classes to implement abstract data types and their services.

10.8.1 Example: Array Abstract Data Type

We discussed arrays in Chapter 7. As described there, an array is not much more than a pointer and some space in memory. This primitive capability is acceptable for performing array operations if the programmer is cautious and undemanding. There are many operations that would be nice to perform with arrays, but that are not built into C++. With C++ classes, the programmer can develop an array ADT that is preferable to "raw" arrays. The array class can provide many helpful new capabilities such as

- subscript range checking

- an arbitrary range of subscripts instead of having to start with 0

- array assignment

- array comparison

- array input/output

- arrays that know their sizes

- arrays that expand dynamically to accommodate more elements

- arrays that can print themselves in neat tabular format.

We create our own array class with many of these capabilities in Chapter 11, Operator Overloading; String and Array Objects. Recall that C++ Standard Library class template vector (introduced in Chapter 7) provides many of these capabilities as well. C++ has a small set of built-in types. Classes extend the base programming language with new types.

Software Engineering Observation 10.12

The programmer is able to create new types through the class mechanism. These new types can be designed to be used as conveniently as the built-in types. Thus, C++ is an extensible language. Although the language is easy to extend with these new types, the base language itself cannot be changed.

New classes created in C++ environments can be proprietary to an individual, to small groups or to companies. Classes can also be placed in standard class libraries intended for wide distribution. ANSI (the American National Standards Institute) and ISO (the International Organization for Standardization) developed a standard version of C++ that includes a standard class library. The reader who learns C++ and object-oriented programming will be ready to take advantage of the new kinds of rapid, component-oriented software development made possible with increasingly abundant and rich libraries.

10.8.2 Example: String Abstract Data Type

C++ is an intentionally sparse language that provides programmers with only the raw capabilities needed to build a broad range of systems (consider it a tool for making tools). The language is designed to minimize performance burdens. C++ is appropriate for both applications programming and systems programming—the latter places extraordinary performance demands on programs. Certainly, it would have been possible to include a string data type among C++'s built-in data types. Instead, the language was designed to include mechanisms for creating and implementing string abstract data types through classes. We introduced the C++ Standard Library class string in Chapter 3, and in Chapter 11 we will develop our own String ADT.

10.8.3 Example: Queue Abstract Data Type

Each of us stands in line from time to time. A waiting line is also called a queue. We wait in line at the supermarket checkout counter, we wait in line to get gasoline, we wait in line to board a bus, we wait in line to pay a highway toll, and students know all too well about waiting in line during registration to get the courses they want. Computer systems use many waiting lines internally, so we need to write programs that simulate what queues are and do.

A queue is a good example of an abstract data type. Queues offer well-understood behavior to their clients. Clients put things in a queue one at a time—invoking the queue's enqueue operation—and the clients get those things back one at a time on demand—invoking the queue's dequeue operation. Conceptually, a queue can become infinitely long. A real queue, of course, is finite. Items are returned from a queue in first-in, first-out (FIFO) order—the first item inserted in the queue is the first item removed from the queue.

The queue hides an internal data representation that somehow keeps track of the items currently waiting in line, and it offers a set of operations to its clients, namely, *enqueue* and *dequeue*. The clients are not concerned about the implementation of the queue. Clients merely want the queue to operate "as advertised." When a client enqueues a new item, the queue should accept that item and place it internally in some kind of first-in, first-out data structure. When the client wants the next item from the front of the queue, the queue should remove the item from its internal representation and deliver it to the outside world (i.e., to the client of the queue) in FIFO order (i.e., the item that has been in the queue the longest should be the next one returned by the next *dequeue* operation).

The queue ADT guarantees the integrity of its internal data structure. Clients may not manipulate this data structure directly. Only the queue member functions have access to its internal data. Clients may cause only allowable operations to be performed on the data representation; operations not provided in the ADT's public interface are rejected in some appropriate manner. This could mean issuing an error message, throwing an exception, terminating execution or simply ignoring the operation request.

10.9 Container Classes and Iterators

Among the most popular types of classes are container classes (also called collection classes), i.e., classes designed to hold collections of objects. Container classes commonly provide services such as insertion, deletion, searching, sorting, and testing an item to determine whether it is a member of the collection. Arrays, stacks, queues, trees and linked lists are examples of container classes; we studied arrays in Chapter 7. We study each of these other data structures in Chapter 21, Data Structures, and Chapter 23, Standard Template Library, of our sister book, *C++ How to Program, 5/e*.

It is common to associate iterator objects—or more simply iterators—with container classes. An iterator is an object that "walks through" a collection, returning the next item (or performing some action on the next item). Once an iterator for a class has been written, obtaining the next element from the class can be expressed simply. Just as a book being shared by several people could have several bookmarks in it at once, a container class can have several iterators operating on it at once. Each iterator maintains its own "position" information. We discuss containers and iterators in detail in Chapter 23, Standard Template Library, of our sister book, *C++ How to Program, 5/e*.

10.10 **Proxy Classes**

Recall that two of the fundamental principles of good software engineering are separating interface from implementation and hiding implementation details. We strive to achieve these goals by defining a class in a header file and implementing its member functions in a separate implementation file. However, as we pointed out in Chapter 9, header files *do* contain some portion of a class's implementation and hints about others. For example, a class's private members are listed in the class definition in a header file, so these members are visible to clients, even though the clients may not access the private members. Revealing a class's private data in this manner potentially exposes proprietary information to clients of the class. We now introduce the notion of a proxy class that allows you to hide even the private data of a class from clients of the class. Providing clients of your class with a proxy class that knows only the public interface to your class enables the clients to use your class's services without giving the client access to your class's implementation details.

Implementing a proxy class requires several steps, which we demonstrate in Figs. 10.24–10.27. First, we create the class definition for the class that contains the proprietary implementation we would like to hide. Our example class, called Implementation, is shown in Fig. 10.24. The proxy class Interface is shown in Figs. 10.25–10.26. The test program and sample output are shown in Fig. 10.27.

Class Implementation (Fig. 10.24) provides a single private data member called value (the data we would like to hide from the client), a constructor to initialize value and functions setValue and getValue.

We define a proxy class called Interface (Fig. 10.25) with an identical public interface (except for the constructor and destructor names) to that of class Implementation.

```
1   // Fig. 10.24: Implementation.h
2   // Header file for class Implementation
3
4   class Implementation
5   {
6   public:
7      // constructor
8      Implementation( int v )
9         : value( v ) // initialize value with v
10     {
11        // empty body
12     } // end constructor Implementation
13
14     // set value to v
15     void setValue( int v )
16     {
17        value = v; // should validate v
18     } // end function setValue
19
20     // return value
21     int getValue() const
22     {
23        return value;
24     } // end function getValue
```

Fig. 10.24 | Implementation class definition. (Part I of 2.)

```
25   private:
26      int value; // data that we would like to hide from the client
27   }; // end class Implementation
```

Fig. 10.24 | Implementation class definition. (Part 2 of 2.)

```
 1   // Fig. 10.25: Interface.h
 2   // Header file for class Interface
 3   // Client sees this source code, but the source code does not reveal
 4   // the data layout of class Implementation.
 5
 6   class Implementation; // forward class declaration required by line 17
 7
 8   class Interface
 9   {
10   public:
11      Interface( int ); // constructor
12      void setValue( int ); // same public interface as
13      int getValue() const; // class Implementation has
14      ~Interface(); // destructor
15   private:
16      // requires previous forward declaration (line 6)
17      Implementation *ptr;
18   }; // end class Interface
```

Fig. 10.25 | Interface class definition.

The only private member of the proxy class is a pointer to an object of class Implementation. Using a pointer in this manner allows us to hide the implementation details of class Implementation from the client. Notice that the only mentions in class Interface of the proprietary Implementation class are in the pointer declaration (line 17) and in line 6, a forward class declaration. When a class definition (such as class Interface) uses only a pointer or reference to an object of another class (such as to an object of class Implementation), the class header file for that other class (which would ordinarily reveal the private data of that class) is not required to be included with #include. You can simply declare that other class as a data type with a forward class declaration (line 6) before the type is used in the file.

The member-function implementation file for proxy class Interface (Fig. 10.26) is the only file that includes the header file Implementation.h (line 5) containing class Implementation. The file Interface.cpp (Fig. 10.26) is provided to the client as a pre-compiled object code file along with the header file Interface.h that includes the function prototypes of the services provided by the proxy class. Because file Interface.cpp is made available to the client only as object code, the client is not able to see the interactions between the proxy class and the proprietary class (lines 9, 17, 23 and 29). Notice that the proxy class imposes an extra "layer" of function calls as the "price to pay" for hiding the private data of class Implementation. Given the speed of today's computers and the fact that many compilers can inline simple function calls automatically, the effect of these extra function calls on performance is often negligible.

```
 1   // Fig. 10.26: Interface.cpp
 2   // Implementation of class Interface--client receives this file only
 3   // as precompiled object code, keeping the implementation hidden.
 4   #include "Interface.h" // Interface class definition
 5   #include "Implementation.h" // Implementation class definition
 6
 7   // constructor
 8   Interface::Interface( int v )
 9      : ptr ( new Implementation( v ) ) // initialize ptr to point to
10   {                                     // a new Implementation object
11      // empty body
12   } // end Interface constructor
13
14   // call Implementation's setValue function
15   void Interface::setValue( int v )
16   {
17      ptr->setValue( v );
18   } // end function setValue
19
20   // call Implementation's getValue function
21   int Interface::getValue() const
22   {
23      return ptr->getValue();
24   } // end function getValue
25
26   // destructor
27   Interface::~Interface()
28   {
29      delete ptr;
30   } // end ~Interface destructor
```

Fig. 10.26 | Interface class member-function definitions.

Figure 10.27 tests class Interface. Notice that only the header file for Interface is included in the client code (line 7)—there is no mention of the existence of a separate class called Implementation. Thus, the client never sees the private data of class Implementation, nor can the client code become dependent on the Implementation code.

Software Engineering Observation 10.13

A proxy class insulates client code from implementation changes.

```
 1   // Fig. 10.27: fig10_27.cpp
 2   // Hiding a class's private data with a proxy class.
 3   #include <iostream>
 4   using std::cout;
 5   using std::endl;
 6
 7   #include "Interface.h" // Interface class definition
 8
```

Fig. 10.27 | Implementing a proxy class. (Part 1 of 2.)

```
 9   int main()
10   {
11      Interface i( 5 ); // create Interface object
12
13      cout << "Interface contains: " << i.getValue()
14         << " before setValue" << endl;
15
16      i.setValue( 10 );
17
18      cout << "Interface contains: " << i.getValue()
19         << " after setValue" << endl;
20      return 0;
21   } // end main
```

```
Interface contains: 5 before setValue
Interface contains: 10 after setValue
```

Fig. 10.27 | Implementing a proxy class. (Part 2 of 2.)

10.11 Wrap-Up

In this chapter, we introduced several advanced topics related to classes and data abstraction. You learned how to specify const objects and const member functions to prevent modifications to objects, thus enforcing the principle of least privilege. You also learned that, through composition, a class can have objects of other classes as members. We introduced the topic of friendship and presented examples that demonstrate how to use friend functions.

You learned that the this pointer is passed as an implicit argument to each of a class's non-static member functions, allowing the functions to access the correct object's data members and other non-static member functions. You also saw explicit use of the this pointer to access the class's members and to enable cascaded member-function calls.

The chapter introduced the concept of dynamic memory management. You learned that C++ programmers can create and destroy objects dynamically with the new and delete operators. We motivated the need for static data members and demonstrated how to declare and use static data members and member functions in your own classes.

You learned about data abstraction and information hiding—two of the fundamental concepts of object-oriented programming. We discussed abstract data types—ways of representing real-world or conceptual notions to some satisfactory level of precision within a computer system. You then learned about three example abstract data types—arrays, strings and queues. We introduced the concept of a container class that holds a collection of objects, as well as the notion of an iterator class that walks through the elements of a container class. Finally, you learned how to create a proxy class to hide the implementation details (including the private data members) of a class from clients of the class.

In Chapter 11, we continue our study of classes and objects by showing how to enable C++'s operators to work with objects—a process called operator overloading. For example, you will see how to "overload" the << operator so it can be used to output a complete array without explicitly using a repetition statement.

Summary

- The keyword const can be used to specify that an object is not modifiable and that any attempt to modify the object should result in a compilation error.
- C++ compilers disallow non-const member function calls on const objects.
- An attempt by a const member function to modify an object of its class (*this) is a compilation error.
- A function is specified as const both in its prototype and in its definition.
- A const object must be initialized, not assigned to.
- Constructors and destructors cannot be declared const.
- const data member and data members that are references *must* be initialized using member initializers.
- A class can have objects of other classes as members—this concept is called composition.
- Member objects are constructed in the order in which they are declared in the class definition and before their enclosing class objects are constructed.
- If a member initializer is not provided for a member object, the member object's default constructor will be called implicitly.
- A friend function of a class is defined outside that class's scope, yet has the right to access the non-public (and public) members of the class. Stand-alone functions or entire classes may be declared to be friends of another class.
- A friend declaration can appear anywhere in the class. A friend is essentially a part of the public interface of the class.
- The friendship relation is neither symmetric nor transitive.
- Every object has access to its own address through the this pointer.
- An object's this pointer is not part of the object itself—i.e., the size of the memory occupied by the this pointer is not reflected in the result of a sizeof operation on the object.
- The this pointer is passed (by the compiler) as an implicit argument to each of the object's non-static member functions.
- Objects use the this pointer implicitly (as we have done to this point) or explicitly to reference their data members and member functions.
- The this pointer enables cascaded member-function calls in which multiple functions are invoked in the same statement.
- Dynamic memory management enables programmers to control the allocation and deallocation of memory in a program for any built-in or user-defined type.
- The free store (sometimes called the heap) is a region of memory assigned to each program for storing objects dynamically allocated at execution time.
- The new operator allocates storage of the proper size for an object, runs the object's constructor and returns a pointer of the correct type. The new operator can be used to dynamically allocate any fundamental type (such as int or double) or class type. If new is unable to find space in memory for the object, it indicates that an error occurred by "throwing" an "exception." This usually causes the program to terminate immediately.
- To destroy a dynamically allocated object and free the space for the object, use the delete operator.
- An array of objects can be allocated dynamically with new as in

```
int *ptr = new int[ 100 ];
```

which allocates an array of 100 integers and assigns the starting location of the array to `ptr`. The preceding array of integers is deleted with the statement

```
delete [] ptr;
```

- A `static` data member represents "class-wide" information (i.e., a property of the class shared by all instances, not a property of a specific object of the class).
- `static` data members have class scope and can be declared `public`, `private` or `protected`.
- A class's `static` members exist even when no objects of that class exist.
- To access a `public` `static` class member when no objects of the class exist, simply prefix the class name and the binary scope resolution operator (`::`) to the name of the data member.
- A class's `public` `static` class members can be accessed through any object of that class.
- A member function should be declared `static` if it does not access non-`static` data members or non-`static` member functions of the class. Unlike non-`static` member functions, a `static` member function does not have a `this` pointer, because `static` data members and `static` member functions exist independently of any objects of a class.
- Abstract data types are ways of representing real-world and conceptual notions to some satisfactory level of precision within a computer system.
- An abstract data type captures two notions: a data representation and the operations that can be performed on those data.
- C++ is an intentionally sparse language that provides programmers with only the raw capabilities needed to build a broad range of systems. C++ is designed to minimize performance burdens.
- Items are returned from a queue in first-in, first-out (FIFO) order—the first item inserted in the queue is the first item removed from the queue.
- Container classes (also called collection classes) are designed to hold collections of objects. Container classes commonly provide services such as insertion, deletion, searching, sorting, and testing an item to determine whether it is a member of the collection.
- It is common to associate iterators with container classes. An iterator is an object that "walks through" a collection, returning the next item (or performing some action on the next item).
- Providing clients of your class with a proxy class that knows only the `public` interface to your class enables the clients to use your class's services without giving the clients access to your class's implementation details, such as its `private` data.
- When a class definition uses only a pointer or reference to an object of another class, the class header file for that other class (which would ordinarily reveal the `private` data of that class) is not required to be included with `#include`. You can simply declare that other class as a data type with a forward class declaration before the type is used in the file.
- The implementation file containing the member functions for a proxy class is the only file that includes the header file for the class whose `private` data we would like to hide.
- The implementation file containing the member functions for the proxy class is provided to the client as a precompiled object code file along with the header file that includes the function prototypes of the services provided by the proxy class.

Terminology

abstract data type (ADT)	collection class
allocate memory	composition
arithmetic overflow	const member function
cascaded member-function calls	const object

container class	host object
data abstraction	information hiding
data representation	iterator
deallocate memory	last-in, first-out (LIFO)
delete operator	member initializer
delete[] operator	member initializer list
dequeue (queue operation)	member object
dynamic memory management	member object constructor
dynamic objects	memory leak
enqueue (queue operation)	new [] operator
first-in, first-out (FIFO)	new operator
forward class declaration	operations in an ADT
free store	proxy class
friend class	queue abstract data type
friend function	static data member
has-a relationship	static member function
heap	this pointer

Self-Review Exercises

10.1 Fill in the blanks in each of the following:

a) _____ must be used to initialize constant members of a class.

b) A nonmember function must be declared as a(n) _____ of a class to have access to that class's private data members.

c) The _____ operator dynamically allocates memory for an object of a specified type and returns a _____ to that type.

d) A constant object must be _____; it cannot be modified after it is created.

e) A(n) _____ data member represents class-wide information.

f) An object's non-static member functions have access to a "self pointer" to the object called the _____ pointer.

g) The keyword _____ specifies that an object or variable is not modifiable after it is initialized.

h) If a member initializer is not provided for a member object of a class, the object's _____ is called.

i) A member function should be declared static if it does not access _____ class members.

j) Member objects are constructed _____ their enclosing class object.

k) The _____ operator reclaims memory previously allocated by new.

10.2 Find the errors in the following class and explain how to correct them:

```cpp
class Example
{
public:
   Example( int y = 10 )
      : data( y )
   {
      // empty body
   } // end Example constructor

   int getIncrementedData() const
   {
      return data++;
   } // end function getIncrementedData
```

```
    static int getCount()
    {
        cout << "Data is " << data << endl;
        return count;
    } // end function getCount
private:
    int data;
    static int count;
}; // end class Example
```

Answers to Self-Review Exercises

10.1   a) member initializers. b) `friend`. c) `new`, pointer. d) initialized. e) `static`. f) `this`.
g) `const`. h) default constructor. i) `non-static`. j) before. k) `delete`.

10.2   Error: The class definition for `Example` has two errors. The first occurs in function `get-IncrementedData`. The function is declared `const`, but it modifies the object.
Correction: To correct the first error, remove the `const` keyword from the definition of
`getIncrementedData`.
Error: The second error occurs in function `getCount`. This function is declared `static`, so
it is not allowed to access any non-static member of the class.
Correction: To correct the second error, remove the output line from the `getCount` definition.

Exercises

10.3   Compare and contrast dynamic memory allocation and deallocation operators `new`, `new []`,
`delete` and `delete []`.

10.4   Explain the notion of friendship in C++. Explain the negative aspects of friendship as described in the text.

10.5   Can a correct `Time` class definition include both of the following constructors? If not, explain why not.

```
Time( int h = 0, int m = 0, int s = 0 );
Time();
```

10.6   What happens when a return type, even `void`, is specified for a constructor or destructor?

10.7   Modify class `Date` in Fig. 10.10 to have the following capabilities:
   a) Output the date in multiple formats such as

```
DDD YYYY
MM/DD/YY
June 14, 1992
```

   b) Use overloaded constructors to create `Date` objects initialized with dates of the formats
       in part (a).
   c) Create a `Date` constructor that reads the system date using the standard library functions
       of the `<ctime>` header and sets the `Date` members. (See your compiler's reference documentation or www.cplusplus.com/ref/ctime/index.html for information on the functions in header `<ctime>`.)

In Chapter 11, we will be able to create operators for testing the equality of two dates and for comparing dates to determine whether one date is prior to, or after, another.

10.8   Create a `SavingsAccount` class. Use a `static` data member `annualInterestRate` to store the
annual interest rate for each of the savers. Each member of the class contains a `private` data member

savingsBalance indicating the amount the saver currently has on deposit. Provide member function calculateMonthlyInterest that calculates the monthly interest by multiplying the balance by annualInterestRate divided by 12; this interest should be added to savingsBalance. Provide a static member function modifyInterestRate that sets the static annualInterestRate to a new value. Write a driver program to test class SavingsAccount. Instantiate two different objects of class SavingsAccount, saver1 and saver2, with balances of $2000.00 and $3000.00, respectively. Set the annualInterestRate to 3 percent. Then calculate the monthly interest and print the new balances for each of the savers. Then set the annualInterestRate to 4 percent, calculate the next month's interest and print the new balances for each of the savers.

10.9 Create class IntegerSet for which each object can hold integers in the range 0 through 100. A set is represented internally as an array of ones and zeros. Array element a[i] is 1 if integer *i* is in the set. Array element a[j] is 0 if integer *j* is not in the set. The default constructor initializes a set to the so-called "empty set," i.e., a set whose array representation contains all zeros.

Provide member functions for the common set operations. For example, provide a unionOfSets member function that creates a third set that is the set-theoretic union of two existing sets (i.e., an element of the third set's array is set to 1 if that element is 1 in either or both of the existing sets, and an element of the third set's array is set to 0 if that element is 0 in each of the existing sets).

Provide an intersectionOfSets member function which creates a third set which is the set-theoretic intersection of two existing sets (i.e., an element of the third set's array is set to 0 if that element is 0 in either or both of the existing sets, and an element of the third set's array is set to 1 if that element is 1 in each of the existing sets).

Provide an insertElement member function that inserts a new integer *k* into a set (by setting a[k] to 1). Provide a deleteElement member function that deletes integer *m* (by setting a[m] to 0).

Provide a printSet member function that prints a set as a list of numbers separated by spaces. Print only those elements that are present in the set (i.e., their position in the array has a value of 1). Print --- for an empty set.

Provide an isEqualTo member function that determines whether two sets are equal.

Provide an additional constructor that receives an array of integers and the size of that array and uses the array to initialize a set object.

Now write a driver program to test your IntegerSet class. Instantiate several IntegerSet objects. Test that all your member functions work properly.

10.10 It would be perfectly reasonable for the Time class of Figs. 10.18–10.19 to represent the time internally as the number of seconds since midnight rather than the three integer values hour, minute and second. Clients could use the same public methods and get the same results. Modify the Time class of Fig. 10.18 to implement the time as the number of seconds since midnight and show that there is no visible change in functionality to the clients of the class. [*Note:* This exercise nicely demonstrates the virtues of implementation hiding.]

11

Operator Overloading; String and Array Objects

The whole difference
between construction and
creation is exactly this:
that a thing constructed
can only be loved after
it is constructed; but a
thing created is loved
before it exists.
—Gilbert Keith Chesterton

The die is cast.
—Julius Caesar

Our doctor would never
really operate unless it was
necessary. He was just that
way. If he didn't need the
money, he wouldn't lay a
hand on you.
—Herb Shriner

OBJECTIVES

In this chapter you will learn:

■ What operator overloading is and how it makes programs more readable and programming more convenient.

■ To redefine (overload) operators to work with objects of user-defined classes.

■ The differences between overloading unary and binary operators.

■ To convert objects from one class to another class.

■ When to, and when not to, overload operators.

■ To create **PhoneNumber**, `Array`, `String` and `Date` classes that demonstrate operator overloading.

■ To use overloaded operators and other member functions of standard library class `string`.

■ To use keyword `explicit` to prevent the compiler from using single-argument constructors to perform implicit conversions.

Outline

11.1 Introduction
11.2 Fundamentals of Operator Overloading
11.3 Restrictions on Operator Overloading
11.4 Operator Functions as Class Members vs. Global Functions
11.5 Overloading Stream Insertion and Stream Extraction Operators
11.6 Overloading Unary Operators
11.7 Overloading Binary Operators
11.8 Case Study: `Array` Class
11.9 Converting between Types
11.10 Case Study: `String` Class
11.11 Overloading ++ and --
11.12 Case Study: A `Date` Class
11.13 Standard Library Class `string`
11.14 `explicit` Constructors
11.15 Wrap-Up

Summary | Terminology | Self-Review Exercises | Answers to Self-Review Exercises | Exercises

11.1 Introduction

Chapters 9–10 introduced the basics of C++ classes. Services were obtained from objects by sending messages (in the form of member-function calls) to the objects. This function call notation is cumbersome for certain kinds of classes (such as mathematical classes). Also, many common manipulations are performed with operators (e.g., input and output). We can use C++'s rich set of built-in operators to specify common object manipulations. This chapter shows how to enable C++'s operators to work with objects—a process called operator overloading. It is straightforward and natural to extend C++ with these new capabilities, but it must be done cautiously.

One example of an overloaded operator built into C++ is <<, which is used both as the stream insertion operator and as the bitwise left-shift operator. Similarly, >> is also overloaded; it is used both as the stream extraction operator and as the bitwise right-shift operator. [*Note:* The bitwise left-shift and bitwise right-shift operators are discussed in detail in Chapter 22 of our sister book, *C++ How to Program, 5/e.*] Both of these operators are overloaded in the C++ Standard Library.

Although operator overloading sounds like an exotic capability, most programmers implicitly use overloaded operators regularly. For example, the C++ language itself overloads the addition operator (+) and the subtraction operator (-). These operators perform differently, depending on their context in integer arithmetic, floating-point arithmetic and pointer arithmetic.

C++ enables the programmer to overload most operators to be sensitive to the context in which they are used—the compiler generates the appropriate code based on the context (in particular, the types of the operands). Some operators are overloaded frequently, especially the assignment operator and various arithmetic operators such as + and -. The jobs performed by overloaded operators can also be performed by explicit function calls, but operator notation is often clearer and more familiar to programmers.

We discuss when to, and when not to, use operator overloading. We implement user-defined classes PhoneNumber, Array, String and Date to demonstrate how to overload operators, including the stream insertion, stream extraction, assignment, equality, relational, subscript, logical negation, parentheses and increment operators. The chapter ends with an example of C++'s Standard Library class string, which provides many overloaded operators that are similar to our String class that we present earlier in the chapter. In the exercises, we ask you to implement several classes with overloaded operators. The exercises also use classes Complex (for complex numbers) and HugeInt (for integers larger than a computer can represent with type long) to demonstrate overloaded arithmetic operators + and - and ask you to enhance those classes by overloading other arithmetic operators.

II.2 Fundamentals of Operator Overloading

C++ programming is a type-sensitive and type-focused process. Programmers can use fundamental types and can define new types. The fundamental types can be used with C++'s rich collection of operators. Operators provide programmers with a concise notation for expressing manipulations of objects of fundamental types.

Programmers can use operators with user-defined types as well. Although C++ does not allow new operators to be created, it does allow most existing operators to be overloaded so that, when these operators are used with objects, the operators have meaning appropriate to those objects. This is a powerful capability.

Software Engineering Observation II.1

Operator overloading contributes to C++'s extensibility—one of the language's most appealing attributes.

Good Programming Practice II.1

Use operator overloading when it makes a program clearer than accomplishing the same operations with function calls.

Good Programming Practice II.2

Overloaded operators should mimic the functionality of their built-in counterparts—for example, the + operator should be overloaded to perform addition, not subtraction. Avoid excessive or inconsistent use of operator overloading, as this can make a program cryptic and difficult to read.

An operator is overloaded by writing a non-static member function definition or global function definition as you normally would, except that the function name now becomes the keyword operator followed by the symbol for the operator being overloaded. For example, the function name operator+ would be used to overload the addition operator (+). When operators are overloaded as member functions, they must be non-static, because they must be called on an object of the class and operate on that object.

To use an operator on class objects, that operator *must* be overloaded—with three exceptions. The assignment operator (=) may be used with every class to perform memberwise assignment of the data members of the class—each data member is assigned from the "source" object to the "target" object of the assignment. We will soon see that such default memberwise assignment is dangerous for classes with pointer members; we will explicitly overload the assignment operator for such classes. The address (&) and comma (,) operators may also be used with objects of any class without overloading. The address operator returns the address of the object in memory. The comma operator evaluates the expression to its left then the expression to its right. Both of these operators can also be overloaded.

Overloading is especially appropriate for mathematical classes. These often require that a substantial set of operators be overloaded to ensure consistency with the way these mathematical classes are handled in the real world. For example, it would be unusual to overload only addition for a complex number class, because other arithmetic operators are also commonly used with complex numbers.

Operator overloading provides the same concise and familiar expressions for user-defined types that C++ provides with its rich collection of operators for fundamental types. Operator overloading is not automatic—you must write operator-overloading functions to perform the desired operations. Sometimes these functions are best made member functions; sometimes they are best as friend functions; occasionally they can be made global, non-friend functions. We discuss these issues throughout the chapter.

11.3 Restrictions on Operator Overloading

Most of C++'s operators can be overloaded. These are shown in Fig. 11.1. Figure 11.2 shows the operators that cannot be overloaded.

 Common Programming Error 11.1

Attempting to overload a nonoverloadable operator is a syntax error.

Precedence, Associativity and Number of Operands

The precedence of an operator cannot be changed by overloading. This can lead to awkward situations in which an operator is overloaded in a manner for which its fixed precedence is inappropriate. However, parentheses can be used to force the order of evaluation of overloaded operators in an expression.

Operators that can be overloaded							
+	-	*	/	%	^	&	|
~	!	=	<	>	+=	-=	*=
/=	%=	^=	&=	|=	<<	>>	>>=
<<=	==	!=	<=	>=	&&	||	++
--	->*	,	->	[]	()	new	delete
new[]	delete[]						

Fig. 11.1 | Operators that can be overloaded.

Operators that cannot be overloaded			
.	.*	::	?:

Fig. 11.2 | Operators that cannot be overloaded.

The associativity of an operator (i.e., whether the operator is applied right-to-left or left-to-right) cannot be changed by overloading.

It is not possible to change the "arity" of an operator (i.e., the number of operands an operator takes): Overloaded unary operators remain unary operators; overloaded binary operators remain binary operators. C++'s only ternary operator (?:) cannot be overloaded. Operators &, *, + and - all have both unary and binary versions; these unary and binary versions can each be overloaded.

Common Programming Error 11.2

Attempting to change the "arity" of an operator via operator overloading is a compilation error.

Creating New Operators

It is not possible to create new operators; only existing operators can be overloaded. Unfortunately, this prevents the programmer from using popular notations like the ** operator used in some other programming languages for exponentiation. [*Note:* You could overload the ∧ operator to perform exponentiation—as it does in some other languages.]

Common Programming Error 11.3

Attempting to create new operators via operator overloading is a syntax error.

Operators for Fundamental Types

The meaning of how an operator works on objects of fundamental types cannot be changed by operator overloading. The programmer cannot, for example, change the meaning of how + adds two integers. Operator overloading works only with objects of user-defined types or with a mixture of an object of a user-defined type and an object of a fundamental type.

Software Engineering Observation 11.2

At least one argument of an operator function must be an object or reference of a user-defined type. This prevents programmers from changing how operators work on fundamental types.

Common Programming Error 11.4

Attempting to modify how an operator works with objects of fundamental types is a compilation error.

Related Operators

Overloading an assignment operator and an addition operator to allow statements like

        object2 = object2 + object1;

does not imply that the += operator is also overloaded to allow statements such as

        object2 += object1;

Such behavior can be achieved only by explicitly overloading operator += for that class.

Common Programming Error 11.5

Assuming that overloading an operator such as + overloads related operators such as += or that overloading == overloads a related operator like != can lead to errors. Operators can be overloaded only explicitly; there is no implicit overloading.

11.4 Operator Functions as Class Members vs. Global Functions

Operator functions can be member functions or global functions; global functions are often made `friends` for performance reasons. Member functions use the `this` pointer implicitly to obtain one of their class object arguments (the left operand for binary operators). Arguments for both operands of a binary operator must be explicitly listed in a global function call.

Operators That Must Be Overloaded as Member Functions

When overloading (), [], -> or any of the assignment operators, the operator overloading function must be declared as a class member. For the other operators, the operator overloading functions can be class members or global functions.

Operators as Member Functions and Global Functions

Whether an operator function is implemented as a member function or as a global function, the operator is still used the same way in expressions. So which implementation is best?

When an operator function is implemented as a member function, the leftmost (or only) operand must be an object (or a reference to an object) of the operator's class. If the left operand must be an object of a different class or a fundamental type, this operator function must be implemented as a global function (as we will do in Section 11.5 when overloading << and >> as the stream insertion and stream extraction operators, respectively). A global operator function can be made a `friend` of a class if that function must access `private` or `protected` members of that class directly.

Operator member functions of a specific class are called (implicitly by the compiler) only when the left operand of a binary operator is specifically an object of that class, or when the single operand of a unary operator is an object of that class.

Why Overloaded Stream Insertion and Stream Extraction Operators Are Overloaded as Global Functions

The overloaded stream insertion operator (<<) is used in an expression in which the left operand has type `ostream &`, as in `cout << classObject`. To use the operator in this manner where the right operand is an object of a user-defined class, it must be overloaded as a global function. To be a member function, operator << would have to be a member of the `ostream` class. This is not possible for user-defined classes, since we are not allowed to modify C++ Standard Library classes. Similarly, the overloaded stream extraction operator (>>) is used in an expression in which the left operand has type `istream &`, as in `cin >> classObject`, and the right operand is an object of a user-defined class, so it, too, must be a global function. Also, each of these overloaded operator functions may require access to the `private` data members of the class object being output or input, so these overloaded operator functions can be made `friend` functions of the class for performance reasons.

Performance Tip 11.1

It is possible to overload an operator as a global, non-`friend` function, but such a function requiring access to a class's `private` or `protected` data would need to use set *or* get *functions provided in that class's `public` interface. The overhead of calling these functions could cause poor performance, so these functions can be inlined to improve performance.*

Commutative Operators

Another reason why one might choose a global function to overload an operator is to enable the operator to be commutative. For example, suppose we have an object, number, of type long int, and an object bigInteger1, of class HugeInteger (a class in which integers may be arbitrarily large rather than being limited by the machine word size of the underlying hardware; class HugeInteger is developed in the chapter exercises). The addition operator (+) produces a temporary HugeInteger object as the sum of a HugeInteger and a long int (as in the expression bigInteger1 + number), or as the sum of a long int and a HugeInteger (as in the expression number + bigInteger1). Thus, we require the addition operator to be commutative (exactly as it is with two fundamental-type operands). The problem is that the class object must appear on the left of the addition operator if that operator is to be overloaded as a member function. So, we overload the operator as a global function to allow the HugeInteger to appear on the right of the addition. The operator+ function, which deals with the HugeInteger on the left, can still be a member function.

11.5 Overloading Stream Insertion and Stream Extraction Operators

C++ is able to input and output the fundamental types using the stream extraction operator >> and the stream insertion operator <<. The class libraries provided with C++ compilers overload these operators to process each fundamental type, including pointers and C-like char * strings. The stream insertion and stream extraction operators also can be overloaded to perform input and output for user-defined types. The program of Figs. 11.3–11.5 demonstrates overloading these operators to handle data of a user-defined telephone number class called PhoneNumber. This program assumes telephone numbers are input correctly.

```
1   // Fig. 11.3: PhoneNumber.h
2   // PhoneNumber class definition
3   #ifndef PHONENUMBER_H
4   #define PHONENUMBER_H
5
6   #include <iostream>
7   using std::ostream;
8   using std::istream;
9
10  #include <string>
11  using std::string;
12
13  class PhoneNumber
14  {
15     friend ostream &operator<<( ostream &, const PhoneNumber & );
16     friend istream &operator>>( istream &, PhoneNumber & );
17  private:
18     string areaCode; // 3-digit area code
19     string exchange; // 3-digit exchange
```

Fig. 11.3 | PhoneNumber class with overloaded stream insertion and stream extraction operators as friend functions. (Part 1 of 2.)

```
20      string line; // 4-digit line
21   }; // end class PhoneNumber
22
23   #endif
```

Fig. 11.3 | PhoneNumber class with overloaded stream insertion and stream extraction operators as friend functions. (Part 2 of 2.)

```
 1   // Fig. 11.4: PhoneNumber.cpp
 2   // Overloaded stream insertion and stream extraction operators
 3   // for class PhoneNumber.
 4   #include <iomanip>
 5   using std::setw;
 6
 7   #include "PhoneNumber.h"
 8
 9   // overloaded stream insertion operator; cannot be
10   // a member function if we would like to invoke it with
11   // cout << somePhoneNumber;
12   ostream &operator<<( ostream &output, const PhoneNumber &number )
13   {
14      output << "(" << number.areaCode << ") "
15         << number.exchange << "-" << number.line;
16      return output; // enables cout << a << b << c;
17   } // end function operator<<
18
19   // overloaded stream extraction operator; cannot be
20   // a member function if we would like to invoke it with
21   // cin >> somePhoneNumber;
22   istream &operator>>( istream &input, PhoneNumber &number )
23   {
24      input.ignore(); // skip (
25      input >> setw( 3 ) >> number.areaCode; // input area code
26      input.ignore( 2 ); // skip ) and space
27      input >> setw( 3 ) >> number.exchange; // input exchange
28      input.ignore(); // skip dash (-)
29      input >> setw( 4 ) >> number.line; // input line
30      return input; // enables cin >> a >> b >> c;
31   } // end function operator>>
```

Fig. 11.4 | Overloaded stream insertion and stream extraction operators for class PhoneNumber.

```
 1   // Fig. 11.5: fig11_05.cpp
 2   // Demonstrating class PhoneNumber's overloaded stream insertion
 3   // and stream extraction operators.
 4   #include <iostream>
 5   using std::cout;
 6   using std::cin;
 7   using std::endl;
```

Fig. 11.5 | Overloaded stream insertion and stream extraction operators. (Part 1 of 2.)

```
 8
 9    #include "PhoneNumber.h"
10
11    int main()
12    {
13       PhoneNumber phone; // create object phone
14
15       cout << "Enter phone number in the form (123) 456-7890:" << endl;
16
17       // cin >> phone invokes operator>> by implicitly issuing
18       // the global function call operator>>( cin, phone )
19       cin >> phone;
20
21       cout << "The phone number entered was: ";
22
23       // cout << phone invokes operator<< by implicitly issuing
24       // the global function call operator<<( cout, phone )
25       cout << phone << endl;
26       return 0;
27    } // end main
```

```
Enter phone number in the form (123) 456-7890:
(800) 555-1212
The phone number entered was: (800) 555-1212
```

Fig. 11.5 | Overloaded stream insertion and stream extraction operators. (Part 2 of 2.)

The stream extraction operator function operator>> (Fig. 11.4, lines 22–31) takes istream reference input and PhoneNumber reference num as arguments and returns an istream reference. Operator function operator>> inputs phone numbers of the form

```
(800) 555-1212
```

into objects of class PhoneNumber. When the compiler sees the expression

```
cin >> phone
```

in line 19 of Fig. 11.5, the compiler generates the global function call

```
operator>>( cin, phone );
```

When this call executes, reference parameter input (Fig. 11.4, line 22) becomes an alias for cin and reference parameter number becomes an alias for phone. The operator function reads as strings the three parts of the telephone number into the areaCode (line 25), exchange (line 27) and line (line 29) members of the PhoneNumber object referenced by parameter number. Stream manipulator setw limits the number of characters read into each character array. When used with cin and strings, setw restricts the number of characters read to the number of characters specified by its argument (i.e., setw(3) allows three characters to be read). The parentheses, space and dash characters are skipped by calling istream member function ignore (Fig. 11.4, lines 24, 26 and 28), which discards the specified number of characters in the input stream (one character by default). Function operator>> returns istream reference input (i.e., cin). This enables input operations on

PhoneNumber objects to be cascaded with input operations on other PhoneNumber objects or on objects of other data types. For example, a program can input two PhoneNumber objects in one statement as follows:

```
cin >> phone1 >> phone2;
```

First, the expression `cin >> phone1` executes by making the global function call

```
operator>>( cin, phone1 );
```

This call then returns a reference to cin as the value of cin >> phone1, so the remaining portion of the expression is interpreted simply as cin >> phone2. This executes by making the global function call

```
operator>>( cin, phone2 );
```

The stream insertion operator function (Fig. 11.4, lines 12–17) takes an ostream reference (output) and a const PhoneNumber reference (number) as arguments and returns an ostream reference. Function operator<< displays objects of type PhoneNumber. When the compiler sees the expression

```
cout << phone
```

in line 25 of Fig. 11.5, the compiler generates the global function call

```
operator<<( cout, phone );
```

Function operator<< displays the parts of the telephone number as strings, because they are stored as string objects.

Error-Prevention Tip 11.1

Returning a reference from an overloaded << or >> operator function is typically successful because cout, cin and most stream objects are global, or at least long-lived. Returning a reference to an automatic variable or other temporary object is dangerous—creating "dangling references" to nonexisting objects.

Note that the functions operator>> and operator<< are declared in PhoneNumber as global, friend functions (Fig. 11.3, lines 15–16). They are global functions because the object of class PhoneNumber appears in each case as the right operand of the operator. Remember, overloaded operator functions for binary operators can be member functions only when the left operand is an object of the class in which the function is a member. Overloaded input and output operators are declared as friends if they need to access non-public class members directly for performance reasons or because the class may not offer appropriate *get* functions. Also note that the PhoneNumber reference in function operator<<'s parameter list (Fig. 11.4, line 12) is const, because the PhoneNumber will simply be output, and the PhoneNumber reference in function operator>>'s parameter list (line 22) is non-const, because the PhoneNumber object must be modified to store the input telephone number in the object.

Software Engineering Observation 11.3

New input/output capabilities for user-defined types are added to C++ without modifying C++'s standard input/output library classes. This is another example of the extensibility of the C++ programming language.

11.6 Overloading Unary Operators

A unary operator for a class can be overloaded as a non-static member function with no arguments or as a global function with one argument; that argument must be either an object of the class or a reference to an object of the class. Member functions that implement overloaded operators must be non-static so that they can access the non-static data in each object of the class. Remember that static member functions can access only static data members of the class.

Later in this chapter, we will overload unary operator ! to test whether an object of the String class we create (Section 11.10) is empty and return a bool result. Consider the expression !s, in which s is an object of class String. When a unary operator such as ! is overloaded as a member function with no arguments and the compiler sees the expression !s, the compiler generates the call s.operator!(). The operand s is the class object for which the String class member function operator! is being invoked. The function is declared in the class definition as follows:

```
class String
{
public:
    bool operator!() const;
    ...
}; // end class String
```

A unary operator such as ! may be overloaded as a global function with one argument in two different ways—either with an argument that is an object (this requires a copy of the object, so the side effects of the function are not applied to the original object), or with an argument that is a reference to an object (no copy of the original object is made, so all side effects of this function are applied to the original object). If s is a String class object (or a reference to a String class object), then !s is treated as if the call operator!(s) had been written, invoking the global operator! function that is declared as follows:

```
bool operator!( const String & );
```

11.7 Overloading Binary Operators

A binary operator can be overloaded as a non-static member function with one argument or as a global function with two arguments (one of those arguments must be either a class object or a reference to a class object).

Later in this chapter, we will overload < to compare two String objects. When overloading binary operator < as a non-static member function of a String class with one argument, if y and z are String-class objects, then y < z is treated as if y.operator<(z) had been written, invoking the operator< member function declared below

```
class String

public:
    bool operator<( const String & ) const;
    ...
}; // end class String
```

If binary operator < is to be overloaded as a global function, it must take two arguments—one of which must be a class object or a reference to a class object. If y and z are

String-class objects or references to String-class objects, then y < z is treated as if the call operator<(y, z) had been written in the program, invoking global-function operator< declared as follows:

```
bool operator<( const String &, const String & );
```

11.8 Case Study: Array Class

Pointer-based arrays have a number of problems. For example, a program can easily "walk off" either end of an array, because C++ does not check whether subscripts fall outside the range of an array (the programmer can still do this explicitly though). Arrays of size *n* must number their elements 0, …, *n* – 1; alternate subscript ranges are not allowed. An entire non-char array cannot be input or output at once; each array element must be read or written individually. Two arrays cannot be meaningfully compared with equality operators or relational operators (because the array names are simply pointers to where the arrays begin in memory and, of course, two arrays will always be at different memory locations). When an array is passed to a general-purpose function designed to handle arrays of any size, the size of the array must be passed as an additional argument. One array cannot be assigned to another with the assignment operator(s) (because array names are const pointers and a constant pointer cannot be used on the left side of an assignment operator). These and other capabilities certainly seem like "naturals" for dealing with arrays, but pointer-based arrays do not provide such capabilities. However, C++ does provide the means to implement such array capabilities through the use of classes and operator overloading.

In this example, we create a powerful array class that performs range checking to ensure that subscripts remain within the bounds of the Array. The class allows one array object to be assigned to another with the assignment operator. Objects of the Array class know their size, so the size does not need to be passed separately as an argument when passing an Array to a function. Entire Arrays can be input or output with the stream extraction and stream insertion operators, respectively. Array comparisons can be made with the equality operators == and !=.

This example will sharpen your appreciation of data abstraction. You will probably want to suggest other enhancements to this Array class. Class development is an interesting, creative and intellectually challenging activity—always with the goal of "crafting valuable classes."

The program of Figs. 11.6–11.8 demonstrates class Array and its overloaded operators. First we walk through main (Fig. 11.8). Then we consider the class definition (Fig. 11.6) and each of the class's member-function and friend-function definitions (Fig. 11.7).

```
1   // Fig. 11.6: Array.h
2   // Array class for storing arrays of integers.
3   #ifndef ARRAY_H
4   #define ARRAY_H
5
```

Fig. 11.6 | Array class definition with overloaded operators. (Part 1 of 2.)

```
 6  #include <iostream>
 7  using std::ostream;
 8  using std::istream;
 9
10  class Array
11  {
12     friend ostream &operator<<( ostream &, const Array & );
13     friend istream &operator>>( istream &, Array & );
14  public:
15     Array( int = 10 ); // default constructor
16     Array( const Array & ); // copy constructor
17     ~Array(); // destructor
18     int getSize() const; // return size
19
20     const Array &operator=( const Array & ); // assignment operator
21     bool operator==( const Array & ) const; // equality operator
22
23     // inequality operator; returns opposite of == operator
24     bool operator!=( const Array &right ) const
25     {
26        return ! ( *this == right ); // invokes Array::operator==
27     } // end function operator!=
28
29     // subscript operator for non-const objects returns modifiable lvalue
30     int &operator[]( int );
31
32     // subscript operator for const objects returns rvalue
33     int operator[]( int ) const;
34  private:
35     int size; // pointer-based array size
36     int *ptr; // pointer to first element of pointer-based array
37  }; // end class Array
38
39  #endif
```

Fig. 11.6 | Array class definition with overloaded operators. (Part 2 of 2.)

```
 1  // Fig 11.7: Array.cpp
 2  // Member-function definitions for class Array
 3  #include <iostream>
 4  using std::cerr;
 5  using std::cout;
 6  using std::cin;
 7  using std::endl;
 8
 9  #include <iomanip>
10  using std::setw;
11
12  #include <cstdlib> // exit function prototype
13  using std::exit;
```

Fig. 11.7 | Array class member- and friend-function definitions. (Part 1 of 4.)

```
14
15   #include "Array.h" // Array class definition
16
17   // default constructor for class Array (default size 10)
18   Array::Array( int arraySize )
19   {
20      size = ( arraySize > 0 ? arraySize : 10 ); // validate arraySize
21      ptr = new int[ size ]; // create space for pointer-based array
22
23      for ( int i = 0; i < size; i++ )
24         ptr[ i ] = 0; // set pointer-based array element
25   } // end Array default constructor
26
27   // copy constructor for class Array;
28   // must receive a reference to prevent infinite recursion
29   Array::Array( const Array &arrayToCopy )
30      : size( arrayToCopy.size )
31   {
32      ptr = new int[ size ]; // create space for pointer-based array
33
34      for ( int i = 0; i < size; i++ )
35         ptr[ i ] = arrayToCopy.ptr[ i ]; // copy into object
36   } // end Array copy constructor
37
38   // destructor for class Array
39   Array::~Array()
40   {
41      delete [] ptr; // release pointer-based array space
42   } // end destructor
43
44   // return number of elements of Array
45   int Array::getSize() const
46   {
47      return size; // number of elements in Array
48   } // end function getSize
49
50   // overloaded assignment operator;
51   // const return avoids: ( a1 = a2 ) = a3
52   const Array &Array::operator=( const Array &right )
53   {
54      if ( &right != this ) // avoid self-assignment
55      {
56         // for Arrays of different sizes, deallocate original
57         // left-side array, then allocate new left-side array
58         if ( size != right.size )
59         {
60            delete [] ptr; // release space
61            size = right.size; // resize this object
62            ptr = new int[ size ]; // create space for array copy
63         } // end inner if
64
```

Fig. 11.7 | Array class member- and friend-function definitions. (Part 2 of 4.)

```
65           for ( int i = 0; i < size; i++ )
66               ptr[ i ] = right.ptr[ i ]; // copy array into object
67       } // end outer if
68
69       return *this; // enables x = y = z, for example
70  } // end function operator=
71
72  // determine if two Arrays are equal and
73  // return true, otherwise return false
74  bool Array::operator==( const Array &right ) const
75  {
76      if ( size != right.size )
77          return false; // arrays of different number of elements
78
79      for ( int i = 0; i < size; i++ )
80          if ( ptr[ i ] != right.ptr[ i ] )
81              return false; // Array contents are not equal
82
83      return true; // Arrays are equal
84  } // end function operator==
85
86  // overloaded subscript operator for non-const Arrays;
87  // reference return creates a modifiable lvalue
88  int &Array::operator[]( int subscript )
89  {
90      // check for subscript out-of-range error
91      if ( subscript < 0 || subscript >= size )
92      {
93          cerr << "\nError: Subscript " << subscript
94              << " out of range" << endl;
95          exit( 1 ); // terminate program; subscript out of range
96      } // end if
97
98      return ptr[ subscript ]; // reference return
99  } // end function operator[]
100
101 // overloaded subscript operator for const Arrays
102 // const reference return creates an rvalue
103 int Array::operator[]( int subscript ) const
104 {
105     // check for subscript out-of-range error
106     if ( subscript < 0 || subscript >= size )
107     {
108         cerr << "\nError: Subscript " << subscript
109             << " out of range" << endl;
110         exit( 1 ); // terminate program; subscript out of range
111     } // end if
112
113     return ptr[ subscript ]; // returns copy of this element
114 } // end function operator[]
115
```

Fig. 11.7 | Array class member- and friend-function definitions. (Part 3 of 4.)

```
116   // overloaded input operator for class Array;
117   // inputs values for entire Array
118   istream &operator>>( istream &input, Array &a )
119   {
120      for ( int i = 0; i < a.size; i++ )
121         input >> a.ptr[ i ];
122
123      return input; // enables cin >> x >> y;
124   } // end function
125
126   // overloaded output operator for class Array
127   ostream &operator<<( ostream &output, const Array &a )
128   {
129      int i;
130
131      // output private ptr-based array
132      for ( i = 0; i < a.size; i++ )
133      {
134         output << setw( 12 ) << a.ptr[ i ];
135
136         if ( ( i + 1 ) % 4 == 0 ) // 4 numbers per row of output
137            output << endl;
138      } // end for
139
140      if ( i % 4 != 0 ) // end last line of output
141         output << endl;
142
143      return output; // enables cout << x << y;
144   } // end function operator<<
```

Fig. 11.7 | Array class member- and friend-function definitions. (Part 4 of 4.)

```
1    // Fig. 11.8: fig11_08.cpp
2    // Array class test program.
3    #include <iostream>
4    using std::cout;
5    using std::cin;
6    using std::endl;
7
8    #include "Array.h"
9
10   int main()
11   {
12      Array integers1( 7 ); // seven-element Array
13      Array integers2; // 10-element Array by default
14
15      // print integers1 size and contents
16      cout << "Size of Array integers1 is "
17         << integers1.getSize()
18         << "\nArray after initialization:\n" << integers1;
19
```

Fig. 11.8 | Array class test program. (Part 1 of 3.)

```
20    // print integers2 size and contents
21    cout << "\nSize of Array integers2 is "
22       << integers2.getSize()
23       << "\nArray after initialization:\n" << integers2;
24
25    // input and print integers1 and integers2
26    cout << "\nEnter 17 integers:" << endl;
27    cin >> integers1 >> integers2;
28
29    cout << "\nAfter input, the Arrays contain:\n"
30       << "integers1:\n" << integers1
31       << "integers2:\n" << integers2;
32
33    // use overloaded inequality (!=) operator
34    cout << "\nEvaluating: integers1 != integers2" << endl;
35
36    if ( integers1 != integers2 )
37       cout << "integers1 and integers2 are not equal" << endl;
38
39    // create Array integers3 using integers1 as an
40    // initializer; print size and contents
41    Array integers3( integers1 ); // invokes copy constructor
42
43    cout << "\nSize of Array integers3 is "
44       << integers3.getSize()
45       << "\nArray after initialization:\n" << integers3;
46
47    // use overloaded assignment (=) operator
48    cout << "\nAssigning integers2 to integers1:" << endl;
49    integers1 = integers2; // note target Array is smaller
50
51    cout << "integers1:\n" << integers1
52       << "integers2:\n" << integers2;
53
54    // use overloaded equality (==) operator
55    cout << "\nEvaluating: integers1 == integers2" << endl;
56
57    if ( integers1 == integers2 )
58       cout << "integers1 and integers2 are equal" << endl;
59
60    // use overloaded subscript operator to create rvalue
61    cout << "\nintegers1[5] is " << integers1[ 5 ];
62
63    // use overloaded subscript operator to create lvalue
64    cout << "\n\nAssigning 1000 to integers1[5]" << endl;
65    integers1[ 5 ] = 1000;
66    cout << "integers1:\n" << integers1;
67
68    // attempt to use out-of-range subscript
69    cout << "\nAttempt to assign 1000 to integers1[15]" << endl;
70    integers1[ 15 ] = 1000; // ERROR: out of range
71    return 0;
72 } // end main
```

Fig. 11.8 | Array class test program. (Part 2 of 3.)

```
Size of Array integers1 is 7
Array after initialization:
            0            0            0            0
            0            0            0

Size of Array integers2 is 10
Array after initialization:
            0            0            0            0
            0            0            0            0
            0            0

Enter 17 integers:
1 2 3 4 5 6 7 8 9 10 11 12 13 14 15 16 17

After input, the Arrays contain:
integers1:
            1            2            3            4
            5            6            7
integers2:
            8            9           10           11
           12           13           14           15
           16           17

Evaluating: integers1 != integers2
integers1 and integers2 are not equal

Size of Array integers3 is 7
Array after initialization:
            1            2            3            4
            5            6            7

Assigning integers2 to integers1:
integers1:
            8            9           10           11
           12           13           14           15
           16           17
integers2:
            8            9           10           11
           12           13           14           15
           16           17

Evaluating: integers1 == integers2
integers1 and integers2 are equal

integers1[5] is 13

Assigning 1000 to integers1[5]
integers1:
            8            9           10           11
           12         1000           14           15
           16           17

Attempt to assign 1000 to integers1[15]

Error: Subscript 15 out of range
```

Fig. 11.8 | Array class test program. (Part 3 of 3.)

*Creating **Arrays**, Outputting Their Size and Displaying Their Contents*
The program begins by instantiating two objects of class Array—integers1 (Fig. 11.8, line 12) with seven elements, and integers2 (Fig. 11.8, line 13) with the default Array size—10 elements (specified by the Array default constructor's prototype in Fig. 11.6, line 15). Lines 16–18 use member function getSize to determine the size of integers1 and output integers1, using the Array overloaded stream insertion operator. The sample output confirms that the Array elements were set correctly to zeros by the constructor. Next, lines 21–23 output the size of Array integers2 and output integers2, using the Array overloaded stream insertion operator.

*Using the Overloaded Stream Insertion Operator to Fill an **Array***
Line 26 prompts the user to input 17 integers. Line 27 uses the Array overloaded stream extraction operator to read these values into both arrays. The first seven values are stored in integers1 and the remaining 10 values are stored in integers2. Lines 29–31 output the two arrays with the overloaded Array stream insertion operator to confirm that the input was performed correctly.

Using the Overloaded Inequality Operator
Line 36 tests the overloaded inequality operator by evaluating the condition

```
integers1 != integers2
```

The program output shows that the Arrays indeed are not equal.

*Initializing a New **Array** with a Copy of an Existing **Array**'s Contents*
Line 41 instantiates a third Array called integers3 and initializes it with a copy of Array integers1. This invokes the Array copy constructor to copy the elements of integers1 into integers3. We discuss the details of the copy constructor shortly. Note that the copy constructor can also be invoked by writing line 41 as follows:

```
Array integers3 = integers1;
```

The equal sign in the preceding statement is *not* the assignment operator. When an equal sign appears in the declaration of an object, it invokes a constructor for that object. This form can be used to pass only a single argument to a constructor.

Lines 43–45 output the size of integers3 and output integers3, using the Array overloaded stream insertion operator to confirm that the Array elements were set correctly by the copy constructor.

Using the Overloaded Assignment Operator
Next, line 49 tests the overloaded assignment operator (=) by assigning integers2 to integers1. Lines 51–52 print both Array objects to confirm that the assignment was successful. Note that integers1 originally held 7 integers and was resized to hold a copy of the 10 elements in integers2. As we will see, the overloaded assignment operator performs this resizing operation in a manner that is transparent to the client code.

Using the Overloaded Equality Operator
Next, line 57 uses the overloaded equality operator (==) to confirm that objects integers1 and integers2 are indeed identical after the assignment.

Using the Overloaded Subscript Operator

Line 61 uses the overloaded subscript operator to refer to integers1[5]—an in-range element of integers1. This subscripted name is used as an *rvalue* to print the value stored in integers1[5]. Line 65 uses integers1[5] as a modifiable *lvalue* on the left side of an assignment statement to assign a new value, 1000, to element 5 of integers1. We will see that operator[] returns a reference to use as the modifiable *lvalue* after the operator confirms that 5 is a valid subscript for integers1.

Line 70 attempts to assign the value 1000 to integers1[15]—an out-of-range element. In this example, operator[] determines that the subscript is out of range, prints a message and terminates the program. Note that we highlighted line 70 of the program in red to emphasize that it is an error to access an element that is out of range. This is a runtime logic error, not a compilation error.

Interestingly, the array subscript operator [] is not restricted for use only with arrays; it also can be used, for example, to select elements from other kinds of container classes, such as linked lists, strings and dictionaries. Also, when operator[] functions are defined, subscripts no longer have to be integers—characters, strings, floats or even objects of user-defined classes also could be used. Note that the C++ Standard Template Library provides the map class, which allows noninteger subscripts.

Array Class Definition

Now that we have seen how this program operates, let us walk through the class header (Fig. 11.6). As we refer to each member function in the header, we discuss that function's implementation in Fig. 11.7. In Fig. 11.6, lines 35–36 represent the private data members of class Array. Each Array object consists of a size member indicating the number of elements in the Array and an int pointer—ptr—that points to the dynamically allocated pointer-based array of integers managed by the Array object.

Overloading the Stream Insertion and Stream Extraction Operators as **friends**

Lines 12–13 of Fig. 11.6 declare the overloaded stream insertion operator and the overloaded stream extraction operator to be friends of class Array. When the compiler sees an expression like cout << arrayObject, it invokes global function operator<< with the call

```
operator<<( cout, arrayObject )
```

When the compiler sees an expression like cin >> arrayObject, it invokes global function operator>> with the call

```
operator>>( cin, arrayObject )
```

We note again that these stream insertion and stream extraction operator functions cannot be members of class Array, because the Array object is always mentioned on the right side of the stream insertion operator and the stream extraction operator. If these operator functions were to be members of class Array, the following awkward statements would have to be used to output and input an Array:

```
arrayObject << cout;
arrayObject >> cin;
```

Such statements would be confusing to most C++ programmers, who are familiar with cout and cin appearing as the left operands of << and >>, respectively.

Function `operator<<` (defined in Fig. 11.7, lines 127–144) prints the number of elements indicated by `size` from the integer array to which `ptr` points. Function `operator>>` (defined in Fig. 11.7, lines 118–124) inputs directly into the array to which `ptr` points. Each of these operator functions returns an appropriate reference to enable cascaded output or input statements, respectively. Note that each of these functions has access to an `Array`'s `private` data because these functions are declared as `friend`s of class `Array`. Also, note that class `Array`'s `getSize` and `operator[]` functions could be used by `operator<<` and `operator>>`, in which case these operator functions would not need to be `friend`s of class `Array`. However, the additional function calls might increase execution-time overhead.

Array Default Constructor
Line 15 of Fig. 11.6 declares the default constructor for the class and specifies a default size of 10 elements. When the compiler sees a declaration like line 13 in Fig. 11.8, it invokes class `Array`'s default constructor (remember that the default constructor in this example actually receives a single `int` argument that has a default value of 10). The default constructor (defined in Fig. 11.7, lines 18–25) validates and assigns the argument to data member `size`, uses `new` to obtain the memory for the internal pointer-based representation of this array and assigns the pointer returned by `new` to data member `ptr`. Then the constructor uses a `for` statement to set all the elements of the array to zero. It is possible to have an `Array` class that does not initialize its members if, for example, these members are to be read at some later time; but this is considered to be a poor programming practice. `Array`s, and objects in general, should be properly initialized and maintained in a consistent state.

Array Copy Constructor
Line 16 of Fig. 11.6 declares a copy constructor (defined in Fig. 11.7, lines 29–36) that initializes an `Array` by making a copy of an existing `Array` object. Such copying must be done carefully to avoid the pitfall of leaving both `Array` objects pointing to the same dynamically allocated memory. This is exactly the problem that would occur with default memberwise copying, if the compiler is allowed to define a default copy constructor for this class. Copy constructors are invoked whenever a copy of an object is needed, such as in passing an object by value to a function, returning an object by value from a function or initializing an object with a copy of another object of the same class. The copy constructor is called in a declaration when an object of class `Array` is instantiated and initialized with another object of class `Array`, as in the declaration in line 41 of Fig. 11.8.

Software Engineering Observation 11.4

The argument to a copy constructor should be a `const` reference to allow a `const` object to be copied.

Common Programming Error 11.6

Note that a copy constructor must receive its argument by reference, not by value. Otherwise, the copy constructor call results in infinite recursion (a fatal logic error) because receiving an object by value requires the copy constructor to make a copy of the argument object. Recall that any time a copy of an object is required, the class's copy constructor is called. If the copy constructor received its argument by value, the copy constructor would call itself recursively to make a copy of its argument!

The copy constructor for `Array` uses a member initializer (Fig. 11.7, line 30) to copy the `size` of the initializer `Array` into data member `size`, uses `new` (line 32) to obtain the memory for the internal pointer-based representation of this `Array` and assigns the pointer returned by `new` to data member `ptr`.[1] Then the copy constructor uses a `for` statement to copy all the elements of the initializer `Array` into the new `Array` object. Note that an object of a class can look at the `private` data of any other object of that class (using a handle that indicates which object to access).

Common Programming Error 11.7

If the copy constructor simply copied the pointer in the source object to the target object's pointer, then both objects would point to the same dynamically allocated memory. The first destructor to execute would then delete the dynamically allocated memory, and the other object's `ptr` would be undefined, a situation called a dangling pointer—*this would likely result in a serious run-time error (such as early program termination) when the pointer was used.*

Array Destructor
Line 17 of Fig. 11.6 declares the destructor for the class (defined in Fig. 11.7, lines 39–42). The destructor is invoked when an object of class `Array` goes out of scope. The destructor uses `delete []` to release the memory allocated dynamically by `new` in the constructor.

getSize Member Function
Line 18 of Fig. 11.6 declares function `getSize` (defined in Fig. 11.7, lines 45–48) that returns the number of elements in the `Array`.

Overloaded Assignment Operator
Line 20 of Fig. 11.6 declares the overloaded assignment operator function for the class. When the compiler sees the expression `integers1 = integers2` in line 49 of Fig. 11.8, the compiler invokes member function `operator=` with the call

```
integers1.operator=( integers2 )
```

The implementation of member function `operator=` (Fig. 11.7, lines 52–70) tests for self assignment (line 54) in which an object of class `Array` is being assigned to itself. When `this` is equal to the address of the `right` operand, a self-assignment is being attempted, so the assignment is skipped (i.e., the object already is itself; in a moment we will see why self-assignment is dangerous). If it is not a self-assignment, then the member function determines whether the sizes of the two arrays are identical (line 58); in that case, the original array of integers in the left-side `Array` object is not reallocated. Otherwise, `operator=` uses `delete` (line 60) to release the memory originally allocated to the target array, copies the `size` of the source array to the `size` of the target array (line 61), uses `new` to allocate memory for the target array and places the pointer returned by `new` into the array's `ptr` member.[2] Then the `for` statement at lines 65–66 copies the array elements from the source array to the target array. Regardless of whether this is a self-assignment, the member function returns the current object (i.e., `*this` at line 69) as a constant reference; this enables cascaded `Array` assignments such as x = y = z. If self-assignment occurs, and function `operator=` did not test for this case, `operator=` would delete the dynamic memory associated

---

1. Note that `new` could fail to obtain the needed memory.
2. Once again, `new` could fail.

with the `Array` object before the assignment was complete. This would leave `ptr` pointing to memory that had been deallocated, which could lead to fatal runtime errors.

Software Engineering Observation 11.5

A copy constructor, a destructor and an overloaded assignment operator are usually provided as a group for any class that uses dynamically allocated memory.

Common Programming Error 11.8

Not providing an overloaded assignment operator and a copy constructor for a class when objects of that class contain pointers to dynamically allocated memory is a logic error.

Software Engineering Observation 11.6

It is possible to prevent one object of a class from being assigned to another. This is done by declaring the assignment operator as a `private` member of the class.

Software Engineering Observation 11.7

It is possible to prevent class objects from being copied; to do this, simply make both the overloaded assignment operator and the copy constructor of that class `private`.

Overloaded Equality and Inequality Operators

Line 21 of Fig. 11.6 declares the overloaded equality operator (`==`) for the class. When the compiler sees the expression `integers1 == integers2` in line 57 of Fig. 11.8, the compiler invokes member function `operator==` with the call

```
integers1.operator==( integers2 )
```

Member function `operator==` (defined in Fig. 11.7, lines 74–84) immediately returns `false` if the `size` members of the arrays are not equal. Otherwise, `operator==` compares each pair of elements. If they are all equal, the function returns `true`. The first pair of elements to differ causes the function to return `false` immediately.

Lines 24–27 of the header file define the overloaded inequality operator (`!=`) for the class. Member function `operator!=` uses the overloaded `operator==` function to determine whether one `Array` is equal to another, then returns the opposite of that result. Writing `operator!=` in this manner enables the programmer to reuse `operator==`, which reduces the amount of code that must be written in the class. Also, note that the full function definition for `operator!=` is in the `Array` header file. This allows the compiler to inline the definition of `operator!=` to eliminate the overhead of the extra function call.

Overloaded Subscript Operators

Lines 30 and 33 of Fig. 11.6 declare two overloaded subscript operators (defined in Fig. 11.7 at lines 88–99 and 103–114, respectively). When the compiler sees the expression `integers1[ 5 ]` (Fig. 11.8, line 61), the compiler invokes the appropriate overloaded `operator[]` member function by generating the call

```
integers1.operator[]( 5 )
```

The compiler creates a call to the `const` version of `operator[]` (Fig. 11.7, lines 103–114) when the subscript operator is used on a `const Array` object. For example, if `const` object `z` is instantiated with the statement

```
const Array z( 5 );
```

then the `const` version of `operator[]` is required to execute a statement such as

```
cout << z[ 3 ] << endl;
```

Remember, a program can invoke only the `const` member functions of a `const` object.

Each definition of `operator[]` determines whether the subscript it receives as an argument is in range. If it is not, each function prints an error message and terminates the program with a call to function `exit` (header `<cstdlib>`).[3] If the subscript is in range, the non-`const` version of `operator[]` returns the appropriate array element as a reference so that it may be used as a modifiable *lvalue* (e.g., on the left side of an assignment statement). If the subscript is in range, the `const` version of `operator[]` returns a copy of the appropriate element of the array. The returned character is an *rvalue*.

11.9 Converting between Types

Most programs process information of many types. Sometimes all the operations "stay within a type." For example, adding an `int` to an `int` produces an `int` (as long as the result is not too large to be represented as an `int`). It is often necessary, however, to convert data of one type to data of another type. This can happen in assignments, in calculations, in passing values to functions and in returning values from functions. The compiler knows how to perform certain conversions among fundamental types (as we discussed in Chapter 6). Programmers can use cast operators to force conversions among fundamental types.

But what about user-defined types? The compiler cannot know in advance how to convert among user-defined types, and between user-defined types and fundamental types, so the programmer must specify how to do this. Such conversions can be performed with conversion constructors—single-argument constructors that turn objects of other types (including fundamental types) into objects of a particular class. In Section 11.10, we use a conversion constructor to convert ordinary `char *` strings into `String` class objects.

A conversion operator (also called a cast operator) can be used to convert an object of one class into an object of another class or into an object of a fundamental type. Such a conversion operator must be a non-`static` member function. The function prototype

```
A::operator char *() const;
```

declares an overloaded cast operator function for converting an object of user-defined type `A` into a temporary `char *` object. The operator function is declared `const` because it does not modify the original object. An overloaded cast operator function does not specify a return type—the return type is the type to which the object is being converted. If `s` is a class object, when the compiler sees the expression `static_cast< char * >( s )`, the compiler generates the call

```
s.operator char *()
```

The operand `s` is the class object `s` for which the member function `operator char *` is being invoked.

---

3. Note that it is more appropriate when a subscript is out of range to "throw an exception" indicating the out-of-range subscript. Then the program can "catch" that exception, process it and possibly continue execution.

Overloaded cast operator functions can be defined to convert objects of user-defined types into fundamental types or into objects of other user-defined types. The prototypes

```
A::operator int() const;
A::operator OtherClass() const;
```

declare overloaded cast operator functions that can convert an object of user-defined type A into an integer or into an object of user-defined type OtherClass, respectively.

One of the nice features of cast operators and conversion constructors is that, when necessary, the compiler can call these functions implicitly to create temporary objects. For example, if an object s of a user-defined String class appears in a program at a location where an ordinary char * is expected, such as

```
cout << s;
```

the compiler can call the overloaded cast-operator function operator char * to convert the object into a char * and use the resulting char * in the expression. With this cast operator provided for our String class, the stream insertion operator does not have to be overloaded to output a String using cout.

11.10 Case Study: String Class

As a capstone exercise to our study of overloading, we will build our own String class to handle the creation and manipulation of strings (Figs. 11.9–11.11). The C++ standard library provides a similar, more robust class string as well. Recall that we introduced standard class string in Chapter 3. We present an additional example using string in Section 11.13. For now, we will make extensive use of operator overloading to craft our own class String.

First, we present the header file for class String. We discuss the private data used to represent String objects. Then we walk through the class's public interface, discussing each of the services the class provides. We discuss the member-function definitions for the class String. For each of the overloaded operator functions, we show the code in the program that invokes the overloaded operator function, and we provide an explanation of how the overloaded operator function works.

String Class Definition

Now let us walk through the String class header file in Fig. 11.9. We begin with the internal pointer-based representation of a String. Lines 55–56 declare the private data members of the class. Our String class has a length field, which represents the number of characters in the string, not including the null character at the end, and has a pointer sPtr that points to the dynamically allocated memory representing the character string.

```
1   // Fig. 11.9: String.h
2   // String class definition.
3   #ifndef STRING_H
4   #define STRING_H
5
6   #include <iostream>
7   using std::ostream;
8   using std::istream;
```

Fig. 11.9 | String class definition with operator overloading. (Part 1 of 2.)

```
 9
10   class String
11   {
12      friend ostream &operator<<( ostream &, const String & );
13      friend istream &operator>>( istream &, String & );
14   public:
15      String( const char * = "" ); // conversion/default constructor
16      String( const String & ); // copy constructor
17      ~String(); // destructor
18
19      const String &operator=( const String & ); // assignment operator
20      const String &operator+=( const String & ); // concatenation operator
21
22      bool operator!() const; // is String empty?
23      bool operator==( const String & ) const; // test s1 == s2
24      bool operator<( const String & ) const; // test s1 < s2
25
26      // test s1 != s2
27      bool operator!=( const String &right ) const
28      {
29         return !( *this == right );
30      } // end function operator!=
31
32      // test s1 > s2
33      bool operator>( const String &right ) const
34      {
35         return right < *this;
36      } // end function operator>
37
38      // test s1 <= s2
39      bool operator<=( const String &right ) const
40      {
41         return !( right < *this );
42      } // end function operator <=
43
44      // test s1 >= s2
45      bool operator>=( const String &right ) const
46      {
47         return !( *this < right );
48      } // end function operator>=
49
50      char &operator[]( int ); // subscript operator (modifiable lvalue)
51      char operator[]( int ) const; // subscript operator (rvalue)
52      String operator()( int, int = 0 ) const; // return a substring
53      int getLength() const; // return string length
54   private:
55      int length; // string length (not counting null terminator)
56      char *sPtr; // pointer to start of pointer-based string
57
58      void setString( const char * ); // utility function
59   }; // end class String
60
61   #endif
```

Fig. 11.9 | String class definition with operator overloading. (Part 2 of 2.)

```
1   // Fig. 11.10: String.cpp
2   // Member-function definitions for class String.
3   #include <iostream>
4   using std::cerr;
5   using std::cout;
6   using std::endl;
7
8   #include <iomanip>
9   using std::setw;
10
11  #include <cstring> // strcpy and strcat prototypes
12  using std::strcmp;
13  using std::strcpy;
14  using std::strcat;
15
16  #include <cstdlib> // exit prototype
17  using std::exit;
18
19  #include "String.h" // String class definition
20
21  // conversion (and default) constructor converts char * to String
22  String::String( const char *s )
23     : length( ( s != 0 ) ? strlen( s ) : 0 )
24  {
25     cout << "Conversion (and default) constructor: " << s << endl;
26     setString( s ); // call utility function
27  } // end String conversion constructor
28
29  // copy constructor
30  String::String( const String &copy )
31     : length( copy.length )
32  {
33     cout << "Copy constructor: " << copy.sPtr << endl;
34     setString( copy.sPtr ); // call utility function
35  } // end String copy constructor
36
37  // Destructor
38  String::~String()
39  {
40     cout << "Destructor: " << sPtr << endl;
41     delete [] sPtr; // release pointer-based string memory
42  } // end ~String destructor
43
44  // overloaded = operator; avoids self assignment
45  const String &String::operator=( const String &right )
46  {
47     cout << "operator= called" << endl;
48
49     if ( &right != this ) // avoid self assignment
50     {
51        delete [] sPtr; // prevents memory leak
52        length = right.length; // new String length
```

Fig. 11.10 | String class member-function and friend-function definitions. (Part 1 of 4.)

```
53          setString( right.sPtr ); // call utility function
54      } // end if
55      else
56         cout << "Attempted assignment of a String to itself" << endl;
57
58      return *this; // enables cascaded assignments
59   } // end function operator=
60
61   // concatenate right operand to this object and store in this object
62   const String &String::operator+=( const String &right )
63   {
64      size_t newLength = length + right.length; // new length
65      char *tempPtr = new char[ newLength + 1 ]; // create memory
66
67      strcpy( tempPtr, sPtr ); // copy sPtr
68      strcpy( tempPtr + length, right.sPtr ); // copy right.sPtr
69
70      delete [] sPtr; // reclaim old space
71      sPtr = tempPtr; // assign new array to sPtr
72      length = newLength; // assign new length to length
73      return *this; // enables cascaded calls
74   } // end function operator+=
75
76   // is this String empty?
77   bool String::operator!() const
78   {
79      return length == 0;
80   } // end function operator!
81
82   // Is this String equal to right String?
83   bool String::operator==( const String &right ) const
84   {
85      return strcmp( sPtr, right.sPtr ) == 0;
86   } // end function operator==
87
88   // Is this String less than right String?
89   bool String::operator<( const String &right ) const
90   {
91      return strcmp( sPtr, right.sPtr ) < 0;
92   } // end function operator<
93
94   // return reference to character in String as a modifiable lvalue
95   char &String::operator[]( int subscript )
96   {
97      // test for subscript out of range
98      if ( subscript < 0 || subscript >= length )
99      {
100        cerr << "Error: Subscript " << subscript
101           << " out of range" << endl;
102        exit( 1 ); // terminate program
103     } // end if
104
```

Fig. 11.10 | String class member-function and friend-function definitions. (Part 2 of 4.)

```
105        return sPtr[ subscript ]; // non-const return; modifiable lvalue
106    } // end function operator[]
107
108    // return reference to character in String as rvalue
109    char String::operator[]( int subscript ) const
110    {
111        // test for subscript out of range
112        if ( subscript < 0 || subscript >= length )
113        {
114            cerr << "Error: Subscript " << subscript
115                 << " out of range" << endl;
116            exit( 1 ); // terminate program
117        } // end if
118
119        return sPtr[ subscript ]; // returns copy of this element
120    } // end function operator[]
121
122    // return a substring beginning at index and of length subLength
123    String String::operator()( int index, int subLength ) const
124    {
125        // if index is out of range or substring length < 0,
126        // return an empty String object
127        if ( index < 0 || index >= length || subLength < 0 )
128            return ""; // converted to a String object automatically
129
130        // determine length of substring
131        int len;
132
133        if ( ( subLength == 0 ) || ( index + subLength > length ) )
134            len = length - index;
135        else
136            len = subLength;
137
138        // allocate temporary array for substring and
139        // terminating null character
140        char *tempPtr = new char[ len + 1 ];
141
142        // copy substring into char array and terminate string
143        strncpy( tempPtr, &sPtr[ index ], len );
144        tempPtr[ len ] = '\0';
145
146        // create temporary String object containing the substring
147        String tempString( tempPtr );
148        delete [] tempPtr; // delete temporary array
149        return tempString; // return copy of the temporary String
150    } // end function operator()
151
152    // return string length
153    int String::getLength() const
154    {
155        return length;
156    } // end function getLength
```

Fig. 11.10 | String class member-function and friend-function definitions. (Part 3 of 4.)

```
157
158   // utility function called by constructors and operator=
159   void String::setString( const char *string2 )
160   {
161      sPtr = new char[ length + 1 ]; // allocate memory
162
163      if ( string2 != 0 ) // if string2 is not null pointer, copy contents
164         strcpy( sPtr, string2 ); // copy literal to object
165      else // if string2 is a null pointer, make this an empty string
166         sPtr[ 0 ] = '\0'; // empty string
167   } // end function setString
168
169   // overloaded output operator
170   ostream &operator<<( ostream &output, const String &s )
171   {
172      output << s.sPtr;
173      return output; // enables cascading
174   } // end function operator<<
175
176   // overloaded input operator
177   istream &operator>>( istream &input, String &s )
178   {
179      char temp[ 100 ]; // buffer to store input
180      input >> setw( 100 ) >> temp;
181      s = temp; // use String class assignment operator
182      return input; // enables cascading
183   } // end function operator>>
```

Fig. 11.10 | `String` class member-function and `friend`-function definitions. (Part 4 of 4.)

```
1    // Fig. 11.11: fig11_11.cpp
2    // String class test program.
3    #include <iostream>
4    using std::cout;
5    using std::endl;
6    using std::boolalpha;
7
8    #include "String.h"
9
10   int main()
11   {
12      String s1( "happy" );
13      String s2( " birthday" );
14      String s3;
15
16      // test overloaded equality and relational operators
17      cout << "s1 is \"" << s1 << "\"; s2 is \"" << s2
18         << "\"; s3 is \"" << s3 << '\"'
19         << boolalpha << "\n\nThe results of comparing s2 and s1:"
20         << "\ns2 == s1 yields " << ( s2 == s1 )
21         << "\ns2 != s1 yields " << ( s2 != s1 )
```

Fig. 11.11 | `String` class test program. (Part 1 of 4.)

```
22          << "\ns2 >  s1 yields " << ( s2 > s1 )
23          << "\ns2 <  s1 yields " << ( s2 < s1 )
24          << "\ns2 >= s1 yields " << ( s2 >= s1 )
25          << "\ns2 <= s1 yields " << ( s2 <= s1 );
26
27
28          // test overloaded String empty (!) operator
29          cout << "\n\nTesting !s3:" << endl;
30
31          if ( !s3 )
32          {
33             cout << "s3 is empty; assigning s1 to s3;" << endl;
34             s3 = s1; // test overloaded assignment
35             cout << "s3 is \"" << s3 << "\"";
36          } // end if
37
38          // test overloaded String concatenation operator
39          cout << "\n\ns1 += s2 yields s1 = ";
40          s1 += s2; // test overloaded concatenation
41          cout << s1;
42
43          // test conversion constructor
44          cout << "\n\ns1 += \" to you\" yields" << endl;
45          s1 += " to you"; // test conversion constructor
46          cout << "s1 = " << s1 << "\n\n";
47
48          // test overloaded function call operator () for substring
49          cout << "The substring of s1 starting at\n"
50             << "location 0 for 14 characters, s1(0, 14), is:\n"
51             << s1( 0, 14 ) << "\n\n";
52
53          // test substring "to-end-of-String" option
54          cout << "The substring of s1 starting at\n"
55             << "location 15, s1(15), is: "
56             << s1( 15 ) << "\n\n";
57
58          // test copy constructor
59          String *s4Ptr = new String( s1 );
60          cout << "\n*s4Ptr = " << *s4Ptr << "\n\n";
61
62          // test assignment (=) operator with self-assignment
63          cout << "assigning *s4Ptr to *s4Ptr" << endl;
64          *s4Ptr = *s4Ptr; // test overloaded assignment
65          cout << "*s4Ptr = " << *s4Ptr << endl;
66
67          // test destructor
68          delete s4Ptr;
69
70          // test using subscript operator to create a modifiable lvalue
71          s1[ 0 ] = 'H';
72          s1[ 6 ] = 'B';
73          cout << "\ns1 after s1[0] = 'H' and s1[6] = 'B' is: "
74             << s1 << "\n\n";
```

Fig. 11.11 | String class test program. (Part 2 of 4.)

```
75
76      // test subscript out of range
77      cout << "Attempt to assign 'd' to s1[30] yields:" << endl;
78      s1[ 30 ] = 'd'; // ERROR: subscript out of range
79      return 0;
80   } // end main
```

```
Conversion (and default) constructor: happy
Conversion (and default) constructor:  birthday
Conversion (and default) constructor:
s1 is "happy"; s2 is " birthday"; s3 is ""

The results of comparing s2 and s1:
s2 == s1 yields false
s2 != s1 yields true
s2 >  s1 yields false
s2 <  s1 yields true
s2 >= s1 yields false
s2 <= s1 yields true

Testing !s3:
s3 is empty; assigning s1 to s3;
operator= called
s3 is "happy"

s1 += s2 yields s1 = happy birthday

s1 += " to you" yields
Conversion (and default) constructor:  to you
Destructor:  to you
s1 = happy birthday to you

Conversion (and default) constructor: happy birthday
Copy constructor: happy birthday
Destructor: happy birthday
The substring of s1 starting at
location 0 for 14 characters, s1(0, 14), is:
happy birthday

Destructor: happy birthday
Conversion (and default) constructor: to you
Copy constructor: to you
Destructor: to you
The substring of s1 starting at
location 15, s1(15), is: to you

Destructor: to you
Copy constructor: happy birthday to you

*s4Ptr = happy birthday to you

assigning *s4Ptr to *s4Ptr
operator= called
Attempted assignment of a String to itself
```

(continued at top of next page...)

Fig. 11.11 | String class test program. (Part 3 of 4.)

```
                                         (...continued from bottom of previous page)
*s4Ptr = happy birthday to you
Destructor: happy birthday to you

s1 after s1[0] = 'H' and s1[6] = 'B' is: Happy Birthday to you

Attempt to assign 'd' to s1[30] yields:
Error: Subscript 30 out of range
```

Fig. 11.11 | String class test program. (Part 4 of 4.)

Overloading the Stream Insertion and Stream Extraction Operators as *friends*

Lines 12–13 (Fig. 11.9) declare the overloaded stream insertion operator function operator<< (defined in Fig. 11.10, lines 170–174) and the overloaded stream extraction operator function operator>> (defined in Fig. 11.10, lines 177–183) as friends of the class. The implementation of operator<< is straightforward. Note that operator>> restricts the total number of characters that can be read into array temp to 99 with setw (line 180); the 100th position is reserved for the string's terminating null character. [*Note:* We did not have this restriction for operator>> in class Array (Figs. 11.6–11.7), because that class's operator>> read one array element at a time and stopped reading values when the end of the array was reached. Object cin does not know how to do this by default for input of character arrays.] Also, note the use of operator= (line 181) to assign the C-style string temp to the String object to which s refers. This statement invokes the conversion constructor to create a temporary String object containing the C-style string; the temporary String is then assigned to s. We could eliminate the overhead of creating the temporary String object here by providing another overloaded assignment operator that receives a parameter of type const char *.

String Conversion Constructor

Line 15 (Fig. 11.9) declares a conversion constructor. This constructor (defined in Fig. 11.10, lines 22–27) takes a const char * argument (that defaults to the empty string; Fig. 11.9, line 15) and initializes a String object containing that same character string. Any single-argument constructor can be thought of as a conversion constructor. As we will see, such constructors are helpful when we are doing any String operation using char * arguments. The conversion constructor can convert a char * string into a String object, which can then be assigned to the target String object. The availability of this conversion constructor means that it is not necessary to supply an overloaded assignment operator for specifically assigning character strings to String objects. The compiler invokes the conversion constructor to create a temporary String object containing the character string; then the overloaded assignment operator is invoked to assign the temporary String object to another String object.

> **Software Engineering Observation 11.8**
>
> *When a conversion constructor is used to perform an implicit conversion, C++ can apply only one implicit constructor call (i.e., a single user-defined conversion) to try to match the needs of another overloaded operator. The compiler will not match an overloaded operator's needs by performing a series of implicit, user-defined conversions.*

The String conversion constructor could be invoked in such a declaration as String s1("happy"). The conversion constructor calculates the length of its character-string argument and assigns it to data member length in the member-initializer list. Then, line 26 calls utility function setString (defined in Fig. 11.10, lines 159–167), which uses new to allocate a sufficient amount of memory to private data member sPtr and uses strcpy to copy the character string into the memory to which sPtr points.[4]

String Copy Constructor

Line 16 in Fig. 11.9 declares a copy constructor (defined in Fig. 11.10, lines 30–35) that initializes a String object by making a copy of an existing String object. As with our class Array (Figs. 11.6–11.7), such copying must be done carefully to avoid the pitfall in which both String objects point to the same dynamically allocated memory. The copy constructor operates similarly to the conversion constructor, except that it simply copies the length member from the source String object to the target String object. Note that the copy constructor calls setString to create new space for the target object's internal character string. If it simply copied the sPtr in the source object to the target object's sPtr, then both objects would point to the same dynamically allocated memory. The first destructor to execute would then delete the dynamically allocated memory, and the other object's sPtr would be undefined (i.e., sPtr would be a dangling pointer), a situation likely to cause a serious runtime error.

String Destructor

Line 17 of Fig. 11.9 declares the String destructor (defined in Fig. 11.10, lines 38–42). The destructor uses delete [] to release the dynamic memory to which sPtr points.

Overloaded Assignment Operator

Line 19 (Fig. 11.9) declares the overloaded assignment operator function operator= (defined in Fig. 11.10, lines 45–59). When the compiler sees an expression like string1 = string2, the compiler generates the function call

```
string1.operator=( string2 );
```

The overloaded assignment operator function operator= tests for self-assignment. If this is a self-assignment, the function does not need to change the object. If this test were omitted, the function would immediately delete the space in the target object and thus lose the character string, such that the pointer would no longer be pointing to valid data—a classic example of a dangling pointer. If there is no self-assignment, the function deletes the memory and copies the length field of the source object to the target object. Then operator= calls setString to create new space for the target object and copy the character

---

4. There is a subtle issue in the implementation of this conversion constructor. As implemented, if a null pointer (i.e., 0) is passed to the constructor, the program will fail. The proper way to implement this constructor would be to detect whether the constructor argument is a null pointer, then "throw an exception." We can make classes more robust in this manner. Also, note that a null pointer (0) is not the same as the empty string (""). A null pointer is a pointer that does not point to anything. An empty string is an actual string that contains only a null character ('\0').

string from the source object to the target object. Whether or not this is a self-assignment, `operator=` returns `*this` to enable cascaded assignments.

Overloaded Addition Assignment Operator
Line 20 of Fig. 11.9 declares the overloaded string-concatenation operator += (defined in Fig. 11.10, lines 62–74). When the compiler sees the expression s1 += s2 (line 40 of Fig. 11.11), the compiler generates the member-function call

```
s1.operator+=( s2 )
```

Function operator+= calculates the combined length of the concatenated string and stores it in local variable newLength, then creates a temporary pointer (tempPtr) and allocates a new character array in which the concatenated string will be stored. Next, operator+= uses strcpy to copy the original character strings from sPtr and right.sPtr into the memory to which tempPtr points. Note that the location into which strcpy will copy the first character of right.sPtr is determined by the pointer-arithmetic calculation tempPtr + length. This calculation indicates that the first character of right.sPtr should be placed at location length in the array to which tempPtr points. Next, operator+= uses delete [] to release the space occupied by this object's original character string, assigns tempPtr to sPtr so that this String object points to the new character string, assigns newLength to length so that this String object contains the new string length and returns *this as a const String & to enable cascading of += operators.

Do we need a second overloaded concatenation operator to allow concatenation of a String and a char *? No. The const char * conversion constructor converts a C-style string into a temporary String object, which then matches the existing overloaded concatenation operator. This is exactly what the compiler does when it encounters line 44 in Fig. 11.11. Again, C++ can perform such conversions only one level deep to facilitate a match. C++ can also perform an implicit compiler-defined conversion between fundamental types before it performs the conversion between a fundamental type and a class. Note that, when a temporary String object is created in this case, the conversion constructor and the destructor are called (see the output resulting from line 45, s1 += " to you", in Fig. 11.11). This is an example of function-call overhead that is hidden from the client of the class when temporary class objects are created and destroyed during implicit conversions. Similar overhead is generated by copy constructors in call-by-value parameter passing and in returning class objects by value.

Performance Tip 11.2
*Overloading the += concatenation operator with an additional version that takes a single argument of type const char * executes more efficiently than having only a version that takes a String argument. Without the const char * version of the += operator, a const char * argument would first be converted to a String object with class String's conversion constructor, then the += operator that receives a String argument would be called to perform the concatenation.*

Software Engineering Observation 11.9
Using implicit conversions with overloaded operators, rather than overloading operators for many different operand types, often requires less code, which makes a class easier to modify, maintain and debug.

Overloaded Negation Operator
Line 22 of Fig. 11.9 declares the overloaded negation operator (defined in Fig. 11.10, lines 77–80). This operator determines whether an object of our String class is empty. For example, when the compiler sees the expression !string1, it generates the function call

```
string1.operator!()
```

This function simply returns the result of testing whether length is equal to zero.

Overloaded Equality and Relational Operators
Lines 23–24 of Fig. 11.9 declare the overloaded equality operator (defined in Fig. 11.10, lines 83–86) and the overloaded less-than operator (defined in Fig. 11.10, lines 89–92) for class String. These are similar, so let us discuss only one example, namely, overloading the == operator. When the compiler sees the expression string1 == string2, the compiler generates the member-function call

```
string1.operator==( string2 )
```

which returns true if string1 is equal to string2. Each of these operators uses function strcmp (from <cstring>) to compare the character strings in the String objects. Many C++ programmers advocate using some of the overloaded operator functions to implement others. So, the !=, >, <= and >= operators are implemented (Fig. 11.9, lines 27–48) in terms of operator== and operator<. For example, overloaded function operator>= (implemented at lines 45–48 in the header file) uses the overloaded < operator to determine whether one String object is greater than or equal to another. Note that the operator functions for !=, >, <= and >= are defined in the header file. The compiler inlines these definitions to eliminate the overhead of the extra function calls.

 Software Engineering Observation 11.10

By implementing member functions using previously defined member functions, the programmer reuses code to reduce the amount of code that must be written and maintained.

Overloaded Subscript Operators
Lines 50–51 in the header file declare two overloaded subscript operators (defined in Fig. 11.10, lines 95–106 and 109–120, respectively)—one for non-const Strings and one for const Strings. When the compiler sees an expression like string1[0], the compiler generates the member-function call

```
string1.operator[]( 0 )
```

(using the appropriate version of operator[] based on whether the String is const). Each implementation of operator[] first validates the subscript to ensure that it is in range. If the subscript is out of range, each function prints an error message and terminates the program with a call to exit.[5] If the subscript is in range, the non-const version of operator[] returns a char & to the appropriate character of the String object; this char & may be used as an *lvalue* to modify the designated character of the String object. The const version of operator[] returns the appropriate character of the String object; this can be used only as an *rvalue* to read the value of the character.

---

5. Again, it is more appropriate when a subscript is out of range to "throw an exception" indicating the out-of-range subscript.

Error-Prevention Tip 11.2

Returning a non-const char reference from an overloaded subscript operator in a String class is dangerous. For example, the client could use this reference to insert a null ('\0') anywhere in the string.

Overloaded Function Call Operator

Line 52 of Fig. 11.9 declares the overloaded function call operator (defined in Fig. 11.10, lines 123–150). We overload this operator to select a substring from a String. The two integer parameters specify the start location and the length of the substring being selected from the String. If the start location is out of range or the substring length is negative, the operator simply returns an empty String. If the substring length is 0, then the substring is selected to the end of the String object. For example, suppose string1 is a String object containing the string "AEIOU". For the expression string1(2, 2), the compiler generates the member-function call

```
string1.operator()( 2, 2 )
```

When this call executes, it produces a String object containing the string "IO" and returns a copy of that object.

Overloading the function call operator () is powerful, because functions can take arbitrarily long and complex parameter lists. So we can use this capability for many interesting purposes. One such use of the function call operator is an alternate array-subscripting notation: Instead of using C's awkward double-square-bracket notation for pointer-based two-dimensional arrays, such as in a[b][c], some programmers prefer to overload the function call operator to enable the notation a(b, c). The overloaded function call operator must be a non-static member function. This operator is used only when the "function name" is an object of class String.

String Member Function getLength

Line 53 in Fig. 11.9 declares function getLength (defined in Fig. 11.10, lines 153–156), which returns the length of a String.

Notes on Our String Class

At this point, you should step through the code in main, examine the output window and check each use of an overloaded operator. As you study the output, pay special attention to the implicit constructor calls that are generated to create temporary String objects throughout the program. Many of these calls introduce additional overhead into the program that can be avoided if the class provides overloaded operators that take char * arguments. However, additional operator functions can make the class harder to maintain, modify and debug.

11.11 Overloading ++ and --

The prefix and postfix versions of the increment and decrement operators can all be overloaded. We will see how the compiler distinguishes between the prefix version and the postfix version of an increment or decrement operator.

To overload the increment operator to allow both prefix and postfix increment usage, each overloaded operator function must have a distinct signature, so that the compiler will be able to determine which version of ++ is intended. The prefix versions are overloaded exactly as any other prefix unary operator would be.

Overloading the Prefix Increment Operator

Suppose, for example, that we want to add 1 to the day in Date object d1. When the compiler sees the preincrementing expression ++d1, the compiler generates the member-function call

```
d1.operator++()
```

The prototype for this operator function would be

```
Date &operator++();
```

If the prefix increment operator is implemented as a global function, then, when the compiler sees the expression ++d1, the compiler generates the function call

```
operator++( d1 )
```

The prototype for this operator function would be declared in the Date class as

```
Date &operator++( Date & );
```

Overloading the Postfix Increment Operator

Overloading the postfix increment operator presents a challenge, because the compiler must be able to distinguish between the signatures of the overloaded prefix and postfix increment operator functions. The convention that has been adopted in C++ is that, when the compiler sees the postincrementing expression d1++, it generates the member-function call

```
d1.operator++( 0 )
```

The prototype for this function is

```
Date operator++( int )
```

The argument 0 is strictly a "dummy value" that enables the compiler to distinguish between the prefix and postfix increment operator functions.

If the postfix increment is implemented as a global function, then, when the compiler sees the expression d1++, the compiler generates the function call

```
operator++( d1, 0 )
```

The prototype for this function would be

```
Date operator++( Date &, int );
```

Once again, the 0 argument is used by the compiler to distinguish between the prefix and postfix increment operators implemented as global functions. Note that the postfix increment operator returns Date objects by value, whereas the prefix increment operator returns Date objects by reference, because the postfix increment operator typically returns a temporary object that contains the original value of the object before the increment occurred. C++ treats such objects as *rvalues*, which cannot be used on the left side of an assignment. The prefix increment operator returns the actual incremented object with its new value. Such an object can be used as an *lvalue* in a continuing expression.

Performance Tip 11.3

The extra object that is created by the postfix increment (or decrement) operator can result in a significant performance problem—especially when the operator is used in a loop. For this reason, you should use the postfix increment (or decrement) operator only when the logic of the program requires postincremnting (or postdecrementing).

Everything stated in this section for overloading prefix and postfix increment operators applies to overloading predecrement and postdecrement operators. Next, we examine a `Date` class with overloaded prefix and postfix increment operators.

11.12 Case Study: A Date Class

The program of Figs. 11.12–11.14 demonstrates a `Date` class. The class uses overloaded prefix and postfix increment operators to add 1 to the day in a `Date` object, while causing appropriate increments to the month and year if necessary. The `Date` header file (Fig. 11.12) specifies that `Date`'s `public` interface includes an overloaded stream insertion operator (line 11), a default constructor (line 13), a `setDate` function (line 14), an overloaded prefix increment operator (line 15), an overloaded postfix increment operator (line 16), an overloaded `+=` addition assignment operator (line 17), a function to test for leap years (line 18) and a function to determine whether a day is the last day of the month (line 19).

```
1    // Fig. 11.12: Date.h
2    // Date class definition.
3    #ifndef DATE_H
4    #define DATE_H
5
6    #include <iostream>
7    using std::ostream;
8
9    class Date
10   {
11      friend ostream &operator<<( ostream &, const Date & );
12   public:
13      Date( int m = 1, int d = 1, int y = 1900 ); // default constructor
14      void setDate( int, int, int ); // set month, day, year
15      Date &operator++(); // prefix increment operator
16      Date operator++( int ); // postfix increment operator
17      const Date &operator+=( int ); // add days, modify object
18      bool leapYear( int ) const; // is date in a leap year?
19      bool endOfMonth( int ) const; // is date at the end of month?
20   private:
21      int month;
22      int day;
23      int year;
24
25      static const int days[]; // array of days per month
26      void helpIncrement(); // utility function for incrementing date
27   }; // end class Date
28
29   #endif
```

Fig. 11.12 | `Date` class definition with overloaded increment operators.

```
 1   // Fig. 11.13: Date.cpp
 2   // Date class member-function definitions.
 3   #include <iostream>
 4   #include "Date.h"
 5
 6   // initialize static member at file scope; one classwide copy
 7   const int Date::days[] =
 8      { 0, 31, 28, 31, 30, 31, 30, 31, 31, 30, 31, 30, 31 };
 9
10   // Date constructor
11   Date::Date( int m, int d, int y )
12   {
13      setDate( m, d, y );
14   } // end Date constructor
15
16   // set month, day and year
17   void Date::setDate( int mm, int dd, int yy )
18   {
19      month = ( mm >= 1 && mm <= 12 ) ? mm : 1;
20      year = ( yy >= 1900 && yy <= 2100 ) ? yy : 1900;
21
22      // test for a leap year
23      if ( month == 2 && leapYear( year ) )
24         day = ( dd >= 1 && dd <= 29 ) ? dd : 1;
25      else
26         day = ( dd >= 1 && dd <= days[ month ] ) ? dd : 1;
27   } // end function setDate
28
29   // overloaded prefix increment operator
30   Date &Date::operator++()
31   {
32      helpIncrement(); // increment date
33      return *this; // reference return to create an lvalue
34   } // end function operator++
35
36   // overloaded postfix increment operator; note that the
37   // dummy integer parameter does not have a parameter name
38   Date Date::operator++( int )
39   {
40      Date temp = *this; // hold current state of object
41      helpIncrement();
42
43      // return unincremented, saved, temporary object
44      return temp; // value return; not a reference return
45   } // end function operator++
46
47   // add specified number of days to date
48   const Date &Date::operator+=( int additionalDays )
49   {
50      for ( int i = 0; i < additionalDays; i++ )
51         helpIncrement();
52
```

Fig. 11.13 | Date class member- and friend-function definitions. (Part 1 of 2.)

```
53       return *this; // enables cascading
54    } // end function operator+=
55
56    // if the year is a leap year, return true; otherwise, return false
57    bool Date::leapYear( int testYear ) const
58    {
59       if ( testYear % 400 == 0 ||
60          ( testYear % 100 != 0 && testYear % 4 == 0 ) )
61          return true; // a leap year
62       else
63          return false; // not a leap year
64    } // end function leapYear
65
66    // determine whether the day is the last day of the month
67    bool Date::endOfMonth( int testDay ) const
68    {
69       if ( month == 2 && leapYear( year ) )
70          return testDay == 29; // last day of Feb. in leap year
71       else
72          return testDay == days[ month ];
73    } // end function endOfMonth
74
75    // function to help increment the date
76    void Date::helpIncrement()
77    {
78       // day is not end of month
79       if ( !endOfMonth( day ) )
80          day++; // increment day
81       else
82          if ( month < 12 ) // day is end of month and month < 12
83          {
84             month++; // increment month
85             day = 1; // first day of new month
86          } // end if
87          else // last day of year
88          {
89             year++; // increment year
90             month = 1; // first month of new year
91             day = 1; // first day of new month
92          } // end else
93    } // end function helpIncrement
94
95    // overloaded output operator
96    ostream &operator<<( ostream &output, const Date &d )
97    {
98       static char *monthName[ 13 ] = { "", "January", "February",
99          "March", "April", "May", "June", "July", "August",
100         "September", "October", "November", "December" };
101      output << monthName[ d.month ] << ' ' << d.day << ", " << d.year;
102      return output; // enables cascading
103   } // end function operator<<
```

Fig. 11.13 | Date class member- and friend-function definitions. (Part 2 of 2.)

```
1    // Fig. 11.14: fig11_14.cpp
2    // Date class test program.
3    #include <iostream>
4    using std::cout;
5    using std::endl;
6
7    #include "Date.h" // Date class definition
8
9    int main()
10   {
11       Date d1; // defaults to January 1, 1900
12       Date d2( 12, 27, 1992 ); // December 27, 1992
13       Date d3( 0, 99, 8045 ); // invalid date
14
15       cout << "d1 is " << d1 << "\nd2 is " << d2 << "\nd3 is " << d3;
16       cout << "\n\nd2 += 7 is " << ( d2 += 7 );
17
18       d3.setDate( 2, 28, 1992 );
19       cout << "\n\n  d3 is " << d3;
20       cout << "\n++d3 is " << ++d3 << " (leap year allows 29th)";
21
22       Date d4( 7, 13, 2002 );
23
24       cout << "\n\nTesting the prefix increment operator:\n"
25            << "  d4 is " << d4 << endl;
26       cout << "++d4 is " << ++d4 << endl;
27       cout << "  d4 is " << d4;
28
29       cout << "\n\nTesting the postfix increment operator:\n"
30            << "  d4 is " << d4 << endl;
31       cout << "d4++ is " << d4++ << endl;
32       cout << "  d4 is " << d4 << endl;
33       return 0;
34   } // end main
```

```
d1 is January 1, 1900
d2 is December 27, 1992
d3 is January 1, 1900

d2 += 7 is January 3, 1993

  d3 is February 28, 1992
++d3 is February 29, 1992 (leap year allows 29th)

Testing the prefix increment operator:
  d4 is July 13, 2002
++d4 is July 14, 2002
  d4 is July 14, 2002

Testing the postfix increment operator:
  d4 is July 14, 2002
d4++ is July 14, 2002
  d4 is July 15, 2002
```

Fig. 11.14 | Date class test program.

Function main (Fig. 11.14) creates three Date objects (lines 11–13)—d1 is initialized by default to January 1, 1900; d2 is initialized to December 27, 1992; and d3 is initialized to an invalid date. The Date constructor (defined in Fig. 11.13, lines 11–14) calls setDate to validate the month, day and year specified. An invalid month is set to 1, an invalid year is set to 1900 and an invalid day is set to 1.

Lines 15–16 of main output each of the constructed Date objects, using the overloaded stream insertion operator (defined in Fig. 11.13, lines 96–103). Line 16 of main uses the overloaded operator += to add seven days to d2. Line 18 uses function setDate to set d3 to February 28, 1992, which is a leap year. Then, line 20 preincrements d3 to show that the date increments properly to February 29. Next, line 22 creates a Date object, d4, which is initialized with the date July 13, 2002. Then line 26 increments d4 by 1 with the overloaded prefix increment operator. Lines 24–27 output d4 before and after the preincrement operation to confirm that it worked correctly. Finally, line 31 increments d4 with the overloaded postfix increment operator. Lines 29–32 output d4 before and after the postincrement operation to confirm that it worked correctly.

Overloading the prefix increment operator is straightforward. The prefix increment operator (defined in Fig. 11.13, lines 30–34) calls utility function helpIncrement (defined in Fig. 11.13, lines 76–93) to increment the date. This function deals with "wraparounds" or "carries" that occur when we increment the last day of the month. These carries require incrementing the month. If the month is already 12, then the year must also be incremented and the month must be set to 1. Function helpIncrement uses function endOfMonth to increment the day correctly.

The overloaded prefix increment operator returns a reference to the current Date object (i.e., the one that was just incremented). This occurs because the current object, *this, is returned as a Date &. This enables a preincremented Date object to be used as an *lvalue*, which is how the built-in prefix increment operator works for fundamental types.

Overloading the postfix increment operator (defined in Fig. 11.13, lines 38–45) is trickier. To emulate the effect of the postincrement, we must return an unincremented copy of the Date object. For example, that int variable x has the value 7, the statement

```
cout << x++ << endl;
```

outputs the original value of variable x. So we'd like our postfix increment operator to operate the same way on a Date object. On entry to operator++, we save the current object (*this) in temp (line 40). Next, we call helpIncrement to increment the current Date object. Then, line 44 returns the unincremented copy of the object previously stored in temp. Note that this function cannot return a reference to the local Date object temp, because a local variable is destroyed when the function in which it is declared exits. Thus, declaring the return type to this function as Date & would return a reference to an object that no longer exists. Returning a reference (or a pointer) to a local variable is a common error for which most compilers will issue a warning.

11.13 Standard Library Class string

In this chapter, you learned that you can build a String class (Figs. 11.9–11.11) that is better than the C-style, char * strings that C++ absorbed from C. You also learned that you can build an Array class (Figs. 11.6–11.8) that is better than the C-style, pointer-based arrays that C++ absorbed from C.

Building useful, reusable classes such as `String` and `Array` takes work. However, once such classes are tested and debugged, they can be reused by you, your colleagues, your company, many companies, an entire industry or even many industries (if they are placed in public or for-sale libraries). The designers of C++ did exactly that, building class `string` (which we have been using since Chapter 3) and class template `vector` (which we introduced in Chapter 7) into standard C++. These classes are available to anyone building applications with C++. The C++ Standard Library provides several predefined class templates for use in your programs.

To close this chapter, we redo our `String` (Figs. 11.9–11.11) example, using the standard C++ `string` class. We rework our example to demonstrate similar functionality provided by standard class `string`. We also demonstrate three member functions of standard class `string`—empty, `substr` and `at`—that were not part of our `String` example. Function `empty` determines whether a `string` is empty, function `substr` returns a `string` that represents a portion of an existing `string` and function `at` returns the character at a specific index in a `string` (after checking that the index is in range).

Standard Library Class *string*

The program of Fig. 11.15 reimplements the program of Fig. 11.11, using standard class `string`. As you will see in this example, class `string` provides all the functionality of our class `String` presented in Figs. 11.9–11.10. Class `string` is defined in header `<string>` (line 7) and belongs to namespace `std` (line 8).

```cpp
 1   // Fig. 11.15: fig11_15.cpp
 2   // Standard Library string class test program.
 3   #include <iostream>
 4   using std::cout;
 5   using std::endl;
 6
 7   #include <string>
 8   using std::string;
 9
10   int main()
11   {
12      string s1( "happy" );
13      string s2( " birthday" );
14      string s3;
15
16      // test overloaded equality and relational operators
17      cout << "s1 is \"" << s1 << "\"; s2 is \"" << s2
18         << "\"; s3 is \"" << s3 << '\"'
19         << "\n\nThe results of comparing s2 and s1:"
20         << "\ns2 == s1 yields " << ( s2 == s1 ? "true" : "false" )
21         << "\ns2 != s1 yields " << ( s2 != s1 ? "true" : "false" )
22         << "\ns2 >  s1 yields " << ( s2 > s1 ? "true" : "false" )
23         << "\ns2 <  s1 yields " << ( s2 < s1 ? "true" : "false" )
24         << "\ns2 >= s1 yields " << ( s2 >= s1 ? "true" : "false" )
25         << "\ns2 <= s1 yields " << ( s2 <= s1 ? "true" : "false" );
26
```

Fig. 11.15 | Standard Library class `string`. (Part 1 of 3.)

```
27      // test string member-function empty
28      cout << "\n\nTesting s3.empty():" << endl;
29
30      if ( s3.empty() )
31      {
32         cout << "s3 is empty; assigning s1 to s3;" << endl;
33         s3 = s1; // assign s1 to s3
34         cout << "s3 is \"" << s3 << "\"";
35      } // end if
36
37      // test overloaded string concatenation operator
38      cout << "\n\ns1 += s2 yields s1 = ";
39      s1 += s2; // test overloaded concatenation
40      cout << s1;
41
42      // test overloaded string concatenation operator with C-style string
43      cout << "\n\ns1 += \" to you\" yields" << endl;
44      s1 += " to you";
45      cout << "s1 = " << s1 << "\n\n";
46
47      // test string member function substr
48      cout << "The substring of s1 starting at location 0 for\n"
49         << "14 characters, s1.substr(0, 14), is:\n"
50         << s1.substr( 0, 14 ) << "\n\n";
51
52      // test substr "to-end-of-string" option
53      cout << "The substring of s1 starting at\n"
54         << "location 15, s1.substr(15), is:\n"
55         << s1.substr( 15 ) << endl;
56
57      // test copy constructor
58      string *s4Ptr = new string( s1 );
59      cout << "\n*s4Ptr = " << *s4Ptr << "\n\n";
60
61      // test assignment (=) operator with self-assignment
62      cout << "assigning *s4Ptr to *s4Ptr" << endl;
63      *s4Ptr = *s4Ptr;
64      cout << "*s4Ptr = " << *s4Ptr << endl;
65
66      // test destructor
67      delete s4Ptr;
68
69      // test using subscript operator to create lvalue
70      s1[ 0 ] = 'H';
71      s1[ 6 ] = 'B';
72      cout << "\ns1 after s1[0] = 'H' and s1[6] = 'B' is: "
73         << s1 << "\n\n";
74
75      // test subscript out of range with string member function "at"
76      cout << "Attempt to assign 'd' to s1.at( 30 ) yields:" << endl;
77      s1.at( 30 ) = 'd'; // ERROR: subscript out of range
78      return 0;
79   } // end main
```

Fig. 11.15 | Standard Library class `string`. (Part 2 of 3.)

```
s1 is "happy"; s2 is " birthday"; s3 is ""

The results of comparing s2 and s1:
s2 == s1 yields false
s2 != s1 yields true
s2 >  s1 yields false
s2 <  s1 yields true
s2 >= s1 yields false
s2 <= s1 yields true

Testing s3.empty():
s3 is empty; assigning s1 to s3;
s3 is "happy"

s1 += s2 yields s1 = happy birthday

s1 += " to you" yields
s1 = happy birthday to you

The substring of s1 starting at location 0 for
14 characters, s1.substr(0, 14), is:
happy birthday

The substring of s1 starting at
location 15, s1.substr(15), is:
to you

*s4Ptr = happy birthday to you

assigning *s4Ptr to *s4Ptr
*s4Ptr = happy birthday to you

s1 after s1[0] = 'H' and s1[6] = 'B' is: Happy Birthday to you

Attempt to assign 'd' to s1.at( 30 ) yields:

abnormal program termination
```

Fig. 11.15 | Standard Library class `string`. (Part 3 of 3.)

Lines 12–14 create three `string` objects—s1 is initialized with the literal "happy", s2 is initialized with the literal " birthday" and s3 uses the default string constructor to create an empty `string`. Lines 17–18 output these three objects, using `cout` and operator `<<`, which the `string` class designers overloaded to handle `string` objects. Then lines 19–25 show the results of comparing s2 to s1 by using class `string`'s overloaded equality and relational operators.

Our class `String` (Figs. 11.9–11.10) provided an overloaded `operator!` that tested a `String` to determine whether it was empty. Standard class `string` does not provide this functionality as an overloaded operator; instead, it provides member function *empty*, which we demonstrate on line 30. Member function `empty` returns `true` if the `string` is empty; otherwise, it returns `false`.

Line 33 demonstrates class `string`'s overloaded assignment operator by assigning s1 to s3. Line 34 outputs s3 to demonstrate that the assignment worked correctly.

Line 39 demonstrates class `string`'s overloaded += operator for string concatenation. In this case, the contents of s2 are appended to s1. Then line 40 outputs the resulting string that is stored in s1. Line 44 demonstrates that a C-style string literal can be appended to a `string` object by using operator +=. Line 45 displays the result.

Our class `String` (Figs. 11.9–11.10) provided overloaded `operator()` to obtain substrings. Standard class `string` does not provide this functionality as an overloaded operator; instead, it provides member function `substr` (lines 50 and 55). The call to `substr` in line 50 obtains a 14-character substring (specified by the second argument) of s1 starting at position 0 (specified by the first argument). The call to `substr` in line 55 obtains a substring starting from position 15 of s1. When the second argument is not specified, `substr` returns the remainder of the `string` on which it is called.

Line 58 dynamically allocates a `string` object and initializes it with a copy of s1. This results in a call to class `string`'s copy constructor. Line 63 uses class `string`'s overloaded = operator to demonstrate that it handles self-assignment properly.

Lines 70–71 used class `string`'s overloaded [] operator to create *lvalues* that enable new characters to replace existing characters in s1. Line 73 outputs the new value of s1. In our class `String` (Figs. 11.9–11.10), the overloaded [] operator performed bounds checking to determine whether the subscript it received as an argument was a valid subscript in the string. If the subscript was invalid, the operator printed an error message and terminated the program. Standard class `string`'s overloaded [] operator does not perform any bounds checking. Therefore, the programmer must ensure that operations using standard class `string`'s overloaded [] operator do not accidentally manipulate elements outside the bounds of the `string`. Standard class `string` does provide bounds checking in its member function `at`, which "throws an exception" if its argument is an invalid subscript. By default, this causes a C++ program to terminate. If the subscript is valid, function `at` returns the character at the specified location as a modifiable *lvalue* or an unmodifiable *lvalue* (i.e., a `const` reference), depending on the context in which the call appears. Line 77 demonstrates a call to function `at` with an invalid subscript.

11.14 explicit Constructors

In Section 11.8 and Section 11.9, we discussed that any single-argument constructor can be used by the compiler to perform an implicit conversion—the type received by the constructor is converted to an object of the class in which the constructor is defined. The conversion is automatic and the programmer need not use a cast operator. In some situations, implicit conversions are undesirable or error-prone. For example, our `Array` class in Fig. 11.6 defines a constructor that takes a single `int` argument. The intent of this constructor is to create an `Array` object containing the number of elements specified by the `int` argument. However, this constructor can be misused by the compiler to perform an implicit conversion.

 Common Programming Error 11.9

Unfortunately, the compiler might use implicit conversions in cases that you do not expect, resulting in ambiguous expressions that generate compilation errors or resulting in execution-time logic errors.

Accidentally Using a Single-Argument Constructor as a Conversion Constructor
The program (Fig. 11.16) uses the Array class of Figs. 11.6–11.7 to demonstrate an improper implicit conversion.

Line 13 in main instantiates Array object integers1 and calls the single argument constructor with the int value 7 to specify the number of elements in the Array. Recall from Fig. 11.7 that the Array constructor that receives an int argument initializes all the array elements to 0. Line 14 calls function outputArray (defined in lines 20–24), which receives as its argument a const Array & to an Array. The function outputs the number of elements in its Array argument and the contents of the Array. In this case, the size of the Array is 7, so seven 0s are output.

Line 15 calls function outputArray with the int value 3 as an argument. However, this program does not contain a function called outputArray that takes an int argument. So, the compiler determines whether class Array provides a conversion constructor that can convert an int into an Array. Since any constructor that receives a single argument is considered to be a conversion constructor, the compiler assumes the Array constructor that receives a single int is a conversion constructor and uses it to convert the argument 3 into a temporary Array object that contains three elements. Then, the compiler passes the

```cpp
// Fig. 11.16: Fig11_16.cpp
// Driver for simple class Array.
#include <iostream>
using std::cout;
using std::endl;

#include "Array.h"

void outputArray( const Array & ); // prototype

int main()
{
   Array integers1( 7 ); // 7-element array
   outputArray( integers1 ); // output Array integers1
   outputArray( 3 ); // convert 3 to an Array and output Array's contents
   return 0;
} // end main

// print Array contents
void outputArray( const Array &arrayToOutput )
{
   cout << "The Array received has " << arrayToOutput.getSize()
      << " elements. The contents are:\n" << arrayToOutput << endl;
} // end outputArray
```

```
The Array received has 7 elements. The contents are:
           0           0           0           0
           0           0           0

The Array received has 3 elements. The contents are:
           0           0           0
```

Fig. 11.16 | Single-argument constructors and implicit conversions.

temporary `Array` object to function `outputArray` to output the `Array`'s contents. Thus, even though we do not explicitly provide an `outputArray` function that receives an `int` argument, the compiler is able to compile line 15. The output shows the contents of the three-element `Array` containing 0s.

Preventing Accidental Use of a Single-Argument Constructor as a Conversion Constructor

C++ provides the keyword **explicit** to suppress implicit conversions via conversion constructors when such conversions should not be allowed. A constructor that is declared explicit cannot be used in an implicit conversion. Figure 11.17 declares an `explicit` constructor in class `Array`. The only modification to `Array.h` was the addition of the key-

```
1   // Fig. 11.17: Array.h
2   // Array class for storing arrays of integers.
3   #ifndef ARRAY_H
4   #define ARRAY_H
5
6   #include <iostream>
7   using std::ostream;
8   using std::istream;
9
10  class Array
11  {
12     friend ostream &operator<<( ostream &, const Array & );
13     friend istream &operator>>( istream &, Array & );
14  public:
15     explicit Array( int = 10 ); // default constructor
16     Array( const Array & ); // copy constructor
17     ~Array(); // destructor
18     int getSize() const; // return size
19
20     const Array &operator=( const Array & ); // assignment operator
21     bool operator==( const Array & ) const; // equality operator
22
23     // inequality operator; returns opposite of == operator
24     bool operator!=( const Array &right ) const
25     {
26        return ! ( *this == right ); // invokes Array::operator==
27     } // end function operator!=
28
29     // subscript operator for non-const objects returns lvalue
30     int &operator[]( int );
31
32     // subscript operator for const objects returns rvalue
33     const int &operator[]( int ) const;
34  private:
35     int size; // pointer-based array size
36     int *ptr; // pointer to first element of pointer-based array
37  }; // end class Array
38
39  #endif
```

Fig. 11.17 | Array class definition with `explicit` constructor.

word explicit to the declaration of the single-argument constructor at line 15. No modifications are required to the source-code file containing class Array's member-function definitions.

Figure 11.18 presents a slightly modified version of the program in Fig. 11.16. When this program is compiled, the compiler produces an error message indicating that the integer value passed to outputArray at line 15 cannot be converted to a const Array &. The compiler error message is shown in the output window. Line 16 demonstrates how the explicit constructor can be used to create a temporary Array of 3 elements and pass it to function outputArray.

Common Programming Error 11.10

Attempting to invoke an explicit constructor for an implicit conversion is a compilation error.

Common Programming Error 11.11

Using the explicit keyword on data members or member functions other than a single-argument constructor is a compilation error.

```cpp
1   // Fig. 11.18: Fig11_18.cpp
2   // Driver for simple class Array.
3   #include <iostream>
4   using std::cout;
5   using std::endl;
6
7   #include "Array.h"
8
9   void outputArray( const Array & ); // prototype
10
11  int main()
12  {
13     Array integers1( 7 ); // 7-element array
14     outputArray( integers1 ); // output Array integers1
15     outputArray( 3 ); // convert 3 to an Array and output Array's contents
16     outputArray( Array( 3 ) ); // explicit single-argument constructor call
17     return 0;
18  } // end main
19
20  // print array contents
21  void outputArray( const Array &arrayToOutput )
22  {
23     cout << "The Array received has " << arrayToOutput.getSize()
24        << " elements. The contents are:\n" << arrayToOutput << endl;
25  } // end outputArray
```

```
c:\scpphtp5_examples\ch11\Fig11_17_18\Fig11_18.cpp(15) : error C2664:
'outputArray' : cannot convert parameter 1 from 'int' to 'const Array &'
        Reason: cannot convert from 'int' to 'const Array'
        Constructor for class 'Array' is declared 'explicit'
```

Fig. 11.18 | Demonstrating an explicit constructor.

Error-Prevention Tip 11.3

Use the explicit *keyword on single-argument constructors that should not be used by the compiler to perform implicit conversions.*

11.15 Wrap-Up

In this chapter, you learned how to build more robust classes by defining overloaded operators that enable programmers to treat objects of your classes as if they were fundamental C++ data types. We presented the basic concepts of operator overloading, as well as several restrictions that the C++ standard places on overloaded operators. You learned reasons for implementing overloaded operators as member functions or as global functions. We discussed the differences between overloading unary and binary operators as member functions and global functions. With global functions, we showed how to enable objects of our classes to be input and output using the overloaded stream extraction and stream insertion operators, respectively. We showed a special syntax that is required to differentiate between the prefix and postfix versions of the increment (++) operator. We also demonstrated standard C++ class string, which makes extensive use of overloaded operators to create a robust, reusable class that can replace C-style, pointer-based strings. Finally, you learned how to use keyword explicit to prevent the compiler from using a single-argument constructor to perform implicit conversions. In the next chapter, we continue our discussion of classes by introducing a form of software reuse called inheritance. We will see that classes often share common attributes and behaviors. In such cases, it is possible to define those attributes and behaviors in a common "base" class and "inherit" those capabilities into new class definitions.

Summary

- C++ enables the programmer to overload most operators to be sensitive to the context in which they are used—the compiler generates the appropriate code based on the context (in particular, the types of the operands).

- Many of C++'s operators can be overloaded to work with user-defined types.

- One example of an overloaded operator built into C++ is operator <<, which is used both as the stream insertion operator and as the bitwise left-shift operator. Similarly, >> is also overloaded; it is used both as the stream extraction operator and as the bitwise right-shift operator. Both of these operators are overloaded in the C++ Standard Library.

- The C++ language itself overloads + and -. These operators perform differently, depending on their context in integer arithmetic, floating-point arithmetic and pointer arithmetic.

- The jobs performed by overloaded operators can also be performed by function calls, but operator notation is often clearer and more familiar to programmers.

- An operator is overloaded by writing a non-static member-function definition or global function definition in which the function name is the keyword operator followed by the symbol for the operator being overloaded.

- When operators are overloaded as member functions, they must be non-static, because they must be called on an object of the class and operate on that object.

- To use an operator on class objects, that operator *must* be overloaded—with three exceptions: the assignment operator (=), the address operator (&) and the comma operator (,).

- You cannot change the precedence and associativity of an operator by overloading.
- You cannot change the "arity" of an operator (i.e., the number of operands an operator takes).
- You cannot create new operators; only existing operators can be overloaded.
- You cannot change the meaning of how an operator works on objects of fundamental types.
- Overloading an assignment operator and an addition operator for a class does not imply that the += operator is also overloaded. Such behavior can be achieved only by explicitly overloading operator += for that class.
- Operator functions can be member functions or global functions; global functions are often made friends for performance reasons. Member functions use the this pointer implicitly to obtain one of their class object arguments (the left operand for binary operators). Arguments for both operands of a binary operator must be explicitly listed in a global function call.
- When overloading (), [], -> or any of the assignment operators, the operator overloading function must be declared as a class member. For the other operators, the operator overloading functions can be class members or global functions.
- When an operator function is implemented as a member function, the leftmost (or only) operand must be an object (or a reference to an object) of the operator's class.
- If the left operand must be an object of a different class or a fundamental type, this operator function must be implemented as a global function.
- A global operator function can be made a friend of a class if that function must access private or protected members of that class directly.
- The overloaded stream insertion operator (<<) is used in an expression in which the left operand has type ostream &. For this reason, it must be overloaded as a global function. To be a member function, operator << would have to be a member of the ostream class, but this is not possible, since we are not allowed to modify C++ Standard Library classes. Similarly, the overloaded stream extraction operator (>>) must be a global function.
- Another reason to choose a global function to overload an operator is to enable the operator to be commutative.
- When used with cin and strings, setw restricts the number of characters read to the number of characters specified by its argument.
- istream member function ignore discards the specified number of characters in the input stream (one character by default).
- Overloaded input and output operators are declared as friends if they need to access non-public class members directly for performance reasons.
- A unary operator for a class can be overloaded as a non-static member function with no arguments or as a global function with one argument; that argument must be either an object of the class or a reference to an object of the class.
- Member functions that implement overloaded operators must be non-static so that they can access the non-static data in each object of the class.
- A binary operator can be overloaded as a non-static member function with one argument or as a global function with two arguments (one of those arguments must be either a class object or a reference to a class object).
- A copy constructor initializes a new object of a class by copying the members of an existing object of that class. When objects of a class contain dynamically allocated memory, the class should provide a copy constructor to ensure that each copy of an object has its own separate copy of the dynamically allocated memory. Typically, such a class would also provide a destructor and an overloaded assignment operator.

- The implementation of member function `operator=` should test for self-assignment, in which an object is being assigned to itself.

- The compiler calls the `const` version of `operator[]` when the subscript operator is used on a `const` object and calls the non-`const` version of the operator when it is used on a non-`const` object.

- The array subscript operator (`[]`) is not restricted for use with arrays. It can be used to select elements from other types of container classes. Also, with overloading, the index values no longer need to be integers; characters or strings could be used, for example.

- The compiler cannot know in advance how to convert among user-defined types, and between user-defined types and fundamental types, so the programmer must specify how to do this. Such conversions can be performed with conversion constructors—single-argument constructors that turn objects of other types (including fundamental types) into objects of a particular class.

- A conversion operator (also called a cast operator) can be used to convert an object of one class into an object of another class or into an object of a fundamental type. Such a conversion operator must be a non-`static` member function. Overloaded cast-operator functions can be defined for converting objects of user-defined types into fundamental types or into objects of other user-defined types.

- An overloaded cast operator function does not specify a return type—the return type is the type to which the object is being converted.

- One of the nice features of cast operators and conversion constructors is that, when necessary, the compiler can call these functions implicitly to create temporary objects.

- Any single-argument constructor can be thought of as a conversion constructor.

- Overloading the function call operator () is powerful, because functions can take arbitrarily long and complex parameter lists.

- The prefix and postfix increment and decrement operator can all be overloaded.

- To overload the increment operator to allow both preincrement and postincrement usage, each overloaded operator function must have a distinct signature, so that the compiler will be able to determine which version of ++ is intended. The prefix versions are overloaded exactly as any other prefix unary operator would be. Providing a unique signature to the postfix increment operator is accomplished by providing a second argument, which must be of type `int`. This argument is not supplied in the client code. It is used implicitly by the compiler to distinguish between the prefix and postfix versions of the increment operator.

- Standard class `string` is defined in header `<string>` and belongs to namespace `std`.

- Class `string` provides many overloaded operators, including equality, relational, assignment, addition assignment (for concatenation) and subscript operators.

- Class `string` provides member function `empty`, which returns `true` if the `string` is empty; otherwise, it returns `false`.

- Standard class `string` member function `substr` obtains a substring of a length specified by the second argument, starting at the position specified by the first argument. When the second argument is not specified, `substr` returns the remainder of the `string` on which it is called.

- Class `string`'s overloaded `[]` operator does not perform any bounds checking. Therefore, the programmer must ensure that operations using standard class `string`'s overloaded `[]` operator do not accidentally manipulate elements outside the bounds of the `string`.

- Standard class `string` provides bounds checking with member function `at`, which "throws an exception" if its argument is an invalid subscript. By default, this causes a C++ program to terminate. If the subscript is valid, function `at` returns the character at the specified location as an *lvalue* or an *rvalue*, depending on the context in which the call appears.

- C++ provides the keyword `explicit` to suppress implicit conversions via conversion constructors when such conversions should not be allowed. A constructor that is declared `explicit` cannot be used in an implicit conversion.

Terminology

"arity" of an operator
`Array` class
assignment-operator functions
associativity not changed by overloading
cast operator function
commutative operation
const version of `operator[]`
conversion between fundamental and class types
conversion constructor
conversion operator
copy constructor
empty member function of `string`
`explicit` constructor
function call operator ()
global function to overload an operator
`ignore` member function of `istream`
implicit user-defined conversions
lvalue ("left value")
operator function
operator keyword
operator overloading
`operator!`
`operator!=`
`operator()`
`operator+`
`operator++`
`operator++( int )`
`operator<`
`operator<<`
`operator=`
`operator==`

`operator>=`
`operator>>`
`operator[]`
overloadable operators
overloaded `!` operator
overloaded `!=` operator
overloaded `()` operator
overloaded `+` operator
overloaded `++` operator
overloaded `++( int )` operator
overloaded `+=` operator
overloaded `<` operator
overloaded `<<` operator
overloaded `<=` operator
overloaded `==` operator
overloaded `>` operator
overloaded `>=` operator
overloaded `>>` operator
overloaded assignment (=) operator
overloaded `[]` operator
overloaded stream insertion and stream extrac-
    tion operators
overloading a binary operator
overloading a unary operator
self-assignment
`string` (standard C++ class)
`string` concatenation
`substr` member function of `string`
substring
user-defined conversion
user-defined type

Self-Review Exercises

11.1   Fill in the blanks in each of the following:
   a) Suppose a and b are integer variables and we form the sum a + b. Now suppose c and d are floating-point variables and we form the sum c + d. The two + operators here are clearly being used for different purposes. This is an example of _____.
   b) Keyword _____ introduces an overloaded-operator function definition.
   c) To use operators on class objects, they must be overloaded, with the exception of operators _____, _____ and _____.
   d) The _____, _____ and _____ of an operator cannot be changed by overloading the operator.

11.2   Explain the multiple meanings of the operators << and >> in C++.

11.3   In what context might the name `operator/` be used in C++?

11.4 (True/False) In C++, only existing operators can be overloaded.

11.5 How does the precedence of an overloaded operator in C++ compare with the precedence of the original operator?

Answers to Self-Review Exercises

11.1 a) operator overloading. b) operator. c) assignment (=), address (&), comma (,). d) precedence, associativity, "arity."

11.2 Operator >> is both the right-shift operator and the stream extraction operator, depending on its context. Operator << is both the left-shift operator and the stream insertion operator, depending on its context.

11.3 For operator overloading: It would be the name of a function that would provide an overloaded version of the / operator for a specific class.

11.4 True.

11.5 The precedence is identical.

Exercises

11.6 Give as many examples as you can of operator overloading implicit in C++. Give a reasonable example of a situation in which you might want to overload an operator explicitly in C++.

11.7 The operators that cannot be overloaded are _____, _____, _____ and _____.

11.8 String concatenation requires two operands—the two strings that are to be concatenated. In the text, we showed how to implement an overloaded concatenation operator that concatenates the second String object to the right of the first String object, thus modifying the first String object. In some applications, it is desirable to produce a concatenated String object without modifying the String arguments. Implement operator+ to allow operations such as

```
string1 = string2 + string3;
```

11.9 *(Ultimate operator overloading exercise)* To appreciate the care that should go into selecting operators for overloading, list each of C++'s overloadable operators, and for each, list a possible meaning (or several, if appropriate) for each of several classes you have studied in this text. We suggest you try:
   a) Array
   b) Stack
   c) String

After doing this, comment on which operators seem to have meaning for a wide variety of classes. Which operators seem to be of little value for overloading? Which operators seem ambiguous?

11.10 Now work the process described in Exercise 11.9 in reverse. List each of C++'s overloadable operators. For each, list what you feel is perhaps the "ultimate operation" the operator should be used to represent. If there are several excellent operations, list them all.

11.11 One nice example of overloading the function call operator () is to allow another form of double-array subscripting popular in some programming languages. Instead of saying

```
chessBoard[ row ][ column ]
```

for an array of objects, overload the function call operator to allow the alternate form

```
chessBoard( row, column )
```

Create a class DoubleSubscriptedArray that has similar features to class Array in Figs. 11.6–11.7. At construction time, the class should be able to create an array of any number of rows and any number of columns. The class should supply operator() to perform double-subscripting operations. For example, in a 3-by-5 DoubleSubscriptedArray called a, the user could write a(1, 3) to access the element at row 1 and column 3. Remember that operator() can receive any number of arguments (see class String in Figs. 11.9–11.10 for an example of operator()). The underlying representation of the double-subscripted array should be a single-subscripted array of integers with *rows* * *columns* number of elements. Function operator() should perform the proper pointer arithmetic to access each element of the array. There should be two versions of operator()—one that returns int & (so that an element of a DoubleSubscriptedArray can be used as an *lvalue*) and one that returns const int & (so that an element of a const DoubleSubscriptedArray can be used only as an *rvalue*). The class should also provide the following operators: ==, !=, =, << (for outputting the array in row and column format) and >> (for inputting the entire array contents).

11.12 Overload the subscript operator to return the largest element of a collection, the second largest, the third largest, and so on.

11.13 Consider class Complex shown in Figs. 11.19–11.21. The class enables operations on so-called *complex numbers*. These are numbers of the form realPart + imaginaryPart * *i*, where *i* has the value

$$\sqrt{-1}$$

   a) Modify the class to enable input and output of complex numbers through the over-loaded >> and << operators, respectively (you should remove the print function from the class).

   b) Overload the multiplication operator to enable multiplication of two complex numbers as in algebra.

   c) Overload the == and != operators to allow comparisons of complex numbers.

```
1   // Fig. 11.19: Complex.h
2   // Complex class definition.
3   #ifndef COMPLEX_H
4   #define COMPLEX_H
5
6   class Complex
7   {
8   public:
9      Complex( double = 0.0, double = 0.0 ); // constructor
10     Complex operator+( const Complex & ) const; // addition
11     Complex operator-( const Complex & ) const; // subtraction
12     void print() const; // output
13  private:
14     double real; // real part
15     double imaginary; // imaginary part
16  }; // end class Complex
17
18  #endif
```

Fig. 11.19 | Complex class definition.

```
1   // Fig. 11.20: Complex.cpp
2   // Complex class member-function definitions.
3   #include <iostream>
4   using std::cout;
5
6   #include "Complex.h" // Complex class definition
7
8   // Constructor
9   Complex::Complex( double realPart, double imaginaryPart )
10     : real( realPart ),
11       imaginary( imaginaryPart )
12   {
13     // empty body
14   } // end Complex constructor
15
16   // addition operator
17   Complex Complex::operator+( const Complex &operand2 ) const
18   {
19     return Complex( real + operand2.real,
20        imaginary + operand2.imaginary );
21   } // end function operator+
22
23   // subtraction operator
24   Complex Complex::operator-( const Complex &operand2 ) const
25   {
26     return Complex( real - operand2.real,
27        imaginary - operand2.imaginary );
28   } // end function operator-
29
30   // display a Complex object in the form: (a, b)
31   void Complex::print() const
32   {
33     cout << '(' << real << ", " << imaginary << ')';
34   } // end function print
```

Fig. 11.20 | Complex class member-function definitions.

```
1   // Fig. 11.21: fig11_21.cpp
2   // Complex class test program.
3   #include <iostream>
4   using std::cout;
5   using std::endl;
6
7   #include "Complex.h"
8
9   int main()
10  {
11     Complex x;
12     Complex y( 4.3, 8.2 );
13     Complex z( 3.3, 1.1 );
```

Fig. 11.21 | Complex numbers. (Part 1 of 2.)

```
14
15      cout << "x: ";
16      x.print();
17      cout << "\ny: ";
18      y.print();
19      cout << "\nz: ";
20      z.print();
21
22      x = y + z;
23      cout << "\n\nx = y + z:" << endl;
24      x.print();
25      cout << " = ";
26      y.print();
27      cout << " + ";
28      z.print();
29
30      x = y - z;
31      cout << "\n\nx = y - z:" << endl;
32      x.print();
33      cout << " = ";
34      y.print();
35      cout << " - ";
36      z.print();
37      cout << endl;
38      return 0;
39   } // end main
```

```
x: (0, 0)
y: (4.3, 8.2)
z: (3.3, 1.1)

x = y + z:
(7.6, 9.3) = (4.3, 8.2) + (3.3, 1.1)

x = y - z:
(1, 7.1) = (4.3, 8.2) - (3.3, 1.1)
```

Fig. 11.21 | Complex numbers. (Part 2 of 2.)

11.14 A machine with 32-bit integers can represent integers in the range of approximately –2 billion to +2 billion. This fixed-size restriction is rarely troublesome, but there are applications in which we would like to be able to use a much wider range of integers. This is what C++ was built to do, namely, create powerful new data types. Consider class HugeInt of Figs. 11.22–11.24. Study the class carefully, then answer the following:

   a) Describe precisely how it operates.
   b) What restrictions does the class have?
   c) Overload the * multiplication operator.
   d) Overload the / division operator.
   e) Overload all the relational and equality operators.

[*Note:* We do not show an assignment operator or copy constructor for class HugeInteger, because the assignment operator and copy constructor provided by the compiler are capable of copying the entire array data member properly.]

```
 1   // Fig. 11.22: Hugeint.h
 2   // HugeInt class definition.
 3   #ifndef HUGEINT_H
 4   #define HUGEINT_H
 5
 6   #include <iostream>
 7   using std::ostream;
 8
 9   class HugeInt
10   {
11      friend ostream &operator<<( ostream &, const HugeInt & );
12   public:
13      HugeInt( long = 0 ); // conversion/default constructor
14      HugeInt( const char * ); // conversion constructor
15
16      // addition operator; HugeInt + HugeInt
17      HugeInt operator+( const HugeInt & ) const;
18
19      // addition operator; HugeInt + int
20      HugeInt operator+( int ) const;
21
22      // addition operator;
23      // HugeInt + string that represents large integer value
24      HugeInt operator+( const char * ) const;
25   private:
26      short integer[ 30 ];
27   }; // end class HugetInt
28
29   #endif
```

Fig. 11.22 | HugeInt class definition.

11.15   Create a class RationalNumber (fractions) with the following capabilities:
   a)   Create a constructor that prevents a 0 denominator in a fraction, reduces or simplifies fractions that are not in reduced form and avoids negative denominators.
   b)   Overload the addition, subtraction, multiplication and division operators for this class.
   c)   Overload the relational and equality operators for this class.

11.16   Study the C string-handling library functions and implement each of the functions as part of class String (Figs. 11.9–11.10). Then, use these functions to perform text manipulations.

11.17   Develop class Polynomial. The internal representation of a Polynomial is an array of terms. Each term contains a coefficient and an exponent. The term

$$2x^4$$

has the coefficient 2 and the exponent 4. Develop a complete class containing proper constructor and destructor functions as well as *set* and *get* functions. The class should also provide the following overloaded operator capabilities:
   a)   Overload the addition operator (+) to add two Polynomials.
   b)   Overload the subtraction operator (-) to subtract two Polynomials.
   c)   Overload the assignment operator to assign one Polynomial to another.
   d)   Overload the multiplication operator (*) to multiply two Polynomials.
   e)   Overload the addition assignment operator (+=), subtraction assignment operator (-=), and multiplication assignment operator (*=).

```
1   // Fig. 11.23: Hugeint.cpp
2   // HugeInt member-function and friend-function definitions.
3   #include <cctype> // isdigit function prototype
4   #include <cstring> // strlen function prototype
5   #include "Hugeint.h" // HugeInt class definition
6
7   // default constructor; conversion constructor that converts
8   // a long integer into a HugeInt object
9   HugeInt::HugeInt( long value )
10  {
11     // initialize array to zero
12     for ( int i = 0; i <= 29; i++ )
13        integer[ i ] = 0;
14
15     // place digits of argument into array
16     for ( int j = 29; value != 0 && j >= 0; j-- )
17     {
18        integer[ j ] = value % 10;
19        value /= 10;
20     } // end for
21  } // end HugeInt default/conversion constructor
22
23  // conversion constructor that converts a character string
24  // representing a large integer into a HugeInt object
25  HugeInt::HugeInt( const char *string )
26  {
27     // initialize array to zero
28     for ( int i = 0; i <= 29; i++ )
29        integer[ i ] = 0;
30
31     // place digits of argument into array
32     int length = strlen( string );
33
34     for ( int j = 30 - length, k = 0; j <= 29; j++, k++ )
35
36        if ( isdigit( string[ k ] ) )
37           integer[ j ] = string[ k ] - '0';
38  } // end HugeInt conversion constructor
39
40  // addition operator; HugeInt + HugeInt
41  HugeInt HugeInt::operator+( const HugeInt &op2 ) const
42  {
43     HugeInt temp; // temporary result
44     int carry = 0;
45
46     for ( int i = 29; i >= 0; i-- )
47     {
48        temp.integer[ i ] =
49           integer[ i ] + op2.integer[ i ] + carry;
50
51        // determine whether to carry a 1
52        if ( temp.integer[ i ] > 9 )
53        {
```

Fig. 11.23 | HugeInt class member-function and friend-function definitions. (Part 1 of 2.)

```
54            temp.integer[ i ] %= 10;  // reduce to 0-9
55            carry = 1;
56         } // end if
57         else // no carry
58            carry = 0;
59      } // end for
60
61      return temp; // return copy of temporary object
62   } // end function operator+
63
64   // addition operator; HugeInt + int
65   HugeInt HugeInt::operator+( int op2 ) const
66   {
67      // convert op2 to a HugeInt, then invoke
68      // operator+ for two HugeInt objects
69      return *this + HugeInt( op2 );
70   } // end function operator+
71
72   // addition operator;
73   // HugeInt + string that represents large integer value
74   HugeInt HugeInt::operator+( const char *op2 ) const
75   {
76      // convert op2 to a HugeInt, then invoke
77      // operator+ for two HugeInt objects
78      return *this + HugeInt( op2 );
79   } // end operator+
80
81   // overloaded output operator
82   ostream& operator<<( ostream &output, const HugeInt &num )
83   {
84      int i;
85
86      for ( i = 0; ( num.integer[ i ] == 0 ) && ( i <= 29 ); i++ )
87         ; // skip leading zeros
88
89      if ( i == 30 )
90         output << 0;
91      else
92
93         for ( ; i <= 29; i++ )
94            output << num.integer[ i ];
95
96      return output;
97   } // end function operator<<
```

Fig. 11.23 | HugeInt class member-function and friend-function definitions. (Part 2 of 2.)

11.18 In the program of Figs. 11.3–11.5, Fig. 11.4 contains the comment "overloaded stream insertion operator; cannot be a member function if we would like to invoke it with cout << somePhoneNumber;." Actually, the stream insertion operator could be a PhoneNumber class member function if we were willing to invoke it either as somePhoneNumber.operator<<(cout); or as some-PhoneNumber << cout;. Rewrite the program of Fig. 11.5 with the overloaded stream insertion operator<< as a member function and try the two preceding statements in the program to demonstrate that they work.

```
1   // Fig. 11.24: fig11_24.cpp
2   // HugeInt test program.
3   #include <iostream>
4   using std::cout;
5   using std::endl;
6
7   #include "Hugeint.h"
8
9   int main()
10  {
11     HugeInt n1( 7654321 );
12     HugeInt n2( 7891234 );
13     HugeInt n3( "99999999999999999999999999999" );
14     HugeInt n4( "1" );
15     HugeInt n5;
16
17     cout << "n1 is " << n1 << "\nn2 is " << n2
18        << "\nn3 is " << n3 << "\nn4 is " << n4
19        << "\nn5 is " << n5 << "\n\n";
20
21     n5 = n1 + n2;
22     cout << n1 << " + " << n2 << " = " << n5 << "\n\n";
23
24     cout << n3 << " + " << n4 << "\n= " << ( n3 + n4 ) << "\n\n";
25
26     n5 = n1 + 9;
27     cout << n1 << " + " << 9 << " = " << n5 << "\n\n";
28
29     n5 = n2 + "10000";
30     cout << n2 << " + " << "10000" << " = " << n5 << endl;
31     return 0;
32  } // end main
```

```
n1 is 7654321
n2 is 7891234
n3 is 99999999999999999999999999999
n4 is 1
n5 is 0

7654321 + 7891234 = 15545555

99999999999999999999999999999 + 1
= 100000000000000000000000000000

7654321 + 9 = 7654330

7891234 + 10000 = 7901234
```

Fig. 11.24 | Huge integers.

12

Object-Oriented Programming: Inheritance

Featuring... Early Classes & Objects with the UML™ 2

OBJECTIVES

In this chapter you will learn:

- To create classes by inheriting from existing classes.

- How inheritance promotes software reuse.

- The notions of base classes and derived classes and the relationships between them.

- The **protected** member access specifier.

- The use of constructors and destructors in inheritance hierarchies.

- The differences between **public**, **protected** and **private** inheritance.

- The use of inheritance to customize existing software.

Say not you know another entirely, till you have divided an inheritance with him.
—Johann Kasper Lavater

This method is to define as the number of a class the class of all classes similar to the given class.
—Bertrand Russell

Good as it is to inherit a library, it is better to collect one.
—Augustine Birrell

Save base authority from others' books.
—William Shakespeare

Outline

12.1 Introduction

12.2 Base Classes and Derived Classes

12.3 protected Members

12.4 Relationship between Base Classes and Derived Classes

    12.4.1 Creating and Using a CommissionEmployee Class

    12.4.2 Creating a BasePlusCommissionEmployee Class Without Using Inheritance

    12.4.3 Creating a CommissionEmployee–BasePlusCommissionEmployee Inheritance Hierarchy

    12.4.4 CommissionEmployee–BasePlusCommissionEmployee Inheritance Hierarchy Using protected Data

    12.4.5 CommissionEmployee–BasePlusCommissionEmployee Inheritance Hierarchy Using private Data

12.5 Constructors and Destructors in Derived Classes

12.6 public, protected and private Inheritance

12.7 Software Engineering with Inheritance

12.8 Wrap-Up

Summary | Terminology | Self-Review Exercises | Answers to Self-Review Exercises | Exercises

12.1 Introduction

This chapter continues our discussion of object-oriented programming (OOP) by introducing another of its key features—inheritance. Inheritance is a form of software reuse in which the programmer creates a class that absorbs an existing class's data and behaviors and enhances them with new capabilities. Software reusability saves time during program development. It also encourages the reuse of proven, debugged, high-quality software, which increases the likelihood that a system will be implemented effectively.

When creating a class, instead of writing completely new data members and member functions, the programmer can designate that the new class should inherit the members of an existing class. This existing class is called the base class, and the new class is referred to as the derived class. (Other programming languages, such as Java, refer to the base class as the superclass and the derived class as the subclass.) A derived class represents a more specialized group of objects. Typically, a derived class contains behaviors inherited from its base class plus additional behaviors. As we will see, a derived class can also customize behaviors inherited from the base class. A direct base class is the base class from which a derived class explicitly inherits. An indirect base class is inherited from two or more levels up in the class hierarchy. In the case of single inheritance, a class is derived from one base class. C++ also supports multiple inheritance, in which a derived class inherits from multiple (possibly unrelated) base classes. Single inheritance is straightforward—we show several examples that should enable the reader to become proficient quickly. Multiple inheritance can be complex and error prone. We cover multiple inheritance in Chapter 24, Other Topics, of our sister book, *C++ How to Program, 5/e.*

C++ offers three kinds of inheritance—public, protected and private. In this chapter, we concentrate on public inheritance and briefly explain the other two. In some cases, `private` inheritance can be used as an alternative to composition. The third form, `protected` inheritance, is rarely used. With `public` inheritance, every object of a derived class is also an object of that derived class's base class. However, base-class objects are not objects of their derived classes. For example, if we have vehicle as a base class and car as a derived class, then all cars are vehicles, but not all vehicles are cars. As we continue our study of object-oriented programming in Chapter 12 and Chapter 13, we take advantage of this relationship to perform some interesting manipulations.

Experience in building software systems indicates that significant amounts of code deal with closely related special cases. When programmers are preoccupied with special cases, the details can obscure the big picture. With object-oriented programming, programmers focus on the commonalities among objects in the system rather than on the special cases.

We distinguish between the *is-a relationship* and the *has-a* relationship. The *is-a* relationship represents inheritance. In an *is-a* relationship, an object of a derived class also can be treated as an object of its base class—for example, a car *is a* vehicle, so any properties and behaviors of a vehicle are also properties of a car. By contrast, the *has-a* relationship represents composition. (Composition was discussed in Chapter 10.) In a *has-a* relationship, an object contains one or more objects of other classes as members. For example, a car includes many components—it *has a* steering wheel, *has a* brake pedal, *has a* transmission and *has* many other components.

Derived-class member functions might require access to base-class data members and member functions. A derived class can access the non-`private` members of its base class. Base-class members that should not be accessible to the member functions of derived classes should be declared `private` in the base class. A derived class can effect state changes in `private` base-class members, but only through non-`private` member functions provided in the base class and inherited into the derived class.

Software Engineering Observation 12.1

Member functions of a derived class cannot directly access `private` members of the base class.

Software Engineering Observation 12.2

If a derived class could access its base class's `private` members, classes that inherit from that derived class could access that data as well. This would propagate access to what should be `private` data, and the benefits of information hiding would be lost.

One problem with inheritance is that a derived class can inherit data members and member functions it does not need or should not have. It is the class designer's responsibility to ensure that the capabilities provided by a class are appropriate for future derived classes. Even when a base-class member function is appropriate for a derived class, the derived class often requires that member function to behave in a manner specific to the derived class. In such cases, the base-class member function can be redefined in the derived class with an appropriate implementation.

12.2 Base Classes and Derived Classes

Often, an object of one class *is an* object of another class, as well. For example, in geometry, a rectangle *is a* quadrilateral (as are squares, parallelograms and trapezoids). Thus, in C++, class `Rectangle` can be said to *inherit* from class `Quadrilateral`. In this context, class `Quadrilateral` is a base class, and class `Rectangle` is a derived class. A rectangle *is a* specific type of quadrilateral, but it is incorrect to claim that a quadrilateral *is a* rectangle—the quadrilateral could be a parallelogram or some other shape. Figure 12.1 lists several simple examples of base classes and derived classes.

Because every derived-class object *is an* object of its base class, and one base class can have many derived classes, the set of objects represented by a base class typically is larger than the set of objects represented by any of its derived classes. For example, the base class Vehicle represents all vehicles, including cars, trucks, boats, airplanes, bicycles and so on. By contrast, derived class Car represents a smaller, more specific subset of all vehicles.

Inheritance relationships form treelike hierarchical structures. A base class exists in a hierarchical relationship with its derived classes. Although classes can exist independently, once they are employed in inheritance relationships, they become affiliated with other classes. A class becomes either a base class—supplying members to other classes, a derived class—inheriting its members from other classes, or both.

Let us develop a simple inheritance hierarchy with five levels (represented by the UML class diagram in Fig. 12.2). A university community has thousands of members.

Base class	Derived classes
Student	GraduateStudent, UndergraduateStudent
Shape	Circle, Triangle, Rectangle, Sphere, Cube
Loan	CarLoan, HomeImprovementLoan, MortgageLoan
Employee	Faculty, Staff
Account	CheckingAccount, SavingsAccount

Fig. 12.1 | Inheritance examples.

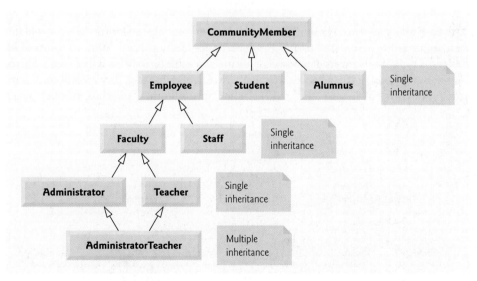

Fig. 12.2 | Inheritance hierarchy for university CommunityMembers.

These members consist of employees, students and alumni. Employees are either faculty members or staff members. Faculty members are either administrators (such as deans and department chairpersons) or teachers. Some administrators, however, also teach classes. Note that we have used multiple inheritance to form class AdministratorTeacher. Also note that this inheritance hierarchy could contain many other classes. For example, students can be graduate or undergraduate students. Undergraduate students can be freshmen, sophomores, juniors and seniors.

Each arrow in the hierarchy (Fig. 12.2) represents an *is-a* relationship. For example, as we follow the arrows in this class hierarchy, we can state "an Employee *is a* Community-Member" and "a Teacher *is a* Faculty member." CommunityMember is the direct base class of Employee, Student and Alumnus. In addition, CommunityMember is an indirect base class of all the other classes in the diagram. Starting from the bottom of the diagram, the reader can follow the arrows and apply the *is-a* relationship to the topmost base class. For example, an AdministratorTeacher *is an* Administrator, *is a* Faculty member, *is an* Employee and *is a* CommunityMember.

Now consider the Shape inheritance hierarchy in Fig. 12.3. This hierarchy begins with base class Shape. Classes TwoDimensionalShape and ThreeDimensionalShape derive from base class Shape—Shapes are either TwoDimensionalShapes or ThreeDimensional-Shapes. The third level of this hierarchy contains some more specific types of TwoDimensionalShapes and ThreeDimensionalShapes. As in Fig. 12.2, we can follow the arrows from the bottom of the diagram to the topmost base class in this class hierarchy to identify several *is-a* relationships. For instance, a Triangle *is a* TwoDimensionalShape and *is a* Shape, while a Sphere *is a* ThreeDimensionalShape and *is a* Shape. Note that this hierarchy could contain many other classes, such as Rectangles, Ellipses and Trapezoids, which are all TwoDimensionalShapes.

To specify that class TwoDimensionalShape (Fig. 12.3) is derived from (or inherits from) class Shape, class TwoDimensionalShape could be defined in C++ as follows:

```
class TwoDimensionalShape : public Shape
```

This is an example of **public inheritance**, the most commonly used form. We also will discuss **private inheritance** and **protected inheritance** (Section 12.6). With all forms of inheritance, private members of a base class are not accessible directly from that class's derived classes, but these private base-class members are still inherited (i.e., they are still considered parts of the derived classes). With public inheritance, all other base-class members retain

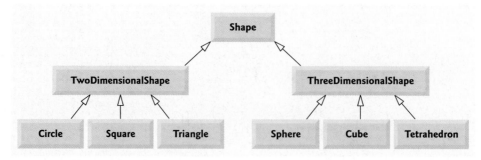

Fig. 12.3 | Inheritance hierarchy for Shapes.

their original member access when they become members of the derived class (e.g., public members of the base class become public members of the derived class, and, as we will soon see, protected members of the base class become protected members of the derived class). Through these inherited base-class members, the derived class can manipulate private members of the base class (if these inherited members provide such functionality in the base class). Note that friend functions are not inherited.

Inheritance is not appropriate for every class relationship. In Chapter 10, we discussed the *has-a* relationship, in which classes have members that are objects of other classes. Such relationships create classes by composition of existing classes. For example, given the classes Employee, BirthDate and TelephoneNumber, it is improper to say that an Employee *is a* BirthDate or that an Employee *is a* TelephoneNumber. However, it is appropriate to say that an Employee *has a* BirthDate and that an Employee *has a* TelephoneNumber.

It is possible to treat base-class objects and derived-class objects similarly; their commonalities are expressed in the members of the base class. Objects of all classes derived from a common base class can be treated as objects of that base class (i.e., such objects have an *is-a* relationship with the base class). In Chapter 13, Object-Oriented Programming: Polymorphism, we consider many examples that take advantage of this relationship.

12.3 protected Members

Chapter 3 introduced access specifiers public and private. A base class's public members are accessible within the body of that base class and anywhere that the program has a handle (i.e., a name, reference or pointer) to an object of that base class or one of its derived classes. A base class's private members are accessible only within the body of that base class and the friends of that base class. In this section, we introduce an additional access specifier: protected.

Using protected access offers an intermediate level of protection between public and private access. A base class's protected members can be accessed within the body of that base class, by members and friends of that base class, and by members and friends of any classes derived from that base class.

Derived-class member functions can refer to public and protected members of the base class simply by using the member names. When a derived-class member function redefines a base-class member function, the base-class member can be accessed from the derived class by preceding the base-class member name with the base-class name and the binary scope resolution operator (::). We discuss accessing redefined members of the base class in Section 12.4 and using protected data in Section 12.4.4.

12.4 Relationship between Base Classes and Derived Classes

In this section, we use an inheritance hierarchy containing types of employees in a company's payroll application to discuss the relationship between a base class and a derived class. Commission employees (who will be represented as objects of a base class) are paid a percentage of their sales, while base-salaried commission employees (who will be represented as objects of a derived class) receive a base salary plus a percentage of their sales. We divide our discussion of the relationship between commission employees and base-salaried commission employees into a carefully paced series of five examples:

1. In the first example, we create class `CommissionEmployee`, which contains as `private` data members a first name, last name, social security number, commission rate (percentage) and gross (i.e., total) sales amount.

2. The second example defines class `BasePlusCommissionEmployee`, which contains as `private` data members a first name, last name, social security number, commission rate, gross sales amount and base salary. We create the latter class by writing every line of code the class requires—we will soon see that it is much more efficient to create this class simply by inheriting from class `CommissionEmployee`.

3. The third example defines a new version of class `BasePlusCommissionEmployee` class that inherits directly from class `CommissionEmployee` (i.e., a `BasePlusCommissionEmployee` *is a* `CommissionEmployee` who also has a base salary) and attempts to access class `CommissionEmployee`'s `private` members—this results in compilation errors, because the derived class does not have access to the base class's `private` data.

4. The fourth example shows that if `CommissionEmployee`'s data is declared as `protected`, a new version of class `BasePlusCommissionEmployee` that inherits from class `CommissionEmployee` *can* access that data directly. For this purpose, we define a new version of class `CommissionEmployee` with `protected` data. Both the inherited and noninherited `BasePlusCommissionEmployee` classes contain identical functionality, but we show how the version of `BasePlusCommissionEmployee` that inherits from class `CommissionEmployee` is easier to create and manage.

5. After we discuss the convenience of using `protected` data, we create the fifth example, which sets the `CommissionEmployee` data members back to `private` to enforce good software engineering. This example demonstrates that derived class `BasePlusCommissionEmployee` can use base class `CommissionEmployee`'s `public` member functions to manipulate `CommissionEmployee`'s `private` data.

12.4.1 Creating and Using a CommissionEmployee Class

Let us first examine `CommissionEmployee`'s class definition (Figs. 12.4–12.5). The `CommissionEmployee` header file (Fig. 12.4) specifies class `CommissionEmployee`'s `public` services, which include a constructor (lines 12–13) and member functions `earnings` (line 30) and `print` (line 31). Lines 15–28 declare `public` *get* and *set* functions for manipulating the class's data members (declared in lines 33–37) `firstName`, `lastName`, `socialSecurityNumber`, `grossSales` and `commissionRate`. The `CommissionEmployee` header file specifies each of these data members as `private`, so objects of other classes cannot directly access this data. Declaring data members as `private` and providing non-`private` *get* and *set* functions to manipulate and validate the data members helps enforce good software engineering. Member functions `setGrossSales` (defined in lines 57–60 of Fig. 12.5) and `setCommissionRate` (defined in lines 69–72 of Fig. 12.5), for example, validate their arguments before assigning the values to data members `grossSales` and `commissionRate`, respectively.

The `CommissionEmployee` constructor definition purposely does not use member-initializer syntax in the first several examples of this section, so that we can demonstrate how `private` and `protected` specifiers affect member access in derived classes. As shown in Fig. 12.5, lines 13–15, we assign values to data members `firstName`, `lastName` and

```
1   // Fig. 12.4: CommissionEmployee.h
2   // CommissionEmployee class definition represents a commission employee.
3   #ifndef COMMISSION_H
4   #define COMMISSION_H
5
6   #include <string> // C++ standard string class
7   using std::string;
8
9   class CommissionEmployee
10  {
11  public:
12     CommissionEmployee( const string &, const string &, const string &,
13        double = 0.0, double = 0.0 );
14
15     void setFirstName( const string & ); // set first name
16     string getFirstName() const; // return first name
17
18     void setLastName( const string & ); // set last name
19     string getLastName() const; // return last name
20
21     void setSocialSecurityNumber( const string & ); // set SSN
22     string getSocialSecurityNumber() const; // return SSN
23
24     void setGrossSales( double ); // set gross sales amount
25     double getGrossSales() const; // return gross sales amount
26
27     void setCommissionRate( double ); // set commission rate (percentage)
28     double getCommissionRate() const; // return commission rate
29
30     double earnings() const; // calculate earnings
31     void print() const; // print CommissionEmployee object
32  private:
33     string firstName;
34     string lastName;
35     string socialSecurityNumber;
36     double grossSales; // gross weekly sales
37     double commissionRate; // commission percentage
38  }; // end class CommissionEmployee
39
40  #endif
```

Fig. 12.4 | CommissionEmployee class header file.

```
1   // Fig. 12.5: CommissionEmployee.cpp
2   // Class CommissionEmployee member-function definitions.
3   #include <iostream>
4   using std::cout;
5
6   #include "CommissionEmployee.h" // CommissionEmployee class definition
7
```

Fig. 12.5 | Implementation file for CommissionEmployee class that represents an employee who is paid a percentage of gross sales. (Part 1 of 3.)

```cpp
8   // constructor
9   CommissionEmployee::CommissionEmployee(
10     const string &first, const string &last, const string &ssn,
11     double sales, double rate )
12  {
13     firstName = first; // should validate
14     lastName = last;   // should validate
15     socialSecurityNumber = ssn; // should validate
16     setGrossSales( sales ); // validate and store gross sales
17     setCommissionRate( rate ); // validate and store commission rate
18  } // end CommissionEmployee constructor
19
20  // set first name
21  void CommissionEmployee::setFirstName( const string &first )
22  {
23     firstName = first; // should validate
24  } // end function setFirstName
25
26  // return first name
27  string CommissionEmployee::getFirstName() const
28  {
29     return firstName;
30  } // end function getFirstName
31
32  // set last name
33  void CommissionEmployee::setLastName( const string &last )
34  {
35     lastName = last; // should validate
36  } // end function setLastName
37
38  // return last name
39  string CommissionEmployee::getLastName() const
40  {
41     return lastName;
42  } // end function getLastName
43
44  // set social security number
45  void CommissionEmployee::setSocialSecurityNumber( const string &ssn )
46  {
47     socialSecurityNumber = ssn; // should validate
48  } // end function setSocialSecurityNumber
49
50  // return social security number
51  string CommissionEmployee::getSocialSecurityNumber() const
52  {
53     return socialSecurityNumber;
54  } // end function getSocialSecurityNumber
55
56  // set gross sales amount
57  void CommissionEmployee::setGrossSales( double sales )
58  {
```

Fig. 12.5 | Implementation file for CommissionEmployee class that represents an employee who is paid a percentage of gross sales. (Part 2 of 3.)

```
59        grossSales = ( sales < 0.0 ) ? 0.0 : sales;
60     } // end function setGrossSales
61
62     // return gross sales amount
63     double CommissionEmployee::getGrossSales() const
64     {
65        return grossSales;
66     } // end function getGrossSales
67
68     // set commission rate
69     void CommissionEmployee::setCommissionRate( double rate )
70     {
71        commissionRate = ( rate > 0.0 && rate < 1.0 ) ? rate : 0.0;
72     } // end function setCommissionRate
73
74     // return commission rate
75     double CommissionEmployee::getCommissionRate() const
76     {
77        return commissionRate;
78     } // end function getCommissionRate
79
80     // calculate earnings
81     double CommissionEmployee::earnings() const
82     {
83        return commissionRate * grossSales;
84     } // end function earnings
85
86     // print CommissionEmployee object
87     void CommissionEmployee::print() const
88     {
89        cout << "commission employee: " << firstName << ' ' << lastName
90           << "\nsocial security number: " << socialSecurityNumber
91           << "\ngross sales: " << grossSales
92           << "\ncommission rate: " << commissionRate;
93     } // end function print
```

Fig. 12.5 | Implementation file for `CommissionEmployee` class that represents an employee who is paid a percentage of gross sales. (Part 3 of 3.)

`socialSecurityNumber` in the constructor body. Later in this section, we will return to using member-initializer lists in the constructors.

Note that we do not validate the values of the constructor's arguments `first`, `last` and `ssn` before assigning them to the corresponding data members. We certainly could validate the first and last names—perhaps by ensuring that they are of a reasonable length. Similarly, a social security number could be validated to ensure that it contains nine digits, with or without dashes (e.g., 123-45-6789 or 123456789).

Member function `earnings` (lines 81–84) calculates a `CommissionEmployee`'s earnings. Line 83 multiplies the `commissionRate` by the `grossSales` and returns the result. Member function `print` (lines 87–93) displays the values of a `CommissionEmployee` object's data members.

Figure 12.6 tests class `CommissionEmployee`. Lines 16–17 instantiate object `employee` of class `CommissionEmployee` and invoke `CommissionEmployee`'s constructor to initialize the object with "Sue" as the first name, "Jones" as the last name, "222-22-2222" as the social security number, 10000 as the gross sales amount and .06 as the commission rate. Lines 23–29 use employee's *get* functions to display the values of its data members. Lines 31–32 invoke the object's member functions setGrossSales and setCommissionRate to change the values of data members grossSales and commissionRate, respectively. Line 36 then calls employee's print member function to output the updated CommissionEmployee information. Finally, line 39 displays the CommissionEmployee's earnings, calculated by the object's earnings member function using the updated values of data members gross-Sales and commissionRate.

```cpp
1   // Fig. 12.6: fig12_06.cpp
2   // Testing class CommissionEmployee.
3   #include <iostream>
4   using std::cout;
5   using std::endl;
6   using std::fixed;
7
8   #include <iomanip>
9   using std::setprecision;
10
11  #include "CommissionEmployee.h" // CommissionEmployee class definition
12
13  int main()
14  {
15     // instantiate a CommissionEmployee object
16     CommissionEmployee employee(
17        "Sue", "Jones", "222-22-2222", 10000, .06 );
18
19     // set floating-point output formatting
20     cout << fixed << setprecision( 2 );
21
22     // get commission employee data
23     cout << "Employee information obtained by get functions: \n"
24        << "\nFirst name is " << employee.getFirstName()
25        << "\nLast name is " << employee.getLastName()
26        << "\nSocial security number is "
27        << employee.getSocialSecurityNumber()
28        << "\nGross sales is " << employee.getGrossSales()
29        << "\nCommission rate is " << employee.getCommissionRate() << endl;
30
31     employee.setGrossSales( 8000 ); // set gross sales
32     employee.setCommissionRate( .1 ); // set commission rate
33
34     cout << "\nUpdated employee information output by print function: \n"
35        << endl;
36     employee.print(); // display the new employee information
37
38     // display the employee's earnings
39     cout << "\n\nEmployee's earnings: $" << employee.earnings() << endl;
40
41     return 0;
42  } // end main
```

Fig. 12.6 | CommissionEmployee class test program. (Part 1 of 2.)

```
Employee information obtained by get functions:

First name is Sue
Last name is Jones
Social security number is 222-22-2222
Gross sales is 10000.00
Commission rate is 0.06

Updated employee information output by print function:

commission employee: Sue Jones
social security number: 222-22-2222
gross sales: 8000.00
commission rate: 0.10

Employee's earnings: $800.00
```

Fig. 12.6 | CommissionEmployee class test program. (Part 2 of 2.)

12.4.2 Creating a BasePlusCommissionEmployee Class Without Using Inheritance

We now discuss the second part of our introduction to inheritance by creating and testing (a completely new and independent) class BasePlusCommissionEmployee (Figs. 12.7–12.8), which contains a first name, last name, social security number, gross sales amount, commission rate and base salary.

Defining Class BasePlusCommissionEmployee

The BasePlusCommissionEmployee header file (Fig. 12.7) specifies class BasePlusCommissionEmployee's public services, which include the BasePlusCommissionEmployee constructor (lines 13–14) and member functions earnings (line 34) and print (line 35).

```
1   // Fig. 12.7: BasePlusCommissionEmployee.h
2   // BasePlusCommissionEmployee class definition represents an employee
3   // that receives a base salary in addition to commission.
4   #ifndef BASEPLUS_H
5   #define BASEPLUS_H
6
7   #include <string> // C++ standard string class
8   using std::string;
9
10  class BasePlusCommissionEmployee
11  {
12  public:
13     BasePlusCommissionEmployee( const string &, const string &,
14        const string &, double = 0.0, double = 0.0, double = 0.0 );
15
16     void setFirstName( const string & ); // set first name
17     string getFirstName() const; // return first name
18
```

Fig. 12.7 | BasePlusCommissionEmployee class header file. (Part 1 of 2.)

```
19    void setLastName( const string & ); // set last name
20    string getLastName() const; // return last name
21
22    void setSocialSecurityNumber( const string & ); // set SSN
23    string getSocialSecurityNumber() const; // return SSN
24
25    void setGrossSales( double ); // set gross sales amount
26    double getGrossSales() const; // return gross sales amount
27
28    void setCommissionRate( double ); // set commission rate
29    double getCommissionRate() const; // return commission rate
30
31    void setBaseSalary( double ); // set base salary
32    double getBaseSalary() const; // return base salary
33
34    double earnings() const; // calculate earnings
35    void print() const; // print BasePlusCommissionEmployee object
36  private:
37    string firstName;
38    string lastName;
39    string socialSecurityNumber;
40    double grossSales; // gross weekly sales
41    double commissionRate; // commission percentage
42    double baseSalary; // base salary
43  }; // end class BasePlusCommissionEmployee
44
45  #endif
```

Fig. 12.7 | BasePlusCommissionEmployee class header file. (Part 2 of 2.)

Lines 16–32 declare public *get* and *set* functions for the class's private data members (declared in lines 37–42) firstName, lastName, socialSecurityNumber, grossSales, commissionRate and baseSalary. These variables and member functions encapsulate all the necessary features of a base-salaried commission employee. Note the similarity between this class and class CommissionEmployee (Figs. 12.4–12.5)—in this example, we will not yet exploit that similarity.

Class BasePlusCommissionEmployee's earnings member function (defined in lines 96–99 of Fig. 12.8) computes the earnings of a base-salaried commission employee. Line 98 returns the result of adding the employee's base salary to the product of the commission rate and the employee's gross sales.

Testing Class *BasePlusCommissionEmployee*
Figure 12.9 tests class BasePlusCommissionEmployee. Lines 17–18 instantiate object employee of class BasePlusCommissionEmployee, passing "Bob", "Lewis", "333-33-3333", 5000, .04 and 300 to the constructor as the first name, last name, social security number, gross sales, commission rate and base salary, respectively. Lines 24–31 use BasePlusCommissionEmployee's *get* functions to retrieve the values of the object's data members for output. Line 33 invokes the object's setBaseSalary member function to change the base salary. Member function setBaseSalary (Fig. 12.8, lines 84–87) ensures that data member baseSalary is not assigned a negative value, because an employee's base salary cannot be negative. Line 37 of Fig. 12.9 invokes the object's print member function to output

the updated BasePlusCommissionEmployee's information, and line 40 calls member function earnings to display the BasePlusCommissionEmployee's earnings.

```
1   // Fig. 12.8: BasePlusCommissionEmployee.cpp
2   // Class BasePlusCommissionEmployee member-function definitions.
3   #include <iostream>
4   using std::cout;
5
6   // BasePlusCommissionEmployee class definition
7   #include "BasePlusCommissionEmployee.h"
8
9   // constructor
10  BasePlusCommissionEmployee::BasePlusCommissionEmployee(
11     const string &first, const string &last, const string &ssn,
12     double sales, double rate, double salary )
13  {
14     firstName = first; // should validate
15     lastName = last; // should validate
16     socialSecurityNumber = ssn; // should validate
17     setGrossSales( sales ); // validate and store gross sales
18     setCommissionRate( rate ); // validate and store commission rate
19     setBaseSalary( salary ); // validate and store base salary
20  } // end BasePlusCommissionEmployee constructor
21
22  // set first name
23  void BasePlusCommissionEmployee::setFirstName( const string &first )
24  {
25     firstName = first; // should validate
26  } // end function setFirstName
27
28  // return first name
29  string BasePlusCommissionEmployee::getFirstName() const
30  {
31     return firstName;
32  } // end function getFirstName
33
34  // set last name
35  void BasePlusCommissionEmployee::setLastName( const string &last )
36  {
37     lastName = last; // should validate
38  } // end function setLastName
39
40  // return last name
41  string BasePlusCommissionEmployee::getLastName() const
42  {
43     return lastName;
44  } // end function getLastName
45
46  // set social security number
47  void BasePlusCommissionEmployee::setSocialSecurityNumber(
48     const string &ssn )
49  {
```

Fig. 12.8 | BasePlusCommissionEmployee class represents an employee who receives a base salary in addition to a commission. (Part 1 of 3.)

```cpp
50        socialSecurityNumber = ssn; // should validate
51   } // end function setSocialSecurityNumber
52
53   // return social security number
54   string BasePlusCommissionEmployee::getSocialSecurityNumber() const
55   {
56        return socialSecurityNumber;
57   } // end function getSocialSecurityNumber
58
59   // set gross sales amount
60   void BasePlusCommissionEmployee::setGrossSales( double sales )
61   {
62        grossSales = ( sales < 0.0 ) ? 0.0 : sales;
63   } // end function setGrossSales
64
65   // return gross sales amount
66   double BasePlusCommissionEmployee::getGrossSales() const
67   {
68        return grossSales;
69   } // end function getGrossSales
70
71   // set commission rate
72   void BasePlusCommissionEmployee::setCommissionRate( double rate )
73   {
74        commissionRate = ( rate > 0.0 && rate < 1.0 ) ? rate : 0.0;
75   } // end function setCommissionRate
76
77   // return commission rate
78   double BasePlusCommissionEmployee::getCommissionRate() const
79   {
80        return commissionRate;
81   } // end function getCommissionRate
82
83   // set base salary
84   void BasePlusCommissionEmployee::setBaseSalary( double salary )
85   {
86      baseSalary = ( salary < 0.0 ) ? 0.0 : salary;
87   } // end function setBaseSalary
88
89   // return base salary
90   double BasePlusCommissionEmployee::getBaseSalary() const
91   {
92        return baseSalary;
93   } // end function getBaseSalary
94
95   // calculate earnings
96   double BasePlusCommissionEmployee::earnings() const
97   {
98        return baseSalary + ( commissionRate * grossSales );
99   } // end function earnings
100
```

Fig. 12.8 | BasePlusCommissionEmployee class represents an employee who receives a base salary in addition to a commission. (Part 2 of 3.)

```
101  // print BasePlusCommissionEmployee object
102  void BasePlusCommissionEmployee::print() const
103  {
104     cout << "base-salaried commission employee: " << firstName << ' '
105        << lastName << "\nsocial security number: " << socialSecurityNumber
106        << "\ngross sales: " << grossSales
107        << "\ncommission rate: " << commissionRate
108        << "\nbase salary: " << baseSalary;
109  } // end function print
```

Fig. 12.8 | BasePlusCommissionEmployee class represents an employee who receives a base salary in addition to a commission. (Part 3 of 3.)

```
1   // Fig. 12.9: fig12_09.cpp
2   // Testing class BasePlusCommissionEmployee.
3   #include <iostream>
4   using std::cout;
5   using std::endl;
6   using std::fixed;
7
8   #include <iomanip>
9   using std::setprecision;
10
11  // BasePlusCommissionEmployee class definition
12  #include "BasePlusCommissionEmployee.h"
13
14  int main()
15  {
16     // instantiate BasePlusCommissionEmployee object
17     BasePlusCommissionEmployee
18        employee( "Bob", "Lewis", "333-33-3333", 5000, .04, 300 );
19
20     // set floating-point output formatting
21     cout << fixed << setprecision( 2 );
22
23     // get commission employee data
24     cout << "Employee information obtained by get functions: \n"
25        << "\nFirst name is " << employee.getFirstName()
26        << "\nLast name is " << employee.getLastName()
27        << "\nSocial security number is "
28        << employee.getSocialSecurityNumber()
29        << "\nGross sales is " << employee.getGrossSales()
30        << "\nCommission rate is " << employee.getCommissionRate()
31        << "\nBase salary is " << employee.getBaseSalary() << endl;
32
33     employee.setBaseSalary( 1000 ); // set base salary
34
35     cout << "\nUpdated employee information output by print function: \n"
36        << endl;
37     employee.print(); // display the new employee information
38
```

Fig. 12.9 | BasePlusCommissionEmployee class test program. (Part 1 of 2.)

```
39      // display the employee's earnings
40      cout << "\n\nEmployee's earnings: $" << employee.earnings() << endl;
41
42      return 0;
43   } // end main
```

```
Employee information obtained by get functions:

First name is Bob
Last name is Lewis
Social security number is 333-33-3333
Gross sales is 5000.00
Commission rate is 0.04
Base salary is 300.00

Updated employee information output by print function:

base-salaried commission employee: Bob Lewis
social security number: 333-33-3333
gross sales: 5000.00
commission rate: 0.04
base salary: 1000.00

Employee's earnings: $1200.00
```

Fig. 12.9 | BasePlusCommissionEmployee class test program. (Part 2 of 2.)

Exploring the Similarities Between Class BasePlusCommissionEmployee and Class CommissionEmployee

Note that much of the code for class BasePlusCommissionEmployee (Figs. 12.7–12.8) is similar, if not identical, to the code for class CommissionEmployee (Figs. 12.4–12.5). For example, in class BasePlusCommissionEmployee, private data members firstName and lastName and member functions setFirstName, getFirstName, setLastName and get-LastName are identical to those of class CommissionEmployee. Classes CommissionEmployee and BasePlusCommissionEmployee also both contain private data members socialSecurityNumber, commissionRate and grossSales, as well as *get* and *set* functions to manipulate these members. In addition, the BasePlusCommissionEmployee constructor is almost identical to that of class CommissionEmployee, except that BasePlusCommission-Employee's constructor also sets the baseSalary. The other additions to class BasePlus-CommissionEmployee are private data member baseSalary and member functions setBaseSalary and getBaseSalary. Class BasePlusCommissionEmployee's print member function is nearly identical to that of class CommissionEmployee, except that BasePlus-CommissionEmployee's print also outputs the value of data member baseSalary.

We literally copied code from class CommissionEmployee and pasted it into class BasePlusCommissionEmployee, then modified class BasePlusCommissionEmployee to include a base salary and member functions that manipulate the base salary. This "copy-and-paste" approach is often error prone and time consuming. Worse yet, it can spread many physical copies of the same code throughout a system, creating a code-maintenance nightmare. Is there a way to "absorb" the data members and member functions of a class in a way that makes them part of other classes without duplicating code? In the next several examples, we do exactly this, using inheritance.

Software Engineering Observation 12.3

Copying and pasting code from one class to another can spread errors across multiple source code files. To avoid duplicating code (and possibly errors), use inheritance, rather than the "copy-and-paste" approach, in situations where you want one class to "absorb" the data members and member functions of another class.

Software Engineering Observation 12.4

With inheritance, the common data members and member functions of all the classes in the hierarchy are declared in a base class. When changes are required for these common features, software developers need to make the changes only in the base class—derived classes then inherit the changes. Without inheritance, changes would need to be made to all the source code files that contain a copy of the code in question.

12.4.3 Creating a CommissionEmployee–BasePlusCommissionEmployee Inheritance Hierarchy

Now we create and test a new version of class BasePlusCommissionEmployee (Figs. 12.10–12.11) that derives from class CommissionEmployee (Figs. 12.4–12.5). In this example, a BasePlusCommissionEmployee object *is a* CommissionEmployee (because inheritance passes on the capabilities of class CommissionEmployee), but class BasePlusCommissionEmployee

```
1   // Fig. 12.10: BasePlusCommissionEmployee.h
2   // BasePlusCommissionEmployee class derived from class
3   // CommissionEmployee.
4   #ifndef BASEPLUS_H
5   #define BASEPLUS_H
6
7   #include <string> // C++ standard string class
8   using std::string;
9
10  #include "CommissionEmployee.h" // CommissionEmployee class declaration
11
12  class BasePlusCommissionEmployee : public CommissionEmployee
13  {
14  public:
15     BasePlusCommissionEmployee( const string &, const string &,
16        const string &, double = 0.0, double = 0.0, double = 0.0 );
17
18     void setBaseSalary( double ); // set base salary
19     double getBaseSalary() const; // return base salary
20
21     double earnings() const; // calculate earnings
22     void print() const; // print BasePlusCommissionEmployee object
23  private:
24     double baseSalary; // base salary
25  }; // end class BasePlusCommissionEmployee
26
27  #endif
```

Fig. 12.10 | BasePlusCommissionEmployee class definition indicating inheritance relationship with class CommissionEmployee.

also has data member baseSalary (Fig. 12.10, line 24). The colon (:) in line 12 of the class definition indicates inheritance. Keyword public indicates the type of inheritance. As a derived class (formed with public inheritance), BasePlusCommissionEmployee inherits all the members of class CommissionEmployee, except for the constructor—each class provides its own constructors that are specific to the class. [Note that destructors, too, are not inherited.] Thus, the public services of BasePlusCommissionEmployee include its constructor (lines 15–16) and the public member functions inherited from class CommissionEmployee—although we cannot see these inherited member functions in BasePlusCommissionEmployee's source code, they are nevertheless a part of derived class BasePlusCommissionEmployee. The derived class's public services also include member functions setBaseSalary, getBaseSalary, earnings and print (lines 18–22).

Figure 12.11 shows BasePlusCommissionEmployee's member-function implementations. The constructor (lines 10–17) introduces base-class initializer syntax (line 14), which uses a member initializer to pass arguments to the base-class (CommissionEmployee) constructor. C++ requires a derived-class constructor to call its base-class constructor to initialize the base-class data members that are inherited into the derived class. Line 14 accomplishes this task by invoking the CommissionEmployee constructor by name, passing the constructor's parameters first, last, ssn, sales and rate as arguments to initialize base-class data members firstName, lastName, socialSecurityNumber, grossSales and commissionRate. If BasePlusCommissionEmployee's constructor did not invoke class CommissionEmployee's constructor explicitly, C++ would attempt to invoke class CommissionEmployee's default constructor—but the class does not have such a constructor, so the compiler would issue an error. Recall from Chapter 3 that the compiler provides a default constructor with no parameters in any class that does not explicitly include a constructor. However, CommissionEmployee *does* explicitly include a constructor, so a default constructor is not provided and any attempts to implicitly call CommissionEmployee's default constructor would result in compilation errors.

```cpp
1   // Fig. 12.11: BasePlusCommissionEmployee.cpp
2   // Class BasePlusCommissionEmployee member-function definitions.
3   #include <iostream>
4   using std::cout;
5
6   // BasePlusCommissionEmployee class definition
7   #include "BasePlusCommissionEmployee.h"
8
9   // constructor
10  BasePlusCommissionEmployee::BasePlusCommissionEmployee(
11     const string &first, const string &last, const string &ssn,
12     double sales, double rate, double salary )
13     // explicitly call base-class constructor
14     : CommissionEmployee( first, last, ssn, sales, rate )
15  {
16     setBaseSalary( salary ); // validate and store base salary
17  } // end BasePlusCommissionEmployee constructor
18
```

Fig. 12.11 | BasePlusCommissionEmployee implementation file: private base-class data cannot be accessed from derived class. (Part 1 of 3.)

```
19   // set base salary
20   void BasePlusCommissionEmployee::setBaseSalary( double salary )
21   {
22      baseSalary = ( salary < 0.0 ) ? 0.0 : salary;
23   } // end function setBaseSalary
24
25   // return base salary
26   double BasePlusCommissionEmployee::getBaseSalary() const
27   {
28      return baseSalary;
29   } // end function getBaseSalary
30
31   // calculate earnings
32   double BasePlusCommissionEmployee::earnings() const
33   {
34      // derived class cannot access the base class's private data
35      return baseSalary + ( commissionRate * grossSales );
36   } // end function earnings
37
38   // print BasePlusCommissionEmployee object
39   void BasePlusCommissionEmployee::print() const
40   {
41      // derived class cannot access the base class's private data
42      cout << "base-salaried commission employee: " << firstName << ' '
43         << lastName << "\nsocial security number: " << socialSecurityNumber
44         << "\ngross sales: " << grossSales
45         << "\ncommission rate: " << commissionRate
46         << "\nbase salary: " << baseSalary;
47   } // end function print
```

```
C:\scpphtp5_examples\ch12\Fig12_10_11\BasePlusCommission-Employee.cpp(35) :
   error C2248: 'CommissionEmployee::commissionRate' :
   cannot access private member declared in class 'CommissionEmployee'
      C:\scpphtp5_examples\ch12\Fig12_10_11\CommissionEmployee.h(37) :
         see declaration of 'CommissionEmployee::commissionRate'
      C:\scpphtp5e_examples\ch12\Fig12_10_11\CommissionEmployee.h(10) :
         see declaration of 'CommissionEmployee'

C:\scpphtp5_examples\ch12\Fig12_10_11\BasePlusCommission-Employee.cpp(35) :
   error C2248: 'CommissionEmployee::grossSales' :
   cannot access private member declared in class 'CommissionEmployee'
      C:\scpphtp5_examples\ch12\Fig12_10_11\CommissionEmployee.h(36) :
         see declaration of 'CommissionEmployee::grossSales'
      C:\scpphtp5_examples\ch12\Fig12_10_11\CommissionEmployee.h(10) :
         see declaration of 'CommissionEmployee'

C:\scpphtp5_examples\ch12\Fig12_10_11\BasePlusCommission-Employee.cpp(42) :
   error C2248: 'CommissionEmployee::firstName' :
   cannot access private member declared in class 'CommissionEmployee'
      C:\scpphtp5_examples\ch12\Fig12_10_11\CommissionEmployee.h(33) :
         see declaration of 'CommissionEmployee::firstName'
      C:\scpphtp5_examples\ch12\Fig12_10_11\CommissionEmployee.h(10) :
         see declaration of 'CommissionEmployee'
```

Fig. 12.11 | BasePlusCommissionEmployee implementation file: private base-class data cannot be accessed from derived class. (Part 2 of 3.)

```
C:\scpphtp5_examples\ch12\Fig12_10_11\BasePlusCommission-Employee.cpp(43) :
   error C2248: 'CommissionEmployee::lastName' :
   cannot access private member declared in class 'CommissionEmployee'
      C:\scpphtp5_examples\ch12\Fig12_10_11\CommissionEmployee.h(34) :
         see declaration of 'CommissionEmployee::lastName'
      C:\scpphtp5_examples\ch12\Fig12_10_11\CommissionEmployee.h(10) :
         see declaration of 'CommissionEmployee'

C:\scpphtp5_examples\ch12\Fig12_10_11\BasePlusCommission-Employee.cpp(43) :
   error C2248: 'CommissionEmployee::socialSecurity-Number' :
   cannot access private member declared in class 'CommissionEmployee'
      C:\scpphtp5_examples\ch12\Fig12_10_11\CommissionEmployee.h(35) :
         see declaration of 'CommissionEmployee::socialSecurityNumber'
      C:\scpphtp5_examples\ch12\Fig12_10_11\CommissionEmployee.h(10) :
         see declaration of 'CommissionEmployee'

C:\scpphtp5_examples\ch12\Fig12_10_11\BasePlusCommission-Employee.cpp(44) :
   error C2248: 'CommissionEmployee::grossSales' :
   cannot access private member declared in class 'CommissionEmployee'
      C:\scpphtp5_examples\ch12\Fig12_10_11\CommissionEmployee.h(36) :
         see declaration of 'CommissionEmployee::grossSales'
      C:\scpphtp5_examples\ch12\Fig12_10_11\CommissionEmployee.h(10) :
         see declaration of 'CommissionEmployee'

C:\scpphtp5_examples\ch12\Fig12_10_11\BasePlusCommission-Employee.cpp(45) :
   error C2248: 'CommissionEmployee::commissionRate' :
   cannot access private member declared in class 'CommissionEmployee'
      C:\scpphtp5_examples\ch12\Fig12_10_11\CommissionEmployee.h(37) :
         see declaration of 'CommissionEmployee::commissionRate'
      C:\scpphtp5_examples\ch12\Fig12_10_11\CommissionEmployee.h(10) :
         see declaration of 'CommissionEmployee'
```

Fig. 12.11 | BasePlusCommissionEmployee implementation file: private base-class data cannot be accessed from derived class. (Part 3 of 3.)

Common Programming Error 12.1

A compilation error occurs if a derived-class constructor calls one of its base-class constructors with arguments that are inconsistent with the number and types of parameters specified in one of the base-class constructor definitions.

Performance Tip 12.1

In a derived-class constructor, initializing member objects and invoking base-class constructors explicitly in the member initializer list prevents duplicate initialization in which a default constructor is called, then data members are modified again in the derived-class constructor's body.

The compiler generates errors for line 35 of Fig. 12.11 because base class CommissionEmployee's data members commissionRate and grossSales are private—derived class BasePlusCommissionEmployee's member functions are not allowed to access base class CommissionEmployee's private data. Note that we used red text in Fig. 12.11 to indicate erroneous code. The compiler issues additional errors at lines 42–45 of BasePlusCommissionEmployee's print member function for the same reason. As you can see, C++ rigidly enforces restrictions on accessing private data members, so that even a derived class (which is intimately related to its base class) cannot access the base class's private data. [*Note:* To save space, we show only the error messages from Visual C++ .NET in this example. The error messages produced by your compiler may differ from those shown here. Also notice that we highlight key portions of the lengthy error messages in bold.]

We purposely included the erroneous code in Fig. 12.11 to demonstrate that a derived class's member functions cannot access its base class's private data. The errors in BasePlusCommissionEmployee could have been prevented by using the *get* member functions inherited from class CommissionEmployee. For example, line 35 could have invoked getCommissionRate and getGrossSales to access CommissionEmployee's private data members commissionRate and grossSales, respectively. Similarly, lines 42–45 could have used appropriate *get* member functions to retrieve the values of the base class's data members. In the next example, we show how using protected data also allows us to avoid the errors encountered in this example.

Including the Base Class Header File in the Derived Class Header File with `#include`
Notice that we #include the base class's header file in the derived class's header file (line 10 of Fig. 12.10). This is necessary for three reasons. First, for the derived class to use the base class's name in line 12, we must tell the compiler that the base class exists—the class definition in CommissionEmployee.h does exactly that.

The second reason is that the compiler uses a class definition to determine the size of an object of that class (as we discussed in Section 3.8). A client program that creates an object of a class must #include the class definition to enable the compiler to reserve the proper amount of memory for the object. When using inheritance, a derived-class object's size depends on the data members declared explicitly in its class definition *and* the data members inherited from its direct and indirect base classes. Including the base class's definition in line 10 allows the compiler to determine the memory requirements for the base class's data members that become part of a derived-class object and thus contribute to the total size of the derived-class object.

The last reason for line 10 is to allow the compiler to determine whether the derived class uses the base class's inherited members properly. For example, in the program of Figs. 12.10–12.11, the compiler uses the base-class header file to determine that the data members being accessed by the derived class are private in the base class. Since these are inaccessible to the derived class, the compiler generates errors. The compiler also uses the base class's function prototypes to validate function calls made by the derived class to the inherited base-class functions—you will see an example of such a function call in Fig. 12.16.

Linking Process in an Inheritance Hierarchy
In Section 3.9, we discussed the linking process for creating an executable GradeBook application. In that example, you saw that the client's object code was linked with the object code for class GradeBook, as well as the object code for any C++ Standard Library classes used in either the client code or in class GradeBook.

The linking process is similar for a program that uses classes in an inheritance hierarchy. The process requires the object code for all classes used in the program and the object code for the direct and indirect base classes of any derived classes used by the program. Suppose a client wants to create an application that uses class BasePlusCommission-Employee, which is a derived class of CommissionEmployee (we will see an example of this in Section 12.4.4). When compiling the client application, the client's object code must be linked with the object code for classes BasePlusCommissionEmployee and Commission-

Employee, because BasePlusCommissionEmployee inherits member functions from its base class CommissionEmployee. The code is also linked with the object code for any C++ Standard Library classes used in class CommissionEmployee, class BasePlusCommission-Employee or the client code. This provides the program with access to the implementations of all of the functionality that the program may use.

12.4.4 CommissionEmployee-BasePlusCommissionEmployee Inheritance Hierarchy Using protected Data

To enable class BasePlusCommissionEmployee to directly access CommissionEmployee data members firstName, lastName, socialSecurityNumber, grossSales and commission-Rate, we can declare those members as protected in the base class. As we discussed in Section 12.3, a base class's protected members can be accessed by members and friends of the base class and by members and friends of any classes derived from that base class.

 Good Programming Practice 12.1

Declare public members first, protected members second and private members last.

Defining Base Class CommissionEmployee with protected Data
Class CommissionEmployee (Figs. 12.12–12.13) now declares data members firstName, lastName, socialSecurityNumber, grossSales and commissionRate as protected (Fig. 12.12, lines 33–37) rather than private. The member-function implementations in Fig. 12.13 are identical to those in Fig. 12.5.

```
1    // Fig. 12.12: CommissionEmployee.h
2    // CommissionEmployee class definition with protected data.
3    #ifndef COMMISSION_H
4    #define COMMISSION_H
5
6    #include <string> // C++ standard string class
7    using std::string;
8
9    class CommissionEmployee
10   {
11   public:
12      CommissionEmployee( const string &, const string &, const string &,
13         double = 0.0, double = 0.0 );
14
15      void setFirstName( const string & ); // set first name
16      string getFirstName() const; // return first name
17
18      void setLastName( const string & ); // set last name
19      string getLastName() const; // return last name
20
21      void setSocialSecurityNumber( const string & ); // set SSN
22      string getSocialSecurityNumber() const; // return SSN
23
```

Fig. 12.12 | CommissionEmployee class definition that declares protected data to allow access by derived classes. (Part 1 of 2.)

```
24     void setGrossSales( double ); // set gross sales amount
25     double getGrossSales() const; // return gross sales amount
26
27     void setCommissionRate( double ); // set commission rate
28     double getCommissionRate() const; // return commission rate
29
30     double earnings() const; // calculate earnings
31     void print() const; // print CommissionEmployee object
32  protected:
33     string firstName;
34     string lastName;
35     string socialSecurityNumber;
36     double grossSales; // gross weekly sales
37     double commissionRate; // commission percentage
38  }; // end class CommissionEmployee
39
40  #endif
```

Fig. 12.12 | CommissionEmployee class definition that declares protected data to allow access by derived classes. (Part 2 of 2.)

```
1   // Fig. 12.13: CommissionEmployee.cpp
2   // Class CommissionEmployee member-function definitions.
3   #include <iostream>
4   using std::cout;
5
6   #include "CommissionEmployee.h" // CommissionEmployee class definition
7
8   // constructor
9   CommissionEmployee::CommissionEmployee(
10     const string &first, const string &last, const string &ssn,
11     double sales, double rate )
12  {
13     firstName = first; // should validate
14     lastName = last; // should validate
15     socialSecurityNumber = ssn; // should validate
16     setGrossSales( sales ); // validate and store gross sales
17     setCommissionRate( rate ); // validate and store commission rate
18  } // end CommissionEmployee constructor
19
20  // set first name
21  void CommissionEmployee::setFirstName( const string &first )
22  {
23     firstName = first; // should validate
24  } // end function setFirstName
25
26  // return first name
27  string CommissionEmployee::getFirstName() const
28  {
29     return firstName;
30  } // end function getFirstName
31
```

Fig. 12.13 | CommissionEmployee class with protected data. (Part 1 of 3.)

```
32   // set last name
33   void CommissionEmployee::setLastName( const string &last )
34   {
35      lastName = last; // should validate
36   } // end function setLastName
37
38   // return last name
39   string CommissionEmployee::getLastName() const
40   {
41      return lastName;
42   } // end function getLastName
43
44   // set social security number
45   void CommissionEmployee::setSocialSecurityNumber( const string &ssn )
46   {
47      socialSecurityNumber = ssn; // should validate
48   } // end function setSocialSecurityNumber
49
50   // return social security number
51   string CommissionEmployee::getSocialSecurityNumber() const
52   {
53      return socialSecurityNumber;
54   } // end function getSocialSecurityNumber
55
56   // set gross sales amount
57   void CommissionEmployee::setGrossSales( double sales )
58   {
59      grossSales = ( sales < 0.0 ) ? 0.0 : sales;
60   } // end function setGrossSales
61
62   // return gross sales amount
63   double CommissionEmployee::getGrossSales() const
64   {
65      return grossSales;
66   } // end function getGrossSales
67
68   // set commission rate
69   void CommissionEmployee::setCommissionRate( double rate )
70   {
71      commissionRate = ( rate > 0.0 && rate < 1.0 ) ? rate : 0.0;
72   } // end function setCommissionRate
73
74   // return commission rate
75   double CommissionEmployee::getCommissionRate() const
76   {
77      return commissionRate;
78   } // end function getCommissionRate
79
80   // calculate earnings
81   double CommissionEmployee::earnings() const
82   {
83      return commissionRate * grossSales;
84   } // end function earnings
```

Fig. 12.13 | CommissionEmployee class with protected data. (Part 2 of 3.)

```
85
86   // print CommissionEmployee object
87   void CommissionEmployee::print() const
88   {
89      cout << "commission employee: " << firstName << ' ' << lastName
90         << "\nsocial security number: " << socialSecurityNumber
91         << "\ngross sales: " << grossSales
92         << "\ncommission rate: " << commissionRate;
93   } // end function print
```

Fig. 12.13 | CommissionEmployee class with protected data. (Part 3 of 3.)

Modifying Derived Class BasePlusCommissionEmployee

We now modify class BasePlusCommissionEmployee (Figs. 12.14–12.15) so that it inherits from the version of class CommissionEmployee in Figs. 12.12–12.13. Because class BasePlusCommissionEmployee inherits from this version of class CommissionEmployee, objects of class BasePlusCommissionEmployee can access inherited data members that are declared protected in class CommissionEmployee (i.e., data members firstName, lastName, socialSecurityNumber, grossSales and commissionRate). As a result, the compiler does not generate errors when compiling the BasePlusCommissionEmployee earnings and print member-function definitions in Fig. 12.15 (lines 32–36 and 39–47, respectively).

```
 1   // Fig. 12.14: BasePlusCommissionEmployee.h
 2   // BasePlusCommissionEmployee class derived from class
 3   // CommissionEmployee.
 4   #ifndef BASEPLUS_H
 5   #define BASEPLUS_H
 6
 7   #include <string> // C++ standard string class
 8   using std::string;
 9
10   #include "CommissionEmployee.h" // CommissionEmployee class declaration
11
12   class BasePlusCommissionEmployee : public CommissionEmployee
13   {
14   public:
15      BasePlusCommissionEmployee( const string &, const string &,
16         const string &, double = 0.0, double = 0.0, double = 0.0 );
17
18      void setBaseSalary( double ); // set base salary
19      double getBaseSalary() const; // return base salary
20
21      double earnings() const; // calculate earnings
22      void print() const; // print BasePlusCommissionEmployee object
23   private:
24      double baseSalary; // base salary
25   }; // end class BasePlusCommissionEmployee
26
27   #endif
```

Fig. 12.14 | BasePlusCommissionEmployee class header file.

```cpp
 1   // Fig. 12.15: BasePlusCommissionEmployee.cpp
 2   // Class BasePlusCommissionEmployee member-function definitions.
 3   #include <iostream>
 4   using std::cout;
 5
 6   // BasePlusCommissionEmployee class definition
 7   #include "BasePlusCommissionEmployee.h"
 8
 9   // constructor
10   BasePlusCommissionEmployee::BasePlusCommissionEmployee(
11      const string &first, const string &last, const string &ssn,
12      double sales, double rate, double salary )
13      // explicitly call base-class constructor
14      : CommissionEmployee( first, last, ssn, sales, rate )
15   {
16      setBaseSalary( salary ); // validate and store base salary
17   } // end BasePlusCommissionEmployee constructor
18
19   // set base salary
20   void BasePlusCommissionEmployee::setBaseSalary( double salary )
21   {
22      baseSalary = ( salary < 0.0 ) ? 0.0 : salary;
23   } // end function setBaseSalary
24
25   // return base salary
26   double BasePlusCommissionEmployee::getBaseSalary() const
27   {
28      return baseSalary;
29   } // end function getBaseSalary
30
31   // calculate earnings
32   double BasePlusCommissionEmployee::earnings() const
33   {
34      // can access protected data of base class
35      return baseSalary + ( commissionRate * grossSales );
36   } // end function earnings
37
38   // print BasePlusCommissionEmployee object
39   void BasePlusCommissionEmployee::print() const
40   {
41      // can access protected data of base class
42      cout << "base-salaried commission employee: " << firstName << ' '
43         << lastName << "\nsocial security number: " << socialSecurityNumber
44         << "\ngross sales: " << grossSales
45         << "\ncommission rate: " << commissionRate
46         << "\nbase salary: " << baseSalary;
47   } // end function print
```

Fig. 12.15 | BasePlusCommissionEmployee implementation file for
BasePlusCommissionEmployee class that inherits protected data from CommissionEmployee.

This shows the special privileges that a derived class is granted to access protected base-class data members. Objects of a derived class also can access protected members in any of that derived class's indirect base classes.

Class `BasePlusCommissionEmployee` does not inherit class `CommissionEmployee`'s constructor. However, class `BasePlusCommissionEmployee`'s constructor (Fig. 12.15, lines 10–17) calls class `CommissionEmployee`'s constructor explicitly (line 14). Recall that `BasePlusCommissionEmployee`'s constructor must explicitly call the constructor of class `CommissionEmployee`, because `CommissionEmployee` does not contain a default constructor that could be invoked implicitly.

Testing the Modified ***BasePlusCommissionEmployee*** *Class*

Figure 12.16 uses a `BasePlusCommissionEmployee` object to perform the same tasks that Fig. 12.9 performed on an object of the first version of class `BasePlusCommissionEmployee` (Figs. 12.7–12.8). Note that the outputs of the two programs are identical. We created the first class `BasePlusCommissionEmployee` without using inheritance and created this version of `BasePlusCommissionEmployee` using inheritance; however, both classes provide the same functionality. Note that the code for class `BasePlusCommissionEmployee` (i.e., the header and implementation files), which is 74 lines, is considerably shorter than the

```
1   // Fig. 12.16: fig12_16.cpp
2   // Testing class BasePlusCommissionEmployee.
3   #include <iostream>
4   using std::cout;
5   using std::endl;
6   using std::fixed;
7
8   #include <iomanip>
9   using std::setprecision;
10
11  // BasePlusCommissionEmployee class definition
12  #include "BasePlusCommissionEmployee.h"
13
14  int main()
15  {
16     // instantiate BasePlusCommissionEmployee object
17     BasePlusCommissionEmployee
18        employee( "Bob", "Lewis", "333-33-3333", 5000, .04, 300 );
19
20     // set floating-point output formatting
21     cout << fixed << setprecision( 2 );
22
23     // get commission employee data
24     cout << "Employee information obtained by get functions: \n"
25        << "\nFirst name is " << employee.getFirstName()
26        << "\nLast name is " << employee.getLastName()
27        << "\nSocial security number is "
28        << employee.getSocialSecurityNumber()
29        << "\nGross sales is " << employee.getGrossSales()
30        << "\nCommission rate is " << employee.getCommissionRate()
31        << "\nBase salary is " << employee.getBaseSalary() << endl;
32
33     employee.setBaseSalary( 1000 ); // set base salary
34
```

Fig. 12.16 | `protected` base-class data can be accessed from derived class. (Part 1 of 2.)

```
35        cout << "\nUpdated employee information output by print function: \n"
36           << endl;
37        employee.print(); // display the new employee information
38
39        // display the employee's earnings
40        cout << "\n\nEmployee's earnings: $" << employee.earnings() << endl;
41
42        return 0;
43     } // end main
```

```
Employee information obtained by get functions:

First name is Bob
Last name is Lewis
Social security number is 333-33-3333
Gross sales is 5000.00
Commission rate is 0.04
Base salary is 300.00

Updated employee information output by print function:

base-salaried commission employee: Bob Lewis
social security number: 333-33-3333
gross sales: 5000.00
commission rate: 0.04
base salary: 1000.00

Employee's earnings: $1200.00
```

Fig. 12.16 | protected base-class data can be accessed from derived class. (Part 2 of 2.)

code for the noninherited version of the class, which is 154 lines, because the inherited version absorbs part of its functionality from CommissionEmployee, whereas the noninherited version does not absorb any functionality. Also, there is now only one copy of the CommissionEmployee functionality declared and defined in class CommissionEmployee. This makes the source code easier to maintain, modify and debug, because the source code related to a CommissionEmployee exists only in the files of Figs. 12.12–12.13.

Notes on Using protected Data
In this example, we declared base-class data members as protected, so that derived classes could modify the data directly. Inheriting protected data members slightly increases performance, because we can directly access the members without incurring the overhead of calls to *set* or *get* member functions. In most cases, however, it is better to use private data members to encourage proper software engineering, and leave code optimization issues to the compiler. Your code will be easier to maintain, modify and debug.

Using protected data members creates two major problems. First, the derived-class object does not have to use a member function to set the value of the base-class's protected data member. Therefore, a derived-class object easily can assign an invalid value to the protected data member, thus leaving the object in an inconsistent state. For example, with CommissionEmployee's data member grossSales declared as protected, a derived-class (e.g., `BasePlusCommissionEmployee`) object can assign a negative value to `grossSales`. The second problem with using `protected` data members is that derived-class member functions are more likely to be written so that they depend on the base-class implementation. In practice, derived classes should depend only on the base-class services (i.e., non-private member functions) and not on the base-class implementation. With `protected` data members in the base class, if the base-class implementation changes, we may need to modify all derived classes of that base class. For example, if for some reason we were to change the names of data members `firstName` and `lastName` to `first` and `last`, then we would have to do so for all occurrences in which a derived class references these base-class data members directly. In such a case, the software is said to be fragile or brittle, because a small change in the base class can "break" derived-class implementation. The programmer should be able to change the base-class implementation while still providing the same services to derived classes. (Of course, if the base-class services change, we must reimplement our derived classes—good object-oriented design attempts to prevent this.)

Software Engineering Observation 12.5

It is appropriate to use the `protected` access specifier when a base class should provide a service (i.e., a member function) only to its derived classes (and `friend`s), not to other clients.

Software Engineering Observation 12.6

Declaring base-class data members `private` (as opposed to declaring them `protected`) enables programmers to change the base-class implementation without having to change derived-class implementations.

Error-Prevention Tip 12.1

When possible, avoid including `protected` data members in a base class. Rather, include non-private member functions that access `private` data members, ensuring that the object maintains a consistent state.

12.4.5 CommissionEmployee–BasePlusCommissionEmployee Inheritance Hierarchy Using private Data

We now reexamine our hierarchy once more, this time using the best software engineering practices. Class `CommissionEmployee` (Figs. 12.17–12.18) now declares data members `firstName`, `lastName`, `socialSecurityNumber`, `grossSales` and `commissionRate` as private (Fig. 12.17, lines 33–37) and provides `public` member functions `setFirstName`, `getFirstName`, `setLastName`, `getLastName`, `setSocialSecurityNumber`, `getSocialSecurityNumber`, `setGrossSales`, `getGrossSales`, `setCommissionRate`, `getCommissionRate`, `earnings` and `print` for manipulating these values. If we decide to change the data member names, the `earnings` and `print` definitions will not require modification—only the definitions of the *get* and *set* member functions that directly manipulate the data members will need to change. Note that these changes occur solely within the base class—no changes to the derived class are needed. Localizing the effects of changes like this is a good software engineering practice. Derived class `BasePlusCommissionEmployee` (Figs. 12.19–12.20) inherits `CommissionEmployee`'s non-private member functions and can access the `private` base-class members via those member functions.

```cpp
1   // Fig. 12.17: CommissionEmployee.h
2   // CommissionEmployee class definition with good software engineering.
3   #ifndef COMMISSION_H
4   #define COMMISSION_H
5
6   #include <string> // C++ standard string class
7   using std::string;
8
9   class CommissionEmployee
10  {
11  public:
12     CommissionEmployee( const string &, const string &, const string &,
13        double = 0.0, double = 0.0 );
14
15     void setFirstName( const string & ); // set first name
16     string getFirstName() const; // return first name
17
18     void setLastName( const string & ); // set last name
19     string getLastName() const; // return last name
20
21     void setSocialSecurityNumber( const string & ); // set SSN
22     string getSocialSecurityNumber() const; // return SSN
23
24     void setGrossSales( double ); // set gross sales amount
25     double getGrossSales() const; // return gross sales amount
26
27     void setCommissionRate( double ); // set commission rate
28     double getCommissionRate() const; // return commission rate
29
30     double earnings() const; // calculate earnings
31     void print() const; // print CommissionEmployee object
32  private:
33     string firstName;
34     string lastName;
35     string socialSecurityNumber;
36     double grossSales; // gross weekly sales
37     double commissionRate; // commission percentage
38  }; // end class CommissionEmployee
39
40  #endif
```

Fig. 12.17 | CommissionEmployee class defined using good software engineering practices.

```cpp
1   // Fig. 12.18: CommissionEmployee.cpp
2   // Class CommissionEmployee member-function definitions.
3   #include <iostream>
4   using std::cout;
5
6   #include "CommissionEmployee.h" // CommissionEmployee class definition
7
```

Fig. 12.18 | CommissionEmployee class implementation file: CommissionEmployee class uses member functions to manipulate its private data. (Part 1 of 3.)

```
 8    // constructor
 9    CommissionEmployee::CommissionEmployee(
10       const string &first, const string &last, const string &ssn,
11       double sales, double rate )
12       : firstName( first ), lastName( last ), socialSecurityNumber( ssn )
13    {
14       setGrossSales( sales ); // validate and store gross sales
15       setCommissionRate( rate ); // validate and store commission rate
16    } // end CommissionEmployee constructor
17
18    // set first name
19    void CommissionEmployee::setFirstName( const string &first )
20    {
21       firstName = first; // should validate
22    } // end function setFirstName
23
24    // return first name
25    string CommissionEmployee::getFirstName() const
26    {
27       return firstName;
28    } // end function getFirstName
29
30    // set last name
31    void CommissionEmployee::setLastName( const string &last )
32    {
33       lastName = last; // should validate
34    } // end function setLastName
35
36    // return last name
37    string CommissionEmployee::getLastName() const
38    {
39       return lastName;
40    } // end function getLastName
41
42    // set social security number
43    void CommissionEmployee::setSocialSecurityNumber( const string &ssn )
44    {
45       socialSecurityNumber = ssn; // should validate
46    } // end function setSocialSecurityNumber
47
48    // return social security number
49    string CommissionEmployee::getSocialSecurityNumber() const
50    {
51       return socialSecurityNumber;
52    } // end function getSocialSecurityNumber
53
54    // set gross sales amount
55    void CommissionEmployee::setGrossSales( double sales )
56    {
57       grossSales = ( sales < 0.0 ) ? 0.0 : sales;
58    } // end function setGrossSales
```

Fig. 12.18 | CommissionEmployee class implementation file: CommissionEmployee class uses member functions to manipulate its **private** data. (Part 2 of 3.)

```
59
60   // return gross sales amount
61   double CommissionEmployee::getGrossSales() const
62   {
63      return grossSales;
64   } // end function getGrossSales
65
66   // set commission rate
67   void CommissionEmployee::setCommissionRate( double rate )
68   {
69      commissionRate = ( rate > 0.0 && rate < 1.0 ) ? rate : 0.0;
70   } // end function setCommissionRate
71
72   // return commission rate
73   double CommissionEmployee::getCommissionRate() const
74   {
75      return commissionRate;
76   } // end function getCommissionRate
77
78   // calculate earnings
79   double CommissionEmployee::earnings() const
80   {
81      return getCommissionRate() * getGrossSales();
82   } // end function earnings
83
84   // print CommissionEmployee object
85   void CommissionEmployee::print() const
86   {
87      cout << "commission employee: "
88         << getFirstName() << ' ' << getLastName()
89         << "\nsocial security number: " << getSocialSecurityNumber()
90         << "\ngross sales: " << getGrossSales()
91         << "\ncommission rate: " << getCommissionRate();
92   } // end function print
```

Fig. 12.18 | CommissionEmployee class implementation file: CommissionEmployee class uses member functions to manipulate its private data. (Part 3 of 3.)

In the CommissionEmployee constructor implementation (Fig. 12.18, lines 9–16), note that we use member initializers (line 12) to set the values of members firstName, lastName and socialSecurityNumber. We show how derived-class BasePlusCommissionEmployee (Figs. 12.19–12.20) can invoke non-private base-class member functions (setFirstName, getFirstName, setLastName, getLastName, setSocialSecurityNumber and getSocialSecurityNumber) to manipulate these data members.

Performance Tip 12.2

Using a member function to access a data member's value can be slightly slower than accessing the data directly. However, today's optimizing compilers are carefully designed to perform many optimizations implicitly (such as inlining set and get member-function calls). As a result, programmers should write code that adheres to proper software engineering principles, and leave optimization issues to the compiler. A good rule is, "Do not second-guess the compiler."

Class `BasePlusCommissionEmployee` (Figs. 12.19–12.20) has several changes to its member-function implementations (Fig. 12.20) that distinguish it from the previous version of the class (Figs. 12.14–12.15). Member functions `earnings` (Fig. 12.20, lines 32–35) and

```
1   // Fig. 12.19: BasePlusCommissionEmployee.h
2   // BasePlusCommissionEmployee class derived from class
3   // CommissionEmployee.
4   #ifndef BASEPLUS_H
5   #define BASEPLUS_H
6
7   #include <string> // C++ standard string class
8   using std::string;
9
10  #include "CommissionEmployee.h" // CommissionEmployee class declaration
11
12  class BasePlusCommissionEmployee : public CommissionEmployee
13  {
14  public:
15     BasePlusCommissionEmployee( const string &, const string &,
16        const string &, double = 0.0, double = 0.0, double = 0.0 );
17
18     void setBaseSalary( double ); // set base salary
19     double getBaseSalary() const; // return base salary
20
21     double earnings() const; // calculate earnings
22     void print() const; // print BasePlusCommissionEmployee object
23  private:
24     double baseSalary; // base salary
25  }; // end class BasePlusCommissionEmployee
26
27  #endif
```

Fig. 12.19 | `BasePlusCommissionEmployee` class header file.

```
1   // Fig. 12.20: BasePlusCommissionEmployee.cpp
2   // Class BasePlusCommissionEmployee member-function definitions.
3   #include <iostream>
4   using std::cout;
5
6   // BasePlusCommissionEmployee class definition
7   #include "BasePlusCommissionEmployee.h"
8
9   // constructor
10  BasePlusCommissionEmployee::BasePlusCommissionEmployee(
11     const string &first, const string &last, const string &ssn,
12     double sales, double rate, double salary )
13     // explicitly call base-class constructor
14     : CommissionEmployee( first, last, ssn, sales, rate )
15  {
```

Fig. 12.20 | `BasePlusCommissionEmployee` class that inherits from class `CommissionEmployee` but cannot directly access the class's `private` data. (Part 1 of 2.)

```
16        setBaseSalary( salary ); // validate and store base salary
17   } // end BasePlusCommissionEmployee constructor
18
19   // set base salary
20   void BasePlusCommissionEmployee::setBaseSalary( double salary )
21   {
22        baseSalary = ( salary < 0.0 ) ? 0.0 : salary;
23   } // end function setBaseSalary
24
25   // return base salary
26   double BasePlusCommissionEmployee::getBaseSalary() const
27   {
28        return baseSalary;
29   } // end function getBaseSalary
30
31   // calculate earnings
32   double BasePlusCommissionEmployee::earnings() const
33   {
34        return getBaseSalary() + CommissionEmployee::earnings();
35   } // end function earnings
36
37   // print BasePlusCommissionEmployee object
38   void BasePlusCommissionEmployee::print() const
39   {
40        cout << "base-salaried ";
41
42        // invoke CommissionEmployee's print function
43        CommissionEmployee::print();
44
45        cout << "\nbase salary: " << getBaseSalary();
46   } // end function print
```

Fig. 12.20 | `BasePlusCommissionEmployee` class that inherits from class `CommissionEmployee` but cannot directly access the class's `private` data. (Part 2 of 2.)

print (lines 38–46) each invoke member function getBaseSalary to obtain the base salary value, rather than accessing baseSalary directly. This insulates earnings and print from potential changes to the implementation of data member baseSalary. For example, if we decide to rename data member baseSalary or change its type, only member functions set-BaseSalary and getBaseSalary will need to change.

Class BasePlusCommissionEmployee's earnings function (Fig. 12.20, lines 32–35) redefines class CommissionEmployee's earnings member function (Fig. 12.18, lines 79–82) to calculate the earnings of a base-salaried commission employee. Class BasePlusCommissionEmployee's version of earnings obtains the portion of the employee's earnings based on commission alone by calling base-class CommissionEmployee's earnings function with the expression CommissionEmployee::earnings() (Fig. 12.20, line 34). BasePlusCommissionEmployee's earnings function then adds the base salary to this value to calculate the total earnings of the employee. Note the syntax used to invoke a redefined base-class member function from a derived class—place the base-class name and the binary scope resolution operator (::) before the base-class member-function name. This member-function invocation is a good software engineering practice: Recall from Software Engineering Observation 9.9 that, if an object's member function performs the actions needed by another object, we should call that member function rather than duplicating its code body. By having BasePlusCommissionEmployee's earnings function invoke Commission-Employee's earnings function to calculate part of a BasePlusCommissionEmployee object's earnings, we avoid duplicating the code and reduce code-maintenance problems.

Common Programming Error 12.2

When a base-class member function is redefined in a derived class, the derived-class version often calls the base-class version to do additional work. Failure to use the :: operator prefixed with the name of the base class when referencing the base class's member function causes infinite recursion, because the derived-class member function would then call itself.

Common Programming Error 12.3

Including a base-class member function with a different signature in the derived class hides the base-class version of the function. Attempts to call the base-class version through the public interface of a derived-class object result in compilation errors.

Similarly, BasePlusCommissionEmployee's print function (Fig. 12.20, lines 38–46) redefines class CommissionEmployee's print member function (Fig. 12.18, lines 85–92) to output information that is appropriate for a base-salaried commission employee. Class BasePlusCommissionEmployee's version displays part of a BasePlusCommissionEmployee object's information (i.e., the string "commission employee" and the values of class CommissionEmployee's private data members) by calling CommissionEmployee's print member function with the qualified name CommissionEmployee::print() (Fig. 12.20, line 43). BasePlusCommissionEmployee's print function then outputs the remainder of a BasePlusCommissionEmployee object's information (i.e., the value of class BasePlus-CommissionEmployee's base salary).

Figure 12.21 performs the same manipulations on a BasePlusCommissionEmployee object as did Fig. 12.9 and Fig. 12.16 on objects of classes CommissionEmployee and BasePlusCommissionEmployee, respectively. Although each "base-salaried commission employee" class behaves identically, class BasePlusCommissionEmployee is the best engineered. By using inheritance and by calling member functions that hide the data and ensure consistency, we have efficiently and effectively constructed a well-engineered class.

```
 1   // Fig. 12.21: fig12_21.cpp
 2   // Testing class BasePlusCommissionEmployee.
 3   #include <iostream>
 4   using std::cout;
 5   using std::endl;
 6   using std::fixed;
 7
 8   #include <iomanip>
 9   using std::setprecision;
10
11   // BasePlusCommissionEmployee class definition
12   #include "BasePlusCommissionEmployee.h"
```

Fig. 12.21 | Base-class private data is accessible to a derived class via public or protected member function inherited by the derived class. (Part 1 of 2.)

```
13
14   int main()
15   {
16       // instantiate BasePlusCommissionEmployee object
17       BasePlusCommissionEmployee
18           employee( "Bob", "Lewis", "333-33-3333", 5000, .04, 300 );
19
20       // set floating-point output formatting
21       cout << fixed << setprecision( 2 );
22
23       // get commission employee data
24       cout << "Employee information obtained by get functions: \n"
25           << "\nFirst name is " << employee.getFirstName()
26           << "\nLast name is " << employee.getLastName()
27           << "\nSocial security number is "
28           << employee.getSocialSecurityNumber()
29           << "\nGross sales is " << employee.getGrossSales()
30           << "\nCommission rate is " << employee.getCommissionRate()
31           << "\nBase salary is " << employee.getBaseSalary() << endl;
32
33       employee.setBaseSalary( 1000 ); // set base salary
34
35       cout << "\nUpdated employee information output by print function: \n"
36           << endl;
37       employee.print(); // display the new employee information
38
39       // display the employee's earnings
40       cout << "\n\nEmployee's earnings: $" << employee.earnings() << endl;
41
42       return 0;
43   } // end main
```

```
Employee information obtained by get functions:

First name is Bob
Last name is Lewis
Social security number is 333-33-3333
Gross sales is 5000.00
Commission rate is 0.04
Base salary is 300.00

Updated employee information output by print function:

base-salaried commission employee: Bob Lewis
social security number: 333-33-3333
gross sales: 5000.00
commission rate: 0.04
base salary: 1000.00

Employee's earnings: $1200.00
```

Fig. 12.21 | Base-class `private` data is accessible to a derived class via `public` or `protected` member function inherited by the derived class. (Part 2 of 2.)

In this section, you saw an evolutionary set of examples that was carefully designed to teach key capabilities for good software engineering with inheritance. You learned how to create a derived class using inheritance, how to use protected base-class members to enable a derived class to access inherited base-class data members and how to redefine base-class functions to provide versions that are more appropriate for derived-class objects. In addition, you learned how to apply software engineering techniques from Chapters 9–10 and this chapter to create classes that are easy to maintain, modify and debug.

12.5   Constructors and Destructors in Derived Classes

As we explained in the preceding section, instantiating a derived-class object begins a chain of constructor calls in which the derived-class constructor, before performing its own tasks, invokes its direct base class's constructor either explicitly (via a base-class member initializer) or implicitly (calling the base class's default constructor). Similarly, if the base class is derived from another class, the base-class constructor is required to invoke the constructor of the next class up in the hierarchy, and so on. The last constructor called in this chain is the constructor of the class at the base of the hierarchy, whose body actually finishes executing first. The original derived-class constructor's body finishes executing last. Each base-class constructor initializes the base-class data members that the derived-class object inherits. For example, consider the CommissionEmployee/BasePlusCommissionEmployee hierarchy from Figs. 12.17–12.20. When a program creates an object of class BasePlusCommissionEmployee, the CommissionEmployee constructor is called. Since class CommissionEmployee is at the base of the hierarchy, its constructor executes, initializing the private data members of CommissionEmployee that are part of the BasePlusCommissionEmployee object. When CommissionEmployee's constructor completes execution, it returns control to BasePlusCommissionEmployee's constructor, which initializes the BasePlusCommissionEmployee object's baseSalary.

> **Software Engineering Observation 12.7**
>
> *When a program creates a derived-class object, the derived-class constructor immediately calls the base-class constructor, the base-class constructor's body executes, then the derived class's member initializers execute and finally the derived-class constructor's body executes. This process cascades up the hierarchy if the hierarchy contains more than two levels.*

When a derived-class object is destroyed, the program calls that object's destructor. This begins a chain (or cascade) of destructor calls in which the derived-class destructor and the destructors of the direct and indirect base classes and the classes' members execute in reverse of the order in which the constructors executed. When a derived-class object's destructor is called, the destructor performs its task, then invokes the destructor of the next base class up the hierarchy. This process repeats until the destructor of the final base class at the top of the hierarchy is called. Then the object is removed from memory.

> **Software Engineering Observation 12.8**
>
> *Suppose that we create an object of a derived class where both the base class and the derived class contain objects of other classes. When an object of that derived class is created, first the constructors for the base class's member objects execute, then the base-class constructor executes, then the constructors for the derived class's member objects execute, then the derived class's constructor executes. Destructors for derived-class objects are called in the reverse of the order in which their corresponding constructors are called.*

Base-class constructors, destructors and overloaded assignment operators (see Chapter 11, Operator Overloading; String and Array Objects) are not inherited by derived classes. Derived-class constructors, destructors and overloaded assignment operators, however, can call base-class constructors, destructors and overloaded assignment operators.

Our next example revisits the commission employee hierarchy by defining class CommissionEmployee (Figs. 12.22–12.23) and class BasePlusCommissionEmployee (Figs. 12.24–12.25) that contain constructors and destructors, each of which prints a message when it is invoked. As you will see in the output in Fig. 12.26, these messages demonstrate the order in which the constructors and destructors are called for objects in an inheritance hierarchy.

```cpp
1   // Fig. 12.22: CommissionEmployee.h
2   // CommissionEmployee class definition represents a commission employee.
3   #ifndef COMMISSION_H
4   #define COMMISSION_H
5
6   #include <string> // C++ standard string class
7   using std::string;
8
9   class CommissionEmployee
10  {
11  public:
12     CommissionEmployee( const string &, const string &, const string &,
13        double = 0.0, double = 0.0 );
14     ~CommissionEmployee(); // destructor
15
16     void setFirstName( const string & ); // set first name
17     string getFirstName() const; // return first name
18
19     void setLastName( const string & ); // set last name
20     string getLastName() const; // return last name
21
22     void setSocialSecurityNumber( const string & ); // set SSN
23     string getSocialSecurityNumber() const; // return SSN
24
25     void setGrossSales( double ); // set gross sales amount
26     double getGrossSales() const; // return gross sales amount
27
28     void setCommissionRate( double ); // set commission rate
29     double getCommissionRate() const; // return commission rate
30
31     double earnings() const; // calculate earnings
32     void print() const; // print CommissionEmployee object
33  private:
34     string firstName;
35     string lastName;
36     string socialSecurityNumber;
37     double grossSales; // gross weekly sales
38     double commissionRate; // commission percentage
39  }; // end class CommissionEmployee
40
41  #endif
```

Fig. 12.22 | CommissionEmployee class header file.

In this example, we modified the CommissionEmployee constructor (lines 10–21 of Fig. 12.23) and included a CommissionEmployee destructor (lines 24–29), each of which outputs a line of text upon its invocation. We also modified the BasePlusCommissionEmployee constructor (lines 11–22 of Fig. 12.25) and included a BasePlusCommissionEmployee destructor (lines 25–30), each of which outputs a line of text upon its invocation.

```cpp
1   // Fig. 12.23: CommissionEmployee.cpp
2   // Class CommissionEmployee member-function definitions.
3   #include <iostream>
4   using std::cout;
5   using std::endl;
6
7   #include "CommissionEmployee.h" // CommissionEmployee class definition
8
9   // constructor
10  CommissionEmployee::CommissionEmployee(
11     const string &first, const string &last, const string &ssn,
12     double sales, double rate )
13     : firstName( first ), lastName( last ), socialSecurityNumber( ssn )
14  {
15     setGrossSales( sales ); // validate and store gross sales
16     setCommissionRate( rate ); // validate and store commission rate
17
18     cout << "CommissionEmployee constructor: " << endl;
19     print();
20     cout << "\n\n";
21  } // end CommissionEmployee constructor
22
23  // destructor
24  CommissionEmployee::~CommissionEmployee()
25  {
26     cout << "CommissionEmployee destructor: " << endl;
27     print();
28     cout << "\n\n";
29  } // end CommissionEmployee destructor
30
31  // set first name
32  void CommissionEmployee::setFirstName( const string &first )
33  {
34     firstName = first; // should validate
35  } // end function setFirstName
36
37  // return first name
38  string CommissionEmployee::getFirstName() const
39  {
40     return firstName;
41  } // end function getFirstName
42
43  // set last name
44  void CommissionEmployee::setLastName( const string &last )
45  {
```

Fig. 12.23 | CommissionEmployee's constructor outputs text. (Part 1 of 3.)

```
46      lastName = last; // should validate
47   } // end function setLastName
48
49   // return last name
50   string CommissionEmployee::getLastName() const
51   {
52      return lastName;
53   } // end function getLastName
54
55   // set social security number
56   void CommissionEmployee::setSocialSecurityNumber( const string &ssn )
57   {
58      socialSecurityNumber = ssn; // should validate
59   } // end function setSocialSecurityNumber
60
61   // return social security number
62   string CommissionEmployee::getSocialSecurityNumber() const
63   {
64      return socialSecurityNumber;
65   } // end function getSocialSecurityNumber
66
67   // set gross sales amount
68   void CommissionEmployee::setGrossSales( double sales )
69   {
70      grossSales = ( sales < 0.0 ) ? 0.0 : sales;
71   } // end function setGrossSales
72
73   // return gross sales amount
74   double CommissionEmployee::getGrossSales() const
75   {
76      return grossSales;
77   } // end function getGrossSales
78
79   // set commission rate
80   void CommissionEmployee::setCommissionRate( double rate )
81   {
82      commissionRate = ( rate > 0.0 && rate < 1.0 ) ? rate : 0.0;
83   } // end function setCommissionRate
84
85   // return commission rate
86   double CommissionEmployee::getCommissionRate() const
87   {
88      return commissionRate;
89   } // end function getCommissionRate
90
91   // calculate earnings
92   double CommissionEmployee::earnings() const
93   {
94      return getCommissionRate() * getGrossSales();
95   } // end function earnings
96
```

Fig. 12.23 | CommissionEmployee's constructor outputs text. (Part 2 of 3.)

```
97   // print CommissionEmployee object
98   void CommissionEmployee::print() const
99   {
100     cout << "commission employee: "
101        << getFirstName() << ' ' << getLastName()
102        << "\nsocial security number: " << getSocialSecurityNumber()
103        << "\ngross sales: " << getGrossSales()
104        << "\ncommission rate: " << getCommissionRate();
105  } // end function print
```

Fig. 12.23 | CommissionEmployee's constructor outputs text. (Part 3 of 3.)

```
1    // Fig. 12.24: BasePlusCommissionEmployee.h
2    // BasePlusCommissionEmployee class derived from class
3    // CommissionEmployee.
4    #ifndef BASEPLUS_H
5    #define BASEPLUS_H
6
7    #include <string> // C++ standard string class
8    using std::string;
9
10   #include "CommissionEmployee.h" // CommissionEmployee class declaration
11
12   class BasePlusCommissionEmployee : public CommissionEmployee
13   {
14   public:
15      BasePlusCommissionEmployee( const string &, const string &,
16         const string &, double = 0.0, double = 0.0, double = 0.0 );
17      ~BasePlusCommissionEmployee(); // destructor
18
19      void setBaseSalary( double ); // set base salary
20      double getBaseSalary() const; // return base salary
21
22      double earnings() const; // calculate earnings
23      void print() const; // print BasePlusCommissionEmployee object
24   private:
25      double baseSalary; // base salary
26   }; // end class BasePlusCommissionEmployee
27
28   #endif
```

Fig. 12.24 | BasePlusCommissionEmployee class header file.

```
1    // Fig. 12.25: BasePlusCommissionEmployee.cpp
2    // Class BasePlusCommissionEmployee member-function definitions.
3    #include <iostream>
4    using std::cout;
5    using std::endl;
6
7    // BasePlusCommissionEmployee class definition
8    #include "BasePlusCommissionEmployee.h"
```

Fig. 12.25 | BasePlusCommissionEmployee's constructor outputs text. (Part 1 of 2.)

```
 9
10   // constructor
11   BasePlusCommissionEmployee::BasePlusCommissionEmployee(
12      const string &first, const string &last, const string &ssn,
13      double sales, double rate, double salary )
14      // explicitly call base-class constructor
15      : CommissionEmployee( first, last, ssn, sales, rate )
16   {
17      setBaseSalary( salary ); // validate and store base salary
18
19      cout << "BasePlusCommissionEmployee constructor: " << endl;
20      print();
21      cout << "\n\n";
22   } // end BasePlusCommissionEmployee constructor
23
24   // destructor
25   BasePlusCommissionEmployee::~BasePlusCommissionEmployee()
26   {
27      cout << "BasePlusCommissionEmployee destructor: " << endl;
28      print();
29      cout << "\n\n";
30   } // end BasePlusCommissionEmployee destructor
31
32   // set base salary
33   void BasePlusCommissionEmployee::setBaseSalary( double salary )
34   {
35      baseSalary = ( salary < 0.0 ) ? 0.0 : salary;
36   } // end function setBaseSalary
37
38   // return base salary
39   double BasePlusCommissionEmployee::getBaseSalary() const
40   {
41      return baseSalary;
42   } // end function getBaseSalary
43
44   // calculate earnings
45   double BasePlusCommissionEmployee::earnings() const
46   {
47      return getBaseSalary() + CommissionEmployee::earnings();
48   } // end function earnings
49
50   // print BasePlusCommissionEmployee object
51   void BasePlusCommissionEmployee::print() const
52   {
53      cout << "base-salaried ";
54
55      // invoke CommissionEmployee's print function
56      CommissionEmployee::print();
57
58      cout << "\nbase salary: " << getBaseSalary();
59   } // end function print
```

Fig. 12.25 | BasePlusCommissionEmployee's constructor outputs text. (Part 2 of 2.)

Figure 12.26 demonstrates the order in which constructors and destructors are called for objects of classes that are part of an inheritance hierarchy. Function main (lines 15–34) begins by instantiating CommissionEmployee object employee1 (lines 21–22) in a separate block inside main (lines 20–23). The object goes in and out of scope immediately (the end of the block is reached as soon as the object is created), so both the CommissionEmployee constructor and destructor are called. Next, lines 26–27 instantiate BasePlusCommissionEmployee object employee2. This invokes the CommissionEmployee constructor to display outputs with values passed from the BasePlusCommissionEmployee constructor, then the output specified in the BasePlusCommissionEmployee constructor is performed. Lines 30–31 then instantiate BasePlusCommissionEmployee object employee3. Again, the CommissionEmployee and BasePlusCommissionEmployee constructors are both called. Note that, in each case, the body of the CommissionEmployee constructor is executed before the body of the BasePlusCommissionEmployee constructor executes. When the end of main is reached, the destructors are called for objects employee2 and employee3. But, because destructors are called in the reverse order of their corresponding constructors, the BasePlusCommissionEmployee destructor and CommissionEmployee destructor are called (in that order) for object employee3, then the BasePlusCommissionEmployee and CommissionEmployee destructors are called (in that order) for object employee2.

```cpp
1   // Fig. 12.26: fig12_26.cpp
2   // Display order in which base-class and derived-class constructors
3   // and destructors are called.
4   #include <iostream>
5   using std::cout;
6   using std::endl;
7   using std::fixed;
8
9   #include <iomanip>
10  using std::setprecision;
11
12  // BasePlusCommissionEmployee class definition
13  #include "BasePlusCommissionEmployee.h"
14
15  int main()
16  {
17     // set floating-point output formatting
18     cout << fixed << setprecision( 2 );
19
20     { // begin new scope
21        CommissionEmployee employee1(
22           "Bob", "Lewis", "333-33-3333", 5000, .04 );
23     } // end scope
24
25     cout << endl;
26     BasePlusCommissionEmployee
27        employee2( "Lisa", "Jones", "555-55-5555", 2000, .06, 800 );
28
```

Fig. 12.26 | Constructor and destructor call order. (Part 1 of 3.)

```
29      cout << endl;
30      BasePlusCommissionEmployee
31         employee3( "Mark", "Sands", "888-88-8888", 8000, .15, 2000 );
32      cout << endl;
33      return 0;
34   } // end main
```

```
CommissionEmployee constructor:
commission employee: Bob Lewis
social security number: 333-33-3333
gross sales: 5000.00
commission rate: 0.04

CommissionEmployee destructor:
commission employee: Bob Lewis
social security number: 333-33-3333
gross sales: 5000.00
commission rate: 0.04


CommissionEmployee constructor:
base-salaried commission employee: Lisa Jones
social security number: 555-55-5555
gross sales: 2000.00
commission rate: 0.06

BasePlusCommissionEmployee constructor:
base-salaried commission employee: Lisa Jones
social security number: 555-55-5555
gross sales: 2000.00
commission rate: 0.06
base salary: 800.00


CommissionEmployee constructor:
commission employee: Mark Sands
social security number: 888-88-8888
gross sales: 8000.00
commission rate: 0.15

BasePlusCommissionEmployee constructor:
base-salaried commission employee: Mark Sands
social security number: 888-88-8888
gross sales: 8000.00
commission rate: 0.15
base salary: 2000.00

BasePlusCommissionEmployee destructor:
base-salaried commission employee: Mark Sands
social security number: 888-88-8888
gross sales: 8000.00
commission rate: 0.15
base salary: 2000.00
```

(continued at top of next page...)

Fig. 12.26 | Constructor and destructor call order. (Part 2 of 3.)

```
                                            (...continued from bottom of previous page)

CommissionEmployee destructor:
commission employee: Mark Sands
social security number: 888-88-8888
gross sales: 8000.00
commission rate: 0.15

BasePlusCommissionEmployee destructor:
base-salaried commission employee: Lisa Jones
social security number: 555-55-5555
gross sales: 2000.00
commission rate: 0.06
base salary: 800.00

CommissionEmployee destructor:
commission employee: Lisa Jones
social security number: 555-55-5555
gross sales: 2000.00
commission rate: 0.06
```

Fig. 12.26 | Constructor and destructor call order. (Part 3 of 3.)

12.6 **public, protected** and **private** Inheritance

When deriving a class from a base class, the base class may be inherited through **public**, **protected** or **private** inheritance. Use of **protected** and **private** inheritance is rare, and each should be used only with great care; we use only **public** inheritance in this book. Figure 12.27 summarizes for each type of inheritance the accessibility of base-class members in a derived class. The first column contains the base-class access specifiers.

When deriving a class from a **public** base class, **public** members of the base class become **public** members of the derived class and **protected** members of the base class become **protected** members of the derived class. A base class's **private** members are never accessible directly from a derived class, but can be accessed through calls to the **public** and **protected** members of the base class.

When deriving from a **protected** base class, **public** and **protected** members of the base class become **protected** members of the derived class. When deriving from a **private** base class, **public** and **protected** members of the base class become **private** members (e.g., the functions become utility functions) of the derived class. Private and protected inheritance are not *is-a* relationships.

12.7 Software Engineering with Inheritance

In this section, we discuss the use of inheritance to customize existing software. When we use inheritance to create a new class from an existing one, the new class inherits the data members and member functions of the existing class, as described in Fig. 12.27. We can customize the new class to meet our needs by including additional members and by redefining base-class members. The derived-class programmer does this in C++ without accessing the base class's source code. The derived class must be able to link to the base class's

Base-class member-access specifier	Type of inheritance		
	`public` inheritance	`protected` inheritance	`private` inheritance
public	`public` in derived class. Can be accessed directly by member functions, `friend` functions and nonmember functions.	`protected` in derived class. Can be accessed directly by member functions and `friend` functions.	`private` in derived class. Can be accessed directly by member functions and `friend` functions.
protected	`protected` in derived class. Can be accessed directly by member functions and `friend` functions.	`protected` in derived class. Can be accessed directly by member functions and `friend` functions.	`private` in derived class. Can be accessed directly by member functions and `friend` functions.
private	Hidden in derived class. Can be accessed by member functions and `friend` functions through `public` or `protected` member functions of the base class.	Hidden in derived class. Can be accessed by member functions and `friend` functions through `public` or `protected` member functions of the base class.	Hidden in derived class. Can be accessed by member functions and `friend` functions through `public` or `protected` member functions of the base class.

Fig. 12.27 | Summary of base-class member accessibility in a derived class.

object code. This powerful capability is attractive to independent software vendors (ISVs). ISVs can develop proprietary classes for sale or license and make these classes available to users in object-code format. Users then can derive new classes from these library classes rapidly and without accessing the ISVs' proprietary source code. All the ISVs need to supply with the object code are the header files.

Sometimes it is difficult for students to appreciate the scope of problems faced by designers who work on large-scale software projects in industry. People experienced with such projects say that effective software reuse improves the software development process. Object-oriented programming facilitates software reuse, thus shortening development times and enhancing software quality.

The availability of substantial and useful class libraries delivers the maximum benefits of software reuse through inheritance. Just as shrink-wrapped software produced by independent software vendors became an explosive-growth industry with the arrival of the personal computer, so, too, interest in the creation and sale of class libraries is growing exponentially. Application designers build their applications with these libraries, and library designers are being rewarded by having their libraries included with the applications. The standard C++ libraries that are shipped with C++ compilers tend to be rather general purpose and limited in scope. However, there is massive worldwide commitment to the development of class libraries for a huge variety of applications arenas.

Software Engineering Observation 12.9

At the design stage in an object-oriented system, the designer often determines that certain classes are closely related. The designer should "factor out" common attributes and behaviors and place these in a base class, then use inheritance to form derived classes, endowing them with capabilities beyond those inherited from the base class.

Software Engineering Observation 12.10

The creation of a derived class does not affect its base class's source code. Inheritance preserves the integrity of a base class.

Software Engineering Observation 12.11

Just as designers of non-object-oriented systems should avoid proliferation of functions, designers of object-oriented systems should avoid proliferation of classes. Proliferation of classes creates management problems and can hinder software reusability, because it becomes difficult for a client to locate the most appropriate class of a huge class library. The alternative is to create fewer classes that provide more substantial functionality, but such classes might provide too much functionality.

Performance Tip 12.3

If classes produced through inheritance are larger than they need to be (i.e., contain too much functionality), memory and processing resources might be wasted. Inherit from the class whose functionality is "closest" to what is needed.

Reading derived-class definitions can be confusing, because inherited members are not shown physically in the derived classes, but nevertheless are present. A similar problem exists when documenting derived-class members.

12.8 Wrap-Up

This chapter introduced inheritance—the ability to create a class by absorbing an existing class's data members and member functions and embellishing them with new capabilities. Through a series of examples using an employee inheritance hierarchy, you learned the notions of base classes and derived classes and used `public` inheritance to create a derived class that inherits members from a base class. The chapter introduced the access specifier `protected`; derived-class member functions can access `protected` base-class members. You learned how to access redefined base-class members by qualifying their names with the base-class name and binary scope resolution operator (`::`). You also saw the order in which constructors and destructors are called for objects of classes that are part of an inheritance hierarchy. Finally, we explained the three types of inheritance—`public`, `protected` and `private`—and the accessibility of base-class members in a derived class when using each type.

In Chapter 13, Object-Oriented Programming: Polymorphism, we build upon our discussion of inheritance by introducing polymorphism—an object-oriented concept that enables us to write programs that handle, in a more general manner, objects of a wide variety of classes related by inheritance. After studying Chapter 13, you will be familiar with classes, objects, encapsulation, inheritance and polymorphism—the essential aspects of object-oriented programming.

Summary

- Software reuse reduces program development time and cost.

- Inheritance is a form of software reuse in which the programmer creates a class that absorbs an existing class's data and behaviors and enhances them with new capabilities. The existing class is called the base class, and the new class is referred to as the derived class.

- A direct base class is the one from which a derived class explicitly inherits (specified by the class name to the right of the : in the first line of a class definition). An indirect base class is inherited from two or more levels up in the class hierarchy.

- With single inheritance, a class is derived from one base class. With multiple inheritance, a class inherits from multiple (possibly unrelated) base classes.

- A derived class represents a more specialized group of objects. Typically, a derived class contains behaviors inherited from its base class plus additional behaviors. A derived class can also customize behaviors inherited from the base class.

- Every object of a derived class is also an object of that class's base class. However, a base-class object is not an object of that class's derived classes.

- The *is-a* relationship represents inheritance. In an *is-a* relationship, an object of a derived class also can be treated as an object of its base class.

- The *has-a* relationship represents composition. In a *has-a* relationship, an object contains one or more objects of other classes as members, but does not disclose their behavior directly in its interface.

- A derived class cannot access the private members of its base class directly; allowing this would violate the encapsulation of the base class. A derived class can, however, access the public and protected members of its base class directly.

- A derived class can effect state changes in private base-class members, but only through non-private member functions provided in the base class and inherited into the derived class.

- When a base-class member function is inappropriate for a derived class, that member function can be redefined in the derived class with an appropriate implementation.

- Single-inheritance relationships form treelike hierarchical structures—a base class exists in a hierarchical relationship with its derived classes.

- It is possible to treat base-class objects and derived-class objects similarly; the commonality shared between the object types is expressed in the data members and member functions of the base class.

- A base class's public members are accessible anywhere that the program has a handle to an object of that base class or to an object of one of that base class's derived classes—or, when using the binary scope resolution operator, whenever the class's name is in scope.

- A base class's private members are accessible only within the definition of that base class or from friends of that class.

- A base class's protected members have an intermediate level of protection between public and private access. A base class's protected members can be accessed by members and friends of that base class and by members and friends of any classes derived from that base class.

- Unfortunately, protected data members often present two major problems. First, the derived-class object does not have to use a *set* function to change the value of the base-class's protected data. Second, derived-class member functions are more likely to depend on base-class implementation details.

- When a derived-class member function redefines a base-class member function, the base-class member function can be accessed from the derived class by qualifying the base-class member function name with the base-class name and the binary scope resolution operator (::).

- When an object of a derived class is instantiated, the base class's constructor is called immediately (either explicitly or implicitly) to initialize the base-class data members in the derived-class object (before the derived-class data members are initialized).

- Declaring data members `private`, while providing non-`private` member functions to manipulate and perform validation checking on this data, enforces good software engineering.

- When a derived-class object is destroyed, the destructors are called in the reverse order of the constructors—first the derived-class destructor is called, then the base-class destructor is called.

- When deriving a class from a base class, the base class may be declared as either `public`, `protected` or `private`.

- When deriving a class from a `public` base class, `public` members of the base class become `public` members of the derived class, and `protected` members of the base class become `protected` members of the derived class.

- When deriving a class from a `protected` base class, `public` and `protected` members of the base class become `protected` members of the derived class.

- When deriving a class from a `private` base class, `public` and `protected` members of the base class become `private` members of the derived class.

Terminology

base class

base-class constructor

base-class default constructor

base-class destructor

base-class initializer

brittle software

class hierarchy

composition

customize software

derived class

derived-class constructor

derived-class destructor

direct base class

fragile software

`friend` of a base class

`friend` of a derived class

has-a relationship

hierarchical relationship

indirect base class

inherit the members of an existing class

inheritance

is-a relationship

multiple inheritance

`private` base class

`private` inheritance

`protected` base class

`protected` inheritance

`protected` keyword

`protected` member of a class

`public` base class

`public` inheritance

qualified name

redefine a base-class member function

single inheritance

subclass

superclass

Self-Review Exercises

12.1   Fill in the blanks in each of the following statements:

a) _____ is a form of software reuse in which new classes absorb the data and behaviors of existing classes and embellish these classes with new capabilities.

b) A base class's _____ members can be accessed only in the base-class definition or in derived-class definitions.

c) In a(n) _____ relationship, an object of a derived class also can be treated as an object of its base class.

d) In a(n) _____ relationship, a class object has one or more objects of other classes as members.

e) In single inheritance, a class exists in a(n) _____ relationship with its derived classes.

f) A base class's _____ members are accessible within that base class and anywhere that the program has a handle to an object of that base class or to an object of one of its derived classes.

g) A base class's `protected` access members have a level of protection between those of `public` and _____ access.

h) C++ provides for _____, which allows a derived class to inherit from many base classes, even if these base classes are unrelated.

i) When an object of a derived class is instantiated, the base class's _____ is called implicitly or explicitly to do any necessary initialization of the base-class data members in the derived-class object.

j) When deriving a class from a base class with `public` inheritance, `public` members of the base class become _____ members of the derived class, and `protected` members of the base class become _____ members of the derived class.

k) When deriving a class from a base class with `protected` inheritance, `public` members of the base class become _____ members of the derived class, and `protected` members of the base class become _____ members of the derived class.

12.2 State whether each of the following is *true* or *false*. If *false*, explain why.
a) Base-class constructors are not inherited by derived classes.
b) A *has-a* relationship is implemented via inheritance.
c) A `Car` class has an *is-a* relationship with the `SteeringWheel` and `Brakes` classes.
d) Inheritance encourages the reuse of proven high-quality software.
e) When a derived-class object is destroyed, the destructors are called in the reverse order of the constructors.

Answers to Self-Review Exercises

12.1 a) Inheritance. b) `protected`. c) *is-a* or inheritance. d) *has-a* or composition or aggregation. e) hierarchical. f) `public`. g) `private`. h) multiple inheritance. i) constructor. j) `public`, `protected`. k) `protected`, `protected`.

12.2 a) True. b) False. A *has-a* relationship is implemented via composition. An *is-a* relationship is implemented via inheritance. c) False. This is an example of a *has-a* relationship. Class `Car` has an *is-a* relationship with class `Vehicle`. d) True. e) True.

Exercises

12.3 Many programs written with inheritance could be written with composition instead, and vice versa. Rewrite class `BasePlusCommissionEmployee` of the `CommissionEmployee–BasePlusCommissionEmployee` hierarchy to use composition rather than inheritance. After you do this, assess the relative merits of the two approaches for designing classes `CommissionEmployee` and `BasePlusCommissionEmployee`, as well as for object-oriented programs in general. Which approach is more natural? Why?

12.4 Discuss the ways in which inheritance promotes software reuse, saves time during program development and helps prevent errors.

12.5 Some programmers prefer not to use `protected` access because they believe it breaks the encapsulation of the base class. Discuss the relative merits of using `protected` access vs. using `private` access in base classes.

12.6 Draw an inheritance hierarchy for students at a university similar to the hierarchy shown in Fig. 12.2. Use `Student` as the base class of the hierarchy, then include classes `UndergraduateStudent` and GraduateStudent that derive from Student. Continue to extend the hierarchy as deep (i.e., as many levels) as possible. For example, Freshman, Sophomore, Junior and Senior might derive from UndergraduateStudent, and DoctoralStudent and MastersStudent might derive from Graduate-Student. After drawing the hierarchy, discuss the relationships that exist between the classes. [*Note:* You do not need to write any code for this exercise.]

12.7   The world of shapes is much richer than the shapes included in the inheritance hierarchy of Fig. 12.3. Write down all the shapes you can think of—both two-dimensional and three-dimensional—and form them into a more complete Shape hierarchy with as many levels as possible. Your hierarchy should have base class Shape from which class TwoDimensionalShape and class ThreeDimensionalShape are derived. [*Note:* You do not need to write any code for this exercise.] We will use this hierarchy in the exercises of Chapter 13 to process a set of distinct shapes as objects of base-class Shape. (This technique, called polymorphism, is the subject of Chapter 13.)

12.8   Draw an inheritance hierarchy for classes Quadrilateral, Trapezoid, Parallelogram, Rectangle and Square. Use Quadrilateral as the base class of the hierarchy. Make the hierarchy as deep as possible.

12.9   (*Package Inheritance Hierarchy*) Package-delivery services, such as FedEx®, DHL® and UPS®, offer a number of different shipping options, each with specific costs associated. Create an inheritance hierarchy to represent various types of packages. Use Package as the base class of the hierarchy, then include classes TwoDayPackage and OvernightPackage that derive from Package. Base class Package should include data members representing the name, address, city, state and ZIP code for both the sender and the recipient of the package, in addition to data members that store the weight (in ounces) and cost per ounce to ship the package. Package's constructor should initialize these data members. Ensure that the weight and cost per ounce contain positive values. Package should provide a public member function calculateCost that returns a double indicating the cost associated with shipping the package. Package's calculateCost function should determine the cost by multiplying the weight by the cost per ounce. Derived class TwoDayPackage should inherit the functionality of base class Package, but also include a data member that represents a flat fee that the shipping company charges for two-day-delivery service. TwoDayPackage's constructor should receive a value to initialize this data member. TwoDayPackage should redefine member function calculate-Cost so that it computes the shipping cost by adding the flat fee to the weight-based cost calculated by base class Package's calculateCost function. Class OvernightPackage should inherit directly from class Package and contain an additional data member representing an additional fee per ounce charged for overnight-delivery service. OvernightPackage should redefine member function calculateCost so that it adds the additional fee per ounce to the standard cost per ounce before calculating the shipping cost. Write a test program that creates objects of each type of Package and tests member function calculateCost.

12.10   (*Account Inheritance Hierarchy*) Create an inheritance hierarchy that a bank might use to represent customers' bank accounts. All customers at this bank can deposit (i.e., credit) money into their accounts and withdraw (i.e., debit) money from their accounts. More specific types of accounts also exist. Savings accounts, for instance, earn interest on the money they hold. Checking accounts, on the other hand, charge a fee per transaction (i.e., credit or debit).

Create an inheritance hierarchy containing base class Account and derived classes Savings-Account and CheckingAccount that inherit from class Account. Base class Account should include one data member of type double to represent the account balance. The class should provide a constructor that receives an initial balance and uses it to initialize the data member. The constructor should validate the initial balance to ensure that it is greater than or equal to 0.0. If not, the balance should be set to 0.0 and the constructor should display an error message, indicating that the initial balance was invalid. The class should provide three member functions. Member function credit should add an amount to the current balance. Member function debit should withdraw money from the Account and ensure that the debit amount does not exceed the Account's balance. If it does, the balance should be left unchanged and the function should print the message "Debit amount exceeded account balance." Member function getBalance should return the current balance.

Derived class SavingsAccount should inherit the functionality of an Account, but also include a data member of type double indicating the interest rate (percentage) assigned to the Account. SavingsAccount's constructor should receive the initial balance, as well as an initial value for the SavingsAccount's interest rate. SavingsAccount should provide a public member function calculateInterest that returns a double indicating the amount of interest earned by an account. Member function calculateInterest should determine this amount by multiplying the interest rate by the account balance. [*Note:* SavingsAccount should inherit member functions credit and debit as is without redefining them.]

Derived class CheckingAccount should inherit from base class Account and include an additional data member of type double that represents the fee charged per transaction. CheckingAccount's constructor should receive the initial balance, as well as a parameter indicating a fee amount. Class CheckingAccount should redefine member functions credit and debit so that they subtract the fee from the account balance whenever either transaction is performed successfully. CheckingAccount's versions of these functions should invoke the base-class Account version to perform the updates to an account balance. CheckingAccount's debit function should charge a fee only if money is actually withdrawn (i.e., the debit amount does not exceed the account balance). [*Hint:* Define Account's debit function so that it returns a bool indicating whether money was withdrawn. Then use the return value to determine whether a fee should be charged.]

After defining the classes in this hierarchy, write a program that creates objects of each class and tests their member functions. Add interest to the SavingsAccount object by first invoking its calculateInterest function, then passing the returned interest amount to the object's credit function.

13

Object-Oriented Programming: Polymorphism

*One Ring to rule them all,
One Ring to find them,
One Ring to bring them all
and in the darkness bind
them.*
—John Ronald Reuel Tolkien

*The silence often of pure
innocence
Persuades when speaking
fails.*
—William Shakespeare

*General propositions do not
decide concrete cases.*
—Oliver Wendell Holmes

*A philosopher of imposing
stature doesn't think in a
vacuum. Even his most
abstract ideas are, to some
extent, conditioned by what
is or is not known in the time
when he lives.*
—Alfred North Whitehead

OBJECTIVES

In this chapter you will learn:

- What polymorphism is, how it makes programming more convenient, and how it makes systems more extensible and maintainable.

- To declare and use **virtual** functions to effect polymorphism.

- The distinction between abstract and concrete classes.

- To declare pure **virtual** functions to create abstract classes.

- How to use run-time type information (RTTI) with downcasting, **dynamic_cast**, **typeid** and **type_info**.

- How C++ implements **virtual** functions and dynamic binding "under the hood."

- How to use **virtual** destructors to ensure that all appropriate destructors run on an object.

13.1 Introduction

13.2 Polymorphism Examples

13.3 Relationships Among Objects in an Inheritance Hierarchy

    13.3.1 Invoking Base-Class Functions from Derived-Class Objects

    13.3.2 Aiming Derived-Class Pointers at Base-Class Objects

    13.3.3 Derived-Class Member-Function Calls via Base-Class Pointers

    13.3.4 Virtual Functions

    13.3.5 Summary of the Allowed Assignments Between Base-Class and Derived-Class Objects and Pointers

13.4 Type Fields and `switch` Statements

13.5 Abstract Classes and Pure `virtual` Functions

13.6 Case Study: Payroll System Using Polymorphism

    13.6.1 Creating Abstract Base Class `Employee`

    13.6.2 Creating Concrete Derived Class `SalariedEmployee`

    13.6.3 Creating Concrete Derived Class `HourlyEmployee`

    13.6.4 Creating Concrete Derived Class `CommissionEmployee`

    13.6.5 Creating Indirect Concrete Derived Class `BasePlusCommissionEmployee`

    13.6.6 Demonstrating Polymorphic Processing

13.7 (Optional) Polymorphism, Virtual Functions and Dynamic Binding "Under the Hood"

13.8 Case Study: Payroll System Using Polymorphism and Run-Time Type Information with Downcasting, `dynamic_cast`, `typeid` and `type_info`

13.9 Virtual Destructors

13.10 Wrap-Up

Summary | Terminology | Self-Review Exercises | Answers to Self-Review Exercises | Exercises

13.1 Introduction

In Chapters 9–12, we discussed key object-oriented programming technologies including classes, objects, encapsulation, operator overloading and inheritance. We now continue our study of OOP by explaining and demonstrating polymorphism with inheritance hierarchies. Polymorphism enables us to "program in the general" rather than "program in the specific." In particular, polymorphism enables us to write programs that process objects of classes that are part of the same class hierarchy as if they are all objects of the hierarchy's base class. As we will soon see, polymorphism works off base-class pointer handles and base-class reference handles, but not off name handles.

Consider the following example of polymorphism. Suppose we create a program that simulates the movement of several types of animals for a biological study. Classes Fish, Frog and Bird represent the three types of animals under investigation. Imagine that each of these classes inherits from base class Animal, which contains a function move and maintains an animal's current location. Each derived class implements function move. Our program maintains a `vector` of pointers to objects of the various `Animal` derived classes. To simulate the animals' movements, the program sends each object the same message once per second—namely, `move`. However, each specific type of `Animal` responds to a `move` message in its own unique way—a `Fish` might swim two feet, a `Frog` might jump three feet and a `Bird` might fly ten feet. The program issues the same message (i.e., `move`) to each animal object generically, but each object knows how to modify its location appropriately for its specific type of movement. Relying on each object to know how to "do the right thing" (i.e., do what is appropriate for that type of object) in response to the same function call is the key concept of polymorphism. The same message (in this case, `move`) sent to a variety of objects has "many forms" of results—hence the term polymorphism.

With polymorphism, we can design and implement systems that are easily extensible—new classes can be added with little or no modification to the general portions of the program, as long as the new classes are part of the inheritance hierarchy that the program processes generically. The only parts of a program that must be altered to accommodate new classes are those that require direct knowledge of the new classes that the programmer adds to the hierarchy. For example, if we create class `Tortoise` that inherits from class `Animal` (which might respond to a `move` message by crawling one inch), we need to write only the `Tortoise` class and the part of the simulation that instantiates a `Tortoise` object. The portions of the simulation that process each `Animal` generically can remain the same.

We begin with a sequence of small, focused examples that lead up to an understanding of `virtual` functions and dynamic binding—polymorphism's two underlying technologies. We then present a case study that revisits Chapter 12's `Employee` hierarchy. In the case study, we define a common "interface" (i.e., set of functionality) for all the classes in the hierarchy. This common functionality among employees is defined in a so-called abstract base class, `Employee`, from which classes `SalariedEmployee`, `HourlyEmployee` and `CommissionEmployee` inherit directly and class `BaseCommissionEmployee` inherits indirectly. We will soon see what makes a class "abstract" or its opposite—"concrete."

In this hierarchy, every employee has an `earnings` function to calculate the employee's weekly pay. These `earnings` functions vary by employee type—for instance, `Salaried-Employees` are paid a fixed weekly salary regardless of the number of hours worked, while `HourlyEmployees` are paid by the hour and receive overtime pay. We show how to process each employee "in the general"—that is, using base-class pointers to call the `earnings` function of several derived-class objects. This way, the programmer needs to be concerned with only one type of function call, which can be used to execute several different functions based on the objects referred to by the base-class pointers.

A key feature of this chapter is its (optional) detailed discussion of polymorphism, `virtual` functions and dynamic binding "under the hood," which uses a detailed diagram to explain how polymorphism can be implemented in C++.

Occasionally, when performing polymorphic processing, we need to program "in the specific," meaning that operations need to be performed on a specific type of object in a hierarchy—the operation cannot be generally applied to several types of objects. We reuse our `Employee` hierarchy to demonstrate the powerful capabilities of run-time type information (RTTI) and dynamic casting, which enable a program to determine the type of an object at execution time and act on that object accordingly. We use these capabilities to determine whether a particular employee object is a `BasePlusCommissionEmployee`, then give that employee a 10 percent bonus on his or her base salary.

13.2 Polymorphism Examples

In this section, we discuss several polymorphism examples. With polymorphism, one function can cause different actions to occur, depending on the type of the object on which the function is invoked. This gives the programmer tremendous expressive capability. If class Rectangle is derived from class Quadrilateral, then a Rectangle object is a more specific version of a Quadrilateral object. Therefore, any operation (such as calculating the perimeter or the area) that can be performed on an object of class Quadrilateral also can be performed on an object of class Rectangle. Such operations also can be performed on other kinds of Quadrilaterals, such as Squares, Parallelograms and Trapezoids. The polymorphism occurs when a program invokes a virtual function through a base-class (i.e., Quadrilateral) pointer or reference—C++ dynamically (i.e., at execution time) chooses the correct function for the class from which the object was instantiated. You will see a code example that illustrates this process in Section 13.3.

As another example, suppose that we design a video game that manipulates objects of many different types, including objects of classes Martian, Venutian, Plutonian, Space-Ship and LaserBeam. Imagine that each of these classes inherits from the common base class SpaceObject, which contains member function draw. Each derived class implements this function in a manner appropriate for that class. A screen-manager program maintains a container (e.g., a vector) that holds SpaceObject pointers to objects of the various classes. To refresh the screen, the screen manager periodically sends each object the same message—namely, draw. Each type of object responds in a unique way. For example, a Martian object might draw itself in red with the appropriate number of antennae. A SpaceShip object might draw itself as a silver flying saucer. A LaserBeam object might draw itself as a bright red beam across the screen. Again, the same message (in this case, draw) sent to a variety of objects has "many forms" of results.

A polymorphic screen manager facilitates adding new classes to a system with minimal modifications to its code. Suppose that we want to add objects of class Mercurian to our video game. To do so, we must build a class Mercurian that inherits from SpaceObject, but provides its own definition of member function draw. Then, when pointers to objects of class Mercurian appear in the container, the programmer does not need to modify the code for the screen manager. The screen manager invokes member function draw on every object in the container, regardless of the object's type, so the new Mercurian objects simply "plug right in." Thus, without modifying the system (other than to build and include the classes themselves), programmers can use polymorphism to accommodate additional classes, including ones that were not even envisioned when the system was created.

Software Engineering Observation 13.1

With virtual functions and polymorphism, you can deal in generalities and let the execution-time environment concern itself with the specifics. You can direct a variety of objects to behave in manners appropriate to those objects without even knowing their types (as long as those objects belong to the same inheritance hierarchy and are being accessed off a common base-class pointer).

Software Engineering Observation 13.2

Polymorphism promotes extensibility: Software written to invoke polymorphic behavior is written independently of the types of the objects to which messages are sent. Thus, new types of objects that can respond to existing messages can be incorporated into such a system without modifying the base system. Only client code that instantiates new objects must be modified to accommodate new types.

13.3 Relationships Among Objects in an Inheritance Hierarchy

Section 12.4 created an employee class hierarchy, in which class `BasePlusCommission-Employee` inherited from class `CommissionEmployee`. The Chapter 12 examples manipulated `CommissionEmployee` and `BasePlusCommissionEmployee` objects by using the objects' names to invoke their member functions. We now examine the relationships among classes in a hierarchy more closely. The next several sections present a series of examples that demonstrate how base-class and derived-class pointers can be aimed at base-class and derived-class objects, and how those pointers can be used to invoke member functions that manipulate those objects. Toward the end of this section, we demonstrate how to get polymorphic behavior from base-class pointers aimed at derived-class objects.

In Section 13.3.1, we assign the address of a derived-class object to a base-class pointer, then show that invoking a function via the base-class pointer invokes the base-class functionality—i.e., the type of the handle determines which function is called. In Section 13.3.2, we assign the address of a base-class object to a derived-class pointer, which results in a compilation error. We discuss the error message and investigate why the compiler does not allow such an assignment. In Section 13.3.3, we assign the address of a derived-class object to a base-class pointer, then examine how the base-class pointer can be used to invoke only the base-class functionality—when we attempt to invoke derived-class member functions through the base-class pointer, compilation errors occur. Finally, in Section 13.3.4, we introduce `virtual` functions and polymorphism by declaring a base-class function as `virtual`. We then assign a derived-class object to the base-class pointer and use that pointer to invoke derived-class functionality—precisely the capability we need to achieve polymorphic behavior.

A key concept in these examples is to demonstrate that an object of a derived class can be treated as an object of its base class. This enables various interesting manipulations. For example, a program can create an array of base-class pointers that point to objects of many derived-class types. Despite the fact that the derived-class objects are of different types, the compiler allows this because each derived-class object *is an* object of its base class. However, we cannot treat a base-class object as an object of any of its derived classes. For example, a `CommissionEmployee` is not a `BasePlusCommissionEmployee` in the hierarchy defined in Chapter 12—a `CommissionEmployee` does not have a `baseSalary` data member and does not have member functions `setBaseSalary` and `getBaseSalary`. The *is-a* relationship applies only from a derived class to its direct and indirect base classes.

13.3.1 Invoking Base-Class Functions from Derived-Class Objects

The example in Figs. 13.1–13.5 demonstrates three ways to aim base-class pointers and derived-class pointers at base-class objects and derived-class objects. The first two are straightforward—we aim a base-class pointer at a base-class object (and invoke base-class functionality), and we aim a derived-class pointer at a derived-class object (and invoke derived-class functionality). Then, we demonstrate the relationship between derived classes and base classes (i.e., the *is-a* relationship of inheritance) by aiming a base-class pointer at a derived-class object (and showing that the base-class functionality is indeed available in the derived-class object).

Class `CommissionEmployee` (Figs. 13.1–13.2), which we discussed in Chapter 12, is used to represent employees who are paid a percentage of their sales. Class `BasePlusCom-`

```
 1   // Fig. 13.1: CommissionEmployee.h
 2   // CommissionEmployee class definition represents a commission employee.
 3   #ifndef COMMISSION_H
 4   #define COMMISSION_H
 5
 6   #include <string> // C++ standard string class
 7   using std::string;
 8
 9   class CommissionEmployee
10   {
11   public:
12      CommissionEmployee( const string &, const string &, const string &,
13         double = 0.0, double = 0.0 );
14
15      void setFirstName( const string & ); // set first name
16      string getFirstName() const; // return first name
17
18      void setLastName( const string & ); // set last name
19      string getLastName() const; // return last name
20
21      void setSocialSecurityNumber( const string & ); // set SSN
22      string getSocialSecurityNumber() const; // return SSN
23
24      void setGrossSales( double ); // set gross sales amount
25      double getGrossSales() const; // return gross sales amount
26
27      void setCommissionRate( double ); // set commission rate
28      double getCommissionRate() const; // return commission rate
29
30      double earnings() const; // calculate earnings
31      void print() const; // print CommissionEmployee object
32   private:
33      string firstName;
34      string lastName;
35      string socialSecurityNumber;
36      double grossSales; // gross weekly sales
37      double commissionRate; // commission percentage
38   }; // end class CommissionEmployee
39
40   #endif
```

Fig. 13.1 | CommissionEmployee class header file.

missionEmployee (Figs. 13.3–13.4), which we also discussed in Chapter 12, is used to represent employees who receive a base salary plus a percentage of their sales. Each Base-PlusCommissionEmployee object *is a* CommissionEmployee that also has a base salary. Class BasePlusCommissionEmployee's earnings member function (lines 32–35 of Fig. 13.4) redefines class CommissionEmployee's earnings member function (lines 79–82 of Fig. 13.2) to include the object's base salary. Class BasePlusCommissionEmployee's print member function (lines 38–46 of Fig. 13.4) redefines class CommissionEmployee's print member function (lines 85–92 of Fig. 13.2) to display the same information as the print function in class CommissionEmployee, as well as the employee's base salary.

```cpp
1   // Fig. 13.2: CommissionEmployee.cpp
2   // Class CommissionEmployee member-function definitions.
3   #include <iostream>
4   using std::cout;
5
6   #include "CommissionEmployee.h" // CommissionEmployee class definition
7
8   // constructor
9   CommissionEmployee::CommissionEmployee(
10     const string &first, const string &last, const string &ssn,
11     double sales, double rate )
12     : firstName( first ), lastName( last ), socialSecurityNumber( ssn )
13  {
14     setGrossSales( sales ); // validate and store gross sales
15     setCommissionRate( rate ); // validate and store commission rate
16  } // end CommissionEmployee constructor
17
18  // set first name
19  void CommissionEmployee::setFirstName( const string &first )
20  {
21     firstName = first; // should validate
22  } // end function setFirstName
23
24  // return first name
25  string CommissionEmployee::getFirstName() const
26  {
27     return firstName;
28  } // end function getFirstName
29
30  // set last name
31  void CommissionEmployee::setLastName( const string &last )
32  {
33     lastName = last;   // should validate
34  } // end function setLastName
35
36  // return last name
37  string CommissionEmployee::getLastName() const
38  {
39     return lastName;
40  } // end function getLastName
41
42  // set social security number
43  void CommissionEmployee::setSocialSecurityNumber( const string &ssn )
44  {
45     socialSecurityNumber = ssn; // should validate
46  } // end function setSocialSecurityNumber
47
48  // return social security number
49  string CommissionEmployee::getSocialSecurityNumber() const
50  {
51     return socialSecurityNumber;
52  } // end function getSocialSecurityNumber
53
```

Fig. 13.2 | CommissionEmployee class implementation file. (Part 1 of 2.)

```
54  // set gross sales amount
55  void CommissionEmployee::setGrossSales( double sales )
56  {
57     grossSales = ( sales < 0.0 ) ? 0.0 : sales;
58  } // end function setGrossSales
59
60  // return gross sales amount
61  double CommissionEmployee::getGrossSales() const
62  {
63     return grossSales;
64  } // end function getGrossSales
65
66  // set commission rate
67  void CommissionEmployee::setCommissionRate( double rate )
68  {
69     commissionRate = ( rate > 0.0 && rate < 1.0 ) ? rate : 0.0;
70  } // end function setCommissionRate
71
72  // return commission rate
73  double CommissionEmployee::getCommissionRate() const
74  {
75     return commissionRate;
76  } // end function getCommissionRate
77
78  // calculate earnings
79  double CommissionEmployee::earnings() const
80  {
81     return getCommissionRate() * getGrossSales();
82  } // end function earnings
83
84  // print CommissionEmployee object
85  void CommissionEmployee::print() const
86  {
87     cout << "commission employee: "
88        << getFirstName() << ' ' << getLastName()
89        << "\nsocial security number: " << getSocialSecurityNumber()
90        << "\ngross sales: " << getGrossSales()
91        << "\ncommission rate: " << getCommissionRate();
92  } // end function print
```

Fig. 13.2 | CommissionEmployee class implementation file. (Part 2 of 2.)

```
1  // Fig. 13.3: BasePlusCommissionEmployee.h
2  // BasePlusCommissionEmployee class derived from class
3  // CommissionEmployee.
4  #ifndef BASEPLUS_H
5  #define BASEPLUS_H
6
7  #include <string> // C++ standard string class
8  using std::string;
9
```

Fig. 13.3 | BasePlusCommissionEmployee class header file. (Part 1 of 2.)

```
10   #include "CommissionEmployee.h" // CommissionEmployee class declaration
11
12   class BasePlusCommissionEmployee : public CommissionEmployee
13   {
14   public:
15      BasePlusCommissionEmployee( const string &, const string &,
16         const string &, double = 0.0, double = 0.0, double = 0.0 );
17
18      void setBaseSalary( double ); // set base salary
19      double getBaseSalary() const; // return base salary
20
21      double earnings() const; // calculate earnings
22      void print() const; // print BasePlusCommissionEmployee object
23   private:
24      double baseSalary; // base salary
25   }; // end class BasePlusCommissionEmployee
26
27   #endif
```

Fig. 13.3 | BasePlusCommissionEmployee class header file. (Part 2 of 2.)

```
1    // Fig. 13.4: BasePlusCommissionEmployee.cpp
2    // Class BasePlusCommissionEmployee member-function definitions.
3    #include <iostream>
4    using std::cout;
5
6    // BasePlusCommissionEmployee class definition
7    #include "BasePlusCommissionEmployee.h"
8
9    // constructor
10   BasePlusCommissionEmployee::BasePlusCommissionEmployee(
11      const string &first, const string &last, const string &ssn,
12      double sales, double rate, double salary )
13      // explicitly call base-class constructor
14      : CommissionEmployee( first, last, ssn, sales, rate )
15   {
16      setBaseSalary( salary ); // validate and store base salary
17   } // end BasePlusCommissionEmployee constructor
18
19   // set base salary
20   void BasePlusCommissionEmployee::setBaseSalary( double salary )
21   {
22      baseSalary = ( salary < 0.0 ) ? 0.0 : salary;
23   } // end function setBaseSalary
24
25   // return base salary
26   double BasePlusCommissionEmployee::getBaseSalary() const
27   {
28      return baseSalary;
29   } // end function getBaseSalary
30
```

Fig. 13.4 | BasePlusCommissionEmployee class implementation file. (Part 1 of 2.)

```
31   // calculate earnings
32   double BasePlusCommissionEmployee::earnings() const
33   {
34      return getBaseSalary() + CommissionEmployee::earnings();
35   } // end function earnings
36
37   // print BasePlusCommissionEmployee object
38   void BasePlusCommissionEmployee::print() const
39   {
40      cout << "base-salaried ";
41
42      // invoke CommissionEmployee's print function
43      CommissionEmployee::print();
44
45      cout << "\nbase salary: " << getBaseSalary();
46   } // end function print
```

Fig. 13.4 | `BasePlusCommissionEmployee` class implementation file. (Part 2 of 2.)

In Fig. 13.5, lines 19–20 create a `CommissionEmployee` object and line 23 creates a pointer to a `CommissionEmployee` object; lines 26–27 create a `BasePlusCommission-Employee` object and line 30 creates a pointer to a `BasePlusCommissionEmployee` object. Lines 37 and 39 use each object's name (`commissionEmployee` and `basePlusCommis-sionEmployee`, respectively) to invoke each object's `print` member function. Line 42 assigns the address of base-class object `commissionEmployee` to base-class pointer `commissionEmployeePtr`, which line 45 uses to invoke member function `print` on that `CommissionEmployee` object. This invokes the version of `print` defined in base class `Com-missionEmployee`. Similarly, line 48 assigns the address of derived-class object `basePlus-CommissionEmployee` to derived-class pointer `basePlusCommissionEmployeePtr`, which line 52 uses to invoke member function `print` on that `BasePlusCommissionEmployee` object. This invokes the version of `print` defined in derived class `BasePlusCommission-Employee`. Line 55 then assigns the address of derived-class object `basePlusCommission-Employee` to base-class pointer `commissionEmployeePtr`, which line 59 uses to invoke member function `print`. The C++ compiler allows this "crossover" because an object of a derived class *is an* object of its base class. Note that despite the fact that the base class

```
1    // Fig. 13.5: fig13_05.cpp
2    // Aiming base-class and derived-class pointers at base-class
3    // and derived-class objects, respectively.
4    #include <iostream>
5    using std::cout;
6    using std::endl;
7    using std::fixed;
8
9    #include <iomanip>
10   using std::setprecision;
11
```

Fig. 13.5 | Assigning addresses of base-class and derived-class objects to base-class and derived-class pointers. (Part 1 of 3.)

```
12   // include class definitions
13   #include "CommissionEmployee.h"
14   #include "BasePlusCommissionEmployee.h"
15
16   int main()
17   {
18      // create base-class object
19      CommissionEmployee commissionEmployee(
20         "Sue", "Jones", "222-22-2222", 10000, .06 );
21
22      // create base-class pointer
23      CommissionEmployee *commissionEmployeePtr = 0;
24
25      // create derived-class object
26      BasePlusCommissionEmployee basePlusCommissionEmployee(
27         "Bob", "Lewis", "333-33-3333", 5000, .04, 300 );
28
29      // create derived-class pointer
30      BasePlusCommissionEmployee *basePlusCommissionEmployeePtr = 0;
31
32      // set floating-point output formatting
33      cout << fixed << setprecision( 2 );
34
35      // output objects commissionEmployee and basePlusCommissionEmployee
36      cout << "Print base-class and derived-class objects:\n\n";
37      commissionEmployee.print(); // invokes base-class print
38      cout << "\n\n";
39      basePlusCommissionEmployee.print(); // invokes derived-class print
40
41      // aim base-class pointer at base-class object and print
42      commissionEmployeePtr = &commissionEmployee; // perfectly natural
43      cout << "\n\n\nCalling print with base-class pointer to "
44         << "\nbase-class object invokes base-class print function:\n\n";
45      commissionEmployeePtr->print(); // invokes base-class print
46
47      // aim derived-class pointer at derived-class object and print
48      basePlusCommissionEmployeePtr = &basePlusCommissionEmployee; // natural
49      cout << "\n\n\nCalling print with derived-class pointer to "
50         << "\nderived-class object invokes derived-class "
51         << "print function:\n\n";
52      basePlusCommissionEmployeePtr->print(); // invokes derived-class print
53
54      // aim base-class pointer at derived-class object and print
55      commissionEmployeePtr = &basePlusCommissionEmployee;
56      cout << "\n\n\nCalling print with base-class pointer to "
57         << "derived-class object\ninvokes base-class print "
58         << "function on that derived-class object:\n\n";
59      commissionEmployeePtr->print(); // invokes base-class print
60      cout << endl;
61      return 0;
62   } // end main
```

Fig. 13.5 | Assigning addresses of base-class and derived-class objects to base-class and derived-class pointers. (Part 2 of 3.)

```
Print base-class and derived-class objects:

commission employee: Sue Jones
social security number: 222-22-2222
gross sales: 10000.00
commission rate: 0.06

base-salaried commission employee: Bob Lewis
social security number: 333-33-3333
gross sales: 5000.00
commission rate: 0.04
base salary: 300.00


Calling print with base-class pointer to
base-class object invokes base-class print function:

commission employee: Sue Jones
social security number: 222-22-2222
gross sales: 10000.00
commission rate: 0.06


Calling print with derived-class pointer to
derived-class object invokes derived-class print function:

base-salaried commission employee: Bob Lewis
social security number: 333-33-3333
gross sales: 5000.00
commission rate: 0.04
base salary: 300.00


Calling print with base-class pointer to derived-class object
invokes base-class print function on that derived-class object:

commission employee: Bob Lewis
social security number: 333-33-3333
gross sales: 5000.00
commission rate: 0.04
```

Fig. 13.5 | Assigning addresses of base-class and derived-class objects to base-class and derived-class pointers. (Part 3 of 3.)

CommissionEmployee pointer points to a derived class BasePlusCommissionEmployee object, the base class CommissionEmployee's print member function is invoked (rather than BasePlusCommissionEmployee's print function). The output of each print member-function invocation in this program reveals that *the invoked functionality depends on the type of the handle (i.e., the pointer or reference type) used to invoke the function, not the type of the object to which the handle points.* In Section 13.3.4, when we introduce virtual functions, we demonstrate that it is possible to invoke the object type's functionality, rather than invoke the handle type's functionality. We will see that this is crucial to implementing polymorphic behavior—the key topic of this chapter.

13.3.2 Aiming Derived-Class Pointers at Base-Class Objects

In Section 13.3.1, we assigned the address of a derived-class object to a base-class pointer and explained that the C++ compiler allows this assignment, because a derived-class object *is a* base-class object. We take the opposite approach in Fig. 13.6, as we aim a derived-class pointer at a base-class object. [*Note*: This program uses classes CommissionEmployee and BasePlusCommissionEmployee of Figs. 13.1–13.4.] Lines 8–9 of Fig. 13.6 create a CommissionEmployee object, and line 10 creates a BasePlusCommissionEmployee pointer. Line 14 attempts to assign the address of base-class object commissionEmployee to derived-class pointer basePlusCommissionEmployeePtr, but the C++ compiler generates an error. The compiler prevents this assignment, because a CommissionEmployee is not a BasePlusCommissionEmployee. Consider the consequences if the compiler were to allow this assignment. Through a BasePlusCommissionEmployee pointer, we can invoke every BasePlusCommissionEmployee member function, including setBaseSalary, for the object to which the pointer points (i.e., the base-class object commissionEmployee). However, the CommissionEmployee object does not provide a setBaseSalary member function, nor does it provide a baseSalary data member to set. This could lead to problems, because member function setBaseSalary would assume that there is a baseSalary data member to set at its "usual location" in a BasePlusCommissionEmployee object. This memory does not belong to the CommissionEmployee object, so member function setBaseSalary might overwrite other important data in memory, possibly data that belongs to a different object.

```cpp
1   // Fig. 13.6: fig13_06.cpp
2   // Aiming a derived-class pointer at a base-class object.
3   #include "CommissionEmployee.h"
4   #include "BasePlusCommissionEmployee.h"
5
6   int main()
7   {
8      CommissionEmployee commissionEmployee(
9         "Sue", "Jones", "222-22-2222", 10000, .06 );
10     BasePlusCommissionEmployee *basePlusCommissionEmployeePtr = 0;
11
12     // aim derived-class pointer at base-class object
13     // Error: a CommissionEmployee is not a BasePlusCommissionEmployee
14     basePlusCommissionEmployeePtr = &commissionEmployee;
15     return 0;
16  } // end main
```

Borland C++ command-line compiler error messages:

```
Error E2034 Fig13_06\fig13_06.cpp 14: Cannot convert 'CommissionEmployee *'
   to 'BasePlusCommissionEmployee *' in function main()
```

GNU C++ compiler error messages:

```
fig13_06.cpp:14: error: invalid conversion from `CommissionEmployee*' to
   `BasePlusCommissionEmployee*'
```

Fig. 13.6 | Aiming a derived-class pointer at a base-class object. (Part 1 of 2.)

Microsoft Visual C++.NET compiler error messages:

```
C:\scpphtp5_examples\ch13\Fig13_06\fig13_06.cpp(14) : error C2440:
   '=' : cannot convert from 'CommissionEmployee *__w64 ' to
   'BasePlusCommissionEmployee *'
        Cast from base to derived requires dynamic_cast or static_cast
```

Fig. 13.6 | Aiming a derived-class pointer at a base-class object. (Part 2 of 2.)

13.3.3 Derived-Class Member-Function Calls via Base-Class Pointers

Off a base-class pointer, the compiler allows us to invoke only bases-class member functions. Thus, if a base-class pointer is aimed at a derived-class object, and an attempt is made to access a derived-class-only member function, a compilation error will occur.

Figure 13.7 shows the consequences of attempting to invoke a derived-class member function off a base-class pointer. [*Note:* We are again using classes CommissionEmployee and BasePlusCommissionEmployee of Figs. 13.1–13.4.] Line 9 creates commissionEmployeePtr—a pointer to a CommissionEmployee object—and lines 10–11 create a BasePlusCommissionEmployee object. Line 14 aims commissionEmployeePtr at derived-class object basePlusCommissionEmployee. Recall from Section 13.3.1 that the C++ compiler allows

```
 1   // Fig. 13.7: fig13_07.cpp
 2   // Attempting to invoke derived-class-only member functions
 3   // through a base-class pointer.
 4   #include "CommissionEmployee.h"
 5   #include "BasePlusCommissionEmployee.h"
 6
 7   int main()
 8   {
 9      CommissionEmployee *commissionEmployeePtr = 0; // base class
10      BasePlusCommissionEmployee basePlusCommissionEmployee(
11         "Bob", "Lewis", "333-33-3333", 5000, .04, 300 ); // derived class
12
13      // aim base-class pointer at derived-class object
14      commissionEmployeePtr = &basePlusCommissionEmployee;
15
16      // invoke base-class member functions on derived-class
17      // object through base-class pointer
18      string firstName = commissionEmployeePtr->getFirstName();
19      string lastName = commissionEmployeePtr->getLastName();
20      string ssn = commissionEmployeePtr->getSocialSecurityNumber();
21      double grossSales = commissionEmployeePtr->getGrossSales();
22      double commissionRate = commissionEmployeePtr->getCommissionRate();
23
24      // attempt to invoke derived-class-only member functions
25      // on derived-class object through base-class pointer
26      double baseSalary = commissionEmployeePtr->getBaseSalary();
27      commissionEmployeePtr->setBaseSalary( 500 );
28      return 0;
29   } // end main
```

Fig. 13.7 | Attempting to invoke derived-class-only functions via a base-class pointer. (Part 1 of 2.)

Borland C++ command-line compiler error messages:

```
Error E2316 Fig13_07\fig13_07.cpp 26: 'getBaseSalary' is not a member of
   'CommissionEmployee' in function main()
Error E2316 Fig13_07\fig13_07.cpp 27: 'setBaseSalary' is not a member of
   'CommissionEmployee' in function main()
```

Microsoft Visual C++.NET compiler error messages:

```
C:\scpphtp5_examples\ch13\Fig13_07\fig13_07.cpp(26) : error C2039:
   'getBaseSalary' : is not a member of 'CommissionEmployee'
      C:\cpphtp5_examples\ch13\Fig13_07\CommissionEmployee.h(10) :
      see declaration of 'CommissionEmployee'
C:\scpphtp5_examples\ch13\Fig13_07\fig13_07.cpp(27) : error C2039:
   'setBaseSalary' : is not a member of 'CommissionEmployee'
      C:\cpphtp5_examples\ch13\Fig13_07\CommissionEmployee.h(10) :
      see declaration of 'CommissionEmployee'
```

GNU C++ compiler error messages:

```
fig13_07.cpp:26: error: `getBaseSalary' undeclared (first use this function)
fig13_07.cpp:26: error: (Each undeclared identifier is reported only once for
   each function it appears in.)
fig13_07.cpp:27: error: `setBaseSalary' undeclared (first use this function)
```

Fig. 13.7 | Attempting to invoke derived-class-only functions via a base-class pointer. (Part 2 of 2.)

this, because a BasePlusCommissionEmployee *is a* CommissionEmployee (in the sense that a BasePlusCommissionEmployee object contains all the functionality of a CommissionEmployee object). Lines 18–22 invoke base-class member functions getFirstName, getLastName, getSocialSecurityNumber, getGrossSales and getCommissionRate off the base-class pointer. All of these calls are legitimate, because BasePlusCommissionEmployee inherits these member functions from CommissionEmployee. We know that commissionEmployeePtr is aimed at a BasePlusCommissionEmployee object, so in lines 26–27 we attempt to invoke BasePlusCommissionEmployee member functions getBaseSalary and setBaseSalary. The C++ compiler generates errors on both of these lines, because these are not member functions of base-class CommissionEmployee. The handle can invoke only those functions that are members of that handle's associated class type. (In this case, off a CommissionEmployee *, we can invoke only CommissionEmployee member functions setFirstName, getFirstName, setLastName, getLastName, setSocialSecurityNumber, getSocialSecurityNumber, setGrossSales, getGrossSales, setCommissionRate, getCommissionRate, earnings and print.)

It turns out that the C++ compiler does allow access to derived-class-only members from a base-class pointer that is aimed at a derived-class object if we explicitly cast the base-class pointer to a derived-class pointer—a technique known as downcasting. As you learned in Section 13.3.1, it is possible to aim a base-class pointer at a derived-class object. However, as we demonstrated in Fig. 13.7, a base-class pointer can be used to invoke only the functions declared in the base class. Downcasting allows a program to perform a derived-class-specific operation on a derived-class object pointed to by a base-class pointer.

After a downcast, the program can invoke derived-class functions that are not in the base class. We will show you a concrete example of downcasting in Section 13.8.

Software Engineering Observation 13.3

If the address of a derived-class object has been assigned to a pointer of one of its direct or indirect base classes, it is acceptable to cast that base-class pointer back to a pointer of the derived-class type. In fact, this must be done to send that derived-class object messages that do not appear in the base class.

13.3.4 Virtual Functions

In Section 13.3.1, we aimed a base-class CommissionEmployee pointer at a derived-class BasePlusCommissionEmployee object, then invoked member function print through that pointer. Recall that the type of the handle determines which class's functionality to invoke. In that case, the CommissionEmployee pointer invoked the CommissionEmployee member function print on the BasePlusCommissionEmployee object, even though the pointer was aimed at a BasePlusCommissionEmployee object that has its own customized print function. *With virtual functions, the type of the object being pointed to, not the type of the handle, determines which version of a virtual function to invoke.*

First, we consider why virtual functions are useful. Suppose that a set of shape classes such as Circle, Triangle, Rectangle and Square are all derived from base class Shape. Each of these classes might be endowed with the ability to draw itself via a member function draw. Although each class has its own draw function, the function for each shape is quite different. In a program that draws a set of shapes, it would be useful to be able to treat all the shapes generically as objects of the base class Shape. Then, to draw any shape, we could simply use a base-class Shape pointer to invoke function draw and let the program determine *dynamically* (i.e., at runtime) which derived-class draw function to use, based on the type of the object to which the base-class Shape pointer points at any given time.

To enable this kind of behavior, we declare draw in the base class as a **virtual function**, and we *override* draw in each of the derived classes to draw the appropriate shape. From an implementation perspective, overriding a function is no different than redefining one (which is the approach we have been using until now). An overridden function in a derived class has the same signature and return type (i.e., prototype) as the function it overrides in its base class. If we do not declare the base-class function as virtual, we can redefine that function. By contrast, if we declare the base-class function as virtual, we can override that function to enable polymorphic behavior. We declare a virtual function by preceding the function's prototype with the keyword virtual in the base class. For example,

```
virtual void draw() const;
```

would appear in base class Shape. The preceding prototype declares that function draw is a virtual function that takes no arguments and returns nothing. The function is declared const because a draw function typically would not make changes to the Shape object on which it is invoked. Virtual functions do not necessarily have to be const functions.

Software Engineering Observation 13.4

Once a function is declared virtual, it remains virtual all the way down the inheritance hierarchy from that point, even if that function is not explicitly declared virtual when a class overrides it.

Good Programming Practice 13.1

Even though certain functions are implicitly virtual *because of a declaration made higher in the class hierarchy, explicitly declare these functions* virtual *at every level of the hierarchy to promote program clarity.*

Error-Prevention Tip 13.1

When a programmer browses a class hierarchy to locate a class to reuse, it is possible that a function in that class will exhibit virtual *function behavior even though it is not explicitly declared* virtual. *This happens when the class inherits a* virtual *function from its base class, and it can lead to subtle logic errors. Such errors can be avoided by explicitly declaring all* virtual *functions* virtual *throughout the inheritance hierarchy.*

Software Engineering Observation 13.5

When a derived class chooses not to override a virtual *function from its base class, the derived class simply inherits its base class's* virtual *function implementation.*

If the program invokes a virtual function through a base-class pointer to a derived-class object (e.g., shapePtr->draw()), the program will choose the correct derived-class draw function dynamically (i.e., at execution time) based on the object type—not the pointer type. Choosing the appropriate function to call at execution time (rather than at compile time) is known as dynamic binding or late binding.

When a virtual function is called by referencing a specific object by name and using the dot member-selection operator (e.g., squareObject.draw()), the function invocation is resolved at compile time (this is called static binding) and the virtual function that is called is the one defined for (or inherited by) the class of that particular object—this is not polymorphic behavior. Thus, dynamic binding with virtual functions occurs only off pointer (and, as we will soon see, reference) handles.

Now let's see how virtual functions can enable polymorphic behavior in our employee hierarchy. Figures 13.8–13.9 are the header files for classes CommissionEmployee and BasePlusCommissionEmployee, respectively. Note that the only difference between these files and those of Fig. 13.1 and Fig. 13.3 is that we specify each class's earnings and print member functions as virtual (lines 30–31 of Fig. 13.8 and lines 21–22 of Fig. 13.9). Because functions earnings and print are virtual in class CommissionEmployee, class BasePlusCommissionEmployee's earnings and print functions override class CommissionEmployee's. Now, if we aim a base-class CommissionEmployee pointer at a derived-class BasePlusCommissionEmployee object, and the program uses that pointer to call either function earnings or print, the BasePlusCommissionEmployee object's corresponding function will be invoked. There were no changes to the member-function implementations of classes CommissionEmployee and BasePlusCommissionEmployee, so we reuse the versions of Fig. 13.2 and Fig. 13.4.

We modified Fig. 13.5 to create the program of Fig. 13.10. Lines 46–57 demonstrate again that a CommissionEmployee pointer aimed at a CommissionEmployee object can be used to invoke CommissionEmployee functionality, and a BasePlusCommissionEmployee pointer aimed at a BasePlusCommissionEmployee object can be used to invoke BasePlusCommissionEmployee functionality. Line 60 aims base-class pointer commissionEmployeePtr at derived-class object basePlusCommissionEmployee. Note that when line 67 invokes member function print off the base-class pointer, the derived-class BasePlusCommissionEmployee's print member function is invoked, so line 67 outputs different text than line 59 does in Fig. 13.5 (when member function print was not declared virtual).

```
1   // Fig. 13.8: CommissionEmployee.h
2   // CommissionEmployee class definition represents a commission employee.
3   #ifndef COMMISSION_H
4   #define COMMISSION_H
5
6   #include <string> // C++ standard string class
7   using std::string;
8
9   class CommissionEmployee
10  {
11  public:
12     CommissionEmployee( const string &, const string &, const string &,
13        double = 0.0, double = 0.0 );
14
15     void setFirstName( const string & ); // set first name
16     string getFirstName() const; // return first name
17
18     void setLastName( const string & ); // set last name
19     string getLastName() const; // return last name
20
21     void setSocialSecurityNumber( const string & ); // set SSN
22     string getSocialSecurityNumber() const; // return SSN
23
24     void setGrossSales( double ); // set gross sales amount
25     double getGrossSales() const; // return gross sales amount
26
27     void setCommissionRate( double ); // set commission rate
28     double getCommissionRate() const; // return commission rate
29
30     virtual double earnings() const; // calculate earnings
31     virtual void print() const; // print CommissionEmployee object
32  private:
33     string firstName;
34     string lastName;
35     string socialSecurityNumber;
36     double grossSales; // gross weekly sales
37     double commissionRate; // commission percentage
38  }; // end class CommissionEmployee
39
40  #endif
```

Fig. 13.8 | CommissionEmployee class header file declares earnings and print functions as virtual.

```
1   // Fig. 13.9: BasePlusCommissionEmployee.h
2   // BasePlusCommissionEmployee class derived from class
3   // CommissionEmployee.
4   #ifndef BASEPLUS_H
5   #define BASEPLUS_H
6
```

Fig. 13.9 | BasePlusCommissionEmployee class header file declares earnings and print functions as virtual. (Part 1 of 2.)

```
7   #include <string> // C++ standard string class
8   using std::string;
9
10  #include "CommissionEmployee.h" // CommissionEmployee class declaration
11
12  class BasePlusCommissionEmployee : public CommissionEmployee
13  {
14  public:
15     BasePlusCommissionEmployee( const string &, const string &,
16        const string &, double = 0.0, double = 0.0, double = 0.0 );
17
18     void setBaseSalary( double ); // set base salary
19     double getBaseSalary() const; // return base salary
20
21     virtual double earnings() const; // calculate earnings
22     virtual void print() const; // print BasePlusCommissionEmployee object
23  private:
24     double baseSalary; // base salary
25  }; // end class BasePlusCommissionEmployee
26
27  #endif
```

Fig. 13.9 | BasePlusCommissionEmployee class header file declares earnings and print functions as virtual. (Part 2 of 2.)

We see that declaring a member function virtual causes the program to dynamically determine which function to invoke based on the type of object to which the handle points, rather than on the type of the handle. The decision about which function to call is an example of polymorphism. Note again that when commissionEmployeePtr points to a CommissionEmployee object (line 46), class CommissionEmployee's print function is invoked, and when CommissionEmployeePtr points to a BasePlusCommissionEmployee object, class BasePlusCommissionEmployee's print function is invoked. Thus, the same message—print, in this case—sent (off a base-class pointer) to a variety of objects related by inheritance to that base class, takes on many forms—this is polymorphic behavior.

```
1   // Fig. 13.10: fig13_10.cpp
2   // Introducing polymorphism, virtual functions and dynamic binding.
3   #include <iostream>
4   using std::cout;
5   using std::endl;
6   using std::fixed;
7
8   #include <iomanip>
9   using std::setprecision;
10
11  // include class definitions
12  #include "CommissionEmployee.h"
13  #include "BasePlusCommissionEmployee.h"
```

Fig. 13.10 | Demonstrating polymorphism by invoking a derived-class virtual function via a base-class pointer to a derived-class object. (Part 1 of 3.)

```
14
15    int main()
16    {
17       // create base-class object
18       CommissionEmployee commissionEmployee(
19          "Sue", "Jones", "222-22-2222", 10000, .06 );
20
21       // create base-class pointer
22       CommissionEmployee *commissionEmployeePtr = 0;
23
24       // create derived-class object
25       BasePlusCommissionEmployee basePlusCommissionEmployee(
26          "Bob", "Lewis", "333-33-3333", 5000, .04, 300 );
27
28       // create derived-class pointer
29       BasePlusCommissionEmployee *basePlusCommissionEmployeePtr = 0;
30
31       // set floating-point output formatting
32       cout << fixed << setprecision( 2 );
33
34       // output objects using static binding
35       cout << "Invoking print function on base-class and derived-class "
36          << "\nobjects with static binding\n\n";
37       commissionEmployee.print(); // static binding
38       cout << "\n\n";
39       basePlusCommissionEmployee.print(); // static binding
40
41       // output objects using dynamic binding
42       cout << "\n\n\nInvoking print function on base-class and "
43          << "derived-class \nobjects with dynamic binding";
44
45       // aim base-class pointer at base-class object and print
46       commissionEmployeePtr = &commissionEmployee;
47       cout << "\n\nCalling virtual function print with base-class pointer"
48          << "\nto base-class object invokes base-class "
49          << "print function:\n\n";
50       commissionEmployeePtr->print(); // invokes base-class print
51
52       // aim derived-class pointer at derived-class object and print
53       basePlusCommissionEmployeePtr = &basePlusCommissionEmployee;
54       cout << "\n\nCalling virtual function print with derived-class "
55          << "pointer\nto derived-class object invokes derived-class "
56          << "print function:\n\n";
57       basePlusCommissionEmployeePtr->print(); // invokes derived-class print
58
59       // aim base-class pointer at derived-class object and print
60       commissionEmployeePtr = &basePlusCommissionEmployee;
61       cout << "\n\nCalling virtual function print with base-class pointer"
62          << "\nto derived-class object invokes derived-class "
63          << "print function:\n\n";
64
```

Fig. 13.10 | Demonstrating polymorphism by invoking a derived-class `virtual` function via a base-class pointer to a derived-class object. (Part 2 of 3.)

```
65      // polymorphism; invokes BasePlusCommissionEmployee's print;
66      // base-class pointer to derived-class object
67      commissionEmployeePtr->print();
68      cout << endl;
69      return 0;
70   } // end main
```

```
Invoking print function on base-class and derived-class
objects with static binding

commission employee: Sue Jones
social security number: 222-22-2222
gross sales: 10000.00
commission rate: 0.06

base-salaried commission employee: Bob Lewis
social security number: 333-33-3333
gross sales: 5000.00
commission rate: 0.04
base salary: 300.00


Invoking print function on base-class and derived-class
objects with dynamic binding

Calling virtual function print with base-class pointer
to base-class object invokes base-class print function:

commission employee: Sue Jones
social security number: 222-22-2222
gross sales: 10000.00
commission rate: 0.06

Calling virtual function print with derived-class pointer
to derived-class object invokes derived-class print function:

base-salaried commission employee: Bob Lewis
social security number: 333-33-3333
gross sales: 5000.00
commission rate: 0.04
base salary: 300.00

Calling virtual function print with base-class pointer
to derived-class object invokes derived-class print function:

base-salaried commission employee: Bob Lewis
social security number: 333-33-3333
gross sales: 5000.00
commission rate: 0.04
base salary: 300.00
```

Fig. 13.10 | Demonstrating polymorphism by invoking a derived-class `virtual` function via a base-class pointer to a derived-class object. (Part 3 of 3.)

13.3.5 Summary of the Allowed Assignments Between Base-Class and Derived-Class Objects and Pointers

Now that you have seen a complete application that processes diverse objects polymorphically, we summarize what you can and cannot do with base-class and derived-class objects and pointers. Although a derived-class object also *is a* base-class object, the two objects are nevertheless different. As discussed previously, derived-class objects can be treated as if they are base-class objects. This is a logical relationship, because the derived class contains all the members of the base class. However, base-class objects cannot be treated as if they are derived-class objects—the derived class can have additional derived-class-only members. For this reason, aiming a derived-class pointer at a base-class object is not allowed without an explicit cast—such an assignment would leave the derived-class-only members undefined on the base-class object. The cast relieves the compiler of the responsibility of issuing an error message. In a sense, by using the cast you are saying, "I know that what I'm doing is dangerous and I take full responsibility for my actions."

In the current section and in Chapter 12, we have discussed four ways to aim base-class pointers and derived-class pointers at base-class objects and derived-class objects:

1. Aiming a base-class pointer at a base-class object is straightforward—calls made off the base-class pointer simply invoke base-class functionality.

2. Aiming a derived-class pointer at a derived-class object is straightforward—calls made off the derived-class pointer simply invoke derived-class functionality.

3. Aiming a base-class pointer at a derived-class object is safe, because the derived-class object *is an* object of its base class. However, this pointer can be used to invoke only base-class member functions. If the programmer attempts to refer to a derived-class-only member through the base-class pointer, the compiler reports an error. To avoid this error, the programmer must cast the base-class pointer to a derived-class pointer. The derived-class pointer can then be used to invoke the derived-class object's complete functionality. However, this technique—called downcasting—is a potentially dangerous operation. Section 13.8 demonstrates how to safely use downcasting.

4. Aiming a derived-class pointer at a base-class object generates a compilation error. The *is-a* relationship applies only from a derived class to its direct and indirect base classes, and not vice versa. A base-class object does not contain the derived-class-only members that can be invoked off a derived-class pointer.

Common Programming Error 13.1

After aiming a base-class pointer at a derived-class object, attempting to reference derived-class-only members with the base-class pointer is a compilation error.

Common Programming Error 13.2

Treating a base-class object as a derived-class object can cause errors.

13.4 Type Fields and `switch` Statements

One way to determine the type of an object that is incorporated in a larger program is to use a `switch` statement. This allows us to distinguish among object types, then invoke an appropriate action for a particular object. For example, in a hierarchy of shapes in which each shape object has a shapeType attribute, a switch statement could check the object's shapeType to determine which print function to call.

However, using switch logic exposes programs to a variety of potential problems. For example, the programmer might forget to include a type test when one is warranted, or might forget to test all possible cases in a switch statement. When modifying a switch-based system by adding new types, the programmer might forget to insert the new cases in all relevant switch statements. Every addition or deletion of a class requires the modification of every switch statement in the system; tracking these statements down can be time consuming and error prone.

Software Engineering Observation 13.6

Polymorphic programming can eliminate the need for unnecessary switch logic. By using the C++ polymorphism mechanism to perform the equivalent logic, programmers can avoid the kinds of errors typically associated with switch logic.

Software Engineering Observation 13.7

An interesting consequence of using polymorphism is that programs take on a simplified appearance. They contain less branching logic and more simple, sequential code. This simplification facilitates testing, debugging and program maintenance.

13.5 Abstract Classes and Pure virtual Functions

When we think of a class as a type, we assume that programs will create objects of that type. However, there are cases in which it is useful to define classes from which the programmer never intends to instantiate any objects. Such classes are called abstract classes. Because these classes normally are used as base classes in inheritance hierarchies, we refer to them as abstract base classes. These classes cannot be used to instantiate objects, because, as we will soon see, abstract classes are incomplete—derived classes must define the "missing pieces." We build programs with abstract classes in Section 13.6.

The purpose of an abstract class is to provide an appropriate base class from which other classes can inherit. Classes that can be used to instantiate objects are called concrete classes. Such classes provide implementations of every member function they define. We could have an abstract base class TwoDimensionalShape and derive such concrete classes as Square, Circle and Triangle. We could also have an abstract base class ThreeDimensionalShape and derive such concrete classes as Cube, Sphere and Cylinder. Abstract base classes are too generic to define real objects; we need to be more specific before we can think of instantiating objects. For example, if someone tells you to "draw the two-dimensional shape," what shape would you draw? Concrete classes provide the specifics that make it reasonable to instantiate objects.

An inheritance hierarchy does not need to contain any abstract classes, but, as we will see, many good object-oriented systems have class hierarchies headed by abstract base classes. In some cases, abstract classes constitute the top few levels of the hierarchy. A good example of this is the shape hierarchy in Fig. 12.3, which begins with abstract base class Shape. On the next level of the hierarchy we have two more abstract base classes, namely, TwoDimensionalShape and ThreeDimensionalShape. The next level of the hierarchy defines concrete classes for two-dimensional shapes (namely, Circle, Square and Triangle) and for three-dimensional shapes (namely, Sphere, Cube and Tetrahedron).

A class is made abstract by declaring one or more of its virtual functions to be "pure." A pure virtual function is specified by placing "= 0" in its declaration, as in

```
virtual void draw() const = 0; // pure virtual function
```

The "= 0" is known as a pure specifier. Pure virtual functions do not provide implementations. Every concrete derived class must override all base-class pure virtual functions with concrete implementations of those functions. The difference between a virtual function and a pure virtual function is that a virtual function has an implementation and gives the derived class the *option* of overriding the function; by contrast, a pure virtual function does not provide an implementation and *requires* the derived class to override the function (for that derived class to be concrete; otherwise the derived class remains abstract).

Pure virtual functions are used when it does not make sense for the base class to have an implementation of a function, but the programmer wants all concrete derived classes to implement the function. Returning to our earlier example of space objects, it does not make sense for the base class SpaceObject to have an implementation for function draw (as there is no way to draw a generic space object without having more information about what type of space object is being drawn). An example of a function that would be defined as virtual (and not pure virtual) would be one that returns a name for the object. We can name a generic SpaceObject (for instance, as "space object"), so a default implementation for this function can be provided, and the function does not need to be pure virtual. The function is still declared virtual, however, because it is expected that derived classes will override this function to provide more specific names for the derived-class objects.

Software Engineering Observation 13.8

An abstract class defines a common public interface for the various classes in a class hierarchy. An abstract class contains one or more pure virtual functions that concrete derived classes must override.

Common Programming Error 13.3

Attempting to instantiate an object of an abstract class causes a compilation error.

Common Programming Error 13.4

Failure to override a pure virtual function in a derived class, then attempting to instantiate objects of that class, is a compilation error.

Software Engineering Observation 13.9

An abstract class has at least one pure virtual function. An abstract class also can have data members and concrete functions (including constructors and destructors), which are subject to the normal rules of inheritance by derived classes.

Although we cannot instantiate objects of an abstract base class, we *can* use the abstract base class to declare pointers and references that can refer to objects of any concrete classes derived from the abstract class. Programs typically use such pointers and references to manipulate derived-class objects polymorphically.

Let us consider another application of polymorphism. A screen manager needs to display a variety of objects, including new types of objects that the programmer will add to the system after writing the screen manager. The system might need to display various shapes, such as Circles, Triangles or Rectangles, which are derived from abstract base class Shape. The screen manager uses Shape pointers to manage the objects that are displayed. To draw any object (regardless of the level at which that object's class appears in the inheritance hierarchy), the screen manager uses a base-class pointer to the object to invoke the object's draw function, which is a pure virtual function in base class Shape; therefore, each concrete derived class must implement function draw. Each Shape object in the inheritance hierarchy knows how to draw itself. The screen manager does not have to worry about the type of each object or whether the screen manager has ever encountered objects of that type.

Polymorphism is particularly effective for implementing layered software systems. In operating systems, for example, each type of physical device could operate quite differently from the others. Even so, commands to *read* or *write* data from and to devices may have a certain uniformity. The *write* message sent to a device-driver object needs to be interpreted specifically in the context of that device driver and how that device driver manipulates devices of a specific type. However, the *write* call itself really is no different from the *write* to any other device in the system—place some number of bytes from memory onto that device. An object-oriented operating system might use an abstract base class to provide an interface appropriate for all device drivers. Then, through inheritance from that abstract base class, derived classes are formed that all operate similarly. The capabilities (i.e., the public functions) offered by the device drivers are provided as pure virtual functions in the abstract base class. The implementations of these pure virtual functions are provided in the derived classes that correspond to the specific types of device drivers. This architecture also allows new devices to be added to a system easily, even after the operating system has been defined. The user can just plug in the device and install its new device driver. The operating system "talks" to this new device through its device driver, which has the same public member functions as all other device drivers—those defined in the abstract base device driver class.

It is common in object-oriented programming to define an iterator class that can traverse all the objects in a container (such as an array). For example, a program can print a list of objects in a vector by creating an iterator object, then using the iterator to obtain the next element of the list each time the iterator is called. Iterators often are used in polymorphic programming to traverse an array or a linked list of pointers to objects from various levels of a hierarchy. The pointers in such a list are all base-class pointers. A list of pointers to objects of base class TwoDimensionalShape could contain pointers to objects of classes Square, Circle, Triangle and so on. Using polymorphism to send a draw message, off a TwoDimensionalShape * pointer, to each object in the list would draw each object correctly on the screen.

13.6 Case Study: Payroll System Using Polymorphism

This section reexamines the CommissionEmployee-BasePlusCommissionEmployee hierarchy that we explored throughout Section 12.4. In this example, we use an abstract class and polymorphism to perform payroll calculations based on the type of employee. We create an enhanced employee hierarchy to solve the following problem:

A company pays its employees weekly. The employees are of four types: Salaried employees are paid a fixed weekly salary regardless of the number of hours worked, hourly employees are paid by the hour and receive overtime pay for all hours worked in excess of 40 hours, commission employees are paid a percentage of their sales and base-salary-plus-commission employees receive a base salary plus a percentage of their sales. For the current pay period, the company has decided to reward base-salary-plus-commission employees by adding 10 percent to their base salaries. The company wants to implement a C++ program that performs its payroll calculations polymorphically.

We use abstract class `Employee` to represent the general concept of an employee. The classes that derive directly from `Employee` are `SalariedEmployee`, `CommissionEmployee` and `HourlyEmployee`. Class `BasePlusCommissionEmployee`—derived from `CommissionEmployee`—represents the last employee type. The UML class diagram in Fig. 13.11 shows the inheritance hierarchy for our polymorphic employee payroll application. Note that abstract class name `Employee` is italicized, as per the convention of the UML.

Abstract base class `Employee` declares the "interface" to the hierarchy—that is, the set of member functions that a program can invoke on all `Employee` objects. Each employee, regardless of the way his or her earnings are calculated, has a first name, a last name and a social security number, so `private` data members `firstName`, `lastName` and `socialSecurityNumber` appear in abstract base class `Employee`.

Software Engineering Observation 13.10

A derived class can inherit interface or implementation from a base class. Hierarchies designed for implementation inheritance tend to have their functionality high in the hierarchy—each new derived class inherits one or more member functions that were defined in a base class, and the derived class uses the base-class definitions. Hierarchies designed for interface inheritance tend to have their functionality lower in the hierarchy—a base class specifies one or more functions that should be defined for each class in the hierarchy (i.e., they have the same prototype), but the individual derived classes provide their own implementations of the function(s).

The following sections implement the `Employee` class hierarchy. The first five each implement one of the abstract or concrete classes. The last section implements a test program that builds objects of all these classes and processes the objects polymorphically.

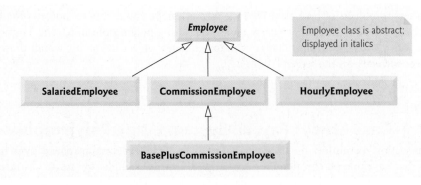

Fig. 13.11 | `Employee` hierarchy UML class diagram.

13.6.1 Creating Abstract Base Class Employee

Class Employee (Figs. 13.13–13.14, discussed in further detail shortly) provides functions earnings and print, in addition to various *get* and *set* functions that manipulate Employee's data members. An earnings function certainly applies generically to all employees, but each earnings calculation depends on the employee's class. So we declare earnings as pure virtual in base class Employee because a default implementation does not make sense for that function—there is not enough information to determine what amount earnings should return. Each derived class overrides earnings with an appropriate implementation. To calculate an employee's earnings, the program assigns the address of an employee's object to a base class Employee pointer, then invokes the earnings function on that object. We maintain a vector of Employee pointers, each of which points to an Employee object (of course, there cannot be Employee objects, because Employee is an abstract class—because of inheritance, however, all objects of all derived classes of Employee may nevertheless be thought of as Employee objects). The program iterates through the vector and calls function earnings for each Employee object. C++ processes these function calls polymorphically. Including earnings as a pure virtual function in Employee forces every direct derived class of Employee that wishes to be a concrete class to override earnings. This enables the designer of the class hierarchy to demand that each derived class provide an appropriate pay calculation, if indeed that derived class is to be concrete.

Function print in class Employee displays the first name, last name and social security number of the employee. As we will see, each derived class of Employee overrides function print to output the employee's type (e.g., "salaried employee:") followed by the rest of the employee's information.

The diagram in Fig. 13.12 shows each of the five classes in the hierarchy down the left side and functions earnings and print across the top. For each class, the diagram shows the desired results of each function. Note that class Employee specifies "= 0" for function earnings to indicate that this is a pure virtual function. Each derived class overrides this function to provide an appropriate implementation. We do not list base class Employee's *get* and *set* functions because they are not overridden in any of the derived classes—each of these functions is inherited and used "as is" by each of the derived classes.

Let us consider class Employee's header file (Fig. 13.13). The public member functions include a constructor that takes the first name, last name and social security number as arguments (line 12); *set* functions that set the first name, last name and social security number (lines 14, 17 and 20, respectively); *get* functions that return the first name, last name and social security number (lines 15, 18 and 21, respectively); pure virtual function earnings (line 24) and virtual function print (line 25).

Recall that we declared earnings as a pure virtual function because we first must know the specific Employee type to determine the appropriate earnings calculations. Declaring this function as pure virtual indicates that each concrete derived class *must* provide an appropriate earnings implementation and that a program can use base-class Employee pointers to invoke function earnings polymorphically for any type of Employee.

Figure 13.14 contains the member-function implementations for class Employee. No implementation is provided for virtual function earnings. Note that the Employee constructor (lines 10–15) does not validate the social security number. Normally, such validation should be provided. An exercise in Chapter 12 asks you to validate a social security number to ensure that it is in the form ###-##-####, where each # represents a digit.

	earnings	print
Employee	= 0	*firstName lastName* social security number: *SSN*
Salaried- Employee	weeklySalary	salaried employee: *firstName lastName* social security number: *SSN* weekly salary: *weeklysalary*

Hourly-
Employee
	If hours <= 40
	   wage * hours
	If hours > 40
	  (40 * wage) +
	  ((hours - 40)
	  * wage * 1.5)
		hourly employee: *firstName lastName*
		social security number: *SSN*
		hourly wage: *wage*; hours worked: *hours*

Commission- Employee	commissionRate * grossSales	commission employee: *firstName lastName* social security number: *SSN* gross sales: *grossSales*; commission rate: *commissionRate*
BasePlus- Commission- Employee	baseSalary + (commissionRate * grossSales)	base salaried commission employee: *firstName lastName* social security number: *SSN* gross sales: *grossSales*; commission rate: *commissionRate*; base salary: *baseSalary*

Fig. 13.12 | Polymorphic interface for the `Employee` hierarchy classes.

```
1   // Fig. 13.13: Employee.h
2   // Employee abstract base class.
3   #ifndef EMPLOYEE_H
4   #define EMPLOYEE_H
5
6   #include <string> // C++ standard string class
7   using std::string;
8
9   class Employee
10  {
11  public:
12     Employee( const string &, const string &, const string & );
13
14     void setFirstName( const string & ); // set first name
15     string getFirstName() const; // return first name
16
17     void setLastName( const string & ); // set last name
18     string getLastName() const; // return last name
19
```

Fig. 13.13 | `Employee` class header file. (Part 1 of 2.)

```
20       void setSocialSecurityNumber( const string & ); // set SSN
21       string getSocialSecurityNumber() const; // return SSN
22
23       // pure virtual function makes Employee abstract base class
24       virtual double earnings() const = 0; // pure virtual
25       virtual void print() const; // virtual
26    private:
27       string firstName;
28       string lastName;
29       string socialSecurityNumber;
30    }; // end class Employee
31
32    #endif // EMPLOYEE_H
```

Fig. 13.13 | Employee class header file. (Part 2 of 2.)

```
1    // Fig. 13.14: Employee.cpp
2    // Abstract-base-class Employee member-function definitions.
3    // Note: No definitions are given for pure virtual functions.
4    #include <iostream>
5    using std::cout;
6
7    #include "Employee.h" // Employee class definition
8
9    // constructor
10   Employee::Employee( const string &first, const string &last,
11      const string &ssn )
12      : firstName( first ), lastName( last ), socialSecurityNumber( ssn )
13   {
14      // empty body
15   } // end Employee constructor
16
17   // set first name
18   void Employee::setFirstName( const string &first )
19   {
20      firstName = first;
21   } // end function setFirstName
22
23   // return first name
24   string Employee::getFirstName() const
25   {
26      return firstName;
27   } // end function getFirstName
28
29   // set last name
30   void Employee::setLastName( const string &last )
31   {
32      lastName = last;
33   } // end function setLastName
34
```

Fig. 13.14 | Employee class implementation file. (Part 1 of 2.)

```
35   // return last name
36   string Employee::getLastName() const
37   {
38      return lastName;
39   } // end function getLastName
40
41   // set social security number
42   void Employee::setSocialSecurityNumber( const string &ssn )
43   {
44      socialSecurityNumber = ssn; // should validate
45   } // end function setSocialSecurityNumber
46
47   // return social security number
48   string Employee::getSocialSecurityNumber() const
49   {
50      return socialSecurityNumber;
51   } // end function getSocialSecurityNumber
52
53   // print Employee's information (virtual, but not pure virtual)
54   void Employee::print() const
55   {
56      cout << getFirstName() << ' ' << getLastName()
57         << "\nsocial security number: " << getSocialSecurityNumber();
58   } // end function print
```

Fig. 13.14 | `Employee` class implementation file. (Part 2 of 2.)

Note that `virtual` function `print` (Fig. 13.14, lines 54–58) provides an implementation that will be overridden in each of the derived classes. Each of these functions will, however, use the abstract class's version of `print` to print information common to all classes in the `Employee` hierarchy.

13.6.2 Creating Concrete Derived Class `SalariedEmployee`

Class `SalariedEmployee` (Figs. 13.15–13.16) derives from class `Employee` (line 8 of Fig. 13.15). The `public` member functions include a constructor that takes a first name, a last name, a social security number and a weekly salary as arguments (lines 11–12); a *set* function to assign a new nonnegative value to data member `weeklySalary` (lines 14); a *get* function to return `weeklySalary`'s value (line 15); a `virtual` function `earnings` that calculates a `SalariedEmployee`'s earnings (line 18) and a `virtual` function `print` that outputs the employee's type, namely, `"salaried employee: "` followed by employee-specific information produced by base class `Employee`'s `print` function and `SalariedEmployee`'s `getWeeklySalary` function (line 19).

Figure 13.16 contains the member-function implementations for `SalariedEmployee`. The class's constructor passes the first name, last name and social security number to the `Employee` constructor (line 11) to initialize the `private` data members that are inherited from the base class, but not accessible in the derived class. Function `earnings` (line 30–33) overrides pure `virtual` function `earnings` in `Employee` to provide a concrete implementation that returns the `SalariedEmployee`'s weekly salary. If we do not implement `earnings`, class `SalariedEmployee` would be an abstract class, and any attempt to instantiate an object of the class would result in a compilation error (and, of course, we

```
1   // Fig. 13.15: SalariedEmployee.h
2   // SalariedEmployee class derived from Employee.
3   #ifndef SALARIED_H
4   #define SALARIED_H
5
6   #include "Employee.h" // Employee class definition
7
8   class SalariedEmployee : public Employee
9   {
10  public:
11     SalariedEmployee( const string &, const string &,
12        const string &, double = 0.0 );
13
14     void setWeeklySalary( double ); // set weekly salary
15     double getWeeklySalary() const; // return weekly salary
16
17     // keyword virtual signals intent to override
18     virtual double earnings() const; // calculate earnings
19     virtual void print() const; // print SalariedEmployee object
20  private:
21     double weeklySalary; // salary per week
22  }; // end class SalariedEmployee
23
24  #endif // SALARIED_H
```

Fig. 13.15 | SalariedEmployee class header file.

```
1   // Fig. 13.16: SalariedEmployee.cpp
2   // SalariedEmployee class member-function definitions.
3   #include <iostream>
4   using std::cout;
5
6   #include "SalariedEmployee.h" // SalariedEmployee class definition
7
8   // constructor
9   SalariedEmployee::SalariedEmployee( const string &first,
10     const string &last, const string &ssn, double salary )
11     : Employee( first, last, ssn )
12  {
13     setWeeklySalary( salary );
14  } // end SalariedEmployee constructor
15
16  // set salary
17  void SalariedEmployee::setWeeklySalary( double salary )
18  {
19     weeklySalary = ( salary < 0.0 ) ? 0.0 : salary;
20  } // end function setWeeklySalary
21
22  // return salary
23  double SalariedEmployee::getWeeklySalary() const
24  {
```

Fig. 13.16 | SalariedEmployee class implementation file. (Part 1 of 2.)

```
25        return weeklySalary;
26    } // end function getWeeklySalary
27
28    // calculate earnings;
29    // override pure virtual function earnings in Employee
30    double SalariedEmployee::earnings() const
31    {
32        return getWeeklySalary();
33    } // end function earnings
34
35    // print SalariedEmployee's information
36    void SalariedEmployee::print() const
37    {
38        cout << "salaried employee: ";
39        Employee::print(); // reuse abstract base-class print function
40        cout << "\nweekly salary: " << getWeeklySalary();
41    } // end function print
```

Fig. 13.16 | SalariedEmployee class implementation file. (Part 2 of 2.)

want SalariedEmployee here to be a concrete class). Note that in class SalariedEmployee's header file, we declared member functions earnings and print as virtual (lines 18–19 of Fig. 13.15)—actually, placing the virtual keyword before these member functions is redundant. We defined them as virtual in base class Employee, so they remain virtual functions throughout the class hierarchy. Recall from Good Programming Practice 13.1 that explicitly declaring such functions virtual at every level of the hierarchy can promote program clarity.

Function print of class SalariedEmployee (lines 36–41 of Fig. 13.16) overrides Employee function print. If class SalariedEmployee did not override print, SalariedEmployee would inherit the Employee version of print. In that case, SalariedEmployee's print function would simply return the employee's full name and social security number, which does not adequately represent a SalariedEmployee. To print a SalariedEmployee's complete information, the derived class's print function outputs "salaried employee: " followed by the base-class Employee-specific information (i.e., first name, last name and social security number) printed by invoking the base class's print using the scope resolution operator (line 39)—this is a nice example of code reuse. The output produced by SalariedEmployee's print function contains the employee's weekly salary obtained by invoking the class's getWeeklySalary function.

13.6.3 Creating Concrete Derived Class HourlyEmployee

Class HourlyEmployee (Figs. 13.17–13.18) also derives from class Employee (line 8 of Fig. 13.17). The public member functions include a constructor (lines 11–12) that takes as arguments a first name, a last name, a social security number, an hourly wage and the number of hours worked; *set* functions that assign new values to data members wage and hours, respectively (lines 14 and 17); *get* functions to return the values of wage and hours, respectively (lines 15 and 18); a virtual function earnings that calculates an HourlyEmployee's earnings (line 21) and a virtual function print that outputs the employee's type, namely, "hourly employee: " and employee-specific information (line 22).

```
 1   // Fig. 13.17: HourlyEmployee.h
 2   // HourlyEmployee class definition.
 3   #ifndef HOURLY_H
 4   #define HOURLY_H
 5
 6   #include "Employee.h" // Employee class definition
 7
 8   class HourlyEmployee : public Employee
 9   {
10   public:
11      HourlyEmployee( const string &, const string &,
12         const string &, double = 0.0, double = 0.0 );
13
14      void setWage( double ); // set hourly wage
15      double getWage() const; // return hourly wage
16
17      void setHours( double ); // set hours worked
18      double getHours() const; // return hours worked
19
20      // keyword virtual signals intent to override
21      virtual double earnings() const; // calculate earnings
22      virtual void print() const; // print HourlyEmployee object
23   private:
24      double wage; // wage per hour
25      double hours; // hours worked for week
26   }; // end class HourlyEmployee
27
28   #endif // HOURLY_H
```

Fig. 13.17 | HourlyEmployee class header file.

```
 1   // Fig. 13.18: HourlyEmployee.cpp
 2   // HourlyEmployee class member-function definitions.
 3   #include <iostream>
 4   using std::cout;
 5
 6   #include "HourlyEmployee.h" // HourlyEmployee class definition
 7
 8   // constructor
 9   HourlyEmployee::HourlyEmployee( const string &first, const string &last,
10      const string &ssn, double hourlyWage, double hoursWorked )
11      : Employee( first, last, ssn )
12   {
13      setWage( hourlyWage ); // validate hourly wage
14      setHours( hoursWorked ); // validate hours worked
15   } // end HourlyEmployee constructor
16
17   // set wage
18   void HourlyEmployee::setWage( double hourlyWage )
19   {
20      wage = ( hourlyWage < 0.0 ? 0.0 : hourlyWage );
21   } // end function setWage
```

Fig. 13.18 | HourlyEmployee class implementation file. (Part 1 of 2.)

```
22
23   // return wage
24   double HourlyEmployee::getWage() const
25   {
26      return wage;
27   } // end function getWage
28
29   // set hours worked
30   void HourlyEmployee::setHours( double hoursWorked )
31   {
32      hours = ( ( ( hoursWorked >= 0.0 ) && ( hoursWorked <= 168.0 ) ) ?
33         hoursWorked : 0.0 );
34   } // end function setHours
35
36   // return hours worked
37   double HourlyEmployee::getHours() const
38   {
39      return hours;
40   } // end function getHours
41
42   // calculate earnings;
43   // override pure virtual function earnings in Employee
44   double HourlyEmployee::earnings() const
45   {
46      if ( getHours() <= 40 ) // no overtime
47         return getWage() * getHours();
48      else
49         return 40 * getWage() + ( ( getHours() - 40 ) * getWage() * 1.5 );
50   } // end function earnings
51
52   // print HourlyEmployee's information
53   void HourlyEmployee::print() const
54   {
55      cout << "hourly employee: ";
56      Employee::print(); // code reuse
57      cout << "\nhourly wage: " << getWage() <<
58         "; hours worked: " << getHours();
59   } // end function print
```

Fig. 13.18 | `HourlyEmployee` class implementation file. (Part 2 of 2.)

Figure 13.18 contains the member-function implementations for class `HourlyEm-ployee`. Lines 18–21 and 30–34 define *set* functions that assign new values to data members `wage` and `hours`, respectively. Function `setWage` (lines 18–21) ensures that `wage` is non-negative, and function `setHours` (lines 30–34) ensures that data member `hours` is between 0 and 168 (the total number of hours in a week). Class `HourlyEmployee`'s *get* functions are implemented in lines 24–27 and 37–40. We do not declare these functions `virtual`, so classes derived from class `HourlyEmployee` cannot override them (although derived classes certainly can redefine them). Note that the `HourlyEmployee` constructor, like the `SalariedEmployee` constructor, passes the first name, last name and social security number to the base class `Employee` constructor (line 11) to initialize the inherited `private` data members declared in the base class. In addition, `HourlyEmployee`'s `print` function calls base-class function print (line 56) to output the Employee-specific information (i.e., first name, last name and social security number)—this is another nice example of code reuse.

13.6.4 Creating Concrete Derived Class CommissionEmployee

Class CommissionEmployee (Figs. 13.19–13.20) derives from class Employee (line 8 of Fig. 13.19). The member-function implementations (Fig. 13.20) include a constructor (lines 9–15) that takes a first name, a last name, a social security number, a sales amount and a commission rate; *set* functions (lines 18–21 and 30–33) to assign new values to data members commissionRate and grossSales, respectively; *get* functions (lines 24–27 and 36–39) that retrieve the values of these data members; function earnings (lines 43–46) to calculate a CommissionEmployee's earnings; and function print (lines 49–55), which outputs the employee's type, namely, "commission employee: " and employee-specific information. The CommissionEmployee's constructor also passes the first name, last name and social security number to the Employee constructor (line 11) to initialize Employee's pri-

```cpp
1   // Fig. 13.19: CommissionEmployee.h
2   // CommissionEmployee class derived from Employee.
3   #ifndef COMMISSION_H
4   #define COMMISSION_H
5
6   #include "Employee.h" // Employee class definition
7
8   class CommissionEmployee : public Employee
9   {
10  public:
11     CommissionEmployee( const string &, const string &,
12        const string &, double = 0.0, double = 0.0 );
13
14     void setCommissionRate( double ); // set commission rate
15     double getCommissionRate() const; // return commission rate
16
17     void setGrossSales( double ); // set gross sales amount
18     double getGrossSales() const; // return gross sales amount
19
20     // keyword virtual signals intent to override
21     virtual double earnings() const; // calculate earnings
22     virtual void print() const; // print CommissionEmployee object
23  private:
24     double grossSales; // gross weekly sales
25     double commissionRate; // commission percentage
26  }; // end class CommissionEmployee
27
28  #endif // COMMISSION_H
```

Fig. 13.19 | CommissionEmployee class header file.

```cpp
1   // Fig. 13.20: CommissionEmployee.cpp
2   // CommissionEmployee class member-function definitions.
3   #include <iostream>
```

Fig. 13.20 | CommissionEmployee class implementation file. (Part 1 of 2.)

```cpp
 4    using std::cout;
 5
 6    #include "CommissionEmployee.h" // CommissionEmployee class definition
 7
 8    // constructor
 9    CommissionEmployee::CommissionEmployee( const string &first,
10       const string &last, const string &ssn, double sales, double rate )
11       : Employee( first, last, ssn )
12    {
13       setGrossSales( sales );
14       setCommissionRate( rate );
15    } // end CommissionEmployee constructor
16
17    // set commission rate
18    void CommissionEmployee::setCommissionRate( double rate )
19    {
20       commissionRate = ( ( rate > 0.0 && rate < 1.0 ) ? rate : 0.0 );
21    } // end function setCommissionRate
22
23    // return commission rate
24    double CommissionEmployee::getCommissionRate() const
25    {
26       return commissionRate;
27    } // end function getCommissionRate
28
29    // set gross sales amount
30    void CommissionEmployee::setGrossSales( double sales )
31    {
32       grossSales = ( ( sales < 0.0 ) ? 0.0 : sales );
33    } // end function setGrossSales
34
35    // return gross sales amount
36    double CommissionEmployee::getGrossSales() const
37    {
38       return grossSales;
39    } // end function getGrossSales
40
41    // calculate earnings;
42    // override pure virtual function earnings in Employee
43    double CommissionEmployee::earnings() const
44    {
45       return getCommissionRate() * getGrossSales();
46    } // end function earnings
47
48    // print CommissionEmployee's information
49    void CommissionEmployee::print() const
50    {
51       cout << "commission employee: ";
52       Employee::print(); // code reuse
53       cout << "\ngross sales: " << getGrossSales()
54          << "; commission rate: " << getCommissionRate();
55    } // end function print
```

Fig. 13.20 | CommissionEmployee class implementation file. (Part 2 of 2.)

vate data members. Function print calls base-class function print (line 52) to display the Employee-specific information (i.e., first name, last name and social security number).

13.6.5 Creating Indirect Concrete Derived Class BasePlusCommissionEmployee

Class BasePlusCommissionEmployee (Figs. 13.21–13.22) directly inherits from class CommissionEmployee (line 8 of Fig. 13.21) and therefore is an indirect derived class of class Employee. Class BasePlusCommissionEmployee's member-function implementations include a constructor (lines 10–16 of Fig. 13.22) that takes as arguments a first name, a last name, a social security number, a sales amount, a commission rate and a base salary. It then passes the first name, last name, social security number, sales amount and commission rate to the CommissionEmployee constructor (line 13) to initialize the inherited members. Base-PlusCommissionEmployee also contains a *set* function (lines 19–22) to assign a new value to data member baseSalary and a *get* function (lines 25–28) to return baseSalary's value. Function earnings (lines 32–35) calculates a BasePlusCommissionEmployee's earnings. Note that line 34 in function earnings calls base-class CommissionEmployee's earnings function to calculate the commission-based portion of the employee's earnings. This is a nice example of code reuse. BasePlusCommissionEmployee's print function (lines 38–43) outputs "base-salaried", followed by the output of base-class CommissionEmployee's print function (another example of code reuse), then the base salary. The resulting output begins with "base-salaried commission employee: " followed by the rest of the Base-

```
1   // Fig. 13.21: BasePlusCommissionEmployee.h
2   // BasePlusCommissionEmployee class derived from Employee.
3   #ifndef BASEPLUS_H
4   #define BASEPLUS_H
5
6   #include "CommissionEmployee.h" // CommissionEmployee class definition
7
8   class BasePlusCommissionEmployee : public CommissionEmployee
9   {
10  public:
11     BasePlusCommissionEmployee( const string &, const string &,
12        const string &, double = 0.0, double = 0.0, double = 0.0 );
13
14     void setBaseSalary( double ); // set base salary
15     double getBaseSalary() const; // return base salary
16
17     // keyword virtual signals intent to override
18     virtual double earnings() const; // calculate earnings
19     virtual void print() const; // print BasePlusCommissionEmployee object
20  private:
21     double baseSalary; // base salary per week
22  }; // end class BasePlusCommissionEmployee
23
24  #endif // BASEPLUS_H
```

Fig. 13.21 | BasePlusCommissionEmployee class header file.

```cpp
1   // Fig. 13.22: BasePlusCommissionEmployee.cpp
2   // BasePlusCommissionEmployee member-function definitions.
3   #include <iostream>
4   using std::cout;
5
6   // BasePlusCommissionEmployee class definition
7   #include "BasePlusCommissionEmployee.h"
8
9   // constructor
10  BasePlusCommissionEmployee::BasePlusCommissionEmployee(
11     const string &first, const string &last, const string &ssn,
12     double sales, double rate, double salary )
13     : CommissionEmployee( first, last, ssn, sales, rate )
14  {
15     setBaseSalary( salary ); // validate and store base salary
16  } // end BasePlusCommissionEmployee constructor
17
18  // set base salary
19  void BasePlusCommissionEmployee::setBaseSalary( double salary )
20  {
21     baseSalary = ( ( salary < 0.0 ) ? 0.0 : salary );
22  } // end function setBaseSalary
23
24  // return base salary
25  double BasePlusCommissionEmployee::getBaseSalary() const
26  {
27     return baseSalary;
28  } // end function getBaseSalary
29
30  // calculate earnings;
31  // override pure virtual function earnings in Employee
32  double BasePlusCommissionEmployee::earnings() const
33  {
34     return getBaseSalary() + CommissionEmployee::earnings();
35  } // end function earnings
36
37  // print BasePlusCommissionEmployee's information
38  void BasePlusCommissionEmployee::print() const
39  {
40     cout << "base-salaried ";
41     CommissionEmployee::print(); // code reuse
42     cout << "; base salary: " << getBaseSalary();
43  } // end function print
```

Fig. 13.22 | BasePlusCommissionEmployee class implementation file.

PlusCommissionEmployee's information. Recall that CommissionEmployee's print displays the employee's first name, last name and social security number by invoking the print function of its base class (i.e., Employee)—yet another example of code reuse. Note that BasePlusCommissionEmployee's print initiates a chain of functions calls that spans all three levels of the Employee hierarchy.

13.6.6 Demonstrating Polymorphic Processing

To test our `Employee` hierarchy, the program in Fig. 13.23 creates an object of each of the four concrete classes `SalariedEmployee`, `HourlyEmployee`, `CommissionEmployee` and `BasePlusCommissionEmployee`. The program manipulates these objects, first with static binding, then polymorphically, using a vector of `Employee` pointers. Lines 31–38 create objects of each of the four concrete `Employee` derived classes. Lines 43–51 output each Employee's information and earnings. Each member-function invocation in lines 43–51 is

```
1   // Fig. 13.23: fig13_23.cpp
2   // Processing Employee derived-class objects individually
3   // and polymorphically using dynamic binding.
4   #include <iostream>
5   using std::cout;
6   using std::endl;
7   using std::fixed;
8
9   #include <iomanip>
10  using std::setprecision;
11
12  #include <vector>
13  using std::vector;
14
15  // include definitions of classes in Employee hierarchy
16  #include "Employee.h"
17  #include "SalariedEmployee.h"
18  #include "HourlyEmployee.h"
19  #include "CommissionEmployee.h"
20  #include "BasePlusCommissionEmployee.h"
21
22  void virtualViaPointer( const Employee * const ); // prototype
23  void virtualViaReference( const Employee & ); // prototype
24
25  int main()
26  {
27     // set floating-point output formatting
28     cout << fixed << setprecision( 2 );
29
30     // create derived-class objects
31     SalariedEmployee salariedEmployee(
32        "John", "Smith", "111-11-1111", 800 );
33     HourlyEmployee hourlyEmployee(
34        "Karen", "Price", "222-22-2222", 16.75, 40 );
35     CommissionEmployee commissionEmployee(
36        "Sue", "Jones", "333-33-3333", 10000, .06 );
37     BasePlusCommissionEmployee basePlusCommissionEmployee(
38        "Bob", "Lewis", "444-44-4444", 5000, .04, 300 );
39
40     cout << "Employees processed individually using static binding:\n\n";
41
42     // output each Employee's information and earnings using static binding
43     salariedEmployee.print();
```

Fig. 13.23 | `Employee` class hierarchy driver program. (Part 1 of 4.)

```
44      cout << "\nearned $" << salariedEmployee.earnings() << "\n\n";
45      hourlyEmployee.print();
46      cout << "\nearned $" << hourlyEmployee.earnings() << "\n\n";
47      commissionEmployee.print();
48      cout << "\nearned $" << commissionEmployee.earnings() << "\n\n";
49      basePlusCommissionEmployee.print();
50      cout << "\nearned $" << basePlusCommissionEmployee.earnings()
51         << "\n\n";
52
53      // create vector of four base-class pointers
54      vector < Employee * > employees( 4 );
55
56      // initialize vector with Employees
57      employees[ 0 ] = &salariedEmployee;
58      employees[ 1 ] = &hourlyEmployee;
59      employees[ 2 ] = &commissionEmployee;
60      employees[ 3 ] = &basePlusCommissionEmployee;
61
62      cout << "Employees processed polymorphically via dynamic binding:\n\n";
63
64      // call virtualViaPointer to print each Employee's information
65      // and earnings using dynamic binding
66      cout << "Virtual function calls made off base-class pointers:\n\n";
67
68      for ( size_t i = 0; i < employees.size(); i++ )
69         virtualViaPointer( employees[ i ] );
70
71      // call virtualViaReference to print each Employee's information
72      // and earnings using dynamic binding
73      cout << "Virtual function calls made off base-class references:\n\n";
74
75      for ( size_t i = 0; i < employees.size(); i++ )
76         virtualViaReference( *employees[ i ] ); // note dereferencing
77
78      return 0;
79   } // end main
80
81   // call Employee virtual functions print and earnings off a
82   // base-class pointer using dynamic binding
83   void virtualViaPointer( const Employee * const baseClassPtr )
84   {
85      baseClassPtr->print();
86      cout << "\nearned $" << baseClassPtr->earnings() << "\n\n";
87   } // end function virtualViaPointer
88
89   // call Employee virtual functions print and earnings off a
90   // base-class reference using dynamic binding
91   void virtualViaReference( const Employee &baseClassRef )
92   {
93      baseClassRef.print();
94      cout << "\nearned $" << baseClassRef.earnings() << "\n\n";
95   } // end function virtualViaReference
```

Fig. 13.23 | Employee class hierarchy driver program. (Part 2 of 4.)

```
Employees processed individually using static binding:

salaried employee: John Smith
social security number: 111-11-1111
weekly salary: 800.00
earned $800.00

hourly employee: Karen Price
social security number: 222-22-2222
hourly wage: 16.75; hours worked: 40.00
earned $670.00

commission employee: Sue Jones
social security number: 333-33-3333
gross sales: 10000.00; commission rate: 0.06
earned $600.00

base-salaried commission employee: Bob Lewis
social security number: 444-44-4444
gross sales: 5000.00; commission rate: 0.04; base salary: 300.00
earned $500.00

Employees processed polymorphically using dynamic binding:

Virtual function calls made off base-class pointers:

salaried employee: John Smith
social security number: 111-11-1111
weekly salary: 800.00
earned $800.00

hourly employee: Karen Price
social security number: 222-22-2222
hourly wage: 16.75; hours worked: 40.00
earned $670.00

commission employee: Sue Jones
social security number: 333-33-3333
gross sales: 10000.00; commission rate: 0.06
earned $600.00

base-salaried commission employee: Bob Lewis
social security number: 444-44-4444
gross sales: 5000.00; commission rate: 0.04; base salary: 300.00
earned $500.00

Virtual function calls made off base-class references:

salaried employee: John Smith
social security number: 111-11-1111
weekly salary: 800.00
earned $800.00

hourly employee: Karen Price
social security number: 222-22-2222
hourly wage: 16.75; hours worked: 40.00
earned $670.00
```

(continued at top of next page...)

Fig. 13.23 | `Employee` class hierarchy driver program. (Part 3 of 4.)

(...continued from bottom of previous page)

```
commission employee: Sue Jones
social security number: 333-33-3333
gross sales: 10000.00; commission rate: 0.06
earned $600.00

base-salaried commission employee: Bob Lewis
social security number: 444-44-4444
gross sales: 5000.00; commission rate: 0.04; base salary: 300.00
earned $500.00
```

Fig. 13.23 | Employee class hierarchy driver program. (Part 4 of 4.)

an example of static binding—at compile time, because we are using name handles (not pointers or references that could be set at execution time), the compiler can identify each object's type to determine which print and earnings functions are called.

Line 54 allocates vector employees, which contains four Employee pointers. Line 57 aims employees[0] at object salariedEmployee. Line 58 aims employees[1] at object hourlyEmployee. Line 59 aims employees[2] at object commissionEmployee. Line 60 aims employee[3] at object basePlusCommissionEmployee. The compiler allows these assignments, because a SalariedEmployee *is an* Employee, an HourlyEmployee *is an* Employee, a CommissionEmployee *is an* Employee and a BasePlusCommissionEmployee *is an* Employee. Therefore, we can assign the addresses of SalariedEmployee, HourlyEmployee, CommissionEmployee and BasePlusCommissionEmployee objects to base-class Employee pointers (even though Employee is an abstract class).

The for statement at lines 68–69 traverses vector employees and invokes function virtualViaPointer (lines 83–87) for each element in employees. Function virtualViaPointer receives in parameter baseClassPtr (of type const Employee * const) the address stored in an employees element. Each call to virtualViaPointer uses baseClassPtr to invoke virtual functions print (line 85) and earnings (line 86). Note that function virtualViaPointer does not contain any SalariedEmployee, HourlyEmployee, CommissionEmployee or BasePlusCommissionEmployee type information. The function knows only about base-class type Employee. Therefore, at compile time, the compiler cannot know which concrete class's functions to call through baseClassPtr. Yet at execution time, each virtual-function invocation calls the function on the object to which baseClassPtr points at that time. The output illustrates that the appropriate functions for each class are indeed invoked and that each object's proper information is displayed. For instance, the weekly salary is displayed for the SalariedEmployee, and the gross sales are displayed for the CommissionEmployee and BasePlusCommissionEmployee. Also note that obtaining the earnings of each Employee polymorphically in line 86 produces the same results as obtaining these employees' earnings via static binding in lines 44, 46, 48 and 50. All virtual function calls to print and earnings are resolved at runtime with dynamic binding.

Finally, another for statement (lines 75–76) traverses employees and invokes function virtualViaReference (lines 91–95) for each element in the vector. Function virtualViaReference receives in its parameter baseClassRef (of type const Employee &) a reference formed by dereferencing the pointer stored in each employees element (line 76). Each call to virtualViaReference invokes virtual functions print (line 93) and earnings (line 94) via reference baseClassRef to demonstrate that polymorphic processing occurs with base-class references as well. Each virtual-function invocation calls the function on the object to which baseClassRef refers at runtime. This is another example of dynamic binding. The output produced using base-class references is identical to the output produced using base-class pointers.

13.7 (Optional) Polymorphism, Virtual Functions and Dynamic Binding "Under the Hood"

C++ makes polymorphism easy to program. It is certainly possible to program for polymorphism in non-object-oriented languages such as C, but doing so requires complex and potentially dangerous pointer manipulations. This section discusses how C++ can implement polymorphism, virtual functions and dynamic binding internally. This will give you a solid understanding of how these capabilities really work. More importantly, it will help you appreciate the overhead of polymorphism—in terms of additional memory consumption and processor time. This will help you determine when to use polymorphism and when to avoid it. Note that the C++ Standard Template Library (STL) components were implemented without polymorphism and virtual functions—this was done to avoid the associated execution-time overhead and achieve optimal performance to meet the unique requirements of the STL.

First, we will explain the data structures that the C++ compiler builds at compile time to support polymorphism at execution time. You will see that polymorphism is accomplished through three levels of pointers (i.e., "triple indirection"). Then we will show how an executing program uses these data structures to execute virtual functions and achieve the dynamic binding associated with polymorphism. Note that our discussion explains one possible implementation; this is not a language requirement.

When C++ compiles a class that has one or more virtual functions, it builds a virtual function table (*vtable*) for that class. An executing program uses the *vtable* to select the proper function implementation each time a virtual function of that class is called. The leftmost column of Fig. 13.24 illustrates the *vtables* for classes Employee, SalariedEmployee, HourlyEmployee, CommissionEmployee and BasePlusCommissionEmployee.

In the *vtable* for class Employee, the first function pointer is set to 0 (i.e., the null pointer). This is done because function earnings is a pure virtual function and therefore lacks an implementation. The second function pointer points to function print, which displays the employee's full name and social security number. [*Note:* We have abbreviated the output of each print function in this figure to conserve space.] Any class that has one or more null pointers in its *vtable* is an abstract class. Classes without any null *vtable* pointers (such as SalariedEmployee, HourlyEmployee, CommissionEmployee and BasePlusCommissionEmployee) are concrete classes.

Class SalariedEmployee overrides function earnings to return the employee's weekly salary, so the function pointer points to the earnings function of class SalariedEmployee. SalariedEmployee also overrides print, so the corresponding function pointer points to the SalariedEmployee member function that prints "salaried employee: " followed by the employee's name, social security number and weekly salary.

The earnings function pointer in the *vtable* for class HourlyEmployee points to HourlyEmployee's earnings function that returns the employee's wage multiplied by the number of hours worked. Note that to conserve space, we have omitted the fact that hourly employees receive time-and-a-half pay for overtime hours worked. The print func-

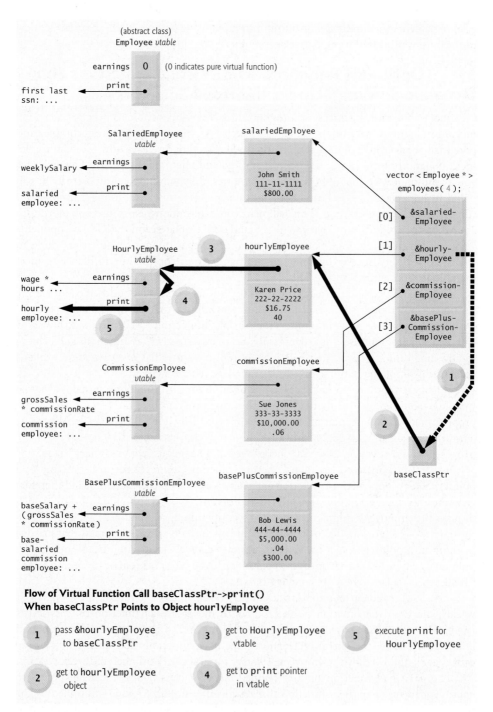

Fig. 13.24 | How virtual function calls work.

tion pointer points to the HourlyEmployee version of the function, which prints "hourly employee: ", the employee's name, social security number, hourly wage and hours worked. Both functions override the functions in class Employee.

The earnings function pointer in the *vtable* for class CommissionEmployee points to CommissionEmployee's earnings function that returns the employee's gross sales multiplied by commission rate. The print function pointer points to the CommissionEmployee version of the function, which prints the employee's type, name, social security number, commission rate and gross sales. As in class HourlyEmployee, both functions override the functions in class Employee.

The earnings function pointer in the *vtable* for class BasePlusCommissionEmployee points to BasePlusCommissionEmployee's earnings function that returns the employee's base salary plus gross sales multiplied by commission rate. The print function pointer points to the BasePlusCommissionEmployee version of the function, which prints the employee's base salary plus the type, name, social security number, commission rate and gross sales. Both functions override the functions in class CommissionEmployee.

Notice that in our Employee case study, each concrete class provides its own implementation for virtual functions earnings and print. You have already learned that each class which inherits directly from abstract base class Employee must implement earnings in order to be a concrete class, because earnings is a pure virtual function. These classes do not need to implement function print, however, to be considered concrete—print is not a pure virtual function and derived classes can inherit class Employee's implementation of print. Furthermore, class BasePlusCommissionEmployee does not have to implement either function print or earnings—both function implementations can be inherited from class CommissionEmployee. If a class in our hierarchy were to inherit function implementations in this manner, the *vtable* pointers for these functions would simply point to the function implementation that was being inherited. For example, if BasePlusCommissionEmployee did not override earnings, the earnings function pointer in the *vtable* for class BasePlusCommissionEmployee would point to the same earnings function as the *vtable* for class CommissionEmployee points to.

Polymorphism is accomplished through an elegant data structure involving three levels of pointers. We have discussed one level—the function pointers in the *vtable*. These point to the actual functions that execute when a virtual function is invoked.

Now we consider the second level of pointers. Whenever an object of a class with one or more virtual functions is instantiated, the compiler attaches to the object a pointer to the *vtable* for that class. This pointer is normally at the front of the object, but it is not required to be implemented that way. In Fig. 13.24, these pointers are associated with the objects created in Fig. 13.23 (one object for each of the types SalariedEmployee, HourlyEmployee, CommissionEmployee and BasePlusCommissionEmployee). Notice that the diagram displays each of the object's data member values. For example, the salariedEmployee object contains a pointer to the SalariedEmployee *vtable*; the object also contains the values John Smith, 111-11-1111 and $800.00.

The third level of pointers simply contains the handles to the objects that receive the virtual function calls. The handles in this level may also be references. Note that Fig. 13.24 depicts the vector employees that contains Employee pointers.

Now let us see how a typical virtual function call executes. Consider the call baseClassPtr->print() in function virtualViaPointer (line 85 of Fig. 13.23). Assume that baseClassPtr contains employees[1] (i.e., the address of object hourlyEmployee in employees). When the compiler compiles this statement, it determines that the call is indeed being made via a base-class pointer and that print is a virtual function.

The compiler determines that print is the *second* entry in each of the *vtables*. To locate this entry, the compiler notes that it will need to skip the first entry. Thus, the compiler compiles an offset or displacement of four bytes (four bytes for each pointer on today's popular 32-bit machines, and only one pointer needs to be skipped) into the table of machine-language object-code pointers to find the code that will execute the virtual function call.

The compiler generates code that performs the following operations [*Note:* The numbers in the list correspond to the circled numbers in Fig. 13.24]:

1. Select the ith entry of employees (in this case, the address of object hourlyEmployee), and pass it as an argument to function virtualViaPointer. This sets parameter baseClassPtr to point to hourlyEmployee.

2. Dereference that pointer to get to the hourlyEmployee object—which, as you recall, begins with a pointer to the HourlyEmployee *vtable*.

3. Dereference hourlyEmployee's *vtable* pointer to get to the HourlyEmployee *vtable*.

4. Skip the offset of four bytes to select the print function pointer.

5. Dereference the print function pointer to form the "name" of the actual function to execute, and use the function call operator () to execute the appropriate print function, which in this case prints the employee's type, name, social security number, hourly wage and hours worked.

The data structures of Fig. 13.24 may appear to be complex, but this complexity is managed by the compiler and hidden from you, making polymorphic programming straightforward. The pointer dereferencing operations and memory accesses that occur on every virtual function call require some additional execution time. The *vtables* and the *vtable* pointers added to the objects require some additional memory. You now have enough information to determine whether virtual functions are appropriate for your programs.

Performance Tip 13.1

Polymorphism, as typically implemented with virtual functions and dynamic binding in C++, is efficient. Programmers may use these capabilities with nominal impact on performance.

Performance Tip 13.2

Virtual functions and dynamic binding enable polymorphic programming as an alternative to switch logic programming. Optimizing compilers normally generate polymorphic code that runs as efficiently as hand-coded switch-based logic. The overhead of polymorphism is acceptable for most applications. But in some situations—real-time applications with stringent performance requirements, for example—the overhead of polymorphism may be too high.

Software Engineering Observation 13.11

Dynamic binding enables independent software vendors (ISVs) to distribute software without revealing proprietary secrets. Software distributions can consist of only header files and object files—no source code needs to be revealed. Software developers can then use inheritance to derive new classes from those provided by the ISVs. Other software that worked with the classes the ISVs provided will still work with the derived classes and will use the overridden virtual functions provided in these classes (via dynamic binding).

13.8 Case Study: Payroll System Using Polymorphism and Run-Time Type Information with Downcasting, dynamic_cast, typeid and type_info

Recall from the problem statement at the beginning of Section 13.6 that, for the current pay period, our fictitious company has decided to reward BasePlusCommissionEmployees by adding 10 percent to their base salaries. When processing Employee objects polymorphically in Section 13.6.6, we did not need to worry about the "specifics." Now, however, to adjust the base salaries of BasePlusCommissionEmployees, we have to determine the specific type of each Employee object at execution time, then act appropriately. This section demonstrates the powerful capabilities of run-time type information (RTTI) and dynamic casting, which enable a program to determine the type of an object at execution time and act on that object accordingly.

Some compilers, such as Microsoft Visual C++ .NET, require that RTTI be enabled before it can be used in a program. Consult your compiler's documentation to determine whether your compiler has similar requirements. To enable RTTI in Visual C++ .NET, select the **Project** menu and then select the properties option for the current project. In the **Property Pages** dialog box that appears, select **Configuration Properties > C/C++ > Language**. Then choose **Yes (/GR)** from the combo box next to **Enable Run-Time Type Info**. Finally, click **OK** to save the settings.

The program in Fig. 13.25 uses the Employee hierarchy developed in Section 13.6 and increases by 10 percent the base salary of each BasePlusCommissionEmployee. Line 31

```
1   // Fig. 13.25: fig13_25.cpp
2   // Demonstrating downcasting and run-time type information.
3   // NOTE: For this example to run in Visual C++ .NET,
4   // you need to enable RTTI (Run-Time Type Info) for the project.
5   #include <iostream>
6   using std::cout;
7   using std::endl;
8   using std::fixed;
9
10  #include <iomanip>
11  using std::setprecision;
12
13  #include <vector>
14  using std::vector;
15
16  #include <typeinfo>
17
18  // include definitions of classes in Employee hierarchy
19  #include "Employee.h"
20  #include "SalariedEmployee.h"
21  #include "HourlyEmployee.h"
22  #include "CommissionEmployee.h"
23  #include "BasePlusCommissionEmployee.h"
24
25  int main()
26  {
```

Fig. 13.25 | Demonstrating downcasting and run-time type information. (Part 1 of 3.)

```
27      // set floating-point output formatting
28      cout << fixed << setprecision( 2 );
29
30      // create vector of four base-class pointers
31      vector < Employee * > employees( 4 );
32
33      // initialize vector with various kinds of Employees
34      employees[ 0 ] = new SalariedEmployee(
35         "John", "Smith", "111-11-1111", 800 );
36      employees[ 1 ] = new HourlyEmployee(
37         "Karen", "Price", "222-22-2222", 16.75, 40 );
38      employees[ 2 ] = new CommissionEmployee(
39         "Sue", "Jones", "333-33-3333", 10000, .06 );
40      employees[ 3 ] = new BasePlusCommissionEmployee(
41         "Bob", "Lewis", "444-44-4444", 5000, .04, 300 );
42
43      // polymorphically process each element in vector employees
44      for ( size_t i = 0; i < employees.size(); i++ )
45      {
46         employees[ i ]->print(); // output employee information
47         cout << endl;
48
49         // downcast pointer
50         BasePlusCommissionEmployee *derivedPtr =
51            dynamic_cast < BasePlusCommissionEmployee * >
52               ( employees[ i ] );
53
54         // determine whether element points to base-salaried
55         // commission employee
56         if ( derivedPtr != 0 ) // 0 if not a BasePlusCommissionEmployee
57         {
58            double oldBaseSalary = derivedPtr->getBaseSalary();
59            cout << "old base salary: $" << oldBaseSalary << endl;
60            derivedPtr->setBaseSalary( 1.10 * oldBaseSalary );
61            cout << "new base salary with 10% increase is: $"
62               << derivedPtr->getBaseSalary() << endl;
63         } // end if
64
65         cout << "earned $" << employees[ i ]->earnings() << "\n\n";
66      } // end for
67
68      // release objects pointed to by vector's elements
69      for ( size_t j = 0; j < employees.size(); j++ )
70      {
71         // output class name
72         cout << "deleting object of "
73            << typeid( *employees[ j ] ).name() << endl;
74
75         delete employees[ j ];
76      } // end for
77
78      return 0;
79   } // end main
```

Fig. 13.25 | Demonstrating downcasting and run-time type information. (Part 2 of 3.)

```
salaried employee: John Smith
social security number: 111-11-1111
weekly salary: 800.00
earned $800.00

hourly employee: Karen Price
social security number: 222-22-2222
hourly wage: 16.75; hours worked: 40.00
earned $670.00

commission employee: Sue Jones
social security number: 333-33-3333
gross sales: 10000.00; commission rate: 0.06
earned $600.00

base-salaried commission employee: Bob Lewis
social security number: 444-44-4444
gross sales: 5000.00; commission rate: 0.04; base salary: 300.00
old base salary: $300.00
new base salary with 10% increase is: $330.00
earned $530.00

deleting object of class SalariedEmployee
deleting object of class HourlyEmployee
deleting object of class CommissionEmployee
deleting object of class BasePlusCommissionEmployee
```

Fig. 13.25 | Demonstrating downcasting and run-time type information. (Part 3 of 3.)

declares four-element vector employees that stores pointers to Employee objects. Lines 34–41 populate the vector with the addresses of dynamically allocated objects of classes SalariedEmployee (Figs. 13.15–13.16), HourlyEmployee (Figs. 13.17–13.18), CommissionEmployee (Figs. 13.19–13.20) and BasePlusCommissionEmployee (Figs. 13.21–13.22).

The for statement at lines 44–66 iterates through the employees vector and displays each Employee's information by invoking member function print (line 46). Recall that because print is declared virtual in base class Employee, the system invokes the appropriate derived-class object's print function.

In this example, as we encounter BasePlusCommissionEmployee objects, we wish to increase their base salary by 10 percent. Since we process the employees generically (i.e., polymorphically), we cannot (with the techniques we've learned) be certain as to which type of Employee is being manipulated at any given time. This creates a problem, because BasePlusCommissionEmployee employees must be identified when we encounter them so they can receive the 10 percent salary increase. To accomplish this, we use operator **dynamic_cast** (line 51) to determine whether the type of each object is BasePlusCommissionEmployee. This is the downcast operation we referred to in Section 13.3.3. Lines 50–52 dynamically downcast employees[i] from type Employee * to type BasePlusCommissionEmployee *. If the vector element points to an object that *is a* BasePlusCommissionEmployee object, then that object's address is assigned to commissionPtr; otherwise, 0 is assigned to derived-class pointer derivedPtr.

If the value returned by the dynamic_cast operator in lines 50–52 is not 0, the object is the correct type and the if statement (lines 56–63) performs the special processing required for the BasePlusCommissionEmployee object. Lines 58, 60 and 62 invoke Base-PlusCommissionEmployee functions getBaseSalary and setBaseSalary to retrieve and update the employee's salary.

Line 65 invokes member function earnings on the object to which employees[i] points. Recall that earnings is declared virtual in the base class, so the program invokes the derived-class object's earnings function—another example of dynamic binding.

The for loop at lines 69–76 displays each employee's object type and uses the delete operator to deallocate the dynamic memory to which each vector element points. Operator **typeid** (line 73) returns a reference to an object of class **type_info** that contains the information about the type of its operand, including the name of that type. When invoked, type_info member function **name** (line 73) returns a pointer-based string that contains the type name (e.g., "class BasePlusCommissionEmployee") of the argument passed to typeid. [*Note:* The exact contents of the string returned by type_info member function name may vary by compiler.] To use typeid, the program must include header file <typeinfo> (line 16).

Note that we avoid several compilation errors in this example by downcasting an Employee pointer to a BasePlusCommissionEmployee pointer (lines 50–52). If we remove the dynamic_cast from line 51 and attempt to assign the current Employee pointer directly to BasePlusCommissionEmployee pointer commissionPtr, we will receive a compilation error. C++ does not allow a program to assign a base-class pointer to a derived-class pointer because the *is-a* relationship does not apply—a CommissionEmployee is *not* a BasePlusCommissionEmployee. The *is-a* relationship applies only between the derived class and its base classes, not vice versa.

Similarly, if lines 58, 60 and 62 used the current base-class pointer from employees, rather than derived-class pointer commissionPtr, to invoke derived-class-only functions getBaseSalary and setBaseSalary, we would receive a compilation error at each of these lines. As you learned in Section 13.3.3, attempting to invoke derived-class-only functions through a base-class pointer is not allowed. Although lines 58, 60 and 62 execute only if commissionPtr is not 0 (i.e., if the cast can be performed), we cannot attempt to invoke derived class BasePlusCommissionEmployee functions getBaseSalary and setBas-eSalary on the base class Employee pointer. Recall that, using a base class Employee pointer, we can invoke only functions found in base class Employee—earnings, print and Employee's *get* and *set* functions.

13.9 Virtual Destructors

A problem can occur when using polymorphism to process dynamically allocated objects of a class hierarchy. So far you have seen nonvirtual destructors—destructors that are not declared with keyword virtual. If a derived-class object with a nonvirtual destructor is destroyed explicitly by applying the delete operator to a base-class pointer to the object, the C++ standard specifies that the behavior is undefined.

The simple solution to this problem is to create a virtual destructor (i.e., a destructor that is declared with keyword virtual) in the base class. This makes all derived-class destructors `virtual` *even though they do not have the same name as the base-class destructor.* Now, if an object in the hierarchy is destroyed explicitly by applying the `delete` operator to a base-class pointer, the destructor for the appropriate class is called based on the object to which the base-class pointer points. Remember, when a derived-class object is destroyed, the base-class part of the derived-class object is also destroyed, so it is important for the destructors of both the derived class and base class to execute. The base-class destructor automatically executes after the derived-class destructor.

Good Programming Practice 13.2

If a class has `virtual` functions, provide a `virtual` destructor, even if one is not required for the class. Classes derived from this class may contain destructors that must be called properly.

Common Programming Error 13.5

Constructors cannot be `virtual`. Declaring a constructor `virtual` is a compilation error.

13.10 Wrap-Up

In this chapter we discussed polymorphism, which enables us to "program in the general" rather than "program in the specific," and we showed how this makes programs more extensible. We began with an example of how polymorphism would allow a screen manager to display several "space" objects. We then demonstrated how base-class and derived-class pointers can be aimed at base-class and derived-class objects. We said that aiming base-class pointers at base-class objects is natural, as is aiming derived-class pointers at derived-class objects. Aiming base-class pointers at derived-class objects is also natural because a derived-class object *is an* object of its base class. You learned why aiming derived-class pointers at base-class objects is dangerous and why the compiler disallows such assignments. We introduced `virtual` functions, which enable the proper functions to be called when objects at various levels of an inheritance hierarchy are referenced (at execution time) via base-class pointers. This is known as dynamic or late binding. We then discussed pure `virtual` functions (`virtual` functions that do not provide an implementation) and abstract classes (classes with one or more pure `virtual` functions). You learned that abstract classes cannot be used to instantiate objects, while concrete classes can. We then demonstrated using abstract classes in an inheritance hierarchy. You learned how polymorphism works "under the hood" with *vtables* that are created by the compiler. We discussed downcasting base-class pointers to derived-class pointers to enable a program to call derived-class-only member functions. The chapter concluded with a discussion of `virtual` destructors, and how they ensure that all appropriate destructors in an inheritance hierarchy run on a derived-class object when that object is deleted via a base-class pointer.

You should now be familiar with classes, objects, encapsulation, inheritance and polymorphism—the most essential aspects of object-oriented programming. Well, that's it for now. Congratulations on completing this introduction to C++ programming. We wish you the best and hope that you will continue your study of C++. If you have any questions, please write to us at `deitel@deitel.com` and we will respond promptly.

Summary

- With virtual functions and polymorphism, it becomes possible to design and implement systems that are more easily extensible. Programs can be written to process objects of types that may not exist when the program is under development.

- Polymorphic programming with virtual functions can eliminate the need for switch logic. The programmer can use the virtual function mechanism to perform the equivalent logic automatically, thus avoiding the kinds of errors typically associated with switch logic.

- Derived classes can provide their own implementations of a base-class virtual function if necessary, but if they do not, the base class's implementation is used.

- If a virtual function is called by referencing a specific object by name and using the dot member-selection operator, the reference is resolved at compile time (this is called static binding); the virtual function that is called is the one defined for the class of that particular object.

- In many situations it is useful to define abstract classes for which the programmer never intends to create objects. Because these are used only as base classes, we refer to them as abstract base classes. No objects of an abstract class may be instantiated.

- Classes from which objects can be instantiated are called concrete classes.

- A class is made abstract by declaring one or more of its virtual functions to be pure. A pure virtual function is one with a pure specifier (= 0) in its declaration.

- If a class is derived from a class with a pure virtual function and that derived class does not supply a definition for that pure virtual function, then that virtual function remains pure in the derived class. Consequently, the derived class is also an abstract class.

- C++ enables polymorphism—the ability for objects of different classes related by inheritance to respond differently to the same member-function call.

- Polymorphism is implemented via virtual functions and dynamic binding.

- When a request is made through a base-class pointer or reference to use a virtual function, C++ chooses the correct overridden function in the appropriate derived class associated with the object.

- Through the use of virtual functions and polymorphism, a member-function call can cause different actions, depending on the type of the object receiving the call.

- Although we cannot instantiate objects of abstract base classes, we can declare pointers and references to objects of abstract base classes. Such pointers and references can be used to enable polymorphic manipulations of derived-class objects instantiated from concrete derived classes.

- Dynamic binding requires that at runtime, the call to a virtual member function be routed to the virtual function version appropriate for the class. A virtual function table called the *vtable* is implemented as an array containing function pointers. Each class with virtual functions has a *vtable*. For each virtual function in the class, the *vtable* has an entry containing a function pointer to the version of the virtual function to use for an object of that class. The virtual function to use for a particular class could be the function defined in that class, or it could be a function inherited either directly or indirectly from a base class higher in the hierarchy.

- When a base class provides a virtual member function, derived classes can override the virtual function, but they do not have to override it. Thus, a derived class can use a base class's version of a virtual function.

- Each object of a class with virtual functions contains a pointer to the *vtable* for that class. When a function call is made from a base-class pointer to a derived-class object, the appropriate function pointer in the *vtable* is obtained and dereferenced to complete the call at execution time. This *vtable* lookup and pointer dereferencing require nominal runtime overhead.

- Any class that has one or more 0 pointers in its *vtable* is an abstract class. Classes without any 0 *vtable* pointers are concrete classes.

- New kinds of classes are regularly added to systems. New classes are accommodated by dynamic binding (also called late binding). The type of an object need not be known at compile time for a virtual-function call to be compiled. At runtime, the appropriate member function will be called for the object to which the pointer points.

- Operator dynamic_cast checks the type of the object to which the pointer points, then determines whether this type has an *is-a* relationship with the type to which the pointer is being converted. If there is an *is-a* relationship, dynamic_cast returns the object's address. If not, dynamic_cast returns 0.

- Operator typeid returns a reference to an object of class type_info that contains information about the type of its operand, including the name of the type. To use typeid, the program must include header file <typeinfo>.

- When invoked, type_info member function name returns a pointer-based string that contains the name of the type that the type_info object represents.

- Operators dynamic_cast and typeid are part of C++'s run-time type information (RTTI) feature, which allows a program to determine an object's type at runtime.

- Declare the base-class destructor virtual if the class contains virtual functions. This makes all derived-class destructors virtual, even though they do not have the same name as the base-class destructor. If an object in the hierarchy is destroyed explicitly by applying the delete operator to a base-class pointer to a derived-class object, the destructor for the appropriate class is called. After a derived-class destructor runs, the destructors for all of that class's base classes run all the way up the hierarchy—the root class's destructor runs last.

Terminology

abstract base class
abstract class
base-class pointer to a base-class object
base-class pointer to a derived-class object
concrete class
dangerous pointer manipulation
derived-class pointer to a base-class object
derived-class pointer to a derived-class object
displacement
downcasting
dynamic binding
dynamic casting
dynamic_cast
dynamically determine function to execute
flow of control of a virtual function call
implementation inheritance
interface inheritance
iterator class
late binding
name function of class type_info
nonvirtual destructor
object's *vtable* pointer

offset into a *vtable*
override a function
polymorphic programming
polymorphism
polymorphism as an alternative to switch logic
programming in the general
programming in the specific
pure specifier
pure virtual function
RTTI (run-time type information)
static binding
switch logic
type_info class
typeid operator
<typeinfo> header file
virtual destructor
virtual function
virtual function table (*vtable*)
virtual keyword
vtable
vtable pointer

Self-Review Exercises

13.1   Fill in the blanks in each of the following statements:
   a) Treating a base-class object as a(n) _____ can cause errors.
   b) Polymorphism helps eliminate _____ logic.
   c) If a class contains at least one pure virtual function, it is a(n) _____ class.
   d) Classes from which objects can be instantiated are called _____ classes.
   e) Operator _____ can be used to downcast base-class pointers safely.
   f) Operator typeid returns a reference to a(n) _____ object.
   g) _____ involves using a base-class pointer or reference to invoke virtual functions on base-class and derived-class objects.
   h) Overridable functions are declared using keyword _____.
   i) Casting a base-class pointer to a derived-class pointer is called _____.

13.2   State whether each of the following is *true* or *false*. If *false*, explain why.
   a) All virtual functions in an abstract base class must be declared as pure virtual functions.
   b) Referring to a derived-class object with a base-class handle is dangerous.
   c) A class is made abstract by declaring that class virtual.
   d) If a base class declares a pure virtual function, a derived class must implement that function to become a concrete class.
   e) Polymorphic programming can eliminate the need for switch logic.

Answers to Self-Review Exercises

13.1   a) derived-class object. b) switch. c) abstract. d) concrete. e) dynamic_cast. f) type_info. g) Polymorphism. h) virtual. i) downcasting.

13.2   a) False. An abstract base class can include virtual functions with implementations. b) False. Referring to a base-class object with a derived-class handle is dangerous. c) False. Classes are never declared virtual. Rather, a class is made abstract by including at least one pure virtual function in the class. d) True. e) True.

Exercises

13.3   How is it that polymorphism enables you to program "in the general" rather than "in the specific"? Discuss the key advantages of programming "in the general."

13.4   Discuss the problems of programming with switch logic. Explain why polymorphism can be an effective alternative to using switch logic.

13.5   Distinguish between inheriting interface and inheriting implementation. How do inheritance hierarchies designed for inheriting interface differ from those designed for inheriting implementation?

13.6   What are virtual functions? Describe a circumstance in which virtual functions would be appropriate.

13.7   Distinguish between static binding and dynamic binding. Explain the use of virtual functions and the *vtable* in dynamic binding.

13.8   Distinguish between virtual functions and pure virtual functions.

13.9   Suggest one or more levels of abstract base classes for the Shape hierarchy discussed in this chapter and shown in Fig. 12.3. (The first level is Shape, and the second level consists of the classes TwoDimensionalShape and ThreeDimensionalShape.)

13.10   How does polymorphism promote extensibility?

13.11 You have been asked to develop a flight simulator that will have elaborate graphical outputs. Explain why polymorphic programming would be especially effective for a problem of this nature.

13.12 *(Payroll System Modification)* Modify the payroll system of Figs. 13.13–13.23 to include private data member birthDate in class Employee. Use class Date from Figs. 11.12–11.13 to represent an employee's birthday. Assume that payroll is processed once per month. Create a vector of Employee references to store the various employee objects. In a loop, calculate the payroll for each Employee (polymorphically), and add a $100.00 bonus to the person's payroll amount if the current month is the month in which the Employee's birthday occurs.

13.13 *(Shape Hierarchy)* Implement the Shape hierarchy designed in Exercise 12.7 (which is based on the hierarchy in Fig. 12.3). Each TwoDimensionalShape should contain function getArea to calculate the area of the two-dimensional shape. Each ThreeDimensionalShape should have member functions getArea and getVolume to calculate the surface area and volume of the three-dimensional shape, respectively. Create a program that uses a vector of Shape pointers to objects of each concrete class in the hierarchy. The program should print the object to which each vector element points. Also, in the loop that processes all the shapes in the vector, determine whether each shape is a TwoDimensionalShape or a ThreeDimensionalShape. If a shape is a TwoDimensionalShape, display its area. If a shape is a ThreeDimensionalShape, display its area and volume.

13.14 *(Polymorphic Screen Manager Using Shape Hierarchy)* Develop a basic graphics package. Use the Shape hierarchy implemented in Exercise 13.13. Limit yourself to two-dimensional shapes such as squares, rectangles, triangles and circles. Interact with the user. Let the user specify the position, size, shape and fill characters to be used in drawing each shape. The user can specify more than one of the same shape. As you create each shape, place a Shape * pointer to each new Shape object into an array. Each Shape class should now have its own draw member function. Write a polymorphic screen manager that walks through the array, sending draw messages to each object in the array to form a screen image. Redraw the screen image each time the user specifies an additional shape.

13.15 *(Package Inheritance Hierarchy)* Use the Package inheritance hierarchy created in Exercise 12.9 to create a program that displays the address information and calculates the shipping costs for several Packages. The program should contain a vector of Package pointers to objects of classes TwoDayPackage and OvernightPackage. Loop through the vector to process the Packages polymorphically. For each Package, invoke *get* functions to obtain the address information of the sender and the recipient, then print the two addresses as they would appear on mailing labels. Also, call each Package's calculateCost member function and print the result. Keep track of the total shipping cost for all Packages in the vector, and display this total when the loop terminates.

13.16 *(Polymorphic Banking Program Using Account Hierarchy)* Develop a polymorphic banking program using the Account hierarchy created in Exercise 12.10. Create a vector of Account pointers to SavingsAccount and CheckingAccount objects. For each Account in the vector, allow the user to specify an amount of money to withdraw from the Account using member function debit and an amount of money to deposit into the Account using member function credit. As you process each Account, determine its type. If an Account is a SavingsAccount, calculate the amount of interest owed to the Account using member function calculateInterest, then add the interest to the account balance using member function credit. After processing an Account, print the updated account balance obtained by invoking base class member function getBalance.

Operator Precedence and Associativity Chart

A.1 Operator Precedence

Operators are shown in decreasing order of precedence from top to bottom (Fig. A.1).

Operator	Type	Associativity
: :	binary scope resolution	left to right
: :	unary scope resolution	
()	parentheses	left to right
[]	array subscript	
.	member selection via object	
->	member selection via pointer	
++	unary postfix increment	
--	unary postfix decrement	
typeid	runtime type information	
dynamic_cast < *type* >	runtime type-checked cast	
static_cast< *type* >	compile-time type-checked cast	
reinterpret_cast< *type* >	cast for nonstandard conversions	
const_cast< *type* >	cast away const-ness	

Fig. A.1 | Operator precedence and associativity chart. (Part 1 of 3.)

Operator	Type	Associativity
++	unary prefix increment	right to left
--	unary prefix decrement	
+	unary plus	
-	unary minus	
!	unary logical negation	
~	unary bitwise complement	
sizeof	determine size in bytes	
&	address	
*	dereference	
new	dynamic memory allocation	
new[]	dynamic array allocation	
delete	dynamic memory deallocation	
delete[]	dynamic array deallocation	
(*type*)	C-style unary cast	right to left
.*	pointer to member via object	left to right
->*	pointer to member via pointer	
*	multiplication	left to right
/	division	
%	modulus	
+	addition	left to right
-	subtraction	
<<	bitwise left shift	left to right
>>	bitwise right shift	
<	relational less than	left to right
<=	relational less than or equal to	
>	relational greater than	
>=	relational greater than or equal to	
==	relational is equal to	left to right
!=	relational is not equal to	
&	bitwise AND	left to right
^	bitwise exclusive OR	left to right
|	bitwise inclusive OR	left to right
&&	logical AND	left to right
||	logical OR	left to right
?:	ternary conditional	right to left

Fig. A.1 | Operator precedence and associativity chart. (Part 2 of 3.)

Operator	Type	Associativity
=	assignment	right to left
+=	addition assignment	
-=	subtraction assignment	
*=	multiplication assignment	
/=	division assignment	
%=	modulus assignment	
&=	bitwise AND assignment	
^=	bitwise exclusive OR assignment	
|=	bitwise inclusive OR assignment	
<<=	bitwise left-shift assignment	
>>=	bitwise right-shift assignment	
,	comma	left to right

Fig. A.1 | Operator precedence and associativity chart. (Part 3 of 3.)

B

ASCII Character Set

ASCII character set										
	0	1	2	3	4	5	6	7	8	9
0	nul	soh	stx	etx	eot	enq	ack	bel	bs	ht
1	lf	vt	ff	cr	so	si	dle	dc1	dc2	dc3
2	dc4	nak	syn	etb	can	em	sub	esc	fs	gs
3	rs	us	sp	!	"	#	$	%	&	'
4	(	)	*	+	,	-	.	/	0	1
5	2	3	4	5	6	7	8	9	:	;
6	<	=	>	?	@	A	B	C	D	E
7	F	G	H	I	J	K	L	M	N	O
8	P	Q	R	S	T	U	V	W	X	Y
9	Z	[	\	]	^	_	`	a	b	c
10	d	e	f	g	h	i	j	k	l	m
11	n	o	p	q	r	s	t	u	v	w
12	x	y	z	{	|	}	~	del		

Fig. B.1 | ASCII character set.

The digits at the left of the table are the left digits of the decimal equivalent (0–127) of the character code, and the digits at the top of the table are the right digits of the character code. For example, the character code for "F" is 70, and the character code for "&" is 38.

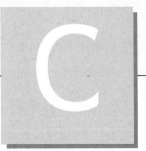

Fundamental Types

Figure C.1 lists C++'s fundamental types. The C++ Standard Document does not provide the exact number of bytes required to store variables of these types in memory. However, the C++ Standard Document does indicate how the memory requirements for fundamental types relate to one another. By order of increasing memory requirements, the signed integer types are `signed char`, `short int`, `int` and `long int`. This means that a `short int` must provide at least as much storage as a `signed char`; an `int` must provide at least as much storage as a `short int`; and a `long int` must provide at least as much storage as an `int`. Each signed integer type has a corresponding unsigned integer type that has the same memory requirements. Unsigned types cannot represent negative values, but can represent twice as many positive values than their associated signed types. By order of increasing

Integral Types	Floating-Point Types
bool	float
char	double
signed char	long double
unsigned char	
short int	
unsigned short int	
int	
unsigned int	
long int	
unsigned long int	
wchar_t	

Fig. C.1 | C++ fundamental types.

memory requirements, the floating-point types are float, double and long double. Like integer types, a double must provide at least as much storage as a float and a long double must provide at least as much storage as a double.

The exact sizes and ranges of values for the fundamental types are implementation dependent. The header files <climits> (for the integral types) and <cfloat> (for the floating-point types) specify the ranges of values supported on your system.

The range of values a type supports depends on the number of bytes that are used to represent that type. For example, consider a system with 4 byte (32 bits) ints. For the signed int type, the nonnegative values are in the range 0 to 2,147,483,647 ($2^{31} - 1$). The negative values are in the range -1 to $-2,147,483,648$ (-2^{31}). This is a total of 2^{32} possible values. An unsigned int on the same system would use the same number of bits to represent data, but would not represent any negative values. This results in values in the range 0 to 4,294,967,295 ($2^{32} - 1$). On the same system, a short int could not use more than 32 bits to represent its data and a long int must use at least 32 bits.

C++ provides the data type bool for variables that can hold only the values true and false.

D

Number Systems

Here are only numbers ratified.
—William Shakespeare

Nature has some sort of arithmetic-geometrical coordinate system, because nature has all kinds of models. What we experience of nature is in models, and all of nature's models are so beautiful.
It struck me that nature's system must be a real beauty, because in chemistry we find that the associations are always in beautiful whole numbers—there are no fractions.

—Richard Buckminster Fuller

OBJECTIVES

In this appendix you will learn:

■ To understand basic number systems concepts, such as base, positional value and symbol value.

■ To understand how to work with numbers represented in the binary, octal and hexadecimal number systems.

■ To abbreviate binary numbers as octal numbers or hexadecimal numbers.

■ To convert octal numbers and hexadecimal numbers to binary numbers.

■ To convert back and forth between decimal numbers and their binary, octal and hexadecimal equivalents.

■ To understand binary arithmetic and how negative binary numbers are represented using two's complement notation.

Outline

D.1 Introduction
D.2 Abbreviating Binary Numbers as Octal and Hexadecimal Numbers
D.3 Converting Octal and Hexadecimal Numbers to Binary Numbers
D.4 Converting from Binary, Octal or Hexadecimal to Decimal
D.5 Converting from Decimal to Binary, Octal or Hexadecimal
D.6 Negative Binary Numbers: Two's Complement Notation

Summary | Terminology | Self-Review Exercises | Answers to Self-Review Exercises | Exercises

D.1 Introduction

In this appendix, we introduce the key number systems that C++ programmers use, especially when they are working on software projects that require close interaction with machine-level hardware. Projects like this include operating systems, computer networking software, compilers, database systems and applications requiring high performance.

When we write an integer such as 227 or –63 in a C++ program, the number is assumed to be in the decimal (base 10) number system. The digits in the decimal number system are 0, 1, 2, 3, 4, 5, 6, 7, 8 and 9. The lowest digit is 0 and the highest is 9—one less than the base of 10. Internally, computers use the binary (base 2) number system. The binary number system has only two digits, namely 0 and 1. Its lowest digit is 0 and its highest is 1—one less than the base of 2.

As we will see, binary numbers tend to be much longer than their decimal equivalents. Programmers who work in assembly languages, and in high-level languages like C++ that enable them to reach down to the machine level, find it cumbersome to work with binary numbers. So two other number systems—the octal number system (base 8) and the hexadecimal number system (base 16)—are popular primarily because they make it convenient to abbreviate binary numbers.

In the octal number system, the digits range from 0 to 7. Because both the binary and the octal number systems have fewer digits than the decimal number system, their digits are the same as the corresponding digits in decimal.

The hexadecimal number system poses a problem because it requires 16 digits—a lowest digit of 0 and a highest digit with a value equivalent to decimal 15 (one less than the base of 16). By convention, we use the letters A through F to represent the hexadecimal digits corresponding to decimal values 10 through 15. Thus in hexadecimal we can have numbers like 876 consisting solely of decimal-like digits, numbers like 8A55F consisting of digits and letters and numbers like FFE consisting solely of letters. Occasionally, a hexadecimal number spells a common word such as FACE or FEED—this can appear strange to programmers accustomed to working with numbers. The digits of the binary, octal, decimal and hexadecimal number systems are summarized in Fig. D.1–Fig. D.2.

Each of these number systems uses positional notation—each position in which a digit is written has a different positional value. For example, in the decimal number 937 (the 9, the 3 and the 7 are referred to as symbol values), we say that the 7 is written in the ones position, the 3 is written in the tens position and the 9 is written in the hundreds position. Note that each of these positions is a power of the base (base 10) and that these powers begin at 0 and increase by 1 as we move left in the number (Fig. D.3).

Binary digit	Octal digit	Decimal digit	Hexadecimal digit
0	0	0	0
1	1	1	1
	2	2	2
	3	3	3
	4	4	4
	5	5	5
	6	6	6
	7	7	7
		8	8
		9	9
			A (decimal value of 10)
			B (decimal value of 11)
			C (decimal value of 12)
			D (decimal value of 13)
			E (decimal value of 14)
			F (decimal value of 15)

Fig. D.1 | Digits of the binary, octal, decimal and hexadecimal number systems.

Attribute	Binary	Octal	Decimal	Hexadecimal
Base	2	8	10	16
Lowest digit	0	0	0	0
Highest digit	1	7	9	F

Fig. D.2 | Comparing the binary, octal, decimal and hexadecimal number systems.

Positional values in the decimal number system			
Decimal digit	9	3	7
Position name	Hundreds	Tens	Ones
Positional value	100	10	1
Positional value as a power of the base (10)	10^2	10^1	10^0

Fig. D.3 | Positional values in the decimal number system.

For longer decimal numbers, the next positions to the left would be the thousands position (10 to the 3rd power), the ten-thousands position (10 to the 4th power), the hundred-thousands position (10 to the 5th power), the millions position (10 to the 6th power), the ten-millions position (10 to the 7th power) and so on.

In the binary number 101, the rightmost 1 is written in the ones position, the 0 is written in the twos position and the leftmost 1 is written in the fours position. Note that each position is a power of the base (base 2) and that these powers begin at 0 and increase by 1 as we move left in the number (Fig. D.4). So, $101 = 2^2 + 2^0 = 4 + 1 = 5$.

For longer binary numbers, the next positions to the left would be the eights position (2 to the 3rd power), the sixteens position (2 to the 4th power), the thirty-twos position (2 to the 5th power), the sixty-fours position (2 to the 6th power) and so on.

In the octal number 425, we say that the 5 is written in the ones position, the 2 is written in the eights position and the 4 is written in the sixty-fours position. Note that each of these positions is a power of the base (base 8) and that these powers begin at 0 and increase by 1 as we move left in the number (Fig. D.5).

For longer octal numbers, the next positions to the left would be the five-hundred-and-twelves position (8 to the 3rd power), the four-thousand-and-ninety-sixes position (8 to the 4th power), the thirty-two-thousand-seven-hundred-and-sixty-eights position (8 to the 5th power) and so on.

In the hexadecimal number 3DA, we say that the A is written in the ones position, the D is written in the sixteens position and the 3 is written in the two-hundred-and-fifty-sixes position. Note that each of these positions is a power of the base (base 16) and that these powers begin at 0 and increase by 1 as we move left in the number (Fig. D.6).

For longer hexadecimal numbers, the next positions to the left would be the four-thousand-and-ninety-sixes position (16 to the 3rd power), the sixty-five-thousand-five-hundred-and-thirty-sixes position (16 to the 4th power) and so on.

Positional values in the binary number system			
Binary digit	1	0	1
Position name	Fours	Twos	Ones
Positional value	4	2	1
Positional value as a power of the base (2)	2^2	2^1	2^0

Fig. D.4 | Positional values in the binary number system.

Positional values in the octal number system			
Decimal digit	4	2	5
Position name	Sixty-fours	Eights	Ones
Positional value	64	8	1
Positional value as a power of the base (8)	8^2	8^1	8^0

Fig. D.5 | Positional values in the octal number system.

Positional values in the hexadecimal number system			
Decimal digit	3	D	A
Position name	Two-hundred-and-fifty-sixes	Sixteens	Ones
Positional value	256	16	1
Positional value as a power of the base (16)	16^2	16^1	16^0

Fig. D.6 | Positional values in the hexadecimal number system.

D.2 Abbreviating Binary Numbers as Octal and Hexadecimal Numbers

The main use for octal and hexadecimal numbers in computing is for abbreviating lengthy binary representations. Figure D.7 highlights the fact that lengthy binary numbers can be expressed concisely in number systems with higher bases than the binary number system.

A particularly important relationship that both the octal number system and the hexadecimal number system have to the binary system is that the bases of octal and hexadecimal (8 and 16 respectively) are powers of the base of the binary number system (base 2).

Decimal number	Binary representation	Octal representation	Hexadecimal representation
0	0	0	0
1	1	1	1
2	10	2	2
3	11	3	3
4	100	4	4
5	101	5	5
6	110	6	6
7	111	7	7
8	1000	10	8
9	1001	11	9
10	1010	12	A
11	1011	13	B
12	1100	14	C
13	1101	15	D
14	1110	16	E
15	1111	17	F
16	10000	20	10

Fig. D.7 | Decimal, binary, octal and hexadecimal equivalents.

Consider the following 12-digit binary number and its octal and hexadecimal equivalents. See if you can determine how this relationship makes it convenient to abbreviate binary numbers in octal or hexadecimal. The answer follows the numbers.

Binary number	Octal equivalent	Hexadecimal equivalent
100011010001	4321	8D1

To see how the binary number converts easily to octal, simply break the 12-digit binary number into groups of three consecutive bits each, starting from the right, and write those groups over the corresponding digits of the octal number as follows:

100	011	010	001
4	3	2	1

Note that the octal digit you have written under each group of thee bits corresponds precisely to the octal equivalent of that 3-digit binary number, as shown in Fig. D.7.

The same kind of relationship can be observed in converting from binary to hexadecimal. Break the 12-digit binary number into groups of four consecutive bits each, starting from the right, and write those groups over the corresponding digits of the hexadecimal number as follows:

1000	1101	0001
8	D	1

Notice that the hexadecimal digit you wrote under each group of four bits corresponds precisely to the hexadecimal equivalent of that 4-digit binary number as shown in Fig. D.7.

D.3 Converting Octal and Hexadecimal Numbers to Binary Numbers

In the previous section, we saw how to convert binary numbers to their octal and hexadecimal equivalents by forming groups of binary digits and simply rewriting them as their equivalent octal digit values or hexadecimal digit values. This process may be used in reverse to produce the binary equivalent of a given octal or hexadecimal number.

For example, the octal number 653 is converted to binary simply by writing the 6 as its 3-digit binary equivalent 110, the 5 as its 3-digit binary equivalent 101 and the 3 as its 3-digit binary equivalent 011 to form the 9-digit binary number 110101011.

The hexadecimal number FAD5 is converted to binary simply by writing the F as its 4-digit binary equivalent 1111, the A as its 4-digit binary equivalent 1010, the D as its 4-digit binary equivalent 1101 and the 5 as its 4-digit binary equivalent 0101 to form the 16-digit 1111101011010101.

D.4 Converting from Binary, Octal or Hexadecimal to Decimal

We are accustomed to working in decimal, and therefore it is often convenient to convert a binary, octal, or hexadecimal number to decimal to get a sense of what the number is "really" worth. Our diagrams in Section D.1 express the positional values in decimal. To convert a number to decimal from another base, multiply the decimal equivalent of each digit by its positional value and sum these products. For example, the binary number 110101 is converted to decimal 53 as shown in Fig. D.8.

To convert octal 7614 to decimal 3980, we use the same technique, this time using appropriate octal positional values, as shown in Fig. D.9.

To convert hexadecimal AD3B to decimal 44347, we use the same technique, this time using appropriate hexadecimal positional values, as shown in Fig. D.10.

D.5 Converting from Decimal to Binary, Octal or Hexadecimal

The conversions in Section D.4 follow naturally from the positional notation conventions. Converting from decimal to binary, octal, or hexadecimal also follows these conventions.

Suppose we wish to convert decimal 57 to binary. We begin by writing the positional values of the columns right to left until we reach a column whose positional value is greater than the decimal number. We do not need that column, so we discard it. Thus, we first write:

Positional values: 64   32   16   8   4   2   1

Then we discard the column with positional value 64, leaving:

Positional values: 32   16   8   4   2   1

Converting a binary number to decimal					
Positional values:	32	16	8	4	2	1
Symbol values:	1	1	0	1	0	1
Products:	1*32=32	1*16=16	0*8=0	1*4=4	0*2=0	1*1=1
Sum:	= 32 + 16 + 0 + 4 + 0s + 1 = 53					

Fig. D.8 | Converting a binary number to decimal.

Converting an octal number to decimal			
Positional values:	512	64	8	1
Symbol values:	7	6	1	4
Products	7*512=3584	6*64=384	1*8=8	4*1=4
Sum:	= 3584 + 384 + 8 + 4 = 3980			

Fig. D.9 | Converting an octal number to decimal.

Converting a hexadecimal number to decimal			
Positional values:	4096	256	16	1
Symbol values:	A	D	3	B
Products	A*4096=40960	D*256=3328	3*16=48	B*1=11
Sum:	= 40960 + 3328 + 48 + 11 = 44347			

Fig. D.10 | Converting a hexadecimal number to decimal.

Next we work from the leftmost column to the right. We divide 32 into 57 and observe that there is one 32 in 57 with a remainder of 25, so we write 1 in the 32 column. We divide 16 into 25 and observe that there is one 16 in 25 with a remainder of 9 and write 1 in the 16 column. We divide 8 into 9 and observe that there is one 8 in 9 with a remainder of 1. The next two columns each produce quotients of 0 when their positional values are divided into 1, so we write 0s in the 4 and 2 columns. Finally, 1 into 1 is 1, so we write 1 in the 1 column. This yields:

```
Positional values:  32   16    8    4    2    1
Symbol values:       1    1     1    0    0    1
```

and thus decimal 57 is equivalent to binary 111001.

To convert decimal 103 to octal, we begin by writing the positional values of the columns until we reach a column whose positional value is greater than the decimal number. We do not need that column, so we discard it. Thus, we first write:

```
Positional values:       512      64     8     1
```

Then we discard the column with positional value 512, yielding:

```
Positional values:                64     8     1
```

Next we work from the leftmost column to the right. We divide 64 into 103 and observe that there is one 64 in 103 with a remainder of 39, so we write 1 in the 64 column. We divide 8 into 39 and observe that there are four 8s in 39 with a remainder of 7 and write 4 in the 8 column. Finally, we divide 1 into 7 and observe that there are seven 1s in 7 with no remainder, so we write 7 in the 1 column. This yields:

```
Positional values:  64     8     1
Symbol values:       1     4     7
```

and thus decimal 103 is equivalent to octal 147.

To convert decimal 375 to hexadecimal, we begin by writing the positional values of the columns until we reach a column whose positional value is greater than the decimal number. We do not need that column, so we discard it. Thus, we first write:

```
Positional values:  4096   256    16     1
```

Then we discard the column with positional value 4096, yielding:

```
Positional values:         256    16     1
```

Next we work from the leftmost column to the right. We divide 256 into 375 and observe that there is one 256 in 375 with a remainder of 119, so we write 1 in the 256 column. We divide 16 into 119 and observe that there are seven 16s in 119 with a remainder of 7 and write 7 in the 16 column. Finally, we divide 1 into 7 and observe that there are seven 1s in 7 with no remainder, so we write 7 in the 1 column. This yields:

```
Positional values:  256    16     1
Symbol values:       1      7      7
```

and thus decimal 375 is equivalent to hexadecimal 177.

D.6 Negative Binary Numbers: Two's Complement Notation

The discussion so far in this appendix has focused on positive numbers. In this section, we explain how computers represent negative numbers using *two's complement notation*. First we explain how the two's complement of a binary number is formed, then we show why it represents the negative value of the given binary number.

Consider a machine with 32-bit integers. Suppose

```
int value = 13;
```

The 32-bit representation of value is

```
00000000 00000000 00000000 00001101
```

To form the negative of value we first form its *one's complement* by applying C++'s bitwise complement operator (~):

```
onesComplementOfValue = ~value;
```

Internally, ~value is now value with each of its bits reversed—ones become zeros and zeros become ones, as follows:

```
value:
00000000 00000000 00000000 00001101

~value  (i.e., value's ones complement):
11111111 11111111 11111111 11110010
```

To form the two's complement of value, we simply add 1 to value's one's complement. Thus

```
Two's complement of value:
11111111 11111111 11111111 11110011
```

Now if this is in fact equal to −13, we should be able to add it to binary 13 and obtain a result of 0. Let us try this:

```
  00000000 00000000 00000000 00001101
+ 11111111 11111111 11111111 11110011
-------------------------------------
  00000000 00000000 00000000 00000000
```

The carry bit coming out of the leftmost column is discarded and we indeed get 0 as a result. If we add the one's complement of a number to the number, the result will be all 1s. The key to getting a result of all zeros is that the twos complement is one more than the one's complement. The addition of 1 causes each column to add to 0 with a carry of 1. The carry keeps moving leftward until it is discarded from the leftmost bit, and thus the resulting number is all zeros.

Computers actually perform a subtraction, such as

```
x = a - value;
```

by adding the two's complement of value to a, as follows:

```
x = a + (~value + 1);
```

Suppose a is 27 and value is 13 as before. If the two's complement of value is actually the negative of value, then adding the two's complement of value to a should produce the result 14. Let us try this:

```
a (i.e., 27)      00000000 00000000 00000000 00011011
+(~value + 1)    +11111111 11111111 11111111 11110011
                 -----------------------------------
                  00000000 00000000 00000000 00001110
```

which is indeed equal to 14.

Summary

- An integer such as 19 or 227 or −63 in a C++ program is assumed to be in the decimal (base 10) number system. The digits in the decimal number system are 0, 1, 2, 3, 4, 5, 6, 7, 8 and 9. The lowest digit is 0 and the highest is 9—one less than the base of 10.
- Internally, computers use the binary (base 2) number system. The binary number system has only two digits, namely 0 and 1. Its lowest digit is 0 and its highest is 1—one less than the base of 2.
- The octal number system (base 8) and the hexadecimal number system (base 16) are popular primarily because they make it convenient to abbreviate binary numbers.
- The digits of the octal number system range from 0 to 7.
- The hexadecimal number system poses a problem because it requires 16 digits—a lowest digit of 0 and a highest digit with a value equivalent to decimal 15 (one less than the base of 16). By convention, we use the letters A through F to represent the hexadecimal digits corresponding to decimal values 10 through 15.
- Each number system uses positional notation—each position in which a digit is written has a different positional value.
- A particularly important relationship of both the octal and the hexadecimal number systems to the binary system is that their bases (8 and 16 respectively) are powers of the base of the binary number system (base 2).
- To convert an octal to a binary number, replace each octal digit with its three-digit binary equivalent.
- To convert a hexadecimal to a binary number, simply replace each hexadecimal digit with its four-digit binary equivalent.
- Because we are accustomed to working in decimal, it is convenient to convert a binary, octal or hexadecimal number to decimal to get a sense of the number's "real" worth.
- To convert a number to decimal from another base, multiply the decimal equivalent of each digit by its positional value and sum the products.
- Computers represent negative numbers using two's complement notation.
- To form the negative of a value in binary, first form its one's complement by applying C++'s bitwise complement operator (~). This reverses the bits of the value. To form the two's complement of a value, simply add one to the value's one's complement.

Terminology

base
base 2 number system
base 8 number system
base 10 number system

base 16 number system
binary number system
bitwise complement operator (~)
conversions

decimal number system	one's complement notation
digit	positional notation
hexadecimal number system	positional value
negative value	symbol value
octal number system	two's complement notation

Self-Review Exercises

D.1   The bases of the decimal, binary, octal and hexadecimal number systems are _____, _____, _____ and _____ respectively.

D.2   In general, the decimal, octal and hexadecimal representations of a given binary number contain (more/fewer) digits than the binary number contains.

D.3   (*True/False*) A popular reason for using the decimal number system is that it forms a convenient notation for abbreviating binary numbers simply by substituting one decimal digit per group of four binary bits.

D.4   The (octal / hexadecimal / decimal) representation of a large binary value is the most concise (of the given alternatives).

D.5   (*True/False*) The highest digit in any base is one more than the base.

D.6   (*True/False*) The lowest digit in any base is one less than the base.

D.7   The positional value of the rightmost digit of any number in either binary, octal, decimal or hexadecimal is always _____.

D.8   The positional value of the digit to the left of the rightmost digit of any number in binary, octal, decimal or hexadecimal is always equal to _____.

D.9   Fill in the missing values in this chart of positional values for the rightmost four positions in each of the indicated number systems:

decimal	1000	100	10	1
hexadecimal	...	256	...	...
binary	...	...	...	...
octal	512	...	8	...

D.10   Convert binary 110101011000 to octal and to hexadecimal.

D.11   Convert hexadecimal FACE to binary.

D.12   Convert octal 7316 to binary.

D.13   Convert hexadecimal 4FEC to octal. [*Hint:* First convert 4FEC to binary, then convert that binary number to octal.]

D.14   Convert binary 1101110 to decimal.

D.15   Convert octal 317 to decimal.

D.16   Convert hexadecimal EFD4 to decimal.

D.17   Convert decimal 177 to binary, to octal and to hexadecimal.

D.18   Show the binary representation of decimal 417. Then show the one's complement of 417 and the two's complement of 417.

D.19   What is the result when a number and its two's complement are added to each other?

Answers to Self-Review Exercises

D.1   10, 2, 8, 16.

D.2   Fewer.

D.3   False. Hexadecimal does this.

D.4   Hexadecimal.

D.5   False. The highest digit in any base is one less than the base.

D.6   False. The lowest digit in any base is zero.

D.7   1 (the base raised to the zero power).

D.8   The base of the number system.

D.9   Fill in the missing values in this chart of positional values for the rightmost four positions in each of the indicated number systems:

decimal	1000	100	10	1
hexadecimal	4096	256	16	1
binary	8	4	2	1
octal	512	64	8	1

D.10   Octal 6530; Hexadecimal D58.

D.11   Binary 1111 1010 1100 1110.

D.12   Binary 111 011 001 110.

D.13   Binary 0 100 111 111 101 100; Octal 47754.

D.14   Decimal 2+4+8+32+64=110.

D.15   Decimal 7+1*8+3*64=7+8+192=207.

D.16   Decimal 4+13*16+15*256+14*4096=61396.

D.17   Decimal 177
to binary:

```
256 128 64 32 16 8 4 2 1
128 64 32 16 8 4 2 1
(1*128)+(0*64)+(1*32)+(1*16)+(0*8)+(0*4)+(0*2)+(1*1)
10110001
```

to octal:

```
512 64 8 1
64 8 1
(2*64)+(6*8)+(1*1)
261
```

to hexadecimal:

```
256 16 1
16 1
(11*16)+(1*1)
(B*16)+(1*1)
B1
```

D.18   Binary:

```
512 256 128 64 32 16 8 4 2 1
256 128 64 32 16 8 4 2 1
(1*256)+(1*128)+(0*64)+(1*32)+(0*16)+(0*8)+(0*4)+(0*2)+(1*1)
110100001
```

One's complement: 001011110
Two's complement: 001011111
Check: Original binary number + its two's complement

```
110100001
001011111
---------
000000000
```

D.19   Zero.

Exercises

D.20   Some people argue that many of our calculations would be easier in the base 12 number system because 12 is divisible by so many more numbers than 10 (for base 10). What is the lowest digit in base 12? What would be the highest symbol for the digit in base 12? What are the positional values of the rightmost four positions of any number in the base 12 number system?

D.21   Complete the following chart of positional values for the rightmost four positions in each of the indicated number systems:

decimal	1000	100	10	1
base 6	...	...	6	...
base 13	...	169	...	...
base 3	27	...	...	...

D.22   Convert binary 100101111010 to octal and to hexadecimal.

D.23   Convert hexadecimal 3A7D to binary.

D.24   Convert hexadecimal 765F to octal. [*Hint:* First convert 765F to binary, then convert that binary number to octal.]

D.25   Convert binary 1011110 to decimal.

D.26   Convert octal 426 to decimal.

D.27   Convert hexadecimal FFFF to decimal.

D.28   Convert decimal 299 to binary, to octal and to hexadecimal.

D.29   Show the binary representation of decimal 779. Then show the one's complement of 779 and the two's complement of 779.

D.30   Show the two's complement of integer value −1 on a machine with 32-bit integers.

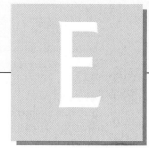

C++ Internet and Web Resources

This appendix contains a list of C++ resources that are available on the Internet and the World Wide Web. These resources include FAQs (Frequently Asked Questions), tutorials, links to the ANSI/ISO C++ standard, information about popular C++ compilers and access to free compilers, demos, books, tutorials, software tools, articles, interviews, conferences, journals and magazines, online courses, newsgroups and career resources. For additional information about the American National Standards Institute (ANSI) and its activities related to C++, visit `www.ansi.org`. You can also purchase a copy of the C++ Standard Document from this site.

E.1 Resources

`www.cplusplus.com`
This site contains information about the history and development of C++ as well as tutorials, documentation, reference material, source code and forums.

`www.possibility.com/Cpp/CppCodingStandard.html`
The *C++ Coding Standard* site examines the C++ standard and the standardizing process. The site includes such topics as standards enforcement, formatting, portability and documentation and offers links to additional C++ Web resources.

`http://www.research.att.com/~bs/bs_faq2.html`
The C++ Style and Technique FAQ by Bjarne Stroustrup, the creator of the language, provides answers to common questions about C++.

`help-site.com/cpp.html`
Help-site.com provides links to C++ resources on the Web, including tutorials and a C++ FAQ.

`www.glenmccl.com/tutor.htm`
This reference site discusses topics such as object-oriented design and writing robust code. The site provides introductions to C++ language topics, including keyword `static`, data type `bool`, namespaces, the Standard Template Library and memory allocation.

www.programmersheaven.com/zone3

This site provides links to articles, tutorials, development tools, an extensive collection of free C++ libraries and source code.

www.hal9k.com/cug

The *C/C++ Users Group (CUG)* site contains C++ resources, journals, shareware and freeware.

www.devx.com

DevX is a comprehensive resource for programmers that provides the latest news, tools and techniques for various programming languages. The *C++ Zone* offers tips, discussion forums, technical help and online newsletters.

www.cprogramming.com

This site contains interactive tutorials, quizzes, articles, journals, compiler downloads, book recommendations and free source code.

www.acm.org/crossroads/xrds3-2/ovp32.html

The Association for Computing Machinery's (ACM) site offers a comprehensive listing of C++ resources, including recommended texts, journals and magazines, published standards, newsletters, FAQs and newsgroups.

www.comeaucomputing.com/resources

Comeau Computing's site links to technical discussions, FAQs (including one devoted to templates), user groups, newsgroups and an online C++ compiler.

www.exciton.cs.rice.edu/CppResources

The site provides a document that summarizes the technical aspects of C++. The site also discusses the differences between Java and C++.

www.accu.informika.ru/resources/public/terse/cpp.htm

The Association of C & C++ Users (ACCU) site contains links to C++ tutorials, articles, developer information, discussions and book reviews.

www.cuj.com

The *C/C++ User's Journal* is an online magazine that contains articles, tutorials and downloads. The site features news about C++, forums and links to information about development tools.

directory.google.com/Top/Computers/Programming/Languages/C++/Resources/Directories

Google's C++ resources directory ranks the most useful C++ sites.

www.compinfo-center.com/c++.htm

This site provides links to C++ FAQs, newsgroups and magazines.

www.apl.jhu.edu/~paulmac/c++-references.html

This site contains book reviews and recommendations for introductory, intermediate and advanced C++ programmers and links to online C++ resources, including books, magazines and tutorials.

www.cmcrossroads.com/bradapp/links/cplusplus-links.html

This site divides links into categories, including Resources and Directories, Projects and Working Groups, Libraries, Training, Tutorials, Publications and Coding Conventions.

www.codeproject.com

Articles, code snippets, user discussions, books and news about C++, C# and .NET programming are available at this site.

www.austinlinks.com/CPlusPlus

Quadralay Corporation's site links to numerous C++ resources, including Visual C++/MFC Libraries, C++ programming information, C++ career resources and a list of tutorials and other online tools for learning C++.

www.csci.csusb.edu/dick/c++std

Links to the ANSI/ISO C++ Standard and the comp.std.c++ Usenet group are available at this site.

www.research.att.com/~bs/homepage.html

This is the home page for Bjarne Stroustrup, designer of the C++ programming language. This site provides a list of C++ resources, FAQs and other useful C++ information.

E.2 Tutorials

www.cprogramming.com/tutorial.html

This site offers a step-by-step tutorial, with sample code, that covers file I/O, recursion, binary trees, template classes and more.

www.programmersheaven.com/zone3/cat34

Free tutorials that are appropriate for many skill levels are available at this site.

www.programmershelp.co.uk/c%2B%2Btutorials.php

This site contains free online courses and a comprehensive list of C++ tutorials. This site also provides FAQs, downloads and other resources.

www.codeproject.com/script/articles/beginners.asp

This site lists tutorials and articles available for C++ beginners.

www.eng.hawaii.edu/Tutor/Make

This site provides a tutorial that describes how to create makefiles.

www.cpp-home.com

Free tutorials, discussions, chat rooms, articles, compilers, forums and online quizzes related to C++ are available at this site. The C++ tutorials cover such topics as ActiveX/COM, MFC and graphics.

www.codebeach.com

Code Beach contains source code, tutorials, books and links to major programming languages, including C++, Java, ASP, Visual Basic, XML, Python, Perl and C#.

www.kegel.com/academy/tutorials.html

This site provides links to tutorials on C, C++ and assembly languages.

E.3 FAQs

www.faqs.org/faqs/by-newsgroup/comp/comp.lang.c++.html

This site consists of links to FAQs and tutorials gathered from the Comp.Lang.C++ newsgroup.

www.eskimo.com/~scs/C-faq/top.html

This C FAQ list contains topics such as pointers, memory allocation and strings.

www.technion.ac.il/technion/tcc/usg/Ref/C_Programming.html

This site contains C/C++ programming references, including FAQs and tutorials.

www.faqs.org/faqs/by-newsgroup/comp/comp.compilers.html

This site contains a list of FAQs generated in the comp.compilers newsgroup.

E.4 Visual C++

msdn.microsoft.com/visualc

Microsoft's Visual C++ page provides information about the latest release of Visual C++ .NET.

www.freeprogrammingresources.com/visualcpp.html

This site contains free programming resources for Visual C++ programmers, including tutorials and sample programming applications.

www.mvps.org/vcfaq

The *Most Valuable Professional (MVP)* site contains a Visual C++ FAQ.

www.onesmartclick.com/programming/visual-cpp.html

This site contains Visual C++ tutorials, online books, tips, tricks, FAQs and debugging.

E.5 Newsgroups

ai.kaist.ac.kr/~ymkim/Program/c++.html

This site offers tutorials, libraries, popular compilers, FAQs and newsgroups, including comp.lang.c++.

www.coding-zone.co.uk/cpp/cnewsgroups.shtml

This site includes links to several C++ newsgroups including comp.lang.c, comp.lang.c++ and comp.lang.c++.moderated, to name a few.

E.6 Compilers and Development Tools

msdn.microsoft.com/visualc

The *Microsoft Visual C++* site provides product information, overviews, supplemental materials and ordering information for the Visual C++ compiler.

lab.msdn.microsoft.com/express/visualc/

You can download the Microsoft Visual C++ Express Beta for free from this Web site.

msdn.microsoft.com/visualc/vctoolkit2003/

Visit this site to download the Visual C++ Toolkit 2003

www.borland.com/bcppbuilder

This is a link to the *Borland C++ Builder 6*. A free command-line version is available for download.

www.thefreecountry.com/developercity/ccompilers.shtml

This site lists free C and C++ compilers for a variety of operating systems.

www.faqs.org/faqs/by-newsgroup/comp/comp.compilers.html

This site lists FAQs generated within the comp.compilers newsgroup.

www.compilers.net/Dir/Free/Compilers/CCpp.htm

Compilers.net is designed to help users locate compilers.

developer.intel.com/software/products/compilers/cwin/index.htm

The *Intel® C++ Compiler 8.1 for Windows* is available at this site.

www.intel.com/software/products/compilers/clin/index.htm

The *Intel® C++ Compiler 8.1 for Linux* is available at this site.

www.symbian.com/developer/development/cppdev.html

Symbian provides a C++ Developer's Pack and links to various resources, including code and development tools for C++ programmers (particularly those working with the Symbian operating system).

www.gnu.org/software/gcc/gcc.html

The *GNU Compiler Collection (GCC)* site includes links to download GNU compilers for C++, C, Objective C and other languages.

www.bloodshed.net/devcpp.html

Bloodshed Dev-C++ is a free integrated development environment for C++.

Third Party Vendors That Provide Libraries for Precise Financial Calculations

www.roguewave.com/products/sourcepro/analysis/

RogueWave Software's SourcePro Analysis libraries include classes for precise monetary calculations, data analysis and essential mathematical algorithms.

www.boic.com/numorder.htm

Base One International Corporation's Bas/1 Number class implements highly precise mathematical calculations.

F

Featuring...
Early
Classes &
Objects
with the
UML™ 2

And so shall I catch the fly.
—William Shakespeare

*We are built to make
mistakes, coded for error.*
—Lewis Thomas

*What we anticipate seldom
occurs; what we least expect
generally happens.*
—Benjamin Disraeli

He can run but he can't hide.
—Joe Louis

*It is one thing to show a man
that he is in error, and
another to put him in
possession of truth.*
—John Locke

Using the
Visual Studio
.NET Debugger

OBJECTIVES

In this appendix you will learn:

- To set breakpoints to debug programs.
- To run a program through the debugger.
- To set, disable and remove a breakpoint.
- To use the **Continue** command to continue execution.
- To use the **Locals** window to view and modify the values of variables.
- To use the **Watch** window to evaluate expressions.
- To use the **Step Into**, **Step Out** and **Step Over** commands to control execution.
- To use the **Autos** window to view variables that are used in the surrounding statements.

Outline

F.1 Introduction
L.2 Breakpoints and the **Continue** Command
L.3 The **Locals** and **Watch** Windows
L.4 Controlling Execution Using the **Step Into**, **Step Over**, **Step Out** and **Continue** Commands
L.5 The **Autos** Window
F.6 Wrap-Up

Summary | Terminology | Self-Review Exercises | Answers to Self-Review Exercises

F.1 Introduction

In Chapter 2, you learned that there are two types of errors—compilation errors and logic errors—and you learned how to eliminate compilation errors from your code. Logic errors (also called bugs) do not prevent a program from compiling successfully, but do cause the program to produce erroneous results when it runs. Most C++ compiler vendors provide software called a debugger, which allows you to monitor the execution of your programs to locate and remove logic errors. The debugger will be one of your most important program development tools. This appendix demonstrates key features of the Visual Studio .NET debugger. Appendix G discusses the features and capabilities of the GNU C++ debugger. We provide several free *Dive Into™ Series* publications to help students and instructors familiarize themselves with the debuggers provided with various other development tools. These publications are available on the CD that accompanies the text and can be downloaded from `www.deitel.com/books/downloads`.

F.2 Breakpoints and the Continue Command

We begin our study of the debugger by investigating breakpoints, which are markers that can be set at any executable line of code. When program execution reaches a breakpoint, execution pauses, allowing you to examine the values of variables to help determine whether logic errors exist. For example, you can examine the value of a variable that stores the result of a calculation to determine whether the calculation was performed correctly. Note that attempting to set a breakpoint at a line of code that is not executable (such as a comment) will actually set the breakpoint at the next executable line of code in that function.

To illustrate the features of the debugger, we use the program listed in Fig. F.3, which creates and manipulates an object of class Account (Figs. F.1–F.2). Execution begins in main (lines 12–30 of Fig. F.3). Line 14 creates an Account object with an initial balance of $50.00. Account's constructor (lines 10–22 of Fig. F.2) accepts one argument, which specifies the Account's initial balance. Line 17 of Fig. F.3 outputs the initial account balance using Account member function getBalance. Line 19 declares a local variable withdrawalAmount, which stores a withdrawal amount read from the user. Line 21 prompts the user for the withdrawal amount, and line 22 inputs the amount into withdrawalAmount. Line 25 subtracts the withdrawal from the Account's balance using its debit member function. Finally, line 28 displays the new balance.

```
 1   // Fig. F.1: Account.h
 2   // Definition of Account class.
 3
 4   class Account
 5   {
 6   public:
 7      Account( int ); // constructor initializes balance
 8      void credit( int ); // add an amount to the account balance
 9      void debit( int ); // subtract an amount from the account balance
10      int getBalance(); // return the account balance
11   private:
12      int balance; // data member that stores the balance
13   }; // end class Account
```

Fig. F.1 | Header file for the Account class.

```
 1   // Fig. F.2: Account.cpp
 2   // Member-function definitions for class Account.
 3   #include <iostream>
 4   using std::cout;
 5   using std::endl;
 6
 7   #include "Account.h" // include definition of class Account
 8
 9   // Account constructor initializes data member balance
10   Account::Account( int initialBalance )
11   {
12      balance = 0; // assume that the balance begins at 0
13
14      // if initialBalance is greater than 0, set this value as the
15      // balance of the Account; otherwise, balance remains 0
16      if ( initialBalance > 0 )
17         balance = initialBalance;
18
19      // if initialBalance is negative, print error message
20      if ( initialBalance < 0 )
21         cout << "Error: Initial balance cannot be negative.\n" << endl;
22   } // end Account constructor
23
24   // credit (add) an amount to the account balance
25   void Account::credit( int amount )
26   {
27      balance = balance + amount; // add amount to balance
28   } // end function credit
29
30   // debit (subtract) an amount from the account balance
31   void Account::debit( int amount )
32   {
33      if ( amount <= balance ) // debit amount does not exceed balance
34         balance = balance - amount;
35
```

Fig. F.2 | Definition for the Account class. (Part 1 of 2.)

```
36      else // debit amount exceeds balance
37          cout << "Debit amount exceeded account balance.\n" << endl;
38   } // end function debit
39
40   // return the account balance
41   int Account::getBalance()
42   {
43      return balance; // gives the value of balance to the calling function
44   } // end function getBalance
```

Fig. F.2 | Definition for the Account class. (Part 2 of 2.)

```
1    // Fig. F.3: figF_03.cpp
2    // Create and manipulate Account objects.
3    #include <iostream>
4    using std::cin;
5    using std::cout;
6    using std::endl;
7
8    // include definition of class Account from Account.h
9    #include "Account.h"
10
11   // function main begins program execution
12   int main()
13   {
14      Account account1( 50 ); // create Account object
15
16      // display initial balance of each object
17      cout << "account1 balance: $" << account1.getBalance() << endl;
18
19      int withdrawalAmount; // stores withdrawal amount read from user
20
21      cout << "\nEnter withdrawal amount for account1: "; // prompt
22      cin >> withdrawalAmount; // obtain user input
23      cout << "\nattempting to subtract " << withdrawalAmount
24         << " from account1 balance\n\n";
25      account1.debit( withdrawalAmount ); // try to subtract from account1
26
27      // display balances
28      cout << "account1 balance: $" << account1.getBalance() << endl;
29      return 0; // indicate successful termination
30   } // end main
```

Fig. F.3 | Test class for debugging.

In the following steps, you will use breakpoints and various debugger commands to examine the value of the variable withdrawalAmount declared in Fig. F.3.

1. *Enabling the debugger.* The debugger is enabled by default. If it is not enabled, you have to change the settings of the *Solution Configurations* combo box (Fig. F.4) in the toolbar. To do this, click the combo box's down arrow to access the *Solution Configurations* combo box, then select **Debug**. The toolbar will display **Debug** in the *Solution Configurations* combo box.

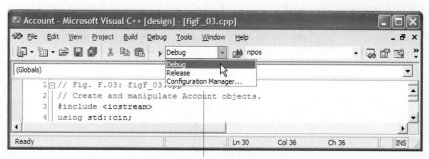

Solution Configurations combo box

Fig. F.4 | Enabling the debugger.

2. *Inserting breakpoints in Visual Studio .NET.* To insert a breakpoint in Visual Studio .NET, click inside the margin indicator bar (the gray margin at the left of the code window in Fig. F.5) next to the line of code at which you wish to break or right click that line of code and select **Insert Breakpoint.** You can set as many breakpoints as necessary. Set breakpoints at lines 21 and 25 of your code. A solid maroon circle appears in the margin indicator bar where you clicked, indicating that a breakpoint has been set (Fig. F.5). When the program runs, the debugger suspends execution at any line that contains a breakpoint. The program is said to be in break mode when the debugger pauses the program's execution. Breakpoints can be set before running a program, in break mode and while a program is running.

3. *Beginning the debugging process.* After setting breakpoints in the code editor, select **Build > Build Solution** to compile the program, then select **Debug > Start** to begin the debugging process. During debugging of a C++ program, a **Command Prompt** window appears (Fig. F.6), allowing program interaction (input and output). The program pauses when execution reaches the breakpoint at line 21. At this point, the title bar of the IDE will display **[break]** (Fig. F.7), indicating that the IDE is in break mode.

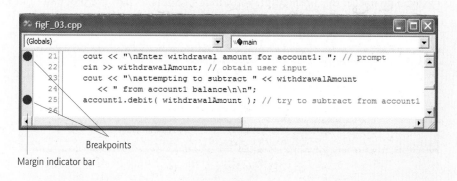

Breakpoints

Margin indicator bar

Fig. F.5 | Setting two breakpoints.

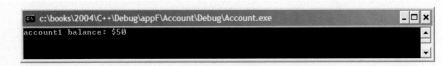

Fig. F.6 | **Inventory** program running.

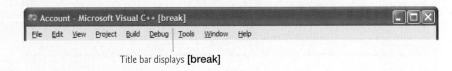

Title bar displays **[break]**

Fig. F.7 | Title bar of the IDE displaying **[break]**.

4. ***Examining program execution.*** Program execution suspends at the first breakpoint (line 21), and the IDE becomes the active window (Fig. F.8). The yellow arrow to the left of line 21 indicates that this line contains the next statement to execute. [*Note:* We have added the yellow highlighting to these images. Your code will not contain this highlighting.]

5. ***Using the Continue command to resume execution.*** To resume execution, select **Debug > Continue**. The Continue command will execute any statements between the next executable statement and the next breakpoint or the end of main, whichever comes first. The program continues executing and pauses for input at line 22. Input 13 as the withdrawal amount. The program executes until it stops at the next breakpoint, line 25. Notice that when you place your mouse pointer over the variable name withdrawalAmount, the value that the variable stores is displayed in a *Quick Info* box (Fig. F.9). In a sense, you are peeking inside the computer at the value of one of your variables. As you'll see, this can help you spot logic errors in your programs.

6. ***Setting a breakpoint at the return statement.*** Set a breakpoint at line 29 in the source code by clicking in the margin indicator bar to the left of line 29 (Fig. F.9). This will prevent the program from closing immediately after displaying its result. When there are no more breakpoints at which to suspend execution, the program will execute to completion and the **Command Prompt** window will close. If you do not set this breakpoint, you will not be able to view the program's output before the console window closes.

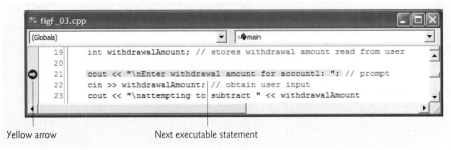

Yellow arrow   Next executable statement

Fig. F.8 | Program execution suspended at the first breakpoint.

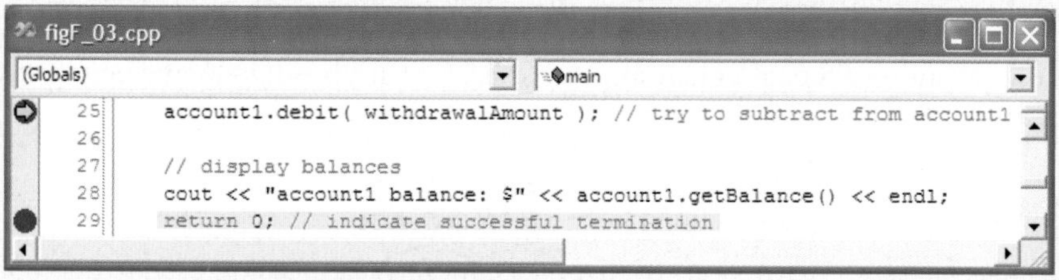

Fig. F.9 | Setting a breakpoint at line 29.

7. *Continuing program execution.* Use the **Debug > Continue** command to execute line 25. The program displays the result of its calculation (Fig. F.10).

8. *Disabling a breakpoint.* To disable a breakpoint, right click a line of code on which a breakpoint has been set (or the breakpoint itself) and select **Disable Breakpoint**. The disabled breakpoint is indicated by a hollow maroon circle (Fig. F.11). Disabling rather than removing a breakpoint allows you to re-enable the breakpoint (by clicking inside the hollow circle) in a program. This also can be done by right clicking the line marked by the hollow maroon circle (or the maroon circle itself) and selecting **Enable Breakpoint**.

9. *Removing a breakpoint.* To remove a breakpoint that you no longer need, right click a line of code on which a breakpoint has been set and select **Remove Breakpoint**. You also can remove a breakpoint by clicking the maroon circle in the margin indicator bar.

10. *Finishing program execution.* Select **Debug > Continue** to execute the program to completion.

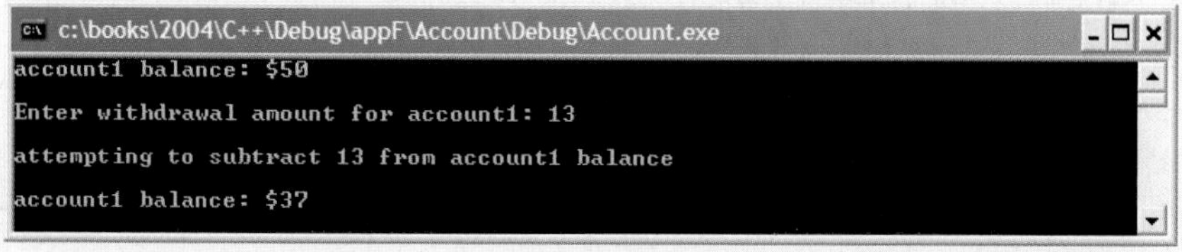

Fig. F.10 | Program output.

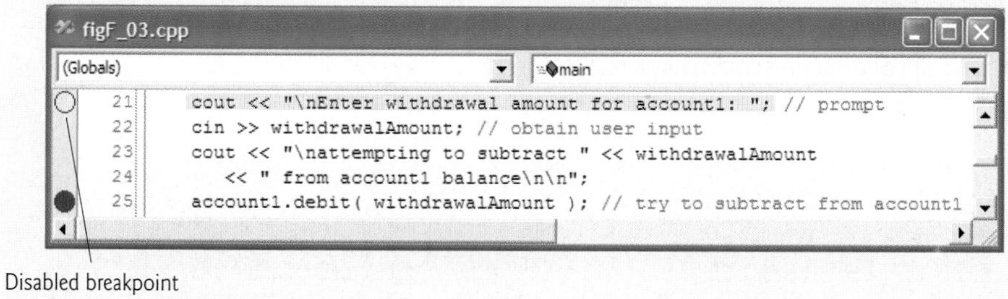

Fig. F.11 | Disabled breakpoint.

In this section, you learned how to enable the debugger and set breakpoints so that you can examine the results of code while a program is running. You also learned how to continue execution after a program suspends execution at a breakpoint and how to disable and remove breakpoints.

F.3 The Locals and Watch Windows

In the preceding section, you learned that the *Quick Info* feature allows you to examine the value of a variable. In this section, you will learn how to use the Locals window to assign new values to variables while your program is running. You will also use the Watch window to examine the value of more complex expressions.

1. *Inserting breakpoints.* Set a breakpoint at line 25 in the source code by clicking in the margin indicator bar to the left of line 25 (Fig. F.12). Set another breakpoint at line 28 of the code by clicking in the margin indicator bar to the left of line 28.

2. *Starting debugging.* Select **Debug > Start**. Type 13 at the **Enter withdrawal amount for account1:** prompt (Fig. F.13) and press *Enter* so that your program reads the value you just entered. The program executes until the breakpoint at line 25.

3. *Suspending program execution.* When the program reaches line 25, Visual C++ .NET suspends program execution and switches the program into break mode (Fig. F.14). At this point, the statement in line 22 (Fig. F.3) has input the withdrawalAmount that you entered (13), the statement in lines 23–24 has output that the program will attempt to withdraw money and the statement in line 25 is the next statement that will be executed.

4. *Examining data.* Once the program has entered break mode, you can explore the values of your local variables using the debugger's **Locals** window. To view the **Locals** window, select **Debug > Windows > Locals**. The values for account1 and withdrawalAmount (13) are displayed (Fig. F.15).

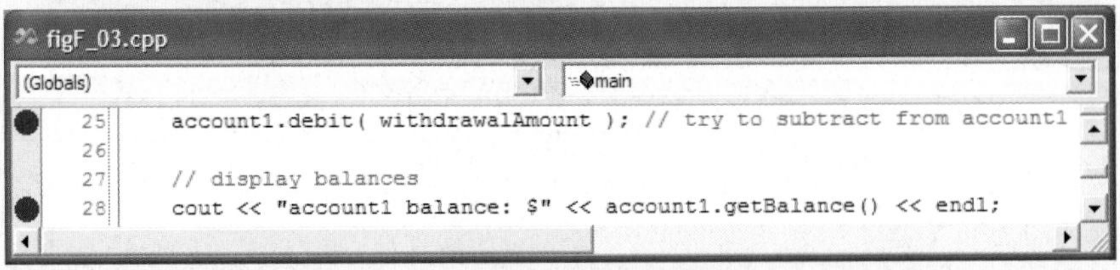

Fig. F.12 | Setting breakpoints at lines 25 and 28.

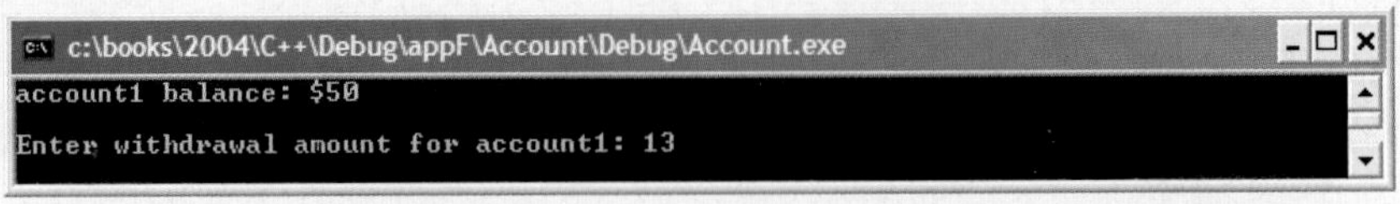

Fig. F.13 | Entering withdrawal amount before breakpoint is reached.

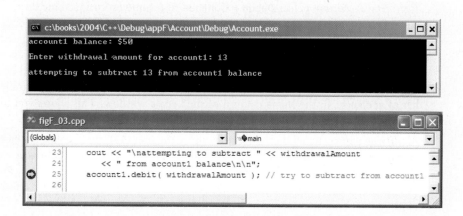

Fig. F.14 | Program execution suspended when debugger reaches the breakpoint at line 25.

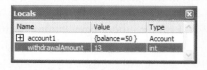

Fig. F.15 | Examining variable `withdrawalAmount`.

5. *Evaluating arithmetic and boolean expressions.* Visual Studio .NET allows you to evaluate arithmetic and boolean expressions using the **Watch** window. There are four different **Watch** windows, but we will be using only the first window. Select **Debug > Windows > Watch > Watch 1**. In the first row of the **Name** column (which should be blank initially), type `(withdrawalAmount + 3) * 5`, then press *Enter*. Notice that the **Watch** window can evaluate arithmetic expressions. In this case, it displays the value 80 (Fig. F.16). In the next row of the **Name** column in the **Watch** window, type `withdrawalAmount == 3`, then press *Enter*. This expression determines whether the value contained in `withdrawalAmount` is 3. Expressions containing the `==` symbol are treated as boolean expressions. The value returned is `false` (Fig. F.16), because `withdrawalAmount` does not currently contain the value 3.

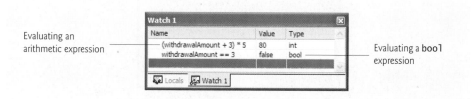

Evaluating an arithmetic expression

Evaluating a `bool` expression

Fig. F.16 | Examining the values of expressions.

6. *Resuming execution.* Select **Debug > Continue** to resume execution. Line 25 executes, debiting the account with the withdrawal amount, and the program is once again suspended at line 28. Select **Debug > Windows > Locals**. The updated account1 value is now displayed in red to indicate that it has been modified since the last breakpoint (Fig. F.17). The value in withdrawalAmount is not in red because it has not been updated since the last breakpoint. Click the plus box to the left of account1 in the **Name** column of the **Locals** window. This allows you to view each of account1's data member values individually.

7. *Modifying values.* Based on the value input by the user (13), the account balance output by the program should be $37. However, you can use the debugger to change the values of variables in the middle of the program's execution. This can be valuable for experimenting with different values and for locating logic errors in programs. You can use the **Locals** window to change the value of a variable. In the **Locals** window, click the **Value** field in the balance row to select the value 37. Type 33, then press *Enter*. The debugger changes the value of balance and displays its new value in red (Fig. F.18).

8. *Setting a breakpoint at the **return** statement.* Set a breakpoint at line 29 in the source code by clicking in the margin indicator bar to the left of line 29 (Fig. F.19). This will prevent the program from closing immediately after displaying its result. If you do not set this breakpoint, you will not be able to view the program's output before the console window closes.

9. *Viewing the program result.* Select **Debug > Continue** to continue program execution. Function main executes until the return statement on line 29 and displays the result. Notice that the result is $33 (Fig. F.20). This shows that the previous step changed the value of balance from the calculated value (37) to 33.

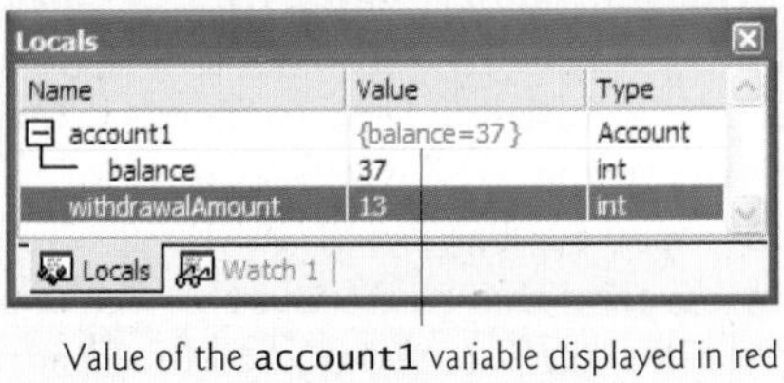

Value of the account1 variable displayed in red

Fig. F.17 | Displaying the value of local variables.

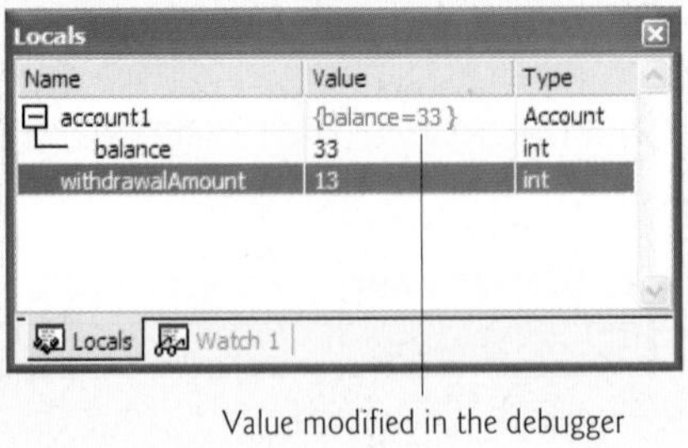

Value modified in the debugger

Fig. F.18 | Modifying the value of a variable.

```
figF_03.cpp                                                    _ □ X
(Globals)                              ▼   main                          ▼
   28       cout << "account1 balance: $" << account1.getBalance() << endl;
   29       return 0; // indicate successful termination
   30  } // end main
```

Fig. F.19 | Setting a breakpoint at line 29.

```
c:\books\2004\C++\Debug\appF\Account\Debug\Account.exe           _ □ X
account1 balance: $50

Enter withdrawal amount for account1: 13

attempting to subtract 13 from account1 balance

account1 balance: $33
```

Fig. F.20 | Output displayed after modifying the `account1` variable.

10. *Stopping the debugging session.* Select **Debug > Stop Debugging**. This will close the **Command Prompt** window. Remove all remaining breakpoints.

In this section, you learned how to use the debugger's **Watch** and **Locals** windows to evaluate arithmetic and boolean expressions. You also learned how to modify the value of a variable during your program's execution.

F.4 Controlling Execution Using the Step Into, Step Over, Step Out and Continue Commands

Sometimes you will need to execute a program line by line to find and fix logic errors. Walking through a portion of your program this way can help you verify that a function's code executes correctly. In this section, you will learn how to use the debugger for this task. The commands you learn in this section allow you to execute a function line by line, execute all the statements of a function at once or execute only the remaining statements of a function (if you have already executed some statements within the function).

1. *Setting a breakpoint.* Set a breakpoint at line 25 by clicking in the margin indicator bar (Fig. F.21).

Fig. F.21 | Setting a breakpoint in the program

2. *Starting the debugger.* Select **Debug > Start.** Enter the value 13 at the **Enter with-drawal amount for account1:** prompt. Execution will halt when the program reaches the breakpoint at line 25.

3. *Using the Step Into command.* The Step Into command executes the next state-ment in the program (the yellow highlighted line of Fig. F.24) and immediately halts. If the statement to be executed as a result of the **Step Into** command is a function call, control is transferred to the called function. The **Step Into** com-mand allows you to enter a function and confirm its execution by individually executing each statement inside the function. Select **Debug > Step Into** to enter the debit function (Fig. F.22). If the debugger is not at line 33, select **Debug > Step Into** again to reach that line.

4. *Using the Step Over command.* Select **Debug > Step Over** to execute the current statement (line 33 in Fig. F.22) and transfer control to line 34 (Fig. F.23). The Step Over command behaves like the **Step Into** command when the next state-ment to execute does not contain a function call. You will see how the **Step Over** command differs from the **Step Into** command in *Step 10.*

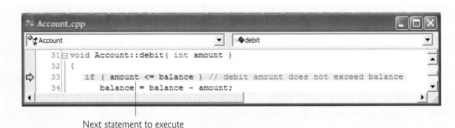

Next statement to execute

Fig. F.22 | Stepping into the debit function.

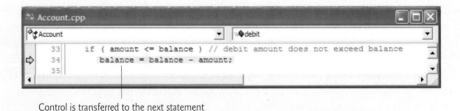

Control is transferred to the next statement

Fig. F.23 | Stepping over a statement in the debit function.

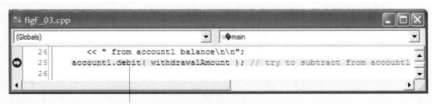

Next statement to execute is a function call

Fig. F.24 | Using the **Step Into** command to execute a statement.

5. *Using the **Step Out** command.* Select **Debug > Step Out** to execute the remaining statements in the function and return control to the next executable statement (line 28 in Fig. F.3), which contains the function call. Often, in lengthy functions, you will want to look at a few key lines of code, then continue debugging the caller's code. The **Step Out** command is useful for such situations, where you do not want to continue stepping through the entire function line by line.

6. *Setting a breakpoint.* Set a breakpoint (Fig. F.25) at the `return` statement of `main` at line 29 of Fig. F.3. You will make use of this breakpoint in the next step.

7. *Using the **Continue** command.* Select **Debug > Continue** to exectue until the next breakpoint is reached at line 29. This feature saves time when you do not want to step line by line through many lines of code to reach the next breakpoint.

8. *Stopping the debugger.* Select **Debug > Stop Debugging** to end the debugging session. This will close the **Command Prompt** window.

9. *Starting the debugger.* Before we can demonstrate the next debugger feature, you must start the debugger again. Start it, as you did in *Step 2*, and enter as input the same value (13). The debugger pauses execution at line 25.

10. *Using the **Step Over** command.* Select **Debug > Step Over** (Fig. F.26) Recall that this command behaves like the **Step Into** command when the next statement to execute does not contain a function call. If the next statement to execute contains a function call, the called function executes in its entirety (without pausing execution at any statement inside the function), and the yellow arrow advances to the next executable line (after the function call) in the current function. In this case, the debugger executes line 25, located in `main` (Fig. F.3). Line 25 calls the `debit` function. The debugger then pauses execution at line 28, the next executable line in the current function, `main`.

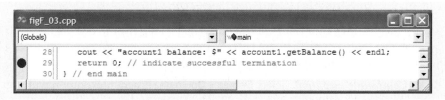

Fig. F.25 | Setting a second breakpoint in the program.

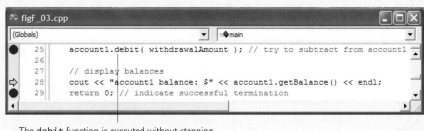

The `debit` function is executed without stepping into it when the **Step Over** command is selected

Fig. F.26 | Using the debugger's **Step Over** command.

11. *Stopping the debugger.* Select **Debug > Stop Debugging**. This will close the **Command Prompt** window. Remove all remaining breakpoints.

In this section, you learned how to use the debugger's **Step Into** command to debug functions called during your program's execution. You saw how the **Step Over** command can be used to step over a function call. You used the **Step Out** command to continue execution until the end of the current function. You also learned that the **Continue** command continues execution until another breakpoint is found or the program exits.

F.5 The Autos Window

In this section, we present the Autos window, which displays the variables used in the previous statement executed and the next command to execute. The **Autos** window allows you to focus on variables that were just used, and those that will be used and modified in the next statement.

1. *Setting breakpoints.* Set breakpoints at lines 14 and 22 by clicking in the margin indicator bar (Fig. F.27).

2. *Using the Autos window.* Start the debugger by selecting **Debug > Start**. When execution halts at the breakpoint at line 14, open the **Autos** window (Fig. F.28) by selecting **Debug > Windows > Autos**. The **Autos** window allows you to view the contents of the variables used in the last statement that was executed. This allows you to verify that the previous statement executed correctly. The **Autos** window also lists the values in the next statement to be executed. Notice that the **Autos** window lists the account1 variable, its value and its type. Viewing the values stored in an object lets you verify that your program is manipulating these variables correctly. Notice that account1 contains a large negative value. This value, which may be different each time the program executes, is account1's uninitialized value. This unpredictable (and often undesirable) value demonstrates why it is important to initialize all C++ variables before use.

3. *Using the Step Over command.* Select **Debug > Step Over** to execute line 14. The **Autos** window (Fig. F.29) updates the value of account1 after it is initialized. The value of account1 is displayed in red to indicate that it changed.

4. *Continuing execution.* Select **Debug > Continue**. Program execution will stop at the second breakpoint, set at line 22. The **Autos** window (Fig. F.30) displays uninitialized local variable withdrawalAmount, which has a large negative value.

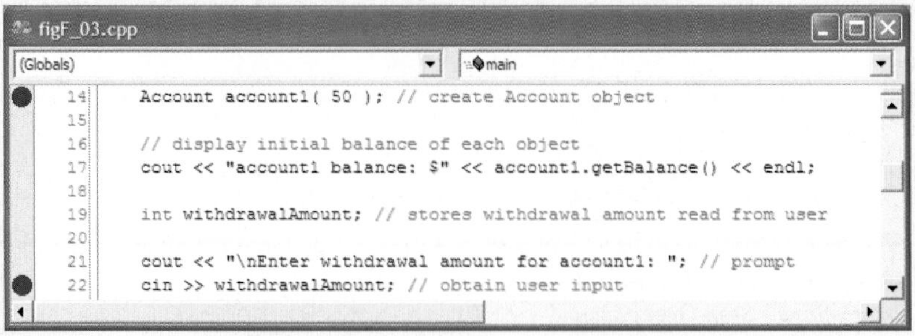

Fig. F.27 | Setting breakpoints in the program.

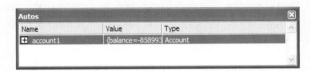

Fig. F.28 | **Autos** window displaying the state of `account1` object.

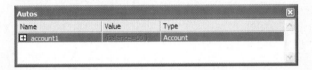

Fig. F.29 | **Autos** window displaying the state of `account1` object after initialization.

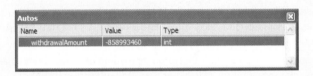

Fig. F.30 | **Autos** window displaying local variable `withdrawalAmount`.

5. *Entering data.* Select **Debug > Step Over** to execute line 22. At the program's input prompt, enter a value for the withdrawal amount. The **Autos** window (Fig. F.29) will update the value of local variable `withdrawalAmount` with the value you entered. [*Note:* The first line of the **Autos** window contains the `istream` object (`cin`) you used to input data.]

6. *Stopping the debugger.* Select **Debug > Stop Debugging** to end the debugging session. Remove all remaining breakpoints.

In this section, you learned about the **Autos** window, which allows you to view the variables used in the most recent command.

F.6 Wrap-Up

In this appendix, you learned how to insert, disable and remove breakpoints in the Visual Studio .NET debugger. Breakpoints allow you to pause program execution so you can examine variable values. This capability will help you locate and fix logic errors in your programs. You saw how to use the **Locals** and **Watch** windows to examine the value of an expression and how to change the value of a variable. You also learned debugger com-

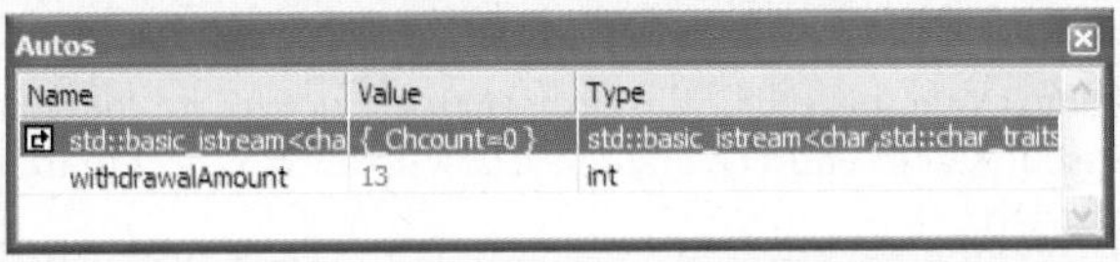

Fig. F.31 | **Autos** window displaying updated local variable `withdrawalAmount`.

mands **Step Into, Step Over, Step Out** and **Continue** that can be used to determine whether a function is executing correctly. Finally, you learned how to use the **Autos** window to examine variables used specifically in the previous and next commands.

Summary

- Most C++ compiler vendors provide software called a debugger, which allows you to monitor the execution of your programs to locate and remove logic errors.

- Breakpoints are markers that can be set at any executable line of code. When program execution reaches a breakpoint, execution pauses.

- The debugger is enabled by default. If it is not enabled, you have to change the settings of the *Solution Configurations* combo box.

- To insert a breakpoint, either click inside the margin indicator bar next to the line of code or right click that line of code and select **Insert Breakpoint**. A solid maroon circle appears where you clicked, indicating that a breakpoint has been set.

- When the program runs, it suspends execution at any line that contains a breakpoint. It is then said to be in break mode, and the title bar of the IDE will display **[break]**.

- A yellow arrow indicates that this line contains the next statement to execute.

- When you place your mouse pointer over a variable name, the value that the variable stores is displayed in a *Quick Info* box.

- To disable a breakpoint, right click a line of code on which a breakpoint has been set and select **Disable Breakpoint**. The disabled breakpoint is indicated by a hollow maroon circle.

- To remove a breakpoint that you no longer need, right click a line of code on which a breakpoint has been set and select **Remove Breakpoint**. You also can remove a breakpoint by clicking the maroon circle in the margin indicator bar.

- Once the program has entered break mode, you can explore the values of your variables using the debugger's **Locals** window. To view the **Locals** window, select **Debug > Windows > Locals**.

- You can evaluate arithmetic and boolean expressions using one of the **Watch** windows. The first **Watch** window is displayed by selecting **Debug > Windows > Watch > Watch 1**.

- Updated variables are displayed in red to indicate that they have been modified since the last breakpoint.

- Clicking the plus box next to an object in the **Name** column of the **Locals** window allows you to view each of object's data member values individually.

- You can click the **Value** field of a variable to change its value in the **Locals** window.

- The **Step Into** command executes the next statement (the yellow highlighted line) in the program. If the next statement is to execute a function call and you select **Step Into**, control is transferred to the called function.

- The **Step Over** command behaves like the **Step Into** command when the next statement to execute does not contain a function call. If the next statement to execute contains a function call, the called function executes in its entirety, and the yellow arrow advances to the next executable line in the current function.

- Select **Debug > Step Out** to execute the remaining statements in the function and return control to the function call.

- The **Continue** command will execute any statements between the next executable statement and the next breakpoint or the end of `main`, whichever comes first.
- The **Autos** window allows you to view the contents of the variables used in the last statement that was executed. The **Autos** window also lists the values in the next statement to be executed.

Terminology

Autos window	margin indicator bar
break mode	*Quick Info* box
breakpoint	*Solution Configurations* combo box
bug	**Step Into** command
Continue command	**Step Out** command
debugger	**Step Over** command
disabling a breakpoint	**Watch** window
Locals window	yellow arrow in break mode

Self-Review Exercises

F.1 Fill in the blanks in each of the following statements:

    a) When the debugger suspends program execution at a breakpoint, the program is said to be in _____ mode.

    b) The _____ feature in Visual Studio .NET allows you to "peek into the computer" and look at the value of a variable.

    c) You can examine the value of an expression by using the debugger's _____ window.

    d) The _____ command behaves like the **Step Into** command when the next statement to execute does not contain a function call.

F.2 State whether each of the following is *true* or *false*. If *false*, explain why.

    a) When program execution suspends at a breakpoint, the next statement to be executed is the statement after the breakpoint.

    b) When a variable's value is changed, it becomes yellow in the **Autos** and **Locals** windows.

    c) During debugging, the **Step Out** command executes the remaining statements in the current function and returns program control to the place where the function was called.

Answers to Self-Review Exercises

F.1   a) break. b) *Quick Info* box. c) **Watch**. d) **Step Over**.

F.2   a) False. When program execution suspends at a breakpoint, the next statement to be executed is the statement at the breakpoint. b) False. A variable turns red when its value is changed. c) True.

G

Using the GNU C++ Debugger

And so shall I catch the fly.
—William Shakespeare

We are built to make mistakes, coded for error.
—Lewis Thomas

What we anticipate seldom occurs; what we least expect generally happens.
—Benjamin Disraeli

He can run but he can't hide.
—Joe Louis

It is one thing to show a man that he is in error, and another to put him in possession of truth.
—John Locke

OBJECTIVES

In this appendix you will learn:

- To use the **run** command to run a program in the debugger.

- To use the **break** command to set a breakpoint.

- To use the **continue** command to continue execution.

- To use the **print** command to evaluate expressions.

- To use the **set** command to change variable values during program execution.

- To use the **step**, **finish** and **next** commands to control execution.

- To use the **watch** command to see how a data member is modified during program execution.

- To use the **delete** command to remove a breakpoint or a watchpoint.

Outline

G.1 Introduction
G.2 Breakpoints and the run, stop, continue and print Commands
G.3 The print and set Commands
G.4 Controlling Execution Using the step, finish and next Commands
G.5 The watch Command
G.6 Wrap-Up

Summary | Terminology | Self-Review Exercises | Answers to Self-Review Exercises

G.1 Introduction

In Chapter 2, you learned that there are two types of errors—compilation errors and logic errors—and you learned how to eliminate compilation errors from your code. Logic errors do not prevent a program from compiling successfully, but they do cause the program to produce erroneous results when it runs. GNU includes software called a debugger that allows you to monitor the execution of your programs so you can locate and remove logic errors.

The debugger will be one of your most important program development tools. Many IDEs provide their own debuggers similar to the one included in GNU or provide a graphical user interface to GNU's debugger. This appendix demonstrates key features of GNU's debugger. Appendix F discusses the features and capabilities of the Visual Studio .NET debugger. We provide several free *Dive Into™ Series* publications to help students and instructors familiarize themselves with the debuggers provided with various development tools. These publications are available on the CD that accompanies the text and can be downloaded from www.deitel.com/books/downloads.

G.2 Breakpoints and the run, stop, continue and print Commands

We begin our study of the debugger by investigating breakpoints, which are markers that can be set at any executable line of code. When program execution reaches a breakpoint, execution pauses, allowing you to examine the values of variables to help determine whether logic errors exist. For example, you can examine the value of a variable that stores the result of a calculation to determine whether the calculation was performed correctly. Note that attempting to set a breakpoint at a line of code that is not executable (such as a comment) will actually set the breakpoint at the next executable line of code in that function.

To illustrate the features of the debugger, we use the program listed in Fig. G.3, which creates and manipulates an object of class Account (Figs. G.1–G.2). Execution begins in main (lines 12–30 of Fig. G.3). Line 14 creates an Account object with an initial balance of $50.00. Account's constructor (lines 10–22 of Fig. G.2) accepts one argument, which specifies the Account's initial balance. Line 17 of Fig. G.3 outputs the initial account balance using Account member function getBalance. Line 19 declares a local variable withdrawalAmount which stores a withdrawal amount read from the user. Line 21 prompts the user for the withdrawal amount; line 22 inputs the amount into withdrawalAmount. Line 25 subtracts the withdrawal from the Account's balance using its debit member function. Finally, line 28 displays the new balance.

```
 1   // Fig. G.1: Account.h
 2   // Definition of Account class.
 3
 4   class Account
 5   {
 6   public:
 7      Account( int ); // constructor initializes balance
 8      void credit( int ); // add an amount to the account balance
 9      void debit( int ); // subtract an amount from the account balance
10      int getBalance(); // return the account balance
11   private:
12      int balance; // data member that stores the balance
13   }; // end class Account
```

Fig. G.1 | Header file for the Account class.

```
 1   // Fig. G.2: Account.cpp
 2   // Member-function definitions for class Account.
 3   #include <iostream>
 4   using std::cout;
 5   using std::endl;
 6
 7   #include "Account.h" // include definition of class Account
 8
 9   // Account constructor initializes data member balance
10   Account::Account( int initialBalance )
11   {
12      balance = 0; // assume that the balance begins at 0
13
14      // if initialBalance is greater than 0, set this value as the
15      // balance of the Account; otherwise, balance remains 0
16      if ( initialBalance > 0 )
17         balance = initialBalance;
18
19      // if initialBalance is negative, print error message
20      if ( initialBalance < 0 )
21         cout << "Error: Initial balance cannot be negative.\n" << endl;
22   } // end Account constructor
23
24   // credit (add) an amount to the account balance
25   void Account::credit( int amount )
26   {
27      balance = balance + amount; // add amount to balance
28   } // end function credit
29
30   // debit (subtract) an amount from the account balance
31   void Account::debit( int amount )
32   {
33      if ( amount <= balance ) // debit amount does not exceed balance
34         balance = balance - amount;
35
```

Fig. G.2 | Definition for the Account class. (Part 1 of 2.)

```
36        else // debit amount exceeds balance
37            cout << "Debit amount exceeded account balance.\n" << endl;
38    } // end function debit
39
40    // return the account balance
41    int Account::getBalance()
42    {
43        return balance; // gives the value of balance to the calling function
44    } // end function getBalance
```

Fig. G.2 | Definition for the Account class. (Part 2 of 2.)

```
1    // Fig. G.3: figG_03.cpp
2    // Create and manipulate Account objects.
3    #include <iostream>
4    using std::cin;
5    using std::cout;
6    using std::endl;
7
8    // include definition of class Account from Account.h
9    #include "Account.h"
10
11   // function main begins program execution
12   int main()
13   {
14       Account account1( 50 ); // create Account object
15
16       // display initial balance of each object
17       cout << "account1 balance: $" << account1.getBalance() << endl;
18
19       int withdrawalAmount; // stores withdrawal amount read from user
20
21       cout << "\nEnter withdrawal amount for account1: "; // prompt
22       cin >> withdrawalAmount; // obtain user input
23       cout << "\nattempting to subtract " << withdrawalAmount
24           << " from account1 balance\n\n";
25       account1.debit( withdrawalAmount ); // try to subtract from account1
26
27       // display balances
28       cout << "account1 balance: $" << account1.getBalance() << endl;
29       return 0; // indicate successful termination
30   } // end main
```

Fig. G.3 | Test class for debugging.

In the following steps, you will use breakpoints and various debugger commands to examine the value of the variable withdrawalAmount declared in line 19 of Fig. G.3.

1. *Compiling the program for debugging.* The GNU debugger works only with executable files that were compiled with the -g compiler option, which generates information that is used by the debugger to help you debug your programs. Compile the program with the -g command-line option by typing g++ -g -o figG_03 figG_03.cpp Account.cpp.

2. *Starting the debugger.* Type gdb figG_03 (Fig. G.4). This command will start the GNU debugger and display the (gdb) prompt at which you can enter commands.

3. *Running a program in the debugger.* Run the program through the debugger by typing run (Fig. G.5). If you do not set any breakpoints before running your program in the debugger, the program will run to completion.

4. *Inserting breakpoints using the GNU debugger.* You set a breakpoint at a specific line of code in your program. The line numbers used in these steps are from the source code in Fig. G.3. Set a breakpoint at line 17 in the source code by typing break 17. The break command inserts a breakpoint at the line number specified after the command. You can set as many breakpoints as necessary. Each breakpoint is identified in terms of the order in which it was created. The first breakpoint created is known as Breakpoint 1. Set another breakpoint at line 25 by typing break 25 (Fig. G.6). When the program runs, it suspends execution at any line that contains a breakpoint and the program is said to be in break mode. Breakpoints can be set even after the debugging process has begun. [*Note:* If you do not have a numbered listing for your code, you can use the list command to output your code with line numbers. For more information about the list command type help list from the gdb prompt.]

```
~/Debug$ gdb figG_03
GNU gdb 6.1-debian
Copyright 2004 Free Software Foundation, Inc.
GDB is free software, covered by the GNU General Public License, and you are
welcome to change it and/or distribute copies of it under certain conditions.
Type "show copying" to see the conditions.
There is absolutely no warranty for GDB.  Type "show warranty" for details.
This GDB was configured as "i386-linux"...Using host libthread_db library "/
lib/libthread_db.so.1".

(gdb)
```

Fig. G.4 | Starting the debugger to run the program.

```
(gdb) run
Starting program: /home/student/Debug/figG_03
account1 balance: $50

Enter withdrawal amount for account1: 13

attempting to subtract 13 from account1 balance

account1 balance: $37

Program exited normally.
(gdb)
```

Fig. G.5 | Running the program with no breakpoints set.

```
(gdb) break 17
Breakpoint 1 at 0x80487d8: file figG_03.cpp, line 17.
(gdb) break 25
Breakpoint 2 at 0x8048871: file figG_03.cpp, line 25.
(gdb)
```

Fig. G.6 | Setting two breakpoints in the program.

5. *Running the program and beginning the debugging process.* Type run to execute your program and begin the debugging process (Fig. G.7). The program pauses when execution reaches the breakpoint at line 17. At this point, the debugger notifies you that a breakpoint has been reached and displays the source code at that line (17). That line of code contains the next statement that will execute.

6. *Using the continue command to resume execution.* Type continue. The continue command causes the program to continue running until the next breakpoint is reached (line 25). Enter 13 at the prompt. The debugger notifies you when execution reaches the second breakpoint (Fig. G.8). Note that figG_03's normal output appears between messages from the debugger.

```
(gdb) run
Starting program: /home/student/Debug/figG_03

Breakpoint 1, main () at figG_03.cpp:17
17          cout << "account1 balance: $" << account1.getBalance() << endl;
(gdb)
```

Fig. G.7 | Running the program until it reaches the first breakpoint.

```
(gdb) continue
Continuing.
account1 balance: $50

Enter withdrawal amount for account1: 13

attempting to subtract 13 from account1 balance

Breakpoint 2, main () at figG_03.cpp:25
25          account1.debit( withdrawalAmount ); // try to subtract from
account1
(gdb)
```

Fig. G.8 | Continuing execution until the second breakpoint is reached.

7. *Examining a variable's value.* Type print withdrawalAmount to display the current value stored in the withdrawalAmount variable (Fig. G.9). The print command allows you to peek inside the computer at the value of one of your variables. This command will help you find and eliminate logic errors in your code. Note that the value displayed is 13—the value read in and assigned to withdrawalAmount in line 22 of Fig. G.3. Use the print command to output the contents of the account1 object. When an object is output through the debugger with the print command, the object is output with braces surrounding the object's data members. In this case, there is a single data member—balance—which has a value of 50.

8. *Using convenience variables.* When the print command is used, the result is stored in a convenience variable such as $1. Convenience variables, which are temporary variables, named using a dollar sign followed by an integer, are created by the debugger as you print values during your debugging session. A convenience variable can be used in the debugging process to perform arithmetic and evaluate boolean expressions. Type print $1. The debugger displays the value of $1 (Fig. G.10), which contains the value of withdrawalAmount. Note that printing the value of $1 creates a new convenience variable—$3.

9. *Continuing program execution.* Type continue to continue the program's execution. The debugger encounters no additional breakpoints, so it continues executing and eventually terminates (Fig. G.11).

```
(gdb) print withdrawalAmount
$1 = 13
(gdb) print account1
$2 = {balance = 50}
(gdb)
```

Fig. G.9 | Printing the values of variables.

```
(gdb) print $1
$3 = 13
(gdb)
```

Fig. G.10 | Printing a convenience variable.

```
(gdb) continue
Continuing.
account1 balance: $37

Program exited normally.
(gdb)
```

Fig. G.11 | Finishing execution of the program.

10. *Removing a breakpoint.* You can display a list of all of the breakpoints in the program by typing `info break`. To remove a breakpoint, type `delete`, followed by a space and the number of the breakpoint to remove. Remove the first breakpoint by typing `delete 1`. Remove the second breakpoint as well. Now type `info break` to list the remaining breakpoints in the program. The debugger should indicate that no breakpoints are set (Fig. G.12).

11. *Executing the program without breakpoints.* Type run to execute the program. Enter the value 13 at the prompt. Because you successfully removed the two breakpoints, the program's output is displayed without the debugger entering break mode (Fig. G.13).

12. *Using the `quit` command.* Use the `quit` command to end the debugging session (Fig. G.14). This command causes the debugger to terminate.

```
(gdb) info break
Num Type           Disp Enb Address    What
1   breakpoint     keep y   0x080487d8 in main at figG_03.cpp:17
        breakpoint already hit 1 time
2   breakpoint     keep y   0x08048871 in main at figG_03.cpp:25
        breakpoint already hit 1 time
(gdb) delete 1
(gdb) delete 2
(gdb) info break
No breakpoints or watchpoints.
(gdb)
```

Fig. G.12 | Viewing and removing breakpoints.

```
(gdb) run
Starting program: /home/student/Debug/figG_03
account1 balance: $50

Enter withdrawal amount for account1: 13

attempting to subtract 13 from account1 balance

account1 balance: $37

Program exited normally.
(gdb)
```

Fig. G.13 | Program executing with no breakpoints set.

```
(gdb) quit
~/Debug$
```

Fig. G.14 | Exiting the debugger using the `quit` command.

In this section, you learned how to enable the debugger using the gdb command and run a program with the run command. You saw how to set a breakpoint at a particular line number in the main function. The break command can also be used to set a breakpoint at a line number in another file or at a particular function. Typing break, then the filename, a colon and the line number will set a breakpoint at a line in another file. Typing break, then a function name will cause the debugger to enter the break mode whenever that function is called.

Also in this section, you saw how the help list command will provide more information on the list command. If you have any questions about the debugger or any of his commands, type help or help followed by the command name for more information.

Finally, you learned to examine variables with the print command and remove breakpoints with the delete command. You learned how to use the continue command to continue execution after a breakpoint is reached and the quit command to end the debugger.

G.3 The print and set Commands

In the preceding section, you learned how to use the debugger's print command to examine the value of a variable during program execution. In this section, you will learn how to use the print command to examine the value of more complex expressions. You will also learn the **set command**, which allows the programmer to assign new values to variables. We assume you are working in the directory containing this appendix's examples and have compiled for debugging with the -g compiler option.

1. *Starting debugging.* Type gdb figG_03 to start the GNU debugger.

2. *Inserting a breakpoint.* Set a breakpoint at line 25 in the source code by typing break 25 (Fig. G.15).

3. *Running the program and reaching a breakpoint.* Type run to begin the debugging process (Fig. G.16). This will cause main to execute until the breakpoint at line 25 is reached. This suspends program execution and switches the program into break mode. The statement in line 25 is the next statement that will execute.

4. *Evaluating arithmetic and boolean expressions.* Recall from Section G.2 that once the program has entered break mode, you can explore the values of the program's variables using the debugger's print command. You can also use the print command to evaluate arithmetic and boolean expressions. Type print withdrawalAmount - 2. Note that the print command returns the value 11 (Fig. G.17). However, this command does not actually change the value of withdrawalAmount. Type print withdrawalAmount == 11. Expressions containing the == symbol are treated as boolean expressions. The value returned is false (Fig. G.17) because withdrawalAmount does not currently contain the value 11—withdrawalAmount is still 13.

```
(gdb) break 25
Breakpoint 1 at 0x8048871: file figG_03.cpp, line 25.
(gdb)
```

Fig. G.15 | Setting a breakpoint in the program.

```
(gdb) run
Starting program: /home/student/Debug/figG_03
account1 balance: $50

Enter withdrawal amount for account1: 13

attempting to subtract 13 from account1 balance


Breakpoint 1, main () at figG_03.cpp:25
25          account1.debit( withdrawalAmount ); // try to subtract from
account1
(gdb)
```

Fig. G.16 | Running the program until the breakpoint at line 25 is reached.

```
(gdb) print withdrawalAmount - 2
$1 = 11
(gdb) print withdrawalAmount == 11
$2 = false
(gdb)
```

Fig. G.17 | Printing expressions with the debugger.

5. *Modifying values.* The debugger allows you to change the values of variables during the program's execution. This can be valuable for experimenting with different values and for locating logic errors in programs. You can use the debugger's set command to change the value of a variable. Type set withdrawalAmount = 42. The debugger changes the value of withdrawalAmount. Type print withdrawalAmount to display its new value (Fig. G.18).

6. *Viewing the program result.* Type continue to continue program execution. Line 25 of Fig. G.3 executes, passing withdrawalAmount to Account member function debit. Function main then displays the new balance. Note that the result is $8 (Fig. G.19). This shows that the preceding step changed the value of withdrawalAmount from its initial value (13) to 42.

7. *Using the quit command.* Use the quit command to end the debugging session (Fig. G.20). This command causes the debugger to terminate.

In this section, you learned how to use the debugger's print command to evaluate arithmetic and boolean expressions. You also learned how to use the set command to modify the value of a variable during your program's execution.

```
(gdb) set withdrawalAmount = 42
(gdb) print withdrawalAmount
$3 = 42
(gdb)
```

Fig. G.18 | Setting the value of a variable while in break mode.

```
(gdb) continue
Continuing.
account1 balance: $8

Program exited normally.
(gdb)
```

Fig. G.19 | Using a modified variable in the execution of a program.

```
(gdb) quit
~/Debug$
```

Fig. G.20 | Exiting the debugger using the quit command.

G.4 Controlling Execution Using the step, finish and next Commands

Sometimes you will need to execute a program line by line to find and fix errors. Walking through a portion of your program this way can help you verify that a function's code executes correctly. In this section, you will learn how to use the debugger for this task. The commands you learn here allow you to execute a function line by line, execute all the statements of a function at once or execute only the remaining statements of a function (if you have already executed some statements within the function). Once again, we assume you are working in the directory containing this appendix's examples and have compiled for debugging with the -g compiler option.

1. *Starting the debugger.* Start the debugger by typing gdb figG_03.

2. *Setting a breakpoint.* Type break 25 to set a breakpoint at line 25.

3. *Running the program.* Run the program by typing run. After the program displays its two output messages, the debugger indicates that the breakpoint has been reached and displays the code at line 25. The debugger and program then pause and wait for the next command to be entered.

4. *Using the step command.* The step command executes the next statement in the program. If the next statement to execute is a function call, control transfers to the called function. The step command enables you to enter a function and study the individual statements of that function. For instance, you can use the print and set commands to view and modify the variables within the function. Type step to enter the debit member function of class Account (Fig. G.2). The debugger indicates that the step has been completed and displays the next executable statement (Fig. G.21)—in this case, line 33 of class Account (Fig. G.2).

5. *Using the finish command.* After you have stepped into the debit member function, type finish. This command executes the remaining statements in the function and returns control to the place where the function was called. The finish command executes the remaining statements in member function debit, then pauses at line 28 in main (Fig. G.22). In lengthy functions, you may want to look at a few key lines of code, then continue debugging the caller's code. The finish

```
(gdb) step
Account::debit (this=0xbffffd70, amount=13) at Account.cpp:33
33          if ( amount <= balance ) // debit amount does not exceed balance
(gdb)
```

Fig. G.21 | Using the `step` command to enter a function.

```
(gdb) finish
Run till exit from #0  Account::debit (this=0xbffffd70, amount=13)
    at Account.cpp:33
main () at figG_03.cpp:28
28          cout << "account1 balance: $" << account1.getBalance() << endl;
(gdb)
```

Fig. G.22 | Using the `finish` command to complete execution of a function and return to the calling function.

command is useful for situations in which you do not want to continue stepping through the entire function line by line.

6. *Using the* **continue** *command to continue execution.* Enter the `continue` command to continue execution. No additional breakpoints are reached, so the program terminates.

7. *Running the program again.* Breakpoints persist until the end of the debugging session in which they are set—even after execution of the program, all breakpoints are maintained. The breakpoint you set in *Step 2* will be there in the next execution of the program. Type `run` to run the program. As in *Step 3*, the program runs until the breakpoint at line 25 is reached, then the debugger pauses and waits for the next command (Fig. G.23).

8. *Using the* **next** *command.* Type `next`. This command behaves like the `step` command, except when the next statement to execute contains a function call. In that case, the called function executes in its entirety and the program advances to the next executable line after the function call (Fig. G.24). In *Step 4*, the `step` com-

```
(gdb) run
Starting program: /home/student/Debug/figG_03
account1 balance: $50

Enter withdrawal amount for account1: 13

attempting to subtract 13 from account1 balance

Breakpoint 1, main () at figG_03.cpp:25
25          account1.debit( withdrawalAmount ); // try to subtract from
account1
(gdb)
```

Fig. G.23 | Restarting the program.

```
(gdb) next
28          cout << "account1 balance: $" << account1.getBalance() << endl;
(gdb)
```

Fig. G.24 | Using the next command to execute a function in its entirety.

mand enters the called function. In this example, the next command causes Ac-count member function debit to execute, then the debugger pauses at line 28.

9. *Using the quit command.* Use the quit command to end the debugging session (Fig. G.25). While the program is running, this command causes the program to immediately terminate rather than execute the remaining statements in main.

In this section, you learned how to use the debugger's step and finish commands to debug functions called during your program's execution. You saw how the next command can be used to step over a function call. You also learned that the quit command ends a debugging session.

G.5 The watch Command

In this section, we present the watch command, which tells the debugger to watch a data member. When that data member is about to change, the debugger will notify you. In this section, you will learn how to use the watch command to see how the Account object's data member balance is modified during the execution of the program.

1. *Starting the debugger.* Start the debugger by typing gdb figG_03.

2. *Running the program.* Type break 14 to set a breakpoint at line 14. Run the program with the command run. The debugger and program will pause at the breakpoint at line 14 (Fig. G.26).

3. *Watching a class's data member.* Set a watch on account1's balance data member by typing watch account1.balance (Fig. G.27). This watch is labeled as watchpoint 2 because watchpoints are labeled with the same numbers as breakpoints. You can set a watch on any variable or data member of an object currently in scope during execution of the debugger. Whenever the value of a watched variable changes, the debugger enters break mode and notifies you that the value has changed.

4. *Continuing the program.* Step into the Account constructor with the command step. The debugger will display line 12 of Fig. G.2, which is the first line in the constructor. Use the step command again to execute this line of code. The debugger will now notify you that data member balance's value will change (Fig. G.28). When the program begins, an instance of Account is created. When

```
(gdb) quit
The program is running.  Exit anyway? (y or n) y
~/Debug$
```

Fig. G.25 | Exiting the debugger using the quit command.

```
(gdb) run
Starting program: /home/student/Debug/figG_03

Breakpoint 1, main () at figG_03.cpp:14
14          Account account1( 50 ); // create Account object
(gdb)
```

Fig. G.26 | Running the program until the first breakpoint.

```
(gdb) watch account1.balance
Hardware watchpoint 2: account1.balance
(gdb)
```

Fig. G.27 | Setting a watchpoint on a data member.

```
(gdb) step
Account (this=0xbffffd70, initialBalance=50) at Account.cpp:12
12          balance = 0; // assume that the balance begins at 0
(gdb) step
Hardware watchpoint 2: account1.balance

Old value = 1073833120
New value = 0
Account (this=0xbffffd70, initialBalance=50) at Account.cpp:16
16          if ( initialBalance > 0 )
(gdb)
```

Fig. G.28 | Stepping into the constructor.

the constructor for this object runs, data member balance is first assigned the value 0. The debugger notifies you that the value of balance has been changed.

5. *Finishing the constructor.* Type step to execute line 16, then type step again to execute line 17. The debugger will notify you that data member balance's value has changed from 0 to 50 (Fig. G.29).

```
(gdb) step
17              balance = initialBalance;
(gdb) step
Hardware watchpoint 2: account1.balance

Old value = 0
New value = 50
Account (this=0xbffffd70, initialBalance=50) at Account.cpp:20
20          if ( initialBalance < 0 )
(gdb)
```

Fig. G.29 | Reaching a watchpoint notification.

6. *Withdrawing money from the account.* Type continue to continue execution and enter a withdrawal value at the prompt. The program executes normally. Line 25 of Fig. G.3 calls Account member function debit to reduce the Account object's balance by a specified amount. Line 34 of Fig. G.2 inside function debit changes the value of balance. The debugger notifies you of this change and enters break mode (Fig. G.30).

7. *Continuing execution.* Type continue—the program will finish executing function main because the program does not attempt any additional changes to balance. The debugger removes the watch on account1's balance data member because the variable goes out of scope when function main ends. Removing the watchpoint causes the debugger to enter break mode. Type continue again to finish execution of the program (Fig. G.31).

8. *Restarting the debugger and resetting the watch on the variable.* Type run to restart the debugger. Once again, set a watch on account1 data member balance by typing watch account1.balance. This watchpoint is labeled as watchpoint 3. Type continue to continue execution (Fig. G.32).

```
(gdb) continue
Continuing.
account1 balance: $50

Enter withdrawal amount for account1: 13

attempting to subtract 13 from account1 balance

Hardware watchpoint 2: account1.balance

Old value = 50
New value = 37
0x08048a01 in Account::debit (this=0xbffffd70, amount=13) at Account.cpp:34
34              balance = balance - amount;
(gdb)
```

Fig. G.30 | Entering break mode when a variable is changed.

```
(gdb) continue
Continuing.
end of function
account1 balance: $37

Watchpoint 2 deleted because the program has left the block in
which its expression is valid.
0x4012fa65 in exit () from /lib/libc.so.6
(gdb) continue
Continuing.

Program exited normally.
(gdb)
```

Fig. G.31 | Continuing to the end of the program.

```
(gdb) run
Starting program: /home/student/Debug/figG_03

Breakpoint 1, main () at figG_03.cpp:14
14          Account account1( 50 ); // create Account object
(gdb) watch account1.balance
Hardware watchpoint 3: account1.balance
(gdb) continue
Continuing.
Hardware watchpoint 3: account1.balance

Old value = 1073833120
New value = 0
Account (this=0xbffffd70, initialBalance=50) at Account.cpp:16
16          if ( initialBalance > 0 )
(gdb)
```

Fig. G.32 | Resetting the watch on a data member.

9. ***Removing the watch on the data member.*** Suppose you want to watch a data member for only part of a program's execution. You can remove the debugger's watch on variable balance by typing delete 3 (Fig. G.33). Type continue—the program will finish executing without reentering break mode.

In this section, you learned how to use the watch command to enable the debugger to notify you of changes to the value of a data member throughout the life of a program. You also learned how to use the delete command to remove a watch on a data member before the end of the program.

G.6 Wrap-Up

In this appendix, you learned how to insert and remove breakpoints in the debugger. Breakpoints allow you to pause program execution so you can examine variable values with the debugger's print command. This capability will help you locate and fix logic errors in your programs. You saw how to use the print command to examine the value of an ex-

```
(gdb) delete 3
(gdb) continue
Continuing.
account1 balance: $50

Enter withdrawal amount for account1: 13

attempting to subtract 13 from account1 balance

end of function
account1 balance: $37

Program exited normally.
(gdb)
```

Fig. G.33 | Removing a watch.

pression, and you learned how to use the set command to change the value of a variable. You also learned debugger commands (including the step, finish and next commands) that can be used to determine whether a function is executing correctly. You learned how to use the watch command to keep track of a data member throughout the scope of that data member. Finally, you learned how to use the info break command to list all the breakpoints and watchpoints set for a program and the delete command to remove individual breakpoints and watchpoints.

Summary

- GNU includes software called a debugger, which allows you to monitor the execution of your programs to locate and remove logic errors.
- The GNU debugger works only with executable files that were compiled with the -g compiler option, which generates information that is used by the debugger to help you debug your programs.
- The gdb command will start the GNU debugger and enable you to use its features. The run command will run a program through the debugger.
- Breakpoints are markers that can be set at any executable line of code. When program execution reaches a breakpoint, execution pauses.
- The break command inserts a breakpoint at the line number specified after the command.
- When the program runs, it suspends execution at any line that contains a breakpoint and is said to be in break mode.
- The continue command causes the program to continue running until the next breakpoint is reached.
- The print command allows you to peek inside the computer at the value of one of your variables.
- When the print command is used, the result is stored in a convenience variable such as $1. Convenience variables are temporary variables that can be used in the debugging process to perform arithmetic and evaluate boolean expressions.
- You can display a list of all of the breakpoints in the program by typing info break.
- To remove a breakpoint, type delete, followed by a space and the number of the breakpoint to remove.
- Use the quit command to end the debugging session.
- The set command allows the programmer to assign new values to variables.
- The step command executes the next statement in the program. If the next statement to execute is a function call, control transfers to the called function. The step command enables you to enter a function and study the individual statements of that function.
- The finish command executes the remaining statements in the function and returns control to the place where the function was called.
- The next command behaves like the step command, except when the next statement to execute contains a function call. In that case, the called function executes in its entirety and the program advances to the next executable line after the function call.
- The watch command sets a watch on any variable or data member of an object currently in scope during execution of the debugger. Whenever the value of a watched variable changes, the debugger enters break mode and notifies you that the value has changed.

Terminology

break command	info break command
break mode	next command
breakpoint	print command
continue command	quit command
debugger	run command
delete command	set command
finish command	step command
-g compiler option	watch command
gdb command	

Self-Review Exercises

G.1 Fill in the blanks in each of the following statements:

a) A breakpoint cannot be set at a(n) _____.

b) You can examine the value of an expression by using the debugger's _____ command.

c) You can modify the value of a variable by using the debugger's _____ command.

d) During debugging, the _____ command executes the remaining statements in the current function and returns program control to the place where the function was called.

e) The debugger's _____ command behaves like the step command when the next statement to execute does not contain a function call.

f) The watch debugger command allows you to view all changes to a(n) _____.

G.2 State whether each of the following is *true* or *false*. If *false*, explain why.

a) When program execution suspends at a breakpoint, the next statement to be executed is the statement after the breakpoint.

b) Watches can be removed using the debugger's remove command.

c) The -g compiler option must be used when compiling programs for debugging.

Answers to Self-Review Exercises

G.1 a) non-executable line. b) print. c) set. d) finish. e) next. f) data member.

G.2 a) False. When program execution suspends at a breakpoint, the next statement to be executed is the statement at the breakpoint. b) False. Watches can be removed using the debugger's delete command. c) True.

Bibliography

Alhir, S. *UML in a Nutshell*. Cambridge, MA: O'Reilly & Associates, Inc., 1998.

Allison, C. "Text Processing I." *The C Users Journal* Vol. 10, No. 10, October 1992, 23–28.

Allison, C. "Text Processing II." *The C Users Journal* Vol. 10, No. 12, December 1992, 73–77.

Allison, C. "Code Capsules: A C++ Date Class, Part I," *The C Users Journal* Vol. 11, No. 2, February 1993, 123–131.

Allison, C. "Conversions and Casts." *The C/C++ Users Journal* Vol. 12, No. 9, September 1994, 67–85.

Almarode, J. "Object Security." *Smalltalk Report* Vol. 5, No. 3 November/December 1995, 15–17.

American National Standard, Programming Language C++. (ANSI Document ISO/IEC 14882), New York, NY: American National Standards Institute, 1998.

Anderson, A. E. and W. J. Heinze. *C++ Programming and Fundamental Concepts*. Englewood Cliffs, NJ: Prentice Hall, 1992.

Baker, L. *C Mathematical Function Handbook*. New York, NY: McGraw Hill, 1992.

Bar-David, T. *Object-Oriented Design for C++*. Englewood Cliffs, NJ: Prentice Hall, 1993.

Beck, K. "Birds, Bees, and Browsers–Obvious Sources of Objects." *The Smalltalk Report* Vol. 3, No. 8, June 1994,13.

Becker, P. "Shrinking the Big Switch Statement." *Windows Tech Journal* Vol. 2, No. 5, May 1993, 26–33.

Becker, P. "Conversion Confusion." *C++ Report* October 1993, 26–28.

Berard, E. V. *Essays on Object-Oriented Software Engineering: Volume I*. Englewood Cliffs, NJ: Prentice Hall, 1993.

Binder, R. V. "State-Based Testing." *Object Magazine* Vol. 5, No. 4, August 1995, 75–78.

Binder, R. V. "State-Based Testing: Sneak Paths and Conditional Transitions." *Object Magazine* Vol. 5, No. 6, October 1995, 87–89.

Blum, A. *Neural Networks in C++: An Object-Oriented Framework for Building Connectionist Systems*. New York, NY: John Wiley & Sons, 1992.

Booch, G. *Object Solutions: Managing the Object-Oriented Project*. Reading, MA: Addison-Wesley, 1996.

Booch, G. *Object-Oriented Analysis and Design with Applications, Third Edition*. Reading: MA: Addison-Wesley, 2005.

Booch, G., J. Rumbaugh, and I. Jacobson. *The Unified Modeling Language User Guide*. Reading, MA: Addison-Wesley, 1999.

Cargill, T. *C++ Programming Style*. Reading, MA: Addison-Wesley, 1993.

Carroll, M. D. and M. A. Ellis. *Designing and Coding Reusable C++*. Reading, MA: Addison-Wesley, 1995.

Coplien, J. O. and D. C. Schmidt. *Pattern Languages of Program Design*. Reading, MA: Addison-Wesley, 1995.

Deitel, H. M, P. J. Deitel and D. R. Choffnes. *Operating Systems, Third Edition*. Upper Saddle River, NJ: Prentice Hall, 2004.

Deitel, H. M and P. J. Deitel. *Java How to Program, Sixth Edition*. Upper Saddle River, NJ: Prentice Hall, 2005.

Deitel, H. M. and P. J. Deitel. *C How to Program, Fourth Edition*. Upper Saddle River, NJ: Prentice Hall, 2004.

Duncan, R. "Inside C++: Friend and Virtual Functions, and Multiple Inheritance." *PC Magazine* 15 October 1991, 417–420.

Ellis, M. A. and B. Stroustrup. *The Annotated C++ Reference Manual*. Reading, MA: Addison-Wesley, 1990.

Embley, D. W., B. D. Kurtz and S. N. Woodfield. *Object-Oriented Systems Analysis: A Model-Driven Approach*. Englewood Cliffs, NJ: Yourdon Press, 1992.

Entsminger, G. and B. Eckel. *The Tao of Objects: A Beginner's Guide to Object-Oriented Programming*. New York, NY: Wiley Publishing, 1990.

Firesmith, D.G. and B. Henderson-Sellers. "Clarifying Specialized Forms of Association in UML and OML." *Journal of Object-Oriented Programming* May 1998: 47–50.

Flamig, B. *Practical Data Structures in C++*. New York, NY: John Wiley & Sons, 1993.

Fowler, M. *UML Distilled: A Brief Guide to the Standard Object Modeling Language, Third Edition*. Reading, MA: Addison-Wesley, 2004.

Gehani, N. and W. D. Roome. *The Concurrent C Programming Language*. Summit, NJ: Silicon Press, 1989.

Giancola, A. and L. Baker. "Bit Arrays with C++." *The C Users Journal* Vol. 10, No. 7, July 1992, 21–26.

Glass, G. and B. Schuchert. *The STL <Primer>*. Upper Saddle River, NJ: Prentice Hall PTR, 1995.

Gooch, T. "Obscure C++." *Inside Microsoft Visual C++* Vol. 6, No. 11, November 1995, 13–15.

Hansen, T. L. *The C++ Answer Book*. Reading, MA: Addison-Wesley, 1990.

Henricson, M. and E. Nyquist. *Industrial Strength C++: Rules and Recommendations*. Upper Saddle River, NJ: Prentice Hall, 1997.

International Standard: Programming Languages—C++. ISO/IEC 14882:1998. New York, NY: American National Standards Institute, 1998.

Jacobson, I. "Is Object Technology Software's Industrial Platform?" *IEEE Software Magazine* Vol. 10, No. 1, January 1993, 24–30.

Jaeschke, R. *Portability and the C Language*. Indianapolis, IN: Sams Publishing, 1989.

Johnson, L.J. "Model Behavior." *Enterprise Development* May 2000: 20–28.

Josuttis, N. *The C++ Standard Library: A Tutorial and Reference*. Boston, MA: Addison-Wesley, 1999.

Knight, A. "Encapsulation and Information Hiding." *The Smalltalk Report* Vol. 1, No. 8 June 1992, 19–20.

Koenig, A. "What is C++ Anyway?" *Journal of Object-Oriented Programming* April/May 1991, 48–52.

Koenig, A. "Implicit Base Class Conversions." *The C++ Report* Vol. 6, No. 5, June 1994, 18–19.

Koenig, A. and B. Stroustrup. "Exception Handling for C++ (Revised)," *Proceedings of the USENIX C++ Conference,* San Francisco, CA, April 1990.

Koenig, A. and B. Moo. *Ruminations on C++: A Decade of Programming Insight and Experience.* Reading, MA: Addison-Wesley, 1997.

Kruse, R. L. and A. J. Ryba. *Data Structures and Program Design in C++.* Upper Saddle River, NJ: Prentice Hall, 1999.

Langer, A. and K. Kreft. *Standard C++ IOStreams and Locales: Advanced Programmer's Guide and Reference.* Reading, MA: Addison-Wesley, 2000.

Lejter, M., S. Meyers and S. P. Reiss. "Support for Maintaining Object-Oriented Programs," *IEEE Transactions on Software Engineering* Vol. 18, No. 12, December 1992, 1045–1052.

Lippman, S. B. and J. Lajoie. *C++ Primer, Third Edition,* Reading, MA: Addison-Wesley, 1998.

Lorenz, M. *Object-Oriented Software Development: A Practical Guide.* Englewood Cliffs, NJ: Prentice Hall, 1993.

Lorenz, M. "A Brief Look at Inheritance Metrics." *The Smalltalk Report* Vol. 3, No. 8 June 1994, 1, 4–5.

Martin, J. *Principles of Object-Oriented Analysis and Design.* Englewood Cliffs, NJ: Prentice Hall, 1993.

Martin, R. C. *Designing Object-Oriented C++ Applications Using the Booch Method.* Englewood Cliffs, NJ: Prentice Hall, 1995.

Matsche, J. J. "Object-Oriented Programming in Standard C." *Object Magazine* Vol. 2, No. 5, January/February 1993, 71–74.

McCabe, T. J. and A. H. Watson. "Combining Comprehension and Testing in Object-Oriented Development." *Object Magazine* Vol. 4, No. 1, March/April 1994, 63–66.

McLaughlin, M. and A. Moore. "Real-Time Extensions to the UML." *Dr. Dobb's Journal* December 1998: 82–93.

Melewski, D. "UML Gains Ground." *Application Development Trends* October 1998: 34–44.

Melewski, D. "UML: Ready for Prime Time?" *Application Development Trends* November 1997: 30–44.

Melewski, D. "Wherefore and What Now, UML?" *Application Development Trends* December 1999: 61–68.

Meyer, B. *Object-Oriented Software Construction, Second Edition.* Englewood Cliffs, NJ: Prentice Hall, 1997.

Meyer, B. *Eiffel: The Language.* Englewood Cliffs, NJ: Prentice Hall, 1992.

Meyer, B. and D. Mandrioli. *Advances in Object-Oriented Software Engineering.* Englewood Cliffs, NJ: Prentice Hall, 1992.

Meyers, S. "Mastering User-Defined Conversion Functions." *The C/C++ Users Journal* Vol. 13, No. 8, August 1995, 57–63.

Meyers, S. *More Effective C++: 35 New Ways to Improve Your Programs and Designs.* Reading, MA: Addison-Wesley, 1996.

Meyers, S. *Effective C++: 50 Specific Ways to Improve Your Programs and Designs, Second Edition.* Reading, MA: Addison-Wesley, 1998.

Meyers, S. *Effective STL: 50 Specific Ways to Improve Your Use of the Standard Template Library.* Reading, MA: Addison-Wesley, 2001.

Muller, P. *Instant UML.* Birmingham, UK: Wrox Press Ltd, 1997.

Murray, R. *C++ Strategies and Tactics.* Reading, MA: Addison-Wesley, 1993.

Musser, D. R. and A. A. Stepanov. "Algorithm-Oriented Generic Libraries." *Software Practice and Experience* Vol. 24, No. 7, July 1994.

Musser, D. R., G. J. Derge and A. Saini. *STL Tutorial and Reference Guide: C++ Programming with the Standard Template Library, Second Edition.* Reading, MA: Addison-Wesley, 2001.

Nerson, J. M. "Applying Object-Oriented Analysis and Design." *Communications of the ACM,* Vol. 35, No. 9, September 1992, 63–74.

Nierstrasz, O., S. Gibbs and D. Tsichritzis. "Component-Oriented Software Development." *Communications of the ACM* Vol. 35, No. 9, September 1992, 160–165.

Perry, P. "UML Steps to the Plate." *Application Development Trends* May 1999: 33–36.

Pinson, L. J. and R. S. Wiener. *Applications of Object-Oriented Programming.* Reading, MA: Addison-Wesley, 1990.

Pittman, M. "Lessons Learned in Managing Object-Oriented Development." *IEEE Software Magazine* Vol. 10, No. 1, January 1993, 43–53.

Plauger, P. J. *The Standard C Library.* Englewood Cliffs, NJ: Prentice Hall, 1992.

Plauger, D. "Making C++ Safe for Threads." *The C Users Journal* Vol. 11, No. 2, February 1993, 58–62.

Pohl, I. *C++ Distilled: A Concise ANSI/ISO Reference and Style Guide.* Reading, MA: Addison-Wesley, 1997.

Press, W. H., S. A. Teukolsky, W. T. Vetterling and B. P. Flannery. *Numerical Recipes in C: The Art of Scientific Computing.* Cambridge, MA: Cambridge University Press, 1992.

Prieto-Diaz, R. "Status Report: Software Reusability." *IEEE Software* Vol. 10, No. 3, May 1993, 61–66.

Prince, T. "Tuning Up Math Functions." *The C Users Journal* Vol. 10, No. 12, December 1992.

Prosise, J. "Wake Up and Smell the MFC: Using the Visual C++ Classes and Applications Framework." *Microsoft Systems Journal* Vol. 10, No. 6, June 1995, 17–34.

Rabinowitz, H. and C. Schaap. *Portable C.* Englewood Cliffs, NJ: Prentice Hall, 1990.

Reed, D. R. "Moving from C to C++." *Object Magazine* Vol. 1, No. 3, September/October 1991, 46–60.

Ritchie, D. M. "The UNIX System: The Evolution of the UNIX Time-Sharing System." *AT&T Bell Laboratories Technical Journal* Vol. 63, No. 8, Part 2, October 1984, 1577–1593.

Ritchie, D. M., S. C. Johnson, M. E. Lesk and B. W. Kernighan. "UNIX Time-Sharing System: The C Programming Language." *The Bell System Technical Journal* Vol. 57, No. 6, Part 2, July/ August 1978, 1991–2019.

Rosler, L. "The UNIX System: The Evolution of C—Past and Future." *AT&T Laboratories Technical Journal* Vol. 63, No. 8, Part 2, October 1984, 1685–1699.

Robson, R. *Using the STL: The C++ Standard Template Library.* New York, NY: Springer Verlag, 2000.

Rubin, K. S. and A. Goldberg. "Object Behavior Analysis." *Communications of the ACM* Vol. 35, No. 9, September 1992, 48–62.

Rumbaugh, J., M. Blaha, W. Premerlani, F. Eddy and W. Lorensen. *Object-Oriented Modeling and Design.* Englewood Cliffs, NJ: Prentice Hall, 1991.

Rumbaugh, J., Jacobson, I. and G. Booch. *The Unified Modeling Language Reference Manual, Second Edition.* Reading, MA: Addison-Wesley, 2005.

Saks, D. "Inheritance." *The C Users Journal* May 1993, 81–89.

Schildt, H. *STL Programming from the Ground Up.* Berkeley, CA: Osborne McGraw-Hill, 1999.

Schlaer, S. and S. J. Mellor. *Object Lifecycles: Modeling the World in States.* Englewood Cliffs, NJ: Prentice Hall, 1992.

Sedgwick, R. *Bundle of Algorithms in C++, Parts 1–5: Fundamentals, Data Structures, Sorting, Searching, and Graph Algorithms (Third Edition).* Reading, MA: Addison-Wesley, 2002.

Sessions, R. *Class Construction in C and C++: Object-Oriented Programming.* Englewood Cliffs, NJ: Prentice Hall, 1992.

Skelly, C. "Pointer Power in C and C++." *The C Users Journal* Vol. 11, No. 2, February 1993, 93–98.

Snyder, A. "The Essence of Objects: Concepts and Terms." *IEEE Software Magazine* Vol. 10, No. 1, January 1993, 31–42.

Stepanov, A. and M. Lee. "The Standard Template Library." 31 October 1995 <www.cs.rpi.edu/ ~musser/doc.ps>.

Stroustrup, B. "The UNIX System: Data Abstraction in C." *AT&T Bell Laboratories Technical Journal* Vol. 63, No. 8, Part 2, October 1984, 1701–1732.

Stroustrup, B. "What is Object-Oriented Programming?" *IEEE Software* Vol. 5, No. 3, May 1988, 10–20.

Stroustrup, B. "Parameterized Types for C++." *Proceedings of the USENIX C++ Conference* Denver, CO, October 1988.

Stroustrup, B. "Why Consider Language Extensions?: Maintaining a Delicate Balance." *The C++ Report* September 1993, 44–51.

Stroustrup, B. "Making a vector Fit for a Standard." *The C++ Report* October 1994.

Stroustrup, B. *The Design and Evolution of C++.* Reading, MA: Addison-Wesley, 1994.

Stroustrup, B. *The C++ Programming Language, Special Third Edition.* Reading, MA: Addison-Wesley, 2000.

Taligent's Guide to Designing Programs: Well-Mannered Object-Oriented Design in C++. Reading, MA: Addison-Wesley, 1994.

Taylor, D. *Object-Oriented Information Systems: Planning and Implementation.* New York, NY: John Wiley & Sons, 1992.

Tondo, C. L. and S. E. Gimpel. *The C Answer Book.* Englewood Cliffs, NJ: Prentice Hall, 1989.

Urlocker, Z. "Polymorphism Unbounded." *Windows Tech Journal* Vol. 1, No. 1, January 1992, 11–16.

Van Camp, K. E. "Dynamic Inheritance Using Filter Classes." *The C/C++ Users Journal* Vol. 13, No. 6, June 1995, 69–78.

Vilot, M. J. "An Introduction to the Standard Template Library." *The C++ Report* Vol. 6, No. 8, October 1994.

Voss, G. *Object-Oriented Programming: An Introduction.* Berkeley, CA: Osborne McGraw-Hill, 1991.

Voss, G. "Objects and Messages." *Windows Tech Journal* February 1993, 15–16.

Wang, B. L. and J. Wang. "Is a Deep Class Hierarchy Considered Harmful?" *Object Magazine* Vol. 4, No. 7, November/December 1994, 35–36.

Weisfeld, M. "An Alternative to Large Switch Statements." *The C Users Journal* Vol. 12, No. 4, April 1994, 67–76.

Weiskamp, K. and B. Flamig. *The Complete C++ Primer, Second Edition.* Orlando, FL: Academic Press, 1993.

Wiebel, M. and S. Halladay. "Using OOP Techniques Instead of *switch* in C++." *The C Users Journal* Vol. 10, No. 10, October 1993, 105–112.

Wilde, N. and R. Huitt. "Maintenance Support for Object-Oriented Programs." *IEEE Transactions on Software Engineering* Vol. 18, No. 12, December 1992, 1038–1044.

Wilde, N., P. Matthews and R. Huitt. "Maintaining Object-Oriented Software." *IEEE Software Magazine* Vol. 10, No. 1, January 1993, 75–80.

Wilson, G. V. and P. Lu. *Parallel Programming Using C++.* Cambridge, MA: MIT Press, 1996.

Wilt, N. "Templates in C++." *The C Users Journal* May 1993, 33–51.

Wirfs-Brock, R., B. Wilkerson and L. Wiener. *Designing Object-Oriented Software.* Englewood Cliffs, NJ: Prentice Hall PTR, 1990.

Wyatt, B. B., K. Kavi and S. Hufnagel. "Parallelism in Object-Oriented Languages: A Survey." *IEEE Software* Vol. 9, No. 7, November 1992, 56–66.

Yamazaki, S., K. Kajihara, M. Ito and R. Yasuhara. "Object-Oriented Design of Telecommunication Software." *IEEE Software Magazine* Vol. 10, No. 1, January 1993, 81–87.

Index

*[Note: Page references for defining occurrences of terms appear in **bold blue**.]*

Symbols

-- (postfix decrement operator) **145**
-- (prefix decrement operator) **145**
! (logical NOT operator) 190, **192**
! (logical NOT) operator truth table 193
!= (inequality operator) 52, 526
% (modulus operator) 48
%= (modulus assignment operator) 145
& (address operator) 363, 365
& and * operators as inverses 364
& in a parameter list 250
& to declare reference 248
&& (logical AND operator) 190, 267
&& (logical AND) operator truth table 191
-g compiler command (GNU Debugger) **735**
* (multiplication operator) 48
* (pointer dereference or indirection operator) **363**, 365
*= (multiplication assignment operator) 145
+ (addition operator) 46, 48
++ (postfix increment operator) **145**
++ (prefix increment operator) **145**
+= (addition assignment operator) **145**, 526
, (comma operator) **170**
.h header file 86, 223
/ (division operator) 48
// single-line comment **37**
/= (division assignment operator) 145
:: (binary scope resolution operator) 92, 504
:: (unary scope resolution operator) **255**
< (less-than operator) 52
<< (stream insertion operator) **39**, 46
<= (less-than-or-equal-to operator) 52
= (assignment operator) 46, 48, 192
-= subtraction assignment operator 145
== (equality operator) 52, 192, 526
> (greater-than operator) 52
>= (greater-than-or-equal-to operator) 52
>> (stream extraction operator) 46
?: (ternary conditional operator) **117**, 267
\" (double-quote-character) escape sequence 40
\\ (backslash-character) escape sequence 40
\' (single-quote-character) escape sequence 40
\a (alert) escape sequence 40
\n (newline) escape sequence 40
\r (carriage-return) escape sequence 40
\t (tab) escape sequence 40

|| (logical OR operator) 190, **191**, 267
|| (logical OR) operator truth table 192
'\0' (null character) **403**
'\n' 403

Numerics

2-D array **328**

A

abbreviating assignment expressions 145
`abort` function **459**
absolute value 215
abstract base class 639, **659**, 660
abstract class **659**, 660, 661, 679
abstract data type (ADT) **510**, 511
access a global variable 255
access function **450**
access non-`static` class data members and member functions 508
access `private` member of a class 78
access privileges 371, 376
access-specifier label
  `private:` 78
  `public:` 70
access specifiers 70, 78, 493
  `private` **78**
  `protected` 442, 589
  `public` **70**, 78
access the caller's data 248
access violation 405
accessing an object's members through each type of object handle 449
accessor **80**
`Account` class (exercise) 106
`Account` inheritance hierarchy (exercise) 635
accumulated outputs 46
accumulator 423, 424
action 3, **109**, 116, 118, 122, 509
action expression **112**, 116, 117, 122, 172, 178, 186
action oriented **23**
action state **112**, 113, 198
action state symbol **112**
action/decision model of programming 116, 117
activation record **242**
active window 720
activity diagram 112, 117, 122, 171, 196
  `do...while` statement 178
  `for` statement 171
  `if` statement 116
  sequence statement 112
  `switch` statement 187

activity of a portion of a software system **112**
Ada Lovelace 10
Ada programming language **10**
add an integer to a pointer 383
addition 4, 47, 48, 49
addition assignment operator (+=) **145**
addition program that displays the sum of two numbers 43
address operator (&) 363, 365, 366, 379, 524
"administrative" section of the computer 4
ADT (abstract data type) **510**, 511
aggregate data type 374
aggregation **446**
aiming a derived-class pointer at a base-class object 649
airline reservation system 352
alert escape sequence ('\a') 40
algebraic expression 48
`<algorithm>` 225
algorithm **109**, 116, 117, 123, 132
  action **109**
  insertion sort **325**
  order in which actions should execute **109**
  procedure **109**
  selection sort **377**
alias for the name of an object 462
allocate memory 225, 501, **502**
alphabetizing strings 409
alter the flow of control 188
ALU (arithmetic and logic unit) **4**
American National Standards Institute (ANSI) 3, 8, 511
American Standard Code for Information Interchange (ASCII) **182**, 410
analysis 24
`Analysis.cpp` 142
`Analysis.h` 142
Analytical Engine 10
angle brackets (< and >) 259
ANSI (American National Standards Institute) 8
ANSI C 15
ANSI/ISO 9899: 1990 8
ANSI/ISO C++ Draft Standard 712
ANSI/ISO C++ Standard, 15
Apple Computer, Inc. 5
arbitrary range of subscripts 511
argument coercion **222**
argument to a function **72**
arguments in correct order 220
arguments passed to member-object constructors 486
arithmetic and logic unit (ALU) 4

arithmetic assignment operators 145
arithmetic calculations 48
arithmetic mean 50
arithmetic operator **48**
arithmetic overflow **510**
"arity" of an operator 526
array **293**, 295, 374, 510, 512
array assignment 511
array bounds 307
array bounds checking 307
`Array` class definition with overloaded operators 533, 570
`Array` class member-function and `friend` function definitions 534
`Array` class test program 537
array comparison 511
array initializer list 298
array input/output 511
array name 386, 387
array name as a constant pointer to beginning of array 375, 386, 387
array notation 387
array of pointers to functions 401, 431
array of strings 390
array size 312
array subscript operator ([]) 541
array subscripting 375, 387
arrays passed by reference 317
arrow 63, 112
arrow member selection operator (->) 448, 496
ASCII (American Standard Code for Information Interchange) **182**, 403, 410
ASCII character set **64**
assembler **7**
assembly language **7**
`<assert.h>` header file 225
assign the value of 52
assigning addresses of base-class and derived-class objects to base-class and derived-class pointers 646
assigning character strings to `String` objects 554
assigning class objects 465
assignment operator (=) **46**, 55, 465, 523, 524
assignment operator functions 543
assignment operators **145**
    %= modulus assignment operator 145
    *= multiplication assignment operator 145
    += addition assignment operator 145
    /= division assignment operator 145
    -= subtraction assignment operator 145
assignment statement 46, 147
associate from left to right 55, 148
associate from right to left 55, 148, 183
association (in the UML) **23**
associativity 192, 194
associativity chart 56
associativity not changed by overloading 526
associativity of operators **49**, 55
asterisk (*) **48**
`at` member function of `vector` **343**
AT&T 11
Attempting to modify a constant pointer to constant data 376

Attempting to modify a constant pointer to nonconstant data 375
Attempting to modify data through a nonconstant pointer to constant data 374
attribute 23, **76**
    in the UML **22**, 71
attributes of a variable 235
`auto` keyword 236
`auto` storage-class specifier **235**
automatic array 296
automatic array initialization 310
automatic local array 310
automatic local object 459
automatic local variable 236, 239, 252
automatic storage class **235**, 236, 293, 312
automatically destroyed 241
Autos window **728**
    displaying state of objects 729
Autos window displaying the state of `withdrawalAmount` (Visual C++ .NET Debugger) 729
average 50
average calculation 123, 132
average of several integers 207
avoid repeating code 456

B

B programming language 8
Babbage, Charles 10
backslash (\) 40
backslash escape sequence (\\) 40
backslash zero 308
bar chart 208, 302, 303
bar chart printing program 302
bar of asterisks 302, 303
base case(s) **262**, 265, 268
base class **585**, 586, 588
base-class constructor 622
base-class member accessibility in derived class 630
base-class pointer to a derived-class object 686
base-class `private` member 589
base *e* 215
base-10 number system 216
base-class initializer syntax **602**
base-class member function redefined in a derived class 619
`BasePlusCommissionEmployee` class header file 673
`BasePlusCommissionEmployee` class implementation file 674
`BasePlusCommissionEmployee` class represents an employee who receives a base salary in addition to a commission 597
`BasePlusCommissionEmployee` class test program 599
`BasePlusCommissionEmployee` class that inherits from class `CommissionEmployee`, which does not provide `protected` data 617
`BasePlusCommissionEmployee` class that inherits `protected` data from `CommissionEmployee` 610

BASIC (Beginner's All-Purpose Symbolic Instruction Code) 11
batch processing **5**
BCPL 8
Beginner's All-Purpose Symbolic Instruction Code (BASIC) 11
behavior 22, 510
behaviors in the UML **22**
Bell Laboratories 8
binary (base 2) number system 699
binary arithmetic operator 138
binary integer 162
binary operator **46**, 48, 192
binary operator + 48
binary scope resolution operator (::) **92**, 504
binary search 324
`<bitset>` 224
bitwise left-shift operator (<<) 523
bitwise right-shift operator (>>) 523
blank character 115
blank line 45, 131
block **54**, 98, **120**, 121, 137, 236, 238, 241
block is active 236
block is exited 236
block scope **238**, 448
block-scope variable 448
body of a class definition **70**
body of a function **39**, 41
body of a loop 122, 166, 171, 210
Böhm, C. 111, 200
"bombing" 131
Booch, Grady 24, 25
`bool` data type **116**
`bool` value `true` 116
`boolalpha` stream manipulator **193**
Borland C++ 14, 257
bounds checking 307
box 63
braces ({}) 41, 54, 98, 120, 121, 137, 184
braces in a `do...while` statement 176
bracket ([]) 295
`break` debugger command (GNU Debugger) **736**
break mode **719**, **736**
`break` statement 184, 188, 210
`break` statement exiting a `for` statement 188
breakpoint (GNU Debugger) **716**, **733**
breakpoints (GNU Debugger)
    inserting 719, 736, 740
breakpoints (Visual C++ .NET Debugger)
    disabling **721**
    inserting 719, 722
    maroon circle, solid 719
    yellow arrow in break mode **720**
brittle software **613**
"brute force" computing **209**
bubble sort **350**
bucket sort **358**
bug **716**
building-block appearance 196
"building blocks" 23
building-block approach 9
built-in type **44**, 510, 511
business software 10

C

.c extension 14
C legacy code 475
C programming language 7
C# programming language 11
C++ career resources 712
C++ compiler 14
C++ development environment 13
C++ environment 13
C++ preprocessor 14, 38
C++ programming environment 213
C++ programming language 6, 7, 8, 11, 15
C++ resources 16, 29, 713
C++ resources on the Web 711
C++ Standard Library 8, 213
   header file location 89
   string class 72
C++ Standard Library class template vector 339
C++ Standard Library header files 223
calculate a salesperson's earnings 158
calculate the value of π 209
call a function 72
call stack 374
calling function (caller) 70, 79, 214
calling functions by reference 366
camel case 69
card dealing algorithm 396
card games 391
card shuffling and dealing simulation 391, 393, 396
career resource 712
carriage-return escape sequence ('\r') 40
carry bit 706
cascaded assignments 556
cascading += operators 556
cascading member function calls 498, 499, 501
cascading stream insertion operations 46
case label 183, 184
case sensitive 44
case study: Date class 560
case study: String class 546
<cassert> header file 225
cast
   downcast 651, 658
cast operator 133, 138, 222, 385, 545, 568
cast operator function 545
cast operators
   dynamic_cast 685
casting 385, 386
cataloging 467
<cctype> header file 224, 372
ceil function 215
Celsius and Fahrenheit Temperatures exercise 284
central processing unit (CPU) 4
cerr (standard error unbuffered) 15
<cfloat> header file 225
chaining stream insertion operations 46
char data type 43, 182, 223
character array 308, 389, 403, 530
character array as a string 309
character code 410
character constant 403
character manipulation 213

character presentation 225
character set 64, 188, 410
character string 39, 296, 308
character's numerical representation 182
characters represented as numeric codes 410
checkerboard pattern 63, 162
cin (standard input stream) 14, 45
cin.get function 182
cin.getline function 404
clarity 2, 15, 45, 306
class 8, 22, 23
   attribute 76
   client-code programmer 95
   constructor 82
   data member 67, 76
   default constructor 82, 85
   define a constructor 84
   define a member function 68
   defining 69
   implementation programmer 94
   instance of 77
   interface 90
   interface described by function prototypes 91
   member function 67, 68
   member function implementations in a separate source-code file 92
   naming convention 69
   object of 77
   public services 90
   services 80
class average problem 123, 132
class definition 69
class development 533
class diagram (UML) 71
class hierarchy 585, 660, 686
class-implementation programmer 94
class keyword 260
class libraries 12, 175, 448, 467, 630
class scope 238, 445, 446
class-scope variable is hidden 448
class variable 321
class's object code 448
class's source code 448
classes 72, 492, 511, 524, 565, 567
   Array 533
   Complex 472, 577, 577
   Date 472, 486, 559
   Employee 486, 491
   HugeInt 579
   IntegerSet 521
   PhoneNumber 582
   Polynomial 580
   Rational 472
   RationalNumber 580
   SavingsAccount 520
   string 72, 225, 492, 511, 524, 565, 567
   TicTacToe 473
   Time 472
   type_info 686
   vector 338, 565
client 514
client code 640
client-code programmer 94, 95
client computer 6
client of a class 23
client of a queue 512

client of an object 68, 80
client/server computing 6
<climits> header file 225
<cmath> header file 224
COBOL (COmmon Business Oriented Language) 10
coefficient 580
coin tossing 226, 285
collection classes 512
colon (:) 238, 486
column 328
column headings 296
column subscript 328
combining class Time and class Date exercise 473
combining control statements in two ways 195
comma operator (,) 170, 267, 524
comma-separated list
   of parameters 43, 55, 170, 220, 362
command-and-control software system 10
command-line arguments 391
comment 37, 38, 44
commission worker 209
CommissionEmployee class header file 671
CommissionEmployee class implementation file 671
CommissionEmployee class represents an employee paid a percentage of gross sales 591
CommissionEmployee class test program 594
CommissionEmployee class uses member functions to manipulate its private data 614
CommissionEmployee class with protected data 607
Common Programming Error 9
commutative operation 528
comparing strings 405, 409
compilation error 40
compilation phase 40
compile 12
compile-time error 40
compiler 7, 40, 138
compiler dependent 364
compiler error 40
compiler option 16
compiling multiple-source-file program 96
Complex Class exercise 472
Complex class member-function definitions 578
complex conditions 190
complex numbers 472, 577
component in the UML 23
component-oriented software development 511
components 212, 467
composition 446, 485, 586, 589
compound interest 173, 208, 210
compound interest calculation with for 173, 174
compound statement 54, 120
computation 3
computer 3
computer-assisted instruction (CAI) 285

Computer Assisted Instruction exercise 285
computer network 5
computer networking 6
computer program 3
computer programmer 3
computer simulator 426
Computers in Education exercise 285
computing the sum of the elements of an array 301
concatenated strings 556
concatenating strings 407
concatenation of stream insertion operations 46
concrete class 659
concrete derived class 663
condition 51, 115, 118, 177, 190
conditional expression 117, 118, 444
conditional operator (?:) 117
confusing assignment (=) and equality (==) operators 52
confusing equality (==) and assignment (=) operators 52
confusing equality (==) and assignment (=) operators 195
conserving memory 236
consistent state 98, 442, 455
const char * 373
const keyword 247, 315, 316, 476, 531
const member function 475
const member function on a const object 477
const member function on a non-const object 477
const object 300, 475, 477
const object must be initialized 300
const objects and const member functions 479
const pointer 338, 533
const qualifier 299, 370
const qualifier before type specifier in parameter declaration 250
const type qualifier applied to an array parameter 316
const variables must be initialized 300
const version of operator[] 544
const with function parameters 370
constant 137
constant integral expression 178, 186
constant pointer 386, 496
constant pointer to an integer constant 376
constant pointer to constant data 371, 376
constant pointer to nonconstant data 371, 375
constant reference 543
constant reference parameter 250
constant variable 299, 301
constructed inside out 490
constructor 82
   conversion 545, 554, 570
   copy 542
   default 85
   defining 84
   explicit 570
   function prototype 91
   in a UML class diagram 85

constructor (cont.)
   naming 84
   parameter list 84
   single argument 545, 554, 569, 571
constructor called recursively 542
constructor with default arguments 456
constructors and destructors called automatically 459
constructors cannot be virtual 687
constructors cannot specify a return type 82
container 224
container class 450, 492, 512, 541
continue command (GNU Debugger) 737
Continue command (Visual C++ .NET Debugger) 720
continue statement 188, 210
continue statement terminating a single iteration of a for statement 189
control statement 110, 111, 114, 116
control statement nesting 114
control statement stacking 114, 196
control statements 114, 117
   do...while repetition statement 113, 176, 177, 178, 200
   for repetition statement 113, 167, 168, 169, 200
   if selection statement 51, 54, 200
   if...else selection statement 200
   nested if...else selection statement 120
   nesting 116, 140
   repetition statement 114
   selection statement 114
   sequence statement 114
   stacking 116
   switch 178, 185, 200
   while 113, 136, 166, 176, 200
control variable 167
control-variable name 169
controlling expression 183
converge on the base case 268
conversational computing 45
conversion between a fundamental type and a class 556
conversion constructor 545, 554, 556, 570
conversion operator 545
conversions among fundamental types 545
   by cast 546
convert a binary number to decimal 704
convert a hexadecimal number to decimal 704
convert among user-defined types and built-in types 545
convert an octal number to decimal 704
convert between types 545
convert lowercase letters 224
Converting a string to uppercase 372
converting from a higher data type to a lower data type 223
copy a string using array notation 389
copy a string using pointer notation 389
"copy-and-paste" approach 601
copy constructor 467, 540, 542, 544
copy constructors in pass-by-value parameter passing 556

copy of the argument 371
copying strings 389, 406
core memory 4
correct number of arguments 220
correct order of arguments 220
correctly initializing and using a constant variable 300
cos function 215
cosine 215
counter 124, 141, 159, 236
counter-controlled repetition 123, 124, 129, 136, 140, 141, 165, 166, 268
counter-controlled repetition with the for statement 168
counter variable 127
counting loop 167
counting up by one 129
cout (<<) (the standard output stream) 15, 39, 42, 45
.cpp extension 14
CPU (central processing unit) 4, 14
craps simulation 231, 232, 235, 290
"crashing" 131
create new data types 46, 509, 511
CreateAndDestroy class definition 460
CreateAndDestroy class member-function definitions 460
credit limit on a charge account 157
crossword puzzle generator 438
<cstdio> header file 225
<cstdlib> header file 224, 226
<cstring> header file 224, 406, 557
<ctime> header file 224, 231
<Ctrl>-d 183
Ctrl key 183
<Ctrl>-z 183
<ctype.h> header file 224
cursor 40
.cxx extension 14

D

dangerous pointer manipulation 679
dangling-else problem 119, 161
dangling pointer 543, 555
dangling reference 252
data 3
data abstraction 475, 509, 533
data hiding 78, 80
data member 23, 67, 76, 77, 444
   private 78
data representation 510
data structures 293
data types 510
   bool 116
   char 43, 182, 223
   double 132, 137, 174, 222
   float 43, 132, 223
   int 42
   long 187, 222
   long double 223
   long int 187, 223, 263
   short 187, 222
   short int 187
   unsigned 223, 229
   unsigned char 223
   unsigned int 223, 229, 380
   unsigned long 223, 264
   unsigned long int 223, 264

data types (cont.)
  unsigned short 223
  unsigned short int 223
data types in the UML 75
Date class 472, 486, 559
Date class (exercise) 107
Date class definition 486
Date class definition with overloaded increment operators 560
Date class member function definitions 487
Date class member-function and friend-function definitions 561
Date class test program 563
deallocate memory 501, 502
debug 9, 15
Debug configuration (Visual C++ .NET Debugger) 718
debugger 716
  Autos window displaying state of objects (Visual C++ .NET Debugger) 729
  break command (GNU Debugger) 736
  break mode (GNU Debugger) 736
  break mode (Visual C++ .NET Debugger) 719
  breakpoint (GNU Debugger) 733
  breakpoint (Visual C++ .NET Debugger) 716
  continue command (GNU Debugger) 737
  Continue command (Visual C++ .NET Debugger) 720
  Debug configuration (Visual C++ .NET Debugger) 718
  defined (GNU Debugger) 733
  defined (Visual C++ .NET Debugger) 716
  delete command (GNU Debugger) 739
  finish command (GNU Debugger) 742
  -g compiler option (GNU Debugger) 735
  gdb command (GNU Debugger) 736
  help command (GNU Debugger) 736
  info break command (GNU Debugger) 739
  inserting a breakpoint (GNU Debugger) 736
  inserting a breakpoint (Visual C++ .NET Debugger) 719
  list command (GNU Debugger) 736
  Locals window (Visual C++ .NET Debugger) 722
  logic error (GNU Debugger) 733
  logic error (Visual C++ .NET Debugger) 716
  margin indicator bar (Visual C++ .NET Debugger) 719
  next command (GNU Debugger) 743
  print command (GNU Debugger) 738, 740

debugger (cont.)
  quit command (GNU Debugger) 739
  run command (GNU Debugger) 736
  set command (GNU Debugger) 740, 741
  Solution Configurations ComboBox (Visual C++ .NET Debugger) 718
  step command (GNU Debugger) 742
  Step Into command (Visual C++ .NET Debugger) 726
  Step Out command (Visual C++ .NET Debugger) 727
  Step Over command (Visual C++ .NET Debugger) 726
  suspending program execution (GNU Debugger) 740
  suspending program execution (Visual C++ .NET Debugger) 722
  watch command (GNU Debugger) 744
  Watch window (Visual C++ .NET Debugger) 722, 723
debugging 229
decimal (base 10) number system 699
decimal number 209
decimal point 132, 139, 175
decision 3, 115, 116
decision symbol 115
deck of cards 390, 392
declaration 42, 110
declaration of a function 91
declarations
  using 53
declaring a static member function const 509
decrement a control variable 166
decrement a pointer 383
decrement operator (--) 145, 146
decrement operators 558
deeply nested statements 200
default access mode for class is private 78
default argument 253, 254, 452
default arguments with constructors 454
default case 183, 184, 185, 229
default constructor 82, 85, 455, 491, 540, 542, 560
  provided by the compiler 85
  provided by the programmer 85
default memberwise assignment 465, 524
default memberwise copy 542
default precision 139
defensive programming 169
define a constructor 84
#define preprocessor directive 442
defining a class 69
defining a member function of a class 68
definite repetition 123
Deitel Buzz Online newsletter 28
deitel@deitel.com 3
delay loop 170
delete 543
delete [] (dynamic array deallocation) 503

delete debugger command (GNU Debugger) 739
delete operator 501, 686
deleting dynamically allocated memory 509
delimiter character 404, **411**
DeMorgan's laws 209
Department of Defense (DOD) 10
<deque> header file 224
dequeue operation 512
dereference a null pointer 364
dereference a pointer 364, 367, 371
dereferencing operator (*) 363
derive one class from another **446**
derived class 585, 586, 588, 629
  indirect 673
derived-class destructor 686
design process 24
destructive write 47
destructor 458, 602
destructor calls in reverse order of constructor calls 459
destructor in a derived class 621
destructor overloading 458
destructor receives no parameters and returns no value 458
destructors called in reverse order 621
developer.intel.com/software/products/compilers/cwin/index.htm 28
diagnostics that aid program debugging 225
dialog 45
diamond 63, 210
diamond symbol 112, 115
dice game 231
Die-rolling program using an array instead of switch 304
digit 43, 403, 699
direct base class **585**
directly reference a value 362
disabling a breakpoint 721
disk 14, 15
displacement **682**
distributed client/server applications 6
distributed computing 5
divide-and-conquer approach 212, 213
division 4, 48, 49
division by zero 131, 510
do...while repetition statement 113, 176, 177, 178, 200
document a program 37
dollar amount 175
dot operator (.) 71, 448, 497, 653
dotted line 113
double-array subscripting 576
double data type 132, 174, 222
double-precision floating-point number 137
double quote 39, 40
double-selection statement 113, 178, 200
"doubly initializing" member objects 491
downcasting 651, 658
driver program 87
dummy value 129
dynamic binding 639, **653**, 678, 679, 682
dynamic casting 639
dynamic content 10
dynamic data structures 361

dynamic memory management **501**
dynamic_cast **685**
dynamically allocate array of integers 541
dynamically allocated memory 509, 686
dynamically allocated storage 459, 467, 542, 546, 555
dynamically creates exact amount of space 491
dynamically determine function to execute **652**

E

EBCDIC (Extended Binary Coded Decimal Interchange Code) 410
edit 12
edit phase 14
editing a file 13
editor 13
Eight Queens 357
    brute force approaches 357
element of an array **294**
emacs 14
embedded parentheses 49
Employee class 486, 491
Employee class (Exercise) 107
Employee class definition showing composition 488
Employee class definition with a static data member to track the number of Employee objects in memory 505
Employee class header file 664
Employee class hierarchy driver program 675
Employee class implementation file 665
Employee class member function definitions, including constructor with a member-initializer list 489
Employee class member-function definitions 506
empty function parameter list 245
empty member function of class string 567
empty parentheses 70, 71, 74
empty statement **121**
empty string **80**
encapsulation **22**, 81, 445, 465, 491
encrypted integer 163
encryption 163
end line 46
"end of data entry" 129
end-of-file 183, 404
#endif preprocessor directive **442**
endl 46, 139
English-like abbreviations 7
Enhancing Class Date exercise 472
Enhancing Class Rectangle exercise 473
Enhancing Class Time exercise 471, 472
enqueue operation **512**
Enter key 45, 183, 185
entry point 196
enum keyword **234**
enumeration **234**
enumeration constant **234**
environment 213
equal to 52
equality and relational operators 53
equality operator 51, **52**, 53
equality operator (== and !=) 116, 190

equality operator (==) 533
equation of straight line 50
Erroneous attempt to initialize a constant of a built-in data type by assignment 484
error 14
    off-by-one **129**, 168, 169, 295
error checking 213
error message 14
Error-Prevention Tip **9**
escape character **40**
escape early from a loop 188
escape sequence **40**, 41
escape sequences
    \" (double-quote character) 40
    \" (double-quote-character) 40
    \\ (backslash character) 40
    \\ (backslash-character) 40
    \' (single-quote character) 40
    \' (single-quote-character) 40
    \a (alert) 40
    \n (newline) 40
    \r (carriage return) 40
    \r (carriage-return) 40
    \t (tab) 40, 185
even integer 207
examination-results problem 142
Examples
    Accessing an object's members through each type of object handle 449
    Addition program that displays the sum of two numbers 43
    Aiming a derived-class pointer at a base-class object 649
    Analysis.cpp 142
    Analysis.h 142
    Array class definition with overloaded operators 533, 570
    Array class member-function and friend-function definitions 534
    Array class test program 537
    Array of pointers to functions 401
    Attempting to modify a constant pointer to constant data 376
    Attempting to modify a constant pointer to nonconstant data 375
    Attempting to modify data through a nonconstant pointer to constant data 374
    Bar chart printing program 302
    BasePlusCommissionEmployee class header file 673
    BasePlusCommissionEmployee class implementation file 674
    BasePlusCommissionEmployee class represents an employee who receives a base salary in addition to a commission 597
    BasePlusCommissionEmployee class test program 599
    BasePlusCommissionEmployee class that inherits from class CommissionEmployee, which does not provide protected data 617
    BasePlusCommissionEmployee class that inherits protected data from CommissionEmployee 610

Examples (cont.)
    break statement exiting a for statement 188
    C++ Standard Library class template vector 339
    Cascading member function calls 498, 501
    Character arrays processed as strings 309
    CommissionEmployee class header file 671
    CommissionEmployee class implementation file 671
    CommissionEmployee class represents an employee paid a percentage of gross sales 591
    CommissionEmployee class test program 594
    CommissionEmployee class uses member functions to manipulate its private data 614
    CommissionEmployee class with protected data 607
    Complex class definition 577
    Complex class member-function definitions 578
    Complex numbers 578
    Compound interest calculations with for 174
    Computing the sum of the elements of an array 301
    const objects and const member functions 479
    const type qualifier applied to an array parameter 316
    const variables must be initialized 300
    Constructor with default arguments 456
    continue statement terminating a single iteration of a for statement 189
    Converting a string to uppercase 372
    Copying the Examples folder xlv
    Correctly initializing and using a constant variable 300
    Counter-controlled repetition with the for statement 168
    Craps simulation 232
    CreateAndDestroy class definition 460
    CreateAndDestroy class member-function definitions 460
    Creating and manipulating a Grade-Book object in which the course name is limited to 25 characters in length 99
    Date class definition 486
    Date class definition with overloaded increment operators 560
    Date class member function definitions 487
    Date class member-function and friend-function definitions 561
    Date class test program 563
    Default arguments to a function 253
    Default memberwise assignment 465

Examples (cont.)

Defining and testing class Grade-Book with a data member and *set* and *get* functions 76

Defining class GradeBook with a member function that takes a parameter 73

Defining class GradeBook with a member function, creating a GradeBook object and calling its member function 69

Die-rolling program using an array instead of switch 304

do...while repetition statement 177

Employee class definition showing composition 488

Employee class definition with a static data member to track the number of Employee objects in memory 505

Employee class header file 664

Employee class hierarchy driver program 675

Employee class implementation file 665

Employee class member function definitions, including constructor with a member-initializer list 489

Employee class member-function definitions 506

Equality and relational operators 53

Erroneous attempt to initialize a constant of a built-in data type by assignment 484

Friends can access private members of class 493

Functions that take no arguments 246

Generating values to be placed into elements of an array 299

GradeBook class definition containing function prototypes that specify the interface of the class 91

GradeBook class demonstration after separating its interface from its implementation 94

GradeBook.cpp 125, 133

GradeBook.h 124, 133

HourlyEmployee class header file 669

HourlyEmployee class implementation file 669

Huge integers 583

Implementation class definition 513

Implementing a proxy class 515

Including class GradeBook from file GradeBook.h for use in main 88

Inheritance examples 587

Inheritance hierarchy for university CommunityMembers 587

Initializing a reference 251

Initializing an array's elements to zeros and printing the array 297

Initializing multidimensional arrays 329

Initializing the elements of an array with a declaration 297

Examples (cont.)

inline function to calculate the volume of a cube 247

Instantiating multiple objects of the GradeBook class and using the GradeBook constructor to specify the course name when each GradeBook object is created 83

Interface class definition 514

Interface class member-function definitions 515

Iterative factorial solution 268

Linear search of an array 324

Member initializer used to initialize a constant of a built-in data type 481

Member-function definitions for class GradeBook with a *set* function that validates the length of data member courseName 97

Multipurpose sorting program using function pointers 398

Name mangling to enable type-safe linkage 258

Nested control statements: Examination-results problem 142

Non-friend/non-member functions cannot access private members 495

Overloaded function definitions 256

Overloaded stream insertion and stream extraction operators 529

Pass-by-reference with a pointer argument used to cube a variable's value 368

Pass-by-value used to cube a variable's value 367

Passing arguments by value and by reference 249

Passing arrays and individual array elements to functions 314

Pointer operators & and * 365

Poll analysis program 305

Preincrementing and postincrementing 147

Printing a line of text with multiple statements 41

Printing a string one character at a time using a nonconstant pointer to constant data 373

Printing multiple lines of text with a single statement 42

private base-class data cannot be accessed from derived class 602

protected base-class data can be accessed from derived class 611

Randomizing the die-rolling program 229

Referencing array elements with the array name and with pointers 387

Returning a reference to a private data member 463

Rolling a six-sided die 6000 times 227

SalariedEmployee class header file 667

SalariedEmployee class implementation file 667

SalesPerson class definition 450

Examples (cont.)

SalesPerson class member-function definitions 451

Scoping example 239

Selection sort with call-by-reference 378

Set of recursive calls to method Fibonacci 267

Shifted, scaled integers produced by 1 + rand() % 6 226

sizeof operator used to determine standard data type sizes 382

sizeof operator when applied to an array name returns the number of bytes in the array 381

Standard Library class string 565

static array initialization and automatic array initialization 310

static data member tracking the number of objects of a class 505, 507

strcat and strncat 408

strcmp and strncmp 409

strcpy and strncpy 407

String class definition with operator overloading 546

String class member-function and friend-function definitions 548

String class test program 551

String copying using array notation and pointer notation 389

strlen 412

strtok 411

Summing integers with the for statement 173

Text-printing program 38

this pointer used implicitly and explicitly to access members of an object 496

Time class containing a constructor with default arguments 453

Time class definition 441

Time class definition modified to enable cascaded member-function calls 498

Time class member function definitions, including const member functions 478

Time class member-function definitions 443

Time class member-function definitions including a constructor that takes arguments 454

Time class with const member functions 477

Two-dimensional array manipulations 331

Unary scope resolution operator 255

Uninitialized local reference causes a syntax error 251

User-defined maximum function 216

Using a function template 259

Utility function demonstration 452

<exception> header file 224

exception handling 224

exceptional condition 184

executable image 14

executable statement 45, 110

execute a program 12, 14

Examples (cont.)
execution-time error 15
execution-time overhead 679
Exercises
    `Account` class 106
    `Account` inheritance hierarchy 635
    bubble sort 350
    Celsius and Fahrenheit Temperatures 284
    Combining Class `Time` and Class `Date` 473
    `Complex` Class 472
    Computer Assisted Instruction 285
    Computers in Education 285
    `Date` class 107
    `Employee` class 107
    Enhancing Class `Date` 472
    Enhancing Class `Rectangle` 473
    Enhancing Class `Time` 471, 472
    Fibonacci Series 286
    Guess the Number Game 286
    `HugeInteger` Class 473
    `Invoice` class 106
    Modifying Class `GradeBook` 106
    `Package` Inheritance Hierarchy 691
    `Package` inheritance hierarchy 635
    Payroll System Modification 691
    Perfect Numbers 285
    Polymorphic banking program using `Account` hierarchy 691
    Polymorphic Screen Manager Using `Shape` Hierarchy 691
    Prime Numbers 285
    `Rational` Class 472
    `Rectangle` Class 473
    recursive Eight Queens 270, 359
    recursive factorial function 270
    recursive Fibonacci function 270
    recursive Towers of Hanoi 270
    Returning Error Indicators from Class `Time`'s *set* Functions 473
    Reverse Digits 285
    `Shape` hierarchy 691
    `TicTacToe` class 473
exhaust memory 265
exit a function **40**
exit a loop 210
`exit` function 459
exit point of a control statement 196
`exp` function 215
`explicit` constructor **570**
explicit conversion **138**
`explicit` keyword 571
explicit use of the `this` pointer 496
exponent 580
exponential "explosion" of calls 268
exponential complexity **268**
exponential function 215
exponentiation 50, 174
expression 116, 117, 138, 169, 170
extend the base programming language 511
Extended Binary Coded Decimal Interchange Code (EBCDIC) 410
extensibility of C++ 531, 640
extensible language **25**, **71**, 265, 307, 511
`extern` keyword 237
`extern` storage-class specifier **235**

F

`fabs` function 215
face values of cards 391
factorial 163, 208, 262, 263, 265
`false` **116**, 118, 268
FAQs 29, 713
fatal error 15, 131, 428
fatal logic error **52**, **131**
fatal runtime error 131
Fibonacci series 265, 267
Fibonacci Series exercise 286
field width **176**, 296
FIFO (first-in first-out) **512**
file scope **238**, **446**, 504
file server **6**
filename extensions 14
    `.cpp` 14
    `.cxx` 14
    `.h` 86
fill character **444**
final state **113**, 196
final value of a control variable **166**, 171
`finish` debugger command (GNU Debugger) **742**
first-in first-out (FIFO) **512**
first refinement 130, 140, 393
fixed-point format **139**
fixed-point value 176
`fixed` stream manipulator **139**
fixed word size 510
flag value **129**
flight simulator 691
`float` data type 43, **132**, 223
`<float.h>` header file 225
floating-point arithmetic 523
floating-point constant **137**
floating-point division 138
floating-point literal
    `double` by default 137
floating-point number **132**, **139**
    `double` data type **132**
    double precision **137**
    `float` data type **132**
    single precision **137**
floating-point size limits 225
`floor` function 215, 282
flow of control 122, 136
flow of control in the `if...else` statement 117
flow of control of a `virtual` function call 680
flush output buffer 46
`fmod` function 215
`for` repetition statement **113**, 167, 168, 169, 200
`for` repetition statement examples 171
formal parameter **220**
formal type parameter **260**
formulating algorithms 123, 129
FORTRAN (FORmula TRANslator) 10
forward class declaration **514**
fractional parts 138
fractions 580
fragile software **613**
`friend` function 492, 525, 533, 589
`friend` functions to enhance performance 492
`friend` keyword 527
`friend`s are not member functions 492

Friends can access `private` members of class 493
friendship granted, not taken 493
friendship not symmetric 493
friendship not transitive 493
front of a queue 512
`<fstream>` header file 225
`<fstream.h>` header file 225
function 9, 14, 23, **39**, 221
    argument 72
    empty parentheses 70, 71, 74
    header 70
    local variable 75
    multiple parameters 74
    parameter 72, 74
    parameter list 74
    prototype **91**
    return a result 79
function body 70
function call 72, 214, 220
function call operator () 558, 682
function-call overhead 246, 556
function call stack **241**, 374
function declaration 221
function definition 74, 220, 238
function header 380
function name 237, 397
function overloading **256**
function parameter as a local variable 75
function pointer 397, 679, 682
function prototype **91**, 175, 220, 221, 238, 248, 367, 492
    parameter names optional 92
    semicolon at end 92
function prototype for `rand` in `<cstdlib>` 226
function prototype for `srand` in `<cstdlib>` 229
function prototype for `time` in `<ctime>` 231
function prototype scope **238**
function prototypes are mandatory 221
function scope **238**
function signature **221**, 257
`function template` 259, **259**, 260
function template `max` 291
function template `min` 290
function template specialization **259**
function that calls itself 261
function that takes no arguments 246
`<functional>` header file 225
functional structure of a program 41
functions for manipulating data in the standard library containers 225
functions with empty parameter lists 245, 246
fundamental type **44**

G

`-g` command-line compiler option (GNU Debugger) **735**
game of "guess the number" 286
game of chance 231
game of craps 232, 235
game playing 225
"garbage" value **127**
`gcd` function 288
`gdb` command (GNU Debugger) **736**

general class average problem 129
generating mazes of any size 270
generating mazes randomly 270
generating values to be placed into ele-
    ments of an array 299
get a value 80
get and *set* functions 80
get function 80
getline function of cin 404
getline function of the string header
    file 72, 80
gets the value of 52
global function 214
global function to overload an operator
    528
global object constructors 459
global scope 461
global variable 237, 238, 241, 255, 313
global, friend function 531
global, non-friend function 525
golden mean 265
golden ratio 265
Good Programming Practices 9, 15
goto elimination 111
goto-less programming 111
goto statement 111, 238
grade-point average 208
GradeBook.cpp 125, 133
GradeBook.h 124, 133
graph 208
graph information 303
graphics package 691
greater-than operator (>) 52
greater-than-or-equal-to operator (>=) 52
greatest common divisor (GCD) 285,
    288
gross pay 159
guard condition 115, 116, 117, 122, 172,
    178, 186
Guess the Number Game exercise 286
guillemets (« and ») in the UML 85

H

handle on an object 446
hard disk 4, 5
hardcopy printer 15
hardware 3, 4, 6
hardware platform 8
has-a relationship 485, 586
header file 86, 95, 223, 225, 442, 630,
    682
header files
    <assert.h> 225
    <cassert> 225
    <cctype> 224, 372
    <climits> 225
    <cmath> 224
    <cstdio> 225
    <cstdlib> 224, 226
    <ctime> 224, 231
    <ctype.h> 224
    <exception> 224
    <float.h> 225
    <fstream.h> 225
    <fstream> 225
    <functional> 225
    <iomanip.h> 139, 224
    <iomanip> 224

header files (cont.)
    <iostream.h> 224
    <iostream> 38, 183, 224
    <iterator> 225
    <limits.h> 225
    <limits> 225
    <list> 224
    <locale> 225
    <map> 224
    <math.h> 224
    <memory> 225
    <queue> 224
    <set> 224
    <sstream> 225
    <stack> 224
    <stdexcept> 224
    <stdio.h> 225
    <stdlib.h> 224
    <string.h> 224
    <string> 72, 225
    <time.h> 224
    <typeinfo> 224, 686
    <vector> 224, 338
    location 89
    name enclosed in angle brackets (<
        >) 89
    name enclosed in quotes (" ") 89
heap 502
help debugger command (GNU Debug-
    ger) 736
helper function 450
help-site.com 711
heuristic 355
hexadecimal 209
hexadecimal (base 16) number system
    699
hexadecimal integers 364
hide an internal data representation 512
hide implementation details 214, 509,
    514
hide names in outer scopes 239
hide private data from clients 450
hiding 491
hierarchical boss function/worker func-
    tion relationship 214
hierarchy of shapes 659
high-level language 7
highest level of precedence 49
"highest" type 222
horizontal tab ('\t') 40
host object 486
HourlyEmployee class header file 669
HourlyEmployee class implementation
    file 669
Huge integers 583
HugeInt class 579
HugeInteger 473
HugeInteger Class exercise 473
hypotenuse 278, 283
Hypotenuse exercise

I

IBM Corporation 5, 10
IBM Personal Computer 5
identifier 44, 113, 238
identifiers for variable names 235
if single-selection statement 51, 54, 113,
    115, 116, 200

if statement activity diagram 116
if...else double-selection statement
    113, 116, 117, 200
#ifndef preprocessor directive 442
ignore function 530
Implementation class definition 513
implementation file 514
implementation inheritance 662
implementation of a member function
    changes 456
implementing a proxy class 515
implicit compiler-defined conversion be-
    tween fundamental types 556
implicit conversion 138, 554, 568, 570,
    571
    via conversion constructors 570
implicit first argument 496
implicit handle 447
implicit pointer 491
implicit, user-defined conversions 554
implicitly virtual 653
imprecision of floating-point numbers
    175
improper implicit conversion 569
#include <iomanip> 139
#include <iostream> 38
#include preprocessor directive 221
including a header file multiple times 442
increment a control variable 166, 170,
    171
increment a pointer (++) 383
increment operator (++) 145, 558
indefinite postponement 392
indefinite repetition 129
indentation 54, 115, 117, 119, 167
independent software vendor (ISV) 8,
    448, 630, 682
index 294
indirect base class 585, 588
indirect derived class 673
indirection 362
indirection operator (*) 363, 366
indirectly reference a value 362
ineqality operator (!=) 533
infinite loop 122, 137, 162, 170, 265
infinite recursion 542
info break debugger command (GNU
    Debugger) 739
information hiding 22, 378, 509
inherit implementation 690
inherit interface 659, 690
inherit members of an existing class 585
inheritance 22, 442, 446, 585, 588, 629,
    682
    implementation vs. interface inherit-
        ance 662
inheritance examples 587
inheritance hierarchy 652, 661
Inheritance hierarchy for university Com-
    munityMembers 587
inheriting interface versus inheriting im-
    plementation 690
initial state in the UML 113, 196
initial value of a control variable 165, 167
initialization phase 130
initialize a constant of a built-in data type
    481
initialize a pointer 363
initialize to a consistent state 455

initialize with an assignment statement 483
initializer **296**
initializer list **296**, 298, 403
initializing a pointer declared const 376
initializing a reference 251
initializing an array's elements to zeros and printing the array 297
initializing multidimensional arrays 329
initializing the elements of an array with a declaration 297
inline function **246**
inline function definition 448
inline function to calculate the volume of a cube 247
inline keyword **246**, 247, 445, 527, 544, 557
inner block 238
innermost pair of parentheses 49
input data 14
input device 4
input from string in memory 225
input line of text into an array 404
input/output (I/O) 213
input/output library functions 225
input/output operations 112
input/output stream header file <iostream> **38**
input stream object (cin) 42, **45**
input unit 4
inserting a breakpoint 719
insertion 512
insertion sort algorithm **325**
instance of a class 77
instantiated 23
instruction 14
instruction execution cycle 426
int & 248
int keyword 39, 44, 222
int operands promoted to double 138
integer 39, **42**, 162
integer arithmetic 523
integer division **48**, 138
integer promotion **138**
integerPower 283
IntegerSet class 521
integral size limits 225
integrity of an internal data structure 512
interactive computing **45**
interchangeability of arrays and pointers 389
interest on deposit 210
interest rate 173, 208
interface **22**, **90**, 639
    inheritance **662**
Interface class definition 514
Interface class member-function definitions 515
interface inheritance **662**
interface of a class **90**
internal character string 555
internal representation of a string 546
internal stream manipulator 427
International Organization for Standardization (ISO) 511
International Standards Organization (ISO) 3, 8
Internet 6, 16
interpreter 7

interrupt handler 405
Intranet 11
intToFloat 278
Invoice class (exercise) 106
invoke a method 214
invoking a non-const member function on a const object 476
<iomanip> header file 224
<iomanip.h> header file 139, 224
<iostream> header file 38, 183, 224
<iostream.h> header file 224
is-a relationship (inheritance) **586**, 629, 640
islower function (<cctype>) 371
ISO 3
istream member function ignore 530
ISV 682
iterating **128**
iteration 123, 268, 269
iterations of a loop **123**
Iterative factorial solution 268
iterative solution **262**, 269
<iterator> header file 225
iterator **512**, **661**
iterator class 492, **661**
iterator object 512

J

Jacobson, Ivar 24, 25
Jacopini, G. 111, 200
Java 9, 12
job 5

K

keyboard 4, 5, 15, 45, 182, 185, 424
keyboard input 136
keyword **39**, 113
    table of keywords 114
keyword const in parameter list of function 247
keywords 114
    auto 236
    class 260
    const 247, 315, 316, 476, 531
    enum 234
    explicit 570, 571
    extern 237
    friend 527
    inline 246, 247, 445, 527, 544, 557
    int 39, 44, 222
    operator 524
    private 78
    public 70, 78
    return 214
    static 237
    template 259
    void 70, 80, 385
KIS ("keep it simple") 15
Knight's Tour 354
    brute force approaches 356
    closed tour test 357

L

label **238**
labels in a switch statement 238

Lady Ada Lovelace 10
LAN local area network) 5
large object 250
largest element of a collection 577
last-in, first-out (LIFO) **241**
late binding **653**
left brace ({) 39, 42
left justification 176, 396
left shift operator (<<) 523
left side of an assignment 195, 294, 462, 541
left stream manipulator 176
left-to-right associativity 55, 148
left value 195
left-to-right evaluation 49, 50
legacy code 370
length member function of class string 96
length of a string 308, 404
length of a substring 558
less-than operator 52
less-than-or-equal-to operator 52
level of indentation 117
licensing classes 467
LIFO (last-in, first-out) 241
limerick 434
<limits> header file 225
<limits.h> header file 225
line 50
linear search of an array 324
link to a class's object code 448
linkage 235
linked list 512
linker 14
linking 12, 14
Linux 6
    shell prompt 16
<list> header file 224
list debugger command (GNU Debugger) **736**
literal 45
live-code approach 2
loading 12, 14
local area network (LAN) 5
local automatic object 461
local variable 75, 236, 237, 241
<locale> header file 225
Locals window (Visual C++ .NET Debugger) 722
location in memory 46
log 10 function 216
log function 215
logarithm 215
logic error **52**, 716, 733
logical AND (&&) 190, 209
logical decision 3
logical negation 190, 192
logical NOT (!) 190, **192**, 209
logical operators 190
logical OR (||) 190, **191**, 209
logical unit 4
Logo language 353
long data type 187, 222
long double data type 223
long int data type 187, 223, 263
loop **113**, 121, 122, 123, 131
loop-continuation condition **113**, 166, 167, 168, 171, 176, 177
loop-continuation test 210

loop counter 165
loop iterations 123
loop nested within a loop 141
loop-continuation condition fails 268
looping statement 113, 121
Lord Byron 10
Lovelace, Ada 10
lowercase letters 44, 64, 114, 224, 372
"lowest type" 222
lvalue ("left value") 195, 251, 294, 342, 363, 364, 418, 462, 541, 545, 557, 568
*lvalue*s as *rvalue*s 195

M

m-by-*n* array 328
Mac OS X 6
machine dependent 7, 383, 510
machine language 6, 236
machine-language code 176
machine-language programming 423
magic numbers 301
main 39, 42
mainframe 3
maintenance of software 12
"make your point" 231
mandatory function prototypes 221
mangled function name 257
manipulator 176
"manufacturing" section of the computer 4
<map> header file 224
margin indicator bar (Visual C++ .NET Debugger) 719
maroon breakpoint circle, solid (Visual C++ .NET Debugger) 719
math library 224
math library functions 175, 215, 277
   ceil 215
   cos 215
   exp 215
   fabs 215
   floor 215
   fmod 215
   log 215
   log10 216
   pow 216
   sin 216
   sqrt 216
   tan 216
<math.h> header file 224
mathematical calculation 213
mathematical classes 523
mathematical computations 10
maximum function 216
mean 50
meaningful names 75
member function 23, 67, 68
   implementation in a separate source-code file 92
   parameter 72
member function argument 72
member function automatically inlined 445
member function call 67, 523
member function calls for const objects 476
member function calls often concise 445

member function defined in a class definition 445
member functions that take no arguments 445
member initializer 480, 481, 482, 483, 543, 555
member initializer for a const data member 483
member-initializer list 482, 486, 489
member-initializer syntax 480
Member initializer used to initialize a constant of a built-in data type 481
member-object initializer 490
member object's default constructor 491
member selection operator (.) 448, 497, 653
memberwise assignment 465, 524
memberwise copy 542
<memory> header file 225
memory 4, 42, 46, 236
memory access violation 405
memory address 362
memory consumption 679
memory leak 502
memory location 46, 47, 124
memory unit 4
menu driven system 402
merge symbol 122
message 22, 39, 523
message (send to an object) 67
method 23, 213
metric conversion program 438
MFC (Microsoft Foundation Classes) 12
Microsoft Visual C++ 14
Microsoft Visual C++ home page 28, 714
Microsoft Windows 183
Microsoft's .NET Framework Class Library 12
Microsoft's Windows-based systems 6
mileage obtained by automobiles 157
minus sign, – (UML) 82
mixed-type expression 222
model 426
modifiable 342
modifiable *lvalue* 342, 541, 545, 568
modify a constant pointer 375
modify address stored in pointer variable 375
Modifying Class GradeBook (Exercise) 106
modularizing a program with functions 213
modulus operator (%) 48, 49, 63, 162, 226, 231
monetary calculations 175
monetary formats 225
mouse 4
multidimensional array 328, 329, 330
multiple function 283
multiple inheritance 585, 588
multiple parameters to a function 74
multiple-selection statement 113, 178
multiple-source file program compilation and linking process 94
multiple-statement body 54
multiplication 48, 49
multiplicative operators (*, /, %) 138
multiprocessor 4
multiprogramming 5

Multipurpose sorting program using function pointers 398
multitasking 10
multithreading 10
mutable storage-class specifier 235
mutator 80
mystery recursive exercise 270

N

name decoration 257
name function of class type_info 686
name handle 446, 508
name mangling 257
name mangling to enable type-safe linkage 258
name of a control variable 165
name of a user-defined class 69
name of a variable 46, 235
name of an array 294, 366
named constant 299
namespace scope 238
natural language of a computer 6
natural logarithm 215
nested blocks 238
nested building block 200
nested control statement 140, 199
nested for statement 303, 330, 335
nested if...else statement 118, 119, 120
nested parentheses 49
nesting 116, 117, 167, 200
nesting rule 199
.NET platform 11
new calls the constructor 502
new operator 501, 543
newline ('\n') escape sequence 40, 46, 55, 403
newline character 115, 185
nickname 363
non-static member function 545
non-const member function 480
non-const member function called on a const object 478
non-const member function on a non-const object 477
nonconstant pointer to constant data 371, 373, 374
nonconstant pointer to nonconstant data 371
nondestructive read 47
nonfatal logic error 52
nonfatal runtime error 15
Non-friend/non-member functions cannot access private members 495
nonmodifiable function code 446
nonparameterized stream manipulator 139
non-static member function 496, 508
nonvirtual destructor 686
nonzero treated as true 195
noshowpos stream manipulator 427
not equal 52
note in the UML 113
nouns in a system specification (UML) 23
NULL 362
null character ('\0') 308, 373, 390, 403, 404, 406, 412
null pointer 363, 364

null statement 121
null-terminated string 309, 390
number of arguments 220
number of elements in an array 381
numerical data type limits 225

O

object 8, 11, 67
object (or instance) 3, 22
object code 7, 14, 95, 448
object file 682
object handle 449, 508
object leaves scope 458
Object Management Group (OMG) 25
object module 448
object of a derived class 641, 646
object of a derived class is instantiated 621
object orientation 22
object-oriented analysis and design
    (OOAD) 24
object-oriented design (OOD) 22, 493
object-oriented language 12, 23
object-oriented programming (OOP) 3,
    4, 8, 16, 23, 24, 442, 585
object's *vtable* pointer 682
object-oriented programming (OOP) 2
objects contain only data 446
octal 209
octal number system (base 8) 699
odd integer 207
odd number 210
off-by-one error 129, 168, 169, 295
offset 682
offset to a pointer 386
"old-style" header files 223
OMG (Object Management Group) 25
one's complement 706
ones position 699
OOAD (object-oriented analysis and de-
    sign) 24
OOD (object-oriented design) 22
OOP (object-oriented programming) 2,
    3, 4, 8, 16, 23, 24, 585
operand 39, 46, 48, 118, 423
operating system 5, 6, 8, 405
operation code 423
operation in the UML 22, 71
operation parameter in the UML 75
operations that can be performed on data
    510
operator associativity 194
operator functions 527
operator keyword 524
operator overloading 46, 259, 523
    decrement operators 558
    increment operators 558
operator precedence 49, 148, 194
operator precedence and associativity
    chart 56
operator! member function 532
operator!= function 544
operator() function 577
operator+ function 524
operator++ function 559, 564
operator< function 557
operator<< function 531, 541, 554,
    582
operator= function 543

operator== function 544, 557
operator>= function 557
operator>> function 530, 541, 554
operator[]
    const version 544
operators
    ! (logical NOT operator) 190, 192
    != (inequality operator) 52
    % (modulus operator) 48
    %= modulus assignment 145
    && (logical AND operator) 190
    * (multiplication operator) 48
    * (pointer dereference or indirection)
        363, 365
    *= (multiplication assignment) 145
    + (addition operator) 46, 48
    += addition assignment 145
    / (division operator) 48
    /= (division assignment) 145
    < (less-than operator) 52
    << (stream insertion operator) 39, 46
    <= (less-than-or-equal-to operator)
        52
    = (assignment operator) 46, 48, 192
    -= (subtraction assignment) 145
    == (equality operator) 52, 192
    > (greater-than operator) 52
    >= (greater-than-or-equal-to opera-
        tor) 52
    >> (stream extraction operator) 46
    || (logical OR operator) 190, 191
    addition assignment (+=) 145
    address (&) 365
    arithmetic 145
    arrow member selection (->) 448,
        496
    assignment 145
    binary scope resolution (::) 92
    conditional (?:) 117
    decrement (--) 145, 146
    delete 501, 686
    dot (.) 71
    increment (++) 145, 146
    member selection (.) 448
    multiplicative (*, /, %) 138
    new 501, 543
    postfix decrement 146
    postfix increment 146, 148
    prefix decrement 146
    prefix increment 145, 146, 148
    sizeof 380, 382, 446, 496
    ternary 117
    typeid 686
    unary minus (-) 138
    unary plus (+) 138
    unary scope resolution (::) 255
operators that can be overloaded 525
optimizations on constants 476
optimizing compiler 176, 237, 476
order in which actions should execute
    109, 123
order in which constructors and destruc-
    tors are called 459, 461
order in which operators are applied to
    their operands 266
order of evaluation 267
order of evaluation of operators 49, 62
out-of-range element 541, 557
out of scope 241

outer block 238
outer for statement 330
output data 14
output device 4
output to string in memory 225
output unit 4
oval 63
overflow error 510
overhead of an extra function call 544
overload an operator as a non-member,
    non-friend function 527
overload the addition operator (+) 524
overload unary operator ! 532
overloaded += concatenation operator
    556
overloaded << operator 527, 557
overloaded [] operator 541
overloaded addition assignment operator
    (+=) 560
overloaded assignment (=) operator 540,
    543, 554, 555
overloaded binary operators 526
overloaded cast operator function 545
overloaded concatenation operator 556
overloaded equality operator (==) 540,
    544, 557
overloaded function call operator () 558
overloaded function definitions 256, 257
overloaded increment operator 560
overloaded inequality operator 540, 544
overloaded less than operator 557
overloaded negation operator 557
overloaded operator += 564
overloaded operator[] member func-
    tion 544
overloaded postfix increment operator
    560, 564
overloaded prefix increment operator
    560, 564
overloaded stream insertion and stream
    extraction operators 529
overloaded string concatenation operator
    556
overloaded subscript operator 541, 544,
    558, 577
overloaded unary operators 526
overloading 46, 256
overloading + 526
overloading += 526
overloading << and >> 259
overloading a member function 448
overloading an assignment operator 526
overloading binary operator < 532
overloading binary operators 532
overloading function call operator ()
    558, 576
overloading operators 259
overloading prefix and postfix decrement
    operators 560
overloading prefix and postfix increment
    operators 560
overloading stream insertion and stream
    extraction operators 528, 540, 541,
    554, 560, 564
override a function 652

P

π 209

Package inheritance hierarchy 691
Package inheritance hierarchy exercise 635
page layout software 402
pair of braces {} 54, 98
parallel activities 10
parallelogram 586
parameter 72, 74, 236
parameter in the UML 75
parameter list 74, 84
parameterized stream manipulator 139, 176
parentheses operator (()) 49, 138
parentheses to force order of evaluation 56
partitioning step 430
Pascal, Blaise 10
pass-by-reference 248, 313, 361, 367, 368, 370, 377
   with reference parameters 249
pass-by-reference with a pointer argument used to cube a variable's value 368
pass-by-reference with pointer arguments 250, 366
pass-by-reference with reference arguments 366
pass-by-value 248, 249, 313, 366, 367, 368, 369, 379
pass-by-value used to cube a variable's value 367
pass size of an array as an argument 313, 380
passing an array element 314
passing an entire array 314
passing an object by value 467
passing arguments by value and by reference 249
passing arrays and individual array elements to functions 314
passing arrays to functions 312
passing large objects 250
passing options to a program 391
Payroll System Modification exercise 691
percent sign (%) (modulus operator) 48
perfect number 285
Perfect Numbers exercise 285
perform a task 70
perform an action 39
performance 9
Performance Tip 9
personal computer 3, 5
Peter Minuit problem 176, 210
phases of a program 130
PhoneNumber class 582
pi 63
Pig Latin 434
platform 15
Plauger, P.J. 8
playing cards 391
plus sign, + (UML) 72
pointer 361, 383
pointer arithmetic 372, 383, 385, 387
pointer arithmetic is machine dependent 383
pointer arithmetic on a character array 384
pointer assignment 385
pointer-based strings 403
pointer comparison 386

pointer dereference (*) operator 363, 365
pointer exercises 428
pointer expression 383, 386
pointer handle 446
pointer manipulation 679
pointer notation 387
pointer operators & and * 365
pointer subtraction 383
pointer to a function 397, 398
pointer to an object 374, 445
pointer to **void** (**void** *) 385
pointer values as hexadecimal integers 364
pointer/offset notation 386
pointer/subscript notation 387
pointers and array subscripting 386, 387
pointers and arrays 386
pointers declared **const** 375
pointers to dynamically allocated storage 497, 544
poker playing program 421
poll analysis program 305
Polymorphic banking program exercise using **Account** hierarchy 691
polymorphic programming 659, 661, 682
polymorphic screen manager 640
Polymorphic screen manager exercise using **Shape** hierarchy 691
polymorphism 187, 631, 638, 639, 640, 655
polymorphism and references 679
polymorphism as an alternative to **switch** logic 690
polynomial 51
Polynomial class 580
pop off a stack 241
portability 15
Portability Tip 9, 15
portable 8
portable code 8
portable language 15
position number 294
positional notation 699
positional value 162, 700
positional values in the decimal number system 700
postdecrement 146, 148
postfix decrement operator 146
postfix increment operator 146, 148
postincrement 146, 564
pow function 50, 174, 176, 216
power 216
power 153
precedence 49, 50, 55, 148, 170, 192, 266
precedence chart 56
precedence not changed by overloading 525
precedence of the conditional operator 118
precision 139
precision of a floating-point value 133, 139
precompiled object file 514
predecrement 146, 148
predicate function 450
prefix decrement operator 146
prefix increment operator 145, 146, 148
preincrement 146, 564
"prepackaged" functions 213

preprocess 12
preprocessor 14, 221
preprocessor directives 14, 38, 42
   #define 442
   #endif 442
   #ifndef 442
preprocessor wrapper 442
prevent class objects from being copied 544
prevent one class object from being assigned to another 544
preventing header files from being included more than once 442
primary memory 4, 14
prime 285
Prime Numbers exercise 285
primitive data type promotion 138
primitive type 44
principle of least privilege 236, 306, 317, 368, 370, 380, 390, 450, 475, 476
print debugger command (GNU Debugger) 738
printer 15
printing a line of text with multiple statements 41
Printing a string one character at a time using a nonconstant pointer to constant data 373
printing dates 436
printing multiple lines of text with a single statement 42
private access specifier 78
private base class 629
private base-class data cannot be accessed from derived class 602
private data member 463
private inheritance 586, 588, 629
private libraries 14
private members of a base class 588
private static data member 505
probability 226
procedural programming language 23
procedure 109, 213
processing phase 130
processing unit 4
product of odd integers 208
program 3
program control 110
program development environment 12
program development tool 115, 132
program execution stack 241
program in the general 638, 690
program in the specific 638
program termination 461, 462
programmer 3
programming environment 213
promotion 138
promotion hierarchy for built-in data types 223
promotion rules 222
prompt 45, 136
proprietary classes 630
protected access specifier 442, 589
protected base class 629
protected base-class data can be accessed from derived class 611
protected inheritance 586, 588, 629
protection mechanism 467

proxy class 450, 513, 515
pseudocode 24, 110, 115, 117, 124, 140, 394
   first refinement 130
   second refinement 130
   top 130
   top-down, stepwise refinement 132
   two levels of refinement 132
pseudorandom numbers 229
public access specifier 70, 78
public base class 629
public inheritance 585, 588
public interface 78
public keyword 70, 78
public member of a derived class 589
public services of a class 90
public static class member 504
public static member function 505
punctuation mark 411
pure procedure 446
pure specifier 660
pure virtual function 660, 679
purpose of the program 38
push onto a stack 241
Pythagorean triples 209

Q

Quadralay Corporation's Web site 712
qualified name 619
qualityPoints function 285
<queue> header file 224
queue 511, 512
Quick Info box 720
quicksort 430
quit debugger command (GNU Debugger) 739
quotation marks 39

R

radians 215
radius of a circle 163
raise to a power 204, 216
rand function 226, 351
RAND_MAX symbolic constant 226
random integers in range 1 to 6 226
random number 229
randomizing 229
randomizing the die-rolling program 229
range checking 533
rapid application development (RAD) 467
Rational class 472
Rational Class exercise 472
Rational Software Corporation 25
RationalNumber class 580
raw array 510
read a line of text 74
read characters with getline 74
read-only variable 299
readability 115, 141
real number 132
reassign a reference 252
"receiving" section of the computer 4
Rectangle Class
Rectangle Class exercise 473
recursion 261, 268, 269, 287
recursion examples and exercises 270

recursion step 262, 265
recursive binary search 270
recursive call 262, 265
recursive Eight Queens 270, 359
recursive factorial function 270
recursive Fibonacci function 270
recursive function 261
recursive greatest common divisor 270
recursive linear search 270, 324, 359
recursive maze traversal 270
recursive quicksort 270
recursive selection sort 270, 358
recursive solution 269
recursive step 430
recursive sum of two integers 270
recursive Towers of Hanoi 270
recursively calculate minimum value in an array 270
recursively check if a string is a palindrome 270
recursively determine whether a string is a palindrome 358
recursively print a string backward 270, 359
recursively print an array 270, 359
recursively raising an integer to an integer power 270
redundant parentheses 51, 191
reentrant code 446
reference 361
reference argument 366
reference parameter 248, 248, 250
reference to a constant 250
reference to a private data member 462
reference to an automatic variable 252
reference to an int 249
reference to an object 445
reference to constant data 374
references must be initialized 252
referencing array elements 387
referencing array elements with the array name and with pointers 387
refinement process 130
register declaration 237
register storage-class specifier 235
reinventing the wheel 9
relational operator 52, 53
relational operators >, <, >=, and <= 168, 190
release dynamically allocated memory 543
remainder after integer division 48
repeatability of function rand 229
repetition 200
   counter controlled 123, 124, 136
   definite 123
   indefinite 129
   sentinel controlled 129, 132
repetition statement 111, 114, 121, 131
   do…while 176, 177, 178, 200
   for 167, 168, 169, 200
   while 121, 136, 166, 176, 200
repetition terminates 121, 122
replace == operator with = 195
requesting a service from an object 67
requirements 15, 24
return a result 221
return a value 39
Return key 45
return keyword 214

return statement 40, 214, 221, 262
return type 70
   void 70, 80
return type in a function header 221
returning a reference from a function 252
returning a reference to a private data member 463
Returning Error Indicators from Class Time's *set* Functions exercise 473
reusability 380
reusable software component 8, 12, 467
reuse 23, 86, 446
reusing components 12
Reverse Digits exercise 285
Richards, Martin 8
right brace (}) 39, 40, 136
right justification 176, 396
right operand 39
right shift operator (>>) 523
right stream manipulator 176
right-to-left associativity 55, 148
right triangle 163, 209
right value (*rvalue*) 195
rightmost (trailing) arguments 253
rise-and-shine algorithm 109
Ritchie, D. 8
Rogue Wave 12
rolling a die 227
rolling a six-sided die 6000 times 227
rolling two dice 231, 351
round a floating-point number for display purposes 139
rounding 139
rounding numbers 215
row subscript 328
rows 328
RTTI (runtime type information) 639, 683
rule of thumb 190
rules for forming structured programs 196
rules of operator precedence 49
Rumbaugh, James 24, 25
run debugger command (GNU Debugger) 736
running total 130
runtime error 15
runtime type information (RTTI) 224, 639, 683
rvalue ("right value") 195, 251, 541, 545

S

SalariedEmployee class header file 667
SalariedEmployee class implementation file 667
SalesPerson class definition 450
SalesPerson class member-function definitions 451
savings account 173
SavingsAccount class 520
scalable 301
scalar 313, 379
scalar quantity 313
scale 301
scaling 226
scaling factor 226, 231
scanning images 4
scientific notation 139
scope 169

scope of an identifier 235, 237
scope resolution operator (::) 504
scopes
    block 238
    class 238
    file 238
    function 238
    function prototype 238
    namespace 238
scoping example 239
screen 4, 5, 15, 38
screen cursor 40
screen-manager program 640
scrutinize data 443
search key 324
searching 512
searching arrays 324
searching strings 405
second-degree polynomial 50, 51
second refinement 130, 131, 141, 393
secondary storage device 13
secondary storage unit 5
security 467
seed 230
seed function rand 229
select a substring 558
selection 199, 200
selection sort 358
selection sort algorithm 377
selection sort with call-by-reference 378
selection statement 111, 114
self assignment 543, 555
self-assignment 497, 543
self-documenting 44
semicolon (;) 39, 55, 74, 121
sentinel-controlled repetition 131, 132, 136
sentinel value 129, 131, 136, 183
separate interface from implementation 90
sequence 198, 200
sequence of integers 207
sequence of random numbers 229
sequence statement 111, 112, 114
sequence-statement activity diagram 112
sequential execution 111
services of a class 80
<set> header file 224
set a value 80
set and *get* functions 80
set debugger command (GNU Debugger) 740
set function 80, 491
set of recursive calls to function Fibonacci 267
set the value of a private data member 81
setfill parameterized stream manipulator 427, 444
setprecision stream manipulator 139, 175
setw parameterized stream manipulator 176, 296, 404, 530
Shakespeare, William 435
Shape class hierarchy 588, 635
Shape hierarchy exercise 691
shell prompt on Linux 16
shift a range of numbers 226
shifted, scaled integers 227

shifted, scaled integers produced by 1 + rand() % 6 226
shiftingValue 231
"shipping" section of the computer 4
short-circuit evaluation 192
short data type 187, 222
short int data type 187
showpoint stream manipulator 139
showpos stream manipulator 427
shrink-wrapped software 630
shuffle cards 392
side effect 248
side effect of an expression 237, 248, 267
sides of a right triangle 163
sides of a square 209
sides of a triangle 163
Sieve of Eratosthenes 357
signal value 129
signature 221, 257, 558
signatures of overloaded prefix and postfix increment operators 559
simple condition 190, 191
simplest activity diagram 196, 198
Simpletron Machine Language (SML) 432
Simpletron Simulator 432
Simula 11
simulated deck of cards 392
simulation 426
Simulation: Tortoise and the Hare 422
sin function 216
sine 216
single-argument constructor 545, 554, 569, 571
single entry point 196
single-entry/single-exit control statement 114, 116, 196
single exit point 196
single inheritance 585
single-line comment 37
single-precision floating-point number 137
single quote 40
single quote (') character 403
single selection 200
single-selection if statement 113, 115, 119
single-selection statement 178
six-sided die 226
size member function of vector 313, 342
size of a variable 46, 235
size of an array 309, 380
size_t type 380
sizeof operator 380, 382, 446, 496
sizeof operator used to determine standard data type sizes 382
sizeof operator when applied to an array name returns the number of bytes in the array 381
skip remainder of switch statement 188
skip remaining code in loop 189
small circle symbol 112
smaller integer sizes 188
smallest 278
smallest of several integers 208
"smart array" 308
SML 423
SML operation code 423

"sneakernet" 5
software 3, 4
software asset 24
software engineering 69, 89, 90
    data hiding 78, 80
    encapsulation 81
    reuse 86, 89
    separate interface from implementation 90
    set and *get* functions 80
Software Engineering Observation 9
software reuse 9, 40, 213, 585
solid circle symbol 113
Solution Configurations ComboBox 718
sort algorithms
    insertion sort 325
    selection sort 377
sorting 512
sorting arrays 325
sorting strings 225
source code 13, 448, 629
source-code file 86
space (' ') 43
speaking to a computer 4
special characters 43, 403
Special Section: Building Your Own Computer 423
specifics 640
spiral 265
sqrt function of <cmath> header file 216
square 162
square function 222
square root 216
srand function 229, 231
srand(time(0)) 230
<sstream> header file 225
<stack> header file 224
stack 241, 512
stack frame 242
stack overflow 242
stacked building blocks 200
stacking 116, 117, 200
stacking rule 196
stacks implemented with arrays 509
"stand-alone" units 5
standard class libraries 511
standard data type sizes 382
standard error stream (cerr) 15
standard input object (cin) 45
Standard Library 213
Standard Library header files 225
standard output object (cout) 39
"standardized, interchangeable parts" 24
"warehouse" section of the computer 5
starvation 392
statement 39, 70
statement spread over several lines 55
statement terminator (;) 39
statements
    break 184, 188, 210
    continue 188, 210
    do...while 176, 177, 178, 200
    for 167, 168, 169, 200
    if 51, 54, 200
    if...else 200
    return 40, 214
    switch 178, 185, 200

statements (cont.)
    `while` 166, 176, 200
`static` array initialization 310
static binding 653
`static_cast<int>` 182
`static` data member 321, 503, 505
`static` data member tracking the number of objects of a class 507
`static` data members save storage 504
`static` keyword 237
`static` local object 459, 461
`static` local variable 239, 241, 310
`static` member 504
`static` member function 508
static storage class 235, 236, 238
`static` storage-class specifier 235
`static_cast` 148, 194
`static_cast` (compile-time type-checked cast) 295
`std::cin` 42, 45
`std::cout` 39
`std::endl` stream manipulator 46
`<stdexcept>` header file 224
`<stdio.h>` header file 225
`<stdlib.h>` header file 224
`step` debugger command (GNU Debugger) 742
Step Into command (Visual C++ .NET Debugger) 726
Step Out command (Visual C++ .NET Debugger) 727
Step Over command (Visual C++ .NET Debugger) 726
stepwise refinement 393
"sticky" setting 176, 444
storage class 235, 237
storage-class specifiers 235
    `auto` 235
    `extern` 235
    `mutable` 235
    `register` 235
    `static` 235
straight-line form 48, 50
straight-time 159
`strcat` function of header file `<cstring>` 405, 407
`strcmp` function of header file `<cstring>` 405, 409
`strcpy` function of header file `<cstring>` 405, 406
stream extraction operator >> ("get from") 42, 45, 54, 259, 523, 528, 541
stream input/output 38
stream insertion operator << ("put to") 39, 41, 46, 259, 523, 528, 541
stream manipulator 46, 139, 176
stream manipulators
    `boolalpha` 193
    `fixed` 139
    `left` 176
    `right` 176
    `setprecision` 139, 175
    `setw` 176
    `showpoint` 139
    `std::endl` (end line) 46
stream of characters 39
`<string>` header file 225
string 402
`string` 492, 567

string array 390
string being tokenized 412
`string` class 72, 225, 492, 511, 524, 565, 567
    `length` member function 96
    `substr` member function 98, 568
`String` class definition with operator overloading 546
`String` class member-function and `friend`-function definitions 548
`String` class test program 551
string constant 403
string copying 389
string copying using array notation and pointer notation 389
string data type 511
`<string>` header file 72
string is a constant pointer 403
string length 412
string literal 39, 45, 308, 309, 403, 404
string manipulation 213
`string` object
    empty string 80
    initial value 80
string of characters 39
string processing 361
`<string.h>` header file 224
`<string>` header file 72, 89, 565
strings as full-fledged objects 402
`strlen` function of header file `<cstring>` 406, 412
`strncat` function of header file `<cstring>` 405, 408
`strncmp` function of header file `<cstring>` 406, 409
`strncpy` function of header file `<cstring>` 405, 406
Stroustrup, B. 8, 11, 29, 713
`strtok` function of header file `<cstring>` 406, 411
structure 293
structured program 196
structured programming 3, 4, 10, 11, 109, 111, 190
structured programming summary 196
structured systems analysis and design 11
student-poll-analysis program 305
subclass 585
subproblem 262
subscript 294
subscript 0 (zero) 294
subscript range checking 511
subscripted name of an array element 313
subscripted name used as an *rvalue* 541
subscripting with a pointer and an offset 387
`substr` member function of class `string` 98, 568
substring 558
substring length 558
subtract an integer from a pointer 383
subtract one pointer from another 383
subtraction 4, 48, 49
suit values of cards 391
sum of the elements of an array 301
summing integers with the `for` statement 173
superclass 585
supercomputer 3

survey 305, 307
swapping values 325, 377
`switch` logic 187, 659, 688
`switch` multiple-selection statement 178, 185, 200
`switch` multiple-selection statement activity diagram with `break` statements 187
synonym 363, 366
syntax 40
syntax error 40

T

tab 55
tab character 115
tab escape sequence \t 185
Tab key 41
tab stop 40
table of values 328
tabular format 296
tails 226
`tan` function 216
tangent 216
task 5
telephone 163
template definition 260
template function 260
`template` keyword 259
template parameter list 259
temporary object 546
temporary `String` object 556
temporary value 138, 222
terminal 5
terminate a loop 131
terminate successfully 40
terminating condition 263
terminating execution 512
terminating null character 308, 310, 403, 404, 406, 412
terminating null character, '0', of a string 491
terminating right brace (}) of a block 238
termination condition 307
termination housekeeping 458
termination phase 130
termination test 268
ternary conditional operator (`?:`) 267, 526
ternary operator 117
test characters 224
text analysis 435
text editor 402
text-printing program 38
third refinement 393
`this` pointer 491, 496, 497, 508, 527, 543
`this` pointer used explicitly 496
`this` pointer used implicitly and explicitly to access members of an object 496
Thompson, Ken 8
throughput 5
`TicTacToe` class exercise 473
tilde character (~) 458
time-and-a-half 159, 209
`Time` class 472
`Time` class containing a constructor with default arguments 453
`Time` class definition 441

Time class definition modified to enable cascaded member-function calls 498

Time class member function definitions, including const member functions 478

Time class member-function definitions 443

Time class member-function definitions, including a constructor that takes arguments 454

Time class with const member functions 477

time function 231

<time.h> header file 224

timesharing 5, 11

token 406, 411

tokenizing strings 405, 411

top 130

top-down, stepwise refinement 130, 132, 393

Tortoise and the Hare 422

total 124, 130, 236

toupper function (<cctype>) 372

Towers of Hanoi 287

transfer of control 111

transition 113

transition arrow 112, 113, 115, 117, 122

translate 14

translation 6

translator program 7

transmit securely 163

trapezoid 586

tree 512

trigonometric cosine 215

trigonometric sine 216

trigonometric tangent 216

tripleByReference 290

tripleCallByValue 290

true 51

true 115, 116, 118, 166

truncate 48, 129, 138, 491, 501

truncate fractional part of a double 222

truth table 191

    ! (logical NOT) operator 193

    && (logical AND) operator 191

    || (logical OR) operator 192

Turing Machine 111

turtle graphics 353

two-dimensional array 328, 331

two-dimensional array manipulations 331

two largest values 159

two levels of refinement 132

two's complement 706

twos position 701

type name (enumerations) 234

type of a variable 46, 235

type of the this pointer 496

type parameter 260

type qualifier 316

type-safe linkage 257

type_info class 686

typeid operator 686

<typeinfo> header file 224, 686

typename 260

u

ultimate operator overloading exercise 576

UML 71

    action expression 112, 116, 122

    action state 112, 113

    activity diagram 112, 117, 122, 171

    arrow 112

    attribute 71

    class diagram 71

    constructor in a class diagram 85

    data types 75

    decision 116

    decision symbol 115

    diamond symbol 112, 115

    dotted line 113

    final state 113

    guard condition 115, 116, 122

    guillemets (« and ») 85

    initial state 113

    merge symbol 122

    minus sign (–) 82

    note 113

    plus sign (+) 72

    public operation 72

    small circle symbol 112

    solid circle symbol 113

    String type 75

    transition 113

    transition arrow 112, 113, 115, 117, 122

UML (Unified Modeling Language) 22, 24, 112

UML activity diagram 112

UML class diagram

    constructor 85

UML Partners 25

unary cast operator 138

unary decrement operator (--) 145

unary increment operator (++) 145

unary minus (-) operator 138

unary operator 138, 192, 363

unary operator overload 526, 532

unary plus (+) operator 138

unary scope resolution operator (::) 255

undefined value 127

underscore (_) 44

Unified Modeling Language (UML) 22, 24, 112

unincremented copy of an object 564

uninitialized local reference causes a syntax error 251

uninitialized variable 127

universal-time format 444

UNIX 6, 8, 11

unmodifiable 342, 568

unmodifiable lvalue 342, 568

unsigned char data type 223

unsigned data type 223, 229

unsigned int data type 223, 229, 380

unsigned long data type 223, 264

unsigned long int data type 223, 264

unsigned short data type 223

unsigned short int data type 223

uppercase letter 43, 64, 224, 372

user-defined class name 69

user-defined function 213, 216

    maximum 216

user-defined type 23, 71, 234, 545

using a function template 259

Using a static data member to maintain a count of the number of objects of a class 505

using arrays instead of switch 304

using declaration 53

<utility> header file 225

utility function demonstration 452

V

validation 96

validity checking 96

value 45

value of a variable 46, 235

value of an array element 294

variable 42

variable name 46

    argument 74

    parameter 74

variable size 46

variable type 46

<vector> header file 224, 338

vector class 338, 565

verbs in a system specification 23

vertical spacing 115, 167

vi 14

virtual destructor 686, 687

virtual function 639, 652, 679, 681

virtual function call 681

virtual function call illustrated 680

virtual function table (vtable) 679

virtual memory operating systems 11

Visual Basic .NET 11

Visual C++ .NET 11

Visual C++ home page 28, 714

Visual Studio .NET

    Quick Info box 720

visualizing recursion 270

void keyword 70, 80, 385

void return type 222

volume of a cube 247

vtable (virtual function table) 679, 681, 682

vtable pointer 682

W

"walk off" either end of an array 533

warning 40

watch debugger command (GNU Debugger) 744

Watch window (Visual C++ .NET debugger) 722, 723

webstore.ansi.org/ansidocstore/default.asp 15

while repetition statement 113, 121, 136, 166, 176, 200

white space 38

white-space characters 39, 55, 115, 185, 309

    blank 115

    newline 115

    tab 115

whole number 42

width of random number range 231

Windows 183

word 423

word equivalent of a check amount 437

word processing 402, 436

workflow of a portion of a software system 112

workstation 6

World Wide Web (WWW) 6

wraparound 564

www.accu.informika.ru/resources/public/terse/cpp.htm 29

www.acm.org/crossroads/xrds3-2/ovp32.html 29

www.borland.com 14

www.borland.com/bcppbuilder 28

www.codearchive.com/list.php?go=0708 29

www.compilers.net 28

www.cuj.com 29

www.deitel.com 2, 28

www.deitel.com/newsletter/subscribe.html 3, 28

www.devx.com 29

www.forum.nokia.com/main/0,6566,050_20,00.html 29

www.gametutorials.com/Tutorials/GT/GT_Pg1.htm 29

www.hal9k.com/cug 29

www.kai.com/C_plus_plus 29

www.mathtools.net/C_C__/Games/ 29

www.metrowerks.com 14

www.msdn.microsoft.com/visualc/ 14

www.omg.org 25

www.prenhall.com/deitel 28

www.research.att.com/~bs/homepage.html 29

www.symbian.com/developer/development/cppdev.html 29

www.thefreecountry.com/developercity/ccompilers.shtml 28

www.uml.org 25

y

yellow arrow in break mode 720

z

zero-based counting 169

zeroth element 294

End User License Agreements

Prentice Hall License Agreement and Limited Warranty

READ THE FOLLOWING TERMS AND CONDITIONS CAREFULLY BEFORE OPENING THIS SOFTWARE PACKAGE. THIS LEGAL DOCUMENT IS AN AGREEMENT BETWEEN YOU AND PRENTICE-HALL, INC. (THE "COMPANY"). BY OPENING THIS SEALED SOFT-WARE PACKAGE, YOU ARE AGREEING TO BE BOUND BY THESE TERMS AND CONDI-TIONS. IF YOU DO NOT AGREE WITH THESE TERMS AND CONDITIONS, DO NOT OPEN THE SOFTWARE PACKAGE. PROMPTLY RETURN THE UNOPENED SOFTWARE PACKAGE AND ALL ACCOMPANYING ITEMS TO THE PLACE YOU OBTAINED THEM FOR A FULL REFUND OF ANY SUMS YOU HAVE PAID.

1.GRANT OF LICENSE: In consideration of your purchase of this book, and your agreement to abide by the terms and conditions of this Agreement, the Company grants to you a nonexclusive right to use and display the copy of the enclosed software program (hereinafter the "SOFTWARE") on a single computer (i.e., with a single CPU) at a single location so long as you comply with the terms of this Agreement. The Company reserves all rights not expressly granted to you under this Agreement.

2.OWNERSHIP OF SOFTWARE: You own only the magnetic or physical media (the enclosed media) on which the SOFTWARE is recorded or fixed, but the Company and the software developers retain all the rights, title, and ownership to the SOFTWARE recorded on the original media copy(ies) and all subsequent copies of the SOFTWARE, regardless of the form or media on which the original or other copies may exist. This license is not a sale of the original SOFTWARE or any copy to you.

3.COPY RESTRICTIONS: This SOFTWARE and the accompanying printed materials and user manual (the "Documentation") are the subject of copyright. The individual programs on the media are copyrighted by the authors of each program. Some of the programs on the media include separate licensing agreements. If you intend to use one of these programs, you must read and follow its accompa-nying license agreement. You may not copy the Documentation or the SOFTWARE, except that you may make a single copy of the SOFTWARE for backup or archival purposes only. You may be held legally responsible for any copying or copyright infringement which is caused or encouraged by your failure to abide by the terms of this restriction.

4.USE RESTRICTIONS: You may not network the SOFTWARE or otherwise use it on more than one computer or computer terminal at the same time. You may physically transfer the SOFTWARE from one computer to another provided that the SOFTWARE is used on only one computer at a time. You may not distribute copies of the SOFTWARE or Documentation to others. You may not reverse engi-neer, disassemble, decompile, modify, adapt, translate, or create derivative works based on the SOFT-WARE or the Documentation without the prior written consent of the Company.

5. TRANSFER RESTRICTIONS: The enclosed SOFTWARE is licensed only to you and may not be transferred to any one else without the prior written consent of the Company. Any unauthorized transfer of the SOFTWARE shall result in the immediate termination of this Agreement.

6. TERMINATION: This license is effective until terminated. This license will terminate automat-ically without notice from the Company and become null and void if you fail to comply with any provi-sions or limitations of this license. Upon termination, you shall destroy the Documentation and all copies of the SOFTWARE. All provisions of this Agreement as to warranties, limitation of liability, remedies or damages, and our ownership rights shall survive termination.

7. MISCELLANEOUS: This Agreement shall be construed in accordance with the laws of the United States of America and the State of New York and shall benefit the Company, its affiliates, and assignees.

8.LIMITED WARRANTY AND DISCLAIMER OF WARRANTY: The Company warrants that the SOFTWARE, when properly used in accordance with the Documentation, will operate in substantial conformity with the description of the SOFTWARE set forth in the Documentation. The Company does not warrant that the SOFTWARE will meet your requirements or that the operation of the SOFTWARE will be uninterrupted or error-free. The Company warrants that the media on which the SOFTWARE is delivered shall be free from defects in materials and workmanship under normal use for a period of thirty

(30) days from the date of your purchase. Your only remedy and the Company's only obligation under these limited warranties is, at the Company's option, return of the warranted item for a refund of any amounts paid by you or replacement of the item. Any replacement of SOFTWARE or media under the warranties shall not extend the original warranty period. The limited warranty set forth above shall not apply to any SOFTWARE which the Company determines in good faith has been subject to misuse, neglect, improper installation, repair, alteration, or damage by you. EXCEPT FOR THE EXPRESSED WARRANTIES SET FORTH ABOVE, THE COMPANY DISCLAIMS ALL WARRANTIES, EXPRESS OR IMPLIED, INCLUDING WITHOUT LIMITATION, THE IMPLIED WARRANTIES OF MERCHANTABILITY AND FITNESS FOR A PARTICULAR PURPOSE. EXCEPT FOR THE EXPRESS WARRANTY SET FORTH ABOVE, THE COMPANY DOES NOT WARRANT, GUARANTEE, OR MAKE ANY REPRESENTATION REGARDING THE USE OR THE RESULTS OF THE USE OF THE SOFTWARE IN TERMS OF ITS CORRECTNESS, ACCURACY, RELIABILITY, CURRENTNESS, OR OTHERWISE.

IN NO EVENT, SHALL THE COMPANY OR ITS EMPLOYEES, AGENTS, SUPPLIERS, OR CONTRACTORS BE LIABLE FOR ANY INCIDENTAL, INDIRECT, SPECIAL, OR CONSEQUENTIAL DAMAGES ARISING OUT OF OR IN CONNECTION WITH THE LICENSE GRANTED UNDER THIS AGREEMENT, OR FOR LOSS OF USE, LOSS OF DATA, LOSS OF INCOME OR PROFIT, OR OTHER LOSSES, SUSTAINED AS A RESULT OF INJURY TO ANY PERSON, OR LOSS OF OR DAMAGE TO PROPERTY, OR CLAIMS OF THIRD PARTIES, EVEN IF THE COMPANY OR AN AUTHORIZED REPRESENTATIVE OF THE COMPANY HAS BEEN ADVISED OF THE POSSIBILITY OF SUCH DAMAGES. IN NO EVENT SHALL LIABILITY OF THE COMPANY FOR DAMAGES WITH RESPECT TO THE SOFTWARE EXCEED THE AMOUNTS ACTUALLY PAID BY YOU, IF ANY, FOR THE SOFTWARE.

SOME JURISDICTIONS DO NOT ALLOW THE LIMITATION OF IMPLIED WARRANTIES OR LIABILITY FOR INCIDENTAL, INDIRECT, SPECIAL, OR CONSEQUENTIAL DAMAGES, SO THE ABOVE LIMITATIONS MAY NOT ALWAYS APPLY. THE WARRANTIES IN THIS AGREEMENT GIVE YOU SPECIFIC LEGAL RIGHTS AND YOU MAY ALSO HAVE OTHER RIGHTS WHICH VARY IN ACCORDANCE WITH LOCAL LAW.

ACKNOWLEDGMENT
YOU ACKNOWLEDGE THAT YOU HAVE READ THIS AGREEMENT, UNDERSTAND IT, AND AGREE TO BE BOUND BY ITS TERMS AND CONDITIONS. YOU ALSO AGREE THAT THIS AGREEMENT IS THE COMPLETE AND EXCLUSIVE STATEMENT OF THE AGREEMENT BETWEEN YOU AND THE COMPANY AND SUPERSEDES ALL PROPOSALS OR PRIOR AGREEMENTS, ORAL, OR WRITTEN, AND ANY OTHER COMMUNICATIONS BETWEEN YOU AND THE COMPANY OR ANY REPRESENTATIVE OF THE COMPANY RELATING TO THE SUBJECT MATTER OF THIS AGREEMENT.

Should you have any questions concerning this Agreement or if you wish to contact the Company for any reason, please contact in writing at the address below.

Robin Short
Prentice Hall PTR
One Lake Street
Upper Saddle River, New Jersey 07458

The DEITEL® Suite of Products...

HOW TO PROGRAM BOOKS

C++ How to Program Fifth Edition

BOOK / CD-ROM

©2005, 1500 pp., paper
(0-13-185757-6)

The complete authoritative DEITEL® LIVE-CODE introduction to programming with C++! The Fifth Edition takes a new easy-to-follow, carefully developed early classes and early objects approach to programming in C++. The text includes comprehensive coverage of the fundamentals of object-oriented programming in C++. It includes a a new optional automated teller machine (ATM) case study that teaches the fundamentals of software engineering and object-oriented design with the UML 2.0 in Chapters 1-7, 9 and 13. Additional integrated case studies appear throughout the text, including the `Time` class (Chapter 9), the `Employee` class (Chapters 12 and 13) and the `GradeBook` class (Chapters 3-7). The book also includes a new interior design including updated colors, new fonts, new design elements and more.

Small C++ How to Program Fifth Edition

BOOK / CD-ROM

©2005, 900 pp., paper
(0-13-185758-4)

Based on chapters 1-13 (except the optional OOD/UML case study) and appendices of *C++ How to Program, Fifth Edition, Small C++* features a new early classes and early objects approach and comprehensive coverage of the fundamentals of object-oriented programming in C++. Key topics include applications, variables, memory concepts, data types, control statements, functions, arrays, pointers and strings, inheritance and polymorphism.

Coming in Spring 2005 for both *C++ How to Program, 5/e* and *Small C++ How to Program, 5/e:* FREE C++ Web-based *Cyber Classroom* with the purchase of a new textbook. The *Cyber Classroom* includes a complete e-book, audio walkthroughs of the code examples, a FREE Lab Manual and selected student solutions. See pages 7–8 of this advertorial for more information.

Java™ How to Program Sixth Edition

BOOK / CD-ROM

©2005, 1500 pp., paper
(0-13-148398-6)

The complete authoritative DEITEL® LIVE-CODE introduction to programming with the new Java™ 2 Platform Standard Edition 5.0! New early classes and early objects approach. *Java How to Program, Sixth Edition* is up-to-date with J2SE™ 5.0 and includes comprehensive coverage of the fundamentals of object-oriented programming in Java; a new interior design including new colors, new fonts, new design elements and more; and a new optional automated teller machine (ATM) case study that teaches the fundamentals of software engineering and object oriented design with the UML 2.0 in Chapters 1-8 and 10. Additional integrated case studies appear throughout the text, including GUI and graphics (Chapters 3-12), the `Time` class (Chapter 8), the `Employee` class (Chapters 9 and 10) and the `GradeBook Employee` (Chapters 3-8). New J2SE 5.0 topics covered included input/output, enhanced `for` loop, autoboxing, generics, new collections APIs and more.

Small Java™ How to Program, Sixth Edition

BOOK / CD-ROM

©2005, 700 pp., paper
(0-13-148660-8)

Based on chapters 1-10 of *Java™ How to Program, Sixth Edition, Small Java* is up-to-date with J2SE™ 5.0, features a new early classes and early objects approach and comprehensive coverage of the fundamentals of object-oriented programming in Java. Key topics include applications, variables, data types, control statements, methods, arrays, object-based programming, inheritance and polymorphism.

Coming in Spring 2005 for both *Java How to Program, 6/e* and *Small Java How to Program, 6/e:* Free Java Web-based *Cyber Classroom* with the purchase of a new textbook. The *Cyber Classroom* includes a complete e-book, audio walkthroughs of the code examples, a FREE Lab Manual and selected student solutions. See pages 7–8 of this advertorial for more information.

Sign up now for the FREE *DEITEL® Buzz Online* newsletter at:
www.deitel.com/newsletter/subscribe.html

C How to Program
Fourth Edition

BOOK / CD-ROM

*©2004, 1255 pp., paper
(0-13-142644-3)*

C How to Program, Fourth Edition—the world's best-selling C text—is designed for introductory through intermediate courses as well as programming languages survey courses. This comprehensive text is aimed at readers with little or no programming experience through intermediate audiences. Highly practical in approach, it introduces fundamental notions of structured programming and software engineering and gets up to speed quickly.

A Student Solutions Manual is also available is for use with this text. Use ISBN 0-13-145245-2 to order.

Getting Started with Microsoft® Visual C++™ 6 with an Introduction to MFC

BOOK / CD-ROM

*©2000, 163 pp., paper
(0-13-016147-0)*

Visual C++ .NET® How To Program

BOOK / CD-ROM

*©2004, 1400 pp., paper
(0-13-437377-4)*

Written by the authors of the world's best-selling introductory/intermediate C and C++ textbooks, this comprehensive book thoroughly examines Visual C++® .NET. *Visual C++®.NET How to Program* begins with a strong foundation in the introductory and intermediate programming principles students will need in industry, including fundamental topics such as arrays, functions and control statements. Readers learn the concepts of object-oriented programming. The text then explores such essential topics as networking, databases, XML and multimedia. Graphical user interfaces are also extensively covered, giving students the tools to build compelling and fully interactive programs using the "drag-and-drop" techniques provided by Visual Studio .NET 2003.

Advanced Java™ 2 Platform How to Program

BOOK / CD-ROM

*©2002, 1811 pp., paper
(0-13-089560-1)*

Expanding on the world's best-selling Java textbook—*Java™ How to Program*—*Advanced Java™ 2 Platform How To Program* presents advanced Java topics for developing sophisticated, user-friendly GUIs; significant, scalable enterprise applications; wireless applications and distributed systems. Primarily based on Java 2 Enterprise Edition (J2EE), this textbook integrates technologies such as XML, JavaBeans, security, JDBC™, JavaServer Pages (JSP™), servlets, Remote Method Invocation (RMI), Enterprise JavaBeans™ (EJB), design patterns, Swing, J2ME™, Java 2D and 3D, XML, design patterns, CORBA, Jini™, JavaSpaces™, Jiro™, Java Management Extensions (JMX) and Peer-to-Peer networking with an introduction to JXTA.

C# How to Program

BOOK / CD-ROM

*©2002, 1568 pp., paper
(0-13-062221-4)*

C# How to Program provides a comprehensive introduction to Microsoft's C# object-oriented language. C# enables students to create powerful Web applications and components—ranging from XML-based Web services on Microsoft's .NET platform to middle-tier business objects and system-level applications. *C# How to Program* begins with a strong foundation in the introductory- and intermediate-programming principles students will need in industry. It then explores such essential topics as object-oriented programming and exception handling. Graphical user interfaces are extensively covered, giving readers the tools to build compelling and fully interactive programs. Internet technologies such as XML, ADO .NET and Web services are covered as well as topics including regular expressions, multithreading, networking, databases, files and data structures.

Visual Basic® .NET How to Program Second Edition

BOOK / CD-ROM

©2002, 1400 pp., paper
(0-13-029363-6)

Learn Visual Basic .NET programming from the ground up! This book provides a comprehensive introduction to Visual Basic .NET—featuring extensive updates and increased functionality. *Visual Basic .NET How to Program, Second Edition* covers introductory programming techniques as well as more advanced topics, featuring enhanced treatment of developing Web-based applications. Other topics discussed include XML and wireless applications, databases, SQL and ADO .NET, Web forms, Web services and ASP .NET.

Internet & World Wide Web How to Program Third Edition

BOOK / CD-ROM

©2004, 1250 pp., paper
(0-13-145091-3)

This book introduces students with little or no programming experience to the exciting world of Web-based applications. This text provides in-depth coverage of introductory programming principles, various markup languages (XHTML, Dynamic HTML and XML), several scripting languages (JavaScript, JScript .NET, ColdFusion, Flash ActionScript, Perl, PHP, VBScript and Python), Web servers (IIS and Apache) and relational databases (MySQL)—all the skills and tools needed to create dynamic Web-based applications. The text contains a comprehensive introduction to ASP .NET and the Microsoft .NET Framework. A case study illustrating how to build an online message board using ASP .NET and XML is also included. New in this edition are chapters on Macromedia ColdFusion, Macromedia Dreamweaver and a much enhanced treatment of Flash, including a case study on building a video game in Flash. After mastering the material in this book, students will be well prepared to build real-world, industrial-strength, Web-based applications.

Wireless Internet & Mobile Business How to Program

©2002, 1292 pp., paper
(0-13-062226-5)

This book offers a thorough treatment of both the management and technical aspects of this growing area, including coverage of current practices and future trends. The first half explores the business issues surrounding wireless technology and mobile business. The book then turns to programming for the wireless Internet, exploring topics such as WAP (including 2.0), WML, WMLScript, XML, XHTML™, wireless Java programming (J2ME™) and more. Other topics covered include career resources, wireless marketing, accessibility, Palm™, PocketPC, Windows CE, i-mode, Bluetooth, MIDP, MIDlets, ASP, Microsoft .NET Mobile Framework, BREW™, multimedia, Flash™ and VBScript.

Python How to Program

BOOK / CD-ROM

©2002, 1376 pp., paper
(0-13-092361-3)

This exciting textbook provides a comprehensive introduction to Python—a powerful object-oriented programming language with clear syntax and the ability to bring together various technologies quickly and easily. This book covers introductory-programming techniques and more advanced topics such as graphical user interfaces, databases, wireless Internet programming, networking, security, process management, multithreading, XHTML, CSS, PSP and multimedia. Readers will learn principles that are applicable to both systems development and Web programming.

e-Business & e-Commerce for Managers

©2001, 794 pp., cloth
(0-13-032364-0)

This comprehensive overview of building and managing e-businesses explores topics such as the decision to bring a business online, choosing a business model, accepting payments, marketing strategies and security, as well as many other important issues (such as career resources). The book features Web resources and online demonstrations that supplement the text and direct readers to additional materials. The book also includes an appendix that develops a complete Web-based shopping-cart application using HTML, JavaScript, VBScript, Active Server Pages, ADO, SQL, HTTP, XML and XSL. Plus, company-specific sections provide "real-world" examples of the concepts presented in the book.

XML How to Program

BOOK / CD-ROM

©2001, 934 pp., paper (0-13-028417-3)

This book is a comprehensive guide to programming in XML. It teaches how to use XML to create customized tags and includes chapters that address markup languages for science and technology, multimedia, commerce and many other fields. Concise introductions to Java, JavaServer Pages, VBScript, Active Server Pages and Perl/CGI provide readers with the essentials of these programming languages and server-side development technologies to enable them to work effectively with XML. The book also covers topics such as XSL, DOM™, SAX, a real-world e-commerce case study and a complete chapter on Web accessibility that addresses Voice XML. Other topics covered include XHTML, CSS, DTD, schema, parsers, XPath, XLink, namespaces, XBase, XInclude, XPointer, XSLT, XSL Formatting Objects, JavaServer Pages, XForms, topic maps, X3D, MathML, OpenMath, CML, BML, CDF, RDF, SVG, Cocoon, WML, XBRL and BizTalk™ and SOAP™ Web resources.

Perl How to Program

BOOK / CD-ROM

©2001, 1057 pp., paper (0-13-028418-1)

This comprehensive guide to Perl programming emphasizes the use of the Common Gateway Interface (CGI) with Perl to create powerful, dynamic multi-tier Web-based client/server applications. The book begins with a clear and careful introduction to programming concepts at a level suitable for beginners, and proceeds through advanced topics such as references and complex data structures. Key Perl topics such as regular expressions and string manipulation are covered in detail. The authors address important and topical issues such as object-oriented programming, the Perl database interface (DBI), graphics and security. Also included is a treatment of XML, a bonus chapter introducing the Python programming language, supplemental material on career resources and a complete chapter on Web accessibility.

e-Business & e-Commerce How to Program

BOOK / CD-ROM

©2001, 1254 pp., paper (0-13-028419-X)

This book explores programming technologies for developing Web-based e-business and e-commerce solutions, and covers e-business and e-commerce models and business issues. Readers learn a full range of options, from "build-your-own" to turnkey solutions. The book examines scores of the top e-businesses (examples include Amazon, eBay, Priceline, Travelocity, etc.), explaining the technical details of building successful e-business and e-commerce sites and their underlying business premises. Learn how to implement the dominant e-commerce models—shopping carts, auctions, name-your-own-price, comparison shopping and bots/intelligent agents—by using markup languages (HTML, Dynamic HTML and XML), scripting languages (JavaScript, VBScript and Perl), server-side technologies (Active Server Pages and Perl/CGI) and database (SQL and ADO), security and online payment technologies.

Visual Basic® 6 How to Program

BOOK / CD-ROM

©1999, 1015 pp., paper (0-13-456955-5)

ORDER INFORMATION

For ordering information,
visit us on the Web at www.prenhall.com.

INTERNATIONAL ORDERING INFORMATION

CANADA:
Pearson Education Canada
26 Prince Andrew Place
PO Box 580
Don Mills, Ontario M3C 2T8 Canada
Tel.: 416-925-2249; Fax: 416-925-0068
e-mail: phcinfo.pubcanada@pearsoned.com

EUROPE, MIDDLE EAST, AND AFRICA:
Pearson Education
Edinburgh Gate
Harlow, Essex CM20 2JE UK
Tel: 01279 623928; Fax: 01279 414130
e-mail: enq.orders@pearsoned-ema.com

BENELUX REGION:
Pearson Education
Concertgebouwplein 25
1071 LM Amsterdam
The Netherlands
Tel: 31 20 5755 800; Fax: 31 20 664 5334
e-mail: amsterdam@pearsoned-ema.com

ASIA:
Pearson Education Asia Pte. Ltd.
23/25 First Lok Yang Road
Jurong, 629733 Singapore
Tel: 65 476 4688; Fax: 65 378 0370

JAPAN:
Pearson Education Japan
Ogikubo TM Bldg. 6F. 5-26-13 Ogikubo
Suginami-ku, Tokyo 167-0051 Japan
Tel: 81 3 3365 9001; Fax: 81 3 3365 9009

INDIA:
Pearson Education
Indian Branch
482 FIE, Patparganj
Delhi – 110092 India
Tel: 91 11 2059850 & 2059851
Fax: 91 11 2059852

AUSTRALIA:
Pearson Education Australia
Unit 4, Level 2, 14 Aquatic Drive
Frenchs Forest, NSW 2086, Australia
Tel: 61 2 9454 2200; Fax: 61 2 9453 0089
e-mail: marketing@pearsoned.com.au

NEW ZEALAND/FIJI:
Pearson Education
46 Hillside Road
Auckland 10, New Zealand
Tel: 649 444 4968; Fax: 649 444 4957
E-mail: sales@pearsoned.co.nz

SOUTH AFRICA:
Maskew Miller Longman
Central Park Block H
16th Street Midrand 1685
South Africa
Tel: 27 21 686 6356; Fax: 27 21 686 4590

LATIN AMERICA:
Pearson Education Latin America
Attn: Tina Sheldon
1 Lake Street
Upper Saddle River, NJ 07458

The SIMPLY SERIES!

The Deitels' *Simply Series* takes an engaging new approach to teaching programming languages from the ground up. The pedagogy of this series combines the DEITEL® signature *LIVE-CODE Approach* with an *APPLICATION-DRIVEN Tutorial Approach* to teach programming with outstanding pedagogical features that help students learn. We have merged the notion of a lab manual with that of a conventional textbook, creating a book in which readers build and execute complete applications from start to finish, while learning the fundamental concepts of programming!

Simply C++
An APPLICATION-DRIVEN Tutorial Approach

©2005, 800 pp., paper
(0-13-142660-5)

Simply C++ An APPLICATION-DRIVEN Tutorial Approach guides readers through building real-world applications that incorporate C++ programming fundamentals. Learn methods, functions, data types, control statements, procedures, arrays, object-oriented programming, strings and characters, pointers, references, templates, operator overloading and more in this comprehensive introduction to C++.

Simply Java™ Programming
An APPLICATION-DRIVEN Tutorial Approach

©2004, 950 pp., paper
(0-13-142648-6)

Simply Java™ Programming An APPLICATION-DRIVEN Tutorial Approach guides readers through building real-world applications that incorporate Java programming fundamentals. Learn GUI design, components, methods, event-handling, types, control statements, arrays, object-oriented programming, exception-handling, strings and characters, sequential files and more in this comprehensive introduction to Java. We also include higher-end topics such as database programming, multimedia, graphics and Web applications development.

Simply C#
An APPLICATION-DRIVEN Tutorial Approach

©2004, 850 pp., paper
(0-13-142641-9)

Simply C# An APPLICATION-DRIVEN Tutorial Approach guides readers through building real-world applications that incorporate C# programming fundamentals. Learn GUI design, controls, methods, functions, data types, control statements, procedures, arrays, object-oriented programming, strings and characters, sequential files and more in this comprehensive introduction to C#. We also include higher-end topics such as database programming, multimedia and graphics and Web applications development.

Simply Visual Basic® .NET
An APPLICATION-DRIVEN Tutorial Approach

Visual Studio .NET 2002 Version:
©2003, 830 pp., paper
(0-13-140553-5)

Visual Studio .NET 2003 Version:
©2004, 960 pp., paper
(0-13-142640-0)

Simply Visual Basic® .NET An APPLICATION-DRIVEN Tutorial Approach guides readers through building real-world applications that incorporate Visual Basic .NET programming fundamentals. Learn GUI design, controls, methods, functions, data types, control statements, procedures, arrays, object-oriented programming, strings and characters, sequential files and more in this comprehensive introduction to Visual Basic .NET. We also include higher-end topics such as database programming, multimedia and graphics and Web applications development. If you're using Visual Studio® .NET 2002, choose *Simply Visual Basic .NET*; or, if you're using Visual Studio .NET 2003, you can use *Simply Visual Basic .NET 2003*, which includes updated screen captures and line numbers consistent with Visual Studio .NET 2003.

Sign up now for the FREE *DEITEL® Buzz Online* newsletter at:
www.deitel.com/newsletter/subscribe.html

The DEITEL® DEVELOPER SERIES!

Deitel & Associates is recognized worldwide for its best-selling *How to Program Series* of books for college and university students and its signature *LIVE-CODE Approach* to teaching programming languages. Now, for the first time, Deitel & Associates brings its proven teaching methods to a series of books specifically designed for professionals.

THREE TYPES OF BOOKS FOR THREE DISTINCT AUDIENCES

> **A Technical Introduction**

A Technical Introduction books provide programmers, technical managers, project managers and other technical professionals with introductions to broad new technology areas.

> **A Programmer's Introduction**

A Programmer's Introduction books offer focused treatments of programming fundamentals for practicing programmers. These books are also appropriate for novices.

> **For Experienced Programmers**

For Experienced Programmers books are for experienced programmers who want a detailed treatment of a programming language or technology. These books contain condensed introductions to programming language fundamentals and provide extensive intermediate level coverage of high-end topics.

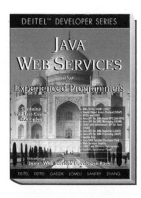

Java™ Web Services for Experienced Programmers

©2003, 700 pp., paper (0-13-046134-2)

Java™ Web Services for Experienced Programmers covers industry standards including XML, SOAP, WSDL and UDDI. Learn how to build and integrate Web services using the Java API for XML RPC, the Java API for XML Messaging, Apache Axis and the Java Web Services Developer Pack. Develop and deploy Web services on several major Web services platforms. Register and discover Web services through public registries and the Java API for XML Registries. Build Web services clients for several platforms, including J2ME. Significant Web services case studies also are included.

Web Services: A Technical Introduction

©2003, 400 pp., paper (0-13-046135-0)

Web Services: A Technical Introduction familiarizes programmers, technical managers and project managers with key Web services concepts, including what Web services are and why they are revolutionary. The book covers the business case for Web services—the underlying technologies, ways in which Web services can provide competitive advantages and opportunities for Web services-related lines of business. Readers learn the latest Web-services standards, including XML, SOAP, WSDL and UDDI; learn about Web services implementations in .NET and Java; benefit from an extensive comparison of Web services products and vendors; and read about Web services security options. Although this is not a programming book, the appendices show .NET and Java code examples to demonstrate the structure of Web services applications and documents. In addition, the book includes numerous case studies describing ways in which organizations are implementing Web services to increase efficiency, simplify business processes, create new revenue streams and interact better with partners and customers.

MULTIMEDIA CYBER CLASSROOMS

Premium content available FREE with *Java™* and *Small Java™ How to Program, Sixth Edition* and *C++* and *Small C++ How to Program, Fifth Edition!*

Java and *Small Java How to Program, 6/e* and *C++* and *Small C++ How to Program, 5/e* will soon be available with a **FREE** Web-based *Multimedia Cyber Classroom* for students who purchase new copies of these books! The *Cyber Classroom* is an interactive, multimedia, tutorial version of DEITEL textbooks. *Cyber Classrooms* are a great value, giving students additional hands-on experience and study aids.

COMING SOON for *Java and Small Java How to Program, 6/e* and *C++ and Small C++ How to Program, 5/e* (with purchase of book)

DEITEL® Multimedia Cyber Classrooms *feature the complete text of their corresponding* How to Program *titles.*

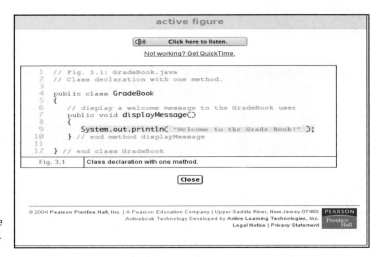

Unique audio "walkthroughs" of code examples reinforce key concepts.

MULTIMEDIA CYBER CLASSROOMS

DEITEL® *Multimedia Cyber Classrooms* include:

- The full text, illustrations and program listings of its corresponding *How to Program* book.

- Hours of detailed, expert audio descriptions of hundreds of lines of code that help to reinforce important concepts.

- An abundance of self-assessment material, including practice exams, hundreds of programming exercises and self-review questions and answers.

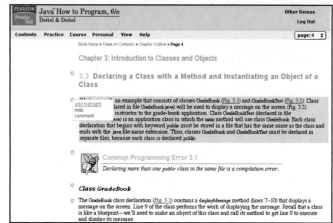

DEITEL® Multimedia Cyber Classrooms *offer a host of interactive features, such as highlighting of key sections of the text...*

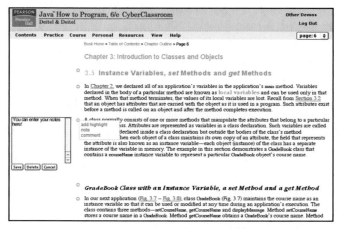

- Intuitive browser-based interface designed to be easy and accessible.

- A Lab Manual featuring lab exercises as well as pre- and post-lab activities.

- Student Solutions to approximately one-half of the exercises in the textbook.

...and the ability to write notes in the margin of a given page for future reference.

Students receive access to a protected Web site via access code cards packaged, for FREE, automatically with these new textbooks. (Simply tear the strip on the inside of the *Cyber Classroom* package to reveal access code.)

To redeem your access code or for more information, please visit:
www.prenhall.com/deitel/ cyberclassroom

PearsonChoices

For Instructors and Students using DEITEL® Publications!

Today's students have increasing demands on their time and money, and they need to be resourceful about how, when and where they study. Pearson Education has responded to that need by creating PearsonChoices, which allows faculty and students to choose from a variety of formats and prices.

Visit www.pearsonchoices.com for more information!

We are pleased to announce PearsonChoices this fall for our brand new DEITEL publications:

- *Small Java How to Program, Sixth Edition* and *Small C++ How to Program, Fifth Edition*—our alternative print editions to *Java How to Program, Sixth Edition* and *C++ How to Program, Fifth Edition* at a competitive price!

Small Java How to Program and *Small C++ How to Program* bring the solid and proven pedagogy of our fully updated *Java How to Program 6/E* and *C++ How to Program 5/E* to new, smaller texts that are purely focused on CS1 courses and priced lower than our full and comprehensive *How to Program* texts and other competing texts in the CS1 market. See the first page of this advertorial for more on these compelling new Java and C++ titles!

- SafariX WebBooks—We are pleased to offer students five NEW DEITEL SafariX WebBooks available for Fall 2005 at 50% off the print version's price!
    - *Java How to Program, Sixth Edition*
    - *Small Java How to Program, Sixth Edition*
    - *C++ How to Program, Fifth Edition*
    - *Small C++ How to Program, Fifth Edition*
    - *Simply C++: An Application-Driven Tutorial Approach*

SafariX Textbooks Online is an exciting new service for college students looking to save money on required or recommended textbooks for academic courses!

This secure WebBooks platform creates a new option in the higher education market; an additional choice for students alongside conventional textbooks and online learning services. By eliminating the costs relating to printing, manufacturing and retail distribution for the physical textbook, Pearson provides students with a WebBook at 50% of the cost of its conventional print equivalent. Beginning spring 2005, students can choose to purchase a print edition textbook or subscribe to the same textbook content through SafariX Textbooks Online.

SafariX WebBooks are digital versions of print textbooks enhanced with features such as high-speed search, note taking and bookmarking. SafariX WebBooks are viewed through a Web browser connected to the Internet. SafariX Textbooks Online requires no special plug-ins and no applications download to your computer. Students just log in, purchase access and begin studying!

With SafariX Textbooks Online students will be able to search the text, make notes online, print out reading assignments that incorporate your lecture notes and bookmark important passages they want to review later. They can navigate easily to a page number, reading assignment or chapter. The Table of Contents of each WebBook appears in the left hand column alongside the text.

Visit www.safarix.com for more information!

Sign up now for the FREE *DEITEL® Buzz Online* newsletter at:
w w w . d e i t e l . c o m / n e w s l e t t e r / s u b s c r i b e . h t m l

The *DEITEL® BUZZ ONLINE* e-mail newsletter is now sent to over 38,000 opt-in subscribers. This free publication is designed to keep you updated on our publishing program, instructor-led corporate training courses, the latest industry topics and trends and more.

Each issue of our newsletter includes:

- Highlights and announcements on our products available for professionals, students and instructors.

- Sample chapters from our forthcoming publications.

- Information on our instructor-led corporate training courses taught worldwide.

- Detailed ordering information for instructors, professors, students and professionals, along with additional book resources and downloads.

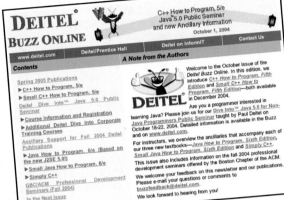

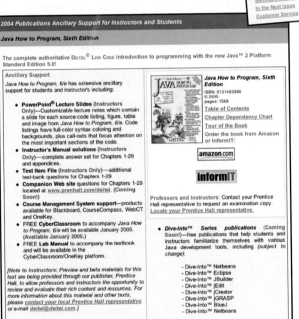

- Available in both full-color HTML or plain-text format.

- Approximately 6–8 issues per year.

- Your e-mail address will not be distributed or sold.

Turn the page to find out more about Deitel & Associates!

To sign up for the *DEITEL® BUZZ ONLINE* newsletter, visit **www.deitel.com/newsletter/subscribe.html**.

Deitel & Associates, Inc. provides intensive, lecture-and-laboratory courses to organizations worldwide. The programming courses use our signature LIVE-CODE Approach, presenting complete working programs.

Deitel & Associates, Inc. has trained over one million students and professionals worldwide through Dive Into Series™ corporate training courses, public seminars, university teaching, How to Program Series textbooks, DEITEL® Developer Series books, Simply Series textbooks, Cyber Classroom Series multimedia packages, Complete Training Course Series textbook and multimedia packages, broadcast-satellite courses and Web-based training.

Educational Consulting

Deitel & Associates, Inc. offers complete educational consulting services for corporate training programs and professional schools including:

- Curriculum design and development
- Preparation of Instructor Guides
- Customized courses and course materials
- Design and implementation of professional training certificate programs
- Instructor certification
- Train-the-trainers programs
- Delivery of software-related corporate training programs

Visit our Web site for more information on our Dive Into™ Series corporate training curriculum and to purchase our training products.

www.deitel.com/training

Would you like to review upcoming publications?

If you are a professor or senior industry professional interested in being a reviewer of our forthcoming publications, please contact us by email at **deitel@deitel.com**. Insert "Content Reviewer" in the subject heading.

Are you interested in a career in computer education, publishing and training?

We offer a limited number of full-time positions available for college graduates in computer science, information systems, information technology and management information systems. Please check our Web site for the latest job postings or contact us by email at **deitel@deitel.com**. Insert "Full-time Job" in the subject heading.

Are you a Boston-area college student looking for an internship?

We have a limited number of competitive summer positions and 20-hr./week school-year opportunities for computer science, IT/IS and MIS majors. Students work at our worldwide headquarters west of Boston. We also offer full-time internships for students taking a semester off from school. This is an excellent opportunity for students looking to gain industry experience and earn money to pay for school. Please contact us by email at **deitel@deitel.com**. Insert "Internship" in the subject heading.

Would you like to explore contract training opportunities with us?

Deitel & Associates, Inc. is looking for contract instructors to teach software-related topics at our clients' sites in the United States and worldwide. Applicants should be experienced professional trainers or college professors. For more information, please visit **www.deitel.com** and send your resume to Abbey Deitel at **abbey.deitel@deitel.com**.

Are you a training company in need of quality course materials?

Corporate training companies worldwide use our How to Program Series textbooks, Complete Training Course Series book and multimedia packages, Simply Series textbooks and our DEITEL® Developer Series books in their classes. We have extensive ancillary instructor materials for many of our products. For more details, please visit **www.deitel.com** or contact us by email at **deitel@deitel.com**.

PROGRAMMING LANGUAGE TEXTBOOK AUTHORS

Check out our Dive Into Series™ Corporate On-site Seminars...

Java™
- Java for Nonprogrammers
- Java for VB/COBOL Programmers
- Java for C/C++ Programmers

Advanced Java™
- Java™ Web Services
- J2ME™
- J2EE
- Enterprise JavaBeans (EJB™) and Design Patterns
- Advanced Swing GUI
- RMI
- JDBC
- CORBA
- JavaBeans™

Internet & World Wide Web Programming
- Client-Side Internet & World Wide Web Programming
- Server-Side Internet & World Wide Web Programming
- Perl/CGI, Python, PHP

C/C++
- C and C++ Programming: Part 1 (for Nonprogrammers)
- C and C++ Programming: Part 2 (for Non-C Programmers)
- C++ and Object-Oriented Programming
- Advanced C++ and Object-Oriented Programming

XML
- XML Programming for programmers with Java, Web or other programming experience

.NET Programming
- C# Programming
- Visual Basic .NET Programming
- Visual C++ .NET Programming

Other Topics
- Object-Oriented Analysis and Design with the UML
- SQL Server
- e-Business and e-Commerce

For Detailed Course Descriptions, Visit Our Web Site: www.deitel.com

Through our worldwide network of trainers, we would be happy to attempt to arrange corporate on-site courses for you in virtually any software-related field.

For Additional Information about Our Dive Into Series™ Corporate On-Site Courses, contact:

Abbey Deitel, President
Email: abbey.deitel@deitel.com
Phone: (978) 461-5880/Fax: (978) 461-5884

Our training clients include:

3Com
Argonne National Laboratories
Art Technology
Avid Technology
Bank of America
BEA Systems
BlueCross BlueShield
Boeing
Bristol-Myers Squibb
Cambridge Technology Partners
Cap Gemini
Concord Communications
Dell
Dunn & Bradstreet
Eastman Kodak
EMC^2
Federal Reserve Bank of Chicago
Fidelity
GE
General Dynamics Electric Boat Corporation
Gillette
GTE
Hitachi
IBM
Invensys
JPL Laboratories
Lockheed Martin
Lucent
MapInfo Corporation
MCI
Motorola
NASA's Kennedy Space Center
NASDAQ
National Oceanographic and Atmospheric Administration
Nortel Networks
Omnipoint
One Wave
Open Market
Oracle
Pacific Capital Bank Corporation
PalmSource
Pragmatics
Primavera
Progress Software
Rogue Wave Software
Schlumberger
Sun Microsystems
Symmetrix
Teleflora
Thompson Technology
Tivoli Systems
TJX Companies
Toys "R" Us
U.S. Army at Ft. Leavenworth
Visa International
Washington Post Newsweek Interactive
White Sands Missile Range
and more!

www.deitel.com   www.prenhall.com/deitel

License Agreement and Limited Warranty

The software is distributed on an "AS IS" basis, without warranty. Neither the authors, the software developers, nor Prentice Hall make any representation, or warranty, either express or implied, with respect to the software programs, their quality, accuracy, or fitness for a specific purpose. Therefore, neither the authors, the software developers, nor Prentice Hall shall have any liability to you or any other person or entity with respect to any liability, loss, or damage caused or alleged to have been caused directly or indirectly by the programs contained on the media. This includes, but is not limited to, interruption of service, loss of data, loss of classroom time, loss of consulting or anticipatory profits, or consequential damages from the use of these programs. If the media itself is defective, you may return it for a replacement. Use of this software is subject to the Binary Code License terms and conditions at the back of this book. Read the licenses carefully. By opening this package, you are agreeing to be bound by the terms and conditions of these licenses. If you do not agree, do not open the package.
Please refer to end-user license agreements on the CD-ROM for further details.

Using the CD-ROM

The interface to the contents of this CD is designed to start automatically through the **AUTORUN.EXE** file. If a startup screen does not pop up automatically when you insert the CD into your computer, double click on the welcome.htm file to launch the Student CD or refer to the file **readme.txt** on the CD.

Contents of the CD-ROM

- Software downloads: links to free C++ compilers and development tools
- Examples
- Web Resources

Software and Hardware System Requirements

- 450 MHz (minimum) Pentium II or faster processor
- Microsoft® Windows® Server 2003, XP Professional, XP Home Edition, XP Media Center Edition, XP Tablet PC Edition, 2000 Professional (SP3 or later required for installation), 2000 Server (SP3 or later required for installation), or
- One of the following Linux distributions: Fedora Core 3 (Formally Red Hat Linux), Mandrakelinux 10.1 Official, Red Hat 9.0, SUSE LINUX Professional 9.2, or Turbolinux 10 Desktop
- Other than the minimum amount of RAM required by the items listed above, there are no additional RAM requirements for this CD-ROM
- CD-ROM drive
- Internet connection
- C++ environment
- Web browser, Adobe® Acrobat® Reader® and a Zip decompression utility